LONDON

WordWise

DICTIONARY

ACKNOWLEDGEMENTS

Director
Della Summers

Editorial Director
Adam Gadsby

Publisher
Laurence Delacroix

Managing Editor
Stephen Bullon

Senior Editor
Michael Murphy

Lexicographers
Elizabeth Beizai
Rosalind Combley
Sheila Dignen
Elizabeth Manning
Evadne Adrian-Vallance
Laura Wedgeworth
Deborah Yuill

Production Editors
Andrew Taylor
Michael Brooks

Pronunciation Editor
Dinah Jackson

Design
Jenny Fleet
Alex Ingr

Illustrators
Jeremy Banx
Andrew Clark
Emma Dodd
 (Black Hat Company)
Sam Thompson
 (Eikon Design Company)
Neil Stanton
 (Eikon Design Company)

Project Manager
Alan Savill

Production
Clive McKeough

Project Administrator
Denise Denney

Exercises
Andrew Taylor

Proofreader
Gerard Delaney

PEARSON EDUCATION LIMITED
Edinburgh Gate, Harlow, Essex CM20 2JE, England
and Associated Companies throughout the world

Visit our website at: http://www.longman-elt.com/dictionaries

First published 2001
010 008 006 004 005 007 009

British Library Cataloguing-in-Publication Data
A catalogue record for this book is available from the British Library

Library of Congress Cataloging-in-Publication Data
A catalog record for this book is available from the
Library of Congress

ISBN
0 582 344565

Typeset in Formata by RefineCatch Ltd, Bungay, Suffolk
Printed and bound in Great Britain by William Clowes Ltd, Beccles and London

LABELS USED IN THE DICTIONARY

AmE	American English
BrE	British English
formal	used in formal or official situations, but not usually in ordinary conversation
informal	used in conversations with friends and people who you know well, but not suitable for formal speech or writing
spoken	used mostly in spoken English
written	used mostly in written English
trademark	used as the official name of a product by a company

PARTS OF SPEECH

noun	*adjective*	*preposition*	*number*
verb	*adverb*	*plural*	*negative*
pronoun	*modal verb*	*past tense*	*past participle*
present participle			

CONTENTS

spelling

pronunciation

part of speech

important word

difficult past tenses

grammar patterns of important words

definition

examples

phrases

different meanings

spelling in British and American English

nouns that do not have a plural

different entries for words that have different parts of speech

be·fore·hand /bɪˈfɔːhænd $ bɪ-ˈfɔrhænd/ *adverb* formal before a particular time or event: *You should have told me about this **beforehand**.*

be·gin /bɪˈɡɪn/ *verb* **began** /bɪˈɡæn/ **begun** /bɪˈɡʌn/ **beginning**

GRAMMAR

begin to do something
begin doing something
begin with something
begin by doing something

to start doing something, or to start to happen ⇨ *same meaning* START: *She **began to** cry.* | *The exam will begin at 9:00.* | *When did you begin having these headaches?* | *The band **began with** one of their most famous hits.* | *Let's **begin by** looking at page 25.*

PHRASE

to begin with **1)** used to introduce the first or most important point: *They made a lot of mistakes. **To begin with**, they spelt my name wrong.* **2)** at the start of something: *To begin with, we all introduced ourselves.*

be·have /bɪˈheɪv/ *verb*
1 to do or say things in a particular way: *Some boys behaved badly at the party.*
2 to act politely and not cause trouble: *Children, please behave.*

be·hav·iour *BrE* **behavior** *AmE* /bɪˈheɪvjə $ bɪˈheɪvjər/ *noun* [no plural] your behaviour is the way that you act or do things

be·hind¹ /bɪˈhaɪnd/ *preposition, adverb*
at or near the back of something: *The car behind us was driving too close.* | *His diary had fallen behind the sofa.*

be·hind² *adjective*
behind with if you are behind with your work, you have not done as much work as you should have done: *I can't come out – I'm a bit behind with my homework this week.*

be·long /bɪˈlɒŋ $ bɪˈlɔːŋ/ *verb*

GRAMMAR
belong in a place
if something belongs somewhere, it is in the correct place or situation: *This kind of picture does not **belong in** a teenage magazine.* | *Where does this book belong?*

PHRASAL VERB ← phrasal verbs
belong to
1 belong to something if you belong to a group, you are a member of it: *I don't **belong to** any political parties.*
2 belong to someone if something belongs to you, you own it: *That bike **belongs to** my sister.*

be·lov·ed /bɪˈlʌvɪd/ *adjective* written ← information on usage
loved very much: *She was the beloved wife of Tom Smith.*

bench /bentʃ/ *noun, plural* benches
long wooden seat for two or more people: *a garden bench* ← difficult plurals of nouns

best² *adverb*
1 most: *Which bit of the film did you **like best?*** | *His brother **knew** him **best***.
2 in a way that is better than any other: *Which of the children draws best?* | *Michael **did best** in the spelling test* (=was most successful).

← words that often go with other words

bite¹ /baɪt/ *verb* bit /bɪt/ bitten /ˈbɪtn/

GRAMMAR
bite into something
1 to cut or crush something with your teeth: *Sophie was bitten by a dog.* | *I can't stop **biting my fingernails**.* | *James **bit into** the apple.*
2 if an insect bites you, it pushes a sharp point into your skin and it hurts: *I think I've been bitten by ants.*

USAGE ← usage note
Insects such as fleas and mosquitos **bite** you, but bees and wasps **sting** you.

boast /bəʊst $ boʊst/ *verb* to talk too proudly about yourself and tell other people how good or clever you are : same meaning BRAG: *He's always boasting about his rich friends.*

← information about other words with the same meaning

INTRODUCTION

The new *Longman WordWise Dictionary* provides new practical solutions for students at pre-intermediate to intermediate level. It contains 35,000 words, phrases, and examples that will help students learn the language more quickly and effectively.

▶ **Learn 2000 key words and you will be able to understand 80% of the language**
Research has shown that if students learn 2000 basic words of English, they will be able to understand 80% of the English language. Based on their frequency in the 300 million-word Longman Corpus Network, including the Learners' Corpus, we have carefully selected 2000 words that form the core vocabulary of English. These 2000 *WordWise* words include difficult words such as *place* and *time*, and difficult verbs such as *see*, *get*, and *feel* that students need to fully master to progress in English.

▶ **Easy access** to the different meanings helps you get to the meaning you are looking for more quickly. The basic meanings are explained in a different, more pedagogical way using the Longman 2000-word Defining Vocabulary, so that all the definitions are easy to understand. Typical structures and collocations are highlighted to make these words easier to use.

▶ **Learn by example: authentic written and spoken English**
Thousands of authentic example sentences clearly show how words are really used in speech and writing. All the examples in this dictionary were selected for intermediate learners by teachers of English, based on their classroom experience.

▶ **An easy way to remember grammar structures**
Most of the 2000 key words show grammar structures, which can be difficult for students to remember because the patterns are different from their own language. We are showing these structures in grammar boxes at the beginning of the entries so students can access them quickly and avoid making grammar mistakes. For example:

> **GRAMMAR**
> **begin to do something**
> **begin doing something**
> **begin with something**
> **begin by doing something**

▶ **Get natural with idiomatic expressions**
Common English phrases are highlighted to show which words are used together, so students can reuse them easily and sound more natural, for example: *leave a message*, *take place*, *break the news*, *have a bath*, *have breakfast*, *do your homework*, *do the cooking*, *make an effort* etc.

▶ **No more mistakes with phrasal verbs**
Phrasal verbs are notoriously difficult for students of English because the meaning of a phrasal verb cannot be understood by putting together the meaning of its parts. When a verb is combined with a preposition or an adverb (e.g. *get up*, *take off*, *give back* etc) it can have a different meaning from the main meaning of the verbs *get*, *take*, *give* etc. For example, *take off* has nothing to do with 'taking something' but has three meanings that are different from the main meanings of *take*:

take off
1 to move clothes off your body: ⇨ *opposite* PUT ON: *Jane took off her coat and hung it up.* | *I bent down and took my shoes off.*
2 if a plane takes off, it leaves the ground and goes into the air: ⇨ *opposite* LAND *The plane took off at 8:45.*
3 to not go to work for a period of time: *Emma took three days off school last week when she was ill.*

The grammar structures are clearly shown in the examples so that students can see immediately that they can say, for example, *take your clothes off*, and also *take off your clothes*, but that *a plane takes off*, and that you cannot say *'take a plane off'*!

We wish you rapid progress and every success with the new *Longman WordWise Dictionary*!

Laurence Delacroix
PUBLISHER

WORKBOOK EXERCISES

▸ WORDBUILDING

Exercise 1

Compound nouns are formed from a noun + another noun. This dictionary contains many common compound nouns listed as separate entries so they are easy to find.

Match the words below to form compound nouns. *Example:* cassette player

cassette	bear
polar	phone
middle	dish
classical	class
mobile	music
satellite	player
pay	phone

Use the dictionary to check your answers.

Exercise 2

Now, form more compound words using the following words as the first part. Use your dictionary to help you.

Example: fire → fireplace

post
air
battle
bed
space
foot
water

▸ CHOOSING THE CORRECT WORD

Exercise 3

It is sometimes difficult in English to be sure you are using the correct word(s). Some words are presented differently in the dictionary to help you choose the correct word.

Look at the full-page entry for 'make' on page 380.

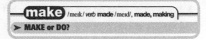

make /meɪk/ *verb* **made** /meɪd/, **made, making**
▸ **MAKE or DO?**

It gives you the rule that you usually MAKE something, but you DO an action or activity.

Use this rule to put the following nouns in the correct column below.

housework	cooking	a cake
homework	a plan	shopping

Do	Make

Exercise 4

Sometimes, however, it isn't always possible in English to follow a rule. Some words are always used with each other. Look again at the entry for 'make':

Most common words used with **make**:

make a mistake
make a statement
make a noise
make an appointment
make a suggestion
make a difference
make a note
make a decision
make an effort
make progress
make a choice
make breakfast/lunch etc

Fill in the gaps in the following sentences, using the phrases from the list above. Look up the individual words in the dictionary if you are not sure of their meaning.

Exercises

1 I mustn't forget her telephone number. I'll
▉▉▉▉▉ ▉▉ of it.

2 I've got a terrible headache. I'll ▉▉▉▉▉
▉▉ ▉▉▉▉▉▉▉▉ with the doctor.

3 I've been working on this essay all day but
I haven't written anything. I've ▉▉▉▉▉
no ▉▉▉▉▉ at all.

4 He's been thinking about buying the flat
all day. He needs to ▉▉▉▉▉ ▉▉
▉▉▉▉▉ , or they'll sell it to someone
else.

Exercise 5

Read the sentences below and choose one
of the words in *italics* to fill each gap. Use the
dictionary entries for the words in *italics* to
help you, and with verbs remember to use
the correct tense.

1 "I'll have a glass of orange, please, and a
▉▉▉▉▉ of crisps."
(*package/packet*)

2 "I can't make any decisions at work – my
boss has all the ▉▉▉▉▉."
(*power/energy*)

3 Last year, a lot of ▉▉▉▉▉ visited
the United Kingdom.
(*strangers/foreigners*)

4 "Can you ▉▉▉▉▉ me to buy some
milk at the supermarket?"
(*remind/remember*)

5 She ▉▉▉▉▉ me all about her holiday.
(*talk/tell*)

6 Agassi picked up a serious ▉▉▉▉▉ half
way through the third game.
(*wound/injury*)

7 "Let me give you some ▉▉▉▉▉ . Don't
buy any more food from that supermarket."
(*advise/advice*)

8 "I can't believe that he could do such a
stupid thing! He's far too ▉▉▉▉▉."
(*sensible/sensitive*)

▶ FINDING AND USING THE CORRECT MEANING

Exercise 6

Some words are confusing because they have
a number of different meanings, depending
on where they are used. Look at the full-page
entry for 'get' on page 249. Each numbered
box shows you a different meaning. Read
through each box to check you understand it.
Then read through each sentence below and
write the meaning number that matches most
closely the meaning of 'get' as it is being used.

Example: He got the car repaired. **7**

1 "Can you get me a carton of juice from the
shop?" ▉

2 He didn't get back from the office until 9
o'clock. ▉

3 Simon got a brand new bicycle for his 16th
birthday. ▉

4 "I'm afraid, Mrs Smith, that your husband's
illness isn't getting any better." ▉

5 "Get away from that fire! It's dangerous."
▉

Exercise 7

Now use the correct form of 'get' to help you
complete the following sentences. In some of
the sentences, you will also need to add one
or two more words to give the sentence
meaning.

Example: If you go outside in winter without
a sweater, you'll *get cold* .

1 "If you don't behave well during the year,
you won't ▉▉▉▉▉ ▉▉▉▉▉ for
Christmas."

2 "I'm sorry. I can't come out tonight. I have to

my homework   by tomorrow."

3 "He wasn't very happy at all. In fact, he
     very   when he saw what
had happened."

4 "You'll never be able to lift that on your
own. You should   to
help you."

5 "What time do you think you'll
     tonight? I need to know what
time to   started on the dinner."

Exercise 8

Now look at the entry for 'play':

---

play¹ /pleɪ/ *verb*

GRAMMAR
**play (against) something/some-
one**
play with something/someone
play for something/someone

1 to take part in a sport or game: *Do
you know how to play tennis?* | *The
boys were playing computer
games.* | *England **played against**
France in the final.* | *The USA will
play Norway.* | *He **plays for** the Chi-
cago Bulls* (=he is on their team).

2 if you play a musical instrument, you
use it to produce music: *I'm learning
to play the piano.* | *He played me a
tune on his guitar.*

USAGE
Always use 'the' after the verb **play**
and before the names of musical instruments:
*Anna plays the piano, and Sam plays the
trumpet.* Never use 'the' after the verb **play**
and before the name of a particular sport:
*In the winter I play football, and in the
summer I play tennis.*

3 if children play, they have fun doing
things with toys or with their friends:
*Henry loves **playing with** his toy
cars.* | *When you've finished your
lunch, you can go and play.*

4 if you play a record, radio etc, or it
plays, it produces music or sounds:
The DJ played some great records. |
*My favourite song was playing on
the radio.*

5 to take part in a film, programme,
or play as one of the characters in
it: *Brad Pitt played the hero in the
film.*

Study the different meanings of 'play' listed by
sense number. Then write down the correct
sense number in the space provided for each
of the following sentences.

Example: Anthony spends all day playing with
his toys. **3**

1 He'll be playing Macbeth next year on
Broadway.

2 Adams played football for Arsenal his
entire career.

3 The boys played on the beach for the
whole afternoon.

4 She's been playing the guitar since she was
5 years old.

5 "You two kids should go out and play. Get
some fresh air!"

6 The band played its tape to the record
company executive.

▸ WORDBUILDING

Exercise 9

Look at the 'Most common words used with
….' section in the full-page entries for GIVE,
MAKE, and DO in the dictionary. These show
words used frequently with a particular word.

Now fill in the gaps below. You'll find answers
in the 'Most common words used with…'
sections.

1 "Hello. Is that the Doctor's surgery?" "Yes?"
"I'd like to   an appointment, please."

2 "He's missed all the trains. Can anybody
     him a lift home?"

3 His boss   him permission to take a
day off work to visit his sick mother.

4 When she crashed into that tree, she
     some real   to her car.

5 I don't have enough information for my
essay – I need to   some   .

6 She was really sorry that they were always arguing. She decided to ▮▮▮▮▮ real ▮▮▮▮▮ to improve the relationship.

Exercise 10

Use the dictionary to complete the words and phrases below:

Example: **absent-minded** = a person who often forgets things

1 post▮▮▮▮ (someone who is studying at a university who has already done a degree)

2 body▮▮▮ (someone whose job is to protect an important person)

3 earth▮▮▮ (a sudden shaking of the earth's surface)

4 hair▮▮▮ (a thin piece of metal, used to hold a woman's hair in place)

5 neck▮▮ (a piece of jewellery that you wear around your neck)

6 pick▮▮▮ (someone who steals from people's pockets in public places)

7 pull▮▮ (another word for a sweater)

▸ DEFINITIONS

Definitions in *Longman WordWise* tell you much more than just what a word means. For example, look at the definition for *saddle* and the question and answer below.

saddle = a leather seat on a horse or bicycle

1 Q Name two places where you'd expect to find a **saddle**.

A On a horse or bicycle.

Exercise 11

Now answer the following questions. Look up the definition of the word in **bold** to help you.

1 Q Write down four facts about an **owl**.

2 Q How is the sky when it is **overcast**?

3 Q If an animal **hibernates**, when does it wake up?

Exercise 12

Longman WordWise definitions also provide useful extra information and vocabulary. Fill in the gaps in the sentences below. Then check your answers by looking up the word in **bold**.

Example: A **croak** is a deep low *sound* in your throat.

1 An **engine** is a ▮▮▮▮ that uses oil, petrol, or electricity to make it move.

2 A **dome** is a ▮▮▮▮ with a round roof.

3 A **clarinet** is a wooden musical ▮▮▮▮▮▮ like a long black tube, which you play by blowing into it.

4 A **cauliflower** is a ▮▮▮▮ with green leaves on the outside and a large firm white centre.

5 **Pepper** is a hot-tasting ▮▮▮▮ made from the seeds of a plant.

6 A **car** is a ▮▮▮▮ with four wheels and an engine, which carries a small number of people.

7 A **beetle** is an ▮▮▮▮ with a hard round back.

Exercise 13

Look at the meaning and example sentences in the dictionary entries for the words in **bold** below, and then answer the questions.

1 Where is **saliva** produced?

2 Describe a situation when you might show **gratitude**.

3 Where might you find a **misprint**?

4 If you are **overdrawn**, how much money do you have?

5 What kinds of food might **sizzle** when being cooked?

6 If somebody remembers your birthday, are they **thoughtful** or **thoughtless**?

Exercise 14

Read the definitions and fill in the gaps for the words below.

1 sa_ _er: a small round plate that you put a cup on

2 li_ _id: a substance such as water which flows and is not solid or a gas

3 re_ _ _ _gle: a shape with four straight sides with two longer and two shorter sides

4 sn_ _ze: to sleep for a short time

5 co_ _ _ter: someone who travels to work each day

6 ti_ _ _e: if you stand or walk on your toes

▸ HOW TO SAY THE WORD

If a word has more than one syllable, when we speak, we put stress on one of the syllables (we speak that syllable more strongly or louder).

Look at the entry for *permission*:

per•mis•sion /pə'mɪʃən $ pɚ'mɪ-ʃən/ *noun [no plural]*

The small ' shows you which syllable should be stressed.

Exercise 15

Now look at the stress patterns of these words and circle the correct stress. You may find speaking the word out loud helps you to decide.

1 ACTor *or* actOR

2 BREAKdown *or* breakDOWN

3 ENGine *or* engINE

4 Alive *or* aLIVE

5 UNDerneath *or* underNEATH

6 EXaggerate *or* exAGGerate

Check your answers in the dictionary.

Each dictionary entry is given a pronunciation. The symbols used to show this are based on the International Phonetic Alphabet (IPA). A list of the symbols is given on the inside front cover. Look again at the entry for *permission*.

Exercise 16

Try to guess these words from their phonetic representations.

1 kʊk

2 'bɔɪ-ɪʃ

3 ɪ'klɪps

4 kwiːn

5 ə'griːmənt

6 jʌŋ

In English, the same letters can sometimes be pronounced in different ways, or different letters can be pronounced in the same way. For example, the **bold** letters in **c**ity, **ps**ychic, and **s**oon all produce the sound s.

Exercise 17

Put the following words under the correct sound in the table below (the **bold** letters show the sound). The numbers under the pronunciation symbol tell you how many different spellings of the same sound there are in the list (so, for example, for the sound k, there are four words to find from the list).

pilot	decide	chord	come
aisle	caller	capture	know
generous	chauffeur	while	awkward
citrus	photo	kill	wrote
the	psychology		

Vowels	Consonants
ə	ʃ
1 about	1 shone
2	2
3	dʒ
ɪ	1 joke
1 pick	2
2	s
ʌ	1 sit
1 mum	2
2	3
aɪ	f
1 eye	1 fall
2	2
3	k
ɔːɔ	1 quarter
1 taught	2
2	3
3	4
	r
	1 ripple
	2
	n
	1 not
	2

▸ CONFUSING WORDS

Sometimes, two words have the same spelling but very different meanings and sometimes different pronunciations. Look at the words *refuse*[1] and *refuse*[2] below.

- *refuse*[1] means 'to say firmly that you will not do something' or that you will not allow someone to do something
- *refuse*[2] means 'waste material such as old food or paper'

The dictionary lists the two words separately under separate entry numbers so that the words cannot be confused.

Exercise 18

Use the dictionary to find out which separate entry correctly explains the use of the **bold** word in each of the sentences below. Write the number of the entry in the space provided.

1 When I came in late for the fifth day in a row, my boss gave me the **sack**.

2 He was given a good **blow** on the head and fell unconscious.

3 He looked very **grave** after he spoke to the doctor.

4 Sam **booked** a table for 8.00 pm in the restaurant.

5 They **ducked** under the table.

6 She couldn't **bear** to be without him.

Some words sound the same, but are spelt differently and have different meanings. For example, *prise* means 'to force something open or away from something else', while *prize* means 'something that is given to someone who is successful in a competition, race etc'.

Exercise 19

Choose the correct words in **bold** below to complete the sentences. Look them up in the dictionary if you need help.

1 She had blue eyes and a beautiful   skin.

"Don't forget to take some money for your bus   home." **fare/fair**

2 "He's ▨▨▨▨ so much since I last saw him."

As the ball hit him, he let out a long ▨▨▨▨. **grown/groan**

3 "What time are you going to ▨▨▨▨ him?"

"I didn't enjoy the meal at all. The ▨▨▨▨ was horribly overcooked."

meat/meet

4 After five years of terrible warfare, the entire population was ready for ▨▨▨▨.

"I'd like a ▨▨▨▨ of the chocolate cake, please." **piece/peace**

5 "Lower the ▨▨▨▨ or the boat will capsize in this strong wind!"

"I'm going shopping – there's a 50% off ▨▨▨▨ down at the department store."

(sale/sail)

6 "I was so ▨▨▨▨ I could barely pick up my bag."

Top football teams now play games at least two or three times a ▨▨▨▨.

(week/weak)

▸ PHRASAL VERBS

In English, verbs that are made up of two or three words are called 'phrasal' verbs. Sometimes, their meaning may be very different from that of the main verb. For example, look at the phrasal verb entries for **point** and **check** below:

> **PHRASAL VERB**
> **point out**
> 1 **point something out** to tell someone about a mistake that they had not noticed or a fact they had not thought about: *She **pointed out** that I had made a mistake.*
> 2 **point something/someone out** to point at a person or thing so that people will know who they are or where they are: *Geoff **pointed out** his sister on the dance floor.*

> **PHRASAL VERBS**
> **check in/into**
> **check into something** to go to the desk at a hotel, airport etc and say that you have arrived ⇨ *same meaning* BOOK IN: *We have to **check in** an hour before the flight leaves.* | *We **checked into** a motel.*
> **check up on**
> **check up on someone** to get information about someone, for example to make sure that they are honest: *We always **check up on** new employees.*
> **check out**
> 1 **check something out** *informal* to get information in order to discover whether something is true, correct, or acceptable: *If you're not sure about the spelling, **check** it **out**.* | *Roy went in to **check out** the menu.*
> 2 **check out** to pay the bill and leave a hotel: *What time did he **check out**?*

Exercise 20

Use the dictionary to check the meaning of the following phrasal verbs. Then fill in the spaces in the sentences below with the correct form of the correct phrasal verb.

Example: She *pointed* *out* all the problems with the essay.

> think over   check out   tell off
> come back   scare off   mix (something) up

1 He was ▨▨▨▨ for breaking the window.

2 I'm really not sure whether to buy a new car or not. I'll have to ▨▨▨▨ it ▨▨▨▨.

3 I think we ▨▨▨▨ the burglar when we put the key in the lock.

4 She knew that once she left the country, she would probably never ▨▨▨▨.

5 He ▨▨▨▨ of the hotel at 11 am and drove to the airport.

6 Sally had so many pairs of socks, she got them all ▨▨▨▨.

Exercises

▸ USING THE DICTIONARY

To benefit most from using this dictionary, it is important you are sure what each part of an entry means. Look at the 'How to use *Longman WordWise*' section on pages IV and V for a full explanation.

Exercise 21

The elements of the entry below are mixed up and in the wrong order. Reorder them so that they are listed as they would appear in an entry.

/'ruːθləs/

cruel and not caring about other people

– **ruthlessly**

ruth·less

The judge described Marshall as a ruthless killer.

adjective

Now label each word or sentence with its correct descriptive term from the list below:

part of speech   definition   headword
example sentence   pronunciation
adverb

Exercise 22

Now use the dictionary to help answer the following questions:

1 If you stop doing something that you do regularly, do you?

a give it away
b give it out
c give it up

2 Do you say?

a I said about the holiday
b I told about the holiday
c I talked about the holiday

3 Do you **hold someone's hand** because...?

a you want to make sure they don't escape.
b you want to give them something.
c you love them or want to keep them safe.

4 What part of speech is the word **savagely** in the sentence below?

She was *savagely* attacked by the dogs.

a adjective
b preposition
c adverb

5 If you **give way** to somebody, do you?

a allow them to use your map
b allow their car on another road to go first
c allow them to use your car

6 Which of the following will you find at the top of a mountain?

a peak   **b** pique   **c** peek

7 Which of the following words rhyme with queue?

a though   **b** through   **c** stew

8 Where does the main stress fall in the word **satisfactory**?

a on the 1st syllable
b on the 2nd syllable
c on the 3rd syllable

9 What part of speech is the word **mistake** in the sentence below?

"I don't think you'll have a problem finding it. You can't **mistake** it – it's the largest building in the street."

a adjective   **b** verb   **c** adverb

Aa

a /ə; strong eɪ/, **an** (before a vowel sound) /ən; strong æn/
1 before a noun to show that you are talking about a general type of person or thing: *I saw **a** young boy on **a** bicycle.* | *Do you need **a** pencil?* | *Lucy wants to be **a** teacher.* | *We went to see **a** movie on Friday.*
2 to mean the number 'one': *a thousand pounds* | *Add **an** egg to the mixture.*
3 before words that show how much of something there is: *There were **a** lot of people there.* | *A few magazines were on the table.* | *I like **a** little milk in my tea.*
4 **once a week, £5 an hour etc** one time each week, £5 each hour etc: *Henry makes £21,000 **a** year.*
⇨ compare THE

USAGE a or an?
If a noun starts with a consonant sound, use 'a': *a car* | *I bought a CD today.* If a noun starts with a vowel sound (the sounds made by the letters a, e, i, o, or u), use 'an': *an apple* | *I waited an hour.*

a·ban·don /əˈbændən/ verb to leave someone or something and never return to them: *She abandoned her baby outside the police station.*

ab·bey /ˈæbi/ noun, plural **abbies** a large church: *Westminster Abbey*

ab·bre·vi·a·tion /əˌbriːviˈeɪʃən/ noun a shorter way of writing a word: *Rd. is a written abbreviation for Road.*

ab·do·men /ˈæbdəmən/ noun formal the part of your body between your chest and the top of your legs: *I felt a sharp pain in my abdomen.*

ab·duct /əbˈdʌkt/ verb written to take someone to a place, using force: *Anna believes her ex-husband may have abducted their daughter.*

a·bil·i·ty /əˈbɪləti/ noun, plural **abilities**

GRAMMAR
the ability to do something
power or knowledge that makes you able to do something ⇨ opposite INABILITY: *He **has the ability to** understand difficult ideas.* | *students of different ages and abilities*

a·blaze /əˈbleɪz/ adjective written burning with a lot of flames: *Soon the whole building was ablaze.*

a·ble /ˈeɪbəl/ adjective
1 **be able to do something** if you are able to do something, you can do it: *She might not **be able to** reach the top shelf.* | *You'll **be able to** meet all my friends at the party.*
2 formal intelligent: *Jo is a very able student.*

ab·norm·al /æbˈnɔːməl $ æbˈnɔːrməl/ adjective not normal, especially in a way that is strange or dangerous: *The doctors found some abnormal cells in her body.*

a·board /əˈbɔːd $ əˈbɔrd/ adverb, preposition on or onto a ship, plane, train, or bus: *"Welcome aboard," the Captain said.* | *Thirty passengers were aboard the plane when it crashed.*

a·bol·ish /əˈbɒlɪʃ $ əˈbɑlɪʃ/ verb to officially stop or end something, using a law: *A lot of people think we should abolish fox-hunting.*

a·bor·tion /əˈbɔːʃən $ əˈbɔrʃən/ noun an operation to stop a baby developing inside its mother, by removing the baby while it is too small to live: *She might not have an abortion.*

a·bout¹ /əˈbaʊt/ preposition
1 the subject of a book, talk, or film: *a book about dinosaurs* | *The film is about a group of people who get lost in a jungle.* | *We were talking about you.*

A

2 why you are happy, worried, upset etc: *I'm quite worried about Jack.* | *She's upset about missing the party.*

PHRASE
what about, how about *spoken* used to make a suggestion: *"I don't know what to give him." "What about a book?"* | *How about going by train?*

about² *adverb, adjective*

1 showing an approximate amount or time: *There were about 40 people at the party.* | *It costs about £200.* | *Come over to my house at about 7.*
2 everywhere in a place *BrE*: *The kids were running about in the yard.*
3 somewhere in a place *BrE*: *"Is Colin about?" "Yes, he's here somewhere."*

PHRASES
be about to do something if you are about to do something, you are going to do it very soon: *I was about to leave when the phone rang.* | *She looked as if she was about to cry.*
just about almost: *We've just about finished.*

a·bove /əˈbʌv/ *preposition, adverb*

1 higher than something, or on top of it: *There was a light above the door.* | *We lived in a flat above the shop.* | *His office is on the floor above.* ⇨ see picture on page 354
2 more than a particular amount: *In summer the temperature often rises above 40 degrees.*

PHRASE
above all *formal* used to say strongly that something is more important than anything else: *I would like to thank my teachers, my friends, and above all, my parents.*

a·broad /əˈbrɔːd/ *adverb*

in a foreign country or going to a foreign country: *Have you travelled abroad much?* | *Jane is interested in working or studying abroad.*

a·brupt /əˈbrʌpt/ *adjective* sudden and unexpected: *It was a very abrupt decision.*

ab·sence /ˈæbsəns/ *noun* [no plural] when you are not in the place where you usually are or where you should be: *Did the teacher noticed my absence?*

ab·sent /ˈæbsənt/ *adjective* someone who is absent is not where they usually are or where they should be: *Your parents must send a letter if you are absent from school.*

ab·sen·tee /ˌæbsənˈtiː/ *noun* *formal* someone who is not where they usually are or where they should be: *There were several absentees.*

ab·sen·tee·is·m /ˌæbsənˈtiːɪzəm/ *noun* [no plural] *formal* when people are often not at work or at school when they should be there: *Absenteeism at the school is becoming a real problem.*

absent-mind·ed /ˌ.. ˈ../ *adjective* an absent-minded person often forgets things or does not notice things: *He's a bit absent-minded; he never even knows what day it is!*

ab·so·lute /ˈæbsəluːt/ *adjective* complete and total: *Jodie, you are an absolute idiot for coming here today.*

ab·so·lute·ly /ˈæbsəluːtli/ *adverb*

1 completely or totally: *I'll be absolutely amazed if we win.* | *You will absolutely adore Venice.*
2 **absolutely nothing, absolutely anything**: *There's absolutely nothing* (=nothing at all) *to do in this town.* | *We can do absolutely anything* (=anything at all) *we like.*

absorb

sponge

ab·sorb /əbˈsɔːb $ əbˈsɔːrb/ *verb* **1** if an object absorbs water or a similar substance, the water goes into it through its surface and stays there: *Your skin will absorb most of the cream very quickly.*
2 **be absorbed in something** to be very interested in something that you are doing, watching, or reading: *The kids were completely absorbed in their game.*

ab·sor·bent /əbˈsɔːbənt $ əbˈsɔːrbənt/ *adjective* absorbent material easily takes in water through its surface: *absorbent towels*

A

ab·stain /əb'steɪn/ *verb* **1** *formal* if you abstain from doing something, you do not do it even though you want to: *Please abstain from smoking.* **2** if you abstain during a vote on something, you deliberately do not vote: *Four members of the committee abstained.*

ab·stract /'æbstrækt/ *adjective* abstract ideas are difficult to describe because they are about things that you cannot see or things that are not real: *This lecture discusses abstract concepts, such as justice, morals, and the law.*

ab·surd /əb's3ːd $ əb'sɜ·d/ *adjective formal* very silly: *Don't be so absurd!* | *an absurd idea*

a·bun·dant /ə'bʌndənt/ *adjective* if something is abundant, there is a large amount of it: *abundant supplies of clean water*

a·buse¹ /ə'bjuːs/ *noun* **1** when someone uses their power or authority in a way that is wrong: *This was an abuse of your power as a doctor.* **2** *[no plural]* bad or cruel treatment of someone: *He was put in prison for child abuse.* **3** *[no plural]* rude things that someone says to another person: *The truck driver shouted abuse at us.*

a·buse² /ə'bjuːz/ *verb* **1** to treat someone very badly or cruelly: *The man had abused his wife, both physically and mentally.* **2** if someone abuses their power or authority, they use it in a way that is wrong: *She had abused her position as a teacher.*

a·bu·sive /ə'bjuːsɪv/ *adjective* abusive words are rude: *He used very abusive language.*

ac·a·dem·ic¹ /ˌækə'demɪk/ *adjective* **1** connected with education: *The school has excellent academic results.* **2 academic year** the period of time, usually from September to July, when colleges and universities are open

academic² *noun* someone who teaches and studies in a college or university

a·cad·e·my /ə'kædəmi/ *noun, plural* **academies** a school or college where students learn a special subject or skill: *the Royal Academy of Art*

ac·cel·e·rate /ək'seləreɪt/ *verb* if the driver of a car accelerates, they make the car go faster: *I accelerated and passed the truck in front.*

ac·cel·e·ra·tor /ək'seləreɪtə $ ək'selə‑ˌreɪtɚ/ *noun* the thing that you press with your foot in a car to make it go faster

ac·cent /'æksənt $ 'æksent/ *noun* your accent is the way that you speak a language. Your accent often shows where you were born or where you live: *She speaks English with a strong French accent.*

ac·cept /ək'sept/ *verb*

GRAMMAR
accept that

1 to say 'yes' when someone gives or offers you something: *Are you going to accept the job?* | *It is a generous gift, but I can't accept it.* | *Mary decided to accept the invitation to the party.*
2 to agree that something is true: *He will not accept that he has done anything wrong.*
3 to treat someone in a friendly way: *The other children did not accept him because he was different.*
4 accept responsibility, accept the blame *formal* to admit that you did something bad: *No one has yet accepted responsibility for the attack.* | *I am not going to accept the blame for something I didn't do.*

ac·cept·a·ble /ək'septəbəl/ *adjective formal*
1 if your work is acceptable, it is satisfactory ⇨ *opposite* UNACCEPTABLE: *This work is not of an acceptable standard.*
2 if something is acceptable, most people approve of it or think it is normal ⇨ *opposite* UNACCEPTABLE: *Do you think smoking in restaurants is acceptable?*

ac·cept·ed /ək'septɪd/ *adjective formal* an accepted idea or way of doing something is one that most people agree is right: *the accepted rules of the game*

ac·cess¹ /'ækses/ *noun [no plural]* if you have access to something, you have the chance or ability to use it: *The Internet gives us access to all the latest information.* | *The building is being adapted to allow access for wheelchair users* (=so that people in wheelchairs can get into it).

A

access² *verb* to find and use information, especially on a computer: *Students can access this information via their computers.*

ac·ces·si·ble /ək'sesəbəl/ *adjective* an accessible place is easy to get to: *Some beaches are only accessible by boat.*

ac·ces·so·ry /ək'sesəri/ *noun, plural* **accessories** something such as a belt or jewellery that you wear because it looks nice with your clothes

ac·ci·dent /'æksədənt/ *noun*

GRAMMAR
have an accident
1 if someone has an accident, they are hurt, for example when their car crashes: *What would you do if I **had an accident**? | I saw a **bad accident** on my way to school. | A man has died in a **car accident**.
2 if something is an accident, no one planned it or wanted it to happen: *They said my father's death **was an accident**, but I did not believe them.*
3 **by accident** if something happens by accident, no one planned it or expected it to happen: *We met **by accident** in the street.*

ac·ci·den·tal /ˌæksə'dentl/ *adjective* happening by chance, without being planned: *The drug was an accidental discovery.*

ac·ci·den·tal·ly /ˌæksə'dentl-i/ *adverb* if you accidentally do something, you do it without meaning to do it or planning to do it: *I'm so sorry, I accidentally deleted your files from the computer last night. | The police think the fire was started accidentally.*

ac·com·mo·date /ə'kɒmədeɪt $ə'kɑmə,deɪt/ *verb formal* to have enough space for a particular number of people or things: *The school can only accommodate about seventy children.*

ac·com·mo·da·tion /əˌkɒmə'deɪʃən $ə,kɑmə'deɪʃən/ *noun, also* plural **accommodations** *AmE* a place that you can live or stay in: *I*

need to find some cheap accommodation. | The price includes flights and hotel accommodation.

USAGE
In British English, there is no plural form of **accommodation**. In American English, the plural **accommodations** is very common, and the singular form is rare: *The accommodations are plain but comfortable.*

ac·com·pa·ny /ə'kʌmpəni/ **accompanied, accompanies** *verb* **1** *formal* to go with someone to a place: *Will your husband accompany you to the hospital?* **2** to play a musical instrument while someone else plays or sings the main tune: *Simon accompanied me on the guitar.*

ac·com·plish /ə'kʌmplɪʃ $ə'kɑmplɪʃ/ *verb formal* to succeed in doing something: *He took about one hour to accomplish the task.*

ac·com·plished /ə'kʌmplɪʃt $ə'kɑmplɪʃt/ *adjective* very good at doing a particular thing: *Sam is an accomplished violinist.*

ac·com·plish·ment /ə'kʌmplɪʃmənt $ə'kɑmplɪʃmənt/ *noun* **1** [no plural] when you succeed in doing something difficult: *We all felt a great sense of accomplishment when we finished the project.* **2** *formal* something that you can do well: *Singing was one of her many accomplishments.*

ac·cord /ə'kɔːd $ə'kɔrd/ *noun* **do something of your own accord** if you do something of your own accord, you do it even though no one has asked you or told you to do it: *She didn't lose her job; she left of her own accord.*

ac·cord·ance /ə'kɔːdns $ə'kɔrdns/ *noun* **in accordance with** *formal* if something happens in accordance with a particular rule or law, it happens in the way the rule or law says it should: *The company delivered the video recorders in accordance with the contract.*

ac·cord·ing·ly /ə'kɔːdɪŋli $ə'kɔrdɪŋli/ *adverb formal* in a way that is suitable for a particular situation: *He broke the law and was punished accordingly.*

according to /.'... ./ *preposition* showing who said something: *According to Rachel, Keith started the fight* (=Rachel says that Keith

▼ started the fight). | *According to this book, all artists are mad* (=this book says that all artists are mad).

ac·count¹ /ə'kaʊnt/ *noun*

GRAMMAR
give an account of something
1 if you give an account of something, you describe what happened: *He gave an account of his conversation with Jane.*
2 if you have an account with a bank, you can leave money there or take it out, pay bills etc: *a bank account | She took ten pounds out of her account. | I will pay the money straight into my account.*
3 **accounts** a record of the money that a business or person has received and spent during a particular time: *the company's annual accounts*

PHRASES
open an account to start to use a bank account: *I would like to open a new account.*
take something into account, take account of something to think about a particular fact when you are deciding what to do, so that it affects what you decide: *We will take your age into account. | What should I take account of when I rent an apartment?*

account² *verb* **account for something** to give a reason for something that is unusual or wrong: *How do you account for these figures?*

ac·count·a·ble /ə'kaʊntəbəl/ *adjective formal* if you are accountable for the things that you do, you are responsible for them, and you must be able to explain why you did them: *At what age is a person legally accountable for their actions?*

ac·coun·tan·cy /ə'kaʊntənsi/ *noun [no plural] BrE* the job of being an accountant ⇨ *same meaning* ACCOUNTING

ac·coun·tant /ə'kaʊntənt/ *noun* someone whose job is to keep records of how much money a business has received and spent

ac·count·ing /ə'kaʊntɪŋ/ ACCOUNTANCY

ac·cu·mu·late /ə'kjuːmjəleɪt/ *verb*
1 to gradually get more and more of something: *During his life he had accumulated a huge amount of money.*

2 if something accumulates, it gradually increases: *Her problems started to accumulate after the baby was born.*

ac·cu·ra·cy /'ækjərəsi/ *noun [no plural]* when something is exactly correct: *I was amazed at the accuracy of his answers.*

ac·cu·rate /'ækjərət/ *adjective* exactly correct ⇨ *opposite* INACCURATE: *The police gave an accurate description of the man.*
– **accurately** *adverb*: *This watch keeps time very accurately.*

ac·cu·sa·tion /ˌækjə'zeɪʃən/ *noun* when someone says that another person has done something wrong: *She made accusations of violence against him.*

ac·cuse /ə'kjuːz/ *verb* to say that someone has done something wrong: *They accused her of trying to poison his drink.*
– **accuser** *noun*: *His accusers say he is lying.*

ac·cus·ing /ə'kjuːzɪŋ/ *adjective* showing that you think someone has done something wrong: *"Where have you been?" asked Jenny in an accusing voice.*
– **accusingly** *adverb*: *He looked at me accusingly.*

ac·cus·tomed /ə'kʌstəmd/ *adjective formal* if you are accustomed to something, it is not strange or unusual to you: *I am not accustomed to hot weather.*

ace¹ /eɪs/ *adjective informal* excellent: *He's an ace goalkeeper.*

ace² *noun* one of four playing cards in a pack that can have either the highest or lowest value in a game of cards: *the ace of diamonds*

ache¹ /eɪk/ *verb* if part of your body aches, it hurts slightly for a long time: *Driving long distances makes your legs ache.*

ache² *noun* a slight pain that does not go away quickly: *My body felt full of aches and pains.*

USAGE
You can use **ache** after other words to describe a pain in a particular part of your body: *toothache | earache | headache | I've got a terrible stomachache.*

a·chieve /ə'tʃiːv/ *verb*
to succeed in doing or getting something you want: *Our local team achieved another win last* ▼

weekend. | *He achieved a lot in his life.*

a·chieve·ment /əˈtʃiːvmənt/ noun

something important or difficult that you do successfully: *Learning to drive is a great achievement.*

ac·id /ˈæsɪd/ noun a strong chemical that can burn things: *sulphuric acid*

acid rain /ˌ.. ˈ./ noun [no plural] rain that contains acid and that damages plants, trees, and rivers

ac·knowl·edge /əkˈnɒlɪdʒ $ əkˈnɑl-ɪdʒ/ verb to say or show that something is true or correct: *He finally acknowledged that I was right.* | *She refused to acknowledge the problem.*

ac·knowl·edge·ment or **acknowl-edgment** /əkˈnɒlɪdʒmənt $ əkˈnɑl-ɪdʒmənt/ noun when you show that you agree that something is true or correct: *Maggie listened and nodded in acknowledgement.*

ac·ne /ˈækni/ noun [no plural] a skin disease that makes a lot of red spots appear on your face: *I had terrible acne in my teens.*

ac·quaint·ance /əˈkweɪntəns/ noun someone you have met but do not know well: *There were several acquaintances of mine at the party.*

ac·quaint·ed /əˈkweɪntɪd/ adjective formal if you are acquainted with someone, you know them but not very well: *I see that you two are acquainted with each other already.*

ac·quire /əˈkwaɪə $ əˈkwaɪɚ/ verb formal to get or buy something: *She'd acquired some valuable furniture over the years.*

a·cre /ˈeɪkə $ ˈeɪkɚ/ noun a measure-ment of land, equal to 4047 square metres or 4840 square YARDS

ac·ro·bat /ˈækrəbæt/ noun someone who performs in a CIRCUS, doing difficult jumps or balancing their body in difficult positions

ac·ro·nym /ˈækrənɪm/ noun a word that is made from the first letters of a group of words. For example, EFL is an acronym for English as a Foreign Lan-guage

a·cross /əˈkrɒs $ əˈkrɔs/ adverb, preposition

1 from one side of something to the other: *A boy suddenly ran across the road.* | *They are building a bridge across the river.*
2 on the other side of something: *Her best friend lived across the road from her.*

act¹ /ækt/ verb

GRAMMAR
act like something

1 to do something: *When someone has a heart attack, you need to act quickly.*
2 to behave in a particular way: *Stop acting like a child.* | *Peter is acting very strangely.*
3 to perform in a play or film: *We were both acting in 'Carmen' when we fell in love.*

act² noun

GRAMMAR
an act of something **1** some-thing that you do, especially some-thing that shows how you feel: *As an act of rebellion, she refused to go to school.* | *acts of kindness* **2** a law that the government has made: *the Employment Act of 1989* **3** one of the main parts of a play: *The ghost appears in Act 1, Scene 2* **4** a short piece of entertainment in a television or theatre show: *a comedy act*

act·ing /ˈæktɪŋ/ noun [no plural] perform-ing in plays or films: *He's brilliant at acting.*

ac·tion /ˈækʃən/ noun

something that you do: *He said he was sorry for his actions.* | *Sally's quick action stopped the fire from spreading.*

PHRASES
take action if you take action, you do something in order to deal with a problem: *The police are **taking action** against car crime.*
course of action formal something that you do to deal with a situation: *We need to think about our best **course of action**.*
put something into action to start using a plan: *It's time to **put** our plans **into action**.*

action re·play /ˌ.. ˈ../ noun BrE when

an interesting part of a sports event is shown again on film or television immediately after it happens; INSTANT REPLAY AmE: *The action replay showed that the ball crossed the line.*

ac·tiv·ate /'æktəveɪt/ *verb formal* to make something start to work: *Pressing this button will activate the car alarm.*

ac·tive¹ /'æktɪv/ *adjective*
1 someone who is active can move and do things easily: *Although Bob is over 70, he's still active, and manages a long walk most days. | Having three very active teenagers in the house sure keeps us busy.*
2 in grammar, if a verb or sentence is active, the person or thing doing the action is the SUBJECT of the verb. In the sentence 'The boy kicked the ball', the verb 'kick' is active ➪ compare PASSIVE¹ (2)

active² *noun* **the active (voice)** the active form of a verb

ac·tive·ly /'æktɪvli/ *adverb* if you are actively doing something, you are doing things to try and make something happen: *Are you actively trying to find work?*

ac·tiv·ist /'æktəvɪst/ *noun* someone who works hard to change society or a political situation they do not agree with: *a political activist*

ac·tiv·i·ty /æk'tɪvəti/ *noun, plural activities*
the things that someone does: *Do you enjoy sporting activities? | Criminal activity in the area is increasing.*

ac·tor /'æktə $'æktɚ/ *noun* someone who performs in plays or films: *He wants to be an actor when he grows up.*

ac·tress /'æktrəs/ *noun, plural actresses* a woman who performs in plays or films: *Elizabeth Taylor is a famous actress.*

ac·tu·al /'æktʃuəl/ *adjective*
real, rather than what you believed or expected: *Our guess was much higher than the actual number.*

ac·tu·al·ly /'æktʃuəli/ *adverb*
1 really: *Do you actually believe that? | I wish I knew what she was actually thinking.*
2 used to say in a polite way that someone is wrong: *"Hi Jo." "My name is Jane, actually."*

a·cute /ə'kjuːt/ *adjective* 1 very serious or bad: *patients who suffer acute pain* 2 an acute angle is less than 90 degrees

AD /ˌeɪ 'diː/ an abbreviation for Anno Domini; used in dates to mean after the birth of Christ: *the first century AD*

ad /æd/ *informal* an ADVERTISEMENT

ad·a·mant /'ædəmənt/ *adjective formal* determined not to change your opinion or decision: *She was adamant that she would stay.*

a·dapt /ə'dæpt/ *verb* 1 to change the way you do things because you are in a new situation: *She never really adapted to living abroad.* 2 to change something so that you can use it for a different purpose: *We can adapt your computer to make it easier to log on.*

a·dapt·a·ble /ə'dæptəbəl/ *adjective* someone who is adaptable is good at changing the way they do things when they are in a new situation: *We're looking for someone lively and adaptable to join our team.*

ad·ap·ta·tion /ˌædæp'teɪʃən/ *noun* a play or film that is based on a book: *The film is a modern adaptation of 'Romeo and Juliet'.*

a·dapt·er or **adaptor** /ə'dæptə $ə'dæptɚ/ *noun* something that you use to connect two pieces of equipment when you cannot connect them together directly: *an electrical adapter*

add /æd/ *verb*

GRAMMAR
add something to something
add that
1 to put something with another thing: ***Add** more garlic **to** the sauce. | Fluoride **is added to** water to prevent tooth decay.*
2 also **add up** to put numbers together to get the total: *Add the two numbers together and divide them by three. | **Add up** the prices of all the things you bought.*
3 to say more about something: *He told me what Sue had done but **added that** it was not her fault. | "Come to my house – and don't be late," he added.*

ad·dict /'ædɪkt/ *noun* **1** someone who cannot stop taking harmful drugs: *a drug addict* **2** *informal* someone who likes something very much and does it a lot: *I'm a TV addict.*

ad·dic·ted /ə'dɪktɪd/ *adjective* not able to stop doing something, especially taking a harmful drug: *He was addicted to heroin.*

ad·dic·tion /ə'dɪkʃən/ *noun* the problem someone has when they need to take alcohol or harmful drugs regularly: *the problem of heroin addiction*

ad·dic·tive /ə'dɪktɪv/ *adjective* an addictive drug is one that makes you need it more and more: *Cocaine is addictive.*

ad·di·tion /ə'dɪʃən/ *noun* [no plural] **1** adding numbers or amounts together to get the total: *Mark's very good at addition and subtraction.* **2 in addition to** as well as: *We won a holiday for four, in addition to the prize money.*

ad·di·tion·al /ə'dɪʃənəl/ *adjective* additional numbers or amounts of something are more than you already have: *We always need additional staff over the New Year.*

ad·dress¹ /ə'dres $ 'ædres/ *noun*, *plural* **addresses**
the number of the house and the name of the street and town where you live: *My address is 37 King Street, London.*

address² /ə'dres/ *verb*
1 *formal* to speak to a group of people: *Mandela addressed a crowd of thousands of people.*
2 be addressed to someone if a letter is addressed to someone, their name is on it because it is for them: *The official-looking letter* **was addressed to** *my mother.*
3 *formal* to try to deal with a problem: *There are serious problems that we need to address.*

ad·ept /'ædept $ ə'dept/ *adjective formal* good at doing something: *I'm not very adept at typing.*

ad·e·quate /'ædɪkwət/ *adjective* good enough for a particular purpose ⇨ *opposite* INADEQUATE: *The government should provide adequate public transport.*

ad·ja·cent /ə'dʒeɪsənt/ *adjective formal* next to something: *The garden is adjacent to the river.*

ad·jec·tive /'ædʒəktɪv/ *noun*
a word that describes something. 'Big', 'funny', and 'hot' are all adjectives

ad·join·ing /ə'dʒɔɪnɪŋ/ *adjective formal* next to or connected to another building, room etc: *She hurried into the adjoining room.*

ad·just /ə'dʒʌst/ *verb* to change or move something slightly to make it better: *How do you adjust the colour on the TV? | You may need to adjust your seat belt.*

ad·just·a·ble /ə'dʒʌstəbəl/ *adjective* something that is adjustable can be changed or moved slightly to make it better: *adjustable car seats*

ad·just·ment /ə'dʒʌstmənt/ *noun* a small change that you make to something: *We had to make a few adjustments to our plan.*

ad·min·is·ter /əd'mɪnəstə $ əd'mɪnəstɚ/ *verb formal* to organize or manage something: *A special committee will administer the scheme.*

ad·min·is·tra·tion /əd,mɪnə'streɪʃən/ *noun* [no plural] the work of organizing or managing the work in a company or organization: *a career in university administration*

ad·min·is·tra·tive /əd'mɪnəstrətɪv $ əd'mɪnə,streɪtɪv/ *adjective* connected with organizing or managing the work in a company or organization: *The company has thirteen administrative staff.*

ad·min·is·tra·tor /əd'mɪnəstreɪtə $ əd'mɪnə,streɪtɚ/ *noun* someone whose job is to help organize a particular area of work in a company or organization

ad·mi·ra·ble /'ædmərəbəl/ *adjective formal* something that is admirable is good and deserves your respect: *He had many admirable qualities, especially honesty.*

ad·mi·ral /'ædmərəl/ *noun* an officer who has a very high rank in the Navy

ad·mi·ra·tion /,ædmə'reɪʃən/ *noun* [no plural] when you admire something or someone: *I have great admiration for his skill as a player.*

ad·mire /əd'maɪə $ əd'maɪər/ verb

GRAMMAR
admire someone for (doing) something

1 to think that someone is very good or clever: *Many people admired Margaret Thatcher.* | *I admired her for being honest with her father.*
2 to look at something and think that it is very good: *We stopped for a moment to admire the view.*

ad·mis·sion /əd'mɪʃən/ noun **1** [no plural] the amount of money you have to pay to go to a film, sports event, concert etc: *Admission to the exhibition is $9.50.* **2** when you are allowed to study at a university or get treatment in a hospital: *Lucy is applying for admission to Harvard next year.*

ad·mit /əd'mɪt/ verb **admitted, admitting**

GRAMMAR
admit (that)
admit to something

1 to accept and say that something is true, although you do not want to: *We know you stole the money. Why won't you admit it?* | *I admit that I did not like Sarah when I first met her.* | *Ian will never admit to being afraid.*
2 to allow someone to go into a place or join a college, university etc: *The club admits women for half price on Wednesdays.*

ad·o·les·cence /ˌædə'lesəns/ noun [no plural] the time when a young person is developing into an adult, usually between the ages of 12 and 17: *Adolescence is a difficult time for young people.*

ad·o·les·cent /ˌædə'lesənt/ noun a young person between the ages of about 12 and 17, who is developing into an adult
–**adolescent** adjective: *Many adolescent girls worry about their appearance.*

a·dopt /ə'dɒpt $ ə'dɑpt/ verb to legally make someone else's child your own son or daughter: *They adopted Sam when he was a baby.*
–**adopted** adjective: *their adopted son*

a·dop·tion /ə'dɒpʃən $ ə'dɑpʃən/ noun when someone adopts a child

a·dor·a·ble /ə'dɔːrəbəl/ adjective very attractive: *What an adorable baby girl!*

a·dore /ə'dɔː $ ə'dɔr/ verb to love someone very much, or to like something very much: *She had always adored her father.* | *I just adore pizza!*

a·dren·a·lin /ə'drenl-ɪn/ noun [no plural] a substance that your body produces when you are frightened, excited, or angry, and which gives you more energy

ad·ult /'ædʌlt $ ə'dʌlt/ noun a person or animal that has finished growing: *When you are an adult you have a lot of responsibilities.*
–**adult** adjective: *I've lived in London all my adult life.*

a·dul·ter·y /ə'dʌltəri/ noun [no plural] when someone who is married has sex with someone who is not their husband or wife: *She accused her husband of adultery.*

ad·vance¹ /əd'vɑːns $ əd'væns/ noun **1 in advance** before a particular time or event starts: *You should always plan your journey in advance.* **2** something new and important that someone discovers: *There have been great advances in technology.*

advance² verb written to move forward to a new position: *The animal advanced slowly towards her.*

advance³ adjective before an event happens: *For advance tickets, call the number below.* | *We got no advance warning that there was a problem.*

ad·vanced /əd'vɑːnst $ əd'vænst/ adjective
very modern and new: *the most advanced medical equipment*

ad·van·tage /əd'vɑːntɪdʒ $ əd'væntɪdʒ/ noun

GRAMMAR
an advantage of something
an advantage over something

something that makes things better or easier for you: *The **advantage of** living in a town is that there is lots to do.* | *The new system **has** many **advantages over** the old one.* | *Did having a famous father **give** you an **advantage** as an actor?*

PHRASES
take advantage of something to use a situation to help you get what

you want: *The thief **took advantage of** a door that someone left open.*
take advantage of someone to behave unfairly towards someone to help you get what you want: *Because she's a kind person, people often **take advantage of** her.*

ad·van·ta·geous /ˌædvən'teɪdʒəs/ *adjective formal* helpful to you and likely to make you more successful: *an advantageous deal*

ad·vent /'ædvent/ *noun [no plural]* when something important first starts to exist: *Since the advent of computers, offices have changed completely.*

ad·ven·ture /əd'ventʃə $əd'ventʃɚ/ *noun* an unusual, exciting, or dangerous thing that happens to someone: *It's a book about Johnson's adventures at sea.*

ad·ven·tur·ous /əd'ventʃərəs/ *adjective* an adventurous person likes doing new and exciting things: *an adventurous little boy*

ad·verb /'ædvɜːb $'ædvɚb/ *noun* a word that describes or adds to the meaning of a verb, an adjective, another adverb, or a sentence. For example, 'quietly' is an adverb in 'He spoke quietly' and 'very' is an adverb in 'It was very difficult'

ad·verse /'ædvɜːs $əd'vɚs/ *adjective formal* bad and causing problems: *The illness has had an adverse effect on her schoolwork.* | *Adverse weather conditions caused the accident.*

ad·vert /'ædvɜːt $'ædvɚt/ *BrE* an ADVERTISEMENT: *Have you seen that advert for Nike sportswear?*

ad·ver·tise /'ædvətaɪz $'ædvɚˌtaɪz/ *verb* **1** to put pictures and information about something in newspapers, on television, on walls etc in order to persuade people to buy it or use it: *They're advertising the new car on TV.* **2** to put a notice in a newspaper saying that you are looking for someone to do a particular job: *The school is advertising for a new head teacher.*

ad·ver·tise·ment /əd'vɜːtɪsmənt $ˌædvɚ'taɪzmənt/ *noun* **1** a notice in a newspaper, a short film on television etc, which tries to persuade people to buy something: *an advertisement for a cellphone* **2** a notice in a

newspaper that gives information about a job that is available: *I saw an advertisement for a driver in the paper.*

ad·ver·tis·ing /'ædvətaɪzɪŋ $'ædvɚˌtaɪzɪŋ/ *noun [no plural]* the business of advertising things on television, in newspapers etc: *My father works in advertising.*

ad·vice /əd'vaɪs/ *noun [no plural]*

GRAMMAR
advice about/on something
when you suggest what someone should do: *I need some **advice about** boys.* | *Do you have any **advice** on how to remove coffee stains?* | *My mother is always **giving** me **advice**.*

PHRASES
take someone's advice, follow someone's advice to do what someone suggests you should do: *I **took** your **advice** and phoned her.* | *If you **follow** my **advice**, you will be alright.*
ask someone's advice to ask someone what they think you should do: *Can I **ask** your **advice about** something?*

USAGE
Do not say 'an advice' or 'some advices'. Say **some advice**, **a lot of advice**, or **a piece of advice**: *I need **some advice** on what to wear for the wedding.* | *My Mum gave me a really good **piece of advice**.*

ad·vis·a·ble /əd'vaɪzəbəl/ *adjective formal* something that is advisable is something that you should do in order to avoid problems: *It's advisable to book your ticket early.*

ad·vise /əd'vaɪz/ *verb*

GRAMMAR
advise someone to do something
advise someone against something
advise someone on something
to tell someone what you think they should do: *His lawyer **advised** him to say nothing.* | *We all **advised** him **against** (=said he should not) going into business with Kamal.* | *Accountants **advise** people **on** tax matters.*

ad·vis·er or **advisor** /əd'vaɪzə $əd'vaɪzɚ/ *noun* someone whose job is to give advice to a company, government etc: *a financial adviser*

ad·vo·cate¹ /'ædvəkeɪt/ *verb formal* to say that you support a particular plan or method: *We have never advocated the use of violence.*

ad·vo·cate² /'ædvəkət/ *noun formal* **1** someone who supports a particular plan or method: *He was an advocate of fascism.* **2** a lawyer who tries to show that someone is not guilty of a crime

aer·i·al¹ /'eəriəl $ 'eriəl/ *adjective* from a plane or happening in the air: *an aerial photograph of the island*

aerial² *noun BrE* an object on top of a building or television that sends or receives radio or television signals; ANTENNA *AmE: The TV aerial blew down in the storm.* ⇨ *see picture on page 343*

ae·ro·bic /eə'rəʊbɪk $ ə'roʊbɪk/ *adjective* aerobic exercise is any exercise that makes your heart and lungs strong, such as running or swimming: *an aerobic workout*

aerobics

aer·o·bics /eə'rəʊbɪks $ ə'roʊbɪks/ *plural noun* a type of physical exercise that you do with music, especially in a class: *She teaches aerobics.*

aer·o·plane /'eərəpleɪn $ 'erə,pleɪn/ *noun BrE* a vehicle with wings and an engine that flies in the air; AIRPLANE *AmE* ⇨ *same meaning* PLANE: *We've been on this aeroplane for 11 hours.* ⇨ *see picture on page 349*

aer·o·sol /'eərəsɒl $ 'erə,sɔl/ *noun* a small metal container with a liquid inside. You press a button on the container to make the liquid come out: *an aerosol deodorant spray* ⇨ *see picture at* SPRAY¹

af·fair /ə'feə $ ə'fer/ *noun* **1** if two people have an affair, they have a sexual

relationship, especially one that is secret because they are married to other people: *She had an affair with her husband's best friend.* **2** a situation that everyone knows about, especially one that involves bad things that important people have done: *Several teachers had to resign over the affair.* **3** **affairs** things that are connected with a particular subject, especially business or politics: *He never talked about his business affairs.*

af·fect /ə'fekt/ *verb*

to make something or someone different or change in some way: *I hope this new job will not affect your schoolwork.* | *How did the divorce affect the children?*

af·fec·tion /ə'fekʃən/ *noun* a feeling of liking someone and caring about them: *I've always had a great affection for Tim.*

af·fec·tion·ate /ə'fekʃənət/ *adjective* showing that you like or love someone: *He gave her an affectionate hug.*
—**affectionately** *adverb: He patted his son on the head affectionately.*

af·fin·i·ty /ə'fɪnəti/ *noun* a feeling that you like and understand a person or animal: *He had a remarkable affinity with horses.*

af·fir·ma·tive /ə'fɜːmətɪv $ ə'fɚ-mətɪv/ *adjective formal* meaning 'yes': *an affirmative reply*

af·flict /ə'flɪkt/ *verb formal* **be afflicted by something** to be badly affected by a serious disease or problem: *a country that is afflicted by disease and famine*

af·flic·tion /ə'flɪkʃən/ *noun formal* something that makes people suffer: *Bad eyesight is a common affliction.*

af·flu·ent /'æfluənt/ *adjective* having a lot of money and possessions: *our affluent western society*

af·ford /ə'fɔːd $ ə'fɔrd/ *verb*

can afford (to do) something to have enough money to buy something: *I want to go on holiday but I can't afford it.* | *Can you afford to buy a computer?*

af·ford·a·ble /ə'fɔːdəbəl $ ə'fɔrdəbəl/ *adjective* something that is affordable is not too expensive, and you are able to buy it: *It was difficult to find affordable accommodation.*

af·front /ə'frʌnt/ *noun* [no plural] *formal* something that someone says or does that offends or upsets you: *The people saw the remark as an affront to their religion.*

a·fraid /ə'freɪd/ *adjective*

GRAMMAR
afraid of something
afraid that
afraid of doing something
1 frightened: *Don't be afraid – I won't hurt you.* | *Some people are afraid of spiders.*
2 worried that something may happen: *I was afraid that no one would like my paintings.* | *He was afraid of offending my father.*

a·fresh /ə'freʃ/ *adverb* **start afresh** to start again from the beginning: *You'd better start afresh on a clean piece of paper.*

A·fri·can A·mer·i·can /ˌæfrɪkən ə'merɪkən/ *noun* an American whose family originally came from Africa
– African-American *adjective*

af·ter¹ /'ɑːftə $ 'æftɚ/ *preposition*
1 when something has happened or finished: *I felt much better after my holiday.* | *I'll meet you after school* (=when the school day has finished).
2 when a period of time has passed: *We left after half an hour.*
3 used when telling the time AmE: *It's ten after five* (=it's ten minutes after five o'clock).
4 following someone: *His little sister ran after him.*

PHRASES
after all 1) used to say that what you expected did not happen: *It didn't rain after all.* 2) used when saying something that shows why you are right: *The accident could have been worse – after all no one was killed.*
one after the other with each person or animal following the one in front: *The children went downstairs, one after the other.*
day after day, year after year etc *written* used to say that something happens for a long time: *Day after*

day he stayed in his room, studying.

after²
when you have done something or something has finished: *I'll come and talk to you after I've finished this.* | *After we'd had lunch, we all went out in the garden.*

after-ef·fect /'.. ˌ./ *noun* the after-effects of a bad event are the unpleasant results that stay after it has ended: *the after-effects of the war*

af·ter·noon /ˌɑːftə'nuːn $ ˌæftɚ-'nun/ *noun*
1 the period of time between 12 o'clock and the evening: *I'll see you on Sunday afternoon.* | *There's a good film on TV tomorrow afternoon.* | *Come to my house this afternoon* (=today in the afternoon). | *He sometimes has a sleep in the afternoon.* | *She's been crying all afternoon.*
2 **(Good) Afternoon** *spoken* used when you meet someone in the afternoon: *Good afternoon, everyone.*

af·ter·shave /'ɑːftəʃeɪv $ 'æftɚˌʃeɪv/ *noun* a liquid with a nice smell that a man puts on his skin: *Are you wearing aftershave?*

af·ter·thought /'ɑːftəθɔːt $ 'æftɚ-ˌθɔt/ *noun* if you do something as an afterthought, you do it after doing other things, because you forgot to do it earlier: *She invited me to the party, but only as an afterthought.*

af·ter·wards /'ɑːftəwədz $ 'æftɚ-wɚdz/ also **afterward** AmE, *adverb* after something has happened: *There will be party games and a disco afterwards.* | *She became ill in 1997 and died two years afterwards.*

a·gain /ə'gen/ *adverb*
1 one more time: *I'd like to see that film again.* | *I don't think I'll go there again – it was too crowded.*
2 when you do something or feel something as before: *He should be back at school again soon* (=he should return to school soon). | *I'll*

come *and visit you when I'm well again* (=when I'm no longer ill).

PHRASES

all over again used to say that you have to do something for a second time, and that this is a bad thing: *We're going to have to paint the room **all over again**.*

again and again very many times: *I've tried calling him **again and again** but he's never home.*

a·gainst /ə'genst/ *preposition*

1 not agreeing with something: *Philip was against the idea of selling the house.* | *I'm against testing chemicals on animals* (=I do not think it should be done).

2 fighting or competing with someone: *the war against Spain* | *Italy will play in the final against Brazil.* | *the war against drugs*

3 trying to stop something from happening: *The government must take action against homelessness.*

4 touching or passing on a surface: *He leaned his bike against a tree.* | *The cat rubbed itself against my legs.*

PHRASES

against the law, against the rules: *You can't park here – it's **against the law*** (=not allowed by the law).

have nothing against someone to not dislike someone: *I **have nothing against** him personally, but I do not think he is right for the job.*

age¹ /eɪdʒ/ *noun*

your age is the number of years you have lived: *What age were you when your father died?* | *Louise is the same age as me.* | *When you get to my age, you'll understand.* | *people of all different ages*

PHRASES

10, 40 etc years of age *formal* if someone is 10, 40 etc years of age, they have been alive for 10, 40 etc years: *When I was 14 **years of age**, my sister was born.*

for your age if someone is big, clever etc for their age, they are bigger, more clever etc than other people who are the same age: *Grace is not very big **for her age**.*

under age not old enough to do something legally: *You cannot drink alcohol if you are **under age**.*

age² *verb* if someone ages, they become older and weaker: *Jim had aged a lot since I last saw him.*
–**ageing** *BrE*, **aging** *AmE adjective*: *the country's ageing population*

aged¹ /eɪdʒd/ *adjective* **aged 5, aged 15 etc** 5, 15 etc years old: *His son is now aged 4.*

a·ged² /'eɪdʒɪd/ *adjective formal* very old: *his aged mother*

a·gen·cy /'eɪdʒənsi/ *noun, plural* **agencies** a business that arranges services for people: *I went to a travel agency to book my holiday.*

a·gen·da /ə'dʒendə/ *noun* a list of the things that people are going to discuss at a meeting: *The next item on the agenda is the school trip.*

a·gent /'eɪdʒənt/ *noun* **1** a person or company that arranges services or does work for other people: *Our company has an agent in Madrid.* **2** someone who tries to get secret information about another government or organization: *a secret agent*

ag·gra·vate /'æɡrəveɪt/ *verb formal* to annoy someone: *Some students try to aggravate the tutor deliberately.*
–**aggravating** *adjective*: *Having the radio on all day at work is really aggravating.*

ag·gres·sion /ə'ɡreʃən/ *noun [no plural]* angry or violent behaviour or feelings: *You need to learn how to control your aggression.*

ag·gres·sive /ə'ɡresɪv/ *adjective* behaving angrily, as if you want to fight or attack someone: *He is very aggressive when he plays football.*
–**aggressively** *adverb*: *He shouted at me aggressively.*

a·gile /'ædʒaɪl $ 'ædʒəl/ *adjective* able to move quickly and easily: *In spite of her size, Sara is very agile.*

a·gi·ta·ted /'ædʒəteɪtɪd/ *adjective* very worried or upset: *Mum gets very agitated when I'm late.*

a·go /ə'ɡəʊ $ ə'ɡoʊ/ *adverb*

use **ago** after a period of time to say how far back in the past something happened: *Rob and Di got married* two years ago. | Carl left a few moments ago. | A very long time ago, this area was covered with trees and grass.

USAGE for, since, and ago
For, since, and **ago** are used to talk about time. **For** is used with the present perfect or simple past tense. It is always followed by periods of time: *She's been here for three days.* | *The party lasted for five hours.* **Since** is always used with the present perfect tense and with exact days, dates, and times: *He's been here since Sunday.* | *I've been working here since 1998.* **Ago** is always used with the simple past tense. It tells you how far back in the past something happened or began: *My grandfather died two years ago.*

ag·o·nize also **agonise** *BrE* /'ægənaɪz/ *verb* to think and worry for a long time about something you have to do: *Don't agonize for too long about any of the exam questions.*

ag·o·niz·ing also **agonising** *BrE* /'ægənaɪzɪŋ/ *adjective* **1** very painful: *an agonizing injury* **2** making you feel very worried or nervous: *Waiting for the result was agonizing.*

ag·o·ny /'ægəni/ *noun* very bad pain: *I was in agony before the operation.*

a·gree /ə'griː/ *verb*

GRAMMAR
agree on/about something
agree with someone/something
agree to something
agree to do something
1 to have the same opinion as someone else: *Paul and I don't **agree on** everything.* | *I **agree about** the colour – it's awful.* | *I want you to tell me if you don't **agree with** me.* | *We all **agreed that** it was a bad idea.*
2 to say 'yes' when someone asks you to do something: *Do you think she will **agree to** our plan?* | *Tracy **agreed to** help her mother.*
3 to think that something is right: *I don't **agree with** hitting children.*

a·gree·a·ble /ə'griːəbəl/ *adjective formal* pleasant or enjoyable: *a very agreeable meal*

a·greed /ə'griːd/ *adjective* **1** an agreed amount or arrangement is one that people have all accepted: *The agreed price for the bike was $50.*

2 be agreed on if people are agreed on something, they all accept it: *Are we all agreed on the date for the party?*

a·gree·ment /ə'griːmənt/ *noun*

GRAMMAR
an agreement between people
an arrangement or promise between people, countries, or organizations, agreeing to do something: *a trade **agreement between** Europe and the US* | *We **made an agreement** to help each other.*

PHRASES
come to an agreement, reach an agreement if two or more people come to an agreement, or if they reach an agreement, they agree about what they are going to do: *I'm sure that we can **come to an agreement** about this.* | *Britain and France have not yet **reached an agreement** about British beef.*
in agreement if two or more people are in agreement, they have the same opinion: *If we are all **in agreement**, we can start the work tomorrow.*

ag·ri·cul·tural /ˌægrɪ'kʌltʃərəl/ *adjective* related to or used in agriculture: *agricultural machinery*

ag·ri·cul·ture /'ægrɪˌkʌltʃə $'ægrɪˌkʌltʃɚ/ *noun* [no plural] growing crops and keeping animals on farms: *Agriculture in Britain is changing.*

a·head /ə'hed/ *adverb*
1 in front of someone or further forward than someone: *Lucy and Dave ran on ahead.* | *I could see the mountains **ahead of** us.*
2 going to happen in the future: *I think we have a lot of problems ahead.* | *We have a busy day **ahead of** us tomorrow.*
3 more successful than someone else in a competition: *The Reds are **ahead of** us in the championship* (=the Reds are more successful than us).

aid /eɪd/ *noun* **1** [no plural] help such as money or food that an organization gives to people: *We are sending aid to the victims of the war.* **2** with the aid of something using something to help you: *I opened the jar with the aid of a* knife. **3** a thing that helps you do something: *We use computers as a teaching aid.*

AIDS /eɪdz/ noun [no plural] Acquired Immune Deficiency Syndrome; a very serious disease that stops your body from protecting itself against other diseases

ail·ment /'eɪlmənt/ noun an illness that is not very serious: *He misses too much school because of minor ailments.*

aim¹ /eɪm/ verb

> **GRAMMAR**
> aim for something
> aim to do something
> aim something at something

1 to plan or want to do something: *The government is **aiming for** 100% employment.* | *He says he's **aiming to** win the competition.*

2 to point something in a particular direction: ***Aim** the arrow **at** the target.*

> **PHRASES**

be aimed at someone if something is aimed at a particular group of people, it has been made or designed for them: *Many magazines **are aimed at** teenagers.*

be aimed at doing something if something is aimed at getting a particular result, it is done in a way that will get that result: *The course **is aimed at** building up people's self-confidence.*

aim² noun

something that you want to do or get: *My aim is to start my own business.* | *organizations whose main aim is to make money*

ain't /eɪnt/ spoken a short form of 'am not', 'is not', 'are not', 'has not', or 'have not' that many people think is not correct: *It ain't true!*

air¹ /eə $ er/ noun [no plural]

the gases around the Earth which we breathe: *The air is very clean in the mountains.*

> **PHRASES**

fresh air air from outside: *Open the window – I need some **fresh air**.*

the air the space above the ground or around things: *I threw my hat into the air.*

an air of something a general appearance or feeling: *There was **an air of** tension in the room.*

air² verb formal to tell other people your opinions or feelings: *Everyone got a chance to air their complaints.*

air con·di·tion·ing /'. ...../ noun [no plural] a system that keeps the air in a building or vehicle at the correct temperature

air·craft /'eəkrɑːft $ 'erkræft/ plural aircraft noun a plane or any vehicle that can fly: *a military aircraft*

air·fare /'eəfeə $ 'erfer/ noun the price of a plane trip: *I couldn't afford the airfare to go see him.*

air force /'. ./ noun the part of a country's military organization that uses planes to fight: *He's an officer in the air force.*

air host·ess /'. ,../ noun BrE, plural air hostesses a woman whose job is to help and serve the passengers on a plane

air·line /'eəlaɪn $ 'erlaɪn/ noun a company that carries passengers by plane: *The airline sent us our plane tickets.*

air·mail /'eəmeɪl $ 'ermeɪl/ noun [no plural] the system of sending letters and packages by plane: *It's quicker to send letters by airmail.*

air·plane /'eəpleɪn $ 'erpleɪn/ the American word for AEROPLANE

air·port /'eəpɔːt $ 'erpɔrt/ noun the place where you arrive and leave when you travel by plane: *I got a taxi to the airport.*

air·strip /'eə,strɪp $ 'er,strɪp/ noun a long narrow piece of land where planes can come down: *The plane took off from a small airstrip.*

air·tight /'eə,taɪt $ 'er,taɪt/ adjective completely closed so that air cannot get in or out: *an airtight jar*

aisle /aɪl/ noun a long space between rows of seats in a theatre, church, or plane: *Please do not block the aisle.*

a·jar /ə'dʒɑː $ ə-'dʒɑr/ adjective a door or window that is ajar is not completely closed: *The door was slightly ajar.*

ajar

a·larm¹ /ə'lɑːm $ə'lɑrm/ noun 1 [no plural] a feeling of fear because something dangerous might happen: *The police told us there was no cause for alarm.* 2 something that makes a loud noise or produces a bright light that warns people of danger: *The fire alarm started to ring.* | *I'm having an alarm fitted to the house to stop burglars.* 3 **false alarm** a warning that something dangerous will happen that you discover later was a mistake or not true: *We thought there was a fire, but it was a false alarm.*

alarm² verb to make someone feel very worried or frightened
–**alarmed** adjective: *Please don't be alarmed – I'm fine.*
–**alarming** adjective: *We heard an alarming bang.*

alarm clock /. '. ./ noun a clock that makes a noise to wake you up

al·bum /'ælbəm/ noun 1 a record, CD, or TAPE that has several songs on it: *Do you have Madonna's new album?* 2 a book with special pages where you can stick photographs or stamps

al·co·hol /'ælkəhɒl $'ælkə,hɔl/ noun [no plural] drinks such as beer and wine, that can make you drunk: *I never drink alcohol.*

al·co·hol·ic¹ /,ælkə'hɒlɪk $,ælkə-'hɔlɪk/ adjective containing alcohol ⇨ opposite NON-ALCOHOLIC: *an alcoholic drink*

alcoholic² noun someone who cannot stop drinking too much alcohol: *He won't admit he's an alcoholic.*

al·co·hol·is·m /'ælkəhɒlɪzəm $'ælkə-hɔ,lɪzəm/ noun [no plural] the medical condition of being an alcoholic: *Alcoholism is a serious problem.*

a·lert¹ /ə'lɜːt $ə'lɚt/ adjective always watching and ready to act: *The danger seems to have passed, but we must remain alert.*

alert² verb to warn someone about a problem or danger: *Police found a bomb and alerted the public.*

alert³ noun **be on the alert** to be ready to notice and deal with a problem: *Teachers are on the alert after drug dealers were seen in the school.*

A lev·el /'eɪ ,levəl/ noun an examination in a particular subject that students take when they are 18 in England, Wales, and Northern Ireland: *I have A levels in French and English.*

al·ge·bra /'ældʒəbrə/ noun [no plural] a type of mathematics that uses letters and signs to show amounts

a·li·as¹ /'eɪliəs/ preposition used to give another name that someone uses, after giving their real name: *the writer Eric Blair, alias George Orwell*

alias² noun, plural **aliases** a false name, usually used by a criminal: *Bates sometimes uses the alias John Smith.*

al·i·bi /'æləbaɪ/ noun proof that someone was not at the place where a crime happened: *He has an alibi for the night of the murder.*

a·li·en¹ /'eɪliən/ adjective very different and strange: *Their culture is completely alien to me.*

alien² noun 1 a creature that comes from another world: *a film about aliens from Mars* 2 formal someone who is not a citizen of the country where they live: *He lives in Chicago as an illegal alien.*

a·li·en·ate /'eɪliəneɪt/ verb to make someone feel that they do not belong to your group: *We don't want to alienate young people.*

a·light /ə'laɪt/ adjective **set something alight** to make something start burning: *The crowd set the building alight.*

a·like /ə'laɪk/ adjective similar or the same: *All the sisters look alike.*

a·live /ə'laɪv/ adjective
living and not dead: *The doctors struggled to keep him alive.* | *A man was brought out of the wreckage alive.*

all¹ /ɔːl/ pronoun
1 the whole of an amount: *Have you done all your homework?* | *I've spent all my money.*
2 every person or thing: *All children are different.* | *This affects all of us.* | *We all felt sorry for him.* | *I've lost all my books.*

PHRASES
all day, all year etc for the whole of a day, year etc: *I lay awake all night.* | *It's the best film I've seen all year.*
not at all, none at all etc: *I wasn't at all worried* (=I wasn't even slightly

A

worried). | *We had **no** money **at all*** (=we didn't have any money).
all the time continuously or very often: *I think about him **all the time.***

> **USAGE**
> Use **all** with a singular verb when you are talking about a noun that you cannot count: *All the wine is finished.* Use **all** with a plural verb when you are talking about a noun that you can count: *All my friends are coming to the party.*

all[2] *adverb* **1** completely or very *spoken*: *They were **all alone**. | She got **all upset**.* **2** used to show that two players or teams have an equal amount of points or goals: *The score was two all at half time.*

> **PHRASES**

all over in every part of a place: *We looked for him **all over** the house. | He had chocolate **all over** his face.*
all along from the beginning: *I knew **all along** that we could win.*
all through through the whole time that something continues: *They talked **all through** the film.*

all-a·round /ˌ. .ˈ./ the American word for ALL-ROUND

al·lay /əˈleɪ/ *verb* **allay someone's worries, allay someone's fears** *formal* to make someone feel less worried or frightened: *I tried to allay his fears by telling him the facts.*

all clear /ˌ. ˈ./ *noun* **the all clear** when someone tells you that it is safe to do something: *The pilot got the all clear to take off.*

al·le·ga·tion /ˌælɪˈgeɪʃən/ *noun* if you make an allegation about something, you say that someone has done something bad but you do not prove that it is true: *There were allegations that he stole the money.*

al·lege /əˈledʒ/ *verb* to say that someone has done something bad, but not to prove that it is true: *She alleges that he was violent towards her.*

al·le·giance /əˈliːdʒəns/ *noun* loyalty to a leader, country, or team: *They swore allegiance to the king.*

al·ler·gic /əˈlɜːdʒɪk $ əˈlɚdʒɪk/ *adjective* if you are allergic to something, you become ill if you touch, eat, or breathe it: *I am allergic to peanuts.*

al·ler·gy /ˈælədʒi $ ˈælɚdʒi/ *noun, plural* **allergies** a medical condition that makes you ill when you eat, touch, or breathe a particular thing: *He has an allergy to cats.*

al·ley /ˈæli/ also **al·ley·way** /ˈæliweɪ/ *noun* a narrow path between buildings

al·li·ance /əˈlaɪəns/ *noun* an agreement between countries or groups of people to support each other: *Environmental groups formed an alliance to stop the new road being built.*

al·li·ga·tor /ˈæləgeɪtə $ ˈælə,geɪtɚ/ *noun* a large animal with a long body, sharp teeth, and short legs, that lives in hot wet areas

al·lo·cate /ˈæləkeɪt/ *verb formal* to decide to use an amount of money, time etc for a particular purpose: *The school has allocated £5,000 for new computers.*

al·low /əˈlaʊ/ *verb*

> **GRAMMAR**
> **allow someone to do something**
> **1** to say that someone can do something because they have permission: *My father won't **allow** me **to** sit in his chair. | Are you **allowed to** smoke in here? | I'd love to come to your party, but I'm not allowed.*
> **2** to make it possible for something to happen: *How could you **allow** the house **to** get so dirty?*

> **USAGE allow, let, permit**
> Compare **allow, let,** and **permit. Let** is informal and is used a lot in spoken English: *Mum wouldn't let me go to the party.* **Permit** is formal and is mainly used in written English: *Smoking is not permitted anywhere in the airport buildings.* **Allow** is used in both formal and informal English: *You're not allowed to wear earrings to school.*

al·low·ance /əˈlaʊəns/ *noun* **1** money that someone gives you regularly or for a special purpose: *Her parents give her a clothes allowance.* **2** **make allowances for someone/something** to be kinder than usual towards someone when you judge their behaviour because they have a problem: *They made no allowances for her age.*

all right /ˌ. ˈ./ also **alright** *adjective spoken* **1** satisfactory or acceptable, but not good ⇨ *same meaning* OK (1): *"How was your holiday?" "It was all right, but it did rain quite a lot."* **2** safe and not hurt or upset ⇨ *same meaning* OK (2):

A

Don't worry, I'm sure the kids will be all right. **3** used to say that you agree to do something ⇨ *same meaning* OK (3): *"I think we should leave." "All right, we'll go now if you want to."* **4 that's all right** **1)** used to reply to someone who has just thanked you: *"Thanks for the lift." "That's all right."* **2)** used to tell someone you are not angry when they tell you something or say they are sorry: *"I'm sorry, but I don't really want to go to a club." "That's all right!"*

all-round /'. ./ *adjective* BrE good at doing many different things, especially in sports; ALL-AROUND AmE: *an all-round athlete*

al·lude /ə'luːd/ *verb formal* **allude to something** to mention something, without saying it directly or clearly: *I think he was alluding to your problems at school.*

al·ly /'ælaɪ/ *noun, plural* **allies** a country that helps another country, especially in a war: *the US and its European allies*

al·most /'ɔːlməʊst $ 'ɔlmoʊst/ *adverb*
nearly: *Almost everyone did well in the test* (=only a few people didn't do well). | *I almost forgot to go to my music lesson* (=I remembered just in time). | *I've almost finished* (=I will finish soon). | *It was almost dark.*

a·lone /ə'ləʊn $ ə'loʊn/ *adjective, adverb*
1 without anyone else: *She didn't like being alone in the house. | He lives alone now. | We can't do this alone* (=without other people helping us). | *She was all alone* (=completely alone) *in a strange country.*
2 without anything else: *This disease cannot be cured by drugs alone.*

USAGE alone, lonely
Use **alone** to describe a situation in which you are not with other people: *Lisa sometimes spends hours alone in her room.* Use **lonely** to describe the unhappy feeling that you sometimes have when you are not with other people, or when you feel that you have no friends: *I felt lonely when I first went away to university, but I don't any more.* You can use **lonely** before a noun, but **alone** is never used before a noun: *a very lonely man*

a·long¹ /ə'lɒŋ $ ə'lɒŋ/ *preposition*
following a road, river, or line: *We were walking along the road, talking. | the path along the river | Cut along this line.*

along² *adverb*
1 going forward: *He was driving along quite quickly.*
2 going somewhere with someone *spoken*: *Can I come along* (=come with you)? *| She'd brought a couple of friends along* (=she'd brought a couple of friends with her).

PHRASES
along with someone or something *written* with someone or something else, at the same time: *The boy was killed, along with seven other children.*

a·long·side /ə,lɒŋ'saɪd $ ə,lɒŋ'saɪd/ *adverb, preposition* close to the side of something: *A police car stopped alongside us.*

a·loud /ə'laʊd/ *adverb* speaking so that people can hear you: *We read our essays aloud.*

al·pha·bet /'ælfəbet/ *noun* a set of letters that you use to write a language: *the Russian alphabet*

al·pha·bet·i·cal /,ælfə'betɪkəl/ *adjective* arranged in the order of the letters of the alphabet: *The words in this dictionary are in alphabetical order.*
–alphabetically /-kli/ *adverb*: *The books are arranged alphabetically.*

al·read·y /ɔːl'redi/ *adverb*
1 before: *I've seen that film already. | He's already won three titles this year. | When they went in the shop, they had already decided what to buy.*
2 now, rather than later: *I can't wait for Christmas – I'm getting excited already. | Pat was already feeling hungry, although lunch was hours away.*

al·right /,ɔːl'raɪt/ another spelling of ALL RIGHT

al·so /'ɔːlsəʊ $ 'ɔlsoʊ/ *adverb*
use **also** when you want to add a new fact to what you have said or to

show that something is true about two people or things: *Jan plays the guitar, and she **also** plays the piano.* | *I would **also** like some water.* | *The sports centre has a large swimming pool, and it **also** has a small pool for children.* | *"I'm really hungry." "I am **also** hungry."*
⇨ compare TOO

USAGE
• **Also** comes before a verb: *Ron **also** speaks Italian.* **Also** comes after the verb be: *James is **also** very tall.* If there are two verbs, **also** comes after the first one: *Patty can **also** speak Italian.*
• **also, too, or either?**
Also is more formal than **too**, and is used more often in writing than in speech: *I am **also** hungry.* **Too** is less formal and more often used in spoken English: *I am hungry **too**.*
• Do not say *I am also not hungry.* Say *I am not hungry **either**.* Do not say *She doesn't smoke. She also doesn't drink.* Say *She doesn't smoke. She doesn't drink either.*

al·tar /ˈɔːltə $ ˈɔːltɚ/ *noun* a raised area or table that someone uses to perform a religious ceremony, for example in a church

al·ter /ˈɔːltə $ ˈɔːltɚ/ *verb* to change, or to make something or someone change: *Her tone of voice altered slightly.* | *They had to alter their plans.*

al·ter·a·tion /ˌɔːltəˈreɪʃən $ ˌɔːltəˈreɪʃən/ *noun* if you make an alteration, you change something slightly: *She made a few alterations to the letter.*

al·ter·nate¹ /ɔːlˈtɜːnət $ ˈɔːltɚnət/ *adjective* **1** happening or arranged in a regular way, first one thing, then the other thing: *alternate stripes of red and black* **2** **alternate days**, **alternate weeks etc** if you do something on alternate days, weeks etc, you do it on one of every two days, weeks etc: *We visit my grandma on alternate weekends.* **3** an American word for ALTERNATIVE
– **alternately** *adverb*: *We spend the summers in France and England alternately.*

al·ter·nate² /ˈɔːltəneɪt $ ˈɔːltɚˌneɪt/ *verb* if two things alternate, first one thing happens, then the other, and this process continues: *She alternated between shouting and crying.*
– **alternating** *adjective*: *alternating periods of sun and rain*

al·ter·na·tive¹ /ɔːlˈtɜːnətɪv $ ɔːlˈtɚ-nətɪv/ *adjective* **1** an alternative plan, idea etc can be used instead of another one: *Leave your car at home and use an alternative method of transport.* **2** different from what is usual or accepted: *alternative medicine, such as aromatherapy*

alternative² *noun* something you can choose to do or use instead of something else: *Milk is a healthier alternative to cream.*

al·ter·na·tive·ly /ɔːlˈtɜːnətɪvli $ ɔːlˈtɚ-nətɪvli/ *adverb* used to suggest something that someone could do or use instead of something else: *I could call you, or alternatively I could come to your house.*

al·though /ɔːlˈðəʊ $ ɔːlˈðoʊ/
1 in spite of something: *Although she is only seven, she can speak three languages.* | *He lent his friend £20 although he didn't have much money himself.*
2 but: *You can copy my answers, although I'm not sure they're right.*

USAGE although, though
You can use **although** and **though** in the same way, but **though** is more informal.

al·ti·tude /ˈæltɪtjuːd $ ˈæltəˌtuːd/ *noun* the height of something above sea level: *Breathing is more difficult at high altitudes.*

al·to /ˈæltəʊ $ ˈæltoʊ/ *noun* a female singer with a low voice or a male singer with a high voice

al·to·geth·er /ˌɔːltəˈgeðə $ ˌɔːltə-ˈgeðɚ/ *adverb* **1** completely: *Should we allow smoking in certain areas, or ban it altogether?* | *I'm not altogether sure that you're right.* **2** considering everything or including the whole amount: *The bill came to $45 altogether.*

USAGE altogether, all together
Altogether does not mean the same as **all together**. Use **all together** to say that people or things are together in a group, or do something together in a group: *It was lovely for the family to be all together again.* | *The children jumped up all together, and ran towards the door.*

al·u·min·i·um /ˌæljəˈmɪniəm/ *BrE*, **a·lu·mi·num** /əˈluːmənəm/ *AmE*, *noun* [no plural] a light silver metal

al·ways /'ɔːlwəz $ 'ɔlweɪz/ adverb
1 every time: *You should always clean your teeth after eating sweet things.* | *I always forget her name* (=I never remember her name).
2 for a long time: *I've always wanted to visit Australia.*
3 for ever: *You'll always be my friend.*
4 happening very often: *My parents are always criticizing me*

USAGE always
Use **always** before the main verb in a sentence unless it is the verb 'to be': *We always go on holiday in August.* | *I have always lived in this town.* | *Jeff's always late for school.*

am /əm; *strong* æm/ the first person singular present tense of the verb BE

am or **a.m.** /ˌeɪ 'em/7am, 9 am etc 7 or 9 o'clock in the morning, not in the afternoon or evening: *I get up at 8 am.* | *It's 5 a.m.*

am·a·teur /'æmətə $ 'æmətʃɚ/ noun someone who does a particular activity because they enjoy it, not because it is their job ⇨ *opposite* PROFESSIONAL²: *He's not a professional athlete, but he's a very good amateur.*
–**amateur** adjective: *an amateur photographer*

a·maze /ə'meɪz/ verb if something amazes you, it surprises you a lot: *Her skill amazed me.*
–**amazed** adjective: *I'm amazed that she invited you.*

a·maze·ment /ə'meɪzmənt/ noun [no plural] the feeling of being very surprised: *To my amazement, he remembered me.*

a·maz·ing /ə'meɪzɪŋ/ adjective very surprising or very good: *Their apartment is amazing.*
–**amazingly** adverb: *an amazingly high score*

am·bas·sa·dor /æm'bæsədə $ æm-'bæsədɚ/ noun an important person who lives and works in a foreign country, and whose job is to represent their own country and people there: *the Dutch ambassador to Brazil*

am·bi·ence or **ambiance** /'æmbiəns/ noun [no plural] the type of feeling you have because of the place you are in and the people who are there ⇨ *same meaning* ATMOSPHERE (1): *The club has a friendly ambience.*

am·big·u·ous /æm'bɪgjuəs/ adjective something that is ambiguous has more than one possible meaning: *His comment was rather ambiguous.*

am·bi·tion /æm'bɪʃən/ noun 1 something that you want to achieve in the future: *My ambition is to become a doctor.* 2 [no plural] a strong determination to be successful or powerful: *You need a lot of ambition to succeed as a musician.*

am·bi·tious /æm'bɪʃəs/ adjective determined to be successful or powerful: *We are looking for ambitious, hard-working young people.*

am·biv·a·lent /æm'bɪvələnt/ adjective formal if you feel ambivalent about something, you are not sure whether you like it or not: *I feel somewhat ambivalent about leaving home.*

am·bu·lance /'æmbjələns/ noun a special vehicle for taking ill people to hospital: *I asked a neighbour to call an ambulance.*

am·bush /'æmbʊʃ/ noun, plural ambushes a sudden attack by people who have been waiting and hiding: *We were afraid we might be attacked in an ambush.*
–**ambush** verb: *Two men ambushed him in the forest.*

a·mend /ə'mend/ verb formal to make small changes to a piece of writing: *The school rules had to be amended.*

a·mend·ment /ə'mendmənt/ noun a change made in a law or document: *We made a few amendments to the contract.*

a·mends /ə'mendz/ noun make amends to do something to show that you are sorry for hurting or upsetting someone: *I sent my mom chocolates to make amends for not visiting her.*

a·me·ni·ty /ə'miːnəti $ ə'menəti/ noun formal, plural amenities something useful or enjoyable in a place that makes it nice to live there: *The town's amenities include a sports ground and cinemas.*

A·mer·i·can¹ /ə'merəkən/ adjective 1 from or connected with the United States: *American cars* 2 North American, South American from or connected with one of the countries in North America or South America

American² noun someone from the United States: *She married an American.*

American foot·ball /.,... '../ *noun* [*no plural*] *BrE* a game played in the US in which two teams wearing special clothes to protect them carry, kick, and throw a ball; FOOTBALL *AmE* ⇨ *see picture on page 351*

am·i·ca·ble /'æmɪkəbəl/ *adjective formal* done in a friendly way, without arguing: *My parents' divorce was quite amicable.*

a·miss /ə'mɪs/ *adjective* **be amiss** *formal* if something is amiss, there is a problem: *I checked the house, but nothing was amiss.*

am·mu·ni·tion /,æmjə'nɪʃən/ *noun* [*no plural*] bullets that people fire from a weapon such as a gun: *The soldiers had no ammunition left.*

am·nes·ty /'æmnəsti/ *noun, plural* amnesties a period of time when a government lets some people leave prison or does not punish people: *The new government announced an amnesty for political prisoners.*

a·mong /ə'mʌŋ/ also **a·mongst** /ə'mʌŋst/ *preposition*
1 saying which group of people is affected by something: *The disease is quite common among young people.* | *There is a lot of concern among parents about this problem.*
2 surrounded by things *written*: *He hid among the bushes.*
3 giving something to each person in a group: *She shared the sweets among the children.*

PHRASE
among yourselves with each other: *Just talk among yourselves* (=talk to each other) *until I'm ready to begin the lesson.* | *The soldiers ended up fighting among themselves* (=fighting with each other). ⇨ *see usage note at* BETWEEN

a·mount¹ /ə'maʊnt/ *noun*
GRAMMAR
an amount of something
a quantity of something, for example money: *A large amount of jewellery was stolen.* | *Kevin gets £5 a week from his parents, but Jo gets half that amount.*

USAGE
Use **amount** with nouns that you cannot count: *a huge amount of food* | *a small*

amount of money. Use **number** with the plural of nouns that you can count: *the number of road accidents in a year* | *a large number of animals*

amount² *verb* **amount to** 1) to be the same as something or to have the same effect: *What she said amounted to a criticism of the other teachers.* 2) to add up to a particular total: *My debts amount to over £500.*

amp /æmp/ *noun* 1 also **am·pere** /'æmpeə $ æmpɪr/ a unit for measuring an electric current 2 *informal* an AMPLIFIER

am·ple /'æmpəl/ *adjective* more than enough: *There was ample food for everyone.*

am·pli·fi·er /'æmpləfaɪə $ 'æmplə,faɪɚ/ *noun* a piece of electronic equipment that you use to make music louder

am·pu·tate /'æmpjəteɪt/ *verb* to cut off a part of someone's body for medical reasons: *After trying to repair his leg, the surgeons eventually decided they had to amputate it.*

a·muse /ə'mjuːz/ *verb* if something amuses you, it makes you laugh or smile: *His jokes don't amuse me.*
– **amused** *adjective*: *He was highly amused by my story.*
– **amusing** *adjective*: *an amusing joke*

a·muse·ment /ə'mjuːzmənt/ *noun* [*no plural*] the feeling that you want to laugh or smile: *They watched with amusement as I tried to catch the cat.*

amusement park /.'.. ,./ *noun* a large park where people can enjoy themselves, for example by riding on big machines such as ROLLER COASTERS

an·aes·thet·ic *BrE*, **anesthetic** *AmE* /,ænəs'θetɪk/ *noun* a drug that stops you feeling pain, used during a medical operation: *Sometimes anaesthetics can make the patient feel ill for a couple of days after the operation.*

a·naes·the·tist *BrE*, **anesthetist** *AmE* /ə'niːsθətɪst $ ə'nestətɪst/ *noun* a doctor whose job is to give anaesthetics to people

an·a·gram /'ænəgræm/ *noun* a word or phrase that you make by changing the order of the letters in another word or phrase: *'Dear' is an anagram of 'read'.*

a·nal·o·gy /ə'nælədʒi/ *noun, plural* analogies a way of explaining one thing by showing how it is similar to another thing: *He made an analogy between the brain and a computer.*

an·a·lyse *BrE*, **analyze** *AmE* /'ænl-aɪz/ verb to examine something carefully so that you understand what it is or why it happens: *We're trying to analyse why students fail.*

a·nal·y·sis /ə'næləsəs/ noun, plural analyses /-siːz/ a careful examination of something so that you understand more about it: *an analysis of blood samples*

an·a·lyst /'ænl-ɪst/ noun **1** someone whose job is to analyse a subject and explain it to other people: *a political analyst* **2** a PSYCHOANALYST

an·ar·chist /'ænəkɪst $'ænɚkɪst/ noun someone who believes that there should be no government or laws

an·ar·chy /'ænəki $'ænɚki/ noun [no plural] a situation in which people do not obey the rules or laws and no one has control: *The situation in the school is close to anarchy.*

a·nat·o·my /ə'nætəmi/ noun [no plural] the scientific study of the structure of the body

an·ces·tor /'ænsəstə $'æn,sestɚ/ noun a person in your family who lived a very long time ago: *Her ancestors came from Ireland.*

an·ces·try /'ænsəstri $'æn,sestri/ noun [no plural] your ancestors, or the place they came from: *He is of Welsh ancestry.*

an·chor /'æŋkə $'æŋkɚ/ noun **1** a heavy metal object on a chain or rope that you put into the water to stop a ship or boat moving: *They raised the anchor and sailed with the tide.* **2** a NEWSREADER

anchor

an·cient /'eɪnʃənt/ adjective many hundreds of years old: *an ancient temple*

and /ən, ənd; strong ænd/
1 used when adding something to what you are saying: *I have one brother and two sisters.* | *The house was large and very old.* | *She fin-*

ished *her homework and went to bed.* | *He fell over and hurt his arm.*
2 used when adding numbers: *What's eight and seventeen* (=eight plus seventeen)?

an·ec·dote /'ænɪkdəʊt $'ænɪk,doʊt/ noun an interesting or funny story about something that really happened: *He told a funny anecdote about his work.*

an·es·thet·ic /,ænəs'θetɪk/ the American spelling of ANAESTHETIC

a·nes·the·tist /ə'niːsθətɪst $ə'nes-θətɪst/ the American spelling of ANAES-THETIST

an·gel /'eɪndʒəl/ noun **1** in the Christian religion, an angel is a spirit who lives with God in heaven **2** *spoken* someone who is very good or kind: *Joe is such a little angel.*

an·ger¹ /'æŋgə $'æŋgɚ/ noun [no plural] a strong feeling of wanting to shout at someone or hurt them because they have done something bad: *I felt such anger when I saw what the burglars had done.*

anger² verb formal to make someone feel angry: *The school's decision has angered parents.*

an·gle /'æŋgəl/ noun **1** the space between two lines or surfaces that meet, measured in degrees: *an angle of 45°* **2** at an angle not straight or flat: *The painting was hanging at an angle.* **3** a way of thinking about something: *Let's look at the problem from a different angle.*

an·gling /'æŋglɪŋ/ noun [no plural] the activity of trying to catch fish with a hook on the end of a line

an·gry /'æŋgri/ adjective angrier, angriest

GRAMMAR
angry about something
angry with someone
angry (that)

if you are angry, you feel anger towards someone who has done something bad: *I am very angry with you.* | *My father was angry about the broken window.* | *Will Simon be angry that I forgot his birthday?*
– **angrily** adverb: *"It's not funny,"* my mother said angrily.

USAGE

Compare **angry**, **furious**, **bad-tempered**, and **mad**. Someone who is **furious** is very angry: *She was furious when she saw what happened to the car.* Someone who is **bad-tempered** becomes annoyed or angry easily: *Matthew is such a bad-tempered boy.* **Mad** is an informal word that means 'very angry': *He'll be mad at you when he finds out.*

an·guish /'æŋgwɪʃ/ *noun [no plural] written* very great pain or worry: *She suffered the anguish of losing her baby in the accident.*

an·gu·lar /'æŋgjələ $ 'æŋgjələ/ *adjective* something that is angular has sharp corners

an·i·mal /'ænəməl/ *noun* a living thing that can move around and is not a bird, insect, or fish: *farm animals* | *I feel sorry for animals that are kept in zoos.*

animal rights /ˌ... ˈ./ *noun* the idea that people should not hurt animals or use them to do things such as test medicines etc

an·i·mat·ed /'ænəmeɪtɪd/ *adjective* **1** interesting and with lots of energy: *We had a lively and animated discussion about music.* **2** an animated film is one in which drawings of people or things seem to move and talk

an·i·ma·tion /ˌænəˈmeɪʃən/ *noun [no plural]* the process of making films or computer games with drawings that seem to move and talk

an·kle /'æŋkəl/ *noun* the part of your body where your foot joins your leg: *I tripped and hurt my ankle.* ➪ *see picture at BODY*

an·nexe *BrE*, **annex** *AmE* /'æneks/ *noun* a separate building that is attached to a bigger one: *The toilets are in an annexe.*

an·ni·hi·late /ə'naɪəleɪt/ *verb formal* to destroy something or defeat someone completely: *In 1314, the English army was annihilated by the Scots.*

an·ni·ver·sa·ry /ˌænəˈvɜːsəri $ ˌænə-ˈvɚsəri/ *noun, plural* **anniversaries** a date that is special because it is exactly a year or a number of years after an important event: *Today is my parents' 25th wedding anniversary* (=today, it is exactly 25 years since their wedding).

an·nounce /ə'naʊns/ *verb*

GRAMMAR
announce that

to say something in public: *The judges are ready to announce the winner.* | *He suddenly* **announced** *that he was leaving.*

an·nounce·ment /ə'naʊnsmənt/ *noun* an official statement about something important: *They're going to make an announcement this afternoon.*

an·noy /ə'nɔɪ/ *verb* if someone or something annoys you, they make you feel slightly angry: *Stop annoying your father.* | *It really annoys me when people are late.*

— **annoying** *adjective*: *She has an annoying laugh.*

an·noy·ance /ə'nɔɪəns/ *noun [no plural]* the feeling of being annoyed: *I tried not to show my annoyance.*

an·noyed /ə'nɔɪd/ *adjective* slightly angry: *She gets annoyed with me for being untidy.* | *I'm annoyed that he didn't reply.*

an·nu·al /'ænjuəl/ *adjective* happening once each year: *the school's annual concert* | *The annual fee is £25.*

a·non·y·mous /ə'nɒnəməs $ ə'nɑn-əməs/ *adjective* someone who is anonymous does not tell you what their name is: *The person who complained wishes to remain anonymous.*

— **anonymously** *adverb*: *He wrote anonymously to the newspaper.*

an·o·rex·i·a /ˌænəˈreksiə/ *noun [no plural]* a mental illness that makes someone stop eating because they believe they are fat: *Many teenage girls suffer from anorexia.*

an·o·rex·ic /ˌænəˈreksɪk/ *adjective* someone who is anorexic is very thin and ill because they have anorexia

an·oth·er /ə'nʌðə $ ə'nʌðɚ/

1 an additional thing or person: *Have another biscuit.* | *I think we will stay for another week.*

2 a different thing or person: *She's trying to find another job.* | *students from another country*

an·swer¹ /'ɑːnsə $ 'ænsɚ/ *verb*

GRAMMAR
answer that

1 to say something after someone has

asked you a question: *"How old is Brian?" "I don't know,"* Mary answered. | *He refused to* **answer** *my questions.* | *Answer me!* | *When I asked his name, she* **answered** *that she could not remember.*
2 to say or write something in reply to a question in a test or competition: *I didn't have time to answer all the questions.*

PHRASES

answer the telephone to pick up the telephone when it rings and speak into it
answer the door to go to open the door when someone knocks or rings the bell

answer² *noun*

GRAMMAR
an answer to someone/something

1 a reply to something that someone asks you: *I don't know the* **answer to** *your question.* | *I will* **give** *you my* **answer** *tomorrow.*
2 a reply to a question in a test or competition: *What is the* **answer to** *the first question?*
3 something that solves a problem: *Could this be the* **answer to** *all our problems?*

answering ma·chine /'... .../ also **an·swer·phone** /'ɑ:nsəfəʊn $ 'ænsə,fəʊn/ *BrE, noun* a machine that answers the telephone for you and records messages from the people who are calling: *I left a message on his answering machine.*

ant /ænt/ *noun* a small red or black insect that lives in large groups ⇨ *see picture at* INSECT

An·tarc·tic /æn'tɑ:ktɪk $ æn'tɑrktɪk/ *noun* the Antarctic the most southern part of the world, where it is very cold

an·ten·na /æn'tenə/ *noun* 1 *plural* antennae one of two long thin parts on an insect's head that it uses to feel things 2 the American word for AERIAL

an·them /'ænθəm/ *noun* a serious song that people sing at special events: *We stood up to sing the national anthem* (=a song that belongs to a country and its people).

an·thro·pol·o·gy /,ænθrə'pɒlədʒi $,ænθrə'pɑlədʒi/ *noun* [no plural] the scientific study of people and their origins, customs, beliefs etc: *an expert in anthropology*

an·ti·bi·ot·ic /,æntɪbaɪ'ɒtɪk $,æntɪbaɪ'ɑtɪk/ *noun* a medicine that doctors give to people who are ill with an infection, to make them better again: *The doctor gave me some antibiotics for my cold.*

an·tic·i·pate /æn'tɪsəpeɪt/ *verb* to expect something to happen: *We anticipate about 1,000 visitors at the exhibition.*

an·tic·i·pa·tion /æn,tɪsə'peɪʃən/ *noun* [no plural] a hopeful or slightly nervous feeling that you have when something exciting is going to happen: *The audience waited in eager anticipation.*

an·ti·cli·max /,æntɪ'klaɪmæks/ *noun,* *plural* anticlimaxes something that is not as exciting as you expected: *The end of the exams is always an anticlimax.*

an·ti·clock·wise /,æntɪ'klɒkwaɪz $,æntɪ'klɑkwaɪz/ *adjective, adverb BrE* moving in the opposite direction to the hands of a clock; COUNTER-CLOCKWISE *AmE* ⇨ *opposite* CLOCKWISE: *Turn the handle anticlockwise.*

an·tics /'æntɪks/ *plural noun* funny, silly, or annoying behaviour: *We laughed at the childrens' antics.*

an·ti·dote /'æntɪdəʊt $ 'æntɪ,dəʊt/ *noun* 1 something that makes a bad situation better: *Laughter can be an antidote to stress.* 2 a substance that stops a poison harming or killing someone

an·tique /,æn'ti:k/ *noun* an old and unusual piece of furniture, jewellery etc that costs a lot of money: *Do you think this table might be an antique?*
– antique *adjective: an antique chair*

an·ti·sep·tic /,æntɪ'septɪk/ *noun* a substance that kills harmful BACTERIA, for example on your skin
– antiseptic *adjective: antiseptic cream*

an·ti·so·cial /,æntɪ'səʊʃəl $,æntɪ'səʊʃəl/ *adjective* antisocial behaviour upsets or annoys other people: *It's considered very antisocial to drop litter in Singapore.*

ant·ler /'æntlə $ 'æntlə/ *noun* one of the two horns on the head of male DEER

a·nus /'eɪnəs/ *noun formal* the hole near your bottom from which solid waste material leaves your body

anx·i·e·ty /æŋ'zaɪəti/ noun, plural anxieties a strong feeling of worry that something bad may happen: He has caused his family a lot of anxiety.

anx·ious /'æŋkʃəs/ adjective

> **GRAMMAR**
> anxious for someone to do something
> anxious to do something
> anxious that

1 very worried: Many students get **anxious about** exams. | the children's anxious faces
2 wanting something to happen very much: She was **anxious for** everyone to enjoy the food. | Police are **anxious to** interview a man who was seen running away. | We are **anxious that** nobody should be upset.

an·y¹ /'eni/

1 use **any** in negative statements to mean 'none': There weren't any children playing in the street. | I don't have any money with me. | No thanks, I don't want any. | She didn't eat **any of** her dinner.

> **USAGE a or any?**
> Use **any** about things that you cannot count, or when there are several of something you can count. Use **a** when there is only one thing that you can count: "Do you have any money?" | "Do you have a 10 pence coin?"

2 use **any** in questions to mean 'some', when you do not know what the answer will be: Is there any cake left? | Did he bring any pictures of his holiday.
3 use **any** to talk about each one of the people or things in a group, when it is not important to say exactly which one: You can buy the magazine at any good bookstore. | I'm sure any student would use this a lot. | If **any of** you are interested in going, call Debbie. ⇨ compare SOME

> **USAGE**
> Do not say Any parents love their children. Say **All** parents love their children. Do not say Any teacher must deal with these problems. Say **Every** teacher must deal with these problems.

any² adverb

1 use **any** in negative sentences to emphasize what you are saying: I couldn't walk any further. | It doesn't make the job any easier.
2 use **any** in questions to mean 'at all' or 'in any way': Are you feeling any better?

an·y·bod·y /'eni,bɒdi $ 'eni,bɑdi/ pronoun
anyone

an·y·how /'enihaʊ/ informal ANYWAY

any more or **anymore** /,eni'mɔr/ adverb not anymore if something used to not happen any more, it used to happen in the past but it does not happen now: I don't go out with him any more.

an·y·one /'eniwʌn/ pronoun
any person: Would anyone like some more cake? | I cannot see anyone I know. | Don't tell **anyone else** (=any other person) about this. | It's easy – anyone can do it.

an·y·place /'enipleɪs/ AmE ANYWHERE

an·y·thing /'eniθɪŋ/ pronoun
one thing of any kind: Did he seem worried about anything? | Do you need **anything else** (=any other thing)? | She couldn't think of anything to say. | I'll do anything that needs doing.

an·y·way /'eniweɪ/ also **anyhow** adverb

1 in spite of something: Catherine wasn't sure the book was the right one, but she bought it anyway. | We might not take any pictures, but we'll take the camera anyway.
2 used when changing the subject you are talking about: So we all had a great time. Anyway, what have you been doing?
3 used when adding another reason for something: I didn't buy the suit because I couldn't afford it, and anyway it was the wrong colour.

an·y·where /'eniweə $ 'eni,wer/ adverb
in any one place: I can't find my purse anywhere. | You can sit anywhere you like. | If you could travel anywhere in the world, where would you go?

a·part /ə'pɑːt $ ə'pɑrt/ *adverb*

not together: *I get very sad when we are apart.* | *My mother and father live apart.* | *Kim **sat apart from** the rest of the children.*

PHRASES

apart from except for: *Everyone came to the party **apart from** Sue.* | ***Apart from** a wooden table, the room was empty.*

5 cm apart, 3 days apart etc separated by 5 cm, 3 days etc: *Plant the seeds three inches apart.* | *Our birthdays are only two days apart.*

take something apart to separate something into parts: *The mechanic **took** the engine **apart**.*

fall apart, come apart to break into many pieces: *She wore the coat until it **fell apart**.*

a·part·ment /ə'pɑːtmənt $ ə'pɑrtmənt/ *noun* a set of rooms on one floor of a large building, where someone lives; FLAT *BrE: Let's meet at your apartment.*

ap·a·thet·ic /ˌæpə'θetɪk/ *adjective* not interested in anything and not wanting to try: *People here are too apathetic to run a youth club.*

ap·a·thy /'æpəθi/ *noun* [no plural] when people are not interested and do not want to try: *young people's apathy towards politics*

ape /eɪp/ *noun* a large monkey without a tail, such as a GORILLA

a·pol·o·get·ic /əˌpɒlə'dʒetɪk $ əˌpɑlə'dʒetɪk/ *adjective* saying that you are sorry for something bad you have done: *He was really apologetic about the mess.*
– **apologetically** /-kli/ *adverb*

a·pol·o·gize also **apologise** *BrE*
/ə'pɒlədʒaɪz $ ə'pɑləˌdʒaɪz/ *verb*

apologize

GRAMMAR
apologize for something
apologize to someone

to tell someone that you are sorry for something bad that you did: *I have behaved very badly, and I apologize.* | *He didn't even **apologize for** breaking my cup.* | *I think you should **apologize to** your teacher.*

USAGE

When you apologize to someone, the words you usually say are "I'm sorry."

a·pol·o·gy /ə'pɒlədʒi $ ə'pɑlədʒi/ *noun, plural* **apologies** something that you say or write to show that you are sorry for something bad you have done: *You made me late and I want an apology.* | *a letter of apology*

a·pos·tro·phe /ə'pɒstrəfi $ ə'pɑstrəfi/ *noun* **1** the sign (') used to show that one or more letters are missing, such as in the word 'don't' (=do not) **2** the sign (') used before or after the letter 's' to show that something belongs to someone: *Lucy's friends* | *my parents' house*

ap·pal *BrE*, **appall** *AmE* /ə'pɔːl/ *verb* **appalled, appalling** if something appals you, it shocks you because it is so unpleasant: *The idea of killing animals appals me.*
– **appalled** *adjective: We were appalled at the price of the meal.*
– **appalling** *adjective: appalling cruelty*

ap·pa·ra·tus /ˌæpə'reɪtəs $ ˌæpə'rætəs/ *noun, plural* **apparatus** or **apparatuses** a set of equipment or tools that you use for a particular purpose: *The school needs new science apparatus.*

ap·par·ent /ə'pærənt/ *adjective* **1** easy to see or understand: *It was apparent that she had never ridden a bike before.* **2** seeming to be true or real: *He found the apparent cause of the problem.*

ap·par·ent·ly /ə'pærəntli/ *adverb* used to say that something seems to be true or you have heard it is true: *Apparently, he doesn't like his job.*

ap·peal¹ /ə'piːl/ *verb*

GRAMMAR
appeal for something
appeal to someone to do something
appeal to someone

1 to ask people for something publicly: *The police are **appealing for***

A

witnesses. | They **appealed to** local people **to** help.
2 if something appeals to you, you like it: *Camping has never appealed to me.*

appeal² noun

GRAMMAR
an appeal for something
the appeal of something
1 when an organization asks for something such as money or help: *Oxfam launched* (=announced) *an appeal for the earthquake victims.* | *The appeal for information was very successful.*
2 the quality of something that makes you like it or want it: *Just what is the appeal of fast motorbikes?*

ap·peal·ing /əˈpiːlɪŋ/ adjective attractive or interesting: *That's an appealing idea.*

ap·pear /əˈpɪə $ əˈpɪr/ verb

GRAMMAR
appear to do something
1 to seem: *She appeared to change her mind.* | *You appear to be very nervous.* | *Everyone appeared very relaxed.*
2 if something appears, you see it for the first time: *Clouds started to appear in the sky.*

ap·pear·ance /əˈpɪərəns $ əˈpɪrəns/ noun
1 your appearance is what you look like, for example your hair colour and height: *He worries about his appearance.* | *The wig completely changed her appearance.*
2 when someone or something arrives: *The crowd cheered as the band made their appearance on stage.*

ap·pen·di·ci·tis /ə,pendəˈsaɪtəs/ noun [no plural] an illness in which your appendix hurts a lot

ap·pen·dix /əˈpendɪks/ noun 1 a small organ inside your body, near your stomach 2 plural appendixes or appendices /-dɪsiːz/ a part at the end of a book that has additional information: *There is a list of dates in the appendix.*

ap·pe·tite /ˈæpətaɪt/ noun the feeling that makes you want to eat: *That walk has given me an appetite.*

ap·plaud /əˈplɔːd/ verb to hit your hands together to show that you have enjoyed a performance ➪ same meaning CLAP: *Everyone applauded after the speech.*

ap·plause /əˈplɔːz/ noun [no plural] the sound of people hitting their hands together to show that they have enjoyed a performance: *There was applause from the fans as the team left the field.*

ap·ple /ˈæpəl/ noun a hard round red or green fruit that is white inside ➪ see picture on page 345

ap·pli·ance /əˈplaɪəns/ noun a piece of electrical equipment that people use in their homes: *kitchen appliances*

ap·plic·a·ble /əˈplɪkəbəl $ ˈæplɪkəbəl/ adjective concerning or involving a particular person or situation: *Question 8 on the form is only applicable to married people.*

ap·pli·cant /ˈæplɪkənt/ noun someone who has formally asked for a job, a place at a college etc: *We have too many applicants for the course.*

ap·pli·ca·tion /,æplɪˈkeɪʃən/ noun 1 a letter or other document in which someone officially asks for a job, place at a college etc: *The college lost my application.* 2 a way in which something can be used: *His new invention has many different applications.* 3 a computer PROGRAM

application form /,..ˈ.. ,./ noun a printed piece of paper on which you write the answers to questions about yourself. You complete an application form when you are asking for something officially: *Please fill in the job application form and return it to our personnel department.* | *I had to complete an application form to get my passport.*

ap·ply /əˈplaɪ/ verb applied, applies

GRAMMAR
apply for something
apply to someone
apply something to something
1 to ask for something in writing, such as a job, a place at a college etc: *I*

28

applied for *a place on the computing course.*
2 to concern or affect a particular person or situation: *This rule applies to
both girls and boys.*
3 to spread something such as paint or
a cream on a surface: *Don't forget to
apply sun cream.* | *Stir the paint
well, then apply it to the wall.*

ap·point /ə'pɔɪnt/ *verb* to choose
someone for an important job: *They
have appointed a new school principal.*

ap·point·ment /ə'pɔɪntmənt/ *noun*
1 a meeting that has been arranged for
a particular time and place: *I made an
appointment with the doctor.* **2** when
someone is chosen for an important
job: *the appointment of a new Finance
Minister*

ap·pre·ci·ate /ə'priːʃieɪt/ *verb* **1** to
understand what something is really
like, especially how good it is: *Being
away made me appreciate my family
more.* **2** to be grateful for something:
Thanks – I appreciate your help.

ap·pre·ci·a·tion /ə'priːʃi'eɪʃən/ *noun*
the feeling of being grateful to someone
because they have helped you: *I gave
her some flowers to show my appreci-
ation.*

ap·pre·cia·tive /ə'priːʃətɪv/ *adjective*
showing that you have enjoyed something or feel grateful for it: *The audience
was very appreciative.*

ap·pre·hen·sive /ˌæprɪ'hensɪv/ *adjective* worried or nervous about something
you have to do in the future: *I'm appre-
hensive about taking my driving test.*

ap·pren·tice /ə'prentɪs/ *noun* someone who works for an employer for an
agreed amount of time in order to learn
a skill

ap·proach[1] /ə'prəʊtʃ $ ə'proʊtʃ/ *verb*
1 to move closer to someone or something: *A man approached me and asked
me the time.* **2** *formal* to ask someone
for something: *I approached my father
for some money.*

approach[2] *noun, plural* **approaches** a
way of doing something or dealing with
a problem: *a new approach to language
teaching*

ap·proach·a·ble /ə'prəʊtʃəbəl
$ ə'proʊtʃəbəl/ *adjective* friendly and
easy to talk to: *Our school principal is
very approachable.*

ap·pro·pri·ate /ə'prəʊpri-ət $ ə'proʊ-
pri-ət/ *adjective* suitable or right for a
particular time, situation, or purpose
⇨ *opposite* INAPPROPRIATE: *It is not ap-
propriate to make jokes at a funeral.* | *I
chose an appropriate gift.* | *Do you think
that you're wearing appropriate clothes
for a long walk?*
– **appropriately** *adverb*: *Make sure you
are dressed appropriately.*

ap·prov·al /ə'pruːvəl/ *noun* [no
plural]

GRAMMAR
approval for something

1 an official statement saying that
someone allows you to do something: *We are waiting for approval
for our project.*
2 someone's approval is their opinion
that someone or something is good:
*She was desperate for her teacher's
approval.*

ap·prove /ə'pruːv/ *verb*

GRAMMAR
approve of something

1 if you approve of something, you
think that it is good or right: *She
doesn't approve of eating meat.* |
*Mum has never approved of any of
my girlfriends.*
2 to officially agree to something: *The
committee approved the plan.*

ap·prox /ə'prɒks $ ə'prɑːks/ *adverb* the
written abbreviation of 'approximately'
ap·prox·i·mate /ə'prɒksəmət
$ ə'prɑːksəmət/ *adjective* nearly right but
not exact: *The approximate cost of the
building will be £500,000.*
ap·prox·i·mate·ly /ə'prɒksəmətli
$ ə'prɑːksəmətli/ *adverb* a little more or
less than an exact number, amount etc
⇨ *same meaning* ABOUT[2] (1): *It will take
approximately 15 minutes to walk to the
station.*

A·pril /'eɪprəl/ *written abbreviation* **Apr**
noun the fourth month of the year

a·pron /'eɪprən/ *noun* a piece of
clothing that you wear to protect your
clothes, for example when you are
cooking

ap·ti·tude /'æptətjuːd $ 'æptə,tud/
noun a natural ability to do something
well: *They tested our aptitude for computing.*

a·quar·i·um /ə'kweəriəm $ ə'kwer-iəm/ *noun* **1** a clear glass container that you use to keep fish or other water animals **2** a building where people go to look at fish or other water animals

Ar·ab /'ærəb/ *noun* someone whose family comes from the Middle East or North Africa

Ar·a·bic /'ærəbɪk/ *noun* the language of Arab people or the religious language of ISLAM

ar·bi·tra·ry /'ɑːbətrəri $ 'ɑrbə,treri/ *adjective* arbitrary decisions seem unfair because there is no rule or plan behind them: *Age limits for films are rather arbitrary because they vary in different countries.*

arc /ɑːk $ ɑrk/ *noun* a curved line

ar·cade /ɑː'keɪd $ ɑr'keɪd/ *noun* **1** a large room or building where people go to play VIDEO GAMES etc **2** *BrE* a building where there are many shops: *a new shopping arcade*

arch /ɑːtʃ $ ɑrtʃ/ *noun, plural* arches a curved structure at the top of a door, bridge etc, or something that has this curved shape

arch

ar·chae·o·log·i·cal also **archeo·logical** *AmE* /,ɑːkiə'lɒdʒɪkəl $,ɑrkiə-'lɑdʒɪkəl/ *adjective* relating to archaeology: *an archaeological dig*

ar·chae·ol·o·gist also **archeologist** *AmE* /,ɑːki'ɒlədʒɪst $,ɑrki'ɑlədʒɪst/ *noun* someone who digs up and examines ancient buildings and objects in order to study them

ar·chae·ol·o·gy also **archeology** *AmE* /,ɑːki'ɒlədʒi $,ɑrki'ɑlədʒi/ *noun* [*no plural*] the study of ancient societies by digging up and examining ancient buildings and objects: *She wants to study archaeology.*

ar·cha·ic /ɑː'keɪ-ɪk $ ɑr'keɪ-ɪk/ *adjective* very old-fashioned: *the archaic language of Shakespeare*

arch·bish·op /,ɑːtʃ'bɪʃəp $,ɑrtʃ-'bɪʃəp/ *noun* the most important priest in a country, in some Christian religions

archeologist the American spelling of ARCHAEOLOGIST

archeology the American spelling of ARCHAEOLOGY

ar·cher·y /'ɑːtʃəri $ 'ɑrtʃəri/ *noun* [*no plural*] the sport of shooting ARROWS from a BOW

ar·chi·tect /'ɑːkətekt $ 'ɑrkə,tekt/ *noun* someone whose job is to design buildings: *Her dad is an architect.*

ar·chi·tec·tur·al /,ɑːkə'tektʃərəl $,ɑrkə'tektʃərəl/ *adjective* relating to architecture

ar·chi·tec·ture /'ɑːkətektʃə $ 'ɑrkə-,tektʃɚ/ *noun* [*no plural*] **1** the style and design of buildings: *The city has some beautiful architecture.* **2** the skill or job of designing buildings: *He's studying architecture.*

Arc·tic /'ɑːktɪk $ 'ɑrktɪk/ *noun* the Arctic the most northern part of the world, where it is very cold

ar·dent /'ɑːdənt $ 'ɑrdnt/ *adjective* admiring or supporting something very strongly: *an ardent fan of Manchester United*

ar·du·ous /'ɑːdjuəs $ 'ɑrdʒuəs/ *adjective* needing a lot of effort and hard work: *an arduous journey*

are /ə $ ɚ; *strong* ɑː $ ɑr/ the present tense plural and second person singular of BE

ar·e·a /'eəriə $ 'eriə/ *noun* **1** part of a place or building: *Camden is my favourite area of London.* | *a room with an area for children to play* **2** the size of a flat surface that you calculate by multiplying its length by its width: *The area of the room is six square metres.*

area code /'... ,./ another phrase for DIALING CODE

a·re·na /ə'riːnə/ *noun* a building with a large flat area inside with seats all around it, used for watching something such as a sports game: *The concert will be at Wembley arena.*

aren't /ɑːnt $ 'ɑrənt/ **1)** the short form of 'are not': *We aren't going to the party.* **2)** the short form of 'am not', used when asking questions: *I'm lucky, aren't I?*

A

ar·gue /'ɑːgjuː $ 'ɑrgju/ *verb*

GRAMMAR
argue about something
argue with someone
argue that
argue for/against something

1 if people argue, they shout or say angry things because they do not agree about something: *I hate it when Mum and Dad argue.* | *Some of the kids started arguing about which was the best band.* | *He always argues with the teacher.*

2 to explain why you think something is true: *Joe argued that the new road would just create more traffic.* | *The students argued for more time to prepare for the exam.*

argument

ar·gu·ment /'ɑːgjəmənt $ 'ɑrgjəmənt/ *noun*

GRAMMAR
an argument with someone
an argument about something
an argument for/against some-thing
an argument that

1 if you have an argument with someone, you shout or say angry things to them because you do not agree with them: *I had a big argument with my girlfriend.* | *There was an argument about who was going to pay for the meal.*

2 the reasons that you give to show that something is right or wrong: *Kate explained her arguments for banning smoking.* | *So what are the arguments against experiments on animals?* | *She doesn't accept the argument that 16-year-olds are not old enough to vote.*

ar·gu·men·ta·tive /ˌɑːgjə'mentətɪv $ ˌɑrgjə'mentətɪv/ *adjective* someone who is argumentative often argues with other people: *Don't be so argumentative.*

a·rise /ə'raɪz/ *verb formal* **arose** /ə'rəʊz $ ə'roʊz/ **arisen** /ə'rɪzən/ **arising** if a problem arises, it begins to happen: *We are prepared for any difficulties that arise.*

ar·is·toc·ra·cy /ˌærə'stɒkrəsi $ ˌærə'stɑkrəsi/ *noun* the people belonging to the highest social class in some countries, who usually have a lot of land, money, and power

ar·is·to·crat /'ærɪstəkræt $ ə'rɪstə,kræt/ *noun* someone who is a member of the aristocracy

a·rith·me·tic /ə'rɪθmətɪk/ *noun* [no plural] the skill of working with numbers by adding, dividing, multiplying etc: *I'm no good at arithmetic.*

arm¹ /ɑːm $ ɑrm/ *noun*

1 the long part of your body between your shoulder and your hand: *He put his arms around me.* ⇨ *see picture at* BODY

2 the part of a piece of clothing that covers your arm: *It's a nice jacket but the arms are too long.*

3 **arms** weapons: *Britain still sells arms to some countries.*

arm² *verb* to give someone weapons: *Should we arm the police?*

arm·chair /'ɑːmtʃeə $ 'ɑrmtʃer/ *noun* a comfortable chair with sides where you can rest your arms ⇨ *see picture at* CHAIR¹

armed /ɑːmd $ ɑrmd/ *adjective* carrying weapons: *armed police* | *Armed with a knife, the man stole jewellery worth £2,000.*

armed forc·es /ˌ. '../ *plural noun* the armed forces a country's military organizations such as its army

ar·mour *BrE*, **armor** *AmE* /'ɑːmə $ 'ɑrmɚ/ *noun* [no plural] metal or leather clothing that men wore in the past to protect themselves in fights: *a knight's armour*

ar·moured *BrE*, **armored** *AmE* /'ɑːməd $ 'ɑrməd/ *adjective* an armoured vehicle has a strong layer of metal on it to protect it against bullets or bombs

arm·pit /'ɑːm,pɪt $ 'ɑrm,pɪt/ *noun* the hollow place under your arm where it joins your body: *The dress is too tight under my armpits.*

ar·my /'ɑːmi $ 'ɑrmi/ *noun, plural* armies the part of a country's military force that is trained to fight on land: *My brother joined the army.*

a·ro·ma /ə'rəʊmə $ə'roʊmə/ *noun* a strong pleasant smell: *the aroma of baking bread*

arose the past tense of ARISE

a·round /ə'raʊnd/ *adverb, preposition*

1 also **round** *BrE* surrounding something: *There was a high fence around the school.* | *She had a gold chain around her neck.*

2 also **round** *BrE* in many parts of a place: *The puppy ran around the sitting room.* | *They showed us around their new house* (=took us to every part of their new house). | *People around the world* (=in every part of the world) *admire his singing.*

3 somewhere in a place *informal*: *I've got a pen around here somewhere.* | *I went to the house, but there was no one around* (=no one was there).

4 also **round** *BrE* moving in a circle: *The Earth goes around the sun.* | *The wheels spin around very quickly.* ⇨ *see picture on page 354*

5 used when giving an approximate amount or time: *These machines cost around £60 in the shops.* | *We should be ready by around 10 o'clock.*

ar·range /ə'reɪndʒ/ *verb*

GRAMMAR
arrange for someone to do something
arrange to do something

1 to make plans so that something can happen: *I've arranged a football practice for tomorrow.* | *Susan arranged for the whole class to go out for a meal.* | *Sorry I can't come – I've arranged to go to a movie tonight.*

2 to put things in a particular order or pattern: *We arranged the chairs so that everyone could see the screen.*

ar·range·ment /ə'reɪndʒmənt/ *noun*

1 if you make arrangements, you organize things so that something can happen: *He is in charge of security arrangements for the concert.* | *Have you made all the arrangements for the party?* | *What are your travel arrangements?*

2 something that two people or groups have agreed to do: *My sister* and I **have an arrangement** where we share some of our clothes.

ar·rears /ə'rɪəz $ə'rɪrz/ *plural noun* be in arrears to owe someone money and not make a payment when you should: *The family are in arrears with the rent.*

ar·rest¹ /ə'rest/ *verb* if the police arrest someone, they take them away because they believe that the person is guilty of a crime: *They arrested her for stealing.*

arrest² *noun* 1 when a police officer takes someone away and guards them because they may have done something illegal: *He was interviewed for two hours after his arrest.* 2 be under arrest if someone is under arrest, the police have arrested them: *The policewoman told me that I was under arrest.*

ar·riv·al /ə'raɪvəl/ *noun* [no plural]

1 when you get to a place you were going to: *Julie met Mike a few days after her arrival at college.*

2 the arrival of someone/something when a new thing or person first starts to exist: *The arrival of the World Wide Web changed everything.* | *the arrival of a new baby*

ar·rive /ə'raɪv/ *verb*

GRAMMAR
arrive in
arrive at

1 to get to a place after a journey: *We arrived at the party just as Lee was leaving.* | *The next train to arrive at platform 2 is the 10:10 to London.* | *The parcel took two weeks to arrive.* | *If the train is on time, we will arrive in Oxford by eight.*

2 if a particular event or time arrives, it comes or happens: *At last the day of the party arrived.* | *The time has arrived for me to leave.*

3 to begin to exist: *Before email arrived, a lot of people never wrote letters.*

ar·ro·gant /'ærəgənt/ *adjective* believing that you are very important, clever etc: *He's so arrogant that he thought he would win.*

ar·row /'ærəʊ $'æroʊ/ *noun* 1 a thin straight weapon with a point at one end that you shoot from a BOW 2 a sign (→), used to show the direction or position of something

ar·son /'ɑːsən $ 'ɑrsən/ *noun* [no plural] the crime of deliberately burning something, especially a building: *He was accused of arson.*

art /ɑːt $ ɑrt/ *noun*

1 [no plural] things that you can look at such as drawings or paintings, that are beautiful or express ideas: *She went to college to study art.* | *Do you like modern art?*
2 arts school subjects such as history and English, that are not sciences
3 the arts art, music, theatre, film, literature etc: *I am interested in the arts.*

PHRASE

a work of art something such as a painting that is an example of art: *The building is full of expensive works of art.*

ar·te·ry /'ɑːtəri $ 'ɑrtəri/ *noun, plural* arteries one of the tubes that takes blood from your heart to the rest of your body

ar·thri·tis /ɑː'θraɪtəs $ ɑr'θraɪtɪs/ *noun* [no plural] a disease that causes pain and swelling in the joints of your body: *She suffers from arthritis.*

ar·ti·cle /'ɑːtɪkəl $ 'ɑrtɪkəl/ *noun*
1 a piece of writing in a newspaper, magazine etc: *I read an interesting article about drugs.* 2 a thing, especially one of a group of things: *an article of clothing* 3 in grammar, the word 'the' (=the definite article), or the word 'a' or 'an' (=the indefinite article)

ar·tic·u·late¹ /ɑː'tɪkjələt $ ɑr'tɪk-jələt/ *adjective* able to express your thoughts and feelings clearly: *He's clever, but not very articulate.*

ar·tic·u·late² /ɑː'tɪkjəleɪt $ ɑr'tɪk-jə‚leɪt/ *verb* to be able to say what you think or feel: *Men can find it hard to articulate their feelings.*

ar·ti·fi·cial /‚ɑːtə'fɪʃəl $ ‚ɑrtə-'fɪʃəl/ *adjective*
not real or natural, but made by people: *The room was decorated with artificial flowers.*

artificial in·tel·li·gence /‚.... .'.../ *noun* [no plural] the science of making

computers do things that people can do, such as understand language

art·ist /'ɑːtɪst $ 'ɑrtɪst/ *noun* someone who makes art, for example a painter, musician, or dancer: *It is hard to make money as an artist.*

ar·tis·tic /ɑː'tɪstɪk $ ɑr'tɪstɪk/ *adjective*
1 good at making things such as paintings or drawings: *I'm not very artistic.* 2 connected with art or with being an artist: *Denis is the film's artistic director.*

as /əz; strong æz/ *adverb, preposition*
1 used when comparing people or things: *He's as tall as his father now* (=he and his father are now the same height). | *Her hands were as cold as ice* (=her hands were very cold, like ice). | *I worked as hard as I could.*
2 what job someone does: *She worked as a teacher for a while.*
3 how something is used: *He used the piece of wood as a bridge across the stream.*
4 when something happens written: *He fell as he was walking up the steps.* | *Mary arrived just as I was leaving* (=I was just leaving when Mary arrived).
5 because: *As we've got some time left, I'll give you a short test.*

PHRASES

as if, as though: *She looked as though she'd been crying* (=the way she looked made me think she'd been crying). | *It looks as if it's been raining.*
as well also: *Can I have a drink as well?*

asap /‚eɪ es eɪ 'piː/ *adverb informal* the abbreviation of 'as soon as possible': *I will let you know asap.*

as·cend /ə'send/ *verb formal* to move up or towards the top of something ⇨ opposite DESCEND: *The plane ascended rapidly.*

as·cent /ə'sent/ *noun formal* when someone moves or climbs up or to the top of something ⇨ opposite DESCENT: *a successful ascent of Mount Everest*

ash /æʃ/ *noun, plural* ashes the soft grey powder that is left after something has burned: *cigarette ash*

a·shamed /ə'ʃeɪmd/ *adjective*

GRAMMAR
ashamed of something
ashamed to do something
feeling embarrassed or guilty about
something: *I felt **ashamed of** the
way I had lied to him.* | *Don't be
ashamed to ask for help.*

a·shore /ə'ʃɔː $ə'ʃɔr/ *adverb* onto or
towards the side of a lake, river, or
ocean: *We swam ashore.*

ash·tray /'æʃtreɪ/ *noun* a small dish
where you put finished cigarettes

a·side /ə'saɪd/ *adverb* **1** move aside,
step aside to move to the side: *She
moved aside to let me pass.* **2** put
something aside, set something aside
to keep or save something so that you
can use it later: *We set aside some of the
fruit to eat later.*

ask /ɑːsk $æsk/ *verb*

GRAMMAR
ask someone something
ask (someone) about something
ask (someone) why/when etc
ask (someone) for something
ask (someone) to do something
1 to say to someone that you want
them to tell you something: *"Where
have you been?" asked my mother.* |
*Can I **ask a question**?* | *He wanted
to ask his girlfriend something.* | *Tess
kept **asking** me **about** you.* | *Just
ask him **why** he doesn't want to
come.* | *The police **asked** her
whether she had seen him before.*
2 to say to someone that you want
them to help you or give your some-
thing: *She often asks my advice.* | *If
you don't understand, just ask.* | *I
had to **ask** my parents **for** money.* |
*He **asked** me **to** go to the cinema
with him.*

PHRASES
ask someone in to invite someone
to come into your house: *She **asked**
me **in** for coffee.*
ask someone out to ask someone
to go with you for a meal, drink etc
because you like them: *Leo **asked**
me **out** but I said no.*

USAGE **ask, demand, request**
Compare **ask**, **demand**, and **request**. If
you **demand** something, you ask for it
very strongly: *Teachers are demanding a*

pay rise. If you **request** something, you
ask someone in authority if you can have
it: *I've requested three days' holiday next
week.*

a·sleep /ə'sliːp/ *adjective* **1** sleeping:
Dad was asleep in his chair. **2** fall
asleep to begin to sleep: *I fell asleep in
class.*

as·pect /'æspekt/ *noun* one of the separate parts of something: *My work and
my family are two important aspects of
my life.*

as·phyx·i·ate /æs'fɪksieɪt/ *verb formal*
to stop someone breathing: *The thick
smoke asphyxiated three children in an
upstairs bedroom.*

as·pir·in /'æsprɪn/ *noun* [no plural] a drug
that stops pain: *She took some aspirin
for her headache.*

as·sai·lant /ə'seɪlənt/ *noun formal* someone who attacks another person: *He did
not know his assailant.*

as·sas·sin·ate /ə'sæsəneɪt $ə'sæsn-
ˌeɪt/ *verb* to murder an important person: *a plot to assassinate the Pope*

as·sas·sin·ation /ˌsæsə'neɪʃən
$ə,sæsə'neɪʃən/ *noun* when someone
murders an important person: *the
assassination of John F Kennedy*

as·sault¹ /ə'sɔːlt/ *noun* a violent attack:
*He was accused of several assaults on
women.*

assault² *verb* to attack someone violently: *A gang of boys assaulted him.*

as·sem·ble /ə'sembəl/ *verb* to come
together in the same place: *The students
assembled in the school yard.*

as·sem·bly /ə'sembli/ *noun, plural*
assemblies **1** a regular meeting of all
the students and teachers in a school:
Assembly begins at 9.30. **2** a group of
people who have come together for a
particular purpose: *the United Nations
General Assembly*

as·sert /ə'sɜːt $ə'sɚt/ *verb* **1** assert
your rights, assert your authority *formal*
to say strongly that you have rights or
authority: *My father decided to assert his
authority by refusing to let me go out.*
2 assert yourself to say what you think
or ask for what you want in a confident
and determined way

as·ser·tive /ə'sɜːtɪv $ə'sɚtɪv/ *adjec-
tive* saying what you think or asking for
what you want in a confident and determined way: *Be polite but assertive when
you make a complaint.*

as·sess /ə'ses/ *verb* to examine something and make a decision about it: *We assess the students' work throughout the year.*

as·set /'æset/ *noun* something or someone that helps you to succeed: *Tom is a real asset to the team.*

as·sign·ment /ə'saɪnmənt/ *noun* a piece of work that someone gives you to do: *a homework assignment*

as·sist /ə'sɪst/ *verb formal* to help someone to do something: *The porter will assist you with your bags.*

as·sist·ance /ə'sɪstəns/ *noun [no plural] formal* help: *Students can get financial assistance from the government.*

as·sis·tant /ə'sɪstənt/ *noun* 1 someone whose job is to help customers in a shop: *I asked the assistant for a bigger size.* 2 someone who helps someone else to do their work: *My assistant answers the phone and arranges meetings.*

as·so·ci·ate /ə'səʊʃieɪt $ ə'soʊʃi,eɪt/ *verb* be associated with to be connected or related to something: *A lot of health problems are associated with smoking.*

as·so·ci·a·tion /ə,səʊsi'eɪʃən $ ə,soʊsi'eɪʃən/ *noun* 1 an organization for people who do the same work or have the same interests: *the Association of University Teachers* 2 in association with someone working with another organization or person: *The school is building a new library in association with local companies.*

as·sort·ment /ə'sɔːtmənt $ ə'sɔrtmənt/ *noun* a mixture of various different types of thing: *an assortment of cookies*

as·sume /ə'sjuːm $ ə'sum/ *verb* to think that something is true although you have no proof: *I assume his girlfriend went to the party with him.*

as·sump·tion /ə'sʌmpʃən/ *noun* something that you think is true although you have no proof: *We made the assumption that people would come by car.*

as·sur·ance /ə'ʃʊərəns $ ə'ʃʊrəns/ *noun* a definite statement or promise: *Can you give me an assurance that the plane is safe?*

as·sure /ə'ʃʊə $ ə'ʃʊr/ *verb* to tell someone that something will definitely happen or is definitely true, so that they ▼ are less worried: *The doctor assured me that the injection would not hurt.*

as·te·risk /'æstərɪsk/ *noun* a mark like a star (*), used to show that there is a note about a particular word or phrase

asth·ma /'æsmə $ 'æzmə/ *noun [no plural]* an illness that makes it difficult for you to breathe: *Both sisters suffer from asthma.*

as·ton·ish /ə'stɒnɪʃ $ ə'stɑnɪʃ/ *verb* to surprise someone very much: *He astonished everybody with his skill.*

as·ton·ished /ə'stɒnɪʃt $ ə'stɑnɪʃt/ *adjective* very surprised: *I was astonished at how easy it was.*

as·ton·ish·ing /ə'stɒnɪʃɪŋ $ ə'stɑnɪʃɪŋ/ *adjective* very surprising: *It is astonishing that so many students failed.*
– astonishingly *adverb*: *It was astonishingly simple.*

as·ton·ish·ment /ə'stɒnɪʃmənt $ ə'stɑnɪʃmənt/ *noun [no plural]* very great surprise: *My parents stared at me in astonishment.*

as·tound /ə'staʊnd/ *verb* to surprise or shock someone very much: *Her confidence astounded me.*
– astounded *adjective*: *They were astounded at his decision to leave.*

as·tound·ing /ə'staʊndɪŋ/ *adjective* very surprising or shocking: *The news was astounding.*

a·stray /ə'streɪ/ *adverb* 1 go astray to become lost: *My letter went astray in the post.* 2 lead someone astray to make someone do bad things by encouraging them: *Don't let the older girls lead you astray.*

as·trol·o·gy /ə'strɒlədʒi $ ə'strɑlədʒi/ *noun [no plural]* the study of the position of stars and PLANETS, and the effect that they might have on people's lives: *Do you believe in astrology?*

as·tro·naut /'æstrənɔːt/ *noun* someone who travels in a SPACECRAFT

as·tron·o·my /ə'strɒnəmi $ ə'strɑnəmi/ *noun [no plural]* the scientific study of stars and PLANETS

as·tute /ə'stjuːt $ ə'stut/ *adjective* clever and quick to understand situations and people: *an astute politician*

at /ət; strong æt/ *preposition*
1 where someone or something is: *Her auntie met her at the station.* | *You should be at school.* | *His mother was standing at the bottom of the stairs.*

2 what time something happens: *OK, I'll see you at half past five.* | *We arrived at three o'clock.*

3 when something happens: *I'll see you at the weekend.* | *Simon's coming home at Christmas.*

4 where something is thrown, kicked etc: *She threw the cushion at him.* | *The two men shot at police officers.*

5 the person someone is looking or shouting towards: *The man was staring at her.* | *Don't shout at me!*

6 how fast something is moving: *The car was going at about sixty miles an hour* (=its speed was about sixty miles an hour).

ate the past tense of EAT

a·the·ist /'eɪθi-ɪst/ *noun* someone who does not believe that God exists: *She believed in God when she was a child but now she's an atheist.*
– **atheism** *noun*

ath·lete /'æθliːt/ *noun* someone who takes part in sports such as running: *Athletes have to be careful with their diet.*

ath·let·ic /æθ'letɪk/ *adjective* physically strong and good at sport

ath·let·ics /æθ'letɪks/ *noun* **1** BrE sports such as running races and jumping: *We play hockey in winter and do athletics in summer.* **2** AmE sports and physical exercise in general ⇨ see picture on page 351

at·las /'ætləs/ *noun,* plural **atlases** a book of maps: *an atlas of Europe*

ATM /ˌeɪ tiː 'em/ Automated Teller Machine; the American word for CASHPOINT

at·mo·sphere /'ætməsfɪə $ 'ætməs-ˌfɪr/ *noun [no plural]* **1** the kind of feeling that you get when you are in a place: *The town has a nice friendly atmosphere.* **2 the atmosphere** the mixture of gases that surrounds the Earth

at·om /'ætəm/ *noun* the smallest part that a substance can be divided into

a·tom·ic /ə'tɒmɪk $ ə'tɑmɪk/ *adjective* **1** using the power that is produced by dividing atoms: *an atomic bomb* **2** related to atoms

a·tro·cious /ə'trəʊʃəs $ ə'troʊʃəs/ *adjective* very bad: *His handwriting is atrocious.*

a·troc·i·ty /ə'trɒsəti $ ə'trɑsəti/ *noun*

formal, plural **atrocities** a very cruel and violent action: *Both sides in the war committed atrocities.*

at·tach /ə'tætʃ/ *verb*

> **GRAMMAR**
> **attach something to something**

to fix one thing to another: *I attached a copy of the article to my letter.* | *The cat had a bell attached to its collar.*

at·tached /ə'tætʃt/ *adjective* **be attached to someone/something** to like someone or something very much: *Billy is very attached to his teddy bear.*

at·tach·ment /ə'tætʃmənt/ *noun* **1** formal a strong feeling of liking or loving someone or something: *He had a close attachment to his family.* **2** a document or FILE that you send with an EMAIL

at·tack¹ /ə'tæk/ *verb* **1** to try to hurt or kill someone: *Two men attacked him and took his car.* | *The soldiers planned to attack the village at night.* **2** to say strongly that you do not agree with someone or something: *She attacked politicians for not doing enough for young people.* | *The prince has attacked society's values of greed and envy.* **3** to kick or throw a ball forward during a game in order to get a GOAL or point

at·tack² *noun* **1** a violent action that someone does to hurt or kill someone: *Two men were killed in the attack.* **2** a strong statement that someone makes, saying that they do not agree with someone or something: *In his speech he made an attack on all journalists.* **3** a sudden short period of illness: *an attack of coughing* **4** BrE the players in a game such as football who try to get points

at·tack·er /ə'tækə $ ə'tækɚ/ *noun* someone who attacks someone else: *Her attacker ran off.*

at·tempt¹ /ə'tempt/ *verb*

> **GRAMMAR**
> **attempt to do something**

to try to do something difficult or dangerous: *You should attempt to answer all the questions.* | *Few people have climbed this mountain, although many have attempted it.*

A

attempt² *noun*

GRAMMAR
an attempt to do something
if you make an attempt to do something, you try to do it: *Despite all our **attempts to** stop him, he decided to leave school.* | *She **made no attempt to** (=did not try to) explain what she was doing there.*

at·tend /əˈtend/ *verb* **1** *formal* to go to a meeting, school, church etc: *300 students attended the lecture.* **2** attend to someone/something to give care or attention to something or someone: *The doctor will attend to you in a moment.*

at·tend·ance /əˈtendəns/ *noun* when you go to a meeting, school, church etc: *Your attendance at classes is obligatory.*

at·ten·tion /əˈtenʃən/ *noun* [no plural]

GRAMMAR
attention to something/someone
when you watch, listen to, or think about something carefully: *Can I have your attention please, class.* | *She **gives** a lot of **attention to** her clothes.*

PHRASES
pay attention to listen or watch carefully: *Jodie never **pays attention to** the teacher.*
attract attention if someone or something attracts attention, people notice them: *I waved to try and **attract** his **attention**.* | *Her new dress was **attracting** a lot of **attention**.*
draw attention to something to make people notice or think about something: *We are trying to **draw attention to** the problem of drugs in schools.*
the centre of attention the person that everyone is looking at: *Naomi is shy and hates being **the centre of attention**.*

at·ten·tive /əˈtentɪv/ *adjective* listening or watching carefully: *The students were very attentive.*
–**attentively** *adverb*: *They all listened attentively.*

at·tic /ˈætɪk/ *noun* a room at the top of a house, inside the roof: *I keep my old clothes in the attic.*

at·ti·tude /ˈætətjuːd $ ˈætəˌtuːd/ *noun*

GRAMMAR
an attitude to/towards someone/ something
what you think and feel about something, and how you show this in your behaviour: *I think it's best to have a relaxed **attitude to** money.* | *I don't like her **attitude towards** me.* | *The team coach encourages players to have a positive attitude before the match.*

at·tor·ney /əˈtɜːni $ əˈtɜˌni/ the American word for LAWYER

at·tract /əˈtrækt/ *verb*

GRAMMAR
attract someone to something/ someone
1 if something attracts you, you like it or feel interested in it: *It wasn't the money that **attracted** me to the job.* | *She **was attracted by** the idea of living in a big city.*
2 be attracted to someone to feel interested in someone in a sexual way: *I like him, but I **am** not **attracted to** him.*
3 if something attracts people, it makes them want to see it: *The exhibition is attracting a lot of tourists.*

at·trac·tion /əˈtrækʃən/ *noun* **1** something that people like to see or do because it is interesting or enjoyable: *Buckingham Palace is one of London's most popular tourist attractions.* **2** when you feel interested in someone in a sexual way: *There was a strong physical attraction between us.*

at·trac·tive /əˈtræktɪv/ *adjective*

GRAMMAR
attractive to someone
1 pretty or pleasant to look at: *His new girlfriend is very attractive.*
2 if something is attractive, people want to see it, go to it, or have it: *The new theatre will make the town more **attractive to** tourists.*

au·ber·gine /ˈəʊbəʒiːn $ ˈoʊbəˌʒiːn/ *noun* a large vegetable with smooth shiny purple skin; EGGPLANT *AmE* ⇨ see picture on page 345

automatic

au·burn /'ɔːbən $ 'ɔbən/ *adjective* auburn hair is a reddish brown colour

auc·tion /'ɔːkʃən/ *noun* an event at which things are sold to the person who offers the most money: *We bought the furniture at an auction.*

au·di·ble /'ɔːdəbəl/ *adjective* loud enough to be heard: *His words were clearly audible.*

au·di·ence /'ɔːdiəns/ *noun* the people who watch or listen to a performance: *The audience stood up and cheered at the end of the performance.*

au·di·o /'ɔːdiəʊ $ 'ɔdioʊ/ *adjective* used to record sounds: *an audio cassette*

au·di·o·vis·u·al /ˌɔːdiəʊ'vɪʒuəl $ ˌɔdi-oʊ'vɪʒuəl/ *adjective* having recorded pictures and sound: *Our teacher uses a lot of audiovisual aids.*

au·di·tion /ɔː'dɪʃən/ *noun* a short performance to test whether an actor or singer is good enough to be in a play or concert: *I have an audition for a part in 'Annie' tomorrow.*

au·di·to·ri·um /ˌɔːdɪ'tɔːriəm/ *noun* the part of a theatre where people sit

Au·gust /'ɔːɡəst/ *written abbreviation* **Aug** *noun* the eighth month of the year: *It's Friday August 10th. | My birthday's in August.*

aunt /ɑːnt $ ænt/ *also* **aunt·ie** /'ɑːnti $ 'ænti/ *noun* the sister of your father or mother, or the wife of your UNCLE: *I'm going to stay with my aunt. | Auntie Mary is here.*

au pair /əʊ 'peə $ oʊ 'per/ *noun* a young woman who stays with a family in a foreign country and cares for their children: *I worked for a year as an au pair.*

au·ral /'ɔːrəl/ *adjective* connected with hearing and listening: *visual and aural sensations*

aus·tere /ɔː'stɪə $ ɔ'stɪr/ *adjective formal* plain and simple: *The room was very austere.*

aus·ter·i·ty /ɔː'sterəti/ *noun* [no plural] *formal* bad economic conditions in which people do not have enough money: *There was a period of austerity after the war.*

au·then·tic /ɔː'θentɪk/ *adjective* not copying or pretending to be something else: *The restaurant serves authentic Chinese food. | Is it an authentic Van Gogh painting?*

au·thor /'ɔːθə $ 'ɔθər/ *noun* the writer

of a book: *Who is the author of 'Pride and Prejudice?'*

au·thor·i·tar·i·an /ɔːˌθɒrə'teəriən $ əˌθɔrə'teriən/ *adjective* strict and not allowing people much freedom: *Her father is very authoritarian.*

au·thor·i·ty /ɔː'θɒrəti $ ə'θɔrəti/ *noun*

GRAMMAR
authority to do something
authority over someone

1 [no plural] if someone has authority, they have the right to make important decisions and control people: *The manager has the authority to refuse to allow people into the club. | My father wanted complete authority over us.*

2 an organization or government department that controls something: *the local health authority*

PHRASES
in authority with the right to make important decisions and control people: *Only leave the building if you are told to do so by someone in authority.*
the authorities organizations such as the police who control people: *If you see anything suspicious, inform the airport authorities.*

au·thor·ize *also* **authorise** *BrE* /'ɔːθəraɪz/ *verb* to officially allow someone to do something: *You can't go in unless I authorize it.*

au·to·bi·o·graph·i·cal /ˌɔːtəbaɪə-'ɡræfɪkəl/ *adjective* about someone's own life: *The film is based on the autobiographical novel by Joseph Ackerley.*

au·to·bi·og·ra·phy /ˌɔːtəbaɪ'ɒɡrəfi $ ˌɔtəbaɪ'ɑɡrəfi/ *noun, plural* **autobiographies** a book that someone writes about their own life: *His autobiography caused a lot of embarrassment to the government.*

au·to·graph /'ɔːtəɡrɑːf $ 'ɔtə,ɡræf/ *noun* if a famous person gives you their autograph, they sign their name for you: *Can I have your autograph?*

au·to·mat·ic /ˌɔːtə'mætɪk/ *adjective* an automatic machine works by itself without much human control: *an automatic washing machine*
–automatically /-kli/ *adverb*: *The camera flashes automatically.*

au·to·mo·bile /'ɔːtəməbiːl/ the American word for CAR

au·top·sy /'ɔːtɒpsi $'ɔ,tɑpsi/ noun, plural **autopsies** an examination of a dead body to discover why the person died: *Doctors performed an autopsy on the body.*

au·tumn /'ɔːtəm/ noun

the season when the leaves fall off the trees; FALL AmE

aux·il·ia·ry /ɔːg'zɪljəri $ɔg'zɪləri/ adjective **auxiliary nurse, auxiliary worker** someone whose job is to give additonal help to other nurses or other workers

auxiliary verb /,.,... '. / noun a verb used with another verb to make questions, negative sentences, and tenses. In English the auxiliary verbs are 'be', 'do', and 'have'.

a·vail·a·bil·i·ty /ə,veɪlə'bɪləti/ noun when you can get, buy, or use something: *I rang to ask about the availability of tickets.*

a·vail·a·ble /ə'veɪləbəl/ adjective

GRAMMAR
available to someone
available for something
available from someone/somewhere
if something is available, you can buy it, use it, or have it: *Tickets are not available to the public.* | *Have you got any bikes available for sale?* | *The books are available from all good booksellers.*

av·a·lanche /'æv-
əlɑːnʃ $'ævə-
,læntʃ/ noun a
large amount of
snow that falls
down a mountain:
*He was killed in
an avalanche.*

avalanche

av·e·nue /'ævə-
njuː $'ævə,nu/
noun a road in a
town: *The hotel is
on 11th Avenue.*

av·e·rage¹ /'ævərɪdʒ/ noun

GRAMMAR
an average of something
the amount that you get when you add several figures together and then divide the result by the number of figures: *The girls spend an average of £10 a week on clothes.*

PHRASES
on average: *I see my grandmother once a month on average* (=I usually see her once a month).
above average, below average higher or lower than the usual level or amount: *Her intelligence is well above average.*

average² adjective **1** the average amount is the amount you get when you add several figures together and then divide the result by the number of figures: *The average age of the students is 14.* **2** typical or normal: *The average person doesn't know much about computers.* ⇨ see picture on page 353

average³ verb to be a particular amount as an average: *Her test results average 60%.*

a·vert /ə'vɜːt $ə'vɚt/ verb written to stop something unpleasant from happening: *How can we avert the crisis?*

a·vi·a·tion /,eɪvi'eɪʃən/ noun [no plural] formal the activity of flying in planes, or making planes: *an expert in aviation*

av·id /'ævɪd/ adjective liking something a lot, or doing a lot of something: *Doug's an avid fan of American football.*

av·o·ca·do /,ævə'kɑːdəʊ $,ævə'kɑdoʊ/ noun a fruit with a thick green or purple skin and a soft green part inside that you eat

a·void /ə'vɔɪd/ verb

GRAMMAR
avoid doing something
1 if you avoid something bad, you try to make sure it does not happen: *She avoided trouble by keeping quiet.* | *I left early to avoid getting stuck in traffic.*
2 to deliberately try not to see or meet someone: *Were you trying to avoid me at the party?*
3 to deliberately not do something: *Avoid using informal language when you are writing an essay.*

a·wait /ə'weɪt/ verb formal to wait for something to happen or arrive: *We're still awaiting news of our application for a visa.*

a·wake¹ /ə'weɪk/ *adjective*

not sleeping: *Mum was still awake when I got home.* | *His music kept me **awake** all night.* | *I tried to **stay awake** to watch the film but couldn't.*

PHRASES

lie awake to be unable to sleep when you are in bed, especially because you are worried: *She **lay awake** wondering what to tell Toby.*
wide awake: *I was **wide awake** (=completely awake) at five this morning.*

awake² *verb written* **awoke** /ə'wəʊk $ ə'woʊk/ **awoken** /ə'wəʊkən $ ə-'woʊkən/ to stop sleeping: *I will be there when you awake.*

a·ward¹ /ə'wɔːd $ ə'wɔrd/ *verb* to officially give someone a prize: *She was awarded the Nobel Peace Prize.*

award² *noun* a prize for something good that you have done: *The fireman won an award for bravery.*

a·ware /ə'weə $ ə'wer/ *adjective*

GRAMMAR

aware of something/someone
aware (that)
if you are aware of something, you know about it or realize that it is there ⇨ opposite UNAWARE: *I **was aware of** someone standing behind me.* | *Are you **aware that** it is illegal to park here?*

a·wash /ə'wɒʃ $ ə'wɑʃ/ *adjective written* covered with water: *The streets were awash with flood water.*

a·way /ə'weɪ/ *adverb*

1 moving further from a place: *We walked **away from** the building.* | *She waved goodbye before driving*
▼ *away.* | *The paper boat floated away down the river.* | *Go away! I'm busy!*
2 showing how far something is from a place: *The nearest town was 10 miles away.* | *The huge animal was only two metres **away from** me.*
3 not at home, work, or school: *He's away on holiday at the moment.* | *Fiona's been **away from** school for a week.* ⇨ see picture on page 354
4 showing how long it will be before something happens: *The exams are only two weeks away* (=they will happen after two weeks).

awe /ɔː/ *noun* **in awe, with awe** when you feel that you admire something or someone a lot: *I looked back in awe across the mountains.*

awe·some /'ɔːsəm/ *adjective* very big or important: *It's an awesome achievement.*

aw·ful /'ɔːfəl/ *adjective* very bad or unpleasant: *What awful food!* | *My hair looks awful.*

awk·ward /'ɔːkwəd $ 'ɔkwəd/ *adjective* **1** difficult to deal with: *He kept asking awkward questions.* **2** embarrassed and shy: *I felt awkward going there by myself.*
−**awkwardness** *noun* [no plural]: *She looked away quickly to hide her awkwardness.*

awoke the past tense of AWAKE

awoken the past participle of AWAKE

axe also **ax** *AmE* /æks/ *noun* a tool that you use for breaking wood into smaller pieces, or for cutting down trees

ax·is /'æksɪs/ *noun, plural* **axes** /'æksiːz/ a line at the side or bottom of a GRAPH, where you write the measurements

ax·le /'æksəl/ *noun* the bar that joins two wheels on a vehicle

Bb

BA /ˌbiː 'eɪ/ noun Bachelor of Arts; a university degree in a subject such as history or literature: *She has a BA in French.*

ba·by /'beɪbi/ noun, plural **babies** **1** a very young child who has not learned to talk yet: *The baby's crying.* ⇨ see usage note at CHILD **2** have a baby to give birth to a baby: *Lucy recently had a baby.*

baby car·riage /'.. ˌ../ also **baby bug·gy** /'.. ˌ../ the American word for a PRAM

baby·sit /'beɪbisɪt/ verb **babysat** /-sæt/, **babysitting** to look after children while their parents go out: *Can you babysit tomorrow night?*
–**babysitter** noun: *I'm Sarah's babysitter.*

bach·e·lor /'bætʃələ $ 'bætʃələʳ/ noun **1** a man who is not married: *His son is 32 and still a bachelor.* **2** Bachelor of Arts, Bachelor of Science the title of a first university degree

back¹ /bæk/ noun

> **GRAMMAR**
> **the back of something**

1 the part of your body from your neck and shoulders down to your bottom: *Billy lay on his back and looked at the sky.* | *I hurt my back when I was moving the computer.* | *Jilly leapt lightly onto the horse's back.*

2 the part of something that is furthest away from the front ⇨ opposite FRONT¹ (2): *Sam and Steve always sit at the back of the class.* | *Put your bags in the back of the car.*

> **PHRASES**

back to front BrE in the wrong position, so that the front is where the back should be: *He's got his shirt on back to front.*

in back of something AmE if something is in back of another thing, it is behind it: *There's a football field in back of the school.*

out back AmE if a person is out back, they are outside, behind a building: *Mom's out back in the yard.*

behind someone's back if you do something unkind behind someone's back, you do it secretly, so that they do not know you did it: *Carole's been talking about me to the teacher behind my back.*

back² adverb

1 returning to the place where someone or something was before: *Tracey ran back to the house* (=ran to the house she had just left) *to get her umbrella.* | *She put the magazine back in her bag* (=she put the magazine in the bag she had taken it from).

2 in the direction that is behind you: *He stepped back from the edge of the road.* | *Jane turned and looked back.*

3 doing the same thing to someone that they have done to you: *Stephanie waved to me, and I waved back.* | *I'll phone you back later.* | *When are you going to give me that money back?*

back³ verb

1 to support someone or something, for example by voting for them or agreeing with them in a meeting: *I'm backing Peter in the election for school president.*

2 to make a vehicle move in the direction that is behind you: *I can't back the car into that tiny space!* | *Joe backed his truck out of the garage.*

> **PHRASAL VERBS**
> **back away**
> to move slowly backwards because you are afraid, shocked etc: *When he*

saw the dog, he started to **back away**.

back down
to stop saying that you are right about something and admit that you are wrong: *She had to **back down** because I knew she was lying.*

back off
to move away from someone in order to avoid a problem: *I thought he was going to hit me but he **backed off**.*

back out
if you back out of something that you agreed to do, you decide not to do it: *You can't **back out of** the holiday now.*

back up
1 back someone/something up to support someone or show that what they are saying is true: *Will you **back** me **up** in the meeting?*
2 back something up to make a copy of information on a computer: *You should **back up** all your data at least once a week.*

back⁴ *adjective* **1** behind or furthest from the front of something: *There's someone at the back door.* | *Tim and I always sit on the back row at the cinema.* **2** back street, back road a street or road that is away from the main streets of a town

back·ache /ˈbækeɪk/ *noun* pain in your back: *I've got terrible backache.*

back·bone /ˈbækbəʊn $ ˈbækboʊn/ *noun* the bone down the middle of your back ⇨ *same meaning* SPINE: *He damaged his backbone in a car accident.*

back·break·ing /ˈbæk‚breɪkɪŋ/ *adjective* backbreaking work is very difficult physical work that makes you tired: *Moving the piano was backbreaking work.*

back·fire /‚bækˈfaɪə $ ˈbækfaɪəʳ/ *verb* if something you do backfires, it has the opposite result to the one you wanted: *The plan backfired when I realised I didn't have enough money.*

back·ground /ˈbækgraʊnd/ *noun* **1** your background is the type of education you had and the family you belong to: *Jo and I come from very different backgrounds.* **2** in the background in the part of a picture or scene that is behind the main part ⇨ *opposite*

FOREGROUND: *In the background of the painting there is a river.*

back·ing /ˈbækɪŋ/ *noun* [no plural] money or support that a person or organization gives you in order to help you achieve something: *The government gives financial backing to many small businesses.*

back·log /ˈbæklɒg $ ˈbæklɔɡ/ *noun* a lot of work that you should have done earlier: *We have a huge backlog of letters to answer.*

back·pack /ˈbækpæk/ *noun* a large bag that you carry on your back when you go walking or camping: *I carried everything including my tent in a backpack.*
–**backpacker** *noun*: *a hostel for backpackers*

back·pack·ing /ˈbæk‚pækɪŋ/ *noun* [no plural] an occasion when you go walking and camping carrying a backpack: *We're going backpacking in Nepal.*

back·side /ˈbæksaɪd/ *noun informal* the part of your body that you sit on

back·stage /‚bækˈsteɪdʒ/ *adverb, adjective* in the area behind the stage in a theatre: *We're hoping to go backstage and talk to the actors.*

back·stroke /ˈbækstrəʊk $ ˈbækstroʊk/ *noun* [no plural] a style of swimming on your back: *Can you do backstroke?*

back-to-back /‚. . ˈ./ *adjective, adverb* with the backs of two people or things facing each other: *Stand back-to-back and we'll see who's tallest.*

back·up /ˈbækʌp/ *noun* a copy of a document, especially a computer FILE, that you can use if you lose or damage the original one: *Do you have a backup of this file?*

back·ward /ˈbækwəd $ ˈbækwəʳd/ *adjective* towards the direction that is behind you: *a backward glance*

back·wards /ˈbækwədz $ ˈbækwəʳdz/ also **backward** *adverb*
1 towards the direction that is behind you ⇨ *opposite* FORWARD¹: *He fell over backwards.*
2 starting at the end, instead of the beginning: *'Pan' spelled backwards is 'nap'.*
3 backwards and forwards first in one direction, then in the other direction, many times: *I travel **backwards and forwards** to London several times a week.*

back·yard /ˌbæk'jɑːd $ ˌbæk'jɑrd/ noun a small area behind a house: *The kids are playing in the backyard.*

ba·con /'beɪkən/ noun [no plural] long thin pieces of meat from a pig: *Would you like bacon and eggs for breakfast?*

bac·te·ri·a /bæk'tɪəriə $ bæk'tɪriə/ plural noun very small living things that can cause disease: *This cleaning product kills bacteria.*

bad /bæd/ adjective **worse** /wɜːs $ wɜˑs/ **worst** /wɜːst $ wɚst/

GRAMMAR
bad at something
bad for someone

1 not enjoyable or pleasant ⇨ opposite GOOD[1] (2): *bad weather* | *I've had a really bad day.* | *Unfortunately, I've got some bad news for you.*
2 of a low standard or quality ⇨ opposite GOOD[1] (1): *I've never read such a bad essay.* | *That was the worst party I've ever been to.*
3 not useful or suitable ⇨ opposite GOOD[1] (4): *That's a bad idea.*
4 someone who is bad at something is not skilful at doing it ⇨ opposite GOOD[1] (3): *I'm pretty **bad at** saying I'm sorry, but here goes.* | *Gary's much **worse at** maths than he is **at** English.*
5 serious or severe: *She had a bad cough.* | *Was the traffic bad this morning?*
6 a bad person does not behave well and is not morally good ⇨ opposite GOOD[1] (5): *I don't think she's a bad girl; she's just a little confused right now.*
7 something that is bad for you is not healthy for your body or mind ⇨ opposite GOOD[1] (6): *Smoking is bad for you.*

PHRASES
be bad for you if something is bad for you, it can harm you because it is not healthy: *Too much chocolate is bad for your skin.* | *There can't be anyone who doesn't know that smoking is bad for you.*
not bad spoken: *"Was the food good?" "Not bad (=it was fairly good; okay)."*
too bad spoken BrE used to say that you do not care about someone's feelings: *"I don't want to go to a club!" "Too bad, everybody else does!"*

feel bad to feel ashamed or sorry: *I feel bad that I wasn't there when you needed me.*

badge /bædʒ/ noun a piece of metal or plastic with a sign or writing on it that you wear on your clothes: *The policeman showed me his badge.*

bad·ger /'bædʒə $ 'bædʒɚ/ noun an animal with black and white fur that lives under the ground

bad·ly /'bædli/ adverb **worse** /wɜːs $ wɜˑs/ **worst** /wɜːst $ wɚst/
1 not done in the correct or a good way ⇨ opposite WELL[1] (1): *The team played badly.* | *badly made clothes*
2 very much or very seriously: *She needs some sleep badly.* | *Was anyone badly injured?*

bad·min·ton /'bædmɪntən/ noun [no plural] a game in which you hit a SHUTTLECOCK (=a small object with feathers) over a net: *Who wants a game of badminton?*

bad-tem·pered /ˌ. '../ adjective someone who is bad-tempered gets annoyed easily: *Why is Tim so bad-tempered today?* ⇨ see usage note at ANGRY

baf·fle /'bæfəl/ verb if something baffles you, you cannot understand it: *Question 4 baffled the whole class.*
– baffled adjective: *We were completely baffled by her behaviour.*

bag /bæg/ noun

GRAMMAR
a bag of something

1 a container made of paper, plastic, cloth etc that you use for carrying things: *She brought her lunch in a paper bag.* | *You can take one bag on the plane with you.*

bags

toilet bag — carrier bag — handbag

rucksack — holdall

2 the amount that you can fit in a bag: *He put a whole **bag of** sugar in the cake.*

bag·gage /'bægɪdʒ/ *noun* [no plural] the bags that you carry when you are travelling ⇨ *same meaning* LUGGAGE: *The porter will help you with your baggage.*

USAGE
Baggage does not have a plural form. You can say **some baggage**, **any baggage**, or **a piece of baggage**: *Do you have any baggage? | She lost her baggage.*

bag·gy /'bægi/ *adjective* **baggier, baggiest** baggy clothes are big and loose: *She wore a baggy T-shirt.*

bail¹ /beɪl/ *noun* [no plural] money that you pay to a court so that a prisoner does not have to stay in prison before the TRIAL starts: *They released him on £10,000 bail this morning.*

bail² *verb* **bail someone out** to help someone who is in trouble, especially by giving them money: *She asked her dad to **bail** her **out**.*

bait /beɪt/ *noun* food that you use to attract fish or animals so that you can catch them: *We used worms for bait.*

bake /beɪk/ *verb* to make things such as bread and cakes: *Mom bakes her own bread.*

baked beans /ˌ ˈ./ *plural noun* white beans cooked with TOMATO SAUCE and sold in TINS

bak·er /'beɪkə $ 'beɪkɚ/ *noun* **1** someone whose job is making bread **2** baker's a shop that sells bread and cakes: *Is there a baker's near here?*

bak·er·y /'beɪkəri/ *noun, plural* bakeries a place where people make or sell bread

bal·ance¹ /'bæləns/ *noun* [no plural]

GRAMMAR
a balance between things
1 when you are able to stay steady while you are standing up: *These drugs may affect your balance.*
2 when you give the right amount of attention to two different things, rather than giving too much attention to one of them: *It's important to find a balance between work and play.*

PHRASES
lose your balance: *I lost my bal-*

ance (=was unable to stay steady) *and fell off the wall.*
off balance when you are not steady, for example because you are standing on one leg: *The wind caught him **off balance** and he fell over.*
on balance used to tell someone your opinion after considering all the facts: ***On balance**, the new test is probably fairer.*

balance² *verb* to stay in a steady position, without falling to one side or the other: *Can you balance on this beam?*

bal·anced /'bælənst/ *adjective* **1** a balanced opinion, view etc is sensible and fair: *He has a very balanced attitude to the situation.* **2** a balanced meal, way of living etc includes a variety of different things that you need to make you healthy or happy: *a balanced diet with plenty of fresh fruit and vegetables*

bal·co·ny /'bælkəni/ *noun, plural* balconies a small area outside an upstairs window, where you can sit or stand: *The room had a balcony overlooking the harbour.* ⇨ *see picture on page 343*

bald /bɔːld/ *adjective* having little or no hair on your head: *He's going bald.* ⇨ *see picture on page 353*

bale /beɪl/ *noun* a large amount of dried grass that has been tied together: *a bale of hay*

ball /bɔːl/ *noun*

GRAMMAR
a ball of something
1 a round object that you throw, hit, or kick in a game: *She threw a tennis ball at me. | a golf ball*
2 any round object: *a ball of string*
3 a large formal party where people dance: *a Christmas ball*

bal·lad /'bæləd/ *noun* a long song that tells a story

bal·le·ri·na /ˌbælə'riːnə/ *noun* a female ballet dancer: *I wanted to be a ballerina when I grew up.*

bal·let /'bæleɪ $ bæ'leɪ/ *noun* **1** [no plural] a type of dancing that dancers do on a stage in a theatre, which tells a story with music and actions but no words: *I've been doing ballet for a year.* **2** a dance done in this style: *Swan Lake is my favourite ballet.*

B

balloon
44

B

bal·loon /bəˈluːn/ *noun* a coloured rubber object that you fill with air and use as a decoration

bal·lot /ˈbælət/ *verb* to find out what a group of people wants by asking them to vote in secret: *The trade union will ballot its members next week, asking them if they want to take strike action* (=asking them if they want to officially stop working).
– **ballot** *noun*: *We held a ballot to decide who would be the new chairman.*

ball·park /ˈbɔːlpɑːk $ ˈbɔlˌpɑrk/ *noun* AmE a field for playing BASEBALL, with seats for people to watch the game

ball·point pen /ˌbɔːlpɔɪnt ˈpen/ *noun* a pen with a very small ball in the end that controls the flow of ink

ball·room /ˈbɔːlruːm/ *noun* a large room for formal dances: *the hotel ballroom*

bam·boo /ˌbæmˈbuː/ *noun* a tall plant with hard hollow stems that are used to make furniture: *a set of bamboo chairs*

ban¹ /bæn/ *noun* an official order saying that people cannot do something: *They put a ban on nuclear tests.*

ban² *verb* **banned, banning** to officially say that people cannot do something: *He has banned us from smoking in his house.*

ba·nal /bəˈnɑːl $ bəˈnæl/ *adjective* formal ordinary and not interesting: *a banal conversation*

ba·na·na /bəˈnɑːnə $ bəˈnænə/ *noun* a long curved yellow fruit: *a bunch of bananas* ⇨ *see picture on page 345*

band¹ /bænd/ *noun*
1 a group of musicians who play popular music together: *He plays drums in a band.* | *Which is your favourite band?*
2 a thin flat piece of material that you use to keep something in a particular position: *She wore a white hair band.* | *a pack of rubber bands*

band² *verb* **band together (to do something)** to join with other people to do something: *We all banded together to organize the party.*

ban·dage /ˈbændɪdʒ/ *noun* a long piece of cloth that you use to cover a wound
– **bandage** *verb*: *The nurse bandaged my leg.*

Band-Aid /ˈ. ./ AmE trademark the American word for a PLASTER¹

ban·dit /ˈbændɪt/ *noun* someone who robs people who are travelling: *The bandits stole money and cameras from the tourists.*

bang¹ /bæŋ/ *verb*

GRAMMAR
bang something on something
bang on something

1 to make a loud noise by hitting something hard: *He banged his fists on the table.* | *Someone's banging on the door.* | *The door banged shut* (=it made a loud sound as it closed).
2 to hit a part of your body against something by mistake: *Don't bang your head on the ceiling.*

bang² *noun*

GRAMMAR
a bang on something

1 a sudden loud noise: *He slammed the door with a loud bang.* | *I heard a bang, and the car engine started smoking.* ⇨ *see picture on page 350*
2 when you hit part of your body against something hard by mistake: *a painful bang on the knee*
3 **bangs** the American word for FRINGE: *My bangs are getting long.*

bang³ *adverb* informal exactly: *He arrived bang on time.*

ban·gle /ˈbæŋɡəl/ *noun* a band of metal or wood that you wear around your wrist: *silver bangles* ⇨ *see picture at* JEWELLERY

ban·ish /ˈbænɪʃ/ *verb* to punish someone by making them go away somewhere: *My mother banished me to my bedroom.*

ban·is·ter /ˈbænəstə $ ˈbænəstər/ *noun* the long piece of wood at the side of stairs that you can hold onto as you go up them

ban·jo /ˈbændʒəʊ $ ˈbændʒoʊ/ *noun* a musical instrument with four or more strings and a round body

bank¹ /bæŋk/ *noun*
1 an organization where you can keep your money safely until you need it. You can also borrow or change money in a bank: *I need to go to the bank to get some money.*

B

2 land along the side of a river or lake: *We went for a walk along the **river bank**.*

3 a place where a large amount of something is kept until someone needs it: *a **data bank***

bank² *verb* **bank on someone/ something** to depend on someone for something: *We were banking on your help.*

bank·er /'bæŋkə $ 'bæŋkəʳ/ *noun* someone who works in a bank at a high level

bank hol·i·day /ˌ. '.../ *noun BrE* an official holiday when banks and most companies are closed; PUBLIC HOLIDAY *AmE: Next Monday is a bank holiday.*

bank·ing /'bæŋkɪŋ/ *noun [no plural]* the business that is done by a bank: *I'd like a career in banking.*

bank·note /'bæŋknəʊt $ 'bæŋkˌnoʊt/ *noun* a piece of paper money; BILL *AmE*

bank·rupt /'bæŋkrʌpt/ *adjective* not able to pay your debts, and therefore not able to continue in business: *Many small businesses go bankrupt.*
–**bankrupt** *verb*: *This tax increase could bankrupt us.*

bank·rupt·cy /'bæŋkrʌptsi/ *noun,* *plural* **bankruptcies** when someone goes bankrupt: *A series of business failures led to bankruptcy.*

ban·ner /'bænə $ 'bænəʳ/ *noun* a long piece of cloth with writing on it: *They waved banners reading 'Welcome home'.*

ban·quet /'bæŋkwɪt/ *noun* a very formal meal for a lot of people: *a state banquet*

bap·tis·m /'bæptɪzəm/ *noun* a religious ceremony in which a priest puts water on someone to make them a member of the Christian Church

bap·tize also **baptise** *BrE* /bæp'taɪz $ 'bæptaɪz/ *verb* to put water on someone in a religious ceremony to make them a member of the Christian Church: *This is the priest who baptized me.*

bar¹ /bɑː $ bɑr/ *noun*

GRAMMAR
a bar of something

1 a place where you can buy and drink alcohol: *We met at a bar near the station. | I just saw Michael Jackson standing in the hotel bar* (=a place in a hotel where you can buy drinks).

2 **coffee bar/sandwich bar etc** a place where you can buy and drink coffee, buy and eat a sandwich, etc: *a coffee bar*

3 a small block of something solid: *a **bar of** soap | a chocolate bar*

4 a long thin piece of metal or wood: *The man attacked us with an iron bar.*

5 a group of notes in music: *She played a few **bars of** the song on her guitar.*

USAGE
Bars, pubs, restaurants, cafes, cafeterias, and **canteens** are all places where people go to drink and eat. A **restaurant** is a place where you sit at a table and eat a meal that is brought to you. **Bars** and **pubs** are places where people go to drink beer or wine, but sometimes they have food too. A **cafe** is a place where you go to drink tea or coffee and have a small meal, a sandwich etc. A **cafeteria** is a place in a school or company where people can go to eat lunch during the day. In British English, this is also called a **canteen**. When you eat in a **cafeteria** or **canteen**, you collect your food from where it is served and take it back to a table to eat it.

bar² *verb* **barred, barring** to officially stop someone from doing something: *He was barred from playing football for six months.*

bar·bar·ic /bɑː'bærɪk $ bɑr'bærɪk/ *adjective* violent and cruel: *This was a barbaric crime.*

bar·be·cue /'bɑː- bɪkjuː $ 'bɑrbɪ- ˌkjuː/ *noun* **1** an occasion when you cook and eat hot food outdoors, on a fire or on a special piece of equipment: *We had a barbecue on the beach.* **2** a piece of equipment that you use for cooking food outdoors: *Put some more sausages on the barbecue.*
–**barbecue** *verb*: *Dad barbecued all the food.*

barbecue

barbed wire /ˌ. './ *noun [no plural]* wire with short sharp points on it, to stop people from getting into a place: *a fence with barbed wire on top*

bar·ber /'bɑːbə $ 'bɑrbɚ/ noun a man whose job is to cut men's hair

bar code /'. ./ noun a row of black lines printed on products sold in a shop, that a computer reads when you buy the product

bare /beə $ ber/ adjective **1** not covered by clothes: It's too cold to go out with bare legs. **2** empty: The classroom looked very bare without any desks.

bare·foot /ˌbeə'fʊt $ 'berfʊt/ adjective, adverb not wearing any shoes or socks: They walked barefoot on the grass.

bare·ly /'beəli $ 'berli/ adverb almost not: I could barely understand her.

bar·gain¹ /'bɑːgən $ 'bɑrgən/ noun something you buy for a price that is cheaper than normal: These shorts were a bargain.

bargain² verb to discuss with someone how much you are willing to pay for something, or how much money you want to be paid for something, until you both agree about it ⇨ same meaning HAGGLE: In Egypt they expect you to bargain over the price you pay.

barge¹ /bɑːdʒ $ bɑrdʒ/ noun a long narrow boat with a flat bottom

barge² verb informal to walk somewhere quickly, pushing past people or things: He barged past me into the room.

bark¹ /bɑːk $ bɑrk/ verb if a dog barks, it makes several short loud sounds: I knocked on the door and a dog barked inside.

bark² noun **1** the sound that a dog makes **2** [no plural] the material that covers the surface of a tree

bar·ley /'bɑːli $ 'bɑrli/ noun [no plural] a grain used to make food and alcoholic drinks

bar·maid /'bɑːmeɪd $ 'bɑrmeɪd/ noun BrE a woman whose job is to serve drinks in a bar; BARTENDER AmE

bar·man /'bɑːmən/ noun BrE, plural barmen /-mən/ a man whose job is to serve drinks in a bar; BARTENDER AmE

barn /bɑːn $ bɑrn/ noun a building on a farm for keeping crops or animals in

bar·racks /'bærəks/ plural noun a group of buildings where soldiers live

bar·rage /'bærɑːʒ $ bə'rɑʒ/ noun when there are a lot of complaints, questions, sounds etc that happen very quickly after each other: We faced a barrage of criticism after announcing the winner.

bar·rel /'bærəl/ noun a large container for liquids such as beer: I've ordered ten barrels of beer. ⇨ see picture at CONTAINER

bar·ren /'bærən/ adjective if land is barren, plants cannot grow on it: a barren desert

bar·ri·cade /'bærəkeɪd/ noun an object that is put across a road or a door to stop people from going through: They put a barricade across the front door.

–barricade verb: The kids had barricaded themselves into their bedroom.

bar·ri·er /'bæriə $ 'bæriɚ/ noun a fence that stops people from entering an area: The police put up barriers to hold back the crowds.

bar·tend·er /'bɑːˌtendə $ 'bɑrˌtendɚ/ noun AmE someone whose job is to serve drinks in a bar; BARMAN, BARMAID BrE

bar·ter /'bɑːtə $ 'bɑrtɚ/ verb to pay for goods or services by giving other goods or services, instead of using money: They bartered food for coal.

base¹ /beɪs/ verb

GRAMMAR
based in/at a place
to live somewhere most of the time, or use it as your main place of business: The actress was born in Wales but **is based in** Los Angeles now. | The New York City ballet **is based at** the Lincoln Center. | Where **are** you **based**?

PHRASAL VERB
base on
base something on something to develop an idea, story etc from particular information or facts: The film **is based on** events in the director's life.

base² noun

GRAMMAR
the base of something
a base for (doing) something
1 the lowest part of something: They planted flowers around **the base of** the tree. | We had to repair the base of the boat.
2 a place where people in the army, navy etc live and work: There is a US **military base** near here.

3 a place that you stay in because it is close to other places that you want to go to: *We used the campsite as a base for exploring the mountains.*
4 one of the four places that a player must run to in order to get a point in the game of BASEBALL

base·ball /'beɪsbɔːl/ *noun* **1** *[no plural]* a game in which two teams try to get points by hitting a ball and running around four bases: *Who's your favourite baseball player?* ➪ *see picture on page 351* **2** the ball used in this game

base·ment /'beɪsmənt/ *noun* the rooms in a building that are below the level of the ground: *We keep our wine in the basement.* ➪ *see picture on page 343*

bases the plural of BASIS

bash /bæʃ/ *verb* to hit something hard: *I bashed my leg on the table.*

bash·ful /'bæʃfəl/ *adjective* embarrassed and shy: *Why are you looking so bashful?*

ba·sic /'beɪsɪk/ *adjective*
1 you use **basic** to describe things that are the simplest and most important part of something: *I know some basic vocabulary in Greek.* | *His basic problem is that he's lazy.*
2 if something is basic, it has only the things you need and nothing more: *The science equipment in the school is very basic.*

ba·sic·ally /'beɪsɪkli/ *adverb*
1 *spoken* you use **basically** to explain a situation or describe something simply: *Basically, the team didn't play well enough.*
2 in the most important ways: *She gave basically the right answer.*

ba·sics /'beɪsɪks/ *plural noun* the most important skills or facts of something: *I don't even know the basics of first aid.*

ba·sin /'beɪsən/ *noun BrE* the round container in a bathroom for washing your hands and face; WASHBASIN

ba·sis /'beɪsəs/ *noun, plural bases* /-siːz/
1 on the basis of something for a particular reason or because of a particular piece of information: *On the basis of her interview she got a place at college.* | *The doctor decided to admit Jean to hospital on the basis of her symptoms.*
2 on a weekly basis, on a regular basis etc: *We meet regularly, on a monthly basis* (=we meet every month). | *He runs several miles on a daily basis* (=every day). | *I go swimming on a regular basis* (=regularly).
3 the basis for something the information or ideas that you use to develop an idea or plan: *The work he did at university formed the basis for his first book.*

bask /bɑːsk $bæsk/ *verb* to enjoy lying somewhere warm: *The cat was basking in the sun.*

bas·ket /'bɑːskɪt $'bæskɪt/ *noun* a container made from thin pieces of wood, plastic, or wire: *She brought me a basket of fruit.*

bas·ket·ball /'bɑːskɪtbɔːl $'bæskɪt,bɔːl/ *noun* **1** a game in which two teams try to win points by throwing a ball through a net: *I'm not very good at basketball.* ➪ *see picture on page 351* **2** the ball used in this game

bass¹ /beɪs/ *adjective* a bass instrument plays low musical notes: *He plays the bass guitar.*

bass² /beɪs/ *noun* **1** a singer or instrument that sings or plays notes that are the lowest in the range **2** a DOUBLE BASS

bas·soon /bə'suːn/ *noun* a long wooden musical instrument that makes a low sound

bat¹ /bæt/ *noun* **1** a piece of wood that you use to hit the ball in some games: *a baseball bat* **2** a small animal like a mouse with wings, that flies around at night

bat² *verb* **batted, batting** to hit the ball with a bat in a game: *It's your turn to bat.*

batch /bætʃ/ *noun, plural batches* a group of things that arrive together: *I've just received my first batch of replies.*

bath¹ /bɑːθ $bæθ/ *noun*
BrE a long container that you sit in to wash yourself; BATHTUB *AmE: Sally's in the bath.*

B

▼ **PHRASE**
have a bath *BrE*, take a bath *AmE*
to wash yourself in a bath: *I think I'll
have a nice hot bath.*

bath² *verb BrE* to wash someone in a
bath: *I'll help you bath the baby.*

bathe /beɪð/ *verb* **1** to wash a wound
or a part of your body: *Bathe the cut with
warm water.* **2** *AmE* to wash yourself in
a bath: *I usually bathe in the morning.*

bathing suit /'beɪðɪŋ ˌsuːt/ *noun* a
SWIMSUIT

bath·robe /'bɑːθrəʊb/ $ 'bæθroʊb/
noun a piece of clothing like a coat that
you wear after you have a bath

bath·room /'bɑːθruːm/ $ 'bæθrum/
noun **1** the room in a house where
you wash yourself **2** go to the bathroom *AmE* to use the toilet

bath·tub /'bɑːθtʌb/ $ 'bæθtʌb/ an
American word for a BATH¹

bat·tal·ion /bə'tæljən/ *noun* a large
group of soldiers that consists of several
smaller groups

bat·ter¹ /'bætə $ 'bætər/ *noun* **1** a
mixture of flour, milk, and eggs: *They
served fish in batter.* **2** the person who
is trying to hit the ball in BASEBALL

batter² *verb* to hit something many
times: *The waves battered against the
rocks.*

bat·tered /'bætəd $ 'bætərd/ *adjective*
old and damaged: *a battered old book*

bat·ter·y /'bætəri/ *noun, plural*
batteries
an object that provides the electrical
power for a machine, toy, car etc:
*The radio cassette needs new bat-
teries.* | *The car's got a **flat battery**
(=one that doesn't work anymore).*

bat·tle¹ /'bætl/ *noun* **1** a fight between two armies: *Many soldiers were
killed in the battle.* **2** a situation in
which people try to do something difficult: *Scientists have not yet won the
battle against AIDS.*

battle² *verb* to try very hard to do or get
something: *We had to battle to get new
computers for the school.*

bat·tle·field /'bætlfiːld/ also **battle-
ground** /'bætlɡraʊnd/ *noun* a place
where a battle has been fought

bat·tle·ship /'bætlˌʃɪp/ *noun* a very
large ship used in wars

bawl /bɔːl/ *verb informal* to shout or cry
loudly: *Stop that child bawling!*

bay /beɪ/ *noun* a part of the coast where
the land curves inwards: *This is a beautiful sandy bay.*

ba·zaar /bə'zɑː $ bə'zɑr/ *noun* a sale to
collect money for an organization: *I
bought this book at a school bazaar.*

BC /ˌbiː 'siː/ *adverb* an abbreviation for
Before Christ; used in dates to mean be-
fore the birth of Christ: *Alexander the
Great died in 323 BC.*

be ⇨ *see box on next page*

beach /biːtʃ/ *noun, plural* **beaches** an
area of sand next to the sea: *Shall we
go to the beach?* ⇨ *see picture on page
348*

bea·con /'biːkən/ *noun* a light that
flashes to guide boats or planes

bead /biːd/ *noun* a small round ball of
plastic or glass used in jewellery: *She
wore a string of beads around her
neck.*

bead·y /'biːdi/ *adjective* **beadier,
beadiest** beady eyes are small and dark:
an old woman with beady eyes

beak /biːk/ *noun* the hard pointed
mouth of a bird

beam¹ /biːm/ *noun* **1** a line of light
shining from something: *A beam of light
shone through the curtains.* **2** a long
heavy piece of wood or metal that is
used to support something in a building: *I banged my head on a wooden
beam.*

beam² *verb* to smile very happily: *Gary
beamed at us as he went to collect his
prize.*

bean /biːn/ *noun* **1** the seed of a plant
that you can cook and eat, or the seed
and the case together: *green beans*
2 the seed of a plant that is used to
make a drink: *coffee beans* ⇨ *see picture
on page 345*

bear¹ /beə $ ber/ *verb* bore /bɔː
$ bɔr/ borne /bɔːn $ bɔrn/

GRAMMAR
bear to do something
bear doing something
1 to be able to accept or deal with
something unpleasant: *The noise
was more than I could bear.* | *She
couldn't bear to leave her
husband.* | *Switch the TV off now — I*

➤ VERB FORMS

PRESENT TENSE

Singular	Plural
I **am** (I'**m**)	we **are** (we'**re**)
you **are** (you'**re**)	you **are** (you'**re**)
he, she, it **is**	they **are** (they'**re**)
(he'**s**, she'**s**, it'**s**)	

PAST TENSE

Singular	Plural
I **was**	we **were**
you **were**	you **were**
he, she, it **was**	they **were**

present participle ➤ **being**
past participle ➤ **been**
negative short forms ➤ **aren't, isn't, wasn't, weren't**

➤ BE

be

❶ used to describe or give information about people or things
*Donald **was** nine years old when his mother died.* | *I'**m** really tired.* | *The movie **was** really good.* | *When **is** Laura's birthday party?* | *"What do your parents do?" "They'**re** both dentists."* | *Robert De Niro **wasn't** in that film.*

❷ used with other verbs to show that something is or was happening at a particular time
*It **is** raining.* | ***Are** you **feeling** better?* | *What **are** you **doing**?* | *His brother **is** still **living** in Boston.* | *We **were** both **working** at the bookstore.* | *Why **aren't** you **eating** anything?*

❸ used with other verbs to show that something happens or happened to a person or thing
*The room **is painted** yellow.* | *What **was** that film **called**?* | *These houses **were built** 50 years ago.* | *Our dog **was hit** by a car.* | *The chocolates **are wrapped** in coloured paper.*

❹ there is, there are, there were etc
***There was** a story about it in the newspaper.* | ***Is there** any coffee left?* | ***There were** a lot of little girls standing together.* | ***There isn't** any milk in the fridge.* | *You can't leave at nine – **there aren't** any trains.*

B

don't know how you **can bear** watching such rubbish.
2 to turn or go in a particular direction: *Go straight on until you reach a church, then* **bear right**.
3 *formal* to carry or bring something: *George came in bearing a message.*

PHRASES
bear in mind that, bear something in mind to not forget an important fact when you decide something: **Bear in mind that** *the journey may take longer in bad weather.* | *I hope you'll* **bear** *me* **in mind** *if any jobs do come up.*
can't bear (doing) something to hate something very much: *I* **can't bear** *the food we get at school.* | *Mum* **can't bear** *travelling by plane.*
bear the blame, bear the responsibility to accept that you are responsible for something bad that has happened: *The school must* **bear some responsibility for** *the accident.*
bear a grudge to feel angry with someone for a long time because of something they have done: *Mustaq was the sort of person who* **bore a grudge** *for months after an argument.*

PHRASAL VERB
bear out
bear something out to show that something is true: *There is no evidence to* **bear out** *this idea.*

bear² *noun* a large strong animal with thick fur: *There are wild bears around here.* ⇨ *see picture on page 339*
bear·a·ble /ˈbeərəbəl $ ˈberəbəl/ *adjective* if a situation is bearable, it is difficult but you are able to accept it or deal with it: *I don't enjoy the work but it is bearable.*
beard /bɪəd $ bɪrd/ *noun* the hair that grows on a man's chin: *He has shaved his beard off.* ⇨ *see picture on page 353*
bear·ing /ˈbeərɪŋ $ ˈberɪŋ/ *noun*
1 **have a bearing on something** to affect something: *Recent events have had a bearing on his decision.* 2 **lose your bearings** to become lost: *The boat lost its bearings in the fog.*
beast /biːst/ *noun written* a wild or dangerous animal

beat¹ /biːt/ *verb* beat, beaten /ˈbiːtn/

GRAMMAR
beat someone at something
1 to defeat someone in a game or competition: *I* **beat** *Dad* **at** *tennis for the first time today.*
2 to hit someone or something many times with your hand, a stick etc: *They* **beat** *him and robbed him.* | *One man marched in front* **beating** *a drum.*
3 to mix food together quickly using a fork, spoon etc: **Beat** *the eggs and pour them into a pan.*
4 to make a regular sound or movement: *I can hear your* **heart beating.** | *The rain* **beat** *all night on the roofs of the little houses.*

PHRASAL VERB
beat up
beat someone up to hit someone many times so that they are badly hurt: *A gang of men* **beat** *him* **up** *for no reason.*

beat² *noun* a regular movement or sound: *the slow beat of a drum*
beat·en /ˈbiːtn/ *adjective* **off the beaten track** far away from places that people usually visit: *We want to stay somewhere off the beaten track.*

beau·ti·ful /ˈbjuːtəfəl/ *adjective*
1 a woman, girl, or child who is beautiful is very attractive: *Some of the models were incredibly beautiful.*
2 something that is beautiful is very attractive or pleasant: *That's a beautiful picture.* | *The music was really beautiful.* ⇨ *see usage note at* PRETTY²
– **beautifully** *adverb*: *She sings beautifully.*

beau·ty /ˈbjuːti/ *noun [no plural]* the quality of being beautiful: *He was amazed by her beauty.* | *the beauty of the morning sunrise*
became the past tense of BECOME
be·cause /bɪˈkɒz, bɪkəz $ bɪˈkɔz, bɪkəz/ giving the reason for something: *I like history because it's interesting.* | *She left the party early because she felt ill.* | *He did badly in his exams* **because of** *problems at home.*

beck·on /'bekən/ *verb formal* to move your hand or arm to show that you want someone to come to you: *He beckoned me over to him.*

be·come /bɪ'kʌm/ *verb* **became** /bɪ'keɪm/ **become**

1 *formal* to start to be or do something ⇨ *same meaning* GET *spoken*: *The weather had become colder.* | *It is becoming difficult to find a parking space.* | *Dad started to become angry.*

2 if someone becomes a doctor, teacher etc, they start to be a doctor, teacher etc: *At the age of only 35 he became a judge.*

bed /bed/ *noun* **1** a piece of furniture that you sleep on at night: *It's time to go to bed.* | *I bought a new bed.* **2** the ground at the bottom of the sea or a river: *The boat's now lying on the sea bed.*

bed·clothes /'bedkləʊðz $ 'bedkloʊðz/ *plural noun* the sheets and other covers that are on a bed

bed·rid·den /'bed,rɪdn/ *adjective* unable to get out of bed because you are old or ill: *My grandmother's bedridden and can't go out.*

bed·room /'bedruːm/ *noun* a room that you sleep in at night: *a house with four bedrooms*

bed·side /'bedsaɪd/ *noun* the area next to a bed: *His mother stayed at his bedside all night.*

bed·sit /,bed'sɪt/ also **bedsitter** /,bed'sɪtə $,bed'sɪtɚ/ *noun BrE* a room that you rent to live and sleep in: *I had a bedsit in London.*

bed·spread /'bedspred/ *noun* a large cloth cover that goes on top of a bed

bed·time /'bedtaɪm/ *noun* the time when you usually go to bed: *It's past my bedtime.*

bee /biː/ *noun* a black and yellow flying insect that makes HONEY

bee

beef /biːf/ *noun [no plural]* meat from a cow

beef·bur·ger /'biːf bɜːgə $ 'bif,bɚgɚ/ *noun BrE* a BURGER

bee·hive /'biːhaɪv/ *noun* a place where you keep BEES to make HONEY

been /biːn, bɪn $ bɪn/ the past participle of BE

beep /biːp/ *verb* to make a short high noise: *The computer beeps when you make a mistake.*
–beep *noun*: *I heard the beep of a car horn.*

beep·er /'biːpə $ 'bipɚ/ *noun* a PAGER

beer /bɪə $ bɪr/ *noun [no plural]* a drink that contains alcohol, made from grain: *a bottle of beer*

bee·tle /'biːtl/ *noun* an insect with a hard round black back ⇨ *see picture at* INSECT

beet·root /'biːtruːt/ *BrE*, **beet** /biːt/ *AmE noun* a dark red root of a plant that you can cook and eat ⇨ *see picture on page 345*

be·fore¹ /bɪ'fɔː $ bɪ'fɔr/ *preposition*

1 earlier than: *I got up before 7 o'clock.* | *We arrived before the others.*

2 when something has not yet happened or started: *I felt very tired before my holiday.* | *We met in a pub before the show.*

before² *adverb*

showing that something has already happened once, at an earlier time: *I had seen the film before.* | *I think I've met you before.*

PHRASES

the day before, the year before etc the previous day, year etc: *I had mailed the letter the day before.* | *His mother had died the year before.*

the same as before if something is the same as before, it has not changed: *The method used was the same as before.*

before³

if you do something before doing something else, you do the first thing at an earlier time than the second thing: *You should wash the walls before you paint them.* | *I always brush my teeth before I go to bed.*

be·fore·hand /bɪ'fɔːhænd $ bɪ'fɔr,hænd/ *adverb formal* before a particular time or event: *You should have told me about this beforehand.*

beg /beg/ *verb*   **beg**
begged, begging
1 to ask for something in a way that shows you want or need it very much: *She begged me to stay.* **2** to ask someone for food or money because you are very poor: *Children were begging in the street.*

began the past tense of BEGIN

beg·gar /ˈbegə $ ˈbegɚ/ *noun* someone who lives by asking people for food and money

be·gin /bɪˈgɪn/ *verb* **began** /bɪˈgæn/ **begun** /bɪˈgʌn/ **beginning**

> **GRAMMAR**
> **begin to do something**
> **begin doing something**
> **begin with something**
> **begin by doing something**

to start doing something, or to start to happen ⇨ *same meaning* START: *She began to cry.* | *The exam will begin at 9:00.* | *When did you begin having these headaches?* | *The band began with one of their most famous hits.* | *Let's begin by looking at page 25.*

> **PHRASE**
> **to begin with**   **1)** used to introduce the first or most important point: *They made a lot of mistakes. To begin with, they spelt my name wrong.* **2)** at the start of something: *To begin with, we all introduced ourselves.*

be·gin·ner /bɪˈgɪnə $ bɪˈgɪnɚ/ *noun* someone who has just started to do or learn something: *This French class is for complete beginners.*

be·gin·ning /bɪˈgɪnɪŋ/ *noun*

> **GRAMMAR**
> **the beginning of something**
> the start or first part of something: *We moved house at the beginning of the year.* | *We were late and we missed the beginning of the film.*

be·grudge /bɪˈgrʌdʒ/ *verb* if you begrudge someone something, you do not want them to have it, usually because it is something you want: *I don't begrudge him his money.*

begun the past participle of BEGIN

be·half /bɪˈhɑːf $ bɪˈhæf/ *noun* **on behalf of someone, on someone's behalf** instead of someone, or in order to help someone: *Will you go to the meeting on my behalf?*

be·have /bɪˈheɪv/ *verb*
1 to do or say things in a particular way: *Some boys behaved badly at the party.*
2 to act politely and not cause trouble: *Children, please behave.* | *I hope you behave yourself while your mother is away.*

be·hav·iour BrE, **behavior** AmE /bɪˈheɪvjə $ bɪˈheɪvjɚ/ *noun* [no plural] your behaviour is the way that you act or do things: *The children's behaviour is always worse with a new teacher.*

be·hind¹ /bɪˈhaɪnd/ *preposition, adverb*
1 at or near the back of something: *The car behind us was driving too close.* | *His diary had fallen behind the sofa.* | *There are some empty seats in the row behind.* ⇨ *see picture on page 354*
2 less successful than someone in a competition: *Our team is still behind theirs in the championship.*
3 responsible for something that has happened: *Who is behind the bombing?*

behind² *adjective*
behind with if you are behind with your work, you have not done as much work as you should have done: *I can't come out – I'm a bit behind with my homework this week.*

beige /beɪʒ/ *adjective, noun* a pale brown colour: *a beige carpet*

be·ing /ˈbiːɪŋ/ *noun* **1** a creature or person: *The film is about beings from outer space.* **2** **come into being** to begin to exist: *When did the Soviet Union come into being?*

be·lat·ed /bɪ'leɪtɪd/ adjective a belated letter, action etc is sent or done late: *Myra sent me a belated birthday card.*

belch /beltʃ/ BURP

be·lief /bə'liːf/ noun

> **GRAMMAR**
> **belief that**
> **a belief in something/someone**

1 [no plural] the feeling that something is true or right: *There is a general belief that parents know what is best for their children.* | *We share a belief in the importance of education.*
2 [no plural] a feeling of respect or trust for someone or something, because you think that they are good: *She never lost her belief in him.*
3 an idea that you think is true: *What are your religious beliefs?*

be·liev·a·ble /bə'liːvəbəl/ adjective easy to believe: *His story is very believable.*

be·lieve /bə'liːv/ verb

> **GRAMMAR**
> **believe (that)**
> **believe someone/something to be something**

1 to feel sure that something is true: *We all believed that Martyn was the killer.* | *I can't believe they're brothers.* | *His family believed him to be dead.*
2 if you believe someone, you are sure that they are telling the truth: *I told her what happened, but she didn't believe me.*
3 to think that something might be true, without being completely sure: *I believe that her name is Lucy Gray.*

> **PHRASAL VERB**
> **believe in**

believe in something/someone
1) to feel sure that something or someone exists: *Do you believe in love at first sight?* **2)** to trust or respect someone or something because you think that they are good: *We believe in you.* | *The revolutionaries believed in liberty, freedom and equality.*

bell /bel/ noun **1** a piece of electrical equipment that makes a noise as a signal or warning: *Just then, I heard the* door bell. | *At last the bell rang and the lesson was over.* **2** a metal object that makes a musical sound when you move it: *He rang a bell to attract our attention.* | church bells

bel·low /'beləʊ $ 'beloʊ/ verb to shout something in a very loud low voice: *"Come here," he bellowed.*

bell pep·per /'. ,../ the American word for a PEPPER

bel·ly /'beli/ noun informal, plural bellies your stomach: *I've got a pain in my belly.*

belly but·ton /'.. ,../ noun informal NAVEL

be·long /bɪ'lɒŋ $ bɪ'lɔːŋ/ verb

> **GRAMMAR**
> **belong in a place**

if something belongs somewhere, it is in the correct place or situation: *This kind of picture does not belong in a teenage magazine.* | *Where does this book belong?*

> **PHRASAL VERB**
> **belong to**

1 belong to something if you belong to a group, you are a member of it: *I don't belong to any political parties.*
2 belong to someone if something belongs to you, you own it: *That bike belongs to my sister.*

be·long·ings /bɪ'lɒŋɪŋz $ bɪ'lɔːŋɪŋz/ plural noun the things that you own or take with you somewhere: *She packed her belongings into a suitcase.*

be·lov·ed /bɪ'lʌvɪd/ adjective written loved very much: *She was the beloved wife of Tom Smith.*

be·low /bɪ'ləʊ $ bɪ'loʊ/ adverb, preposition

1 lower than something, or under it: *When I looked out of the plane window, I could see the fields below us.* | *They skied down the mountain to the valley below.*
2 less than a particular amount: *The temperature dropped to below zero at night.*

belt /belt/ noun a band of leather or cloth that you wear around your waist, for example to stop your trousers or skirt from falling down: *I tightened my belt.*
⇨ see picture on page 352

be·mused /bɪˈmjuːzd/ *adjective written* slightly confused: *She looked bemused by what he was saying.*

bench /bentʃ/ *noun, plural* **benches** a long wooden seat for two or more people: *a garden bench*

bend¹ /bend/ *verb, past tense and past participle* **bent** /bent/

GRAMMAR
bend down/over

1 to move the top part of your body and your head down: *His back hurts when he bends.* | *She **bent down** to pat the dog.* | *In this exercise you have to **bend over** and touch your toes.* ⇨ *see picture on page 340*

2 to move a part of your body so that it is no longer straight: *This jacket's so tight that I can't bend my arms.*

3 if something bends, or if you bend it, it does not have its normal shape any more: *You've bent the wheel.* | *Plastic bends easily.*

bend

bend² *noun* a curve in a road or river: *There was a sharp bend in the road.*

be·neath /bɪˈniːθ/ *adverb, preposition written*
under or below something: *These animals live in tunnels beneath the ground.* | *We stood on the hill and looked down at the fields beneath.*

ben·e·fi·cial /ˌbenəˈfɪʃəl/ *adjective formal* helpful or useful: *It might be beneficial to talk to someone about your problems.*

ben·e·fit¹ /ˈbenəfɪt/ *noun*

1 an advantage that you get from something: *Exercising regularly gives you great benefits.*

2 money that the government gives you when you are ill or when you do not have a job: *Her boyfriend is unemployed and **on benefit** (=receiving this money).*

PHRASES
for someone's benefit, for the benefit of someone: *For the benefit of people who arrived late* (=in order to help them), *I'll repeat what I said.*

give someone the benefit of the doubt to believe what someone says even though they might be wrong or not telling the truth: *It all seems a bit suspicious to me John, but I'll **give** you **the benefit of the doubt** this time.*

benefit² *verb* **benefited, benefiting** also **benefitted, benefitting** if something benefits someone, it helps them: *Will the changes in the law benefit us?*

bent¹ the past tense and past participle of BEND¹

bent² /bent/ *adjective* curved and no longer flat or straight: *I can't sew with this needle – it's bent.*

be·reaved /bɪˈriːvd/ *adjective formal* if you are bereaved, someone that you love has died: *a support group for bereaved parents*

be·reave·ment /bɪˈriːvmənt/ *noun* the situation when someone you love has died: *He is away from work because of a family bereavement.*

be·ret /ˈbereɪ $ bəˈreɪ/ *noun* a soft round flat hat

ber·ry /ˈberi/ *noun, plural* **berries** a small soft fruit with very small seeds

ber·serk /bɜːˈsɜːk $ bɚˈsɚk/ *adjective* **go berserk** *informal* to become very angry and violent in a crazy way: *He went berserk and started hitting Sue.*

be·set /bɪˈset/ *verb formal* **beset, besetting** if someone is beset by problems, they have a lot of problems: *The company has been beset by financial difficulties.*

be·side /bɪˈsaɪd/ *preposition*
next to or very close to someone or something: *His dog walked beside him.* | *There is a picnic area beside the river.* ⇨ *see picture on page 354*

be·sides /bɪˈsaɪdz/ *adverb, preposition* in addition to someone or something:

Besides painting, she enjoys reading and sewing. | Who will be there besides you and me?

be·siege /bɪˈsiːdʒ/ *verb* if you are besieged by people or things, you have to deal with a lot of them: *They were besieged by journalists as they left the building.*

best¹ /best/ *adjective*

1 better than anyone or anything else: *This is the best Chinese restaurant in town.* | *Where's the best place to leave my bike?*

2 **your best friend, her best friend etc** the friend someone knows and likes the most: *Susan's my best friend.*

best² *adverb*

1 most: *Which bit of the film did you like best?* | *His brother knew him best.*

2 in a way that is better than any other: *Which of the children draws best?* | *Michael did best in the spelling test* (=was most successful).

best³ *noun* 1 **the best** the person or thing that is better than any others: *Which song is the best?* 2 **do your best, try your best** to try very hard to succeed: *She tried her best but she still didn't pass the exam.*

best man /ˌ. ˈ./ *noun* a friend of a man who is getting married, who helps him to get ready and stands next to him during the wedding

best·sel·ler /ˌbestˈselə $ ˌbestˈselɚ/ *noun* a book that a lot of people have bought

bet¹ /bet/ *verb, past tense and past participle* **bet, betting**

1 to try to win money by saying what the result of a game or competition will be: *I bet him five pounds that he wouldn't win, but I lost and had to give him the money.* | *My Dad used to bet on the horses* (=on the result of horse races).

I bet *spoken* used to say that you are sure something is true or happened: *I wonder what time it is? I bet it's*

past midnight. | *I bet she was surprised when she saw you at the party!*
You bet! *spoken* used to say 'yes' in a very definite way: *"Would you like to come?" "You bet!"*

bet² *noun*

if you have a bet on something, you try to win money by saying what the result of a game or competition will be. You can also place or lay a bet: *I might have a bet on the match.* | *Tom won his bet.*

a good bet something that is likely to be useful or successful: *This shop is always a good bet for presents.*

be·tray /bɪˈtreɪ/ *verb* to behave dishonestly towards someone who loves you or trusts you: *She felt her husband had betrayed her by lying to her.*

be·tray·al /bɪˈtreɪəl/ *noun* when someone betrays you: *The film is a story of betrayal and murder.*

better¹ /ˈbetə $ ˈbetɚ/ *adjective*

1 more useful, interesting, skilful etc than something or someone else: *We need a better computer.* | *My sister's got much better at maths since she moved to a new school.* | *Sitting on the beach is definitely better than working!*

2 less ill than you were, or no longer ill: *Are you feeling a bit better today?* | *I had a cold, but I'm better now.*

get better to improve: *His English is getting better.*
the sooner the better, the bigger the better: *He should stop smoking – the sooner the better* (=as soon as possible). | *Fetch a large bowl, the bigger the better* (=as big as possible).

better² *adverb*

1 more: *I think this jacket suits me better.* | *I knew her better than anyone else did.*

2 in a more skilful way: *He speaks English better than I do.*

B

PHRASE

you'd better, we'd better etc *spoken* used to tell someone what you think they should do: *You'd better not annoy him.* | *We'd better start packing up now.*

better³ *noun* **get the better of someone** if a feeling gets the better of you, you do not control it when you should: *His anger got the better of him and he lashed out at me.*

better off /ˌ.. '. / *adjective* **1 be better off doing something** *informal* if you say that someone would be better off doing something, you are advising them to do it: *You'd be better off sitting the exam next year, when you're ready for it.* **2** if you are better off, you have more money now than you did in the past: *We plan to reduce taxes and make all families better off.*

be·tween /bɪ'twiːn/ *preposition, adverb*

1 also **in between** with one thing or person on each side: *He sat between the two women on the sofa.* ⇨ see picture on page 354
2 showing that a place is in the middle, with other places at a distance from it: *Oxford is between London and Birmingham.*
3 also **in between** after one event or time and before another: *I didn't see my parents at all between Christmas and Easter.* | *He had a year off between leaving school and going to university.* | *You shouldn't eat in between meals.* | *I have a lesson at nine o'clock and another at three o'clock, but nothing in between.*
4 also **in between** showing a range of amounts, by giving the largest and smallest: *My journey to school takes between 30 and 40 minutes.* | *children aged between 7 and 11*
5 showing who is involved in a relationship, agreement, fight etc: *There has always been a friendly relationship between these two countries.* | *an agreement between the company and the trade unions* | *the war between England and France*
6 giving something to each person in a group: *They shared the prize money between the three winners.*

PHRASE

have something between you if people have an amount of money between them, that is the total amount they have: *We only had ten dollars between us.*

USAGE between, among
Use **between** and **among** to talk about the position of someone or something. Use **between** when there is one other person or thing on each side of someone or something: *I sat between Alex and Sarah.* Use **among** when there are two or more people or things on each side of someone or something: *It would be easy to get lost among all these trees.*

bev·er·age /'bevərɪdʒ/ *noun formal written* a drink: *We do not sell alcoholic beverages.*

be·ware /bɪ'weə $bɪ'wer/ *verb* used to warn someone to be careful: *Beware of the dog!* | *There are some very difficult questions, so beware.*

be·wil·dered /bɪ'wɪldəd $bɪ'wɪldɚd/ *adjective* confused and not sure what to do or think: *The children looked bewildered and scared.*

be·yond /bɪ'jɒnd $bɪ'jɑnd/ *preposition*

1 if something is beyond a place, it is on the side of it that is farthest away from you: *Beyond the stream was a small wood.*
2 past a particular time or date: *The project will continue beyond 2003.*
3 if something is beyond repair, beyond control etc, you cannot repair it, control it etc: *The television is beyond repair.* | *The evidence proves beyond doubt* (=there is no doubt at all) *that she could not have committed the crime.*

PHRASE

it's beyond me *informal spoken*: *It's beyond me* (=I can't understand) *why she's so popular.*

bi·as /'baɪəs/ *noun* **have a bias against someone** to have an unfair opinion about someone that affects the way you treat them: *Some employers have a bias against women.*

bi·ased /'baɪəst/ *adjective* showing that your personal opinions have unfairly affected your judgement ⇨ *opposite*

IMPARTIAL: *Some newspapers are biased in favour of the government.*

bib /bɪb/ *noun* a piece of cloth or plastic that you tie under a baby's chin to protect its clothes while it is eating

bi·ble /'baɪbəl/ *noun* the holy book of the Christian religion: *Do you ever read the bible?*

bib·li·og·ra·phy /ˌbɪbli'ɒgrəfi $ ˌbɪb-li'ɑgrəfi/ *noun, plural* **bibliographies** a list of books on a particular subject

bick·er /'bɪkə $ 'bɪkɚ/ *verb* to argue about something that is not very important: *The kids were bickering about who was the fastest runner.*

bi·cy·cle /'baɪsɪkəl/ *noun* a vehicle with two wheels that you ride by pushing the PEDALS with your feet ⇨ *same meaning* BIKE: *Did you come by bicycle?* ⇨ *see picture on page 349*

bid /bɪd/ *verb, past tense and past participle* **bid**, **bidding** to offer to pay a particular price for one particular thing that several people want to buy: *Mr Jones bid $50,000 for the painting.*
−**bid** *noun*: *We received three bids on the house.*

big /bɪg/ *adjective* **bigger, biggest**
1 large ⇨ *opposite* SMALL (1): *a big black car* | *the biggest city in the world*
2 important or serious ⇨ *opposite* SMALL (2): *We have some pretty big problems.* | *It was the biggest mistake of my life.*
3 *informal* very successful: *His last film was a big hit.* | *That band is not as big as it used to be.*

big·head·ed /ˌbɪg'hedɪd/ *adjective* someone who is bigheaded thinks that they are better than other people

big·ot /'bɪgət/ *noun* a person who has strong and unreasonable opinions about people who are different from them

big·ot·ed /'bɪgətɪd/ *adjective* someone who is bigoted has strong and unreasonable opinions about people who belong to a different race, religion, or political group: *Some people are very bigoted about the Irish.* | *a bigoted old man*

bike /baɪk/ *noun* a bicycle or a MOTOR-CYCLE: *He fell off his bike.* | *I came here by bike.*

bik·er /'baɪkə $ 'baɪkɚ/ *noun informal* someone who rides a MOTORCYCLE, especially as part of a group: *This road is popular with bikers.*

bi·ki·ni /bɪ'kiːni/ *noun* a piece of clothing in two parts that women wear on the beach when it is hot

bi·lin·gual /baɪ'lɪŋgwəl/ *adjective*
1 able to speak two languages very well: *Philippe and Jane's children are bilingual.* 2 spoken or written in two languages: *a bilingual dictionary*

bill¹ /bɪl/ *noun*
1 a list of things that you have bought or that someone has done for you, showing how much you have to pay for them: *Have you paid the electricity bill?* | *I'm expecting to get a big phone bill* (=a bill asking for a lot of money to pay for your phone calls).
2 the American word for NOTE: *a ten-dollar bill*
3 a plan for a new law: *The new education bill was passed* (=became law) *last week.*

bill·board /'bɪlbɔːd $ 'bɪlbɔrd/ *noun* a big sign next to a road, that is used to advertise something

bill·fold /'bɪlfəʊld $ 'bɪlˌfoʊld/ the American word for WALLET

bil·lion /'bɪljən/ *number plural* **billion** or **billions** 1,000,000,000: *The government spends billions of dollars on defence.*

bil·low /'bɪləʊ $ 'bɪloʊ/ *verb* if smoke billows, a lot of it rises into the air: *Smoke billowed out of the chimneys.*

bin /bɪn/ *noun*
1 a large container where you put small things that you no longer want: *She threw the letter in the bin.*
2 a container that you use to store things: *a flour bin* | *We put our baggage in the overhead bins.*

bind /baɪnd/ *verb, past tense and past participle* **bound** /baʊnd/ to tie something together firmly, with string or rope: *They bound his legs with a rope.*

binge /bɪndʒ/ *noun* an occasion when you eat or drink a lot in a very short time: *He goes on alcohol binges that last all weekend.*
−**binge** *verb*: *Sometimes I binge on chocolate and sweets.*

B

bi·noc·u·lars /bɪˈnɒkjələz $bɪˈnɑk-jələˑz/ *plural noun* an object like a large pair of glasses that you hold up and look through to see things that are far away: *a pair of binoculars* ➪ *see picture at* GLASSES

bi·o·de·grad·a·ble /ˌbaɪəʊdɪˈɡreɪdəbəl $ˌbaɪoʊdɪˈɡreɪdəbəl/ *adjective* able to be destroyed by natural processes, in a way that does not harm the environment: *Plastic is not biodegradable.*

bi·og·ra·pher /baɪˈɒɡrəfə $baɪˈɑɡrəfɚ/ *noun* a person who writes someone's biography

bi·og·ra·phy /baɪˈɒɡrəfi $baɪˈɑɡrəfi/ *noun, plural* **biographies** a book about a person's life: *He wrote a biography of Princess Diana.*

bi·o·lo·gi·cal /ˌbaɪəˈlɒdʒɪkəl $ˌbaɪə-ˈlɑdʒɪkəl/ *adjective* connected with biology: *The company does biological research.*

bi·ol·o·gist /baɪˈɒlədʒɪst $baɪˈɑlə-dʒɪst/ *noun* someone whose job involves studying biology

bi·ol·o·gy /baɪˈɒlədʒi $baɪˈɑlədʒi/ *noun [no plural]* the scientific study of living things: *Biology is my favourite subject.*

bird /bɜːd $bɚd/ *noun* an animal with wings and feathers that can usually fly. Female birds produce eggs

bird of prey /ˌ. . ˈ./ *noun, plural* **birds of prey** a bird that kills and eats other birds and small animals: *The eagle is a bird of prey.*

bi·ro /ˈbaɪərəʊ $ˈbaɪroʊ/ *noun BrE trademark* a type of pen

birth /bɜːθ $bɚθ/ *noun*

the time when a baby comes out of its mother's body: *She weighed 3 kg at birth* (=when she was born). | *the birth of her second child*

PHRASES
give birth if a woman gives birth, she produces a baby from her body: *Jenni gave birth on Tuesday.* | *She's just given birth to her fifth son.*
date of birth: *Write down your name, address, and date of birth* (=the date when you were born).

birth con·trol /ˈ. .ˌ./ *noun [no plural]* methods of stopping a woman becoming PREGNANT

birth·day /ˈbɜːθdeɪ $ˈbɚθdeɪ/ *noun*

the date in each year on which you were born: *It's my birthday next week.* | *I got ten birthday cards.* | *Happy Birthday!* (=said to someone on their birthday)

birth·mark /ˈbɜːθmɑːk $ˈbɚθmɑrk/ *noun* an unusual mark on someone's skin that is there when they are born

birth·place /ˈbɜːθpleɪs $ˈbɚθpleɪs/ *noun* the place where someone was born: *Stratford-upon-Avon is the birthplace of William Shakespeare.*

bis·cuit /ˈbɪskɪt/ *noun* **1** *BrE* a thin dry sweet cake; COOKIE *AmE*: *Who wants a chocolate biscuit?* **2** *AmE* a kind of bread that you bake in small round shapes

bi·sex·u·al /baɪˈsekʃuəl/ *noun* someone who is sexually attracted to men and women
– **bisexual** *adjective*

bish·op /ˈbɪʃəp/ *noun* a priest with a high rank who is in charge of the churches and priests in a large area: *The Bishop of Durham conducted the service.*

bi·son /ˈbaɪsən/ *noun* an animal that looks like a large cow with long hair on the front part of its body, and lives in the United States; BUFFALO

bit¹ /bɪt/ *noun*

GRAMMAR
a bit of something
1 a small piece or amount of something: *Can I have a bit of paper to write on?* | *I've got a bit of work to do.* | *All I want is a bit of fun.*
2 a part of something: *The best bit in the film was when they all fell in the swimming pool.*

PHRASES
a bit slightly: *I felt a bit embarrassed.* | *It tastes a bit like cabbage.* | *Turn the sound up a bit.* | *I hadn't seen Yolanda for 20 years – and she hadn't changed a bit* (=she hadn't changed, not even slightly).
a bit of a shock, a bit of a surprise *BrE spoken*: *The news came as a bit of a shock* (=a slight shock).
for a bit, after a bit *informal* following or taking a short amount of time: *After a bit, he got used to the idea.* |

*I waited **for a bit** and then tried phoning again.*
tear something to bits, smash something to bits, blow something to bits to destroy something completely: *The car **was blown to bits** in the explosion.*

bit² the past tense of BITE¹

bite¹ /baɪt/ bit/bɪt/ bitten/'bɪtn/ *verb*

GRAMMAR
bite into something

1 to cut or crush something with your teeth: *Sophie was bitten by a dog.* | *I can't stop **biting my fingernails**.* | *James **bit into** the apple.*
2 if an insect bites you, it pushes a sharp point into your skin and it hurts: *I think I've been bitten by ants.*

USAGE
Insects such as fleas and mosquitos **bite** you, but bees and wasps **sting** you.

bite² *noun*

GRAMMAR
a bite of something
a bite out of something

1 if you take a bite of something, you use your teeth to remove part of it: *Can I have **a bite of** your sandwich?* | *He **took a big bite** out of his apple.*
2 a wound made when an animal or insect bites you: *Have you got any cream for mosquito bites?*

bitten the past participle of BITE¹

bit·ter /'bɪtə $'bɪtɚ/ *adjective*
1 angry for a long time because you feel that something bad or unfair has happened to you: *She's very bitter about losing her job.* 2 having a strong taste, like coffee without sugar
– **bitterness** *noun* [no plural]

bit·ter·ly /'bɪtəli $'bɪtɚli/ *adverb*
1 in a way that shows that you are very unhappy: *"You tricked me," she said bitterly.* 2 very bad: *It's bitterly cold outside.* | *We were bitterly disappointed to lose.*

bi·zarre /bɪ'zɑː $bɪ'zɑr/ *adjective* very unusual and strange: *The drugs caused his bizarre behaviour.*
– **bizarrely** *adverb*

black¹ /blæk/ *adjective*
1 something that is black is as dark as it can be, like the colour of the sky at night: *a black horse*
2 someone who is black has dark skin: *two young black kids*
3 black coffee or tea does not have milk in it: *I'll have two black coffees and one white* (=with milk in it), *please.*

black² *noun*
the darkest colour, like the colour of the sky at night: *He was dressed in black.*

black·ber·ry /'blækbəri $'blæk,beri/ *noun, plural* **blackberries** a small sweet black fruit that grows on a bush ⇨ *see picture on page 345*

black·board /'blækbɔːd $'blæk,bɔrd/ *noun* a dark smooth board that you write on with CHALK: *The teacher wrote the date on the blackboard.*

black·cur·rant/,blæk'kʌrənt $,blæk-'kɚ·ənt/ *noun* a small black fruit, often used to make drinks: *blackcurrant juice*

black eye /,. './ *noun* an area of dark skin around someone's eye where someone has hit them: *How did you get that black eye?*

black mag·ic /,. '../ *noun* [no plural] a type of magic used to do bad or evil things

black·mail /'blækmeɪl/ *noun* [no plural] when someone makes you do what they want by saying that they will tell secrets about you: *"End your relationship with her, and I might be prepared to forget about it." "That's blackmail!"*
– **blackmail** *verb:* *Jeremy tried to blackmail his boss.*

black mar·ket /,. '../ *noun* when people buy and sell things illegally: *They buy drugs on the black market.*

black·out /'blækaʊt/ *noun* when you suddenly cannot see, hear, or feel anything for a short time, for example because you are ill or have hit your head: *I had a blackout and couldn't remember anything.*

black·smith /'blæk,smɪθ/ *noun* someone who makes and repairs metal things

blad·der /'blædə $'blædɚ/ *noun* the part of your body where URINE stays before it leaves your body

B

blade /bleɪd/ *noun* **1** the flat sharp cutting part of a knife or tool: *The blade of this knife is completely blunt* (=not sharp). **2** a single piece of grass

blame¹ /bleɪm/ *verb*

GRAMMAR

blame someone for something
blame something on someone

if you blame someone, you say or think that they are responsible for something bad that has happened: *They **blamed** the captain **for** the team's defeat.* | *He **blamed** his bad results **on** his teachers.* | *Don't blame yourself. You tried to stop him.*

PHRASE

1 I don't blame you *spoken* used to say that you think that someone is being reasonable, although other people might criticize them: *"I was so angry!" "I **don't blame you**. He treated you really badly."*
2 be to blame to be responsible for something bad: *I know who's **to blame for** this.*

blame² *noun* [no plural]

GRAMMAR

blame for something

if you get the blame for something bad, other people say you are responsible for it: *I always **get the blame** when things go wrong.* | *He tried to **put the blame on** his brother* (=he said that his brother was responsible). | *She **took the blame for** her boss's mistake* (=people said that she was responsible).

bland /blænd/ *adjective* bland food has very little taste: *Some people think English food is very bland.*
– blandness *noun* [no plural]

blank¹ /blæŋk/ *adjective* **1** a blank sheet of paper, CASSETTE etc has nothing written or recorded on it: *She started writing on a blank page.* **2 go blank** if your mind goes blank, you suddenly cannot remember something: *When she saw the exam questions, her mind went blank.*

blank² *noun* an empty space on a piece of paper, for you to write a word or letter in: *Fill in the blanks on this quiz.*

blan·ket /'blæŋkɪt/ *noun* **1** a thick warm cover for a bed **2** *written* a thick layer of something: *A blanket of snow covered the mountains.*

blare /bleə $ bler/ also **blare out** *verb* to make a very loud unpleasant noise: *Music blared out from the house next door.*

blast¹ /blɑːst $ blæst/ *noun* an explosion: *Five people were killed in the blast.*

blast² *verb* to break rock into pieces using explosives: *They blasted a tunnel through the side of the mountain.*

bla·tant /'bleɪtnt/ *adjective* easy to notice, in a way that is shocking: *What a blatant insult!*
– blatantly *adverb*: *It was blatantly obvious he was lying.*

blaze¹ /bleɪz/ *noun* a large fire: *The blaze was caused by a cigarette.*

blaze² *verb written* to burn or shine very brightly and strongly: *A fire was blazing in the hearth.*

bleach¹ /bliːtʃ/ *noun* [no plural] a chemical used to clean things or make them whiter

bleach² *verb* to make something white or lighter in colour, using bleach: *She's bleached her hair.*

bleach·ers /'bliːtʃəz $ 'bliːtʃəz/ *plural noun* AmE long rows of wooden seats where people sit to watch sports games: *We could only afford to sit in the bleachers.*

bleak /bliːk/ *adjective* **1** cold and unattractive: *It was a bleak December day.* **2** a bleak situation seems very bad and is not likely to get better: *Without a job, the future seemed bleak.*

blear·y-eyed /ˌblɪəri 'aɪd $ ˌblɪri 'aɪd/ *adjective* someone who is bleary-eyed looks tired or as if they have been crying: *She came down to breakfast looking bleary-eyed.*

bleat /bliːt/ *verb* if a sheep or goat bleats, it makes a high noise

bled the past tense and past participle of BLEED

bleed /bliːd/ *verb, past tense and past participle* **bled** /bled/ if you bleed, blood comes out of a cut on your body: *The wound on his arm started bleeding again.*

bleed·ing /'bliːdɪŋ/ *noun* [no plural] the flow of blood from a wound: *She pressed on the wound to stop the bleeding.*

bleep /bliːp/ *verb* to make a high electronic sound: *The alarm clock was bleeping.*
–**bleep** *noun*: *When you hear a bleep, you have new email.*

bleep·er /'bliːpə $ 'blipɚ/ *noun* BrE a PAGER

blem·ish /'blemɪʃ/ *noun* formal, plural **blemishes** a small mark that spoils something: *My new dress had a small blemish on the collar.*

blend /blend/ *verb* to mix two or more things together thoroughly: *Blend the butter and the flour.*
–**blend** *noun*: *You have to get the right blend of flavours.*

blend·er /'blendə $ 'blendɚ/ *noun* a small electric machine that you use to mix food

bless /bles/ *verb* 1 to ask God to make something holy: *The priest blessed the bread and wine.* 2 **bless you!** spoken what you say to someone when they SNEEZE

blew the past tense of BLOW¹

blind¹ /blaɪnd/ *adjective*
a blind person cannot see because their eyes are damaged: *She is going* (=becoming) *blind.* | *Some of the children were born blind* (=they were blind when they were born).
–**blindness** *noun* [no plural]: *a new treatment for some forms of blindness*

PHRASE
turn a blind eye to pretend you have not noticed something bad that is happening: *The teacher turned a blind eye to the students' smoking.*

blind² *verb* to make someone unable to see: *She was blinded for a moment by the bright light.*

blind³ *noun* a flat piece of cloth that you pull down to cover a window: *We closed all the blinds.* ↪ see picture on page 342

blind·fold¹ /'blaɪndfəʊld $ 'blaɪndfoʊld/ *verb* to cover someone's eyes with a piece of cloth so that they cannot see: *They blindfolded him and locked him in a room.*

blindfold² *noun* a piece of cloth that you put over someone's eyes to stop them being able to see

blind·ing /'blaɪndɪŋ/ *adjective* very

bright: *There was a blinding flash as the car exploded.*

blink /blɪŋk/ *verb* 1 to open and close your eyes quickly: *He blinked as he stepped into the sunlight.* 2 if a light blinks, it goes on and off: *The red warning light was blinking.*

bliss /blɪs/ *noun* [no plural] complete happiness: *A hot bath and a glass of wine is my idea of bliss.*

blis·ter¹ /'blɪstə $ 'blɪstɚ/ *noun* a small area of raised skin that is painful and full of liquid because something has rubbed or burnt it: *After walking five miles, I had blisters on my feet.*

blister² *verb* to become covered with blisters: *The chemicals made my hands blister.* | *The sun had blistered the skin on her back.*

blitz /blɪts/ *noun* when you use a lot of effort to do something in a short time: *We had a blitz on cleaning the house.*

bliz·zard /'blɪzəd $ 'blɪzɚd/ *noun* a storm with a lot of wind and snow

bloat·ed /'bləʊtɪd $ 'bloʊtɪd/ *adjective* feeling very full and uncomfortable: *I'd eaten so much I felt bloated.*

blob /blɒb $ blɑb/ *noun* a small drop of a thick liquid: *Put a blob of glue on the back of the picture.*

block¹ /blɒk $ blɑk/ *noun*

GRAMMAR
a block of something
1 a large piece of heavy solid material with straight sides: *a block of concrete* | *a block of ice*
2 BrE a large building with many homes or offices in it: *a block of flats* | *a new office block*
3 AmE a group of buildings with streets on all four sides: *I lived two blocks away from Woody Allen.*

block² *verb*
1 also **block up** if something blocks a space, it is there, stopping things coming through: *Two large men were blocking the entrance.* | *I've got a cold and my nose is blocked up.*
2 if something blocks your view, it stops you from seeing something because it is in front of you: *A big man was blocking my view of the screen.*
3 to stop something being done or

being finished: *The President tried to block the investigation.*

PHRASAL VERB
block off
block something off to completely close a road or entrance: *The police **blocked off** the road where the accident happened.*

block·ade /blɒˈkeɪd $blɑˈkeɪd/ *noun* when an army or navy surrounds a place to stop people getting in or out

block·age /ˈblɒkɪdʒ $ˈblɑkɪdʒ/ *noun* something that blocks a tube or pipe

block·bust·er /ˈblɒkˌbʌstə $ˈblɑkˌbʌstəʳ/ *noun informal* a book or film that is very successful: *the latest Hollywood blockbuster*

block cap·i·tals /ˌ. ˈ.../ also **block let·ters** /ˌ. ˈ../ *noun* big letters, for example 'A' instead of 'a'

bloke /bləʊk/ *noun BrE informal* a man

blonde¹ also **blond** /blɒnd $blɑnd/ *adjective* **1** blonde hair is pale or yellow ➪ *see picture on page 353* **2** someone who is blonde has pale or yellow hair: *She's small, blonde, and very attractive.*

USAGE
The spelling 'blonde' is usually used for a woman and the spelling 'blond' for a man.

blonde² *noun informal* a woman who has pale or yellow hair: *All his girlfriends have been blondes.*

blood /blʌd/ *noun* [no plural] the red liquid that your heart pushes around your body: *I cut my finger and there was blood everywhere!* | *I saw dried blood on his shirt.*

blood·bath /ˈblʌdbɑːθ $ˈblʌdbæθ/ *noun* when a lot of people are killed violently

blood·cur·dling /ˈblʌdˌkɜːdlɪŋ $ˈblʌdˌkɜʳdlɪŋ/ *adjective* bloodcurdling sounds are very frightening: *a bloodcurdling scream*

blood·shed /ˈblʌdʃed/ *noun* [no plural] *formal* when people are killed in fighting: *The army has surrendered to avoid further bloodshed.*

blood·shot /ˈblʌdʃɒt $ˈblʌdʃɑt/ *adjective* bloodshot eyes look slightly red

blood·stream /ˈblʌdstriːm/ *noun* your blood as it flows around your body: *The*

drugs get into your bloodstream very quickly.*

blood·thirst·y /ˈblʌdˌθɜːsti $ˈblʌdˌθɜʳsti/ *adjective* someone who is bloodthirsty enjoys violence

blood ves·sel /ˈ. ˌ.../ *noun* one of the tubes in your body that blood flows through

blood·y /ˈblʌdi/ *adjective* **1** covered in blood: *Her hands were all bloody.* **2** violent, and killing or wounding a lot of people: *a bloody battle*

bloom¹ /bluːm/ *noun* **in bloom** a plant that is in bloom has flowers that are fully open: *The roses are in bloom.*

bloom² *verb* if plants bloom, their flowers open: *Roses bloom in the summer.*

blos·som¹ /ˈblɒsəm $ˈblɑsəm/ *noun* the flowers on a tree or bush: *apple blossom*

blossom² *verb* **1** if trees blossom, they produce flowers **2** if someone blossoms, they become happier, more successful, more attractive etc: *Mary has blossomed into a beautiful young lady.*

blot¹ /blɒt $blɑt/ *verb* **blotted, blotting**; **blot something out** to stop yourself from thinking about something: *She managed to blot out the memory of the accident.*

blot² *noun* a drop of liquid such as ink that has fallen on a piece of paper: *His essay was covered in ink blots.*

blotch /blɒtʃ $blɑtʃ/ *noun, plural* **blotches** a mark on something: *There were red blotches on his face.*

blouse /blaʊz $blaʊs/ *noun* a shirt for women ➪ *see picture on page 352*

blow¹ /bləʊ $bloʊ/ *verb* **blew** /bluː/ **blown** /bləʊn $bloʊn/

GRAMMAR
blow something down/away etc
blow on/through/etc something
blow from somewhere
blow towards someone

1 if the wind blows something somewhere, or if it blows there, the wind moves it there: *It was so windy the tent nearly blew away!* | *The door blew shut.* | *The wind blew the fence down.*
2 if the wind blows, the air moves: *A cold wind was blowing from the north.* | *The breeze blew towards us.*

3 to send a thin stream of air out through your mouth: *She blew through the tube.* | *John blew on his cold fingers.*

4 if a musical instrument or whistle blows, or if you blow it, it makes a sound when you send air through it from your mouth: *Joe blew the trumpet as hard as he could.* | *The guard's whistle blew and the train started to leave.*

5 to violently move or destroy something with an explosion or bullet: *The explosion blew the windows out.* | *The bomb blew a hole in the wall.*

PHRASES

blow your nose to force air through your nose in order to clear it

blow it, blow a chance *informal* to lose a good opportunity because you make a mistake: *He had a great chance of scoring a goal but he blew it.*

blow money on something *informal* to spend a lot of money quickly in a careless way: *He blew all his money on presents for his new girlfriend.* | *I blew £140 on a new pair of trainers.*

PHRASAL VERBS

blow out

blow something out if you blow out a flame, or if a flame blows out, your breath or the wind stops it burning: *She blew out the candle.* | *All the matches blew out almost as soon as I lit them.*

blow over

if an argument blows over, it ends: *Don't worry – it'll soon blow over.*

blow up

1 blow something up if something blows up, or if someone blows it up, it is destroyed in an explosion: *They had only just escaped when the car blew up.* | *The soldiers blew up the bridge.*

2 blow something up if you blow up a BALLOON or car tyre, you fill it with air

blow² *noun* **1** a hard hit: *He gave the handle several blows with his hammer.* **2** something that disappoints or upsets you: *Her mother's death was a terrible blow.*

blow dry /'. ./ *verb* **blow dries, blow** dried to dry your hair using a HAIRDRYER

blown the past participle of BLOW¹

blue¹ /blu:/ *adjective*

something that is blue is the colour of a clear sky on a nice day: *She had blue eyes.* | *a dark-blue sweater*

blue² *noun* **1** the colour of a clear sky on a nice day: *Blue is my favourite colour.* **2** blues a slow sad style of music that came from the southern US: *I like jazz and blues.*

blue-col·lar /ˌ. '../ *adjective* blue-collar workers do jobs such as repairing machines and making things in factories

bluff /blʌf/ *verb* to pretend that you are going to do something, when this is not true: *She was only bluffing when she said she would leave college.*
– **bluff** *noun*: *He said he would go to the police, but it was just a bluff.*

blun·der /'blʌndə $ 'blʌndɚ/ *noun* a careless or stupid mistake that causes serious problems

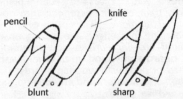

blunt

pencil   knife

blunt   sharp

blunt /blʌnt/ *adjective* **1** a blunt object is not sharp: *This knife's blunt!* **2** someone who is blunt says exactly what they think, even if it upsets people: *John can be very blunt sometimes.*

blur /blɜ: $ blɜr/ *noun* something that you cannot see or remember clearly: *The crash is all a blur in my mind.*

blurred /blɜ:d $ blɜrd/ *adjective* blurred shapes, pictures, or thoughts are not clear: *The photograph was rather blurred.*

blurt /blɜ:t $ blɜrt/ **blurt something out** *verb informal* to say something suddenly and without thinking, especially something you should have tried to keep quiet or secret: *I blurted out his name without realising my parents were listening.*

blush /blʌʃ/ *verb* if you blush, your face becomes red because you feel embarrassed: *a shy child who blushes easily*

B

blus·ter·y /'blʌstəri/ *adjective* blustery weather is very windy

board¹ /bɔːd $ bɔrd/ *noun*

1 a flat piece of wood or plastic that is fixed on a wall and used to show information for everyone to see: *He* **pinned** *the notice* **up on the board.** | *Copy the picture from the board.*

2 a thin flat piece of wood or plastic that is used for a particular purpose: *a* **chess board**

3 the group of people in an organization who make the rules and important decisions: *He's* **on the board** *of two companies.* | *a board meeting*

PHRASE

on board on a plane, ship, train, or bus: *Everyone* **on board** *the plane survived the crash.*

board² *noun* **board and lodging** *BrE* a room to sleep in and meals to eat; ROOM AND BOARD *AmE*: *They charge £100 a week for board and lodging.*

board³ *verb* **1** *formal* to get on a plane, ship, train, or bus: *Passengers may now board the plane.* **2** if a plane or ship is boarding, passengers are getting on it: *Flight 207 for Paris is now boarding.* **3** board something up to cover a window or door with wooden boards: *The shop is now empty and boarded up.*

boarding school /'.. ./ *noun* a school where students live as well as study

board·room /'bɔːdruːm $ 'bɔrdrum/ *noun* a room where the important people in an organization have meetings

boast /bəust $ boust/ *verb* to talk too proudly about yourself and tell other people how good or clever you are ⇨ *same meaning* BRAG: *He's always boasting about his rich friends.*

boast·ful /'bəustfəl $ 'boustfəl/ *adjective* if you are boastful, you talk too proudly about yourself and tell other people how good or clever you are: *He was not popular at school because he was very boastful.*

boat /bəut $ bout/ *noun*

GRAMMAR
by boat

something that people sit in to travel across water: *a sailing boat* | *We went to the island* **by boat**. ⇨ *see picture on page 349*

bob /bɒb $ bab/ *verb* **bobbed, bobbing; bob up and down** to move up and down in water

bod·i·ly /'bɒdəli $ 'badl-i/ *adjective written* related to someone's body: *He did not suffer any bodily harm.*

body

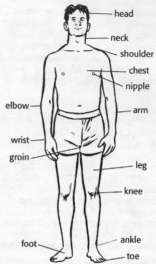

head
neck
shoulder
chest
nipple
elbow
arm
wrist
groin
leg
knee
foot
ankle
toe

bod·y /'bɒdi $ 'badi/ *noun, plural* bodies

1 the physical structure of a person or animal: *Our bodies need vitamins to stay healthy.* | *the human body*

2 a dead person: *Two bodies were found in the car.*

3 *formal* an official group of people who work together: *the public body responsible for safety at work*

body build·ing /'.. ,../ *noun* [no plural] physical exercises you do to make your muscles bigger and stronger

bod·y·guard /'bɒdigaːd $ 'badi,gard/ *noun* someone whose job is to protect an important person

bog /bɒg $ bag/ *noun* an area of soft wet muddy ground

bo·gus /'bəugəs $ 'bougəs/ *adjective informal* false, but pretending to be real: *a bogus doctor*

boil¹ /bɔil/ *verb*

1 if you boil a container of liquid, or if liquid boils, the liquid becomes so

hot that it starts changing into steam: *I'll just **boil the kettle** and we can have a cup of tea.* | *Wait for the water to boil before adding the pasta.* | *a pan of boiling water* **2** to cook food in boiling water: *Boil the potatoes for twenty minutes.* | *a boiled egg*

PHRASE
it all boils down to something: *It **all boils down** to trust* (=the most important thing is trust).

boil² noun **1 bring something to the boil** BrE, **bring something to a boil** AmE to heat something in a pan until it boils: ***Bring** the potatoes **to the boil**.* **2** a small area of your skin that has become red and painful because it is infected: *He has a boil on his chin.*

boil·er /'bɔɪlə $ 'bɔɪlɚ/ noun a piece of equipment that heats a large amount of water for people to use

boil·ing /'bɔɪlɪŋ/ adjective **boiling hot** very hot: *a boiling hot day*

boiling point /'.. ,./ noun the temperature at which a liquid gets so hot that it starts changing into steam: *The boiling point of water is 100 degrees Celsius.*

bois·ter·ous /'bɔɪstərəs/ adjective noisy, cheerful, and full of energy: *a boisterous four-year old*

bold /bəʊld $ boʊld/ adjective **1** confident and willing to take risks: *a very bold robbery* | *Guevara was a bold soldier and a great leader of men.* **2** writing, shapes, or colours that are bold are very clear or bright
– **boldly** adverb

bol·lard /'bɒləd $ 'bɑlɚd/ noun BrE a thick post that is fixed in the ground to stop cars going onto a piece of land or road

bolt¹ /bəʊlt $ boʊlt/ noun **1** a metal bar that you slide across in order to keep a door or window shut **2** a type of screw, which is used with a NUT to hold pieces of metal or wood together

bolt² verb **1** to run away suddenly: *The man bolted before the police could catch him.* **2** to close a door or window with a bolt **3** also **bolt down** to eat something very quickly: *I bolted down my breakfast.*

bomb¹ /bɒm $ bɑm/ noun a container filled with a substance that will explode: *a nuclear bomb*

bomb² verb **1** to attack a place with bombs: *The city was bombed during the war.* **2** informal if a play or film bombs, it is not successful

bom·bard /bɒm'bɑːd $ bɑm'bɑrd/ verb **1** to attack a place with guns and bombs: *The city was bombarded from all sides.* **2 bombard someone with questions, bombard someone with information** to ask someone too many questions or give them too much information

bomb·er /'bɒmə $ 'bɑmɚ/ noun **1** a plane that drops bombs **2** informal someone who puts a bomb somewhere: *the hunt for the bombers*

bond¹ /bɒnd $ bɑnd/ noun a shared feeling or interest that makes people feel love and loyalty towards each other: *There's a strong bond between the two brothers.*

bond² verb **1** to develop a special loving relationship with someone: *It takes time to bond with a new baby.* **2** to join or glue things together firmly

bone /bəʊn $ boʊn/ noun one of the hard parts in the frame of your body: *She broke a bone in her leg.*

bone dry /, . './ adjective completely dry: *After the long, hot summer, the ground was bone dry.*

bon·fire /'bɒnfaɪə $ 'bɑn,faɪɚ/ noun a large outdoor fire that someone has under their control

bon·net /'bɒnɪt $ 'bɑnɪt/ noun **1** BrE the part at the front of a car that covers the engine; HOOD AmE ⇨ *see picture at* CAR **2** a hat that you tie under your chin

bo·nus /'bəʊnəs $ 'boʊnəs/ noun **1** money that is added to someone's usual pay: *All members of staff get a Christmas bonus.* **2** something good that you did not expect: *Getting a free printer with the computer was a bonus.*

bon·y /'bəʊni $ 'boʊni/ adjective informal **bonier, boniest** bony people are very thin

boo /buː/ verb to shout 'boo' to show that you do not like someone's performance or speech
– **boo** noun

boo·by prize /'buːbi ˌpraɪz/ noun a prize given as a joke to the person who finishes last in a competition

booby trap /'.. ,./ noun a bomb or other dangerous thing that is hidden in something that seems harmless

book¹ /bʊk/ noun

> **GRAMMAR**
> **a book of something**
> **a book on/about something**

1 a set of printed pages fastened together in a cover so that you can read them: *Have you read any good books recently?* | *The new dictionary is a useful reference book* (=a book that you use for finding information). | *a book on shells and fishes* | *Jim had some school books* (=books that you use at school) *under his arm.*
2 small sheets of paper fastened together in a thin cover: *a cheque book* | *an address book* | *a book of stamps*
3 **books** written records of the financial accounts of a business

book² verb

1 *BrE* to arrange to have or do something at a particular time: *He booked a table at the restaurant for 8 o'clock.* | *We've booked a band to play at the wedding.* | *The hotel was fully booked* (=all the rooms were being used).
2 *informal* to ARREST someone: *The policeman booked me for speeding.*

> **PHRASAL VERB**
> **book in** also **book into something** *BrE* to arrive at a hotel and collect your key ⇨ *same meaning* CHECK IN: *We booked into a hotel for the night.* | *I'll call you as soon as I've booked in.*

book·case /'bʊk-keɪs/ noun a piece of furniture with shelves for books

book·ing /'bʊkɪŋ/ noun BrE an arrangement that you make to have a hotel room, a seat on a plane etc at a future time: *Please can I make a booking?*

book·let /'bʊklət/ noun a small book that contains information

book·mak·er /'bʊkmeɪkə $ 'bʊk-,meɪkɚ/ noun someone whose job is to serve people who want to BET on the result of a game or competition

book·mark /'bʊkmɑːk $ 'bʊkmɑrk/ noun a piece of paper that you put in a book so that you can find the page you want

book·shelf /'bʊkʃelf/ noun, plural **bookshelves** /-ʃelvz/ a shelf that has books on it ⇨ *see picture on page 342*

book·shop /'bʊkʃɒp $ 'bʊkʃɑp/ BrE, **book·store** /'bʊkstɔː $ 'bʊkstɔr/ AmE, noun a shop that sells books

boom /buːm/ verb to become very successful or popular: *Britain's economy is booming.*
–**boom** noun: *Films had a boom in popularity in the 1990s.*

boost¹ /buːst/ noun something that helps you become more successful or feel more confident and happy: *The visit by the queen gave a great boost to local people.*

boost² verb to increase the value or amount of something: *The hot weather boosted sales of ice cream* (=more people bought ice cream than usual).

boot¹ /buːt/ noun 1 a type of strong shoe that covers your foot and the lower part of your leg: *a pair of boots* ⇨ *see picture on page 352* 2 *BrE* a covered space in the back of a car, used for carrying bags, boxes etc; TRUNK AmE 3 **get the boot, give someone the boot** *informal* to be forced to leave your job, or to force someone to leave their job

boot² verb *informal* to kick something hard: *She booted the ball as hard as she could.*

booth /buːð $ buːθ/ noun a small space surrounded by thin walls: *a telephone booth*

booze /buːz/ noun [no plural] *informal* alcoholic drink

bor·der¹ /'bɔːdə $ 'bɔrdɚ/ noun

1 the official line that separates two countries: *We were not allowed to cross the border between the two parts of the island.*
2 a narrow area or piece around the edge of something: *The flag was blue with a white border.*

border² verb 1 to be in a line along the edge of something: *Large trees border the park.* 2 to be next to another country: *A small Jewish settlement borders on Iran.* 3 **border on** to be very nearly something bad or unpleasant: *His behaviour bordered on rudeness.*

bore¹ /bɔː $ bɔr/ verb 1 to make someone feel bored: *I won't bore you with all the details.* | *Sorry, am I boring*

you? **2 bore a hole** to make a deep round hole in the ground or under the sea

bore² *noun* someone or something that you find dull and uninteresting: *I'm not asking that bore to the party!*

bore³ the past tense of BEAR¹

bored

bored /bɔːd $ bɔrd/ *adjective*

GRAMMAR
bored with something
unhappy and impatient because something is not interesting or you have nothing to do: *She soon got bored with the game.* | *Most of the students looked bored.*

PHRASE
be bored stiff, be bored to tears to be very bored

bore·dom /'bɔːdəm $ 'bɔrdəm/ *noun* [no plural] the feeling you have when you are bored

bor·ing /'bɔːrɪŋ/ *adjective*
not interesting in any way: *The programme was so boring she fell asleep.*

born¹ /bɔːn $ bɔrn/ *verb*

GRAMMAR
be born
to come out of your mother and begin life: *I was born in 1986.* | *Where were you born?*

born² *adjective* a born leader, teacher etc is someone who has a natural ability to lead, teach etc

borne /bɔːn $ bɔrn/ the past participle of BEAR¹

bor·row /'bɒrəʊ $ 'bɑroʊ/ *verb*

GRAMMAR
borrow something from someone
to take and use something that belongs to someone who has agreed to let you have it for a short time: *He borrowed £2,000 from his father.* | *She borrowed her friend's jacket.*
⇨ see usage note at LEND

bos·om /'bʊzəm/ *noun formal* a woman's breasts

boss¹ /bɒs $ bɔs/ *noun, plural* **bosses** your boss at work is the person who tells you what work to do: *I get on well with my boss.*

boss² *verb* **boss someone around** to tell someone to do things in an unfriendly way, especially when you have no authority over them

boss·y /'bɒsi $ 'bɔsi/ *adjective* **bossier, bossiest** always telling other people what to do, in a way that is annoying

both¹ /bəʊθ $ boʊθ/
two people or things: *Both the boys had dark hair.* | *I like both of you.* | *Jump with both feet together.* | *They are both learning to play the piano.*

both²
showing that two things or people are involved: *She's good at both tennis and golf.* | *The idea is both simple and brilliant.* | *Both Nick and Mike were in the team.*

both·er¹ /'bɒðə $ 'bɑðɚ/ *verb*

GRAMMAR
bother to do something
1 to make someone stop what they are doing in order to ask them for something: *How can I work when people keep bothering me?* | *Sorry to bother you – have you seen Ian anywhere?*
2 if something bothers you, it makes you feel slightly worried or upset: *Something's obviously bothering her.*
3 to make the effort to do something: *He didn't bother to lock the door.*

PHRASES
can't be bothered to do something *BrE informal* to not have enough interest or energy to do something: *I can't be bothered to go out tonight.*

not bothered *spoken* if you are not bothered about something, it is not important to you: *"Do you want tea or coffee?" "I'm not bothered."*

bother² *noun* [no plural] problems or trouble that you have to spend time and effort on: *This new car has caused me a lot of bother.*

bot·tle¹ /'bɒtl $ 'bɑtl/ *noun* a glass or plastic container with a narrow top, used for liquids: *a wine bottle*

bottle² *verb* **1** to put a liquid into a bottle: *This wine is bottled in France.* **2 bottle something up** to keep a feeling hidden and not show it: *Don't bottle your anger up.*

bottle bank /'.. ,./ *noun* a large container in a public place where people leave empty glass bottles so that the glass can be used again

bot·tled /'bɒtld $ 'bɑtld/ *adjective* bottled water has been put in a bottle so that people can buy it and drink it

bot·tle·neck /'bɒtlnek $ 'bɑtl,nek/ *noun* a place in a road where the traffic cannot pass easily, so that cars are delayed

bot·tom¹ /'bɒtəm $ 'bɑtəm/ *noun*
1 the lowest part of something ⇨ opposite TOP¹: *Her mother was standing at the bottom of the stairs. | The bucket had a hole in the bottom.*
2 *informal* the part of your body that you sit on

bottom² *adjective*
in the lowest place or position ⇨ opposite TOP² (2): *The juice is on the bottom shelf.*

bought the past tense and past participle of BUY

boul·der /'bəʊldə $ 'bəʊldɚ/ *noun* a very large rock

boule·vard /'buːlvɑːd $ 'bʊləvɑrd/ *noun* a wide road in a town or city

bounce¹ /baʊns/
verb **1** if something hits a surface, it then immediately moves away from it again: *The ball bounced off the wall.* **2** if you write a cheque and

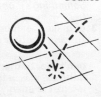

bounce

it bounces, your bank will not pay the amount written on the cheque because there is not enough money in your bank account **3** to run or walk quickly because you are happy: *She bounced into the office.*

bounce² *noun* when something bounces: *You have to hit the ball after the first bounce.*

bounc·er /'baʊnsə $ 'baʊnsɚ/ *noun informal* someone whose job is to keep people who behave badly out of a club or bar

bounc·y /'baʊnsi/ *adjective* **bouncier, bounciest** something that is bouncy bounces easily: *a bouncy ball*

bound¹ the past tense and past participle of BIND

bound² /baʊnd/ *adjective*

> **GRAMMAR**
> **be bound to do something**
> **be bound for somewhere**
> **be bound up with something**

1 to be certain to do something: *Fiona is bound to win the competition – she's brilliant!*
2 *written* a ship, plane etc that is bound for a particular place is going there: *A ship bound for Singapore had just left. | a Paris-bound flight*
3 to be closely connected with something: *Her success was bound up with the success of the team.*

bound³ *noun* **1** *written* a long or high jump **2 out of bounds** if somewhere is out of bounds, you are not allowed to go there: *This area is out of bounds to the prisoners.*

bound·a·ry /'baʊndəri/ *noun, plural* **boundaries** the line that marks the edge of an area of land: *The river forms the boundary between the two states.*

bou·quet /bəʊ'keɪ $ boʊ'keɪ/ *noun* a number of flowers fastened together, that you give to someone

bout /baʊt/ *noun* a short period of illness: *a bout of flu*

bou·tique /buː'tiːk/ *noun* a small shop that sells fashionable clothes

bow¹ /baʊ/ *verb* **1** to bend your head or the top part of your body forward: *The musicians stood up and bowed.* **2 bow to something** to finally agree to do something that other people want you to do: *The school has bowed to* public pressure and agreed to allow the pop concert.

bow² /baʊ/ noun **1** when someone bows **2** also **bows** the front part of a ship

bow³ /bəʊ $boʊ/ noun **1** a thin band of cloth or string that you tie to form two circles and use as a decoration or to tie your shoes: *Jenny had a big red bow in her hair.* **2** a weapon that you use for shooting ARROWS **3** a thing that you use for playing instruments with strings, such as a VIOLIN

bow·el /'baʊəl/ noun the part inside your body that carries solid waste food away from your stomach and out of your body

bowl¹ /bəʊl $boʊl/ noun **1** a round container in which you put food or liquid: *a bowl of rice* **2 bowls** an outdoor game, in which you roll large wooden balls towards a smaller ball

bowl² verb to throw a ball towards the BATSMAN in CRICKET
— **bowler** noun

bow-legged /'bəʊ‚legɪd $ 'boʊ‚legɪd/ adjective a bow-legged person has legs that curve out at their knees

bowl·ing /'bəʊlɪŋ $ 'boʊlɪŋ/ also **ten pin bowling** noun [no plural] an indoor game in which you roll a heavy ball along a wooden track in order to knock over pieces of wood

bow tie /‚bəʊ 'taɪ $ 'boʊ taɪ/ noun a man's tie that he fastens to form two small circles at the front of his neck

box¹ /bɒks $baks/ noun, plural **boxes**
1 a container for putting things in, especially one with four straight sides: *a large cardboard box | a box of chocolates* ➪ see picture at CONTAINER **2** a small space surrounded by thin walls: *a telephone box* **3** a small square on a page where you write a figure or other information: *Sign your name in the box below.* **4 the box** BrE informal television: *What's on the box tonight?*

box² verb to take part in the sport of BOXING

box·er /'bɒksə $ 'baksɚ/ noun someone who does boxing as a sport

boxer shorts /'.. ‚./ noun loose cotton underwear for men

box·ing /'bɒksɪŋ $ 'baksɪŋ/ noun [no plural] a sport in which two people wearing big leather GLOVEs hit each other ➪ see picture on page 351

Boxing Day /'.. ‚./ noun BrE the 26th December, the day after Christmas Day, which is a national holiday in the UK

box of·fice /'. ‚../ noun a place in a theatre, cinema etc where you buy tickets

boy /bɔɪ/ noun a male child or a young man: *She is married now and has two boys.*

boy·cott /'bɔɪkɒt $ 'bɔɪkɑt/ verb to refuse to buy or use something as a protest: *The US has threatened to boycott French wine.*
— **boycott** noun

boy·friend /'bɔɪfrend/ noun a boy or man with whom you have a romantic relationship

boy·hood /'bɔɪhʊd/ noun [no plural] the time during a man's life when he is a boy

boy·ish /'bɔɪ-ɪʃ/ adjective like a young man: *She had a slim figure and a boyish face.*

bra /brɑː/ noun a piece of underwear that a woman wears on her breasts

brace /breɪs/ verb **brace yourself** to prepare yourself for something unpleasant

brace·let /'breɪslət/ noun a piece of jewellery that you wear around your wrist ➪ see picture at JEWELLERY

bra·ces /'breɪsɪz/ plural noun **1** BrE two narrow bands that you wear over your shoulders and fasten to your trousers to stop them from falling down; SUSPENDERS AmE: *a pair of red braces* ➪ see picture on page 352 **2** also **brace** BrE a wire frame that some children wear to make their teeth straight

brack·et /'brækɪt/ noun **1** one of the pairs of signs [] or () that you sometimes put around less important words: *Please give your age (in brackets) after your name.* **2** a piece of metal or wood fixed to a wall to support a shelf

brag /bræg/ verb **bragged, bragging** to talk too proudly about yourself ➪ same meaning BOAST: *He's always bragging about how much he earns.*

braid /breɪd/ verb to twist three long pieces of hair, rope etc together to make one long piece; PLAIT BrE
— **braid** noun

Braille /breɪl/ noun [no plural] a type of printing that blind people can read by touching the page

brain /breɪn/ *noun*

1 the part of your body inside your head which you use to think and control everything you do: *The baby had permanent brain damage.* | *His brain couldn't cope with all the new information.*

2 brains the ability to think well

brain·storm /'breɪnstɔːm $ breɪn-ˌstɔrm/ the American word for BRAIN-WAVE

brain·wash /'breɪnwɒʃ $ 'breɪnwɑʃ/ *verb* to force someone to believe something that is not true by telling them many times that it is true

brain·wave /'breɪnweɪv/ *noun* BrE a very good idea that you have suddenly; BRAINSTORM *AmE*

brain·y /'breɪni/ *adjective informal* brainier, brainiest clever and good at learning

brake¹ /breɪk/ *noun* the part of a vehicle that makes it go more slowly or stop

brake² *verb* to make a vehicle go more slowly or stop, using its brake: *The car in front braked suddenly.*

bran /bræn/ *noun* [no plural] the crushed skin of wheat and other grain, often used in bread

branch¹ /brɑːntʃ $ bræntʃ/ *noun*, *plural* branches

1 a part of a tree that grows out from the main part: *branches covered in blossom*

2 one part of an organization: *There's a branch of that shop in most big towns.*

branch² *verb* branch off to leave a main road or path: *We branched off the main road onto a small track.*

brand¹ /brænd/ *noun* **1** a product that a particular company makes: *What brand of washing powder do you use?* **2** a particular type of something: *He has his own special brand of humour.*

brand² *verb* brand someone as something to describe someone as a very bad type of person: *You can't brand all football fans as violent.*

bran·dish /'brændɪʃ/ *verb written* to wave a weapon around in a dangerous and threatening way: *He ran into the room brandishing a knife.*

brand-new /ˌ. './ *adjective* completely new and not used at all: *a brand-new house*

bran·dy /'brændi/ *noun* a strong alcoholic drink made from wine

brash /bræʃ/ *adjective* a brash person seems too confident and speaks too loudly

brass /brɑːs $ bræs/ *noun* **1** [no plural] a shiny yellow metal that is a mixture of COPPER and ZINC **2** the brass (section) the part of a band that plays instruments made of brass, such as TRUMPETS

brat /bræt/ *noun informal* a badly behaved child

bra·va·do /brə'vɑːdəʊ $ brə'vadoʊ/ *noun* [no plural] *formal* behaviour that is meant to show that you feel brave and confident, even though you do not

brave¹ /breɪv/ *adjective*

behaving with courage in a frightening situation: *He wasn't brave enough to dive into the deep water.* – bravely *adverb*: *She bravely tried to ignore her pain.*

brave² *verb written* to be brave enough to do something difficult, dangerous, or unpleasant: *We braved the cold weather to go and watch the match.*

brav·e·ry /'breɪvəri/ *noun* [no plural] the quality of being brave ⇨ *opposite* COW-ARDICE: *He was awarded a medal for his bravery.*

bra·vo /'brɑːvəʊ $ 'brɑvoʊ/ a word you shout to show that you like something

brawl /brɔːl/ *noun* a noisy fight – brawl *verb*: *two drunken men brawling in the street*

breach /briːtʃ/ *noun* when you break a law, rule, or agreement: *If he leaves, he will be in breach of his contract.*

bread /bred/ *noun* [no plural]

a common food made by baking a mixture of FLOUR and water: *He bought a loaf of bread.* | *She cut another slice of bread.*

breadth /bredθ/ *noun* [no plural] the distance from one side of something to the other: *Jilly swam the breadth of the pool, and she's only five.*

bread·win·ner /'bred,wɪnə $ 'bred-ˌwɪnɚ/ *noun* the person in a family who earns most of the money that the family needs: *Mum was the breadwinner after Dad became ill.*

break¹ /breɪk/ ⇨ see box on pages 72 and 73

break² noun

a break in something
1 if you take a break, you stop what you are doing for a short time in order to rest or eat: *OK, let's take a break for a few minutes.* | *It's time for my lunch break.*
2 a short holiday: *I need a break.* | *a weekend break by the sea*
3 a pause or opening in the middle of something: *He stopped to wait for a break in the traffic.*
4 a chance to become successful: *Her big break was being chosen to star in a TV series.*
5 a part of something where it has been broken: *My arm always hurts where I had that break in my elbow.*

break·age /'breɪkɪdʒ/ noun written something that has been broken or when something is broken: *You will have to pay for any breakages.*

break·down /'breɪkdaʊn/ noun
1 when something stops working successfully: *a breakdown in the relationship between the two countries*
2 when a car stops working 3 if someone has a breakdown, they become seriously ill in their mind because they cannot deal with the problems in their life: *After his wife left he had a breakdown.*

break·fast /'brekfəst/ noun
the meal that you eat when you get up in the morning: *I haven't had breakfast yet.* | *What would you like for breakfast?*

break-in /'. ./ noun when someone breaks a door or window to enter a building and steal things: *There was a break-in at the school over the weekend.*

break·through /'breɪkθruː/ noun an important new discovery or change: *a breakthrough in the treatment of cancer*

break·up /'breɪkʌp/ noun 1 when a marriage or romantic relationship ends
2 when an organization or country is forced to separate into smaller parts: *the fighting that followed the breakup of Yugoslavia*

breast /brest/ noun 1 one of the two round raised parts on a woman's chest that can produce milk for babies 2 the

front of a bird's body, or the meat from this: *chicken breast*

breast·stroke /'brest-strəʊk $ 'brest-stroʊk/ noun [no plural] a way of swimming on your front in which you push your arms forward and move them round towards your sides

breath /breθ/ noun
the air that comes out of your lungs when you breathe: *I could smell garlic on his breath.*

take a breath to take air into your lungs: *He **took** a deep **breath** and dived into the water.*
be out of breath to have difficulty breathing, for example because you have been running: *You'd be **out of breath** too if you'd climbed all those stairs.*
hold your breath to deliberately stop breathing for a short time while keeping air in your lungs: *I **held** my **breath** and swam under the boat.*
get your breath back, catch your breath to rest after doing something such as running until you can breathe normally again: *I'll have to stop for a moment and **get** my **breath back**.*
under your breath if you say something under your breath, you say it quietly, so that other people cannot hear: *He always mutters something **under his breath** as he is leaving.*

breathe /briːð/ verb
to take air in through your nose or mouth and let it out again: *The room was so crowded I could hardly breathe.* | *"Is she still breathing?" asked Doctor May.*

breathe in
breathe in, breathe something in to take air in through your nose or mouth: *I tried not to **breathe in** the smoke.*
breathe out
to let air out through your nose or mouth: *Now **breathe out** slowly.*

breath·er /'briːðə $ 'briːðɚ/ noun informal a short rest: *Let's stop for a breather.*

breath·less /'breθləs/ adjective if you are breathless, you are finding it difficult to breathe normally

break /breɪk/ *verb* **broke** /brəʊk $ broʊk/ **broken** /ˈbrəʊkən $ ˈbroʊkən/

➤ BREAK, CUT, or TEAR?

BREAK you **break** something made of a hard material such as glass, wood etc. When things **break**, they make a loud noise.

CUT you **cut** something using a knife or scissors.

TEAR you **tear** something using your hands.

I dropped the plate and it **broke** *into pieces.*

I **cut** *the paper into squares.*

I **tore** *the letter into pieces.*

⇨ *see also* SMASH, BURST

BREAK

❶ to be damaged
if something breaks, or if you break it, it separates into pieces because it has been damaged: *She accidentally dropped the bowl and* **broke** *it.* | *The chair* **broke** *when he sat on it.* | *If you leave your watch there, it'll* **get broken**. | *He fell off his bike and* **broke** *his arm.* | *A branch had* **broken off** *the tree.*

break

❸ to disobey a law or rule
You are **breaking the law.** | *He* **broke the rules** *by touching the ball with his hand.*

❷ to stop working properly
if you break a machine, or if it breaks, it no longer works properly: *He* **broke** *the washing machine by putting too many clothes in it.*

PHRASES

break a record
to do something faster or better than anyone has ever done it before: *Linford **broke the** 100 metres **record**.*

break the news
to tell someone about something bad that has happened: *How are we going to **break the news** to Mum?*

break someone's heart
to make someone very unhappy: *He **broke my heart** when he left me.*

break your promise
if you break your promise, you do not do what you promised to do: *You've **broken your promise** again!*

break loose, break free *written*
to escape: *He managed to **break free** of his attacker.*

PHRASAL VERBS

break down
1 if a car or a machine breaks down, it stops working: *The car **broke down** on the way home.*

2 if someone breaks down, they start crying: *He **broke down** in tears.*

*He **broke down** in tears.*

break in
to use force to get into a building: *Burglars **broke in** last night and took everything.*

break into
to use force to get into a building: *Someone **broke into** our house and stole the TV.*

*Someone **broke into** our house and stole the TV.*

break out
if a disease, fire, war etc breaks out, it starts: *A fire had **broken out** in the school.*

break through
to use force to get through something that is stopping you from moving forward: *The crowd **broke through** the police barriers.*

*The crowd **broke through** the police barriers.*

break up
1 to separate something into many pieces: ***Break** the chocolate **up** into pieces.*

2 to end a relationship with a husband, wife, BOYFRIEND etc: *She and her boyfriend **broke up** last week. | I've **broken up** with Gary.*

B

breath·tak·ing /'breθ,teɪkɪŋ/ *adjective* very beautiful, exciting, or surprising: *a breathtaking view of the Grand Canyon*

bred the past tense and past participle of BREED[1]

breed[1] /briːd/ *verb, past tense and past participle* **bred** /bred/ **1** if animals breed, they have babies **2** if you breed animals, you keep them in order to produce young ones

breed[2] *noun* a particular type of dog, horse etc

breeze /briːz/ *noun* a light gentle wind

breez·y /'briːzi/ *adjective* **breezier, breeziest** with quite a strong wind: *a warm but rather breezy day*

brew[1] /bruː/ *verb* **1** if something bad is brewing, it will happen soon: *I could see that there was trouble brewing.* **2** to make beer

brew·er·y /'bruːəri/ *noun, plural* **breweries** a place where beer is made, or a company that makes beer

bribe[1] /braɪb/ *noun* money that someone gives to a person in an official position to persuade them to do something dishonest

bribe[2] *verb* to pay money to someone to persuade them to help you by doing something dishonest: *He was sent to prison for trying to bribe the judge.*

brib·er·y /'braɪbəri/ *noun [no plural]* when someone offers or accepts bribes

brick /brɪk/ *noun* a hard block of baked clay used for building

brid·al /'braɪdl/ *adjective* connected to a bride or a wedding: *a bridal shop*

bride /braɪd/ *noun* a woman who is getting married

bride·groom /'braɪdgruːm/ *noun* a man who is getting married

brides·maid /'braɪdzmeɪd/ *noun* a woman or girl who helps a BRIDE at her wedding

bridge /brɪdʒ/ *noun*
a special road that is built over a river or a busy road so that people or vehicles can cross the river or busy road: *They are building a new bridge over the river.* ⇨ *see picture on page 348*

brief /briːf/ *adjective written*
1 continuing for only a short time: *There was a brief silence.* **2** using only a few words: *She gave the police a brief description of the man.* | *There isn't much time, so I'll be brief.*
– **briefly** *adverb*: *He told us briefly what had happened.*

brief·case /'briːfkeɪs/ *noun* a thin flat case that you use to carry papers or books to work or college

briefs /briːfs/ *plural noun* underwear that you wear between your waist and the top of your legs: *a pair of cotton briefs*

bri·gade /brɪ'geɪd/ *noun* a large group of soldiers who are part of an army

bright /braɪt/ *adjective*
1 something that is bright shines a lot or has a lot of light: *the bright flames of the candles* | *a nice bright room*
2 bright colours are strong and not dark: *a bunch of bright yellow flowers*
3 intelligent: *Maria is one of the brightest students in the school.*
– **brightness** *noun [no plural]*

bright·en /'braɪtn/ also **brighten up** *verb* to become brighter or happier and more cheerful: *I put some flowers in the room to brighten it up.* | *The weather brightened up in the afternoon.* | *Kate brightened up a bit when Tim arrived.*

bril·liant /'brɪljənt/ *adjective* **1** very bright: *brilliant yellows and reds* **2** very intelligent or skilful: *a brilliant mathematician* **3** *BrE spoken* very good or enjoyable: *We had a brilliant time!*
– **brilliantly** *adverb*: *brilliantly coloured flowers* | *a brilliantly sunny day*

brim[1] /brɪm/ *noun* **1** the bottom part of a hat that turns out **2** be full to the brim to be as full as possible: *The club was absolutely full to the brim.*

brim[2] *verb* **brimmed, brimming** **1** be brimming with confidence, be brimming with excitement to be very confident or very excited: *The children were brimming with confidence.* **2** brim over if a bowl or cup brims over, it is so full that liquid is coming out

bring ⇨ *see box on next page*

brink /brɪŋk/ *noun* be on the brink of something if you are on the brink of something exciting or terrible, it will happen soon: *The country is on the brink of war.*

B

➤ VERB FORMS

BRING use **bring** when someone has something with them when they come to the place where you are: *Elena **brought** some photographs to show us.* | *Will everyone please **bring** a packed lunch on Thursday.*

TAKE use **take** when you have something with you when you go to a place: *Are you **taking** your camera to Ben's party?* | *I **took** some cakes to class on my birthday.*

BRING

❶ to have something with you when you arrive at a place
*Don't forget to **bring** your camera.* | *Her dad **brought** her back a present from France.* | *She had **brought** a friend **with** her.* | *Could you **bring** me an ashtray please?*

> **GRAMMAR**
> bring someone something
> bring someone with someone
> bring something to a place

❸ to move something somewhere *written*
*She **brought out** a newspaper from her bag.* | *We **brought** the box from the upstairs bedroom.*

> **GRAMMAR**
> bring something out/down/up etc

bring

❷ to make something happen or cause a particular result
*New technology **brings** new problems.* | *The death of her son **brought** her **to** the edge of despair.*

> **GRAMMAR**
> bring someone to something

PHRASAL VERBS

bring back
1 to start using something again that was used in the past: *They should **bring back** the old system.* | *a vote on whether to **bring** the death penalty **back***

2 to make someone remember something: *That song **brought back** some happy memories for me.* | *Talking about it just **brings** it all **back** again.*

bring down
to reduce the number or amount of something: *Doctors want to **bring down** the number of deaths from this disease.* | *Competition has **brought** the price of mobile phones **down**.*

bring forward
to arrange for something to happen at an earlier time than you originally planned: *The match has been **brought forward** to Wednesday.*

bring up
1 **bring someone up** to care for children until they are adults: *She was **brought up** by her grandmother.* | *It's not easy **bringing** kids **up** on your own.*

2 **bring something up** to start to talk about something: *He wasn't sure how to **bring up** the subject.* | *Did you have to **bring** that **up** right now?*

brisk /brɪsk/ adjective quick and determined: *She walked at a brisk pace.*

bris·tle[1] /'brɪsəl/ noun one of many short stiff hairs, wires etc growing or placed together: *the bristles on a toothbrush*

Brit·ish[1] /'brɪtɪʃ/ adjective from or connected with Great Britain

British[2] plural noun the British the people of Great Britain

Brit·on /'brɪtn/ noun someone from Great Britain

brit·tle /'brɪtl/ adjective hard and easily broken: *The wood was dry and brittle.*

broach /brəʊtʃ $ broʊtʃ/ verb broach a subject to mention a subject that may be embarrassing or unpleasant: *Parents often find it hard to broach the subject of sex.*

broad /brɔːd/ adjective

1 wide ⇨ opposite NARROW[1]: *He had a broad smile on his face.* | *a long, broad river*

2 including many different things or people: *The university offers a broad range of subjects.*

3 concerning the main ideas or parts of something, rather than the small details: *I support the broad aims of the group.*

broad·cast[1] /'brɔːdkɑːst $ 'brɔdkæst/ noun a programme on radio or television: *a live broadcast of the concert*

broadcast[2] verb broadcast to send out a radio or television programme
– **broadcaster** noun

broad·en /'brɔːdn/ verb 1 to make something include more kinds of things or people: *The course will broaden your knowledge of computers.* 2 also **broaden out** to become wider: *The river broadens out here.*

broad·ly /'brɔːdli/ adverb in a general way: *I broadly agree with what you are saying.*

broad·mind·ed /ˌbrɔːd'maɪndɪd/ adjective willing to accept behaviour or ideas that are different from your own

broc·co·li /'brɒkəli $ 'brɑkəli/ noun [no plural] a thick green vegetable with green or purple flowers that you cook ⇨ see picture on page 345

bro·chure /'brəʊʃə $ broʊ'ʃʊr/ noun a thin book that gives information or advertises something: *a holiday brochure*

broke[1] /brəʊk $ broʊk/ adjective informal if you are broke, you have no money at all

broke[2] the past tense of BREAK[1]

bro·ken[1] /'brəʊkən $ 'broʊkən/ adjective **broken**

1 something that is broken is damaged or in pieces because it has been dropped etc: *a broken window* | *Their best player now has a broken leg.*

2 a machine or piece of equipment that is broken does not work: *a broken TV set*

broken[2] the past participle of BREAK[1]

broken-heart·ed /ˌ.. '../ adjective very sad, especially because someone you love has died or left you

bro·ker /'brəʊkə $ 'broʊkɚ/ noun someone whose job is to buy and sell property, insurance etc for other people

bronze /brɒnz $ brɑnz/ noun [no plural] a metal that is a mixture of COPPER and TIN

brooch /brəʊtʃ $ broʊtʃ/ noun, plural **brooches** a piece of jewellery that you fasten to your clothes with a pin ⇨ see picture at JEWELLERY

brood /bruːd/ verb to think about something angrily or sadly for a long time

broom /bruːm/ noun a brush with a long handle that you use for sweeping floors ⇨ see picture at BRUSH[1], SWEEP[1]

broth·el /'brɒθəl $ 'brɑθəl/ noun a house where men pay to have sex with women

broth·er /'brʌðə $ 'brʌðɚ/ noun
a boy or man who has the same parents as you: *This is my brother Dave.* | *She has two **older brothers**.* | *My **big brother** (=older brother) is coming home from America.* | *My **little brother** (=younger brother) is very annoying.*

brother-in-law /'.. . ,./ noun 1 the brother of your husband or wife 2 the husband of your sister

brought the past tense and past participle of BRING

brow /braʊ/ noun written your FOREHEAD

brown /braʊn/ *adjective*
something that is brown is the colour of chocolate or wood: *He had light brown hair.*
– **brown** *noun*

browse /braʊz/ *verb* **1** to spend time looking at things in a shop without buying anything and without hurrying **2** to look through a book or magazine without reading it carefully **3** browse the Internet, browse the Web to look for information on the INTERNET: *I couldn't find what I wanted on the library shelves, so I browsed the Web.*

brows·er /'braʊzə $ 'braʊzər/ *noun* computer SOFTWARE that you use to look at information on the INTERNET

bruise¹ /bruːz/ *noun* a dark mark on your skin where you have hurt yourself: *She had a nasty bruise on her face.*

bruise² *verb* to cause a bruise on someone's skin: *He fell and bruised his leg.*

bru·nette /bruː'net/ *noun* a woman who has dark brown hair

brunt /brʌnt/ *noun* **bear the brunt of something** to suffer the worst part of something unpleasant: *The south coast bore the brunt of the storm.*

brushes

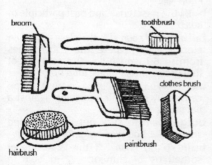

broom
toothbrush
clothes brush
paintbrush
hairbrush

brush¹ /brʌʃ/ *noun, plural* **brushes**
a thing that you use for cleaning, painting etc, consisting of hairs fastened onto a handle: *a paint brush | a brush and comb*

brush² *verb*

1 to clean or tidy something with a brush: *She brushed her hair.*
2 to remove something by moving a brush or your hand across a surface: *He brushed the mud off his boots. | She brushed away her tears.*
3 to touch someone or something lightly as you go past them: *She felt something brush her leg. | His coat brushed against her arm.*

brush up
brush up on something to try to reach again the level of skill or knowledge that you had in the past: *I must brush up on my English before our British visitors come.*

brus·sels sprout /ˌbrʌsəlz 'spraʊt/ *noun* a small round green vegetable ⇨ *see picture on page 345*

bru·tal /'bruːtl/ *adjective* very cruel and violent: *a brutal murder*
– **brutally** *adverb*: *She was brutally murdered.*

brute¹ /bruːt/ *noun* **1** a cruel violent man **2** a large strong animal

brute² *adjective* **brute force, brute strength** physical strength: *He uses brute force to get what he wants.*

BSc /ˌbiː es 'siː/ *BrE*, **B.S.** /ˌbiː 'es/ *AmE*, *noun* Bachelor of Science; a university degree in a science subject

bub·ble¹ /'bʌbəl/ *noun* a ball of air in a liquid: *The bubbles rise to the surface as the water boils.*

bubble² *verb* if a liquid bubbles, it produces bubbles, especially when it boils: *When the water bubbles, put in the pasta.*

bub·bly /'bʌbli/ *adjective* **1** full of bubbles **2** cheerful and full of energy: *a bright, bubbly girl*

buck /bʌk/ *noun AmE spoken* a dollar: *It cost me 50 bucks.*

buck·et /'bʌkɪt/ *noun* a large round container, used for carrying liquids

buck·le¹ /'bʌkəl/ *verb* **1** also **buckle up** to fasten something with a buckle: *He buckled his belt.* **2** if your knees buckle, they become weak and you fall down **3** if metal buckles, it bends because of heat or pressure

buckle² *noun* a thing made of metal used for fastening a belt, shoe, bag etc

bud /bʌd/ noun a young flower or leaf before it opens

Bud·dhis·m /'bʊdɪzəm $ 'bʊdɪzəm/ noun [no plural] a very old religion that started in Asia, which teaches people to want fewer things so that they can be happy

Bud·dhist /'bʊdɪst $ 'bʊdɪst/ noun someone whose religion is Buddhism

bud·dy /'bʌdi/ noun informal, plural **buddies** a friend

budge /bʌdʒ/ verb informal to move: I pushed on the door but it wouldn't budge.

bud·get¹ /'bʌdʒɪt/ noun an amount of money that is available, or a careful plan of how to spend an amount of money: We had a budget of £150 for the party.

budget² verb to carefully plan and control how you will spend your money: Have you budgeted for a holiday this year?

budget³ adjective very low in price: budget air tickets

buf·fa·lo /'bʌfələʊ $ 'bʌfəloʊ/ noun, plural **buffalos**, **buffaloes** or **buffalo**
1 an animal that looks like a cow with very long horns that lives in Africa or Asia
2 a BISON ⇨ see picture on page 339

buf·fet /'bʊfeɪ $ bə'feɪ/ noun a meal in which people take food that is on a table and then move away to eat

bug¹ /bʌg/ noun 1 informal a small insect 2 informal a very small living thing that gets into your body and makes you ill: We've all been ill with this horrible flu bug. 3 a small mistake in a computer PROGRAM that stops it from working correctly 4 a small piece of electronic equipment for listening to people secretly

bug² verb **bugged, bugging** 1 to use electronic equipment to listen to people secretly: Someone had bugged my telephone. 2 spoken to annoy someone: Go away, you're bugging me.

bug·gy /'bʌgi/ noun, plural **buggies** a light folding chair on wheels that you push small children in; STROLLER AmE

build¹ /bɪld/ verb, past tense and past participle **built** /bɪlt/

to make something large and strong such as a building, road, bridge etc, using special materials: They are going to build a hotel near the beach. | When was this house built?

PHRASAL VERBS

build on
build on something if you build on something, you use it to make more progress or be more successful: The students will **build on** the writing skills they learned last year.

build up
build something up, build up if you build something up, or if it builds up, it gradually becomes bigger: He **has built up** a large collection of model cars. | The amount of work I had to do each week seemed to **build up**.

build² noun [no plural] the shape and size of someone's body: He is tall with a heavy build.

build·er /'bɪldə $ 'bɪldɚ/ noun a person or a company that builds and repairs buildings

build·ing /'bɪldɪŋ/ noun
a place such as a house that has a roof and walls: The science laboratory is in this building.

building so·ci·e·ty /'.. .,.../ noun BrE an organization similar to a bank, where you can save money or borrow money to buy a house; SAVINGS AND LOAN ASSOCIATION AmE

built the past tense and past participle of BUILD¹

bulb /bʌlb/ noun 1 the glass part of an electric light, where the light shines from: a 60 watt bulb 2 a round root that grows into a plant: tulip bulbs

bulge¹ /bʌldʒ/ noun a curved shape caused by something pushing against a flat surface

bulge² verb to stick out in a rounded shape: Her bag was bulging.

bulk /bʌlk/ noun 1 the large size of something or someone 2 in bulk in large quantities: We buy all our food in bulk.

bulk·y /'bʌlki/ adjective big and difficult to move

bull /bʊl/ noun a male cow, or the male of some other large animals such as an ELEPHANT

bull·doz·er /'bʊldəʊzə $ 'bʊl,doʊzɚ/ noun a large powerful vehicle that can push over buildings and move rocks

bul·let /'bʊlɪt/ noun a small piece of metal that is fired from a gun

bul·le·tin /'bʊlətɪn/ *noun* a short news report

bulletin board /'... ,./ *noun* **1** a board on a wall where you can put information for people to see **2** a place on a computer system where a group of people can leave and read messages

bul·ly¹ /'bʊli/ *verb* bullied, bullies to frighten or threaten to hurt someone who is smaller or weaker than you

bully² *noun, plural* bullies someone who frightens or threatens to hurt people who are smaller or weaker than them

bum /bʌm/ *noun informal* **1** *BrE* the part of your body that you sit on **2** *AmE* someone who has no home or job

bump¹ /bʌmp/ *verb* **1** to hit or knock against something, especially by accident: *I fell and bumped my head.* | *He nearly bumped into the door.* **2 bump into** to meet someone when you were not expecting to: *Oh, I bumped into Martha this morning.*

bump² *noun* **1** a small raised area on a surface **2** a sudden movement in which one thing hits against another thing: *Sorry, Dad, I had a little bump in the car last night.*

bump·er /'bʌmpə $ 'bʌmpɚ/ *noun* the part across the front and back of a car that protects it if it hits anything ⇨ see *picture at* CAR

bumpy   flat

bump·y /'bʌmpi/ *adjective* bumpier, bumpiest a bumpy surface has a lot of raised parts on it: *The road was narrow and very bumpy.*

bun /bʌn/ *noun* **1** *BrE* a small round sweet cake **2** bread that is made in a small round shape: *hamburger buns* **3** a way of arranging long hair by fastening it on top of your head in a small round shape

bunch¹ /bʌntʃ/ *noun, plural* bunches

GRAMMAR
a bunch of things

1 a group of similar things that are fastened together: *He gave her a* **bunch of** *flowers.* | *I bought two* **bunches of** *bananas.*

2 *informal* a group of people: *I invited a* **bunch of** *friends round.* | *They're an odd bunch.*

3 *AmE informal* a large number of things or amount of something: *We visited a whole* **bunch of** *places.*

bun·dle¹ /'bʌndl/ *noun* a group of things that are fastened or tied together: *a bundle of old clothes*

bundle² *verb* **1** to move someone or something quickly and roughly into a place: *They bundled him out of the room.* **2 bundle something up** to tie things into a bundle

bung /bʌŋ/ *verb BrE informal* to put something somewhere: *Just bung your coat on the chair.*

bun·ga·low /'bʌŋgələʊ $ 'bʌŋgə,loʊ/ *noun* a house that has only one level and no stairs ⇨ see *picture on page 343*

bunk /bʌŋk/ *noun* **1** a bed on a train or ship **2 bunk beds** two beds arranged so that one is above the other

bun·ker /'bʌŋkə $ 'bʌŋkɚ/ *noun* a strongly built room or building where people can shelter from bombs

buoy /bɔɪ $ 'buːi/ *noun* an object that floats on the water to show ships which areas are safe and which areas are dangerous

bur·den /'bɜːdn $ 'bɚdn/ *noun formal* something difficult or worrying that you have to deal with: *the financial burden involved in sending your children to college*

bu·reau /'bjʊərəʊ $ 'bjʊroʊ/ *noun, plural* bureaux *or* bureaus **1** an office, department, or organization: *the Federal Bureau of Investigation* **2** *AmE* a piece of furniture with drawers, used for keeping clothes in

bu·reauc·ra·cy /bjʊəˈrɒkrəsi $ bjʊ-ˈrɑkrəsi/ *noun* an official system that annoys and confuses people because it has too many rules

bu·reau·crat /'bjʊərəkræt $ 'bjʊrə-,kræt/ *noun* a person who works for a government organization and who uses the rules in a way that annoys people

bu·reau·crat·ic /ˌbjʊərəˈkrætɪk $ ˌbjʊrəˈkrætɪk/ *adjective* involving or using too many rules

burg·er /ˈbɜːɡə $ ˈbɝɡɚ/ *noun* meat that has been pressed into a round flat shape and cooked ⇨ *same meaning* HAMBURGER

bur·glar /ˈbɜːɡlə $ ˈbɝɡlɚ/ *noun* someone who goes into buildings in order to steal things

bur·glar·ize /ˈbɜːɡləraɪz $ ˈbɝɡləˌraɪz/ the American word for BURGLE

bur·glar·y /ˈbɜːɡləri $ ˈbɝɡləri/ *noun*, *plural* **burglaries** the crime of going into a building to steal things

bur·gle /ˈbɜːɡəl $ ˈbɝɡəl/ *BrE*, **burglarize** *AmE*, *verb* to go into a place and steal things

bur·i·al /ˈberiəl/ *noun* when a dead body is put into the ground

burn¹ /bɜːn $ bɝn/ *verb*, *past tense and past participle* **burned** or **burnt** /bɜːnt $ bɝnt/

GRAMMAR
burn something on/in something

1 if you burn something, or if it burns, it is damaged by fire or heat: *She burned the letter.* | *I burned my hand on the hot pan.* | *These dry sticks should burn well.*

2 if a fire burns, it produces heat and flames

3 if a part of your body is burning, it hurts and feels very hot: *Her sore throat was burning.*

PHRASAL VERB
burn down
burn down if a building burns down, it is destroyed by fire: *The old house burned down a long time ago.*

burn² *noun* an injury to your skin caused by fire or heat

burnt¹ a past tense and past participle of BURN¹

burnt² *adjective* damaged or hurt by burning: *The meat was dry and burnt.*

burp /bɜːp $ bɝp/ *verb informal* to let air come out noisily from your stomach ⇨ *same meaning* BELCH
– **burp** *noun*

bur·row¹ /ˈbʌrəʊ $ ˈbɝoʊ/ *verb* to make a hole in the ground by digging: *Rabbits had burrowed under the fence.*

burrow² *noun* a hole in the ground made by an animal such as a rabbit

burst¹ /bɜːst $ bɝst/ *verb*

1 if something bursts, or if you burst it, it breaks open suddenly and something such as air or water comes out of it: *A water pipe had burst upstairs and water was coming through the ceiling.* | *I burst the balloon with a pin.*

2 to move suddenly, with a lot of energy or violence: *The door burst open and four men ran in.* | *A woman on a horse burst out of the woods.* | *The class had already started when Sheila burst in late.*

PHRASES
be bursting with energy to have a lot of energy: *The kids are always bursting with energy.*

burst into tears, **burst into flames** to suddenly start to cry or burn: *She put her head on his shoulder and burst into tears.*

burst out laughing, **burst out crying** to suddenly start to laugh or cry: *Everyone in the room burst out laughing, even the teachers.*

burst² *noun* a short sudden period of activity or noise: *a burst of gunfire*

burst³ *adjective* broken or torn apart: *a burst pipe*

bur·y /ˈberi/ *verb* **buried**, **buries**

GRAMMAR
bury someone/something somewhere

1 to put a dead body into a GRAVE (=a hole that has been dug in the ground for this purpose): *We buried my brother in a small country churchyard.* | *We visited the grave where Bob Marley is buried.*

2 to cover something so that no one can see it: *The wall collapsed, burying him under a pile of bricks.* | *We found the treasure buried underground.*

PHRASE
bury your face in something, **bury your head in something** to hide your face by pressing it into something, usually because you are upset: *She buried her face in her hands and began to cry.*

bus /bʌs/ noun, plural **buses**

GRAMMAR
by bus

a large vehicle that people pay to travel on. You can catch a bus, or go somewhere by bus: *I usually catch a bus to college.* | *We went to the nightclub by bus.* | *We missed the bus* (=we were too late, so it went without us). | *a London bus driver* (=someone whose job is to drive a bus) ⇨ *see picture on page 349*

bush /bʊʃ/ noun, plural **bushes**
1 a plant like a small tree with a lot of branches: *a rose bush* ⇨ *see picture on page 348*
2 **the bush** areas of Australia and Africa that are still wild: *We got lost in the bush.*

bush·y /ˈbʊʃi/ adjective bushy hair or fur grows thickly

bus·i·ly /ˈbɪzəli/ adverb in a busy way: *chefs busily preparing dinner*

busi·ness /ˈbɪznəs/ noun
1 *[no plural]* making, buying, or selling things: *You need a lot of money to succeed in business.* | *The village shop is open for business again.*
2 *[no plural]* the amount of work a company is doing, or the amount of money it is making: *The local shops have lost business since the new supermarket opened.*
3 *plural* **businesses** an organization that produces or sells things: *James runs a publishing business.* | *a small family business*
4 *[no plural]* the work that you do as your job to earn money: *The next day, Tim went to Paris on business* (=as part of his job). | *Information on new products is always useful in my business.*

PHRASES
go out of business to close a company because it is not making enough money: *Many small firms went out of business last year.*
the film business, the music business etc all the companies and people that are involved in making films, music etc: *Richard Branson has made a lot of money from the music business.*

do business (with someone) if one company does business with another company, it buys things from the other company, or sells things to it: *Our firm has been doing business with Frank for years.*
mind your own business spoken used to tell someone in a rude way that something is private: *"Where are you going?" "Mind your own business!"*

busi·ness·like /ˈbɪznəs-laɪk/ adjective sensible and practical in the way you do things

busi·ness·man /ˈbɪznəsmən/ noun, plural **businessmen** /-mən/ a man who works at a high level in a company or who owns his own company

busi·ness·wom·an /ˈbɪznəs,wʊmən/ noun, plural **businesswomen** /-,wɪmɪn/ a woman who works at a high level in a company or who owns her own company

bus stop /ˈ. ./ noun a place at the side of a road where buses stop for passengers

bust[1] /bʌst/ verb informal, past tense and past participle **bust** or **busted** to break: *Someone's bust my ruler!*

bust[2] noun the measurement around a woman's breasts and back

bust[3] adjective informal **1 go bust** a business that goes bust has to close because it has lost so much money **2** broken: *This TV is bust.*

bus·tle[1] /ˈbʌsəl/ noun busy and noisy activity

bus·y /ˈbɪzi/ adjective **busier, busiest**
1 someone who is busy has a lot of things that they must do: *a busy mother of three small children* | *Dad was too busy with work to spend much time with us.* | *Our tutor keeps us busy in class.*
2 a busy time is a time when you have a lot of things that you must do: *Christmas is always the busiest time of year.* | *Have you had a busy day at work?*
3 full of people, vehicles etc: *We live on a very busy road.* | *It was busy in the city centre today.*
4 a telephone number that is busy is being used; ENGAGED BrE: *The line's busy; I'll ring back later.*

B

but¹ /bət; *strong* bʌt/

1 used when adding something different or surprising: *He's not much good at schoolwork but he is good at sport.* | *I was very tired, but I still enjoyed the party.*
2 used when giving the reason why something did not happen: *I'd like to go, but I've got to finish my homework.*

but² *preposition*

except: *Everyone but me went on the trip.*

butch·er /ˈbʊtʃə $ ˈbʊtʃɚ/ *noun*
1 someone who owns or works in a shop that sells meat 2 **butcher's** a shop that sells meat

butt /bʌt/ *noun* 1 the person that other people often make jokes about: *Why am I always the butt of their jokes?* 2 *AmE informal* your BOTTOM 3 the end of a cigarette after it has been smoked

but·ter¹ /ˈbʌtə $ ˈbʌtɚ/ *noun [no plural]*

a solid yellow food made from cream that you spread on bread or use in cooking: *Fry the onions in butter.* ⇨ *see picture on page 344*

butter² *verb* to put butter on something

but·ter·fly /ˈbʌtəflaɪ $ ˈbʌtɚˌflaɪ/ *noun, plural* **butterflies** an insect with large coloured wings

butterfly

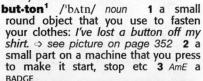

but·tocks /ˈbʌtəks/ *plural noun* the part of your body that you sit on

but·ton¹ /ˈbʌtn/ *noun* 1 a small round object that you use to fasten your clothes: *I've lost a button off my shirt.* ⇨ *see picture on page 352* 2 a small part on a machine that you press to make it start, stop etc 3 *AmE* BADGE

button² *verb* **button something up** to fasten something with buttons

but·ton·hole /ˈbʌtnhəʊl $ ˈbʌtnˌhoʊl/ *noun* a hole in a shirt, jacket etc that you push a button through to fasten it

buy /baɪ/ *verb* **bought** /bɔːt/

if you buy something, you give someone money and they give you the thing in return: *I **buy** my computer games **from** a shop in the high street.* | *Ken **bought** a box of chocolates **for** his girlfriend.* | *We **bought** the apartment **for** $460,000.* | *Can I buy you a drink?*

buyer /ˈbaɪə $ ˈbaɪɚ/ *noun* someone who wants to buy something from another person: *Have you found a buyer for your car yet?*

buzz¹ /bʌz/ *verb* to make a low steady noise like the sound an insect makes: *A fly was buzzing round the bedroom.* ⇨ *see picture on page 350*

buzz² *noun* a low steady noise like the sound an electric bell makes: *There was a buzz at the door.*

buz·zer /ˈbʌzə $ ˈbʌzɚ/ *noun* a piece of electrical equipment that makes a sudden sound to tell you that something has happened

by¹ /baɪ/ *preposition*

1 who or what does something: *She was bitten by a dog* (=a dog bit her). | *I was frightened by the sudden noise.* | *The room was heated by three electric fires.* | *a book by Jane Austen* (=a book that Jane Austen wrote)
2 next to something: *There's a garage by the side of the house.* | *I'll see you by the park gates at 9.* | *the house by the river* ⇨ *see picture on page 354*
3 saying which part of something you hold: *Always hold a knife by the handle, not the blade.* | *He grabbed me by the arm.*
4 saying the latest time when something must be done or finished: *You must finish this piece of homework by Friday.* | *We need to get to the airport by 6.*
5 showing how big a difference in amount something is: *We won by ten points* (=we had ten points more than the other team). | *Prices have increased by 4% this year.*

6 used when giving measurements: *The room was 12 foot by 10 foot* (=the room was 12 foot long and 10 foot wide).

PHRASES

by bus, by train, by car etc travelling in a bus, train etc: *Most of the children go to school by bus.*

by phone, by email etc using the telephone etc: *He contacted me by email.*

by cash, by credit card etc using money etc to pay for something: *We paid for the holiday by credit card.*

by yourself without anyone else: *Alec made supper for six of us all by himself* (=without help from anyone else). | *He lives by himself* (=alone).

by² *adverb*

moving past someone/something: *They watched the cars going by.*

bye /baɪ/ also **bye-bye** /. './ *spoken*

goodbye: *Bye Max! It was nice meeting you!*

byte /baɪt/ *noun* a unit for measuring the amount of information a computer can use: *There are one million bytes in one megabyte.*

B

Cc

C the written abbreviation of CELSIUS or CENTIGRADE

cab /kæb/ *noun* a car with a driver who you pay to take you somewhere ⇨ *same meaning* TAXI: *We took a cab to the airport.*

cab·bage /'kæbɪdʒ/ *noun* a large round vegetable with thick green leaves that you cook and eat ⇨ *see picture on page 345*

cab·in /'kæbɪn/ *noun* **1** a room on a ship where you sleep **2** the area inside a plane where the passengers or pilots sit

cab·i·net /'kæbənət/ *noun* **1** a piece of furniture with shelves or drawers, that you keep things in: *a filing cabinet* **2** the Cabinet a group of the most important members of the government

ca·ble /'keɪbəl/ *noun* **1** wires that carry electricity or telephone signals: *electricity cables* **2** CABLE TELEVISION

cable tel·e·vi·sion /ˌ.. '..../ also **cable TV** /ˌ.. .'./ or **cable** *noun* [no plural] a way of showing television programmes by sending signals through wires under the ground: *The hotel has cable TV. | The game was on cable.*

cac·tus /'kæktəs/ *noun, plural* **cacti** /-taɪ/ or **cactuses** a plant that grows in hot dry places and is covered with small sharp points

cactus

ca·fe or **café** /'kæfeɪ $ kæ'feɪ/ *noun* a small restaurant: *We had a cup of tea in the cafe.*

caf·e·te·ri·a /ˌkæfə'tɪəriə $ ˌkæfə-'tɪriə/ *noun* a restaurant where you collect your own food and take it to a table to eat it: *a self-service cafeteria*

caf·feine /'kæfiːn $ kæ'fin/ *noun* [no plural] the substance in coffee, tea, and some other drinks that makes people feel more awake

cage /keɪdʒ/ *noun* a box that you can keep birds or animals in, and which is made of metal bars or wires

cake /keɪk/ *noun* a sweet food that is made by mixing flour, butter, sugar, eggs etc together, and baking it: *a chocolate cake | Who wants a piece of cake?*

cal·ci·um /'kælsiəm/ *noun* [no plural] a substance that helps bones and teeth to grow strongly: *Milk contains a lot of calcium.*

cal·cu·late /'kælkjəleɪt/ *verb* to find out something by using numbers, for example how big something is: *Have you calculated what the cost will be?*

cal·cu·la·tion /ˌkælkjə'leɪʃən/ *noun* when you add, multiply, or divide numbers, for example to find out the answer to a sum: *I did a quick calculation in my head.*

cal·cu·la·tor /'kælkjəleɪtə $ 'kælkjəˌleɪtɚ/ also **pocket calculator** *noun* a small electronic machine that you use for adding, multiplying etc numbers

calculator

cal·en·dar /'kæləndə $ 'kæləndɚ/ *noun* a list that shows the days and months of a year

calf /kɑːf $ kæf/ *noun, plural* **calves** /kɑːvz $ kævz/ **1** a young cow **2** the back of your leg between your knee and foot: *She had strong calf muscles.*

call[1] ⇨ *see box on next page*

call[2] *noun*
1 a telephone conversation: *Could I*

C

1 to telephone someone
⇨ *same meaning* PHONE[2], RING[2]: *I called Sue at her office in London.* | *Someone call the police!* | *Call this number for careers advice.*

2 to give someone or something a name or title
If my baby's a boy, I'm going to call him William. | *I have a dog called Blackie.* | *What's the new Spice Girls album called?*

GRAMMAR
call someone/something something

call

3 to describe someone or something using a particular word or phrase
Critics have called his latest film a great success. | *Are you calling me a liar?*

4 also call out
to say something loudly because you want someone to hear you: *He called out in agony.* | *"I'll see you later," she called.*

PHRASAL VERBS

call at
if a train, bus etc calls at a place, it stops there to let passengers get on or off: *This train calls at all local stations.*

call back
to telephone someone, after they have telephoned you: *I'm just about to eat – can I call you back later?*

call off
to decide that a planned event will not happen: *The match was called off due to bad weather.* | *I don't know what he did, but she called the wedding off!*

call out
1 to shout something: *As the bus drove past, she waved and called out his name.* | *I heard Jimmy call out in pain*
2 to ask someone to come to a place to help you because something bad has happened: *Firefighters were called out to a fire in a factory.*

call up
to telephone someone: *I think you should call her up to thank her.* | *Call up a few builders and ask them how much it costs.*

use your phone to **make a call** please? | **Give** me **a call** later. | My job involves **taking calls** (=answering phone calls) *from members of the public*. | She will not **return** my **calls** (=telephone me back after I telephoned her).

2 a shout or cry: We could hear calls from behind the door.

call·er /'kɔːlə $ 'kɔlɚ/ noun someone who makes a telephone call: There was one caller but he didn't give me his name.

calm¹ /kɑːm/ adjective

1 relaxed and not worried, angry, or upset: I took a deep breath and tried to **keep calm**. | Gradually, she began to **feel calmer**.

2 if an area of water or the weather is calm, there is no wind: a calm sunny day

−**calmness** noun [no plural]: the calmness of the sea

calm² verb **calm down, calm someone down** to become quiet again instead of being angry, excited, or upset, or to make someone do this: She was very shocked and it took me a long time to calm her down.

calm·ly /'kɑːmli/ adverb

in a calm way that shows you are not upset, angry, or worried: Dad **took** the news very **calmly**. | Joe was very angry, but Liz smiled calmly.

cal·o·rie /'kæləri/ noun a unit that measures the amount of energy a particular food can produce: Don't eat high-calorie food if you're trying to lose weight.

calves the plural of CALF

cam·cor·der /'kæm,kɔːdə $ 'kæm,kɔrdɚ/ noun a camera that you can carry with you and use for recording moving pictures and sound

camcorder

came the past tense of COME

cam·el /'kæməl/ noun a large animal that lives in the desert and is used for

carrying people and things ⇨ see picture on page 339

cam·e·ra /'kæmərə/ noun a piece of equipment that you use for taking photographs or making films ⇨ see picture on page 342

cam·e·ra·man /'kæmərəmæn/ noun, plural cameramen /-men/ someone whose job is to use the camera when people are making a film or television programme

camouflage

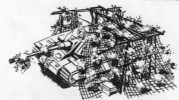

cam·ou·flage /'kæməflɑːʒ/ noun [no plural] clothes or colours that hide people, animals, or things by making them look the same as the things around them: All the soldiers were in camouflage.

−**camouflage** verb: The zebra is camouflaged by its stripes.

camp¹ /kæmp/ noun 1 a place where children go to stay for a short time and do special activities: The kids all go to summer camp in the vacation. 2 an area of land where people sleep in tents

camp² verb to put up a tent and sleep in it, especially when you are travelling somewhere: That night we camped in the forest.

cam·paign¹ /kæm'peɪn/ noun a number of things that people do in order to get a particular result, especially people in business or government: an anti-drugs campaign

campaign² verb to do things to try to achieve a particular result, especially in politics: She campaigned for nuclear disarmament.

−**campaigner** noun: a human rights campaigner

camp·ing /'kæmpɪŋ/ noun [no plural] the activity of sleeping in a tent, especially for a holiday: We went camping in France in the summer.

camp·site /'kæmpsaɪt/ BrE, **campground** /'kæmpgraʊnd/ AmE, noun a piece of land where you can stay in a tent

cam·pus /'kæmpəs/ noun, plural campuses an area of land where the main buildings of a university or college are: the campus at Atlanta University

can¹ /kən; strong kæn/ modal verb, negative cannot or can't

1 being able to do something **1)** use **can** to talk about ability in the present: Pete can speak Spanish well. | Can you swim? | I can't run any faster. **2)** use **could** to talk about ability in the past: I woke up in hospital and couldn't move. **3)** use **be able to** to talk about ability in the future: The new computers will be able to recognise your voice.

2 likely to be possible or true **1)** use **can** to talk about possibility in the present: Too much fat can be bad for you. | If a doctor makes a mistake, it can have terrible results. | She's married? That can't be true! **2)** use **could** to talk about possibility in the past or the future: This time next week we could be in France. | I could have been rich if I'd married Sam.

3 asking or giving permission **1)** use **can** to talk about permission in the present: Can Sally stay the night with us? | All citizens who are over 18 can vote. | I'm sorry, you cannot leave your bag there. **2)** use **be allowed to** to talk about permission on one particular occasion in the past: We were not allowed to leave until we'd finished our work.

4 asking for something: Can I have another slice of cake? | Can my boyfriend use the computer tomorrow? | Can you take me home?

5 offering to do something: Can I help you?

6 feeling or knowing something use **can** with verbs such as 'see', 'hear', 'feel', 'think', and 'believe' to say what you feel: I cannot understand why Julie doesn't like me. | I can't believe you've never watched 'The X Files'! | Can you smell gas?

can² /kæn/ noun a metal container containing food or drink: a can of cola ⇨ see picture at CONTAINER

ca·nal /kə'næl/ noun a long narrow area of water that has been cut into a piece of

land so that boats can travel along it: Venice is famous for its canals.

can·cel /'kænsəl/ verb cancelled, cancelling BrE, canceled canceling AmE if you cancel an event, meeting etc, you say that it will not happen: We had to cancel the picnic because of the bad weather.

can·cel·la·tion /ˌkænsə'leɪʃən/ noun when someone decides that they will not do something they were going to do, or that a planned event will not happen: airport delays and flight cancellations

can·cer /'kænsə $ 'kænsər/ noun a very serious illness in which cells in some parts of the body grow in a way that is not normal: He died of lung cancer.

can·di·date /'kændədət $ 'kændəˌdeɪt/ noun **1** someone who tries to get a political position or a particular job: the Republican party's candidate for president **2** BrE someone who takes an examination: Candidates should write their names at the top.

can·dle /'kændl/ noun a long piece of WAX with a piece of string through the middle, which you burn to use as a light

can·dle·stick /'kændlˌstɪk/ noun an object that you put a candle in so that it stands up

can·dy /'kændi/ noun, plural candies the American word for a SWEET

cane /keɪn/ noun **1** a long thin stick that people use to help them walk or to hit someone **2** the long hard stem of some plants that people use, for example to make furniture: cane furniture

can·na·bis /'kænəbɪs/ noun [no plural] an illegal drug that some people smoke

canned /kænd/ adjective canned food is in a special metal container called a can ⇨ same meaning TINNED BrE: canned pears

can·non /'kænən/ noun a large gun, usually on wheels, that was used in battles in the past

can·not /'kænɒt $ 'kænɑt/ the negative of CAN¹

ca·noe /kə'nuː/ noun a long narrow boat for one or two people that you push through the water using a short flat piece of wood called an OAR ⇨ see picture on page 349

ca·noe·ing /kə'nuːɪŋ/ noun [no plural] the sport or activity of using a canoe: We could go canoeing this weekend.

can o·pen·er /'. ˌ.../ *noun* a tool for opening cans of food

can't /kɑːnt $ kænt/ the short form of CANNOT: *I'm sorry I can't come to your party.*

can·teen /kæn'tiːn/ *noun* a place where the people who work in a school, factory, or office go to eat: *the staff canteen*

can·vas /'kænvəs/ *noun* **1** [no plural] a type of strong cloth that is used to make tents, bags etc **2** a piece of canvas on which a picture is painted

can·vass /'kænvəs/ *verb* to try to persuade people to vote for your political party in an election: *Someone came to the house canvassing for the Labour Party.*

can·yon /'kænjən/ *noun* a deep narrow valley with steep sides: *the Grand Canyon*

cap /kæp/ *noun*

1 a soft hat with a curved part at the front: *a Red Sox baseball cap* ⇨ see picture on page 352
2 something that covers the end or top of something, and stops other things from getting in it: *I can't get the fuel cap off my car.* ⇨ see picture at CAR

ca·pa·ble /'keɪpəbəl/ *adjective* **1** if you are capable of doing something, you are able to do it because you have the right skills or knowledge ⇨ opposite IN-CAPABLE: *Our team is certainly capable of winning.* **2** a capable worker is skilful and good at their job: *He's a very capable teacher.*

ca·pac·i·ty /kə'pæsəti/ *noun* the amount that something can contain: *The theatre has a capacity of 500.*

cap·i·tal /'kæpətl/ *noun*

GRAMMAR
the capital of a country or state
1 the most important city in a country, where the government and other big organizations are: *London is the capital of England.*
2 also **capital letter** the large form of a letter of the alphabet, that you use at the beginning of a name or sentence: *The days of the week always begin with a capital letter.*

USAGE
Use **capital letters** for the names of people, places, and special dates in the year: *Richard Wright | Paris, France | Christmas.* Use them for the days of the week and the months of the year: *Monday, the 25th April.* Write words like French, Italian, Russian etc with a capital letter. Write spring, summer, autumn, and winter with a small letter.

cap·i·tal·is·m /'kæpətl-ɪzəm/ *noun* [no plural] an economic system in which businesses and industry are owned by private owners and not by the government

capital pun·ish·ment /ˌ... '.../ *noun* [no plural] when people are killed as an official punishment for a serious crime

capsize

cap·size /kæp'saɪz $ 'kæpsaɪz/ *verb* if a boat capsizes, or if you capsize it, it turns over in the water

captain¹ /'kæptən/ *noun* **1** someone who leads a team or group: *the captain of the football team* **2** the most important person working on a ship or plane **3** an officer in the army or NAVY

captain² *verb* to be the captain of a team or group: *She captained the school's hockey team.*

cap·tion /'kæpʃən/ *noun* a few words that are written under a photograph or drawing to explain what or who it is

cap·tive /'kæptɪv/ *noun written* someone who is kept as a prisoner: *The captives were released after six hours.*

cap·tiv·i·ty /kæp'tɪvəti/ *noun* [no plural] when a person or animal is not free: *It's sad to see beautiful wild animals in captivity.*

capture /'kæptʃə $ 'kæptʃɚ/ *verb* **1** to catch a person or animal and to keep them somewhere as a prisoner: *Murray was captured in Italy, two days after his escape from a British gaol.* **2** *written* to get control of a place during a war: *The* *army has captured many towns and villages from the rebels.*

car

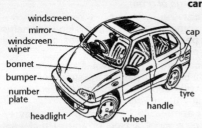

- windscreen
- mirror
- windscreen wiper
- bonnet
- bumper
- number plate
- headlight
- cap
- tyre
- handle
- wheel

car /kɑː $ kɑr/ *noun*

GRAMMAR
by car

1 a vehicle with four wheels and an engine, that carries a small number of people: *We decided to travel by car* (=in a car). | *I parked my car outside the house.* ⇨ *see picture on page 349*
2 one of the separate carriages on a train: *the dining car*

car·at also **karat** *AmE* /'kærət/ *noun* a unit for measuring how pure gold is, or how heavy jewels are: *an eighteen carat gold ring*

car·a·van /'kærəvæn/ *noun BrE* a vehicle that can be pulled by a car, and that you can cook and sleep in when you are on holiday ⇨ *see picture on page 349*

car·bo·hy·drate /ˌkɑːbəʊ'haɪdreɪt $ ˌkɑrboʊ'haɪdreɪt/ *noun* a substance in some foods that gives your body energy: *Bread and rice contain a lot of carbohydrates.*

car·bon /'kɑːbən $ 'kɑrbən/ *noun [no plural]* a chemical ELEMENT that is found in coal and petrol

carbon di·ox·ide /ˌkɑːbən daɪ'ɒksaɪd $ ˌkɑrbən daɪ'ɑksaɪd/ *noun [no plural]* the gas that people and animals produce when they breathe out

card /kɑːd $ kɑrd/ *noun*

1 a small piece of plastic or thick paper with information written on it: *Here's my business card* (=a card showing your name and the place you work for). | *I paid by credit card.*
2 a piece of thick folded paper with a picture on the front and a message inside that you send to people on their birthday, at Christmas etc: *a Christmas card*
3 one of a set of small pieces of thick paper with pictures or numbers on them, that you use to play games
4 **cards** a game that you play using a set of cards: *Do you want to play cards?* | *a game of cards*

card·board /'kɑːdbɔːd $ 'kɑrdbɔrd/ *noun [no plural]* very stiff thick paper, used especially for making boxes

car·di·gan /'kɑːdɪgən $ 'kɑrdɪgən/ *noun* a piece of clothing that you wear on the top half of your body, and that you fasten down the front with buttons ⇨ *see picture on page 352*

care¹ /keə $ ker/ *verb*

GRAMMAR
care about someone/something
care whether/if/what etc

if you care about someone or something, you feel concerned about them because you like or love them, or they are important to you: *Most young people care about the environment.* | *She didn't seem to care whether she passed the exam or not.* | *I don't care if I never see you again.*

PHRASE
who cares? *spoken* used to say that you do not think that something is important: *We came last in the race, but who cares? It was fun.*

PHRASAL VERB
care for

care for someone to make sure that someone who is ill, old, or very young has the attention, food etc they need ⇨ *same meaning* LOOK AFTER, TAKE CARE OF: *He gave up his job to care for his elderly mother.* | *women who stay at home to care for their children*

care² *noun*

1 when you do something carefully in order to avoid making a mistake: *Choose your university with care.* | *He doesn't take enough care over his homework.*
2 medical care, dental care etc: *Your father needs expert medical care* (=medical treatment).

PHRASES
take care of someone to make sure that someone who is ill, old, or very young has the attention, food etc

▼ they need: *Can you **take care of** the children while I'm out?*

take care of something **1)** to make sure that you do not damage something, by being careful: *If you **take care of** your CDs, they will last for years.* **2)** to be responsible for the work or effort that is needed to get a particular result: *I'll **take care of** all the travel arrangements.*

ca·reer /kə'rɪə $kə'rɪr/ *noun* a job or profession that you do for a long time, especially one in which you can move to a higher position: *careers in business and finance.* ⇨ *see usage note at* JOB

care·free /'keəfriː $'kerfriː/ *adjective* without any problems or worries: *At that time we were young and carefree.*

care·ful /'keəfəl $'kerfəl/ *adjective*

GRAMMAR
careful to do something
if you are careful, you do something with a lot of attention, to avoid making a mistake or damaging something: *Be careful crossing the road.* | *Sally **was careful** not to tear her dress.* | *Try to keep a careful record of your spending.*
– **carefully** *adverb*: *Please listen carefully to the instructions.*

PHRASE
careful with money not spending more money than you need to

care·less /'keələs $'kerləs/ *adjective*
if you are careless, you do not give enough attention to what you are doing, and you often make a mistake or damage something: *Try not to be so careless in future.* | *a careless mistake* | *He was found guilty of **careless driving**.*
– **carelessly** *adverb*: *This essay is very carelessly written.*
– **carelessness** *noun* [no plural]: *He might lose his job because of your carelessness.*

care·tak·er /'keə,teɪkə $'ker,teɪkɚ/ *noun BrE* someone whose job is to look after a building, especially a school; JANITOR *AmE*

car·go /'kɑːgəʊ $'kɑrgoʊ/ *noun, plural* ▼ **cargoes** the things that a ship, plane etc carries from one place to another: *a cargo of grain*

car·ing /'keərɪŋ $'kerɪŋ/ *adjective* someone who is caring is kind and helps people: *She was a warm and caring person, always ready to help.*

car·ni·val /'kɑːnəvəl $'kɑrnəvəl/ *noun* a big public party in the streets of a town with dancing, drinking, and entertainment: *the Venice carnival*

car·ni·vore /'kɑːnəvɔː $'kɑrnəvɔr/ *noun formal* a type of animal that eats meat: *Lions are carnivores.*

car·ol /'kærəl/ *noun* a song that people sing at Christmas

car park /'. ./ *noun BrE* a large area or building where people can park their cars; PARKING LOT *AmE*: *I parked in the underground car park.*

car·pen·ter /'kɑːpəntə $'kɑrpəntɚ/ *noun* someone whose job is making and repairing wooden things

car·pen·try /'kɑːpəntri $'kɑrpəntri/ *noun* [no plural] the work of a carpenter: *He is good at carpentry.*

car·pet /'kɑːpɪt $'kɑrpɪt/ *noun* a material for covering the floor, that is often made of wool: *a thick bedroom carpet*

car·riage /'kærɪdʒ/ *noun* **1** *BrE* one of the several connected parts of a train, where the passengers sit; CAR *AmE*: *I prefer sitting in a front carriage.* **2** a vehicle pulled by a horse, that people in the past travelled in

car·ri·er bag /'kæriə ,bæg $'kæriɚ ,bæg/ *noun BrE* a plastic or paper bag for carrying things that you buy in a shop ⇨ *see picture at* BAG

car·rot /'kærət/ *noun* a long thin orange vegetable that grows under the ground ⇨ *see pictures on pages 344 and 345*

car·ry /'kæri/ *verb* **carried, carries**

GRAMMAR
carry something to/into/down etc a place
1 to hold something in your hands or arms and to take it somewhere: *Steve **carried** a tray of drinks **into** the room.* | *Kim picked up the baby and **carried** her **back** inside.* | *Would you like me to carry your bag?*
▼**2** if vehicles, pipes etc carry things

somewhere, they take them from one place to another: *The trucks were carrying emergency food supplies.* | *A system of channels carries the water to the fields.* ⇨ see picture on page 340

PHRASE

get carried away to become so excited that you do or say things that you would not normally do or say: *We both got carried away by our feelings for each other.*

PHRASAL VERBS

carry on
to continue doing something: *I tried to ask a question, but he just carried on talking.*

carry out
carry something out to do something that has been planned and organized, or that someone has told you to do: *We carried out a research project on drug use in colleges.* | *Please carry out my instructions.*

cart /kɑːt $ kɑrt/ *noun* **1** a wooden vehicle on wheels, that a horse pulls: *a farmer with his horse and cart* **2** the American word for a TROLLEY

car·ton /ˈkɑːtn $ ˈkɑrtn/ *noun* a small strong container of thick paper that contains food or drink: *a carton of orange juice* ⇨ see picture at CONTAINER

car·toon /kɑːˈtuːn $ kɑrˈtun/ *noun* **1** a film that is made with characters that are drawn, rather than real actors: *a Walt Disney cartoon* **2** a drawing, especially in a newspaper or magazine, that makes a joke about something or tells a story

carve /kɑːv $ kɑrv/ *verb* **1** to cut wood, stone etc into a particular shape: *The statue is carved from marble.* **2** to cut cooked meat into pieces, using a large knife: *Will you carve the chicken?* ⇨ see picture on page 344

carv·ing /ˈkɑːvɪŋ $ ˈkɑrvɪŋ/ *noun* an object that has been carved from wood, stone etc: *a wooden carving*

case /keɪs/ *noun*
1 an example of a particular situation or problem: *This is the worst case of animal cruelty I have ever seen.* | *In some cases, the illness caused by the HIV virus develops into AIDS.*
2 a crime that the police deal with: *The police are investigating three murder cases.*
3 something that must be decided in a court of law: *The court case will continue next week.*
4 a container for storing or carrying something: *a guitar case*
5 *BrE* a SUITCASE: *Have you packed your case?*

PHRASES

in case, just in case: *I brought some food, in case we get hungry later* (=because we might get hungry later). | *Just in case you don't know* (=because you might not know), *all our classes are cancelled today.*
in any case used to give another reason for something: *I don't feel like going out to a bar, and in any case I can't afford it.*
in my case, in her case etc in my, her etc particular situation: *In my case, the tutor agreed that I could finish the essay later.*

cash¹ /kæʃ/ *noun* [no plural] money in the form of coins and paper notes: *I haven't got much cash. Can I pay by cheque?*

cash² *verb* to change a cheque for money: *I went to the bank to cash some traveller's cheques.*

cash·ier /kæˈʃɪə $ kæˈʃɪr/ *noun* someone whose job is to take money from customers in a shop, or give money to customers in a bank etc

cash·point /ˈkæʃpɔɪnt/ *noun BrE* a machine that you can use to get money from your bank account without going into the bank; ATM *AmE*: *There are several cashpoints at the next railway station.*

ca·si·no /kəˈsiːnəʊ $ kəˈsinoʊ/ *noun* a place where people try to win money by playing games with numbers, cards etc

cas·sette /kəˈset/ *noun* a small plastic container with TAPE (=thin plastic material) inside, that you use for playing or recording sound or pictures: *a video cassette*

cassette play·er /ˈ.. ˌ../ *noun* a machine that you use for playing and recording cassettes

cast¹ /kɑːst $ kæst/ *verb, past tense and past participle* **cast** to give an actor a particular part in a film, play etc: *As usual, Hugh Grant was cast as the typical Englishman.*

cast² *noun* all of the actors in a film or play: *The film has a brilliant cast.*

cas·tle /ˈkɑːsəl $ ˈkæsəl/ *noun* a large strong building that was built in the past to defend the people inside from attack

cas·u·al /ˈkæʒuəl/ *adjective* **1** relaxed and not very serious: *He bent to kiss her in a casual sort of way.* **2** casual clothes are comfortable and you wear them in informal situations: *casual trousers* **3** casual work is temporary work that you do for a short time: *a casual part-time job*

cas·u·al·ty /ˈkæʒuəlti/ *noun, plural* **casualties 1** someone who is hurt in an accident, a war etc: *There have been 20 casualties following an accident on the motorway.* **2** [no plural] BrE the part of a hospital that people are taken to when they need urgent treatment; EMERGENCY ROOM AmE

cat /kæt/ *noun* a small animal with four legs, fur, and sharp teeth and CLAWS, that people often keep in their house as a pet

cat·a·logue BrE, **catalog** AmE /ˈkætəlɒg $ ˈkætl̩ˌɔg/ *noun* a book with pictures and information about the things you can buy from a particular shop: *a children's clothes catalogue*

catapult

cat·a·pult /ˈkætəpʌlt/ *verb written* to make someone or something move through the air very quickly: *The car stopped suddenly, catapulting the boy through the window.*

ca·tas·tro·phe /kəˈtæstrəfi/ *noun* a terrible event that causes a lot of damage or death: *the danger of a nuclear catastrophe*

throw

catch

catch¹ /kætʃ/ *verb, past tense and past participle* **caught** /kɔːt/

GRAMMAR
catch someone doing something

1 to get hold of something that is moving or moving through the air, using your hands: *Bill threw the ball and Joe caught it.* ⇨ *see picture on page 340*

2 to stop a person or animal from running or moving away from you: *All the other boys were trying to catch George.* | *I caught a fish in the river today.*

3 if the police catch someone who has done something illegal, they find that person: *Police officers say they need help to catch the killers.*

4 to see someone doing something wrong: *I caught him reading through my letters.*

5 to get an illness that is passed from one person to another: *Lots of students catch a cold at the beginning of term.*

PHRASES
catch a bus, catch a train etc to get on a bus, train etc: *We caught a cab (=taxi) to Grand Central station.*

catch fire to start burning, especially by mistake: *The car crashed into a tree and caught fire.*

PHRASAL VERBS
catch on
to become popular or fashionable: *Salsa music has really caught on in Britain.*

catch out
catch someone out to ask someone a question that will show that they have been lying: *The boy was far too clever to be caught out by his father's questions.*

catch up
1 catch someone up to get to the same place as someone who is in front of you by moving faster than

them: *We ran to* **catch up with** *our friends.* | *Ahmed was winning the race but then his brother started to* **catch** *him* **up**.
2 to reach the same standard or level that someone else has reached: *After my illness, it took a long time to* **catch up with** *the rest of the class.*
catch up on
catch up on something *informal* to do something that you have not yet had time to do: *I'm going to* **catch up on** *some reading during the Christmas break.*

catch² *noun, plural* **catches** when you catch something that someone has thrown or hit: *Good catch, Paul!*

catch·ing /ˈkætʃɪŋ/ *adjective* an illness that is catching passes easily from one person to another

cat·e·go·ry /ˈkætəgəri $ ˈkætə,gɔri/ *noun, plural* **categories** a group of people or things that are similar in some way: *These animals can be divided into four categories.*

ca·ter /ˈkeɪtə $ ˈkeɪtɚ/ *verb* **cater to** also **cater for** *BrE* to provide a particular group of people with what they need or want: *We chose the hotel because it caters for small children.*

cat·er·pil·lar /ˈkætə,pɪlə $ ˈkætɚ,pɪlɚ/ *noun* a small garden creature that eats leaves. A caterpillar later becomes a BUTTERFLY (=a flying insect with large beautiful wings).

ca·the·dral /kəˈθiːdrəl/ *noun* a very large church that is the most important one in a particular area

Cath·o·lic /ˈkæθəlɪk/ ROMAN CATHOLIC

cat·sup /ˈkætsəp/ an American word for KETCHUP

cat·tle /ˈkætl/ *plural noun* male and female cows: *a cattle ranch*

caught the past tense and past participle of CATCH¹

cau·li·flow·er /ˈkɒlɪ,flaʊə $ ˈkɒli,flaʊɚ/ *noun* a vegetable with green leaves on the outside and a large firm white centre ⇨ *see picture on page 345*

cause¹ /kɔːz/ *verb written*

GRAMMAR
cause someone to do something
cause someone something
to make something happen: *Smok-*

ing causes cancer. | *The floods were caused by heavy rain.* | *I wonder what caused her to leave so early.* | *I don't want to cause you any trouble.*

cause² *noun*

GRAMMAR
a/the cause of something
a person, event, or thing that makes something happen: *Police are trying to find the cause of the fire.* | *What are the causes of this illness?*

PHRASES
have cause for something, have cause to do something to have reasons for feeling or behaving in a particular way: *You have no cause for worry because your illness is not serious.* | *We have cause to think that the President is lying.*

for a good cause, in a good cause if you do something kind or helpful for a good cause, you do it to help people who need and deserve help: *Would you like to give a donation (=money) to the Children's Charity? It's all in a good cause.*

cau·tion /ˈkɔːʃən/ *noun* [no plural] *formal* great care when you are doing something, because it is dangerous: *The sign said 'Caution. Dangerous cliffs.'*

cau·tious /ˈkɔːʃəs/ *adjective* careful not to hurt or harm yourself
–**cautiously** *adverb*: *He began to climb cautiously down the tree.*

cav·al·ry /ˈkævəlri/ *noun* [no plural] soldiers who fought on horses in the past

cave /keɪv/ *noun* a large natural hole under the ground, or in the side of a mountain or rock ⇨ *see picture on page 348*

cave·man /ˈkeɪvmæn/ *noun, plural* **cavemen** /-men/ someone who lived many thousands of years ago, when people lived in caves

cav·i·ty /ˈkævəti/ *noun, plural* **cavities** a hole in a tooth: *The dentist said I had a cavity.*

CD /,siː ˈdiː/ *noun* an abbreviation for COMPACT DISC; a small round piece of hard plastic with music or words recorded on it: *I'm going to buy Radiohead's latest CD.* ⇨ *see picture on page 342*

CD play·er /.ˈ. ,../ *noun* a piece of electric equipment that you play CDs on

CD-ROM /ˌsiː diː 'rɒm $ˌsi di 'rɑm/ noun a CD with a lot of information stored on it, which you look at using a computer

cease /siːs/ verb formal to stop doing something or stop happening: The company ceased trading in 1924.

cease·fire /'siːsfaɪə $'sis,faɪəʳ/ noun an agreement between two countries or enemy groups to stop fighting

cei·ling /'siːlɪŋ/ noun the flat surface above your head in a room: It was a big room with a high ceiling.

cel·e·brate /'seləbreɪt/ verb to do something nice because it is a special occasion, or because something good has happened: The team celebrated by opening some bottles of champagne.

cel·e·bra·tion /ˌseləˈbreɪʃən/ noun a party, meal, dance etc when you celebrate something special or good: The wedding celebrations went on all through the night.

ce·leb·ri·ty /səˈlebrəti/ noun, plural celebrities a famous person, especially an actor or entertainer: There were lots of TV celebrities at the party.

cel·e·ry /'seləri/ noun a long thin hard green vegetable that you eat in a SALAD

cell /sel/ noun 1 a small room in a police station or prison for keeping prisoners: They locked him in a cell. 2 the smallest living part of an animal or plant: brain cells

cel·lar /'selə $'seləʳ/ noun a room under the ground in a house, used especially for storing things: He got a bottle of wine from the cellar.

cel·lo /'tʃeləʊ $'tʃeloʊ/ noun a large wooden musical instrument that you hold between your knees and play by pulling a special stick across four strings

cell phone /'. ./ or **cel·lu·lar phone** /ˌseljələ 'fəʊn $ˌseljələʳ 'foʊn/ the American word for MOBILE PHONE

Cel·si·us /'selsiəs/ abbreviation **C** noun [no plural] a scale for measuring temperature, in which water freezes at 0° and boils at 100°

ce·ment /sɪˈment/ noun [no plural] a substance that is mixed with sand and water to make CONCRETE (=a substance for building walls and making hard surfaces): You have to wait for the cement to dry.

cem·e·tery /'semətri $'semə,teri/ noun, plural cemeteries an area of land where dead people are buried

cen·sor /'sensə $'sensəʳ/ verb to look at books, films etc and remove anything that might offend or harm people: It was obvious that the television reports were being censored.

cen·sor·ship /'sensəʃɪp $'sensəʳʃɪp/ noun when a government or other authority censors books, films, newspapers etc: She believes that censorship is wrong.

cen·sus /'sensəs/ noun, plural censuses an official event when a government collects information about the number of people in the country and their ages, jobs etc

cent /sent/ noun a small coin used in the US. There are 100 cents in a dollar ($)

cen·te·na·ry /sen'tiːnəri/ BrE, **cen·ten·ni·al** /sen'teniəl/ AmE noun, plural centenaries BrE, the day or year exactly one hundred years after an important event: We will be celebrating the school's centenary in 2003.

cen·ter /'sentə $sentəʳ/ the American spelling of CENTRE

Cen·ti·grade /'sentəgreɪd/ CELSIUS

cen·ti·me·tre BrE, **centimeter** AmE /'sentəˌmiːtə $sentə,mitəʳ/ written abbreviation **cm** noun

a unit for measuring length in the METRIC system. There are 100 centimetres in a metre

cen·tral /'sentrəl/ adjective
1 in the middle of a place: Central Europe | The central shopping area has the best shops.
2 more important than anything else: A central theme in my talk will be the development of Islam.

central heat·ing /ˌ.. '../ noun [no plural] a system of heating buildings in which pipes carry the heat to every part of the building: Most of these houses have central heating.

cen·tre¹ BrE, **center** AmE /'sentə/ noun

GRAMMAR
the centre of something
1 the middle part or point of something: He took her hand and led her to the centre of the room. | Find the

▼ **centre of** *the circle using your ruler.*
2 a building where people go for a particular purpose: *a sports centre* | *I have an appointment at the Health Centre this afternoon.*
3 the part in the middle of a city or town where most of the shops, restaurants, clubs etc are: *We took a bus to* **the centre of** *Cairo.* | *a busy city centre*

centre² *BrE,* **center** *AmE, verb* **centre on, centre around** to have something or someone as the most important part: *The town centres on the university.* | *Her whole life centres around her family.*

cen·tu·ry /'sentʃəri/ *noun, plural* **centuries**
a period of 100 years, used especially for dates: *the 21st century* | *at the beginning of the last century* | *The rocks were formed many centuries ago.*

ce·ram·ics /sə'ræmɪks/ *noun [no plural]*
the art of making pots, bowls etc from clay, or the things that are made from clay: *Sonia teaches ceramics at Columbia College.*

ce·re·al /'sɪəriəl $ 'sɪriəl/ *noun* **1** a food you eat for breakfast that contains a mixture of wheat, rice, nuts etc, and that you usually mix with milk **2** a plant such as wheat or rice that is grown for food

cer·e·mo·ny /'serəməni $ 'serə-ˌmoʊni/ *noun, plural* **ceremonies** a formal event, when people do or say something special in public: *The opening ceremony for the new theatre was performed by the Queen.* | *a wedding ceremony*

cer·tain /'sɜːtn $ 'sɜ˞tn/ *adjective*

GRAMMAR
certain about/of something
certain what/whether/if/how etc
certain (that)

1 if you are certain, you are completely sure about something: *One day we will be married – I* **feel certain about** *that.* | *The manager wants to* **be certain of** *Beckham's fitness before he starts playing again.* | *Phil isn't quite* **certain what** *he wants to do next year.* | *Everyone seems to* **be certain** ▼

▼ **that** *he'll win the race.* ⇨ opposite UNCERTAIN
2 used to talk about people or things without saying exactly who or what they are: *Certain people have been stealing books from the library – you probably know who I mean.*

cer·tain·ly /'sɜːtnli $ 'sɜ˞tnli/ *adverb*
without any doubt: *This match will certainly be difficult for us to win.*

cer·tif·i·cate /sə'tɪfɪkət $ sə˞'tɪfəkət/ *noun* an official document showing that something is true or correct: *We need to see your birth certificate before you can get a passport.*

ce·sar·e·an /sə'zeəriən $ sə'zeriən/ another spelling of CAESAREAN

chain¹ /tʃeɪn/ *noun* **1** a line of metal rings that are connected to each other: *She wore a gold chain around her neck.* **2** a group of shops that one person or company owns: *a chain of menswear shops*

chain² *verb* to fasten one thing to another with a chain: *I chained my bicycle to a tree.*

chairs

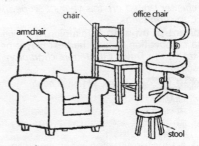

chair¹ /tʃeə $ tʃer/ *noun* a piece of furniture for one person to sit on: *a kitchen chair* ⇨ see picture on page 342

chair² *verb* to be the chairperson of a meeting or official group: *Mrs Dolan will chair the meeting.*

chair·per·son /'tʃeəˌpɜːsən $ 'tʃer-ˌpɜ˞sən/ *also* **chair·man** /'tʃeəmən $ 'tʃermən/ *or* **chair·wom·an** /'tʃeə-ˌwʊmən $ 'tʃerˌwʊmən/ *noun* someone who manages a meeting, official group, or company: *They elected a new chairperson.*

chalk /tʃɔːk/ noun [no plural] **1** soft white rock that you buy in small sticks and use for writing on a board: *Take a piece of chalk and write your name on the blackboard.* **2** soft white rock: *the chalk cliffs of Dover*

chal·lenge¹ /'tʃæləndʒ/ noun

something new, exciting, or difficult that you will need a lot of determination and effort to do: *Getting students interested is a challenge for most teachers.* | *Phillip gets bored easily, and enjoys meeting new challenges.*

challenge² verb **1** to say that you disagree with a decision or judgement and try to change it: *She's always challenging my decisions.* **2** to invite someone to compete against you: *Sam challenged me to a game of tennis.*

chal·leng·ing /'tʃæləndʒɪŋ/ adjective difficult but interesting or enjoyable: *Teaching is a very challenging job.*

cham·pagne /ʃæm'peɪn/ noun [no plural] a type of wine containing gas, that people often drink on special occasions: *Who would like a glass of champagne?*

cham·pi·on /'tʃæmpiən/ noun a person or team that wins a competition: *Manchester United are this year's European Cup champions.*

cham·pi·on·ship /'tʃæmpiənʃɪp/ noun a competition to find the best player or team: *the Davis Cup tennis championship*

chance /tʃɑːns $ tʃæns/ noun

> **GRAMMAR**
> a/the chance to do something
> chance of doing something
> a chance (that)

1 a time or situation when you can do something you wanted to do ⇨ *same meaning* OPPORTUNITY: *Have you had a chance to read the paper yet?* | *Fans got the chance to meet the band after the concert.* | *"Did you explain why you were late?" "She didn't give me a chance (=give me time to explain)."*

2 something that may happen ⇨ *same meaning* POSSIBILITY: *I don't think we have much chance of winning.* | *There's a chance that it might rain later today.* | *What are England's*

chances in the World Cup (=is England likely to win or not)?

> **PHRASES**

by chance if something happens by chance, it happens even though you did not plan or expect it: *We got lost, and found this house quite by chance.*

take a chance to do something that may be dangerous or may fail: *Lock the car – I don't want to take any chances.*

chan·cel·lor /'tʃɑːnsələ $ 'tʃænsələr/ noun **1** the head of a university or government: *the Chancellor of York University* | *The German Chancellor has arrived in Britain.* **2** also **Chancellor of the Exchequer** in Britain, the government minister who is in charge the money the government spends

chan·de·lier /ˌʃændə'lɪə $ ˌʃændə'lɪr/ noun a large decoration made of glass that holds lights and hangs from the ceiling

change¹ /tʃeɪndʒ/ verb

> **GRAMMAR**
> change from something to something
> change into/out of something
> change something into something

1 if someone or something changes, or if you change them, they become different: *As we travelled, the view changed from mountains to fields.* | *Getting married has changed him.* | *You can change the settings on your computer.*

2 to replace something that is old, used, or not working properly: *It's important to be able to change a tyre on your car.* | *The hotel staff haven't changed the sheets on the bed.*

3 to remove the clothes you are wearing and put on different ones: *She went upstairs to change into some dry clothes.* | *Nell had already changed and was ready to go to bed.*

4 if you change some money, you give it to someone and they give back the same amount to you, but in different notes or coins: *Could you change $200 into lira, please?* | *She asked the shop assistant to change a £20 note.*

▼**5** to get out of one bus, train, or plane and get into another one: *Does this train go direct to London, or do I have to change?* | *We had to change planes in Kuwait.*

PHRASES

change your mind to change your decision, plan, or opinion: *Has Carol changed her mind about having children?*
change the subject to stop talking about one thing and start talking about something else: *Ruth looked upset, so I quickly changed the subject.*

change² *noun*

GRAMMAR
a change in something

1 when something becomes different to what it was before: *There have been huge changes in technology in the past five years.* | *There has been little change in the weather.*
2 a change of clothes, a change of address etc a different set of clothes, a different address etc to the one you have now or had before: *Take a change of clothes in case it rains.* | *Sandy sent out cards to tell people about her change of address.*
3 something that is interesting or enjoyable because it is different from what you usually do: *It makes a change to eat in a restaurant.* | *Let's walk to college for a change.*
4 [no plural] the money someone gives back to you when you pay for something with more money than it costs: *You've given me the wrong change* (= too much or not enough money).
5 [no plural] money in the form of coins: *I need 50p in change for the parking meter.* | *Have you got change for a £10 note?*

chan·nel /'tʃænl/ *noun* **1** a television station: *Which channel is the film on?* | *Can we change channels to watch the football?* **2** a long narrow area that water can go along: *There are channels at the edge of the road for flood water.*

chant /tʃɑːnt $tʃænt/ *noun* words or phrases that people sing or shout many times: *There were chants of "We want more!"*
–**chant** *verb*: *The crowd chanted his name.*

cha·os /'keɪɒs $'keɪɑs/ *noun* [no plural] when there is no organization or order: *I left the kids alone for 10 minutes and when I came back it was chaos.*

cha·ot·ic /keɪ'ɒtɪk $keɪ'ɑtɪk/ *adjective* without any organization or plan: *Tina has a very chaotic lifestyle.*

chap /tʃæp/ *noun BrE informal* a man: *Frank seems a friendly chap.*

chap·el /'tʃæpəl/ *noun* a small Christian church

chap·e·rone /'ʃæpərəʊn $'ʃæpəroʊn/ *noun* an older person who in the past went to places with a young person, to protect and take care of them: *Your aunt will go with you as your chaperone.*

chap·lain /'tʃæplən/ *noun* a priest who works for the army, a hospital, or a college: *the college chaplain*

chap·ter /'tʃæptə $'tʃæptɚ/ *noun* one of the parts that a book is divided into: *Chapter 7 is about space travel.*

char·ac·ter /'kærɪktə $'kærɪktɚ/ *noun*
1 the particular qualities that a person, place, or thing has: *The new road will spoil the quiet character of the village.*
2 a person in a book, play, film etc: *Brad Pitt plays an evil character who becomes a Christian.*
3 a letter, mark, or sign that is used in writing, printing, or COMPUTING: *The software can read Japanese characters.*

char·ac·ter·is·tic /ˌkærɪktə'rɪstɪk/ *noun* a particular quality or feature that someone or something has: *There's one characteristic I like about you – you never stop trying.*
–**characteristic** *adjective*: *He showed none of his characteristic charm.*

char·coal /'tʃɑːkəʊl $'tʃɑrkoʊl/ *noun* [no plural] a black substance made of burned wood, that you can burn to make heat: *Ada put some more charcoal on the barbecue.*

charge¹ /tʃɑːdʒ $ tʃɑrdʒ/ noun

GRAMMAR
a charge of something

1 the amount of money that you must pay for a service, or to use something: *There's **a charge of** $350 for hiring the room.* | *The bank will no longer **make a charge** (=make you pay something) each time you use the cash machine.* | *The student guide is available **free of charge** (=you do not have to pay for it).*
2 an official statement by the police, saying that someone might be guilty of a crime: *The police arrested him **on a charge of** murder.*

PHRASES
be in charge if you are in charge, you control something or you are responsible for something: *Jack **is in charge of** lighting for the disco.* | *Who's **in charge** here?*
take charge to take control of someone or something: *A police officer arrived and **took charge of** the situation.*

charge² verb

GRAMMAR
charge someone something
charge for something
charge someone with something

1 to ask someone to pay a particular amount of money for something: *The university is charging students £200 in fees each term.* | *Do you **charge for** bike hire?* | *Some companies charge extra (=ask for more money) for supplying the software.*
2 if the police charge someone, they say officially that he or she might be guilty of a crime: *He appeared in court, **charged with** murder.*
3 to run towards someone very quickly in order to attack them: *The elephant lowered its head and started to charge.* | *Police with batons charged the demonstrators.*

cha·ris·ma /kəˈrɪzmə/ noun [no plural] a natural ability to make people like you: *He is a man of great charisma.*

char·is·mat·ic /ˌkærɪzˈmætɪk/ adjective having charisma: *President Clinton was a very charismatic leader.*

char·i·ty /ˈtʃærəti/ noun, plural **charities** an organization that collects money and provides help for people who need it: *She works for the charity Oxfam.* | *I'm collecting money for charity.*

charm /tʃɑːm $ tʃɑrm/ noun the special quality someone or something has that makes people like them: *Oxford has a lot of charm.*

charm·ing /ˈtʃɑːmɪŋ $ ˈtʃɑrmɪŋ/ adjective having qualities which people think are pleasing or attractive: *What a charming child!*

chart¹ /tʃɑːt $ tʃɑrt/ noun a picture or DIAGRAM that shows information: *Look at the chart to find your ideal weight.*

chart² verb formal to record information about something over a period of time: *The teacher will chart your progress over the year.*

char·ter /ˈtʃɑːtə $ ˈtʃɑrtɚ/ noun a statement of the beliefs, duties, and purposes of an organization: *The United Nations published its charter.*

charter flight /ˈ.. ˌ./ noun a flight that you buy from a travel company, and that is often cheaper than a flight you buy directly from an AIRLINE: *We managed to get a charter flight to Istanbul.*

chase /tʃeɪs/ verb

GRAMMAR
chase someone/something somewhere

to try to catch someone or something by following them or running towards them: *The dog **chased** the rabbit **across** the field.* | *Mr Twee always **chased away** children who played near his house.*

chat /tʃæt/ verb informal **chatted, chatting**
to talk in a friendly and informal way: *Pete and I were chatting in the bar.* | *What are you two chatting about?*
–**chat** noun: *Let's meet for coffee and have a chat.*

PHRASAL VERB
chat up
chat someone up BrE informal to talk to someone in a way that shows you think they are sexually attractive: *Eric was trying to **chat up** my girlfriend.*

châ·teau /ˈʃætəʊ $ ʃæˈtoʊ/ noun, plural **châteaux** /-təʊz $ -toʊz/ a castle or large country house in France

chat show /ˈ. ./ noun BrE a television or

radio show on which someone talks to famous or interesting people; TALK SHOW AmE: *Brosnan appeared as a guest on her chat show.*

chat·ter /'tʃætə $ 'tʃætɚ/ verb **1** to talk a lot about things that are not important: *Stop chattering and listen to me.* **2** if your teeth chatter, they knock together because you are cold or afraid

chat·ty /'tʃæti/ adjective informal **chattier, chattiest** a chatty person is friendly and easy to talk to: *She was very chatty on the telephone.*

chauf·feur /'ʃəʊfə $ 'ʃəʊfɚ/ noun someone whose job is to drive another person's car, and take that person to the places they want to go: *My chauffeur drove me to the airport.*

cheap /tʃiːp/ adjective **cheaper, cheapest**

something that is cheap does not cost very much money, or costs less money than you expect ⇨ *opposite* EXPENSIVE: *cheap rail fares | CDs are much cheaper in the US.*
– **cheaply** adverb: *You can buy fruit and vegetables more cheaply in the market.*

cheat

cheat /tʃiːt/ verb

to do something that is not fair, honest, or truthful, especially in order to win or get something you want: *Kylie and Grant cheated in the spelling test.*
– **cheat** noun: *You're a cheat, changing the score like that!*

check¹ /tʃek/ verb

GRAMMAR
check what/whether/if etc
check (that)
check with someone
1 to do something in order to make

sure that everything is safe, correct, or working properly: *The firemen check all the equipment daily. | If your computer fails to start, check that you have entered your password correctly. | Bill is checking whether the trains are running on Sunday.*
2 to ask someone's advice or permission before you do something: *Before starting a diet, you should check with your doctor.*

PHRASAL VERBS
check in/into
check into something to go to the desk at a hotel, airport etc and say that you have arrived ⇨ *same meaning* BOOK IN: *We have to check in an hour before the flight leaves. | We checked into a motel.*
check up on
check up on someone to get information about someone, for example to make sure that they are honest: *We always check up on new employees.*
check out
1 check something out informal to get information in order to discover whether something is true, correct, or acceptable: *If you're not sure about the spelling, check it out. | Roy went in to check out the menu.*
2 check out to pay the bill and leave a hotel: *What time did he check out?*

check² noun
1 an examination to find out if something is correct, true, or safe: *The police are doing road safety checks. | We ran a check on the network after we found a computer virus.*
2 the American spelling of CHEQUE
3 the American word for BILL
4 the American word for TICK

check·book /'tʃekbʊk/ the American spelling of CHEQUEBOOK
checked /tʃekt/ also **check** adjective a checked shirt, a checked cloth etc a checked shirt, cloth etc has a regular pattern of different coloured squares: *a red and white checked tablecloth*
check·ers /'tʃekəz $ 'tʃekɚz/ the American word for DRAUGHTS

check·list /'tʃek,lɪst/ *noun* a list of all the things you have to do for a job or activity: *Read the checklist to make sure you haven't forgotten anything.*

check·out /'tʃek-aʊt/ also **checkout coun·ter** /'.. ,../ *AmE, noun* the place in a SUPERMARKET (=large shop) where you go to pay for the things you want to buy: *Sally was working on the checkout.*

check·point /'tʃekpɔɪnt/ *noun* a place where an official person stops people and vehicles to examine them: *There are several checkpoints along the border.*

check·up or **check-up** /'tʃek-ʌp/ *noun* when a doctor or DENTIST examines you to see if you are healthy: *You should have regular checkups with your dentist.*

cheek /tʃiːk/ *noun*

1 your cheeks are the two soft round parts of your face below your eyes: *He kissed her gently on the cheek.* ⇨ *see picture at* HEAD[1]

2 *[no plural] BrE informal* when someone says or does something that shows no respect for another person: *Tom had the cheek to ask me for some more money.*

cheek·y /'tʃiːki/ *adjective BrE* **cheekier, cheekiest** someone who is cheeky says or does things that show a lack of respect for someone who is older, in a higher position at work etc: *He's a cheeky little boy.*

cheer[1] /tʃɪə $ tʃɪr/ *verb* **1** to shout in order to encourage someone or because you are enjoying what they are doing: *The crowd cheered as the players ran onto the field.* **2 cheer someone up** to make someone who is unhappy feel happier: *He bought her some flowers to cheer her up.*

cheer[2] *noun* a shout that shows you are happy or pleased with something: *You could hear the cheers from outside the theatre.*

cheer·ful /'tʃɪəfəl $ 'tʃɪrfəl/ *adjective* happy and showing this by your behaviour: *Tom seems a very cheerful child.*

cheer·lead·er /'tʃɪə,liːdə $ 'tʃɪr,liːdɚ/ *noun* a member of a group of young women that encourages the crowd at a sports event to cheer for a particular team

cheers /tʃɪəz $ tʃɪrz/ something you

say just before you drink a glass of alcohol with someone, to show friendly feelings

cheese /tʃiːz/ *noun [no plural]* a solid white or yellow food made from milk: *cheese on toast* ⇨ *see picture on page 344*

cheese·cake /'tʃiːzkeɪk/ *noun [no plural]* a sweet cake made with soft white cheese and fruit: *strawberry cheesecake*

chef /ʃef/ *noun* the most important cook in a restaurant

chem·i·cal[1] /'kemɪkəl/ *noun* a substance used in chemistry: *Some of these chemicals are very dangerous.*

chemical[2] *adjective* related to chemicals: *Chemical weapons were used in the war.*

chem·ist /'kemɪst/ *noun* **1** also **chemist's** *BrE* a shop where you can buy medicines, soap, TOOTHPASTE etc; DRUGSTORE *AmE* **2** *BrE* someone whose job is to prepare drugs and medicines for sale in a shop; PHARMACIST *AmE* **3** a scientist who studies chemistry

chem·is·try /'keməstri/ *noun [no plural]* the science of studying chemicals and what happens to them when they change or combine with each other

cheque *BrE*, **check** *AmE* /tʃek/ *noun*

a special printed form that you use to pay for things, using the money in your bank account. You write the amount of money, the date, and the name of the person you are paying on the cheque, and then you sign it: *a check for $300* | *I'd like to pay by cheque.* | *Do you mind if I write you a cheque* (=pay for something with a cheque)?

cheque·book /'tʃekbʊk/ *noun BrE* a small book of cheques; CHECKBOOK *AmE*

cher·ry /'tʃeri/ *noun, plural* **cherries** a small round soft red fruit with a large seed

chess /tʃes/ *noun [no plural]* a board game for two players in which you must catch your opponent's king in order to win: *a game of chess*

chest /tʃest/ *noun* **1** the front part of your body between your neck and stomach: *He has a very broad chest.* ⇨ *see picture at* BODY **2** a large strong box with a lid, that you use to keep things in: *I took two blankets out of the chest.*

chest of drawers /ˌ. . './ noun a piece of furniture with drawers, used for keeping clothes in; BUREAU AmE: *The room had only a bed and a small chest of drawers.*

chew /tʃuː/ verb to crush food with your teeth before you swallow it: *He was chewing a tough piece of meat.*

chewing gum /'.. ˌ./ also **gum** noun [no plural] a type of sweet that you chew for a long time, but do not swallow: *a stick of chewing gum*

chic /ʃiːk/ adjective fashionable and showing good style: *We had lunch at a chic little cafe.*

chick /tʃɪk/ noun a baby bird: *You can hear the chicks in the nest.*

chick·en¹ /'tʃɪkən/ noun **1** a farm bird that you keep for its meat and eggs **2** [no plural] the meat from a chicken: *a chicken sandwich* ⇨ see picture on page 344

chicken² verb **chicken out** to decide not to do something because you do not feel brave enough: *I was going to do a bunjee jump, but I chickened out.*

chicken pox /'tʃɪkən ˌpɒks $ 'tʃɪkən ˌpɑːks/ noun [no plural] an illness that children get, that causes a fever and red spots on their skin: *Ruth's got chicken pox.*

chief¹ /tʃiːf/ adjective
1 highest in rank: *the company's chief executive*
2 the most important ⇨ same meaning MAIN: *I've made a list of the chief points from the lecture.*

chief² noun the leader of a group or organization: *The chief of police appeared on television.*

chief·ly /'tʃiːfli/ adverb mainly: *The book is aimed chiefly at women.*

child /tʃaɪld/ noun, plural **children** /'tʃɪldrən/
1 a young person who is not yet fully grown: *I lived in the US when I was a child. | The children were coming out of the school gates.*
2 a son or daughter: *Lynda has three grown-up children.*

USAGE **child, baby, toddler, teenager, kid**
When you are first born, you are a **baby**. A child who has just learnt to walk is a **toddler**. Between 13 and 19, you are a **teenager**. **Kid** is an informal word for a child or a young person.

child·birth /'tʃaɪldbɜːθ $ 'tʃaɪldbɚθ/ noun [no plural] the process by which a baby is born: *Childbirth is very painful.*

child·care /'tʃaɪldkeə $ 'tʃaɪldˌker/ noun [no plural] when someone is responsible for the care of children whose parents are at work: *The government should provide free childcare.*

child·hood /'tʃaɪldhʊd/ noun the time when you are a child: *I had a happy childhood.*

child·ish /'tʃaɪldɪʃ/ adjective an adult who is childish behaves in a silly way, like a small child: *Stop being so childish.*

child·less /'tʃaɪldləs/ adjective having no children: *The new treatment offers hope to childless couples.*

child·mind·er /'tʃaɪldˌmaɪndə $ 'tʃaɪldˌmaɪndɚ/ noun BrE someone who is responsible for the care of young children while their parents are at work

child·mind·ing /'tʃaɪldˌmaɪndɪŋ/ noun BrE the job of being a childminder: *I do a little childminding.*

children /'tʃɪldrən/ noun the plural of CHILD

chill¹ /tʃɪl/ verb **1** to make something cold: *Chill the champagne before you serve it.* **2** also **chill out** informal to relax and rest, especially after going to a party, club etc: *We stayed till about 3.00, then back to our place to chill.*

chill² noun a feeling of coldness: *There was a chill in the air.*

chil·li BrE also **chili** AmE /'tʃɪli/ noun a small thin red or green vegetable with a very hot taste

chill·y /'tʃɪli/ adjective **chillier, chilliest** cold: *It's a bit chilly today.*

chime /tʃaɪm/ verb written if a clock or bell chimes, it makes a sound like a bell: *The clock chimed six o'clock.*
– **chime** noun: *The chimes of the church bells woke me up.*

chim·ney /'tʃɪmni/ noun a wide pipe that takes smoke from a fire through the roof ⇨ see picture on page 343

chim·pan·zee /ˌtʃɪmpænˈziː/ also **chimp** /tʃɪmp/ informal noun an African APE (=an animal that looks like a monkey) ⇨ see picture on page 339

chin /tʃɪn/ noun

the front part of your face below your mouth: *a pointed chin* ⇨ see picture at HEAD¹

chi·na /ˈtʃaɪnə/ noun [no plural] the hard white substance that cups and plates are made of: *a china teapot*

chip¹ /tʃɪp/ noun **1** BrE a long thin piece of potato that has been cooked in oil; FRENCH FRY AmE: *Would you like chips with your burger?* **2** the American word for a CRISP **3** a mark on something where a small piece has broken off it: *This cup has a chip in it.*

chip² verb **chipped, chipping** to break a small piece off something: *I've chipped my tooth.*

chip·munk /ˈtʃɪpmʌŋk/ noun a small brown animal like a SQUIRREL, that has black and white lines on its fur

chirp /tʃɜːp $ tʃɚp/ verb if a bird chirps, it makes short high sounds

chirp·y /ˈtʃɜːpi $ ˈtʃɚpi/ adjective informal **chirpier, chirpiest** cheerful: *You're very chirpy this morning,*

chis·el /ˈtʃɪzəl/ noun a metal tool with a sharp end, used for cutting and shaping wood or stone ⇨ see picture at TOOL

choc·o·late /ˈtʃɒklət $ ˈtʃɑklɪt/ noun [no plural] a sweet hard brown food: *Can I have a piece of chocolate?* | *chocolate ice cream*

choice /tʃɔɪs/ noun

> **GRAMMAR**
> **a choice between things/people**
> **a choice of things**

1 a decision to choose one thing or person rather than another: *It's a difficult choice, but I think I like the red dress best.* | *I had to **make a choice between** a quiet evening at home or going to the concert.* | *You have two choices for dinner: pasta or chicken.*

2 [no plural] the opportunity or right to choose between two or more things: *We **had a choice of** five questions in the exam.* | *I accepted the job because I **had no choice** and I needed the money.*

3 a person or thing that you choose: *Spain is a good choice, if you want to go somewhere hot.*

choir /kwaɪə $ kwaɪɚ/ noun a group of people who sing together: *Sue sings in the school choir.*

choke /tʃəʊk $ tʃoʊk/ verb if you choke, or if something chokes you, you cannot breathe properly because you are not getting enough air into your lungs: *I choked on a small piece of bone.* | *Your cigarette smoke is choking me!*

choose /tʃuːz/ verb **chose** /tʃəʊz $ tʃoʊz/ **chosen** /ˈtʃəʊzən $ ˈtʃoʊzən/

> **GRAMMAR**
> **choose which/whether/what etc**
> **choose from things/people**

to decide to have or do one of several things that are available or possible: *Lucy chose a red dress with a white collar.* | *We were able to **choose from** over a dozen films.* | *Students can **choose whether** to study abroad or stay at home.* | *"Where would you like to go tonight?" "I'm not sure – you choose!"*

choos·y /ˈtʃuːzi/ adjective **choosier, choosiest** someone who is choosy only likes certain things: *I'm very choosy about my food.*

chop¹ /tʃɒp $ tʃɑp/ verb **chopped, chopping** also **chop up** to cut something into small pieces: *He's outside chopping firewood.* | *Shall I chop the carrots up?* ⇨ see picture on pages 341 and 344

chop² noun **lamb chop, pork chop** a small flat piece of lamb or PORK on a bone

chop·per /ˈtʃɒpə $ ˈtʃɑpɚ/ noun informal a HELICOPTER

chop·sticks /ˈtʃɒpstɪks $ ˈtʃɑpstɪks/ plural noun a pair of thin sticks used for eating food in China and Japan

chord /kɔːd $ kɔrd/ noun two or more musical notes that you play at the same time: *I can play a few chords on the guitar.*

chore /tʃɔː $ tʃɔr/ noun a job that you have to do, especially a boring one in the house or garden: *You can't go out until you've finished your chores.*

chor·e·og·ra·pher /ˌkɒriˈɒɡrəfə $ˌkɔriˈɑɡrəfɚ/ *noun* someone who does the choreography for a performance

chor·e·og·ra·phy /ˌkɒriˈɒɡrəfi $ˌkɔriˈɑɡrəfi/ *noun [no plural]* the art of arranging how dancers should move during a performance

cho·rus /ˈkɔːrəs/ *noun* the part of a song that is repeated after each VERSE: *Everyone join in the chorus.*

chose the past tense of CHOOSE

chosen the past participle of CHOOSE

Christ /kraɪst/ *noun* Jesus Christ, who Christians believe is the son of God

chris·ten /ˈkrɪsən/ *verb* if a priest christens someone, he gives them their name in a religious ceremony

chris·ten·ing /ˈkrɪsənɪŋ/ *noun* a Christian ceremony in which a priest gives a baby its name

Chris·tian¹ /ˈkrɪstʃən/ *adjective* related to Christianity: *We don't go to church, but we have Christian values.*

Christian² *noun* someone whose religion is Christianity

Chris·ti·an·i·ty /ˌkrɪstiˈænəti/ *noun [no plural]* the religion that is based on the life and teachings of Jesus Christ

Christian name /ˈ.. ./ *noun* your first name: *His Christian name is David.*

Christ·mas /ˈkrɪsməs/ *noun* the period around December 25th when people celebrate the birth of Christ and give and receive gifts: *We're going to my parents' house this Christmas.*

Christmas Day /ˌ.. ˈ./ *noun* December 25th, the day on which Christians celebrate the birth of Christ

Christmas Eve /ˌ.. ˈ./ *noun* the evening or the day before Christmas Day

Christmas stock·ing /ˌ.. ˈ../ *noun* a long sock that children leave out on the night before Christmas to be filled with presents

chrome /krəʊm $kroʊm/ *also* **chro·mi·um** /ˈkrəʊmiəm $ˈkroʊmiəm/ *noun [no plural]* a hard shiny silver metal that is used for covering objects: *The door has chrome handles.*

chron·ic /ˈkrɒnɪk $ˈkrɑnɪk/ *adjective* if a situation or illness is chronic, it is serious and likely to continue for a long time: *There is a chronic shortage of teachers.*

chron·o·log·i·cal /ˌkrɒnəˈlɒdʒɪkəl $ˌkrɑnlˈɑdʒɪkəl/ *adjective* arranged in the same order as events happened: *The children had to put the events of the war in chronological order.*

chub·by /ˈtʃʌbi/ *adjective* *informal* chubbier, chubbiest slightly fat: *He's a chubby little baby.*

chuck /tʃʌk/ *verb* *informal* to throw something: *I chucked the ball over the fence.*

chuck·le /ˈtʃʌkəl/ *verb* *informal* to laugh quietly: *He chuckled to himself as he read his book.*
– **chuckle** *noun*: *"This is funny," he said with a chuckle.*

chunk /tʃʌŋk/ *noun* a large piece of something solid: *She broke off a large chunk of bread.*

church /tʃɜːtʃ $tʃɚtʃ/ *noun, plural* churches
a building where Christians go to pray: *We always go to church on Sundays.* ⇨ *see picture on page 343*

church·yard /ˈtʃɜːtʃjɑːd $ˈtʃɚtʃjɑrd/ *noun* a piece of land around a church where dead people are buried

ci·der /ˈsaɪdə $ˈsaɪdɚ/ *noun* a drink containing alcohol that is made from apples

ci·gar /sɪˈɡɑː $sɪˈɡɑr/ *noun* a large brown cigarette

cig·a·rette /ˌsɪɡəˈret $ˈsɪɡəˌret/ *noun* a paper tube filled with tobacco that people smoke: *Would you like a cigarette?*

cin·e·ma /ˈsɪnəmə/ *noun*
BrE a building where you go to see films; MOVIE THEATER AmE: *Shall we go to the cinema tonight?*

circle¹ /ˈsɜːkəl $ˈsɚkəl/ *noun*
1 a round flat shape like the letter O, or a group of people or things arranged in this shape: *Draw a circle on this piece of paper.* | *We sat in a circle round the table.* ⇨ *see picture at* SHAPE¹
2 political circles, literary circles etc the people who are involved in politics, literature etc

PHRASE
go round (and round) in circles to think or talk etc about something a lot without achieving anything

circle² *verb* **1** to move in a circle around something: *Our plane circled the airport for hours, waiting for the fog to clear.* **2** to draw a circle around something: *Circle the right answer.*

cir·cuit /'sɜːkɪt $ 'sɚkɪt/ *noun* **1** a track where people race cars, bicycles etc: *The racing cars go three times round the circuit.* **2** the complete circle that an electric current flows around: *an electrical circuit*

cir·cu·lar¹ /'sɜːkələ $ 'sɚkjələ/ *adjective* shaped like a circle: *a circular table*

circular² *noun* a printed advertisement or notice that a lot of people receive at the same time: *The school sent out a circular to all the parents.*

cir·cu·late /'sɜːkjəleɪt $ 'sɚkjə,leɪt/ *verb* to go around something: *Your blood circulates around your body.*

cir·cu·la·tion /,sɜːkjə'leɪʃən $,sɚkjə'leɪʃən/ *noun* [no plural] the movement of blood around your body: *Exercise can improve your circulation.*

cir·cum·cise /'sɜːkəmsaɪz $ 'sɚkəm,saɪz/ *verb* if a man or boy is circumcised, a doctor or priest has removed the skin at the end of his PENIS

cir·cum·ci·sion /,sɜːkəm'sɪʒən $,sɚkəm'sɪʒən/ *noun* when someone is circumcised

cir·cum·fer·ence /sə'kʌmfrəns $ sɚ'kʌmfrəns/ *noun* the distance around the outside of a circle

cir·cum·stance /'sɜːkəmstæns $ 'sɚkəm,stæns/ *noun* formal something such as a particular fact that affects what happens in a situation: *We hope the circumstances of her death will eventually be discovered.*

PHRASE
in the circumstances, under the circumstances: *In certain circumstances* (=in particular conditions), *students will receive money towards their course fees.*

cir·cus /'sɜːkəs $ 'sɚkəs/ *noun, plural* **circuses** a group of performers and animals that travel to different places doing tricks and other kinds of entertainment

cit·i·zen /'sɪtəzən/ *noun* **1** someone who has the legal right to live and work in a particular country: *American citizens*

2 someone who lives in a particular town, state, or country

cit·i·zen·ship /'sɪtəzənʃɪp/ *noun* [no plural] the legal right to belong to a particular country: *Peter has British citizenship.*

cit·rus fruit /'sɪtrəs ,fruːt/ *noun* a fruit such as an orange or LEMON

cit·y /'sɪti/ *noun, plural* **cities**
a large important town: *What is the capital city of England?*

civ·il /'sɪvəl/ *adjective* **1** not connected with military or religious organizations: *The company makes civil aircraft.* | *We were married in a civil ceremony, not in church.* **2** related to laws that deal with people's rights, not laws that are related to crimes: *This is a civil case, not a criminal one.*

ci·vil·ian /sə'vɪljən/ *noun* anyone who is not a member of a military organization or the police: *He left the army and became a civilian again.*

civ·i·li·za·tion also **civilisation** BrE /,sɪvəlaɪ'zeɪʃən $,sɪvələ'zeɪʃən/ *noun* a society that is well organized and developed: *We will study the ancient civilizations of Greece and Rome.*

civ·i·lized also **civilised** BrE /'sɪvəlaɪzd/ *adjective* **1** a civilized society is well organized and has laws and customs **2** behaving politely and sensibly: *Can't we discuss this in a civilized way?*

civil rights /,.. './ *plural noun* the legal rights that every person has

civil ser·vant /,.. '../ *noun* someone who works in the civil service

civil ser·vice /,.. '../ *noun* the civil service all the government departments and the people who work in them

civil war /,.. './ *noun* a war between groups of people from the same country

claim¹ /kleɪm/ *verb*

GRAMMAR
claim (that)
claim to be someone/something
claim for something
1 to say that something is true, even though it might not be: *The manufacturers* **claim that** *the car is the safest you can buy.* | *Several refugees* **claimed to be** *from Albania.*
2 to ask for something because you

have a right to have it or because it belongs to you: *Have you **claimed** for your travel costs?* | *Many lost dogs are never claimed by their owners.*

claim² *noun*

GRAMMAR
a claim that

1 a statement that something is true, even though it may not be: *The police are investigating **claims that** she stole the car.*
2 a demand for something that you have a right to have: *Insurance companies receive hundreds of false claims.*

clair·voy·ant /kleə'vɔɪənt $ kler-'vɔɪənt/ *noun* someone who says they can see what will happen in the future

clam·ber /'klæmbə $ 'klæmbɚ/ *verb* to climb over something with difficulty, using your hands and feet: *I clambered over the rocks.*

clam·my /'klæmi/ *adjective* **clammier, clammiest** wet and sticky in an unpleasant way: *clammy hands*

clam·our *BrE*, **clamor** *AmE* /'klæmə $ 'klæmɚ/ *verb* to demand something loudly: *All the reporters were clamouring for his attention.*

clamp /klæmp/ *verb* **1** to hold something tightly in a particular position so that it does not move: *He clamped his hand over her mouth.* **2 clamp down** to become very strict in order to stop people from doing something: *The police are clamping down on drivers who go too fast.*

clang /klæŋ/ *verb* to make a loud sound like metal being hit: *The heavy gate clanged shut.*

clap /klæp/ *verb* **clapped, clapping** to hit your hands together several times to show that you enjoyed something or approve of something: *We all clapped and cheered.* ⟿ *see picture on page 341*
– clap *noun*

clar·i·fy /'klærəfaɪ/ *verb formal* **clarified, clarifies** to make something easier to understand: *Can you clarify exactly what you mean?*

clar·i·net /ˌklærə'net/ *noun* a wooden musical instrument like a long black tube, which you play by blowing into it

clash /klæʃ/ *verb* **1** to fight, argue, or disagree: *The demonstrators clashed with police.* **2** if colours or clothes clash, they do not look nice together: *That tie clashes with your shirt.* **3** if two events clash, they happen at the same time, so you cannot go to one of them: *The concert clashes with my evening class.*
– clash *noun*: *There was a violent clash between rival groups of supporters.*

clasp¹ /klɑːsp $ klæsp/ *noun* a small metal object used to fasten a bag or piece of jewellery: *The clasp on my necklace is broken.*

clasp² *verb written* to hold something tightly in your hands: *He clasped the book to his chest.*

class¹ /klɑːs $ klæs/ *noun, plural* **classes**
1 a group of students who learn together: *Mary is in the same class* (=belongs to the same group of students) *as me.*
2 a period of time when a group of students learn together: *I've got a French class this afternoon.* | *We are not supposed to talk **in class**.*
3 the social group that you belong to: *They live in a **working class** area.* | *Class still has a big effect on education in Britain.*

class² *verb* to decide that something belongs in a particular group: *They class his music as jazz.*

clas·sic¹ /'klæsɪk/ *adjective* very typical: *Confusing 'their' and 'there' is a classic mistake.*

classic² *noun* an important book or film that has been popular for a long time: *I enjoy reading classics.*

classical mu·sic /ˌ... '../ *noun* music by people such as Beethoven and Mozart that is serious and important

clas·si·fied /'klæsəfaɪd/ *adjective* officially secret: *I can't tell you where they live – that's classified information.*

clas·si·fy /'klæsəfaɪ/ *verb* **classified, classifies** to put things into groups according to their type, size, age etc: *They classified Bill as a problem child.*

class·mate /'klɑːsmeɪt $ 'klæsmeɪt/ *noun* someone who is in the same class as you: *His classmates don't like him.*

class·room /'klɑːs-ruːm $'klæs-rum/ *noun*
a room in a school where students learn with a teacher

class·work /'klɑːswɜːk $'klæswɚk/ *noun [no plural]* school work that you do in class, not at home: *Do exercises 1–4 as classwork.*

clat·ter /'klætə $'klætɚ/ *verb* if hard objects clatter, they make a loud unpleasant noise when they hit against each other: *The saucepans clattered as they fell to the floor.*
–**clatter** *noun*: *I heard the clatter of dishes coming from the kitchen.*

clause /klɔːz/ *noun* 1 a part of a legal document: *Read the first clause in the contract.* 2 a group of words that contains a subject and a verb, which may be a sentence or part of a sentence

claus·tro·pho·bi·a /ˌklɔːstrə'fəubiə $ˌklɔstrə'foubiə/ *noun* fear of being in a small space: *People who suffer from claustrophobia hate going in caves.*

claus·tro·pho·bic /ˌklɔːstrə'fəubɪk $ˌklɔstrə'foubɪk/ *adjective* someone who is claustrophobic suffers from claustrophobia

claw /klɔː/ *noun* a sharp curved hard part on the toe of an animal or bird: *a lion's claw*

clay /kleɪ/ *noun [no plural]* a type of heavy soil that is used for making pots: *He made a figure out of clay.*

clean¹ /kliːn/ *adjective*
not dirty: *He put on a clean shirt.* | *The room looked very neat and clean.* | *The city is much cleaner now.*

clean² *verb*
GRAMMAR
clean something off/from something
clean something with something
also **clean up** to remove dirt from something, for example by washing it: *I need to clean my boots.* | *Clean the wound **with** warm water.* | *It took us two hours to **clean up** all the mess after the party.*

clean·er /'kliːnə $'klinɚ/ *noun* 1 someone whose job is to clean houses or offices: *The cleaner will tidy*

your desk. 2 **the cleaner's** the DRY CLEANER'S

clean·li·ness /'klenlinəs/ *noun [no plural]* when you keep things clean: *Cleanliness is very important in the kitchen.*

cleanse /klenz/ *verb formal* to clean something: *The nurse cleansed the wound with warm water.*

clean-shav·en /ˌ. '../ *adjective* a man who is clean-shaven does not have a BEARD

clear¹ /klɪə $klɪr/ *adjective*
1 easy to see, hear, or understand: *His writing isn't very clear.* | *Some of the exam questions weren't very clear.*
2 if something is clear, it is certain and people cannot doubt it: *It soon **became clear** that John was lying to us.* | *Sarah **made it clear** that she wanted to come with us.* | *It's not clear how many people were hurt.*
3 if a substance or liquid is clear, you can see through it: *clear glass*
4 a clear sky has no clouds

clear² *verb*
GRAMMAR
clear something off/from something
clear something away
1 also **clear up** to make a place tidy or empty by removing things from it: *We **cleared** the snow **off** the path.* | *Sammy helped me clear the table when we had finished eating.* | *I asked the children to come and **clear** their toys **away**.* | *Who's going to help me **clear up** all this mess?*
2 *written* to jump over something such as a fence or wall without touching it: *He cleared the wall easily.*

clear³ *adverb* away from something: *Stand clear of the doors.*

clear-cut /ˌ. './ *adjective* certain or definite: *There's no clear-cut answer to your question.*

clear·ing /'klɪərɪŋ $'klɪrɪŋ/ *noun* a small area in a forest where there are no trees

clear·ly /'klɪəli $'klɪrli/ *adverb*
1 without any doubt: *Clearly, you will have to work harder if you want to pass your exam.*
2 if you say or show something clearly, you do it in a way that is easy to see

or understand: *The teacher ex-*
plained everything very clearly.
3 if you cannot think clearly, you are
confused

cleav·age /ˈkliːvɪdʒ/ *noun* the space
between a woman's breasts: *She wore a*
dress that showed her cleavage.

clench /klentʃ/ *verb* to close your
hands or your mouth tightly, especially
because you are angry: *He clenched his*
fists and started banging the door. |
Clenching her teeth she said, "Go
away!"

cler·gy /ˈklɜːdʒi $ˈklɚdʒi/ *plural noun*
priests and other religious leaders:
Catholic clergy are not allowed to marry.

cler·gy·man /ˈklɜːdʒimən $ˈklɚdʒi-
mən/ *noun, plural* **clergymen** /-mən/ a
male member of the clergy

cler·i·cal /ˈklerɪkəl/ *adjective* connected with office work: *We need some*
more clerical staff.

clerk /klɑːk $klɚk/ *noun* 1 someone
whose job is to keep the records or
accounts in an office: *A bank clerk was*
counting money. 2 *AmE* someone
whose job is to deal with people arriving
at a hotel: *The desk clerk will give you*
your room keys.

clev·er /ˈklevə $ˈklevɚ/ *adjective*

1 someone who is clever is able to
learn and understand things quickly:
⇨ *same meaning* INTELLIGENT: *Paul is*
good-looking, clever, and charm-
ing. | *a very clever student*
2 something that is clever has been
made or done in an intelligent way,
so that it is useful and effective:
What a clever idea!

cli·ché /ˈkliːʃeɪ $kliˈʃeɪ/ *noun* an ex-
pression that is used too often and no
longer has any real meaning: *His speech*
was full of clichés like "We must take
one day at a time."

click /klɪk/ *verb* 1 to make a short
hard sound: *The door clicked open.*
2 if you click on something on a computer screen, you press a button on the
MOUSE in order to do something: *Double*
click on the file manager to open it up.
3 **click your fingers** to make a short
hard sound by moving your thumb
quickly across your second finger ⇨ *see*
picture on page 350

– **click** *noun*: *I heard the click of the gate*
closing.

cli·ent /ˈklaɪənt/ *noun* someone who
pays a person or organization for a service or advice: *Mr Dolan is an important*
client of this law firm. ⇨ *see usage note*
at CUSTOMER

cli·en·tele /ˌkliːənˈtel $ˌklaɪənˈtel/
noun [no plural] the people who regularly
go to a shop or restaurant: *The shop's*
clientele is mainly women.

cliff /klɪf/ *noun* a high piece of land with
a very steep side, usually next to the sea:
Don't go near the edge of the cliff. ⇨ *see*
picture on page 348

cli·mate /ˈklaɪmət/ *noun* the typical
weather conditions in an area: *The cli-*
mate in the Maldives is hot and sunny.

cli·max /ˈklaɪmæks/ *noun* the most
important or exciting part of something: *The poetry competition reaches its*
climax tomorrow.

climb /klaɪm/　　　　　**climb**
verb

GRAMMAR
climb up/into/
over etc some-
thing

1 to move to-
wards the top of
something: *She*
slowly climbed
the stairs. | *We*
climbed up to
the top of the
hill. | *He* **climbed up** the ladder.
⇨ *see picture on page 340*
2 to move somewhere by bending
your body and using your hands and
feet: *He* **climbed into** the truck. | *We*
had to **climb out of** the window. |
She managed to **climb over** the
fence.
– **climb** *noun*: *It was a long climb up*
to the top of the hill.

climb·er /ˈklaɪmə $ˈklaɪmɚ/ *noun*
someone who climbs mountains or
rocks as a sport

climb·ing /ˈklaɪmɪŋ/ *noun* [no plural] the
sport of climbing mountains or rocks:
We go climbing most weekends.

cling /klɪŋ/ *verb, past tense and past*
participle **clung** /klʌŋ/ to hold someone
tightly, especially because you do not
feel safe: *She clung to her mother.*

cling·film /ˈklɪŋfɪlm/ *noun [no plural]* BrE *trademark* thin clear plastic that is used for wrapping food; SARAN WRAP AmE *trademark*

clin·ic /ˈklɪnɪk/ *noun* a place where people go for medical treatment: *I went to the clinic to see the doctor.*

clin·i·cal /ˈklɪnɪkəl/ *adjective* connected with medical treatment and tests: *The drug needs to have clinical trials.*

clink /klɪŋk/ *noun* the sound made when glass or metal touch each other

clip¹ /klɪp/ *noun* **1** a small metal or plastic object used to hold things together: *a hair clip* **2** a short part of a film or television programme that is shown separately: *a clip from Toystory 2*

clip² *verb* **clipped, clipping** to fasten things together using a clip: *I clipped my papers into a file.*

clip·pers /ˈklɪpəz $ ˈklɪpərz/ *plural noun* a tool used for cutting small pieces off something: *a pair of nail clippers*

clip·ping /ˈklɪpɪŋ/ *noun* a piece of writing that you cut from a newspaper or magazine: *I found a newspaper clipping about Madonna.*

clique /kliːk/ *noun* a small group of people who know each other well and are not very friendly to other people: *Jane has become part of their clique.*

cloak /kləʊk $ kloʊk/ *noun* a warm piece of clothing like a coat without SLEEVES that hangs from your shoulders

cloak·room /ˈkləʊkruːm $ ˈkloʊkrum/ *noun* a room in a public building where people can leave their coats

clock /klɒk $ klɑk/ *noun* an object that shows the time: *You could hear the clock ticking.*

clock·wise /ˈklɒk-waɪz $ ˈklɑk-waɪz/ *adverb, adjective* in the same direction as the moving parts on the face of a clock ⇨ *opposite* ANTICLOCKWISE: *The ring of dancers turned clockwise.* | *Turn the key in a clockwise direction.*

clock·work /ˈklɒk-wɜːk $ ˈklɑk-wərk/ *noun [no plural]* a type of machinery that starts when you turn a key: *The child was playing with a clockwork mouse.*

clog /klɒg $ klɑg/ *verb* **clogged, clogging** also **clog up** to block something: *Leaves can clog drains.*

clone¹ /kləʊn $ kloʊn/ *noun formal* an exact copy of a plant or animal that a scientist develops from one of its cells

clone² *verb* to produce a plant or an animal that is a clone: *Scientists have successfully cloned a sheep.*

close¹ /kləʊz $ kloʊz/ *verb*
1 if you close something such as a door or window, or if it closes, it shuts: *Please could you close the window?* | *Jude lay on the bed and closed her eyes.* | *I heard the door close behind him as he left.*
2 if a shop, bank, or other public place closes, it is not available for people to use: *The shops close at 5:30.* | *The school is closed for the summer.*

PHRASAL VERB
close down if a shop of business closes down, it stops working permanently
close off **close something off** if the police close off a road, street etc, they stop people going there: *It was a bad accident, and the police closed the road off for three hours.* ⇨ *see usage note at* OPEN²

close² /kləʊs $ kloʊs/ *adjective, adverb*
GRAMMAR
close to something/someone
1 near to a place or person: *We live quite close to the school.* | *She came a bit closer.* | *Don't get too close to the fire.* | *The two boys were standing quite close together.*
2 about to happen, or happening very soon: *The day of the exam was coming closer.* | *The shops were busy because it was so close to Christmas.*
3 if two people are close, they like or love each other very much: *We are very close friends.* | *I'm very close to my parents.*
4 if a competition or race is close, someone wins by a very small amount: *It was a very close game.*

close³ /kləʊz $ kloʊz/ *noun* the end of an event or period of time: *We brought the party to a close.*

closed /kləʊzd $ kloʊzd/ *adjective*
1 if a shop or school is closed, it is not open to the public: *The school is closed for six weeks in the summer.*
2 not open: *The door was closed and*

▼ locked. | *Her eyes are closed, but I don't think she's asleep.*

open
closed
closed

close·ly /'kləʊsli $'kloʊsli/ *adverb*
1 if you look at something closely, you look at it very carefully: *The teacher was watching the students closely.*
2 people who are closely related are members of the same family, for example brothers or sisters
3 if people work closely together, they work together and help each other a lot: *We have worked closely with the police to solve this crime.*

clos·et /'klɒzɪt $'klɑzɪt/ the American word for WARDROBE

close-up /'kləʊs ʌp $'kloʊs ʌp/ *noun* a photograph of a person that you take when you are standing very near to them: *a close-up of the actor's face*

clos·ing /'kləʊzɪŋ $'kloʊzɪŋ/ *adjective* the closing part of something is the final part: *In the closing chapter of the book, Max dies.*

clo·sure /'kləʊʒə $'kloʊʒəʳ/ *noun* when a factory, company, school etc closes permanently: *Workers are angry at the closure of their factory.*

clot /klɒt $klɑt/ *noun* a place where blood or another liquid has become almost solid: *She has a blood clot in her leg.*

cloth /klɒθ $klɔθ/ *noun* 1 [no plural] material: *The bag is made from thick cloth.* 2 a piece of material that is used for cleaning: *I wiped the table with a damp cloth.*

clothe /kləʊð $kloʊð/ *verb* written to provide clothes for someone: *We don't have enough money to clothe our children.*

clothed /kləʊðd $kloʊðd/ *adjective* fully clothed, partly clothed with all your clothes on or with only some of your clothes on: *She got into bed fully clothed.* | *He was only partly clothed.*

clothes /kləʊðz $kloʊðz/ *plural noun*
the things such as shirts, skirts, or trousers that you wear: *She was wearing smart clothes.* | *He put on some clean clothes.* | *I'm shy about taking my clothes off in front of other people.*

USAGE
There is no singular form of **clothes**. You have to say **a piece of clothing** or **an article of clothing**: *She picked up each piece of clothing and folded it carefully.*

clothes·line /'kləʊðzlaɪn $'kloʊzlaɪn/ *noun* a rope that you hang clothes on so that they will dry

clothes peg /'. ./ *BrE*, **clothes·pin** /'kləʊðzpɪn $'kloʊzpɪn/ *AmE noun* a small object that you use to fasten clothes to a clothesline ⇨ see picture at PEG

cloth·ing /'kləʊðɪŋ $'kloʊðɪŋ/ *noun* [no plural] clothes: *You'll need to take some warm clothing.*

cloud¹ /klaʊd/ *noun* a white or grey shape in the sky that is made of small drops of water: *There were no clouds in the sky.*

cloud² *verb* 1 to make something less easy to understand, or make someone less able to think clearly: *His own experiences had clouded his judgement.* 2 **cloud up** if glass or a mirror clouds up, it becomes covered in small drops of water, and you cannot see it properly: *Steam had clouded up the mirror.*

cloud·y /'klaʊdi/ *adjective* **cloudier, cloudiest** if it is cloudy, there are a lot of clouds in the sky: *It's very cloudy today.* | *a cloudy, overcast sky*

clove /kləʊv $kloʊv/ *noun* 1 one of the parts that a GARLIC plant is made up of: *Chop up two cloves of garlic.* 2 a small dried black flower with a strong sweet smell, used in cooking

clo·ver /'kləʊvə $'kloʊvəʳ/ *noun* a small plant with white or purple flowers and three round leaves on each stem

clown /klaʊn/ *noun* someone who entertains people by dressing in strange clothes, painting their face, and doing funny things, especially in a CIRCUS

club¹ /klʌb/ *noun*
▼1 an organization for people who have

the same interest or enjoy similar activities: *a football club* | *Are you going to **join** the film **club?***
2 a place where young people go in the evening to dance: *We had a few drinks in the pub, then went to a club.*
3 a special long stick that you use in the game of GOLF to hit the ball
4 **clubs** a group of playing cards with black shapes like rounded leaves on them: *the ace of clubs*

club² *verb* **clubbed, clubbing, club together** if a group of people club together, they all share the cost of something: *We all clubbed together to buy him a leaving present.*

club·bing /'klʌbɪŋ/ *noun* [no plural] when you go to a club to dance: *When we were in Ibiza, we went out clubbing every night.*

clue /kluː/ *noun*

GRAMMAR
a clue to something
a small piece of information or an object that helps you to understand something or know something: *The police searched the area for clues.* | *This note could be a **clue to** the identity of the murderer.* | *I don't know the answer to question 6 – can you **give** me a **clue** (=give me a piece of information that will help me know the answer)?*

PHRASE
not have a clue *informal* if you do not have a clue about something, you do not know what to do about it or you do not understand it at all: *I **haven't got a clue** what I'm going to wear.*

clump /klʌmp/ *noun* a group of trees, bushes, plants etc that are close together: *a clump of trees*

clum·sy /'klʌmzi/ *adjective* **clumsier, clumsiest** a clumsy person often damages things by accidentally hitting them: *I'm always breaking cups – I'm so clumsy.*
– **clumsily** *adverb*
– **clumsiness** *noun* [no plural]

clung the past tense and past participle of CLING

clus·ter /'klʌstə $ 'klʌstɚ/ *verb* to form a group of people or things: *Everyone clustered around the television.*

– **cluster** *noun*: *There's a cluster of restaurants on the main street.*

clutch¹ /klʌtʃ/ *verb* written to hold something tightly: *She was clutching a black bag.*

clutch² *noun, plural* **clutches** the part of a car that you press with your foot when you change GEAR

clut·ter¹ /'klʌtə $ 'klʌtɚ/ *also* **clutter up** *verb* to make something untidy by covering. or filling it with things: *Books and papers cluttered his desk.*

clutter² *noun* [no plural] a lot of things scattered in an untidy way: *I hate clutter – let's put these toys away.*

cm the written abbreviation of CENTIMETRE

Co. /kəʊ $ koʊ/ the abbreviation of 'company': *Hilton, Brooks & Co.*

c/o the written abbreviation of 'care of'; used as part of an address when you send a letter to someone who is staying away from their home for a short time: *Michael Miles, c/o the Grand Hotel, Park Lane, London*

coach¹ /kəʊtʃ $ koʊtʃ/ *noun, plural* **coaches** 1 someone who trains a person or team in a sport: *Jack's my tennis coach.* 2 BrE a bus with comfortable seats, that you go on for long journeys; BUS AmE: *Everyone get back on the coach.* | *It will take us two days, if we go by coach.* 3 another word for CARRIAGE

coach² *verb* 1 to train a person or team in a sport: *Who coaches your football team?* 2 to give a student special lessons in a subject, especially to help them in an examination: *Tim earned some extra money by coaching students in French.*

coal /kəʊl $ koʊl/ *noun* [no plural] a hard black substance that comes from under the ground and that you burn to produce heat: *Put some more coal on the fire.*

coarse /kɔːs $ kɔrs/ *adjective* rough and thick, not smooth or fine: *She dried herself on a coarse old towel.*

coast /kəʊst $ koʊst/ *noun* the land next to the sea: *It gets quite cold on the coast.* | *the southern coast of the USA* ⇨ *see picture on page 348*

coast·al /'kəʊstl $ 'koʊstl/ *adjective* in the sea or on the land near the sea: *the coastal regions of Italy*

C

coast guard /'. ./ *noun* a person or group of people who help boats and swimmers that are in danger

coast·line /'kəʊstlaɪn $ 'koʊstlaɪn/ *noun* the edge of the coast: *You can see the rocky coastline from here.*

coat¹ /kəʊt $ koʊt/ *noun*

GRAMMAR
a coat of something

1 a piece of clothing that you wear over your other clothes to keep you warm: *Put your coat on before you go out.* ⇨ *see picture on page 352*

2 a layer of paint that covers a surface: *The doors will need two **coats of paint**. | I think the ceiling needs another coat.*

3 an animal's fur, wool, or hair: *Your dog has a lovely shiny coat.*

coat² *verb* to cover a surface with a thin layer of something: *Coat the chicken with oil.*

coax /kəʊks $ koʊks/ *verb* to persuade someone to do something by talking to them gently and kindly: *Mom managed to coax me into going.*

cob·web /'kɒbweb $ 'kɑbweb/ *noun* a structure made by a SPIDER, consisting of fine threads: *The ceiling is covered in cobwebs.*

co·caine /kə'keɪn $ koʊ'keɪn/ *noun* [no plural] a drug that stops pain. Some people take cocaine illegally for pleasure

cock /kɒk $ kɑk/ *noun* BrE a male chicken; ROOSTER AmE

cock·e·rel /'kɒkərəl $ 'kɑkərəl/ *noun* a young male chicken

cock·pit /'kɒk,pɪt $ 'kɑk,pɪt/ *noun* the part of a plane where the pilot sits

cock·roach /'kɒk-rəʊtʃ $ 'kɑk-roʊtʃ/ *noun, plural* **cockroaches** a large black or brown insect that lives where food is kept

cock·tail /'kɒkteɪl $ 'kɑkteɪl/ *noun* an alcoholic drink made from a mixture of different drinks

cock·y /'kɒki $ 'kɑki/ **cockier, cockiest** *adjective informal* too proud or confident about yourself, in a way that annoys other people: *He could be a bit too cocky at times, almost arrogant.*

co·coa /'kəʊkəʊ $ 'koʊkoʊ/ *noun* [no plural] 1 a dark brown powder used to make chocolate and to make food taste

of chocolate: *You need cocoa powder to make a chocolate cake.* 2 a drink made from cocoa powder: *I always have a cup of cocoa before I go to bed.*

co·co·nut /'kəʊkənʌt $ 'koʊkə,nʌt/ *noun* a large brown nut with white flesh, which is filled with a liquid ⇨ *see picture on page 345*

code /kəʊd $ koʊd/ *noun* a system of words, letters, or signs that are used for sending secret messages: *They sent the message in code, so that I would be the only person who understood it.*

co·ed /,kəʊ'ed $,koʊ'ed/ *adjective* co-ed schools and colleges are ones where male and female students study together

co·erce /kəʊ'ɜːs $ koʊ'ɚs/ *verb formal* to force someone to do something by threatening them: *They coerced him into confessing.*

cof·fee /'kɒfi $ 'kɔfi/ *noun*

1 [no plural] a brown powder that is made by crushing the beans of the coffee tree

2 a drink made from coffee powder: *a cup of coffee | Two coffees, please.*

coffee ta·ble /'.. ,../ *noun* a low table in a LIVING ROOM

cof·fin /'kɒfɪn $ 'kɔfɪn/ *noun* the box in which a dead person is buried

coil¹ /kɔɪl/ *verb* to wind or twist something into a round shape: *The snake coiled itself around the branch of the tree.*

coil² *noun* a piece of wire, rope etc that someone has made into a circular shape: *a coil of wire*

coin /kɔɪn/ *noun* a piece of money made of metal: *He put a fifty pence coin into the drinks machine.*

co·in·cide /,kəʊɪn'saɪd $,koʊɪn'saɪd/ *verb* if one event coincides with another, the two things happen at the same time: *My birthday coincides with Paul's.*

co·in·ci·dence /kəʊ'ɪnsədəns $ koʊ'ɪnsədəns/ *noun* when two things happen at the same time without being planned or an occasion in which two things are the same by chance: *What a coincidence – my name's Laura too!*

cold¹ /kəʊld $ koʊld/ *adjective*

1 something that is cold has a low temperature and is not warm or hot:

▼ *This room's really cold!* | *Drink your soup before it* ***goes cold.*** | *Hurry up – I'm* ***getting cold.*** | *It's* ***freezing cold*** *outside today.* | *Would you like coffee, or would you prefer a cold drink?*

2 cold food is cooked, but is not eaten while it is hot: *a salad of cold chicken and rice*

3 a cold person is not very friendly or kind: *He was a cold, unsympathetic man.*

USAGE cold, freezing, cool

Cold usually describes a temperature that is unpleasant: *My coffee's cold.* | *a* ***cold winter.*** **Freezing** is even colder, and more unpleasant, and is usually used about the weather: *It's freezing outside!* **Cool** means fairly cold, and usually describes a temperature that is pleasant: *a nice cool drink*

cold² *noun* 1 a common illness that makes you cough and SNEEZE: *I've got a bad cold.* | *Be careful not to catch a cold.* 2 **the cold** a very low temperature because the weather is cold: *He made me stay outside in the cold.*

cold-blood·ed /ˌ. '../ *adjective* cruel and showing no feelings: *This was a cold-blooded murder.*

col·lab·o·rate /kəˈlæbəreɪt/ *verb* to work together to produce or achieve something: *Two companies collaborated on this project.*

col·lab·o·ra·tion /kəˌlæbəˈreɪʃən/ *noun* when people work together to achieve something

col·lage /ˈkɒlɑːʒ $ kəˈlɑːʒ/ *noun* a picture that you make by sticking pieces of paper and cloth onto a surface, or putting different photographs together: *The children made a collage of their visit to the zoo.*

col·lapse /kəˈlæps/ *verb* to fall down suddenly: *The building collapsed in the earthquake.* | *He collapsed after running a marathon.*
– **collapse** *noun*: *What caused the collapse of the bridge?*

col·lar /ˈkɒlə $ ˈkɑlɚ/ *noun* the part of a shirt, coat, or dress that fits around your neck: *Your shirt collar is dirty.* ⇨ *see picture on page 352*

col·lar·bone /ˈkɒləbəʊn $ ˈkɑlɚˌboʊn/ *noun* one of two bones that go from the base of your neck to your shoulders: *I broke my collarbone playing rugby.*

col·league /ˈkɒliːɡ $ ˈkɑliɡ/ *noun* someone who you work with: *This is Ian, a colleague of mine.*

col·lect¹ /kəˈlekt/ *verb*

GRAMMAR
collect something for something
collect for something
collect someone from somewhere

1 also **collect up** to get things from different places and bring them all to one place: *Can you collect all the books and put them on my desk?* | *She* ***collected up*** *all the dirty glasses.*

2 to get and keep things that are the same in some way, because you like them and find them interesting: *He* ***collects stamps.***

3 if you collect money, you ask people to give it for a particular purpose: *The school is* ***collecting*** *money* ***for*** *the Children in Need appeal.*

4 *BrE* to go to a place and get someone or something: *I've got to go and* ***collect*** *Jane* ***from*** *the station.*

collect² *adverb AmE* if you call someone collect, the person who gets the telephone call pays for it: *Phone me tonight – you can call collect, if you need to.*
– **collect** *adjective*: *Will you accept a collect call from Chicago?*

col·lec·tion /kəˈlekʃən/ *noun*

GRAMMAR
a collection of something
a collection for someone/something

1 a set of similar things that you keep together: *She's got a wonderful collection of CDs.* | *a stamp collection*

2 when you ask people for money for a particular purpose: *We* ***had a collection for*** *local children's homes.*

col·lec·tive /kəˈlektɪv/ *adjective* a collective decision, effort etc is shared by all the members of a group together: *It was a collective decision to give you the money.*
– **collectively** *adverb*

col·lege /ˈkɒlɪdʒ $ ˈkɑlɪdʒ/ *noun* a place where students study after they leave school: *I want to go to art college.*

col·lide /kəˈlaɪd/ *verb* to hit something violently by crashing into it: *The car collided with a lorry.*

col·li·sion /kə'lɪʒən/ noun a violent crash in which one vehicle hits another: *Two trains were involved in a head-on collision.*

co·lon /'kəʊlən $ 'koʊlən/ noun the mark (:), used in writing to introduce a list or examples

colo·nel /'kɜːnl $ 'kɜ·nl/ noun an officer with a high rank in the Army, Marines, or the US Air Force

col·o·ny /'kɒləni $ 'kɑːləni/ noun, plural **colonies** a country or area that a more powerful country controls: *Senegal was once a French colony.*

color the American spelling of COLOUR

color-blind the American spelling of COLOUR-BLIND

colorful the American spelling of COLOURFUL

colorless the American spelling of COLOURLESS

co·los·sal /kə'lɒsəl $ kə'lɑːsəl/ adjective very big: *Global warming is a colossal problem.*

colour¹ BrE, **color** AmE /'kʌlə $ 'kʌlə·/ noun
1 green, blue, yellow, red etc: *The room was painted in bright colours.* | *a beautiful dark red colour* | *What colour is her hair?* | *The leaves are dark green in colour.*
2 [no plural] a colour photograph, film etc shows all the different colours, not just black and white: *a colour TV* | *Is the film in black and white or in colour?*
3 how dark or light someone's skin is: *The carnival brought together people of all colors.*

colour² BrE, **color** AmE, verb 1 to make something a different colour: *I want to colour my hair.* 2 also **colour something in** to put colour onto a drawing or picture using coloured pencils: *He drew a picture of a house and coloured it in.*

colour-blind BrE, **color-blind** AmE /'.. ,./ adjective not able to see the difference between particular colours

col·oured BrE, **colored** AmE /'kʌləd $ 'kʌlə·d/ adjective having a colour such as blue, red, or yellow: *A black dress looks good with a coloured scarf.*

col·our·ful BrE, **colorful** AmE /'kʌləfəl ▼

$ 'kʌlə·fəl/ adjective having a lot of bright colours: *I prefer colourful clothes.*

col·our·ing BrE, **coloring** AmE /'kʌlərɪŋ/ noun [no plural] the colour of someone's hair, skin, eyes etc: *She has the same pale colouring as her sister.*

col·our·less BrE, **colorless** AmE /'kʌlələs $ 'kʌlə·ləs/ adjective not having any colour: *Water is a colourless liquid.*

col·umn /'kɒləm $ 'kɑːləm/ noun
1 numbers or words written under each other down a page: *There were six columns of names.* 2 a tall thin stone structure that supports something: *Four marble columns support the roof.*

co·ma /'kəʊmə $ 'koʊmə/ noun when someone is UNCONSCIOUS (=not awake and not able to see, hear, speak etc) for a long time, especially after an accident: *She's been in a coma for weeks.*

comb¹ /kəʊm $ koʊm/ noun a piece of plastic or metal with a row of thin teeth, that you use to make your hair tidy

comb² verb to make your hair tidy with a comb: *Have you combed your hair?*

com·bat¹ /'kɒmbæt $ 'kɑːmbæt/ noun fighting during a war: *Many soldiers were killed in combat.*

com·bat² /'kɒmbæt $ kəm'bæt/ verb **combated, combating** also **combatted, combatting** to try to stop something bad from happening or getting worse: *What is the best way to combat crime?*

com·bi·na·tion /ˌkɒmbə'neɪʃən $ ˌkɑːmbə'neɪʃən/ noun

GRAMMAR
a combination of things
two or more things that you use or mix together: *Doctors use a combination of drugs to treat the disease.*

com·bine /kəm'baɪn/ verb

GRAMMAR
combine (something) with something
1 if you combine two or more different things, you mix or do them together: *Combine the eggs with a small amount of oil.* | *She manages to combine her career and family life quite successfully.* | *I like the way the painter has combined different shades of purple together.*

C

➤ COME or GO?

Are you **coming** to the party? (=the party will be in a place where you are)

Are you **going** to the party? (=the party will be at someone else's house, in a different place from where you are)

➤ COME

1 to move towards a place or person
*It would be nice if Chris could **come**. | Bob is **coming from** Seattle for the wedding. | He **came** to class without his books. | Is Sara **coming** to get those photographs today? | Why don't you **come with** me?*

> **GRAMMAR**
> come to/from/towards etc
> come to do something

2 to arrive at a place
*Jean was really tired when she **came home**. | Mom said she sent us a package, but it hasn't **come** yet.*

3 time, event
if a time or event comes, it arrives or starts to happen: *Spring **came** early.*

come

6 come loose, come apart, come open etc
to start being loose, broken, open etc: *The box **came open** as I was carrying it upstairs. | One of the bicycle's wheels had **come loose**, causing the accident.*

4 to reach a particular position
*The snow **came up to** my knees. | Marty's jacket was too big and the sleeves **came down to** his fingertips.*

5 to have a position
*Jodi **came first** in the 100 meter race. | In the set '2, 4, 6, 8', what number **comes next**?*

PHRASES

come on *spoken*
a say this when you want someone to hurry: *Come on, Linda, we're going to be late!*
b say this when you want to encourage someone: *Come on, you can do it – just keep your eye on the ball.*
c say this when you do not believe someone: *Oh, come on! He'd never do that!*

how come? *spoken*
say this when you want to know why something has happened: *I just gave her £20 – how come she doesn't have any money?* | *"I didn't pass the exam." "How come?"*

here comes Ted/Jo/Sue etc *spoken*
say this when someone is coming towards you: *Here comes your mother now.*

PHRASAL VERBS

come back
to return to a place: *What time are you coming back tonight?*

come down
to move from the top of something to the bottom: *Skiers come down this part of the mountain really fast.*

Skiers come down this part of the mountain really fast.

come from
used to talk about the place where you were born or where you first lived: *Where does Enrico come from?* | *My mother comes from Canada.*

come in
to enter a room or house: *It was just starting to rain when we came in.* | *Hi, Charles, come in.*

come off
to start being separate or removed from something: *A button came off my coat.*

come out
when the sun, moon, or stars come out, you can see them in the sky: *Finally the clouds cleared and the sun came out.*

The sun came out.

come over
if someone comes over, they move to the place where you are: *Why don't you and Ron come over for dinner?* | *Jane came over to talk to me.*

come round *BrE*
to visit someone: *Aunt Flora came round last night.*

come up
1 to move to the front or the top of something: *When I call your names, please come up to get your essays.*
2 be coming up
if an event or time is coming up, it will happen soon: *The summer holidays are coming up in July.*
3 when the sun or the moon comes up, you can see it in the sky for the first time in the morning or the night: *The sun doesn't come up until 9 o'clock in the winter.*

2 if two things combine, they join together and have a particular effect: *The two telephone companies combined to make the world's biggest telecommunications provider.* | *A very hot year combined with a lack of rain led to a very poor harvest.*

come ⇨ see box on pages 114 and 115

come·back /'kʌmbæk/ *noun* when someone or something becomes popular or successful again: *Do you think miniskirts will ever make a comeback?*

co·me·di·an /kə'miːdiən/ *noun* someone whose job is to tell jokes and make people laugh

com·e·dy /'kɒmədi $ 'kɑmədi/ *noun, plural* **comedies** a funny film or play: *All my favourite films are comedies.*

com·et /'kɒmɪt $ 'kɑmɪt/ *noun* a very bright object in the sky like a star with a tail: *A comet flew across the sky.*

com·fort¹ /'kʌmfət $ 'kʌmfɚt/ *noun*

1 *[no plural]* when you feel physically relaxed, happy, and without pain: *I buy shoes for comfort rather than for their appearance.* | *We were able to sit and watch the play in comfort.* | *You can now use the Internet to do your shopping from the comfort of your own home.*

2 *[no plural]* when you feel calm and less unhappy: *Support from friends and family brought us a lot of comfort after the death of our daughter.*

3 *[no plural]* when you have enough money to buy all the things that you need: *They now had enough money to live in comfort for the rest of their lives.*

4 **comforts** all the things that make your life easier and more comfortable: *I really missed all the home comforts while I was travelling.*

comfort² *verb* to make someone feel happier or less worried by being kind to them: *Ruth always comforted him when he was upset.*

– **comforting** *adjective*: *It's very comforting to know you're here.*

com·forta·ble /'kʌmftəbəl $ 'kʌmftɚbəl/ *adjective*

1 if you are comfortable, you feel phys-

ically relaxed ⇨ opposite UNCOMFORTABLE (1): *Are you comfortable sitting on the floor?*

2 something that is comfortable makes you feel physically relaxed ⇨ opposite UNCOMFORTABLE (2): *a comfortable bed*

3 emotionally relaxed and not worried ⇨ opposite UNCOMFORTABLE (3): *I feel very comfortable with Paul whenever we're together.*

com·for·ta·bly /'kʌmftəbli $ 'kʌmftɚbli/ *adverb* if you are sitting or lying comfortably, you are sitting or lying in a comfortable way and feeling relaxed

com·ic /'kɒmɪk $ 'kɑmɪk/ *noun*
1 someone whose job is to tell jokes and make people laugh: *Steve Martin is a great comic.* **2** *BrE* a magazine that tells a story using sets of pictures; COMIC BOOK *AmE*: *I love reading comics, especially Judge Dread.*

com·i·cal /'kɒmɪkəl $ 'kɑmɪkəl/ *adjective* funny in a strange or unexpected way: *It was comical to watch him trying to ride a bike.*

comic book /'.. ,./ the American word for a COMIC

comic strip /'.. ,./ *noun* a set of pictures in a newspaper or magazine that tell a short funny story

com·ing /'kʌmɪŋ/ *adjective formal* a coming event or period of time is happening soon: *We will be very busy over the coming months.*

com·ma /'kɒmə $ 'kɑmə/ *noun* the mark (,) used in writing or printing to show a short pause

com·mand¹ /kə'mɑːnd $ kə'mænd/ *noun*

1 an order that must be obeyed: *The sergeant shouted commands to his men.*

2 *[no plural]* if you are in command, you are responsible for deciding what people should do: *I need to talk to the officer in command.* | *Judith was left in command while the others were out of the office.* | *Who will take command while you are away?*

3 an instruction to a computer to do something: *The program is very similar to the old one, but some of the commands are different.*

command² *verb* **1** to order someone to do something: *The king commanded him to stay.* **2** to control an army or group of soldiers: *Major Fish will command the troops.*

com·mand·er /kə'mɑːndə $ kə-'mændɚ/ *noun* an officer who is in charge of a military organization or group

com·mem·o·rate /kə'meməreɪt/ *verb* if something commemorates an event or group of people, it exists so that people will remember them with respect: *The monument commemorates the war.*

com·mence /kə'mens/ *verb formal* to begin: *The new system will commence next week.*

com·men·da·ble /kə'mendəbəl/ *adjective formal* deserving praise and admiration: *It is commendable that you want to help.*

com·ment¹ /'kɒment $ 'kɑment/ *noun*
an opinion that you give about someone or something: *My tutor made some very useful comments about my work.* | *If you have any comments on our ideas, we would be glad to hear them.*

comment² *verb*

> **GRAMMAR**
> **comment on something**
> **comment that**

to give your opinion about someone or something: *The England manager refused to comment on rumours that he was about to resign.* | *Paul commented that the food was a bit disappointing.*

com·men·ta·ry /'kɒmənteri $ 'kɑmən,teri/ *noun, plural* **commentaries** a description of an event that is on the television or radio, while the event is happening: *There will be a live commentary on the football match.*

com·men·tate /'kɒmənteɪt $ 'kɑmən,teɪt/ *verb* to describe an event on television or radio at the same time as the event happens: *John McEnroe is here to commentate on the event for the BBC.*

com·men·ta·tor /'kɒmənteɪtə $ 'kɑmən,teɪtɚ/ *noun* someone whose job is to describe an event on television or radio at the same time as it happens: *a sports commentator*

com·merce /'kɒmɜːs $ 'kɑmɚs/ *noun* [no plural] *formal* the activity of buying and selling things in business: *We want to encourage commerce between Britain and France.*

com·mer·cial¹ /kə'mɜːʃəl $ kə'mɚ-ʃəl/ *adjective* connected with the buying and selling of things and with making money: *Not all good films are a commercial success.*
– **commercially** *adverb*

commercial² *noun* an advertisement on television or radio: *He appeared in a Pepsi commercial.*

com·mer·cial·ized also **comercial·ised** *BrE* /kə'mɜːʃəlaɪzd $ kə'mɚ·ʃə-,laɪzd/ *adjective* too concerned with making money: *The holiday resort has become too commercialized.*

com·mis·sion¹ /kə'mɪʃən/ *noun* **1** an official group whose job is to find out about something or control an activity: *The International Whaling Commission decides the limits on catching whales.* **2** money that a person or organization is paid when they sell something: *The bank charges commission for cashing traveller's cheques.*

commission² *verb formal* to ask someone to do a particular piece of work for you: *The government commissioned the report.*

com·mit /kə'mɪt/ *verb* **committed, committing**
to do something wrong or illegal: *The police are still looking for the gang that committed this crime.* | *Most murders are committed by men.* | *We were worried that George might commit suicide* (=kill himself).

com·mit·ment /kə'mɪtmənt/ *noun* **1** a promise to do something: *They made a commitment to work together.* **2** [no plural] determination to work hard and continue with something: *You need commitment to succeed in this sport.*

com·mit·ted /kə'mɪtɪd/ *adjective* wanting to work hard at something: *He seems committed to his work.*

com·mit·tee /kə'mɪti/ *noun* an official group of people who have meetings to decide what needs to be done about something: *Nick and Bob are both on the tennis club committee.*

com·mon¹ /'kɒmən $'kamən/ adjective

GRAMMAR
common to someone/something

1 something that is common is often seen or often happens: *Rabbits are the most common wild animal in this area.* | *This is a very common spelling mistake.*
2 shared by two or more people or things: *We have a common interest in old films.* | *These problems are common to all schools and colleges.*

common² noun

have something in common if two people or things have something in common, they are similar in some way: *I don't have a lot in common with my brothers.* | *The two towns have many things in common.*

com·mon·ly /'kɒmənli $'kamənli/ adverb often: *People with this illness commonly complain of headaches.*

com·mon·place /'kɒmənpleɪs $'ka-mən,pleɪs/ adjective very common and not unusual: *Divorce is now commonplace.*

common sense /ˌ.. './ noun [no plural] the ability to do sensible things: *Just use your common sense.*

com·mo·tion /kə'məʊʃən $kə'moʊ-ʃən/ noun [no plural] formal sudden noise or activity

com·mu·ni·cate /kə'mjuːnə-keɪt/ verb

GRAMMAR
communicate with someone

if people communicate with each other, they give each other information, for example by writing letters, speaking on the telephone etc: *It can be difficult to communicate with people if you don't speak their language.* | *We usually communicate by email.*

com·mu·ni·ca·tion /kəˌmjuːnə-'keɪʃən/ noun [no plural]

GRAMMAR
communication between people

when people talk to each other or give each other information using letters, telephones etc: *There should* be better **communication between** teachers and parents.

PHRASE
means of communication: *The Internet is now an important means of communication* (=way of talking to someone or sending information).

Com·mun·ism /'kɒmjənɪzəm $'kam-jənɪzəm/ noun [no plural] a political system based on the idea that people are equal and that the state should own companies

Com·mu·nist /'kɒmjənɪst $'kam-jənɪst/ noun someone who believes in Communism
– **Communist** adjective: *the Communist Party*

com·mu·ni·ty /kə'mjuːnəti/ noun, plural communities

1 a group of people who live in the same town or area: *a small rural community* (=people who live in the countryside) | *The club has had a lot of help from the local community.*
2 a group of people who are similar in some way, for example because they have the same religion or do the same job: *The city has quite a large Jewish community.* | *the business commuity*

com·mute /kə'mjuːt/ verb to regularly travel a long distance to work: *My Dad commutes from Oxford to London every day.*

com·mut·er /kə'mjuːtə $kə'mjutɚ/ noun someone who travels to work each day: *The train was packed with commuters.*

com·pact /kəm'pækt $'kampækt/ adjective small and neat

compact disc /ˌ.. './ noun a CD ⇨ see picture on page 342

com·pan·ion /kəm'pænjən/ noun someone who travels somewhere with you: *One of her travelling companions became ill.*

com·pan·ion·ship /kəm'pænjənʃɪp/ noun [no plural] when you are not alone but have a friend with you: *She joined the club for companionship.*

com·pa·ny /'kʌmpəni/ noun, plural companies

1 an organization that makes or sells

▼ things: *My father **runs** his own company.* | *an insurance company*
2 [no plural] when someone is with you and you are not alone: *She has a dog for company.* | *I really **enjoy** his company* (=like being with him).

keep someone company to spend time with someone so that they are not alone: *I'll stay here to **keep** you company.*

com·pa·ra·ble /'kɒmpərəbəl $ 'kɑmpərəbəl/ *adjective* formal similar in size or importance: *He was offered a comparable job at another branch of the company.*

com·par·a·tive¹ /kəm'pærətɪv/ *adjective* compared with something else: *the Prime Minister's comparative youth*

comparative² *noun* the comparative the form of an adjective or adverb that you use when saying that something is bigger, better, more expensive etc than another thing or than before

com·par·a·tive·ly /kəm'pærətɪvli/ *adverb* compared with something else: *Houses in that area are comparatively cheap.*

com·pare /kəm'peə $ kəm'per/ *verb*

compare something with something
compare something to something

1 if you compare things, you examine them in order to find out how they are similar or different: *We went to three different shops to compare their prices.* | *Look at this list and **compare** it **with** yours.* | *It would be interesting to **compare** this computer **to** one from ten years ago.* | ***Compared to** Harry, Jamie is very tall.*
2 if you compare two things, you say that they are similar in some way: *Film critics have **compared** him **to** some of the great stars of the 1970s.* | *Oasis are often **compared with** the Beatles.*

com·pa·ri·son /kəm'pærəsən/ *noun* when you compare things or people: *a comparison of this year's results with last year's*

com·part·ment /kəm'pɑːtmənt $ kəm'pɑrtmənt/ *noun* a separate space or area inside something: *a purse with several compartments*

com·pass /'kʌmpəs/ *noun, plural* compasses **1** an instrument that shows the direction you are travelling in, with an arrow that always points north **2** also **compasses** an instrument that you use for drawing circles

compass

com·pas·sion /kəm'pæʃən/ *noun* [no plural] sympathy for someone who is suffering

com·pas·sion·ate /kəm'pæʃənət/ *adjective* feeling sympathy for people who are suffering

com·pat·i·ble /kəm'pætəbəl/ *adjective* **1** two people who are compatible have similar ideas or interests, and are able to have a good relationship ⇨ *opposite* INCOMPATIBLE **2** two things that are compatible are able to exist or be used together without problems ⇨ *opposite* INCOMPATIBLE: *Is the new software compatible with the old version?*

com·pel /kəm'pel/ *verb* formal **compelled, compelling** to force someone to do something: *The bad weather compelled them to turn back.*

com·pel·ling /kəm'pelɪŋ/ *adjective* **1** very interesting or exciting: *a compelling TV drama* **2** a compelling argument, reason etc is one which you can believe or accept because it is probably correct

com·pen·sate /'kɒmpənseɪt $ 'kɑmpən,seɪt/ *verb* to do something so that something bad has a smaller effect: *He bought his kids presents to compensate for being away so much.*

com·pen·sa·tion /ˌkɒmpən'seɪʃən $ ˌkɑmpən'seɪʃən/ *noun* **1** [no plural] money that someone is given because they have been injured or badly treated, or have lost something: *The holiday company had to pay the Taylors £1500 compensation.* **2** something that makes a bad situation seem better: *Being unemployed has its compensations, like not having to get up early.*

C

com·pete /kəmˈpiːt/ verb

GRAMMAR
compete with someone
compete against someone
compete in something

to try to win something or to be more successful than someone else: *Ten runners will be* **competing in** *the race.* | *Our team* **competes with** *teams from other villages.* | *Small companies cannot* **compete against** *large international companies.*

com·pe·tence /ˈkɒmpətəns $ˈkɑːmpətəns/ noun when someone is able to do their job correctly ⇨ opposite INCOMPETENCE

com·pe·tent /ˈkɒmpətənt $ˈkɑːmpətənt/ adjective good at your work or able to do a job well ⇨ opposite INCOMPETENT: *a highly competent doctor*

com·pe·ti·tion /ˌkɒmpəˈtɪʃən $ˌkɑːmpəˈtɪʃən/ noun 1 an organized event in which people or teams compete against each other: *Who won the poetry competition?* 2 [no plural] a situation in which people or organizations compete with each other: *There is a lot of competition for places at this university.*

com·pet·i·tive /kəmˈpetətɪv/ adjective determined to be more successful than other people: *Boys are usually more competitive than girls.*
– **competitiveness** noun [no plural]

com·pet·i·tor /kəmˈpetɪtə $kəmˈpetɪtər/ noun a person, team, or company that competes with another

com·pi·la·tion /ˌkɒmpəˈleɪʃən $ˌkɑːmpəˈleɪʃən/ noun a collection of songs or pieces of writing that were originally sold on several different records or in several different books: *The new CD is a compilation of David Bowie's hit singles.*

com·pile /kəmˈpaɪl/ verb to make a book, list etc, using different pieces of information: *They compiled a list of the most popular activities.*

com·pla·cen·cy /kəmˈpleɪsənsi/ noun when you are too pleased with what you have achieved so that you no longer try to improve

com·pla·cent /kəmˈpleɪsənt/ adjective too pleased with what you have achieved so that you no longer try to improve: *You should do well in your exams but you mustn't get complacent.*

com·plain /kəmˈpleɪn/ verb

GRAMMAR
complain about someone/something
complain that
complain to someone
complain of something

to say that you are not satisfied with something or not happy about something: *The children all* **complained about** *the food.* | *Teachers often* **complain that** *they do not get enough support from parents.* | *I'm going to* **complain to** *the manager!* | *He* **complained of** *a pain in his stomach.*

com·plaint /kəmˈpleɪnt/ noun

GRAMMAR
a complaint about someone/something
a complaint to someone

something that you say or write when you are not satisfied with something or not happy about something: *We have received a lot of* **complaints about** *noise.* | *My biggest complaint is that we had to wait for two hours before we saw a doctor.* | *I* **made a complaint** *to the manager.*

com·plete¹ /kəmˈpliːt/ adjective
1 something that is complete has all the parts that it should have ⇨ opposite INCOMPLETE: *the complete works of Shakespeare* | *The collection is nearly complete.*
2 finished ⇨ opposite INCOMPLETE: *Work on the new bridge is almost complete.*
3 used when you are emphasizing something: *The play was a complete failure!*

complete² verb
to finish doing or making something: *We hope to complete the work by next month.*

com·plete·ly /kəmˈpliːtli/ adverb
in every way: *She set out to invent a completely new language.* | *He completely ignored me!*

com·plex¹ /'kɒmpleks $ kɑm'pleks/ adjective something that is complex has a lot of different parts and is often difficult to understand: *This is a very complex problem.*

com·plex² /'kɒmpleks $ 'kɑmpleks/ noun, plural complexes a group of buildings or rooms used for a particular purpose: *a new shopping complex*

com·plex·ion /kəm'plekʃən/ noun the appearance of the skin on your face: *She had a lovely complexion.*

com·pli·cate /'kɒmpləkeɪt $ 'kɑmplə,keɪt/ verb to make something more difficult to do: *Bad weather complicated the attempt to rescue the climbers.*

com·pli·cat·ed /'kɒmpləkeɪtɪd $ 'kɑmplə,keɪtɪd/ adjective not simple or easy to understand: *These instructions are too complicated.* | *a complicated mathematical equation*

com·pli·ca·tion /,kɒmplə'keɪʃən $,kɑmplə'keɪʃən/ noun a problem that makes something more difficult to do: *We don't expect any further complications in the travel arrangements.*

com·pli·ment /'kɒmpləment $ 'kɑmplə,ment/ verb to say something to someone that shows you admire them: *Mr Green complimented her on her taste in music.*
–compliment /-mənt/ noun: *She felt embarrassed when people paid her compliments.*

com·ply /kəm'plaɪ/ complied, complies verb formal to obey an order or request: *He has to comply with the Queen's wishes.*

com·po·nent /kəm'pəʊnənt $ kəm'poʊnənt/ noun one of the different parts of a machine

com·pose /kəm'pəʊz $ kəm'poʊz/ verb 1 to write a piece of music 2 be composed of things/people to consist of particular things or people: *The class is composed of students of various abilities.*

com·pos·er /kəm'pəʊzə $ kəm'poʊzɚ/ noun someone who writes music, especially CLASSICAL music (=serious and important music)

com·po·si·tion /,kɒmpə'zɪʃən $,kɑmpə'zɪʃən/ noun formal 1 a piece of music that someone wrote: *a composition by Debussy* 2 [no plural] the things that something is made of: *the chemical composition of this new material*

com·pound /'kɒmpaʊnd $ 'kɑmpaʊnd/ noun 1 a chemical substance that consists of two or more substances 2 compound noun, compound adjective, compound word a noun or adjective made from two or more words. 'Compact disc' is a compound noun and 'blue-eyed' is a compound adjective

com·pre·hen·sion /,kɒmprɪ'henʃən $,kɑmprɪ'henʃən/ noun 1 BrE a test of how well students understand written or spoken language 2 [no plural] the ability to understand something: *The students want to improve their reading comprehension skills.*

com·pre·hen·sive /,kɒmprɪ'hensɪv $,kɑmprɪ'hensɪv/ adjective including everything that is needed: *a comprehensive range of books*

comprehensive school /..'.. ,./ also **comprehensive** noun a school in Britain which teaches students aged between 11 and 18, who are of all levels of ability

com·prise /kəm'praɪz/ verb formal to consist of particular people or things: *The club comprises myself and twelve other members.*

com·pro·mise /'kɒmprəmaɪz $ 'kɑmprə,maɪz/ noun when people or groups who are trying to agree on something both accept less than they really want: *Eventually the two sides reached a compromise.*
–compromise verb: *If you don't learn to compromise, you'll never succeed.*

com·pul·so·ry /kəm'pʌlsəri/ adjective something that is compulsory must be done because of a rule or law: *Some countries have compulsory military service.*

com·put·er /kəm'pjuːtə $ kəm'pjutɚ/ noun an electronic machine that can store and arrange information and that you can use to do many different things: *I do a lot of my work on the computer.* | *Do you like playing* **computer games***?* | *a new* **computer program** ➪ see picture on page 342

con /kɒn $kɑn/ verb informal **conned, conning** to trick someone in order to get something you want: *They conned me into paying for all the tickets.*
– **con** noun: *It was just a big con.*

con·ceal /kənˈsiːl/ verb formal to hide something: *He tried to conceal the book under his jacket.*

con·cede /kənˈsiːd/ verb **concede defeat** formal to admit that you are not going to win a game, argument etc

con·ceit·ed /kənˈsiːtɪd/ adjective too proud of how good, clever, or attractive you are: *He's so conceited about his looks.*

con·ceiv·a·ble /kənˈsiːvəbəl/ adjective possible: *We tried every conceivable way of getting the lid off the jar.*

con·ceive /kənˈsiːv/ verb to become PREGNANT

con·cen·trate /ˈkɒnsəntreɪt $ˈkɑnsənˌtreɪt/ verb

GRAMMAR
concentrate on something
concentrate on doing something

1 to think very carefully about what you are doing: *Sometimes I find it hard to concentrate when I'm driving long distances.* | *Try to concentrate on what you are doing.*
2 to give most of your time and attention to one thing: *I gave up the piano so that I could concentrate on the violin.* | *We must concentrate on getting the most important tasks done first.*

con·cen·trat·ed /ˈkɒnsəntreɪtɪd $ˈkɑnsənˌtreɪtɪd/ adjective a concentrated liquid is thick and strong because it does not contain much water

con·cen·tra·tion /ˌkɒnsənˈtreɪʃən $ˌkɑnsənˈtreɪʃən/ noun

GRAMMAR
a concentration of something

1 [no plural] when you think very carefully about what you are doing: *The job requires a lot of concentration.* | *I lost concentration* (=did not think carefully) *for a moment, and that's when I crashed the car.*
2 formal a large number of things in a small area: *The area has a high concentration of good schools.*

con·cept /ˈkɒnsept $ˈkɑnsept/ noun ▼

formal a general idea: *Many films have been based on the concept of time travel.*

con·cep·tion /kənˈsepʃən/ noun [no plural] formal when a woman or female animal becomes PREGNANT

con·cern¹ /kənˈsɜːn $kənˈsɝn/ noun

GRAMMAR
concern about someone/something
concern for someone
concern that

worry that you feel about something important: *Some parents have expressed their concern about the number of cars entering and leaving the school yard.* | *a radio programme on the growing concern for young people who experiment with drugs* | *There is concern that he will not be fit enough to play in Monday's match.* | *My only concern* (=the only thing I am worried about) *is your safety.*

PHRASE
be of concern to someone formal if something is of concern to you, it is important to you and worries you: *This problem is of concern to all of us.*

concern² verb **1** if something concerns you, it affects or involves you: *"What were you talking about?" "It doesn't concern you."* **2** to worry someone: *Helen's odd behaviour was beginning to concern us.* **3** formal to be about something: *Much of his work concerned the way the brain works.*

con·cerned /kənˈsɜːnd $kənˈsɝnd/ adjective

GRAMMAR
concerned about someone/something
concerned that
concerned for someone

1 the people concerned are the people involved in something or affected by it: *The fire has been a very upsetting experience for everyone concerned.*
2 worried about something important: *The police are very concerned about the amount of crime in the area.* | *I'm concerned that she's*

▼ *getting too thin.* | *She* **is concerned for** *her children.*

con·cern·ing /kənˈsɜːnɪŋ $ kənˈsɚnɪŋ/ preposition formal
about someone or something: *I'm afraid I have some bad news for you, concerning your son.*

con·cert /ˈkɒnsət $ ˈkɑːnsɚt/ noun a performance given by musicians or singers: *We went to a concert last night.*

con·ces·sion /kənˈseʃən/ noun something that you agree to in order to end an argument: *She wasn't prepared to make any concessions.*

con·cise /kənˈsaɪs/ adjective not using too many words: *He gave a concise explanation of the problem.*

con·clude /kənˈkluːd/ verb **1** to decide that something is true after considering all the information you have: *The police concluded that the man was already dead when he was thrown in the river.* **2** formal to finish a meeting or discussion: *They concluded the meeting soon after two o'clock.*

con·clu·sion /kənˈkluːʒən/ noun

GRAMMAR
the conclusion (that)
1 if you come to a conclusion or reach a conclusion, you decide something after considering all the information you have: *I've* **come to the conclusion that** *most people don't actually enjoy Christmas.* | *It took scientists two years to* **reach** *this* **conclusion**. **2** formal the end or final part of something: *I've nearly finished my essay – I've just got to write the conclusion.*

con·clu·sive /kənˈkluːsɪv/ adjective proving that something is definitely true: *There is now conclusive evidence that smoking causes cancer.*
– **conclusively** adverb: *The marks on his jacket prove conclusively that he was present at the scene of the crime.*

con·crete¹ /ˈkɒnkriːt $ ˈkɑːnkriːt/ noun [no plural] a substance used for building that is made by mixing sand, water, small stones, and CEMENT

con·crete² /ˈkɒnkriːt $ kɑːnˈkriːt/ adjective **1** made of concrete: *a concrete floor* **2** based on facts: *We need concrete evidence before we accuse him of stealing.*

con·cus·sion /kənˈkʌʃən/ noun slight damage to your brain that is caused when you hit your head on something

con·demn /kənˈdem/ verb written **1** to say very strongly that you do not approve of someone or something: *Doctors have condemned the government's plans to change the hospital system.* **2** to give a severe punishment to a criminal: *He was condemned to death for bringing drugs into the country.*

con·dem·na·tion /ˌkɒndəmˈneɪʃən $ ˌkɑːndəmˈneɪʃən/ noun written a statement of very strong disapproval: *There has been widespread condemnation of the bombing.*

con·den·sa·tion /ˌkɒndenˈseɪʃən $ ˌkɑːndenˈseɪʃən/ noun [no plural] small drops of water that appear on a cold surface when warm air touches it

con·de·scend·ing /ˌkɒndɪˈsendɪŋ $ ˌkɑːndɪˈsendɪŋ/ adjective someone who is condescending shows that they think they are better or more important than other people

con·di·tion /kənˈdɪʃən/ noun
something that you must do first, before something else can be done: *One of the* **conditions for** *getting a student grant is that you must already have been accepted by a college.* | *I'll come with you* **on one condition**: *you pay for everything.*

PHRASES
in good condition, in bad condition etc if something is in good condition, it works and there is nothing wrong with it: *The car's engine is still* **in good condition**. | *The dog was* **in a terrible condition** *when we found her.* | *He was drunk, and* **in no condition to** *drive.*

working conditions, living conditions the situation in which people work or live: *The people are very poor, and their* **living conditions** *are very bad.*

weather conditions what the weather is like on a particular day: *The* **weather conditions** *made the rescue difficult.*

on condition that: *You can go out tonight* **on condition that** *you're back by eleven* (=only if you will be back by eleven).

con·di·tion·al /kənˈdɪʃənəl/ adjective a conditional part of a sentence begins with 'if' or 'unless'

con·di·tion·er /kənˈdɪʃənə $ kənˈdɪʃ-ənɚ/ noun a liquid that you put on your hair after you have washed it to keep it in good condition

con·dom /ˈkɒndəm $ ˈkɑndəm/ noun a thin piece of rubber that a man wears over his PENIS during sex

con·done /kənˈdəʊn $ kənˈdoʊn/ verb formal to allow or accept behaviour that most people think is wrong: I cannot condone lying.

con·duct¹ /kənˈdʌkt/ verb
1 to do something in an organized way in order to find out information or achieve something: The government is conducting a survey into the effects of smoking on young children.
2 if a material conducts heat or electricity, it allows heat or electricity to pass along it
3 to stand in front of a large group of musicians and direct them as they play a piece of music: the Birmingham Symphony Orchestra, with Simon Rattle conducting

con·duct² /ˈkɒndʌkt $ ˈkɑndʌkt/ noun [no plural] formal the way that someone behaves: His conduct has been disgraceful.

con·duc·tor /kənˈdʌktə $ kənˈdʌktɚ/ noun 1 someone who stands in front of a large group of musicians and directs them as they play a piece of music 2 someone who works on a bus or train

cone /kəʊn $ koʊn/ noun 1 an object which is round at one end and pointed at the other: There were traffic cones preventing drivers using one side of the road. | an ice-cream cone 2 a brown egg-shaped object containing seeds that grows on a PINE or FIR tree

con·fed·e·ra·tion /kənˌfedəˈreɪʃən/ also **con·fed·e·ra·cy** /kənˈfedərəsi/ noun an official group of people, organizations, or states

con·fer /kənˈfɜː $ kənˈfɚ/ conferred, conferring verb formal 1 to discuss something with other people: I will have to confer with my colleagues about this. 2 to officially give someone a degree, honour etc: His old university conferred a special degree on him.

con·fe·rence /ˈkɒnfərəns $ ˈkɑn-frəns/ noun a large formal meeting in which people discuss important things: Five hundred people attended a recent conference on the environment.

con·fess /kənˈfes/ verb to admit that you have done something wrong or stupid: Eventually Mitchell confessed to the murder. | She confessed that she had forgotten to post the letter.

con·fes·sion /kənˈfeʃən/ noun a statement saying that you have done something wrong

con·fet·ti /kənˈfeti/ noun [no plural] small pieces of paper that you throw over a man and woman who have just got married

con·fide /kənˈfaɪd/ verb if you confide in someone, you tell them a secret: She chose to confide in her sister.

con·fi·dence /ˈkɒnfədəns $ ˈkɑn-fədəns/ noun [no plural]
1 belief in your ability to do things well: This success will **give** the team more **confidence**. | a shy child who **lacks confidence**
2 a feeling of trust: It takes a new teacher quite a long time to **gain** the children's **confidence**.

con·fi·dent /ˈkɒnfədənt $ ˈkɑn-fədənt/ adjective

GRAMMAR
confident about something
confident of doing something
confident (that)

1 sure that you can do something well: Jenny **seems** very **confident about** her exam. | We **were** quite **confident of** winning. | a very confident swimmer
2 sure that something good is true or will happen: I am **confident that** this is the right course for you.

con·fi·den·tial /ˌkɒnfəˈdenʃəl $ ˌkɑn-fəˈdenʃəl/ adjective confidential information is secret: The envelope was marked 'Confidential'.

con·fine /kənˈfaɪn/ verb 1 be confined to someone/something to happen in only one place, or to affect only one group of people: This illness is not confined to older people. 2 if you confine your activities to one thing, you do something using only that thing: He confined his research to monkeys.

con·firm /kən'fɜːm $ kən'fɝm/ *verb formal* **1** to say or show that something is definitely true: *He confirmed that the dead woman was his wife.* **2** to tell someone that an arrangement is now definite: *Have you confirmed the hotel booking?*

con·fir·ma·tion /ˌkɒnfə'meɪʃən $ ˌkɑnfɝ'meɪʃən/ *noun* something telling you that something is definitely true or will definitely happen: *We think Matt will be well enough to play in tomorrow's game, but we're waiting for confirmation.*

con·fis·cate /'kɒnfəskeɪt $ 'kɑnfə,skeɪt/ *verb* if someone in authority confiscates something, they take it away from you: *The teacher confiscated the boy's knife.*

con·flict¹ /'kɒnflɪkt $ 'kɑn,flɪkt/ *noun* a disagreement or fighting: *There was often conflict between him and his brother.*

con·flict² /kən'flɪkt/ *verb* if two ideas or statements conflict, they are different and cannot both be true: *Her description of the man conflicted with the others that the police had received.*
– conflicting *adjective*: *The people who saw the accident gave conflicting descriptions of what happened.*

con·form /kən'fɔːm $ kən'fɔrm/ *verb* **1** to behave in the way that most other people behave: *Kids feel they have to conform.* **2** *formal* if something conforms to a rule or standard, it obeys or matches it: *Does this cycle helmet conform to the European standard?*

con·front /kən'frʌnt/ *verb* **1** if you confront a problem or difficult situation, you deal with it rather than ignoring it: *You've got to confront this problem.* **2** if you confront someone, you talk to them and try to make them admit they have done something wrong: *Richard confronted his sister about her lies.*

con·fron·ta·tion /ˌkɒnfrən'teɪʃən $ ˌkɑnfrən'teɪʃən/ *noun* a situation in which there is a lot of angry disagreement: *I try to avoid confrontations.*

con·fuse /kən'fjuːz/ *verb*

GRAMMAR
confuse someone/something with someone/something
1 if someone or something confuses you, you cannot think clearly or can-not understand something: *When they called the wrong name it really confused me.*
2 to think wrongly that one person or thing is someone or something else: *I'm always confusing Joe with his brother.*

con·fused /kən'fjuːzd/ *adjective*

GRAMMAR
confused about something
if you are confused, you do not understand something clearly: *I'm slightly confused about what we're supposed to be doing. | I got confused when Sam tried to explain what had happened.*

con·fus·ing /kən'fjuːzɪŋ/ *adjective* difficult to understand: *I find some of the maths a bit confusing.*

con·fu·sion /kən'fjuːʒən/ *noun [no plural]* **1** when people do not understand what is happening or what something means: *There was some confusion about whether the goal was allowed.* **2** when people are moving about and making a lot of noise in a confused way: *The man who fired the shot escaped in the confusion.*

con·ges·tion /kən'dʒestʃən/ *noun [no plural] formal* when a road is too full of vehicles: *There is a lot of congestion on the roads today.*

con·grat·u·late /kən'grætʃəleɪt/ *verb*

GRAMMAR
congratulate someone on something
to tell someone that you are happy because they have done something well, or something good has happened to them: *James congratulated me on passing my driving test.*

con·grat·u·la·tions /kən,grætʃə'leɪʃənz/ *plural noun*

GRAMMAR
congratulations on something
something you say to tell someone that you are happy because they have done something well, or something good has happened to them: *Congratulations on passing your*

exams. | **Give** him my **congratu-
lations**. | "I got that job I applied
for." "Congratulations! Well done!"

con·gre·ga·tion /ˌkɒŋgrəˈgeɪʃən
$ ˌkɑŋgrəˈgeɪʃən/ noun the people who
are in a church for a religious ceremony

co·ni·fer /ˈkəʊnəfə $ ˈkɑnəfɚ/ noun a
tree that keeps its leaves in winter and
which has CONEs containing its seeds

con·junc·tion /kənˈdʒʌŋkʃən/ noun a
word such as 'but', 'and', or 'while' that
connects parts of sentences

con·jur·er or **conjuror** /ˈkʌndʒərə
$ ˈkʌndʒɚɚ/ noun someone who does
magic tricks

con·man /ˈkɒnmæn $ ˈkɑnmæn/ noun
informal, plural **conmen** /-men/ someone
who tries to get money by tricking
people

con·nect /kəˈnekt/ verb
GRAMMAR
connect something to something
connect something/someone
with something/someone
1 to join two things or places together:
Connect this wire **to** the back of the
machine. | the road connecting the
two cities
2 if you connect two pieces of information, events, or things, you realize
that they are related or similar in
some way: The police **have** not **con-
nected** him **with** the murder. | I
wouldn't have connected bikes and
guitars, but there's a shop selling
both in the high street.

con·nect·ed /kəˈnektɪd/ adjective
GRAMMAR
connected with something
connected to something
1 if one thing is connected with another, they are related or similar in
some way: The disease may **be connected with** the type of work you do.
2 if one thing is connected to another,
it is joined to it: The car park **is connected to** the airport by a tunnel.

con·nec·tion /kəˈnekʃən/ noun
GRAMMAR
a connection between things
a connection with/to something
1 a relationship between things: There

is a strong **connection between**
happiness and health.
2 when two or more things are joined
together, especially by an electrical
wire: Some villages still have no
connection to an electricity supply.
3 a bus, train, or plane that leaves
shortly after the one you are on
arrives, and that you must get on to
continue your journey: What time is
your connection? | We missed the
connection and had to wait two
hours for the next train.
PHRASE
in connection with something if
something happens in connection
with something, it happens because
of that thing: A man has been
arrested **in connection with** the
murder.

con·quer /ˈkɒŋkə $ ˈkɑŋkɚ/ verb to get
control of a country by fighting: The
Romans conquered Britain.
con·quest /ˈkɒŋkwest $ ˈkɑŋkwest/
noun when people from another country
get control of a country by fighting
con·science /ˈkɒnʃəns $ ˈkɑnʃəns/
noun 1 the feeling that tells you
whether what you are doing is morally
right or wrong: He had a guilty conscience about forgetting to feed the
rabbit. 2 **on someone's conscience**
if you have something on your conscience, you feel guilty about it: I know
the mistake is still on his conscience.
con·sci·en·tious /ˌkɒnʃiˈenʃəs
$ ˌkɑnʃiˈenʃəs/ adjective careful to do
the things that need doing
con·scious /ˈkɒnʃəs $ ˈkɑnʃəs/ adjec-
tive 1 awake and able to understand
what is happening ⇨ opposite UN-
CONSCIOUS: The injured man was still
conscious. 2 knowing of something or
always thinking about it: She was always
conscious of her weight. | fashion con-
scious teenagers
con·scious·ness /ˈkɒnʃəsnəs $ ˈkɑn-
ʃəsnəs/ noun **lose consciousness,
regain consciousness** if someone
who is ill loses consciousness, they
stop being awake and are not able to
understand what is happening: He
was bleeding heavily and soon lost
consciousness. | Will she ever regain
consciousness?

con·sec·u·tive /kən'sekjətɪv/ adjective happening one after the other: *He was late for school on three consecutive days.*

con·sen·sus /kən'sensəs/ noun [no plural] formal agreement between all or most people in a group: *There was consensus on the need for change.*

con·sent /kən'sent/ noun [no plural] formal permission: *She had taken the car without the owner's consent.*

con·se·quence /'kɒnsəkwəns $'kɑnsə,kwens/ noun something that happens as a result of something else: *You don't think about the consequences of your actions!*

con·se·quent·ly /'kɒnsəkwəntli $'kɑnsə,kwentli/ adverb formal as a result: *He lost his coat and consequently his wallet.*

con·ser·va·tion /,kɒnsə'veɪʃən $,kɑnsɚ'veɪʃən/ noun [no plural] the protection of natural things

con·ser·va·tion·ist /,kɒnsə'veɪʃənɪst $,kɑnsɚ'veɪʃənɪst/ noun someone who tries to protect natural things

con·ser·va·tive /kən'sɜːvətɪv $kən'sɚvətɪv/ adjective someone who is conservative likes to continue doing things in the way they are already done, rather than making changes

con·ser·va·to·ry /kən'sɜːvətəri $kən'sɚvə,tɔri/ noun, plural conservatories a room made of glass that is joined to the side of a house

con·sid·er /kən'sɪdə $kən'sɪdɚ/ verb

> **GRAMMAR**
> **consider doing something**
> **consider how/what/whether etc**
> **consider someone/something (to be) something**

1 to think about something carefully, especially before deciding what to do: *Anna is considering studying languages at university.* | *It sounds a great idea, but* **have** *you* **considered how much** *it will cost?*
2 to think of someone or something in a particular way: *He seemed to* **consider** *himself* **to be** *better than other people.*

con·sid·e·ra·ble /kən'sɪdərəbəl/ adjective great or large in amount: *I spent*

a considerable amount of time trying to persuade him to come.
– **considerably** adverb: *He is considerably older than his girlfriend.*

con·sid·er·ate /kən'sɪdərət/ adjective a considerate person thinks about other people's feelings and needs ⇨ opposite INCONSIDERATE

con·sid·e·ra·tion /kən,sɪdə'reɪʃən/ noun [no plural] **1** when someone thinks about other people's feelings and needs: *He shows no consideration for others.* **2** careful thought: *After much consideration, he decided to study history at university.*

con·sid·er·ing /kən'sɪdərɪŋ/ preposition

> **GRAMMAR**
> **considering (that)**

used to remind people of a fact that they should think about: *Maria's doing very well,* **considering that** *she's the youngest in her class.*

con·sist /kən'sɪst/ verb **consist of, consist of** things if something consists of other things, those things are the different parts of it: *The class consists of children from a wide range of countries.*

con·sis·ten·cy /kən'sɪstənsi/ noun **1** [no plural] when someone always behaves in the same way ⇨ opposite INCONSISTENCY: *You have to admire his consistency as a player.* **2** how thick or firm a mixture is: *Stir the mixture until it is the consistency of thick cream.*

con·sis·tent /kən'sɪstənt/ adjective always happening or behaving in the same way ⇨ opposite INCONSISTENT: *His school work is consistent.*
– **consistently** adverb: *Their results are consistently good.*

con·so·la·tion /,kɒnsə'leɪʃən $,kɑnsə'leɪʃən/ noun something that makes you feel better when you are sad or disappointed: *My only consolation is that everyone else found the exam hard too.*

con·sole¹ /kən'səʊl $kən'soʊl/ verb if you console someone who is sad or disappointed, you try to make them feel better

con·sole² /'kɒnsəʊl $'kɑnsoʊl/ noun a piece of equipment with buttons on it that you connect to a computer and use when you play a game on the computer: *a games console that connects to a computer*

con·so·nant /ˈkɒnsənənt $ˈkɑnsənənt/ *noun* any letter of the English alphabet except a, e, i, o, and u

con·spic·u·ous /kənˈspɪkjuəs/ *adjective* very easy to notice: *Her red hair made her very conspicuous.*

con·spi·ra·cy /kənˈspɪrəsi/ *noun, plural* conspiracies a secret plan made by several people to do something bad or illegal

con·sta·ble /ˈkʌnstəbəl $ˈkɑnstəbəl/ *noun* a British police officer of the lowest rank

con·stant /ˈkɒnstənt $ˈkɑnstənt/ *adjective* **1** happening regularly or all the time: *We couldn't get any work done because there were constant interruptions.* **2** a constant speed, temperature etc is always the same: *The medicine must be kept at a constant temperature.*

con·stant·ly /ˈkɒnstəntli $ˈkɑnstəntli/ *adverb*
regularly or all the time: *It had been raining constantly all weekend.*

con·stel·la·tion /ˌkɒnstəˈleɪʃən $ˌkɑnstəˈleɪʃən/ *noun* a group of stars that has a name

con·ster·na·tion /ˌkɒnstəˈneɪʃən $ˌkɑnstəˈneɪʃən/ *noun* [no plural] written a feeling of shock or worry

con·sti·pa·tion /ˌkɒnstəˈpeɪʃən $ˌkɑnstəˈpeɪʃən/ *noun* [no plural] when someone is unable to remove waste food from inside their body

con·sti·tu·ent /kənˈstɪtʃuənt/ *noun* formal one of the substances in a mixture: *The main constituent of this type of paint is oil.*

con·sti·tute /ˈkɒnstətjuːt $ˈkɑnstəˌtut/ *verb* formal to be or form something: *His action constitutes a criminal offence.* | *the people who constitute the committee*

con·sti·tu·tion /ˌkɒnstəˈtjuːʃən $ˌkɑnstəˈtuʃən/ *noun* the written laws and principles of a government or organization

con·straint /kənˈstreɪnt/ *noun* formal something that stops you doing the

things you want to do: *the constraints that were placed on Victorian women*

con·struct /kənˈstrʌkt/ *verb* to build something: *They have not finished constructing the new airport.*

con·struc·tion /kənˈstrʌkʃən/ *noun* **1** [no plural] the process of building something: *The construction of the road will take two years.* **2** something that has been built: *He had built a wooden construction to keep chickens in.* **3** a way in which words are put together in a sentence: *We learned a new grammatical construction.*

con·struc·tive /kənˈstrʌktɪv/ *adjective* helpful or useful: *The teacher wrote some constructive comments on Gary's essay.*

con·sult /kənˈsʌlt/ *verb*

GRAMMAR
consult someone about something
to ask someone for advice or information: *You should consult your teacher about which course is best for you.*

con·sul·tant /kənˈsʌltənt/ *noun* someone whose job is to give advice about a subject: *a management consultant*

con·sul·ta·tion /ˌkɒnsəlˈteɪʃən $ˌkɑnsəlˈteɪʃən/ *noun* when someone is asked for their opinion or advice: *The decision was made after consultations with the students.*

con·sume /kənˈsjuːm $kənˈsum/ *verb* to use energy, products etc: *We are still consuming too much coal and oil.*

con·sum·er /kənˈsjuːmə $kənˈsumɚ/ *noun* someone who buys things or uses a service that a company provides: *Consumers are now more aware of their rights.*

con·sump·tion /kənˈsʌmpʃən/ *noun* [no plural] the amount of electricity, gas etc that something uses: *This car has very low fuel consumption.*

con·tact¹ /ˈkɒntækt $ˈkɑntækt/ *noun*
1 keep in contact, stay in contact to meet, telephone, or write to someone regularly: *I try to keep in contact with all my old friends from school.*
2 get in contact, make contact: *I wanted to get in contact with her*

▼ (=talk or write to her) *but she was on holiday.*

3 lose contact *I **lost contact with** Simon* (=stopped meeting and telephoning him) *when he moved to a different town.*

4 come into contact *You catch a cold by **coming into contact with** someone* (=meeting someone) *who already has one.*

5 be in contact if one thing is in contact with another, it is touching it: *Make sure the wire **is not in contact with** metal.*

contact² *verb*

to telephone or write to someone: *In an emergency, you should contact the police immediately.*

contact lens /'.. ,./ *noun, plural* **contact lenses** one of a pair of small pieces of plastic that you put on your eyes to help you see clearly

con·ta·gious /kən'teɪdʒəs/ *adjective* a contagious disease can pass from one person to another

con·tain /kən'teɪn/ *verb*

if something contains things, those things are in it: *The suitcase contained a lot of old clothes.* | *Monday's newspaper contained several articles about the train crash.*

containers

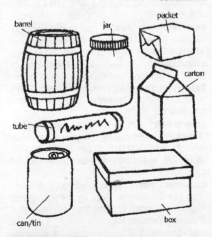

barrel

jar

packet

carton

tube

can/tin

box

con·tain·er /kən'teɪnə $kən-'teɪnɚ/ *noun*

▼ something that you can put things in, for example a box or can: *She put the food in plastic containers.*

con·tam·i·nate /kən'tæmənaɪt/ *verb* to add a substance that makes something dirty or dangerous: *The water was contaminated with chemicals.*

con·tam·i·na·tion /kən,tæmə'neɪ-ʃən/ *noun* [no plural] when a substance is added that makes something dirty or dangerous

con·tem·plate /'kɒntəmpleɪt $'kɑn-təm,pleɪt/ *verb* to think about something that you might do: *She even contemplated killing herself.*

con·tem·po·ra·ry¹ /kən'tempərəri $kən'tempə,reri/ *adjective* **1** modern and belonging to the present time: *She is one of this country's best contemporary artists.* **2** happening or existing in the same period of time: *This information comes from a contemporary record of those events.*

contemporary² *noun, plural* **contemporaries** a person living at the same time as someone else: *Many of Darwin's contemporaries did not agree with his theories.*

con·tempt /kən'tempt/ *noun* [no plural] a feeling that someone or something does not deserve any respect: *He showed complete contempt for the people who worked for him.*

con·tend /kən'tend/ *verb* **contend with** to try to do something in a difficult situation: *The players had to contend with very windy conditions.*

con·tend·er /kən'tendə $kən'tendɚ/ *noun* someone who is competing to win a title, prize, or political job

con·tent¹ /kən'tent/ *adjective*

> **GRAMMAR**
> **content with something**
> **content to do something**

happy and satisfied: *She **seems** very **content with** her life.* | *The children **were content to** spend the afternoon drawing and painting.*

con·tent² /'kɒntent $'kɑntent/ *noun*

> **GRAMMAR**
> **the contents of something**

▼ **1** the amount of a substance that

C

▼ something contains: *Choose foods with a lower fat content.*

2 the ideas or information in a book, programme etc: *The content of the programme was quite upsetting.*

3 contents 1) the things that are inside a box, bag, house etc: *All the contents of the house were destroyed in a fire.* 2) the list at the beginning of a book saying what things are in the book: *The table of contents is at the beginning of a book.*

con·tent·ed /kən'tentɪd/ *adjective* written happy and satisfied ⇨ opposite DISCONTENTED: *He was contented with what he had.*

con·tents /'kɒntents $'kɑn-tents/ *plural noun*

GRAMMAR
the contents of something

1 the things that are inside a box, bag, house etc: *All the contents of the house were destroyed in a fire.*

2 the list at the beginning of a book saying what things are in the book

con·test /'kɒntest $'kɑntest/ *noun* a competition: *She won first prize in a beauty contest.*

con·tes·tant /kən'testənt/ *noun* someone who enters a competition

con·text /'kɒntekst $'kɑntekst/ *noun* **1** the situation within which something happens: *Think about the historical context of these events.* **2** the words around a word or phrase that help you understand its meaning: *What do you think the word means in this context?*

con·ti·nent /'kɒntənənt $'kɑntənənt/ *noun* **1** one of the large areas of land in the world, such as Africa, Asia, or Europe **2 the Continent** BrE Europe, not including Britain: *The situation is different on the Continent.*

con·ti·nen·tal /ˌkɒntə'nentl $ˌkɑn-tə'nentl/ *adjective* BrE in or belonging to Europe, not including Britain

con·tin·u·al /kən'tɪnjuəl/ *adjective* happening often or all the time: *He was in continual pain.*
– **continually** *adverb*: *The phone rang continually.*

con·tin·ue /kən'tɪnjuː/ *verb*

GRAMMAR
continue to do something
continue along/down etc something

1 to do something or happen for a period of time without stopping: *Lisa's continuing to make good progress with her French.* | *The bad weather will continue for another week.*

2 to start again, or start something again, after stopping: *The film will continue after the news.* | *We can continue our conversation later.*

3 to go further in the same direction: *Continue along this road until you come to a church.*

con·ti·nu·i·ty /ˌkɒntə'njuːəti $ˌkɑn-tə'nuəti/ *noun* [no plural] when something continues for a long period of time without change

con·tin·u·ous /kən'tɪnjuəs/ *adjective* **1** continuing without stopping: *Long periods of continuous study are very tiring.* **2** the continuous form of a verb consists of 'be' and the present participle, as in 'she was reading'

con·tin·u·ous·ly /kən'tɪnjuəsli/ *adverb* without stopping: *It rained continuously for three days.*

con·tra·cep·tion /ˌkɒntrə'sepʃən $ˌkɑntrə'sepʃən/ *noun* [no plural] methods of stopping a woman becoming PREGNANT

con·tra·cep·tive /ˌkɒntrə'septɪv $ˌkɑntrə'septɪv/ *noun* something that stops a woman becoming PREGNANT

con·tract¹ /'kɒntrækt $'kɑntrækt/ *noun* a formal written agreement between two people, companies etc: *She's just signed a contract with a record company.*

con·tract² /kən'trækt/ *verb* formal **1** to become smaller ⇨ opposite EXPAND: *Metal contracts as it becomes cooler.* **2** to get a serious illness: *How did he contract the disease?*

con·trac·tor /kən'træktə $'kɑn-ˌtræktɚ/ *noun* a person or company that does work for another company: *a building contractor*

con·tra·dict /ˌkɒntrə'dɪkt $ˌkɑntrə-'dɪkt/ *verb* **1** if one statement contradicts another, the two are different and cannot both be true: *Their stories contradicted each other.* **2** if you contradict someone, you say that what they have just said is not true: *Don't contradict your mother!*

con·tra·dic·tion /ˌkɒntrəˈdɪkʃən $ ˌkɑntrəˈdɪkʃən/ *noun* a difference between two statements or facts, that shows they cannot both be true: *There were some obvious contradictions in what he said.*

con·tra·dic·to·ry /ˌkɒntrəˈdɪktəri $ ˌkɑntrəˈdɪktəri/ *adjective* if two statements are contradictory, they are different and cannot both be true

con·tra·ry¹ /ˈkɒntrəri $ ˈkɑnˌtreri/ *noun formal* **on the contrary** used to emphasize that the opposite of something is true: *He's not a strict teacher. On the contrary, he lets us do anything we like.*

contrary² *adverb* **contrary to something** used to say that something is not correct: *Contrary to earlier reports, the team captain has not resigned.*

con·trast¹ /ˈkɒntrɑːst $ ˈkɑntræst/ *noun*

GRAMMAR
a contrast between things
in contrast to something

a big difference between people, things, or situations: *There was a great **contrast between** the rich and the poor areas of the city.* | ***In contrast to** her brother, Tina is small and fair-haired.*

con·trast² /kənˈtrɑːst $ kənˈtræst/ *verb*

GRAMMAR
contrast something with something
contrast something and something
contrast with something

1 to compare two things, situations etc in order to show how they are different from each other: *I'd like to **contrast** Picasso's early work **with** his later style.* | *We **contrasted** brown mice **and** white mice, and found that the white mice were more intelligent.*
2 if one thing contrasts with another, it is very different from it: *We chose patterned curtains, to **contrast with** the plain walls.*

con·trib·ute /kənˈtrɪbjuːt/ *verb*

GRAMMAR
contribute to/towards something
contribute something to/towards something

1 to be one of the causes of something that happens: *He thanked everyone who **had contributed to** the success of the company.* | *Smoking **contributed towards** his death.*
2 to give money or things to help pay for or achieve something: *Would you like to **contribute towards** a present for Linda's birthday?* | *Jerry **contributed £5 to** the fund.*

con·tri·bu·tion /ˌkɒntrəˈbjuːʃən $ ˌkɑntrəˈbjuːʃən/ *noun* if you make a contribution to something, you do or give something to help it: *Would you like to make a contribution to charity?* | *Linford Christie's outstanding contribution to sport.*

con·trol¹ /kənˈtrəʊl $ kənˈtroʊl/ *noun*
one of the parts of a machine that you press or move to make it work: *The pilot checks all the controls before take-off.*

PHRASES
have control, be in control to have the ability to make people do what you want, or to make things happen in the way you want: *Some parents feel that they **have no control over** their children.* | *It's important that you **are in control of** your life.*
be under control, keep something under control if something is under control, you are succeeding in controlling it, or making it do what you want: *Don't worry, everything **is under control**.* | *Please **keep** your dog **under control**.*
be out of control, get out of control: *The fighting got worse, and the situation **was** soon **out of control*** (=not possible to manage or control).
lose control to be unable to stay calm or manage a difficult situation any more: *The teacher **lost control** and started to shout.*
take control to start to organize and make decisions about something that someone else was organizing before: *When Rose became ill, Jim **took control of** the farm.*

C

control² controlled, controlling *verb*

1 to make someone or something do what you want: *The little girl was unable to control her horse.*

2 to have the power in an organization or place: *Britain controlled India for many years.*

3 to limit something or stop it increasing: *It was no longer possible to control the disease.*

4 control yourself to make yourself behave calmly, even though you feel angry, upset, excited etc: *I couldn't control myself any longer and I started to laugh.*

con·tro·ver·sial /ˌkɒntrəˈvɜːʃəl $ˌkɑntrəˈvɚʃəl/ *adjective* something that is controversial causes arguments because people do not agree about it: *Homosexuality is still a very controversial topic.*

con·tro·ver·sy /ˈkɒntrəvɜːsi $kənˈtrɒvəsi $ˈkɑntrəˌvɚsi/ *noun, plural* **controversies** a lot of argument about something important: *The book has caused a great deal of controversy.*

con·ve·ni·ent /kənˈviːniənt/ *adjective*

1 suitable or easy to do ⇨ *opposite* IN-CONVENIENT: *What would be a convenient time for me to come and see you? | Shopping by computer is convenient for many people.*

2 a place that is convenient is close to you: *The shops are very convenient.*

con·vent /ˈkɒnvənt $ˈkɑnvent/ *noun* a place where NUNS live and work

con·ven·tion·al /kənˈvenʃənəl/ *adjective* conventional ideas, things, and ways of behaving are of the normal or usual kind: *Conventional medicine could not help her, so she tried using herbs.*

con·ver·sa·tion /ˌkɒnvəˈseɪʃən $ˌkɑnvɚˈseɪʃən/ *noun*

> **GRAMMAR**
> **a conversation with someone**
> **a conversation about something**

a talk between two or more people, especially friends: *I had an interesting conversation with Alice yesterday. | We had a long conversation about music.*

con·ver·sion /kənˈvɜːʃən $kənˈvɜʒən/ *noun* when something changes from one form or system to another: *the conversion of the sun's heat into energy*

con·vert /kənˈvɜːt $kənˈvɚt/ *verb* to change something from one form or system to another, or to change like this: *The old barn has been converted into apartments. | Water converts to steam when it is heated.*

con·vey /kənˈveɪ/ *verb* formal to try to help other people understand your feelings or ideas: *I tried to convey my excitement to the rest of the class.*

con·vict /kənˈvɪkt/ *verb* if someone is convicted of a crime, a court of law decides that they are guilty of it: *He was convicted of murder.*

con·vic·tion /kənˈvɪkʃən/ *noun*

1 when someone is convicted of a crime: *He has three convictions for theft.*

2 a strong belief or opinion

con·vince /kənˈvɪns/ *verb*

> **GRAMMAR**
> **convince someone (that)**
> **convince yourself**

to make someone believe that something is true: *In the end Mark convinced me that he was right. | You have to convince yourself that you can succeed.*

con·vinced /kənˈvɪnst/ *adjective*

> **GRAMMAR**
> **convinced (that)**

sure that something is true: *I became convinced that Mara was lying to me. | I'm convinced we're going the wrong way.*

con·vinc·ing /kənˈvɪnsɪŋ/ *adjective* a convincing argument, story etc makes you believe that something is true or right: *There was convincing evidence that he was guilty.*

con·voy /ˈkɒnvɔɪ $ˈkɑnvɔɪ/ *noun* a group of vehicles or ships travelling together

cook¹ /kʊk/ *verb*

1 to prepare food to eat, by heating it, mixing things together etc: *Shall I cook an omelette for you? | You*

▼ *should learn to cook while you're young.*
2 if food cooks, you heat it until it is ready to eat: *How long does the rice take to cook?*

cook² *noun* someone who prepares and cooks food: *My sister is an excellent cook.*

cook·er /'kʊkə $'kʊkɚ/ *noun* BrE a large piece of kitchen equipment that you use for cooking food; STOVE AmE

cook·e·ry /'kʊkəri/ *noun* [no plural] BrE the skill or activity of cooking food: *I really enjoyed cookery at school.*

cook·ie /'kʊki/ the American word for BISCUIT

cook·ing /'kʊkɪŋ/ *noun* [no plural] the activity of cooking food: *I love cooking!*

cool¹ /kuːl/ *adjective*

1 slightly cold, especially in a nice way ⇨ *opposite* WARM¹ (1): *It was hot in the day, but pleasantly cool at night. | After his run, he had a shower and a long, cool drink.* ⇨ *see usage note at* COLD¹
2 calm, rather than nervous or excited: *She tried to **stay cool** and not panic.*
3 *spoken informal* if you say that someone or something is cool, you like or admire them: *It was a really cool party last night.*

cool² *verb* **1** also **cool down** to become colder, or to make something do this: *Let the engine cool before adding the water.* **2 cool down** to become calm after being angry: *By the time we got home, I had cooled down.*

cooped up /ˌkuːpt 'ʌp/ *adjective* if you are cooped up somewhere, you are kept for too long in a place that is too small: *He kept his dogs cooped up in a kennel.*

co·op·e·rate also **co-operate** BrE /kəʊ'ɒpəreɪt $koʊ'ɑpəˌreɪt/ *verb* to work with someone to achieve something together: *Parents are co-operating with teachers to deal with the problem of drugs in schools.*

co·op·e·ra·tion also **co-operation** BrE /kəʊˌɒpə'reɪʃən $koʊˌɑpə'reɪʃən/ *noun* [no plural] when people work together to achieve something: *Thank you for your co-operation.*

co·op·e·ra·tive also **co-operative** BrE /kəʊ'ɒpərətɪv $koʊ'ɑprətɪv/ *adjec-*

tive willing to help: *The children were all cooperative and polite.*

co·or·di·nate¹ also **co-ordinate** BrE /kəʊ'ɔːdɪneɪt $koʊ'ɔrdnˌeɪt/ *verb* to organize all the different things and people involved in an activity: *I'm responsible for co-ordinating training courses.*

co·or·di·nate² also **co-ordinate** BrE /kəʊ'ɔːdənət $koʊ'ɔrdənət/ *noun* one of a set of numbers that give an exact position on a map

cop /kɒp $kɑp/ *noun informal* a police officer

cope /kəʊp $koʊp/ *verb*

> **GRAMMAR**
> **cope with something**

to manage a difficult situation successfully: *It isn't easy, **coping with** four kids and a job. | If you're having problems with college work, we're here to help you cope.*

cop·per /'kɒpə $'kɑpɚ/ *noun* **1** [no plural] a brown metal: *copper pipes* **2** BrE informal a police officer

cop·y¹ /'kɒpi $'kɑpi/ *noun, plural* copies

> **GRAMMAR**
> **a copy of something**

something that is exactly the same as another thing, because someone has made it like that: *Could you **make a copy of** this report?*

copy² *verb* copied, copies

1 to do exactly the same thing as someone else has done: *Other companies are likely to copy the idea.*
2 to make something that is exactly the same as another thing: *She was copying a picture from a book.*

cor·al /'kɒrəl $'kɔrəl/ *noun* [no plural] a hard substance formed from the bones of small sea animals: *Many fish live around this **coral reef** (=large area of coral).*

cord /kɔːd $kɔrd/ *noun* **1** a type of strong thick string **2** *plural* **cords** cotton cloth etc **3** AmE an electrical wire that you use to connect a piece of equipment to a supply of electricity

core /kɔː $kɔr/ *noun* **1** the central or most important part of something: *the*

Earth's core | *The core subjects we teach are English and maths.* **2** the hard part in the middle of an apple or similar fruit

co·ri·an·der /ˌkɒri'ændə $'kɔːri-ˌændɚ/ *noun [no plural] BrE* a plant with leaves or seeds that you add to food to give it a pleasant fresh taste; CILANTRO *AmE*

cork

corkscrew

cork

cork /kɔːk $kɔrk/ *noun* a round piece of soft wood, used to close a bottle

cork·screw /'kɔːkskruː $'kɔrkskru/ *noun* the tool you use to pull a cork out of a bottle ⇨ *see picture at* CORK

corn /kɔːn $kɔrn/ *noun* **1** [no plural] *BrE* plants such as wheat that produce seeds for making flour, or the seeds they produce: *a field of corn* **2** the American word for MAIZE ⇨ *see picture on page 345*

cor·ner /'kɔːnə $'kɔrnɚ/ *noun*
1 the place where two edges, surfaces, or walls join each other at an angle: *Mick was sitting on his own in a corner of the room.*
2 the place where two roads join each other at an angle: *There's a cake shop on the corner of Church Lane and Mill Street.* | *Sam was waiting for me just around the corner.*

corn·flakes /'kɔːnfleɪks $'kɔrnfleɪks/ *plural noun* small pieces of dried corn that you eat mixed with milk, usually as a breakfast food

cor·o·na·tion /ˌkɒrə'neɪʃən $ˌkɔrə-'neɪʃən/ *noun* a ceremony to make someone king or queen: *the coronation of Elizabeth II*

cor·po·ral /'kɔːpərəl $'kɔrpərəl/ *noun* a soldier who has a low rank in the army

cor·po·ra·tion /ˌkɔːpə'reɪʃən $ˌkɔrpə'reɪʃən/ *noun* a large business organization

corpse /kɔːps $kɔrps/ *noun* a dead body

cor·rect¹ /kə'rekt/ *adjective*
right or without a mistake ⇨ *opposite* INCORRECT: *In the test all my answers were correct.* | *Have you filled in the correct form?*

correct² *verb*
if a teacher corrects a student's work, they make marks on it to show where it is wrong: *Mrs Young was correcting the class's maths papers.*

cor·rec·tions /kə'rekʃənz/ *plural noun*
changes that need to be made to a piece of writing: *"Please do your corrections for homework,"* Mr Murray said. | *The editor of the newspaper published a correction, apologising for the mistake.*

cor·re·spond /ˌkɒrə'spɒnd $ˌkɔrə-'spand/ *verb formal* **1** if two things correspond, they are similar in some way: *Sally's description of the accident corresponded with mine.* **2** if two people correspond, they write to each other: *We started to correspond in 1989.*

cor·re·spon·dence /ˌkɒrə'spɒndəns $ˌkɔrə'spandəns/ *noun [no plural] formal* letters that people write: *The company has not replied to my correspondence.*

cor·re·spon·dent /ˌkɒrə'spɒndənt $ˌkɔrə'spandənt/ *noun* a news reporter: *an overseas correspondent*

cor·ri·dor /'kɒrədɔː $'kɔrədɚ/ *noun* a long narrow passage in a building

cor·rupt¹ /kə'rʌpt/ *adjective* **1** a corrupt person or organization is dishonest: *a corrupt government* **2** if a computer FILE is corrupt, the information in it is damaged and you cannot read it

corrupt² *verb* **1** to encourage someone to behave in way that is bad, not honest, or not fair: *I think that television corrupts the young.* **2** if a computer FILE is corrupted, the information in it is damaged and you cannot read it: *A message came up on the screen: "File corrupted; please restart."*

cor·rup·tion /kə'rʌpʃən/ *noun [no plural]* behaviour that is not honest or fair: *The President was accused of corruption.*

cos·met·ic /kɒz'metɪk $kɑz'metɪk/ *adjective* cosmetic products or medical treatments are designed to improve your appearance: *He had cosmetic surgery to make his nose smaller.*

cos·met·ics /kɒz'metɪks $ kɑz'met-ɪks/ *plural noun* products that you put on your skin to improve your appearance: *She spends a lot on cosmetics, especially lipstick.*

cost¹ /kɒst $ kɔst/ *noun*

GRAMMAR
the cost of something
the amount of money that you have to pay for something: *The cost of accommodation in the city centre is very high.*

PHRASE
the cost of living the amount of money that people need in order to buy things they need: *The cost of living is increasing all the time.*

cost² *verb, past tense and past participle* **cost**

GRAMMAR
cost someone something
if something costs a particular amount, that is the amount you have to pay for it: *How much do these jeans cost?* | *This coat only cost me $30.* | *It costs ten pounds to get into the club.*

co-star /'kəʊ stɑː $ 'koʊ stɑr/ *verb* **co-starred, co-starring** if a film co-stars two people, or they co-star in it, they both have important parts in the film: *'A Fish called Wanda', co-starring John Cleese and Michael Palin*
– **co-star** *noun*: *The two co-stars hated each other.*

cos·tume /'kɒstjʊm $ 'kɑstum/ *noun* the clothes that an actor wears in a play or film

co·sy *BrE*, **cozy** *AmE* /'kəʊzi $ 'koʊzi/ *adjective* **cosier, cosiest** warm and comfortable: *It's really cosy in this bed.*

cot /kɒt $ kɑt/ *noun* **1** *BrE* a baby's bed with high sides; CRIB *AmE* **2** the American word for CAMP BED

cot·tage /'kɒtɪdʒ $ 'kɑtɪdʒ/ *noun* a small house in the country ⇨ *see picture on page 348*

cot·ton /'kɒtn $ 'kɑtn/ *noun* [no plural] **1** cloth or thread made from the cotton plant: *a cotton dress* **2** the American word for COTTON WOOL

cotton wool /ˌ.. '../ *noun BrE* a soft piece of cotton that you use for cleaning your skin or putting things on it; COTTON *AmE*: *Wipe the wound with damp cotton wool.*

couch /kaʊtʃ/ *noun, plural* **couches** a long comfortable seat that you can sit or lie on

cough /kɒf $ kɔf/ *verb* if you cough, air suddenly comes out of your throat with a short harsh sound, for example because you are ill: *Smoking makes you cough.*
– **cough** *noun*: *Tom's got a really bad cough – he should see a doctor.*

could /kəd; *strong* kʊd/ *modal verb, negative* **couldn't** *or* **could not**
1 being able to do something in the past: *My brother couldn't read or write until he was eight.* | *Ellis drank his tea as fast as he could.* | *Nothing could change Dad's mind once he'd decided something.*
2 saying that something is possible **1)** if something **could** happen, it is possible in the present: *Scientists say that no life could exist on Mars.* | *Don't park the car there – it could cause an accident.* **2)** if something **could have** happened, it was possible in the past, but it did not happen: *What a silly thing to do! I could have been killed!* | *You could have told me you were leaving.*
3 asking politely for something: *Could I have another coffee please?* | *Could I start by asking everyone their name?*
4 suggesting something: *"We could go to see a film."* | *You could ask your teacher for help.*
5 feeling or knowing something: use **could** with verbs such as 'see', 'taste', 'feel', 'hear', and 'believe' to say what you felt in the past: *I could hear someone in the garden last night.* | *I couldn't understand what he was saying.*

could·n't /'kʊdnt/ the short form of 'could not': *I couldn't open the door.*

could·'ve /'kʊdəv/ the short form of 'could have': *I wish I could've spent more time with my sister.*

coun·cil /'kaʊnsəl/ *noun* a group of

people that have been elected to do a particular job: *the UN Security Council*

coun·cil·lor *BrE*, **councilor** *AmE* /'kaʊnsələ $ 'kaʊnsələ/ *noun* a member of a council: *Councillor Bill Roberts*

coun·sel·ling *BrE*, **counseling** *AmE* /'kaʊnsəlɪŋ/ *noun [no plural]* the job of giving people help and advice about their personal problems: *She is trained in counselling and therapy.*

coun·sel·lor *BrE*, **counselor** *AmE* /'kaʊnsələ $ 'kaʊnsələ/ *noun* someone whose job is to help and advise people with personal problems

count¹ /kaʊnt/ *verb*

> GRAMMAR
> **count to something**

1 also **count up** to discover the exact number of things or people in a group by adding them together: *I counted up the number of hours I watched TV each day.* | *There were so many cars in the car park, I couldn't count them all.*
2 to say numbers one after another in the right order: *Tom was only two, but he could already count to twenty.*
3 to include something when you are adding up a total amount: *I have 23 CDs, counting these new ones.*
4 if something counts, it is important or accepted in a situation: *Everyone's opinion counts.*

> PHRASAL VERB
> **count on**

count on someone/something to expect or be sure that someone will do what you need them to do or that something will happen: *If you need any help you can count on me.*

count² *noun* **1** lose count if you lose count when you are counting something, you forget the number you reached, and so do not know what the total is: *She's lost count of the number of boyfriends she's had.* **2** a man from Europe with a high social rank: *the Count of Luxembourg*

count·a·ble /'kaʊntəbəl/ *adjective* in grammar, a countable noun has a singular and a plural form. 'Table' (plural 'tables') and 'man' (plural 'men') are examples of countable nouns ⇨ *opposite* UNCOUNTABLE

count·down /'kaʊntdaʊn/ *noun* when numbers are counted backwards to one or zero: *Did you listen to the MTV countdown yesterday?*

coun·ter /'kaʊntə $ 'kaʊntə/ *noun* **1** a long table in a shop where someone working in the shop serves you **2** a small round object used in some games

coun·ter·clock·wise /ˌkaʊntə'klɒkwaɪz $ ˌkaʊntə'klɑkwaɪz/ the American word for ANTICLOCKWISE

coun·tess /'kaʊntəs/ *noun, plural* countesses a woman from Europe with a high social rank

count·less /'kaʊntləs/ *adjective* very many: *Countless lives are lost on our roads each year.*

coun·try /'kʌntri/ *noun, plural* countries
1 an area of land that has its own government and people: *How many countries are there in Europe?*
2 the country areas that are not near towns or cities: *Do you prefer living in the town or the country?*

country mu·sic /'.. ˌ../ also **country and west·ern** /ˌ... '.../ *noun [no plural]* a type of popular music from the US

coun·try·side /'kʌntrisaɪd/ *noun [no plural]* land that is not near towns or cities: *a walk in the countryside*

coun·ty /'kaʊnti/ *noun, plural* counties an area in Britain, Ireland, or the US with its own local government

coup /kuː/ *noun* **1** also **coup d'é·tat** /ˌkuː deɪˈtɑː $ ˌkuː deˈtɑ/ when a group of people take control of a country by force: *a military coup* **2** a very good achievement: *Getting a place at college was a real coup for me.*

cou·ple /'kʌpəl/ *noun*
two people who are married or having a romantic relationship: *Sally and Dave are a very attractive couple, aren't they?*

> PHRASE

a couple of people/things *spoken* two people, or a few things: *There were a couple of men standing at the door.* | *Linda appeared a couple of minutes later.*

cou·pon /'kuːpɒn $ 'kupɑn/ *noun* **1** a ticket that you can use instead of money: *Collect three coupons for a free jar of coffee.* **2** a printed form in a newspaper or magazine that you fill in and send to a company to order things, enter a competition etc

cour·age /'kʌrɪdʒ $ 'kɜ·ɪdʒ/ *noun* [no plural] the ability to manage difficult or dangerous situations without being afraid ➪ *same meaning* BRAVERY: *It takes courage to admit that you are wrong.*

cou·ra·geous /kə'reɪdʒəs/ *adjective* very brave: *a courageous man*
– **courageously** *adverb*: *The firefighters acted courageously.*

cour·gette /kuə'ʒet $ kur'ʒet/ *noun* BrE a long green vegetable; ZUCCHINI *AmE* ➪ *see picture on page 345*

cou·ri·er /'kuriə $ 'kuriə·/ *noun* **1** someone whose job is to take and deliver letters and packages **2** BrE someone whose job is to help people who are on holiday with a travel company

course /kɔːs $ kɔrs/ *noun*
1 a set of lessons about a subject: *I'd like to take a course in business studies.*
2 one of the parts of a meal: *We had soup for the first course.* | *a three-course meal*
3 a place where people play GOLF or races take place: *We stood on the edge of the race course as the horses galloped past.*
4 the direction that a plane, ship etc moves in: *The ship changed course and headed west.*
5 during the course of something, in the course of something while something is happening: *We got to know each other really well during the course of the holiday.*

PHRASE
of course, of course not *spoken* used to say 'yes' or 'no' in a strong way: *"Can I come in?" "Of course, sit down."* | *"Is something wrong?" "No, of course not."*

course-book /'. ./ *noun* a book that students use to learn a subject and that is divided into separate lessons

court /kɔːt $ kɔrt/ *noun* **1** the people who make a legal judgement, for example about whether someone is guilty of a crime, or a place where these judgements are made: *The court re-*

jected the charges against him.* | *Would you be willing to say that in court?* **2** an area where you play a sport such as tennis: *I've booked a squash court for tonight.*

cour·te·sy /'kɜːtəsi $ 'kɜ·təsi/ *noun* [no plural] *formal* polite behaviour

court·house /'kɔːthaus $ 'kɔrthaus/ *noun* AmE a building containing a room or rooms in which people make legal judgements

court·room /'kɔːtruːm $ 'kɔrtrum/ *noun* a room in which people make legal judgements

court·yard /'kɔːtjɑːd $ 'kɔrtjɑrd/ *noun* an outdoor area surrounded by walls or buildings

cous·in /'kʌzən/ *noun* the son or daughter of your aunt or uncle

cov·er¹ /'kʌvə $ 'kʌvə·/ *verb*
1 also **cover up** to put something over the top of another thing, for example to protect or hide it: *She quickly covered the child with a blanket.*
2 be covered with/in something if something is covered with something, it has that thing over its whole surface: *The walls of her room are covered with pictures of pop stars.*
3 to lie or fit over the top or surface of something: *the cloth covering the table*
4 to include something: *Does the course cover nineteenth century literature?*

cover² *noun*
1 something that fits over another thing to protect it, keep it clean etc: *Where's the cover for this record?*
2 the front or back part on the outside of a book or magazine: *The price is usually on the back cover.*
3 covers the sheet and other pieces of cloth that cover you when you are in bed

PHRASE
take cover to go somewhere in order to be protected from bad weather or attack: *When the storm started we took cover in a barn.*

cov·er·age /'kʌvərɪdʒ/ *noun* [no plural] the amount and type of attention that television, radio, and newspaper reports give to a news event: *The television coverage of the race was excellent.*

cov·er·ing /'kʌvərɪŋ/ *noun* something that covers something else: *wooden floor coverings*

cover-up /'... ./ *noun* an attempt to stop people finding out the truth: *The government says there has not been a cover-up.*

cow /kaʊ/ *noun* a large animal that is kept on farms for its milk and meat

cow·ard /'kaʊəd $ 'kaʊəd/ *noun* someone who is not brave and who avoids dangerous or difficult situations: *They called me a coward because I wouldn't fight.*

cow·ard·ice /'kaʊədɪs $ 'kaʊədɪs/ *noun* [no plural] behaviour that shows you are not brave ⇨ opposite BRAVERY: *She accused him of cowardice.*

cow·boy /'kaʊbɔɪ/ *noun* a man whose job is to look after cattle in North America

cozy the American spelling of COSY

crab /kræb/ *noun* a sea animal with a shell and ten legs that walks to the side, not forwards: *a rock pool full of tiny crabs* ⇨ see picture on page 339

crack¹ /kræk/ *verb* **1** if something cracks, or if you crack it, it starts to break and a line appears on its surface: *I dropped the cup and it cracked.* **2 crack down** to deal very firmly with a particular crime or bad behaviour: *The government plans to crack down on drug dealers.*

crack² *noun* **1** a thin line on something that shows that it is starting to break: *There's a crack in this mug.* **2** a very narrow space: *The coin fell down a crack in the sidewalk.* **3** a sudden short noise: *the crack of a whip*

crack·down /'krækdaʊn/ *noun* a serious and firm attempt to stop a particular crime or bad behaviour: *The government announced a crackdown on drugs.*

cracked /krækt/ *adjective* a cracked object is damaged and has thin lines on its surface: *These plates are all cracked.*

crack·le /'krækəl/ *verb* written to make a lot of short sharp noises: *The fire crackled in the hearth.* ⇨ see picture on page 350
– **crackle** *noun*: *the crackle of a microphone*

cra·dle /'kreɪdl/ *noun* a small bed for a baby: *He made her a cradle for her doll.*

craft /krɑːft $ kræft/ *noun* a skilled activity in which you make something using your hands: *traditional crafts such as woodwork and pottery*

crafts·man /'krɑːftsmən $ 'kræftsmən/ *noun*, *plural* **craftsmen** /-mən/ someone whose job is making things skilfully with their hands: *violins made by the country's finest craftsmen*

craft·y /'krɑːfti $ 'kræfti/ *adjective* **craftier, craftiest** a crafty person deceives people in a clever way to get what they want: *A crafty football fan had got into the game without paying.*
– **craftily** *adverb*: *She had craftily hidden all her sweets.*

cram /kræm/ *verb* **crammed, cramming** **1** if you cram things into a small space, you put them there so that they completely fill it: *Sally crammed a huge slice of cake into her mouth.* **2** if a place is crammed with things or people, it is full of them: *The bus was crammed with people.*

cramp /kræmp/ *noun* a bad pain in your muscles

cramped /kræmpt/ *adjective* a cramped place is not big enough for the people or things in it: *Six of us lived in a tiny, cramped apartment.*

crane¹ /kreɪn/ *noun* a large machine with a long metal arm for lifting heavy things: *A crane lifted the box onto the boat.*

crane² *verb* to stretch your neck forwards in order to see something: *Mark craned forward to get a better look.*

crap /kræp/ *noun* [no plural] informal a rude word for something that you think is of very bad quality: *The last game I saw was crap.*

crash¹ /kræʃ/ *verb*

GRAMMAR
crash into something

1 if a car, plane etc crashes, it hits something very hard and stops: *The truck ran off the road and crashed into a tree.*

2 if a computer crashes, it suddenly stops working: *My computer keeps crashing and I don't know what's wrong with it.*

crash² *noun*, *plural* **crashes**

1 an accident in which a car, plane etc hits something hard and stops:

There was a bad crash on the motorway and two people were killed.
2 a loud noise, like something suddenly falling down or breaking: *Just then we heard a loud crash in the kitchen.* ⇨ see picture on page 350

crash course /'. ,./ *noun* a short course in a subject where you study the most important things very quickly: *I had a crash course in French before I went to live in Paris.*

crash hel·met /'. ,../ *noun* a hard hat that people wear on their heads when they are riding MOTORCYCLES (=bicycles with engines): *By law, motorcyclists must wear crash helmets.*

crash-land /'. ./ *verb* to land a damaged plane: *The pilot crash-landed in a field.*

crass /kræs/ *adjective* stupid and rude: *Paul made crass comments throughout the film.*

crate /kreɪt/ *noun* a large wooden box: *a crate of champagne*

cra·ter /'kreɪtə $ 'kreɪtɚ/ *noun* a large hole in the ground or at the top of a VOLCANO: *Hot lava flowed from the crater.*

crawl¹ /krɔːl/ *verb*
1 to move on your hands and knees: *The baby crawled towards the fire.* ⇨ see picture on page 340 **2** if an insect crawls, it moves using its legs: *There's a spider crawling on your arm.*

crawl² *noun* [no plural] a way of swimming in which you move each arm in turn over your head and kick your legs: *Can you do the crawl?*

cray·on /'kreɪən $ 'kreɪɑn/ *noun* a coloured pencil: *a picture drawn in crayon*

craze /kreɪz/ *noun* something that is very popular for a short time: *the latest fashion craze*

cra·zy /'kreɪzi/ *adjective* **crazier, craziest**
strange or silly: *a crazy idea* | *He must be crazy to drive his car so fast.*

PHRASES
be crazy about *informal* to like some-

one or something very much: *She's crazy about one of the boys in her class.*
go crazy *informal* to become very angry or excited: *The crowd went crazy when the team scored.*

creak /kriːk/ *verb* if something creaks, it makes a long high noise when it moves: *The gate creaked in the wind.* ⇨ see picture on page 350
– **creak** *noun*: *She heard a creak on the stairs.*

cream¹ /kriːm/ *noun* **1** [no plural] a thick white liquid produced from milk: *coffee with cream* **2** a thick smooth substance that you put on your skin: *shaving cream*

cream² *noun, adjective* a yellowish-white colour: *a cream suit*

cream·y /'kriːmi/ *adjective* **creamier, creamiest** containing or looking like cream: *creamy soup*

crease /kriːs/ *verb* if you crease something, or if it creases, lines or folds appear in it: *Try not to crease your skirt.* | *The new dollar bills had creased in his pocket.*
– **crease** *noun*: *an old man with creases around his eyes*

cre·ate /kri'eɪt/ *verb*
to make something happen or exist: *The new rules will create a lot of problems.*

cre·a·tion /kri'eɪʃən/ *noun* **1** something new and different that someone has made: *Her latest fashion creation is a leather skirt.* **2** when something new is made or formed: *the creation of the Scottish parliament*

cre·a·tive /kri'eɪtɪv/ *adjective* **1** a creative person has a lot of new ideas: *a very creative artist* **2** using your imagination: *creative writing*
– **creatively** *adverb*: *the ability to think creatively*

cre·a·tiv·i·ty /ˌkriːeɪ'tɪvəti/ *noun* [no plural] the ability to use your imagination: *Many of the children show great creativity in class.*

cre·a·tor /kri'eɪtə $ kri'eɪtɚ/ *noun* someone who makes or invents something: *Ian Fleming, the creator of James Bond*

crater

moon

crater

crea·ture /ˈkriːtʃə $ ˈkritʃɚ/
noun

an animal, fish, or insect: *A pond like this is full of all sorts of living creatures.*

crèche /kreʃ/ noun BrE a place where someone is responsible for babies whose parents are away for a short time: *Many shopping centres now have a crèche.*

cred·i·bil·i·ty /ˌkredəˈbɪləti/ noun [no plural] if someone has credibility, other people believe and trust them: *The company lost credibility with its customers.*

cred·it¹ /ˈkredɪt/ noun 1 [no plural] a system in which you receive things and pay for them later: *She was refused credit by all the major banks.* 2 [no plural] praise you give to someone for doing something: *They deserve a lot of credit for finishing the project on time.* 3 be in credit if your bank account is in credit, there is money in it: *My account hasn't been in credit for months.* 4 the credits a list of the people who made a television programme or film

credit² verb if someone is credited with doing something good, people say that they did it: *The film's success can be credited to its director, Stephen Spielberg.*

credit card /ˈ.. ˌ./ noun a small plastic card that you use to buy things and pay for them later: *You can pay by cash or by credit card.*

creep /kriːp/ verb, past tense and past participle **crept** /krept/ 1 to move very quietly and slowly: *She crept outside.* 2 **creep up** written to increase slowly: *The number of people without jobs crept up to 2 million.*

creeps /kriːps/ plural noun **give someone the creeps** informal to make someone feel nervous or frightened: *That man gives me the creeps!*

creep·y /ˈkriːpi/ adjective **creepier, creepiest** slightly frightening: *a creepy ghost story*

cre·mate /krəˈmeɪt $ ˈkriːmeɪt/ verb to burn the body of a dead person: *He will be cremated on Saturday.*

cre·ma·tion /krɪˈmeɪʃən/ noun when a dead person's body is burned: *a cremation service*

crept the past tense and past participle of CREEP

cres·cent /ˈkresənt/ noun 1 a curved shape that is wider in the middle and pointed at the ends: *The moon was a perfect cresent shape.* ⇨ see picture at SHAPE¹ 2 **Crescent** used in the names of some small streets in towns and cities: *number 5, Cherry Crescent*

crest /krest/ noun the top of a hill or wave: *We reached the crest of the hill and looked down.*

crev·ice /ˈkrevɪs/ noun a narrow crack, especially in rock: *A climber fell into a crevice on the moutain.*

crew /kruː/ noun a group of people who work together: *The crew of the plane are trained in fire safety procedures.*

crib /krɪb/ the American word for COT

crick·et /ˈkrɪkɪt/ noun 1 [no plural] a game in which two teams of eleven players each get points by hitting a ball and running between two sets of sticks: *Shall we play cricket?* ⇨ see picture on page 351 2 an insect that makes a short loud noise by rubbing its wings together

crime /kraɪm/ noun

if someone COMMITS a crime, they do something that is illegal: *Anyone who **commits a crime** must be punished.* | *Crime in our cities is increasing.*

crim·i·nal¹ /ˈkrɪmənəl/ adjective related to crime: *criminal activities*

criminal² noun someone who is proved guilty of a crime: *Some criminals will do anything to get what they want.*

crim·son /ˈkrɪmzən/ adjective, noun a dark red colour: *crimson lipstick*

cringe /krɪndʒ/ verb to feel embarrassed by something: *Some of the things she says make me cringe.*

crip·ple /ˈkrɪpəl/ verb 1 to hurt someone so they can no longer walk: *She was crippled in a car accident.* 2 to damage something or make it much weaker: *These policies have crippled the education system.*

cri·sis /ˈkraɪsɪs/ noun, plural **crises** /-siːz/

a situation in which someone or something has very bad problems: *an economic crisis* | *He had to go and deal with a crisis at home.*

crisp¹ /krɪsp/ *adjective* **1** fresh, firm, and pleasant to eat: *Bake the pie until the top is crisp and golden.* **2** pleasantly clean and fresh: *crisp new dollar bills*

crisp² *noun BrE* a very thin piece of potato cooked in hot oil and eaten cold; CHIP *AmE*: *a bag of crisps*

crisp·y /'krɪspi/ *adjective* crispier, crispiest crispy food is pleasantly hard: *crispy fried rice*

cri·te·ri·a /kraɪ'tɪəriə $kraɪ'tɪriə/ *plural noun formal* facts or standards that you use to help you decide something: *What are the college's criteria for measuring each student's ability?*

crit·ic /'krɪtɪk/ *noun* someone whose job is to give their opinion about a film or book: *The critics praised the play highly.*

crit·i·cal /'krɪtɪkəl/ *adjective* **1** saying that you think a person or thing is bad or wrong: *Dad's very critical of the way I dress.* **2** very serious or important: *It's critical that you get your essays in on time.*
— **critically** /-kli/ *adverb*: *He looked critically at my crumpled dress.* | *Ged was critically ill in hospital.*

crit·i·cis·m /'krɪtəsɪzəm/ *noun*

GRAMMAR
criticism of something
when you say that a person or thing is bad in some way: *She is upset by criticism.* | *He disagreed with the teacher's criticisms of his work.*

crit·i·cize also **criticise** *BrE* /'krɪtəsaɪz/ *verb*

GRAMMAR
criticize someone for doing something
to say that someone or something is bad in some way: *My parents are always criticizing me for spending too much money.* | *She criticizes everything I do.*

croak /krəʊk $kroʊk/ *verb written* to make a deep low sound in your throat: *"My throat is sore," she croaked.*

crock·e·ry /'krɒkəri $'krɑkəri/ *noun* [no plural] cups, plates, dishes etc

croc·o·dile /'krɒkədaɪl $'krɑkə‚daɪl/ *noun* a large animal with a long body, short legs, a big mouth, and very sharp

teeth, that lives mainly in water ⇨ see picture on page 339

crook /krʊk/ *noun informal* a criminal: *Don't trust Ben – he's a crook.*

crook·ed /'krʊkɪd/ *adjective* something that is crooked is not straight but it should be: *The picture on the wall was crooked.*

crop¹ /krɒp $krɑp/ *noun* a plant that a farmer grows: *The main crop grown here is barley.*

crop² *verb* cropped, cropping; **crop up** *informal* to happen suddenly: *A problem has just cropped up.*

cross¹ /krɒs $krɔs/ *verb*

GRAMMAR
cross over (something)
1 to go from one side of a road, river, room etc to the other: *Hold Daddy's hand while we cross the road.* | *Thousands of refugees had crossed the border.* | *We had crossed over the bridge safely.* | *A small boy was waiting to cross, so I stopped the car.*
2 if roads or lines cross, they go across each other: *Draw two lines that cross each other at an angle of 60 degrees.*

PHRASE
cross your legs to put one leg on top of the other: *She sat down and crossed her legs.*

PHRASAL VERB
cross off
cross something off (something) to remove something from a list: *I asked the committee to cross my name off the list of volunteers.* | *We've tidied the bookshelves and cleaned the desks, so we can cross them off the list.*
cross out
cross something out to draw a line through something that you have written because it is wrong: *If you make a mistake, just cross it out.*

cross² *noun, plural* **crosses**
1 *BrE* a mark (X) that you make on paper, especially to show that something that is written is not correct: *The teacher had put a cross by three of my answers.*
2 a shape (†) or object that is an important sign for Christians, which has a long upright part with a shorter

▼ part crossing it near the top: *He always wore a gold cross round his neck.*

cross³ *adjective* BrE angry: *Please don't be cross with me.*

cross-coun·try /ˌ. ˈ../ *adjective* cross-country running involves running across fields and not along a road or track: *a cross-country race*

cross-ex·am·ine /ˌ. .ˈ../ *verb* to ask someone questions about something they have just said in a court of law: *The lawyer cross-examined the witness for an hour.*

cross-eyed /ˌ. ˈ. $ ˈ. ./ *adjective* if someone is cross-eyed, their eyes look towards their nose

cross·ing /ˈkrɒsɪŋ $ ˈkrɔsɪŋ/ *noun* **1** a place where you can safely cross a road: *We waited at the crossing.* **2** a journey across the sea: *It was a rough crossing.*

cross-leg·ged /ˌkrɒs ˈleɡɪd $ ˌkrɔs ˈleɡɪd/ *adverb, adjective* sitting with your knees wide apart and your feet crossed: *We sat cross-legged on the floor.*

cross-ref·er·ence /ˌ. ˈ.... $ ˈ. ˌ.../ *noun* a note in a book that tells you to where to look in the same book for more information

cross·roads /ˈkrɒsrəʊdz $ ˈkrɔsroʊdz/ *noun, plural* **crossroads** a place where two roads cross each other: *Turn right at the crossroads.*

cross sec·tion or **cross-section** /ˈ. ˌ../ *noun* **1** a drawing of what something looks like inside by showing it as if it has been cut into two pieces: *a cross section of the ship showing all the levels* **2** a group of people or things that is similar to a larger group: *The students here are a cross-section of the local community.*

cross·walk /ˈkrɒswɔːk $ ˈkrɔswɔk/ the American word for PEDESTRIAN CROSSING

cross·word /ˈkrɒswɜːd $ ˈkrɔsˌwɚd/ also **crossword puz·zle** /ˈ.. ˌ../ *noun* a game in which you try to write the correct words in a pattern of spaces: *I love doing crosswords.*

crouch /kraʊtʃ/ also **crouch down** *verb* to bend your knees and back so that you are close to the ground: *He crouched behind a bush so that he*

couldn't be seen. ➔ see picture on page 340

crowd /kraʊd/ *noun*

GRAMMAR
a crowd of people
a large number of people in one place: *There was a crowd of people waiting for the film star to come out.*

crowd·ed /ˈkraʊdɪd/ *adjective* a place that is crowded is full of people: *a crowded beach*

crown¹ /kraʊn/ *noun* a circle made of gold and jewels that a king or queen wears on their head: *The Queen only wears her crown on official occasions.*

crown² *verb* to place a crown on someone's head, so that they officially become king or queen: *They crowned him King of England.*

cru·cial /ˈkruːʃəl/ *adjective* very important: *It is crucial that we act quickly.*

Cru·ci·fix·ion /ˌkruːsəˈfɪkʃən/ *noun* **the Crucifixion** the death of Christ on the cross

crude /kruːd/ *adjective* **1** rude, especially about sex: *crude jokes* **2** made in a simple way from simple parts: *They made a crude shelter out of branches.*

cru·el /ˈkruːəl/ *adjective* **crueller, cruellest** someone who is cruel deliberately treats people or animals in a very unkind way: *I think it's cruel to keep wild animals in zoos.* | *That was a really cruel thing to say.*

cru·el·ty /ˈkruːəlti/ *noun*

GRAMMAR
cruelty to someone
actions that deliberately hurt people or animals: *Cruelty to animals is against the law.*

cruise¹ /kruːz/ *verb* **1** to sail along slowly: *They spent the summer cruising the Mediterranean Sea.* **2** to move along at a steady speed in a car, plane etc: *The plane will be cruising at 30,000 feet.*

cruise² *noun* a holiday on a large ship: *They went on a Caribbean cruise.*

crumb /krʌm/ *noun* a very small piece of bread, cake etc: *She wiped the crumbs off the table.*

cuff

crum·ble /'krʌmbəl/ verb to break into small pieces: The rocks here are crumbling into the sea.

crum·ple /'krʌmpəl/ verb to crush paper or cloth so that it is folded in an untidy way: You're crumpling my shirt. – crumpled adjective: a crumpled handkerchief

crunch¹ /krʌntʃ/ verb to make a noise like something being crushed: The snow crunched under our feet.

crunch² noun [no plural] 1 a noise like something being crushed: There was a crunch as the car hit the post. ⇨ see picture on page 350 2 **the crunch** informal the moment when you must make an important decision or a special effort: The crunch came when her husband asked her to leave her job.

crunch·y /'krʌntʃi/ adjective crunchier, crunchiest food that is crunchy is pleasantly hard: a crunchy apple

crush¹ /krʌʃ/ verb to press something so hard that it breaks or is damaged: He crushed the paper cup and threw it in the bin. ⇨ see picture on page 344

crush² noun, plural crushes 1 when a young person feels love someone they are unlikely to have a relationship with: Ben has a crush on his teacher. 2 a crowd of people very close together: There was a real crush by the door.

crust /krʌst/ noun the hard part on the outside of something, especially bread: He cut the crust off his sandwiches. | the Earth's crust

crutch /krʌtʃ/ noun, plural crutches a stick that you use to help you walk when you have hurt your leg: Ian was on crutches for a month after the accident.

cry¹ /kraɪ/ verb cried, cries

GRAMMAR
cry for something
1 if you are crying, tears are coming from your eyes because you are sad or hurt: Maria read the letter and started to cry.
2 also **cry out** written to shout something: "Help!" he cried. "I can't swim!" | Mandy **cried for** help, but no-one could hear her.
3 **cry out** written to make a loud sound, for example because you are afraid or hurt: Sam fell over and **cried out** in pain.

cry² noun written, plural cries a loud sound that a person or bird makes: We could hear the cries of the people who were trapped in the burning building.

cryp·tic /'krɪptɪk/ adjective having a meaning that is not clear: a cryptic message

crys·tal /'krɪstl/ noun 1 an amount of a substance in a regular shape that forms naturally: sugar crystals 2 [no plural] high quality glass: a crystal vase

cub /kʌb/ noun a young bear, lion etc

cube¹ /kjuːb/ noun 1 a solid object with six equal square sides: ice cubes ⇨ see picture at SHAPE¹ 2 the number you get when you multiply a number by itself twice: 27 is the cube of 3.

cube² verb to multiply a number by itself twice: 4 cubed is 64.

cu·bic /'kjuːbɪk/ adjective a measurement of space which is calculated by multiplying the length of something by its width and height: The room measures 10 cubic metres.

cu·bi·cle /'kjuːbɪkəl/ noun a small room for one person to change their clothes in: the changing cubicles at the swimming pool

cu·cum·ber /'kjuːkʌmbə $'kjuːˌkʌmbɚ/ noun a long round vegetable with a dark green skin that you do not cook: a cucumber and tomato salad ⇨ see picture on page 345

cud·dle /'kʌdl/ verb to hold your arms around someone or something that you love: The little girl was cuddling a doll. – cuddle noun: His mother gave him a cuddle.

cue /kjuː/ noun 1 a long thin stick used for hitting the ball in games such as POOL 2 an action or event that is a sign for something else to happen: His girlfriend's arrival was our cue to leave.

cuff /kʌf/ noun the end of a SLEEVE: The cuffs of his shirt were dirty.

cul·de·sac /'kʌl də ˌsæk/ *noun* a street which is closed at one end

cul·mi·nate /'kʌlmənet/ *verb formal* **culminate in** to have an important event at the end: *The holiday culminated in a terrible argument.*

cul·prit /'kʌlprɪt/ *noun* a person who has done something wrong: *The man whose car was damaged was determined to find the culprits.*

cult /kʌlt/ *noun* **1** a small religion whose members have unusual views: *a member of an extreme religious cult* **2** [no plural] a fashion, film etc that has become very popular among a particular group of people: *It has become a cult film among students.*

cul·ti·vate /'kʌltəveɪt/ *verb* to prepare and use land for growing plants for food

cul·tu·ral /'kʌltʃərəl/ *adjective* **1** connected with a particular society and its way of life: *the cultural differences between England and Pakistan* **2** related to art, literature, music etc: *There aren't many cultural events in this town.*
– culturally *adverb*: *a culturally diverse society*

cul·ture /'kʌltʃə $ 'kʌltʃɚ/ *noun* **1** the ideas, behaviour, beliefs etc of a particular society: *You have to spend time in a country if you want to understand its culture.* | *the many differences between the two cultures* **2** [no plural] art, music, literature etc: *I prefer living in a big city, where there's plenty of culture.*

cul·tured /'kʌltʃəd $ 'kʌltʃɚd/ *adjective* knowing a lot about art, literature, music etc

cum·ber·some /'kʌmbəsəm $ 'kʌmbɚsəm/ *adjective* difficult to move or use: *a large, cumbersome bag*

cun·ning /'kʌnɪŋ/ *adjective* clever, especially in a rather dishonest way: *a cunning plan*
– cunningly *adverb*: *He cunningly persuaded his wife to stay at home.*

cup /kʌp/ *noun* **1** a small container with a handle that you drink from: *Would you like a cup of tea?* **2** a metal container that is given as a prize in a competition, or the competition itself: *Who do you think will win the European Cup?*

cup·board /'kʌbəd $ 'kʌbɚd/ *noun* a piece of furniture with a door and shelves for storing things: *I'm going to clean the kitchen cupboards.*

curb¹ /kɜːb $ kɚb/ the American spelling of KERB

curb² *verb* to control or limit something: *You must curb your spending.*

cure¹ /kjʊə $ kjʊr/ *verb* to remove an illness or injury: *The doctors are sure they can cure him.*

cure² *noun* a medicine or treatment that can remove an illness: *We have not yet found a cure for cancer.*

cu·ri·os·i·ty /ˌkjʊəri'ɒsəti $ ˌkjʊri'ɑsəti/ *noun* [no plural] the wish to know about something: *His parents showed no curiosity about where he had been.*

cu·ri·ous /'kjʊəriəs $ 'kjʊriəs/ *adjective*

> **GRAMMAR**
> **curious about something**

1 if you are curious about something, you want to know or learn about it: *I was **curious about** how the system worked.* | *The children were excited and curious.* **2** strange or unusual: *There was a curious blue light in the sky.*

curl

curl¹ /kɜːl $ kɚl/ *noun* a piece of hair which curves around: *She has beautiful blond curls.*

curl² *verb* **1** to make hair curve around: *She curled her hair around her finger and smiled.* **2 curl up 1)** to lie or sit comfortably with your legs bent close to your body: *She decided to curl up with a book.* **2)** if paper, leaves etc curl up, the edges bend upwards: *The bottom leaves began to curl up and drop off.*

curl·y /'kɜːli $ 'kɚli/ *adjective* **curlier, curliest** curly hair has a lot of curls: *I had very curly hair when I was a baby.*

cur·ren·cy /'kʌrənsi $ 'kɜ·ənsi/ noun, plural **currencies** the type of money that a country uses: *We need to get some of the local currency before we go on holiday.*

cur·rent¹ /'kʌrənt $ 'kɜ·ənt/ adjective happening or existing at the present time: *Who is her current boyfriend?* – **currently** adverb: *He is currently on holiday.*

current² noun **1** a flow of water or air in a particular direction: *The current swept the boat away.* **2** a flow of electricity through a wire: *an electric current that passes through a coil of wire*

cur·ric·u·lum /kə'rɪkjələm/ noun, plural **curricula** /-lə/ or **curriculums** the subjects that students learn at a school or college: *Greek will be on the curriculum next term.*

cur·ry /'kʌri $ 'kɜ·i/ noun, plural **curries** meat or vegetables cooked in a hot-tasting SAUCE: *chicken curry*

curse¹ /kɜːs $ kɜ·s/ verb written to swear in an angry way: *He put the phone down angrily and cursed.*

curse² noun **1** written a word or words that you use when you are angry: *I could hear his curses from the next room.* **2** magical words that bring someone bad luck: *The witch put a curse on him.*

cur·sor /'kɜːsə $ 'kɜ·sə·/ noun a shape on a computer screen that moves to show where you are writing: *Put the cursor on the icon and click the mouse.*

cur·tain /'kɜːtn $ 'kɜ·tn/ noun a piece of cloth that hangs above a window, and that you can pull across the window, for example at night time: *Close the curtains.*

curve¹ /kɜːv $ kɜ·v/ noun a line or shape which gradually bends like part of a circle: *They came to a curve in the river.*

curve² verb to bend or move in the shape of a curve: *The ball curved through the air into the net.*

curved /kɜːvd $ kɜ·vd/ adjective having the shape of a curve: *a Japanese sword with a curved blade*

cush·ion /'kʊʃən/ noun a bag filled with soft material that you sit or lie on: *She removed the cushions from the sofa.* ⇨ *see picture on page 342*

cush·y /'kʊʃi/ adjective informal **cushier**, **cushiest** a cushy job or situation is very easy or pleasant: *Teaching is not a cushy job.*

cus·tard /'kʌstəd $ 'kʌstə·d/ noun BrE a thick SAUCE that is poured over sweet foods

cus·to·dy /'kʌstədi/ noun [no plural] the right to be responsible and care for a child: *His ex-wife has custody of the kids.*

cus·tom /'kʌstəm/ noun

1 something that people in a particular group or society have done for a long time, and which they continue doing because it is important to them ⇨ *same meaning* TRADITION: *She follows Islamic custom by covering her hair.*

2 customs the place where officials examine your bags to make sure you do not have anything illegal in them before you enter or leave a country: *All baggage must **go through customs**.*

cus·tom·a·ry /'kʌstəməri $ 'kʌstə-ˌmeri/ adjective usual or normal: *She caught her customary train.*

cus·tom·er /'kʌstəmə $ 'kʌstəmə·/ noun someone who buys things from a shop or company: *We try to keep our customers happy.*

USAGE customer, client
Compare **customer** and **client**. A **customer** buys things in a shop. A **client** pays someone such as a lawyer to do something for them.

cut¹ /kʌt/ verb, past tense and past participle **cut**, present participle **cutting**

GRAMMAR
cut comething into something

1 to use a knife or scissors to divide something into two or more pieces: *Lisa had her hair cut really short.* | *Cut the cheese into cubes.* | *Cut off a corner of the paper.*

2 to hurt yourself with a knife or something else that is sharp: *I cut my finger chopping carrots.*

3 to make something smaller, especially a number or amount of money: *Politicians have promised to cut taxes.*

PHRASAL VERBS
cut back
cut something back to make an

amount, number, cost etc smaller: *Bradley **cut back** the number of hours he was working.*

cut down
cut something down to do something less or use less of something: *Recycling bottles helps **cut down on** waste.*

cut off
1 cut something off to stop supplying something to someone: *The US **cut off** aid to the country.*
2 be cut off 1) if a place is cut off, it is separated from other places, usually because of bad weather or because it is a long way from other places: *The town was **cut off** by floods.* 2) if you are talking on the telephone and you are cut off, the telephone stops working: *I was just asking her where she was, and we **were cut off**.*

cut out
1 cut something out to remove something by cutting it with a knife or scissors: *Beth **cut out** pictures of movie stars from the magazine.*
2 cut it out, cut that out *spoken* used when you want someone to stop doing something that is annoying you: *Hey, Kate, **cut it out!** That really hurts!*

cut up
cut something up to cut something into small pieces: ***Cut up** the fruit into bite-sized pieces.* ⇨ *see usage note at* BREAK

cut² *noun*

GRAMMAR
a cut in something
1 a wound that you get when something sharp cuts your skin: *Mum put a plaster over the cut.*
2 when the size, number, or amount of something becomes smaller: *a **cut in** school fees*

cute /kjuːt/ *adjective* pretty or attractive: *her cute little nose*

cut·le·ry /ˈkʌtləri/ *noun* [no plural] knives, forks, and spoons; SILVERWARE *AmE*

cut-price also **cut-rate** /ˌ. ˈ./ *adjective* cheaper than normal: *a shop selling cut-price books*

cut·ting /ˈkʌtɪŋ/ *noun BrE* a piece of writing that you cut from a newspaper or magazine; CLIPPING *AmE*: *He keeps newspaper cuttings about his favourite football team.*

cutting edge /ˌ.. ˈ./ *noun* if you are at the cutting edge of an activity, you are involved in the most recent and most exciting part of its development: *Dr Campbell's work is at the cutting edge of medical science.*
– **cutting-edge** *adjective*: *cutting-edge scientific discoveries*

CV /ˌsiː ˈviː/ *noun BrE* a list of the education and previous jobs you have had that you show companies when you are trying to get a new job; RESUMÉ *AmE*: *Please send an up-to-date CV with your job application.*

cy·ber·space /ˈsaɪbəspeɪs $ ˈsaɪbɚ-ˌspeɪs/ *noun* [no plural] a place that is not real, that people use to talk about where electronic messages go when they travel from one computer to another: *He said his email had got lost in cyberspace.*

cy·cle¹ /ˈsaɪkəl/ *noun* 1 a number of events that happen many times in the same order: *the life cycle of the frog* 2 a bicycle or MOTORCYCLE: *He went for a cycle ride.*

cycle² *verb* to ride a bicycle: *She cycled over to Jane's house.* ⇨ *see pictures on pages 349 and 351*
– **cycling** *noun*

cy·clist /ˈsaɪklɪst/ *noun* someone who rides a bicycle: *This part of the road is for cyclists only.*

cy·clone /ˈsaɪkləʊn $ ˈsaɪkloʊn/ *noun* a very strong wind that moves in a circle

cyl·in·der /ˈsɪləndə $ ˈsɪləndɚ/ *noun* an object or container with circular ends and straight sides

cym·bal /ˈsɪmbəl/ *noun* one of a pair of round metal plates that you hit together or hit with a stick to make a musical sound: *There was a clash of cymbals.*

cyn·ic /ˈsɪnɪk/ *noun* someone who is cynical: *Don't be such a cynic!*

cyn·i·cal /ˈsɪnɪkəl/ *adjective* believing that no one does things for good or honest reasons: *I'm rather cynical about journalists who claim to be helping the public.*

Dd

dab /dæb/ *verb* **dabbed, dabbing** to lightly touch something several times in order to dry it or put something on it: *He dabbed at the mark on his trousers.*

dad /dæd/ *noun informal* father: *My dad took me to the zoo.* | *Dad, can I borrow the car?*

dad·dy /'dædi/ *noun, plural* **daddies** a word for father, used by children: *When is daddy coming home?*

daf·fo·dil /'dæfədɪl/ *noun* a tall yellow flower that grows in early spring

daft /dɑːft $ dæft/ *adjective BrE informal* silly: *I think it's a daft idea.*

dag·ger /'dægə $ 'dægər/ *noun* a short knife used as a weapon

dai·ly /'deɪli/ *adjective, adverb* happening or produced every day: *a daily newspaper*

dai·ry /'deəri $ 'deri/ *noun, plural* **dairies** **1** a part of a farm where butter and cheese are made **2** a company that sells milk and other foods made from milk

dam /dæm/ *noun* a wall built across a river to make a lake: *Water poured through a hole in the dam.*

dam

dam·age¹ /'dæmɪdʒ/ *noun*

GRAMMAR
damage to something
physical harm that breaks or spoils something: *The bomb caused a lot of damage.* | *After the fire, there was some damage to the ceiling and walls.*

damage² *verb*
to physically harm something, so that it breaks or no longer works

properly: *The water had damaged his extensive record collection.* | *Our suitcase was damaged at the airport.*

damn¹ /dæm/ *also* **damned** /dæmd/ *adverb, adjective spoken* used to emphasize something in a rude way, especially when you are annoyed: *Don't be so damn stupid!* | *The damned thing's broken again.*

damn² *noun* **not give a damn** *spoken* to not care at all about something: *I don't give a damn what he thinks.*

damp /dæmp/ *adjective*

slightly wet, in an unpleasant way: *a cold, damp day* | *This bed feels a bit damp to me.*
–**damp, dampness** *noun* [no plural]: *Protect your computer from extreme cold and damp.* | *As he entered the old house, he could feel a slight dampness in the air.*

dance¹ /dɑːns $ dæns/ *verb*

GRAMMAR
dance with someone
dance to something
to move your body in a way that follows a piece of music: *They danced and drank champagne until two in the morning.* | *Sharon danced with Joe.* | *Witney's only three, but she loves dancing to pop music.*
–**dancer** *noun*: *Ballet dancers practise several hours a day.*

dance² *noun*
1 an event where people go in order to dance with each other: *Did you go to the dance last Friday?*
2 a particular set of movements that you make, following a piece of music: *We learned two dances – the waltz and the tango.*
3 when you dance with someone:

May I **have this dance** (=will you dance with me)?

danc·ing /'dɑːnsɪŋ $ 'dænsɪŋ/ noun [no plural] when people dance together: We went dancing on New Year's Eve.

dan·ger /'deɪndʒə $ 'deɪndʒɚ/ noun

GRAMMAR
danger of something

1 [no plural] the possibility that something bad may happen: There is more **danger of** fire in our homes during the Christmas holidays. | Colin is in hospital and his life is no longer **in danger**. | He's **in danger of** losing his job.
2 plural **dangers** something or someone that may harm you: the dangers of smoking

dan·ger·ous /'deɪndʒərəs/ adjective likely to harm you: Police say the escaped prisoner is a very dangerous man. | Drugs are dangerous.
–**dangerously** adverb: He stood dangerously close to the fire.

dan·gle /'dæŋɡəl/ verb to hang or swing from something: Long earrings dangled from her ears.

dare /deə $ der/ verb

1 to be brave enough to do something: I didn't dare admit what I'd done.
2 to ask someone to do something brave to show they are not afraid: I dare you to ask her out on a date!
3 **how dare you, how dare he, how dare they** spoken used when you are very angry about what someone has done: How dare you speak to me like that!
4 **don't you dare** spoken used to tell someone not to do something: Don't you dare tell Mum!

daren't /deənt $ dernt/ the short form of 'dare not': I daren't be late.

dar·ing /'deərɪŋ $ 'derɪŋ/ adjective very brave: a daring attempt to break the land speed record

dark¹ /dɑːk $ dɑːrk/ adjective

1 **it is dark** when it is dark, it is night

time: It's only five o'clock, and it's already dark. | I want to get home before **it gets dark** (=becomes dark). | Come inside, **it's dark out** (=it is dark outside).
2 a dark place is one where there is little or no light: a dark, quiet room | It was very dark in the forest and we could hardly see.
3 a dark colour is strong and closer to black than to white: a dark blue dress | I'd like a carpet that's a bit darker than this one.
4 someone who is dark or who has dark hair or eyes has black or brown skin, hair, or eyes: a beautiful dark-haired woman | Tony's dad was dark, but his mother had blonde hair.

dark² noun 1 **the dark** when there is no light: When I was little, I was afraid of the dark. 2 **after dark, before dark** if it is after dark, night has begun. If it is before dark, it is still day time, although night will begin soon: The town really gets lively after dark. | You must get home before dark.

dark·en /'dɑːkən $ 'dɑːrkən/ verb written to become darker, or to make something darker: The sky darkened very quickly.

dark·ness /'dɑːknəs $ 'dɑːrknəs/ noun [no plural] when there is no light: The whole house was in darkness.

dar·ling /'dɑːlɪŋ $ 'dɑːrlɪŋ/ noun used when talking to someone you love: You look lovely, darling.

dart¹ /dɑːt $ dɑːrt/ noun 1 a small pointed object that you throw in the game of darts 2 **darts** a game in which you throw small pointed objects at a round board: Let's have a game of darts.

dart² verb to move suddenly and quickly in a particular direction: The fish darted away.

dash¹ /dæʃ/ verb 1 to go somewhere very quickly: When he heard about his father's accident, he dashed to the hospital. 2 **dash someone's hopes** written to destroy someone's hopes completely: His hopes of a career as a footballer were dashed when he injured his leg.

dash² noun, plural **dashes** 1 **make a dash for something** to run very quickly towards something: I made a dash for the door. 2 a small amount of a liquid:

Add a dash of lemon juice. **3** a mark (–) used to separate parts of a sentence

dash·board /'dæʃbɔːd $ 'dæʃbɔrd/ *noun* the part inside a car at the front which has the instruments and controls on it

da·ta /'deɪtə/ *noun, plural* **data** facts: *The scientists do not yet have enough data to say if the pollution problem is serious.* | *computer data*

da·ta·base /'deɪtəˌbeɪs/ *noun* a large amount of information stored in a computer system: *a database of students' names and addresses*

date¹ /deɪt/ *noun*

GRAMMAR
a date with someone

1 a particular day of the month or year, shown by a number. For example, 4 October 2001, 16th May and Tuesday 1 June are all dates: *What was the date yesterday – was it the sixth?* | *I need your full name and your **date of birth** (=the day, month, and year you were born).* | *"What date are you travelling?" "Around the third of August."* | *We must **set a date** (=say which day and month) for the party.* | *Let's **make a date** (=say which date and month) for the next meeting.*

2 an arrangement to go to a restaurant, film etc with someone you like in a romantic way: *Alison **has a date with** Mark on Saturday night.*

3 a small sweet brown fruit

PHRASES
out of date not new or modern: *The clothes she wears are always **out of date**.* | *an **out-of-date** computer network*
up to date new and modern, or having the most recent information: *I'm selling my Nintendo and getting a more **up-to-date** play station.* | *I try to **keep up to date with** all the latest technology developments.*
to date *written* until now: *The movie has made $8.4 million **to date**.*
at a later date *written* at a time in the future: *Details will be given to you **at a later date**.*

date² *verb* **1** to write today's date on something: *The letter was dated May 1st, 1923.* **2** *AmE* to have a romantic relationship with someone: *Do you know* ▼

if he's dating anyone? **3 date from**, **date back to** to have existed since a particular time: *The house dates from the 17th century.*

dat·ed /'deɪtɪd/ *adjective* no longer fashionable or modern: *dated ideas*

daugh·ter /'dɔːtə $ 'dɔtɚ/ *noun* someone's female child

daughter-in-law /'... ˌ./ *noun* the wife of someone's son

daunt·ed /'dɔːntɪd/ *adjective* afraid or worried about something you have to do: *He felt daunted by the size of the job.*

daunt·ing /'dɔːntɪŋ/ *adjective* frightening or worrying: *Being captain of the team is a daunting responsibility.*

dawn¹ /dɔːn/ *noun* [no plural] the time of day when light first appears: *Many farmers get up before dawn.*

dawn² *verb* **it dawns on someone** if something dawns on someone, they suddenly know that something is true: *It suddenly dawned on me that Terry had been lying.*

day /deɪ/ *noun*

1 a period of time equal to 24 hours. There are 7 days in a week: *Dad was away for four days on a business trip.* | *Ella's birthday is on the same day as Sam's.*

2 the time when it is light, between morning and night: *a hot, sunny day* | *I had a headache **all day**.*

PHRASES
a long day a day when you had to get up early and you were busy all day: *Jessie was really tired after **a long day** at work.*
one day **1)** at some time in the future: *I'd like to have children **one day**.* **2)** *written* on a particular day in the past: ***One day**, Henry decided that he wanted an adventure.*
some day at some time in the future: *I'd love to visit India **some day**.*
these days used to talk about now, rather than the past, especially when you want to say how things have changed: *You're looking very slim **these days**. Have you lost weight?*
one of these days *spoken* at some time soon, when you do not know the exact day: *I'll have to give him a call **one of these days**.*
the other day *spoken* a few days ago:

Ted gave me that book **the other day**.

USAGE Talking about days
Use **on** to talk about a particular day in the week: *I'm going to a party* **on Saturday**. Use **next** or **after** to talk about days, weeks etc in the future: *I'm on holiday* **next week**. | *I'll meet you* **next Tuesday**. *He's going to Japan the day after tomorrow* (=in two days). | *The film will be out on video* **the week after next** (=in two weeks). Use **last** to talk about days, weeks etc in the past: *The match was on TV last night*. | *I saw her last week*. Be careful: you do not use **last** with the word 'morning'. You say 'yesterday morning' not 'last morning'.

day·break /'deɪbreɪk/ *noun* [no plural] *written* the time of day when light first appears: *They left at daybreak.*

day·care cen·ter /'deɪkeə ˌsentə $ 'deɪkeɪ ˌsentɚ/ the American word for CRÈCHE

day·dream /'deɪdriːm/ *verb* to think about nice things so that you forget what you should be doing: *She was always daydreaming about being a fashion model.*
– **daydream** *noun*: *He seemed to be in a daydream.*

day·light /'deɪlaɪt/ *noun* [no plural]
1 the light that comes from the sun: *She opened the curtains to let the daylight in.* **2 in broad daylight** if someone does something bad in broad daylight, they do it even though people can see them: *The thieves broke into the house in broad daylight.*

day·time /'deɪtaɪm/ *noun* [no plural] the part of a day when it is light ➔ *opposite* NIGHTTIME

day-to-day /ˌ. . './ *adjective* day-to-day activities happen every day as a regular part of your life or work: *the day-to-day running of the college*

daze /deɪz/ *noun* **in a daze** unable to think clearly: *When I heard I'd won the prize, I just sat there in a daze.*

dazed /deɪzd/ *adjective* unable to think clearly, for example because you have hit your head or you are surprised about something: *I'm still a bit dazed at the news.*

daz·zle /'dæzəl/ *verb* if a light dazzles you, it is so bright that you cannot see clearly for a short time
– **dazzling** *adjective*: *a dazzling light*

dead¹ /ded/ *adjective*
1 no longer alive: *Her mother is dead.* | *There was a dead fox lying in the road.* **2** a machine or piece of equipment that is dead is not working because there is no power: *I'm afraid your car engine is completely dead.* | *Why don't you throw these dead batteries away?* **3** *informal* complete or exact: *the dead center of the road* | *There was dead silence as Guy entered the room.*

USAGE dead, died
Be careful about **dead** and **died**. **Dead** is an adjective that describes things that are not alive any more: *a dead bird* | *This plant's dead*. **Died** is the past tense and past participle of the verb 'to die' and is used to talk about how and when someone stopped living: *He died of cancer when he was only forty-two.*

dead² *adverb* **1** *informal* very: *We were dead tired after the long journey.* | *Mr Sampson's classes are dead boring.* **2** exactly: *You're dead right.* **3 go dead** if a piece of electrical equipment, especially a telephone, goes dead, it stops working suddenly: *We were talking on the telephone, and the line just went dead.* **4 stop dead** to suddenly stop completely: *The woman walking in front of me suddenly stopped dead.*

dead³ *noun* **1 the dead** people who are dead: *You should not say things about the dead.* **2 in the dead of night** *written* in the middle of the night

dead end /ˌ. './ *noun* a street with no way out at one end

dead heat /ˌ. './ *noun* the result of a race in which two people finish at exactly the same time: *The race ended in a dead heat.*

dead·line /'dedlaɪn/ *noun* a date or time by which you must finish something: *Do you think we'll be able to meet the deadline?*

dead·lock /'dedlɒk $ 'dedlɑk/ *noun* [no plural] when groups or countries cannot agree: *The talks ended in deadlock.*

dead·ly¹ /'dedli/ *adjective* **deadlier, deadliest** something that is deadly can kill you: *a deadly spider*

deadly² *adverb* very: *I thought he was joking but he was deadly serious.*

debris

deaf /def/ *adjective*
not able to hear: *There are several deaf students in the class.* | *My grandmother went deaf* (=became deaf) *when she was in her sixties.*
– **deafness** *noun [no plural]*: *A childhood disease caused her deafness.*

deaf·en /'defən/ *verb* to be so loud that it is difficult for you to hear anything: *The music deafened us.*
– **deafening** *adjective*: *a deafening explosion*

deal¹ /diːl/ *noun*
an agreement, especially in business or politics: *He accepted a five-year deal to become the team's coach.* | *The Democrats struck a deal* (=agreed to do something) *with the Republicans to get the bill passed.* | *Perhaps we can make a deal where we are both happy with the result.*

PHRASES
a great deal, a good deal a large amount or quantity: *The students have learned a good deal.* | *After a great deal of thought, I decided to go to university.* | *This computer costs a good deal more than this other one.*
be a good deal a cheap or fair price: *At £3.20, the meal is a good deal.* | *We got a good deal on a new TV* (=we bought it at a good price).

deal² *verb, past tense and past participle* **dealt** /delt/ **1 deal in** to buy and sell a particular type of thing: *The shop deals in high-quality jewelry.* | *The police believe the men were dealing in narcotics.* **2 deal with 1)** if you deal with a problem, you do something to make sure the problem no longer exists: *We are here to deal with customer complaints.* | *There are ways of dealing with stress.* **2)** if a book, film, play etc deals with a particular subject, it is about that subject: *Chapter 2 deals with the history of the area.* **3** also **deal out** to give cards to each player in a card game: *Robert, are you dealing?* | *I'd been dealt some good cards, so I was sure I'd win.*

deal·er /'diːlə $ 'diːlɚ/ *noun* someone who buys and sells a particular kind of thing: *a car dealer*

dealt the past tense and past participle of DEAL²

dear¹ /dɪə $ dɪr/ oh dear *spoken* used when something bad has happened: *Oh dear! We're going to be late.*

dear² *noun spoken* used when talking to someone you like or love: *Thank you, dear.*

dear³ *adjective*
1 Dear Sir, Dear Mr Smith, Dear Mrs Jones etc *written* used before the name of the person you are writing to: *Dear Miss Patterson, I am writing to you about your son.*
2 *BrE* costing a lot of money: ⇨ same meaning EXPENSIVE: *Everything in those designer shops is so dear.*

death /deθ/ *noun* **1** the end of someone's life: *After her husband's death, she lived alone for 20 years.* | *What was the cause of death?* | *The driver of the truck bled to death before the ambulance crew could reach him.* **2 scared to death, bored to death** *informal* very scared or bored: *I would be scared to death if I saw a lion.*

death pen·al·ty /'. ,.../ *noun* the death penalty the legal punishment of being killed: *He was convicted of the murder and sentenced to the death penalty.*

de·ba·ta·ble /dɪ'beɪtəbəl/ *adjective* something that is debatable is not certain: *It is debatable whether the peace will last.*

de·bate¹ /dɪ'beɪt/ *noun* **1** an organized discussion on an important subject: *He took part in a school debate on animal rights.* **2** *[no plural]* the process of discussing a subject or question: *There has been a lot of debate in the newspapers about this matter.*

debate² *verb* to discuss an important subject: *Scientists are still debating whether the new treatment really works.*

deb·it /'debɪt/ *noun* an amount of money that you take out of your bank account: *Your bank statement shows all your debits and credits.*
– **debit** *verb*: *The bank will debit the monthly payments from your account automatically.*

deb·ris /'debriː $ dɪ'briː/ *noun [no plural]* pieces of material that are left after a crash, explosion, or large event: *After the crash, the road was covered with debris.*

D

D

debt /det/ noun
1 money that you owe to someone: credit-card debts | Last year I finally **paid back** all my **debts**.
2 [no plural] when you owe money to someone: Many poor countries are **in debt** to richer countries.

de·but /'deɪbjuː $deɪ'bju/ noun the first time that an actor, sports player etc performs in public: Lee made his debut in the TV film, 'Kung Fu'.

dec·ade /'dekeɪd/ noun a period of ten years: The building is now four decades old.

de·caf·fein·a·ted /diː'kæfəneɪtəd/ adjective decaffeinated drinks do not contain CAFFEINE (=a substance that makes you feel more awake): a cup of decaffeinated coffee

decay /dɪ'keɪ/ verb if something decays, natural processes slowly destroy it: The dead body had already started to decay when the police found it. | a pile of decayed wood
– **decay** noun [no plural]: Eating lots of sweets causes tooth decay.

de·ceit /dɪ'siːt/ noun [no plural] when someone tries to make people believe something that is not true: The government was accused of deliberate deceit.

de·ceive /dɪ'siːv/ verb to make someone believe something that is not true: I felt very upset when I realized that he had deceived me.

De·cem·ber /dɪ'sembə $dɪ'sembər/ written abbreviation **Dec** noun the twelfth month of the year: War began in the middle of December.

de·cent /'diːsənt/ adjective 1 good enough: Everyone should have a decent education. 2 decent people are good and honest

de·cep·tive /dɪ'septɪv/ adjective something that is deceptive makes people believe something that is not true: Advertisements can be very deceptive.

de·cide /dɪ'saɪd/ verb

> **GRAMMAR**
> **decide to do something**
> **decide who/what/when etc**
> **decide (that)**
> to choose what you are going to do after thinking about it: Megan **decided to** go to Denise's party. | Chil-

dren should be allowed to **decide how to** spend their pocket money. | I can't **decide which** dress to wear. | We **decided that** we couldn't afford to go on holiday this year. | The date of the game has not yet been decided.

> **PHRASAL VERB**
> **decide on**
> **decide on something** to choose one thing from a group of things: She decided on teaching as a career.

de·cid·ed·ly /dɪ'saɪdɪdli/ adverb formal very or definitely: When I woke up the next day, I felt decidedly ill.

dec·i·mal[1] /'desəməl/ adjective based on the number ten: the decimal system

decimal[2] noun the part of a number which comes after the mark (.) and is less than one, for example in 3.5 or 1.25

decimal point /ˌ... '. / noun the mark (.) before a decimal

de·ci·sion /dɪ'sɪʒən/ noun
a choice that you make: Ben knew he'd **made** the right **decision**. | The city council has not yet **reached a decision**.

de·ci·sive /dɪ'saɪsɪv/ adjective 1 a decisive event is definite or important: the party's decisive victory in the election 2 able to make decisions quickly ⇨ opposite INDECISIVE: She is an intelligent, decisive woman.

deck /dek/ noun 1 the part of a ship where you can walk or sit outside: Most people were out on deck, sunbathing. 2 one of the levels on a ship or bus: Our cabin was on the top deck. 3 the American word for a PACK of cards

dec·la·ra·tion /ˌdeklə'reɪʃən/ noun
an official statement about something: a declaration of war

de·clare /dɪ'kleə $dɪ'kler/ verb

> **GRAMMAR**
> **declare that**
> 1 to say officially what will happen or what you have decided: In 1943, Italy **declared war on** Germany. | The fire department declared the building unsafe.

2 *written* to say publicly what you think or feel: *"I am very proud of the team,"* *Coach Hall declared.* | *Brown* **declared that** *the situation was very serious.*

de·cline /dɪ'klaɪn/ *verb* to become weaker, smaller, or less good: *Her health declined rapidly.*
– **decline** *noun*: *There has been a slight decline in the company's profits.*

de·cor /'deɪkɔː $ 'deɪkɔr/ *noun* the colours, furniture etc in a room: *The restaurant had changed its decor.*

dec·o·rate /'dekəreɪt/ *verb* **1** to make something look more attractive by adding things to it: *The room was decorated with balloons and coloured lights.* **2** to put paint or paper onto the walls of a room or building: *I'm going to decorate the kitchen this summer.*

dec·o·ra·tion /,dekə'reɪʃən/ *noun* a pretty thing that you use to make something look more attractive: *The shop windows were already full of Christmas decorations.*

dec·o·ra·tive /'dekərətɪv/ *adjective* pretty and used to decorate something: *a decorative vase*

dec·o·ra·tor /'dekəreɪtə $ 'dekə,reɪtɚ/ *noun* BrE someone whose job is to decorate rooms and buildings: *The decorators finished painting the ceiling.*

de·crease /dɪ'kriːs/ *verb* to become smaller in number, amount, size etc, or to make something do this ⇨ *opposite* INCREASE[1]: *The price of computers is decreasing all the time.*
– **decrease** /'diːkriːs/ *noun*: *a decrease in crime*

de·cree /dɪ'kriː/ *noun* an official order that a ruler or government makes

de·crep·it /dɪ'krepɪt/ *adjective* old and in bad condition: *The office buildings were thoroughly decrepit.*

ded·i·cate /'dedəkeɪt/ *verb* if you dedicate a book, film, song etc to someone, you say publicly that you wrote it to show how much you love and respect them: *This song is dedicated to my wife.*

ded·i·cat·ed /'dedəkeɪtɪd/ *adjective* someone who is dedicated works very hard at something because it is important to them: *Our staff are all very dedicated.*

ded·i·ca·tion /,dedə'keɪʃən/ *noun* [no

plural] when you work very hard because you believe that what you are doing is important: *I was impressed by the dedication of the school staff.*

de·duce /dɪ'djuːs $ dɪ'dus/ *verb* *written* to decide that something is true, using what you know or notice: *From his accent, I deduced that he was not English.*

de·duct /dɪ'dʌkt/ *verb* to take an amount away from a larger amount: *The tax is deducted from your salary each month.*

deed /diːd/ *noun* *formal* an action: *She was well known for her good deeds in the community.*

deep¹ /diːp/ *adjective*

1 if something is deep, there is a long distance between the top and the bottom ⇨ *opposite* SHALLOW: *The snow was so deep it was nearly over Kerry's head.* | *at the bottom of the deep blue sea*
2 used to talk about the distance from the top to the bottom of something: *The pool is only three feet deep at this end.* | *How deep is this river?*
3 a deep sound or voice is very low: *Ken has a nice deep voice.*
4 a deep feeling or belief is very strong: *Thompson expressed his deep thanks to the men who had helped him.*

PHRASES
take a deep breath to breathe a lot of air into your lungs, especially before you do something difficult or frightening: *I took a deep breath and climbed onto the horse.*
be in a deep sleep if someone is in a deep sleep, it is difficult to wake them up

deep² *adverb*

a long way into or inside something: *Julian thrust his hands deep into his pockets.* | *a hotel deep in the countryside*

PHRASE
deep down if you feel or know something deep down, it is what you really feel: *Deep down, I guess I'm glad my parents are strict.*

deep·en /'diːpən/ *verb* *written* to become worse, or to make something become worse: *The President's political troubles deepened last week.*

deep·ly /'diːpli/ *adverb* extremely or very much: *She had been deeply affected by what happened.*

deer /dɪə $ dɪr/ *noun, plural* deer a large wild animal that lives in forests. The male has long horns that look like tree branches

de·feat¹ /dɪ'fiːt/ *verb*

if you defeat someone in a game, battle, or election, you win: *The tennis star Seles easily defeated her opponent in the final.*

defeat² *noun* when you lose a game, battle, or election ⇨ *opposite* VICTORY: *The team had their fifth defeat on Saturday.*

de·fect /dɪ'fekt/ *noun* formal a fault in something that stops it working properly: *a defect in the plane engine | He's had a hearing defect since he was a child.*

de·fence *BrE*, **defense** *AmE* /dɪ'fens/ *noun* **1** [no plural] the weapons, soldiers, actions etc that a country uses to protect itself from attack: *How much does Britain spend on defence?* **2** /$ 'diːfens/ the players in a game such as football who try to stop the other team getting points: *The Lazio defence is one of the strongest in the Italian league.* **3** the defence the lawyers who are trying to prove that someone is not guilty of a crime ⇨ *opposite* PROSECUTION: *the defence lawyer*

de·fence·less *BrE*, **defenseless** *AmE* /dɪ'fensləs/ *adjective* if someone is defenceless, they are weak and cannot protect themselves: *The thugs attacked a defenceless old woman.*

de·fend /dɪ'fend/ *verb*

GRAMMAR
defend someone/something against something
defend himself/yourself etc

1 to protect someone or something from harm, danger, or an attack: *The Russian army **has defended** the country **against** foreign armies many times. | He hit me first; I **was defending** myself. | A spokesman for the government has defended the tax rises.*

2 defend the championship, defend the title etc to play in a sports competition that you won in the past to try and win it again: *Stanford **are defending the** volleyball **title** today.*

de·fen·dant /dɪ'fendənt/ *noun* the person in a court of law who the police say is guilty of a crime

defense the American spelling of DEFENCE

de·fens·ive /dɪ'fensɪv/ *adjective* used or suitable for defending against an attack: *We took up a defensive position behind the wall.*

de·fi·ant /dɪ'faɪənt/ *adjective* someone who is defiant will not obey someone who is trying to make them do something
– **defiantly** *adverb*: *"I won't go to school!" shouted Lisa defiantly.*

de·fi·cien·cy /dɪ'fɪʃənsi/ *noun, plural* deficiencies when you do not have something that you need: *a vitamin deficiency*

de·fine /dɪ'faɪn/ *verb* to say exactly what a word means or what something is

def·i·nite /'defɪnət/ *adjective*

1 completely certain and not likely to change: *I don't have any definite plans for the holidays.*
2 clear and easy to notice: *The new laws are having a definite effect.*

definite ar·ti·cle /ˌ... '.../ *noun* in grammar, a phrase meaning the word 'the'

def·i·nite·ly /'defɪnətli/ *adverb* used to make a statement or opinion stronger: *I'll definitely phone you tonight.*

def·i·ni·tion /ˌdefə'nɪʃən/ *noun* a phrase or sentence, for example in a dictionary, that says exactly what a word means or what something is

de·flect /dɪ'flekt/ *verb* be deflected if something is deflected, it hits a surface and then goes in a different direction: *The ball hit the post and was deflected for a corner.*

de·formed /dɪ'fɔːmd $ dɪ'fɔrmd/ *adjective* someone who is deformed has something wrong with the shape of their body: *Mothers who took the drug gave birth to deformed babies.*

de·frost /ˌdiː'frɒst $ dɪ'frɔst/ *verb* if frozen food defrosts, or if you defrost it, it slowly stops being frozen until you can cook or eat it: *Defrost the chicken thoroughly before cooking.*

deft /deft/ *adjective* written movements that are deft are quick and skilful: *Katherine drew a picture with a few deft strokes of her pen.*

de·fy /dɪ'faɪ/ *verb* **defied, defies** to say you will not obey someone: *Don't defy your father.*

de·grad·ing /dɪ'greɪdɪŋ/ *adjective* something that is degrading makes people lose their respect for themselves: *A lot of men say housework is degrading.*

de·gree /dɪ'griː/ *noun*

GRAMMAR
a degree of something
1 the level or amount of something: *The factory has a high degree of safety standards. | There was a small degree of difference in the results of the two experiments. | All the students helped to some degree* (=they all helped, but by different amounts).
2 a unit for measuring temperature, written (°): *It's 10 degrees below zero!*
3 a unit for measuring angles, written (°): *A right angle measures 90 degrees. | Turn the bottle cap 180 degrees.*
4 what you get when you successfully finish a university course: *Robbie has a first-class degree in law. | a history degree*

de·hy·drat·ed /ˌdiːhaɪ'dreɪtɪd $ diː'haɪˌdreɪtɪd/ *adjective* someone who is dehydrated is ill because they do not have enough water in their body

de·lay¹ /dɪ'leɪ/ *verb* **1** to make someone or something late: *I'm sorry I'm late – I was delayed by the traffic.* **2** to do something at a later date than you planned: *We had to delay the project until the following year.*

delay² *noun* a period of time when you have to wait for something to happen: *There was a 12-hour delay before the plane took off. | Please accept my apologies for the delay.*

del·e·gate /'deləgət/ *noun* someone that a country or organization chooses to do something for it, such as speak or vote at a meeting: *UN delegates*

del·e·ga·tion /ˌdelə'geɪʃən/ *noun* a small group of people that a country or organization sends to do something for it, such as vote or find out about something

de·lete /dɪ'liːt/ *verb* to remove a letter, word etc from a piece of writing or from the information stored on a computer: *I deleted a file by mistake.*

de·lib·er·ate /dɪ'lɪbərət/ *adjective* a deliberate action is one that someone wants and has planned, not a mistake or an accident: *The murder was deliberate. | Martin's jokes were a deliberate attempt to embarrass Jean.*

de·lib·er·ate·ly /dɪ'lɪbərətli/ *adverb* if you do something deliberately, you do it because you want to: *You deliberately disobeyed me!*

del·i·ca·cy /'delɪkəsi/ *noun, plural* **delicacies** a rare or expensive food that is especially nice to eat

del·i·cate /'delɪkət/ *adjective* if something is delicate, you have to be careful with it because you can easily damage or break it: *a baby's delicate skin | These silk dresses are very old and delicate. | a delicate piece of equipment*

del·i·ca·tes·sen /ˌdelɪkə'tesən/ *noun* a shop that sells good quality cheese, cooked meat etc, as well as special food from foreign countries

de·li·cious /dɪ'lɪʃəs/ *adjective* delicious food tastes very good: *This soup is delicious!*

de·light¹ /dɪ'laɪt/ *noun* to someone's delight, to the delight of someone a feeling of great happiness and excitement: *There were shouts of delight from the children. | To my delight, I passed the exam. | To the delight of the audience, the concert ended with fireworks.*

delight² *verb* formal to give someone great pleasure and enjoyment: *His music delights people of all ages.*

de·light·ed /dɪ'laɪtɪd/ *adjective* very

D

pleased about something: *We were all really delighted with the news.*

de·light·ful /dɪˈlaɪtfəl/ *adjective* very nice or enjoyable: *a delightful party*

de·lir·i·ous /dɪˈlɪriəs/ *adjective* unable to think clearly because you are ill

de·liv·er /dɪˈlɪvə $ dɪˈlɪvɚ/ *verb*

GRAMMAR
deliver something to someone

to take something such as a letter or a package to a place: *Can you deliver this parcel before Christmas? | He got a job delivering pizzas. | Hot meals **are delivered to** old people in the area.*

de·liv·er·y /dɪˈlɪvəri/ *noun, plural* **deliveries** when someone brings something to your house or office, for example letters or things you have asked for: *There's no postal delivery on Sunday.*

del·ta /ˈdeltə/ *noun* an area of low land near the sea where a large river separates into many smaller rivers

del·uge /ˈdeljuːdʒ/ *noun formal* a large flood, or a period of time when it rains continuously: *Weathermen warned that the deluge could continue for several days.*

de·lu·sion /dɪˈluːʒən/ *noun formal* something you believe, but which is not really true: *I thought he loved me, but it was only a delusion.*

de·luxe /dɪˈlʌks/ *adjective* deluxe things cost more money than others of the same kind because they are better: *We had a deluxe room with a balcony.*

delve /delv/ *verb written* to put your hand deep inside a bag, box etc in order to find something: *He delved into his pockets for his key.*

de·mand¹ /dɪˈmɑːnd $ dɪˈmænd/ *noun*
1 *[no plural]* if there is a demand for something, people want to buy it: *There was a huge demand for concert tickets.*
2 something that someone asks for in a very determined way: *The company refused the workers' demands for more pay.*

demand² *verb*

GRAMMAR
demand to do something
demand something from someone
demand that
demand something of someone

to ask for something in a very strong determined way: *"What," demanded James, "does this mean?" | An officer **demanded to** see my passport. | I **demand** an explanation **from** you. | The hijackers **are demanding that** the plane is allowed to leave. | The manager **demanded** the resignation **of** two members of staff.* ⇨ see usage note at ASK

de·mand·ing /dɪˈmɑːndɪŋ $ dɪˈmændɪŋ/ *adjective* a demanding job is not easy because you need a lot of skill or effort to do it: *It was very demanding work.*

de·moc·ra·cy /dɪˈmɒkrəsi $ dɪˈmɑːkrəsi/ *noun, plural* **democracies** the system in which everyone in a country has the right to choose a government by voting, or a country that has this system: *I believe in freedom and democracy. | We live in a democracy.*

dem·o·crat /ˈdeməkræt/ *noun* someone who believes in or supports democracy

dem·o·crat·ic /ˌdeməˈkrætɪk/ *adjective* a democratic country, government, or system is one in which everyone has the right to choose their government by voting

de·mol·ish /dɪˈmɒlɪʃ $ dɪˈmɑːlɪʃ/ *verb* to deliberately destroy a building: *The old houses were demolished years ago.*

de·mon /ˈdiːmən/ *noun* an evil spirit

dem·on·strate /ˈdemənstreɪt/ *verb*

GRAMMAR
demonstrate that
demonstrate against something
demonstrate how to do something
demonstrate something to someone

1 to show something clearly: *The President demonstrated great leadership. | The evidence **demonstrates that** Farley is guilty.*
2 when people demonstrate, they stand or walk together somewhere to protest about something or to support something: *The students **are demonstrating against** high course fees.*
3 to show someone how to do something by doing it yourself: *Artists will*

demonstrate how to use oil paints. | We **demonstrated** our experiment **to** the rest of the class.

dem·on·stra·tion /ˌdemən'streɪʃən/ noun **1** when a large group of people meet to protest against something or to support something: *Thousands of people took part in the demonstration against the war.* **2** if you give a demonstration, you show a group of people how to do something: *The photography club arranges lectures, demonstrations and trips to art galleries.*

dem·on·stra·tor /'demənstreɪtə $ 'demənˌstreɪtɚ/ noun someone who takes part in a demonstration to protest against something or to support something: *Angry demonstrators marched through the streets.*

de·mor·a·lized also **demoralised** BrE /dɪ'mɒrəlaɪzd $ dɪ'mɔrəˌlaɪzd/ adjective feeling less confident and hopeful than before because of bad things that have happened: *After a year in the job I felt totally demoralized.*

de·mor·a·li·zing also **demoralising** BrE /dɪ'mɒrəlaɪzɪŋ $ dɪ'mɔrəˌlaɪzɪŋ/ adjective making you feel less confident and hopeful than before: *Losing the match was very demoralizing for the team.* | *The announcement had a demoralizing effect on staff.*

den /den/ noun the home of some wild animals such as lions and FOXes

de·ni·al /dɪ'naɪəl/ noun formal a statement that something is not true: *his denial of guilt*

den·im /'denəm/ noun [no plural] a type of strong cotton cloth used for making clothes: *denim jeans*

dense /dens/ adjective **1** containing a lot of trees, people etc close together: *a dense tropical jungle* | *our dense population* **2** dense cloud, FOG etc is thick and difficult to see through

dent /dent/ noun a hollow place in the surface of something, especially metal: *There was a dent in the can of soup.* – **dent** verb: *I dented the side of my car.*

den·tal /'dentl/ adjective connected with teeth: *dental problems*

den·tist /'dentɪst/ noun someone whose job is to look after and repair people's teeth

den·tures /'dentʃəz $ 'dentʃɚz/ plural noun false teeth that people wear because they do not have their own teeth: *a set of dentures*

de·ny /dɪ'naɪ/ verb denied, denies to say that something is not true: *Gary denied being involved in the robbery.*

de·o·do·rant /diː'əʊdərənt $ di'oʊdərənt/ noun a substance that you put under your arms to stop your body smelling unpleasant

de·part /dɪ'pɑːt $ dɪ'pɑrt/ verb formal if a plane, train etc departs from a place, it leaves it: *Your flight will depart from Heathrow Airport at 8.30.*

de·part·ment /dɪ'pɑːtmənt $ dɪ'pɑrtmənt/ noun one of the parts of a large organization such as a college, government, or company: *the Modern Languages department at Cambridge University*

department store /.'.. ./ noun a large shop that sells many different types of things

de·par·ture /dɪ'pɑːtʃə $ dɪ'pɑrtʃɚ/ noun when a person, plane, train etc leaves a place: *Our departure was delayed because of bad weather.*

de·pend /dɪ'pend/ verb

it depends, that depends spoken used to say that you are not sure about something, because you do not know what will happen: *"What time will you be back?" "It depends. I'm not sure what the traffic will be like."*

PHRASAL VERBS
depend on/upon
1 depend on something to change because of other things that happen: *"Is the concert indoors or outdoors?" "It depends on the weather."*
2 depend on someone/something to need help from someone or something in order to do something: *I hate having to depend on her to drive me places.* | *We depend on the rain for a good harvest.*

de·pend·a·ble /dɪ'pendəbəl/ adjective someone or something that is dependable is a person or thing that will always do what you need them to do: *We want our employees to be dependable and loyal.* | *a dependable supply of water*

de·pen·dant *BrE*, **dependent** *AmE* /dɪ-'pendənt/ *noun* formal a child or other person who needs someone to pay for their food, clothes etc

de·pen·dent /dɪ'pendənt/ *adjective* needing someone or something in order to live or to continue ⇨ *opposite* IN-DEPENDENT: *The villages are completely dependent on agriculture.*

de·port /dɪ'pɔːt $ dɪ'pɔrt/ *verb* to force someone to leave a country and return to the country they came from

de·pose /dɪ'pəʊz $ dɪ'poʊz/ *verb* to remove a leader from their position: *an attempt to depose the King*

deposit¹ /dɪ'pɒzɪt $ dɪ'pazɪt/ *noun* **1** part of the price of something, that you pay when you agree to buy it: *We paid a 10% deposit on the house.* **2** an amount of money that you pay into a bank account: *a deposit of £300*

deposit² *verb* to put money into a bank account

dep·ot /'depəʊ $ 'dipoʊ/ *noun* a place where buses, trains, products etc are kept until they are needed: *a bus depot*

de·press /dɪ'pres/ *verb* to make someone feel sad or not hopeful about the future: *The standard of sport in this school depresses me.*

de·pressed /dɪ'prest/ *adjective* feeling sad or not hopeful about the future: *She felt very depressed after losing her job.*

de·press·ing /dɪ'presɪŋ/ *adjective* making you feel sad or not hopeful about the future: *depressing news*

de·pres·sion /dɪ'preʃən/ *noun* a feeling of great sadness that sometimes makes you ill and unable to live normally: *Her mother had depression for many years.*

de·prive /dɪ'praɪv/ *verb* to stop someone having something that they need or that they normally have: *They deprived the prisoners of food.*

de·prived /dɪ'praɪvd/ *adjective* deprived places or people do not have the good things that other places or people have: *Sylvia had a very deprived childhood.* | *deprived inner city areas*

depth /depθ/ *noun* how deep something is, measured from the top to the bottom: *As part of our project, we had to measure the depth of the river.*

dep·u·ty /'depjəti/ *noun, plural* **dep-** uties the person in a business, school etc who has the second most important position: *the deputy head teacher*

derelict

der·e·lict /'derəlɪkt/ *adjective* a derelict building or piece of land is in bad condition because no one has used it for a long time: *derelict factories with broken windows and holes in the roof*

de·scend /dɪ'send/ *verb* formal to go down ⇨ *opposite* ASCEND: *We watched the plane slowly descend.*

de·scen·dant /dɪ'sendənt/ *noun* someone who is related to a particular person who lived long ago: *a descendant of Abraham Lincoln*

de·scent /dɪ'sent/ *noun* formal when a plane, person etc goes down to a lower place ⇨ *opposite* ASCENT: *The climbers began their descent.*

de·scribe /dɪ'skraɪb/ *verb*

> **GRAMMAR**
> **describe someone/something as something**
> **describe how/what/why etc**

to say what someone or something is like or what happened: *The police **have described** him **as** around 25 years old, with brown hair.* | ***Describe how** you felt when you heard the news.* | *I tried to **describe what** happened next.*

de·scrip·tion /dɪ'skrɪpʃən/ *noun*

> **GRAMMAR**
> **a description of something**

something you say or write that shows what someone or something is like: *Carson **gave** the police a **description of** the car.* | *The **description of** Cancun sounds wonderful.*

de·sert¹ /'dezət $ 'dezərt/ *noun* a large area of very hot dry land where few plants grow: *the Sahara desert*

de·sert² /dɪ'zɜːt $ dɪ'zərt/ *verb* if you desert a person or a place, you leave them and never go back: He deserted his family.

de·sert·ed /dɪˈzɜːrtɪd $dɪˈzɚtɪd/ adjective a deserted place is empty and quiet: It was midnight and the streets were deserted. | a deserted house with broken windows

des·ert i·sland /ˌ.. ˈ../ noun a tropical island where nobody lives

de·serve /dɪˈzɜːv $dɪˈzɚv/ verb

> **GRAMMAR**
> **deserve to do something**
> if someone deserves something, they should get it because of something they have done: After all that work, I think we deserve a cup of coffee. | After what he did, he **deserves to** go to prison.

de·sign¹ /dɪˈzaɪn/ noun [no plural]
1 the way that something is planned or made, or the ability to plan or make things: I like the design of this room. | Jill has a natural talent for design.
2 a pattern used to decorate something: Each plate has a different design.

design² verb

> **GRAMMAR**
> **design something for someone/ something**
> **design something to do something**

1 to draw or plan something that you will make, plan, or build: The company is designing a golf course.
2 to make something for a particular purpose or person: Sally **designs** books **for** children. | new computer software **designed to** help you use the Internet

de·sign·er¹ /dɪˈzaɪnə $dɪˈzaɪnɚ/ noun someone whose job is to design new styles of clothes, cars etc: the fashion designer Calvin Klein

designer² adjective designer clothes are expensive because they were designed by a famous designer: designer jeans

de·sir·a·ble /dɪˈzaɪərəbəl $dɪˈzaɪr-əbəl/ adjective written if something is desirable, people want it because it is good or useful: a desirable apartment in the centre of the city

de·sire¹ /dɪˈzaɪə $dɪˈzaɪɚ/ noun a strong feeling that you want something very much: I had a strong desire to hit him.

desire² verb formal to want something

desk /desk/ noun a table, where you sit and write or work ➡ see picture on page 342

de·spair¹ /dɪˈspeə $dɪˈsper/ noun [no plural] a very sad feeling that there is no hope any more: I was in despair, when at last she phoned to say that she was all right.

despair² verb to feel that there is no hope any more: Don't despair – things will get better.

des·per·ate /ˈdespərət/ adjective

> **GRAMMAR**
> **desperate for something**
> **desperate to do something**

1 willing to do anything to change a very bad situation, and not caring about any danger: Many homeless families **are desperate for** a place to live. | **desperate attempts** to escape | After five losses, the team **is desperate to** win.
2 a desperate situation is very bad and must change: After the war, the situation in the country was desperate.
–desperately adverb: Simon was desperately unhappy.

de·spise /dɪˈspaɪz/ verb to not like and to have no respect for someone or something: Laura despised boys; she thought they were all stupid.

de·spite /dɪˈspaɪt/ preposition used to say that something happened or is true, even though this is surprising or not what you expected: He struggled on despite the pain.

des·sert /dɪˈzɜːt $dɪˈzɚt/ noun something sweet that you eat after the main part of a meal: For dessert we had ice-cream and chocolate sauce.

des·ti·na·tion /ˌdestəˈneɪʃən/ noun formal the place that you are travelling to: It took me five hours to reach my destination.

des·tined /ˈdestənd/ adjective someone who is destined to do something will definitely do it: He was destined to become president.

des·ti·ny /'destəni/ noun, plural **des-tinies** the things that will happen to someone in the future ⇨ same meaning FATE: Do you think we can control our own destinies?

de·stroy /dɪ'strɔɪ/ verb
to damage something very badly, so that people can no longer use it, or so that it no longer exists: The bombings have destroyed most of the city. | Unfortunately, all her letters were destroyed in a fire.

de·struc·tion /dɪ'strʌkʃən/ noun [no plural] when something is destroyed: the destruction of the Amazon rain forest

de·tach /dɪ'tætʃ/ verb formal to remove part of something that has been made so that you can remove it: Detach the bottom half of the page by tearing along the dotted line.

de·tached /dɪ'tætʃt/ adjective BrE a detached house is not joined to another house ⇨ see picture on page 343

de·tail /'diːteɪl $ dɪ'teɪl/ noun

GRAMMAR
details of something
a small fact or piece of information about something: You will find more **details of** the program on our website.

PHRASES
in detail: Can you describe **in detail** (=thoroughly) how you did this experiment?
someone's details your details are the facts about you that someone wants to know: Please **fill in your details** below.

de·tailed /'diːteɪld $ dɪ'teɪld/ adjective a detailed description, account etc includes a lot of information: The woman gave a detailed description of the man.

de·tain /dɪ'teɪn/ verb formal if the police detain someone, they keep them somewhere and do not allow them to leave

de·tect /dɪ'tekt/ verb to find or notice something that is not easy to see, hear etc: a machine that can detect alcohol in people's blood

de·tec·tive /dɪ'tektɪv/ noun a police officer whose job is to discover who is responsible for crimes

de·tec·tor /dɪ'tektə $ dɪ'tektər/ noun a piece of equipment that tells you if there is a particular substance somewhere: a smoke detector

de·ten·tion /dɪ'tenʃən/ noun a school punishment in which you have to stay at school after the other students have left

de·ter /dɪ'tɜː $ dɪ'tɜr/ verb formal **deterred, deterring** if something deters you from doing something, it makes you not want to do it: The long working hours deter many young people from becoming doctors.

de·ter·gent /dɪ'tɜːdʒənt $ dɪ'tɜrdʒənt/ noun a liquid or powder that you use for washing clothes, dishes etc

de·te·ri·o·rate /dɪ'tɪəriəreɪt $ dɪ'tɪriə,reɪt/ verb formal to become worse: The weather deteriorated, and by the afternoon it was raining.

de·ter·mi·na·tion /dɪ,tɜːmə'neɪʃən $ dɪ,tɜrmə'neɪʃən/ noun [no plural] the ability you have that makes you continue trying to do something, even when it is difficult: I really admire his determination to succeed!

de·ter·mined /dɪ'tɜːmɪnd $ dɪ'tɜrmɪnd/ adjective

GRAMMAR
determined to do something
determined (that)
very sure that you want to do something, and not letting anyone or anything stop you: No one in my family had ever gone to university, but I **was determined to** go. | We **were determined that** we would win the game.

de·ter·min·er /dɪ'tɜːmənə $ dɪ'tɜrmənər/ noun in grammar, a word you use before a noun to show which thing you mean. In the phrases 'the car' and 'some new cars', 'the' and 'some' are determiners

de·test /dɪ'test/ verb formal to hate someone or something very much: I detest vegetables!

det·o·nate /'detəneɪt $ 'detn,eɪt/ verb if you detonate a bomb, or if it detonates, it explodes

de·tour /'diːtʊə $ 'ditʊr/ noun a way of going somewhere that takes longer than the usual way: On the way home we made a detour to visit some friends.
– **detour** verb

dev·a·state /'devəsteɪt/ verb if bombs, wars, storms etc devastate a place, they damage it very badly: *The storm devastated a large part of the state.*

dev·a·stat·ed /'devəsteɪtɪd/ adjective very sad and shocked about something that has happened: *Andrew and Maria were devasted by their son's death.*

dev·a·stat·ing /'devəsteɪtɪŋ/ adjective causing a lot of damage: *The accident had a devastating effect on Stanley's life.*

de·vel·op /dɪ'veləp/ verb

GRAMMAR
develop into something
develop from something

1 if something develops, or if you develop it, it gets bigger or becomes more important: *Their business has developed into one of the biggest in the country.* | *Most plants develop from seeds.* | *We are developing close ties between our two countries.*
2 to begin to have an illness or feeling: *His wife developed cancer.*
3 to make pictures from photographic film, using special chemicals: *Photographs are developed in a dark room.*

de·vel·op·ment /dɪ'veləpmənt/ noun

GRAMMAR
the development of something

1 the process of growing, changing, or making something: *The company spends a lot on research and development.* | *the development of a baby*
2 a new event that changes a situation: *a new development in the treatment of cancer*
3 a group of new buildings, or the work of building them: *a housing development* | *The environment is being damaged by development.*

de·vice /dɪ'vaɪs/ noun a machine or tool, usually a fairly complicated one ⇨ see usage note at MACHINE

Dev·il /'devəl/ noun the Devil an evil spirit that is God's powerful enemy in some religions

de·vi·ous /'diːviəs/ adjective a devious person is clever but unpleasant and dis-

honest: *Mr Marcham was a very devious man.*

de·vise /dɪ'vaɪz/ verb formal to think of a new way of doing something: *People are constantly devising new exercise programmes.*

de·vote /dɪ'vəʊt $dɪ'voʊt/ verb if you devote your time, energy etc to something, you spend most of your time doing it: *He devoted most of his life to scientific research.*

de·vot·ed /dɪ'vəʊtɪd $dɪ'voʊtɪd/ adjective someone who is devoted to another person, their work etc loves or cares about them a lot: *He is devoted to his family.*

de·vo·tion /dɪ'vəʊʃən $dɪ'voʊʃən/ noun [no plural] when you love or care about someone or something a lot: *her devotion to her job*

de·vour /dɪ'vaʊə $dɪ'vaʊɚ/ verb written to eat something quickly: *Tony had already devoured half a pizza.*

de·vout /dɪ'vaʊt/ adjective very religious: *a devout Catholic*

dew /djuː $duː/ noun [no plural] small drops of water that form on the surfaces of things that are outside during the night: *The grass was covered in dew.*

di·a·be·tes /ˌdaɪə'biːtiːz/ noun [no plural] a disease in which there is too much sugar in your blood

di·a·bet·ic /ˌdaɪə'betɪk/ noun someone who has diabetes: *Diabetics cannot eat a lot of sweet food.*

di·a·bol·i·cal /ˌdaɪə'bɒlɪkəl $ˌdaɪə-'bɑːlɪkəl/ adjective BrE spoken very bad: *This film is diabolical.*

di·ag·nose /'daɪəgnəʊz $ˌdaɪəg'noʊs/ verb to find out what illness someone has: *His doctor diagnosed cancer.*

di·ag·no·sis /ˌdaɪəg'nəʊsəs $ˌdaɪəg-'noʊsəs/ noun, plural **diagnoses** /-siːz/ when a doctor says what illness someone has: *The doctor's diagnosis was wrong.*

di·ag·o·nal /daɪ'ægənəl/ adjective a diagonal line slopes up or down ⇨ see picture at LINE[1]

di·a·gram /'daɪəgræm/ noun a drawing that uses simple lines: *He drew a diagram of the new bridge.*

dial[1] /daɪəl/ verb **dialled, dialling** BrE, **dialed, dialing** AmE to press the buttons or turn the dial on a telephone: *I dialled her number again.*

dial² *noun* a round flat object on a radio or other piece of equipment that you turn to make it do something: *Turn the dial to make the oven hotter.*

di·a·lect /ˈdaɪəlekt/ *noun* a form of a language that people in one part of a country speak: *Chinese people speak many different dialects.*

dialing code /ˈ... ,./ *noun* the part of a telephone number that you have to add when you are telephoning a different town or country; AREA CODE *AmE*: *What's the new dialing code for London?*

di·a·logue *BrE*, **dialog** *AmE* /ˈdaɪəlɒg $ ˈdaɪəˌlɔg/ *noun* a conversation between people in a book, film, or play

di·am·e·ter /daɪˈæmətə $ daɪˈæmətəʳ/ *noun* a line that goes through the middle of a circle, or the length of this line: *The ball is about four inches in diameter.*

di·a·mond /ˈdaɪəmənd/ *noun* **1** a very valuable clear hard stone, used in jewellery: *She wore a diamond ring.* **2** a shape with four straight sides of equal length that stands on one of its points ⇨ *see pictures at* SHAPE¹ *and* SYMMETRICAL **3 diamonds** a group of playing cards with a diamond shape printed on them: *the queen of diamonds*

di·a·per /ˈdaɪəpə $ ˈdaɪpəʳ/ the American word for NAPPY

di·ar·rhoea *BrE*, **diarrhea** *AmE* /ˌdaɪə-ˈrɪə/ *noun* [no plural] an illness in which waste from your body is not solid and comes out often: *Too much fruit can give you diarrhoea.*

di·a·ry /ˈdaɪəri/ *noun*, *plural* **diaries** a book with a space for each day in which you write things that you are planning to do or things that have happened: *I'll check my diary to see if I can come Friday.*

dice¹ /daɪs/ *noun*, *plural* **dice** a small square block with a different number of spots on each side, that you use in games: *The first player rolls the dice.*

dice² *verb* to cut food into small square pieces: *Dice the potato and add it to the oil.*

dice

dic·tate /dɪkˈteɪt $ ˈdɪkteɪt/ *verb* to say words for someone to write on a piece of paper: *I'll dictate the letter, and you can type it.*

dic·ta·tion /dɪkˈteɪʃən/ *noun* when someone says words for someone else to write on a piece of paper: *The exam consists of a written paper and a dictation.*

dic·ta·tor /dɪkˈteɪtə $ ˈdɪkteɪtəʳ/ *noun* a leader who has complete power: *A cruel dictator ruled the country.*

dic·ta·tor·ship /dɪkˈteɪtəʃɪp $ dɪkˈteɪtəʳˌʃɪp/ *noun* a system in which a dictator controls a country

dic·tion·a·ry /ˈdɪkʃənəri $ ˈdɪkʃəˌneri/ *noun*, *plural* **dictionaries** a book that gives a list of words in alphabetical order, with their meanings in the same or another language: *If you don't understand a word, look it up in a dictionary.*

did /dɪd/ the past tense of DO

did·n't /ˈdɪdnt/ the short form of 'did not': *I didn't want to go.*

die /daɪ/ *verb* **dying**

GRAMMAR
die of/from something
to stop living: *Grandmother died last year.* | *The oak trees are **dying from** some sort of disease.* | *Her dad **died of** a heart attack.*

PHRASE
be dying for something, be dying to do something *spoken* to want to have or do something very much: *I'm **dying for** a cigarette.* | *I'm **dying to** see her new movie.*

PHRASAL VERBS
die down
if something such as a wind or fire dies down, it slowly becomes less strong: *The flames **died down** after a few minutes.*
die out
to disappear completely: *Two types of tiger in Indonesia **have died out**.*

die·sel /ˈdiːzəl/ *noun* [no plural] a type of FUEL used in some engines

di·et¹ /ˈdaɪət/ *noun* **1** the kind of food that you eat each day: *a healthy diet* **2** a plan to eat only certain kinds or amounts of food, in order to become thinner: *I'm so fat – I need to go on a diet.*

diet² *verb* to eat less in order to become thinner: *My mother's always dieting.*

dif·fer /'dɪfə $ 'dɪfɚ/ *verb* **1** to be different: *This book differs from his other novels.* **2** *formal* if two people differ, they have different opinions: *My father and I differ on many subjects.*

dif·fe·rence /'dɪfərəns/ *noun*

> GRAMMAR
> **difference between someone/ something**
> **difference in something**

the way in which one person or thing is not the same as another: *The **difference between** the two students is that Ross works harder.* | *The **difference in** age doesn't affect our friendship.* | ***What's the difference between** these two computers?*

> PHRASES

make a difference to have an effect on a situation: *Will it **make a difference** to you if I use chicken instead of turkey?* | *New drugs have **made a big difference** in the treatment of the disease.* | ***It makes no difference*** (=does not have an effect) *whether you're black or white.*
tell the difference to be able to see what makes two things or people different: *I still can't **tell the difference between** her twin sons.*

dif·fe·rent /'dɪfərənt/ *adjective*

> GRAMMAR
> **different from something**
> **different to something** *BrE*
> **different than something** *AmE*

not the same: *I had lived in four different houses before I was ten.* | *Each color was different.* | *Schools in Japan **are different from** schools in England.* | *Boys **are** definitely **different to** girls in the way they behave.* | *This CD **is** quite **different than** their last one.*
–**differently** *adverb: Joe and I think quite differently from each other.*

> **USAGE different from, different than, different to**
> You can use **different from** in both British and American English. But you only use **different than** in American English. In British English, some people also use **different to**. However, many teachers think that this use is wrong.

dif·fi·cult /'dɪfɪkəlt/ *adjective*

> GRAMMAR
> **difficult to do something**

not easy to understand or do: *Skiing isn't difficult, but it takes practice.* | *Philosophy is a difficult subject.* | *It's really **difficult to** find a cheap place to live in London.*

dif·fi·cul·ty /'dɪfɪkəlti/ *noun*

> GRAMMAR
> **have difficulty doing something**
> **do something with difficulty**

1 *[no plural]* when it is not easy to do something: *I **had difficulty** finding Kim's house.* | *He speaks slowly and **with difficulty**.*
2 a problem: *They had mechanical difficulties on the plane.*

dig /dɪg/ *verb*   **dig**
dug /dʌg/ dig-
ging

> GRAMMAR
> **dig in/into/out something**

to make a hole in the ground by moving the earth: *Dig a hole and put the rose bush in it.* | *A dog **was digging in** the dirt.* | *Workers **dug out** the people buried in the avalanche.*

> PHRASAL VERB
> **dig up**

dig something up to take something out of the ground using a tool: *We **dug up** a gold watch.*

di·gest /daɪ'dʒest/ *verb* when you digest food, it changes in your stomach into a form your body can use

di·ges·tion /daɪ'dʒestʃən/ *noun [no plural]* the process of digesting food: *He has problems with his digestion.*

di·git /'dɪdʒɪt/ *noun formal* a single number: *What's the first digit of your phone number?*

di·gi·tal /'dɪdʒɪtl/ *adjective* **1** a **digital watch**, a **digital clock** a watch or clock that shows the time in the form of numbers **2** using a system in which information is in the form of changing electronic SIGNALS: *a digital recording of the concert*

dig·ni·fied /'dɪgnəfaɪd/ *adjective* calm, serious, and proud in a way that makes people respect you: *She remained dignified despite her husband's behaviour.*

dig·ni·ty /'dɪgnəti/ *noun [no plural]* when you act in a calm, serious way, even in difficult situations, and this makes people respect you: *She accepted her fate with great dignity.*

di·lap·i·dat·ed /də'læpədeɪtɪd/ *adjective* a dilapidated building or vehicle is old and in bad condition

di·lem·ma /də'lemə/ *noun* a situation in which you find it difficult to choose between two possible actions: *He's in a dilemma about whether to go to college or not.*

dil·i·gent /'dɪlədʒənt/ *adjective* working very hard: *Mary is a very diligent student.*

di·lute /daɪ'luːt/ *verb* to make a liquid weaker or thinner by mixing another liquid with it: *Dilute the orange juice with water.*

dim /dɪm/ *adjective* **dimmer, dimmest** not bright: *The light was becoming dimmer.*

dime /daɪm/ *noun* a coin used in the US worth 10 CENTS

di·men·sions /daɪ'menʃəns/ *plural noun* the size of something, including its length, width, and height: *Measure the dimensions of the room.*

di·min·ish /dɪ'mɪnɪʃ/ *verb formal* to become smaller: *The problem diminished as time passed.*

dim·ple /'dɪmpəl/ *noun* a small hollow place on your cheek or chin: *She gets two little dimples when she smiles.*

din /dɪn/ *noun informal* a loud continuous unpleasant noise: *Stop making such a din.*

din·er /'daɪnə $'daɪnɚ/ *noun AmE* a small restaurant where you can buy cheap meals: *The diner across the road does good food.*

din·gy /'dɪndʒi/ *adjective* **dingier, dingiest** dingy buildings or places are dirty, dark, and unpleasant: *The room was small and dingy.*

dining room /'.. ,./ *noun* a room in a house or hotel where you sit down at a table to eat

din·ner /'dɪnə $'dɪnɚ/ *noun* the main meal of the day, which most people eat in the evening: *We'll have dinner at 8.* | *Let's go out for dinner* (=eat at a restaurant) *tonight.*

dinner jack·et /'.. ,../ *noun* a jacket that men wear on formal occasions; TUXEDO *AmE*

di·no·saur /'daɪnəsɔː $'daɪnə,sɔr/ *noun* a large animal that lived in very ancient times and no longer exists

dip¹ /dɪp/ *verb* **dipped, dipping** to put something into a liquid and quickly lift it out again: *I dipped my toe in the water.*

dip² *noun* a place where the surface of something goes down suddenly: *a dip in the road*

di·plo·ma /də'pləʊmə $dɪ'ploumə/ *noun* an official document showing that someone has successfully finished a course of study: *I have a diploma in French translation.*

dip·lo·mat /'dɪpləmæt/ *noun* someone who the government employs to live and work in a foreign country. Their job is to help people from their own country who are also living or visiting there

dip·lo·mat·ic /,dɪplə'mætɪk/ *adjective* talking to people in a way that does not offend them: *Tell her she can't come to the party – but be diplomatic.*

dire /daɪə $daɪɚ/ *adjective informal* very serious or terrible: *I'm in dire trouble.*

di·rect¹ /də'rekt/ *adjective*

1 going straight towards a person, place etc ⇨ *opposite* INDIRECT (2): *direct eye contact* | *We got a direct flight to LA.*

2 not involving other events, things, or people ⇨ *opposite* INDIRECT (1): *Over 20,000 people died this year as a direct result of smoking.*

direct² *adverb* **1** without stopping and not going anywhere else first: *Can I fly to Hong Kong direct?* | *This train goes direct from London to Edinburgh.* **2** without asking or involving anyone else: *You can speak to him direct on his mobile phone.*

direct³ *verb*

GRAMMAR
direct something/someone somewhere

1 to tell the actors in a film or play what to do: *Jodi Foster has directed several films.* **2** *formal* to tell someone how to get to a place: *Can you **direct** me **to** the post office?*

di·rec·tion /dəˈrekʃən/ *noun*
1 the place or thing that you are moving or pointing towards: *Are you sure you're **going in the right direction**?* | *Half the group went one way, while the others went **in the opposite direction**.* | *Charles pointed his finger **in my direction** (=he pointed it towards me).* **2** **directions** instructions telling you how to go from one place to another, or how to do something: *A woman gave us directions to the theatre.* | *Cook the pasta according to the directions on the package.*

di·rect·ly /dəˈrektli/ *adverb* **1** without involving any other person or thing: *I bought my computer directly from the manufacturer.* **2** directly in front of someone/something, directly behind someone/something exactly in front of someone or something, behind them etc: *I sat directly in front of Jon.*

direct ob·ject /ˌ. ˈ../ *noun* the person or thing that is directly affected by the verb in a sentence. In the sentence 'Joe ate a sandwich', the direct object is 'sandwich' ⇨ *compare* INDIRECT OBJECT

di·rec·tor /dəˈrektə $dəˈrektɚ/ *noun* **1** someone who controls or manages a company: *a conference for company directors* **2** someone who gives instructions to actors in a film or play: *Who was the director of 'Star Wars'?*

di·rec·to·ry /daɪˈrektəri/ *noun, plural* **directories 1** a book or list of names, facts etc in alphabetical order: *the telephone directory* **2** a place on a computer where you store information: *Do you know what directory the files are in?*

dirt /dɜːt $dɝt/ *noun* [no plural] dust, mud, or soil that makes things dirty: *Don't get any dirt on the carpet.*

dirt·y /ˈdɜːti $ˈdɝti/ *adjective* **dirtier, dirtiest** not clean: *Don't get your clothes dirty.* | *dirty hands*

dis·a·bil·i·ty /ˌdɪsəˈbɪləti/ *noun, plural* **disabilities** a physical or mental condition that makes it difficult for someone to do things that most people do easily, such as walk or see: *children with learning disabilities*

dis·a·bled /dɪsˈeɪbəld/ *adjective* someone who is disabled cannot use a part of their body in the way most people are able to: *There's a lift for disabled people.*

dis·ad·van·tage /ˌdɪsədˈvɑːntɪdʒ $ˌdɪsədˈvæntɪdʒ/ *noun* something that makes things more difficult to do or less pleasant for you: *What are the disadvantages of living in a flat?*

dis·a·gree /ˌdɪsəˈɡriː/ *verb*
> **GRAMMAR**
> **disagree with someone**
> **disagree about/on something**

to say that someone's opinion is wrong and that you do not agree with them: *I'm sorry, but I totally disagree.* | *Many students **disagreed with** their parents on the issue.* | *My dad and I **disagree about** most things.* | *We'd only been married a week, and already we **disagreed on** which car to buy.*

dis·a·gree·ment /ˌdɪsəˈɡriːmənt/ *noun* when you do not agree with someone: *They had a disagreement about money.*

dis·ap·pear /ˌdɪsəˈpɪə $ˌdɪsəˈpɪr/ *verb*
> **GRAMMAR**
> **disappear from somewhere**

1 if someone or something disappears, you cannot see them or cannot find them: *The plane **disappeared from** the radar screens.* | *Some books **have disappeared from** the library.* **2** to stop existing: *The rainforests are disappearing quickly.*

dis·ap·point /ˌdɪsəˈpɔɪnt/ *verb* to make someone unhappy because something good that they expected did not happen: *I don't want to disappoint the children by telling them we can't go on holiday.* —**disappointing** *adjective*: *It was disappointing to lose the match.* | *The England team had a disappointing result against Poland.*

dis·ap·point·ed /ˌdɪsə'pɔɪntɪd/
adjective

GRAMMAR
disappointed (that)
disappointed in someone
disappointed with something

unhappy because something good that you expected did not happen: *Julie was disappointed that her friends couldn't come.* | *I'm very disappointed in you, Mark – I thought you could do better.* | *Thomas was bitterly disappointed with* (=very disappointed with) *our performance.*

dis·ap·point·ment /ˌdɪsə'pɔɪntmənt/ noun 1 [no plural] a feeling of sadness that something good has not happened: *I couldn't hide my disappointment at missing the trip.* 2 someone or something that is not as good as you hoped: *The party was a disappointment.*

dis·ap·prove /ˌdɪsə'pruːv/ verb

GRAMMAR
disapprove of someone/something

to believe that someone or something is not good or acceptable: *Pete's parents disapproved of his new girlfriend.*

dis·ar·ma·ment /dɪs'ɑːməmənt $dɪs'ɑrməmənt/ noun [no plural] when a country reduces the number of soldiers and weapons it has: *nuclear disarmament*

dis·ar·ray /ˌdɪsə'reɪ/ noun be in disarray written to be very untidy or not organized: *After the party, the room was in total disarray.*

di·sas·ter /dɪ'zɑːstə $dɪ'zæstər/ noun 1 an event such as an accident, flood, or storm that causes a lot of harm: *Forty people were killed in the rail disaster.* 2 informal a complete failure: *The meal was a disaster.*

di·sas·trous /dɪ'zɑːstrəs $dɪ'zæstrəs/ adjective very bad or ending in complete failure: *It will be disastrous if we lose.*

dis·be·lief /ˌdɪsbə'liːf/ noun [no plural] written a feeling that something is not true or does not exist: *He stared at the broken window in disbelief.*

disc BrE, **disk** AmE /dɪsk/ noun 1 a round flat shape or object: *A metal disc hung from the dog's collar.* 2 a computer DISK

dis·card /dɪ'skɑːd $dɪ'skɑrd/ verb written to throw something away because you not longer need it: *Don't discard the box.*

dis·charge /dɪs'tʃɑːdʒ $dɪs'tʃɑrdʒ/ verb to officially allow someone to leave a place or organization: *They discharged him from hospital yesterday.*

dis·ci·pline /'dɪsəplɪn/ noun [no plural] when people obey rules and orders: *Discipline is very important in this school.*

disc jock·ey BrE, **disk jockey** AmE /'. ˌ../ a DJ

dis·co /'dɪskəʊ $'dɪskoʊ/ noun a place or event where people dance to popular music: *Are you going to the school disco?*

dis·com·fort /dɪs'kʌmfət $dɪs'kʌmfərt/ noun [no plural] slight pain, or a feeling of being physically uncomfortable: *I have a little discomfort in my back.*

dis·con·cert·ing /ˌdɪskən'sɜːtɪŋ $ˌdɪskən'sərtɪŋ/ adjective formal making you feel slightly embarrassed, confused, or worried: *It's disconcerting when someone keeps staring at you.*

dis·con·nect /ˌdɪskə'nekt/ verb to take out the wire, pipe etc that connects a machine or piece of equipment to something ⇨ opposite CONNECT (1): *Have you disconnected the phone?*

dis·con·tent·ed /ˌdɪskən'tentɪd/ adjective written unhappy or not satisfied: *Are you discontented with your work?*

dis·co·theque /'dɪskətek/ noun a DISCO

dis·count /'dɪskaʊnt/ noun a lower price than usual: *There are discounts of 50% on all hats* (=you can buy hats for 50% less than the usual price).

dis·cour·age /dɪs'kʌrɪdʒ $dɪ'skɜrɪdʒ/ verb to try to make someone want to do something less often ⇨ opposite ENCOURAGE: *The government wants to discourage people from using their cars.*

dis·cour·aged /dɪs'kʌrɪdʒd $dɪs'kɜrɪdʒd/ adjective no longer having the confidence to continue doing something: *She gets discouraged when she doesn't win.*

dis·cov·er /dɪ'skʌvə $dɪ'skʌvər/ verb

GRAMMAR
discover who/what/how etc
discover that

to find or learn something that you did not know about before: *Anna discovered a secret entrance to the old house.* | *Scientists are still trying to discover why the dinosaurs died out.* | *At the end of the film, you discover who killed her.* | *Scientists soon discovered that the gas is lighter than air.*

dis·cov·e·ry /dɪ'skʌvəri/ *noun*, *plural* discoveries

GRAMMAR
the discovery of something

1 a fact or an answer to a question that people did not know before: *Doctors have made important new discoveries about the disease.*

2 *[no plural]* when someone finds something that was hidden: *After the discovery of gold in California, many people went there.*

dis·creet /dɪ'skriːt/ *adjective* careful not to let people know what is happening, to avoid embarrassing or offending them: *They were very discreet about their relationship.*
– discreetly *adverb*

dis·crep·an·cy /dɪ'skrepənsi/ *noun* *formal, plural* discrepancies a difference between two things that should be the same: *There's a discrepancy between your results and mine.*

dis·cre·tion /dɪ'skreʃən/ *noun* *[no plural]* *formal* the authority to decide what is the right thing to do in a situation: *Punishment is at the discretion of your teacher.*

dis·crim·i·nate /dɪ'skrɪməneɪt/ *verb* to unfairly treat one person or group differently from another: *It is illegal to discriminate against people because of their sex.*

dis·crim·i·na·tion /dɪ,skrɪmə'neɪʃən/ *noun* *[no plural]* unfair treatment of someone because of the group they belong to: *The company was found guilty of racial discrimination* (=unfair treatment of someone because of their race).

dis·cus /'dɪskəs/ *noun, plural* discuses a flat heavy object that you throw as a sport

dis·cuss /dɪ'skʌs/ *verb*

GRAMMAR
discuss something with someone
discuss how/whether/what

if you discuss something, you talk

with someone about it: *I can always discuss my problems with my sister.* | *The teachers were discussing how to deal with the situation.* | *Tomorrow we will discuss Chapter 3 in class.*

dis·cus·sion /dɪ'skʌʃən/ *noun*

GRAMMAR
a discussion about/on something

a conversation in which people talk about something: *Several students had a discussion about the homework assignment.* | *The meeting ended with a discussion on the current political situation.*

dis·ease /dɪ'ziːz/ *noun* an illness or serious medical condition: *deaths from heart disease*

USAGE disease, illness
Compare **disease** and **illness**. A **disease** is a particular type of illness which has a name and makes you feel ill: *childhood diseases such as measles and chickenpox.* **Illness** is usually used to describe the general condition of being ill: *She missed two weeks' work because of illness.*

dis·en·chant·ed /,dɪsɪn'tʃɑːntɪd $,dɪsɪn'tʃæntɪd/ *adjective formal* no longer believing that something is good or important: *I'm disenchanted with my job.*

dis·fig·ure /dɪs'fɪgə $ dɪs'fɪgjɚ/ *verb* to damage someone's appearance: *His face was disfigured in the fire.*

dis·grace¹ /dɪs'greɪs/ *noun* 1 *[no plural]* something that is very bad: *Your homework is a disgrace.* 2 in disgrace if you are in disgrace, people disapprove of you because you have done something wrong: *After the fight, Sam went home in disgrace.*

disgrace² *verb* to do something so bad that people lose respect for you, your family, or your group: *You have disgraced yourself and your family.* ·

dis·grace·ful /dɪs'greɪsfəl/ *adjective* very bad: *Your behaviour was disgraceful.*
– disgracefully *adverb*

dis·guise /dɪs'gaɪz/ *verb* disguise yourself (as something) to change your usual appearance so that people will not know who you are: *He disguised himself as a policeman.*

disguise

–disguise *noun: The bank robber was in disguise.*

dis·gust /dɪs'gʌst/ *noun [no plural]* a feeling of strong dislike or disapproval: *He pushed his plate away in disgust.*

dis·gus·ted /dɪs'gʌstɪd/ *adjective* feeling strong dislike or disapproval: *I'm disgusted that you had to wait so long.*

dis·gust·ing /dɪs'gʌstɪŋ/ *adjective* something that is disgusting is very unpleasant, and makes you feel ill: *This stuff tastes disgusting! | There's a disgusting smell in the fridge.*

dish /dɪʃ/ *noun, plural* **dishes**

GRAMMAR
a dish of something
1 a round container with low sides, used for holding food: *a dish of cherry pie with whipped cream*
2 food cooked or prepared in a particular way: *Moussaka is a Greek dish.*

PHRASE
do the dishes, wash the dishes to wash the plates, bowls etc that have been used when eating a meal

dis·heart·ened /dɪs'hɑːtnd $ dɪs-'hɑːrtnd/ *adjective* unhappy because you do not think you will achieve something you have been hoping for: *Don't get disheartened if your experiment doesn't work first time.*

di·shev·elled *BrE*, **disheveled** *AmE* /dɪ'ʃevəld/ *adjective* someone who is dishevelled looks untidy: *Her hair was all dishevelled.*

dis·hon·est /dɪs'ɒnəst $ dɪs'ɑːnɪst/ *adjective* likely to lie, steal, or cheat ⇨ *opposite* HONEST: *a dishonest businessman*
–**dishonestly** *adverb: Philip had behaved very dishonestly towards his classmates.*

dis·hon·est·y /dɪs'ɒnəsti $ dɪs'ɑːnəsti/ *noun [no plural]* when someone lies, steals, or cheats: *They accused me of dishonesty.*

dis·hon·our *BrE*, **dishonor** *AmE* /dɪs'ɒnə $ dɪs'ɑːnɚ/ *noun [no plural] formal* when people no longer respect you or approve of you because you have done something bad: *You have brought dishonour on your family.*

dish·wash·er /'dɪʃˌwɒʃə $ 'dɪʃˌwɑːʃɚ/ *noun* a machine that washes dishes: *Please empty the dishwasher.*

dis·il·lu·sioned /ˌdɪsə'luːʒənd/ *adjective* having lost your belief that someone or something is good or right: *He became disillusioned with religion.*

dis·in·fect /ˌdɪsɪn'fekt/ *verb* to clean something with a chemical that destroys BACTERIA (=small creatures that spread disease): *They disinfected all the surfaces.*

dis·in·fec·tant /ˌdɪsɪn'fektənt/ *noun* a chemical that destroys BACTERIA (=small creatures that spread disease): *The nurse cleaned the floor with disinfectant.*

dis·in·te·grate /dɪs'ɪntəgreɪt/ *verb* to break up into small pieces: *The boat was heading towards land when it hit a rock and disintegrated.*

disk /dɪsk/ *noun* 1 also **hard disk** the part of a computer where you store information: *I think the hard disk is full.* 2 a FLOPPY DISK 3 the American spelling of DISC

disk drive /'. ./ *noun* a piece of equipment in a computer that is used to move information to or from a FLOPPY DISK ⇨ *see picture on page 342*

disk jock·ey /'. ˌ../ *AmE* a DJ

dis·like /dɪs'laɪk/ *verb* to not like someone or something ⇨ *opposite* LIKE: *My mother dislikes all my girlfriends.*
–**dislike** *noun: She's always had a dislike of hard work.*

dis·lo·cate /'dɪsləkeɪt $ dɪs'loʊkeɪt/ *verb* if you dislocate a bone in your body, it comes out of its normal place because of an accident: *He's dislocated his shoulder.*

dis·loy·al /dɪs'lɔɪəl/ *adjective formal* not supporting your friends, family, country etc, or doing things that may harm them ⇨ *opposite* LOYAL: *It would be disloyal of me to complain about my wife.*

dis·loy·al·ty /dɪs'lɔɪəlti/ *noun [no plural]* when you do not support your friends, family, country etc, or do things that may harm them ⇨ opposite LOYALTY: *He was accused of disloyalty to his country.*

dis·mal /'dɪzməl/ adjective making you feel unhappy and without hope: *dismal January weather*

dis·may /dɪs'meɪ/ noun [no plural] written a strong feeling of worry, disappointment, or sadness that you have when something unpleasant happens: *She shook her head in dismay.*

dis·miss /dɪs'mɪs/ verb 1 to refuse to consider someone's ideas or opinions: *Why do you always dismiss my ideas?* 2 formal to make someone leave their job ⇨ same meaning FIRE² (2), SACK²: *The company dismissed him for stealing.*

dis·o·be·di·ent /ˌdɪsə'biːdiənt/ adjective deliberately not doing what someone tells you to do: *You're a very disobedient child.*

dis·o·bey /ˌdɪsə'beɪ/ verb to refuse to do what someone in authority or a rule tells you to do ⇨ opposite OBEY: *He deliberately disobeyed my orders.*

dis·or·der /dɪs'ɔːdə $ dɪs'ɔrdɚ/ noun formal 1 [no plural] when things or people are very untidy: *The classroom was in a state of disorder.* 2 an illness that stops part of your body working properly: *She has a rare blood disorder.*

dis·or·der·ly /dɪs'ɔːdəli $ dɪs'ɔrdɚli/ adjective formal untidy or uncontrolled ⇨ opposite ORDERLY: *The papers were in a disorderly mess.*

dis·or·gan·ized also **disorganised** BrE /dɪs'ɔːgənaɪzd $ dɪs'ɔrgə,naɪzd/ adjective not arranged or planned very well: *The wedding was completely disorganized.*

dis·or·i·ent·ed /dɪs'ɔːriəntɪd/ also **dis·or·i·en·tat·ed** BrE /dɪs'ɔːrien-ˌteɪtɪd/ adjective confused and not knowing what is happening or where you are: *She felt disoriented after the accident.*

di·spatch also **despatch** BrE /dɪ'spætʃ/ verb formal 1 to send someone to a place as part of their job: *The UN troops are being dispatched to protect the airport.* 2 to send a letter, package etc to someone: *Father dispatched an angry letter to 'The Times' immediately.*

dis·pense /dɪ'spens/ verb formal to provide something: *a machine that dispenses chocolate*

di·spens·er /dɪ'spensə $ dɪ'spensɚ/ noun a machine that you can get things such as drinks or money from: *I got a coffee from the drinks dispenser.* | *a cash dispenser*

di·sperse /dɪ'spɜːs $ dɪ'spɚs/ verb formal to make things or people go in different directions: *The police finally managed to disperse the crowd.*

di·spir·ited /dɪ'spɪrɪtɪd/ adjective sad and without hope: *After their defeat, the team felt dispirited.*

di·splay¹ /dɪ'spleɪ/ noun

GRAMMAR
a display of something

1 a set of things that are put somewhere so that people can see them: *There was a* **display of** *modern sculptures in the library.* | *Don't miss the fireworks display in the park tonight!*

2 a part of an electronic machine that shows numbers, words etc: *The number you are calling is shown on the phone's display.*

PHRASE
be on display if things are on display, they are put somewhere so that people can see them: *The paintings will* **be on display** *until November 30.*

display² verb 1 to put things where people can see them: *We will display your pictures on the wall.* 2 to show a particular feeling: *The killer has displayed no sympathy for his victims.*

dis·po·sa·ble /dɪ'spəʊzəbəl $ dɪ'spoʊzəbəl/ adjective disposable things are used for a short time and then thrown away: *disposable razors* | *a disposable lighter*

dis·pos·al /dɪ'spəʊzəl $ dɪ'spoʊzəl/ noun [no plural] formal when you throw something away because you no longer want it: *The council is in charge of waste disposal.*

dis·po·si·tion /ˌdɪspə'zɪʃən/ noun formal someone's usual character: *He has a very trusting disposition.*

dis·prove /dɪs'pruːv/ verb, past participle disproven to show that something is false: *He set out to disprove my theory.*

di·spute¹ /dɪ'spjuːt/ noun a serious argument or disagreement: *We're having a dispute with our neighbours about noise.*

dis·pute² /dɪˈspjuːt/ *verb* to say that you think something is not correct or true: *I don't dispute what you're saying.*

dis·qual·i·fy /dɪsˈkwɒləfaɪ $ dɪsˈkwɑːləˌfaɪ/ *verb* disqualified, disqualifies to stop someone taking part in an activity or competition because they have done something wrong: *The judges disqualified him for taking drugs.*

dis·re·gard /ˌdɪsrɪˈɡɑːd $ ˌdɪsrɪˈɡɑrd/ *verb formal* if you disregard something, you do not give it your attention because you think it is not important: *Why do you always disregard everything I say?*

dis·rupt /dɪsˈrʌpt/ *verb* to stop a situation or event from continuing normally: *I don't want to disrupt your work, but can you come to a meeting?*

dis·rup·tion /dɪsˈrʌpʃən/ *noun* when someone or something stops a situation or event from continuing normally: *After the brief disruption, the game continued.*

dis·sat·is·fied /dɪˈsætəsfaɪd/ *adjective* not satisfied: *Are you dissatisfied with the course?*

dis·sect /dɪˈsekt/ *verb formal* to cut up a plant or animal in order to study it: *In biology, we dissected a rat.*

dis·ser·ta·tion /ˌdɪsəˈteɪʃən $ ˌdɪsɚˈteɪʃən/ *noun* a long piece of writing about a subject, especially one that you write as part of a university degree: *She wrote her dissertation on the Romantic poets.*

dis·si·dent /ˈdɪsədənt/ *noun* someone who publicly criticizes their government

dissolve

dis·solve /dɪˈzɒlv $ dɪˈzɑlv/ *verb* if something solid dissolves, it becomes part of a liquid when you mix it with the liquid: *These tablets dissolve in water.*

dis·tance /ˈdɪstəns/ *noun* the amount of space between two places or things: *Kelly was only able* to run a *short distance.* | *Some people have to drive* **long distances** *to work.*

PHRASES
in the distance far away: *We could see some houses* **in the distance.**
at a distance at or from a place that is far away: *Even* **at a distance,** *we could see that it was Rob.*

dis·tant /ˈdɪstənt/ *adjective*
1 far away, or long ago: *The story takes place on a distant planet.* | *All these things happened in the distant past.*
2 distant relatives are not very closely related to you: *Frances is a distant cousin of mine.*

dis·taste /dɪsˈteɪst/ *noun* [no plural] *formal* a strong dislike of something: *He has a great distaste for foreign films.*

dis·til *BrE,* **distill** *AmE* /dɪˈstɪl/ *verb* distilled, distilling to turn a liquid into gas and then turn the gas into liquid again, in order to make it purer or stronger
– distilled *adjective: distilled water*

dis·tinct /dɪˈstɪŋkt/ *adjective* 1 clearly different or separate: *two distinct groups*
2 very easy to see or hear: *She spoke in a clear distinct voice.*

dis·tinc·tion /dɪˈstɪŋkʃən/ *noun* a clear difference between things: *What's the distinction between an 'error' and a 'mistake'?*

dis·tinc·tive /dɪˈstɪŋktɪv/ *adjective* different from others and easy to recognize: *She has a distinctive style of writing.*

dis·tin·guish /dɪˈstɪŋɡwɪʃ/ *verb formal*
1 if you can distinguish between things or people, you can recognize or understand the difference between them: *He couldn't distinguish red from green.*
2 something that distinguishes a person or thing makes them clearly different from others: *What distinguishes this book from others you have read?*

dis·tin·guished /dɪˈstɪŋɡwɪʃt/ *adjective* successful and respected: *Mr Jones is a distinguished doctor.*

dis·tort /dɪˈstɔːt $ dɪˈstɔrt/ *verb* to change the shape or sound of something so it is strange or unclear: *The heat had distorted the doll's face.*

dis·tract /dɪˈstrækt/ *verb* to take someone's attention away from what they are doing: *Don't distract your sister from her homework.*

dis·tract·ed /dɪ'stræktɪd/ *adjective* anxious and not able to think clearly about what is happening around you: *You seem a little distracted.*

distort

dis·trac·tion /dɪ'strækʃən/ *noun* something that takes your attention away from what you are doing: *I can't work at home – there are too many distractions.*

dis·traught /dɪ'strɔːt/ *adjective* very anxious or upset: *She was distraught because her son was missing.*

dis·tress¹ /dɪ'stres/ *noun* [no plural] very great worry or sadness: *The disagreement caused us a lot of distress.*

distress² *verb* to make someone feel very upset
– **distressed** *adjective*: *Clare seemed very distressed.*
– **distressing** *adjective*: *The funeral was very distressing.*

dis·trib·ute /dɪ'strɪbjuːt/ *verb* to give something to each person in a group: *The children distributed sandwiches.*

dis·trict /'dɪstrɪkt/ *noun* an area of a city or country: *He works in the financial district of London.*

dis·trust /dɪs'trʌst/ *noun* a feeling that you cannot trust someone: *He views all businessmen with distrust.*
– **distrust** *verb*: *My father distrusts all accountants.*

dis·turb /dɪ'stɜːb/ $dɪ'stɚb/ *verb*

1 to stop someone doing something, for example by making a noise, asking a question etc: *Please don't disturb me while I'm working.* | *Dad's asleep, so you'd better not disturb him.*

2 to worry or upset you: *The way he stared at me really disturbed me.*

dis·turb·ance /dɪ'stɜːbəns/ $dɪ'stɚ-bəns/ *noun* something that stops you doing something you would normally do: *The builders said they would cause as little disturbance as possible.*

dis·turb·ing /dɪ'stɜːbɪŋ/ $dɪ-'stɚbɪŋ/ *adjective* making you feel worried or upset: *disturbing news*

ditch /dɪtʃ/ *noun, plural* **ditches** a long narrow hole in the ground at the side of a field or road: *The car ended up in a ditch at the side of the road.*

dit·to /'dɪtəʊ/ $'dɪtoʊ/ *noun* two small marks (") that you write under a word in a list so that you do not have to write the same word again

dive /daɪv/ *verb,* **dive** past tense **dived** or **dove** /dəʊv/ $doʊv/ *AmE* 1 to jump into water with your head and arms first: *I walked to the edge of the pool and dived in.* | *Do you know how to dive?*
2 to swim under water, using special equipment to help you breath
– **dive** *noun*: *He did a perfect dive into the water.*

div·er /'daɪvə $'daɪvɚ/ *noun* someone who swims under water with breathing equipment: *The divers found an old ship that had sunk.*

di·verse /daɪ'vɜːs/ $də'vɚs/ *adjective* *formal* very different from each other: *We show a diverse range of programmes.*

di·ver·sion /daɪ'vɜːʃən/ $də'vɚʒən/ *noun* something that takes your attention away from something else: *One boy created a diversion while the other stole the CDs.*

di·vert /daɪ'vɜːt/ $də'vɚt/ *verb* 1 to change the direction of something: *They diverted the river to avoid a flood.*
2 divert attention from something to stop people giving their attention to something: *The government is trying to divert attention from its mistakes.*

di·vide /dɪ'vaɪd/ *verb*

GRAMMAR

divide something into something
divide into something
divide something between/ among people
divide something by something

if you divide something, or if it

divides, it separates into two or more parts: *Divide the cake into four equal pieces.* | *The class divided into three groups for the game.* | *Brenda divided the candy among all the children.*
2 to calculate how many times a number is contained in a larger number: *21 divided by seven is three (=21/7=3).*

di·vine /dɪ'vaɪn/ *adjective* like God, or coming from God: *She asked for divine help.*

div·ing /'daɪvɪŋ/ *noun [no plural]* **1** the activity of swimming under water, using special equipment to help you breath **2** the activity or sport of jumping into water with your head and arms first: *I practised my diving for two hours this morning.*

di·vis·i·ble /dɪ'vɪzəbəl/ *adjective* be divisible a number that is divisible can be divided by another number exactly: *Even numbers are divisible by 2.*

di·vi·sion /dɪ'vɪʒən/ *noun*

> **GRAMMAR**
> **a division between things**
> **1** *[no plural]* the process of calculating how many times one number is contained in a bigger number: *multiplication and division*
> **2** when you separate something into two or more parts, or the way that you separate it: *the division between work and leisure time*
> **3** a part of a large company or organization: *Tony is the manager of the marketing division.*

di·vorce¹ /dɪ'vɔːs $ dɪ'vɔrs/ *noun* the legal ending of a marriage: *His parents decided to get a divorce.*

divorce² *verb* to legally end a marriage: *Julie divorced her husband.*
– **divorced** *adjective*: *My parents are divorced.*

diz·zy /'dɪzi/ *adjective* **dizzier, dizziest** feeling as if you cannot stand up properly, for example because you are ill: *After we danced I felt dizzy and had to sit down.*
– **dizziness** *noun [no plural]*

DJ /ˌdiː 'dʒeɪ/ *noun* someone who plays popular music records on the radio or at parties or clubs

do ⇨ *see box on pages 174 and 175*

do·cile /'dəʊsaɪl $ 'dɑsəl/ *adjective* quiet and easy to control: *The horse was very docile.*

dock /dɒk $ dɑk/ *noun* **1** a place where things are taken on and off ships **2** the dock *BrE* the place in a court of law where the prisoner stands; THE STAND *AmE*

doc·tor /'dɒktə $ 'dɑktɚ/ *noun* someone whose job is to treat people who are sick. In written titles, you use the abbreviation 'Dr': *Nina had to go to the doctor.* | *Doctor Roberts will see you now.* | *The letter was addressed to Dr Armand.*

doc·u·ment /'dɒkjəmənt $ 'dɑkjəmənt/ *noun* a piece of paper that has official information written on it: *a case full of important legal documents*

doc·u·men·tary /ˌdɒkjə'mentri $ ˌdɑkjə'mentri/ *noun, plural* **documentaries** a serious film or television programme that gives facts about something: *We watched a documentary about dinosaurs.*

doc·u·men·ta·tion /ˌdɒkjəmən'teɪʃən $ ˌdɑkjəmən'teɪʃən/ *noun [no plural] formal* documents that prove or show that something is true: *Have you got any documentation to prove who you are?*

dodge /dɒdʒ $ dɑdʒ/ *verb* to move suddenly to the side in order to avoid someone or something: *Someone threw a stone at me and I dodged.*

dodg·y /'dɒdʒi $ 'dɑdʒi/ *adjective BrE informal* **dodgier, dodgiest** a person or thing that is dodgy is one that you think may be dishonest or bad: *His friend looked a bit dodgy to me.*

dizzy

does /dəz; *strong* dʌz/ the third person singular of the present tense of DO

does·n't /'dʌznt/ the short form of 'does not': *She doesn't speak English.*

dog /dɒg $dɔg/ *noun* an animal with four legs, a tail, and fur that many people keep as a pet or to protect them: *We got a big dog to frighten away burglars.*

dog·mat·ic /dɒg'mætɪk $dɔg'mætɪk/ *adjective* someone who is dogmatic has strong beliefs which they do not want to change: *He is very dogmatic about how languages should be taught.*

doing the present participle of DO

dole /dəʊl $doʊl/ *noun* **be on the dole** *BrE* if you are on the dole, you do not have a job, so the government gives you money to help you buy food, clothes etc: *He left school at 16 and now he's on the dole.*

doll /dɒl $dɑl/ *noun* a toy that looks like a small person: *My little sister was playing with her dolls.*

dol·lar /'dɒlə $'dɑlɚ/ *noun* the unit of money in the US, Australia, Canada, New Zealand etc; written sign $: *Dad gave me $5 (=five dollars) for washing the car.*

dol·phin /'dɒlfɪn $'dɑlfɪn/ *noun* a very intelligent sea animal that looks like a large grey fish

dome /dəʊm $doʊm/ *noun* a building with a round roof

do·mes·tic /də'mestɪk/ *adjective* **1** connected with family relationships and life at home: *They enjoyed 30 years of domestic happiness.* **2** a domestic animal is kept as a pet

dom·i·nant /'dɒmənənt $'dɑmənənt/ *adjective* most important or most noticeable: *The Spice Girls were dominant in the pop charts that year.*

dom·i·nate /'dɒmənɪt $'dɑmə,neɪt/ *verb* to be the most important or most noticeable person or thing: *One or two students always dominate the lesson.*

dom·i·neer·ing /,dɒmə'nɪərɪŋ $,dɑmə'nɪrɪŋ/ *adjective* someone who is domineering tries to control other people: *Her boyfriend was very domineering.*

dom·i·no /'dɒmənəʊ $'dɑmə,noʊ/ *noun, plural* **dominoes** one of a set of small pieces of wood or plastic with spots on, used for playing a game called dominoes

do·nate /dəʊ'neɪt $'doʊneɪt/ *verb* to give something to a person or organiza-

tion that needs help: *A local business donated a minibus to the school.*

do·na·tion /dəʊ'neɪʃən $doʊ'neɪʃən/ *noun* something, especially money, that you give to help a person or organization: *I made a donation to help homeless people.*

done¹ /dʌn/ the past participle of DO

done² *adjective* finished or completed: *Is the work done yet?*

don·key /'dɒŋki $'dɑŋki/ *noun* a grey or brown animal like a small horse with long ears

do·nor /'dəʊnə $'doʊnɚ/ *noun* **1** a person or group that gives something, especially money, to an organization in order to help people: *The youth club received £1,000 from a donor.* **2** someone who lets a doctor take out some of their blood or part of their body so that the doctor can put it in a person who is ill: *a kidney donor*

don't /dəʊnt $doʊnt/ the short form of 'do not': *I don't know.*

donut another spelling of DOUGHNUT

doom /du:m/ *noun* [no plural] a bad situation in the future that you cannot avoid: *I had an awful sense of doom before the exam.*

doomed /du:md/ *adjective* if something is doomed, it will certainly fail: *Our relationship was doomed from the beginning.*

door /dɔ: $dɔr/ *noun*

1 the thing that you open and close to get into or out of a house, room, car etc: *Peter **opened the door** and came in.* | *Be sure to **lock the door** when you leave.*

2 the entrance to a building or room: *the next person who comes through that door* | *Two men were standing **at the door** (=near the entrance, waiting to come in).*

3 **next door** in the room, house, or building next to the one you are in: *The Smiths **live next door** to us.* | *our **next-door neighbours** (=the people who live in the house next to ours)*

door·bell /'dɔ:bel $'dɔrbel/ *noun* a button by the door of a house that makes a sound when you press it and lets the people inside know you are

D

➤ VERB FORMS

PRESENT TENSE

Singular	Plural
I **do**	we **do**
you **do**	you **do**
he, she, it **does**	they **do**

PAST TENSE

Singular	Plural
I **did**	we **did**
you **did**	you **did**
he, she, it **did**	they **did**

present participle ➤ **doing**
past participle ➤ **have done**
negative forms ➤ **do not, does not, did not**
negative short forms ➤ **don't, doesn't, didn't**

➤ DO or MAKE?

DO you **do** an action or an activity: *I did my homework last night.* | *What did you do at school today?*

MAKE you **make** something or cause something to happen: *I made a cake.*

➤ DO

1 to do something
if you do an action or activity, you make it happen: *"What are you doing?" "I'm making a cake."* | *I have so much to do.* | *Jack has done a lot to help us.* | *It's your turn to do the washing-up.* | *Women still do most of the housework.*

2 in negative sentences
They did not understand what he meant. | *I don't know.* | *Michelle doesn't trust me.* | *I didn't want to get up this morning.*

3 in questions
What did you say? | *When did you and Ken first meet?* | *Why do I have to sign all these papers?* | *Doesn't she have an older sister (=you think she has an older sister)?* | *Didn't you tell him what happened (=you think someone should have told him)?*

do

6 used when you do not want to repeat another verb
She's only eight, but she eats more than I do (= she eats more than I eat). | *"I loved the movie." "So did I."*

5 in question tags
used at the end of a sentence to ask a question or to ask someone to agree with you: *You didn't tell him what I said, did you?* | *You went to Mary's yesterday, didn't you?* | *They don't argue all the time, do they?*

4 to tell someone not to do something
Don't touch the iron – it's hot. | *A sign on the fence said 'Do Not Enter.'* | *Don't be nervous. It'll be all right.*

Most common words used with **do**:

do damage	do the shopping	do your job	do business
do the washing	do some work	do your duty	do an experiment
do your homework	do the cooking	do research	

Do your homework

Do the cooking

Do the shopping

PHRASES

do well, do badly
to do something in a way that has a good or bad result: *Susan has always done well in school.* | *The team is doing well this year.* | *The business is doing badly.*

do your best
to do something in the best way that you can: *I hope you will always try to do your best.* | *I did my best to be friends, but she wasn't interested.*

what someone does, what someone does for a living
what someone's job is: *"What does your wife do?" "She's a police officer."* | *I'm not sure what Mike does. I think he works in a bank.* | *Holly's a good artist. Does she do that for a living?*

what did you do with something? *spoken*
say this when asking where someone put something: *Jenny, what did you do with my keys?* | *What did I do with my pen? Oh, there it is.*

could do with something
say this when you want or need something: *I could do with some sleep.* | *He could do with losing some weight.*

How do you do? *formal*
say this when you meet someone for the first time, and want to be very polite. You also say **How do you do?** as a reply, when someone has just said it to you: *"How do you do?, Mr Mason," said Miss Cosby. "How do you do? I'm pleased to meet you," replied Mason.*

What do you do?

How do you do?

there: *Someone rang the doorbell.* | *Was that the doorbell I heard?*

door·step /'dɔːstep $ 'dɔrstep/ *noun* a step just outside the door to a building: *We sat on the doorstep in the sunshine.*

door·way /'dɔːweɪ $ 'dɔrweɪ/ *noun* the space where a door opens into a room or building: *He stood in the doorway watching us.*

dor·mi·to·ry /'dɔːmətəri $ 'dɔrmə-ˌtɔri/ *noun, plural* **dormitories** also **dorm** /dɔːm $ dɔrm/ *informal* **1** a large room where a lot of people sleep **2** the American word for HALL OF RESIDENCE

dose /dəʊs $ doʊs/ *noun* a measured amount of medicine: *You must take four doses a day.*

dot /dɒt $ dɑt/ *noun* **1** a small round mark or spot: *a line of dots* **2** on the **dot** *informal* exactly at a particular time: *The train left at 10 o'clock on the dot.*

dot·ing /'dəʊtɪŋ $ 'doʊtɪŋ/ *adjective* loving someone very much, in a way that seems silly to other people: *His doting parents let him do whatever he likes.*

doub·le¹ /'dʌbəl/ *adjective* **1** twice the usual amount, size, or number: *a double portion of fries* **2** made to be big enough for two people or things: *a double room* **3** consisting of two things of the same kind: *double doors*

double² *verb* to become twice as big, or to make something become twice as big: *The number of girls at the school has doubled.* | *They have doubled the price of cigarettes.*

double³ *pronoun, adverb* an amount that is twice the size of another amount: *I offered him £10 but he wanted double that amount.*

double bass /ˌ.. './ *noun* a very large musical instrument, shaped like a VIOLIN, that you play standing up

double-check /ˌ.. './ *verb* to check something again so that you are completely sure about it: *Could you just double-check that the door is locked?*

double-deck·er /ˌ.. '../ *noun* a bus with two levels
–double-decker *adjective*: *a double-decker bus*

doub·les /'dʌbəlz/ *noun* [no plural] a game of tennis played by two teams of two people: *I prefer playing doubles.*

doub·ly /'dʌbli/ *adverb* twice as much: *The job was doubly difficult because of the rain.*

doubt¹ /daʊt/ *noun*

GRAMMAR
doubt about something
no doubt (that)

the feeling that something may not be true, good, or possible: *I still* **have** *some serious* **doubts about** *Ken's plan.* | *The police* **had no doubt that** *Stevens was lying* (=they were sure he was lying).* | *There is* **no doubt that** *Lorna stole the money* (=it is certain that she stole it).

PHRASES
be in doubt to be uncertain: *Sonia was* **in no doubt about** *what to do.* | *His future as a professional footballer* **is in doubt**.
no doubt *spoken*: **No doubt** *Mike will know what to do* (=it is very likely that he will know what to do).

doubt² *verb*

GRAMMAR
doubt (that)
doubt whether/if

to think that something is not true or not likely: *We had no reason to* **doubt** *Maria's story.* | *I* **doubt that** *many people will come to the fair if it rains.* | *Some people* **doubted** **whether** *the team could win.*

PHRASE
I doubt it *spoken*: *"Do you think Rick will join us?"* **"I doubt it"** (=I don't think he will).*"

doubt·ful /'daʊtfəl/ *adjective* **1** not likely to happen or be true: *It's doubtful whether any of the other runners can beat him.* **2** not certain about something: *Everyone looked doubtful about the idea.*

doubt·less /'daʊtləs/ *adverb formal* used to say that something is very likely: *You will doubtless want to go to college one day.*

dough /dəʊ $ doʊ/ *noun* [no plural] a soft mixture containing flour that you bake to make bread

dough·nut or **donut** /'dəʊnʌt $ 'doʊnʌt/ *noun* a small cake shaped like a ring or a ball

dove¹ /dʌv/ *noun* a type of white bird often used as a sign of peace

D

dove² /dəʊv $ doʊv/ *AmE* a past tense of DIVE

down¹ /daʊn/ *adverb, preposition*
1 towards a lower place: *Alison ran down the hill.* | *Harry bent down to tie his shoelace.* | *Ella put the toys down on the floor.* ⇨ *see picture on page 354*
2 becoming lower in amount: *My weight is now down to 9 stone* (=it used to be more than 9 stone).
3 further along a road or path: *Go down this corridor and turn left at the end.* | *There's a bread shop down the road.*
4 towards the south: *Are you going to fly down to Arizona or drive?*

down² *adjective* 1 *informal* unhappy: *She looked a bit down.* 2 a computer that is down is not working: *The network has been down all afternoon.*

down·fall /'daʊnfɔ:l/ *noun* *written* someone's downfall is the thing that makes them fail: *This mistake led to his downfall.*

down·hill /ˌdaʊn'hɪl/ *adverb, adjective* 1 towards the bottom of a hill ⇨ *opposite* UPHILL: *Cycling downhill is easy.* 2 go downhill to become worse: *After the argument our relationship quickly went downhill.*

down·load /ˌdaʊn'ləʊd $ 'daʊnloʊd/ *verb* to move information from one part of a computer system to another: *I downloaded the anti-virus update from the Internet this morning.*

down·pour /'daʊnpɔ: $ 'daʊnpɔr/ *noun* a lot of rain falling in a short time

down·right /'daʊnraɪt/ *adverb informal* completely: *It was downright stupid to go there on your own.*

down·side /'daʊnsaɪd/ *noun* the downside a bad feature of something that is good in other ways: *The downside of the job is you have to work at weekends.*

down·stairs /ˌdaʊn'steəz $ ˌdaʊn'sterz/ *adverb, adjective* on or towards a lower level of a house ⇨ *opposite* UPSTAIRS: *Michael came downstairs in his pyjamas.* | *the downstairs toilet*

down·stream /ˌdaʊn'stri:m/ *adverb* in the same direction that a river or stream

is flowing: *The boat floated downstream.*

down-to-earth /ˌ. . './ *adjective* sensible and practical: *For a famous pop star, she's very down-to-earth.*

down·town /ˌdaʊn'taʊn/ *adverb, adjective AmE* to or in the centre of a city or town: *She works in a bar downtown.* | *a downtown district of New York*

down·wards /'daʊnwədz $ 'daʊnwɚdz/ also **downward** *adverb* towards a lower position ⇨ *opposite* UPWARDS: *Push the handle downwards.*

doze /dəʊz $ doʊz/ *verb* 1 to sleep lightly for a short time: *Grandma was dozing in her chair.* 2 **doze off** to fall asleep: *It was so boring I almost dozed off.*
–**doze** *noun*: *I had a quick doze in my armchair.*

doz·en /'dʌzən/ *noun* 1 a group of 12 things: *a dozen eggs* 2 **dozens of things/people** *informal* a lot of things or people: *The singer gets dozens of letters from fans every day.*

Dr. the written abbreviation for DOCTOR

drab /dræb/ *adjective* **drabber, drabbest** dull: *The room was painted a drab brown.*

draft¹ /drɑ:ft $ dræft/ *noun* 1 a piece of writing, a drawing, or a plan that you have not finished yet: *This is just a first draft of my essay.* 2 the American spelling of DRAUGHT

draft² *verb* 1 to write a plan, letter, report etc that you will need to change before you finish it: *She drafted a letter of complaint.* 2 *AmE* if someone is drafted, the government orders them to join the army during a war: *He was drafted during the Vietnam war.*

drafty the American spelling of DRAUGHTY

drag¹ /dræg/ *verb* **dragged, dragging** 1 to pull someone or something heavy along the ground: *He dragged the table over to the window.* 2 if an event drags, it is boring and seems to go very slowly: *School always drags on Friday afternoons.* 3 **drag someone into something** to make someone get involved in a situation when they do not want to: *Don't drag me into your arguments with your boyfriend!*

drag² *noun* **be a drag** *informal* to be boring

or annoying: *It's such a drag having to work on a Sunday.*

drag·on /'drægən/ *noun* a large animal in children's stories with wings and a long tail, which can breathe fire

drain¹ /dreɪn/ also **drain away** *verb* if you drain something, or if it drains, you let water flow away from it so that it is less wet: *I think I ought to let these towels drain on the line.* | *I drained the water from the pasta.* ➡ *see picture on page 344*

drain² *noun* **1** a pipe or hole that carries water away from something: *The drain is blocked with leaves again.* ➡ *see picture on page 343* **2** a drain on something something that uses too much money or strength: *Going out too often is a drain on your energy.*

drained /dreɪnd/ *adjective* very tired: *After the exams, I felt completely drained.*

drain·pipe /'dreɪnpaɪp/ *noun BrE* a pipe that carries rain water down from a roof ➡ *see picture on page 343*

dra·ma /'drɑːmə $ 'drɑːmə/ *noun* **1** a story that actors perform as a play in the theatre, or on television or radio: *He has written a new drama for the BBC.* **2** [*no plural*] the study of plays or acting in plays: *Miss Jay is our drama teacher.* | *the history of Greek drama*

dra·mat·ic /drə'mætɪk/ *adjective* **1** very sudden, exciting, or noticeable: *The improvement in his behaviour was dramatic.* | *a dramatic story* **2** related to plays and the theatre: *a dramatic society*
—**dramatically** /-kli/ *adverb*: *She looked dramatically different.* | *We decided to tell our story dramatically.*

dram·a·tist /'dræmətɪst/ *noun* someone who writes plays

dram·a·tize also **dramatise** *BrE* /'dræmətaɪz/ *verb* **1** to use a real event or a story from a book to write a play: *They are dramatizing her life story for TV.* **2** to make an event seem more exciting than it really is: *She tends to dramatize things.*

drank the past tense of DRINK

drapes /dreɪps/ *AmE plural noun* heavy curtains

dras·tic /'dræstɪk/ *adjective* drastic actions or changes are great, sudden, and have a big effect: *The new school* principal is planning to make drastic changes.
—**drastically** /-kli/ *adverb*: *The cost of fuel has increased drastically.*

draught *BrE*, **draft** *AmE* /drɑːft $ dræft/ *noun* **1** cold air blowing through a room: *Could you shut the window – there's a draught.* **2** draughts *BrE* a game played by two people, who each have 12 round pieces on a board with 64 squares; CHECKERS *AmE*

draugh·ty *BrE*, **drafty** *AmE* /'drɑːfti $ 'dræfti/ *adjective* draughtier, draughtiest a draughty room has cold air blowing through it

draw¹ /drɔː/ *verb* drew /druː/ drawn /drɔːn/

1 if you draw something, you use a pen or pencil to make a picture of it: *The kids drew pictures of themselves.* | *I'll draw you a map of how to get there.*
2 *written* to pull something from a container or across something: *She **drew** a large envelope **from** her briefcase.* | *When the bank clerk wouldn't give him the money, the man **drew** a **knife**.* | *Helena **drew** the curtains* (=closed or opened the curtains).
3 *BrE* if two teams or players draw, they both get the same number of points; TIE *AmE*: *Inter **drew with** Juventus last night.*

PHRASAL VERB

draw up
1 draw something up to think of and write a list, plan etc: *Teachers **drew up** a list of equipment they needed.*
2 draw up *written* if a car draws up somewhere, it stops there: *A large car **drew up** outside the house.*

draw² *noun* a game that ends with both teams or players having the same number of points

draw·back /'drɔːbæk/ *noun* something that might be a problem or disadvantage: *The only drawback to living in London is the cost.*

drawer /drɔː $ drɔr/ *noun* part of a piece of furniture that is shaped like a long thin box that slides in and out. You keep things in drawers: *I keep my socks in the top drawer.*

draw·ing /'drɔːɪŋ/ *noun*

GRAMMAR
a drawing of something
1 a picture you make with a pen or pencil: *a **drawing of** a cat*
2 [no plural] when you make pictures with a pen or pencil: *Katrina loves drawing and painting.*

drawing pin /'.. ,./ *noun* BrE a short pin with a wide flat top, used for fastening paper to a board; THUMBTACK AmE

drawl /drɔːl/ *verb* written to speak slowly with long vowel sounds: *"Hi there," he drawled.*
– **drawl** *noun*: *She speaks in a slow drawl.*

drawn /drɔːn/ the past participle of DRAW[1]

dread /dred/ *verb* to feel very worried about something that is going to happen: *I'm really dreading the exams.*

dread·ful /'dredfəl/ *adjective* very bad or unpleasant: *a dreadful accident*

dream[1] /driːm/ *noun*

GRAMMAR
a dream about something
1 the pictures that you see in your mind when you are asleep: *I had a **dream about** my dog last night. | After the accident, he had **bad dreams** (=unpleasant or frightening dreams).*
2 something that you want, or that you hope will happen: *It was her dream to travel around the world.*

dream[2] *verb, past tense and past participle* **dreamed, dreamt** /dremt/

GRAMMAR
dream (that)
dream about someone/something
dream of doing something
1 to see pictures in your mind while you are asleep: *I **dreamed that** I was flying. | I **dreamed about** you last night.*
2 to think about something that you hope will happen: *When I was grow-*ing up, I **dreamed of** being a movie star. | Shelley had always **dreamed that** one day she would meet him again.*

PHRASAL VERB
dream up
dream something up to think of an unusual plan or idea: *I don't know who **dreamed up** the idea of a picnic in the middle of winter!*

dream[3] *adjective* your dream job, house etc is the best one that you can imagine: *My dream job would be testing computer games!*

dreamt a past tense and past participle of DREAM[2]

drear·y /'drɪəri $ 'drɪri/ *adjective* **drearier, dreariest** not exciting: *Life here is so dreary.*

drench /drentʃ/ *verb* to make something very wet
– **drenched** *adjective*: *I got totally drenched in the rain.*

dress[1] /dres/ *verb*
to put clothes on someone or on yourself: *I **got dressed** quickly and ran to the shops to get some milk. | Aren't you dressed yet? It's nearly mid-day! | She dressed the twins and got their breakfast ready. | Tina is three, and is learning to **dress herself** (=put her clothes on for herself).*

PHRASE
be dressed in something: *They **were** all **dressed in** jeans (=they were all wearing jeans). | He usually **dresses in** black (=wears black clothes).*

PHRASAL VERB
dress up
1 to wear your best clothes for a special occasion: *Everybody **dressed up** for the party and looked really nice.*
2 to wear special clothes for fun: *When I was a kid, I loved **dressing up as** a cowboy.*

dress[2] *noun, plural* **dresses**
a piece of clothing that a woman or girl wears, which covers the top of her body and part of her legs: *a summer dress* ⇨ *see picture on page 352*

dress·er /'dresə $ 'dresər/ noun **1** BrE a large piece of furniture with shelves for holding dishes and plates **2** an American word for CHEST OF DRAWERS

dress·ing /'dresɪŋ/ noun **1** a mixture of oil and other things that you pour over SALAD **2** a piece of material that you use to cover a wound: *The doctor put a dressing on my eye.*

dressing gown /'.. ,./ noun BrE a piece of clothing like a long loose coat that you wear in your home before you get dressed; ROBE AmE

dressing room /'.. ,./ noun a room where an actor gets ready before going on stage or on television

drew the past tense of DRAW¹

drool   dribble

drib·ble /'drɪbəl/ verb **1** BrE if you dribble, liquid in your mouth comes out onto your chin; DROOL AmE **2** to move a ball forward by kicking or BOUNCING it several times in football or BASKETBALL

drier another spelling of DRYER

drift¹ /drɪft/ verb **1** to move along slowly in the air or water: *The leaves drifted gently in the wind.* **2** drift apart if people drift apart, they gradually stop being friends

drift² noun **1** snow or sand that the wind has blown into a large pile: *Her car was stuck in a snow drift.* **2** get someone's drift informal to understand the general meaning of what someone says: *I don't know much about computers but I get your drift.*

drill¹ /drɪl/ noun a tool or machine that you use to make small holes in something hard: *an electric drill*

drill

drill² verb to make a hole with a drill: *The dentist drilled a hole in my tooth.*

drink¹ verb /drɪŋk/ **drank** /dræŋk/ **drunk** /drʌŋk/
1 to take liquid into your mouth and swallow it: *Rob was drinking a Coke.* | *Do you want something to drink?*
2 to drink alcohol, especially regularly: *Don't drink and drive.* | *I usually drink white wine rather than red.*

drink² noun

GRAMMAR
a drink of something
an amount of something such as water, juice etc that you drink: *Are you thirsty? Would you like a drink?* | *a **drink of** water*

drip¹ /drɪp/ verb **dripped, dripping**
1 if a liquid drips from something, it falls in drops: *Water was dripping from the ceiling.* **2** if something is dripping, drops of a liquid are falling from it: *The tap is dripping.*

drip² noun a small amount of a liquid that falls from something: *She wiped the drips of paint off the floor.*

drive¹ /draɪv/ verb **drove** /drəʊv $ drouv/ **driven** /'drɪvən/

GRAMMAR
drive to/through/around etc a place
drive someone to/from/around etc a place
1 to make a car move in the direction you want: *I learned to drive when I was seventeen.* | *I think the man was driving a red car.* | *Peggy **drove to** work as usual.* | *I drove over some enormous bumps in the road.* | *People waved as they drove past us.*
2 if you drive someone somewhere, you take them there in a car: *Many parents **drive** their children **to** school.* | *They **drove** us **around** the city for a tour.*

PHRASE
drive someone crazy, drive someone mad to annoy someone a lot: *I can't remember his name, and it's **driving** me **crazy**.*

drive² noun
1 a trip in a car: *It's a three-hour drive to the lake.*

2 a part of a computer that can read or store information: *the **hard drive***
3 *BrE* a DRIVEWAY ⇨ *see picture on page 343*

drive-in /'. ./ *adjective* a drive-in restaurant or cinema is one where you stay in your car to collect food or watch a film – **drive-in** *noun: We saw a movie at the drive-in.*

driv·el /'drɪvəl/ *noun* [no plural] *informal* nonsense: *Don't talk drivel!*

driven the past participle of DRIVE¹

driv·er /'draɪvə $ 'draɪvər/ *noun* someone who drives: *a truck driver*

drive-through /'. ./ *adjective* a drive-through restaurant, bank etc is one that you can use without getting out of your car

drive·way /'draɪvweɪ/ also **drive** *noun* a short road between your house and the street, where you put your car: *There is room to park two cars in his driveway.*

driv·ing¹ /'draɪvɪŋ/ *noun* [no plural] the activity or skill of driving a car: *I love driving. | His driving is terrible sometimes.*

driving² *adjective* driving rain, driving snow rain or snow that is falling very heavily and fast

driving test /'.. ,./ *noun* an official test that you must pass in order to drive a car on the roads

driz·zle /'drɪzəl/ *verb* if it is drizzling, it is raining very lightly: *It was only drizzling so I didn't take an umbrella.*

drool /druːl/ *verb* if you drool, liquid in your mouth comes out onto your chin; DRIBBLE *BrE: The dog keeps drooling.* ⇨ *see picture at DRIBBLE*

droop /druːp/ *verb* if something droops, it hangs down because it is old or weak: *These flowers have started to droop.*

drop¹ /drɒp $ drɑːp/ *verb* dropped, dropping

> **GRAMMAR**
> **drop from/off/onto something**

1 if you drop something you are holding, you let it fall, often by accident: *She dropped a glass when she was drying the dishes. | Don't drop that tray!* ⇨ *see picture on page 340*
2 to fall: *The ground was covered in apples that **had dropped** from the tree. | I think this plant is dying – the leaves are starting to **drop off**.*

3 also **drop someone off** to take someone to a place in a car, before going to another place: *Shall I drop you at the station? | She **drops** the kids **off** at school on her way to work.*
4 to become lower in level or amount: *It's warm during the day, but the temperature drops at night. | Pam's voice **dropped to** a whisper.*

PHRASAL VERBS
drop in also **drop by**
to visit someone who does not know you are coming because you have not arranged it with them: *Doris **dropped in** just before lunchtime.*
drop off
to fall asleep: *Dad's **dropped off** in front of the telly again.*
drop out
to leave school or college before you have finished your course: *My grandfather had to **drop out of** school when he was 13 to help on the farm.*

drop² *noun*

> **GRAMMAR**
> **a drop of something**
> **a drop in something**

1 a very small amount of liquid: *rain drops | Put **a drop of** oil on the wheel.*
2 when the amount or level of something becomes lower: *There has been a **drop in** the price of computers.*

drop·out /'drɒpaʊt $ 'drɑːp-aʊt/ *noun* someone who leaves school or college without finishing their course: *a high-school dropout*

drought /draʊt/ *noun* a long period of dry weather when there is not enough water: *The country has had two years of drought.*

drove the past tense of DRIVE

drown /draʊn/ *verb* if someone drowns, or if they are drowned, they die from being under water for too long: *The fishermen drowned when their boat overturned. | He was drowned in a diving accident.*

drow·sy /'draʊzi/ *adjective* drowsier, drowsiest tired and almost asleep: *During the lesson I started to feel drowsy.*

D

D

drug¹ /drʌg/ *noun*   **1** an illegal substance that people smoke, swallow etc to give themselves a pleasant feeling: *He has never taken drugs.*   **2** a medicine: *a new drug that is being used to treat cancer*

drug² *verb* **drugged, drugging** to give someone drugs, usually to make them sleep: *The kidnappers drugged him and put him into the van.*

drug·store /'drʌgstɔː $ 'drʌgstɔr/ the American word for CHEMIST (1)

drum /drʌm/ *noun*   **1** a round musical instrument which you hit with your hand or a stick: *Clare plays the drums in a band.*   **2** a large round container for storing liquids such as oil or chemicals: *an oil drum*

drum·mer /'drʌmə $ 'drʌmɚ/ *noun* someone who plays the drums: *The band has a great drummer.*

drunk¹ the past participle of DRINK¹

drunk² /drʌŋk/ *adjective* if someone is drunk, they have drunk too much alcohol and it makes them behave strangely: *He got drunk and crashed his car.*

dry¹ /draɪ/ *adjective* **drier, driest**

1 something that is dry has no water in it or on it: *Get a dry towel out of the cupboard.*
2 if your mouth, throat, or skin is dry, it does not have enough of the natural liquid that is usually in it: *My skin gets so dry in the winter.*
3 if the weather is dry, there is no rain: *It's been a very dry summer.*

dry² *verb* **dried, dries**

if you dry something, or if it dries, it no longer has any water in it or on it: *Lynn dried the dishes.* | *Lay the sweater out flat to dry.*

PHRASAL VERBS

dry out
dry out, dry something out if clothing, soil etc dries out, or if you dry it out, it becomes completely dry: *It was so hot our swimsuits **dried out** quickly.*

dry up
1 dry up if a river or lake dries up, there is no longer any water in it: *The stream **dried up** during the very hot summer.*
2 dry something up BrE to move a cloth across dishes that have been

washed so that they become dry: *Can you **dry** these dishes **up** for me?*

dry-clean /ˌ. './ *verb* to clean clothes with chemicals instead of water

dry clean·er's /ˌ. '../ *noun* a shop where you take clothes to be dry-cleaned

dry·er or **drier** /'draɪə $ 'draɪɚ/ *noun* a machine that dries things, especially clothes or hair: *Put the washing in the dryer.*

du·al /'djuːəl $ 'duəl/ *adjective* formal having two of something, or two parts: *The interview has a dual purpose: to find out more about you, and to test your English.*

du·bi·ous /'djuːbiəs $ 'dubiəs/ *adjective*   **1** if you are dubious about something, you are not sure whether it is good or true: *Her parents felt rather dubious about her new friends.*   **2** not seeming real or honest: *a dubious story*

duch·ess /'dʌtʃɪs/ *noun*, *plural* **duchesses** a woman from Europe with the highest social rank below a princess, or the wife of a DUKE

duck

duck¹ /dʌk/ *verb* to lower your body or head very quickly to avoid something: *He threw a book at me and I ducked.*

duck² *noun*   **1** a common bird that lives in water and has short legs and a wide beak   **2** [no plural] the meat from a duck: *duck with orange sauce*

duck·ling /'dʌklɪŋ/ *noun* a baby duck

due /djuː $ du/ *adjective*   **1** expected to happen or arrive at a particular time: *Your essay was due in yesterday.* | *The concert was due to start at 8.00 pm.*   **2** due to something if one thing is due to another, it happens as a result of it: *Her success was due to hard work.* | *The* game was cancelled due to bad weather.

du·et /dju'et $ du'et/ noun a piece of music for two performers: a duet for flute and violin

dug the past tense and past participle of DIG

duke /djuːk $ duk/ noun a man from Europe with the highest social rank below a prince

dull /dʌl/ adjective **duller, dullest**

not interesting or exciting ⇨ same meaning BORING: The book was great, but the movie is dull.

dumb /dʌm/ adjective **1** informal stupid: He's so dumb. **2** not able to speak. Some people think this use is rude and offensive

dum·my /'dʌmi/ noun, plural dummies **1** a plastic figure of a person: a dummy in a shop window **2** BrE a rubber object that you put in a baby's mouth when it is hungry or upset; PACIFIER AmE

dump¹ /dʌmp/ verb **1** to drop or put something somewhere in a careless way: He always just dumps his coat on the floor, instead of hanging it up. **2** to leave something somewhere, because you do not want it: It is illegal to dump rubbish here.

dump² noun **1** a place where you can take things you do not want and leave them there **2** informal a place that is unpleasant because it is dirty, ugly, or boring: Their house is a dump.

dune /djuːn $ dun/ noun a hill made of sand: We walked over the sand dunes to the beach. ⇨ see picture on page 348

dung /dʌŋ/ noun [no plural] solid waste from animals, especially large animals: cow dung

dun·ga·rees /ˌdʌŋgə'riːz/ plural noun BrE trousers with thin pieces that go over your shoulders and a square piece of cloth that covers your chest; OVERALLS AmE: a pair of red dungarees ⇨ see picture on page 352

dunk /dʌŋk/ verb to quickly put something into a liquid and then take it out again: He dunked his biscuit in his coffee.

dun·no /də'nəʊ $ də'noʊ/ spoken an informal way of saying 'I don't know': "Where's Lucy?" "Dunno."

dupe /djuːp $ dup/ verb written to tell lies in order to make someone believe or do something: She was duped into giving the robbers her car keys.

du·pli·cate¹ /'djuːpləkət $ 'dupləkət/ adjective a duplicate copy of something is made so that it is exactly the same: a duplicate copy of the letter
– **duplicate** noun: Don't worry, I've got a duplicate of the door key in my car.

du·pli·cate² /'djuːpləkeɪt $ 'dupləˌkeɪt/ verb formal to copy something: Could you duplicate this letter for me?

du·ra·tion /djʊ'reɪʃən $ dʊ'reɪʃən/ noun [no plural] formal the length of time that something continues: He had to sit in the corner for the duration of the lesson.

dur·ing /'djʊərɪŋ $ 'dʊrɪŋ/ preposition
1 all through a period of time: Foxes sleep during the day and hunt at night. | She kept talking during the lesson.
2 at one time in a period of time: Their car was stolen during the night.

USAGE during, for
During is always followed by a noun and it tells you when something happens: He was sick during the night. **For** is followed by a period of time and it tells you how long something lasts: She was in hospital for two weeks.

dusk /dʌsk/ noun [no plural] when it starts to get dark at the end of the day: The streetlights come on at dusk.

dust¹ /dʌst/ noun [no plural] very small bits of dirt or soil that look like a powder: There was a thick layer of dust on the table.

dust² verb to clean the dust from something with a cloth: He dusted the bookshelves.

dust·bin /'dʌstbɪn/ noun BrE a large container outside your home where you put waste so that it can be taken away; GARBAGE CAN AmE

dust·man /'dʌstmən/ noun BrE, plural dustmen /-mən/ someone whose job is to take away waste that people leave in containers outside their houses; GARBAGE COLLECTOR AmE

dust·y /'dʌsti/ adjective **dustier, dustiest** covered with dust: dusty old books

D

du·ty /'djuːti $'duti/ noun, plural duties

something that you should do because it is right or it is part of your job: *Parents* **have a duty to** *protect their children.* | *On January 10, he will begin his duties as chairman of the company.*

PHRASES

(be) on duty if a doctor, nurse, police officer etc is on duty, they are working: *I'm not* **on duty** *this evening.* | *He lost his job for drinking* **on duty**.
be off duty if a doctor, nurse, police officer etc are off duty, they are not working: *I'm afraid I can't help you – I'm* **off duty**.

du·vet /'duːveɪ $du'veɪ/ noun a thick warm cover that you put on top of you when you are in bed

DVD /ˌdiː viː 'diː/ noun a flat round object like a CD that you use on a computer or a piece of equipment called a DVD player to play films, pictures, and sounds: *'The Matrix' is finally out on DVD, priced £13.99.* ⇨ see picture on page 342

dwell /dwel/ verb, past tense and past participle **dwelt** /dwelt/ or **dwelled**;
dwell on, dwell upon to think or talk for too long about something unpleasant: *I don't want to dwell on all the details of the accident.*

dwelt a past tense and past participle of DWELL

dye¹ /daɪ/ noun a substance you can use to change the colour of hair, cloth etc

dye² verb to change the colour of something using a dye: *She dyes her hair.*

dy·nam·ic /daɪ'næmɪk/ adjective full of energy and ideas: *The new teacher is very dynamic.*

dy·na·mite /'daɪnəmaɪt/ noun [no plural] a substance that can cause powerful explosions: *They blew up the building with dynamite.*

dyn·a·sty /'dɪnəsti $'daɪnəsti/ noun, plural **dynasties** a family of rulers who controlled a country for a long time: *The Ming dynasty ruled China for 300 years.*

D

Ee

E the written abbreviation of EAST or EAST-
ERN

each /iːtʃ/

every person or thing separately: *You
have 20 minutes to answer each
question.* | *Each of her friends gave
her a present.* | *They each arrived
separately.* | *The children were given
£5 each.*

PHRASE
each other: *The two brothers hated
each other* (=each one hated the
other).

ea·ger /'iːgə $ 'iːgɚ/ *adjective*

GRAMMAR
eager to do something

if you are eager to do something,
you want to do it very much: *He was
eager to see the result of his experiment.*
—**eagerly** *adverb*: *She opened the
letter eagerly.*

ea·gle /'iːgəl/ *noun* a big wild bird with
a curved beak that eats small animals

ear /ɪə $ ɪr/ *noun*

your ears are the two things on your
head that you hear with: *She turned
and whispered something in his ear.*
⇨ *see picture at* HEAD¹

ear·ly /'ɜːli $ 'ɚli/ *adjective, adverb*
earlier, earliest

1 near the beginning of a period of
time: *It snowed in early January.* |
*The postman comes early in the
morning.*
2 before the usual or expected time:
*Hi, Jim, you're here a bit earlier than
you were yesterday.* | *I got there
early and had to wait for Debbie.*
3 near the beginning of an event, story,
process etc: *Gretzky scored early in
the game.* | *Tom Cruise's character
gets killed in the early part of the
film.*

earn /ɜːn $ ɚn/ *verb*

1 to get money from the work that you
do: *How much do you earn a week?*
2 to get something good because you
have worked hard or done something well: *Teachers have to earn
their students' respect.* | *I think
you've earned a rest!* ⇨ *see usage
note at* GAIN¹

earn·ings /'ɜːnɪŋz $ 'ɚnɪŋz/ *plural noun*
formal money that you get from working: *I
try not to spend all of my earnings.*

ear·plug /'ɪəplʌg $ 'ɪrplʌg/ *noun* one of
a pair of small pieces of rubber that you
put into your ears to keep out noise

ear·ring /'ɪərɪŋ $ 'ɪrɪŋ/ *noun* a piece of
jewellery that you fasten to your ear: *a
pair of gold earrings* ⇨ *see picture at*
JEWELLERY

ear·shot /'ɪəʃɒt $ 'ɪrʃɑt/ *noun* within
earshot, out of earshot near enough or
not near enough to hear what someone
is saying: *He waited until the teacher
was out of earshot, then he started
laughing.*

earth /ɜːθ $ ɚθ/ *noun* [no plural]

1 the PLANET that we live on: *People
used to believe the Earth was flat,
not round.* | *The blue whale is the
largest animal on earth.*
2 the dark substance on the ground
that plants and trees grow in ⇨ *same
meaning* SOIL: *He knelt on the cold,
wet earth.*

earth·quake /'ɜːθkweɪk $ 'ɚθkweɪk/
noun a sudden shaking of the earth's surface: *200 people were killed in the
earthquake.*

ease /iːz/ *noun*   1 with ease if you do

something with ease, it is very easy: *He won the race with ease.* **2 at ease** comfortable and confident in a situation: *The interviewer made me feel at ease.*

eas·i·ly /'iːzəli/ *adverb* **1** without difficulty: *You can find information easily on the Internet.* **2 easily the best, easily the biggest etc** *informal* much better, bigger etc than the others: *That's easily the funniest film I've seen this year.*

east /iːst/ *noun* **1** [no plural] the direction from which the sun rises **2 the east** the eastern part of a country or area: *We live to the east of the city.*
– **east** *adverb, adjective*: *My bedroom faces east.*

east·bound /'iːstbaʊnd/ *adjective* leading towards the east or travelling towards the east: *Police have closed the eastbound lanes of the expressway.*

Eas·ter /'iːstə $'iːstɚ/ *noun* a holiday in March or April when Christians remember Christ's death and his return to life: *I went to stay with my grandma at Easter.*

eas·ter·ly /'iːstəli $'iːstɚli/ *adjective* **1** towards the east: *The plane was heading in an easterly direction.* **2 easterly wind** an easterly wind blows from the east

east·ern /'iːstən $'iːstɚn/ *adjective* **1** in or from the east part of a country or area: *the former Communist countries of Eastern Europe* **2** also **Eastern** in or from the countries in Asia, especially China and Japan: *Eastern music*

east·ward /'iːstwəd $'iːstwɚd/ also **east·wards** /'iːstwədz $'iːstwɚdz/ *adjective, adverb* towards the east: *We drove in an eastward direction.*

eas·y¹ /'iːzi/ *adjective* **easier, easiest**

GRAMMAR
easy to do
not difficult: *some easy homework | The house **is easy to** find. | I found the exam quite **easy**. | **It's not easy to** stop smoking* (=it's difficult).

easy² *adverb* **take it easy, take things easy** *informal* to relax and not try to do too much: *At her age she should be taking it easy.*

easy·go·ing /ˌiːzi'gəʊɪŋ $ˌiːzi'goʊɪŋ/ *adjective* relaxed and calm, and not often angry or upset: *My girlfriend is*

very easygoing about me seeing my friends.

eat /iːt/ *verb* **ate** /et, eɪt $eɪt/ **eaten** /'iːtn/

1 to take food into your body through your mouth: *Most of the children eat sandwiches for lunch. | I was so hungry I just ate and ate and ate. | Do you want to go and get **something to eat*** (=some food)?
2 to have a meal: *I haven't eaten yet.*

PHRASAL VERBS
eat out
to eat in a restaurant, not at home: *My parents **eat out** a lot.*
eat up *spoken*
eat up, eat something up *spoken* to eat all of something: ***Eat up**, Holly. Dinner's almost over. | **Eat up** your stew before it goes cold.*

eaten the past participle of EAT
ec·cen·tric /ɪk'sentrɪk/ *adjective* someone who is eccentric behaves in an unusual way
– **eccentric** *noun*: *My uncle is quite an eccentric.*
– **eccentrically** /-kli/ *adverb*: *She was dressed eccentrically in a man's coat.*

ech·o¹ /'ekəʊ $'ekoʊ/ *noun, plural* **echoes** a sound that you hear again because it was made, for example, in a large empty room: *If you shout into the valley you will hear an echo.*

echo² *verb* if a sound echoes, you hear it again because it was made, for example, in a large empty room: *Her voice echoed around the hall.*

e·clipse /ɪ'klɪps/ *noun* when the sun or the moon seems to disappear. The eclipse of the sun happens when the moon passes between it and the Earth. The eclipse of the moon happens when the Earth comes between it and the sun: *a total eclipse of the sun*

eclipse

e·co·lo·gi·cal /ˌiːkə'lɒdʒɪkəl $ˌiːkə'lɑːdʒɪkəl/ *adjective* about the relationship between plants, animals, people, and the environment: *These farming methods have caused an ecological disaster.*

e·col·o·gist /ɪ'kɒlədʒɪst $ɪ'kɑːlədʒɪst/ *noun* someone who studies ecology

e·col·o·gy /ɪˈkɒlədʒi $ɪˈkɑlədʒi/ *noun* [no plural] the relationship between plants, animals, people, and the environment, or the study of this: *The ecology of the forest has been damaged by farming.*

ec·o·nom·ic /ˌekəˈnɒmɪk $ˌekəˈnɑmɪk/ *adjective* related to the way that a country makes money from its industries, businesses etc: *Can the government fix the country's economic problems?*

ec·o·nom·i·cal /ˌekəˈnɒmɪkəl $ˌekəˈnɑmɪkəl/ *adjective* using money or things carefully without wasting any: *It is more economical to buy the big packets.*
–**economically** /-kli/ *adverb*: *ways of heating your house more economically*

ec·o·nom·ics /ˌekəˈnɒmɪks $ˌekəˈnɑmɪks/ *noun* [no plural] the study of the way that a country produces money and things to sell: *I want to do economics at college.*

e·con·o·mist /ɪˈkɒnəmɪst $ɪˈkɑnəmɪst/ *noun* someone who studies economics

e·con·o·mize also **economise** *BrE* /ɪˈkɒnəmaɪz $ɪˈkɑnəˌmaɪz/ *verb* to try to spend less money or the amount of something that you use: *Try to economize on water during this dry period.*

e·con·o·my /ɪˈkɒnəmi $ɪˈkɑnəmi/ *noun*, *plural* **economies** 1 the way that money and business are organized in a country or area: *The government has promised to build a strong economy.* | *Closing the factory has affected the local economy very badly.* 2 when you use things carefully so that you do not waste anything or spend too much: *Since Dad lost his job, we've had to make economies.*

economy class /.'... ,./ *adjective* a cheap type of ticket for travel: *an economy class air ticket*

ec·sta·sy /ˈekstəsi/ *noun* [no plural] a feeling of great happiness: *He had a look of ecstasy on his face.*

ec·stat·ic /ɪkˈstætɪk/ *adjective* very happy and excited: *When Beckham scored, the crowd was ecstatic.*

edge¹ /edʒ/ *noun*

GRAMMAR
the edge of something
1 the part of something that is furthest from the middle: *Dana sat on the **edge of** the bed.* | *We walked along **the edge of** the field.* | *We stood at the water's edge and waved to the boat.*
2 the thin sharp side of a tool that you use to cut things: *Make sure the edge of the knife is sharp.*

edge² *verb* to move slowly and carefully, or to make something do this: *People were edging away from him.* | *I edged the car into the parking space.*

ed·i·ble /ˈedəbəl/ *adjective* something that is edible can be eaten: *edible mushrooms*

ed·it /ˈedɪt/ *verb* to prepare a book, film etc by correcting mistakes and removing some parts

e·di·tion /ɪˈdɪʃən/ *noun* 1 the copies of a book, newspaper etc that are all the same: *They are bringing out a new edition of the dictionary.* 2 one of a series of television or radio programmes broadcast regularly with the same name: *the 9 o'clock edition of the news*

ed·i·tor /ˈedətə $ˈedətɚ/ *noun* the person who decides what should be included in a book, newspaper, magazine etc: *an editor of a car magazine*

ed·u·cate /ˈedjʊkeɪt $ˈedʒə,keɪt/ *verb* to teach someone, usually in a school or college: *He was educated at a private school.*

ed·u·cat·ed /ˈedjʊkeɪtɪd $ˈedʒə,keɪtɪd/ *adjective* an educated person has a high standard of knowledge and education: *She is very highly educated.*

ed·u·ca·tion /ˌedjʊˈkeɪʃən $ˌedʒəˈkeɪʃən/ *noun*

GRAMMAR
the education of someone
the process of teaching or learning, usually in a school or college: *The education of small children is very important.* | *My father did not have a good education.* ⇨ see also HIGHER EDUCATION

ed·u·ca·tion·al /ˌedjʊˈkeɪʃənəl $ˌedʒəˈkeɪʃənəl/ *adjective* involved with teaching or learning: *television shows that are supposed to be educational*

eel /iːl/ *noun* a long thin fish that looks like a snake

E

ef·fect /ɪˈfekt/ noun

GRAMMAR
the effect of something
the/an effect on something
a change or result that something causes: *The **effects** of the disease are terrible.* | *What will be **the effect on** the environment?* | *The food we eat **has a** great **effect on** our health.*

PHRASES
special effects clever things that are done in a film to make things that are not real appear to exist or happen: *The **special effects** in 'Star Wars' were brilliant!*
put something into effect formal if you put a plan, idea etc into effect, you do what has been planned: *It is time to **put** our plan **into effect**.*
be in effect, come into effect formal if a law, system etc is in effect or comes into effect, it exists: *The new law **has been in effect** for a year.* | *The changes will **come into effect** immediately.*
take effect to start to have results: *The drug should **take effect** immediately.*

ef·fec·tive /ɪˈfektɪv/ adjective having the result that you want ⇨ opposite INEFFECTIVE: *an effective way to teach reading*
– **effectiveness** noun [no plural]: *They argued about the effectiveness of putting people in jail.*

ef·fec·tive·ly /ɪˈfektɪvli/ adverb in a way that gets the result you want: *She controlled the class very effectively.*

ef·fi·cient /ɪˈfɪʃənt/ adjective working well, without wasting time or energy ⇨ opposite INEFFICIENT: *You have to find an efficient way of organizing your work.*
– **efficiently** adverb: *This heats up the water very efficiently.*

ef·fort /ˈefət $ ˈefɚt/ noun

GRAMMAR
an effort to do something
1 hard work that you do when you are trying to achieve something: *It takes a lot of **effort to** find exactly the right present.* | *Edward **puts** a lot of **effort into** his homework* (=he works very hard).
2 an attempt to do something: *He failed at first, but his second effort was successful.* | *Kim **is making an effort** to lose weight.* | *In an effort*

to *reduce crime, more police are being hired.*

ef·fort·less /ˈefətləs $ ˈefɚtləs/ adjective done in a way that looks easy: *His running looks effortless.*
– **effortlessly** adverb: *She seems to learn new languages effortlessly.*

EFL /ˌiː ef ˈel/ English as a Foreign Language; the teaching of English to people who speak a different language

eg or **e.g.** /ˌiː ˈdʒiː/ an abbreviation that means 'for example': *science subjects, eg chemistry and physics*

egg /eg/ noun 1 a round object with a hard surface that contains a baby bird, insect, snake etc: *Our pet parrot has laid two eggs.* ⇨ see picture on page 344 2 an egg from a chicken, used as food: *Do you like boiled eggs?* 3 a cell produced inside a woman or female animal that can develop into a baby

egg·plant /ˈegplɑːnt $ ˈegplænt/ the American word for AUBERGINE

e·go /ˈiːgəʊ $ ˈiːgoʊ/ noun the opinion that you have about yourself: *Her remarks were not very good for my ego.*

eh /eɪ/ BrE spoken used to ask someone to say something again: *"You need a modem." "Eh?"*

eight /eɪt/ number 8

eigh·teen /ˌeɪˈtiːn/ number 18
– **eighteenth** number

eighth /eɪtθ/ number 1 8th 2 one of the eight equal parts of something; 1/8

eigh·ty /ˈeɪti/ number, plural eighties 1 80 2 **the eighties** the years between 1980 and 1989 3 **be in your eighties** to be aged between 80 and 89
– **eightieth** number: *his eightieth birthday*

ei·ther¹ /ˈaɪðə $ ˈiːðɚ/

showing a choice: *We can **either** have lunch here **or** go out.* | *Your socks must be **either** black, grey, **or** dark blue.*

either²

one of two things or people: *Helen has a British and a Canadian passport so she can live in either country.* | *I don't like **either of** them much.*

PHRASE
on either side on both sides: *There are shops on either side of the road.*

either[3] *adverb* used in negative sentences to mean 'also': *"I don't like him." "I don't either."*

e·ject /ɪ'dʒekt/ *verb* **1** *formal* to make someone leave a place, using force: *A few people were ejected from the club for fighting.* **2** to make something come out of a machine by pressing a button: *Eject the tape and turn it over.*

e·lab·o·rate /ɪ'læbərət/ *adjective* something that is elaborate has a lot of small details or parts that are connected in a complicated way: *The plot of the film was very elaborate.*
– **elaborately** *adverb*: *elaborately decorated furniture*

e·las·tic /ɪ'læstɪk/ *noun* [no plural] a material that can stretch and then go back to its usual size, used to make clothes: *These socks have elastic around the top.*

el·bow[1] /'elbəʊ $ 'elbəʊ/ *noun* the joint where your arm bends: *I've hurt my elbow.* ⇨ *see picture at* BODY

elbow[2] *verb* to push someone with your elbow: *He elbowed me in the ribs.*

el·der /'eldə $ 'eldɚ/ *adjective* someone's elder brother, daughter etc is an older one: *Her elder son is at college.*

el·der·ly /'eldəli $ 'eldɚli/ *adjective* an elderly person is old: *His parents are quite elderly.*

el·dest /'eldəst/ *adjective* the eldest child, boy etc in a family is the oldest one: *My eldest sister lives in Canada.*
– **eldest** *noun* [no plural]: *They have four children and Tom is the eldest.*

e·lect /ɪ'lekt/ *verb* to choose someone for an official position by voting: *The country elected a new government in January.*

e·lec·tion /ɪ'lekʃən/ *noun* an occasion when people vote to choose someone for an official position: *Buffy won the election for school president.*

e·lec·tric /ɪ'lektrɪk/ *adjective* something that is electric works using electricity: *an electric light* | *He plays the electric guitar.*

e·lec·tri·cal /ɪ'lektrɪkəl/ *adjective* using or concerned with electricity: *a store selling electrical equipment*

el·ec·tri·cian /ɪ,lek'trɪʃən/ *noun* someone whose job is to repair electrical equipment

e·lec·tri·ci·ty /ɪ,lek'trɪsəti/ *noun* [no plural] the power that is carried by wires and used to make lights and machines work: *Does your cooker work by gas or electricity?*

electric shock /.,.. './ *noun* a sudden painful feeling you get if you accidentally touch electricity: *I got an electric shock from my hairdryer.*

e·lec·tro·cute /ɪ'lektrəkjuːt/ *verb* to kill someone by passing electricity through their body: *He accidentally electrocuted himself when he touched the damaged wiring.* | *He was electrocuted for the murder of two children* (=killed by the State as punishment).

e·lec·tron·ic /ɪ,lek'trɒnɪk $ɪ,lek-'trɑːnɪk/ *adjective* using electricity and MICROCHIPS: *E-mail stands for electronic mail.* | *He likes electronic music.*
– **electronically** /-kli/ *adverb*: *Now we can communicate electronically.*

e·lec·tron·ics /ɪ,lek'trɒnɪks $ɪ,lek-'trɑːnɪks/ *noun* [no plural] the process of making electronic equipment, such as computers or televisions, or the study of this: *an electronics company*

el·e·gant /'eləgənt/ *adjective* graceful and attractive: *simple but elegant clothes*
– **elegantly** *adverb*: *She was dressed very elegantly.*

el·e·ment /'eləmənt/ *noun* **1** a simple chemical substance that consists of only one kind of atom **2** a small amount of something: *There's an element of risk in every sport.*

el·e·men·tary /,elə'mentri/ *adjective* simple or basic: *The teacher asked a few elementary questions.*

elementary school /..'.. ,./ also **grade school** the American word for PRIMARY SCHOOL

el·e·phant /ˈeləfənt/ noun a very large grey animal with big ears and a very long nose called a TRUNK ⇨ see picture on page 339

el·e·va·tor /ˈeləveɪtə $ ˈeləˌveɪtɚ/ the American word for LIFT²

e·lev·en /ɪˈlevən/ number 11

e·lev·enth /ɪˈlevənθ/ number **1** 11th **2** one of the eleven equal parts of something; 1/11

el·i·gi·ble /ˈelədʒəbəl/ adjective if you are eligible for something, you have the right to have it or do it: You have to be 18 to be eligible to vote.

e·lim·i·nate /ɪˈlɪməneɪt/ verb **1** to completely destroy something or someone so that it no longer exists: We can never eliminate crime from our society. **2** be eliminated if you are eliminated in a sports competition, you can no longer be in it, for example because you lost a game: We were eliminated in the very first game.

else /els/ adverb

used when talking about something or someone who is different from the one already mentioned: Can I get you anything else? | He was sitting in someone else's seat. | Where else could she be?

or else used to threaten someone: You'd better give it back **or else**!

else·where /elsˈweə $ ˈelswer/ adverb in another place or to another place: You will have to smoke that cigarette elsewhere.

ELT /ˌiː el ˈtiː/ noun English Language Teaching; the teaching of English to people whose first language is not English

e·mail or **email** /ˈiː meɪl/ noun **1** [no plural] electronic mail; a system for sending messages by computer: Do you know how to use e-mail? **2** a message sent by computer: I got an email from Josie.
– **e-mail** verb: He e-mailed me every day.

em·bark /ɪmˈbɑːk $ ɪmˈbɑrk/ verb formal **1** to get on a ship **2** embark on something to start something new: She left school to embark on a career as a model.

em·bar·rass /ɪmˈbærəs/ verb to make someone feel ashamed, stupid, or uncomfortable: My parents always embarrass me.

embarrassed

em·bar·rassed /ɪmˈbærəst/ adjective
if you feel embarrassed, you feel nervous or uncomfortable about what other people think of you: I **felt embarrassed** about my dirty shoes.

em·bar·ras·sing /ɪmˈbærəsɪŋ/ adjective
if something is embarrassing, it makes you feel embarrassed: It was very embarrassing because he heard what I said about him. | an embarrassing situation

em·bar·rass·ment /ɪmˈbærəsmənt/ noun [no plural] the feeling of being embarrassed: Eric went red in the face with embarrassment.

em·bas·sy /ˈembəsi/ noun, plural **embassies** a group of officials who live and work in a foreign country, and whose job is to help people from their own country who are also living or visiting there. The building these people work in is also called an embassy: You have to apply to the US Embassy for a visa.

em·brace /ɪmˈbreɪs/ verb formal to put your arms around someone and hold them in a loving way: He embraced his cousin warmly.

embrace

em·broi·der /ɪmˈbrɔɪdə $ ɪmˈbrɔɪdɚ/ verb to decorate cloth by sewing a picture or pattern on it: a dress embroidered with flowers

em·bry·o /ˈembriəʊ $ ˈembriˌoʊ/ noun an animal or human that has just begun to develop inside its mother's body

em·e·rald /ˈemərəld/ noun a bright green jewel

e·merge /ɪ'mɜːdʒ $ɪ'mɚdʒ/ *verb written* **1** to become known: *We are waiting for the facts to emerge.* **2** to appear or come out from somewhere: *The children emerged from their hiding place under the bed.*

e·mer·gen·cy /ɪ'mɜːdʒənsi $ɪ'mɚdʒənsi/ *noun, plural* emergencies
a dangerous situation that happens suddenly: *Make sure your children know what to do in an emergency.*

emergency room /.'... ,./ the American word for CASUALTY

emergency ser·vic·es /.'... ,.../ *noun* official organizations such as the police that deal with crimes, fires, or helping people who are badly hurt

em·i·grate /'emǝgreɪt/ *verb* to leave your own country and go to live in another country: *All of her children have emigrated to Australia.*

USAGE emigrate, immigrate
Use **emigrate** to talk about people who leave their own country to live in another country: *They tried to **emigrate to** the UK, but they were sent back to India.* Use **immigrate** to talk about people who come to a country in order to live there: *Many Cuban people have immigrated to the United States.*

em·i·nent /'emɪnǝnt/ *adjective* famous and respected: *an eminent professor*

em·i·nent·ly /'emɪnǝntli/ *adverb formal* very: *The room was eminently suitable for our purposes.*

e·mo·tion /ɪ'mǝʊʃǝn $ɪ'moʊʃǝn/ *noun*
a strong feeling such as love or hate: *Smythe showed no emotion during the trial.* | *Jennifer struggled to control her emotions.*

e·mo·tion·al /ɪ'mǝʊʃǝnǝl $ɪ'moʊʃǝnǝl/ *adjective* connected with people showing how they feel, especially when they cry: *It was a very emotional reunion.* | *Dad became quite emotional when he watched me accept my gold medal.*
–**emotionally** *adverb*: *She spoke emotionally about her father.*

e·mo·tive /ɪ'mǝʊtɪv $ɪ'moʊtɪv/ *adjective* making people have strong feelings: *She made an emotive speech about animal rights.*

em·pe·ror /'empǝrǝ $'empǝrɚ/ *noun* the ruler of an EMPIRE

em·pha·sis /'emfǝsɪs/ *noun, plural* emphases /-siːz/
GRAMMAR
an emphasis on something
the special importance or attention that you give to something: *The **emphasis** in this class is **on** fun.*

em·pha·size also **emphasise** *BrE* /'emfǝsaɪz/ *verb*
GRAMMAR
emphasize that
to say strongly that something is important: *Cobb **emphasized that** wild flowers should not be picked.* | *The teacher emphasized the importance of correct spelling.*

em·phat·ic /ɪm'fætɪk/ *adjective* said in a strong way that shows you are certain about something: *She was very emphatic that she did not like him.*
–**emphatically** /-kli/ *adverb*: *"No way!" he said emphatically.*

em·pire /'empaɪǝ $'empaɪɚ/ *noun* a group of countries that are controlled by one ruler or government

em·ploy /ɪm'plɔɪ/ *verb* to pay someone to work for you: *The company employs 250 people.* | *She was employed as a cleaner.*

em·ploy·ee /ɪm'plɔɪ-iː/ *noun* someone who is paid to work for someone else: *The canteen is for employees of the company only.*

em·ploy·er /ɪm'plɔɪǝ $ɪm'plɔɪɚ/ *noun* your employer is a person or company that pays you to work for them: *His employer allowed him to take the day off.*

em·ploy·ment /ɪm'plɔɪmǝnt/ *noun* [no plural] *formal* work that you do to earn money: *She had to leave school and find employment.*

emp·ty¹ /'empti/ *adjective* emptier, emptiest
something that is empty has nothing or no one inside ⇨ *opposite* FULL (2): *an empty bottle* | *Many of the office buildings are empty.*

E

empty² verb emptied, empties
1 also **empty** something out to remove everything that is inside a container, cupboard etc: *I'll empty the bins while you sweep the floor.* | *I emptied out my desk drawers looking for a pen.* **2** to become empty: *As soon as the lecture finished, the hall emptied.*

empty   full

empty-hand·ed /ˌ.. '../ adjective without getting anything: *I forgot to take any money to the shops and came back empty-handed.*

en·a·ble /ɪˈneɪbəl/ verb formal to make it possible for someone to do something: *His help enabled me to study at college.*

en·chant·ing /ɪnˈtʃɑːntɪŋ $ ɪnˈtʃæntɪŋ/ adjective very beautiful: *She looked enchanting.*

en·close /ɪnˈkləʊz $ ɪnˈkloʊz/ verb **1** to put something inside an envelope with a letter: *Please enclose a photograph of yourself.* **2** if an area of land is enclosed, it has a wall or fence all the way around it: *The prison yard was enclosed by high walls.*

en·clo·sure /ɪnˈkləʊʒə $ ɪnˈkloʊʒɚ/ noun formal an area that has a wall or fence all the way around it: *You must not enter the lion enclosure.*

en·core /ˈɒŋkɔː $ ˈɑŋkɔr/ noun a piece of music that a performer adds or repeats at the end of a performance because people ask for it: *The band played one of their old hits as an encore.*

en·coun·ter¹ /ɪnˈkaʊntə $ ɪnˈkaʊntɚ/ verb written if you encounter difficulties or problems, they happen and you have to do something about them: *If you encounter any difficulties, give me a call.*

encounter² noun a meeting, especially one that you did not expect or that caused problems: *They survived an encounter with a polar bear.*

en·cour·age /ɪnˈkʌrɪdʒ $ ɪnˈkɜːrɪdʒ/ verb
to give someone hope and confidence in order to persuade them to do something ⇨ opposite DISCOURAGE: *The program encourages kids to stay in school.*

en·cour·ag·ing /ɪnˈkʌrədʒɪŋ $ ɪnˈkɜːrɪdʒɪŋ/ adjective giving you hope and confidence: *She said some encouraging things about my work.*
−**encouragingly** adverb: *"It's great," he said encouragingly.*

en·cy·clo·pe·di·a also **encyclopaedia** BrE /ɪnˌsaɪkləˈpiːdiə/ noun a book that contains facts about many subjects

end¹ /end/ noun

1 the last part of a period of time, activity, book, film etc: *I get paid **at the end of** the month.* | *I finally reached **the end of** the book.*
2 the part of a place or thing that is furthest away from you: *There's a shop **at the end of** the street.* | *John dived into **the** deep **end** of the pool.* | *Hold the rope **at this end** and pull as hard as you can.*
3 when something finishes or stops existing: *The Pope asked for **an end to** the violence.* | *The war has finally **come to an end**.* | *The chairman **brought** the meeting **to an end** (=he ended it).*

PHRASE
in the end after a lot of time or discussion: ***In the end**, all that hard work was worth it.*

end² verb
if something ends, or if you end it, it finishes or stops: *World War II ended in 1945.* | *The priest ended the service with a prayer.*

PHRASAL VERB
end up
if you end up in a particular place or situation, you are in that place or situation after a series of events that you did not plan: *I didn't like him at school, but we **ended up** being really good friends.*

en·dan·ger /ɪnˈdeɪndʒə $ ɪnˈdeɪndʒɚ/ verb formal to put someone or something in a dangerous or harmful situation: *Pollution is endangering our planet.*

end·ing /ˈendɪŋ/ noun **1** the end of a story, film etc: *I like films to have a happy ending.* **2** the last part of a word: *To make a past tense you usually add the ending '-ed'.*

end·less /'endləs/ *adjective* continuing for a very long time, especially in an annoying way: *We had endless conversations about her new job.*
–**endlessly** *adverb*: *They argue endlessly.*

en·dure /ɪn'djʊə $ ɪn'dʊr/ *verb* to suffer pain or be in a difficult situation for a long time: *People had to endure terrible living conditions during the war.*

en·e·my /'enəmi/ *noun, plural* enemies
someone who hates you or who you are fighting against in a war: *Everyone likes him, he doesn't have any enemies.* | *The President has many political enemies.* | *They shot at enemy aircraft.*

en·er·get·ic /ˌenə'dʒetɪk $ ˌenə-'dʒetɪk/ *adjective* showing or using a lot of energy: *Their style of dancing is very energetic.*
–**energetically** /-kli/ *adverb*: *The teacher moved around the classroom energetically.*

en·er·gy /'enədʒi $ 'enə-dʒi/ *noun*
1 *[no plural]* the ability to do a lot of work or activity without feeling tired: *The team was excited and full of energy.* | *After I had the flu, I felt as if I had no energy.*
2 power from oil, coal etc that produces heat and makes machines work: *Energy from the sun can be used to heat homes.*

en·force /ɪn'fɔːs $ ɪn'fɔrs/ *verb* to make people obey a rule or law: *We are finding it difficult to enforce the 'no smoking' rule.*

en·gaged /ɪn'geɪdʒd/ *adjective* 1 if two people are engaged, they have agreed to get married: *Greg wants us to get engaged.* 2 *BrE* if a telephone line is engaged, it is already being used by someone; BUSY *AmE*

en·gage·ment /ɪn'geɪdʒmənt/ *noun* 1 an agreement to get married: *We are having a party to celebrate our engagement.* 2 *formal* an arrangement to do something or meet someone: *I'm sorry, I've got another engagement on that day.*

en·gine /'endʒɪn/ *noun* part of a vehicle or other machine that uses oil, petrol, electricity etc to make it move: *a car engine* ⇨ see picture on page 349

en·gi·neer /ˌendʒə'nɪə $ ˌendʒə'nɪr/ *noun* 1 someone whose job is to design roads, bridges, machines etc 2 *AmE* someone whose job is to drive trains

en·gi·neer·ing /ˌendʒə'nɪərɪŋ $ ˌendʒə'nɪrɪŋ/ *noun [no plural]* the work of designing roads, bridges, machines etc: *The course will introduce young people to engineering.*

En·glish¹ /'ɪŋglɪʃ/ *noun* 1 the language that people speak in Britain, the US, Australia etc: *Do you speak English?* 2 the English the people of England: *The English are very polite to visitors.*

English² *adjective* 1 connected with the English language 2 connected with or coming from England: *the English countryside*

en·grave /ɪn'greɪv/ *verb* to cut words or pictures into metal, stone, or glass: *a silver mug engraved with his name*

en·grossed /ɪn'grəʊst $ ɪn'groʊst/ *adjective* if you are engrossed in something, you are so interested in it that you give it all your attention: *Bill was engrossed in the newspaper.*

en·joy /ɪn'dʒɔɪ/ *verb*

GRAMMAR
enjoy doing something
1 to get pleasure from something: *The park was lovely, and I enjoyed the walk.* | *I enjoy cooking when I have time.*
2 **enjoy yourself, enjoy myself** etc to be happy and have fun: *Did you enjoy yourself at the party?*

en·joy·a·ble /ɪn'dʒɔɪəbəl/ *adjective*
something enjoyable is fun and makes you feel happy: *It's an enjoyable movie.* | *We had a very enjoyable afternoon.*

en·large /ɪn'lɑːdʒ $ ɪn'lɑrdʒ/ *verb* to make something bigger: *There are plans to enlarge the hospital.* | *I had the photograph enlarged.*

e·nor·mous /ɪ'nɔːməs $ ɪ'nɔrməs/ *adjective* very big: *an enormous amount of money*

e·nor·mous·ly /ɪˈnɔːməsli $ɪˈnɔr-
məsli/ *adverb* extremely or very much:
The film was enormously successful.

e·nough /ɪˈnʌf/

as much as is necessary: *Have we
got enough time for another
coffee?* | *We had enough money left
to buy some chocolate.* | *The car was
only big enough for four people.* |
*He's not clever enough to go to
university.* | *You don't practise your
violin enough – you should do an
hour every day.*

PHRASE
have had enough *spoken* if you have
had enough, you are tired of something and want it to stop: *I've **had
enough** of your complaining.* | *I've
had enough – I'm leaving.*

USAGE
Use **enough** before nouns: *There isn't
enough space in this office* or after adjectives or adverbs: *These jeans aren't big
enough.*

en·quire *BrE* another spelling of INQUIRE
en·quiry *BrE* another spelling of INQUIRY
en·rol *BrE*, **enroll** *AmE* /ɪnˈrəʊl $ɪnˈroʊl/
verb **enrolled, enrolling** to become a
member of a particular school, college,
class etc: *I decided to enrol on the
chemistry course.*

en·rol·ment *BrE*, **enrollment** *AmE* /ɪn-
ˈrəʊlmənt $ɪnˈroʊlmənt/ *noun* when
someone becomes a member of a particular school, college, class etc: *Enrollment is scheduled for September 3 to
16.*

en route /ˌɒn ˈruːt $ɑn ˈrut/ *adverb* on
the way to a place: *We bought a bottle of
wine en route to the party.*

en·sue /ɪnˈsjuː $ɪnˈsu/ *verb formal* to
happen soon after something, often as a
result of it: *One man pulled out a knife,
and a fight ensued.*
–**ensuing** *adjective*: *What will happen
over the ensuing months?*

en·sure /ɪnˈʃʊə $ɪnˈʃʊr/ *verb formal* to
make certain that something happens:
Please ensure that you sign the form.

en·ter /ˈentə $ˈentər/ *verb*

1 *written* to go or come into a place: *As
soon as I entered the room, I knew
something was wrong.*

2 to arrange to take part in a competi-

tion, race etc: *He decided to enter
the poetry competition.* | *The horse
was entered in the first race.*
3 to put information somewhere, such
as into a computer or a book: *Enter
your name and password, then
press 'return'.*

en·ter·prise /ˈentəpraɪz $ˈentər-
ˌpraɪz/ *noun* **1** [no plural] the ability to
think of and try new things, especially in
business: *He showed a lot of enterprise
in the way he solved the problem.* **2** a
company or business: *She got a loan to
set up her new enterprise.* **3** something new and difficult that you plan to
do: *Moving to a new city was a huge
enterprise for all of us.*

en·ter·pris·ing /ˈentəpraɪzɪŋ $ˈentər-
ˌpraɪzɪŋ/ *adjective* someone who is enterprising thinks of and does things that
are new: *Some enterprising students
set up a book-lending scheme.*

en·ter·tain /ˌentəˈteɪn $ˌentərˈteɪn/
verb if someone or something entertains
people, people enjoy watching or listening to them: *He has been entertaining
audiences for nearly 20 years.* | *They
switched on the TV to entertain the children.*

en·ter·tain·er /ˌentəˈteɪnə $ˌentər-
ˈteɪnər/ *noun* someone whose job is to
tell jokes or sing to amuse people: *a
nightclub entertainer*

en·ter·tain·ing /ˌentəˈteɪnɪŋ $ˌentər-
ˈteɪnɪŋ/ *adjective* amusing and interesting: *a lively and entertaining speech*

en·ter·tain·ment /ˌentəˈteɪn-
mənt $ˌentərˈteɪnmənt/ *noun* [no
plural]
things such as television, films, and
shows that people like to watch or
listen to: *Video games are a modern
form of entertainment.*

en·thral *BrE*, **enthrall** *AmE* /ɪnˈθrɔːl/
verb **enthralled, enthralling** to keep
someone's attention and interest
completely: *The music enthralled the
audience.*
–**enthralling** *adjective*: *an enthralling
story*

en·thu·si·ast /ɪnˈθjuːziæst $ɪnˈθu-
ziˌæst/ *noun* someone who is very interested in a particular subject or activity:
My brother is a motorbike enthusiast.

en·thu·si·as·tic /ɪn,θjuːziˈæstɪk $ ɪn,θuziˈæstɪk/ adjective

GRAMMAR
enthusiastic about something
someone who is enthusiastic about something likes it a lot and is excited about it: *Her parents were enthusiastic about the idea.*
– **enthusiastically** /-kli/ adverb: *The crowd cheered enthusiastically.*

en·thu·si·as·m /ɪnˈθjuːziæzəm $ ɪnˈθuziˌæzəm/ noun [no plural] a strong feeling of interest or excitement about something: *My teacher was full of enthusiasm for music.*

en·tice /ɪnˈtaɪs/ verb written to persuade someone to do something by offering them something nice: *The shops are already enticing customers with low prices.*
– **enticing** adjective: *an enticing suggestion*

en·tire /ɪnˈtaɪə $ ɪnˈtaɪər/ adjective whole or complete: *We spent the entire evening talking.*
– **entirely** adverb: *It was entirely my decision to leave.*

en·ti·tle /ɪnˈtaɪtl/ verb if you are entitled to something, you have the right to do or have it: *You are entitled to have your money back if you are not satisfied.*

en·trance /ˈentrəns/ noun

GRAMMAR
the entrance of/to something
the way into a place: *I'll meet you outside the main entrance of the shop.* | *near the entrance to the park*

en·tranced /ɪnˈtrɑːnst $ ɪnˈtrænst/ adjective feeling great pleasure and surprise because of something very beautiful: *We were entranced by her singing.*

en·trant /ˈentrənt/ noun formal someone who enters a competition, university, or profession

en·tre·pre·neur /ˌɒntrəprəˈnɜː $ ˌɑntrəprəˈnɜr/ noun someone who starts a company: *the British entrepreneur, Richard Branson*

en·trust /ɪnˈtrʌst/ verb formal if you entrust someone with something, you make them responsible for it: *I was entrusted with the care of the children for two hours.*

en·try /ˈentri/ noun

GRAMMAR
entry to something
1 [no plural] formal when you go into a place: *How did the thieves gain entry to the building* (=get into it)? | *Anyone wearing jeans will be refused entry* (=will not be allowed to go in).
2 plural **entries** something which someone sends to be judged in a competition: *The winning entry comes from Katie Chandler of Birmingham.*
3 plural **entries** one of a number of short pieces of writing in a book: *the last entry in her diary* | *a dictionary entry*

en·ve·lope /ˈenvələup $ ˈenvəˌloup/ noun a folded paper cover, that you put a letter in so that you can send it

en·vi·ous /ˈenviəs/ adjective wishing that you had something that someone else has: *I'm really envious of your CD collection.*
– **enviously** adverb: *"I wish I had a job like yours," she said enviously.*

en·vi·ron·ment /ɪnˈvaɪərənmənt $ ɪnˈvaɪərnmənt/ noun
1 the environment the land, water, and air that people, animals, and plants live in: *We must protect the environment.*
2 the people and things around you that affect your life: *a friendly office environment*

en·vi·ron·ment·al /ɪn,vaɪərənˈmentl $ ɪn,vaɪərnˈmentl/ adjective related to the land, water, and air: *environmental pollution*

en·vi·ron·men·tal·ist /ɪn,vaɪərənˈmentəlɪst $ ɪn,vaɪərnˈmentl-ɪst/ noun someone who wants to protect the environment

environmentally friend·ly /ˌ........ ˈ../ adjective environmentally friendly products will not harm the environment

en·vis·age /ɪnˈvɪzɪdʒ/ verb formal to think that something is likely to happen in the future: *I could envisage some problems in my new job.*

en·vy /ˈenvi/ verb envied, envies if you envy someone, you wish you had something that they have: *I envy her – her parents buy her anything she wants.*

E

—envy noun [no plural]: *I was filled with envy when my best friend won.*

ep·ic /'epɪk/ adjective an epic story or journey is very long, exciting, or impressive: *an epic journey in the Himalayas | an epic novel*

ep·i·dem·ic /ˌepə'demɪk/ noun when a disease spreads very quickly: *the AIDS epidemic*

ep·i·sode /'epəsəʊd ＄'epə,soʊd/ noun one of the parts of a television or radio story that is broadcast separately: *Another episode of 'Star Trek' is on tonight.*

ep·i·taph /'epətɑːf ＄'epə,tæf/ noun a short sentence describing someone who has died, often written on the stone over their GRAVE: *"He did his best" would be my epitaph.*

e·qual¹ /'iːkwəl/ adjective

GRAMMAR
equal to something
two things that are equal are the same size or have the same value: *Plant the seeds equal distances apart. | two apples of equal size | One inch is **equal to** 2.54 centimetres.*

PHRASE
equal rights, equal opportunities
the same legal rights or opportunities for everyone: *Women fought for **equal rights**.*

equal² verb equalled, equalling *BrE*, equaled, equaling *AmE*
1 to be as large as something else: *Four plus four equals eight.*
2 to be as good as something else: *Nothing can equal that feeling.*

equal³ noun someone with the same abilities or rights as someone else: *Young people want adults to treat them as equals.*

e·qual·i·ty /ɪ'kwɒləti ＄ɪ'kwɑləti/ noun [no plural] when people from different groups have the same rights and opportunities ⊃ opposite INEQUALITY: *sexual equality*

e·qual·ize also **equalise** *BrE* /'iːkwəl-aɪz/ verb in a team sport, to get a point or GOAL so that you have the same number as your opponents: *Germany equalized in the last few minutes of the game.*

eq·ual·ly /'iːkwəli/ adverb 1 just as

much: *Jim and his sister are equally talented.* 2 in equal parts or amounts: *We should divide the work equally.*

e·qua·tion /ɪ'kweɪʒən/ noun a statement in mathematics showing that two quantities are equal, for example $2y + 4 = 10$

e·qua·tor /ɪ'kweɪtə ＄ɪ'kweɪtɚ/ noun the equator an imaginary line around the Earth that divides it equally into its northern and southern halves

e·quip /ɪ'kwɪp/ verb equipped, equipping to provide the tools or equipment that someone needs to do something: *We were equipped with calculators for the exam.*

e·quip·ment /ɪ'kwɪpmənt/ noun [no plural]
the things that you use for a particular activity: *using the most modern scientific equipment | an expensive **piece of equipment***

USAGE
Equipment does not have a plural form: *James spent $500 on sports equipment. | The company sells computer equipment.*

e·quiv·a·lent /ɪ'kwɪvələnt/ adjective equal in amount, value, rank etc to something or someone else: *The certificate is equivalent to a High School diploma.*
—equivalent noun: *A car costs the equivalent of a year's pay.*

e·ra /'ɪərə ＄'ɪrə/ noun a period of time in history: *the post-war era*

e·rad·i·cate /ɪ'rædəkeɪt/ verb formal to destroy or remove something completely: *We want to eradicate nuclear weapons by 2030.*

e·rase /ɪ'reɪz ＄ɪ'reɪs/ verb to completely remove written or recorded information: *I erased the file from the computer.*

e·ras·er /ɪ'reɪzə ＄ɪ'reɪzɚ/ the American word for RUBBER

e·rect¹ /ɪ'rekt/ adjective, adverb in a straight upright position: *The winners stood erect on the platform.*

erect² verb formal to build something or put it in position: *It was difficult to erect the tent because of the strong winds.*

e·rode /ɪ'rəʊd ＄ɪ'roʊd/ verb if land is eroded, or if it erodes, it is gradually destroyed by the weather or by water: *The river bank has started to erode.*

e·ro·sion /ɪˈrəʊʒən $ ɪˈrəʊʒən/ *noun [no plural]* the gradual destruction of land by the weather or by water: *Planting trees will help prevent soil erosion.*

e·rot·ic /ɪˈrɒtɪk $ ɪˈrɑtɪk/ *adjective* involving or producing sexual feelings: *an erotic painting*

er·rand /ˈerənd/ *noun* a short trip somewhere, made in order to get or do something for someone: *Are there any errands I can do for you?*

er·rat·ic /ɪˈrætɪk/ *adjective* not following a regular pattern: *Your attendance at college has been rather erratic.*
– **erratically** /-kli/ *adverb*: *She was driving erratically before the accident.*

er·ror /ˈerə $ ˈerɚ/ *noun*

if you make an error, you make a mistake: *Owing to a computer error, his name was left off the list.* | *She had made several spelling errors.*

e·rupt /ɪˈrʌpt/ *verb* **1** if violence erupts, it suddenly happens: *Violence erupted during the President's speech.* **2** if a VOLCANO erupts, it sends smoke and fire into the sky

e·rup·tion /ɪˈrʌpʃən/ *noun* when a VOLCANO erupts and sends smoke and fire into the sky

escalator

es·ca·la·tor /ˈeskəleɪtə $ ˈeskəˌleɪtɚ/ *noun* moving stairs that carry people from one level of a building to another: *We took the escalator to the first floor of the store.*

es·cape¹ /ɪˈskeɪp/ *verb*

GRAMMAR
escape from somewhere
1 to succeed in getting away from an unpleasant place or situation: *He escaped from prison by making a tunnel.* | *an escaped prisoner*
2 *written* if you escape death, punish-

ment etc, you are not killed, punished etc when you could have been: *She narrowly escaped death when a tree fell on her car.*

escape

escape² *noun* when someone escapes from a place or a situation: *We made our escape while the guards were not looking.*

es·cort¹ /ɪˈskɔːt $ ɪˈskɔrt/ *verb* to go somewhere with someone in order to protect or guard them: *The police escorted him from the courtroom to the car.* | *Jeff agreed to escort her back to the hotel.*

es·cort² /ˈeskɔːt $ ˈeskɔrt/ *noun* a person or group of people that goes somewhere with someone to guard or protect them: *The President had a police escort.*

Es·ki·mo /ˈeskəməʊ $ ˈeskəˌmoʊ/ *noun* someone who comes from the far north of Canada, Alaska etc

ESL /ˌiː es ˈel/ English as a Second Language; the teaching of English to students whose first language is not English, but who live in an English-speaking country

es·pe·cial·ly /ɪˈspeʃəli/ *adverb*

used to say that something is more true of one person or thing than of other people or things: *Teenagers can get bored, especially in small towns and villages.* | *He is especially good at maths.*

es·say /ˈeseɪ/ *noun* a short piece of writing about a particular subject: *I had to write an essay on Shakespeare.*

es·sen·tial /ɪˈsenʃəl/ *adjective* important and necessary: *If you live in the country, a car is essential.* | *It's essential to phone us if you are going to be late.*

es·sen·tials /ɪˈsenʃəlz/ *plural noun* things that are important or necessary: *I packed a bag of essentials.*

es·tab·lish /ɪˈstæblɪʃ/ *verb* **1** to start

a company, organization etc that will exist for a long time: *He established the business in 1982.* **2** to find out a fact: *The police established that he was not at work that day.*

es·tab·lish·ment /ɪ'stæblɪʃmənt/ *noun formal* a place for education, training, or RESEARCH: *an educational establishment*

es·tate /ɪ'steɪt/ *noun* **1** a large area of land in the countryside that is owned by one person or organization: *The Prince has a large estate in Cornwall.* **2** *BrE* a place where a lot of the same kind of houses have been built together: *a small housing estate*

estate a·gent /.'. ,../ *noun BrE* someone whose job is to buy and sell houses and land for people; REAL ESTATE AGENT or REALTOR *AmE*

estate car /.'. ./ *noun BrE* a large car with a door at the back; STATION WAGON *AmE*

esthetic an American spelling of AESTHETIC

es·ti·mate¹ /'estəmeɪt/ *verb*

> **GRAMMAR**
> estimate that
> estimate something at some-
> thing
> estimate something to be some-
> thing
> estimate someone to do some-
> thing

to make a reasonable guess at the size, amount, or time of something: *I estimate that the job will be finished by Friday.* | *The time taken for the work is estimated at 3 weeks.* | *We estimate the cost of repairs to be $100,000.* | *He is estimated to have over $50 million.*

es·ti·mate² /'estəmət/ *noun*

> **GRAMMAR**
> an estimate of something

what someone guesses the size, amount, or time of something to be: *What is your estimate of their chances of success?*

etc or **etc.** /et 'setərə/ used at the end of a list to show that you could add similar things: *Bring a coat, hat, spare sweater etc.*

e·ter·nal /ɪ'tɜːnəl $ ɪ'tɜːnl/ *adjective*

written continuing for ever: *They made a promise of eternal love.*
−**eternally** *adverb*: *No one can look eternally young.*

e·ter·ni·ty /ɪ'tɜːnəti $ ɪ'tɜːnəti/ *noun* **1** [*no plural*] time that does not end, especially the time after you die **2** an eternity a very long time: *It was an eternity before the phone rang.*

eth·i·cal /'eθɪkəl/ *adjective* involving beliefs about what is right and wrong: *She's a vegetarian on ethical grounds.*
−**ethically** /-kli/ *adverb*: *We try to run the business ethically.*

eth·ics /'eθɪks/ *plural noun* rules that people use to decide what is right and wrong: *medical ethics*

eth·nic /'eθnɪk/ *adjective* related to a particular race of people: *people from different ethnic groups*

et·i·quette /'etɪket $ 'etɪkət/ *noun* [*no plural*] the rules of polite behaviour

EU /ˌiː 'juː/ *noun* **the EU** the European Union; a political and economic organization of European countries

eu·phe·mis·m /'juːfəmɪzəm/ *noun* a polite word or phrase that you use to avoid saying something that might offend people: *'Passed away' is often used as a euphemism for 'died'.*

eu·ro /'jʊərəʊ $ 'jʊroʊ/ *noun* a unit of money intended to be used by all the EU countries

Eu·ro·pe·an /ˌjʊərə'piːən $ ˌjʊrə-'piːən/ *adjective* from or connected with Europe: *the European Court of Justice*
−**European** *noun*: *Most of the people in my class are Europeans.*

European U·nion /ˌ.... '../ *noun* **the European Union** the EU

eu·tha·na·si·a /ˌjuːθə'neɪziə $ ˌjuθə-'neɪʒə/ *noun* [*no plural*] the practice of killing very old or ill people in a painless way, so that they will not suffer any more: *Euthanasia is illegal in most countries.*

e·vac·u·ate /ɪ'vækjueɪt/ *verb* to move people from a dangerous place to a safer place: *The police evacuated us after they received a bomb warning.*

e·vac·u·a·tion /ɪˌvækju'eɪʃən/ *noun* when people are moved from a dangerous place to a safer place: *the evacuation of children from the area of the fighting*

e·val·u·ate /ɪ'væljueɪt/ *verb formal* to decide how good or bad something or someone is by carefully considering them: *The school inspectors evaluate the quality of teaching.*

e·vap·o·rate /ɪ'væpəreɪt/ *verb* if a liquid evaporates, or if something evaporates it, it changes into steam: *Salt is produced by evaporating sea water.*

e·vap·o·ra·tion /ɪ,væpə'reɪʃən/ *noun* [no plural] the process of removing water from something, usually by heating it

evaporation

eve /iːv/ *noun* **Christmas Eve, New Year's Eve** the night or day before Christmas or New Year: *What are you doing on New Year's Eve?*

e·ven¹ /'iːvən/ *adverb*
1 used when adding something surprising: *Even Mum liked my new hair style.* | *He keeps everything, even old bus tickets.* | *He was very helpful, and even offered to drive us home.* | *The mountains always have snow on them, even in summer.*
2 used when comparing people or things: *Then he bought an even bigger car.* | *The second book is even more exciting than the first!*

PHRASES
even so in spite of this: *He knew he could pass the exam, but even so he felt nervous.*
even though although: *He kept asking her out, even though he knew she didn't like him.*

e·ven² *adjective*
1 not changing much: *The room was kept at an even temperature.* | *Try to keep an even temper when you teach small children.*
2 flat, level, or smooth: *Put the tray on an even surface.*
3 a game or competition that is even is one where the teams are equal and as good as each other: *For the first 45 minutes the game was very even.*

PHRASES
get even *informal* to hurt someone as much as they have hurt you: *He*

wanted to **get even with** the boy who had tricked him.
break even if a business breaks even, it does not lose any money, but neither does it make any money: *Many of the new dot com companies will not **break even** for many years.*
even number an even number is a number that you can divide exactly by two. For example, 2, 4, 6, and 8 are all even numbers ⇨ *opposite* ODD NUMBER

eve·ning /'iːvnɪŋ/ *noun*
1 the end of the day and the early part of the night: *We usually eat at around 7 **in the evening**.* | *Shall we meet **tomorrow evening** after work?* | *an evening performance*
2 **(Good) Evening** *spoken* used to greet someone in the evening: *Good evening, ladies and gentlemen, and welcome.*

even·ly /'iːvənli/ *adverb* divided or spread equally: *Spread the cream evenly over the cake.*

e·vent /ɪ'vent/ *noun*
1 something that happens, especially something important, interesting, or unusual: *He described the events that took place before the fight.*
2 something that has been organized, such as a party, sports game, or show: *We are organizing an event to raise money for charity.*

PHRASE
in the event of something *formal* if something happens: *In the event of a fire, leave the school building at once.*

e·vent·ful /ɪ'ventfəl/ *adjective* full of interesting or important events: *an eventful holiday*

e·ven·tu·al·ly /ɪ'ventʃuəli/ *adverb* after a long time: *We eventually arrived over three hours late.*

ev·er /'evə $ 'evɚ/ *adverb*
at any time: *Have you ever been to New York?* | *It was the best birthday I've ever had.* | *Nothing exciting ever happens here.* | *Don't ever lie to me again!*

E

ever since all the time since something happened: *She's been unhappy **ever since** she moved to this school.*

for ever always, from now: *I'd like to live here **for ever!***

USAGE
You use **ever** when you are asking a question, but not when you answer a question: *Have you ever been to America?*

ev·er·green /'evəgri:n $ 'evəˌgri:n/ *adjective* an evergreen tree or plant does not lose its leaves in winter

ev·ery /'evri/
all the people or things: *Every child has the right to go to school.* | *They cut down every tree in the garden.*

PHRASES
every day, every week etc once each day, each week etc: *He phones his girlfriend **every day**.*

every so often, every now and then *informal* sometimes, not regularly: ***Every so often** we meet up for a chat.*

USAGE every, every one, everyone
Notice that **every** and **every one** are followed by a singular verb: *Almost every house has a computer nowadays. Every one of the boats was destroyed in the storm.* **Every one** means each person or thing in a group: *I've seen every one of his films.* **Everyone** means all the people in a group: *Hello, everyone. I'd like to introduce Denise, your new teacher.*

ev·ery·bod·y /'evribɒdi $ 'evriˌbɑdi/ *pronoun*
EVERYONE

ev·ery·day /'evridei/ *adjective* ordinary, usual, or happening every day: *Make exercise part of your everyday life.*

ev·ery·one /'evriwʌn/ also **everybody** *pronoun*
every person: *She knew everyone at the party.*

ev·ery·thing /'evriθɪŋ/ *pronoun*
each thing or all things: *Everything's going to be fine.* | *He forgot about **everything else** (=all other things) when he was playing computer games.*

PHRASE
be everything to be more important than anything else: *Money **isn't** everything.*

ev·ery·where /'evriweə $ 'evriˌwer/ *adverb*
in every place or to every place: *There was broken glass everywhere.* | *Some people get taxis everywhere they go.*

ev·i·dence /'evədəns/ *noun* [no plural]

GRAMMAR
evidence (that)
evidence of something
evidence against someone

1 things that you see, hear, or discover that make you believe that something exists or is true: *There is clear **evidence that** this disease is caused by eating too much fat.* | *Have you any **evidence of** this happening?* | *She had no evidence to support her statement.*

2 in a court of law, the facts and objects that a lawyer presents to the people there in order to prove that something is true: *The gun was an important **piece of evidence**.* | *The **evidence against** him was weak.*

ev·i·dent /'evədənt/ *adjective* formal clear and easily seen: *It became evident that he was not interested in the subject.* – **evidently** *adverb*: *She was evidently ill.*

e·vil /'i:vəl/ *adjective* very cruel or bad: *an evil killer*

ev·o·lu·tion /ˌi:və'lu:ʃən $ ˌevə'lu:ʃən/ *noun* [no plural] the gradual development of something, especially types of plants and animals: *the evolution of man*

e·volve /ɪ'vɒlv $ ɪ'vɑlv/ *verb* to develop gradually: *The sun is a star that has evolved over billions of years.*

ex·act /ɪg'zækt/ *adjective*
an exact detail, description, or copy is completely correct: *I can remember his **exact** words.* | *The exact cause of the disease is not known.*

PHRASE
the exact opposite something that is completely different from another thing: *If you ask him to do something, he does **the exact opposite!***

ex·act·ly /ɪɡˈzæktli/ *adverb*

1 you use exactly to say strongly that something is completely correct, the same, right etc: *I know **exactly what** is going to happen.* | ***Where exactly** did you leave your bike?* | *I was born **exactly** two years after my sister.* | *Simon looks **exactly like** his father.*

2 *spoken* used to agree completely with someone: *"So it's a secret." "Exactly!"*

PHRASE

not exactly *spoken informal* **1)** used to say that something is not at all true: *I'm **not exactly** the world's best cook* (=I'm not a very good cook)! **2)** used to say that something is only partly true: *"Are they sisters?" "**Not exactly** – they're half-sisters."*

ex·ag·ge·rate /ɪɡˈzædʒəreɪt/ *verb*

to say that something is better, larger, worse etc than it really is: *"This dog was as big as a lion!" "Don't exaggerate!"* | *I think people exaggerate the risks of the sport.*

ex·ag·ge·ra·tion /ɪɡˌzædʒəˈreɪʃən/ *noun* a statement saying that something is better, larger, worse etc than it really is: *It would be an exaggeration to call it a disaster.*

ex·am /ɪɡˈzæm/ *noun*

a written or spoken test to discover how much you know about a particular subject, or how well you can do something. You take, sit, or do an exam: *I'm **taking** my history exam tomorrow.* | *I was amazed when I **passed** my maths exam* (=succeeded in getting a high enough mark). | *I have to **re-sit** the French oral exam tomorrow* (=do the exam again). | *She **failed** all her exams.*

ex·am·i·na·tion /ɪɡˌzæməˈneɪʃən/ *noun* **1** when someone looks at something carefully: *a medical examination* **2** *formal* an exam: *I passed all my examinations.*

ex·am·ine /ɪɡˈzæmɪn/ *verb* to look at something carefully in order to find out or decide something: *The doctor examined me, but could find nothing wrong.*

ex·am·ple /ɪɡˈzɑːmpəl $ ɪɡˈzæm-pəl/ *noun*

GRAMMAR
an example of something
something that you add to what you are saying because it explains what you are trying to say: *The video recorder is a good **example of** a product that became popular quickly.* | *I gave a few **examples of** animals that live in hot countries.* | *This is a **typical example of** 18th century architecture.*

PHRASE
for example used to add something to what you are saying in order to support your argument or opinion: *He's so odd. **For example**, he has a rat as a pet.*

ex·as·pe·rate /ɪɡˈzɑːspəreɪt $ ɪɡˈzæs-pə,reɪt/ *verb* to make you feel very annoyed: *His remarks clearly exasperated her.*
– **exasperating** *adjective*: *It's exasperating when you don't listen.*

ex·as·pe·ra·tion /ɪɡˌzɑːspəˈreɪʃən $ ɪɡˌzæspəˈreɪʃən/ *noun [no plural]* a feeling of great annoyance: *She hit the computer in exasperation.*

ex·ca·vate /ˈekskəveɪt/ *verb* to dig deeply into the ground over a large area, usually to build or find something: *Workers found an unexploded bomb while excavating the tunnel.*

ex·ca·va·tion /ˌekskəˈveɪʃən/ *noun* the activity of digging deep into the ground over a large area: *the archaeological excavation of an ancient city*

ex·ceed /ɪkˈsiːd/ *verb formal* to go or be above a particular number, amount, or limit: *Many drivers exceed the speed limit.* | *The cost of repairs will exceed $200.*

ex·cel /ɪkˈsel/ *verb formal* excelled, excelling to do something very well: *She excels in all scientific subjects.*

ex·cel·lence /ˈeksələns/ *noun [no plural]* the quality of being very good at doing something: *She won a prize for sporting excellence.*

ex·cel·lent /ˈeksələnt/ *adjective*

very good: *He's an excellent player.* | *That was an excellent film.* | *Joe's written French is excellent, but he*

▼ *does not speak the language very well.*

ex·cept¹ /ɪk'sept/ also **except for** *preposition*
not including someone or something: *Everyone was happy except Paul.* | *Put all the ingredients, **except for** the milk, in a pan.*

except² used to add something that is different and does not fit in with what you have just said: *He's always bored except when he's playing computer games* (=the only time he isn't bored is when he's playing computer games). | *I can't remember anything about the film except that it had a sad ending.*

ex·cep·tion /ɪk'sepʃən/ *noun* something that is not included in a general statement: *There are some exceptions to this rule.*

ex·cep·tion·al /ɪk'sepʃənəl/ *adjective* unusually good: *an exceptional pupil* – **exceptionally** *adverb*: *an exceptionally talented musician*

ex·ces·sive /ɪk'sesɪv/ *adjective* too much or too great: *Excessive dieting can be very harmful.*

ex·change¹ /ɪks'tʃeɪndʒ/ *noun*
in exchange for something if you get one thing in exchange for another, you give one thing and receive something else as a result: *She gave me the information I wanted **in exchange for** some food.*

exchange² *verb*
to give something to someone who gives you something similar: *They exchanged addresses.*

exchange rate /.'. ./ *noun* the value of the money of one country when you change it for the money of another country: *The exchange rate for the dollar is 5 French francs.*

ex·cit·ed /ɪk'saɪtɪd/ *adjective*
GRAMMAR
excited about/at something
very happy or interested because something good is happening or is going to happen: *Emma **was** so **excited about** the concert that she couldn't sleep.* | *He **was excited at**
▼ *the prospect of playing in the school team.*

ex·cite·ment /ɪk'saɪtmənt/ *noun* [no plural] the feeling of being excited: *There was great excitement when the music started.*

ex·cit·ing /ɪk'saɪtɪŋ/ *adjective*
something that is exciting makes you feel excited: *It was a pretty exciting game.*

ex·claim /ɪk'skleɪm/ *verb* to speak suddenly and loudly because you are surprised, excited, or angry: *"What a lovely surprise!" he exclaimed.*

ex·cla·ma·tion mark /ˌeksklə'meɪʃən ˌmɑːk $ˌeksklə'meɪʃən ˌmɑrk/ *BrE*, **exclamation point** *AmE* /ˌ..'.. ˌ./ *noun* the mark (!) that you write after words to show that something is sudden or surprising

ex·clude /ɪk'skluːd/ *verb* **1** to not allow someone to enter a place or join an organization: *Should gay men be excluded from the army?* **2** to deliberately not include something: *The price of a hotel room excludes the cost of meals.* | *The price of the car is £19,000, excluding VAT.*

ex·clu·sive /ɪk'skluːsɪv/ *adjective* expensive and only available to certain people: *an exclusive London club*

ex·clu·sive·ly /ɪk'skluːsɪvli/ *adverb* only: *She writes exclusively about her own experiences.*

ex·cur·sion /ɪk'skɜːʃən $ɪk'skɜʒən/ *noun* a short trip: *an excursion by boat to the island of Capri*

ex·cuse¹ /ɪk'skjuːz/ *verb*
1 to forgive someone for something that is not very bad: *You'll have to excuse the mess – I haven't had a chance to tidy.*
2 to allow someone not to do something that they should do: *She asked to **be excused from** games.* | *He was excused classes.*
3 to make someone's bad behaviour seem reasonable: *His situation at home doesn't excuse his violence.*

PHRASE
excuse me *spoken* **1)** used to politely get someone's attention: *Excuse me, do you need any help?* **2)** *AmE* used to ask someone to say

▼ something again: *"Have you heard from Gary?" "Excuse me?"*

excuse² /ɪkˈskjuːs/ *noun*

GRAMMAR
an excuse for something
an excuse to do something

1 a reason that you give to explain why you behaved in a particular way: *What's your **excuse for** not doing your homework? | I don't want to **make excuses**, but my train was very late this morning.*
2 a reason, often one that is not true, that you give in order to do something or avoid doing something: *He tried to think of an **excuse to** speak to her. | I often used my illness as **an excuse for** missing games at school.*

PHRASE
there's no excuse, that's no excuse *spoken* used to say that something is not acceptable: ***There's no excuse for** treating someone like that. | "I didn't mean to upset her!" "**That's no excuse!**"*

ex·e·cute /ˈeksəkjuːt/ *verb* to kill someone as an official punishment
ex·e·cu·tion /ˌeksəˈkjuːʃən/ *noun* the act of killing someone as an official punishment
ex·ec·u·tive /ɪgˈzekjətɪv/ *noun* an important manager in a company: *the chief executive*

ex·er·cise¹ /ˈeksəsaɪz $ˈeksəˌsaɪz/ *noun*
1 physical activities such as sport that you do in order to stay strong and healthy: *You should **take** more **exercise** – you're getting fat. | Walking up and down stairs is **good exercise**. | Try to **get** some **exercise** every day.*
2 a piece of work that you do in order to learn or practise something: *Do exercise 5 in your English course book.*

exercise² *verb* to do physical activities such as sport so that you stay strong and healthy: *I try to exercise each morning. | Cycling is good for exercising your leg muscles.*

ex·haust¹ /ɪgˈzɔːst/ *verb* if something exhausts you, it makes you very tired: *Looking after the kids exhausts me.*

– **exhausting** *adjective*: *a long exhausting day*
exhaust² also **exhaust pipe** /.'. ./ *noun* a pipe on a car that waste gas comes out of
ex·haust·ed /ɪgˈzɔːstɪd/ *adjective* very tired: *I was so exhausted that I fell asleep on the couch.*
ex·hib·it¹ /ɪgˈzɪbɪt/ *verb* to show something in a public place so that people can enjoy looking at it: *The paintings were exhibited in the city's main art gallery. | She exhibits her three dogs at all the big dog shows.*
exhibit² *noun* an object that is shown in a public place: *The British Museum has an enormous number of exhibits.*

ex·hi·bi·tion /ˌeksəˈbɪʃən/ *noun*

GRAMMAR
an exhibition of something

a collection of objects, paintings, photographs etc that are put in a public place so that people can enjoy looking at them: *We went to an **exhibition of** modern paintings at the art gallery.*

ex·hil·a·rat·ed /ɪgˈzɪləreɪtɪd/ *adjective* feeling very happy and excited: *The team were exhilarated at their success.*
ex·hil·a·rat·ing /ɪgˈzɪləreɪtɪŋ/ *adjective* making you feel very happy and excited: *an exhilarating helicopter ride*
ex·ile¹ /ˈeksaɪl $ˈegzaɪl/ *noun* 1 in exile if you are living in exile, you are living in a country that is not your own because the people in authority have forced you to leave your country: *political exiles* 2 someone who has been exiled: *political exiles*
exile² *verb* if someone is exiled from their country, the people in authority force them to leave it: *Napoleon was exiled to the island of Elba.*

ex·ist /ɪgˈzɪst/ *verb*

to be a real thing in the world: *I didn't know books like this existed.*

ex·ist·ence /ɪgˈzɪstəns/ *noun* when something exists: *He tried to prove the existence of God.*
ex·ist·ing /ɪgˈzɪstɪŋ/ *adjective* existing things are the ones that you use or that exist now: *The existing computer network is out of date.*

E

ex·it¹ /'egzɪt/ noun

the way out of a place: *He tried to leave the theatre but couldn't find the exit.*

exit² verb to finish using a computer PROGRAM: *Exit Windows and shut down the machine.*

ex·ot·ic /ɪg'zɒtɪk $ ɪg'zɑtɪk/ adjective something that is exotic is unusual and interesting, often because it comes from a distant place: *the exotic music of the East*

ex·pand /ɪk'spænd/ verb to become bigger ⇨ opposite CONTRACT² (1): *The world population is expanding all the time.*

ex·pect /ɪk'spekt/ verb

GRAMMAR
expect (that)
expect (someone/something) to do something

1 to think that something will happen: *The police are expecting trouble after the match.* | *I expect that Keith will be at the party.* | *We expected John to pass the exam, but he failed.* | *We're expecting to move to the States next year.*
2 to believe that someone should do something because it is fair or right: *I expect everyone to help with the clearing up.*
3 if you are expecting something, you are waiting for it to arrive: *I'm expecting a parcel.* | *She's expecting her third child* (=going to have her third baby soon).

PHRASES
I expect *spoken BrE* used to say that you think something is probably true: *I expect you've heard that I'm leaving.* | *"Do you think she'd go out with me?" "I expect so* (=she probably would)."

ex·pec·tant /ɪk'spektənt/ adjective *written* hoping that something good will happen: *Hundreds of expectant fans waited for him to appear.*
—**expectantly** adverb: *The dog looked up expectantly.*

ex·pec·ta·tion /ˌekspek'teɪʃən/ noun a strong belief or hope that something will happen: *He had no expectation of passing the exam.*

ex·pe·di·tion /ˌekspə'dɪʃən/ noun a carefully organized journey to a place for a particular purpose: *an expedition to the South Pole*

ex·pel /ɪk'spel/ verb expelled, expelling to officially order someone to leave a school, organization, or country: *The head teacher has the power to expel pupils who behave badly.*

ex·pense /ɪk'spens/ noun the amount of money you have to spend on something: *the expense involved in travelling abroad* | *living expenses*

ex·pen·sive /ɪk'spensɪv/ adjective

something that is expensive costs a lot of money ⇨ opposite CHEAP, IN-EXPENSIVE: *We can't afford this – it's too expensive.* | *a very expensive car*

ex·pe·ri·ence¹ /ɪk'spɪəriəns $ ɪk-'spɪriəns/ noun

GRAMMAR
experience of something

1 [no plural] the things that you learn when you do a particular job or activity: *The new principal has a lot of experience.* | *I gained a lot of valuable experience from working at the hospital.* | *Do you have any experience of working with children?*
2 something that happens to you: *Pam had some very bad experiences in the army.* | *It was his first experience of flying.*

experience² verb *formal* to be affected by something: *He experienced some pain in his leg.*

ex·pe·ri·enced /ɪk'spɪəriənst $ ɪk-'spɪriənst/ adjective an experienced person has a lot of skill or knowledge about a particular job because they have done it for a long time ⇨ opposite INEXPERI-ENCED: *a very experienced soldier*

ex·per·i·ment¹ /ɪk'sperəmənt/ noun

a scientific test that you do in order to discover or prove something: *We did an experiment to show the effect that acid has on metal.*

ex·per·i·ment² /ɪk'sperəˌment/ verb to try using different things in order to find out what they are like: *Many young people experiment with drugs.*

ex·pert /'eksp3ːt $'ekspɚt/ *noun* someone with special skills or knowledge: *Bomb experts managed to make the device safe.*
– expert *adjective: an expert sailor*

ex·per·tise /ˌeksp3ː'tiːz $ˌekspɚ'tiz/ *noun [no plural]* special skills or knowledge: *legal expertise*

ex·pire /ɪk'spaɪə $ɪk'spaɪɚ/ *verb formal* if a legal agreement or document expires, the period of time in which you can use it ends: *My passport expires in two weeks.*

ex·plain /ɪk'spleɪn/ *verb*

> **GRAMMAR**
> **explain how/why/what**
> **explain that**
> **explain something to someone**

1 to tell someone about something so that they can understand it: *I tried to **explain how** to play the game.* | *He **explained** the situation **to** me.*

2 to say why something happened: *I've already **explained why** I was late.* | *William **explained that** he had forgotten his key.* | *I just can't **explain it** (=I don't know why it happened).*

3 if a fact explains something, people accept that it is the reason for it: *This **explains why** the treatment only works with some patients.*

ex·pla·na·tion /ˌeksplə'neɪʃən/ *noun*

> **GRAMMAR**
> **an explanation of something**
> **an explanation for something**

the reason for something happening, or what someone says or writes about something that lets other people understand it: *She **gave us** a short **explanation of** the rules before we started.* | *There must be an **explanation for** these unusual results.*

ex·pli·cit /ɪk'splɪsɪt/ *adjective* clear or detailed: *The film contains explicit sex scenes.* | *explicit instructions*

ex·plode /ɪk'spləʊd $ɪk'sploʊd/ *verb* if something explodes, it breaks apart suddenly and violently, causing a loud noise and a lot of damage: *A bomb has exploded in the shopping centre.*

ex·ploit /ɪk'sploɪt/ *verb* to unfairly use someone's ideas, time, work etc without

rewarding them for it: *The company was accused of exploiting workers.*

ex·ploits /'eksploɪts/ *plural noun written* your exploits are the brave or interesting things you have done: *My father loved telling us about his exploits in the army.*

ex·plo·ra·tion /ˌeksplə'reɪʃən/ *noun*

> **GRAMMAR**
> **the exploration of something**

when someone travels through a new or strange place to discover what it is like: *his **exploration of** the Antarctic*

ex·plore /ɪk'splɔː $ɪk'splɔr/ *verb* to travel through a new or strange place to discover what it is like: *They spent the afternoon exploring the town.*

ex·plo·rer /ɪk'splɔːrə $ɪk'splɔrɚ/ *noun* someone who travels to places that no one has ever been to

explosion

ex·plo·sion /ɪk'spləʊʒən $ɪk'sploʊ-ʒən/ *noun* when something explodes, or the loud noise it makes: *People heard the explosion five miles away.*

ex·plo·sive /ɪ'spləʊsɪv $ɪk'sploʊsɪv/ *noun* a substance that can cause an explosion

ex·port¹ /ɪk'spɔːt $ek'spɔrt/ *verb* to send and sell things to another country ⇨ *opposite* IMPORT¹: *The weapons were exported illegally.*
– exporter *noun*

ex·port² /'ekspɔːt $'ekspɔrt/ *noun* the business of selling things to another country ⇨ *opposite* IMPORT²: *We produce computers for export.* | *Cloth is one of India's main exports.*

ex·pose /ɪk'spəʊz $ɪk'spoʊz/ *verb formal* to uncover something so that it can be seen: *Do not expose your skin to the sun for too long.*

ex·po·sure /ɪk'spəʊʒə $ɪk'spoʊʒɚ/ *noun* when someone is not protected from a harmful situation or substance: *Exposure to tobacco smoke can harm your children.*

ex·press[1] /ɪk'spres/ *verb* to tell people what you think or feel: *I want to express my thanks to all of you.* | *Joe finds it difficult to express his feelings.*

express[2] *noun, plural* **expresses** also **express train** /.'. ./ a fast train which stops at only a few stations

ex·pres·sion /ɪk'spreʃən/ *noun*
1 a word or phrase that has a particular meaning: *What does the expression 'by yourself' mean?*
2 the way that your face shows how you feel: *The doctor's expression was serious.* | *Rich looked at me with an expression of surprise.*

ex·pres·sive /ɪk'spresɪv/ *adjective written* showing what someone thinks or feels: *She had expressive brown eyes.*

ex·press·way /ɪk'spreswei/ *noun AmE* a very wide road, used for travelling fast between cities

ex·qui·site /ɪk'skwɪzɪt/ *adjective* very beautiful and delicate: *exquisite jewellery*
–**exquisitely** *adverb*: *The room was exquisitely decorated.*

ex·tend /ɪk'stend/ *verb* 1 to continue over a particular distance or period of time: *The forest extends to the mountains.* 2 to make something bigger or longer: *We had the house extended to give ourselves an extra room.*

ex·ten·sion /ɪk'stenʃən/ *noun* 1 a part that you add to a building to make it bigger: *There's an extension at the back of the house.* 2 a telephone that you use at work, which is part of the company's larger telephone system: *What's your extension number?*

ex·ten·sive /ɪk'stensɪv/ *adjective* large in amount or area: *The bombing caused extensive damage* (=a lot of damage).

ex·tent /ɪk'stent/ *noun [no plural]* the size, amount, or importance of something: *We are trying to discover the extent of the problem.*

ex·te·ri·or /ɪk'stɪəriə $ ɪk'stɪriɚ/ *noun* the outside surface of something ⇨ *opposite* INTERIOR: *The exterior of the church was badly damaged.*

ex·ter·nal /ɪk'stɜːnl $ ɪk'stɚnl/ *adjec-* tive on the outside or related to the outside of something ⇨ *opposite* INTERNAL: *the external walls of the house*

ex·tinct /ɪk'stɪŋkt/ *adjective* a type of animal or plant that is extinct no longer exists

ex·tinc·tion /ɪk'stɪŋkʃən/ *noun [no plural]* when a type of animal or plant no longer exists: *The white tiger is facing extinction.*

ex·tin·guish·er /ɪk'stɪŋgwɪʃə $ ɪk'stɪŋgwɪʃɚ/ *a* FIRE EXTINGUISHER

ex·tra[1] /'ekstrə/ *adjective, adverb* more than the usual amount: *Can I have extra fries with my burger?* | *You have to pay extra for a room with a sea view.*

ex·tract[1] /ɪk'strækt/ *verb formal* to remove something from a place: *I had two teeth extracted by the dentist.*

ex·tract[2] /'ekstrækt/ *noun* a small part of a story, poem, song etc: *She read an extract from her latest book.*

ex·tra·cur·ric·u·lar /ˌekstrəkə'rɪkjələ $ ˌekstrəkə'rɪkjələɚ/ *adjective* extracurricular activities are extra activities that students do, which are not part of the work they usually do in school or college

ex·traor·di·na·ry /ɪk'strɔːdənəri $ ɪk'strɔːrdn,eri/ *adjective* strange, unusual, or surprising: *David told us an extraordinary story.* | *It's extraordinary how well she is doing.*

ex·trav·a·gant /ɪk'strævəgənt/ *adjective* spending or costing too much money: *He has an extravagant lifestyle.* | *Don't be so extravagant with water.*

ex·treme[1] /ɪk'striːm/ *adjective* 1 very great: *Many rivers froze in the extreme cold.* 2 extreme opinions are very strong and unusual: *Some of her ideas are very extreme.* 3 farthest away from the middle of a place: *in the extreme south of the country*

extreme[2] *noun* something that is very different from what is normal or usual: *The animals have to cope with extremes of temperature.*

ex·treme·ly /ɪk'striːmli/ *adverb* very: *I am extremely angry with you.*

E

ex·tro·vert also **extravert** /'ekstrə-vɜːt $ 'ekstrə,vɚt/ *noun* someone who is confident and enjoys being with other people ⇨ *opposite* INTROVERT

eye /aɪ/ *noun*

your eyes are the two things in your face that you see with: *Paul has green eyes and brown hair.* | *She* **closed her eyes** *and went to sleep.* | *You can* **open your eyes** *now.* ⇨ *see picture at* HEAD[1]

PHRASES

keep an eye on someone/something to watch what someone or something does in order to stop something bad happening: *I'll* **keep an eye on** *the baby while you go to the shop.* | **Keep an eye on** *that soup for me, please – I don't want to burn it.*

keep your eyes open to watch carefully so that you will notice something: **Keep your eyes open for** *a petrol station.*

in someone's eyes if something is true, important, wrong etc in someone's eyes, they think it is true etc, although other people may not: *In Steve's* **eyes**, *football is the most important thing in the world.*

cannot take your eyes off someone/something to keep looking at someone you find attractive or something you find interesting: *Drew* **couldn't take his eyes off** *Libby all evening.*

set eyes on someone, lay eyes on someone to see someone for the first time: *As soon as I* **set eyes on** *Ricky, I knew we would get married.*

eye·brow /'aɪbraʊ/ *noun* your eyebrows are the lines of short hairs above your eyes ⇨ *see picture at* HEAD[1]

eye·lash /'aɪlæʃ/ *noun, plural* eyelashes your eyelashes are the small hairs that grow on the edge of your eyelids ⇨ *see picture at* HEAD[1]

eye·lid /'aɪlɪd/ *noun* your eyelids are the pieces of skin that cover your eyes when you close them

eye·shad·ow /'. ,../ *noun* [no plural] a coloured substance that women put on their eyelids ⇨ *see picture at* MAKE-UP

eye·sight /'aɪsaɪt/ *noun* [no plural] how well you can see: *She has very good eyesight.*

eye·sore /'aɪsɔː $ 'aɪsɔr/ *noun* a very ugly building

E

Ff

F the written abbreviation of FAHRENHEIT

fab·ric /'fæbrɪk/ noun cloth: *beautiful cotton fabrics*

fab·u·lous /'fæbjələs/ adjective informal extremely good: *We had a fabulous holiday!*

face¹ /feɪs/ noun

the front part of your head, where your eyes, nose, and mouth are: *You have a beautiful face. | I washed my hands and face. | He had a worried look **on** his **face**.*

PHRASES

make a face, pull a face to make your face have a funny or rude expression: *We **made faces at** the people in the car behind.*

someone's face fell if someone's face fell, they suddenly looked very disappointed: *My mother's **face fell** when I told her I'd failed all my exams.*

keep a straight face to stop yourself from smiling or laughing: *I tried hard to **keep a straight face**, but she looked really funny.*

face to face if two people do something face to face, they meet and speak to each other directly: *I'd like to **speak with** you **face to face** rather than on the phone.*

on the face of it if something seems true on the face of it, it seems true but it might not be: *On the face of it, it sounds like a very good job.*

to someone's face if you say something to someone's face, you say it directly to them rather than to someone else: *He called me a liar **to my face**.*

face² verb

1 if you face a bad situation or problem, you have to accept it or deal with it: *The President is facing a political crisis. | She must face the fact that she will never walk again.*

2 if you face something, you have the front of your body turned towards it: *Turn around and face the wall.*

3 if you have to face someone, you have to talk to them even though you feel upset, nervous, or embarrassed: *How can I ever face Stephen again!*

PHRASES

be faced with something if you are faced with something difficult, you have to do or deal with it: *I was **faced with** an impossible decision.*

can't face doing something spoken if you can't face doing something, you feel that you cannot do it because it is too unpleasant: *I **can't face** going out today.*

face up to something to accept or deal with something difficult or unpleasant instead of ignoring it: *We must **face up to** this problem.*

face·lift /'feɪslɪft/ noun a medical operation to make your face look younger by removing loose skin

face val·ue /ˌ. ˈ../ noun take something at face value to accept something without thinking that it might not be as good as it seems

fa·cil·i·ties /fə'sɪlətiz/ plural noun rooms, equipment, or services that are available in a place: *The school has very good sporting facilities.*

fact /fækt/ noun

GRAMMAR
the fact that
a fact about something
the facts in/of something

something that you know is true or that you know has happened: *They won't make a decision until they* know all the facts. | Children need to learn the **facts about** drugs. | The jury needs to examine the **facts in** the case. | The **facts of** what happened can no longer be hidden. | John mentioned **the fact that** his family was from Germany.

PHRASES

in fact, as a matter of fact especially spoken **a)** say this when you are adding information to what you are saying: His mother just got married again; **in fact**, this is her third marriage. | **As a matter of fact**, I started working when I was sixteen. | **In fact**, the two schools have worked together on this project. **b)** say this when you are correcting what someone else thinks: "Isn't Alice a friend of yours?" "No, **as a matter of fact** I've just met her." | People think Ian's family is rich, but **in fact** they're not. **c)** say this to emphasize that something is true even when it is surprising: **As a matter of fact** it's cheaper to fly than to take the train. | She was, **in fact**, terrified of meeting new people.

the fact is (that) use this to show what your main point is, especially when it shows what is really true in a situation: People just want to turn on a computer and use it, but **the fact is that** computers are complicated machines. | I wanted to do it, but **the fact is**, I was scared.

fac·tor /ˈfæktə $ ˈfæktɚ/ noun one of several things that affect a situation or something that happens: The bad weather was an important factor in the crash.

fac·to·ry /ˈfæktəri/ noun, plural **factories** a building where workers make large numbers of things to be sold: She **works in a** chocolate **factory**. | There was a fire **at a** carpet **factory** just outside the city. | a group of **factory workers**

fac·tu·al /ˈfæktʃuəl/ adjective based on facts: He gave us a factual account of what happened.

fac·ul·ty /ˈfækəlti/ noun, plural **faculties** **1** a group of university departments: the Faculty of Engineering **2** the ▼

faculty AmE all the teachers in a school or college

fad /fæd/ noun something that is popular for only a short time: Most of her special diets are just fads.

fade /feɪd/ verb **1** if clothes or coloured objects fade, they gradually lose their colour or brightness: The curtains have faded. | Her jeans had faded to a very pale blue. **2** also **fade away** written to become weaker and gradually disappear: Hopes of an end to the war are fading. | The memory of that day will never fade away.

fag /fæg/ noun BrE informal a cigarette

Fah·ren·heit /ˈfærənhaɪt/ noun [no plural] a system for measuring temperature, in which water freezes at 32° and boils at 212°

fail¹ /feɪl/ verb

GRAMMAR
fail to do something

1 to not pass a test or exam: She **failed** all her **exams**. | If you fail, you can take the test again.

2 to not be successful: Doctors **failed to** save the young girl's life. | The attempt to save the ship failed.

3 if a machine or a part of someone's body fails, it stops working: If one of the plane's engines fails, the other engine will keep the plane flying. | Her eyesight is beginning to fail.

fail² noun **without fail** **a)** if you do something without fail, you always do it: She visits her aunt every Wednesday, without fail. **b)** used to tell someone firmly that they must do something: You must all give your essays to me by Wednesday, without fail!

fail·ing /ˈfeɪlɪŋ/ noun a fault or weakness that someone has: His only failing is that he's always late!

fail·ure /ˈfeɪljə $ ˈfeɪljɚ/ noun

GRAMMAR
failure to do something
the failure of something

1 when you do not do something that you planned or wanted to do: He went to Australia after his **failure to** get a job in England. | We were very disappointed by **the failure of** the project. | The doctor said the operation had a high risk of failure (=was very likely to fail).

F

2 when you do not do something that you should do: *The accident was caused by the train driver's **failure to** notice the red signal light.*
3 when a machine or part of your body stops working: *The plane crashed because of **engine failure**.* | *He died of **heart failure**.*
4 someone or something that is not successful: *You always make me feel like a failure.* | *The party was a complete failure – no one came.*

faint¹ /feɪnt/ *adjective* **1** a faint smell, sound, or colour is not very strong: *a faint smell of perfume* **2** if you feel faint, you feel weak and as if you are about to become unconscious: *It was very hot, and I began to feel a bit faint.* **3** **not have the faintest idea** to not know something at all: *I haven't got the faintest idea where she is!*

faint² *verb* to become unconscious for a short time: *Some people faint when they see blood.*

fair¹ /feə $ fer/ *adjective*
1 reasonable and acceptable ⇨ opposite UNFAIR: *It's not fair to expect me to do all the work.* | *It doesn't seem fair that some people have so much money!* | *Is £100 a fair price for a bike?*
2 treating everyone in an equal way, or in a way that is right according to a law or rule: *He did not get a fair trial.*
3 fair hair or skin is light in colour: *She had blue eyes and long fair hair.*

fair² *noun* an outdoor event where there are large machines to ride on and games to play: *Mum, can we go to the fair?*

fair·ly /'feəli $ 'ferli/ *adverb*
1 in a reasonable or equal way: *Does your teacher treat everyone fairly?* | *We must share the money out fairly.*
2 more than a little, but not very ⇨ same meaning QUITE (1) *BrE*: *Matt is fairly good at tennis.* | *I am fairly sure that she will come.*

fai·ry /'feəri $ 'feri/ *noun, plural* **fairies** a creature in children's stories that looks like a small person with wings

fairy tale /'.. ,./ *noun* a story for young children in which magical things happen

faith /feɪθ/ *noun* **1** [no plural] if you have faith in someone or something, you believe that you can trust them: *I have great faith in Fergus.* **2** [no plural] belief and trust in God: *Her strong faith helped her to cope.* **3** a religion: *the Jewish faith*

faith·ful /'feɪθfəl/ *adjective* **1** continuing to support a person or an idea ⇨ same meaning LOYAL: *The group has many faithful supporters.* **2** if you are faithful to your husband or wife, you do not have a sexual relationship with anyone else

faith·ful·ly /'feɪθfəli/ *adverb* **1** in a faithful way: *She supported him faithfully.* **2** **Yours faithfully** *BrE* the usual polite way of ending a formal letter which begins 'Dear Sir' or 'Dear Madam'

fake¹ /feɪk/ *noun* a copy of something valuable that someone makes and pretends is real: *The painting was a fake.*

fake² *adjective* made to look like something real: *a fake leather coat*

fake³ *verb* **1** to pretend: *He wasn't really upset – he was just faking.* **2** to make a copy of something and pretend it is real: *Someone had faked my signature.*

fall¹ /fɔːl/ *verb* **fell** /fel/ **fallen** /'fɔːlən/

GRAMMAR
fall into/over/off etc something
1 to drop down towards the ground: *The rain was falling heavily.* | *I slipped and **fell onto** the ice.* | *She danced round and round until she **fell over**.* | *I hurt my knee when I **fell off** my bike.* | *The letter **had fallen down** behind the desk.* ⇨ see picture on page 340
2 if an amount or level falls, it becomes less or lower: *Computer prices are falling all the time.*

PHRASES
fall asleep to start to sleep: *She finally **fell asleep** after midnight.*
fall in love to begin to love someone: *My parents **fell in love** when they were sixteen.* | *I think I'm **falling in love with** you.*
be falling to pieces, be falling to bits *informal* if something is falling to pieces or falling to bits, it is in a very bad condition because it is very old: *I*

▼ *need some new trainers – this pair is **falling to bits**.*

PHRASAL VERBS

fall apart
to separate into small pieces: *When I opened the book, it **fell apart**.*

fall behind
to not make as much progress as other people: *She **is falling behind** in her school work.*

fall for
fall for someone to start to love someone you think is attractive: *I **fell for** George the first time I met him.*

fall out
to have a quarrel with a friend or someone you know well: *Those girls **are** always **falling out with** each other.*

fall² *noun*

GRAMMAR
a fall in something

1 when someone falls: *My grandma **had a fall** and broke her leg.*
2 when an amount or level becomes less or lower ➪ opposite RISE² (1): *There has been **a fall in** the number of people killed on the roads.*
3 when someone or something is defeated or loses power ➪ opposite RISE² (2): *the fall of the Roman empire*
4 *AmE* AUTUMN: *We're getting married **in the fall**.*

fallen the past participle of FALL¹

false /fɔːls/ *adjective*

1 not true or correct: *He gave false information to the police. | He may be using a false name. | The Second World War started in 1939 – true or false?*
2 a false object is not real, although it looks real: *She was wearing false nails. | false teeth*
3 not sincere or honest: *Her enthusiasm seemed false.*

PHRASE
false alarm when you think something bad is going to happen, but then it does not happen: *They warned us that a storm might be coming, but it was a false alarm.*

fame /feɪm/ *noun* [no plural] when everyone knows about you: *Appearing in a*

television series brought him instant fame.

fa·mil·i·ar /fəˈmɪliə $ fəˈmɪljɚ/ *adjective*

GRAMMAR
familiar to someone
familiar with something

1 if something is familiar, you recognize it because you have seen or heard it before: *Do any of these people **look familiar to** you? | His face **is** vaguely **familiar** (=I know his face, but not very well). | 'Tina Jones' – that name **sounds familiar**. | It was nice to see some **familiar faces** (=people I know) again.*
2 if you are familiar with something, you know it well: *I am very **familiar with** London – I've lived there all my life.*

fa·mil·i·ar·i·ty /fəˌmɪliˈærəti/ *noun* [no plural] when you know something well or know a lot about it: *It's useful to have some familiarity with computers.*

fam·i·ly /ˈfæməli/ *noun, plural* families
a group of people who are related to each other, especially parents and their children: *There are four girls and two boys **in my family**. | Who is the oldest **member of** your **family**? | a **family of** four (=a family with four people in it)*

PHRASES
start a family to have your first child: *We're too young to **start a family**.*
run in the family if a quality or an illness runs in the family, several members of the same family have it: *Bad eyesight **runs in the family**.*

fam·ine /ˈfæmɪn/ *noun* when a large number of people become ill and die because they do not have enough food

fa·mous /ˈfeɪməs/ *adjective*

GRAMMAR
famous for something

a famous person or thing is one that everyone knows about: *Many famous actors live in Beverly Hills. | Italy **is famous for** its good food.*

fan¹ /fæn/ *noun* **1** someone who likes a particular sport, kind of music, actor etc very much: *a rugby fan | My brother's*

fans

a big fan of Madonna. **2** a machine, or a flat object that you wave, which makes the air move so that you feel less hot

fan² verb **fanned, fanning; fan yourself** to wave something to make the air near you move, so that you feel less hot: *She fanned herself with her hat.*

fa·nat·ic /fə'nætɪk/ noun **1** someone who has very strong and unreasonable beliefs about religion or politics **2** someone who likes something very much: *a football fanatic*

fan·cy¹ /'fænsi/ adjective **fancier, fanciest** special or unusual, not ordinary: *She didn't like wearing fancy clothes.* | *He took her to a fancy restaurant.*

fancy² verb BrE informal **fancied, fancies** **1** to want something: *Do you fancy going to the cinema?* **2** to feel sexually attracted to someone: *My brother fancies you!*

fancy dress /ˌ.. './ noun [no plural] BrE clothes that make you look like a different person and that you wear for fun or for a party

fan·fare /'fænfeə $ 'fænfer/ noun a short piece of music that is played loudly to introduce an important person or event

fang /fæŋ/ noun an animal's fangs are its long sharp teeth

fan·ta·size also **fantasise** BrE /'fæntəsaɪz/ verb to imagine that something pleasant is happening to you

fan·tas·tic /fæn'tæstɪk/ adjective informal extremely good or enjoyable: *It's a fantastic film!*

fan·ta·sy /'fæntəsi/ noun, plural **fantasies** something that you think about that is pleasant but unlikely to happen: *I had fantasies about becoming a famous actress.*

far¹ /faː $ far/ adverb **further** /'fɜːðə $ 'fɚðɚ/ or **farther** /'faːðə $ 'farðɚ/ **furthest** /'fɜːðəst $ 'fɚðəst/ or **farthest** /'faːðəst $ 'farðəst/

1 used to talk about distance: *We live not far from the station* (=not a great distance from the station). | *How far is it to your house* (=what is the distance between here and your house)? | *I want to get as far away from this place as possible.* | *I can't walk any further – I'm too tired.*

2 very much: *He's far more intelligent* (=much more intelligent) *than I am.* | *It's far too hot to go running.*

PHRASES

spoken **as far as I know** used when you think something is true but are not sure about it: *As far as I know, they still live in Cambridge.*

so far until now: *I've understood everything so far.*

USAGE

When you are talking about distances, you can use **far** in questions and negative sentences: *How far is it to the sea?* | *It's not very far.* You can also use **far** after 'too', 'as', and 'so': *It's too far to walk.* | *I ran as far as I could.* | *I wish he didn't live so far away.* But do not use **far** in positive sentences. For example don't say: *It's far to London from here.* Say: *It's a long way to London from here.*

far² adjective
furthest away: *The principal's office is at the far end of the corridor.* | *I could see the others on the far side of the field.*

farce /faːs $ fars/ noun **1** an event or situation that is very badly organized **2** a funny play in which a lot of silly things happen

fare /feə $ fer/ noun the price that you pay to travel by train, plane, bus etc: *a company that offers cheap air fares*

fare·well /feə'wel $ fer'wel/ noun formal goodbye

far-fetched /ˌ. './ adjective a story that is far-fetched is very strange and not likely to be true

farm¹ /faːm $ farm/ noun an area of land where people keep animals or grow food: *a large pig farm* ⇨ see picture on page 348

farm² verb to use land for growing food and keeping animals

farm·er /'fɑːmə $ 'fɑrmɚ/ noun someone who owns a farm or is in charge of a farm

farther a COMPARATIVE form of FAR

farthest a SUPERLATIVE form of FAR

fas·ci·nate /'fæsəneɪt/ verb if something fascinates you, you think it is extremely interesting: *Computers have always fascinated me.*

fas·ci·nat·ing /'fæsəneɪtɪŋ/ adjective extremely interesting: *This is a fascinating book.*

fas·ci·na·tion /ˌfæsə'neɪʃən/ noun [no plural] when you think that something is extremely interesting: *He has a fascination for old books.*

fas·cis·m /'fæʃɪzəm/ noun [no plural] an extreme political system in which the state has complete power and controls everything

fas·cist /'fæʃɪst/ noun someone who supports fascism

fash·ion /'fæʃən/ noun
the style of clothes, hair etc that is popular at a particular time: *The latest fashion is to wear skirts over trousers.* | *Even young children are now becoming interested in fashion.* | *a fashion magazine*

PHRASES
be in fashion to be popular at a particular time: *Short skirts are always in fashion.* | *Long hair is back in fashion.*
be out of fashion to no longer be popular: *That haircut is just so out of fashion now.* | *These hats went out of fashion years ago!*

fash·ion·a·ble /'fæʃənəbəl/ adjective something that is fashionable is popular at a particular time ⇨ opposite UNFASHIONABLE: *Short hair is fashionable for men now.*

fast¹ /fɑːst $ fæst/ adjective
1 moving or happening quickly ⇨ opposite SLOW¹ (1): *He has always loved fast cars.* | *This computer is much faster than my old one.* | *He is the fastest runner in the world.*
2 a clock that is fast shows a time that is later than the real time ⇨ opposite SLOW¹ (2): *That clock is two minutes fast.*

fast² adverb
quickly ⇨ opposite SLOWLY: *I can't run very fast.* | *You have to work faster.*

PHRASES
be fast asleep to be completely asleep: *The children are fast asleep in bed.*
be stuck fast to be completely stuck somewhere and unable to move: *The car was stuck fast in the sand.*

fast³ verb to eat no food or very little food for a period of time, especially for religious reasons

fas·ten /'fɑːsən $ 'fæsən/ verb

GRAMMAR
fasten something to/onto something
1 if you fasten something, you join together the two sides of it so that it is completely closed: *I can't fasten the zip of these trousers.* | *Fasten your seat belt – the plane is about to take off.*
2 if you fasten something to something else, you put it on the other thing in a firm way, so that it will stay connected: *She fastened a rope to the front of the boat.* | *He fastened the flower onto the side of her hat.*

fas·ten·ing /'fɑːsənɪŋ $ 'fæsənɪŋ/ noun something that you use to hold another thing closed

fast food /'. ./ noun [no plural] hot food that a restaurant cooks and serves very quickly to customers

fast-for·ward /ˌ. '../ verb if you fast-forward a TAPE, you wind it forward quickly without playing it

fat¹ /fæt/ adjective **fatter, fattest**
1 someone who is fat is too wide and round ⇨ opposite THIN (1): *I'm too fat – I must try to eat less chocolate.* | *a small fat man* ⇨ see picture on page 353
2 something that is fat is thick or wide: *a big fat book* | *a fat wallet full of money*

USAGE fat, overweight, large, plump, obese
It is not polite to say that someone is **fat**. It is more polite to say that someone is **overweight** or **large**. In American English, you can also say that someone is **heavy**.

You can use **plump** too, but mostly about women and children. **Obese** is a formal or medical word for **fat**.

fat² noun [no plural] **1** the substance under the skin of people and animals which helps to keep them warm **2** an oily substance that some foods contain: *Doctors tell us we should eat less fat.*

fa·tal /'feɪtl/ adjective something that is fatal causes someone's death: *a fatal road accident*

fate /feɪt/ noun **1** someone's fate is what happens to them: *The government will decide the fate of the refugees.* **2** [no plural] a power that, some people believe, controls what happens to people in their lives: *Fate brought him back to London later that year.*

fa·ther /'fɑːðə $ 'fɑðɚ/ noun
1 your male parent: *My father is German.*
2 a title of a priest, especially in the Roman Catholic Church: *Father Christopher took the mass.*

Father Christ·mas /ˌ.. '../ noun BrE an old man with a red coat and white BEARD who, children believe, brings them presents at Christmas ⇨ same meaning SANTA CLAUS

fa·ther·hood /'fɑːðəhʊd $ 'fɑðɚˌhʊd/ noun [no plural] when someone is a father

father-in-law /'.. . ˌ./ noun the father of your husband or wife

fa·tigue /fə'tiːg/ noun [no plural] formal extreme tiredness

fat·ten·ing /'fætn-ɪŋ/ adjective food that is fattening is likely to make you fat

fat·ty /'fæti/ adjective fattier, fattiest fatty food contains a lot of fat

fau·cet /'fɔːsɪt/ the American word for TAP²

fault /fɔːlt/ noun
1 a problem with a machine or piece of equipment that stops it working correctly: *The fire was caused by an electrical fault.*
2 a bad part of someone's character: *In spite of her faults, Bet is a good friend.*

PHRASE
be someone's fault if a mistake is your fault, you are responsible for it:

The accident was partly my fault. | *These problems are your own fault.*

fault·y /'fɔːlti/ adjective not working properly: *Some of the equipment was faulty.*

fa·vour BrE, **favor** AmE /'feɪvə $ 'feɪvɚ/ noun
something kind or helpful that you do for someone else: *Sarah made my wedding dress for me, as a favour.*

PHRASES
do someone a favour to do something kind or helpful for someone: *Could you do me a favour and lend me your bike?*
ask someone a favour, ask a favour of someone to ask someone to do something kind or helpful for you: *John, can I ask you a favour?*
be in favour of something to support a plan or an idea: *Most of the students are in favour of having an end-of-term party.*
in someone's favour formal if a court or official group makes a decision in your favour, it decides that you are right: *After a long discussion, the judges decided in our favour.*

fa·vou·ra·ble BrE, **favorable** AmE /'feɪvərəbəl/ adjective **1** showing that you like someone or something: *All the comments about her work were favourable.* **2** favourable conditions are good, and likely to make something succeed: *We were lucky because the weather conditions were favourable.*

fa·vou·rite¹ BrE, **favorite** AmE /'feɪvərət/ adjective
your favourite thing or person is the one that you like most: *We chose Joe's favorite music for the party.* | *You're my favourite uncle.*

favourite² BrE, **favorite** AmE, noun
1 the person or thing that you like more than all the others: *Which picture is your favourite?* **2** the team, runner etc that is expected to win a competition: *Steve Colman is the favourite to win the 100 metres.*

fa·vou·ri·tis·m BrE, **favoritism** AmE /'feɪvərətɪzəm/ noun [no plural] when one person or group is unfairly treated better than others

fax /fæks/ noun, plural **faxes** 1 a document that is sent down a telephone line and then printed using a special machine: I'll send you a fax. 2 also **fax machine** a machine that you use for sending and receiving faxes
– fax verb: I'll fax the documents to you.

fear¹ /fɪə $ fɪr/ noun

GRAMMAR
fear of something/someone
fear for something/someone
the feeling that you get when you are very afraid or worried: He does not travel by plane because of his **fear of** flying. | Her mind was full of **fears for** her daughter's safety. | She was afraid to make a noise, **for fear of** being discovered.

fear² verb

GRAMMAR
fear (that)
fear for someone/something
to feel very afraid or worried: The police **fear that** he may have killed himself. | They **feared** the programme would upset people. | Her parents began to **fear for** her safety.

fear·less /'fɪələs $ 'fɪrləs/ adjective not afraid of anything

fea·si·ble /'fiːzəbəl/ adjective possible: Is it feasible to get the work finished by next month?

feast /fiːst/ noun a large meal for a lot of people to celebrate a special occasion

feat /fiːt/ noun something that someone does that shows a lot of strength or skill

fea·ther¹ /'feðə $ 'feðər/ noun one of the light soft things that cover a bird's body

fea·ture¹ /'fiːtʃə $ 'fitʃər/ noun

GRAMMAR
a feature of something
a feature on something
1 an important or interesting part of something: This new software has some very useful features. | The use of very bright colours is a typical **feature of** his paintings.
2 a long article in a newspaper or magazine: The paper published a three-page **feature on** the Internet.
3 **features** your features are your eyes, nose, mouth etc: a pretty woman with small features

feature² verb 1 if a film, magazine etc features someone, they are in it: The film features Dustin Hoffman as a New York lawyer. 2 to be an important part of something: Drugs seem to feature in all his films.

Feb·ru·a·ry /'februəri $ 'febju,eri/ written abbreviation **Feb** noun the second month of the year: We went on holiday at the end of February.

fed the past tense and past participle of FEED¹

fed up /,. './ adjective informal annoyed, bored, or unhappy: I'm fed up with my job! | Jerry was feeling bored and fed up.

fee /fiː/ noun 1 an amount of money that you pay to a professional person for their work 2 an amount of money that you pay to do something: school fees

fee·ble /'fiːbəl/ adjective extremely weak: She is now very old and feeble.

feed¹ /fiːd/ verb, past tense and past participle **fed** /fed/

GRAMMAR
feed something to someone
feed someone something
feed someone on something
feed on something
1 to give food to a person or animal: Have you **fed** the cats this morning? | We **fed** apples to the horses. | She sat next to Simon and fed him grapes. | We **fed** the puppy **on** bread and warm milk.
2 if animals or babies feed, they eat: Some birds **feed on** insects.

feed² noun 1 [no plural] food for animals 2 BrE milk or food that you give to a baby: When did he have his last feed?

feed·back /'fiːdbæk/ noun [no plural] criticism or advice about how well or badly you have done something: The teacher will give you feedback on your work.

feel¹ /fiːl/ verb, past tense and past participle **felt** /felt/

GRAMMAR
feel as if
feel a particular way about something
feel (that)
1 to experience something such as anger, happiness, cold, hunger etc: I felt cold and lonely. | You must feel

very disappointed. | *I feel better now I've had a rest.*

2 used to say how something you touch, or an experience, seems to you: *A snake's skin feels dry, not wet.* | *It felt as if the dentist was using a hammer to take my tooth out.* | *It felt good to be home again.* | *How does it feel to be back in England?*

3 to have an opinion about something, based on your feelings: *Rick feels strongly about animal rights.* | *I felt that I should apologise.* | *How do you feel about going out tonight* (=would you like to go out tonight)?

4 to touch something with your hands: *When she felt the carpet, it was wet.* | *Gill slowly felt her way* (=used her hands to find the way) *to the door.*

PHRASE

feel like something to want something or want to do something: *Do you feel like a walk?* | *Sam was being so annoying I felt like hitting him.*

feel² *noun* **1** the way that something feels when you touch it: *I love the feel of wool.* **2** the way that something seems to people: *The theatre has a very modern feel.*

feel·ing /'fiːlɪŋ/ *noun*

GRAMMAR
a feeling of something
a feeling about something

1 something that you experience in your mind or your body: *I enjoy running – it gives me a good feeling.* | *When I'm angry, it's hard to hide my feelings.* | *a feeling of boredom*

2 your opinion or attitude: *What are your feelings about the plan?*

PHRASE

have a/the feeling that to think that something is probably true or will probably happen: *I had the feeling that Jack was lying to me.* | *I left, with the feeling that I would never see him again.*

feet the plural of FOOT

fell the past tense of FALL¹

fel·low /'feləʊ $ 'feloʊ/ *noun* a man

felt¹ the past tense and past participle of FEEL¹

felt² /felt/ *noun* [no plural] a type of soft thick cloth

felt tip pen /ˌ. . ˈ./ *noun* a pen that has a hard piece of felt at the end that the ink comes through

fe·male¹ /'fiːmeɪl/ *adjective*

belonging to the sex that can have babies or produce eggs: *a female tiger* | *female relatives* | *a female voice*

female² *noun*

a person or animal belonging to the sex that can have babies or produce eggs: *We have three cats – two females and one male.*

fem·i·nine /'femənɪn/ *adjective* **1** having qualities that people think are typical of women: *She never wears very feminine clothes.* **2** belonging to a group of nouns, adjectives etc in some languages that is different from the MASCULINE and NEUTER groups

fem·i·nis·m /'femənɪzəm/ *noun* [no plural] the belief that women should have the same rights and opportunities as men

fem·i·nist /'femənɪst/ *noun* someone who believes in feminism

fence¹ /fens/ *noun*

a line of posts that are joined together around an area of land or between two areas of land: *There was a tall wooden fence around the garden.* | *He jumped easily over the fence.* ⇨ see picture on page 348

fence² *verb* **1** **fence something in** to put a fence around something: *The animals were all fenced in.* **2** **fence something off** to separate an area with a fence

fenc·ing /'fensɪŋ/ *noun* [no plural] a sport in which people fight with long thin swords

fend /fend/ *verb* **fend for yourself** to look after yourself without help from other people: *The children had to fend for themselves while their parents were at work.*

fend·er /'fendə $ 'fendər/ *noun* AmE the part of a car that covers the wheels

fe·ro·cious /fə'rəʊʃəs $fə'roʊʃəs/ adjective extremely violent and dangerous: *a ferocious wild animal*

fer·ry /'feri/ noun, plural **ferries** a boat that regularly carries people across a narrow area of water ⇨ see picture on page 349

fer·tile /'fɜːtaɪl $'fɜ⋅tl/ adjective **1** fertile land or soil produces a lot of healthy plants ⇨ opposite INFERTILE **2** someone who is fertile is able to produce babies ⇨ opposite INFERTILE

fer·ti·lize also **fertilise** BrE /'fɜːtəlaɪz $'fɜ⋅tl,aɪz/ verb if an egg is fertilized, the egg and a SPERM join together so that a new animal or baby can start to develop

fer·ti·liz·er /'fɜːtəlaɪzə $'fɜ⋅tl,aɪzɚ/ noun a chemical or natural substance that you put on the soil to help plants grow

fes·ti·val /'festəvəl/ noun **1** a time when people celebrate something, especially a religious holiday **2** an occasion when there are a lot of concerts, films, or performances: *an international music festival*

fes·tive /'festɪv/ adjective happy or cheerful because people are celebrating something: *a festive occasion*

fes·tiv·i·ties /fe'stɪvəti/ plural noun when people eat, drink, and dance to celebrate something

fetch /fetʃ/ verb

GRAMMAR
fetch someone something
fetch something for someone
fetch something/someone from somewhere

to go and get something or someone and bring them back: *What time is your dad coming to fetch you?* | *Would you mind fetching me some milk?* | *She fetched a newspaper for her grandma.* | *She went off to fetch some water from the well.* | *I've got to fetch Sally from the station.*

fetus the American spelling of FOETUS

feud /fjuːd/ noun an angry argument between two people or groups that continues for a long time: *There has been a feud between the two families for many years.*

fe·ver /'fiːvə $'fivɚ/ noun an illness in which you are very hot

fe·ver·ish /'fiːvərɪʃ/ adjective someone who is feverish has a fever

few /fjuː/

only a small number, not more: *He has very few friends.*

PHRASES
a few a small number of people or things: *We had to wait for **a few** minutes.* | ***A few of** her friends were jealous.*
quite a few a fairly large number of people or things: *I've been to **quite a few** parties recently.*

USAGE few, a few
Use **few** when you mean 'not many' or 'not enough': *Very few people came to the meeting.* Use **a few** when you mean 'some': *There's still **a few** bottles of beer left.* **Few** and **a few** are always used with plural nouns.

fi·an·cé /fi'ɒnseɪ $,fiɑn'seɪ/ noun the man that a woman has promised to marry

fi·an·cée /fi'ɒnseɪ $,fiɑn'seɪ/ noun the woman that a man has promised to marry

fi·as·co /fi'æskəʊ $fi'æskoʊ/ noun, plural **fiascoes** or **fiascos** an event that is completely unsuccessful

fib /fɪb/ noun informal a small unimportant lie

fi·bre BrE, **fiber** AmE /'faɪbə $'faɪbɚ/ noun **1** a material such as cotton or NYLON, which is made of thin threads: *Nylon is a man-made fibre.* **2** one of the threads that form a material **3** [no plural] parts of plants that you eat but do not DIGEST, which help food to move through your body: *The doctor said I need more fibre in my diet.*

fic·tion /'fɪkʃən/ noun [no plural] books and stories about people and events that are not real ⇨ opposite NONFICTION: *Most children enjoy reading fiction.*

fic·tion·al /'fɪkʃənəl/ adjective fictional people or events are from a book or story, and are not real

fid·dle¹ /'fɪdl/ verb fiddle with, fiddle around with to keep touching something or moving it around in your hands: *Stop fiddling with your knife and fork!*

fiddle² noun **1** a VIOLIN **2** BrE a dishonest way of getting money: *a tax fiddle*

fid·dly /'fɪdli/ adjective **fiddlier, fiddliest**

F

informal difficult to do because you have to move very small objects: *a very fiddly job*

fid·get /ˈfɪdʒɪt/ *verb* to keep moving your hands or feet, because you are bored or nervous: *The audience were starting to fidget.*

field /fiːld/ *noun*

GRAMMAR
a field of something

1 an area of land that is used for growing food, keeping animals, or playing a sport: *There were cows in the field.* | *The crowd cheered as the players ran onto the field.* | *We went off to the playing fields to play football.* | *fields of corn* ⇨ see picture on page 348

2 a subject that people study: *There has been a lot of research recently in the field of genetics.*

field·er /ˈfiːldə $ˈfildɚ/ *noun* one of the players who tries to catch the ball in BASEBALL or CRICKET

field hock·ey /ˈ. ˌ../ the American word for HOCKEY

field trip /ˈ. ./ *noun* a trip in which students go somewhere to learn about a subject

field·work /ˈfiːldwɜːk $ˈfildwɚk/ *noun* [no plural] the study of subjects outside, rather than in a building: *The course involves quite a lot of fieldwork.*

fiend·ish /ˈfiːndɪʃ/ *adjective* very clever in an unpleasant way: *a fiendish plot to take control of the company*

fierce /fɪəs $fɪrs/ *adjective*

1 a fierce animal is likely to attack you: *a fierce tiger*

2 a fierce person is angry and likely to shout at people: *Miss Stewart can be quite fierce at times.*

3 involving a lot of energy or violence: *A fierce battle took place between the police and the protesters.* | *The climbers could not come down from the mountain because of a fierce storm.*
　– **fiercely** *adverb*: *The dog showed its teeth fiercely.*

fi·er·y /ˈfaɪəri/ *adjective* full of strong or angry emotion: *John has a fiery temper.*

fif·teen /ˌfɪfˈtiːn/ *number* 15
　– **fifteenth** *number*

fifth /fɪfθ/ *number*   1 5th   2 one of five equal parts of something; 1/5

fif·ty /ˈfɪfti/ *number, plural* **fifties**   1 50   2 **the fifties** the years from 1950 to 1959   3 **be in your fifties** to be aged between 50 and 59
　– **fiftieth** *number*

fifty-fif·ty /ˌ.. ˈ../ *adjective, adverb* *informal*   1 if something is divided fifty-fifty, it is divided equally between two people   2 **a fifty-fifty chance** an equal chance that something will happen or will not happen: *She has a fifty-fifty chance of succeeding.*

fig /fɪg/ *noun* a small soft sweet fruit that is often dried

fight¹ /faɪt/ *verb, past tense and past participle* **fought** /fɔːt/

GRAMMAR
fight with someone
fight for/over something
fight against someone/something
fight to do something

1 if people fight, they hit each other: *My brother and I often fight, but we never really hurt each other.* | *Terry was always fighting with other boys.* | *He said he would fight anyone who said anything about his sister.* | *Lennox Lewis fought Evander Holyfield for the World Boxing title.*

2 to take part in a war: *He fought with great bravery in the war.* | *The English fought against the French at the Battle of Agincourt.* | *The terrorists believe that they are fighting for freedom.* | *The two countries fought a war over this area of land.*

3 to try hard to stop something bad or to make something good happen: *Everyone can help to fight crime.* | *We must fight against these harmful ideas.* | *an organization that fights for improvements in the environment* | *The workers at the factory are fighting to keep their jobs.*

PHRASAL VERBS
fight back
to fight or try hard to defeat someone who has attacked or criticized you: *She fought back against the man who attacked her.*

fight off
fight someone off to fight someone who is attacking you so that you make them go away: *She managed to fight off her attackers.*

fight² *noun* 1 an attempt to do something which is difficult and takes a long time: *the fight for democracy | her long fight against cancer* 2 when two people hit each other, or argue with each other: *He got drunk and got into a fight. | She's had a fight with her father.*

fight·er /'faɪtə $ 'faɪtɚ/ *noun* 1 someone who takes part in a sport in which people fight each other 2 a small fast military plane that can destroy other planes

fig·ure¹ /'fɪgə $ 'fɪgjɚ/ *noun*
1 a number that shows an amount: *The figures show that house prices are rising quickly. | The painting was sold for a figure of around $50,000.*
2 any of the signs between 0 and 9 that you write down as a number: *a four-figure number, such as 2300*
3 the shape of a person, especially one you cannot see very well: *A dark figure was sitting alone on the beach.*
4 *formal* a shape in mathematics: *a three-dimensional figure*

figure² *verb* 1 if a person or thing figures in something, they are included in it 2 *AmE spoken* to believe or think: *I figured I ought to talk to her again.* 3 figure something out *informal* to begin to understand something that is difficult to understand

file¹ /faɪl/ *noun*

GRAMMAR
a file on someone/something
1 a set of papers containing information about a particular person or thing, or the box used to store these papers: *Please fetch the file labelled 'A–E'. | The hospital keeps files on all the people who come there. | All the information you need should be in that file. | We will keep all your details on file (=in a file).*
2 an amount of information that you store on a computer under a particular name: *You need to create a new file. | How do I save the file?*

3 a tool with a rough edge that you use for making things smooth ⇨ *see picture at* TOOL

file² *verb* 1 to store papers or information in a particular place: *Her letter is filed under 'complaints'.* 2 file your nails to rub your nails with a rough tool in order to make them smooth

filet an American spelling of FILLET

fill /fɪl/ *verb*

GRAMMAR
fill something with something
fill with something
1 also **fill up** to put a large amount of something in a container or an area so that it becomes full: *We filled the car's petrol tank before we started our trip. | Fill up the holes with soil so that the seeds are covered. | Mary filled two glasses with champagne.*
2 also **fill up** to become full of something: *The concert hall was starting to fill up with people. | As the fire spread, the building filled with smoke.*

PHRASAL VERBS
fill in
fill something in to write the information that someone wants in the spaces on a printed piece of paper: *You have to fill this form in. | Please fill in your name and address.*
fill out
fill something out to write the information that someone wants in the spaces on a printed piece of paper: *Have you filled out that job application form yet?*

fil·let *BrE*, also **filet** *AmE* /'fɪlɪt $ fɪ'leɪ/ *noun* a piece of meat or fish without any bones

fill·ing¹ /'fɪlɪŋ/ *noun* 1 a small amount of metal that is put into a hole in your tooth 2 food that is put inside other food: *The filling had fallen out of my sandwich.*

filling² *adjective* food that is filling makes your stomach feel full

filling sta·tion /'.. ,../ *noun* a place where you can buy petrol for your car ⇨ *same meaning* PETROL STATION *BrE*, GAS STATION *AmE*

F

film¹ /fɪlm/ *noun*

GRAMMAR
a film about something

1 a story told in moving pictures that is shown in a cinema or on television; MOVIE *AmE*: *'Star Wars' is my favourite film.* | *Have you **seen** any good **films** recently?* | *We **watched** a **film** **about** a Russian ballet dancer.*
2 the roll of thin plastic that you use in a camera to take photographs: *I must buy some film for my camera.*

film² *verb* to record moving pictures of something: *No one has ever filmed these animals before.*

film star /'. ./ *noun* a famous film actor or actress

fil·ter¹ /'fɪltə $ 'fɪltɚ/ *noun* a thing that removes substances that you do not want from a liquid or gas as it flows through: *the oil filter in a car*

filter² *verb* to clean a liquid or gas using a filter: *I filter all my drinking water.*

filth /fɪlθ/ *noun* [no plural] unpleasant dirt: *The old bicycle was completely covered in filth.*

filth·y /'fɪlθi/ *adjective* **filthier, filthiest** extremely dirty: *Your hands are filthy!*

fin /fɪn/ *noun* one of the flat parts that stick out of a fish's body and help it to swim

fi·nal¹ /'faɪnl/ *adjective*

1 the final thing is the one that is last or that happens at the end: *On the final day of our holiday, we all went out for a meal.* | *The final scene of the play has a big surprise.*
2 if a decision or offer is final, it cannot be changed: *The judge's decision is final.* | *£300 is my final offer.*

final² *noun* **1** the last part of a competition: *Tickets for the World Cup Final are hard to get.* | *He reached the finals but only came second.* **2 finals a)** *BrE* the examinations that students take at the end of their last year at university **b)** *AmE* the examinations that students take at the end of each class in high school and college

fi·nal·ist /'faɪnl-ɪst/ *noun* one of the people or teams that reach the last part of a competition

fi·nal·ize also **finalise** *BrE* /'faɪnl-aɪz/ *verb* to decide firmly on the details ▼

of a plan or arrangement: *I haven't finalized the details yet.*

fi·nal·ly /'faɪnl-i/ *adverb*

1 after a long time: *We finally arrived home at 10 o'clock, over three hours late.* | *Mark finally agreed to accept the job.*
2 used when you are saying the last of a series of things: *Finally, we welcome Xavier, who has joined the class today.*

fi·nance¹ /'faɪnæns $ fə'næns/ *noun*
1 [no plural] activities connected with the spending or saving of large amounts of money: *He works in finance.* **2** [no plural] money that you get in order to pay for something important: *The government is offering finance to new small businesses.* **3 finances** the money that a person or organization has: *My finances are pretty good at the moment.*

finance² *verb* to provide money for something: *The school agreed to finance my trip.*

fi·nan·cial /fə'nænʃəl/ *adjective* connected with money: *The film was a financial disaster.*
– **financially** *adverb*

find /faɪnd/ *verb, past tense and past participle* **found** /faʊnd/

GRAMMAR
find something for someone
find someone something
find (that)

1 to discover, see, or get something, especially after you have been looking for it: *The boys found a gold watch buried under a tree.* | *I can't find my socks!* | *Phil's been trying to find a job for three weeks.* | *I've found a house for you.* | *Mark went outside to find us a taxi.*
2 to learn that something is true: *They found that men are better at reading maps than women.*

PHRASES
find something difficult, find something easy: *I find maths very difficult* (=maths is difficult for me). | *Jessica said she found the exam quite easy.* | *Bill finds it difficult to make friends* (=it is difficult for Bill to make friends).
find your way to arrive at a place by discovering the right way to get

there: *I tried to **find my way** back to the station.*

find yourself doing something to realize that you are doing something, even though you did not mean to: *He **found himself** laughing out loud during the film.*

find fault with someone/something to criticize someone or something: *My boss **finds fault with** everything I do.*

PHRASAL VERB
find out

find something out to get information about something: *I'd like to **find out** more **about** the college music courses. | I did the test to **find out** how fit I was. | Can you **find out** what time the film starts?*

find·ings /ˈfaɪndɪŋz/ plural noun the things that people have learned as the result of an official study: *They reported their findings to the Health Minister.*

fine¹ /faɪn/ adjective
1 very good: *We sell fine food from around the world. | The team gave a fine performance.*
2 very thin, or in very small pieces or amounts: *a shampoo for fine hair | a scarf made from very fine silk | The sand here is fine and soft.*
3 spoken good enough: *"I've only got water to drink." "That's fine."*
4 spoken healthy and reasonably happy: *"How is your mother?" "She's fine."*
5 if the weather is fine, it is sunny and not raining: *I hope it stays fine for the picnic.*

fine² verb to make someone pay an amount of money as a punishment: *The judge fined him $500 for stealing.*
– **fine** noun: *He was given a £100 fine for speeding.*

fine³ adverb spoken well: *Everything was going fine until you arrived!*

fine·ly /ˈfaɪnli/ adverb into very small pieces: *Chop the onion finely.*

fin·ger /ˈfɪŋɡə $ ˈfɪŋɡɚ/ noun

one of the five long parts at the end of your hand, including your thumb: *She wore a ring on nearly every finger.*

PHRASE
keep your fingers crossed to hope

that something will happen in the way that you want it to: *The exam results come out tomorrow, so we're **keeping** our **fingers crossed!***

fin·ger·nail /ˈfɪŋɡəneɪl $ ˈfɪŋɡɚˌneɪl/ noun the hard flat part at the end of your finger

fin·ger·print /ˈfɪŋɡəˌprɪnt $ ˈfɪŋɡɚˌprɪnt/ noun a mark that someone's finger made which shows its pattern of lines: *The burglar left his fingerprints on the window.*

fin·ish¹ /ˈfɪnɪʃ/ verb

GRAMMAR
finish doing something
1 to come to the end of doing or making something: *Just let me finish this letter. | I'll finish cleaning the house in the morning.*
2 to come to an end: *What time did the party finish?*
3 to eat, drink, or use all the rest of something: *Who finished the pie?*
4 **finish first, finish second etc** to be the winner, come second etc at the end of a race or competition: *Kate finished last.*

PHRASAL VERBS
finish off
1 **finish something off** to do the last part of something: *David has to **finish off** his homework, and then he can go out.*
2 **finish something off** to eat, drink, or use all the rest of something: *Would you like to **finish off** the sandwiches?*

finish with
1 **finish with something** if you have finished with something, you are no longer using it and no longer need it: *You can have this magazine – I've **finished with** it.*
2 **finish with someone** to end a relationship with someone: *I was really upset when Paul **finished with** me.*

fin·ish² noun, plural **finishes** the end of something, especially a race: *It was a very close finish.*

fin·ished /ˈfɪnɪʃt/ adjective 1 completed: *The finished building will be 200 feet high.* 2 no longer able to be successful: *Most footballers are finished by the time they are 30.*

fir /fɜː $ fɚ/ also **fir·tree** /'fɜːtriː $ 'fɚtri/ noun a tree with very narrow leaves that do not fall off in winter

fire¹ /faɪə $ faɪɚ/ noun

fire

1 the light and heat that something produces when it burns: *The village was completely destroyed by fire.* | *A fire started in the kitchen.*

2 a pile of wood or coal that you burn in order to make a place warm or to cook food: *They sang songs around the fire.*

PHRASES

be on fire to be burning: *One of the plane's engines was on fire.*

catch fire to start burning, especially by mistake: *Somehow the curtains caught fire.*

set fire to something, set something on fire to make something start burning: *A cigarette set fire to a pile of leaves.*

put out a fire to stop something burning: *Firefighters tried for three hours to put out the fire.*

open fire to start shooting: *The soldiers were ordered to open fire.*

fire² verb

GRAMMAR
fire (something) somewhere

1 to shoot bullets from a gun: *Police fired into the air.* | *The man fired two shots at the car.*

2 to tell someone that they must leave their job; SACK² BrE: *The company fired her after she had worked there for only a week.*

fire a·larm /'. .,./ noun a piece of equipment that makes a loud noise when there is a fire in a building, in order to warn people: *The fire alarm went off and we had to leave the building.*

fire·arm /'faɪərɑːm $ 'faɪɚɑrm/ noun formal a gun

fire bri·gade /'. .,./ BrE also **fire de·part·ment** /'. .,./ AmE, noun an organization of people whose job is to stop fires

fire en·gine /'. ,..,/ noun a large vehicle that carries firefighters and their equipment

fire es·cape /'. .,./ noun a set of stairs that is next to the outside wall of a building. People use the fire escape to get out of the building if there is a fire ⇨ see picture on page 343

fire ex·tin·guish·er /'. .,.../ noun a piece of equipment used for stopping small fires

fire·fight·er /'faɪəˌfaɪtə $ 'faɪɚˌfaɪtɚ/ noun someone whose job is to stop fires

fire·man /'faɪəmən $ 'faɪɚmən/ noun, plural firemen /-mən/ a man whose job is to stop fires

fire·place /'faɪəpleɪs $ 'faɪɚpleɪs/ noun in a room, the open place in the wall where you light a fire to heat the room ⇨ see picture at MANTELPIECE

fire truck /'. ./ the American word for FIRE ENGINE

fire·work /'faɪəwɜːk $ 'faɪɚwɚk/ noun an object that you light so that it explodes and produces bright lights in the sky, in order to celebrate a special event

firm¹ /fɜːm $ fɚm/ adjective

GRAMMAR
firm with someone

1 something that is firm is not soft when you press it: *The fruit should be firm and not too ripe.* | *These exercises will give you a firm, flat stomach.*

2 a firm date, decision etc is not likely to change: *We have not agreed a firm date for the party.*

3 if you are firm, you say that someone must do what you want them to do: *You need to be firm with people when you are trying to get your money back.*

4 a tight strong way of holding something: *a strong man with a firm handshake*
– **firmly** adverb: *"No," he said firmly.* | *Glue the pieces of wood firmly together.*

firm² noun a business or company: *My father works for a printing firm.*

first¹ /fɜːst $ fɚst/ number, adverb, adjective

1 before anyone or anything else; 1st: *January is the first month of the*

▼ year. | *The band's first recording was very successful.*

2 before anything else happens, or before doing anything else: *You can borrow my clothes, but you have to ask me first.* | *First I did my homework, then I watched TV.*

3 at the beginning of something: *When Jane first met Steve, he was working in a bar.* | *Using email is easier than I first thought.*

4 the first the first person or thing: *I was the first to answer the question.* | *The second week of the holiday was better than the first.*

come first a) to win a race or competition: *Lee came first in a skateboarding contest.* **b)** to be more important than anything else: *For me, friends come first.*

at first in the beginning: *I didn't like her at first, but now we're friends.*

in the first place at the start of a situation: *Why didn't you tell me the truth in the first place?*

first of all before doing anything else: *First of all, we need to decide who to invite.*

first² *noun* **1** something that has never happened before: *Their surprising victory is a sporting first.* **2** the highest level of university degree you can get in Britain: *He got a first in Economics.*

first aid /ˌ. ˈ./ *noun* [no plural] simple medical treatment that you give quickly to someone who is injured

first-class¹ /ˌ. ˈ./ *adjective* **1** excellent: *a first-class actor* **2** of the best and most expensive type: *a first-class train ticket*

first-class² *adverb* if someone travels or sends something first-class, they do it using the best and most expensive service: *She sent the birthday card first-class.*

first floor /ˌ. ˈ./ *noun* **1** *BrE* the level of a building that is just above the level of the street: *The bathroom is on the first floor.* **2** *AmE* the level of a building that is level with the street; GROUND FLOOR *BrE*

first·hand /ˌfɜːstˈhænd/ $ /ˌfɚ·stˈhænd/ *adjective* firsthand information or knowledge is what you learn or see yourself, not what you hear from other people – **firsthand** *adverb*: *He saw firsthand the*

conditions the poorest people were living in.

first·ly /ˈfɜːstli/ $ /ˈfɚstli/ *adverb* used before saying the first of several things: *"Why did you take up tennis?" "Firstly I needed the exercise and secondly I thought it would be fun."*

first name /ˈ. ˌ./ *noun* the name chosen for you when you were born: *Miss Green's first name is Karen.*

See phrases at NAME.

first per·son /ˌ. ˈ../ *noun* the first person the form of a verb that you use with 'I' and 'we'

fish¹ /fɪʃ/ *noun* **1** *plural* **fish** or **fishes** a creature without legs that swims about in water **2** [no plural] the flesh of a fish that people eat: *We had fish cooked with onions and tomatoes.*

fish² *verb* to try to catch fish: *They are fishing for salmon.*

fish·er·man /ˈfɪʃəmən/ $ /ˈfɪʃɚmən/ *noun, plural* **fishermen** /-mən/ a man who catches fish as a job or a sport

fish·ing /ˈfɪʃɪŋ/ *noun* [no plural] the sport or job of catching fish: *We went fishing at the weekend.*

fishing rod /ˈ.. ˌ./ *also* **fishing pole** *AmE, noun* a long stick with string and a hook that you use for catching fish

fish·y /ˈfɪʃi/ *adjective informal* **fishier, fishiest** seeming bad or dishonest ⇨ *same meaning* SUSPICIOUS (1): *The deal sounds a bit fishy to me.*

fist /fɪst/ *noun* a hand with all the fingers curled tightly: *He banged his fist angrily on the table.*

fit¹ /fɪt/ *verb* **fitted, fitting** *BrE*, **fit, fitting** *AmE*

GRAMMAR
fit (something) somewhere

1 to be the right size and shape for someone or something: *My old jeans still fit me.* | *This cover doesn't fit.*

2 if something fits in a place, or if you can fit it in there, there is enough space for it: *This book is too big to fit in my schoolbag.* | *He managed to fit all our skiing things into his car.*

3 to fix a piece of equipment to something: *Before you can ride that bike you need to fit new brakes.*

F

F

▼ PHRASAL VERB
fit in
1 fit in if you fit in, the other people in a group accept you because you are like them: *I didn't really fit in with the other kids in my class.*
2 fit something in *informal* to have enough time to do something: *How does she fit in all that sport and a part-time job as well?*

fit² *adjective* **fitter, fittest**

GRAMMAR
fit to do something
fit for something
1 suitable or good enough: *He said I was not fit to be the team captain.* | *When will the swimming pool be fit for use again?* | *That car is not in a fit state to be driven.*
2 healthy and strong ⇨ *opposite* UNFIT: *Dancing keeps me fit.* | *Owen should be fit for the game on Saturday.*

fit³ *noun* **1 have a fit, throw a fit** *informal* to be very angry and shout a lot: *Dad will have a fit when he sees what you've done to your hair!* **2** a short period of time when you cannot control what you do, for example because you are ill or angry: *She had a coughing fit.* | *In a fit of anger, he tore up the letter.* **3 be a good fit** if a piece of clothing is a good fit, it fits your body well: *Those jeans are a good fit.*

fit·ness /'fɪtnəs/ *noun* [no plural] when you are healthy and able to run or do physical work for a long time: *He started to go running to improve his fitness.*

five /faɪv/ *number* 5

fix /fɪks/ *verb*

GRAMMAR
fix something to/onto something
1 to repair something: *Harry can fix your bike for you.*
2 to decide on an exact time, place, price etc: *Have you fixed a date for the wedding?*
3 *BrE* to fasten something to something else so that it will not come off: *She fixed a new mirror to her bedroom wall.*
4 *AmE* to get something ready: *Mom was fixing dinner.*

▼ PHRASAL VERB
fix up
fix something up *BrE* to arrange an event or trip: *We need to fix up a meeting with all the parents.*

fix·ture /'fɪkstʃə $ 'fɪkstʃɚ/ *noun* *BrE* a sports event that has been arranged

fiz·zle /'fɪzəl/ *verb* **fizzle out** to gradually end in a weak or disappointing way: *Their relationship just fizzled out.*

fiz·zy /'fɪzi/ *adjective* **fizzier, fizziest** a fizzy drink contains gas: *fizzy mineral water*

flab·ber·gas·ted /'flæbə,gɑːstɪd $ 'flæbɚ,gæstɪd/ *adjective* *informal* extremely surprised

flab·by /'flæbi/ *adjective* **flabbier, flabbiest** a part of your body that is flabby has too much soft loose fat: *her flabby arms*

flag /flæg/ *noun* a piece of cloth with a picture or pattern on it that is used as the sign of a country or as a signal: *The French flag has blue, white, and red stripes.*

flag·pole /'flægpəʊl $ 'flægpoʊl/ *noun* a tall pole for a flag

flair /fleə $ fler/ *noun* a natural ability to do something very well: *She has a real flair for languages.*

flak /flæk/ *noun* [no plural] *informal* criticism: *She got a lot of flak for her decision to move abroad.*

flake /fleɪk/ *noun* a small flat thin piece of something: *The paint was coming off the door in flakes.*

flame /fleɪm/ *noun* **1** a bright moving yellow or orange light that you see when something is burning: *the cheerful flames of a log fire* **2 in flames** burning: *The whole house was in flames.*

flan /flæn/ *noun* a PIE with no lid that is filled with fruit etc

flan·nel /'flænl/ *noun* [no plural] **1** *BrE* a piece of cloth that you use to wash yourself **2** a type of soft cloth that is warm: *flannel sheets*

flap¹ /flæp/ *noun* a flat piece of cloth, paper etc that is fastened by one edge to something: *He stuck down the flap of the envelope.*

flap² *verb* **flapped, flapping** **1** if a bird flaps its wings, it moves them up and down **2** if a piece of cloth flaps, it moves backwards and forwards: *The curtains flapped in the wind.*

flare¹ /fleə $fler/ also **flare up** verb *written* if trouble or anger flares, it suddenly starts or becomes more violent: *Fighting has flared up again in the city.*

flare² noun a thing that produces a bright light and that someone shoots into the air as a sign that they need help

flared /fleəd $flerd/ adjective flared trousers or skirts become wider towards the bottom

flash¹ /flæʃ/ verb to shine brightly for a short time: *the flashing lights of a police car*

flash² noun, plural flashes **1** a sudden quick bright light: *a flash of lightning* **2** a bright light on a camera that you use to take photographs indoors

flash·back /'flæʃbæk/ noun part of a film, play, book etc that shows something that happened earlier in the story

flash·light /'flæʃlaɪt/ the American word for TORCH

flash·y /'flæʃi/ adjective flashier, flashiest too big, bright, or expensive: *She was showing off her flashy engagement ring.*

flask /flɑːsk $flæsk/ noun **1** BrE a type of bottle in which liquids remain hot or cold for a long time: *I've brought a flask of coffee.* **2** a type of bottle used in chemistry

flat¹ /flæt/ adjective flatter, flattest

1 smooth and level, without any raised parts: *I need a flat surface to work on.* | *Holland is good for cycling because it's very flat.* ⇨ see picture at BUMPY

2 a tyre that is flat does not have enough air inside it

3 a drink that is flat has lost its gas: *This soda water has gone flat.*

4 BrE a BATTERY that is flat has lost its electrical power

5 E flat, B flat etc the musical note that is slightly lower than E, B etc ⇨ opposite SHARP¹ (7)

6 a flat shoe has a very low heel: *We have to wear flat shoes at school.*

flat² noun **1** BrE a set of rooms for someone to live in that is part of a larger building; APARTMENT AmE: *They're building a new block of flats opposite us.* ⇨ see picture on page 343 **2** a tyre that does not have enough air inside it

flat³ adverb

straight or smoothly on a surface, with no parts that are raised or standing up: *He lay flat on his back and looked at the stars.* | *My hair just won't stay flat.*

in 10 seconds flat, in two minutes flat etc informal very quickly, in 10 seconds, two minutes etc: *He did all his homework in twenty minutes flat.*

flat out informal as fast as possible: *She had to work **flat out** to get the house clean before her parents came back.*

flat·ly /'flætli/ adverb flatly refuse, flatly deny to say something in a very firm strong way: *She flatly refused to let me borrow her car.*

flat·mate /'flætmeɪt/ noun BrE someone who shares a flat with one or more other people; ROOMMATE AmE

flat·ten /'flætn/ verb to make something flat: *The children had ridden their bikes all over the garden, flattening the flowers.*

flat·ter /'flætə $'flætɚ/ verb **1** to say nice things about someone or show that you admire them, sometimes when you do not really mean it: *George flattered her, saying how attractive she looked.* **2** be flattered, feel flattered to feel pleased because someone has shown that they like or admire you: *When they asked me to join their group, I felt flattered.*

flat·ter·ing /'flætərɪŋ/ adjective something that is flattering makes someone look more attractive: *a flattering dress*

flat·ter·y /'flætəri/ noun [no plural] nice things that you say but do not really mean

flaunt /flɔːnt/ verb if you flaunt your money, success, beauty etc, you try to make other people notice it and admire you for it

fla·vour¹ BrE, **flavor** AmE /'fleɪvə $'fleɪvɚ/ noun

1 the taste that a food or drink has: *The ice cream comes in ten different flavours.*

2 [no plural] when something tastes good: *Salt is used to give food more flavour.*

flavour² BrE, **flavor** AmE, verb to give

food or drink a particular taste: *The sauce is flavoured with herbs.*

fla·vour·ing /ˈfleɪvərɪŋ/ *noun* something used to give food or drink a particular taste: *This drink contains artificial flavourings.*

flaw /flɔː/ *noun* a mistake, mark, or weakness that stops something from being perfect: *She took the material back to the shop because there was a flaw in it.*

flawed /flɔːd/ *adjective* something that is flawed has mistakes or weaknesses and so is not perfect: *His theory is badly flawed.*

flea /fliː/ *noun* a very small jumping insect that bites animals and drinks their blood

fled the past tense and past participle of FLEE

flee /fliː/ *verb written, past tense and past participle* **fled** /fled/ to leave a place very quickly, in order to escape from danger: *People have been fleeing the country to avoid the fighting.*

fleece /fliːs/ *noun* the wool that covers a sheep

fleet /fliːt/ *noun* a group of ships or vehicles: *a fleet of trucks*

flesh /fleʃ/ *noun [no plural]* **1** the soft part of your body, between your skin and your bones **2** the soft part inside a fruit or vegetable: *A peach can have yellow or white flesh.*

flew the past tense of FLY¹

flex·i·ble /ˈfleksəbəl/ *adjective* **1** able to change or be changed easily ⇨ *opposite* INFLEXIBLE: *One good thing about the job is the flexible working hours.* **2** easy to bend: *a flexible plastic tube*

flick /flɪk/ *verb* **1** to send something small through the air with a quick movement of your finger or hand: *He flicked the fly off his sleeve.* **2** **flick something on/off** *informal* to press a SWITCH in order to start or stop electrical equipment: *I flicked on the TV.* **3** **flick through** *BrE informal* to look at a book, magazine etc quickly: *She was flicking through a magazine.*
– **flick** *noun*: *I had a quick flick through the book.*

flick·er /ˈflɪkə $ ˈflɪkɚ/ *verb written* **1** to burn or shine with an unsteady light: *The fire in the sitting room flickered*

gently. **2** *written* if an expression flickers across your face, it appears for a moment: *A smile flickered across her face.*

flight /flaɪt/ *noun*
1 a journey in a plane, or the plane making a particular journey: *It was a very quick flight.* | *They **caught** the next **flight** home.* | *She **booked** a **flight** to New York.*
2 *[no plural]* when a bird, plane etc flies through the air: *We could see seagulls in flight.*

PHRASE
a flight of stairs, a flight of steps a set of stairs: *He climbed up the steep flight of stairs.*

flight at·tend·ant /ˈ. .ˌ../ *noun* someone whose job is to look after passengers on a plane

flim·sy /ˈflɪmzi/ *adjective* **flimsier, flimsiest** **1** not strong, and easily damaged: *Their flimsy boats were destroyed in the storm.* **2** a flimsy argument or excuse is not a good one

flinch /flɪntʃ/ *verb* to make a sudden small backward movement because you are afraid, hurt, or shocked: *The boy flinched when she tried to clean his cuts.*

fling /flɪŋ/ *verb written, past tense and past participle* **flung** /flʌŋ/ to throw or move something quickly and with a lot of force: *She flung the ring back at him.* | *He flung open the door.*

flip /flɪp/ *verb* **flipped, flipping** **1** **flip over** to turn over quickly: *The boat went too fast and flipped over.* **2** also **flip out** *informal* to suddenly become very angry: *I just suggested a few changes and he flipped.* **3** **flip something on/off, flip a switch** *informal* to press a SWITCH in order to start or stop electrical equipment: *He flipped on the light.* | *Just flip this switch and the music comes on.* **4** **flip through** *informal* to look at a book, magazine etc quickly: *He flipped through his diary to find a free day.*

flip chart /ˈ. ./ *noun* large sheets of paper on a board to write facts or ideas on in a meeting or class

flip-flop /ˈ. ./ *noun* a light shoe with a v-shaped band to hold your foot;

flip·pant /ˈflɪpənt/ *adjective* if you are flippant about something, you speak about it in a less serious way than you should: *He was rather flippant about her problems.*

flip·per /'flɪpə $ 'flɪpɚ/ *noun* **1** the flat arm or leg of a sea animal such as a SEAL **2** a large flat rubber shoe that you use for swimming under water

flip·ping /'flɪpɪŋ/ *adjective, adverb BrE spoken informal* used when you are annoyed: *I tried phoning them twenty flipping times!*

flirt /flɜːt $ flɚt/ *verb* to behave as if you are sexually attracted to someone, but not in a very serious way: *She always flirted with other boys at parties.*

float

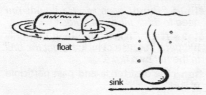

float

sink

float¹ /fləʊt $ floʊt/ *verb*

> **GRAMMAR**
> **float on/in etc something**
> **float to/across etc a place**

1 to stay or move on the surface of a liquid: *Does plastic float?* | *The paper boat floated along on the river.* | *There was all sorts of rubbish floating in the water.*
2 if something very light floats in the air, it stays in the air or moves slowly through the air: *The feather floated slowly to the ground.*

float² *noun* a large vehicle that is decorated to be part of a PARADE

flock¹ /flɒk $ flɑk/ *noun* a group of sheep, goats, or birds

flock² *verb written* if people flock to a place, a lot of them go there: *People flocked to see the exhibition.*

flog /flɒg $ flɑg/ *verb* **flogged, flogging** **1** *BrE informal* to sell something to someone: *I'm still trying to flog my old car.* **2** to hit someone with a whip or stick as a punishment

flood¹ /flʌd/ *verb*

> **GRAMMAR**
> **flood across/into/over a place**

1 if something floods a place or if a place floods, the place becomes covered with water: *A pipe burst and*

flooded the kitchen. | *One corner of the field flooded.*
2 if people or things flood somewhere, a very large number of them go there: *Calls came flooding in from worried members of the public.* | *People flooded across the border, trying to escape.*

> **PHRASE**
> **be flooded with things** to get so many letters, complaints etc that you cannot deal with them all: *We were flooded with complaints about the show.*

flood² *noun* a very large amount of water that covers an area that is usually dry: *Many animals have drowned in the floods.*

flood·ing /'flʌdɪŋ/ *noun* [no plural] when an area that is usually dry becomes covered with water: *The heavy rain caused a lot of flooding.*

flood·light /'flʌd-laɪt/ *noun* a large bright light that is used for lighting sports fields, public buildings etc

floodlight

flood·lit /'flʌdlɪt/ *adjective* lit by floodlights: *floodlit tennis courts*

floor /flɔː $ flɔr/ *noun*
1 the surface that you stand on in a building: *There was a pile of books on the floor.* | *He leaves his clothes all over the floor.*
2 one of the levels in a building: *The toilets are on the top floor.* ➪ see usage note at GROUND¹

floor·board /'flɔːbɔːd $ 'flɔrbɔrd/ *noun* a long piece of wood that is part of a floor

floor·ing /'flɔːrɪŋ/ *noun* [no plural] a material used to make or cover floors: *They chose wooden flooring for the kitchen.*

flop¹ /flɒp $ flɑp/ *verb* **flopped, flopping** to sit down or fall in a loose heavy way: *She flopped down onto the sofa.*

flop² *noun informal* something that is not successful: *The play was a flop.*

flop·py /'flɒpi $ 'flɑpi/ *adjective* **floppier, floppiest** soft and hanging loosely down: *a dog with long floppy ears*

floppy disk /ˌ.. './ also **floppy** noun a flat piece of plastic used for storing information from a computer

flo·ral /'flɔːrəl/ adjective written made of flowers or having a design of flowers: floral wallpaper

flor·ist /'flɒrɪst $ 'flɔrɪst/ also **flor·ist's** noun a shop that sells flowers

floun·der /'flaʊndə $ 'flaʊndɚ/ verb to be unsuccessful or not know what to do: Some of the younger students seemed to be floundering a bit.

flour /flaʊə $ flaʊɚ/ noun [no plural] powder made from grain which you use for making bread, cakes etc

flour·ish /'flʌrɪʃ $ 'flɝɪʃ/ verb to grow well or be successful: This plant will flourish in a sunny place. | a flourishing business

flow¹ /fləʊ $ floʊ/ noun

GRAMMAR
a/the flow of something

1 a steady continuous movement of an amount of something, for example a liquid: The gates can be opened or closed to control the flow of water. | There is a steady flow of traffic through the village.
2 the movement of something such as ideas or money from one person or place to another: We want to encourage the flow of information between countries.

flow² verb

GRAMMAR
flow somewhere

if an amount of something flows somewhere, it moves along in a steady way: The River Don flows through the city centre. | The police tried to keep the traffic flowing.

flow·er /'flaʊə $ 'flaʊɚ/ noun one of the pretty coloured things that a plant or tree produces: There was a vase of yellow flowers by the window.

flow·er·bed /'flaʊəbed $ 'flaʊɚˌbed/ noun an area of ground in which someone grows flowers

flown the past participle of FLY¹

flu /fluː/ also **the flu** noun [no plural] a common illness which is like a very bad cold

fluc·tu·ate /'flʌktʃueɪt/ verb formal if an amount fluctuates, it keeps going up and down: Her weight fluctuated.

flu·en·cy /'fluːənsi/ noun [no plural] formal the ability to speak a language very well

flu·ent /'fluːənt/ adjective able to speak a language quickly and well: Hannah is fluent in three languages.
–fluently adverb: He speaks French fluently.

fluff /flʌf/ noun [no plural] soft fine amounts of thread that come off things: I was covered in fluff from the new carpet.

fluff·y /'flʌfi/ adjective fluffier, fluffiest covered with soft fur or threads: a fluffy toy

flu·id /'fluːɪd/ noun formal a liquid: You need to drink plenty of fluids.

fluke /fluːk/ noun something that only happens because of luck: He got the ball in the net by a fluke.

flung the past tense and past participle of FLING

flunk /flʌŋk/ verb AmE informal to fail a test or course: I flunked all my exams last year.

flu·o·res·cent /fluəˈresənt $ flʊˈresənt/ adjective 1 a fluorescent light consists of a long glass tube containing a special gas 2 fluorescent colours are extremely bright

fluo·ride /'flʊəraɪd $ 'flɔraɪd/ noun [no plural] a chemical that is added to water and TOOTHPASTE to help protect people's teeth

flush /flʌʃ/ verb 1 if you flush a toilet, you make water go through it to clean it 2 if you flush, your face becomes red because you are embarrassed or angry

flushed /flʌʃt/ adjective if someone is flushed, their face is red: She looked hot and flushed.

flus·tered /'flʌstəd $ 'flʌstɚd/ adjective confused because you are nervous or trying to do things too quickly: She got flustered and dropped her papers.

flute /fluːt/ noun a musical instrument shaped like a tube, which you play by blowing across a hole near one end

flut·ter /'flʌtə $ 'flʌtɚ/ verb 1 to wave or move about gently in the air: The flags were fluttering in the wind. 2 if a bird or insect flutters somewhere, it goes there by moving its wings very quickly up and down: The butterfly fluttered across the garden.

fly¹ /flaɪ/ *verb* flew /fluː/ flown /fləʊn/ $ floʊn/ flies

GRAMMAR
fly to/from a place

1 to travel somewhere by plane: *Sam **flew to** New York for his brother's wedding.* | *We are now flying over the Alps.*

2 to move through the air: *Penguins are birds, but they can't fly.*

3 to control a plane: *Have you ever flown this type of aircraft before?*

4 *written* to suddenly move very quickly: *Helen **flew to** the window when she heard the car arrive.* | *The door **flew open** and Tim came in.*

5 also **fly by** if time flies, it seems to pass very quickly: *The weeks flew by until it was time to go back to school.*

6 if a flag is flying, it has been put at the top of a pole so that people can see it: *A white flag was flying above the building.*

fly² *noun, plural* flies 1 a common insect with wings ⇨ *see picture at* INSECT 2 also **flies** *BrE* the ZIP or buttons at the front of a pair of trousers: *Your flies are undone.*

fly·ing¹ /'flaɪ-ɪŋ/ *noun* [no plural] travelling by plane or controlling a plane: *A lot of people are scared of flying.*

flying² *adjective* **with flying colours** if you pass a test with flying colours, you do very well in the test

flying sau·cer /,.. '../ *noun* an object in the sky carrying creatures from space ⇨ *same meaning* UFO

flyover

fly·o·ver /'flaɪ-əʊvə $ 'flaɪ,oʊvɚ/ *noun* *BrE* a bridge that carries one road over another; OVERPASS *AmE*

FM /,ef 'em/ *noun* [no plural] a system used for broadcasting radio programmes

foam /fəʊm $ foʊm/ *noun* [no plural] a substance with a lot of very small BUBBLES of air in it

fo·cus¹ /'fəʊkəs $ 'foʊkəs/ *verb* focused or focussed, focusing or focussing 1 to give all or most of your attention to a particular thing: *In this course we will focus on basic computer skills.* 2 to move part of a camera, TELESCOPE etc so you can see something clearly: *He focused his camera on the nearest of the birds.*

focus² *noun* 1 the person or thing that gets most attention: *The focus of teaching has changed.* | *The new student was the focus of attention.* 2 **in focus, out of focus** if a photograph is in focus it is clear, and if it is out of focus it is not clear

foe·tus *BrE*, **fetus** *AmE* /'fiːtəs/ *noun*, *plural* **foetuses** a human or animal that is growing inside its mother

fog /fɒg $ fɑg/ *noun* cloudy air near the ground, which is difficult to see through: *There was thick fog early this morning.*

USAGE fog, mist
Fog and **mist** are similar in meaning. **Fog** is thicker than **mist**.

fog·gy /'fɒgi $ 'fɑgi/ *adjective* **foggier, foggiest** a foggy day is one when there is fog: *It was so foggy we couldn't see the other side of the road.*

foil /fɔɪl/ *noun* [no plural] very thin metal used for covering and wrapping food

fold¹ /fəʊld $ foʊld/ **fold**
verb

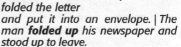

1 also **fold up** to bend something so that one part covers another part and it becomes smaller: *He folded the letter and put it into an envelope.* | *The man **folded up** his newspaper and stood up to leave.*

2 **fold your arms** to bend your arms, so that they are resting across your chest

fold² *noun* a line in paper or cloth where you have folded it: *Cut along the folds in the paper.*

fold·er /'fəʊldə $ 'foʊldɚ/ *noun* 1 a large folded piece of hard paper, in which you keep loose documents or other pieces of paper: *Have you seen my geography folder?* 2 a group of FILES

F

containing information which are stored together on a computer

fo·li·age /ˈfəʊli-ɪdʒ $ ˈfoʊli-ɪdʒ/ noun [no plural] formal the leaves of a plant: *She arranged the flowers and foliage in a vase.*

folk /fəʊk $foʊk/ adjective traditional and typical of the ordinary people who live in an area: *Do you like Scottish folk music?*

folks /fəʊks $foʊks/ plural noun **1** informal your parents or family: *My girlfriend has never met my folks.* **2** spoken used to talk to a group of people in a friendly way: *Hi folks – it's good to see you all.*

fol·low /ˈfɒləʊ $ ˈfɑloʊ/ verb

> **GRAMMAR**
> follow someone/something somewhere

1 to walk or drive behind someone or something: *I **followed** her **into** the house. | Sam had a feeling that someone was following him.*
2 to happen or come after something else: *The floods followed three weeks of heavy rain. | We had roast beef, followed by apple pie.*
3 if you follow a path, road etc, you go along it: *We **followed the path** around the outside of the castle.*
4 to understand something that is said: *Were you able to follow the lecture?*

> **PHRASES**

as follows used to introduce a list: *The team is **as follows**: Williams, Young, Hunter...*
follow advice, follow instructions to do what someone advises or tells you to do: *I think you should **follow** your mum's **advice**.*
follow someone's example, follow someone's lead to do something because someone else has done it: *His friends **followed** his **example** and stopped smoking.*

> **PHRASAL VERB**

follow up
follow something up if you follow up some information, you try to find out more: *The scientists decided to **follow up** this discovery **with** a new set of experiments.*

fol·low·er /ˈfɒləʊə $ ˈfɑloʊɚ/ noun

someone who supports someone or believes in something: *His followers believe he is a god.*

fol·low·ing¹ /ˈfɒləʊɪŋ $ ˈfɑloʊɪŋ/ adjective after the one you have just mentioned: *I was born in 1985, and my sister was born the following year.*

following² noun [no plural] **1** a group of people who support or admire someone such as a singer: *The Spice Girls have a big following all over the world.* **2** the following the people or things that you are going to mention next: *Do you have any of the following: eggs, sugar, or milk?*

following³ preposition after or as a result of something: *Following her death, there was a police investigation.*

fond /fɒnd $fɑnd/ adjective

> **GRAMMAR**
> fond of someone/something

if you are fond of someone or something, you like them very much: *He **was fond of** his sister. | I'm very **fond of** chocolate.*

food /fuːd/ noun [no plural]

things that you eat: *She was out buying food and drink for the party.*

food chain /ˈ. ./ noun a group of different kinds of living thing, in which one kind is eaten by another, which is eaten by another etc: *the plants at the bottom of the food chain*

food poi·son·ing /ˈ. ,.../ noun [no plural] an illness that is caused by eating food that contains harmful BACTERIA (=small creatures that spread disease): *I got food poisoning from eating a beefburger.*

fool¹ /fuːl/ noun **1** a stupid person: *You're behaving like a fool!* **2** make a fool of yourself to do something stupid, which you feel embarrassed about later: *She's always getting drunk and making a fool of herself.*

fool² verb to make someone believe something that is not true: *It was easy to fool the teachers into believing that I was ill.*

fool·ish /ˈfuːlɪʃ/ adjective not sensible: *It was very foolish of you to swim so far out in the sea.*
—**foolishly** adverb: *I've behaved very foolishly.*

fool·proof /ˈfuːlpruːf/ *adjective* certain to be successful: *a foolproof plan*

foot /fʊt/ *noun*

GRAMMAR
the foot of something
1 *plural* **feet** /fiːt/ your feet are the parts at the end of your legs that you stand on: *My feet are cold!* ⇨ see *picture at* BODY
2 *plural* **feet** or **foot** a unit for measuring length, equal to 12 INCHES or 0.3048 metres: *She was sitting a few feet away from us.* | *He was well over six foot tall.*
3 *[no plural]* the bottom of something such as a mountain, tree, or set of stairs: *She went to **the foot of** the stairs and called up to Robin.*

PHRASES
get to your feet, jump to your feet etc to stand up after you have been sitting down: *She **got to her feet** when we came in.*
on foot if you go somewhere on foot, you walk there: *We decided to go **on foot** rather than take the car.*
put your foot down *informal* to say very firmly that someone must not do something: *She wanted to go to the party but her dad **put** his **foot down**.*
put your foot in it *informal* to say something that upsets someone by mistake

foot·ball /ˈfʊtbɔːl/ *noun* **1** *[no plural]* BrE a game in which two teams try to kick a ball between two posts at either end of a field ⇨ same meaning SOCCER: *The children are playing football.* | *Who won the football match?* ⇨ see *picture on page 351* **2** *[no plural]* AmE a game in which two teams wearing special hats and clothes carry, kick, or throw a ball into an area at the end of a field to win points; AMERICAN FOOTBALL BrE: *Would you like to come to the football game with me?* **3** a ball that people use to play football: *He kicked the football over the fence.*

foot·bal·ler /ˈfʊtbɔːlə $ ˈfʊtˌbɔlɚ/ *noun* BrE someone who plays football

foot·note /ˈfʊtnəʊt $ ˈfʊtnoʊt/ *noun* a note at the bottom of a page in a book, which gives more information about something on that page: *He didn't bother reading the footnotes.*

foot·path /ˈfʊtpɑːθ $ ˈfʊtpæθ/ *noun* a path for people to walk along: *Don't ride your bike on the footpath.*

foot·print /ˈfʊtˌprɪnt/ *noun* a mark that your foot or shoe makes on the ground: *The children had made footprints in the snow.*

foot·step /ˈfʊtstep/ *noun* the sound of each step when someone is walking: *Can you hear footsteps?*

foot·wear /ˈfʊtweə $ ˈfʊtwer/ *noun* *[no plural]* things that you wear on your feet, such as shoes or boots: *The store has a big footwear department.*

for /fə $ fɚ; *strong* fɔː $ fɔːr/ *preposition*
1 how long something continues to happen: *I've been at this school for six years.* | *I must have slept for 10 hours.* ⇨ see *usage notes at* AGO *and* DURING
2 who will be given something or who can use something *I have a present for you.* | *Those swings are for little children.*
3 what the purpose of something is: *This knife is for cutting vegetables.* | *I need some money for my train ticket.*
4 who you are helping: *I opened the door for her.* | *We raised some money for the local hospital.* | *I did a few little jobs for my grandmother.*
5 where you are going: *The next morning we set off for London.* | *Is this the train for Cambridge?*
6 how far someone or something goes: *We walked for five miles without seeing anyone.*
7 agreeing with something: *Most people were for the idea of sharing the work* (=most people thought that sharing the work was a good idea).
8 how much you pay: *I bought an old television for £50.*

PHRASES
what for? why: *What did you do that for?*
for your birthday, for Christmas etc because it is your birthday, Christmas etc: *I **got** a puppy **for** my **birthday**.*

USAGE for, since, ago
For, **since**, and **ago** are used to talk about time. **For** is used with the present perfect or simple past tense. It is always followed

by periods of time: *She's been here* for *three days.* | *The party lasted for five hours.* **Since** is always used with the present perfect tense and with exact days, dates, and times: *He's been here since Sunday.* | *I've been working here since 1998.* **Ago** is always used with the simple past tense. It tells you how far back in the past something happened or began: *My grandfather died two years ago.*

forbade the past tense of FORBID

for·bid /fə'bɪd $ fɚ'bɪd/ *verb* formal **forbade** /fə'beɪd $ fɚ'bæd/ **forbidden** /fə'bɪdn $ fɚ'bɪdn/ **forbidding** to order someone not to do something: *My mother has forbidden me to see you.*

for·bid·den[1] /fə'bɪdn $ fɚ'bɪdn/ *adjective* not allowed: *It is forbidden to feed the animals.*

forbidden[2] the past participle of FORBID

force[1] /fɔːs $ fɔrs/ *noun*

GRAMMAR
the force of something

1 an organization or group of people who have been trained to do something, especially military or police work: *the local **police force** | a United Nations **peacekeeping force** | the company's **sales force***

2 [no plural] if you use force, you use physical strength or violence: *He threatened to take the letter from her **by force**.*

3 [no plural] the strength or power of something: *We all felt **the force of** the explosion.*

4 something that has an effect on things: ***the force of** gravity*

PHRASES
be in force, come into force if a law or rule is in force, it exists and people must obey it: *The rules will **be in force** by next summer.* | *The new law **came into force** last month.*
join forces if two people join forces, they start working together: *The university **is joining forces with** a technology company to do research.*

force[2] *verb*

GRAMMAR
force someone to do something

1 to make someone do something that they do not want to do: *His new girlfriend **forced** him **to** stop seeing*

his old friends. | *We **were forced to** go home early when our tent blew away.*

2 to use physical strength to move something or go somewhere: *He **forced open** the box.* | *The soldiers **forced** their **way into** the building.*

forced /fɔːst $ fɔrst/ *adjective* a forced smile or laugh is one that you give because you feel you have to, and not because you really want to

force·ful /'fɔːsfəl $ 'fɔrsfəl/ *adjective* powerful and strong: *She's not very forceful when she argues.*

fore·arm /'fɔːrɑːm $ 'fɔrɑrm/ *noun* the part of your arm between your hand and your elbow: *She has a cut on her left forearm.*

fore·cast[1] /'fɔːkɑːst $ 'fɔrkæst/ *noun* a description of what is likely to happen: *Have you heard the weather forecast?*

forecast[2] *verb*, past tense and past participle **forecast** or **forecasted** to say what is likely to happen: *The government is forecasting that unemployment will fall.*

fore·fa·ther /'fɔː,fɑːðə $ 'fɔr,fɑðɚ/ *noun* written a member of your family who lived a long time ago: *the time when our forefathers arrived in America*

fore·front /'fɔːfrʌnt $ 'fɔrfrʌnt/ *noun* **be at the forefront of something** to do more than other people to make, discover, or cause something new: *a British company that was at the forefront of computer design*

fore·gone con·clu·sion /,fɔːgɒn kən'kluːʒən $,fɔrgɒn kən'kluʒən/ *noun* something that is certain to happen: *War now seemed like a foregone conclusion.*

fore·ground /'fɔːgraʊnd $ 'fɔrgraʊnd/ *noun* **in the foreground** in the part of a picture or scene that is at the front ⇨ opposite BACKGROUND

fore·head /'fɒrəd $ 'fɔrhed/ *noun* the part of your face above your eyes: *You've got a spot in the middle of your forehead.* ⇨ see picture at HEAD[1]

for·eign /'fɒrɪn $ 'fɑrɪn/ *adjective*

1 not from your own country: *He speaks three foreign languages.* | *The university has a lot of foreign students.*

2 dealing with other countries: *Britain's foreign policy*

for·eign·er /'fɒrənə $ 'fɑrənɚ/ noun someone who is not from your own country: *A lot of foreigners visit our town.*

fore·most /'fɔːməʊst $ 'fɔrmoʊst/ adjective formal the most famous or important: *Kasparov is the world's foremost chess player.*

fo·ren·sic /fə'rensɪk/ adjective connected with the use of science to find out who was responsible for a crime: *There is a lot of forensic evidence, including fingerprints.*

fore·saw the past tense of FORESEE

fore·see /fɔː'siː $ fɔr'si/ verb foresaw /fɔː'sɔː $ fɔr'sɔ/ foreseen /fɔː'siːn $ fɔr'sin/ to expect that something will happen in the future: *I don't forsee any problems with the new system.*

fore·seen the past participle of FORESEE

fore·sight /'fɔːsaɪt $ 'fɔrsaɪt/ noun [no plural] the ability to imagine what might happen in the future, and consider this in your plans: *Lucy was glad she had had the foresight to keep her money separate from her husband's.*

for·est /'fɒrɪst $ 'fɔrɪst/ noun a large area of land covered with trees: *He got lost in the forest.* ⇨ see picture on page 348

for·ev·er /fər'evə $ fə'revɚ/ adverb
for all of the future: *I could stay here forever.* | *Those days are gone forever.*

PHRASE
take forever informal to take a very long time: *It's going to take forever to clean all this mess up!*

fore·word /'fɔːwɜːd $ 'fɔrwɚd/ noun a short piece of writing at the beginning of a book about the book or its writer

for·gave the past tense of FORGIVE

forge /fɔːdʒ $ fɔrdʒ/ verb to illegally produce something such as a document or picture and pretend that someone else produced it: *He forged his wife's signature.* | *forged banknotes*

for·ge·ry /'fɔːdʒəri $ 'fɔrdʒəri/ noun, plural forgeries a document, painting etc that someone has forged ⇨ same meaning FAKE[1]: *It was obvious that the painting was a forgery.*

forget /fə'get $ fɚ'get/ verb forgot /fə'gɒt $ fɚ'gɑt/ forgotten /fə'gɒtn $ fɚ'gɑtn/

GRAMMAR
forget (that)
forget what/who/where etc
forget about something/some-one
forget to do something

1 to be or become unable to remember something: *I'll never forget the day I started school.* | *I had forgotten that you know him.* | *I've forgotten what her name is.*
2 if you forget to do something, you do not remember to do it: *Don't forget to feed the fish.* | *We forgot about lunch.*
3 if you forget something, you do not remember to bring it with you: *I've forgotten my purse.*
4 to stop thinking about someone or something: *Forget her – you'll find someone better.*

USAGE forget, leave
If you want to talk about the place where you have left something because you did not remember to take it with you, use **leave** not **forget**. For example, you can say *I forgot my passport.* But you CANNOT say *I forgot my passport at home.* You must say *I left my passport at home.*

for·get·ful /fə'getfəl $ fɚ'getfəl/ adjective someone who is forgetful often forgets things: *I'm getting forgetful in my old age.*

for·give /fə'gɪv $ fɚ'gɪv/ verb forgave /fə'geɪv $ fɚ'geɪv/ forgiven /fə'gɪvən $ fɚ'gɪvən/

GRAMMAR
forgive someone for doing something
to stop being angry with someone who has done something wrong: *He begged her to forgive him.* | *I'll never forgive her for lying to me.*

for·giv·en the past participle of FORGIVE

for·give·ness /fə'gɪvnəs $ fɚ'gɪvnəs/ noun [no plural] when someone forgives another person for doing something wrong: *I begged for her forgiveness.*

for·got the past tense of FORGET

for·got·ten the past participle of FORGET

F

fork /fɔːk $fɔrk/ *noun*
1 a small tool with four points that you use for picking up food when you eat: *He put down his knife and fork.*
2 a tool with four points that you use for breaking up soil in the garden
3 a place where a road divides into two parts: *At the next fork in the road, go left.*

for·lorn /fəˈlɔːn $fərˈlɔrn/ *adjective*
written sad and lonely: *She looked very forlorn sitting alone waiting for a train.*

form¹ /fɔːm $fɔrm/ *noun*

GRAMMAR
a form of something

1 one type of something: *Game shows are a cheap form of entertainment. | We would welcome help in any form.*
2 an official piece of paper with spaces to write information in. You fill in, fill out, or complete a form: *Just fill in the application form* (=write information in the right spaces).
3 *BrE* a class in school: *He's in the sixth form now.*

form² *verb*
1 if something forms, it starts to exist: *A long line of people formed outside the shop.*
2 to make something or start something that is new: *In 1996, he formed a new band called 'Target'.*
3 to be something: *The river forms a natural barrier between the two countries.*

form·al /ˈfɔːməl $ˈfɔrməl/ *adjective*
1 official: *There will be a formal investigation into the accident. | He had no formal qualifications.*
2 formal words or clothes are suitable for serious or important occasions: *'Good evening' is a formal way of saying hello. | He wasn't comfortable wearing formal clothes.*
–**formally** *adverb*: *She has not yet formally applied for the job.*

for·mal·i·ty /fɔːˈmæləti $fɔrˈmæləti/ *noun, plural* **formalities** an official part of a process: *After going through the usual formalities, we got on the plane.*

for·mat¹ /ˈfɔːmæt $ˈfɔrmæt/ *noun* the way that something is organized or designed: *This week the show has a new format.*

format² *verb* **formatted, formatting** to organize the space on a computer DISK so that you can store information on it

for·ma·tion /fɔːˈmeɪʃən $fɔrˈmeɪʃən/ *noun [no plural]* when something starts to exist or develop: *the formation of ice crystals*

for·mer¹ /ˈfɔːmə $ˈfɔrmər/ *adjective* used to say that a person or thing was something in the past but is not that thing now: *his former girlfriend | the former world champion*

former² *noun* **the former** *formal* the first of two people or things that you have just mentioned: *Of the two singers Williams and Barlow, the former is the more popular.*

for·mer·ly /ˈfɔːməli $ˈfɔrmərli/ *adverb* in the past: *the singer formerly known as Prince*

for·mi·da·ble /ˈfɔːmədəbəl $ˈfɔrmədəbəl, fərˈmɪdəbəl/ *adjective* a formidable person is powerful and slightly frightening: *The headmistress was a formidable woman.*

for·mu·la /ˈfɔːmjələ $ˈfɔrmjələ/ *noun, plural* **formulas** or **formulae** /-liː/ a group of numbers or letters that show a mathematical or scientific rule: *What's the formula for calculating the area of a circle?*

for·mu·late /ˈfɔːmjəleɪt $ˈfɔrmjəleɪt/ *verb* to develop a plan and decide all the details: *He soon formulated a plan of escape.*

fort /fɔːt $fɔrt/ *noun* a strong building that soldiers use for defending a place

forth·com·ing /ˌfɔːθˈkʌmɪŋ $ˌfɔrθˈkʌmɪŋ/ *adjective formal* 1 a forthcoming event will happen soon: *Who will win the forthcoming election?* 2 if something is forthcoming, someone gives it to you or offers it to you: *No offers of help have been forthcoming.*

forth·right /ˈfɔːθraɪt $ˈfɔrθraɪt/ *adjective* saying what you think honestly and directly: *She's usually very forthright – I'm surprised she didn't tell you she was annoyed.*

fort·night /ˈfɔːtnaɪt $ˈfɔrtnaɪt/ *noun BrE* two weeks: *The work will take about a fortnight. | She first became ill a fortnight ago.*

for·tress /'fɔːtrɪs $'fɔrtrɪs/ noun, plural fortresses a big strong building that people use for defending a place

for·tu·nate /'fɔːtʃənət $'fɔrtʃənət/ adjective

> **GRAMMAR**
> **fortunate to do something**
> **fortunate in having something**
> **fortunate (that)**

lucky ⇨ opposite UNFORTUNATE: *It was a bad accident – I'm **fortunate to** be alive.* | *You **are fortunate in having** such good friends.* | *It was fortunate that they weren't caught.*

for·tu·nate·ly /'fɔːtʃənətli $'fɔrtʃənətli/ adverb

used to talk about something good or lucky that happens: *Fortunately, the car wasn't damaged much in the accident.*

for·tune /'fɔːtʃən $'fɔrtʃən/ noun 1 a lot of money: *His computer cost a fortune.* 2 chance, or the good and bad things that happen to you: *The team's fortunes changed and they began winning games.*

for·ty /'fɔːti $'fɔrti/ number, plural forties 1 40 2 the forties the years from 1940 to 1949 3 be in your forties to be aged between 40 and 49 – fortieth number

for·ward¹ /'fɔːwəd $'fɔrwəd/ also **forwards** adverb

towards the direction that is in front of you ⇨ opposite BACKWARDS: *They pushed the car forward a couple of feet.* | *Debbie leaned forward to speak to the taxi driver.*

forward² adjective forward planning, forward thinking when you make plans for the future: *With a little forward planning, your party should be a great success.*

for·wards /'fɔːwədz $'fɔrwərdz/ adverb forward: *Can you move your car forwards a little?*

fos·sil /'fɒsəl $'fɑsəl/ noun the shape of an animal or plant from the past that appears in rock

fos·ter¹ /'fɒstə $'fɑstər/ verb 1 to encourage a feeling or skill to develop: *We want to foster a friendly atmosphere*

in the office. 2 to take care of someone else's child for a period of time, without becoming their legal parent: *They fostered two children for nearly a year.*

foster² adjective foster parents, foster children people who foster someone else's child, or children who are fostered: *Pippa and Jo are my foster parents.*

fought the past tense and past participle of FIGHT¹

foul¹ /faʊl/ adjective 1 very dirty or very unpleasant: *What's that foul smell?* 2 foul language language that is rude and offensive: *The film contains a lot of violence and foul language.*

foul² verb if a sports player fouls another player, they do something that is against the rules: *He was sent off for fouling the goalkeeper.*
– **foul** noun: *He committed a foul.*

found¹ the past tense and past participle of FIND

found² /faʊnd/ verb to start an organization: *Our school was founded in 1900.*

foun·da·tion /faʊn'deɪʃən/ noun 1 something basic or important on which something else is based: *Reading and writing are the foundations of learning.* 2 an organization that gives money for special purposes: *The equipment has been paid for the AIDS Foundation.* 3 foundations BrE, foundation AmE the solid base under the ground that supports a building: *They have only built the foundations of the new office block.*

found·er /'faʊndə $'faʊndər/ noun someone who starts an organization: *one of the original founders of the company*

foun·tain /'faʊntən/ noun an object that sends water up into the air

fountain

fountain pen /'.. ,./ noun a pen that you fill with ink

four /fɔː $fɔr/ number 1 4 2 on all fours if you are on all fours, your hands and knees are on the ground: *She was crawling around on all fours under the table.*

four·teen /ˌfɔːˈtiːn $ ˌfɔrˈtin/ *number* 14
–**fourteenth** *number*

fourth /fɔːθ $ fɔrθ/ *number* **1** 4th: *This is the fourth time I've asked you.* **2** the American word for QUARTER

fox /fɒks $ fɑks/ *noun, plural* **foxes** a wild animal like a dog with red-brown fur, a pointed face, and a thick tail ⇨ see picture on page 339

foy·er /ˈfɔɪeɪ $ ˈfɔɪɚ/ *noun* a room at the entrance to a hotel, theatre, or other large building: *I'll meet you in the foyer of the nightclub.*

frac·tion /ˈfrækʃən/ *noun* a number that is smaller than 1, for example ⅓ or ⅝

frac·ture /ˈfræktʃə $ ˈfræktʃɚ/ *verb* to break a bone in your body: *I've fractured my wrist.*
–**fracture** *noun*: *He had a fracture in his foot.*

fra·gile /ˈfrædʒaɪl $ ˈfrædʒəl/ *adjective* easily broken or destroyed: *Some of the works of art are very fragile.*

frag·ment /ˈfrægmənt/ *noun* a small piece of something: *The nurse removed the fragments of glass from my hand.*

fra·grant /ˈfreɪɡrənt/ *adjective written* something that is fragrant smells pleasant: *The room had a fragrant smell of flowers.*

frail /freɪl/ *adjective* thin and weak: *My grandma's getting very old and frail now.*

frame¹ /freɪm/ *noun*

1 the wood, metal etc that is around a picture or window: *a wooden picture frame*
2 the pieces of wood, metal etc that are the main structure of something: *The frame of the chair is made of metal.*

PHRASE
frame of mind your frame of mind is the way you are feeling: *This record will put you in a relaxed **frame of mind**.*

frame² *verb* to put a picture into a frame: *It's a very good photo – why don't you frame it?*

frames /freɪmz/ *plural noun* the part of a pair of glasses that holds the two pieces of glass: *He sat on my glasses and broke the frames.*

frame·work /ˈfreɪmwɜːk $ ˈfreɪmwɚk/ *noun* the main structure around which a building or vehicle is built: *The framework of the car was not strong enough.*

frank /fræŋk/ *adjective* someone who is frank says things in an honest and direct way: *I've always been frank with her.*
–**frankness** *noun* [no plural]: *Some people don't like Sue's frankness.*

fran·tic /ˈfræntɪk/ *adjective* **1** hurrying in a way that is not organized: *There was a frantic rush for tickets.* **2** very anxious or upset: *We've been frantic with worry – where have you been?*
–**frantically** /-kli/ *adverb*: *I tried frantically to put out the fire.*

fraud /frɔːd/ *noun* when someone deceives people to get money: *Tax fraud is a serious offence.*

fraught /frɔːt/ *adjective written* if something is fraught with problems, danger etc, it involves a lot of problems, danger etc: *Firefighting is a job that is fraught with risks.*

fray /freɪ/ *verb* if cloth frays, its threads become loose at the edge: *The legs of his trousers had frayed at the bottom.*

freak¹ /friːk/ *noun* **1** *informal* someone who has a very strong interest in something: *I'm an exercise freak.* **2** someone who is strange or who looks strange

freak² *adjective* a freak event is a very unusual one: *He was injured in a freak accident.*

freck·le /ˈfrekəl/ *noun* a small brown spot on someone's skin: *She has freckles all over her nose.* ⇨ see picture at HEAD¹ and on page 353

free¹ /friː/ *adjective*

GRAMMAR
free to do something
free of/from something

1 something that is free does not cost any money: *a free gift in a magazine* | *Membership of the club is free.*
2 if people are free, they are not controlled and can do what they like: *In a free society, you can say what you like about the government.* | *You are **free to** do whatever you like.*
3 if you are free, you are not being held or kept somewhere: *After six*

▼ years in prison, at last he was free. | She managed to **get free of** the crashed car.

4 not busy doing other things: *I'm free every evening this week.*

5 if something is free, it is not being used: *There's a free table over there. | Carrying a bag on your back leaves your hands free.*

6 something that is free of something harmful or unpleasant does not have it: *These vegetables are free from chemicals.*

PHRASES

feel free *spoken* used to tell someone that they are allowed to do something: *Feel free to make suggestions.*

set someone/something free to allow someone to leave a prison or a wild animal to leave a place such as a zoo: *All the prisoners were set free.*

free of charge something that is free of charge does not cost any money: *This advice is free of charge.*

free² verb

GRAMMAR
free someone from something
free someone to do something

1 if you free someone who has been unable to leave a place, you let them go or get them out: *Should they free this murderer from prison? | They tried to free the people who were trapped inside the burning building.*

2 also **free up** to make a person or thing available: *If nurses treat small injuries, this will free doctors to deal with more serious injuries. | Remove some of the files to free up space on the computer.*

free³ adverb

without having to pay any money: *After four o'clock, you can get into the exhibition free.*

PHRASE

for free **a)** if you do something for free, you do it without being paid: *He offered to appear in the film for free.* **b)** if you get something for free, you get it without having to pay: *I got this jacket for free.*

free·dom /'friːdəm/ *noun* [no plural]

GRAMMAR
freedom of something
the freedom to do something

1 when you are not controlled and are allowed to do what you like: *I believe in freedom of choice* (=I believe people should be able to choose what they like). *| With this diet, you have the freedom to eat as many vegetables as you want.*

2 when you are not held as a prisoner: *his first day of freedom after ten years in jail*

free·lance /'friːlɑːns $'friːlæns/ *adjective, adverb* someone who is freelance works for several different organizations: *I'm a freelance writer. | I'm thinking of going freelance.*

free·ly /'friːli/ *adverb* without anyone trying to control you or stop you doing something: *Children can move freely between classrooms.*

free speech /ˌ. './ *noun* [no plural] the right to express your opinions: *If the government believes in free speech, why does it stop us protesting?*

free·way /'friːweɪ/ the American word for MOTORWAY

freeze /friːz/ froze /frəʊz $frouz/ frozen /'frəʊzən $'froʊzən/ *verb*

1 if water freezes, it becomes hard because it is very cold: *The lake had frozen.*

2 if you freeze food, you make it very cold and hard so that it stays in good condition for a long time: *She froze some of the soup.*
– **frozen** *adjective: a packet of frozen peas*

PHRASE

freeze to death to die because you are so cold: *The climbers froze to death on the mountain.*

freez·er /'friːzə $'friːzɚ/ *noun* a large piece of kitchen equipment where you freeze food and keep it at a very low temperature: *There's some ice-cream in the freezer.*

freez·ing¹ /'friːzɪŋ/ *adjective informal* very cold: *I'm freezing – shall we light the fire? | Put your coat on – it's freezing outside.* ⇨ see usage note at COLD¹

freezing² *noun* [no plural] 32°F or 0°C: *It was 3 degrees below freezing.*

freight /freɪt/ *noun* [no plural] things that are being taken from one place to another by train, road, plane, or ship: *a freight train*

French fry /ˌfrentʃ 'fraɪ/ *noun, plural* French fries a long thin piece of potato cooked in fat; CHIP *BrE*

fren·zy /'frenzi/ *noun* [no plural] when you are so anxious, excited etc that you are unable to control your behaviour: *She was shouting and swearing in a frenzy of rage.*

fre·quen·cy /'friːkwənsi/ *plural* frequencies *noun formal* **1** [no plural] the number of times that something happens: *Her headaches have increased in frequency.* **2** the rate at which a sound or light wave is repeated: *We cannot hear sounds of very high frequency.*

fre·quent /'friːkwənt/ *adjective*

something that is frequent happens often: *She makes frequent visits to the United States.*

fre·quent·ly /'friːkwəntli/ *adverb formal* often: *He's frequently late for school.*

fresh /freʃ/ *adjective*

1 new and different from the previous ones: *The police have received fresh information relating to the murder.* | *people with fresh new ideas*

2 fresh food has been produced or picked recently: *Eat plenty of fresh fruit and vegetables.*

3 pleasantly clean: *the fresh smell of lemons* | *I need some fresh air* (=air outside a building).

4 fresh water contains no salt and can be drunk: *They had a good supply of fresh water on the boat.*

5 if you are fresh, you are not tired: *Let's do as much work as possible while we're still fresh.*

PHRASES
be fresh in your mind, be fresh in your memory if something is fresh in your mind or memory, you remember it clearly, because it happened recently: *The events of that day* **were** still **fresh in** her **mind**.
fresh from somewhere, fresh out of somewhere someone who is fresh from a place has just left that

place: *He joined the company* **fresh from** college.

fresh·ly /'freʃli/ *adverb* very recently: *the smell of freshly baked bread*

fresh·man /'freʃmən/ *noun* AmE, plural freshmen /-mən/ a student in the first year of HIGH SCHOOL or college

fric·tion /'frɪkʃən/ *noun* [no plural] **1** when people disagree with each other and argue in an unfriendly way: *There seemed to be some friction between Jo and Pete.* **2** when one surface rubs against another: *Friction produces heat.*

Fri·day /'fraɪdi/ *written abbreviation* **Fri** *noun* the day of the week between Thursday and Saturday: *See you on Friday!* | *It's Friday June 22nd.*

fridge /frɪdʒ/ *noun* a large piece of kitchen equipment where you keep food at a low temperature but do not freeze it

friend /frend/ *noun*

someone that you know well and like: *She invited all her friends to the party.* | *Everyone needs a few* **close friends.** | *He used to be my* **best friend** (=my closest friend).

PHRASES
make friends to start having someone as a friend, or several people as friends: *I* **made friends with** *a girl in my class.* | *I* **made** *many* **friends** *there.*
be friends if two people are friends, they know each other well and like each other: *We've* **been friends** *for years.*

friend·ly /'frendli/ *adjective* friendlier, friendliest

GRAMMAR
friendly with someone

1 someone who is friendly talks to people or behaves pleasantly towards them ⇨ *opposite* UNFRIENDLY: *Everyone in the village was very friendly to us.*

2 if you are friendly with someone, you are their friend: *She's still* **friendly with** *many people she knew at college.*

friend·ship /'frendʃɪp/ *noun* a relationship in which two people are friends: *Our long friendship began at school.*

fries /fraɪz/ *plural noun* French fries: *I'll have a cheeseburger and fries.*

fright /fraɪt/ *noun* [no plural] a sudden feeling of fear: *You gave me a fright – I didn't realise you were right behind me. | I nearly died of fright!*

fright·en /'fraɪtn/ *verb*
to make someone feel afraid: *Being alone in the dark frightens some people. | If you have a cat, it will **frighten** the birds **away*** (=make them go away because they are afraid).

fright·ened /'fraɪtnd/ *adjective*

> **GRAMMAR**
> **frightened of something/someone**
> **frightened that**
> **frightened to do something**
> afraid that something bad might happen: *Liz has always been **frightened** of spiders. | I **was frightened that** someone would fall and hurt themselves. | He **was frightened to** leave the house.*

fright·en·ing /'fraɪtn-ɪŋ/ *adjective*
something that is frightening makes you feel afraid: *It's a very frightening film.*

frill /frɪl/ *noun* a long piece of cloth with many small folds, which you use to decorate clothing etc: *Her skirt had a frill around the bottom.*

frill·y /'frɪli/ *adjective* **frillier, frilliest** decorated with pieces of cloth which have many small folds: *I don't like frilly dresses.*

fringe /frɪndʒ/ *noun* BrE the part of your hair that hangs over the part of your face above your eyes; BANGS *AmE*: *My fringe needs cutting.* ⇨ *see picture at* HEAD¹

frisk

frisk /frɪsk/ *verb* to feel and search the clothes someone is wearing, to check that they do not have any hidden weapons or drugs: *The security guard frisked me.*

fri·vol·i·ty /frɪ'vɒləti $frɪ'vɑləti/ *noun* when people behave in a way that is not serious or sensible: *My father disapproves of frivolity.*

friv·o·lous /'frɪvələs/ *adjective* behaving in a silly way when you should be sensible: *She kept making frivolous comments.*

frizz·y /'frɪzi/ *adjective* **frizzier, frizziest** frizzy hair is very tightly curled: *My hair's gone all frizzy.*

frog /frɒg $frɔg/ *noun* a small green animal that lives in water or near water and has long legs for jumping

frog·man /'frɒgmən $'frɔgmən/ *noun*, *plural* **frogmen** /-mən/ someone whose job is to work under water wearing a rubber suit and special equipment for breathing: *Frogmen are searching for the body in the river.*

from /frəm; *strong* frɒm $frʌm/ *preposition*
1 where something starts: *He took the train from London to Glasgow* (=he left London and went to Glasgow). | *I ran all the way home from school.*
2 when something starts: *I worked from 4 o'clock until 7* (=I started work at 4 o'clock and finished at 7).
3 where someone was born, lives, or works: *My mother is from Wales* (=she was born in Wales). | *We're all from Glasgow* (=we all live in Glasgow). | *This is Mr Grange from the hospital* (=Mr Grange works in the hospital). | *a group of students from the local college*
4 saying how far away something is: *Our house is 1 kilometre from the station* (=the distance between our house and the station is 1 kilometre). | *The ball stopped two metres from the hole. | She now lives 200 miles **away from** her parents.*
5 who has given or sent something: *I've just had an email from Kurt. | Last Christmas I got a new bike from my parents.*
6 where something is before it is removed: *He took the box from the back of the car. | Can you fetch a chair from the kitchen? | He washed the mud from his shoes.*

front¹ /frʌnt/ *noun*
the front the part of something that is furthest forward, or that is most

important: *Can I sit in **the front of** the car?* | *His name was on **the front of** the book in big letters.*

PHRASES

in front further forward than someone or something else: *The car **in front** stopped suddenly.* | *Tom was sitting **in front of** me in the cinema.*
⇨ *see picture on page 354*

in front of something/someone facing something or near the most important side of it: *She stood **in front of** the mirror.* | *There was a lake **in front of** the house.*

front² *adjective* at or in the front of something: *His brother sat in the front seat.* | *The front door was open.*

fron·tier /ˈfrʌntɪə $ frʌnˈtɪr/ *noun* BrE the place where two countries meet ⇨ *same meaning* BORDER¹: *Strasbourg is on the frontier between France and Germany.*

frost /frɒst $ frɔst/ *noun* [no plural] a white powder of ice, which forms on surfaces outside when it is very cold: *The ground was covered with frost.*

frost·bite /ˈfrɒstbaɪt $ ˈfrɔstbaɪt/ *noun* [no plural] if you get frostbite, your fingers or toes freeze and are badly damaged

frost·ing /ˈfrɒstɪŋ $ ˈfrɔstɪŋ/ the American word for ICING

frost·y /ˈfrɒsti $ ˈfrɔsti/ *adjective* **frostier, frostiest** very cold or covered with FROST: *It was a frosty morning.*

froth /frɒθ $ frɔθ/ *noun* [no plural] a lot of small BUBBLES on top of a liquid: *He blew the froth off his coffee.*

frown /fraʊn/ *verb* to make an angry or unhappy expression, so that lines appear on your face above your eyes: *Her mother frowned when she saw what Ann was wearing.*
–**frown** *noun*: *He had a worried frown on his face.*

frown

froze the past tense of FREEZE

frozen the past participle of FREEZE

fruit /fruːt/ *noun*, *plural* **fruit** or **fruits** something such as an apple or orange

which grows on a plant, tree, or bush, and contains seeds: *Bananas are my favourite fruit.* | *a basket of fruit*

fruit·ful /ˈfruːtfəl/ *adjective* formal producing good results: *Was it a fruitful meeting?*

fruit·less /ˈfruːtləs/ *adjective* formal failing to produce good results, especially after much effort: *It was a fruitless search – they found no one.*

fruit·y /ˈfruːti/ *adjective* **fruitier, fruitiest** tasting or smelling strongly of fruit: *This wine has a fruity smell.*

frus·trate /frʌˈstreɪt $ ˈfrʌstreɪt/ *verb* if something frustrates you, it makes you feel impatient or angry because you are unable to do what you want to do: *It frustrates me when she doesn't listen to me.*
–**frustrated** *adjective*: *I get frustrated when I can't do things straight away.*

frus·trat·ing /frʌˈstreɪtɪŋ $ ˈfrʌstreɪtɪŋ/ *adjective* making you feel disappointed and angry because you try to do something, but cannot do it: *It is so frustrating to play well and still lose.*

frus·tra·tion /frʌˈstreɪʃən/ *noun* the feeling of being impatient or angry because you are unable to do what you want to do: *She threw her pen on the floor in frustration.*

fry /fraɪ/ *verb* **fried, fries** to cook something in hot oil: *I'll fry the onions.*

frying pan /ˈ.. ./ *noun* a round flat pan with a long handle that you use for frying food

ft. the written abbreviation of FOOT or FEET: *The garage is 20 ft. long.*

fu·el¹ /ˈfjuːəl/ *noun* a substance such as coal, gas, or oil, which you can burn to produce heat or power: *The engine had run out of fuel.*

fuel² *verb* written **fuelled, fuelling** BrE, **fueled, fueling** AmE to make a situation worse, or make someone's feelings stronger: *Her behaviour only fuelled his anger.*

fu·gi·tive /ˈfjuːdʒətɪv/ *noun* someone who has escaped and is trying to avoid being caught, especially by the police

ful·fil BrE, **fulfill** AmE /fʊlˈfɪl/ *verb* formal **fulfilled, fulfilling** **1** if you fulfil a promise, aim etc, you do something that you have promised or wanted to do: *I must fulfil my promise.* | *Will he ever fulfil his ambition to be a pilot?* **2** if someone or something fulfils a ROLE or FUNCTION, they do something that is needed: *I think he will fulfil his role as captain well.*

ful·filled /fʊlˈfɪld/ *adjective* completely satisfied with your life or your job: *It is important to feel fulfilled in your work.*

ful·fil·ling /fʊlˈfɪlɪŋ/ *adjective* making you feel satisfied: *Is your relationship a fulfilling one?*

full /fʊl/ *adjective*

1 something that is full of things or people contains a lot of them: *His house is full of interesting books.* | *On Saturday nights the streets are full of young people.*

2 also **full up** *BrE* if something is full, there is no space left in it: *My suitcase was already completely full.* | *The school is full up this year.* ⇨ opposite EMPTY¹ ⇨ *see picture at* EMPTY

3 complete and including everything: *Could you give me your full name and address?* | *For full details of our holidays, write to the address below.*

4 also **full up** *BrE informal* you can say that you are full when you have eaten as much food as you want: *"More ice-cream, Susan?" "No thanks, I'm full."*

PHRASES

full marks *BrE* if you get full marks for work you do at school, you get the highest mark that it is possible to get: *I got full marks in my French test.*

at full speed, at full volume: *The train was going at full speed* (=as quickly as it could) *when the accident happened.* | *He was playing his stereo at full volume* (=as loudly as it could be played).

in full if you pay an amount of money in full, you pay the whole amount

full-blown /ˌ. ˈ./ *adjective* fully developed: *He has full-blown AIDS.*

full-grown /ˌ. ˈ./ *also* **fully-grown** /ˌ.. ˈ./ *adjective* a full-grown animal, plant, or person has developed completely and will not grow any bigger: *A full-grown blue whale can weigh thirty tons.*

full-length /ˌ. ˈ./ *adjective* 1 not shorter than the normal length: *I've seen the full-length version of the film.* 2 a full-length skirt or dress reaches the ground

full moon /ˌ. ˈ./ *noun* the moon when it looks completely round: *There's going to be a full moon tonight.*

full-scale /ˌ. ˈ./ *adjective* 1 a full-scale action or situation uses or includes everything possible: *This disagreement could lead to a full-scale war.* 2 a full-scale model, copy, or picture is the same size as the real thing: *a full-scale model of a human brain*

full stop /ˌ. ˈ./ *noun BrE* a mark (.) that you use to show the end of a sentence; PERIOD *AmE*

full-time /ˌ. ˈ./ *adverb, adjective* if you work or study full-time, you work or study all day during the whole week: *I'm looking for a full-time job.*

ful·ly /ˈfʊli/ *adverb* completely: *I am fully aware of the situation.*

fum·ble /ˈfʌmbəl/ *verb written* to try with difficulty to find, move, or hold something, using your hands in an awkward way: *She fumbled in her bag for her keys.*

fume /fjuːm/ *verb* to be very angry: *I was an hour late coming home, and my mother was fuming.*

fumes

DO NOT
INHALE

fumes /fjuːmz/ *plural noun* gas or smoke with a strong smell that is unpleasant to breathe: *They had breathed in poisonous fumes.*

fun¹ /fʌn/ *noun [no plural]*

if something is fun, you enjoy doing it or being involved in it: *The party was great fun.*

PHRASES

have fun to enjoy yourself doing something nice: *Everyone had fun playing in the snow.*

for fun if you do something for fun, you do it because you enjoy it: *We slept out in the garden, just for fun.*

make **fun** of someone to say unkind things about someone and
laugh at them: *Children often **make
fun of** their teachers.*

USAGE fun, funny
Don't use **fun** and **funny** in the same way.
Use **fun** to talk about situations or activities that you enjoy: *You need to go out
more and have some fun.* **Funny** is used
to describe someone or something that
makes you laugh: *The book was so funny
that I couldn't stop laughing.*

fun² adjective informal enjoyable: *We had a
really fun time.*

func·tion¹ /'fʌŋkʃən/ noun the purpose that something is made for: *The
function of this switch is to make the
screen brighter or darker.*

function² verb if a machine, system etc
is functioning, it is working: *Scientists
are not sure how our brains function.*

fund¹ /fʌnd/ noun **1** an amount of
money that someone keeps for a particular purpose: *I put the money in my
holiday fund.* **2** funds the money that
you need to do something: *We're raising
(=collecting) funds for our school.*

fund² verb to provide money for an event
or activity: *A local business is funding the
competition.*

fun·da·men·tal /ˌfʌndəˈmentl/ adjective related to the most basic and important parts of something: *What are
the fundamental differences between
men and women?*
–**fundamentally** adverb: *The company is
fundamentally changing the way it does
business.*

fund-rais·ing /'. ˌ../ noun [no plural] the
activity of collecting money for a particular purpose: *concerts and other fund-
raising activities*

fu·ne·ral /'fjuːnərəl/ noun a ceremony
for someone who has just died: *I didn't
go to my aunt's funeral.*

fun·fair /'fʌnfeə $ 'fʌnfer/ noun BrE a
noisy outdoor event where you can ride
on machines or play games to win prizes
⇨ same meaning FAIR²

fun·gus /'fʌŋgəs/ noun, plural fungi
/-gaɪ, -dʒaɪ/ or funguses a plant such
as a MUSHROOM or a powder that grows
on things such as old wood or food:
Fungus was growing on the damp walls.

funk·y /'fʌŋki/ adjective informal music

that is funky has a good strong beat and
is enjoyable to listen to

fun·ny /'fʌni/ adjective funnier,
funniest
1 if someone or something is funny,
they make you laugh: *It was one of
the funniest films I've ever seen.*
2 strange or unusual: *There was a
funny smell in the house.*

fur /fɜː $ fɜːr/ noun [no plural] the thick soft
hair that covers the bodies of some ani-
mals: *I stroked the rabbit's soft fur.* | *She
wore a fur coat.*

fu·ri·ous /'fjʊəriəs $ 'fjʊriəs/ adjective
very angry: *She's furious with me for kiss-
ing her boyfriend.* ⇨ see usage note at
ANGRY

fur·nace /'fɜːnɪs $ 'fɜːnɪs/ noun an ob-
ject with a very hot fire in it that is used
for melting metals, burning things, or
producing heat: *They burned the rubbish in a furnace.*

fur·nish /'fɜːnɪʃ $ 'fɜːnɪʃ/ verb to put
furniture into a house or room: *I can't
afford to furnish my new apartment.*

fur·ni·ture /'fɜːnɪtʃə $ 'fɜːnɪtʃɚ/
noun [no plural]
objects such as chairs, tables, and
beds: *All our furniture is old.* | *Do you
sell office furniture?*

USAGE
Furniture does not have a plural form. You
can say **some furniture**, **any furniture**, or
a piece of furniture: *When we first got
married, we didn't have **any furniture** at
all.*

fur·ry /'fɜːri $ 'fɜːi/ adjective furrier,
furriest covered with fur: *a small furry
animal*

fur·ther¹ /'fɜːðə $ 'fɜːðɚ/ adverb
1 a longer distance: *He walked a few
steps further away from me.* | *They
wanted to move to a town further
south.*
2 formal more: *Have you thought about
your plans any further?*

further² adjective formal additional: *Do I
need a further appointment?*

further ed·u·ca·tion /ˌ.. ..ˈ../ noun
[no plural] BrE education for people who
have finished school but are not at a

university: *Do you want to go on to further education?*

fur·thest /'fɜːðəst $ 'fɚðəst/ *adjective, adverb* the longest distance: *the planet that is furthest from the Earth*

fur·tive /'fɜːtɪv $ 'fɚtɪv/ *adjective* behaving as if you want to keep something secret: *She gave him a furtive smile.*
– **furtively** *adverb*

fu·ry /'fjʊəri $ 'fjʊri/ *noun* [no plural] *written* extreme anger: *After reading the letter, she was shaking with fury.*

fuse¹ /fjuːz/ *noun* **1** a short wire inside a piece of electrical equipment that melts if too much electricity passes through it: *This plug needs a new fuse.* **2** a piece of string fixed to explosive that you light to make an explosion happen a short time later

fuse² *verb* if two things fuse, or if you fuse them, they join together and become one thing: *The two pieces of bone fused together.*

fuss¹ /fʌs/ *noun* **1** [no plural] when people become very excited, angry, or upset about something that is not very serious or important: *What's all the fuss about?* **2 make a fuss** to complain about something in a noisy way: *He was making a fuss because the train was late.* **3 make a fuss of someone** BrE, **make a fuss over someone** AmE to pay someone a lot of attention and do nice things for them: *My boyfriend always makes a fuss of me on my birthday.*

fuss² *verb* to behave in a nervous, anxious way, worrying over unimportant things: *Don't fuss – I'm fine.*

fuss·y /'fʌsi/ *adjective* **fussier, fussiest** someone who is fussy only likes a few things and does not accept things that they do not like: *I'm very fussy about what I wear.*

fu·tile /'fjuːtaɪl $ 'fjuːtl/ *adjective* certain not to be effective or successful: *The police made a futile attempt to rescue him.*

fu·ture¹ /'fjuːtʃə $ 'fjuːtʃɚ/ *noun*
1 the future the time that will come after the present time: *Young people often don't think about the future.* | *In the future, almost everyone will have a computer.*
2 what will happen to something or someone: *The future of the band was looking uncertain.* | *We all need to think about our country's future.*

PHRASE
in future starting now and continuing: *In future I'm going to work a lot harder.*

future² *adjective*
future things are things that will happen or exist after the present time: *They discussed possible future projects.* | *He and his future wife* (=the woman who will be his wife) *have bought a house together.*

PHRASE
the future tense the form of a verb that we use to talk about what will happen after the present time

fuzz·y /'fʌzi/ *adjective* **fuzzier, fuzziest** unclear: *The TV picture's gone fuzzy.*

F

Gg

gad·get /'gædʒɪt/ *noun* a small tool or machine that helps you do something: *a handy little gadget for opening bottles*

gag¹ /gæg/ *verb* **gagged, gagging** to cover someone's mouth with a piece of cloth so that they cannot make any noise: *The robbers tied him up and gagged him.*

gag² *noun* a piece of cloth used to gag someone

gain¹ /geɪn/ *verb* **1** to get something that is important, useful, or valuable: *I want to gain more experience with computers.* **2** to get more of something: *She's gained a lot of weight.*

> **USAGE**
> Don't use **gain** to talk about getting money. Instead use **earn** to talk about the money you get by working: *He earns more than £60,000 a year.* Use **win** to talk about getting a prize in a game or competition: *If you get the answer right, you win $20.*

gain² *noun* an increase in the amount or level of something: *What is the reason for his weight gain?*

ga·la /'gɑːlə $ 'gælə/ *noun* a special public performance or celebration: *The theatre is holding a 30th anniversary gala.*

gal·ax·y /'gæləksi/ *noun, plural* **galaxies** a very large group of stars: *The film is set in a distant galaxy.*

gale /geɪl/ *noun* a very strong wind: *Several trees blew down in the gale.*

gall /gɔːl/ *noun* **have the gall to do something** to do something that is rude and not right: *She had the gall to say I was being childish!*

gal·le·ry /'gæləri/ *noun, plural* **galleries** a room or building where you can look at paintings: *an art gallery*

gal·lon /'gælən/ *noun* a unit for measuring liquid, equal to 4.5435 litres in Britain or 3.785 litres in the US: *I need ten gallons of petrol.*

gal·lop /'gæləp/ *verb* if a horse gallops, it runs very quickly

gam·ble¹ /'gæmbəl/ *verb* to try to win money by guessing the result of a competition or race, by playing cards etc: *He used to gamble on the horses* (=horse races).
–gambler *noun: Las Vegas is a gambler's paradise.*

gamble² *noun* something that you are not sure will succeed: *Employing someone with so little experience is a gamble.*

gam·bling /'gæmblɪŋ/ *noun* [no plural] the activity of trying to win money by guessing the result of a competition or race, by playing cards etc: *Many more people are now using the Internet for gambling.*

game /geɪm/ *noun*

> **GRAMMAR**
> **game of something**

1 an activity, such as a sport, in which you obey rules in order to defeat someone or achieve something: *I got a new computer game for Christmas.* | *Would you like a **game** of cards* (=a game using playing cards). | *The boys were out in the garden, playing a game.* | *Manchester United won last night's game against Leeds.*
2 games an important sports event where people play many different sports: *the Olympic Games*

game show /'. ./ *noun* a television programme in which people play games in order to win prizes

gang¹ /gæŋ/ *noun* a group of people, especially a group that causes trouble or does illegal things: *He was beaten up by a gang of youths.*

gang^2 verb **gang up on** to join together in order to criticize or attack someone: *They were always ganging up on the younger children.*

gang·ster /'gæŋstə $ 'gæŋstɚ/ noun a member of a group of violent criminals: *Do you like gangster movies?*

gaol a British spelling of JAIL

gaol·er /'dʒeɪlə $ 'dʒeɪlɚ/ a British spelling of JAILER

gap

gap /gæp/ noun

GRAMMAR
a gap in something
a gap between things

1 an empty space in something or between things: *There was a huge **gap** in the roof.* | *The book had fallen into the **gap between** the couch and the wall.*

2 a difference between people, things, or ideas: *the **gap between** men's pay and women's pay*

gape /geɪp/ verb written to look at something or someone in surprise, with your mouth open: *He just stood there gaping at the mess.*

gap·ing /'geɪpɪŋ/ adjective a gaping hole is very wide: *The crash left a gaping hole in the wall.* | *a gaping wound*

gar·age /'gæraːʒ $ gə'raʒ/ noun **1** a building where you keep your car: *The garage is big enough for two cars.* **2** a place where cars are repaired: *My car's in the garage so I can't take you home.* **3** BrE a place where you buy petrol; a GAS STATION AmE

gar·bage /'gɑːbɪdʒ $ 'gɑrbɪdʒ/ an American word for RUBBISH

garbage can /'.. ,./ the American word for RUBBISH BIN

gar·bled /'gɑːbəld $ 'gɑrbəld/ adjective garbled information is mixed up and difficult to understand: *She left a garbled message about being late.*

gar·den /'gɑːdn $ 'gɑrdn/ noun a piece of land next to your house where there is grass and you can grow flowers; YARD AmE: *The kids are playing in the garden.* ⇨ see picture on page 343

gar·den·er /'gɑːdnə $ 'gɑrdnɚ/ noun someone who works in a garden: *Our gardener cuts the grass.* | *Sam is a keen gardener.*

gar·den·ing /'gɑːdnɪŋ $ 'gɑrdnɪŋ/ noun [no plural] the activity or job of working in a garden: *We did a bit of gardening this afternoon.*

gar·gle /'gɑːgəl $ 'gɑrgəl/ verb to clean your throat with water or a special liquid that you do not swallow: *If you have a sore throat, try gargling with salt water.*

gar·ish /'geərɪʃ $ 'gærɪʃ/ adjective very brightly coloured and unpleasant to look at: *The curtains are very garish.*

garland

gar·land /'gɑːlənd $ 'gɑrlənd/ noun a ring of flowers or leaves, that people wear for decoration: *They put garlands of flowers around our necks.*

gar·lic /'gɑːlɪk $ 'gɑrlɪk/ noun [no plural] a small plant like an onion with a very strong taste, used in cooking: *Your breath smells of garlic.* ⇨ see pictures on pages 344 and 345

gar·ment /'gɑːmənt $ 'gɑrmənt/ noun formal a piece of clothing: *How should you wash woollen garments?*

gar·nish /'gɑːnɪʃ $ 'gɑrnɪʃ/ verb to decorate food with a small piece of a fruit or vegetable: *I garnished the dessert with cherries.*

gas /gæs/ noun

1 plural **gases** any light substance like air that you usually cannot see or feel: *Carbon monoxide is a dangerous gas, produced by cars.*

2 [no plural] a substance like air that we use for cooking and heating: *I prefer to cook with gas rather than electricity.* | *a gas fire*

3 [no plural] the American word for PETROL: *Do we have enough gas?*

gash /gæʃ/ noun, plural **gashes** a deep cut in something: *She had a deep gash in her leg.*
–gash verb: *I've gashed my knee.*

G

gas·o·line /'gæsəliːn/ also **gas** the American word for PETROL

gasp /gɑːsp $ gæsp/ verb written to make a short sudden noise when you breathe in, once or several times: *I gasped when I saw her cut face.* | *She was gasping for breath when she finished the race.*
– **gasp** noun: *Tom let out a gasp of surprise.*

gas sta·tion /'. ,../ the American word for PETROL STATION

gate /geɪt/ noun
the part of a wall or fence that you can open like a door: *We went through the gate and into the field.*

gat·eau /'gætəʊ $ gɑ'toʊ/ noun BrE, plural gateaux /-təʊz $ -'toʊz/ a large cake, often filled and decorated with cream and fruit: *a piece of chocolate gateau*

gate·crash /'geɪtkræʃ/ verb to go to a party or event that you have not been invited to: *People always gatecrash my parties.*
– **gatecrasher** noun: *We don't want any gatecrashers.*

gate·way /'geɪt-weɪ/ noun an opening in a fence or outside wall that can be closed with a gate

gath·er /'gæðə $ 'gæðɚ/ verb

GRAMMAR
gather at a place
gather things together

1 if people gather somewhere, they all come together in that place: *A large crowd had **gathered at** the scene of the accident.* | *The children **gathered round** to hear the story.*
2 also **gather things up** to collect things and put them in one place: *I **gathered** all the clothes **together**.* | *He **gathered up** his papers and walked out.*

PHRASE
I gather (that) spoken: *I gather that* (=someone has told me that) *Mary and Steve aren't going out together any more.*

gath·er·ing /'gæðərɪŋ/ noun formal a group of people meeting together for a particular purpose: *a room for private gatherings*

gau·dy /'gɔːdi/ adjective gaudier, ▼ gaudiest gaudy colours are too bright: *He was wearing a gaudy tie.*

gauge¹ /geɪdʒ/ noun an instrument that measures the amount or size of something: *The temperature gauge tells you how hot the engine is.*

gauge² verb to decide what someone is probably feeling or thinking: *It's difficult to gauge how she's going to react.*

gaunt /gɔːnt/ adjective very thin and pale: *He was looking sick and gaunt.*

gave the past tense of GIVE

gay /geɪ/ adjective someone who is gay is sexually attracted to people of the same sex ⇨ same meaning HOMOSEXUAL

gaze /geɪz/ verb written to look at something for a long time: *She stood gazing at the lovely view.*
– **gaze** noun: *Paul tried to avoid her gaze.*

gear /gɪə $ gɪr/ noun 1 the equipment in a car or other vehicle that turns power from the engine into movement: *It is difficult to shift the gears in this car.* 2 [no plural] special equipment, clothing etc that you need for a particular activity: *I've forgotten my swimming gear.* | *police in riot gear*

geese the plural of GOOSE

gel /dʒel/ noun a thick wet clear substance: *He used lots of hair gel.*

gem /dʒem/ noun a stone used in jewellery: *The crown is covered with precious gems.*

gen·der /'dʒendə $ 'dʒendɚ/ noun 1 formal whether someone is male or female ⇨ same meaning SEX: *You can't tell Jessie's gender from his name.* 2 [no plural] the system in some languages of dividing nouns, PRONOUNS, and adjectives into MASCULINE, FEMININE, or NEUTER

gene /dʒiːn/ noun a part of a CELL in a living thing that controls what it will be like. Parents pass on genes to their children

gen·e·ral¹ /'dʒenərəl/ adjective
1 having only the main parts of something, not the details: *This book should give you a general idea of the subject.* | *We began with a general discussion of the problems.* | *a general knowledge test*
2 including most or all people: *At the meeting, there was general agreement on what should be done.* | *The new medicine will soon be available for general use.*

▼ **PHRASE**

in general used to talk about what usually happens or what is usually true: *In general, April is a wetter month than May.*

general² *noun* an officer with a very high rank in an army, AIR FORCE, or navy: *General Eisenhower*

general e·lec·tion /ˌ... .ˈ../ *noun* an election in which all the voters in a country choose a government: *The Labour Party won the general election.*

gen·e·ral·i·za·tion also **generalisa·tion** /ˌdʒenərəlaɪˈzeɪʃən $ ˌdʒen-ərələˈzeɪʃən/ *noun* a statement about all people or things of a particular kind, which may not be true about every one: *It is silly to make generalizations about all students.*

gen·er·al·ly /ˈdʒenərəli/ *adverb*

usually or mostly: *The food at the Italian restaurant is generally quite good.* | *It is generally accepted that too much fat is bad for you.*

gen·e·rate /ˈdʒenəreɪt/ *verb formal*
1 to make something happen or start: *The violence generated a lot of fear.*
2 to produce heat, electricity, or power: *Even small fires generate a lot of heat.*

gen·e·ra·tion /ˌdʒenəˈreɪʃən/ *noun* all the people who are about the same age: *People of my father's generation don't know much about computers.*

gen·e·ros·i·ty /ˌdʒenəˈrɒsəti $ ˌdʒenə-ˈrɑsəti/ *noun* [no plural] when you willingly give a lot of money to someone: *We appreciate your generosity.*

gen·e·rous /ˈdʒenərəs/ *adjective*

GRAMMAR
it is generous of someone to do something
generous to someone

someone who is generous gives a lot of money, presents, or help to other people: *It was really generous of Jack to take us all on holiday.* | *My parents have always been very generous to me.*
– **generously** *adverb*: *All the bands generously gave the money from the concert to a charity.*

ge·net·ic /dʒəˈnetɪk/ *adjective* related to or caused by GENES: *Heart disease is sometimes a genetic condition.*

genetically mod·i·fied /ˌ.... ˈ.../ *adjective abbreviation* **GM** genetically modified plants have received GENES from another plant in a scientific process: *These burgers contain genetically modified soya.*

ge·net·ics /dʒəˈnetɪks/ *plural noun* the study of GENES

gen·i·tals /ˈdʒenətlz/ also **gen·i·ta·lia** /ˌdʒenəˈteɪljə/ *plural noun formal* the parts on the outside of your body that are used for having sex and producing babies

ge·ni·us /ˈdʒiːniəs/ *noun, plural* geniuses someone who is very intelligent: *Einstein was a genius.*

gen·tle /ˈdʒentl/ *adjective*

GRAMMAR
gentle with someone/something

1 a gentle person is kind and calm, and treats people and things carefully: *You have to be very gentle with young animals.*
2 not strong, loud, or rough: *There was some gentle music playing in the background.* | *a gentle breeze*
– **gently** *adverb*: *"You mustn't worry,"* she said gently.

gen·tle·man /ˈdʒentlmən/ *noun, plural* gentlemen /-mən/ a polite word that you can use when talking about a man: *This gentleman is Mr Wright.*

gents /dʒents/ *noun* **the gents** *BrE* a room in a public building where there are toilets for men; MEN'S ROOM *AmE*

gen·u·ine /ˈdʒenjuɪn/ *adjective*

something that is genuine is real, not pretended, false, or imagined: *Is that a genuine antique?* | *a genuine apology*

ge·og·ra·phy /dʒiˈɒɡrəfi $ dʒiˈɑɡrəfi/ *noun* [no plural] the study of the countries of the world, including their land, rivers, and cities

ge·ol·o·gy /dʒiˈɒlədʒi $ dʒiˈɑlədʒi/ *noun* [no plural] the study of materials such as rocks and soil

ge·o·met·ric /ˌdʒiːəˈmetrɪk/ also **ge·o·met·ric·al** /ˌdʒiːəˈmetrɪkəl/ *adjective* **1** a geometric shape or pattern has regular shapes and lines: *The rugs have geometric designs.* **2** related to geometry

G

ge·om·e·try /dʒi'ɒmətri $dʒi'ɑmətri/ noun [no plural] the study of lines and shapes in mathematics: *You can't do geometry without a ruler.*

germ /dʒɜːm $dʒɜˑm/ noun a very small living thing that can make you ill: *This cleaning fluid kills all household germs.*

German mea·sles /ˌdʒɜːmən 'miːzəlz $ˌdʒɜˑmən 'mizəlz/ plural noun a disease that causes red spots on your body: *Sam's got German measles.*

ger·mi·nate /'dʒɜːməneɪt $'dʒɜˑməˌneɪt/ verb if a seed germinates, it begins to grow

ger·und /'dʒerənd/ noun a noun with the same form as the PRESENT PARTICIPLE of a verb, for example 'reading' in the sentence 'He enjoys reading.'

ges·ture¹ /'dʒestʃə $'dʒestʃɚ/ noun 1 a movement of your head, arm, or hand that shows what you mean or how you feel: *He made a gesture towards the door to show it was time to leave.* 2 something you do to show that you care about someone or something: *It would be a nice gesture if we paid for her meal.*

gesture² verb to tell someone something by moving your arms, hands, or head: *I gestured to my friend to come inside.*

get ⇨ see box on next page

get·a·way /'getəweɪ/ noun **make a getaway** to escape quickly from a place, especially after doing something illegal: *The robbers made a quick getaway after stealing the money.*

get-to·geth·er /'. .ˌ../ noun a friendly informal meeting or party: *We're having a family get-together tomorrow.*

ghast·ly /'gɑːstli $'gæstli/ adjective very unpleasant: *The food in that restaurant is ghastly.*

ghet·to /'getəʊ $'getoʊ/ noun, plural **ghettos** or **ghettoes** a part of a city where people of a particular race or class live, usually in bad conditions: *He came from the ghettos of New York.*

ghost /gəʊst $goʊst/ noun the spirit of a dead person that some people believe they can see: *I don't believe in ghosts.*

gi·ant¹ /'dʒaɪənt/ adjective much larger than other things of the same type: *The band performed on a giant stage.*

giant² noun an extremely tall strong man in children's stories

gib·ber·ish /'dʒɪbərɪʃ/ noun [no plural] things someone says or writes that have no meaning or are difficult to understand: *I tried to read the instruction book, but it was all gibberish.*

gibe another spelling of JIBE

gid·dy /'gɪdi/ adjective **giddier, giddiest** feeling slightly sick and not able to stand up very well ⇨ same meaning DIZZY: *If you feel giddy while exercising, then stop.*

gift /gɪft/ noun

GRAMMAR
a gift for/from someone
a gift for something

1 something that you give to someone as a present: *Did you give your mother **a gift**? | People **exchange gifts** at Christmas. | We received **a** beautiful wedding **gift from** Lisa.*
2 a natural ability to do something: *Sam has **a** great **gift for** acting.*

gift·ed /'gɪftɪd/ adjective very intelligent or having a natural ability to do something very well: *a school for gifted children | Paul's a very gifted artist.*

gig /gɪg/ noun informal a popular music or JAZZ concert

gi·gan·tic /dʒaɪ'gæntɪk/ adjective very big: *He was eating a gigantic ice cream.*

gig·gle /'gɪgəl/ verb to laugh in a silly way, especially because you are nervous or embarrassed: *The little girls wouldn't stop giggling.*
– **giggle** noun: *I could hear giggles coming from the back of the class.*

gim·mick /'gɪmɪk/ noun something unusual that is used to make people interested in something: *The news story was just a gimmick to sell more tickets.*

gin /dʒɪn/ noun [no plural] a strong clear alcoholic drink: *Her favourite drink is gin and tonic.*

gin·ger¹ /'dʒɪndʒə $'dʒɪndʒɚ/ noun [no plural] a light brown root with a strong hot taste, used in cooking

ginger² adjective BrE hair or fur that is ginger is bright orange brown in colour: *a ginger cat*

gin·ger·ly /'dʒɪndʒəli $'dʒɪndʒɚli/ adverb written slowly, carefully, and gently: *She crept gingerly into the room.*

gip·sy /'dʒɪpsi/ a British spelling of GYPSY

gi·raffe /dʒɪ'rɑːf $dʒə'ræf/ noun a tall

get /get/ *verb* **got** /gɒt $ gɑt/ **got** or **gotten** *AmE* /'gɒtn $ 'gɑtn/ **getting**

1 get angry/cold/worse etc
to become angry, cold etc: *It gets very cold at night.* | *Be careful, or someone will get hurt.* | *We got lost on the way to the restaurant.*

2 to buy or have something
Where did you get your bike? | *My dad got a new job.* | *Run and get help!* | *What are you getting your sister for her birthday?*

3 to receive something
He got so many presents at Christmas. | *I got three emails this morning.* | *What did you get for dinner at Annie's?*

7 to do something
You should get your hair cut. | *Did you get your stereo fixed?* | *I have to get this done before tomorrow.*

⇨ *see also* HAVE for how to use *have got* and *have got to*.

4 to bring something or someone
Can I get you a drink? | *Go and get your sister – it's time for dinner.*

get

6 to arrive somewhere
We got there at about seven. | *They didn't get to the hotel until after dark.* | *What time do you usually get home?*

GRAMMAR

get to somewhere

5 to move, or move something
I got down on the floor to look. | *Get off the table, you stupid cat!* | *Will you get the bags out of the car and take them into the house?*

GRAMMAR

get down/across/into etc
get something down/out of etc

G

PHRASAL VERBS

get away
to leave a place or person: *I really need to get away from London for a while.*

get back
to return somewhere: *I'll call her as soon as I get back.* | *They just got back from Japan.* | *Get back in the car!*

get off
to leave a bus, train, plane, or large boat: *Be careful getting off the bus.*

get on
1 to walk onto a bus, train, or plane: *I got on the wrong bus.*
2 *BrE* to be friendly with someone: *We get on really well.* | *I never got on with Jeremy's sister.*

get out
1 to leave or move from a place: *How did the dogs get out of the yard?* | *Get out of the way!*
2 to leave a car, taxi, boat etc: *He fell into the water as he was getting out of the boat.*

get up
1 to wake up and move out of bed: *He has to get up at five a.m. every morning.*
2 to stand up: *Lisa got up and made a cup of tea.*

animal that has a very long neck and dark areas on its fur, and lives in Africa ⇨ *see picture on page 339*

gir·der /ˈɡɜːdə $ ˈɡɚdɚ/ *noun* a long thick piece of iron or steel, used to build bridges or buildings: *Huge iron girders held up the roof.*

girl /ɡɜːl $ ɡɚl/ *noun* a female child: *Lots of girls like riding horses.*

girl·friend /ˈɡɜːlfrend $ ˈɡɚlfrend/ *noun* a girl or woman with whom you have a romantic relationship: *Has Steve got a girlfriend?*

gist /dʒɪst/ *noun* the main points or general meaning of what someone says or writes: *I understood the gist of what he was saying.*

give ⇨ *see box on next page*

give·a·way /ˈɡɪvəweɪ/ *noun* be a giveaway, be a dead giveaway to make it very easy for someone to know that something is true: *I knew it was Jo on the phone – the deep voice was a dead giveaway.*

given the past participle of GIVE

given name /ˈ.. ˌ./ an American word for FIRST NAME: *His given name is Simon.*

gla·ci·er /ˈɡlæsiə $ ˈɡleɪʃɚ/ *noun* a large amount of ice that moves slowly down a mountain

glad /ɡlæd/ *adjective*

> **GRAMMAR**
> **glad (that)**
> **glad to do something**
> if you are glad, you are pleased and happy about something: *I'm **glad that** Mark decided to come with us.* | *My parents **were** very **glad to** see me at last.*

> **USAGE glad, pleased, happy**
> Use **glad** or **pleased** to describe how you feel about a particular event or situation: *I'm glad he telephoned.* You cannot use **glad** or **pleased** before a noun. You cannot say, for example: *a pleased teacher*; rather you must say *The teacher is pleased.* **Happy** is used to describe a general feeling that you have: *Is she happy at school?* You can use **happy** before a noun: *a happy boy*

glad·ly /ˈɡlædli/ *adverb* willingly: *I'll gladly help you.*

glam·or·ous /ˈɡlæmərəs/ *adjective* more attractive and exciting than ordinary people or things: *a glamorous supermodel*

glam·our *BrE*, **glamor** *AmE* /ˈɡlæmə $ ˈɡlæmɚ/ *noun [no plural]* the quality of being attractive and exciting, and connected with wealth or success: *I love the glamour of Hollywood.*

glance[1] /ɡlɑːns $ ɡlæns/ *verb* to look at someone or something for a short time: *He glanced towards the door.*
– **glance** *noun*: *We exchanged glances* (=glanced at each other).

gland /ɡlænd/ *noun* a small part of the body that produces a liquid, such as SWEAT or SALIVA: *The glands in her neck are swollen.*

glare /ɡleə $ ɡler/ *verb* **1** to look at someone or something in an angry way, usually for a long time: *The farmer glared at the men who had walked across his land.* **2** if light glares, it shines so strongly that it hurts your eyes: *The car's headlights glared in the darkness.*
– **glare** *noun*: *She gave him an angry glare.* | *the glare of the sun*

glar·ing /ˈɡleərɪŋ $ ˈɡlerɪŋ/ *adjective* bad and very easy to notice: *The article in the newspaper was full of glaring mistakes.*

glass /ɡlɑːs $ ɡlæs/ *noun*

> **GRAMMAR**
> **a glass of something**
> **1** *[no plural]* a clear hard material that we use for making windows, bottles etc: *The ball hit the window and broke the glass.* | *a glass bowl*
> **2** *plural* **glasses** a cup with no handle that is made of glass: *Could you put the glasses on the table?* | *a wine glass* | *I'd like a **glass of** lemonade, please.*

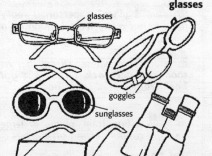

glasses

glasses

goggles

sunglasses

visor binoculars

glass·es /ˈɡlɑːsɪz $ ˈɡlæsɪz/ *plural noun* two pieces of special glass in a plastic or

❶ to put something into someone's hand
Give me the keys – I'll open the door. | A nurse *gave* her some medicine. | Ken *gave* the bags *to* Ellen, who put them on the table.

✗ **Don't say** ➤ give to her the book, give to her a present.

✓ **Say** ➤ give her the book *or* give the book to her, give her a present *or* give a present to her.

❺ to tell someone something
Will you please *give* your name *to* the secretary? | *Give* the doctor as much information as possible.

❷ to let someone have something
What *are* you *giving* Sophie for her birthday? | Their company *gives* money *to* both political parties.

give

❹ to make someone have something
Give me some time to think about it. | The constant noise *gave* me a headache. | The judge *gave* Robbins five years in prison.

❸ to do something
Give me *a call* when you get home. | She's going to Hawaii to *give* a speech at the university. | The program *gives* extra help to students who are having problems. | Mel *is giving* a party (=organizing a party) on New Year's Eve.

G

Most common words used with **give**:

give a speech	give somebody advice	give somebody permission
give help	give somebody a kiss	give an explanation
give somebody a lift	give somebody a chance	give information

PHRASAL VERBS

give away
to give something to someone else, without asking for money: *The radio station is giving away tickets to the concert.* | *We gave three of the kittens away, but we kept the black one.*

give back
to return something to the person who owns it: *I'll be giving you back your essays on Monday.* | *He took twenty dollars, and gave back the change.*

give out
to give something to each person in a group: *Mrs Irvine gave out the awards.* | *The bakery would not give the cookie recipe out to its customers.*

give up
to stop doing something: *I had almost given up hope.* | *Andy had to give up tennis when he hurt his knee.* | *Carol tries really hard – she doesn't give up easily.*

metal frame which you wear in front of your eyes to help you see better ⇨ *same meaning* SPECTACLES: *You might need to wear glasses.* | *a pair of glasses*

glaze /gleɪz/ also **glaze over** *verb* if your eyes glaze or glaze over, they show no expression because you are bored or tired: *As soon as he mentioned football, her eyes started to glaze over.*

gleam /gliːm/ *verb* to shine softly: *She washed the car until it was gleaming.*

glean /gliːn/ *verb* to find out information slowly and with difficulty: *It's difficult to glean any information from Dan.*

glide /glaɪd/ *verb* to move smoothly, quietly, and without effort: *The swan glided through the water.*

glim·mer /ˈglɪmə $ ˈglɪmɚ/ *verb written* to shine with a light that is not very bright or steady: *The stars were glimmering in the sky.*

–**glimmer** *noun*: *the glimmer of street lights*

glimpse /glɪmps/ *verb* to see something for a very short time, or not completely: *I only glimpsed her face.*

–**glimpse** *noun*: *He caught a glimpse of the man* (=glimpsed the man) *as he drove away.*

glint /glɪnt/ *verb written* if something glints, one or more flashes of light come from it: *His glasses glinted in the light.*

–**glint** *noun*: *the glint of sunlight on the sea*

glis·ten /ˈglɪsən/ *verb written* to shine because of being wet or oily: *His face glistened with sweat.*

glit·ter /ˈglɪtə $ ˈglɪtɚ/ *verb written* to shine with a lot of small flashes of light: *The sand on the beach glittered in the sunshine.*

–**glitter** *noun [no plural]*: *the glitter of the Christmas decorations*

gloat /gləʊt $ gloʊt/ *verb* to show in an annoying way that you are happy about your success or about someone else's failure: *He keeps gloating that he's the fastest runner in the school.*

glo·bal /ˈgləʊbəl $ ˈgloʊbəl/ *adjective* affecting or including the whole world: *Pollution is a global problem.*

global warm·ing /ˌ.. ˈ../ *noun [no plural]* an increase in world temperatures, caused by an increase of CARBON DIOXIDE around the Earth: *Maybe the warmer weather is caused by global warming.*

globe /gləʊb $ gloʊb/ *noun* a round object with a map of the Earth drawn on it

gloom /gluːm/ *noun [no plural]* almost complete darkness: *I could see almost nothing in the gloom of the tunnel.*

gloom·y /ˈgluːmi/ *adjective* **gloomier, gloomiest** 1 feeling sad because you do not have a lot of hope: *Why are you so gloomy today?* 2 dark, especially in a way that seems sad: *It was dark and gloomy in the cellar.*

glo·ri·ous /ˈglɔːriəs/ *adjective* 1 very successful: *He left the team after twelve glorious years.* 2 very enjoyable or beautiful: *It was a glorious summer's day.*

glory /ˈglɔːri/ *noun* praise and honour that someone gets because of something good they have done: *the glory of an Olympic victory*

glos·sa·ry /ˈglɒsəri $ ˈglɑsəri/ *noun, plural* **glossaries** a list of unusual words and what they mean, printed at the end of a book: *a glossary of technical terms*

gloss·y /ˈglɒsi $ ˈglɔsi/ *adjective* **glossier, glossiest** shiny and smooth: *a small dog with glossy black fur*

glove /glʌv/ *noun* gloves are pieces of clothing that you wear on your hands, which have separate parts for each finger: *I must buy a new pair of gloves.* ⇨ *see picture on page 352*

glow¹ /gləʊ $ gloʊ/ *noun* a soft light, for example from something that is burning gently: *A fire was burning, giving the whole room a warm glow.*

glow² *verb* to produce a soft light: *It was dark except for one small lamp glowing in the corner.*

glow·er /ˈglaʊə $ ˈglaʊɚ/ *verb written* to look at someone in an angry way: *I started to speak but Chris glowered at me, so I stopped.*

glow·ing /ˈgləʊɪŋ $ ˈgloʊɪŋ/ *adjective* a glowing report, description etc praises someone or something a lot: *Geoff got a glowing report from his teachers last term.*

glue¹ /gluː/ *noun* a sticky substance that you use to join things together

glue² *verb, present participle* **gluing** or **glueing** 1 to join things together using glue: *I tried to glue the broken pieces back together again.* 2 **be glued to something** *informal* to be watching something, especially television, with all your attention: *It was five o'clock and the kids were glued to the television.*

glum /glʌm/ *adjective* **glummer, glummest** sad or disappointed: *Don't look so glum!*

glut /glʌt/ *noun* too many things of the same kind coming at the same time: *There's a glut of violent American films around at the moment.*

gm a written abbreviation for GRAM

gnaw /nɔː/ *verb* to bite something many times in order to break part of it off or make a hole in it: *A dog was gnawing at a bone out in the yard.*

go¹ ➪ *see box on next page*

go² /gəʊ $ goʊ/ *noun, plural* **goes**
1 have a go, give something a go to try doing something: *I'd never been skiing before, but I decided to have a go.*
2 your go your turn to play in a game, try to do something etc: *"It's my go now!" Billy shouted.*

go·a·head /'. .,./ *noun* give someone the go-ahead *informal* to give someone official permission to start doing something: *The council gave them the go-ahead to build the new stadium.*

goal /gəʊl $ goʊl/ *noun* **1** the space between two posts into which you try to kick or hit the ball in some sports, for example football **2** a point that you win when the ball goes into the goal: *The Russians scored three goals in sixteen minutes.*

goal·ie /'gəʊli $ 'goʊli/ *informal* a GOAL-KEEPER

goal·keep·er /'gəʊl,kiːpə $ 'goʊl-,kipɚ/ *BrE*, **goal·tend·er** /'gəʊl,tendə $ 'goʊl,tendɚ/ *AmE, noun* the player in a sports team who tries to stop the ball from going into the GOAL

goal·post /'gəʊlpəʊst $ 'goʊlpoʊst/ *noun* one of the two posts on each side of the GOAL in games such as football

goat /gəʊt $ goʊt/ *noun* a farm animal that has horns and has long hair under its chin

gob·ble /'gɒbəl $ 'gabəl/ also **gobble up** *verb* to eat something very quickly: *Matt gobbled up his dinner and ran back outside.*

gob·lin /'gɒblɪn $ 'gablɪn/ *noun* a small ugly creature in children's stories, who often does bad things

go-cart an American spelling of GO-KART

god /gɒd $ gad/ *noun* **1** God in some religions, the maker and ruler of the world: *She prayed to God for help.* **2** any force that people pray to and consider to be powerful: *In the past, the sun was worshipped as a god.* **3** God, my God *spoken* used to express strong feelings of surprise, anger etc, in a way that offends some people

god·child /'gɒdtʃaɪld $ 'gadtʃaɪld/ *noun, plural* **godchildren** /-,tʃɪldrən/ in the Christian religion, a person's godchild is a child whose parents have chosen that person to be a special friend to the child

god·dess /'gɒdɪs $ 'gadɪs/ *noun, plural* **goddesses** a female god

god·fa·ther /'gɒd,fɑːðə $ 'gad,faðɚ/ *noun* a male godparent

god·moth·er /'gɒd,mʌðə $ 'gad-,mʌðɚ/ *noun* a female godparent

god·pa·rent /'gɒd,peərənt $ 'gad-,perənt/ *noun* in the Christian religion, a person who has been chosen by a child's parents to be a special friend to that child

goes /gəʊz $ goʊz/ the third person singular of the present tense of GO

gog·gles /'gɒgəlz $ 'gagəlz/ *plural noun* large glasses that fit close to your face and protect your eyes: *You should wear goggles when cutting metal.* ➪ *see picture at* GLASSES

going¹ /'gəʊɪŋ $ 'goʊɪŋ/ *noun* be good going, be slow going *informal* to take a shorter time to do than usual, or a longer time to do than usual: *The journey only took two hours, which was very good going.*

going² *adjective* the going rate the usual amount that you have to pay for a service or that you get for doing a job: *What's the going rate for private lessons at the moment?*

goings-on /,.. './ *plural noun informal* things that happen which are strange or interesting: *There have been some interesting goings-on at the house next door.*

go-kart *BrE*, also **go-cart** *AmE* /'gəʊ kɑːt $ 'goʊ kart/ *noun* a low vehicle with no roof and a small engine that people use in races for fun

gold¹ /gəʊld $ goʊld/ *noun* [no plural] a valuable yellow metal that is used for making jewellery, coins etc

➤ GO or COME?

GO to move away from a place: *Are you going to the party?*

COME to move towards a place: *Are you coming to the party?*

➤ GO

❶ go somewhere

to leave one place and move towards another place: *Sam's having a party, and I want* ***to go***. | ***Go through*** *that door and turn left.* | *The little boy wanted to* ***go home***. | *When are you* ***going to*** *Germany?* | *Has Ella* ***gone with*** *Pat to the cinema?* | *"Where's Jim?" "He* ***went to*** *buy some milk."*

GRAMMAR
go to/into/through/out etc | go with someone | go to do something

In British English, you say: *Nick* ***has gone*** *to Paris for the weekend* (=he is still there, he has not come back yet). | *Nick* ***has been*** *to Paris several times this year* (=he has been there, but now he has come back).

❼ belong somewhere

to belong in a particular place: *The toy cars* ***go in*** *the blue box.* | *"Where do you keep these cups?" "They* ***go in*** *the cupboard by the sink."*

❻ go well
go badly
go fine etc

to happen in a particular way: *McConnell's speech* ***went well***. | *What* ***went wrong***? | *"**How did** the game **go**?" "We lost."*

go

❷ go shopping
go swimming
go dancing etc

to go somewhere in order to do something: *Ken and Tina* ***are going skiing*** *in France.* | *We* ***went shopping*** *and found some great clothes.* | *We* ***went camping*** *in the mountains.*

❸ go for a walk
go for a swim
go for a drive etc

to go somewhere and do a particular activity: *We* ***went for a*** *short* ***walk*** *after dinner.* | *Kari and I are* ***going for a swim*** *in the lake.*

❺ go deaf
go grey etc

to become deaf, grey etc: *Her hair has* ***gone*** *completely white.* | *Beethoven* ***went deaf*** *when he was 40 years old.* | *David* ***is going bald*** (=he is losing his hair).

❹ go to school
go to class
go to church etc

to regularly go somewhere in order to take part in something: *Jenny* ***goes to*** *dance lessons every Monday.* | *I've been* ***going to*** *a French class since September.*

G

PHRASES

be going to do something
say this when something will happen:
*Are you **going** to play basketball tonight?* | *It's **going** to rain tomorrow.*

be going, get going *spoken*
say this when you are leaving a place: *It's late – I must **be going**.* | *I'd better **get going**, I have a lot to do today.*

how's it going?, how are things going? *spoken informal*
say this to say hello and ask someone how they are: *"Hi, Ken, **how's it going?**"* *"Fine, thanks. How about you?"*

go and do something *especially BrE spoken*, **go do something** *AmE spoken*
to move somewhere in order to do something: *Please **go and** sit down at your desks.* | *Let's **go see** a movie.*

PHRASAL VERBS

go away
to leave a place or person: *Go away, Jake! I'm busy.*

go back (to)
to return to a place: *I **went back to** the car to get my bag.*

go down
1 when the sun goes down, you can no longer see it in the sky at the end of the day: *The sun doesn't **go down** until 10 o'clock in the summertime.*
2 to become less in amount, price, level etc: *The number of students in the school has **gone down**.*

*The number of students in the school has **gone down**.*

go off
to suddenly make a loud noise or explode: *The alarm clock **went off** at eight a.m.* | *The gun **went off** accidentally.*

*The alarm clock **went off** at eight a.m.*

go on
1 to continue: *I wanted to **go on** learning French.* | *The meeting **went on** for a lot longer than I expected.*
2 to happen: *Parents don't always know **what goes on** at school.* | ***What's going on?*** *Who's making all that noise?*

go out
1 to leave your house to do something: *I'm **going out** for dinner with Lucy.* | *Did you **go out** last Friday?*
2 to have a romantic relationship with someone: *Dana started **going out with** Tim when she was sixteen.* | *They've only been **going out** for a month.*

go up
to become more in amount, level, price etc: *School fees have **gone up**.*

G

gold² *adjective* **1** made of gold: *a gold ring* **2** having the colour of gold: *a gold dress*

gold·en /ˈgəʊldən $ ˈgoʊldən/ *adjective written* **1** having a bright yellow colour: *Shelley was tall with long golden hair.* **2** made of gold: *a golden cup*

gold·fish /ˈgəʊld.fɪʃ $ ˈgoʊld.fɪʃ/ *noun, plural* **goldfish** a small orange fish that people often keep as a pet

golf /gɒlf $ gɑlf/ *noun [no plural]* a game in which you try to hit a small white ball into holes in the ground with a special stick called a CLUB ⇨ *see picture on page 351*

golf course /ˈ. ˌ./ *noun* an area of land where people play golf

gone /gɒn $ gɔn/ the past participle of GO

gon·na /ˈgɒnə $ ˈgɔnə/ *informal* a way of saying or writing 'going to': *We're gonna spend the evening in Bar Rita.*

good¹ /gʊd/ *adjective* **better** /ˈbetə $ ˈbetɚ/ **best** /best/

GRAMMAR
good to do something
good at something
good for someone
good to someone
it is good of someone to do something

1 of a high standard or quality ⇨ *opposite* BAD (2): *I love wearing really good clothes.* | *This is the best hotel in the town.*
2 enjoyable or pleasant ⇨ *opposite* BAD (1): *Did you have a good holiday?* | *I've got some good news!* | *It's really good to be home.*
3 someone who is good at something can do it well ⇨ *opposite* BAD (4): *She's very good at her job, isn't she?* | *Martin's a better driver than I am.*
4 useful or suitable ⇨ *opposite* BAD (3): *That's a good idea!* | *It's a good day for going to the park.*
5 someone who is good behaves well or tries to do what is right ⇨ *opposite* BAD (6): *"You've all been very good today," our teacher said.* | *Mr Hardy was a good, kind man.*
6 something that is good for you makes your body or mind healthy ⇨ *opposite* BAD (7): *Fresh air and exercise are good for you.*
7 if you are good to someone, you are kind to them, especially when they need help: *Everyone was very good to me when my husband died.* | *It's good of you to call.*

PHRASES
good, that's good: *"There's another bus in five minutes." "Oh, good."* (=I am pleased about that)
good luck: *"My exams start tomorrow." "Good luck!"* (=I hope you will be successful)

USAGE good, well
Use **good** to describe the quality of something or someone: *a good teacher*. Use the adverb **well** to talk about the way someone does something: *She plays the piano well.*

good² *noun* **1** be no good, do no good to not improve a situation or not achieve anything: *I've tried to help him but it's no good – he won't listen.* | *Complaining doesn't do any good.* **2** be no good, not be much good to not work well, or not be of a good standard: *Can I borrow your pen? This one's no good any more.* | *I'm not much good at sport.* **3** for good if something happens for good, the situation will not change back again: *Has she stopped working for good?* **4** what is right, compared with what is bad and wrong: *our ideas of good and evil* **5** goods *formal* things that are made for people to buy: *The shop sells a range of household goods.*

good af·ter·noon /ˌ. ..ˈ./ something you say when you meet someone in the afternoon: *Good afternoon, sir.*

good·bye /gʊdˈbaɪ/
a word you say when someone is leaving: *Goodbye Chris! See you Monday.*

good eve·ning /ˌ. ˈ../ something you say when you meet someone in the evening: *Good evening everybody, and welcome!*

good-look·ing /ˌ. ˈ../ *adjective* someone who is good-looking is attractive to look at: *a very good-looking man* ⇨ *see usage note at* PRETTY²

good mor·ning /ˌ. ˈ../ something you say when you meet someone in the morning: *Good morning, class.*

good night /ˌ.ˈ./ also **good·night** /gʊdˈnaɪt/ something you say at night when someone is leaving or when they are going to bed: *Good night. Sleep well.*

goo·ey /ˈguːi/ *adjective informal* **gooier, gooiest** sticky and soft, and usually sweet: *a gooey chocolate cake*

goof /guːf/ also **goof up** *verb AmE informal* to do something silly: *Sorry, I've goofed again!*

goof·y /ˈguːfi/ *adjective informal* **goofier, goofiest** stupid or silly: *Robby looked at me with a goofy expression.*

goose /guːs/ *noun, plural* **geese** /giːs/ a water bird that is like a duck but bigger

gorge /gɔːdʒ $ gɔrdʒ/ *noun* a very narrow valley with steep sides, sometimes with water flowing along the bottom: *The railway runs through a beautiful gorge.*

gor·geous /ˈgɔːdʒəs $ ˈgɔrdʒəs/ *adjective informal* very beautiful or pleasant: *Carlo was gorgeous, with dark hair and eyes.* | *It's a gorgeous day – let's have a picnic!*

go·ril·la /gəˈrɪlə/ *noun* a very large strong animal that looks like a monkey ⇨ *see picture on page 339*

gor·y /ˈgɔːri/ *adjective* **gorier, goriest** a gory film, story etc has a lot of violence in it: *The ending was too gory for me.*

gos·sip[1] /ˈgɒsɪp $ ˈgɑsəp/ *noun* things that people say about other people's behaviour or private lives, especially things that may not be true: *I heard some gossip about Mary, but I don't believe it.*

gossip[2] *verb* to talk about other people's behaviour and private lives, especially in a way that is not kind: *They were gossiping about Lucy's new boyfriend.*

got /gɒt $ gɑt/ the past tense and a past participle of GET

got·ten /ˈgɒtn $ ˈgɑtn/ the usual American past participle of GET

gour·met /ˈguəmeɪ $ gʊrˈmeɪ/ *noun* someone who enjoys good food and drink – **gourmet** *adjective*: *gourmet food shops*

gov·ern /ˈgʌvən $ ˈgʌvərn/ *verb* to officially control a country or state: *The people decide who will govern the country.*

gov·ern·ment /ˈgʌvəmənt $ ˈgʌvərmənt/ *noun* the group of people who govern a

country: *The new government promised not to increase taxes.* | *a socialist government* | *What will the government do to help the poorest people in society?*

USAGE government

In British English, you can use a singular or plural verb after **government**: *The government is determined to reduce unemployment.* | *The government are unlikely to lose the election.* In American English, you can only use the singular form of the verb: *The US government is sending aid to the area.*

---

gov·er·nor /ˈgʌvənə $ ˈgʌvənər/ *noun* **1** a person who officially controls a state, especially in the USA: *the governor of Alabama* **2** a leader or member of a group of people who control an organization: *a meeting of the school governors*

gown /gaʊn/ *noun* a long dress for special occasions: *She wore a pink silk gown.*

GP /ˌdʒiː ˈpiː/ *noun BrE* a doctor who treats people for ordinary health problems: *You should go and see your GP.*

grab /græb/ *verb* **grabbed, grabbing** to suddenly take something or hold someone roughly and with force: *He grabbed my arm and refused to let go.* – **grab** *noun*: *She made a grab for the money* (=tried to take the money).

grace /greɪs/ *noun* [no plural] when you move your body in a smooth and attractive way: *The dancer moved with such grace.*

grace·ful /ˈgreɪsfəl/ *adjective* a person or animal who is graceful moves in a smooth and attractive way: *a tall graceful woman* – **gracefully** *adverb*

graceful

gra·cious /ˈgreɪʃəs/ *adjective formal* polite and kind, especially in a formal way: *The King was gracious to everyone who met him.* – **graciously** *adverb*

grade[1] /greɪd/ *noun* **1** a level that tells you how good the quality of something is or how

G

▼ important it is: *There are five different grades of hotel.*

2 a mark that your teacher gives you for an exam or for school work, to show how good it is: *Martia got grade A in her maths exam. | I got some very poor (=bad) grades when I was at school.*

3 one of the twelve years that you are at school in the US: *Liz is in fifth grade.*

4 **make the grade** to succeed or reach a high level at a particular activity: *Do you think my son will **make the grade** as a professional footballer?*

grade² *verb* **1** to put people or things into groups according to how good, big etc they are: *The students are graded according to their level of English.* **2** the American word for MARK: *Mrs Watts still hasn't graded my homework.*

grade cross·ing /'. ,../ the American word for a LEVEL CROSSING

grade school /'. ,./ an American word for a PRIMARY SCHOOL

gra·di·ent /'greɪdiənt/ *noun* how steep a slope is, especially on a road or railway: *Ringstead Road was on a steep gradient.*

grad·u·al /'grædʒuəl/ *adjective* happening slowly or over a long time: *Learning to walk again after the accident was a very gradual process.*

grad·u·al·ly /'grædʒuəli/ *adverb*
slowly, or over a long period of time: *Her work gradually improved during the year. | Gradually, Dick began to feel a bit better.*

grad·u·ate¹ /'grædʒuət/ *noun* **1** someone who has completed their first course at university and passed the final examinations: *a graduate in physics | law graduates* **2** *AmE* someone who has completed a course at a school, college, or university: *a high school graduate*

grad·u·ate² /'grædʒueɪt/ *verb* **1** to pass your final examinations at university: *Don graduated from York University in 1998.* **2** *AmE* to finish studying at HIGH SCHOOL

graduate stu·dent /'... ,../ the American word for a POSTGRADUATE

grad·u·a·tion /ˌɡrædʒu'eɪʃən/ *noun* when you complete a university degree or your education at an American HIGH SCHOOL: *My parents came to the graduation ceremony.*

graffiti

graf·fi·ti /ɡrə'fiːti/
noun [no plural]
writing and pictures that people draw in public places illegally: *The school walls were covered with graffiti.*

grain /greɪn/ *noun* **1** the seeds of crops such as corn, wheat, or rice, that we grow for food: *The barn was full of grain.* **2** one seed or one very small piece of something: *a grain of salt*

gram or **gramme** /græm/ *written abbreviation* **g** or **gm** *noun* a unit for measuring weight. There are 1,000 grams in a KILOGRAM

gram·mar /'græmə $ 'græmɚ/ *noun* [no plural] the rules of a language: *His pronunciation is good, but his grammar is poor.*

grammar school /'.. ,./ *noun* a school in Britain for children between the ages of 11 and 18, who have to pass an examination to go there

gram·mat·i·cal /ɡrə'mætɪkəl/ *adjective* related to the use of grammar: *a grammatical mistake*
– grammatically /-kli/ *adverb*: *The sentence is not grammatically correct.*

gran /græn/ *BrE informal* a GRANDMOTHER

grand¹ /grænd/ *adjective*
very big, important, or impressive: *She gave a grand party for three hundred people. | Their house is very grand.*

grand² *noun informal*, *plural* **grand** £1,000 (pounds) or $1,000 (dollars): *He earns forty grand a year.*

grand·child /'græntʃaɪld/ *noun*, *plural* **grandchildren** /-ˌtʃɪldrən/ the child of your son or daughter: *Rosa is his youngest grandchild.*

grand·dad /'grændæd/ *informal* a GRANDFATHER

grand·daugh·ter /'græn,dɔːtə $ 'græn,dɔtɚ/ *noun* the daughter of your son or daughter

grand·fa·ther /'græn,fɑːðə $ 'græn-

,faðəʳ/ noun the father of one of your parents: *My grandfather gave me this book.*

grand·ma /'grænmɑː/ *informal* a GRAND-MOTHER

grand·moth·er /'græn,mʌðə $ 'græn-,mʌðəʳ/ noun the mother of one of your parents: *This is a photograph of my grandmother.*

grand·pa /'grænpɑː/ *informal* a GRAND-FATHER

grand·par·ent /'græn,peərənt $ 'græn-,perənt/ noun the parent of your mother or father: *We visited my grandparents at the weekend.*

grand·son /'grænsʌn/ noun the son of your son or daughter

gran·ny /'græni/ noun *informal*, *plural* **grannies** a word for a GRANDMOTHER, used especially by children

grant¹ /grɑːnt $ grænt/ verb **1 take it for granted** to think that something is true even though you have not heard that it is definitely true: *I took it for granted that we would get a pay rise.* **2 take someone for granted** if someone takes you for granted, they expect you to help them and do things for them but they never thank you or praise you for this: *I'm fed up with my boss always taking me for granted.* **3** *formal* to give someone official permission to have or do something: *Everyone was granted an extra day's holiday.*

grant² noun an amount of money that an organization gives someone for a particular purpose: *She got a grant to study at college.*

gran·ule /'grænjuːl/ noun a very small hard piece of something, especially dried coffee: *instant coffee granules*

grape /greɪp/ noun a small round juicy fruit that grows in bunches and is used to make wine: *a bunch of black grapes* ⇨ *see picture on page 345*

grape·fruit /'greɪpfruːt/ noun a yellow fruit like a big orange, but without a sweet taste ⇨ *see picture on page 345*

graph /græf/ noun a drawing or line that shows information about numbers, measurements etc: *The graph showed how the population had increased.*

graph·ic /'græfɪk/ adjective a graphic account, description etc is very clear and gives a lot of details: *She gave a graphic description of the accident.*

graphic de·sign /,.. .'./ noun [no plural] the job or art of combining pictures with the writing in books, magazines etc

graph·ics /'græfɪks/ plural noun drawings or pictures, especially the ones that a computer produces: *The new version of 'Tomb Raider' has brilliant graphics.*

grasp¹ /grɑːsp $ græsp/ verb **1** written to take and hold something firmly in your hands: *Rob grasped the rope and began to climb.* **2** to understand something: *She didn't seem to grasp what I was saying.*

grasp² noun [no plural] the ability to understand something: *You need to have a good grasp of how computers work.*

grass /grɑːs $ græs/ noun [no plural] **1** the green plant that covers the ground in gardens, fields etc: *We lay on the grass by the river.* **2** informal MARIJUANA

grass·hop·per /'grɑːs,hɒpə $ 'græs,hɑpəʳ/ noun an insect with long back legs that it uses to jump and make short loud sounds

grasshopper

grate¹ /greɪt/ verb to break food such as cheese or vegetables into small pieces by rubbing it against a GRATER (=a special kitchen tool with a rough surface): *Put grated cheese on the pizza.* ⇨ *see picture on page 344*

grate² noun the metal part of a fire, where you put the wood, coal etc

grate·ful /'greɪtfəl/ adjective

GRAMMAR
grateful for something
grateful to someone for (doing) something
someone who is grateful wants to thank another person for something ⇨ *opposite* UNGRATEFUL: *I lent him the money but he didn't seem very grateful.* | *We are very grateful for your help.* | *I was really grateful to her for being so kind.*
–gratefully adverb: *"Thank you so much for helping," she said gratefully.*

grat·er /'greɪtə $ 'greɪtəʳ/ noun a special kitchen tool used for breaking food into small pieces

G

grat·i·tude /'grætɪtjuːd $ 'grætə‚tud/ noun [no plural] formal when you want to thank someone for something: *I'd like to express my gratitude to you all for your support.*

gra·tu·i·tous /grə'tjuːɪtəs $ grə'tuːətəs/ adjective gratuitous violence, criticism etc is not necessary and is very unpleasant: *There is too much gratuitous violence on television.*

grave¹ /greɪv/ noun the place in the ground where a dead body is buried: *Joan put some flowers on her father's grave.*

grave² adjective formal very serious or worrying: *Unemployment is a very grave problem.*

grav·el /'grævəl/ noun [no plural] very small stones that are used to make a surface for paths: *His boots crunched on the gravel.*
=**gravel** adjective: *a gravel driveway* (=a path between a house and the road that cars can drive along)

grave·stone /'greɪvstəʊn $ 'greɪvstoʊn/ noun a large stone that is put on a grave, that shows the dead person's name and the dates they were alive

grave·yard /'greɪvjɑːd $ 'greɪvjɑrd/ noun an area of ground where dead people are buried, especially beside a church

grav·i·ty /'grævəti/ noun [no plural] the force that makes objects fall to the ground: *the Earth's gravity*

gra·vy /'greɪvi/ noun [no plural] a liquid that you pour over meat, potatoes etc, that is usually made from the meat's juices: *Would you like some more gravy?*

gray an American spelling of GREY

graze¹ /greɪz/ verb **1** to slightly cut the surface of your skin, for example by falling on a hard surface: *Tim fell off his bicycle and grazed his knees.* **2** if an animal grazes, it eats grass: *The sheep were grazing in a corner of the field.*

graze² noun a small cut in the surface of your skin: *His arms were covered in grazes.*

grease¹ /griːs/ noun [no plural] **1** fat from food that you have cooked: *The pans were all covered in grease.* **2** thick oil that you put on the moving parts of a machine to make them move smoothly

grease² verb to put fat or grease on something: *Grease the cake tin well.*

greas·y /'griːsi/ adjective greasier, greasiest covered in or containing a lot of grease or oil: *greasy fish and chips | a shampoo for greasy hair*

great /greɪt/ adjective
1 a lot of something: *Lily opened the present with great care. | The disco was great fun.*
2 very good or enjoyable: *The kids were having a great time in the sea. | It's really great to be home.*
3 very important, successful, or famous: *I think Tarantino is one of the greatest film directors.*

PHRASES
great, that's great spoken used to say that you are pleased about something: *"We've decided to get married." "Oh, that's great!"*
great big informal very big: *a great big spider*

great·ly /'greɪtli/ adverb formal very much: *I greatly admired him as a teacher.*

greed /griːd/ noun [no plural] when someone always wants more money, food, power etc than they need: *The greed of the logging companies could lead to the destruction of the forest.*

greed·i·ness /'griːdinəs/ noun [no plural] when someone wants more of something than they really need

greed·y /'griːdi/ adjective greedier, greediest someone who is greedy wants more money, food, power etc than they need: *Sometimes I'm rather greedy and I eat more than I should. | greedy businessmen*
=**greedily** adverb: *He looked greedily at the chocolate cake.*

green¹ /griːn/ adjective **1** something that is green is the colour of grass: *a green sweater* **2** covered with grass, trees etc: *Most towns have very few green areas nowadays.*

green² noun **1** the colour of grass: *The skirt is also available in dark green.* **2** **greens** vegetables with green leaves

green card /'. ‚./ noun an official piece of paper that allows you to live and work in the US, although you are not American

green·gro·cer /'griːn,grəʊsə $ 'grin-,grousə/ noun BrE 1 also **greengrocer's** a shop that sells fruit and vegetables ⇨ same meaning GROCER: There is a greengrocer's in the village. 2 someone who owns a shop that sells fruit and vegetables

green·house /'griːnhaʊs/ noun a glass building where you grow plants that must be kept warm: She grows tomatoes in her greenhouse. ⇨ see picture on page 343

greenhouse ef·fect /'.. ,../ noun the greenhouse effect a problem caused by POLLUTION, which stops the sun's heat from escaping and causes the air around the Earth to become warmer

greet /griːt/ verb 1 to welcome someone when you meet them, for example by saying "Hello": The whole family were waiting at the door to greet me. 2 **be greeted with something** if an idea, event etc is greeted with shouts, laughter etc, that is how people react to it: The idea was greeted with great enthusiasm.

greet·ing /'griːtɪŋ/ noun something friendly that you say or do when you meet someone, write to them, or telephone them: The two men **exchanged greetings** (=said "Hello" to each other). | The King raised his hand in greeting.

gre·nade /grə'neɪd/ noun a small bomb that is thrown: a hand grenade

grew the past tense of GROW

grey¹ BrE, **gray** AmE /greɪ/ adjective 1 something that is grey is the colour of dark clouds, neither black nor white: The house was built of old grey stone. 2 weather that is grey is dull and cloudy: a grey day in February

grey² BrE, **gray** AmE, noun the colour you get when you mix black with white: Do you have these skirts in grey?

grid /grɪd/ noun a pattern of straight lines that cross each other and form squares: The teacher told us to draw a grid on a piece of paper.

grief /griːf/ noun [no plural] great sadness, especially because someone you love has died

griev·ance /'griːvəns/ noun formal something that you think is unfair and

that you complain about, especially to someone in authority: The manager called a meeting to try and deal with our grievances.

grieve /griːv/ verb to feel very sad because someone you love has died: It's ten years since her husband died, but she's still grieving for him.

grill¹ /grɪl/ verb to cook meat, fish etc by putting it close to strong heat; BROIL AmE: Grill the steak for about 4 minutes each side.

grill² noun BrE the part of a COOKER which cooks food on a metal shelf, using strong heat: Put the sandwich under the grill until the cheese melts.

grim /grɪm/ adjective grimmer, grimmest 1 making you feel worried or unhappy: The situation here is extremely grim – hundreds of people have lost their homes. 2 a grim place is unattractive, dirty etc: a grim area of the city

gri·mace /grɪ'meɪs $ 'grɪməs/ verb written to twist your face in an ugly way because something is hurting you or because you do not like something: Trevor was grimacing with pain.
– **grimace** noun: She gave a grimace as she tasted the food.

grime /graɪm/ noun [no plural] thick black dirt: The factory walls were covered in grime.

grim·y /'graɪmi/ adjective grimier, grimiest covered in thick black dirt: a row of grimy houses near the railway

grin¹ /grɪn/ verb grinned, grinning to smile widely, showing your teeth: "I've got good news," Sally said, grinning.

grin² noun a wide smile: Simon had a great big grin on his face as he came out of the exam room.

grind /graɪnd/ verb, past tense and past participle **ground** /graʊnd/ to crush something such as coffee beans into small pieces or powder: This machine is for grinding wheat into flour.

grip /grɪp/ verb gripped, gripping 1 to hold something very tightly: I gripped the steering wheel of the car. 2 to keep your attention completely: The audience was gripped. | a gripping film
– **grip** noun: He kept a tight grip on my arm.

G

gris·ly /'grɪzli/ *adjective* grislier, grisliest involving very unpleasant violence and death: *a grisly murder*

grit¹ /grɪt/ *noun* [no plural] very small pieces of stone: *I had a piece of grit stuck in my shoe.*

grit² *verb* gritted, gritting; grit your teeth to decide to keep going in a difficult or painful situation: *He gritted his teeth against the pain.*

groan /grəʊn $ groʊn/ *verb* to make a long low sound to show that you are unhappy or in pain: *Kim groaned with pain as she got up.*
– **groan** *noun*: *The students let out a groan when the teacher announced a test.*

gro·cer /'grəʊsə $ 'groʊsɚ/ also **grocer's** BrE, *noun* 1 a small shop that sells food and other small things you need in your home: *Do you want anything from the grocer's?* 2 someone who owns a grocer's shop

gro·cer·ies /'grəʊsəriz $ 'groʊsəriz/ *plural noun* food and other things that you buy to use in your home: *We can deliver your groceries to your house.*

grog·gy /'grɒgi $ 'grɑgi/ *adjective* groggier, groggiest feeling weak and ill: *The injection made him feel groggy.*
– **groggily** *adverb*

groin /grɔɪn/ *noun* the place where your legs join at the front of your body: *a groin injury* ⇨ see picture at BODY

groom¹ /gruːm/ *verb* to clean and brush an animal: *The first task is to groom the horses.*

groom² *noun* 1 also **bridegroom** a man who is getting married, or has just got married: *a happy bride and groom* 2 someone whose job is to care for horses

groove /gruːv/ *noun* a line cut into a surface: *a pattern of deep grooves*

grope /grəʊp $ groʊp/ *verb* to try to find something or go somewhere using your hands, because you cannot see: *I groped in my handbag for the key.* | *Bob groped his way downstairs in the dark.*

gross /grəʊs $ groʊs/ *adjective* 1 *spoken* very unpleasant to look at or think about: *His jokes are really gross.* 2 *formal* very serious: *children suffering from gross neglect*
– **grossly** *adverb*: *He is grossly overweight.*

gro·tesque /grəʊ'tesk $ groʊ'tesk/ *adjective* ugly in a strange frightening way: *a grotesque monster*
– **grotesquely** *adverb*

grouch·y /'graʊtʃi/ *adjective* informal grouchier, grouchiest someone who is grouchy is cross and complains a lot: *Dad's always grouchy in the morning.*

ground¹ /graʊnd/ *noun*
1 the ground the surface of the earth: *Moira was lying asleep **on the ground**.* | *The dog was smelling **the ground**.* | ***The ground** was frozen.*
2 an area of land, especially one that is used for a special purpose: *The school has its own **sports ground**.* | ***football grounds*** | *We cleared a patch of ground and planted some vegetables.*

PHRASE

above ground, below ground: *The miners are working 1,000 feet below ground* (=1,000 feet under the ground).

USAGE ground, floor
The **ground** is the surface under your feet when you are outside. The **floor** is the surface under your feet when you are inside a building: *the kitchen floor*

ground² *verb* to stop an aircraft or pilot from flying: *All flights are grounded owing to the storms.*

ground³ the past tense and past participle of GRIND

ground beef /ˌ. './ an American word for MINCE

ground floor /ˌ. './ *noun* the part of a building that is on the same level as the ground; FIRST FLOOR AmE: *The men's clothing department is on the ground floor.*

group¹ /gruːp/ *noun*

GRAMMAR
a group of something
1 several people or things that are together in the same place: *a **group** of islands off the coast* | *A fight started between two **groups of** men.* | *Please can the class get into **groups of three** (=three people in each group).*
2 several musicians who play and sing popular music together ⇨ same meaning BAND¹: *'Queen' is my favourite **rock group**.*

group² *verb written* to arrange things in a group: *We grouped our results under two headings.*

grov·el /'grɒvəl $ 'grɑvəl/ *verb* **grovelled, grovelling** *BrE*, **groveled, groveling** *AmE* to try very hard to please someone, because you are frightened of them or you have upset them: *I don't care how important she is, I'm not going to grovel to her.*

grow /grəʊ $ groʊ/ *verb* **grew** /gruː/ **grown** /grəʊn $ groʊn/
1 to get bigger in size or amount: *Babies grow quickly in their first year.* | *The number of overseas students is growing.*
2 if someone grows their hair or grows a beard, they let it get longer and do not cut it: *I think I'd like to grow a beard.* | *Are you growing your hair, or will you have it cut?*
3 if plants grow somewhere or if you grow them there, they are alive in that place: *There were weeds growing everywhere.* | *We grow our own vegetables.*

PHRASES
grow old, grow strong etc to become old, strong etc ⇨ *same meaning* GET OLD, GET STRONG etc: *Grandad was growing old, and becoming forgetful.* | *We were lost, and it was starting to grow dark.*
grow up to gradually change from being a child to being an adult: *Where did you live when you were growing up?*

growl

growl /graʊl/ *verb* if a dog, bear etc growls, it makes a deep angry sound: *The dog started to growl and bark at us.*
– growl *noun*: *I heard a low growl from behind the gate.*

grown the past participle of GROW

grown-up¹ /ˌ. './ *noun* an adult; a word used by children

grown-up² *adjective* someone who is grown-up is an adult: *She has two grown-up daughters.*

growth /grəʊθ $ groʊθ/ *noun* [no plural] when something gets bigger or develops: *The nurse measured the children's growth.* | *The country is in a period of economic growth.*

grub /grʌb/ *noun* [no plural] *informal* food

grub·by /'grʌbi/ *adjective* **grubbier, grubbiest** dirty: *grubby fingers*

grudge /grʌdʒ/ *noun* an unfriendly feeling towards someone because of something they did in the past: *She criticized him months ago, and he still has a grudge against her.*

gru·el·ling *BrE*, **grueling** *AmE* /'gruːəlɪŋ/ *adjective* very difficult and tiring: *a gruelling ten-mile run*

grue·some /'gruːsəm/ *adjective* connected with violence or death: *This castle has a gruesome history.*

grum·ble /'grʌmbəl/ *verb* to complain: *All the hotel guests were grumbling about the food.*

grump·y /'grʌmpi/ *adjective* **grumpier, grumpiest** if someone is grumpy, they show that they feel slightly angry or annoyed: *I'm feeling grumpy because I'm tired.*
– grumpily *adverb*: *"Leave me alone," she said grumpily.*

grunt /grʌnt/ *verb* 1 to make a short, low sound to show that you are not interested in something: *I asked him several times, but he just grunted.* 2 if a pig grunts, it makes a low rough sound
– grunt *noun*: *Alex answered with a grunt.*

guar·an·tee¹ /ˌgærən'tiː/ *verb* to promise something: *We guarantee to repair your computer within 48 hours.* | *Of course, we can't guarantee that you'll pass the exam, but we'll help as much as we can.*

guarantee² *noun* a promise by a company to repair or replace something you have bought from them, for example if it breaks: *a two-year guarantee*

guard¹ /gɑːd $ gɑrd/ *noun*
1 someone whose job is to protect a person or a place, or to make sure that a person does not escape: *A security guard was sitting by the door.* | *Two armed guards* (=guards

carrying guns) *walked behind the President.* | *a prison guard*

2 *BrE* someone whose job is to collect tickets on a train, help the passengers etc: *The guard asked to see our tickets.*

guard

PHRASES

be on guard to be responsible for protecting a place or a person: *A policeman **is** always **on guard** outside the palace.*

be on your guard (against something) to be very careful because you may have to deal with a bad situation: *You have to **be on your guard** **against** thieves in this part of the city.*

catch someone off guard to surprise someone by doing something that they were not expecting: *His question **caught** me **off guard**.*

guard² *verb* to watch someone or something so that they do not escape, or get damaged or stolen: *Three men were sent to guard the prisoner.* | *We have two large dogs guarding the property at night.*

guard·i·an /ˈɡɑːdiən $ ˈɡɑrdiən/ *noun* someone who is legally responsible for someone else's child

guer·ril·la /ɡəˈrɪlə/ *noun* a member of an unofficial army that is fighting for political reasons

guess¹ /ɡes/ *verb*

GRAMMAR
guess (that)
guess how/what/whether/if etc

to answer a question or decide something without being sure whether you are right: *The teacher soon **guessed that** the boys had been smoking.* | ***Guess how much** this dress cost.* | *I could **guess what** Sandra was thinking.* | *I **guessed** her age **correctly**.*

PHRASES

I guess (so) *spoken* used to say that you think something is probably true: *"Is her dad very rich?" "I guess so."* | *My car isn't running, so **I guess** we'll have to get the bus.*

guess what! *spoken* used to tell someone some surprising news: ***Guess what!** I've been picked for the basketball team!*

guess² *noun, plural* **guesses**

an attempt to guess something. You can have or make a guess: *Listen to the tape and then **make a guess** who is speaking.* | *You were wrong the first time, but you **can have** another **guess**.*

guest /ɡest/ *noun* **1** someone that you invite to stay in your home or invite to an event: *How many guests are coming to your party?* **2** someone who is staying in a hotel: *All the guests were given a free meal.*

guid·ance /ˈɡaɪdns/ *noun* [no plural] helpful advice: *People taking the art course will receive expert guidance.*

guide¹ /ɡaɪd/ *noun* **1** someone whose job is to show a place to tourists: *The guide pointed out the cathedral on the left.* **2** also **guidebook** a book that has information and advice on a particular subject: *a guide for new students* | *I've bought you a book called 'The Idiot's Guide to the Internet'.* **3** something that helps you to make a decision: *As a rough guide, you need about 100 grams of meat per person.*

guide² *verb*

GRAMMAR
guide someone to/through/across etc a place

1 to help someone to go somewhere, for example by showing them the right direction: *He took the old lady's arm and **guided** her **across** the road.*

2 to help someone manage a difficult situation: *Your teacher can guide you when you make your college application.*

guide dog /ˈ. ./ *noun BrE* a specially trained dog that blind people use to help them go to places; SEEING EYE DOG *AmE*

guide·lines /ˈɡaɪdlaɪnz/ *plural noun* advice about how to do something: *The teacher gave the students some guidelines on writing essays.*

guilt /ɡɪlt/ *noun* [no plural] **1** a sad feeling you have when you have done something wrong: *a terrible sense of guilt and shame* **2** when someone has broken a law ⇨ *opposite* INNOCENCE: *We were sure he had done it, but could not prove his guilt.*

guilt·y /'gɪlti/ *adjective* **guiltier, guiltiest**

GRAMMAR

guilty about something

1 unhappy and ashamed because you have done something that you know is wrong: *Robyn felt guilty about stealing the pen.* | *The vase was broken, and Billy was looking guilty.*

2 **find someone guilty (of something)** if a court of law finds someone guilty of a crime, it decides that they COMMITTED that crime ⇨ *opposite* INNOCENT (1): *Menzies was found guilty of murder.*

guin·ea pig /'gɪni ˌpɪg/ *noun* a small furry animal with no tail, that is often kept as a pet

gui·tar /gɪ'tɑː $ gɪ'tɑr/ *noun* a wooden musical instrument with strings and a long neck, that you play by pulling the strings: *an electric guitar*

gui·tar·ist /gɪ'tɑːrɪst/ *noun* someone who plays the guitar: *the guitarist, Jimi Hendrix*

gulf /gʌlf/ *noun* a large area of sea that is partly surrounded by land: *the Persian Gulf*

gull /gʌl/ a SEAGULL

gul·li·ble /'gʌləbəl/ *adjective* a gullible person is easy to trick because they always believe what people say: *I was angry with myself for being so gullible.*

gulp /gʌlp/ *verb* 1 also **gulp down** to swallow food or drink quickly: *Sip your drink – don't gulp it.* 2 *written* to swallow suddenly because you are frightened or unhappy: *Nola gulped and tried not to cry.*

–**gulp** *noun*: *He drank the whisky in a single gulp.*

gum /gʌm/ *noun* 1 the pink parts inside your mouth that your teeth grow out of 2 another word for CHEWING GUM

gun /gʌn/ *noun* a weapon that fires bullets: *The police here all carry guns.*

gun·fire /'gʌnfaɪə $ 'gʌnfaɪər/ *noun* [no plural] shots fired from a gun: *the sound of gunfire*

gun·man /'gʌnmən/ *noun, plural* **gunmen** /-mən/ a criminal who uses a

gun: *The gunman was arrested at the airport.*

gun·point /'gʌnpɔɪnt/ *noun* **at gunpoint** if someone does something to you at gunpoint, they do it to you while threatening to shoot you: *The victims were held at gunpoint while the thief stole their car.* | *The man kidnapped her at gunpoint.*

gun·shot /'gʌnʃɒt $ 'gʌnʃɑt/ *noun* the sound made by a gun, or the bullets that are fired from it: *Neighbours said they heard gunshots.* | *a gunshot wound*

gur·gle /'gɜːgəl $ 'gɚgəl/ *verb* to make a sound like flowing water: *The baby gurgled with pleasure.*

gu·ru /'guruː/ *noun* 1 informal someone that people respect because they are very wise or skilful in a particular subject: *a top management guru* 2 a Hindu religious teacher

gush /gʌʃ/ *verb written* if liquid gushes somewhere, a large amount of it flows there: *Blood was gushing from his arm.*

gust /gʌst/ *noun* a sudden strong wind: *A gust of wind nearly knocked her over.*

gut¹ /gʌt/ *adjective informal* **gut feeling, gut reaction** a feeling or idea that you are sure is right, although you cannot say why: *My gut reaction was to refuse.*

gut² *noun informal* 1 also **guts** the tube in your body that food passes through after it leaves your stomach: *I had a pain in my gut.* 2 **guts** courage and determination to do something difficult: *Have you got the guts to ask for a pay rise?*

gut³ *verb* **gutted, gutting** 1 to destroy the inside of a building completely: *The house was gutted by fire.* 2 if you gut a dead fish or animal, you remove the parts that are inside it

gut·ted /'gʌtɪd/ *adjective BrE spoken* very disappointed: *The team were gutted when they lost.*

gut·ter /'gʌtə $ 'gʌtɚ/ *noun* the low part at the edge of a road, or a pipe fixed to a roof, which carries away water: *The gutter was blocked by leaves.*

gutter

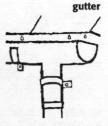

guy /gaɪ/ *noun informal* a MAN

guz·zle /ˈɡʌzəl/ verb informal to drink or eat a lot very quickly: The children were guzzling lemonade.

gym /dʒɪm/ noun 1 a large room or a building containing equipment for doing physical exercise: I go to the gym twice a week. 2 [no plural] exercises done indoors, especially as a school subject: Gym is on Friday afternoons.

gym·na·si·um /dʒɪmˈneɪziəm/ formal a GYM

gym·nast /ˈdʒɪmnæst/ noun someone who performs gymnastics: an Olympic gymnast

gym·nas·tics /dʒɪmˈnæstɪks/ plural noun skilful physical exercises and movements: a gymnastics display ⇨ see picture on page 351

gyp·sy also **gipsy** BrE /ˈdʒɪpsi/ noun, plural gypsies, gipsies a member of a group of people who travel around rather than living in one place

G

Hh

hab·it /'hæbɪt/ noun

> **GRAMMAR**
> **a/the habit of doing something**
> something that you do often or regularly: *Irene **was in the habit of** visiting her uncle every weekend.* | *We **got into the habit of** staying up very late.* | *My tutor **has a habit of** looking over your shoulder while you work.* | *Smoking is a very **bad habit**.* | *Changing your **eating habits** can be really difficult.*

hab·i·tat /'hæbətæt/ noun the habitat of a wild animal or a plant is the type of place in which it lives: *Pollution is damaging many wildlife habitats.*

ha·bit·u·al /hə'bɪtʃuəl/ adjective formal typical or happening often, as a habit: *I'm not happy about your habitual absences from work.* | *a habitual smoker*

hack /hæk/ verb **1** to cut something roughly or violently: *Tom hacked the branches from the tree.* **2** hack into to use a computer to enter someone else's computer system in order to damage it or get secret information: *They hacked into the bank's system and moved money into their accounts.*

hacker /'hækə $ 'hækɚ/ noun someone who uses computers a lot, especially in order to secretly use or change the information in another person's computer system

had /əd; strong hæd/ the past tense and past participle of HAVE

had·n't /'hædnt/ the short form of 'had not': *I hadn't got any money.*

hag /hæg/ noun an ugly unpleasant old woman

hag·gard /'hægəd $ 'hægɚd/ adjective looking tired, thin, and ill: *His face looked haggard and pale.*

hag·gle /'hægəl/ verb to argue about the amount that you will pay for something before agreeing on a price ⇨ same meaning BARGAIN[2]: *The owner of the shop and the tourist were haggling over the price of a rug.*

hail[1] /heɪl/ verb **1** hail a taxi, hail a cab to wave at a taxi to make it stop **2** if it hails, frozen rain falls from the sky

hail[2] noun **1** [no plural] frozen rain that falls from the sky **2** a hail of bullets a lot of bullets travelling through the air at the same time: *Bonnie and Clyde died in a hail of bullets.*

hair /heə $ her/ noun

1 [no plural] your hair is the large number of things like thin threads that grow on your head: *I like girls with ginger hair.* | *Her hair is very long.* ⇨ see picture at HEAD[1]

2 one of the short hairs that grow on the skin of a person or animal: *There are cat hairs all over this chair.*

hair·brush /'heəbrʌʃ $ 'herbrʌʃ/ noun, plural **hairbrushes** a brush you use to tidy your hair ⇨ see picture at BRUSH[1]

hair·cut /'heəkʌt $ 'herkʌt/ noun when someone cuts your hair, or the style in which your hair is cut: *I'm going to have a haircut this week.* | *a short, neat haircut*

hair·dress·er /'heə,dresə $ 'her-,dresɚ/ noun someone whose job is to wash, cut, and arrange people's hair: *an appointment at the hairdresser's*

hair·dry·er /'heə,draɪə $ 'her,draɪɚ/ noun a machine you use to dry your hair that blows hot air onto it

hair·grip BrE /'heəgrɪp/ also **hair·pin** /'heəpɪn $ herpɪn/ noun a thin piece of metal, used to hold a woman's hair in place; BOBBY PIN AmE

hair·rais·ing /'. ,../ adjective informal frightening but exciting: *a hair-raising fairground ride*

H

hair·style /ˈheəstaɪl ˈherstaɪl/ *noun* the way in which your hair is cut and arranged: *I like her new hairstyle.*

hair·y /ˈheəri ˈheri/ *adjective* **hairier, hairiest** a hairy person or animal has a lot of hair on their body: *hairy legs*

half¹ /hɑːf hæf/ *noun, plural* **halves** /hɑːvz hævz/ one of two equal parts: *The first half of the game was pretty dull.* | *Half the pupils in the school are ill.* | *I'll be ready in half an hour.* | *He decided to save* **half of** *the money and spend the rest.* | *Cut the grapes* **in half** (=into two equal pieces).

PHRASE

half past one, half past two etc used when telling the time: *It's* **half past** *two* (=it's half an hour after two o'clock).

half² *adverb* partly but not completely: *His eyes were half closed.* | *a half-empty glass*

half-broth·er /ˈ. ˌ./ *noun* a brother who has either the same mother or the same father as you, but not both

half-heart·ed /ˌ. ˈ../ *adjective informal* a half-hearted attempt is one someone makes without any real effort or interest: *He made a half-hearted attempt to talk to me.*

half-sis·ter /ˈ. ˌ./ *noun* a sister who has either the same mother or the same father as you, but not both

half term /ˌ. ˈ./ *noun BrE* a short holiday in the middle of a school TERM

half time /ˌ. ˈ./ *noun [no plural]* a short period of time between the two parts of a sports game: *The team discussed tactics at half time.*

half·way /ˌhɑːfˈweɪ hæfˈweɪ/ *adjective, adverb* in the middle, between two places or between the beginning and the end of something: *I was at the halfway point when my car broke down.* | *Rosco dies halfway through the film.*

hall /hɔːl/ *noun* **1** also **hallway** the part of a house that you come into through the front door and that leads to the other rooms: *You can hang your coat in the hall.* **2** a large building or room, used for important events: *a concert hall* | *the Albert Hall*

hallo *BrE* HELLO

hall of res·i·dence /ˌ. . ˈ.../ *noun BrE* a college or university building where students live; DORMITORY *AmE*

Hal·low·een /ˌhæləʊˈiːn ˌhæləˈwin/ *noun* the night of October 31, when children dress in strange clothes: *The children dressed up as ghosts and witches for our Halloween party.*

hal·lu·ci·nate /həˈluːsəneɪt/ *verb* to see, feel, or hear something that is not really there: *Jim started hallucinating after he took the drugs.*

hal·lu·ci·na·tion /həˌluːsəˈneɪʃən/ *noun* something you see, feel, or hear that is not really there: *They suffered from strange hallucinations.*

hall·way /ˈhɔːlweɪ/ another word for HALL (1)

ha·lo /ˈheɪləʊ ˈheɪloʊ/ *noun* in paintings, a golden circle above the head of a holy person: *The angel had wings and a halo.*

halt¹ /hɔːlt/ *verb formal* to stop or to make something stop: *The procession halted at the church gates.* | *Police halted traffic after the accident.*

halt² *noun* **come to a halt** to stop moving: *The car came to a halt in front of the house.*

halve /hɑːv hæv/ *verb* to reduce an amount by half, or to make something do this: *Deaths from the disease have been halved.*

halves the plural of HALF

ham /hæm/ *noun [no plural]* meat from a pig's leg, that is usually eaten cold: *ham sandwiches*

ham·burg·er /ˈhæmbɜːgə ˈhæmˌbɚgɚ/ *noun* **1** a flat round piece of cooked BEEF (=meat from a cow), which you eat between two pieces of bread **2** an American word for MINCE

ham·mer¹ /ˈhæmə ˈhæmɚ/ *noun* a tool used for hitting nails into wood ⇨ see picture at TOOL

ham·mer² *verb* to hit something with a hammer: *He hammered two nails into the door.*

ham·mock /ˈhæmək/ *noun* a long piece of material that you hang between two poles or trees and lie on: *They have a hammock in their garden.*

ham·per¹ /ˈhæmpə ˈhæmpɚ/ *verb written* to make it difficult for someone to do something: *Storms hampered* our attempts to reach the crash victims. | *Shearer was hampered by a leg injury.*

hamper² *noun* a large basket with a lid, used for carrying food somewhere: *a picnic hamper*

ham·ster /'hæmstə $'hæmstɚ/ *noun* a small animal like a mouse with soft fur and no tail, often kept as a pet

hand¹ /hænd/ *noun*

1 the part of your body at the end of each of your arms that includes your fingers and thumb: *Polly put her hand on my shoulder.* | *He* **held hands with** *his daughter as they crossed the road.* | *She was carrying a bag in one hand.*

2 one of the parts of a clock that points to the numbers, telling you the time: *The big hand is pointing to three.*

PHRASES

at hand, on hand, to hand near to you and ready to be used: *Keep the tools that you use most often* **close at hand**. | *Luckily, a doctor was* **on hand** *when Lucy collapsed.*

by hand something that is made or done by hand is made or done by a person, not by a machine: *These cushions were sewn* **by hand**. | *I delivered the letter* **by hand**.

shake hands to hold another person's right hand with your right hand and move it up and down as a sign of friendship: *The two men* **shook hands**. | *Marge felt so proud when she* **shook hands with** *the President.*

give someone a hand to help someone to do something: *Will you* **give** *me* **a hand with** *my homework?* | *Tom* **gave** *us* **a hand** *to clean the house.*

get out of hand to become impossible to control: *The party was starting to* **get out of hand**.

have your hands full to have a lot of things that you must do: *You'll have to make your own supper, I've* **got** *my* **hands full** *with the baby.*

in someone's hands, in the hands of someone if something is in your hands, you control it or are responsible for it: *I'll leave the decision* **in** *your* **hands**. | *Power was now* **in the hands of** *the terrorists.*

hand² *verb* 1 to give something to someone: *Could you hand me those scissors please?* 2 **hand something back** to give something back to the person who gave it to you: *Our tutor handed back our essays today.* 3 **hand something in** to give something to someone in authority, usually a teacher: *Hand your test papers in now, please.* 4 **hand something out** to give something to each person in a group: *I handed out the coursebooks to my classmates.*

hand·bag /'hændbæg/ *noun* a small bag that women use to carry money and personal things; PURSE *AmE*: *There's a pen in my handbag.* ➪ *see picture at* BAG

hand·book /'hændbʊk/ *noun* a small book containing advice and information: *the student handbook*

hand·brake /'hændbreɪk/ *noun BrE* the BRAKE in a car that works when you pull a long handle inside the car: EMERGENCY BRAKE *AmE*

hand·cuffs /'hændkʌfs/ *plural noun* two metal rings joined by a chain, used to hold a prisoner's wrists together: *Each officer carries a pair of handcuffs.*

handcuffs

hand·ful /'hændfʊl/ *noun* 1 an amount that you can hold in your hand: *She scattered a handful of seed on the ground.* 2 **a handful of something** a small number or amount: *We employ only a handful of people.*

hand·i·cap /'hændikæp/ *noun* something permanently wrong with someone's mind or body that affects the way that they live

hand·i·capped /'hændikæpt/ *adjective* if someone is handicapped, they have a problem with their body or mind that affects the way they can live their life: *a charity for mentally handicapped children*

hand·ker·chief /'hæŋkətʃɪf $'hæŋkɚtʃɪf/ *noun* a small piece of cloth or paper that you use for drying your nose or eyes

han·dle¹ /'hændl/ *verb*

1 to be responsible for something or to control and organize something:

H

▼ I've handled some difficult situations in my career as a pilot. | Pat's agreed to handle the party invitations.
2 to pick up or touch something: *The metal plate was too hot to handle.*

handle² noun the part of something that you hold when you use it or open it: *The handle of this mug has broken.* | *the door handle* ⇨ see picture at CAR

han·dle·bars /'hændlbɑːz $ 'hændl-,bɑrz/ plural noun the bars at the front of a bicycle that you hold on to

han·dler /'hændlə $ 'hændlɚ/ noun someone whose job is to work or deal with a particular thing: *airport baggage handlers* | *a police dog handler*

hand·made /ˌhænd'meɪd/ adjective made by a person, not a machine: *handmade furniture*

hand·out /'hændaʊt/ noun a piece of paper with information on it that a speaker gives to the people in a class or a meeting: *Have you got a copy of the lecture handout?*

hand·shake /'hændʃeɪk/ noun an action in which two people hold each other's right hand and move it up and down when they make an agreement, meet each other, or leave: *I was given a friendly handshake by the principal.*

hand·some /'hænsəm/ adjective a handsome man is attractive: *He was tall, dark and handsome.* ⇨ see usage note at PRETTY²

hand·writ·ing /'hændˌraɪtɪŋ/ noun [no plural] your handwriting is your style of writing with a pen or a pencil: *I can't read your handwriting.*

hand·y /'hændi/ adjective informal handier, handiest useful: *handy tips on essay writing*

hang¹ /hæŋ/ verb, past tense and past participle **hung** /hʌŋ/

GRAMMAR
hang something above/on/over etc something
hang from somewhere

1 also **hang up** if you hang something somewhere, you fix it above the ground by supporting its top part, but not the bottom part: *Peter hung the mirror above the bed.* | *You can hang your coat on the door.* | *Flags hung from the windows of the house.* | *Mom hung*

▼ up the wet sheets in front of the fire.
2 past tense and past participle **hanged** to kill someone by putting a rope around their neck and then letting them fall, so that they are hanging in the air: *He tried to hang himself with his belt.* | *Some people said the killer should have been hanged for what he did.*

PHRASAL VERBS

hang around also **hang about** BrE informal
to stay in one place without doing very much, often because you are waiting for someone: *Some girls were hanging around outside the cafe.* | *We hung about waiting for Jack but he didn't arrive.*

hang on
1 spoken: *Hang on a minute* (=wait) – *I want to talk to you!*
2 to hold something very firmly: *The dog bit the man's arm and hung on.*

hang onto
hang onto something informal to keep something that is important to you: *I'm surprised Gemma managed to hang onto her job after she was caught stealing.*

hang up
to finish a telephone conversation by putting the telephone down so that it is no longer connected: *Before you hang up, make sure you have written down all the details correctly.*

hang² noun get the hang of something informal to learn how to do something: *Once I got the hang of skiing, it was easy.*

hang·ar /'hæŋə $ 'hæŋɚ/ noun a large building where aircraft are kept

hang·er /'hæŋə $ 'hæŋɚ/ also **coat-hanger** noun a metal, plastic, or wooden object that you put a piece of clothing on to hang it up, for example in a cupboard

hang·o·ver /'hæŋəʊvə $ 'hæŋˌoʊvɚ/ noun when someone feels ill because they drank too much alcohol the evening before: *He had a terrible hangover after the party.*

han·kie or **hanky** /'hæŋki/ noun informal, plural **hankies** a HANDKERCHIEF

hap·haz·ard /ˌhæp'hæzəd $ ˌhæp-'hæzɚd/ adjective not planned or organized: *We work in a very haphazard way.*

–**haphazardly** *adverb: cars parked haphazardly*

hap·pen /'hæpən/ *verb*

1 to start and continue for a period of time: *What happened today at work? | I couldn't see what was happening on the stage. | Thomas was afraid that something terrible had happened. | What happens if you mix the two liquids?*

2 to affect someone: *"What happened to you? Did you fall in the river?" | When you didn't phone, I worried that something had happened to you. | The floods were the worst thing to happen to the country in years.*

3 to do something by chance: *Winchell happened to be a few minutes early. | I happened to have some tissues with me.*

USAGE happen, take place, or occur?
Use **happen** when you talk about things that have not been planned: *A funny thing happened on my way to school. | Accidents like this happen all the time.* Use **take place** when you talk about events that have been planned or that have already happened: *The wedding took place on Saturday afternoon. | When did the robbery take place?* **Occur** means 'to happen', but is formal: *Earthquakes occur without any warning signs. | The accident occurred during rush hour on the freeway.*

hap·pen·ing /'hæpənɪŋ/ *noun* a strange or unusual event: *There have been some bizarre happenings in the old castle.*

hap·pi·ly /'hæpəli/ *adverb* in a happy way: *She laughed happily.*

hap·pi·ness /'hæpinəs/ *noun [no plural]* when someone is happy: *a feeling of great happiness*

hap·py /'hæpi/ *adjective* **happier, happiest**

1 feeling pleased, satisfied, or cheerful ⇨ *opposite* UNHAPPY: *I was so happy to hear about the birth of your baby. | I'm very happy with the results. | Sam was feeling happy because it was his birthday. | The children looked happy as they ate the ice cream.* ⇨ *see usage note at* GLAD

2 making you feel pleased or happy: *The story had a happy ending. | My wedding day was the happiest day of my life.*

3 Happy Birthday, Happy New Year used as a way of greeting someone on a special occasion: *Happy birthday to you, Julie!*

har·ass /'hærəs/ *verb* to deliberately annoy or threaten someone: *She was harassed by her neighbours for two years.*

har·ass·ment /'hærəsmənt/ *noun [no plural]* behaviour that threatens or offends someone: *racial harassment*

har·bour[1] *BrE*, **harbor** *AmE* /'hɑːbə $ 'hɑːbɚ/ *noun* an area of water next to the land where ships can stay safely ⇨ *see picture on page 349*

har·bour[2] *BrE*, **harbor** *AmE*, *verb written* if you harbour an unpleasant feeling or idea, it stays in your mind for a long time: *I began to harbour doubts about my boss.*

hard[1] /hɑːd $ hɑrd/ *adjective*

1 very firm and difficult to cut, break, or bend ⇨ *opposite* SOFT (1): *The chairs were hard and uncomfortable to sit on. | This soil is too hard to dig. | a book with a hard cover*

2 difficult to do or understand ⇨ *opposite* EASY[1]: *She finds it hard to get to sleep sometimes. | That test was much harder than the one we had last week. | That's a very hard question for me to answer. | The government wants to make it harder for foreigners to work in this country.*

3 needing a lot of physical or mental effort: *Clearing the snow was hard work. | Mom's had a really hard day at the office.*

PHRASES

give someone a hard time *informal* to make life difficult or unpleasant for someone, for example by criticizing

H

them or being unkind to them: *Suzie gave Tom **a hard time** when they were married.*

hard² *adverb*

using a lot of effort or force: *Kay **worked hard** all year and came top of the class.* | *You can doing anything if you **try hard enough**.* | *He pulled hard on the rope, but nothing happened, so he pulled harder.*

hard-and-fast /ˌ. . './ *adjective informal* hard-and-fast rule a rule that cannot be changed: *There are no hard-and-fast rules for success.*

hard·back /'hɑːdbæk $ 'hɑrdbæk/ *noun* a book with a strong stiff cover – hardback *adjective*: *a hardback book*

hard-boiled /ˌ. './ *adjective* a hard-boiled egg has been boiled in its shell until the yellow part is firm

hard cop·y /'. ˌ../ *noun [no plural]* information from a computer that is printed on paper: *Can I e-mail the file or do you want it on hard copy?*

hard disk /ˌ. './ *noun* a part fixed inside a computer that you use to store information: *I have no memory left on my hard disk.*

hard·en /'hɑːdn $ 'hɑrdn/ *verb* to become firm: *The plaster will harden in 24 hours.*

hard-head·ed /ˌ. '../ *adjective* practical and able to make difficult decisions: *A businessman needs to be hard-headed to succeed.*

hard-heart·ed /ˌ. '../ *adjective* a hard-hearted person does not care about other people's feelings: *I don't know how you can be so hard-hearted.*

hard·ly /'hɑːdli $ 'hɑrdli/ *adverb*

> **GRAMMAR**
> **can/could hardly do something**
> **hardly any/anyone/anything**
> **hardly ever**

1 almost not or almost none: *Jean was so excited she **could hardly** speak.* | ***Hardly anyone** could remember seeing Bill at the party.* | *He owns a big house, but he's **hardly ever** there.* | *Jill smiled at Jack, but he hardly noticed.*

2 *informal* if something is hardly possible, hardly surprising etc, it is definitely not possible, surprising etc: *He*

was driving very fast, so it was **hard-ly surprising** that the police stopped him.

hard-nosed /ˌ. './ *adjective* a hard-nosed person is determined to get what they want and is not affected by their feelings: *a hard-nosed businessman*

hard·ship /'hɑːdʃɪp $ 'hɑrdˌʃɪp/ *noun* something that makes your life unpleasant: *The family suffered years of poverty and hardship.* | *the hardships of war*

hard shoul·der /ˌ. '../ *noun BrE* the area at the side of a big road where you are allowed to stop if you have a problem with your car; SHOULDER *AmE*

hard up /ˌ. './ *adjective informal* someone who is hard-up does not have enough money: *We were very hard-up when I was young.*

hard·ware /'hɑːdweə $ 'hɑrdwer/ *noun [no plural]* computer machinery and equipment: *The problem is with the hardware, not the program.*

hard-work·ing /ˌ. '../ *adjective* working with a lot of effort: *hard-working pupils*

har·dy /'hɑːdi $ 'hɑrdi/ *adjective* hardier, hardiest strong and able to live in difficult conditions: *a hardy little horse*

hare /heə $ her/ *noun* an animal like a rabbit with long ears, which can run very fast

harm¹ /hɑːm $ hɑrm/ *noun*

1 *[no plural]* damage or physical injury that hurts someone: *We have to protect old people from harm.* | *Staying out late once in a while **does** you **no harm** (=does not hurt you).* | *This new law could **do more harm than good** (=will hurt people more than it will help them).*

2 **there's no harm in doing something** *spoken* used to say that doing something might help a situation, and that it cannot make the situation any worse: *Even if Dad refuses to lend you the car, **there's no harm in** asking.*

harm² *verb* to damage or hurt something or someone: *Luckily, he wasn't harmed by his experiences.*

harm·ful /'hɑːmfəl $ 'hɑrmfəl/ *adjective* something that is harmful causes harm or damage: *products that are harmful to the environment*

harmful

harmful

harmless

harm·less /'hɑːmləs $ 'hɑrmləs/ *adjective* something that is harmless does not cause any harm: *a harmless fly*

har·mon·i·ca /hɑː'mɒnɪkə $ hɑr'mɑnɪkə/ *noun* a small musical instrument with holes along the side that you blow into

har·mo·ny /'hɑːməni $ 'hɑrməni/ *noun* **1** [no plural] when people are not arguing or fighting: *Why can't people live in harmony?* **2** plural **harmonies** musical notes that sound good together

har·ness[1] /'hɑːnɪs $ 'hɑrnɪs/ *noun*, plural **harnesses** **1** a set of bands that you put round a horse so that it can pull a vehicle **2** a set of bands that hold someone or stop them from falling: *The climbers used safety harnesses.*

harness[2] *verb written* to use the energy from something: *ways of harnessing the sun's energy*

harp /hɑːp $ hɑrp/ *noun* a large musical instrument with strings stretched on a frame with three corners

harp

harsh /hɑːʃ $ hɑrʃ/, *adjective* **harsher, harshest** **1** unpleasant and extreme or rough: *a harsh winter* | *the harsh cries of the seabirds* **2** unkind or strict: *harsh laws* | *harsh criticism* –**harshly** *adverb*: *We should not judge him too harshly.*

har·vest[1] /'hɑːvɪst $ 'hɑrvɪst/ *noun* when grain, vegetables etc are collected from the fields, or the amount that you collect: *Harvest is a busy time.* | *The harvest was good this year.*

harvest[2] *verb* to collect grain, vegetables etc from the fields

has /əz, həz; *strong* hæz/ the third person singular of the present tense of HAVE

has-been /'. ./ *noun informal* someone who is no longer important or popular

hash /hæʃ/ *noun* **make a hash of something** *informal* to do something very badly

has·n't /'hæznt/ the short form of 'has not': *Peter hasn't come home yet.*

has·sle[1] /'hæsəl/ *noun informal* something that is annoying because it takes a lot of time or effort: *I didn't want the hassle of moving house again.*

hassle[2] *verb informal* to continuously ask someone to do something, in a way that is annoying: *He keeps hassling me about the money I owe him.*

haste /heɪst/ *noun* [no plural] *formal* when you do something very quickly, because you do not have enough time: *In her haste to leave, she forgot to lock the door.*

has·ten /'heɪsən/ *verb written* to make something happen sooner: *The accident hastened his death.*

hast·y /'heɪsti/ *adjective* **hastier, hastiest** done too quickly, without thinking carefully: *He soon regretted his hasty decision.*

hat /hæt/ *noun* something that you wear on your head ⇨ see picture on page 352

hatch[1] /hætʃ/ *verb* if an egg hatches, it breaks and a baby bird, fish, or insect is born

hatch[2] *noun, plural* **hatches** a small door in a ship, plane, or wall

hatch·et /'hætʃɪt/ *noun* a small tool that you use to cut wood into small pieces

hate[1] /heɪt/ *verb*

GRAMMAR
hate doing something
hate to do something

to have a very strong feeling that you do not like someone or something: *I hate poetry – it's so boring.* | *I hate my boss.* | *Anne hates cleaning the car.* | *We all **hated to** see the Red Sox lose a game.* | *If you eat all those biscuits, you'll hate yourself.*

hate[2] *noun* [no plural] a very strong feeling of not liking someone or something

ha·tred /'heɪtrəd/ *noun* [no plural] *formal* a very strong feeling of not liking someone or something: *her hatred of spiders*

hat trick /'. ./ *noun* if a player SCORES a hat trick in a game of football or HOCKEY, they score three GOALS in one game

H

haul /hɔːl/ *formal noun* a large amount of things that someone has stolen, or that the police have found: *The robbers got away with their haul of jewellery.* | *a drugs haul*

haunt·ed /'hɔːntɪd/ *adjective* a haunted place is one where people believe the spirits of dead people are present: *The old church is haunted.*

haunt·ing /'hɔːntɪŋ/ *adjective* something that is haunting is so beautiful or sad that you remember it: *a haunting picture of a girl in a forest*

have ⇨ see box on pages 276 and 277

have·n't /'hævənt/ the short form of 'have not': *I haven't forgotten.*

hav·oc /'hævək/ *noun* [no plural] a situation in which there is a lot of confusion: *The failure of the airport's computer system caused havoc.*

hawk /hɔːk/ *noun* a wild bird that eats small birds and animals

hay /heɪ/ *noun* [no plural] dried grass that is used to feed farm animals

hay fe·ver /'. ,../ *noun* [no plural] a medical condition which is like a bad COLD that some people get from breathing in dust from plants

haz·ard /'hæzəd $ 'hæzəd/ *noun* something that may be dangerous: *Those piles of boxes are a fire hazard.*

haz·ard·ous /'hæzədəs $ 'hæzədəs/ *adjective* dangerous: *a hazardous journey through the mountains*

haze /heɪz/ *noun* [no plural] smoke, dust, or mist in the air

haz·y /'heɪzi/ *adjective* **hazier, haziest** if something is hazy, you cannot see or remember it clearly: *I only have a hazy memory of my first day at school.*

he /i; *strong* hiː/ *pronoun*
used when talking about a man or boy: *David said he would see us later.* | *He didn't look very happy, did he?*

head¹ /hed/ *noun*

GRAMMAR
the head of something

1 the top part of your body that has your eyes, mouth, brain etc in it: *She rested her head on my shoulder.* | *"No," replied John, shaking his head.* ⇨ see picture at BODY

2 the leader or most important person

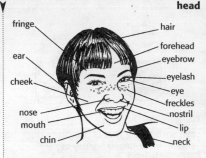

head

fringe
hair
forehead
eyebrow
ear
eyelash
cheek
eye
freckles
nose
nostril
mouth
lip
chin
neck

in a group or organization: *David Hill is **the head of** Sky Sports television.*

3 **the head** in Britain, the teacher who is in charge of a school: *The head wants to see the student who broke the window.*

4 **heads** the side of a coin that has a picture of someone's head on it ⇨ *opposite* TAILS

PHRASES
a head, per head for each person: *The bus to Calais will **cost £15 a head** (=each person will have to pay £15).*

do something in your head to calculate a sum in your mind, rather than writing it down: *I hadn't got a pen, so I added it up **in my head**.*

laugh your head off, scream your head off *informal* to laugh or scream a lot: *When I told him what had happened, he **laughed** his **head off**.*

head² *verb* 1 if you head somewhere, you go towards that place: *I headed back to the house.* | *They headed for the beach.* 2 **be heading for something, be headed for something** if you are heading for a situation, it is likely to happen: *Our team was heading for defeat.*

head·ache /'hedeɪk/ *noun* a pain in your head: *I've got a terrible headache.*

head·ing /'hedɪŋ/ *noun* the title at the top of a piece of writing

head·light /'hedlaɪt/ also **head·lamp** /'hedlæmp/ *BrE noun* one of the large lights at the front of a vehicle ⇨ see picture at CAR

head·line /'hedlaɪn/ *noun* 1 the title of a newspaper report 2 **the headlines** a sentence about each main piece of news on a television or radio news programme: *Here are today's headlines.*

H

head·long /ˈhedlɒŋ $ ˈhedlɒŋ/ *adverb* if you fall or jump headlong, you do it with your head going first: *He fell headlong down the stairs.*

head·mas·ter /ˌhedˈmɑːstə $ ˈhedˌmæstɚ/ *noun BrE* a male teacher who is in charge of a school; PRINCIPAL *AmE*

head·mis·tress /ˌhedˈmɪstrəs $ ˈhedˌmɪstrəs/ *noun, plural* **headmistresses** *BrE* a female teacher who is in charge of a school; PRINCIPAL *AmE*

head-on /ˌ. ˈ./ *adverb* if two vehicles meet head-on, the front part of one vehicle hits the front part of the other – **head-on** *adjective*: *a head-on crash*

head·phones /ˈhedfəʊnz $ ˈhedfoʊnz/ *plural noun* a piece of equipment that you wear over your ears to listen to a radio, recorded music etc: *a pair of headphones*

head·quar·ters /ˈhedˌkwɔːtəz $ ˈhedˌkwɔrtɚz/ also **HQ** *plural noun* the place where the people controlling an organization or military action work

head start /ˌ. ˈ./ *noun* an advantage that helps you to succeed: *With Tony on our team, we had a head start.*

head teach·er /ˌ. ˈ../ *noun BrE* a headmaster or headmistress

head·way /ˈhedweɪ/ *noun* **make headway** to make progress

heal /hiːl/ *verb* if a wound or broken bone heals, it becomes healthy again: *The cut healed quickly.*

health /helθ/ *noun [no plural]*

your health is how well or ill you are: *Exercise is **good for** your **health**. | Do you have any **health problems**?*

> **PHRASE**
>
> **in good health, in poor health** if you are in good health, you are strong and not likely to become ill: *He had been in poor health for some time.*

health club /ˈ. ./ *noun* a place where you pay to use equipment to do physical exercises

health food /ˈ. ˌ./ *noun* food that contains only natural substances

health·y /ˈhelθi/ *adjective* **healthier, healthiest**

1 strong and not likely to become ill ⇨ *opposite* UNHEALTHY (1): *I feel healthier since I stopped smoking.* |

healthy
unhealthy
ill

The puppies looked healthy and strong.

2 healthy food, activities etc are good for you and will help you stay well ⇨ *opposite* UNHEALTHY (2): *a healthy diet | It's healthier to live near the sea.*

heap¹ /hiːp/ *noun* a large untidy pile of things: *a heap of stones*

heap² *verb* to put a lot of things on top of each other in an untidy way

hear ⇨ see box on page 278

hear·ing /ˈhɪərɪŋ $ ˈhɪrɪŋ/ *noun* **1** *[no plural]* the sense that you use to hear sounds: *My Grandpa's hearing is getting worse.* **2** an official meeting to find out the facts about something

hearing aid /ˈ.. ˌ./ *noun* a small object that someone can put in their ear so that they can hear better

hearse /hɜːs $ hɚs/ *noun* a large car for carrying a dead body in a COFFIN at a funeral

heart /hɑːt $ hɑrt/ *noun*

> **GRAMMAR**
> **the heart of something**

1 the part of your body inside your chest that pushes blood around your body: *I could feel her heart beating. | Tom had an operation on his heart last year.*

2 your strongest and most true feelings, especially feelings of love and caring: *His appeal to help the children of Africa has touched the hearts of ordinary people. | I knew **in** my **heart** that we could not win. | Penny believed **with all** her **heart** that Sam was a good man.*

H

➤ **VERB FORMS**

PRESENT TENSE

Singular	Plural
I **have** (I've)	we **have** (we've)
you **have** (you've)	you **have** (you've)
he, she, it **has**	they **have**
(he's, she's, it's)	(they've)

PAST TENSE

Singular	Plural
I **had** (I'd)	we **had** (we'd)
you **had** (you'd)	you **had** (you'd)
he, she, it **had**	they **had**
(he'd, she'd, it'd)	(they'd)

present participle ➤ **having**
past participle ➤ **had**
negative short forms ➤ **haven't, hasn't, hadn't**

➤ **HAVE**

1 in the past

used with the past participle of a verb to say that something happened in the past: *Have you **met** her friend Laura? | He's **seen** 'Star Wars' six times. | I've **been** so worried! | I **haven't written** to her since Christmas. | Eric **hadn't told** the teacher about it.*

2 appearance, qualities, features
also **have got**

used to say what someone or something looks like or what their qualities or features are: *Mark **has** brown hair and green eyes. | London **has** a lot of good restaurants. | She **had** a lot of patience. | Your sweater's **got** a hole in the sleeve.*

✗ Don't say ➤ *I am having, she is having etc*
✓ Say ➤ *I **have**, she **has** etc*

5 to have family or friends
also **have got**

*The Harrisons **have** three children. | Emma **has** a lot of friends. | I've **got** a sister and two brothers. | She's **got** some family in Aberdeen.*

have

4 to do or experience something

*I hope you **have** a good journey. | She **has** an English class on Tuesday nights. | Dad **has** a cup of coffee and toast for breakfast. | We **had** a lot of fun at the park. | Jackie and Doug **had** an argument. | He **hasn't** got the flu – it's just a cold. | Did you **have** a good day?*

3 to own or use something
also **have got**

*It was cold, and I **didn't have** my jacket. | **Do** you **have** a computer? | Philip's **got** a new bike. | **Have** you **got** any tomatoes for the salad? | She said she would help if she **has** time.*

✗ Don't say ➤ *I am having, she is having etc*
✓ Say ➤ *I **have**, she **has** etc*

- ## Have and have got
  In spoken British English, **have got** is more common than **have** and is used to mean the same things. **Have got** and **had got** are usually used in their short forms: *I've got, she's got, we'd got, he'd got* etc.

- ## Questions and negative sentences
  Use **do** with **have**: She *doesn't have* a lot of time. | He *doesn't have* a car. | *Did* she *have* time to finish it? | *Do* you *have* a car?

  You can also use **have got** to form questions and **haven't got** to form negative sentences, especially in British English: She *hasn't got* a lot of time. | He *hasn't got* a car. | *Has* she *got* time to finish it? | *Have* you *got* a car?

Most common words used with **have**:

have fun	have a meeting	have dinner	have an argument
have a problem	have a holiday	have a drink	have a discussion
have trouble	have a bath	have a rest	have a party
have lunch	have a cold	have a dream	have a headache

Have lunch

Have a meeting

Have a party

PHRASES

have (got) to do something
if you have to do something, you must do it: *I have to go to work now.* | *You've got to talk to him.* | *You don't have to answer all the questions.* | *Stan's got to be at the airport by seven.*

had better do something spoken
say this when telling someone what is the best thing to do: *You'd better get dressed – it's almost time to go.* | *I'd better check that the doors are locked.*

may I have...?, could I have...?, I'll have... etc spoken
say this to ask someone politely for something: *Dad, may I have a chocolate bar?* | *I'll have a cheese sandwich, please.*

USAGE
When you are asking someone for something, don't say "I want", because it is not polite. Instead say, **I would like** or **May I have?/Could I have?** People often say **Can I have?**, but many teachers think this is incorrect.

hear /hɪə $ hɪr/ *verb* **heard** /hɜːd $ hɚd/

➤ HEAR or LISTEN?

HEAR you **hear** a sound that has been made: *I **heard** the phone ringing.*

LISTEN you **listen** when you hear and pay attention to what someone says or to sounds or music: *We **were listening to** the radio.*

➤ HEAR

❶ to hear sounds
*I **heard** the girls laughing.* | *Kirsty shouted, but he didn't **hear**.* | *When I woke, I **heard** footsteps in the kitchen.* | *I could **hear** my parents arguing.* | *Do you **hear** that noise?*

> **GRAMMAR**
> **hear someone/something doing something**
> **hear someone/something do something**

> ✗ Don't say ➤ *I am hearing.*
> ✓ Say ➤ *I **hear** or I can **hear**.* But don't say *I can **hear*** when it is something you hear often.

> ✗ Don't say ➤ *Are you hearing?*
> ✓ Say ➤ *Do you **hear**?, Can you **hear**?*

hear

❷ to get information about something
*Did you **hear what** Warren said this morning?* | *I'd **heard** a lot **about** the Greek Islands, but I was still surprised by how beautiful they are.* | *That's the most stupid idea I've ever **heard**.* | *I **heard that** Frank was going to Columbia too.*

> **GRAMMAR**
> **hear (that)**
> **hear about**
> **hear what/where etc**

PHRASAL VERBS

hear from
to get news from someone, in a letter or by telephone: *I **heard from** Barbara at Christmas.* | *She went for a job interview, but she hasn't **heard from** them yet.*

hear of
to know about someone or something: *"Do you know Jerry Tonelli?" "No, never **heard of** him."* | *I've **heard of** the book, but I've never read it.*

H

3 the central or most important part of something: *We sat down to rest in* **the heart of** *the forest.* | *At* **the heart of** *the crisis in Africa is the shortage of clean water and food.*

4 a shape like a heart that is used to mean love: *I drew little hearts all over my school timetable.* ➪ see picture at SYMMETRICAL

5 hearts a group of playing cards with the shape of a red heart printed on them: *the ace of hearts*

PHRASES

learn something by heart, know something by heart if you learn a piece of writing or music by heart, you can remember all of it correctly without having to look at it: *I* **learned** *the song* **by heart** *and sang it for the rest of the class.* | *I think I* **know** *my speech* **by heart** *now.*

heart at·tack /'. .,./ *noun* when a person's heart suddenly stops beating normally, sometimes causing death: *He had a heart attack.*

heart·beat /'hɑːtbiːt $ 'hɑrtbit/ *noun* the movement of your heart: *The baby's heartbeat is irregular.*

heart·break·ing /'hɑːt,breɪkɪŋ $ 'hɑrt,breɪkɪŋ/ *adjective* something that is heartbreaking makes you feel very sad: *The result was heartbreaking news for the fans.*

heart·brok·en /'hɑːt,brəʊkən $ 'hɑrt,broʊkən/ *adjective* very sad because of something that has happened: *When he had to sell his car, he was heartbroken.*

heart·felt /'hɑːtfelt $ 'hɑrtfelt/ *adjective* *written* honest and sincere: *a heartfelt apology*

hearth /hɑːθ $ hɑrθ/ *noun* the area of floor in front of the fire in a house

heart·i·ly /'hɑːtəli $ 'hɑrtl-i/ *adverb written* **1** in a very cheerful or friendly way: *He laughed heartily.* **2** very much or completely: *I heartily agree.*

heart·less /'hɑːtləs $ 'hɑrtləs/ *adjective* cruel: *How can you be so heartless?*

heart·warm·ing /'hɑːt,wɔːmɪŋ $ 'hɑrt,wɔrmɪŋ/ *adjective* a heartwarming story makes you feel happy because something nice happens in it

heart·y /'hɑːti $ 'hɑrti/ *adjective* **heart·ier, heartiest 1** very cheerful or friendly: *hearty laughter* **2** a hearty meal is very large

heat¹ /hiːt/ *noun*

1 [no plural] when something is warm or hot: *The heat of the fire will soon make the room warmer.* | *I could feel the heat from the oven.*

2 the heat very hot weather: *We went into the house to escape from* **the heat** *outside.*

3 the American word for HEATING

4 one of the first races or games in a big competition. The winners of each heat compete against each other in the next race or game until someone wins the final game

PHRASE

in the heat of the moment if you do something in the heat of the moment, you do it without thinking, because you are very excited or angry: *She said some very cruel things* **in the heat of the moment.**

heat² *verb* **1** to make something warmer: *They use gas to heat the house.* **2** heat something up if you heat up food, you make it warmer: *I'll heat up some soup for you.*

heat·ed /'hiːtɪd/ *adjective* a heated argument, discussion etc is one in which people become very angry

heat·er /'hiːtə $ 'hitɚ/ *noun* a piece of equipment in a building, used to heat air or water

heath·er /'heðə $ 'heðɚ/ *noun* a small bush with purple or white flowers that grows on hills

heat·ing /'hiːtɪŋ/ *noun* [no plural] BrE the system in a building that keeps it warm; HEAT AmE: *I'll turn the heating up.*

heat·wave /'hiːt,weɪv/ *noun* a period of unusually hot weather

heave /hiːv/ *verb* to pull, throw, or lift something heavy with a lot of effort: *They heaved the body over the side of the boat.*

heav·en /'hevən/ *noun* [no plural] **1** also **Heaven** the place where many people believe God lives and good people go after they die **2** *informal* a very pleasant situation or experience: *After standing up all day, it was heaven to sit down.* **3** for heaven's sake *spoken* used when you are annoyed: *For heaven's sake, why didn't you telephone me?*

H

heav·ily /'hevəli/ adverb very much or a lot: It was still raining heavily.

heavy

light

heavy

heav·y /'hevi/ adjective **heavier, heaviest**

1 something that is heavy weighs a lot ⇨ opposite LIGHT² (4): The women struggled along carrying their heavy bags. | Take this suitcase – it's not very heavy. | **How heavy** is the parcel?

2 if traffic is heavy, there are a lot of cars and other vehicles on the road ⇨ opposite LIGHT² (6)

3 very thick or warm ⇨ opposite LIGHT² (5): She pulled the heavy blanket tightly over us both.

PHRASES

a heavy drinker, a heavy smoker someone who drinks a lot of alcohol or smokes a lot of cigarettes
heavy rain, heavy snow a lot of rain or snow that falls at once ⇨ opposite LIGHT² (7): There was **heavy rain** in the night, and in the morning some roads were flooded.

heavy-hand·ed /ˌ.. '../ adjective too severe or using too much force: He dealt with the problem in a heavy-handed way.

heav·y·weight /'heviweɪt/ adjective a heavyweight BOXER is in the heaviest weight group
– heavyweight noun

heck /hek/ noun spoken informal used when you are annoyed, surprised etc: Where the heck have you been? | Moving all that furniture will be a heck of a job.

hec·tare /'hektɑː $ 'hekter/ noun a unit for measuring the area of a piece of land, equal to 10,000 square metres

hec·tic /'hektɪk/ adjective very busy or full of activity: I've had a hectic week – I'm exhausted. | Sorry I'm late, but the traffic is really hectic.

he'd /id; strong hiːd/ the short form of 'he would' or 'he had': I knew he'd understand. | He'd made a terrible mess.

hedge /hedʒ/ noun a row of bushes that separates one field or garden from another ⇨ see picture on page 348

hedge·hog /'hedʒhɒg $ 'hedʒhɑg/ noun a small animal whose body is covered in sharp points

heel /hiːl/ noun 1 the back part of your foot 2 the part of a shoe that is under your heel: I can't walk in shoes with high heels.

hef·ty /'hefti/ adjective informal **heftier, heftiest** large, heavy, or strong: He had to pay a hefty fine for stealing.

height /haɪt/ noun

GRAMMAR
the height of something

1 how tall or high someone or something is: We measured **the height of** the building. | My sister is about the same height as me.

2 the height of something is the time when it is busiest or most successful: I would never go to Paris at **the height of the tourist season.** | Jeans are no longer **the height of fashion** (=the most fashionable).

height·en /'haɪtn/ verb written to make a feeling stronger: The rumours heightened people's worries.

heir /eə $er/ noun your heir is the person who will receive your money and property when you die

heir·ess /'eərəs $ 'erəs/ noun, plural heiresses a woman who will receive a lot of money or property when someone dies

heir·loom /'eəluːm $ 'erlum/ noun a valuable object that the same family has owned for many years

held /held/ the past tense and past participle of HOLD

hel·i·cop·ter /'helɪkɒptə $ 'helɪˌkɑptɚ/ noun an aircraft with long metal parts on top which go round very fast to make it fly ⇨ see picture on page 349

he·li·um /'hiːliəm/ noun [no plural] a gas that is lighter than air

he'll /il; strong hiːl/ the short form of 'he will': He'll be so surprised!

hell /hel/ noun 1 also **Hell** the place

where some people believe bad people are punished after they die ₂ *informal* a very difficult or unpleasant situation or experience: *It was hell waiting for the results of the test.* ₃ **what the hell, how the hell** *spoken informal* used to emphasize something in a rude way, usually when you are annoyed or surprised: *What the hell do you want?* ₄ **a hell of a, one hell of a** *spoken informal* used to say in a rude way that something is very big, very good etc: *You were taking a hell of a risk.* | *He's a hell of a guy, isn't he?* ₅ **like hell** *informal* very hard or fast: *We just ran like hell.*

hel·lo also **hallo** /həˈləʊ $ həˈloʊ/ used when you meet or greet someone: *Hello, can I help you?* | *Hello, my name is Jessica.*

hel·met /ˈhelmət/ *noun* a hard hat that protects your head: *You have to wear a helmet when you ride a motorbike.*

help¹ /help/ *verb*

GRAMMAR
help someone (to) do something
help someone with something
1 if you help someone, you do some of their work for them: *Shall I help you clean the car?* | *Sarah helped me to carry the boxes upstairs.* | *Will you help me with the washing up?*
2 to make it easier for someone to do something: *The extra money will help me pay for a new car.*
3 if something helps, it makes a situation better: *Would it help if you had someone to talk to?*
4 **cannot help doing something, could not help doing something** you cannot stop doing something, you cannot stop yourself from doing it: *I couldn't help laughing when I saw him in his costume.*
5 **Help!** *spoken* used to call someone when you are in danger

PHRASE
help yourself to take something that you want, without asking: *Please help yourself to a drink.*

help² *noun* ₁ [no plural] when you help someone: *Thanks for all your help.*
2 *spoken* **be a help, be a lot of help** to be

useful: *"Shall I put these plates away?" "That would be a help."*

help·ful /ˈhelpfəl/ *adjective* ₁ useful: *The teacher made some helpful comments.* ₂ willing to help: *Thank you, you've been very helpful.*

help·ing /ˈhelpɪŋ/ *noun* an amount of food for one person: *a large helping of apple pie*

helping verb /ˈ.. ˌ./ an American phrase for AUXILIARY VERB

help·less /ˈhelpləs/ *adjective* unable to look after yourself: *He was as helpless as a baby.*
—**helplessly** *adverb*: *She lay helplessly on the ground.*

hem /hem/ *noun* the edge of a piece of clothing that is turned under and stitched down

hem·i·sphere /ˈheməsfɪə $ ˈheməsfɪr/ *noun* one of the two halves of the Earth: *the northern hemisphere*

hen /hen/ *noun* a female CHICKEN (1)

hence /hens/ *adverb* formal for this reason: *The school is short of money, hence the need to reduce spending.*

hen·na /ˈhenə/ *noun* a reddish-brown substance used to change the colour of hair or to DYE the skin

her /ə $ ər; strong hɜː $ hər/ *pronoun* ₁ used when talking about a woman or girl: *My mum loves flowers, so I bought these for her.* | *I really like her.* ₂ belonging to a woman or girl: *She put her purse in her pocket.* | *Her name's Caroline.*

herb /hɜːb $ ɜːrb/ *noun* a plant used to improve the taste of food or to make medicine

herb·al /ˈhɜːbəl $ ˈɜːrbəl/ *adjective* made from herbs: *herbal medicine*

herd¹ /hɜːd $ hɜːrd/ *noun* a group of animals such as cows, ELEPHANTS, or DEER: *a herd of cattle*

herd² *verb* to make people or animals move somewhere in a large group: *We were herded into a small room.*

here /hɪə $ hɪr/ *adverb* the place where you are now: *I've lived here all my life.* | *Ben! Come here!* | *It's nice here* (=this is a nice place).

PHRASES

here's, here you are *spoken* something you say when you give or show something to someone: *Here's the magazine I was telling you about.* | *Here you are – you can borrow it over the weekend.*

here it is, here he is etc *spoken* something you say when you find something or see someone: *I've got a pen in my bag somewhere – here it is.* | *"Is John coming too?" "Yes, here he is."*

he·red·i·ta·ry /həˈredətəri $ həˈredəˌteri/ *adjective* a hereditary quality or disease is passed to a child by its parents

her·e·sy /ˈherəsi/ *noun formal*, *plural* **heresies** a belief that a religious or political group thinks is wrong

her·i·tage /ˈherətɪdʒ/ *noun* things from a society's past that people think are valuable: *We must protect our musical heritage.*

he·ro /ˈhɪərəʊ $ ˈhɪroʊ/ *noun*, *plural* **heroes** **1** someone who people admire because they have done something very brave or good: *When the soldiers returned, they were treated as heroes.* **2** the man who is the main character in a book, film, or play

he·ro·ic /hɪˈrəʊɪk $ hɪˈroʊɪk/ *adjective* very brave or determined to succeed: *their heroic attempts to rescue the trapped child*

her·o·in /ˈherəʊɪn $ ˈheroʊɪn/ *noun* [no plural] a very strong illegal drug

her·o·ine /ˈherəʊɪn $ ˈheroʊɪn/ *noun* **1** the woman who is the main character in a book, film, or play **2** a woman who people admire because she has done something very brave or good

her·o·is·m /ˈherəʊɪzəm $ ˈheroʊˌɪzəm/ *noun* [no plural] great courage

hers /hɜːz $ hɜːz/ *pronoun*
a thing belonging to a woman or girl: *My hair is different from hers.* | *Sarah was here earlier, so I think this coat must be hers.*

her·self /hɜːˈself $ hɜˈself/ *pronoun*
1 used when the same woman or girl does an action and receives the action: *She cut herself by accident.* |

y *Sophie bought some flowers for herself.*
2 emphasizing that you are talking about one particular woman or girl: *Zoe arranged the trip for everyone, but she herself had to stay at home.*

PHRASE
by herself alone, or with no one else helping: *She lives by herself.* | *She decorated the whole house by herself.*

he's /iz; *strong* hiːz/ the short form of 'he is' or 'he has': *He's my brother.* | *He's lost his keys.*

hes·i·tant /ˈhezətənt/ *adjective formal* if you are hesitant, you do not do something immediately, because you are nervous or not sure
–**hesitantly** *adverb*: *"I'm not sure," she said hesitantly.*

hes·i·tate /ˈhezəteɪt/ *verb* **1** to stop for a moment before doing or saying something: *She hesitated a moment and then said "Yes".* **2 don't hesitate to do something** *written* used to tell someone that you are very willing for them to do something: *Please do not hesitate to contact me if you need any help.*

hes·i·ta·tion /ˌhezəˈteɪʃən/ *noun* when you hesitate: *He answered without hesitation.*

het·e·ro·sex·u·al /ˌhetərəˈsekʃuəl/ *adjective formal* sexually attracted to people of the opposite sex
–**heterosexual** *noun*

hex·a·gon /ˈheksəgən $ ˈheksəˌgɑn/ *noun* a flat shape with six sides

hey /heɪ/ *spoken informal* used to get someone's attention or when you are surprised or interested: *Hey, that's amazing!*

hi /haɪ/ *spoken informal* HELLO

hi·ber·nate /ˈhaɪbəneɪt $ ˈhaɪbəˌneɪt/ *verb* if an animal hibernates, it sleeps during all of the winter and wakes up in spring

hic·cup[1] or **hiccough** /ˈhɪkʌp/ *noun* **1 hiccups** when your throat makes many short sounds that you cannot control: *I ate too fast and got hiccups.* **2** a small problem: *There were a few small hiccups before the concert began.*

hiccup[2] *verb* **hiccupped, hiccupping** if you hiccup, your throat makes many short sounds that you cannot control

hid the past tense of HIDE

hid·den¹ /'hɪdn/ *adjective* if something is hidden, you cannot see or find it easily: *They were filmed with hidden cameras.*

hidden² the past participle of HIDE

hide /haɪd/
verb hid /hɪd/
hidden /'hɪdn/
hiding

GRAMMAR
hide something in/behind/under etc a place
hide in/behind/under etc a place

1 if you hide something, you put it in a place where no one can find it: *Mary **hid** the money **in** a cupboard.* | *He **hid** the papers **under** his bed.*
2 if you hide, you go to a place where no one can find you: *I **hid behind** the fence.*
3 if you hide your feelings, you do not show them: *Steven tried to hide his disappointment.*

hid·e·ous /'hɪdiəs/ *adjective* very ugly or unpleasant: *a hideous yellow and purple dress*

hid·ing /'haɪdɪŋ/ *noun* be in hiding to be hiding somewhere because you are in danger or you have done something wrong

hi-fi /'haɪ faɪ/ *noun* a piece of electronic equipment that you use to play recorded music ⇨ *see picture on page 342*

high¹ /haɪ/ *adjective* higher, highest

1 something that is high is tall: *a high mountain* | *The walls around the castle are over three metres high.*
2 a long way above the ground: *The shelf is quite high and difficult to reach.* | *We could still see the balloon **high up** in the sky.*
3 used to talk about the height of something: *How **high** is Mount Everest?* | *The fence was about four feet high.*
4 above the usual level, amount, or standard* ⇨ *opposite* LOW (2): *Student fees are quite high at some universities.* | *The temperature is highest at lunch time.*
5 a high sound is near the top of the set of sounds that humans can hear

⇨ *opposite* LOW (3): *I can't sing the high notes.*

PHRASES
be high on something to feel happy or excited after taking an illegal drug: *Police said the driver must **have been high on** drugs.*
high in fat, high in salt etc a food that is high in fat, salt etc contains a lot of fat, salt etc: *Try to avoid foods that are **high in fat**.*

high² *adverb*
a long way above the ground: *The balloon rose high in the sky.*

high-class /ˌ. '.../ *adjective* of good quality: *a high-class hotel*

higher ed·u·ca·tion /ˌ.. ..'.../ *noun* [no plural] education at a college or university rather than a school

high jump /'. ./ *noun* the high jump a sport in which you try to jump over a bar that is raised higher after each attempt

high·lands /'haɪləndz/ *plural noun* an area with a lot of mountains: *the Scottish highlands*

high·light¹ /'haɪlaɪt/ *verb* if you highlight something, you say it is very important: *In his speech, the President highlighted the issue of crime.*

highlight² *noun* the best part of something: *One of the highlights of the holiday was the boat trip.*

high·ly /'haɪli/ *adverb* 1 very: *a highly intelligent girl* 2 if you think highly of someone, you respect and admire them a lot: *His employees think very highly of him.* | *a highly respected musician*

high-pitched /ˌ. '.../ *adjective* a high-pitched sound is high and sharp, and unpleasant to hear: *a high-pitched scream*

high-pow·ered /ˌ. '.../ *adjective* 1 a high-powered machine is very powerful 2 a high-powered job is important with a lot of responsibility

high-rise /'. ./ *adjective* a high-rise building is a very tall modern building: *high-rise apartment blocks*
–**high-rise** *noun*: *We live on the 17th floor of a high-rise.*

high school /'. ./ *noun* 1 a school in the US or Canada for students between

H

14 and 18 years old **2** used in the names of some schools in Britain for students between 11 and 18 years old

high street /ˈ. ./ *noun BrE* the main street in a town, where shops and businesses are: *a busy high street*

high-tech or **hi-tech** /ˌhaɪ ˈtek/ *adjective* high-tech equipment is very modern with the most advanced electronic parts

high·way /ˈhaɪweɪ/ *noun AmE* a wide main road that joins one city to another

hi·jack /ˈhaɪdʒæk/ *verb* to take control of a plane or vehicle by force
– **hijacker** *noun*: *The hijackers told the pilot to fly to Rome.*

hike /haɪk/ *verb* to walk a long way in the countryside for pleasure: *We hiked to the nearest pub.*
– **hike** *noun*

hi·lar·i·ous /hɪˈleəriəs $ hɪˈleriəs/ *adjective* very funny: *a hilarious film*

hill /hɪl/ *noun* an area of high land, like a small mountain ⇨ see picture on page 348

hill·side /ˈhɪlsaɪd/ *noun* the sloping side of a hill

hill·y /ˈhɪli/ *adjective* **hillier, hilliest** a hilly area has a lot of hills

him /ɪm; *strong* hɪm/ *pronoun*
used when talking about a man or boy: *Simon's parents gave him a skateboard for his birthday.* | *He seems friendly, but I don't trust him.* | *What did you say to him?*

him·self /ɪmˈself; *strong* hɪmˈself/ *pronoun*
1 used when the same man or boy does an action and receives an action: *Paul cut himself with the bread knife.* | *He poured himself a glass of orange.*
2 emphasizing that you are talking about one particular man or boy: *Roger loves dogs, but he doesn't own one himself.* | *I spoke to the owner of the shop himself.*

PHRASE
by himself alone, or with no one helping: *He spent the afternoon by himself.* | *He moved all the furniture by himself.*

hin·der /ˈhɪndə $ ˈhɪndɚ/ *verb formal* to make it difficult to do something: *The*

lack of information is hindering the police investigation.*

hind·sight /ˈhaɪndsaɪt/ *noun* [no plural] the ability to understand or judge an event after it has happened: *With hindsight, I should never have let her use my car.*

Hin·du /ˈhɪnduː/ *noun* someone whose religion is Hinduism

Hin·du·is·m /ˈhɪndu-ɪzəm/ *noun* [no plural] the main religion in India, which has many gods and teaches that people live another life on earth after they die

hinge¹ /hɪndʒ/ *noun* a piece of metal that is used to fix a door to a frame or a lid to a box, so that it can open and close

hinge² *verb* **hinge on, hinge upon** to depend on something: *My whole future hinges on my results this term.*

hint¹ /hɪnt/ *noun* **1** something you say in an indirect way, but not plainly: *She had given a few hints that she was leaving.* **2** a small amount of something: *There was a hint of panic in his voice.* **3** a piece of advice on how to do something ⇨ same meaning TIP¹: *helpful hints on passing exams*

hint² *verb* to say something in an indirect way: *Ben had been hinting that he'd like a telescope for his birthday.*

hip¹ /hɪp/ *noun* your hips are the sides of your body between your legs and your waist: *She was standing with her hands on her hips, looking very angry.*

hip² *adjective informal* modern and fashionable

hip·pie or **hippy** /ˈhɪpi/ *noun, plural* **hippies** someone who deliberately does not live or dress like ordinary people and who believes in love and peace

hire¹ /haɪə $ haɪɚ/ *verb* **1** BrE to pay money to borrow something for a short time; RENT AmE: *They hired a car for three days.* **2** to pay someone to work for you: *They hired the best lawyer they could afford.*

hire² *noun* [no plural] BrE an arrangement in which you pay to borrow something for a short time: *Is this car for hire?*

his /ɪz; *strong* hɪz/ *pronoun*
belonging to a man or boy: *He wiped his hands on his shirt.* | *His sister was waiting for him.* | *My hi-fi*

▼ system cost more than his (=than the hi-fi system belonging to him).

Hi·span·ic /hɪˈspænɪk/ adjective connected with people in the US whose families came originally from Latin America

hiss /hɪs/ verb   **1** to make a noise that sounds like 'ssss': *The snake hissed at them.* ⇨ see picture on page 350   **2** written to say something quietly, but in an angry way: *"I hate you!" she hissed.*

his·to·ri·an /hɪˈstɔːriən/ noun someone who studies or writes about history

his·tor·ic /hɪˈstɒrɪk $hɪˈstɔːrɪk/ adjective important in history: *the historic moment when man landed on the moon*

his·tor·i·cal /hɪˈstɒrɪkəl $hɪˈstɔːrɪkəl/ adjective in or related to history: *The film is based on a historical event.* | *historical records from that era*
–**historically** /-kli/ adverb: *Is the book historically accurate?*

his·to·ry /ˈhɪstəri/ noun [no plural]

> **GRAMMAR**
> **the history of something**
> **a history of something**

1 all the things that happened in the past: *She's studying history at university.*
2 the history of something is how it has developed and changed since it started: *the history of pop music*
3 if someone has a history of an illness, they have had that illness in the past: *Do not take this drug if you have a history of heart problems.*

hit¹ /hɪt/ verb, past tense and past participle **hit, hitting**
1 to touch someone or something with a lot of force: *He hit me with his tennis racket!* | *Simon swung his bat and hit the ball as hard as he could.* | *The bullet hit the horse between its eyes.*
2 to crash into something: *The car came off the road and hit a tree.* | *She fell and hit her head on the pavement.*
3 written to reach a particular number or level: *The number of people who are unemployed has hit one million.*
4 to affect someone or something very badly: *The increase in fees will hit students from poorer families.*

▼**5** if a thought hits you, you suddenly realize that it is true: *It suddenly hit me that I might fail the exam.*

hit² noun
1 a film, song, play etc that is very successful: *The group's first album was a big hit.*
2 when something that you throw reaches the place that you are aiming at: *Of the five missiles, three were direct hits on their targets* (=three missiles hit the target exactly).

hit-and-run /ˌ. . ˈ./ adjective a hit-and-run accident is one in which a car driver hits someone but does not stop

hitch¹ /hɪtʃ/ informal another word for HITCHHIKE

hitch² noun, plural **hitches** a small problem that causes a delay

hitchhike

hitch·hike /ˈhɪtʃhaɪk/ verb to travel by getting free rides in other people's cars: *He had hitchhiked down from Glasgow.*
–**hitchhiker** noun: *We picked up three hitchhikers on the way to Glastonbury.*

hi-tech another spelling of HIGH-TECH

HIV /ˌeɪtʃ aɪ ˈviː/ noun [no plural] a VIRUS that can cause the disease AIDS

hive /haɪv/ noun   hive
1 also **beehive** a box that BEES are kept in   **2** be a hive of activity if a place is a hive of activity, everyone there is very busy

h'm or **hmm** /m, hm/ a sound that you make when you are thinking what to say or do

hoard¹ /hɔːd $hɔːrd/ noun a number of things hidden somewhere: *a secret hoard of biscuits*

hoard² verb to get and keep a large amount of food, money etc, and not use it: *People have been hoarding food in case snow blocks the roads.*

hoarse /hɔːs $ hɔrs/ *adjective* a hoarse voice sounds rough, as if the person speaking has a sore throat

hoax /həʊks $ hoʊks/ *noun, plural* hoaxes an attempt to make people believe something that is not true: *He got a phone call saying he'd won $10,000, but it was just a hoax.*

hob /hɒb $ hɑb/ *noun BrE* the flat surface on the top of a COOKER where you cook food in pans

hob·by /ˈhɒbi $ ˈhɑbi/ *noun, plural* hobbies an activity that you enjoy doing in your free time: *My hobbies are playing the guitar and reading.*

hock·ey /ˈhɒki $ ˈhɑki/ *noun [no plural]* BrE a game that you play on grass, in which two teams of players use long curved sticks to hit a ball; FIELD HOCKEY AmE ⇨ *see picture on page 351*

hog /hɒg $ hɔg/ *verb informal* hogged, hogging to use too much or all of something yourself, instead of sharing it: *Lisa was there, hogging the whole sofa as usual.*

hoist /hɔɪst/ *verb* to raise something to a higher position, especially using ropes: *We hoisted the sail and then the boat was ready.*

hold¹ ⇨ *see box on next page*

hold² *noun*
if you take or keep hold of something, you hold it: *Sarah **took hold of** his hand and led him down the corridor.* | *Remember to **keep hold of** your bags as we leave the ship.*

PHRASES
get hold of someone/something to find someone or something when you need them: *I'll be at home later if you need to **get hold of** me.* | *Do you know where we can **get hold of** a map of the town centre?*
have a hold over someone to have power or control over someone
put someone on hold to make someone wait on the telephone: *He **put** me **on hold** while he went to look for the papers.*

hold·all /ˈhəʊld-ɔːl $ ˈhoʊld-ɔl/ *noun* BrE a bag used for carrying clothes, tools etc; CARRYALL AmE ⇨ *see picture at* BAG

hold·er /ˈhəʊldə $ ˈhoʊldɚ/ *noun*
1 someone who has a position, place, or thing: *Butch Reynolds was the world 400 metre record holder.* **2** something that holds or contains something else: *a leather cheque book holder*

hold·up also **hold-up** BrE /ˈhəʊldʌp $ ˈhoʊldʌp/ *noun* **1** a delay, especially one caused by traffic: *There are long hold-ups on the M25 due to an accident.* **2** when someone steals money from a bank, shop etc, by threatening them with a gun: *Two people were injured during the holdup.*

hole /həʊl $ hoʊl/ *noun*

GRAMMAR
a hole in something
an empty space or opening in something: *We dug a **hole in** the garden.* | *Cut a small **hole in** the centre of the paper.* | *The dogs escaped **through a hole in** the fence.*

hol·i·day /ˈhɒlədi $ ˈhɑlədeɪ/ *noun*
1 BrE a period of time when you go to another place for enjoyment; VACATION AmE: *Did you have a nice holiday?* | *Sam isn't here this week – he's **on holiday in** Italy.* | *It's only three weeks until I **go on holiday**.* **2** a day when you do not have to go to work or school: *Next Monday is a holiday.* **3** bank holiday BrE a day when everyone in the country has a holiday and does not have to go to work or school

hol·ler /ˈhɒlə $ ˈhɑlɚ/ *verb* AmE informal to shout loudly: *"Hurry up," Mom hollered up the stairs.*

hol·low /ˈhɒləʊ $ ˈhɑloʊ/ *adjective* something that is hollow has an empty space inside: *a long hollow tube*

hol·ly /ˈhɒli $ ˈhɑli/ *noun [no plural]* a tree with green leaves and red BERRIES that people use as a decoration at Christmas: *We decorated the walls with holly and ivy.*

hol·o·gram /ˈhɒləgræm $ ˈhoʊlə,græm/ *noun* a picture made in a special way so that it does not look flat, and looks more like the real object

➤ HOLD

1 to have something in your hands
*Angela **held** a glass of milk.* | *He was too ill to **hold** the book himself, so she read aloud to him.* | *He put his arms around her and **held** her **tight**.*

2 to keep something in a position
*One woman **held up** a sign that said 'Help now!'.* | *Bates **held** his hand **out**, and I shook it.* | ***Hold down** the computer's control key.* | *Freddie **held** the door **open** for her.*

> **GRAMMAR**
> hold up/out/down something
> hold something up/out/down etc

hold

5 to keep information somewhere
*The addresses of all students **are held on** the school computer.*

3 to have a meeting, party, election etc
*The meeting **was held** in Williamsburg.* | *The school **holds** a dance for the students each year.*

4 to have enough space for something
*I don't think my suitcase will **hold** all of this stuff.*

H

PHRASES

hold hands, hold someone's hand
to hold someone's hand, because you love them or because you want to keep them safe: *They walked along, **holding hands** and laughing.*

hold your breath
to stop breathing for a short time: *I **held my breath** and put my head under the water.*

PHRASAL VERBS

hold on *spoken*
say this when you want someone to wait or stop doing something: ***Hold on** a minute – let me just put this in the car.*

hold out
to hold something in your hand and give it to someone: *She **held** the glass **out** to him.* | *McCloskey **held out** the papers, and I took them.*

hold up
1 to make someone or something late: *The accident **held up** traffic for hours.* | *I don't want to **hold** you **up** – can I phone you later?*

2 to try to steal money from a shop, bank etc using a gun: *A group of men wearing masks **held up** the bank.*

ho·ly /'hǝʊli $ 'hoʊli/ *adjective* **holier,**
holiest **1** connected with God or religion: *Jerusalem is a holy city for Muslims, Christians and Jews.* **2** someone
who is holy is very religious and good

home¹ /hǝʊm $ hoʊm/ *noun*

1 the house or building where you
usually live: *I wasn't feeling very
well, so I stayed at home.* | *When
are you moving into your new
home?* | *This was always such a
happy home for us.* | *Sally left home*
(=stopped living with her parents)
as soon as she was 18.
2 a place where old people or children
with no parents are cared for: *She
was brought up in a children's
home.*

PHRASES
feel at home to feel comfortable,
relaxed, and confident: *I felt quite at
home with my friend's family.*
make yourself at home *spoken* used
to tell someone to relax when they
are visiting your home: *Come in and
sit down – make yourselves at
home.*
play at home, be at home if a
sports team plays at home, it plays at
its own sports field: *Manchester
United are playing at home this
Saturday.*

home² *adverb*

if you go home, you go to the place
where you live: *It's getting late – I
think we ought to go home.* | *We got
home at seven o'clock.* | *When will
Dad be home?* | *We'll arrive home
by ten o'clock.*

home³ *adjective* **1** connected with or
belonging to your home or family: *the
importance of a happy home life*
2 playing on your own sports field rather
than an opponent's: *Newcastle lost their
home match against Sunderland.*
3 connected with your own country, not
other countries: *the minister responsible
for home affairs*
home·land /'hǝʊmlænd $ 'hoʊmlænd/
noun the country where you were born:
She returned to her homeland, Somalia.
home·less /'hǝʊmlǝs $ 'hoʊmlǝs/
adjective someone who is homeless has
no place to live: *Every large city has
homeless people sleeping on the streets.*

home·ly /'hǝʊmli $ 'hoʊmli/ *adjective*
1 *BrE* ordinary and comfortable in a way
that makes you feel relaxed: *a small
family hotel with a homely atmosphere*
2 *AmE* a homely person is not very
attractive

home·made /ˌhǝʊm'meɪd $ ˌhoʊm-
'meɪd/ *adjective* made at home rather
than bought from a shop: *Is this cake
homemade?*

ho·me·op·a·thy /ˌhǝʊmi'ɒpǝθi
$ ˌhoʊmi'ɑpǝθi/ *noun* [*no plural*] a method
of treating illness that involves using very
small amounts of natural substances

home-page /'. ./ *noun* a place on the
INTERNET where you can find information
about a person, company etc: *Visit our
home-page for more information and
links to other sites.*

home·sick /'hǝʊmˌsɪk $ 'hoʊmˌsɪk/
adjective feeling sad because you are a
long way from your home: *Children
often feel homesick when they arrive at
summer camp.*

home·ward /'hǝʊmwǝd $ 'hoʊmwǝrd/
adjective, adverb going towards home:
*The homeward journey took three
hours.*

home·work /'hǝʊmwɜːk $ 'hoʊm-
wǝrk/ *noun* school work that a student
is given to do at home: *Have you finished your homework?*

hom·i·cide /'hɒmɪsaɪd $ 'hɑmǝˌsaɪd/
noun AmE the crime of murder

ho·mo·sex·u·al /ˌhǝʊmǝ'sekʃuǝl
$ ˌhoʊmǝ'sekʃuǝl/ *noun formal* someone
who has sexual relationships with
people of the same sex ⇨ *same meaning*
GAY
– homosexual *adjective*

hon·est /'ɒnɪst $ 'ɑnɪst/ *adjective*

GRAMMAR
honest with someone
honest about something
someone who is honest tells the
truth and does not cheat, lie, or steal
⇨ *opposite* DISHONEST: *My father was
a very honest man.* | *He wouldn't
give me an honest answer to my
question.* | *Please be honest with
me.* | *She was very honest about
her weaknesses.*

hon·est·ly /'ɒnɪstli $ 'ɑnɪstli/ *adverb*
1 in an honest way: *I've earned my
money honestly, through hard work.*

H

2 _spoken_ used to emphasize that you are telling the truth: _I've honestly never met him before._ **3** _spoken_ something you say when you are annoyed: _Honestly! Why can't he get here on time?_

hon·es·ty /'ɒnɪsti $ 'ɑnɪsti/ _noun_ [no plural] the quality of being honest: _I was impressed by his honesty._

hon·ey /'hʌni/ _noun_ [no plural] a sweet substance made by BEES, which people eat: _toast and honey_

hon·ey·moon /'hʌnimuːn/ _noun_ a holiday that people have after their wedding: _We're going to Greece for our honeymoon._

honk /hɒŋk $ hɑŋk/ another word for HOOT (1)

honor the American spelling of honour

honorable the American spelling of honourable

hon·our _BrE,_ **honor** _AmE_ /'ɒnə $ 'ɑnɚ/ _noun_ **1** [no plural] something that makes you feel proud and happy: _To represent your country in any sport is a great honour._ **2** in honour of someone, in someone's honour if you do something in someone's honour, you do it to show special respect for them: _a formal dinner in honour of the Queen_ **3** [no plural] strong beliefs and high standards of behaviour: _We are determined to protect our country's honour._

honour _BrE,_ **honor** _AmE, verb_ **1** be honoured, feel honoured _formal_ to feel very proud and happy, especially because you have been asked to do something important: _I am deeply honoured to be invited here tonight._ **2** to give someone a special title, prize etc, or to treat them with great respect: _He was honoured with the Nobel Peace Prize._

hon·our·a·ble _BrE,_ **honorable** _AmE_ /'ɒnərəbəl $ 'ɑnərəbəl/ _adjective formal_ an honourable person behaves in a way that people think is right: _It was not the honorable way to win an election._

hood /hʊd/ _noun_ **1** a part of a coat or other piece of clothing that you can pull up to cover your head: _a warm jacket with a hood_ **2** the American word for a car BONNET

hoof /huːf $ hʊf/ _noun, plural_ **hoofs** or **hooves** /huːvz $ hʊvz/ the foot of an animal such as a horse

hook /hʊk/ _noun_ a curved piece of metal or plastic that you use for hanging things on, or for catching fish: _Hang your coat on the hook over there._

hooked /hʊkt/ _adjective informal_ if you are hooked on something, you like it a lot and you do not want to stop doing it or using it: _Thousands of children are hooked on computer games._

hoo·li·gan /'huːlɪgən/ _noun_ a noisy person who causes trouble by fighting or damaging things in public places: _a gang of football hooligans_

hoop /huːp/ _noun_ a large ring made of metal, plastic, or wood: _Try and throw the hoops over the post._

hooray HURRAY

hoot /huːt/ _verb_ **1** _BrE_ if a car hoots its HORN, the driver presses it and it makes a loud noise ⊸ _same meaning_ HONK: _All the cars behind me were hooting their horns._ **2** if an OWL hoots, it makes a loud noise

–hoot _noun_

Hoo·ver /'huːvə $ 'huvɚ/ _BrE trademark_ a VACUUM CLEANER

hoo·ver /'huːvə $ 'huvɚ/ _verb BrE_ to clean the floor, using a VACUUM CLEANER

hooves a plural of HOOF

hop /hɒp $ hɑp/ _verb_ **hopped, hopping** **1** to jump on one foot: _The children came hopping towards us, smiling._ ⊸ _see picture on page 340_ **2** if birds and animals hop, they move by jumping with both feet together: _Two frogs hopped into the water with a splash._

–hop _noun_

hope¹ /həʊp $ hoʊp/ _verb_

GRAMMAR
hope (that)
hope to do something

to want something to happen: _I **hope that** Tom will come to the party._ | _I hope you feel better soon._ | _I **hope to** go to college next year._

PHRASES
I hope so _spoken:_ _"Is Tom coming to the party?" "I hope so."_ (=I hope he is coming to the party)
I hope not _spoken:_ _"Are we going to be late?" "I hope not."_ (=I hope we are not going to be late)

hope² _noun_

GRAMMAR
hope that
hope of something

1 when you believe that something

H

▼ good could happen: *I am full of*
hope that *he will get better.* | *I went
to Laura's* **in the hope that** *Julie
would be there* (=because I wanted to
see Julie and hoped she might be
there). | *He* **has hopes of** (=wants to)
studying in the US.

2 a possibility that something will
happen in the way that you want:
There **is no hope of** *getting your
money back now.* | *Is there* **any
hope that** *the police will find your
car?*

PHRASES

lose hope: *You mustn't lose hope*
(=you must not stop believing that
something good will happen).

**someone's only hope, someone's
last hope**: *He's our only hope of
winning the contest* (=he is the only
person who can make us win the contest).

hope·ful /ˈhəʊpfəl $ ˈhoʊpfəl/ *adjective*
feeling fairly confident that what you
want to happen will happen: *Maria
feels quite hopeful that she'll pass her
exams.*

hope·ful·ly /ˈhəʊpfəli $ ˈhoʊpfəli/
adverb **1** used to say what you hope
will happen: *Hopefully, the weather will
be better tomorrow.* **2** in a hopeful
way: *"Can I come with you?" Alec asked
hopefully.*

hope·less /ˈhəʊpləs $ ˈhoʊpləs/ *adjec-
tive* **1** a situation that is hopeless is
very bad and not likely to improve: *Our
relationship was getting worse, and the
situation seemed hopeless.* **2** someone who is hopeless at doing something
is very bad at it: *I was hopeless at sport
at school.*

horde /hɔːd $ hɔrd/ *noun* a very large
crowd: *Hordes of reporters were waiting
at the airport.*

ho·ri·zon /həˈraɪzən/ *noun* **1 the
horizon** the line where the land or sea
seems to meet the sky: *The sun slowly
sank below the horizon.* **2 be on the
horizon** *written* if something is on the
horizon, it will happen soon: *Changes in
the law are on the horizon.*

hor·i·zon·tal /ˌhɒrəˈzɒntl $ ˌhɔrə-
ˈzɑntl/ *adjective* going from side to side,
parallel to the ground ⇨ *opposite* VERTI-
CAL: *a shirt with horizontal stripes* ⇨ *see
picture at* LINE[1]

hor·mone /ˈhɔːməʊn $ ˈhɔrmoʊn/
noun a chemical substance that your
body produces naturally, which makes it
develop in a particular way: *male hor-
mones*

horns

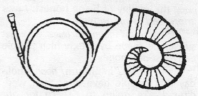

horn /hɔːn $ hɔrn/ *noun* **1** one of the
hard pointed things that some animals,
for example cows, have on their heads
2 the thing in a car, bus etc that you
push to make a sound as a warning: *The
driver behind me kept hooting his horn.*
3 a metal musical instrument shaped
like a long wide tube that you play by
blowing into it and pressing buttons: *the
French horn*

hor·o·scope /ˈhɒrəskəʊp $ ˈhɔrə-
ˌskoʊp/ *noun* a description of what
might happen to you in the future,
based on the position of the stars and
PLANETS when you were born

hor·ren·dous /həˈrendəs/ *adjective*
very bad or unpleasant: *It was a horren-
dous attack on an old lady.*

hor·ri·ble /ˈhɒrəbəl $ ˈhɔrəbəl/ *adjec-
tive* very unpleasant or unkind: *That was
a horrible thing to say.* | *That dress is
horrible.*

hor·rid /ˈhɒrɪd $ ˈhɔrɪd/ *adjective
informal* unpleasant or unkind: *The carpet
was a horrid brown colour.* | *Don't be so
horrid, Brett!*

hor·rif·ic /həˈrɪfɪk/ *adjective formal* very
shocking and unpleasant: *a horrific
crime*

hor·ri·fy /ˈhɒrɪfaɪ $ ˈhɔrəˌfaɪ/ *verb*
horrified, horrifies to shock someone
very much in an unpleasant way: *Everyone was horrified by the news.*

–horrifying *adjective*: *a horrifying accident*

hor·ror /ˈhɒrə $ ˈhɔrɚ/ *noun* **1** a strong
feeling of shock and fear: *I listened in
horror as he described what he had
done.* **2 horror film, horror story** a
film or story which deliberately tries to
shock or frighten people in order to entertain them

horse /hɔːs $ hɔrs/ noun a large animal that people ride on or use for pulling heavy things: *I learnt to ride a horse when I was four.* ⇨ *see picture on page 339*

horse·back /'hɔːsbæk $ 'hɔrsbæk/ noun **1 on horseback** riding a horse: *They did the journey on horseback.* **2 horseback** riding the American word for HORSE-RIDING

horse·rid·ing /'. ,../ noun [no plural] BrE the activity of riding a horse; HORSEBACK RIDING AmE ⇨ *see picture on page 351*

horse·shoe /'hɔːʃ-ʃuː $ 'hɔrʃ-ʃu/ noun a curved piece of iron that is fixed to the bottom of a horse's foot

hose /həʊz $ hoʊz/ also **hose-pipe** /'. ../ noun a long rubber tube that water can flow through and that you use in the garden, or to wash a car, stop a fire etc

hos·pi·ta·ble /'hɒspɪtəbəl $ hɑ'spɪt-əbəl/ adjective friendly to visitors and ready to welcome them: *Greek people are very hospitable.*

hos·pi·tal /'hɒspɪtl $ 'hɑspɪtl/ noun a building where doctors help and treat people who are sick or injured: *We thought Sam had broken his arm, so we took him to the hospital.* | *My mother is in hospital at the moment.* | *She should be out of hospital next week.*

hos·pi·tal·i·ty /ˌhɒspə'tæləti $ ˌhɑspə-'tæləti/ noun [no plural] when you behave in a friendly way towards visitors and make them feel welcome

host¹ /həʊst $ hoʊst/ noun **1** the person at a party who organized it and invited the guests **2** the person who speaks to the guests on a television or radio show: *a chat show host*

host² verb if a country, city etc hosts a special event, that event happens in that country or city: *Several countries competed to host the Olympic Games.*

hos·tage /'hɒstɪdʒ $ 'hɑstɪdʒ/ noun a person who is kept as a prisoner in order to force other people to do something: *After eighteen hours, the hostages were released.*

hos·tel /'hɒstl $ 'hɑstl/ noun a place where people can sleep and eat cheaply for a short time: *an international youth hostel* | *a hostel for the homeless*

host·ess /'həʊstɪs $ 'hoʊstɪs/ noun, plural **hostesses** the woman at a party who organized it and invited the guests

hos·tile /'hɒstaɪl $ 'hɑstl/ adjective **1** very unfriendly: *In some mountain villages, the people can be hostile to strangers.* **2** not agreeing with a particular idea or plan: *Most people are hostile towards the plan.*

hos·til·i·ty /hɒ'stɪləti $ hɑ'stɪləti/ noun unfriendly feelings or behaviour: *There has always been some hostility between the two countries.*

hot¹ /hɒt $ hɑt/ adjective **hotter, hottest**
1 something that is hot has a high temperature: *It was a very hot day.* | *You'll feel better after a hot bath.* | *My coffee is still too hot to drink.*
2 hot food has a burning taste because it has a lot of SPICES in it : *a dish of hot, spicy meat and vegetables*

hot² verb **hotted, hotting; hot up** informal if a situation hots up, it becomes more exciting: *The party scene always begins to hot up around Christmas.*

hot dog /ˌ. '. $ '. ./ noun a long SAUSAGE that people eat in a piece of bread

ho·tel /həʊ'tel $ hoʊ'tel/ noun a building where you pay to sleep and eat: *We stayed in a small hotel in the centre of Paris.*

hot·line /'hɒtlaɪn $ 'hɑtlaɪn/ noun a special telephone number that people can call in order to get or give information: *Anyone with information should call the police hotline immediately.*

hound /haʊnd/ verb to follow someone or ask them questions all the time in an annoying or threatening way: *The press were criticized for hounding the Royal Family.*

hour /aʊə $ aʊɚ/ noun
1 a measure of time that is equal to 60 minutes: *We spent three hours in the museum.* | *I'll see you in about an hour.* | *James was half an hour late.* | *The test should only take a quarter of an hour.* | *The store is now open 24 hours a day* (=all day and all night). | *I often go swimming in my lunch hour* (=the time when I stop working and have my lunch). | *All classes begin on the hour* (=at 1 o'clock, 2 o'clock etc).

2 hours *informal* a very long time: *We wandered around the shops for hours!* | *He takes hours getting ready to go out.*

hour·ly /ˈaʊəli $ ˈaʊəli/ *adjective*
1 happening every hour: *There are hourly trains to London.* **2** an hourly amount of money is the amount you are paid or have to pay each hour: *The minimum hourly wage is £3.40.*

house /haʊs/ *noun, plural* **houses** /ˈhaʊzɪz/
1 a building that you live in: *We spent the evening at Harriet's house.* | *They are buying a new house.*
2 a building that is used for a particular purpose: *the court house*
3 a group of people who make the laws of a country: *He made an important speech to the House of Representatives.*

PHRASE
on the house *spoken* if drinks or food in a restaurant are on the house, they are free

house·bound /ˈhaʊsbaʊnd/ *adjective* unable to leave your house, because you are ill or cannot walk far

house·hold¹ /ˈhaʊshəʊld $ ˈhaʊshoʊld/ *adjective* used in or connected with your home: *household appliances such as washing machines and dishwashers*

household² *noun written* all the people living together in a house or apartment: *Every member of the household helps with the cleaning.*

house·keep·er /ˈhaʊsˌkiːpə $ ˈhaʊsˌkiːpər/ *noun* someone whose job is to cook and clean for another person in their house

house·proud /ˈhaʊspraʊd/ *adjective* BrE someone who is houseproud spends too much time cleaning their home

house-to-house /ˌ. . ˈ./ *adjective* house-to-house collections, inquiries, or searches involve going to every house in an area: *The police are making house-to-house enquiries.*

house·warm·ing /ˈhaʊsˌwɔːmɪŋ $ ˈhaʊsˌwɔːrmɪŋ/ *noun* a party you have to celebrate when you move into a different house

house·wife /ˈhaʊs-waɪf/ *noun, plural* **housewives** /ˈhaʊs-waɪvz/ a woman who works at home doing the cooking, cleaning etc for her family

house·work /ˈhaʊswɜːk $ ˈhaʊswɜrk/ *noun [no plural]* work that you do at home such as cleaning, washing etc: *I usually do the housework at weekends.*

hous·ing /ˈhaʊzɪŋ/ *noun [no plural] formal* houses for people to live in: *More money is needed for housing, education and health.*

hov·er /ˈhɒvə $ ˈhʌvər/ *verb* if an aircraft, especially a HELICOPTER, hovers, it stays in one place in the air while flying: *A helicopter was hovering overhead.*

hov·er·craft /ˈhɒvəkrɑːft $ ˈhʌvərˌkræft/ *noun* a type of boat that travels over land and water by pushing air down and backwards

how /haʊ/ *adverb*
1 asking about the way something is done or happens: *How* (=in what way) *did you get my phone number?* | *How are we going to explain this to Mum?*
2 describing the way something is done or happens: *He explained to us how the machine worked.* | *She showed me how to fill in the form.*
3 asking an amount: *How tall are you?* | *How often do you see her?* | *How much will it cost?* | *How many people do you think will come?*
4 asking about someone's health: *How are you?*
5 asking what something is like: *How was your trip to Italy?* | *"Well, how do I look?" "You look great!"*

PHRASE
how come? *spoken informal* why?: *How come I'm always the one who has to clean the bathroom?*

USAGE
"**How are you?**" and "**How are you doing?**" are friendly ways to greet people. The answer to "How are you?" is usually: "Fine", "Good", "Not too bad" etc: *"Hi, Donna, how are you?" "Just fine, thanks."* "**How do you do?**" is used to formally greet people you have not met before. The usual way to answer someone who has said this to you is to say "How do you do?" to them.

how·ev·er /haʊ'evə $ haʊ'evɚ/ adverb

used when you are adding an opinion or statement which is surprising or different from what you have just said: *Sarah is a very able student. However, she does need to work a bit harder if she wants to get good exam results.*

PHRASES

however long, however big, however careful etc used to say that it makes no difference how long, big etc something is: *I'm determined to get a ticket, however long I have to wait here! | Everyone makes mistakes, however careful they are.*

howl /haʊl/ verb to make a long loud crying sound, like a wild dog or a strong wind: *The wind howled around the house.*
– howl noun

HQ /ˌeɪtʃ 'kjuː/ the abbreviation of HEADQUARTERS

hr the written abbreviation of HOUR

huddle /'hʌdl/ also **huddle together, huddle up** verb to stand or sit closely together: *It was freezing cold so we huddled together to try and keep warm.*

huff /hʌf/ noun **in a huff** informal angry because someone has offended you: *She's in a huff and won't speak to me at the moment.*

hug /hʌg/ verb **hugged, hugging** to put your arms around someone and hold them, because you like or love them
– hug noun: *Come over here and give me a hug.*

huge /hjuːdʒ/ adjective very large: *They have a huge house in the country.*

huge·ly /'hjuːdʒli/ adverb informal very: *That band is hugely popular at the moment.*

hull /hʌl/ noun the main body of a ship

hul·lo /hʌ'ləʊ $ hʌ'loʊ/ a British spelling of HELLO

hum /hʌm/ verb **hummed, humming** **1** to sing a tune with your lips closed: *I didn't know the words, so I just hummed the tune.* **2** to make a low steady noise: *Everything was silent except for a computer humming in the corner.*
– hum noun [no plural] written: *Outside I could hear the hum of traffic.*

hu·man¹ /'hjuːmən/ adjective

related to people rather than to machines or animals: *After two years alone, he longed for human company. | The accident was caused by **human error** (=a mistake made by a person).*

human² also **human be·ing** /ˌ.. '../ noun a man, woman, or child

hu·mane /hjuː'meɪn/ adjective kind rather than cruel: *the humane treatment of animals*

hu·man·i·tar·i·an /hjuːˌmænə'teəriən $ hjuːˌmænə'teriən/ adjective concerned with trying to help people who are ill, hungry etc: *The UN has sent humanitarian aid to help the refugees.*

hu·man·i·ty /hjuː'mænəti/ noun [no plural] formal **1** all the people in the world, as a group: *The attack broke international law and was a crime against humanity.* **2** formal when you act in a kind and respectful way to other people: *He wanted to prove his humanity by helping others.*

human race /ˌ.. '../ noun **the human race** all people, rather than animals or other types of life: *There are many things that threaten the survival of the human race.*

human rights /ˌ.. '../ plural noun the basic rights that everyone has to be free and to be treated fairly, especially by their government: *The government has been accused of **human rights abuses** (=treating people in unfairly or badly).*

humble /'hʌmbəl/ adjective someone who is humble is not proud and does not think that they are better than other people: *The novel is about the friendship between a humble mailman and a famous poet.*

hu·mid /'hjuːmɪd/ adjective a place or weather that is humid is very warm and wet in an unpleasant way: *Florida is extremely humid in the summer.*

hu·mil·i·ate /hjuː'mɪlieɪt/ verb to make someone feel stupid or weak: *He often humiliated other people in meetings.*
– humiliating adjective: *Being arrested was a humiliating experience.*

hu·mor·ous /'hjuːmərəs/ adjective funny: *She made a very humorous speech.*

H

hu·mour[1] _BrE_, **humor** _AmE_ /ˈhjuːmə ＄ˈhjumɚ/ _noun_ **1** sense of humour the ability to see that things are funny and laugh at them: _I really like Sam – he's got a great sense of humour._ **2** [no plural] the quality in something that makes it funny: _Carol can find the humor in almost any situation._

humour[2] _BrE_, **humor** _AmE_, _verb_ to do what someone wants in order to stop them becoming upset: _I humoured Liz rather than getting into an argument with her._

hump

hump /hʌmp/ _noun_ **1** a large lump on a CAMEL'S back **2** a raised part on a road, especially one that is put there in order to make cars go more slowly: _Go slowly – there are humps all along the road._

hunch[1] /hʌntʃ/ _noun_ have a hunch _informal_ to have a feeling that something will happen or is true, although you have no definite information about it: _I had a hunch that something would go wrong._

hunch[2] _verb_ be hunched to be sitting or standing with your back and shoulders bent forwards: _He was sitting in his study, hunched over his books._

hun·dred /ˈhʌndrəd/ _number_ **1** 100: _There were at least a hundred people at the party. | The journey is about five hundred kilometres._ **2** hundreds of a very large number of something: _I have hundreds of tapes._

USAGE

British people always use the word 'and' after the word **hundred**: _one hundred and ten | three thousand, five hundred and sixty._ American people do not usually use 'and': _two thousand one_ (=2001)

hung the past tense and past participle of HANG[1]

hun·ger /ˈhʌŋgə ＄ˈhʌŋgɚ/ _noun_ [no plural] **1** the feeling you have when you want or need to eat: _By one o'clock the_ kids were complaining of hunger. **2** when people do not have enough food, especially for a long period of time: _These refugees are dying of hunger and thirst._

hun·gry /ˈhʌŋgri/ _adjective_
hungrier, hungriest
1 if you are hungry, you need or want to eat: _I'm hungry – is lunch almost ready? | hungry children begging for food_
2 go hungry if you go hungry, you do not have enough food to eat: _We didn't have much money, but we never **went hungry**._

hunk /hʌŋk/ _noun_ **1** _informal_ an attractive man who has a strong body **2** a thick piece of something, especially food: _Dave passed me a hunk of bread._

hunt /hʌnt/ _verb_ **1** to chase wild animals in order to catch and kill them: _They still hunt deer in this forest._ **2** to try to find something or someone by looking carefully: _I've hunted everywhere for my keys but I can't find them._
–hunt _noun_: _Brian Edwards is leading the hunt for the killer._

hunt·er /ˈhʌntə ＄ˈhʌntɚ/ _noun_ someone who hunts wild animals

hunt·ing /ˈhʌntɪŋ/ _noun_ [no plural] the activity of chasing wild animals in order to catch and kill them: _Is foxhunting cruel?_

hur·dle /ˈhɜːdl ＄ˈhɚdl/ _noun_ **1** a small fence that a person or a horse jumps over during a race: _the 100 metres hurdle_ **2** something difficult that you have to do: _Exams are a hurdle that everyone has to face._

hurl /hɜːl ＄hɚl/ _verb_ to throw something using a lot of force: _One of the boys hurled a stone at our car._

hur·ray or **hooray** /huˈreɪ/ something you shout when you are very pleased about something: _Hurray! We've won!_

hur·ri·cane /ˈhʌrɪkən ＄ˈhɚɪˌkeɪn/ _noun_ a violent storm with very strong fast winds

hur·ried /ˈhʌrid ＄ˈhɚid/ _adjective_ written done more quickly than usual, especially because there is not much time: _He said a hurried goodbye and ran for the bus._

hymn

–**hurriedly** adverb: *I got dressed hurriedly.*

hur·ry¹ /'hʌri $ 'həːi/ verb **hurried, hurries**

PHRASE
hurry up! spoken used to tell someone to do something more quickly: *Come on, Katie, hurry up!*
to go somewhere more quickly than usual: *The party doesn't start till eight, so you don't need to hurry. | He picked up his bag and hurried out of the house.*

hurry² noun

1 **be in a hurry** if you are in a hurry, you need to do something very quickly: *She was in a hurry to get to class. | Can I talk to you now, or are you in a hurry?*
2 **there's no hurry** spoken used to tell someone that they do not have to do something immediately: *"When do you need these books back?" "Oh, there's no hurry."*
3 **not be in any hurry, be in no hurry** spoken if you are not in any hurry, you are able to wait because you have a lot of time in which to do something: *"I'll wait for you. I'm in no hurry."*

hurt¹ /hɜːt $ həːt/ verb, past tense and past participle **hurt**

1 to injure someone or make them feel pain: *Let go, you're hurting me! | Ian, sit down before you hurt yourself. | Winnie hurt her back in the accident.*
2 if part of your body hurts, it is painful: *It was so cold my hands started to hurt.*

PHRASE
hurt someone's feelings to make someone feel upset: *I don't want to hurt her feelings by telling her that I don't like the food.*

USAGE
Use **hurt** to talk about damage to the body: *My feet were hurting, so I soaked them. | Stop that! It hurts.* Use **injure** to talk about someone who has been hurt in an accident: *He was seriously injured in the car accident.* Use **wound** to talk about someone who has been hurt by a weapon such as a gun or knife: *He shot and killed two people and wounded two others.*

hurt² adjective

1 if you are hurt, you are injured or feeling pain: *Four people were hurt in the accident.*
2 unhappy because of what someone has said to you: *She looked so hurt, but I had to tell her how I felt.*

hurt·ful /'hɜːtfəl $ 'həːtfəl/ adjective a remark or action that is hurtful makes you feel upset or unhappy: *Some of the things he said were very hurtful.*

hur·tle /'hɜːtl $ 'həːtl/ verb informal to move very fast: *We hurtled down the road at 100 km an hour.*

hus·band /'hʌzbənd/ noun the man that a woman is married to

husky /'hʌski/ adjective **huskier, huskiest** a husky voice is deep and sounds rough but attractive

hustle /'hʌsəl/ verb to make someone move somewhere quickly, often by pushing them: *Steve hustled his son into the house and shut the door.*

hut /hʌt/ noun a small building, often made of wood: *They live in huts in the forest.*

hutch /hʌtʃ/ noun, plural **hutches** a wooden box that people keep rabbits in

hy·draul·ic /haɪ'drɒlɪk $ haɪ'drɔlɪk/ adjective moved or operated by the pressure of water or other liquids: *a hydraulic pump*

hy·dro·e·lec·tric /ˌhaɪdrəʊ-ɪ'lektrɪk $ ˌhaɪdroʊ-ɪ'lektrɪk/ adjective using water power to produce electricity: *The hydroelectric plant provides the town with energy.*

hy·dro·gen /'haɪdrədʒən/ noun [no plural] a gas that is lighter than air

hy·e·na /haɪ'iːnə/ noun a wild animal like a dog that makes a loud laughing sound

hy·giene /'haɪdʒiːn/ noun [no plural] when you keep yourself and the things around you clean in order to avoid diseases: *The children are taught the importance of personal hygiene.*

hy·gien·ic /haɪ'dʒiːnɪk $ haɪ'dʒenɪk/ adjective something that is hygienic is clean and likely to stop diseases spreading: *Conditions in the camps were not very hygienic.*

hymn /hɪm/ noun a religious song that people sing in Christian churches

H

hype /haɪp/ noun [no plural] when something is talked about too much on television, in the newspapers etc and is made to seem important when it is not: *There's been a lot of media hype about the book.*
–**hype** verb

hy·per·mar·ket /'haɪpə,mɑːkɪt $ 'haɪpəˌmɑrkɪt/ noun BrE a very large shop outside a town that sells many different kinds of food and other things

hy·phen /'haɪfən/ noun a short line (-) that joins words or parts of words

hyp·no·sis /hɪp'nəʊsɪs $ hɪp'noʊsɪs/ noun [no plural] when someone is put into a state like a deep sleep, so that another person can control or affect their thoughts: *Under hypnosis, Jean was able to remember exactly what had happened that day.*

hyp·no·tize also **hypnotise** BrE /'hɪpnətaɪz/ verb to make someone go into a state in which they feel they are asleep, so that you can influence what they think or do

hy·poc·ri·sy /hɪ'pɒkrəsi $ hɪ'pɑkrəsi/ noun [no plural] when someone pretends to have particular feelings or opinions, but then behaves in a way that shows that they do not really have them: *The government was accused of hypocrisy.*

hyp·o·crite /'hɪpəkrɪt/ noun someone who says that they have particular feelings or opinions, but then behaves in a way that shows that they do not really have them: *He's such a hypocrite! He tells us to be good, but he behaves badly himself!*

hys·ter·i·cal /hɪ'sterəkəl/ adjective **1** very upset or excited, and not able to control yourself: *She was hysterical and I couldn't stop her screaming* **2** informal very funny: *The movie was hysterical!*

H

Ii

I /aɪ/ pronoun
the person who is speaking: *I don't understand.* | *I was surprised to see him.* | *Have I come to the right room?*

ice /aɪs/ noun [no plural] water that has frozen and become solid: *Would you like some ice in your drink?*

ice·berg /'aɪsbɜːg $ 'aɪsbɚg/ noun a very large piece of ice floating in the sea

ice-cold /ˌ. './ adjective very cold: *an ice-cold lemonade*

ice cream /ˌ. '. $ '. ./ noun a sweet frozen food that is made from milk and sugar

ice cube /'. ./ noun a small block of ice that you put in a drink

ice hock·ey /'. ˌ../ noun [no plural] a game played on ice in which two teams of players use sticks to hit a hard flat object into a GOAL ⇨ see picture on page 351

ice skate¹ /'. ./ verb to slide on ice wearing boots with a metal part on the bottom

ice skate² noun a boot with a metal part on the bottom, used for ice skating

i·ci·cle /'aɪsɪkəl/ noun a thin pointed piece of ice that hangs down

ic·ing /'aɪsɪŋ/ noun [no plural] a sweet mixture made from sugar, water, and butter that you put on a cake to decorate it; FROSTING *AmE*

i·con /'aɪkɒn $ 'aɪkɑn/ noun **1** a small picture on a computer SCREEN that you choose in order to make the computer do something: *Select the print icon, using the right mouse button.* **2** someone or something that many people admire and connect with an important idea: *James Dean is an American film icon.*

ic·y /'aɪsi/ adjective icier, iciest **1** very cold: *an icy winter morning* **2** covered in ice: *an icy highway*

I'd /aɪd/ the short form of 'I had' or 'I would': *I'd like to go, but I can't.*

ID /ˌaɪ 'diː/ noun a document that shows your name, address etc, usually with a photograph: *Do you have any ID?*

i·dea /aɪ'dɪə/ noun
a plan, thought, or suggestion that you have: *I think that's **a good idea**.* | *Emily came up with **an idea for** raising money.* | *Does anyone **have an idea for** a name for the school newspaper?* | *He liked the **idea of** starting a band.*

PHRASES

have an idea (of something) if you have an idea of something, you know about it or understand it: *By the time you've finished school, you'll **have** more of **an idea** of what you want to do.* | *I **have no idea** where David went* (=I do not know at all).

give someone an idea (of something) to give someone information about something: *Can you **give** me some **idea** of the size of the rooms?*

i·deal¹ /ˌaɪ'dɪəl/ adjective the best that something can be: *Being a working mother is not an ideal situation.*

ideal² noun a standard or a way of behaving that you would like to achieve: *the ideals of democracy and freedom*

i·deal·is·tic /ˌaɪˌdɪə'lɪstɪk/ adjective believing in ideals that are difficult to achieve in real life

i·deal·ly /aɪ'dɪəli/ adverb **1** used to say how you would like things to be, even if it is not possible: *Ideally, we would like an extra month to finish this project.* **2** perfectly: *The hotel is ideally located.*

identical

i·den·ti·cal /aɪˈdentɪkəl/ *adjective*
exactly the same: *Childhood pictures of
my dad and my brother are identical. |
identical twins*

i·den·ti·fi·ca·tion /aɪˌdentəfəˈkeɪʃən/
noun [no plural] **1** an official document
that shows your name, address etc, usually with a photograph ⇨ *same meaning*
ID: *You need some identification to travel
across the border.* **2** when you can
recognize someone or something and
are able to say who or what they are

i·den·ti·fy /aɪˈdentəfaɪ/ *verb*
identified, identifies

GRAMMAR
identify someone as something
to be able to say who someone
or something is: *Police identified
the victim of the accident as John
Shelley.*

i·den·ti·ty /aɪˈdentəti/ *noun, plural*
identities **1** who someone is: *Police
have discovered the identity of the
murderer.* **2** [no plural] the qualities that
a person or a group of people have that
make them different from other people:
*Joanna moved to England, but she still
has a strong sense of her Polish identity.*

i·de·ol·o·gy /ˌaɪdiˈɒlədʒi $ ˌaɪdi-
ˈɑːlədʒi/ *noun, plural* ideologies a set of
beliefs or ideas, especially political beliefs: *socialist ideology*

id·i·om /ˈɪdiəm/ *noun* a group of words
that have a special meaning when they
are used together: *'On top of the world'
is an idiom meaning 'extremely happy'.*

id·i·o·mat·ic /ˌɪdiəˈmætɪk/ *adjective*
idiomatic language contains idioms and
is typical of the way people usually talk
and write

id·i·ot /ˈɪdiət/ *noun informal* a stupid person: *He's an idiot.*

id·i·ot·ic /ˌɪdiˈɒtɪk $ ˌɪdiˈɑːtɪk/ *adjective*
very stupid: *Don't ask idiotic questions.*

i·dle /ˈaɪdl/ *adjective* **1** someone who

is idle is lazy and does not do what they
should do: *They are rich, idle women.*
2 *written* not working or being used: *The
computers sit idle after school because
there are no evening classes.*
– **idly** *adverb*

i·dol /ˈaɪdl/ *noun* someone or something
that you admire very much

i·dol·ize also **idolise** *BrE* /ˈaɪdl-aɪz/
verb to admire someone so much that
you think they are perfect: *Herman idol-
ized his father.*

if /ɪf/

1 showing an event that may happen
or could happen: *If you feel hungry, I
can get you something to eat. | You'll
be sick if you eat all that cake. | If
you had worked harder, you could
have passed your exams.*
2 whenever: *If I don't get enough
sleep, I can't concentrate. | I buy a
CD every week, if I can afford it.*
3 asking about something or saying
that you do not know about something: *I asked her if she was all
right. | I wonder if I've upset him
somehow. | I don't know if Sally still
lives there.*

ig·nite /ɪɡˈnaɪt/ *verb formal* to start burning, or to make something start burning

ig·ni·tion /ɪɡˈnɪʃən/ *noun* the part of a
car engine that makes it start working:
He put the key in the ignition.

ig·no·rance /ˈɪɡnərəns/ *noun* [no plural]
lack of knowledge or information about
something: *Her fear is actually based on
ignorance.*

ig·no·rant /ˈɪɡnərənt/ *adjective* not
knowing facts or information that you
should know: *Many older people are
ignorant about computers.*

ig·nore /ɪɡˈnɔː $ ɪɡˈnɔːr/ *verb*

to know that someone or something
is there, but to deliberately not do
anything to show that you know: *I
said hello, but he just ignored me. |
Mike ignored the pain in his ankle
and played football.*

I'll /aɪl/ the short form of 'I will' or 'I shall'

ill /ɪl/ *adjective*

if you are ill, you do not feel well and
are not healthy ⇨ *same meaning* SICK
(1): *Mrs. Jackson has been very ill*

▼ for a long time. ⇨ see picture at
HEALTHY

il·le·gal /ɪ'liːgəl/ adjective not allowed
by law ⇨ opposite LEGAL (1): It is illegal to
sell cigarettes to children.

il·le·gi·ble /ɪ'ledʒ-
əbəl/ adjective dif-
ficult or impossible
to read: Her writ-
ing is illegible.

il·le·git·i·mate
/,ɪlə'dʒɪtəmət/
adjective an il-
legitimate child
has parents who
are not married

il·lit·e·rate /ɪ'lɪt-
ərət/ adjective not
able to read or write

illegible

ill·ness /'ɪlnəs/ noun, plural illnesses

a disease of the body or mind: a
serious **mental illness** | Our grand-
mother died after **a long illness**. |
Illnesses such as mumps are not
very serious. ⇨ see usage note at
DISEASE

il·lo·gi·cal /ɪ'lɒdʒɪkəl/ $ɪ'lɑdʒɪkəl/
adjective not reasonable ⇨ opposite LOGI-
CAL: I have an illogical fear of the dark.

il·lu·sion /ɪ'luːʒən/ noun something
that seems to be true or real but is not: In
expensive cars you get the illusion that
you are floating on air.

il·lus·trate /'ɪləstreɪt/ verb   **1** to explain or show something by giving examples: The graph illustrates what's in
the table below.   **2** to draw or paint pictures for a book: This book is beautifully
illustrated.

il·lus·tra·tion /,ɪlə'streɪʃən/ noun
1 a picture in a book **2** an example
that helps you understand something:
The best illustration of Jackson's coaching ability came in Game 2.

I'm /aɪm/ the short form of 'I am': I'm
hungry.

im·age /'ɪmɪdʒ/ noun

1 if something has a particular image,
that is how it appears to other
people: The Football Association is
trying to improve the image of the
sport.

▼**2** a picture, for example in a news-

▼ paper or on television: The Hubble
telescope sends images of space
back to Earth.

i·ma·gi·na·ry /ɪ'mædʒənəri $ɪ'mæ-
dʒə,neri/ adjective not real, and only
existing in your thoughts: Many children
have imaginary friends.

i·ma·gi·na·tion /ɪ,mædʒə'neɪ-
ʃən/ noun

your imagination is your ability to
form new ideas, and to make pictures in your mind, even of things
that do not exist or that you have
never seen: Toys and games should
encourage a child to **use** their
imagination. | Anna **has** a very
vivid (=strong) **imagination**.

i·ma·gi·na·tive /ɪ'mædʒənətɪv/ adjective having or showing imagination: an
imaginative writer

i·ma·gine /ɪ'mædʒɪn/ verb

> **GRAMMAR**
> **imagine doing something**
> **imagine that**

to think about what something
would be like if it happened: Close
your eyes, and imagine traveling
through space. | No one **imagined**
that Thomas would become a successful writer.

im·i·tate /'ɪməteɪt/ verb to do something in exactly the same way as someone else does, in order to be the same:
He can imitate Caine's voice really well.

im·i·ta·tion[1] /,ɪmə'teɪʃən/ noun when
you do something in exactly the same
way as someone else does, in order to
be the same: Harry can do an excellent
imitation of Elvis.

imitation[2] adjective imitation leather,
wood etc looks like leather, wood etc,
but is not

im·ma·ture /,ɪmə'tʃʊə $,ɪmə'tʃʊr/
adjective   **1** behaving in a way that is
not correct or sensible enough for your
age: Many students are very immature
when they first arrive. **2** not fully
developed: Fishermen must return
immature fish back to the lake.

im·me·di·ate /ɪ'miːdiət/ adjective

▼**1** happening or done now, without

▼ waiting: *The President called for an immediate end to the war.*

2 **immediate family** your parents, children, brothers, and sisters

im·me·di·ate·ly /ɪ'miːdiətli/
adverb
if you do something immediately, you do it now, without waiting: *A restaurant worker immediately came over to clean up the mess. | I need to see you in my office immediately.*

im·mense /ɪ'mens/ *adjective formal* very big: *The problems are immense.*

im·mense·ly /ɪ'mensli/ *adverb formal* to a very great degree: *The movie was immensely popular.*

im·merse /ɪ'mɜːs $ ɪ'mɚs/ *verb* **1** if you immerse yourself in something, or you are immersed in it, you are completely involved in it and do not notice anything else: *Kay missed class because she was immersed in the Internet. | Dad always immerses himself in the paper when he gets home.* **2** *formal* to put something in a liquid so that the liquid covers it completely

im·mi·grant /'ɪmɪgrənt/ *noun* someone who comes to live in a country from another country: *My father came to England as an immigrant. | The U.S. has a lot of illegal immigrants* (=people living in a country without permission).

im·mi·grate /'ɪmɪgreɪt/ *verb* to come to live in another country: *Juan immigrated to the U.S. last year.* ⇨ *see usage note at* EMIGRATE

im·mi·gra·tion /ˌɪmə'greɪʃən/ *noun [no plural]* **1** when people come to a country in order to live there **2** the place at an airport, border etc where your PASSPORT and other documents are checked

im·mor·al /ɪ'mɒrəl $ ɪ'mɔːrəl/ *adjective* bad or evil ⇨ *opposite* MORAL¹: *Stealing is stupid, not to mention immoral.*

–immorally *adverb*: *Do you think Ruth behaved immorally when she left her husband?*

im·mor·tal /ɪ'mɔːtl $ ɪ'mɔːrtl/ *adjective* living or continuing for ever: *man's immortal soul | Her beauty is immortal.*

im·mune /ɪ'mjuːn/ *adjective* not affected by a disease: *Only a few people are immune to tuberculosis.*

im·mu·ni·za·tion /ˌɪmjʊənaɪ'zeɪʃən $ ˌɪmjənə'zeɪʃən/ *noun* the act of immunizing someone: *immunization against polio*

im·mu·nize *also* **immunise** *BrE* /'ɪmjənaɪz/ *verb* to give someone a drug to stop them getting a disease ⇨ *same meaning* VACCINATE: *Children in the U.S. must be immunized before attending school.*

im·pact /'ɪmpækt/ *noun* the effect something or someone has: *Paul has a positive impact on his younger brother.*

im·paired /ɪm'peəd $ ɪm'perd/ *adjective* damaged or made weaker: *She teaches learners who are deaf and hearing impaired* (=not able to hear very well).

im·par·tial /ɪm'pɑːʃəl $ ɪm'pɑːrʃəl/ *adjective formal* not supporting or preferring one person, group, or opinion more than another ⇨ *opposite* BIASED: *A judge must be impartial and fair.*

im·pas·sive /ɪm'pæsɪv/ *adjective formal* not showing any feelings

–impassively *adverb*: *He sat there impassively as the judge read out the verdict.*

im·pa·tience /ɪm'peɪʃəns/ *noun [no plural]* when someone becomes angry because they have to wait

im·pa·tient /ɪm'peɪʃənt/ *adjective*
GRAMMAR

impatient with someone
someone who is impatient becomes angry because they have to wait ⇨ *opposite* PATIENT²: *The officer was rude and impatient when I didn't understand. | My husband is sometimes impatient with the kids. | Don't be so impatient – It's your turn next!*

im·pec·ca·ble /ɪm'pekəbəl/ *adjective formal* perfect and without any mistakes: *She speaks nearly impeccable English.*

–impeccably *adverb*: *She was impeccably dressed.*

im·ped·i·ment /ɪm'pedəmənt/ *noun* **speech impediment, hearing impediment** a problem that makes speaking or hearing difficult

im·pend·ing /ɪm'pendɪŋ/ *adjective formal* an impending event or situation, especially an unpleasant one, will happen very soon: *He sensed the impending danger.*

im·per·a·tive /ɪm'perətɪv/ *noun* the form of a verb you use to give a command. In "Do it now!" the verb 'do' is an imperative

im·per·fect¹ /ɪm'pɜːfɪkt $ɪm'pɚfɪkt/ *adjective* not completely perfect: *We're all imperfect.*

imperfect² *noun* the form of a verb that shows an incomplete action in the past. In 'We were walking down the road' the verb 'were walking' is in the imperfect.

im·per·son·al /ɪm'pɜːsənəl $ɪm-'pɚsənəl/ *adjective* not showing any feelings of kindness, friendliness etc: *Sue complained about the doctor's impersonal manner.*

im·per·so·nate /ɪm'pɜːsəneɪt $ɪm-'pɚsə,neɪt/ *verb* to copy the way someone talks, behaves etc in order to pretend that you are that person, or to make people laugh: *Rick can impersonate many different actors.*

im·per·ti·nent /ɪm'pɜːtɪnənt $ɪm-'pɚtn-ənt/ *adjective* formal rude and not showing respect: *She did not answer the maid's impertinent question.*

im·pet·u·ous /ɪm'petʃuəs/ *adjective* formal doing things quickly, without thinking: *They are young and impetuous.*

im·plau·si·ble /ɪm'plɔːzəbəl/ *adjective* not likely to be true ⇨ *opposite* PLAUSIBLE: *His excuse is totally implausible.*

im·ple·ment /'ɪmpləmənt/ *verb* to begin to use a plan or system: *The school will be implementing changes next year.*

im·pli·cate /'ɪmpləkeɪt/ *verb* formal to show that someone is involved in something bad or illegal: *Howard was implicated in the crime.*

im·pli·ca·tion /,ɪmplə'keɪʃən/ *noun* formal a possible result of a plan, action etc: *This research has many important implications.*

im·ply /ɪm'plaɪ/ *verb* implied, implies to suggest that something is true without saying or showing it directly: *What exactly are you implying?*

im·po·lite /,ɪmpə'laɪt/ *adjective* formal not polite; rude: *It is impolite to leave in the middle of the lecture.*

im·port¹ /ɪm'pɔːt $ɪm'pɔrt/ *verb* to bring something into a country from abroad in order to sell it ⇨ *opposite* EXPORT¹: *The store imports Italian cheeses and meats.*

– **importer** *noun*: *Germany is Europe's biggest importer of organic food.*

im·port² /'ɪmpɔːt $'ɪmpɔrt/ *noun* the business of bringing things into another country to be sold, or the things that are sold ⇨ *opposite* EXPORT²: *The import of wild birds from Africa is restricted.*

im·por·tance /ɪm'pɔːtəns $ɪm-'pɔrtns/ *noun* [no plural]
how important something is: *Good teams understand the importance of working together.*

im·por·tant /ɪm'pɔːtənt $ɪm-'pɔrtnt/ *adjective*
GRAMMAR
important to do something
1 something important has a big effect or influence: *Love and respect are more important than a big car and lots of money.* | *It is important to exercise regularly.* | *There is an important difference between the two experiments we carried out.*
2 someone who is important has a lot of power or influence: *an important businesswoman*

im·pose /ɪm'pəʊz $ɪm'poʊz/ *verb* formal to force people to accept a rule, a tax, beliefs etc: *The king imposed his authority on the whole country.*

im·pos·ing /ɪm'pəʊzɪŋ $ɪm'poʊzɪŋ/ *adjective* large and impressive: *a grand, imposing hotel*

im·pos·si·ble /ɪm'pɒsəbəl $ɪm-'pɑsəbəl/ *adjective*
GRAMMAR
impossible to do something
if something is impossible, it cannot happen or you cannot do it: *an impossible task* | *It was impossible to get tickets for the game.*

im·pos·tor or **imposter** /ɪm'pɒstə $ɪm'pɑstɚ/ *noun* someone who pretends to be someone else in order to trick people

im·po·tent /'ɪmpətənt/ *adjective* a man who is impotent is not able to have sex

im·prac·ti·cal /ɪm'præktɪkəl/ *adjective* not sensible ⇨ *opposite* PRACTICAL¹

im·pre·cise /,ɪmprɪ'saɪs/ *adjective* not exact: *Our measurements were imprecise.*

im·press /ɪm'pres/ *verb* if someone impresses you, they make you admire or respect them: *He spent a lot of money just to try and impress his girlfriend.*

im·pressed /ɪm'prest/ *adjective*

if you are impressed by something, you admire it: *I was really impressed by how well the team played in its first game.*

im·pres·sion /ɪm'preʃən/ *noun*

GRAMMAR
impression of someone/something
impression that

1 the feeling you have about something or someone because of the way they seem: *I don't know what your **impression of** him was, but I didn't like him.* | *I **got the impression that** the food wasn't very good there.* | *Sam **gave the impression that** (=made people think that) he didn't care about his school work.* | *The article is about **making a good impression** on your first date.*
2 when someone copies the way a famous person talks or behaves, in order to make people laugh: *Dawn does a good impression of Marilyn Monroe.*

im·pres·sion·a·ble /ɪm'preʃənəbəl/ *adjective formal* someone who is impressionable is easy to influence: *This TV show isn't appropriate for impressionable young children.*

im·pres·sive /ɪm'presɪv/ *adjective*

if something is impressive, it is very good and you admire it: *Their victory over Toronto was very impressive.* | *The award is an impressive achievement for such a young woman.*

im·print /'ɪmprɪnt/ *noun formal* the mark left by an object that has been pressed onto something: *Fossils are rocks that have imprints of animals on them.*

im·pris·on /ɪm'prɪzən/ *verb* to put someone in prison or to keep them in a place they cannot escape from: *He was arrested and imprisoned.*

im·prop·er /ɪm'prɒpə $ ɪm'prɑpɚ/ *adjective written* not correct according to moral, social, or professional rules

–**improperly** *adverb*: *You will not be allowed in the nightclub if you are improperly dressed.*

im·prove /ɪm'pruːv/ *verb*

1 to make something better: *Digital recording improves the sound quality of the tapes.* | *I'm staying in London to improve my English.*
2 to become better: *The team is improving with every game.* | *The doctor says my mother's health has improved.*

im·prove·ment /ɪm'pruːvmənt/ *noun*

GRAMMAR
improvement in something
an improvement on something

when something becomes better than it was: *There has been a great **improvement in** her work recently.* | *The new house is a **big improvement on** that tiny flat we used to live in.*

im·pro·vise /'ɪmprəvaɪz/ *verb* to do or make something without preparing first, using whatever you have got: *If you do not have a screwdriver, you will have to improvise and use the end of a knife.*

im·pulse /'ɪmpʌls/ *noun* a sudden desire to do something: *My first impulse was to hit him.*

in¹ /ɪn/ *preposition*

1 inside a container or place: *He had a pencil in his pocket.* | *I've left my coat in the car.* | *They live in London.* ⇨ see picture on page 354
2 showing the town or city where someone or something is: *The competition will take place in Manchester.*
3 being part of a group: *Joe's in the army now.* | *She's the smartest girl in our class.*
4 showing the month, year, or time when something happens: *My birthday is in June.* | *They got married in 1968.* | *It is very cold here in the winter.* | *We went out in the evening.*
5 after a period of time: *I'll be back in ten minutes.* | *The photographs will be ready in two hours.* | *In a year's time* (=a year from now) *I'll be going to university.*

6 showing the book, letter etc where something is written: *She says in her letter that she'll see us at Christmas.* | *There's a great description of London in the book.*

7 showing the picture or film where something is shown: *You can see in this picture that she looks ill.* | *In the film, he is left alone on a desert island.*

8 wearing something: *a woman in a smart suit*

9 showing how something is spoken or written: *I think they were speaking in Chinese.* | *Write your name in large letters at the top of the page.*

PHRASE

in his twenties, in her thirties etc used when saying how old someone is: *The police are looking for a dark-haired man in his twenties* (=aged between 20 and 29).

in² *adverb, adjective*

1 into a place: *He opened the door and walked in.* | *Hello, come in.* ⇨ *see picture on page 354*

2 at the place where you live or work: *Mr. Hibbs isn't in today* (=is not at work today). | *I'll be in tomorrow morning.* | *I'm staying in* (=staying at home) *tonight.*

3 given to a teacher: *This homework has to be in by Friday.* | *Have you handed your essay in yet?*

4 fashionable *informal*: *Long skirts are in this winter.*

PHRASES

be in for something *informal* to be going to experience something very good, bad, or surprising: *He's in for a surprise when he opens that door!*

have it in for someone *informal* if someone has it in for you, they do not like you and try to cause problems for you: *My boss really has it in for me!*

in·a·bil·i·ty /ˌɪnəˈbɪləti/ *noun* when you are not able to do something ⇨ *opposite* ABILITY: *They were worried about their child's inability to speak.*

in·ac·cu·rate /ɪnˈækjərət/ *adjective* not correct ⇨ *opposite* ACCURATE: *The newspaper article about the high school was inaccurate.*
–**inaccurately** *adverb*

in·ac·tive /ɪnˈæktɪv/ *adjective formal* not doing anything or not working ⇨ *opposite* ACTIVE¹ (1): *Many children are inactive because they watch too much TV.*

in·ad·e·quate /ɪnˈædəkwət/ *adjective* not enough or not good enough for a particular purpose ⇨ *opposite* ADEQUATE: *The supply of food was inadequate.*
–**inadequately** *adverb*: *He was inadequately prepared for college.*

in·ad·ver·tent·ly /ˌɪnədˈvɜːtəntli $ ˌɪnədˈvɚtntli/ *adverb* if you do something inadvertently, you do it even though you did not intend to: *Sam inadvertently pressed on the car's brake.*

in·ap·pro·pri·ate /ˌɪnəˈprəʊpriət $ ˌɪnəˈproʊpriət/ *adjective* not suitable or correct ⇨ *opposite* APPROPRIATE: *It is inappropriate to wear a T-shirt to a wedding.*
–**inappropriately** *adverb*: *The students acted inappropriately.*

in·au·gu·rate /ɪˈnɔːgjəreɪt/ *verb formal* to have a formal ceremony when someone new starts an important job: *American presidents are always inaugurated in January.*

Inc. the written abbreviation of INCORPORATED, used after names of companies in the US: *Apple Computer Inc.*

in·ca·pa·ble /ɪnˈkeɪpəbəl/ *adjective* not able to do or feel something ⇨ *opposite* CAPABLE (1): *The team seem to be incapable of scoring goals.*

in·car·ce·rate /ɪnˈkɑːsəreɪt $ ɪnˈkɑrsəˌreɪt/ *verb formal* to put someone in prison

in·cense /ˈɪnsens/ *noun [no plural]* a substance that you burn because it has a nice smell

in·cen·tive /ɪnˈsentɪv/ *noun* something that makes you want to work hard or do something new: *Money is a good incentive for hard work.*

in·ces·sant /ɪnˈsesənt/ *adjective written* never stopping: *Incessant rain caused floods and mudslides.*
–**incessantly** *adverb*: *He talks incessantly.*

inch¹ /ɪntʃ/ *noun, plural inches* a unit for measuring length, equal to 2.54 centimetres

inch² *verb written* to move very slowly or carefully: *Prices have inched upwards this year.*

in·ci·dent /'ɪnsədənt/ noun written something unusual, serious, or violent that happens: *The police are investigating the incident.*

in·cite /ɪn'saɪt/ verb formal to deliberately make someone feel so angry or excited that they do something bad: *The opposition leader incited a riot.*

in·cli·na·tion /ˌɪnklə'neɪʃən/ noun formal the desire to do something: *His first inclination was to laugh at Jean's mistake.*

in·cline /'ɪnklaɪn/ noun formal a slope: *The car was parked on an incline.*

in·clined /ɪn'klaɪnd/ adjective likely or wanting to do something: *Families with children are less inclined to move house.*

in·clude /ɪn'kluːd/ verb

if something includes a person or thing, it has that person or thing as one of its parts: *The film festival includes movies from around the world. | Does the price of a hotel room include breakfast? | I noticed that my name had not been included on the list. | The team has twenty people in it, if you include all the managers.*

in·clud·ing /ɪn'kluːdɪŋ/ preposition used to show that the thing or person you are talking about is part of a bigger thing or group of things ⇨ opposite EXCEPT¹: *He was wearing a full army uniform, including the hat. | There will be six people in the car, including the driver.*

in·clu·sion /ɪn'kluːʒən/ noun [no plural] when you include someone or something in a larger group: *Here's the list of books we're considering for inclusion on the reading list.*

in·clu·sive /ɪn'kluːsɪv/ adjective **1** including a particular thing, especially the price of something: *The all-inclusive charge covers meals, rooms, and entertainment.* **2** BrE the first and last number you say, plus all those in between: *He will be on holiday from 22–24 March inclusive.*

in·come /'ɪŋkʌm/ noun money that you receive, for example from your job: *Her annual income is £20,000.* ⇨ see usage note at PAY²

in·com·pat·i·ble /ˌɪnkəm'pætəbəl/ adjective **1** two people who are incompatible have different ideas or interests, and are not able to have a good

relationship ⇨ opposite COMPATIBLE **2** two things that are incompatible cannot exist or be used together ⇨ opposite COMPATIBLE: *Some software may be incompatible with your computer.*

in·com·pe·tence /ɪn'kɒmpətəns $ ɪn'kɑmpətəns/ noun [no plural] when someone is not able to do their job correctly ⇨ opposite COMPETENCE

in·com·pe·tent /ɪn'kɒmpətənt $ ɪn'kɑmpətənt/ adjective not having the ability or skill to do your job correctly ⇨ opposite COMPETENT: *Airlines need to get rid of incompetent pilots.*

in·com·plete /ˌɪnkəm'pliːt/ adjective not finished, or not having all its parts ⇨ opposite COMPLETE: *The drawings of the building were incomplete.*

incomplete

in·com·pre·hen·si·ble /ɪnˌkɒmprɪ'hensəbəl $ ˌɪnkɑmprɪ'hensəbəl/ adjective formal impossible to understand: *The instructions were incomprehensible.*

in·con·clu·sive /ˌɪnkən'kluːsɪv/ adjective formal not leading to any decision or result: *The medical tests were inconclusive.*

in·con·sid·er·ate /ˌɪnkən'sɪdərət/ adjective not caring about other people's needs or feelings ⇨ opposite CONSIDERATE: *Inconsiderate drivers can cause accidents.*

in·con·sis·ten·cy /ˌɪnkən'sɪstənsi/ noun [no plural] something that changes or happens differently each time ⇨ opposite CONSISTENCY: *The team's inconsistency disappointed fans.*

in·con·sis·tent /ˌɪnkən'sɪstənt/ adjective always changing depending on the situation ⇨ opposite CONSISTENT: *Pam's school work has been really inconsistent this term.*
– **inconsistently** adverb: *The team plays inconsistently.*

in·con·ve·ni·ence /ˌɪnkən'viːniəns/ noun when someone has small problems or difficulties: *We're sorry for any inconvenience to our customers.*
– **inconvenience** verb: *The work on the roads has inconvenienced drivers.*

in·con·ve·ni·ent /ˌɪnkən'viːniənt/ adjective causing small problems or difficulties ⇨ opposite CONVENIENT (1): The plane leaves at a very inconvenient time.

in·cor·po·rate /ɪnˈkɔːpəreɪt $ ɪnˈkɔːrpəˌreɪt/ verb formal to include something as part of a group, system etc: This style of karate incorporates kicks, punches, and strikes.

In·cor·po·rat·ed /ɪnˈkɔːpəreɪtɪd $ ɪnˈkɔːrpəˌreɪtɪd/ written abbreviation **Inc.** adjective used after the name of a company to show that it is a CORPORATION

in·cor·rect /ˌɪnkəˈrekt/ adjective wrong or not true ⇨ opposite CORRECT¹: The address on the letter was incorrect.
—incorrectly adverb: She spelled his name incorrectly.

in·crease¹ /ɪnˈkriːs/ verb

GRAMMAR
increase by an amount

1 to become larger in number, amount, size etc ⇨ opposite DECREASE: The price of fuel **has increased by** 5%. | The number of unemployed people **increased to** over 5 million in 1974. | Problems caused by computer viruses have increased dramatically (=a lot).

2 to make something larger in number, amount, size etc ⇨ opposite DECREASE: The government has promised not to increase taxes. | The doctor increased the dose of pain killers.
—increasing adjective: an increasing population
—increased adjective: an increased risk of cancer

in·crease² /ˈɪŋkriːs/ noun

GRAMMAR
increase in something

when an amount or level becomes larger: a tax increase | an **increase in** crime in the area

in·creas·ing·ly /ɪnˈkriːsɪŋli/ adverb formal more and more: Our society is becoming increasingly violent.

in·cred·i·ble /ɪnˈkredəbəl/ adjective
1 very good or large: Winning the game gave me an incredible feeling.
2 strange and difficult to believe: It's incredible that no one questioned the truth of her statement.

in·cred·i·bly /ɪnˈkredəbli/ adverb
1 very: The show is incredibly popular

among teenagers. 2 in a way that is difficult to believe: Incredibly, no one was hurt in the crash.

in·cu·ba·tor /ˈɪŋkjəbeɪtə $ ˈɪŋkjəˌbeɪtər/ noun a machine used in hospitals to keep weak babies alive

in·cur /ɪnˈkɜː $ ɪnˈkɜːr/ verb formal **incurred, incurring** to be punished in some way because of something bad you have done: If the amount is not paid in seven days, you will incur a charge of £15.

in·cur·a·ble /ɪnˈkjʊərəbəl $ ɪnˈkjʊrəbəl/ adjective impossible to cure: an incurable disease

in·de·cent /ɪnˈdiːsənt/ adjective if something is indecent, it is likely to offend or shock people because it is related to sex: indecent photographs

in·de·ci·sive /ˌɪndɪˈsaɪsɪv/ adjective not able to make decisions ⇨ opposite DECISIVE (2): a weak, indecisive leader

in·deed /ɪnˈdiːd/ adverb

used when you want to say something very strongly: The team has done very well indeed this year. | They enjoyed the trip very much indeed.

in·def·i·nite /ɪnˈdefənət/ adjective an indefinite period of time is not fixed and you do not know when it will end: The flood victims will live at the camp for an indefinite period.
—indefinitely adverb: Jack's illness is likely to continue indefinitely.

indefinite ar·ti·cle /ˌ...ˈ.../ noun the word 'a' or 'an' in the English language

in·de·pen·dence /ˌɪndəˈpendəns/ noun [no plural] 1 the freedom to make your own decisions and be responsible for yourself: Women want to keep their independence within a marriage. | The children are starting to show some independence. 2 political freedom from control by another country: When did India gain independence from Britain? | The American war of Independence

in·de·pen·dent /ˌɪndəˈpendənt/ adjective
1 responsible for yourself, making your own decisions, and not needing help from other people ⇨ opposite DEPENDENT: My grandmother is still very independent. | I'd like to be

financially independent instead of relying on my parents.
2 an independent country or organization is not controlled by another country or organization: *Several Soviet states became independent countries in the early 1990s.*
— **independently** *adverb*

in·depth /'. ./ *adjective* considering all the details: *an in-depth interview with the Prime Minister*

in·dex /'ɪndeks/ *noun, plural* **indexes** or **indices** /-dɪsiːz/ an alphabetical list that tells you where you can find information about something. Indexes usually appear as lists at the end of a book: *I looked up 'meat dishes' in the index.*

index fin·ger /'.. ,../ *noun* the finger next to your thumb

In·di·an /'ɪndiən/ *noun* **1** ⇨ NATIVE AMERICAN **2** someone from India
— **Indian** *adjective: Do you like Indian food?*

Indian sum·mer /,... '../ *noun* a period of warm weather in the autumn

in·di·cate /'ɪndəkeɪt/ *verb* **1** *formal* to show that something is likely: *Studies indicate that children from poorer areas are less likely to go to university.* **2** *formal* to say or show what you intend to do: *More than 100 women have indicated they will run for Congress.* **3** *BrE* to show which way you are going to turn when you are driving ⇨ *same meaning* SIGNAL² (2) *AmE: I indicated left.*

in·di·ca·tion /,ɪndə'keɪʃən/ *noun formal* a sign that something is likely: *There was some indication that he had drunk a lot of alcohol.*

in·dic·a·tive /ɪn'dɪkətɪv/ *adjective formal* **1** **be indicative of someone/something** to show that something exists or is likely to be true: *They've lost a few games, but this is not really indicative of the team's ability.* **2** in grammar, an indicative verb expresses a fact or action

in·di·ca·tor /'ɪndəkeɪtə $ 'ɪndə,keɪtɚ/ *noun BrE* one of the lights on a car which show which way it is going to turn; TURN SIGNAL *AmE*

indices a plural of INDEX

in·dif·fer·ence /ɪn'dɪfərəns/ *noun [no plural]* when someone is not interested in or does not care about something or someone: *The factory's indifference to safety rules led to several injuries.*

in·dif·fer·ent /ɪn'dɪfərənt/ *adjective* not interested and not caring: *How could a father be so indifferent to his own children?*

in·di·ges·tion /,ɪndɪ'dʒestʃən/ *noun [no plural]* pain in your stomach that you get when you eat too much or too fast

in·dig·nant /ɪn'dɪgnənt/ *adjective formal* angry because you feel someone has insulted you or treated you unfairly: *Mother was indignant that we didn't believe her.*
— **indignantly** *adverb: "I'm not too fat!" she shouted indignantly.*

in·dig·ni·ty /ɪn'dɪgnəti/ *noun formal, plural* **indignities** a situation that makes you feel ashamed, not important, and not respected: *I hated the indignity of the medical examination.*

in·di·rect /,ɪndə'rekt/ *adjective* **1** not directly caused by something, or not directly connected with it ⇨ *opposite* DIRECT¹: *Scientists have found indirect evidence of other planets.* **2** not following the straightest way between two places: *an indirect route* ⇨ *opposite* DIRECT¹
— **indirectly** *adverb: He had indirectly caused the accident.*

indirect ob·ject /,... '../ *noun* the person or thing that receives something as a result of the action of the verb in a sentence. In the sentence 'Joe gave her a sandwich', 'her' is the indirect object ⇨ *compare* DIRECT OBJECT

indirect speech /,... './ REPORTED SPEECH

in·dis·crim·i·nate /,ɪndɪ'skrɪmənət/ *adjective formal* indiscriminate actions are done without thinking about who or what will be affected or hurt by them: *The government should prevent the indiscriminate cutting down of rain forests.*
— **indiscriminately** *adverb*

in·dis·pens·a·ble /,ɪndɪ'spensəbəl/ *adjective formal* someone or something that is indispensable is so important or useful that you cannot manage without them: *The book is indispensable to anyone using a computer for the first time.*

in·dis·tin·guish·a·ble /,ɪndɪ'stɪŋgwɪʃəbəl/ *adjective* so similar that you cannot see any difference: *The copy was almost indistinguishable from the original.*

individual¹ /,ɪndə'vɪdʒuəl/ *adjective*

related to one person or thing, rather than to a whole group: *Individual schools can make their own rules about what students can wear.*

individual² *noun* a person: *Many individuals who develop this disease need special treatment.* | *Jack is a strange individual.*

in·di·vid·u·al·i·ty /ˌɪndəvɪdʒu'æləti/ *noun* [no plural] the quality that makes someone different from everyone else: *Your clothes can help show your individuality.*

in·di·vid·u·al·ly /ˌɪndə'vɪdʒuəli/ *adverb* separately, not together in a group: *We paid for our meals individually.*

in·door /'ɪndɔː $ 'ɪndɔr/ *adjective* inside a building ⇨ *opposite* OUTDOOR: *an indoor tennis court*

in·doors /ˌɪn'dɔːz $ ˌɪn'dɔrz/ *adverb* into or inside a building ⇨ *opposite* OUTDOORS: *Keep the plant indoors during the winter.*

in·duce /ɪn'djuːs $ ɪn'dus/ *verb formal* to cause someone to do something or cause something to happen: *Can too much exercise induce illness?*

in·dulge /ɪn'dʌldʒ/ *verb* to let yourself do something that you enjoy, especially something that you should not do: *I often indulge myself with chocolates.*

in·dul·gent /ɪn'dʌldʒənt/ *adjective* willing to let someone have whatever they want, even if it is bad for them: *an indulgent grandparent*

in·dus·tri·al /ɪn'dʌstriəl/ *adjective* related to industry or to the people working in industry: *He is meeting industrial leaders and government officials.*
– **industrially** *adverb*

in·dus·tri·al·ized also **industrialised** *BrE* /ɪn'dʌstriəlaɪzd/ *adjective* an industrialized country or area has a lot of industry

in·dus·try /'ɪndəstri/ *noun, plural* **industries** **1** all the companies that make or sell the same kind of thing: *the airline industry* | *the steel industry* **2** the work people do to make things in factories: *The metal is used in industry.*

in·ef·fec·tive /ˌɪnə'fektɪv/ *adjective* not getting the result you want ⇨ *opposite* EFFECTIVE: *The drug has been ineffective against this disease.*
– **ineffectively** *adverb*

in·ef·fi·cient /ˌɪnə'fɪʃənt/ *adjective* a

system, organization, or person that is inefficient does not work well and wastes time, money, or energy ⇨ *opposite* EFFICIENT: *We have an inefficient railway system.*

in·e·qual·i·ty /ˌɪnɪ'kwɒləti $ ˌɪnɪ-'kwɑləti/ *noun, plural* **inequalities** when some groups in society have less money, fewer opportunities etc than others, in a way that seems unfair ⇨ *opposite* EQUALITY: *Inequality between men and women still exists today.*

in·ev·i·ta·ble /ɪ'nevətəbəl/ *adjective* something that is inevitable will definitely happen and you cannot avoid it: *Getting older is inevitable.*

in·ex·cus·a·ble /ˌɪnɪk'skjuːzəbəl/ *adjective formal* inexcusable behaviour is so bad or rude that it is difficult to forgive: *The way you spoke to her was completely inexcusable.*

in·ex·pen·sive /ˌɪnɪk'spensɪv/ *adjective* something that is inexpensive does not cost a lot to buy or use ⇨ *opposite* EXPENSIVE: *inexpensive restaurants and bars*

in·ex·pe·ri·enced /ˌɪnɪk'spɪəriənst $ ˌɪnɪk'spɪriənst/ *adjective* without much experience of doing something ⇨ *opposite* EXPERIENCED: *The team had a number of young inexperienced players.*

in·ex·plic·a·ble /ˌɪnɪk'splɪkəbəl/ *adjective* very strange and impossible to explain or understand: *For some inexplicable reason, he started to laugh.*

in·fal·li·ble /ɪn'fæləbəl/ *adjective* never wrong: *Scientists are not infallible.*

in·fan·cy /'ɪnfənsi/ *noun* [no plural] the period when you are a baby or a young child

in·fant /'ɪnfənt/ *noun formal* a baby or very young child

in·fan·try /'ɪnfəntri/ *noun* [no plural] soldiers who fight on foot, not on horses or in vehicles

in·fat·u·at·ed /ɪn'fætʃueɪtɪd/ *adjective* someone who is infatuated with another person feels very strongly that they love that person, but the feeling does not usually last long: *He's been infatuated with Clare for a couple of weeks now.*

in·fect /ɪn'fekt/ *verb* to give someone an illness: *The local people were infected by the disease through the water supply.*

in·fect·ed /ɪn'fektɪd/ *adjective* a

wound that is infected has become dirty and painful and takes longer to get better: *This cut has become infected.* | *an infected wound*

in·fec·tion /ɪnˈfekʃən/ *noun* an illness that you get from BACTERIA, and which often passes from one person to another: *Infections spread quickly in a school.* | *a chest infection*

in·fec·tious /ɪnˈfekʃəs/ *adjective* an infectious illness can pass from one person to another: *Typhoid is a very infectious disease.*

in·fe·ri·or /ɪnˈfɪəriə $ ɪnˈfɪriɚ/ *adjective* not as good as someone or something else ⇨ *opposite* SUPERIOR: *Luke had a way of looking at me that always made me feel inferior.*

in·fer·tile /ɪnˈfɜːtaɪl $ ɪnˈfɚtl/ *adjective* **1** infertile land is not good enough for growing plants ⇨ *opposite* FERTILE: *infertile stony soil* **2** someone who is infertile is not able to have babies ⇨ *opposite* FERTILE

in·fi·del·i·ty /ˌɪnfəˈdeləti/ *noun* when someone who is married has sex with someone who is not their husband or wife

in·fil·trate /ˈɪnfɪltreɪt $ ɪnˈfɪlˌtreɪt/ *verb* to become part of a group, organization etc, especially a criminal one, in order to get information about it: *Trent was ordered to try and infiltrate the terrorists' group.*

in·fi·nite /ˈɪnfənət/ *adjective* something that is infinite has no end or limit: *Is the universe infinite?*

in·fin·i·tive /ɪnˈfɪnətɪv/ *noun* the basic form of a verb, used with 'to'. In the sentence 'I forgot to buy milk', 'to buy' is an infinitive

in·fin·i·ty /ɪnˈfɪnəti/ *noun* [no plural] space or time that has no end or limit: *It's difficult to understand the idea of infinity.*

in·flamed /ɪnˈfleɪmd/ *adjective* a part of your body that is inflamed is red and painful: *an inflamed throat*

in·flam·ma·ble /ɪnˈflæməbəl/ *adjective* materials or substances that are inflammable burn very easily ⇨ *opposite* NON-FLAMMABLE: *inflammable gases*

in·flam·ma·tion /ˌɪnfləˈmeɪʃən/ *noun* pain and swelling on or in a part of the body: *inflammation of the knee*

in·flat·a·ble /ɪnˈfleɪtəbəl/ *adjective* an inflatable object is one that you fill with air before you use it: *an inflatable boat*

inflate

in·flate /ɪnˈfleɪt/ *verb* to fill something such as a BALLOON or a tyre with air: *Nick inflated the tires of his bike.*

in·flat·ed /ɪnˈfleɪtɪd/ *adjective* **1** inflated prices, figures etc are higher than is usual or reasonable: *Fans are prepared to pay hugely inflated prices for the tickets.* **2** filled with air or gas: *an inflated life-jacket*

in·fla·tion /ɪnˈfleɪʃən/ *noun* [no plural] when the price of things you buy continues to increase, or the rate at which prices increase: *the government's attempts to control inflation*

in·flec·tion or **inflexion** /ɪnˈflekʃən/ *noun* the way the ending of a word changes to show that it is plural, in the past tense etc

in·flex·i·ble /ɪnˈfleksəbəl/ *adjective* not able to change or be changed ⇨ *opposite* FLEXIBLE: *As we get older, our attitudes become more inflexible.*

in·flict /ɪnˈflɪkt/ *verb written* to make a person, place etc suffer something unpleasant: *The earthquake inflicted an enormous amount of damage on the whole area.*

in·flu·ence¹ /ˈɪnfluəns/ *noun*

GRAMMAR

influence **on** someone/something
influence **over** someone/something

if someone has influence, they have the power to change how people or things develop, behave, or think: *The food that you eat **has** an important **influence on** your health.* | *Kate used her influence to get her friend a job.* | *Even though they divorced six years ago, Keith still has a great deal of **influence over** his ex-wife.* | *How much political influence does the Japanese emperor have?*

influence² *verb*
to change how someone or something develops, behaves, or thinks: *His advice influenced my decision to leave.* | *Her music influenced me greatly when I was younger.*

in·flu·en·tial /ˌɪnfluˈenʃəl/ *adjective*
able to influence what happens or what people think: *John is an influential man in the community.* | *influential journalists and critics*

in·flu·en·za /ˌɪnfluˈenzə/ *noun formal* FLU

in·fo /ˈɪnfəʊ $ ˈɪnfoʊ/ *noun informal* ⇨ INFORMATION

in·form /ɪnˈfɔːm $ ɪnˈfɔrm/ *verb formal*

> **GRAMMAR**
> **inform someone about something**
> **inform someone of something**
> **inform someone that**

to formally tell someone about something: *No one **informed** me **about** the change of plan.* | *She was **informed of** the accident by the police.* | *The college **informed** me **that** I had been accepted.*

in·for·mal /ɪnˈfɔːməl $ ɪnˈfɔrməl/ *adjective* **1** relaxed and friendly: *an informal party* **2** suitable for ordinary situations, rather than special ones: *Everyone was told to wear informal clothes.*
– **informally** *adverb*

in·for·ma·tion /ˌɪnfəˈmeɪʃən $ ˌɪnfərˈmeɪʃən/ *noun* [no plural]

> **GRAMMAR**
> **information on/about something**

facts or details about a situation, person, or event: *How can I get more **information about** the sports program?* | *I need more **information on** the course before I decide whether or not to do it.* | *That's a very useful **bit of information**.*

> **USAGE**
> The word **information** is never plural. Do not say 'an information', or 'some informations'. Say **some information, a lot of information**, or a **piece/bit of information**: *I'd like some information about train times, please.* | *That's a useful bit of information.*

information su·per·high·way /ˌɪnfəmeɪʃən ˌsuːpəˈhaɪweɪ $ ˌɪnfəˈmeɪʃən ˌsuːpɚˈhaɪweɪ/ the INTERNET

information tech·nol·o·gy /..ˌ....ˈ.../ *abbreviation* **IT** *noun* [no plural] the use of computers to store and manage information

in·form·a·tive /ɪnˈfɔːmətɪv $ ɪnˈfɔrmətɪv/ *adjective* an informative book, talk etc provides useful information: *The lecture was very informative.*

in·formed /ɪnˈfɔːmd $ ɪnˈfɔrmd/ *adjective* having plenty of knowledge and information about something: *It is important for everyone to keep well informed about what's going on in the world.*

in·form·er /ɪnˈfɔːmə $ ɪnˈfɔrmɚ/ *noun* someone who helps the police by secretly giving them information about crimes and criminals

in·fre·quent /ɪnˈfriːkwənt/ *adjective* not happening often: *The buses from here into town are pretty infrequent.*

in·fu·ri·ate /ɪnˈfjʊərieɪt $ ɪnˈfjʊriˌeɪt/ *verb* to make someone very angry: *It infuriates me when she behaves so badly.*
– **infuriating** *adjective*: *The noise from next door was infuriating.*

in·ge·ni·ous /ɪnˈdʒiːniəs/ *adjective* very clever: *What an ingenious idea!*

in·grat·i·tude /ɪnˈɡrætətjuːd $ ɪnˈɡrætəˌtud/ *noun* [no plural] when someone is not grateful for something, although they should be

in·gre·di·ent /ɪnˈɡriːdiənt/ *noun* one of the things that you use to make a particular type of food: *Mix all the ingredients together in a bowl.*

in·hab·it /ɪnˈhæbɪt/ *verb formal* to live in a particular place: *The desert is still inhabited by tribes of Bedouin.*

in·hab·i·tant /ɪnˈhæbətənt/ *noun formal* the inhabitants of a place are the people who live there: *France has about 57 million inhabitants.*

in·hale /ɪnˈheɪl/ *verb* to breathe air, smoke, or gas into your lungs: *Perce lit a cigarette and inhaled deeply.*

in·her·it /ɪnˈherɪt/ *verb* to receive money, a house etc from someone when they die: *He inherited £100,000 from his aunt.*

in·her·i·tance /ɪnˈherɪtəns/ *noun* money, property etc that you receive from someone when they die: *When his father died, Peter received a large inheritance.*

in·hos·pi·ta·ble /ˌɪnhɒˈspɪtəbəl $ ˌɪn-hɑˈspɪtəbəl/ *adjective* a place that is inhospitable is difficult to live in because it is very hot, cold etc: *Siberia is one of the most inhospitable regions on earth.*

in·hu·man /ɪnˈhjuːmən/ *adjective* very cruel and bad: *inhuman acts of violence and terrorism*

in·hu·mane /ˌɪnhjuːˈmeɪn/ *adjective* inhumane conditions, treatment etc are cruel and not acceptable: *The animals are kept in inhumane conditions, without enough space or light.*

i·ni·tial[1] /ɪˈnɪʃəl/ *adjective* happening at the beginning: *There will be an initial period of training when you start the job.*
– **initially** *adverb*: *Initially, I didn't like him at all.*

initial[2] *noun* the first letter of a name: *His initials are EW – for Ed Williams.*

i·ni·tia·tive /ɪˈnɪʃətɪv/ *noun* [no plural] when you make decisions and do things without waiting for someone to tell you what to do: *We are looking for someone with imagination and initiative to join our sales team.*

in·ject /ɪnˈdʒekt/ *verb* to put a drug into someone's body, using a special needle: *The vaccine is injected into your upper arm.*

in·jec·tion /ɪnˈdʒekʃən/ *noun* when a drug is put into your body, using a special needle: *All children have several injections against tetanus.*

injection
needle

in·jure /ˈɪndʒə $ ˈɪndʒɚ/ *verb* to hurt someone and damage part of their body: *Ten people died, and eight more were injured in the crash.* ⇨ see usage note at HURT[1]
– **injured** *adjective*: *The injured passengers were taken to a nearby hospital.*

injury /ˈɪndʒəri/ *noun*, *plural* injuries
physical harm that someone gets in an accident or attack: *He was lucky to survive with only minor injuries.* | *Laura had internal injuries* (=injuries inside the body) *after the car accident.* | *Matt can't play basketball this season because of a knee injury.*

in·jus·tice /ɪnˈdʒʌstɪs/ *noun* when people are treated in a bad and unfair way: *There is so much poverty and injustice in the world.*

ink /ɪŋk/ *noun* a coloured liquid used for writing, printing, or drawing

in·land /ˈɪnlənd/ *adjective, adverb* away from the coast: *We visited some inland villages.* | *Lake Sabaya lies about six miles inland.*

in-laws /ˈ. ./ *plural noun informal* the parents of your husband or your wife: *We're spending Christmas with my in-laws this year.*

in·ner /ˈɪnə $ ˈɪnɚ/ *adjective* on the inside or near the centre of something: *the castle's inner walls* | *inner London*

inner cit·y /ˌ.. ˈ../ *noun, plural* inner cities the part of a city that is near the centre, especially the part where the buildings are in a bad condition and the people are poor: *the problem of crime in our inner cities*

in·ning /ˈɪnɪŋ/ *noun* one of the nine periods of play in a game of BASEBALL

in·nings /ˈɪnɪŋz/ *noun, plural* innings one of the periods of play in a game of CRICKET

in·no·cence /ˈɪnəsəns/ *noun* **1** the fact that someone is not guilty of a crime ⇨ opposite GUILT: *Her husband is the only one who believes in her innocence.* **2** when someone has not had much experience of life: *the innocence of a child*

in·no·cent /ˈɪnəsənt/ *adjective*

GRAMMAR
innocent of something
1 someone who is innocent has not done anything wrong ⇨ opposite GUILTY (2): *He says he is **innocent of** the murder.* | *The boy was the innocent victim of a gang attack.*
2 someone who is innocent does not not know about the bad things in life: *an innocent child*
– **innocently** *adverb*

in·noc·u·ous /ɪˈnɒkjuəs $ ɪˈnɑkjuəs/ *adjective formal* not likely to harm anyone or cause trouble: *It seemed like a fairly innocuous thing to say.*

in·no·va·tion /ˌɪnəˈveɪʃən/ *noun* an exciting new idea or method that people are using for the first time: *scientific and technological innovations*

in·put /'ɪnpʊt/ *noun [no plural]* the ideas and things that you do to make something succeed: *At the start of a project, everyone's input is very welcome.* | *Thanks for coming to the meeting, Julie – we value your input.*

in·quest /'ɪŋkwest/ *noun* an official process to try and discover why someone has died suddenly

in·quire also **enquire** *BrE* /ɪn-'kwaɪə $ ɪn'kwaɪɚ/ *verb formal*

> **GRAMMAR**
> **inquire about something**
> to ask someone for information: *I called to inquire about changes to the train schedules.*

in·quir·ing also **enquiring** *BrE* /ɪn-'kwaɪərɪŋ/ *adjective* someone who has an inquiring mind wants to learn new things: *a lively boy with a very inquiring mind*

in·quir·y also **enquiry** *BrE* /ɪn'kwaɪəri/ *noun, plural* **inquiries** **1** a question you ask in order to get information: *For further enquiries, please telephone this number.* **2** an official process to try and discover why something bad happened: *There will be a government inquiry into the causes of the disaster.*

in·quis·i·tive /ɪn'kwɪzətɪv/ *adjective* an inquisitive person or animal is very interested in everything: *Cats are very inquisitive animals.*

in·sane /ɪn'seɪn/ *adjective* **1** *informal* very stupid, and often dangerous: *Don't be insane! You can't possibly jump down from here!* **2** not able to think in a normal reasonable way

insects

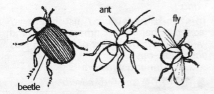

ant
fly
beetle

in·sect /'ɪnsekt/ *noun* any small creature that has six legs, for example a fly

in·se·cure /ˌɪnsɪ'kjʊə $ ˌɪnsɪ'kjʊr/ *adjective* someone who is insecure does not feel confident that other people like

them or confident about their ability to do something: *She was only seventeen and very insecure.*

in·sen·si·tive /ɪn'sensətɪv/ *adjective* someone who is insensitive does not notice other people's feelings and often does or says things that upset them ⇨ *opposite* SENSITIVE (1): *He can be rude and insensitive.* | *insensitive remarks about religion*

in·sep·a·ra·ble /ɪn'sepərəbəl/ *adjective* people who are inseparable are always together and are very friendly with each other: *As children, my brother and I were inseparable.*

in·sert /ɪn'sɜːt $ ɪn'sɜːt/ *verb written* to put something inside or into something else: *Insert the coins in the machine.*

insert

in·side¹ /ɪn'saɪd/ *preposition, adverb*
1 inside a container ⇨ *opposite* OUTSIDE¹: *Is there anything inside the box?* ⇨ *see picture on page 354*
2 in a building ⇨ *opposite* OUTSIDE¹: *The rooms inside the building have just been painted.* | *Let's go inside – it's cold.*

in·side² /ɪn'saɪd/ *noun* the inside the inner part of something: *The inside of the house was much bigger than I'd thought.* | *I bit the inside of my mouth.*

in·side³ /'ɪnsaɪd/ *adjective* on the inside of something: *My new jacket has three inside pockets.*

in·sight /'ɪnsaɪt/ *noun* when you can understand something clearly because you have done it, studied it etc: *The museum gave us a real insight into how people used to live.*

in·sig·nif·i·cant /ˌɪnsɪg'nɪfɪkənt/ *adjective* too small or unimportant to think or worry about ⇨ *opposite* SIGNIFICANT: *I felt small and insignificant beside all these important people.*

in·sin·cere /ˌɪnsɪn'sɪə $ ˌɪnsɪn'sɪr/ *adjective* someone who is insincere pretends to feel or think something that they do not really feel or think ⇨ *opposite* SINCERE: *What a horrible man, thought Maisie, giving him an insincere smile.*

in·sist /ɪnˈsɪst/ *verb*

> **GRAMMAR**
> **insist that**
> **insist on something**

1 to say firmly that something is true: *Don insisted that he hadn't gone out of the house at all.*
2 to say very strongly that you must do something, or that something must happen: *She insisted on paying for the meal herself.* | *"Please don't catch the bus home – I'll give you a lift," she insisted.* | *I insist that you leave the theatre immediately.*

in·sis·tence /ɪnˈsɪstəns/ *noun* [no plural] when you say very firmly that something must happen or be done: *My parents' insistence on good manners was a very good thing.*

in·sis·tent /ɪnˈsɪstənt/ *adjective* saying very firmly that something must happen or be done: *The teachers are all insistent that our homework is done on time.*

in·so·lent /ˈɪnsələnt/ *adjective* rude and not showing someone respect: *Don't be so insolent!*

in·sol·u·ble /ɪnˈsɒljəbəl $ɪnˈsɑljəbəl/ *adjective* an insoluble substance does not disappear when you mix it with water: *Sand is insoluble.*

in·som·ni·a /ɪnˈsɒmniə $ɪnˈsɑmniə/ *noun* [no plural] the problem you have when you often cannot sleep: *Dad's suffered from insomnia for years.*

in·spect /ɪnˈspekt/ *verb* to examine something carefully, especially as an official activity: *The city regularly inspects restaurants for health and safety reasons.*

in·spec·tion /ɪnˈspekʃən/ *noun* when you examine something carefully, especially as an official activity: *Officials completed their inspection of the new building.*

in·spec·tor /ɪnˈspektə $ɪnˈspektɚ/ *noun* **1** someone whose job is to discover whether something is being done in the correct way: *a school inspector* **2** a police officer of middle rank

in·spi·ra·tion /ˌɪnspəˈreɪʃən/ *noun* new ideas about what to do, or the feeling that you can do something: *These gardening programmes give people inspiration for their own homes.*

in·spire /ɪnˈspaɪə $ɪnˈspaɪɚ/ *verb* to make someone feel that they want to do or achieve something: *What exactly inspired you to go back to university at the age of forty?*

in·spired /ɪnˈspaɪəd $ɪnˈspaɪɚd/ *adjective* very skilful and special: *It was an inspired piece of football.*

in·stall /ɪnˈstɔːl/ *verb* to put a piece of equipment somewhere and connect it so that you can use it: *A plumber is coming to install the new washing machine today.*

in·stal·ment BrE, **installment** AmE /ɪnˈstɔːlmənt/ *noun* **1** a payment that you make every week, month etc in order to pay for something: *Would you like to pay for your sofa now or in instalments?* **2** one part of a long story that you can watch or read over a period of time on television, in a magazine etc: *Wait for next week's exciting instalment!*

in·stance /ˈɪnstəns/ *noun* **for instance** for example: *In many countries, for instance Japan, fish is a very important part of the diet.*

in·stant¹ /ˈɪnstənt/ *adjective*

1 something that is instant happens immediately and very quickly: *This type of camera gives you an instant picture.* | *We saw an instant improvement in Sheila's school-work.*
2 instant food can be prepared very quickly, for example because you just mix it with hot water: *instant coffee*
–**instantly** *adverb*: *The doorbell rang, and Joe jumped instantly out of his chair.*

instant² *noun* a very short period of time: *An instant later, the telephone rang.*

in·stan·ta·ne·ous /ˌɪnstənˈteɪniəs/ *adjective* happening immediately and very quickly: *The effect of the drug was instantaneous.*
–**instantaneously** *adverb*

in·stead /ɪnˈsted/ *adverb*

> **GRAMMAR**
> **instead of something**

in the place of someone or something else: *Use yogurt instead of cream and it will be lower in fat.* | *I decided to go in May instead.*

in·stil *BrE*, **instill** *AmE* /ɪnˈstɪl/ *verb* instilled, instilling to make someone think, feel, or behave in a particular way: *It's my job to instil confidence into the whole team.*

in·stinct /ˈɪnstɪŋkt/ *noun* a natural force that makes people or animals do something, without thinking or having to learn it: *All people and animals have a basic instinct to survive.* | *a woman's maternal instinct*

in·sti·tute /ˈɪnstɪtjuːt $ ˈɪnstəˌtuːt/ *noun* an organization where people are studying a particular thing, especially in science or education

in·sti·tu·tion /ˌɪnstɪˈtjuːʃən $ ˌɪnstə-ˈtuːʃən/ *noun* a large important organization such as a university or bank: *financial institutions* (=banks and other organizations that invest money)

in·struct /ɪnˈstrʌkt/ *verb* 1 to officially tell someone to do something: *The government instructed farmers to stop using the chemicals on their crops.* 2 to teach someone how to do something

in·struc·tion /ɪnˈstrʌkʃən/ *noun* information that tells you what to do: *Instructions on how to put the toy together are printed on the box.* | *Follow the instructions carefully.* | *The air stewardess gave us some instruction in using the oxygen masks.*

in·struc·tor /ɪnˈstrʌktə $ ɪnˈstrʌktər/ *noun* someone who teaches a particular activity or sport: *a driving instructor*

in·stru·ment /ˈɪnstrəmənt/ *noun* 1 something such as a piano, GUITAR etc that you play in order to make music: *Do you play any musical instruments?* | *Do you play any musical instruments?* 2 a special piece of equipment that you use to do a particular thing: *An airline pilot must learn how to use all these instruments.* | *medical instruments* ⇨ see usage note at MACHINE

in·stru·men·tal /ˌɪnstrəˈmentl/ *adjective* instrumental music is played on instruments, rather than sung by people's voices
– instrumental *noun*: *The next number the band played was an instrumental.*

in·suf·fi·cient /ˌɪnsəˈfɪʃənt/ *adjective* not enough: *The people here have insufficient food and water.*

in·su·late /ˈɪnsjəleɪt $ ˈɪnsəˌleɪt/ *verb* to cover or protect something with a material that stops electricity, sound, heat etc getting in or out: *Make sure you've insulated the pipes before the cold weather.*

in·su·lin /ˈɪnsjəlɪn $ ˈɪnsələn/ *noun* [no plural] a substance that your body makes so that it can use sugar for energy

in·sult[1] /ɪnˈsʌlt/ *verb* to say or do something rude to someone and offend them: *Sometimes he drinks too much wine, and then insults people.*

in·sult[2] /ˈɪnsʌlt/ *noun* something rude that you say that offends someone: *Rival supporters shouted insults at each other.*

in·sur·ance /ɪnˈʃʊərəns $ ɪnˈʃʊrəns/ *noun* [no plural] an arrangement in which you pay a company money and they pay the costs if you get ill, have an accident in your car etc: *How much does your car insurance cost each year?*

in·sure /ɪnˈʃʊə $ ɪnˈʃʊr/ *verb* 1 to buy or provide insurance for something: *Have you insured your house and its contents?* | *We can insure your car for less.* 2 an American spelling of ENSURE

in·tact /ɪnˈtækt/ *adjective* formal something that is intact is not broken or damaged: *Most of the houses were destroyed, but the church remained intact.*

in·take /ˈɪnteɪk/ *noun* formal 1 the amount of food, liquid etc that you eat or drink: *If you're on a diet, you should reduce your sugar intake.* 2 the number of people that join a school, profession etc at a particular time: *The school has an intake of about 100 children each year.*

in·te·gral /ˈɪntəgrəl/ *adjective* an integral part of something is an important and necessary part of it: *The new leisure centre will form an integral part of the city.*

in·te·grate /ˈɪntəgreɪt/ *verb* to become part of a group or a society, or to help someone do this: *Our neighbours have never really integrated into the local community.*

in·teg·ri·ty /ɪnˈtegrəti/ *noun* [no plural] the quality of being honest and sincere: *Mr Mandela is a man of great integrity.*

in·tel·lect /'ɪntəlekt/ *noun* a person's mind, the things they have learned, and their ability to understand things: *a brilliant intellect*

in·tel·lec·tual /ˌɪntə'lektʃuəl/ *adjective* related to your ability to think, learn, and understand ideas and information: *Mary's intellectual ability is very advanced for her age.*

in·tel·li·gence /ɪn'telədʒəns/ *noun* [no plural] the ability to understand things: *a person of above-average intelligence*

in·tel·li·gent /ɪn'telədʒənt/ *adjective*

someone who is intelligent is able to understand things quickly: *Lisa is very intelligent.* | *That's an intelligent question.*

in·tel·li·gi·ble /ɪn'telədʒəbəl/ *adjective* if something you read or hear is intelligible, you can understand it: *His spelling is poor but his handwriting is perfectly intelligible.*

in·tend /ɪn'tend/ *verb*

> **GRAMMAR**
> **intend to do something**
> **intend that**
> **be intended for something/someone**

1 to plan to do something: *I didn't intend to upset her.* | *We intend to install a lift for disabled people.* | *Pete had intended that I would see him with his new girlfriend.*
2 if something is intended for a particular purpose or person, it has been made especially for that purpose or person: *The film is intended for older children.* | *The extra money was intended as a way of encouraging job applicants.*

in·tense /ɪn'tens/ *adjective* a feeling, reaction etc that is intense is very strong: *He had an intense love of music.* | *The pain in my leg was intense.*

in·ten·si·fy /ɪn'tensəfaɪ/ *verb* intensified, intensifies to increase in strength, size, or amount, or to make something do this: *The pressure at work had slowly intensified.*

in·ten·sive /ɪn'tensɪv/ *adjective* an intensive course, activity etc involves a lot

of work or effort in a short time: *an intensive advertising campaign*

in·tent /ɪn'tent/ *adjective* if you are intent on doing something, you are determined to do it: *The team has been training hard and they're intent on winning.*

in·ten·tion /ɪn'tenʃən/ *noun* something that you plan to do: *My original intention was to study in America.*

in·ten·tion·al /ɪn'tenʃənəl/ *adjective* done deliberately: *The police seemed to think that the killings were intentional.*

in·ter·act /ˌɪntə'rækt/ *verb* to talk to people and make friends with them: *Children need to learn to interact with each other at an early age.*

in·ter·act·ive /ˌɪntə'ræktɪv/ *adjective* involving communication between a computer, television etc and the person who is using it: *interactive CD Roms* | *interactive video materials*

in·ter·cept /ˌɪntə'sept $ ˌɪntɚ'sept/ *verb* to stop someone or something that is moving from one place to another: *The aircraft was intercepted and shot down.*

in·ter·com /'ɪntəkɒm $ 'ɪntɚˌkɑm/ *noun* a system that people in a large building use to speak to people in other parts of the building: *They made the announcement over the intercom.*

in·terest¹ /'ɪntrəst/ *noun*

1 [no plural] the feeling that you want to know more about a subject or activity: *She has shown a lot of interest in learning ballet.* | *When Paul realized how much work was involved, he lost interest* (=stopped being interested).
2 **interests** your interests are the things that you enjoy doing: *We have similar interests.*
3 [no plural] money that you pay a bank when you borrow money from it, or that the bank pays you when you save money: *Some credit cards charge interest of up to 8%.* | *The account pays 6% interest.* | *Interest rates have gone up again.*

interest² *verb* if a subject, activity etc interests you, you want to know more about it: *Cooking doesn't interest me at all.*

in·ter·est·ed /'ɪntrəstɪd/ adjective

GRAMMAR
interested in something
interested in doing something
if you are interested in something, you want to do it more often or know more about it: *Jo has been interested in animals all her life.* | *Would you be interested in going to India this summer?* | *I can show you some other books, if you're interested.* | *I'd be interested to know whether she passes the exam.*

in·ter·est·ing /'ɪntrəstɪŋ/ adjective
unusual or exciting in a way that makes you think, and want to know more: *A good teacher can make any subject interesting.* | *There's a really interesting article about foxes in this month's 'Nature' magazine.*

in·ter·fere /ˌɪntə'fɪə $ ˌɪntɚ'fɪr/ verb

GRAMMAR
interfere in something
interfere with something
1 if someone interferes in a situation, they do something when other people do not want them to: *Her mother has interfered in our marriage from the beginning.*
2 if something interferes with something, it stops it continuing or developing properly: *Playing football must not interfere with your education.*

in·ter·fer·ence /ˌɪntə'fɪərəns $ ˌIntɚ'fɪrəns/ noun [no plural] 1 when someone interferes in something that you are doing or stops you working: *I prefer to work in the library, away from any interference.* 2 when bad weather makes it difficult to hear a radio signal or see a television programme

in·te·ri·or /ɪn'tɪəriə $ ɪn'tɪriɚ/ noun the inside part of something ⇨ opposite EXTERIOR: *I loved the outside of the house, but the interior was disappointing.*

in·ter·jec·tion /ˌɪntə'dʒekʃən $ ˌIntɚ'dʒekʃən/ noun a word or phrase that is used to express surprise, shock, pain etc. In the sentence "Ouch! That hurts!", 'ouch' is an interjection

in·ter·me·di·ate /ˌɪntə'miːdiət $ ˌIntɚ'miːdiət/ adjective an intermediate student has learned about a subject but is not very advanced: *classes for intermediate English students*

in·ter·mis·sion /ˌɪntə'mɪʃən $ ˌIntɚ'mɪʃən/ noun a short period of time when a play, film, game etc stops for a short time before starting again ⇨ same meaning INTERVAL BrE: *We had an ice-cream during the intermission.*

in·tern /'ɪntɜːn $ 'ɪntɚn/ noun AmE
1 someone who works without pay, so that they can learn how to do a job: *Kelly is working this summer as an intern for the senator.* 2 someone who has almost finished training as a doctor and is working in a hospital

in·ter·nal /ɪn'tɜːnl $ ɪn'tɚnl/ adjective on the inside or related to the inside of something ⇨ opposite EXTERNAL: *internal injuries*

in·ter·na·tion·al /ˌɪntə'næʃənəl $ ˌIntɚ'næʃənəl/ adjective involving or existing in many countries: *international football matches* | *an international bank*

In·ter·net /'ɪntənet $ 'ɪntɚˌnet/ noun the Internet a system that allows people using computers around the world to send and receive information: *You can find all the latest information on the Internet.*

in·ter·pret /ɪn'tɜːprɪt $ ɪn'tɚprɪt/ verb to say what someone has just said in one language in another language: *As Mr Bates doesn't speak Polish, I interpreted for him.*

in·ter·pret·er /ɪn'tɜːprɪtə $ ɪn'tɚprɪtɚ/ noun a person whose job is to say what someone has said in one language in another language: *Cairns, a fluent Japanese speaker, acted as interpreter.*

in·ter·ro·gate /ɪn'terəgeɪt/ verb to ask someone a lot of questions, often in an unpleasant way: *Forty people were arrested and interrogated by military police.*

in·ter·rog·a·tive /ˌɪntə'rɒgətɪv $ ˌɪntə'rɑgətɪv/ noun a word or sentence that asks a question
– interrogative adjective

in·ter·ro·gat·or /ɪn'terəgeɪtə $ ɪn'terəˌgeɪtɚ/ noun someone who tries to get information by asking lots of questions, often in an unpleasant way: *She managed to trick her interrogators and escape.*

in·ter·rupt /ˌɪntəˈrʌpt/ verb
1 to say something at the same time as someone else is speaking: *I tried to explain, but people kept interrupting me.* | *"I think you're wrong," interrupted Angela angrily.*
2 to stop something happening for a short time: *The war interrupted his studies.*

in·ter·rup·tion /ˌɪntəˈrʌpʃən/ noun
1 when someone says something while someone else is speaking: *She ignored my interruption, and carried on speaking.*
2 when something is stopped for a short time: *I need a place where I can work without interruption.*

in·ter·sec·tion /ˌɪntəˈsekʃən/ noun a place where two roads, lines etc meet, especially where they cross each other: *Meet me at the intersection of Main Street and Queen Street.*

in·ter·val /ˈɪntəvəl $ ˈɪntɚvəl/ noun
1 a period of time between one thing happening and another: *The buses come at ten-minute intervals.* 2 BrE an INTERMISSION

intervene

in·ter·vene /ˌɪntəˈviːn $ ˌɪntɚˈviːn/ verb to do something to try to stop an argument, problem, war etc: *I could hear them arguing, but decided not to intervene.*

in·ter·view¹ /ˈɪntəvjuː $ ˈɪntɚvju/ noun
1 a meeting in which one or more people ask you questions to discover whether you are suitable for something: *I've got a job interview this afternoon.* | *Do some research about the company before you go to the interview.* | *Could you come for an interview on Tuesday?* | Ad-

mission to Oxford University is by interview.
2 an occasion when someone asks a famous person lots of questions, and the famous person talks about themselves and their life: *In an interview with the newspaper, he discussed his marriage problems.* | *Bob Dylan says he hates giving interviews* (=being asked to talk a lot about himself).

interview² verb
to ask someone questions during an interview: *Later in the programme I will be interviewing the Prime Minister.* | *Fifteen people were interviewed for the job.*

in·ter·view·er /ˈɪntəvjuːə $ ˈɪntɚˌvjuɚ/ noun someone whose job is to interview famous people, especially on television or radio

in·tes·tine /ɪnˈtestɪn/ noun the long tube in your body that carries food away from your stomach

in·ti·mate /ˈɪntəmət/ adjective very private or personal: *She wrote all her most intimate thoughts in her diary.*

in·tim·i·date /ɪnˈtɪmədeɪt/ verb to frighten someone, especially so that they do what you want them to: *Some of the older boys were trying to intimidate him into giving them money.*

in·to /ˈɪntə, before vowels ˈɪntʊ; strong ˈɪntuː/ preposition
1 to the inside of a place or container: *Teresa ran into the house.* | *He packed his clothes into the suitcase.* ⇒ see picture on page 354
2 hitting something by accident: *He drove into another car.* | *He bumped into her desk.*
3 liking something a lot informal: *Ben's really into football.*
4 becoming a shape: *Can everyone please get into a straight line.*

in·tol·e·ra·ble /ɪnˈtɒlərəbəl $ ɪnˈtɑlərəbəl/ adjective very unpleasant or painful: *In the middle of the day, the heat was intolerable.*

in·tol·e·rant /ɪnˈtɒlərənt $ ɪnˈtɑlərənt/ adjective if someone is intolerant, they are not willing to accept ways of thinking and behaving that are different from their own ⇨ *opposite* TOLERANT: *People in this small village are intolerant of progress.*

in·tra·net /ˈɪntrənet/ *noun* a system for sending computer messages between people who work for the same company or organization, which is similar to the Internet but smaller

in·tran·si·tive /ɪnˈtrænsətɪv/ *noun* a verb that does not have an object. In the sentence, 'She was crying,' 'cry' is an intransitive

in·tri·cate /ˈɪntrɪkət/ *adjective* an intricate pattern or design has a lot of details or different parts: *intricate carved statues*

in·trigue /ɪnˈtriːg/ *verb* to interest someone a lot, especially by being strange or mysterious: *The story of the young girl who used to live in the house intrigued me.*

in·tro·duce /ˌɪntrəˈdjuːs $ˌɪntrəˈdus/ *verb*

GRAMMAR
introduce someone to someone
introduce someone to something

1 if you introduce people who are meeting for the first time, you tell them each other's names. If you introduce yourself to someone, you tell them your name: *Eric introduced me to his mother.* | *Please introduce yourself to the person sitting next to you.*
2 to make something happen or start to be used for the first time: *Nintendo introduced the game Pokémon in the late 1990s.*
3 to tell someone about something or show them something for the first time: *I wanted to introduce the kids to jazz.*

in·tro·duc·tion /ˌɪntrəˈdʌkʃən/ *noun*

GRAMMAR
an introduction to something

1 a short explanation at the beginning of a book or speech: *The author's wife wrote the introduction to the book.*
2 something that helps you understand the basic or easiest parts of a subject: *The course provides an introduction to computing.*
3 when you tell people who are meet-

ing for the first time each other's names: *There was no time for formal introductions.*
4 when people start using something new for the first time: *The introduction of MP3 will revolutionize the way we listen to music.*

in·tro·duc·to·ry /ˌɪntrəˈdʌktəri/ *adjective* 1 an introductory remark, CHAPTER etc comes at the beginning of something and introduces the subject: *an introductory lesson in Arabic* 2 an introductory price, offer etc is a cheap price that is available for a short time when something new is being sold: *The software is available at an introductory price of $175.*

in·tro·vert /ˈɪntrəvɜːt $ˈɪntrəˌvɜt/ *noun* someone who is quiet and shy ⇨ *opposite* EXTROVERT

in·tro·vert·ed /ˈɪntrəvɜːtɪd $ˈɪntrəˌvɜtɪd/ *adjective* quiet and shy: *Jake has always been a bit introverted.*

in·trude /ɪnˈtruːd/ *verb* to enter a place or become involved in a situation when you should not, because people do not want you to: *"I hope I'm not intruding,"* Mum said as she opened my bedroom door.

in·trud·er /ɪnˈtruːdə $ɪnˈtrudər/ *noun* someone who enters a building or area without permission or illegally: *The alarm will go off if there's an intruder.*

in·tu·i·tion /ˌɪntjuˈɪʃən $ˌɪntuˈɪʃən/ *noun* the feeling that you know something is correct or true, although you do not have any definite facts: *My intuition told me not to trust him.*

in·vade /ɪnˈveɪd/ *verb* to enter a country with an army in order to take control of it: *Hitler invaded Poland in 1939.*
– invader *noun*

in·va·lid¹ /ɪnˈvælɪd/ *adjective* not acceptable because of a law or rule: *This visa is invalid in this country.*

in·va·lid² /ˈɪnvəliːd $ˈɪnvələd/ *noun* someone who is very ill or old and needs other people to help them do things

in·val·u·a·ble /ɪnˈvæljuəbəl $ɪnˈvæljəbəl/ *adjective* very useful: *I gained invaluable experience while I was working abroad.*

in·var·i·a·bly /ɪnˈveəriəbli $ɪnˈveriəbli/ *adverb* almost always: *The trains are invariably late in the morning.*

in·va·sion /ɪnˈveɪʒən/ noun when a country's army enters another country in order to take control of it: *the Roman invasion of Britain*

in·vent /ɪnˈvent/ verb to think of or make something completely new: *Who invented the first computer?*

in·ven·tion /ɪnˈvenʃən/ noun **1** a completely new thing that someone invents: *They're always developing new inventions and fresh ways of doing things.* **2** [no plural] when someone invents something: *the invention of the telephone*

in·ven·tive /ɪnˈventɪv/ adjective good at thinking of new and interesting ideas: *an inventive solution to an old problem*

in·ven·tor /ɪnˈventə $ ɪnˈventər/ noun someone who thinks of or makes something completely new: *the inventor of the telephone, Alexander Graham Bell*

in·vert·ed com·mas /ɪnˌvɜːtɪd ˈkɒməz $ ɪnˌvɜːtɪd ˈkɑːməz/ plural noun BrE another word for QUOTATION MARKS

in·vest /ɪnˈvest/ verb if you invest money, you put it in a bank or buy something in order to get more money back later when you sell it: *He invested all his money in property.*
– **investor** noun: *Large investors such as banks have invested millions in the project.*

in·ves·ti·gate /ɪnˈvestəɡeɪt/ verb to try to discover the truth about something, especially a crime or accident: *Police are investigating the robbery.*

in·ves·ti·ga·tion /ɪnˌvestəˈɡeɪʃən/ noun an official attempt to discover the truth about something, especially a crime or accident: *There will be an investigation into the train crash.* | *The accident is still under investigation* (=being investigated).

in·vest·ment /ɪnˈvestmənt/ noun when you put money in a bank or buy something in order to get more money back later: *We need more investment in small businesses.*

in·vis·i·ble /ɪnˈvɪzəbəl/ adjective if something is invisible, you cannot see it: *Germs are invisible to humans.*

in·vi·ta·tion /ˌɪnvəˈteɪʃən/ noun

if you get an invitation, someone asks you if you would like to do something nice with them: *We got an invitation to their New Year's party.* | *I did receive an invitation to go, but I will be on holiday.* | *Have you sent the party invitations yet?*

in·vite¹ /ɪnˈvaɪt/ verb

to ask someone to go somewhere, or to do something with you: *Are you going to invite your ex-boyfriend to your birthday party?* | *We were invited over to the Smiths' house for supper.* | *Parents are invited to come to the school and meet the teachers.*

invite in
invite someone in to ask someone to come into your house: *I didn't invite him in because the place was such a mess.*

in·vit·ing /ɪnˈvaɪtɪŋ/ adjective something that is inviting looks nice and makes you want to enjoy it: *The swimming pool looked very inviting.*

in·voice /ˈɪnvɔɪs/ noun a list showing how much money you must pay for things you have received or work that has been done: *You haven't paid these invoices.*

in·volve /ɪnˈvɒlv $ ɪnˈvɑːlv/ verb

1 if something involves you, it includes or affects you: *The celebrations will involve thousands of people across the country.* | *The band like to involve the audience in their performances.*
2 if one thing involves another thing, it includes that thing as a necessary part of it: *Success always involves hard work.* | *Her job involves helping students with their problems.*

in·volved /ɪnˈvɒlvd $ ɪnˈvɑːlvd/

adjective if you are involved in an activity or event, you take part in it: *Were you involved in the fight?*

in·volve·ment /ɪn'vɒlvmənt $ɪn-'vɑlvmənt/ *noun [no plural]* when someone takes part in an activity or event: *They thanked us for our involvement in the project.*

in·wards /'ɪnwədz $'ɪnwɚdz/ BrE, **in·ward** /'ɪnwəd $'ɪnwɚd/ AmE, *adverb* towards the inside of something ➪ opposite OUTWARDS: *The windows open inwards.*

IPA /ˌaɪ piː 'eɪ/ the abbreviation for International Phonetic Alphabet; a system of signs showing the sounds made in speech

i·rate /ˌaɪ'reɪt/ *adjective* formal very angry: *An irate customer complained to the manager.*

irk /ɜːk $ɝk/ *verb* written to annoy someone: *It irks me how he never helps his mother.*

i·ron¹ /'aɪən $'aɪɚn/ *noun* **1** a common heavy strong metal that is used to make steel: *an iron gate* | *The table and chairs were made of iron.* **2** a piece of electrical equipment that you heat and press onto your clothes to make them smooth: *Be careful with that hot iron.*

iron² *verb* to make clothes smooth using an iron: *Did you iron my shirt?*

i·ron·ic /aɪ'rɒnɪk $aɪ'rɑnɪk/ *adjective* if you are ironic, you mean the opposite of what you say, in order to be amusing or show that you are annoyed: *I think when he said "Thanks a lot" he was being ironic.*

i·ron·ing /'aɪənɪŋ $'aɪɚnɪŋ/ *noun [no plural]* when you use an iron to make your clothes smooth: *I've done the ironing.*

i·ron·y /'aɪrəni/ *noun* **1** *[no plural]* a way of saying something that shows that you mean the opposite of what you say: *There was a note of irony in his voice.* **2** an unusual or surprising part of a situation that seems strange or amusing because it is not what you expected: *The irony was that the more the media criticized the film, the more the audiences liked it.*

ir·ra·tion·al /ɪ'ræʃənəl/ *adjective* irrational feelings and behaviour are not sensible or reasonable: *She has an irrational fear of mice.*
– **irrationally** *adverb*

ir·reg·u·lar /ɪ'regjələ $ɪ'regjələr/ *adjective* **1** not happening at regular times: *They have their meals at irregular times.* **2** not following the usual rules in grammar: *an irregular verb*

ir·rel·e·vant /ɪ'reləvənt/ *adjective* something that is irrelevant is not important because it has no effect in a particular situation ➪ opposite RELEVANT: *She thinks my opinion is irrelevant.*

ir·re·sist·i·ble /ˌɪrɪ'zɪstəbəl/ *adjective* impossible not to want, like, enjoy etc: *The chocolate cake was irresistible.*

ir·re·spon·si·ble /ˌɪrɪ'spɒnsəbəl $ˌɪrɪ-'spɑnsəbəl/ *adjective* behaving in a careless way, without thinking of the bad results you might cause: *It's irresponsible to leave small children alone.*

ir·re·vers·i·ble /ˌɪrɪ'vɜːsəbəl $ˌɪrɪ-'vɚsəbəl/ *adjective* if something that has been done is irreversible, it is impossible to change it back to the way it was before ➪ opposite REVERSIBLE (1): *The power cut caused irreversible damage to our computer system.*

ir·ri·ta·ble /'ɪrətəbəl/ *adjective* an irritable person gets annoyed quickly: *She gets irritable when she's tired.*

ir·ri·tate /'ɪrəteɪt/ *verb* to annoy someone: *Her little sister really irritates me.*
– **irritating** *adjective*: *What's that irritating noise?*

is /z, s, əz; strong ɪz/ the third person singular of the present tense of BE

Is·lam /'ɪslɑːm/ *noun [no plural]* the religion that was started by Muhammed and whose holy book is the Koran

Is·lam·ic /ɪz'læmɪk/ *adjective* related to Islam: *Islamic traditions* | *the Islamic faith*

is·land /'aɪlənd/ *noun* a piece of land that is completely surrounded by water: *Britain is an island.* ➪ see picture on page 348

isle /aɪl/ *noun* used in the names of some islands: *Jersey is one of the Channel Isles.*

is·n't /'ɪzənt/ the short form of 'is not': *The hotel isn't far.*

i·so·late /'aɪsəleɪt/ *verb* to keep one person or thing separate from others: *We isolate dangerous prisoners in another part of the prison.*

i·so·lat·ed /'aɪsəleɪtɪd/ *adjective* far away from other places or people: *He lives in an isolated village.* | *Working away from your home and family makes you feel isolated.*

i·so·la·tion /ˌaɪsəˈleɪʃən/ *noun* [no plural] a feeling of being lonely: *Moving to a new town can lead to a sense of isolation.*

is·sue¹ /ˈɪʃuː/ *noun*

1 an important subject or problem that people discuss: *The environment is an issue which is very important to young people.*
2 a magazine or newspaper printed for a particular day, week, or month: *Have you seen this month's issue of 'Wired'?*

issue² *verb* 1 to make an official statement or give an order or warning: *The government issued a warning about British beef.* 2 to officially give people something they need to do a particular job: *All staff are issued with a special uniform.*

IT /ˌaɪ ˈtiː/ the abbreviation of INFORMATION TECHNOLOGY

it /ɪt/ *pronoun*

1 used when talking about a thing: *Where's my mobile phone? I left it here a minute ago.* | *If you've lost your homework, you'll have to do it all again.*
2 used when talking about the weather, time, or date: *It's raining.* | *I hope it stays sunny.* | *It's nearly ten o'clock.* | *It's the twenty-first of June today.*
3 used when talking about an action or situation: *It was nice seeing her again* (=seeing her again was nice). | *It seemed unkind to tell her the truth.* | *It would be awful if she died.* | *It's nice and warm in here.* | *I hated it at school* (=I hated being at school).
4 used when asking or saying which person has done something: *It was me who told them.* | *"Who was that on the phone?" "It was Lauren."*

i·tal·ics /ɪˈtælɪks/ *plural noun* a style of printed letters that slope to the right: *The examples in this dictionary are written in italics.*

itch¹ /ɪtʃ/ *verb* to have an unpleasant feeling on your skin that makes you want to rub it with your hand: *Woollen clothes make me itch.*

itch² *noun, plural* **itches** a slightly unpleasant feeling on your skin that makes

you want to rub it with your hand: *I've got an itch on my nose.*

itch·y /ˈɪtʃi/ *adjective* **itchier, itchiest** if your skin is itchy, it feels slightly unpleasant and you want to rub it with your hand

it'd /ˈɪtəd/ the short form of 'it would' or 'it had': *You said it'd be a short film.* | *It'd be good to live in America.*

i·tem /ˈaɪtəm/ *noun* one thing in a set, group, or list: *What's the first item on the shopping list?*

i·tin·e·ra·ry /aɪˈtɪnərəri $ aɪˈtɪnəˌreri/ *noun, plural* **itineraries** a plan or list of the places you will visit on a trip: *The first stop on our itinerary is Rome.*

it'll /ˈɪtl/ the short form of 'it will': *It'll be a great party.*

it's /ɪts/ the short form of 'it is' or 'it has': *It's time to go.* | *It's fallen down again.*

its /ɪts/
belonging to a thing or animal: *He put the game back in its box.* | *The dog wagged its tail.*

USAGE its, it's

Its as a possessive form does not have (') before the 's': *The dog broke its leg jumping the wall.* When it is written with ('), it means 'it is' or 'it has': *It's raining.* | *It's been raining all day.*

---

it·self /ɪtˈself/ *pronoun*

1 used when the same thing or animal does an action and receives the action: *The machine switches itself off when it is not being used.*
2 emphasizing that you are talking about one particular thing: *The building itself is in good condition, but it needs decorating.* | *The lesson itself was quite boring, but I enjoyed the discussion afterwards.*

PHRASE
by itself alone, or with no one helping: *Did the radio go on by itself?*

I've /aɪv/ the short form of 'I have': *I've got an idea.*

i·vo·ry /ˈaɪvəri/ *noun* the hard smooth white substance that the TUSKs (=the two large front teeth) of an ELEPHANT are made of

i·vy /ˈaɪvi/ *noun* a plant with dark green shiny leaves that grows on the walls of buildings: *The cottage was covered in ivy.*

Jj

jab¹ /dʒæb/ *verb* **jabbed, jabbing** to push something pointed into or towards something else with short quick movements: *I jabbed him in the arm with my pen.*

jab² *noun* **1** a sudden hard push, especially with a pointed object: *I felt a jab in my arm.* **2** *BrE informal* an INJECTION: *I have to have a yellow fever jab.*

jack /dʒæk/ *noun* a playing card with a picture of a young man on it: *Do you have the jack of diamonds?*

jack·et /'dʒækɪt/ *noun* a short light coat: *I like your leather jacket.* ⇨ *see picture on page 352*

jack·pot /'dʒækpɒt/ $'dʒækpɑt/ *noun* a large amount of money that you can win: *The lottery jackpot is £3 million.*

ja·ded /'dʒeɪdɪd/ *adjective* if you feel jaded, you are no longer excited about something because you are tired of it or it no longer interests you: *She felt jaded after the long journey.*

jag·ged /'dʒæg-ɪd/ *adjective* something that is jagged has a rough edge with sharp points: *The rocks were very jagged.*

jagged

jail also **gaol** *BrE* /dʒeɪl/ *noun* a place where criminals are kept as a punishment ⇨ *same meaning* PRISON: *The murderer is still in jail.*

jam¹ /dʒæm/ *noun* a thick sticky sweet food made from fruit: *strawberry jam*

jam² *verb* **jammed, jamming 1** to push something into a small space using force: *I jammed all my things into the bag.* **2** if a machine or door jams, it no longer works because something is stopping one of its parts from moving: *The fax machine has jammed again.*

jan·gle /'dʒæŋgəl/ *verb* to make a noise that sounds like metal objects hitting against each other: *I could hear his keys jangling.*
— **jangle** *noun*: *the jangle of heavy jewellery*

jan·i·tor /'dʒænətə $'dʒænətɚ/ the American word for CARETAKER

Jan·u·a·ry /'dʒænjuəri $'dʒænju,eri/ *written abbreviation* **Jan** *noun* the first month of the year: *It's very cold here in January.* | *His birthday is on January 11th.*

jar /dʒɑː $dʒɑr/ *noun* a round glass container with a lid, used for storing food: *a jar of marmalade* ⇨ *see picture at* CONTAINER

jar·gon /'dʒɑːgən $'dʒɑrgən/ *noun* [no plural] words and phrases that people doing the same type of work use and that other people find difficult to understand: *I can't make any sense of these documents – they're written in legal jargon.*

jav·e·lin /'dʒævəlɪn/ *noun* [no plural] a sport in which you throw a long pointed stick as far as you can

jaw /dʒɔː/ *noun* the bottom part of your face that contains the two bones that your teeth grow in: *My jaw hurts when I eat.*

jazz /dʒæz/ *noun* [no plural] a type of music with a strong beat

jeal·ous /'dʒeləs/ *adjective* **1** angry or unhappy because you want something that someone else has: *She gets jealous when her sister gets new clothes.* **2** angry or unhappy because you think that someone you love likes or loves another person: *She went out with Paul to make Steve jealous.*

jeal·ous·y /'dʒeləsi/ *noun* the feeling of being jealous: *He killed his wife's lover out of jealousy.*

J

jeans /dʒiːnz/ *plural noun* a popular type of trousers made from DENIM: *He was wearing an old pair of jeans.* ⇨ see picture on page 352

Jeep /dʒiːp/ *noun trademark* a vehicle for travelling over rough ground: *They travelled into the bush in a Jeep.*

jeer /dʒɪə $ dʒɪr/ *verb* to say rude things to someone or laugh at them: *The crowed jeered and booed him.*
— **jeer** *noun*: *the angry jeers of demonstrators*

Jell-O /'dʒeləʊ $ 'dʒeloʊ/ *trademark* the American word for JELLY

jel·ly /'dʒeli/ *noun* **1** BrE a soft sweet solid food made with fruit juice that shakes when you move it; Jello AmE: *Kids love jelly and ice-cream.* **2** [no plural] AmE the American word for JAM: *a peanut butter and jelly sandwich*

jerk /dʒɜːk $ dʒɜrk/ *verb* to move with a sudden quick movement: *I jerked the child out of the way.*
— **jerk** *noun*: *He woke up with a jerk.*

jerk·y /'dʒɜːki $ 'dʒɜrki/ *adjective* **jerkier, jerkiest** jerky movements are rough and sudden, not smooth: *We had a very jerky ride in his car.*

jer·sey /'dʒɜːzi $ 'dʒɜrzi/ *noun* a shirt made of soft material: *I need a new football jersey.*

jet /dʒet/ *noun* **1** a very fast plane: *He has his own private jet.* ⇨ see picture on page 349 **2** a thin stream of gas or liquid that is forced out of a small hole: *A jet of water came from the hosepipe.*

jet lag /'. ./ *noun* [no plural] the feeling of being very tired after a long journey in a plane: *Do you get jet-lag after a long flight?*

jet·ty /'dʒeti/ *noun, plural* **jetties** a wide stone or wooden structure used for getting on and off boats: *He got off the boat onto a little wooden jetty.* ⇨ see picture on page 348

Jew /dʒuː/ *noun* someone whose religion is Judaism

jew·el /'dʒuːəl/ *noun* a valuable stone, such as a DIAMOND: *The crown is covered in precious jewels.*

jew·el·ler BrE, **jeweler** AmE /'dʒuːələ $ 'dʒuːələr/ *noun* someone who sells or makes jewellery: *The jeweller fixed my watch.*

jew·el·lery BrE, **jewelry** AmE /'dʒuːəlri/ *noun* things that you wear for decor-

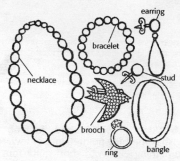

jewellery

ation, such as rings and NECKLACEs: *She wears a lot of gold jewellery.*

Jew·ish /'dʒuːɪʃ/ *adjective* related to Judaism

jibe¹ or **gibe** /dʒaɪb/ *noun* something that you say that criticizes someone or makes them seem silly: *She's always making jibes about my weight.*

jig·saw /'dʒɪgsɔː/ also **jigsaw puz·zle** /'.. ,../ *noun* a game consisting of a picture that has been cut up into many small pieces that you try to fit together again: *Let's do a jigsaw.*

jilt /dʒɪlt/ *verb informal* to suddenly end a romantic relationship with someone: *She jilted him the day before their wedding.*

jin·gle¹ /'dʒɪŋgəl/ *verb* if metal objects jingle, they hit each other, making a noise like small bells: *The coins jingled in his pockets.*
— **jingle** *noun*: *I heard the jingle of bells.*

jit·ter·y /'dʒɪtəri/ *adjective* worried and nervous: *I get very jittery about going to the dentist.*

job /dʒɒb $ dʒɑb/ *noun*

1 your job is work that you do regularly in order to earn money: *Teaching is an interesting job.* | *I had to get a job to pay the rent.* | *I started applying for jobs* (=writing to companies, businesses etc to ask for a job) *as soon as I left college.* | *Graham found a job* (=got a job) *at a local farm.* | *Mark lost his job* (=did not have a job any more) *when the factory closed.* | *Looking for a job* is worse than working. | *a well-paid job*

2 a piece of work that you must do: *Dad asked me to do a few jobs* around the house. | *It's not **my job** to clean your bedroom.*

PHRASES

out of a job not having a job, although you want one: *How long have you been **out of a job**?*

do a good job, do a great job etc to do something very well: *The people who organised the party **did a fantastic job**.*

make a good job of something, make a bad job of something *BrE* to do something well or badly: *She **made a good job** of painting the house.*

it's a good job *BrE spoken* used to say that a situation is fortunate: *It's a good job I'm not vegetarian because all they had to eat was burgers.*

USAGE job, work, occupation, profession
Work is what you do to earn money: *What kind of work does he do?* A **job** is the particular type of work that you do: *Sam's got a job as a waiter.* **Job** can be plural but **work** cannot. **Occupation** is a formal or written word for the type of work you do: *Please state your occupation.* A **profession** is a job such as a doctor, teacher, or lawyer, for which you need a university education and special training: *My parents wanted me to go into the legal profession, but I wanted to be an actor.* A **career** is a professional job that you do for most of your working life: *He's interested in a career in banking.*

jock·ey /ˈdʒɒki $ ˈdʒɑːki/ *noun* someone who rides horses in races: *The jockey was injured when he fell off his horse.*

jog /dʒɒg $ dʒɑːg/   **jog**
verb **jogged, jogging** **1** to run slowly, especially for exercise: *Two girls were jogging around the park.* ➪ *see picture on page 340* **2 jog someone's memory** to make someone remember something that they had forgotten: *A photo might jog your memory about the man.*

jog·ging /ˈdʒɒgɪŋ $ ˈdʒɑːgɪŋ/ *noun* [no

plural] when you run for exercise: *I go jogging every morning.*

join¹ /dʒɔɪn/ *verb*

GRAMMAR
join (things) together

1 to become a member of an organization or group: *Helen has joined a running club to try and get fit.* | *Pete's thinking of joining the army.*

2 if two things join, they come together and are connected in some way: *This is where the pipe joins the tank.* | *The road joins the motorway at Bridge Lane.* | *Several tribal groups **joined together** to fight the soldiers.*

3 if you join two things, you connect them or fasten them together: ***Join** the two pieces of string **together**.*

4 to go somewhere to do something with someone else: *Trevor will join his older brother at university in September.* | *Will you join me in a glass of wine* (=I'm having a glass of wine – would you like one too)?

PHRASAL VERBS
join in
join in, join in something to begin to do an activity with other people: *Everyone started singing, but I didn't feel like **joining in**.* | *Are you going to **join in** the dancing?*
join together
if two organizations join together, they become one organization

join² *noun* a place where two parts of an object join: *You can see the joins in the wallpaper.*

joint¹ /dʒɔɪnt/ *adjective* shared, owned by, or involving two or more people: *This was a joint decision between me and Jo.* | *"Who made the cake?" "It was a joint effort* (=we all helped to make it)."
–**jointly** *adverb: Sam and I own the house jointly.*

joint² *noun* a part of your body where two bones meet: *I've damaged my knee joint.*

joke¹ /dʒəʊk $ dʒoʊk/ *noun*

something funny that you say to make people laugh: *He keeps **making jokes** about my hair.* | *I heard a **funny joke** the other day.* | *He **told a joke** about a man who lost his dog.*

J

get the joke, see the joke: *Sorry, but I just don't **get the joke*** (=understand why the joke is funny).

play a joke on someone to trick someone to make people laugh: *He only bought it to **play a joke on** his friends.*

joke² *verb*

GRAMMAR
joke about something/someone

1 to say funny things to make people laugh: *They all **joke about** the way he speaks.*
2 to say something without meaning it: *I didn't mean to upset you – I was **only joking.***

jol·ly /'dʒɒli $ 'dʒɑli/ *adjective* **jollier, jolliest** happy and cheerful: *It's Christmas so everyone's very jolly.*

jolt /dʒəʊlt $ dʒoʊlt/ *verb* to move suddenly and roughly: *The car jolted forward.*
– jolt *noun: He sat up with a jolt.*

jos·tle /'dʒɒsəl $ 'dʒɑsəl/ *verb* to push against other people in a crowd: *We all jostled towards the front of the stage.*

jot /dʒɒt $ dʒɑt/ *verb* **jotted, jotting; jot something down** to write something quickly on a piece of paper: *Can you jot down your address?*

jour·nal /'dʒɜːnl $ 'dʒɝnl/ *noun* a serious magazine about a particular subject: *I read about the disease in a medical journal.*

jour·nal·is·m /'dʒɜːnəlɪzəm $ 'dʒɝnl,ɪzəm/ *noun* [no plural] the job of writing reports for newspapers, magazines, television, or radio: *I'm interested in a career in journalism.*

jour·nal·ist /'dʒɜːnəlɪst $ 'dʒɝnlɪst/ *noun* someone who writes reports for newspapers, magazines, television, or radio: *There's a journalist on the phone – he wants to interview you.*

jour·ney /'dʒɜːni $ 'dʒɝni/ *noun*

a trip from one place to another, especially in a car or other vehicle: *How long does your journey to school take?* | *I've made several journeys to Ireland already this year.* | *I met him on a train journey.*
⇨ *see usage note at* TRAVEL²

joy /dʒɔɪ/ *noun* a feeling of great happiness and pleasure: *My heart filled with joy when I heard the news.*

joy·ful /'dʒɔɪfəl/ *adjective* formal very happy: *The wedding was a very joyful occasion.*

joy·rid·er /'dʒɔɪ,raɪdə $ 'dʒɔɪ,raɪdɚ/ *noun* someone who steals a car and drives it in a fast and dangerous way

joy·rid·ing /'dʒɔɪ,raɪdɪŋ/ *noun* [no plural] when someone steals a car and drives it in a fast and dangerous way: *He was arrested for joyriding.*

joy·stick /'dʒɔɪ,stɪk/ *noun* a handle used to control a computer game

Ju·da·is·m /'dʒuːdeɪ-ɪzəm $ 'dʒudi,ɪzəm/ *noun* [no plural] the religion that was started in Israel in ancient times, and that is based on a collection of writings and laws. People who believe in Judaism are JEWS

judge¹ /dʒʌdʒ/ *noun*

1 the person in a law court who decides what punishment a criminal should get: *The judge sentenced him to one year in prison.*
2 someone who decides who has won a competition: *The judges decided that Mary's painting was the best.*

judge² *verb*

GRAMMAR
judge someone on something

1 to decide something or form an opinion about someone or something: *It's not right to **judge** him **on** that one exam result.* | *Here are the two pictures – **judge for yourself** (=you decide) which one you prefer.*
2 to decide who has won a competition: *Mrs Taylor will judge the poetry competition.*

PHRASE
judging by something, judging from something used when you are giving a reason for something that you are saying: ***Judging by** his reaction, he still loves Sara.*

judg·ment or **judgement** /'dʒʌdʒmənt/ *noun* **1** [no plural] the ability to make sensible decisions: *Tracy has very good judgment.* **2** a legal decision made by a judge in a court of law: *The judge will give his judgment tomorrow.*

J

ju·do /'dʒuːdəʊ $ 'dʒudoʊ/ *noun* [*no plural*] a sport from Japan in which you try to throw your opponent onto the ground

jug /dʒʌg/ *noun* a container used for pouring liquids: *a jug of water*

jug·gle /'dʒʌgəl/ *verb* to keep objects moving through the air by throwing and catching them very quickly: *He juggled three oranges.*

juggle

juice /dʒuːs/ *noun* the liquid from fruit or vegetables, or a drink made from this: *a glass of **orange juice** | I'd like a **tomato juice**, please.* ⇨ *see picture on page 344*

juic·y /'dʒuːsi/ *adjective* **juicier, juiciest** food that is juicy contains a lot of juice: *a nice, crisp, juicy apple*

Ju·ly /dʒʊ'laɪ/ *written abbreviation* **Jul** *noun* the seventh month of the year: *We got married last July. | It's Saturday 3rd July.*

jum·ble¹ /'dʒʌmbəl/ *noun* an untidy group of things: *The clothes lay in a jumble on her bed.*

jumble² also **jumble up** *verb* to mix things together so that they become untidy: *You've jumbled all my CDs up.*

jum·bo /'dʒʌmbəʊ $ 'dʒʌmboʊ/ *adjective informal* larger than other things of the same type: *jumbo sausages*

jumbo jet /ˌ.. ˌ./ *noun* a very big plane that carries many passengers: *I went to New York on a jumbo jet.*

jump

jump¹ /dʒʌmp/ *verb*

GRAMMAR
jump off/into/out of something
jump over something

1 to push yourself off the ground using your legs: *Jordan jumped but the ball flew over his head. | A man **jumped off** the bridge into the river.* ⇨ *see picture on page 340*

2 to get over something by jumping: *He **jumped over** the gate and ran off. | None of the horses managed to jump the fence.*

3 to move somewhere quickly and suddenly: *When the police arrived, the two men **jumped in** the car and drove off. | She **jumped out of** bed.*

PHRASES

make someone jump if something makes you jump, it makes you feel suddenly afraid: *A loud bang in the street **made me jump**.*

jump at the chance, jump at the opportunity to accept an opportunity as soon as you get it: *I would **jump at the chance of** going out with Peter.*

jump² *noun* when you push yourself off the ground using your legs

jump·er /'dʒʌmpə $ 'dʒʌmpɚ/ *noun BrE* a piece of clothing made of wool that covers the upper part of your body and your arms ⇨ *same meaning* SWEATER ⇨ *see picture on page 352*

junc·tion /'dʒʌŋkʃən/ *noun* a place where roads or railway lines join: *a very busy motorway junction*

June /dʒuːn/ *written abbreviation* **Jun** *noun* the sixth month of the year: *We're going on holiday in June. | On the 7th of June, I'll be fifteen.*

jun·gle /'dʒʌŋgəl/ *noun* a large tropical forest with trees and large plants growing very close together

ju·ni·or¹ /'dʒuːniə $ 'dʒunjɚ/ *adjective* a junior person has a low rank in an organization or profession: *Junior members of staff cannot use this dining room.*

junior² *noun* **1** *AmE* a student in the third year of HIGH SCHOOL or college **2** *BrE* a child who goes to a junior school

junior col·lege /ˌ... '../ *noun* a college in the US or Canada where students do a course for two years

junior high school /ˌ... '. ./ also **junior high** /ˌ... './ *noun* a school in the US or Canada for students who are between 12 and 15 years old

junior school /'... ˌ./ *noun* a school in

Britain for children between the ages of 7 and 11: *I learnt all this stuff in junior school.*

junk /dʒʌŋk/ *noun* [no plural] *informal* old things that have no use or value: *Let's get rid of some of this junk.*

junk food /'. ./ *noun* [no plural] *informal* food that is not healthy because it contains a lot of fat or sugar: *You eat too much junk food.*

junk mail /'. ./ *noun informal* letters that companies send to your house to tell you about the things they sell: *I get far too much junk mail, and most of goes in the bin.*

ju·ror /'dʒʊərə $'dʒʊrɚ/ *noun* a member of a jury: *The jurors must decide whether or not he is guilty.*

ju·ry /'dʒʊəri $'dʒʊri/ *noun*, *plural* **juries**
1 a group of people in a court who decide whether someone is guilty of a crime: *Has the jury reached its verdict?*
2 a group of people who choose the winner of a competition: *Here are the votes of the French jury.*

just¹ /dʒəst; *strong* dʒʌst/ *adverb*
1 only: *It's not serious – it's just a scratch.* | *Calls cost just five pence a minute.* | *I just wanted to say I'm sorry.*
2 only a short time ago: *I've just had a very odd experience.* | *She had just driven off when I realized she'd left her purse behind.*
3 doing something now: *"Have you done all your packing?" "I'm just doing it."* | *I'm just on my way there now.*
4 used to show that you achieve something, but almost do not manage it: *I just managed to catch the bottle before it hit the ground.* | *I just passed the test.*
5 *spoken* used for emphasizing something you are saying: *It just doesn't seem possible.* | *I just knew that was going to happen!*

PHRASES
just before, just after etc a short time before, after etc: *I got home just after twelve o'clock.*
just behind, just in front of etc a short way behind, in front of etc: *Emma was sitting just behind me.*

just like exactly like: *Jo looks just like her sister.*
just as good, just as big etc equally as good, big etc: *This computer is just as good as the other one.*
just as at the very time you are doing something: *Just as I was leaving, the phone rang.*
just about to, just going to going to do something very soon: *I was just about to have a bath when Steve called round.*
just a second, just a minute *spoken* used to ask someone to wait for a short time: *Just a minute – you forgot your receipt.*
just now **a)** a very short time ago: *When I saw him just now he seemed a bit upset.* **b)** now: *Things are a bit complicated just now.*
it's just as well *spoken* used to say that something is lucky: *It's just as well you didn't give him any money.*

just² /dʒʌst/ *adjective formal* morally right and fair: *Is this a just war?*

jus·tice /'dʒʌstəs/ *noun* [no plural]
1 when people are treated in a way that is fair and right: *We are fighting for justice for everyone.*
2 the laws of a country and how they are used: *This sentence is a miscarriage of justice* (=a legal decision that is wrong).

jus·ti·fi·a·ble /'dʒʌstə,faɪəbəl $,dʒʌstə'faɪəbəl/ *adjective* if a feeling or action is justifiable, you feel it or do it for a good reason: *She has justifiable pride in her son.*

jus·ti·fi·ca·tion /,dʒʌstəfə'keɪʃən/ *noun* a good reason for doing something: *There's no justification for violence.*

jus·ti·fied /'dʒʌstəfaɪd/ *adjective* if something is justified, there are good reasons for it: *Her criticism is justified.*

jus·ti·fy /'dʒʌstəfaɪ/ *verb* **justified**, **justifies** to give a good reason for doing something that other people think is unreasonable: *He keeps trying to justify his bad behaviour.*

ju·ve·nile /'dʒuːvənaɪl $'dʒuvənl/ *adjective formal* related to young people: *There has been an increase in juvenile crime.*

Kk

kan·ga·roo /ˌkæŋgə'ruː/ *noun* a large Australian animal that moves by jumping and carries its babies in a special place on its stomach

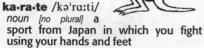
kangaroo

ka·ra·te /kə'rɑːti/ *noun* [no plural] a sport from Japan in which you fight using your hands and feet

keen /kiːn/ *adjective*

> **GRAMMAR**
> **keen to do something**
> **keen on doing something**
> **keen on something**

1 if you are keen to do something, you want to do it very much: *She seemed **keen to** meet my brother.*
2 If you are keen on doing something, or keen on it, you like doing it: *She's not very **keen on** going out to clubs.* | *a keen gardener*

keep ⇨ *see box on next page*

ken·nel /'kenl/ *noun* a small outdoor house for a dog to sleep in

kept /kept/ the past tense and past participle of KEEP

kerb *BrE*, **curb** *AmE* /kɜːb $ kɝb/ *noun* the edge of the PAVEMENT, where it joins the road: *You're driving too close to the kerb.* ⇨ *see picture on page 343*

ketch·up /'ketʃəp/ *noun* [no plural] a thick liquid made from TOMATOES that you put on food: *Do you want ketchup on your burger?*

ket·tle /'ketl/ *noun* a container with a lid that you use to boil water in: *I'll put the kettle on* (=make it start boiling water, usually to make a hot drink).

key¹ /kiː/ *noun*

1 a small object with a special shape that you use to open or close a lock, for example on a door or in a car: *This is the key for the front door.* | *I can't find my **house keys** (=the keys to lock or unlock the door on my house).* | *I turned the key but the car wouldn't start.*

key
key
keyring
keyhole

2 one of the parts of a KEYBOARD on a computer or piano that you press to make it work: *Where's the **'Shift' key** on your PC?*
3 the answers to an exercise, usually found at the back of a school book: *The answer key is on page 92.*
4 **the key to something** the most important thing that helps you to do something: *Hard work is **the key to** doing well in exams.*

key² *adjective* very important and necessary: *Research is a key part of our work.*

key³ *verb* **key something in** to type information into a computer: *Now key in your name.*

key·board /'kiːbɔːd $ 'kibɔrd/ *noun*
1 all the keys on a computer or piano that you press to make it work ⇨ *see picture on page 342* 2 a musical instrument like a small electric piano: *Guy plays the guitar, and I'm on the keyboard.*

key·hole /'kiːhəʊl $ 'kihoʊl/ *noun* the hole where you put a key into a lock ⇨ *see picture at* KEY¹

key ring /'. ./ *noun* a metal ring that you keep keys on ⇨ *see picture at* KEY¹

kg the written abbreviation of KILOGRAM

K

1 to continue to have something

*I **kept** all the letters he wrote me from Europe. | "Do you want your book back?" "No, you can **keep** it." | **Keep** a copy of the form for your records.*

2 keep quiet, keep warm, keep calm etc

***Keep** calm and call the doctor immediately. | School **is keeping** me busy right now. | **Keep** the door **closed** – it's cold outside. | People **kept warm** by staying close together near the fire.*

*People **kept warm** by staying close together near the fire.*

5 to make someone stay in a place

*Chris wasn't feeling well, so I **kept** him home from school. | They're **keeping** her **in** hospital until tomorrow.*

> GRAMMAR
> keep someone in/at etc

keep

4 to have something always in the same place

*Where do you keep the sugar? | **Keep** your passport **in** a safe place.*

> GRAMMAR
> keep something in/on/ under etc something

3 to continue to do something often or for a long time

*I **keep losing** my keys. | Come on, **keep moving** – only a mile to go! | If he **keeps on growing** like this, he'll be really tall. | She **kept saying** she couldn't do it.*

> GRAMMAR
> keep doing something
> keep on doing something

K

PHRASES

keep a promise
to do what you have promised to do:
He fails to **keep** *his* **promises** *to his son.*

keep a secret
to not tell anyone about a secret you know: *They* **kept** *their marriage a secret from their parents.*

keep a diary, keep a record etc
to regularly write down information in a book, on a computer etc: *Many students* **keep** *a vocabulary* **diary**.

keep in mind
to remember something because it might be important or useful later: **Keep in mind** *that teachers have a strong influence on their students.*

keep an eye on someone/ something
to watch someone or something carefully, so that nothing bad happens: *Will you* **keep an eye on** *the baby for me while I'm upstairs?*

keep in touch (with)
to continue to talk to someone you do not see very often any more: *We* **keep in touch** *by e-mail.* | *I've* **kept in touch with** *a lot of people from school.*

PHRASAL VERBS

keep away
to make someone not go close to someone or something: **Keep** *plastic bags* **away** *from small children.* | *The smoke* **keeps** *the mosquitoes* **away**.

The smoke **keeps** *the mosquitoes away.*

keep from
to stop someone from doing something, or to stop something happening: *Susy covered her mouth to* **keep from** *laughing.* | *His friends* **kept** *him* **from** *feeling lonely.*

keep off
to stop something or someone from doing something, going somewhere etc: *Try to* **keep** *the cat* **off** *the sofa.* | **Keep off** *the grass.*

keep out
1 keep out! used on signs to tell people they are not allowed in a place: *Danger!* **Keep out!**

2 to stop someone or something from going into a place or doing something: *The heavy curtains* **kept out** *the sunshine.* | *Smith's injury* **kept** *him* **out** *of the game.*

keep up
1 to continue to do something that is good: *They* **kept up** *their friendship with phone calls and letters.* | *That's good work –* **keep it up!**

2 to do something as well or as quickly as other people: *Paul had to run to* **keep up**. | *I don't know if I'll be able to* **keep up with** *all the reading in the course.*

K

kick¹ /kɪk/ verb

GRAMMAR
kick something down/around etc
kick something into something
to hit someone or something with your foot: *A group of boys were kicking a stone around outside.* | *Tom just kicked me.* | *He **kicked the ball into** the back of the net.* | *The police had to **kick** the door **down** (=kick it until it opened) to get in the flat.* ⇨ see picture on page 340

kick

PHRASE
kick a habit
to stop doing something bad such as smoking: *I hope you've kicked smoking by now.*

PHRASAL VERB
kick out
kick someone out to make someone leave a place because they have done something wrong: *He **was kicked out** of school for fighting.*

kick² noun the action of hitting something or someone with your foot: *Gaye gave him a sharp kick on his ankle.*

kick·off /'kɪk-ɒf $ 'kɪk-ɔf/ noun when a game of football begins: *Kickoff is at 3pm.*

kid¹ /kɪd/ noun informal a child or young person: *Do you want to have kids?* | *She's just a kid.* ⇨ see usage note at CHILD

kid² verb informal kidded, kidding to say something that is not true as a joke: *I was only kidding when I said you were ugly.*

kid·nap /'kɪdnæp/ verb kidnapped, kidnapping to take someone and keep them as your prisoner until people give you money or things you want: *They kidnapped the bank manager's wife.*
– **kidnapper** noun: *The kidnappers are demanding £50,000 for the release of Mr Emmery.*

kid·ney /'kɪdni/ noun one of the two things inside in your body that remove waste liquid from your blood

kill¹ /kɪl/ verb
to cause someone to die: *They*

accused him of killing his wife. | *Hundreds of people were killed in the earthquake.* | *Smoking kills.*

PHRASES
I'll kill you, she'll kill him etc spoken used to say that someone will be very angry with another person: *Mum will **kill us** if we're late again.*
be killing you spoken if a part of your body is killing you, it is very painful: *I need to sit down for a minute – my feet **are killing me**.*
kill time, have time to kill to spend time doing something while you wait for something more important to happen: *We've **got** an hour **to kill** before the train leaves, so let's have some lunch.*

kill² noun when an animal is killed: *The lion moved in for the kill.*

kill·er /'kɪlə $ 'kɪlɚ/ noun written someone who has killed a person: *Police are looking for the man's killer.*

kill·ing /'kɪlɪŋ/ noun written a murder: *The killing took place outside a nightclub.*

ki·lo /'kiːləʊ $ 'kiloʊ/ noun a KILOGRAM: *The package weighs 30 kilos.*

kil·o·byte /'kɪləbaɪt/ noun a unit for measuring computer information, equal to 1024 BYTES

kil·o·gram also **kilogramme** BrE /'kɪləgræm/ written abbreviation **kg** noun a unit for measuring weight, equal to 1000 grams

kil·o·me·tre BrE, **kilometer** AmE /'kɪlə‚miːtə $ kɪ'lɑmətɚ/ written abbreviation **km** noun a unit for measuring length, equal to 1000 metres: *The town is 3 kilometres from the hotel.*

kilt /kɪlt/ noun a skirt traditionally worn by Scottish men

kin /kɪn/ noun **next of kin** formal the person in your family who you are most closely related to: *We should inform his next of kin of his death.*

kind¹ /kaɪnd/ noun

GRAMMAR
a kind of person/thing
a type of person or thing: *What **kind of** music do you like?* | *It's a great place, and **all kinds of** people go there.* | *"I'm buying a dog." "What kind?"*

kind² *adjective*

kin·der·gar·ten /'kɪndəgɑːtn $ 'kɪndəˌgɑrtn/ *noun* **1** *BrE* a school for children aged between 2 and 5 **2** *AmE* a class for young children, usually aged around 5, that prepares them for school

kind-heart·ed /ˌ. '../ *adjective* kind and generous: *A kind-hearted neighbour did her shopping.*

kind·ly /'kaɪndli/ *adverb* used when someone has done something kind or generous: *Mr Smith kindly offered to lend us his car.*

kind·ness /'kaɪndnəs/ *noun* [no plural] behaviour that is kind and generous: *How can I thank you for your kindness?*

king /kɪŋ/ *noun* **1** a man who belongs to a royal family and who rules a country: *The King of Spain is visiting England.* | *King George IV* **2** a playing card with a picture of a king on it: *the king of diamonds*

king·dom /'kɪŋdəm/ *noun* a country that has a king or queen: *The queen ruled a vast kingdom.*

ki·osk /'kiːɒsk $ 'kiɑsk/ *noun* a small shop where you can buy things such as newspapers or tickets through a window

kiss /kɪs/ *verb* to touch someone with your lips, to show that you love them or when you are saying hello or goodbye: *She kissed the children goodnight.*
– **kiss** *noun*: *Give me a kiss.*

kit /kɪt/ *noun* a set of clothes or equipment that you use for a particular purpose or activity: *a sports kit | a tool kit*

kitch·en /'kɪtʃən/ *noun* the room where you prepare and cook food: *Jo is in the kitchen making a sandwich.*

kite /kaɪt/ *noun* a toy that you fly in the air on the end of a long string: *Children love flying kites.*

kit·ten /'kɪtn/ *noun* a young cat

kit·ty /'kɪti/ *noun, plural* **kitties** money that a group of people have collected for a particular purpose: *We only had £3 in the kitty.*

ki·wi fruit /'kiːwi ˌfruːt/ *noun, plural* kiwi fruit or kiwi fruits a small round green fruit with a rough skin ⇨ see picture on page 345

Kleen·ex /'kliːneks/ *noun* trademark a TISSUE

km the written abbreviation of KILOMETRE

knack /næk/ *noun* informal the ability to do something well: *Elton John has a real knack for writing memorable songs.*

knee /niː/ *noun* **1** the middle part of your leg, where it bends: *I have very weak knees.* ⇨ see picture at BODY **2** the part of your trousers that covers your knees: *The knees of his jeans were torn.* **3** bring something to its knees if something brings a country or organization to its knees, it almost destroys it: *The ban on British beef almost brought the farming industry to its knees.*

knee·cap /'niːkæp/ *noun* the bone at the front of your knee

knee-deep /ˌ. '../ *adjective* something such as water that is knee-deep is deep enough to reach your knees: *We were knee-deep in water.*

knee-high /ˌ. '../ *adjective* something that is knee-high is tall enough to reach your knees: *a pair of knee-high boots*

kneel /niːl/ *verb, past tense and past participle* **knelt** /nelt/ or **kneeled** also **kneel down** to bend your legs so that your knees are on the ground and supporting the weight of your body: *I knelt down to stroke the cat.* ⇨ see picture on page 340

knelt a past tense and past participle of KNEEL

knew /njuː $ nuː/ the past tense of KNOW

knick·ers /'nɪkəz $ 'nɪkərz/ *plural noun* *BrE* a piece of clothing that women wear under their clothes, which covers the area between their waist and the top of their legs; PANTIES *AmE*: *a pair of silk knickers*

knife /naɪf/ *noun, plural* **knives** /naɪvz/ a tool used for cutting or as a weapon: *This knife is very sharp.* | *She stabbed him with a knife.* ⇨ see picture at BLUNT

knight /naɪt/ *noun* a soldier with a high rank in the Middle Ages

knight·hood /'naɪthʊd/ *noun* in Britain,

a special title that the King or Queen gives to a man: *Cliff Richard received a knighthood, making him 'Sir Cliff Richard'.*

knit /nɪt/ *verb, past tense and past participle* **knitted** or **knit** *present participle* **knitting** to make clothes by twisting wool together, using long sticks: *My mom's knitting me a hat.* | *I'm knitting a sweater for Dad.*

knives the plural of KNIFE

knob /nɒb $ nɑb/ *noun* **1** a small handle on a door or drawer that you use to open it **2** a round control button on a piece of electrical equipment: *the volume knob*

knob·bly /'nɒbli $ 'nɑbli/ *BrE*, **knob·by** /'nɒbi $ 'nɑbi/ *AmE, adjective* **knobblier, knobbliest** something that is knobbly is not smooth, but has hard parts that stick out: *knobbly knees*

knock¹ /nɒk $ nɑk/ *verb*

1 to make a noise by hitting a door or window with your hand, usually in order to ask someone to open it: *Who's that knocking at the door?* | *A policeman knocked on the car window.* | *The sign read 'Please knock and enter'.*

2 also **knock over** to hit someone or something so that they move or fall down: *Someone knocked my arm and I spilled my drink.* | *I accidentally knocked the bowl off the shelf.* | *I slipped and knocked over a jug of water.*

knock down
1 knock something down to destroy a building or wall by hitting it: *They are going to knock down this apartment block.*
2 knock someone down to hit and injure someone with a car: *Jack was knocked down while he was crossing the road.*
knock out
knock someone out **a)** to hit someone very hard so that they cannot get up: *The punch knocked out his opponent.* **b)** to defeat a person or team so that they cannot stay in a competition: *England were knocked out of the World Cup in the semi-final.*

knock² *noun* the sound that you make when you hit something hard: *Did you hear a knock at the door?*

knock·out /'nɒk-aʊt $ 'nɑk-aʊt/ *noun* when a BOXER hits another boxer so that he falls on the ground and cannot get up: *Tyson won in 15 minutes with a knockout.*

knot¹ /nɒt $ nɑt/ **knot** *noun* a join in two pieces of string, rope etc where they have been tied together: *There's a knot in my shoelaces.*

knot

knot² *verb* **knotted, knotting** to join two pieces of string, rope etc together by tying them: *Amber knotted the rope firmly to the boat.*

know¹ ⇨ *see box on next page*

know² /nəʊ $ noʊ/ *noun* **be in the know** if you are in the know, you have information that most people do not have: *Those in the know are saying that 'American Beauty' will win Oscars.*

know-all /'. ./ *BrE*, **know-it-all** /'. . ./ *AmE, noun informal* an annoying person who thinks they know more than everyone else

know-how /'. ./ *noun [no plural] informal* knowledge that you need to do something: *We don't have the know-how to build our own house.*

know·ing·ly /'nəʊɪŋli $ 'noʊɪŋli/ *adverb* written formal if you knowingly do something wrong, you do it even though you know that it is wrong: *He claimed he'd never knowingly sold alcohol to teenagers.*

knowl·edge /'nɒlɪdʒ $ 'nɑlɪdʒ/ *noun [no plural]*

things that you know about a particular subject: *Her knowledge of music is amazing.* | *advances in scientific knowledge* | *Our knowledge about this disease is quite limited* (=we do not know very much about it).

have no knowledge: *I had no knowledge that* (=I did not know that) *he was planning to leave.*

K

➤ KNOW or CAN?

KNOW to have the facts or information about something in your mind: *I know that song. We sang it in school.*

CAN to have the ability to do something: *Some birds, such as ostriches, can't fly.*

➤ KNOW

❶to have facts or information in your mind
He knows a lot of funny stories. | Doctors do not know much about the disease. | I knew that Carrie would help us. | We don't know what effect the changes will have. | Do you know where Nelson went?

> **GRAMMAR**
> know about something
> know (that)
> know who/what/where etc

know

❸person, place
if you know a person or a place, you have met them or been there before: *Do you know Nancy? | I knew your father well. | I don't know Manchester well.*

- ✗ Don't say ➤ *I am knowing, she was knowing etc*
- ✓ Say ➤ *I know, she knew etc*

❷to be able to do something
Do you know how to drive? | By age six, children should know how to tie their shoes.

> **GRAMMAR**
> know how to do something

PHRASES

you know *spoken*
a say this to check that someone understands what you are saying or that they are listening: *You push this button to make it start, you know?*
b say this when you want to start talking about something: *You know that girl in my English class? She's going to England in June.*
c people say this when they cannot quickly think of what to say next: *I think it's time to, you know, get things tidied up.*

I know *spoken*
say this to show that you agree with or understand what someone is saying: *"Sam was so nice to us when we visited" "I know."*

I don't know *spoken*
say this when you do not know the answer to a question: *"What time does the game start?" "I don't know."*

as far as I know *spoken*
say this when you think something is true, but you are not sure: *She'll be back this afternoon, as far as I know.*

get to know someone
to meet someone and find out about them: *It takes time to get to know people when you start at a new school.*

let someone know *informal*
to tell someone about something: *If you need any help, just let me know.*

K

knowledgeable 334

knowl·edge·a·ble /ˈnɒlɪdʒəbəl $ ˈnɑl-ɪdʒəbəl/ *adjective* a knowledgeable person knows a lot about a particular subject: *Sal's very knowledgable about computers.*

known /nəʊn $ noʊn/ the past participle of KNOW

knuck·le /ˈnʌkəl/ *noun* one of the joints where your fingers join your hand and which you bend to move your fingers

ko·a·la /kəʊˈɑːlə $ koʊˈɑlə/ also **koala bear** /.ˌ.. ˈ./ *noun* an Australian animal like a small bear that climbs trees

Ko·ran, Qur'an /kɔːˈrɑːn $ kəˈræn/ *noun* **the Koran** the holy book of the ISLAMIC religion

ko·sher /ˈkəʊʃə $ ˈkoʊʃɚ/ *adjective* kosher food is prepared according to JEWISH law

kung fu /ˌkʌŋ ˈfuː/ *noun [no plural]* a sport from China in which you fight using your hands and feet

kw the written abbreviation of KILOWATT

l the written abbreviation of LITRE

lab /læb/ *informal* a LABORATORY

la·bel¹ /ˈleɪbəl/ *noun*
1 a piece of paper or cloth with information on it that is fixed to an object: *The label tells you how the dress should be washed.* | *There's no price label on this book.*
2 the name of a company that makes something such as records or clothes: *Their new album is on the 'Atlanta' label.* | *She only wears clothes from famous designer labels.*

label² *verb* **labelled, labelling** *BrE,* **labeled, labeling** *AmE* to fix a label to something to show what it is: *We labelled the boxes so we would know what was in them.*

labor the American spelling of LABOUR

la·bor·a·tory /ləˈbɒrətri $ˈlæbrəˌtɔri/ *noun, plural* **laboratories** also **lab** /læb/
1 a room or building in which people do scientific work **2 language laboratory** a room in a school or college where students can listen to TAPES of a foreign language and practise speaking it

laborer the American spelling of LABOURER

lab·or·i·ous /ləˈbɔːriəs/ *adjective* taking a lot of time and effort to do: *the laborious task of repairing the bridge*

labor u·nion /ˈ.. ˌ../ the American word for TRADE UNION

la·bour *BrE,* **labor** *AmE* /ˈleɪbə $ˈleɪbər/ *noun [no plural]* **1** hard physical work: *This job involves a lot of heavy labour.* **2** workers: *We need additional labour to complete the building.*

la·bour·er *BrE,* **laborer** *AmE* /ˈleɪbərə $ˈleɪbər/ *noun* someone who does a lot of physical work in their job: *farm labourers*

lace /leɪs/ *noun [no plural]* a type of cloth with a pattern of small holes that is often used to make clothes look attractive: *a lace collar*

lac·es /ˈleɪsɪz/ *plural noun* strings that you tie to fasten your shoes: *a pair of black laces* ➪ *see picture on page 352*

lack /læk/ *noun [no plural]* when you do not have enough of something: *She was suffering from lack of sleep.*
—**lack** *verb*: *The school lacks modern equipment.*

lad·der /ˈlædə $ˈlædər/ *noun* a piece of equipment for climbing up to high places. A ladder has two long bars that are connected by short bars that you use as steps

ladder

la·den /ˈleɪdn/ *adjective written* carrying a lot of heavy things: *a truck laden with supplies*

la·dies /ˈleɪdiz/ *noun* **the ladies** *BrE* a room in a public building where there are toilets for women; LADIES ROOM *AmE*

la·dle /ˈleɪdl/ *noun* a big deep spoon with a long handle that you use for putting soup into bowls

la·dy /ˈleɪdi/ *noun, plural* **ladies** **1** a polite word for a woman: *Ask that lady if you can help.* | *Good evening, ladies and gentlemen.* **2 Lady** in Britain, a title for a woman of a high social rank: *Lady Katherine Dugdale*

L

la·dy·bird /'leɪdi-
bɜːrd $ 'leɪdi,bɜˑd/
BrE,   **la·dy·bug**
/'leɪdibʌg/   AmE,
noun a small round
insect that is red
with black spots

lag¹ /læg/ verb
**lagged, lagging;
lag behind** informal
to move or develop more slowly than
other people: Gina lagged behind, waiting for Rob. | My daughter is lagging
behind in her studies.

lag² also **time lag** noun the period of
time between one event and another
event that is connected with it

la·ger /'lɑːgə $ 'lɑgɚ/ noun BrE a type of
light yellow beer: a pint of lager

la·goon /lə'guːn/ noun an area of sea
water that is separated from the sea by
sand

laid the past tense and past participle of
LAY¹

laid-back /ˌ. './ adjective informal relaxed and not worried about anything:
She seems very laid-back about her
exams.

lain the past participle of LIE¹

lake /leɪk/ noun a large area of water
that is surrounded by land ⇨ see picture
on page 348

lamb /læm/ noun   1 a young sheep
2 the meat from a lamb

lame /leɪm/ adjective if a person or animal is lame, they cannot walk properly
because they have hurt their leg: His
horse was lame because a stone had injured its foot.

lamp /læmp/ noun a thing that produces
light using electricity, oil, or gas: a table
lamp ⇨ see picture on page 342

lamp-post /'. ./ noun a tall pole in the
street with a lamp on top

lamp·shade /'læmpʃeɪd/ noun a cover
over a lamp

land¹ /lænd/ noun
1 [no plural] an area of ground: His fam-
ily own a lot of land. | They have
bought a piece of land.
2 [no plural] the solid dry part of the
Earth's surface, rather than the
water or the air: This is the fastest
that anyone has ever travelled on
land.

ladybird

3 literary a country: He was one of the
best actors **in the land.**

land² verb

> **GRAMMAR**
> **land in/at a place**
> **land on/in something**

1 if a plane lands, or if a pilot lands a
plane, the plane moves down until it
is safely on the ground: Our flight
landed at Heathrow airport at 9.30.
2 to fall onto something after moving
through the air: I slipped and **land-
ed on** something sharp. | She drop-
ped the cake and it **landed in** a
puddle.
3 to arrive somewhere by boat or
plane: We **landed in** Southampton
on Friday.

land·ing /'lændɪŋ/ noun   1 the area at
the top of a set of stairs in a house
2 when a plane comes down from the
air onto the ground: The pilot made an
emergency landing.

land·la·dy /'lænd,leɪdi/ noun, plural
landladies a woman that you rent a
room or house from

land·lord /'lændlɔːd $ 'lændlɔrd/ noun
a man that you rent a room or house
from

land·mark /'lændmɑːk $ 'lændmɑrk/
noun something that helps you recognize
where you are, such as a famous building: The Eiffel Tower is a well-known
landmark in Paris.

land·own·er /'lænd,əʊnə $ 'lænd-
,oʊnɚ/ noun someone who owns a lot
of land

land·scape /'lændskeɪp/ noun a view
across an area of land: a city landscape

land·slide /'lændslaɪd/ noun   1 when
soil and rocks fall down the side of a hill
or mountain: The village was destroyed
in a landslide.   2 when a person or political party wins a lot more votes than the
others in an election: It was a landslide
victory for the Labour Party.

lane /leɪn/ noun   1 a narrow country
road   2 one of the parts that a road,
sports track, or swimming pool is divided
into: You need to change lanes here to
turn right.

lan·guage /'læŋgwɪdʒ/ noun
1 the words that are used by the
people who live in a particular

L

country: *She* **speaks** *three* **languages**, *including Japanese.*
2 [no plural] words, especially words of a particular kind: *the kind of technical language that scientists use*

lan·tern /'læntən $ 'læntərn/ *noun* a lamp in a glass or metal container that you can carry

lap[1] /læp/ *noun* **1** the flat area at the top of your legs when you sit down: *A black cat sat on her lap.* **2** one trip around a race track during a long race: *The runners are on the last lap.*

lap[2] *verb* **lapped, lapping 1** if water laps against something, it keeps hitting it gently: *Waves lapped against the side of the boat.* **2** also **lap up** if an animal laps up a drink, it drinks it with quick movements of its tongue: *The cat lapped up all the milk.*

la·pel /lə'pel/ *noun* one of the parts at the front of a coat that join the collar and fold back on each side

lapse /læps/ *noun* when someone makes a mistake or forgets something, for only a short time or only once or twice: *a memory lapse* | *I've had a few lapses in my diet.*

lap·top /'læptɒp $ 'læptɑp/ *noun* a small computer that you can carry: *I use a laptop if I'm travelling by train.* ⇨ see picture on page 342

large /lɑːdʒ $ lɑrdʒ/ *adjective* big in size, number, or amount ⇨ opposite SMALL: *a large house with 15 rooms* | *Have you got this coat in a larger size?* | *They offered him a large amount of money for the information.*

large·ly /'lɑːdʒli $ 'lɑrdʒli/ *adverb* mostly or mainly: *The film was made largely in Mexico.*

large-scale /ˌ. './ *adjective* large-scale situations or activities happen over a large area or involve a lot of people: *modern large-scale industry*

la·ser /'leɪzə $ 'leɪzər/ *noun* a narrow line of powerful light, or the equipment that produces it

lash /læʃ/ *verb written* if rain, wind, or waves lash against something, they hit it hard: *Storms lashed the coast.*

lash·es /'læʃɪz/ EYELASHES

last[1] /lɑːst $ læst/ *adjective, adverb, pronoun*
1 most recent or most recently: *Her spelling has improved over the last few months.* | *When did you last wash your hair?*
2 after all the other things or people: *How are you going to celebrate your last day at school?* | *He dies in the last chapter of the book.* | *Hilary was the last to arrive.* | *He came last in every race.* | *This part of the building was built last.*
3 the last one is the only remaining one: *Who ate the last biscuit?* | *That's the last of the boxes we have to move.*

PHRASES
last night, last week etc during the most recent night, week etc: *Did you go out last night?* | *I saw James last week.* | *I went swimming last Tuesday.*
the week before last, the year before last etc during the week, year etc before the most recent one: *I got a letter from Yvonne the week before last* (=two weeks ago).
at last after a long time: *Good – you've finished at last.* | *At last the bus arrived.*
the last person, the last thing etc a person or thing that you really do not expect or want: *He's the last person I'd invite!* | *The last thing I expected her to do was run away.*

USAGE last, latest
Compare **last** and **latest**. Use **latest** when you mean 'new and most recent': *Have you heard the latest news?* Use **last** when you mean 'the one before the present one': *Our last house was much smaller than this one.* Or when you mean 'final': *Tomorrow's the last day of August.*

last[2] *verb*
GRAMMAR
last for something
1 to continue to happen or exist: *His first marriage lasted 10 years.* | *The pain lasted for only a few seconds.*
2 to continue to be in good condition and suitable for use: *A good carpet will last for years.* | *Vegetables last longer if they are kept in the fridge.*

L

last·ing /'lɑːstɪŋ $ 'læstɪŋ/ *adjective* continuing for a long time: *a lasting friendship*

last·ly /'lɑːstli $ 'læstli/ *adverb* used to show that the next thing you say will be the last thing you say: *Lastly, I'd like to thank all my tutors.*

last-min·ute /ˌ. '../ *adjective* a last-minute action is done very near to the end of a period of time: *His last-minute goal saved the match.*

last name /'. ./ SURNAME

late /leɪt/ *adjective, adverb*

> **GRAMMAR**
> **late for something**

1 after the expected time: *I got up late.* | *Jack **was late for** school again today.* | *The train was twenty minutes late.*
2 near the end of a period of time: *The school was built in the late 1970s.*
3 near the end of the day: *It's getting late and I'm tired.*
4 *formal* used to talk about someone who died fairly recently: *the late Princess of Wales*

> **PHRASE**
> **too late** if it is too late to do something, it is after the time when it should or could have been done: *It's too late to change your mind.*

late·ly /'leɪtli/ *adverb* recently: *I haven't seen her lately.*

lat·er¹ /'leɪtə $ 'leɪtə-/ *adverb* after the present time or after a time that you are talking about: *You'll have to finish that later.* | *A couple of months later, I met her again at a party.*

> **PHRASE**
> **later on** at some time in the future, or at some time after something else: *He kept things he thought might be useful **later on**.* | *Later on, we can go shopping, if you like.*

later² *adjective* happening or coming after something else: *Her later books weren't so popular.*

lat·est¹ /'leɪtəst/ *adjective* the most recent: *the latest news*

latest² *noun* **at the latest** used to tell someone that something will or must happen before a particular time: *Applications must get here by tomorrow at the latest.*

Lat·in¹ /'lætɪn $ 'lætn/ *noun* the language that was used in ancient Rome

Latin² *adjective* **1** written in Latin: *a Latin poem* **2** connected with a nation that speaks a language such as Italian or Spanish: *Latin music*

Latin A·mer·i·can /ˌ... '.../ *adjective* related to South or Central America: *Latin American countries*

laugh¹ /lɑːf $ læf/ *verb*

> **GRAMMAR**
> **laugh at something**
> **laugh at someone**

1 to make a sound with your voice when you think that something is funny: *We couldn't stop laughing.* | *The audience **laughed at** all the jokes.*
2 if people laugh at someone, they laugh or make jokes about that person in an unkind way: *It's not kind to **laugh at** people who make mistakes.*

laugh² *noun* the sound you make when you laugh: *He **gave** a short **laugh**.*

> **PHRASES**
> **be a laugh** *BrE informal* to be fun: *Come on – it'll **be a laugh**!*

laugh·ter /'lɑːftə $ 'læftə-/ *noun* [no plural] when you laugh, or the sound of people laughing: *We heard laughter outside.* | *The audience roared with laughter.*

launch /lɔːntʃ/ *verb* **1** to start a big important series of actions: *The government has launched an anti-racism campaign.* **2** to make a new product available: *The book will be launched next week.* **3** to send a SPACECRAFT into the sky or to put a boat into the water –**launch** *noun: a film launch*

laun·der·ette /ˌlɔːndə'ret/ *BrE*, **laundromat** /'lɔːndrəmæt/ *AmE*, *noun* a public place where you pay to wash your clothes in a machine

laun·dry /'lɔːndri $ 'lɔːndri/ *noun* [no plural] clothes, sheets etc that need to be washed, or that have just been washed: *Do you have any dirty laundry?*

L

polar
bear

penguin

gorilla

wolf

horse

tiger

fox

chimpanzee

snake

giraffe

elephant

camel

rhinoceros

lion

zebra

buffalo

crocodile

hippopotamus

bear

octopus

crab

turtle

climb

fall

kick

throw

catch

pick up

put down

crawl

run

pull

push

jog

tiptoe

march

lift

bend

carry

drop

stretch

kneel

crouch

skip

jump

hop

trip

slip

chop

wave

punch

pinch

point

push

clap

tickle

shake hands

slap

poke

stroke

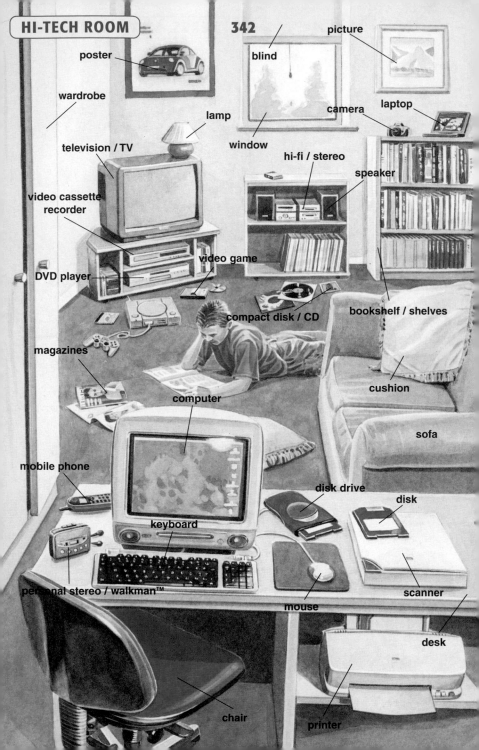

HI-TECH ROOM

342

poster

picture

blind

wardrobe

camera

laptop

lamp

window

television / TV

hi-fi / stereo

speaker

video cassette recorder

DVD player

video game

bookshelf / shelves

compact disk / CD

magazines

cushion

computer

sofa

mobile phone

disk drive

disk

keyboard

personal stereo / walkman™

scanner

mouse

desk

chair

printer

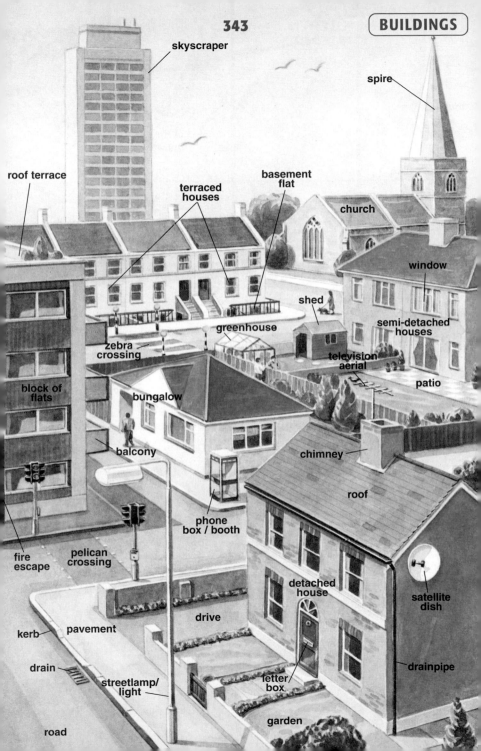

BUILDINGS

skyscraper

spire

roof terrace

terraced houses

basement flat

church

window

semi-detached houses

shed

greenhouse

zebra crossing

block of flats

bungalow

television aerial

patio

balcony

chimney

roof

phone box / booth

fire escape

pelican crossing

satellite dish

drive

detached house

kerb

pavement

drain

drainpipe

streetlamp/ light

letter box

road

garden

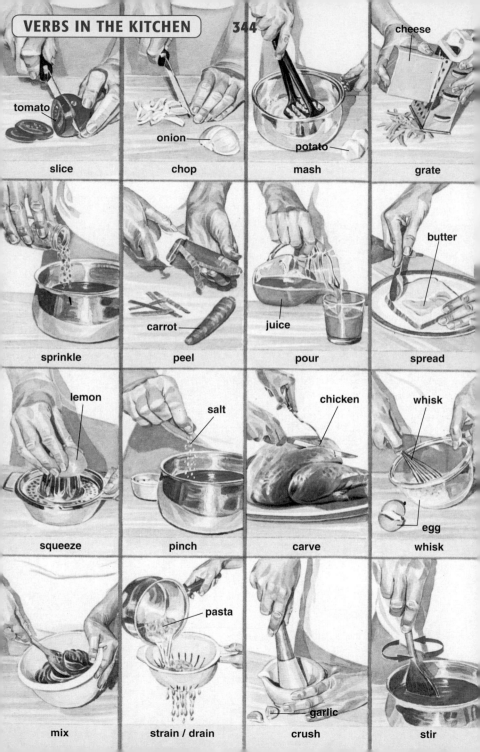

cheese

tomato

onion

potato

grate

slice   **chop**   **mash**   **grate**

butter

carrot

juice

sprinkle   **peel**   **pour**   **spread**

lemon

salt

chicken

whisk

egg

squeeze   **pinch**   **carve**   **whisk**

pasta

garlic

mix   **strain / drain**   **crush**   **stir**

FRUIT and VEGETABLES

1 watermelon	11 lemons	20 broccoli	29 cucumber
2 melon	12 oranges	21 cabbage	30 onions
3 pineapple	13 peaches	22 peas	31 garlic
4 coconut	14 plums	23 beans	32 peppers
5 grapes	15 blackberries	24 brussels sprouts	33 aubergine
6 bananas	16 raspberries	25 corn	34 mushrooms
7 grapefruit	17 strawberries	26 leeks	35 potatoes
8 kiwi fruit	18 cauliflower	27 courgettes	36 beetroot
9 apples	19 pumpkin	28 lettuce	37 carrots
10 pears			

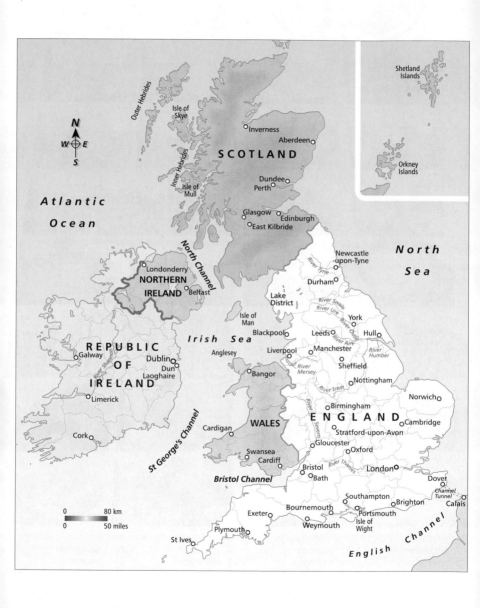

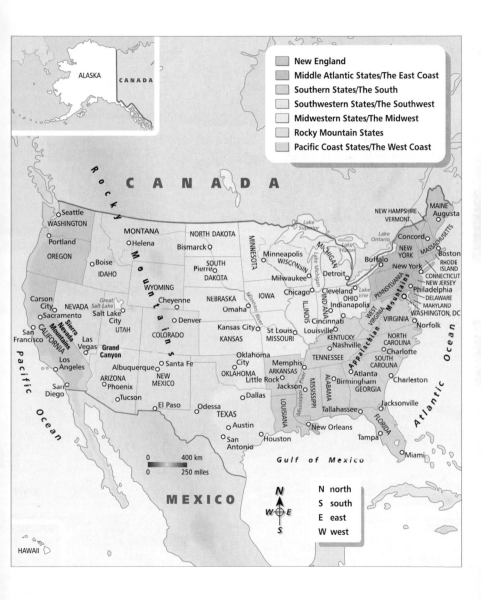

New England
Middle Atlantic States/The East Coast
Southern States/The South
Southwestern States/The Southwest
Midwestern States/The Midwest
Rocky Mountain States
Pacific Coast States/The West Coast

ALASKA   CANADA

CANADA

Rocky   C A N A D A

Seattle
WASHINGTON
Portland
OREGON
Boise
IDAHO

MONTANA
Helena
Bismarck
NORTH DAKOTA
SOUTH
Pierre
DAKOTA
WYOMING
Cheyenne
NEBRASKA
Omaha

Lake
Superior
MINNESOTA
Minneapolis
WISCONSIN
Milwaukee
IOWA
Chicago

Lake
Huron
MICHIGAN
Lake Michigan
Detroit

Lake
Ontario
Buffalo
NEW
YORK
New York

NEW HAMPSHIRE
VERMONT
Concord
MAINE
Augusta
MASSACHUSETTS
Boston
RHODE
ISLAND
CONNECTICUT
NEW JERSEY
Philadelphia
DELAWARE

Carson
City
NEVADA
Sacramento
San
Francisco
CALIFORNIA
Los
Angeles
San
Diego

Great
Salt Lake
Sierra
Nevada
Mountains
Las
Vegas
Grand
Canyon

Salt Lake
City
UTAH
Denver
COLORADO

Kansas City
KANSAS
Albuquerque
Santa Fe
NEW
MEXICO
ARIZONA
Phoenix
Tucson
El Paso
Odessa
TEXAS

Austin
San
Antonio
Houston

Dallas

Cincinnati
OHIO
Indianapolis
INDIANA
ILLINOIS

St Louis
MISSOURI
Louisville
KENTUCKY
Nashville
TENNESSEE

Cleveland
Lake
Erie
PENNSYLVANIA
Appalachian Mountains
WEST
VIRGINIA
VIRGINIA
Norfolk
WASHINGTON, DC
MARYLAND

NORTH
CAROLINA
Charlotte
SOUTH
CAROLINA
Charleston

Oklahoma
City
OKLAHOMA
Memphis
ARKANSAS
Little Rock
Jackson
MISSISSIPPI
ALABAMA
Birmingham
GEORGIA
Atlanta

Tallahassee
Jacksonville
FLORIDA

LOUISIANA
New Orleans
Tampa

Miami

Pacific Ocean

Atlantic Ocean

0   400 km
0   250 miles

Gulf of Mexico

M E X I C O

N north
S south
E east
W west

N
W E
S

HAWAII

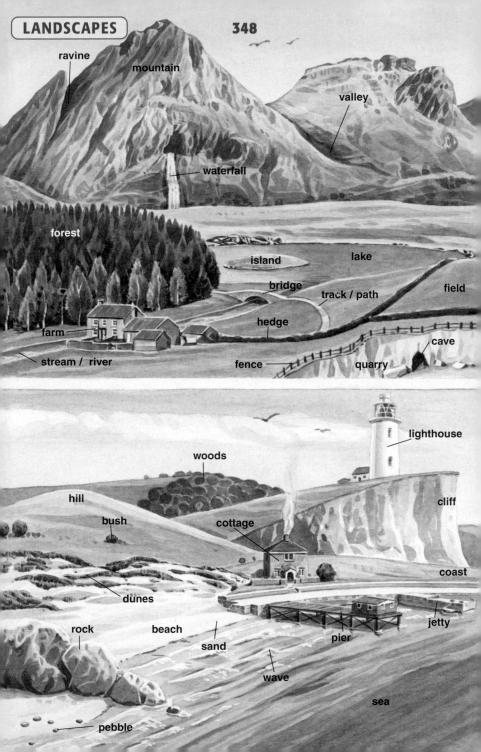

ravine

mountain

valley

waterfall

forest

island

lake

bridge

track / path

field

farm

hedge

stream / river

fence

quarry

cave

lighthouse

woods

hill

cliff

bush

cottage

coast

dunes

rock

beach

sand

pier

jetty

wave

pebble

sea

TRANSPORT

terminal

aeroplane

helicopter

wing

runway

jet engine

station

platform

level crossing

train

car

caravan

lorry

zebra crossing

van

bus

bus stop

roundabout

bicycle

motorbike

taxi

ferry

ship

submarine

harbour

yacht

speedboat

rowing boat

canoe

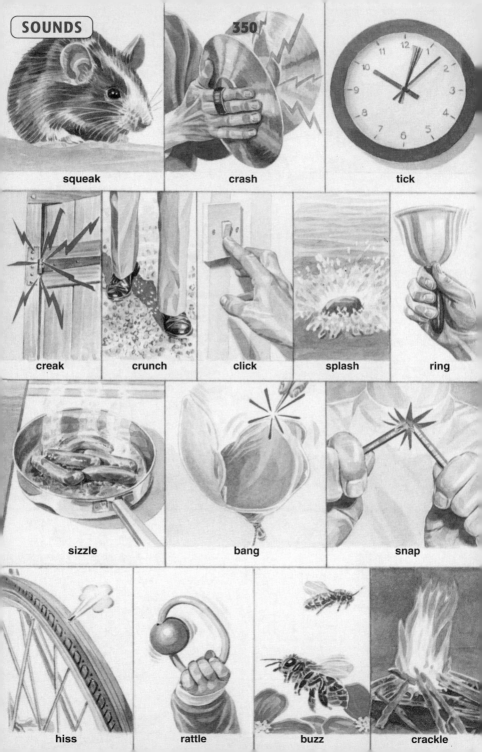

SOUNDS

350

squeak

crash

tick

creak

crunch

click

splash

ring

sizzle

bang

snap

hiss

rattle

buzz

crackle

football

American football

rugby

cricket

baseball

golf

tennis

hockey

swimming

ice hockey

gymnastics

athletics

horse-riding

cycling

basketball

boxing

skiing

CLOTHES

352

- turban
- cap
- overalls
- hat
- tracksuit
- T-shirt
- dress
- cardigan
- shorts
- belt
- leggings
- socks
- zip
- sari
- sweater / jumper
- dungarees
- blouse
- jeans
- scarf
- braces
- boots
- collar
- sandals
- shirt
- jacket
- tie
- suit
- button
- waistcoat
- coat
- trousers
- sleeve
- skirt
- shoes
- glove
- laces

Susan is small with red permed hair, and she wears glasses.

David is overweight/fat with receding hair and has a beard.

Colin is tall with short black hair and he wears glasses.

Robin is well-built/muscular with short spiky brown hair, sideburns, and stubble.

Ashok is of average height, is bald, and wears glasses.

Lucy is slim with shoulder-length wavy blonde hair.

Zoe is thin with brown hair in a ponytail and has freckles.

Phillip is short with straight grey hair and a moustache.

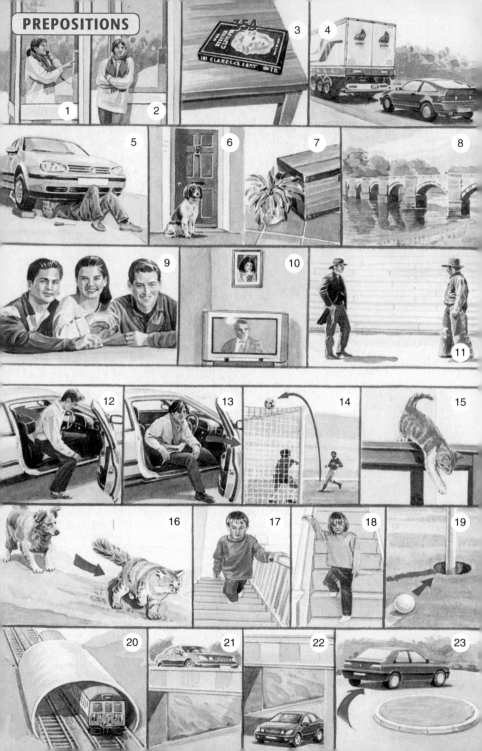

PREPOSITIONS

la·va /ˈlɑːvə/ *noun* [*no plural*] hot liquid rock that comes out of a VOLCANO

lav·a·to·ry /ˈlævətəri $ ˈlævəˌtɔːri/ *noun* formal, plural **lavatories** a TOILET

law /lɔː/ *noun*

GRAMMAR
a law against something
the law of something

1 [*no plural*] the system of rules that people in a country must obey: *The* **law** *says that you must not sell alcohol to people under the age of 18.* | *according to international law*

2 a rule that people in a country must obey: *tough new anti-drug laws* | *There should be a* **law against** *it!*

3 [*no plural*] the study of laws: *He did law at university.*

4 a scientific rule that explains why something happens: *the* **law of** *gravity*

PHRASES
be against the law: *Driving without a licence* **is against the law** (=is illegal).
break the law to do something illegal: *I didn't know I was* **breaking the law**.
law and order when people obey the law and do not act violently: *The local police are trying to keep* **law and order**.

lawn /lɔːn/ *noun* an area of grass that is cut short: *children playing on the lawn*

lawn mow·er /ˈ. ˌ../ *noun* a machine that you use to cut grass

law·yer /ˈlɔːjə $ ˈlɔːjɚ/ *noun* someone whose job is to advise people about the law and speak for them in court

lay¹ /leɪ/ *verb, past tense and past participle* **laid** /leɪd/

GRAMMAR
lay something on something

1 to put something on a surface in a careful way so that it is lying flat: *She* **laid** *her gloves* **on** *the table.* | *He* **laid down** *his knife and fork.*

2 if you lay bricks, CARPETS, electrical wires etc, you put them down in the place where they will stay: *Men are digging up the road to* **lay** *television cables.*

3 if a bird, insect etc lays eggs, it produces them from its body

PHRASE
lay the table to put knives, forks etc on a table before a meal

PHRASAL VERBS
lay down
lay down something to say officially what people should do: *The school* **laid down** *strict rules about appearance.*

USAGE **lay, lie**
Lay and **lie** are not the same. **Lay** means to put something somewhere: *She laid her head on his shoulder.* **Lie** has two different meanings. It can mean to be in a flat position on a surface: *He was lying on the bed.* The past tense for this meaning of **lie** is **lay**. **Lie** can also mean to say something that is not true: *Why did you lie to me?* The past tense for this meaning of **lie** is **lied**.

Prepositions

1. She's in/inside the booth.
2. She's outside the booth.
3. The book's on the table.
4. The car's behind the lorry.
5. He's under the car.
6. The dog's sitting in front of the door.
7. The plant is beside/by the chest.
8. There's a bridge over the river.
9. Sally sat between her brothers.
10. The picture hangs above the tv.
11. They stood opposite each other.
12. Frank got into the car.
13. Bob got out of the car.
14. He kicked the ball onto the net.
15. The cat jumped off the table.
16. The cat ran away from the dog.
17. David went up the stairs.
18. Sophie went down the stairs.
19. The ball rolled towards the hole.
20. The train went through the tunnel.
21. He drove over the bridge.
22. He drove under the bridge.
23. The car went round the roundabout.

L

lay² the past tense of LIE¹

lay-by /ˈ. ./ noun BrE an area at the side of a road where vehicles can stop: We pulled into a lay-by for a rest.

lay·er /ˈleɪə $ ˈleɪɚ/ noun a flat amount or piece of something that is covering a surface or between other things: a layer of dust | Wear several layers of clothing.

lay·out /ˈleɪaʊt/ noun the arrangement of the rooms or objects in a place: a picture showing the layout of Buckingham Palace

laze /leɪz/ also **laze around** verb to relax and not do very much: two cats lazing in the sun

la·zy /ˈleɪzi/ adjective lazier, laziest a lazy person does not like working or doing things that need effort: Don't be so lazy – come and help me clean up. – laziness noun

lb. the written abbreviation of POUND¹

lead¹ /liːd/ verb, past tense and past participle **led** /led/

> **GRAMMAR**
> **lead someone to/from a place**

1 to take someone somewhere by going with them or in front of them: She **led** me **into** the kitchen. | The man was **led away** by the police.
2 if a door, road etc leads somewhere, you can get there by using it: He walked down the corridor that **led to** the exit. | the door **leading into** the sitting room
3 to be in charge of an activity or organization: She led the campaign to save the school from being closed.
4 if you are leading, you are winning a game or competition: At half-time, Manchester United were leading 2–0.

> **PHRASES**

lead a busy life, lead a normal life etc to have a particular kind of life: He **had led an interesting life**.

lead the way a) to go in front so that someone can follow you somewhere: She **led the way** up a flight of stairs. **b)** to be the first to do something: American doctors **led the way** in using this new treatment.

lead someone to do something to be the reason why someone does something: What **led you to** make this decision?

> **PHRASAL VERBS**

lead to
lead to something to cause something to happen: His laziness **led to** arguments with his parents.

lead up to
lead up to something if events lead up to something, they come before it and may be a cause of it: The police are investigating the events **leading up to** the murder.

lead² noun

1 the distance, number of points etc by which one team or person is ahead of another: Germany had an early two-goal lead. | The team managed to increase their lead.
2 BrE a long piece of leather that you fasten to a dog's collar to keep it near you ⇨ same meaning LEASH
3 BrE an electric wire that you use to connect a piece of equipment to a supply of electricity; CORD AmE

> **PHRASES**

in the lead, into the lead if someone in a race, game, or competition is in the lead, they are winning at that time: The Kenyan was **in the lead** at the first bend. | John's team raced **into the lead** by scoring 10 points in the first round.

take the lead to start winning a race, game, or competition: France **took the lead** when they scored a goal after ten minutes.

lead³ /led/ noun 1 [no plural] a heavy soft grey metal 2 the grey substance in the middle of a pencil

lead·er /ˈliːdə $ ˈliːdɚ/ noun the person who is in charge of a country or group: a meeting of world leaders

lead·er·ship /ˈliːdəʃɪp $ ˈliːdɚˌʃɪp/ noun the position of being in charge of a country or group, or the people who are in charge: Owen took over the leadership of the party in 1995.

lead·ing /ˈliːdɪŋ/ adjective best or most important: one of Britain's leading sportsmen

leaf /liːf/ noun, plural **leaves** /liːvz/ one of the flat green things that grow on a plant: The leaves on the trees fall off in autumn.

least

leaf·let /ˈliːflət/ *noun* a piece of paper with information printed on it: *We handed out leaflets about the meeting.*

league /liːɡ/ *noun* **1** a group of sports teams or players who compete against each other: *the football league* **2** a group of people or countries that work together because they have similar aims: *the League of Nations*

leak /liːk/ *verb*
1 if something leaks, there is a hole in it that lets liquid or gas come out or in: *My shoes are leaking.* | *The tank was leaking petrol.* **2** if liquid or gas leaks from something, it comes out of it through a hole: *Water was leaking out of the pipes.*
– **leak** *noun*: *a gas leak*

leak

lean¹ /liːn/ *verb, past tense and past participle* **leaned** or **leant** /lent/ *BrE*

GRAMMAR
lean against/on something
lean something against/on something

1 to bend your body forwards, backwards, or to the side: *Jane leaned forwards to look out of the train window.* | *He leaned back in his chair.* | *Antony leaned over and kissed her.*
2 to stand or sit with part of your body resting against something: *He stood leaning against the wall.* | *He leaned his elbows on the table.*
3 to put an object in a sloping position against something else so that it will stay there: *He leaned his bicycle against the wall.*

lean² *adjective* thin, in an attractive healthy way: *a lean, muscular runner*

leant a past tense and past participle of LEAN¹

leap /liːp/ *verb, past tense and past participle* **leaped** or **leapt** /lept/ to jump somewhere: *The dog leapt the fence.* | *Joe leapt out of bed.*
– **leap** *noun*: *With one leap, he was on the horse's back.*

leapt a past tense and past participle of LEAP

leap year /ˈ. ./ *noun* a year when February has 29 days instead of 28

learn /lɜːn $ lɜːn/ *verb, past tense and past participle* **learned** or **learnt** /lɜːnt $ lɜːnt/ *BrE*

GRAMMAR
learn to do something
learn how/what etc
learn about something
learn from something
learn (that)
learn of something

1 to get knowledge or a skill by studying or training: *How long have you been learning English?* | *I want to learn to drive when I'm seventeen.* | *They learned how to ski when they lived in Switzerland.* | *Today we learned all about dinosaurs.* | *I have learned from my mistakes.*
2 *formal* to hear some news or information: *The next day, I learned that I had passed the exam.* | *I only learned of the change of plan yesterday.*
3 if you learn a poem, part of a play etc, you read it many times so that you can remember it all exactly

USAGE **learn, teach**
You **learn** a subject or skill if you study or practise it: *Greg's learning to drive.* If you **teach** someone a subject or skill, you help them to learn it: *My mother taught me how to cook.*

learn·er /ˈlɜːnə $ ˈlɜːnɚ/ *noun* someone who is learning a language, skill etc: *a course for advanced learners of English* | *Teresa's a slow learner.*

learn·ing /ˈlɜːnɪŋ $ ˈlɜːnɪŋ/ *noun* [no plural] knowledge that you get by reading and studying, or the activity of reading and studying: *Learning should be fun.*

learnt a past tense and past participle of LEARN

leash /liːʃ/ *noun, plural* **leashes** a long piece of leather that you fasten to a dog's collar to keep it near you ⇨ *same meaning* LEAD²: *I have to keep my dog on a leash.*

least /liːst/ *adverb, pronoun*
the smallest amount: *It's the part of the world I know least about.* | *He answered the least difficult*

L

questions. | He always did the thing that required the least effort. | Let me pay for the meal – **it's the least I can do** after you've helped me so much.

PHRASE

at least a) not less than a particular number or amount: The bridge will take **at least** two years to build. | Her dress must have cost **at least** $2000. b) spoken used when mentioning a good part of a bad situation: **At least** we now know what the problem is. c) spoken used before correcting or changing what you have said: He said he'd been swimming – **at least** I think that's what he said. d) used to say what someone should do, even if they do nothing more: If you can't stay for lunch, **at least** stay for a cup of coffee.

leath·er /'leðə $ 'leðɚ/ noun [no plural] animal skin that is used to make shoes, coats etc: a leather bag

leave¹ ⇨ see box on next page

leave² /liːv/ noun [no plural] time that you are allowed to spend away from your job: Our tutor is on leave. | The maximum maternity leave (=leave that a woman can have when she has a new baby) is three months.

leaves the plural of LEAF

lec·ture¹ /'lektʃə $ 'lektʃɚ/ noun a talk to a group of people that teaches them about a subject: What time is the lecture? | a lecture on Beethoven

lecture² verb to teach a group of people about a subject: Dr Marks lectures in biology.
—**lecturer** noun: Miss Jones is a university lecturer.

led the past tense and past participle of LEAD¹

ledge /ledʒ/ noun a narrow flat surface sticking out from the side of a building or a mountain

leek /liːk/ noun a long white and green vegetable that tastes like an onion ⇨ see picture on page 345

left¹ /left/ adjective
your left side is on or near the side of your body that contains your heart ⇨ opposite RIGHT¹ (2): She wore a gold bracelet on her left wrist.

left² adverb
turn left, look left etc to turn, look etc towards your right side: Turn left at the traffic lights and then the school is straight ahead of you. ⇨ opposite RIGHT² (1)

left³ noun
1 **on the left, to your left** etc in the direction of the left side of your body: The Taylors' house is on the left. | To your left you can see the church tower.
2 **the Left** political groups that believe that money should be shared out more equally, for example Socialists

left⁴ the past tense and past participle of LEAVE

left-hand /ˌ. './ adjective on the left: The house is on the left-hand side of the street.

left-hand·ed /ˌ. '../ adjective a left-handed person uses their left hand to do things such as writing or throwing a ball

left·o·vers /'leftəʊvəz $ 'left,oʊvɚz/ plural noun food that has not been eaten during a meal: We gave the leftovers to the dog.

left-wing /ˌ. './ adjective supporting the political ideas of groups such as Socialists and Communists: left-wing voters

leg /leg/ noun
1 one of the long parts of your body that you use for walking and standing: She broke her leg in a riding accident. ⇨ see picture at BODY
2 one of the parts that support a table, chair etc
3 one of the parts of a pair of trousers that cover your legs: My jeans have a hole in the left leg.

le·gal /'liːgəl/ adjective
1 allowed by the law or done correctly according to the law ⇨ opposite ILLEGAL: Is the contract legal?
2 related to the law: the legal system | You should go to a lawyer for legal advice.
—**legally** adverb: The school is legally responsible for the safety of its students.

le·gal·ize also **legalise** BrE /'liːgəlaɪz/ verb to change the law so that something

► LEAVE or FORGET?

LEAVE when you have not brought something with you, either because you did not want to or because you have forgotten it: *I **left** my coursebook at home.*

FORGET when you have not brought something because you have not remembered it: *I **forgot** to bring my coursebook.*

► LEAVE

1 to go away from a place
*We **left** the party at about midnight.* | *Bruce **left** on Monday morning.* | *It's a good college, but Mark doesn't really want to **leave** California.* | *I have to **leave** for the airport at seven.* | *The ferry **leaves from** Dover.*

2 to not take something with you
*Oh no! I **left** my keys **in** the car!* | *I'll **leave** my stuff here until we get back.*

3 to let something stay the same as it is now
*Who **left** the door **open**?* | ***Leave** your shoes **on** – we're going out again soon.*

GRAMMAR
leave something on/off/open/closed etc

6 to end a relationship with your husband or wife
*They were fighting a lot and he finally just **left**.* | *She **left** her husband after five years of marriage.*

leave

5 to stop doing a job, going to school etc
*Many British children **leave** school at sixteen.* | *She **left** her job when she had a baby.*

4 to put something somewhere
*You can **leave** the coats in the bedroom.* | *I **left** a copy of the report on your desk.*

PHRASES

leave someone alone
to stop annoying someone: *Holly, **leave** Becky **alone** – she's doing her homework.*

leave something alone
to stop touching something: *Ruff! Bad dog. **Leave** the plants **alone**!*

leave a message
to give information to one person so that they can give it to another person: *"He isn't home right now." "Oh, can I **leave a message** for him, then?"*

be left, be left over
if something is left or left over, it is still there after other things have been eaten or used: *Is there any cake **left**?* | *If there's any pasta **left over**, put it in the fridge.*

L

is made legal: *They want the government to legalize the drug.*

le·gend /'ledʒənd/ *noun* **1** an old well-known story about people who lived in the past: *ancient Greek legends* **2** someone who is famous for being very good at something: *rock 'n' roll legend, Elvis Presley*

le·gen·da·ry /'ledʒəndəri $'ledʒən,deri/ *adjective* very famous and admired: *the legendary singer, Frank Sinatra*

leg·gings /'legɪŋz/ *plural noun* a piece of women's clothing that fits closely around the legs: *She wore a pair of red leggings.* ➾ *see picture on page 352*

le·gi·ble /'ledʒəbəl/ *adjective* writing that is legible is clear enough for you to read ➾ *opposite* ILLEGIBLE

le·git·i·mate /lə'dʒɪtəmət/ *adjective* *formal* not illegal: *a legitimate business agreement*

lei·sure /'leʒə $'liʒɚ/ *noun* [no plural] time when you are not working and can do things that you enjoy: *How do you spend your leisure time?*

lei·sure·ly /'leʒəli $'liʒɚli/ *adjective* done in a fairly slow relaxed way: *a leisurely walk*

lem·on /'lemən/ *noun* a yellow fruit that tastes sour ➾ *see picture on page 345*

lem·on·ade /,lemə'neɪd/ *noun* [no plural] **1** *BrE* a clear sweet drink with lots of BUBBLES: *a glass of lemonade* **2** a drink made from lemons, water, and sugar

lend /lend/ *verb, past tense and past participle* **lent** /lent/

GRAMMAR
lend someone something
lend something to someone
to let someone borrow something that you own: *I can lend you £10.* | *I had lent my best jacket to a friend.*

USAGE
If you **lend** something **to** someone, you give it to them so that they can use it for a short time: *I've lent that computer game to Rick.* If you **borrow** something **from** someone, you take something that belongs to them, use it for a short time, and then give it back to them: *Can I borrow your car this afternoon?* | *I borrowed the money from the bank.*

length /leŋθ/ *noun*

GRAMMAR
the length of something
a length of something
1 how long something is: *They measured the length of the garden.* | *The snake was 2 metres in length.*
2 the amount of time that something continues for: *The length of the course is ten weeks.* | *The length of time that people have to wait varies.*
3 a long piece of something: *She cut off a length of thread.*

PHRASE
go to any lengths to do something, go to great lengths to do something to do everything you can to achieve something: *She went to great lengths to hide the fact that she couldn't read.*

length·en /'leŋθən/ *verb* to make something longer or to become longer: *I need to lengthen these trousers.* | *In the summer, the days lengthen and everyone seems happier.*

length·ways /'leŋθweɪz/ also **length·wise** /'leŋθwaɪz/ *adverb* in the direction of the longest side: *Cut the carrots lengthways.*

length·y /'leŋθi/ *adjective* **lengthier, lengthiest** continuing for a long time: *a lengthy performance*

lens /lenz/ *noun, plural* **lenses** **1** a piece of curved glass or plastic that makes things look bigger or smaller: *a camera with a zoom lens* | *glasses with tinted lenses* **2** the part of your eye that bends the light coming in

Lent /lent/ *noun* the 40 days before Easter, when some Christians stop doing something that they enjoy

lent the past tense and past participle of LEND

leop·ard /'lepəd $'lepɚd/ *noun* a large wild cat with yellow fur and black spots

le·o·tard /'liːətɑːd $'liːə,tɑrd/ *noun* a piece of clothing that covers the main part of the body, which women wear when dancing or exercising

les·bi·an /'lezbiən/ *noun* a woman who is sexually attracted to other women: *lesbian and gay rights*

less /les/ *adverb, pronoun* a smaller amount: *I wish it was less* cold! | *Catching the train is less effort than driving.* | *You should try to worry less.* | *Could you put less milk in my tea next time?* | *It cost less than £10.*

PHRASES

less and less: *Computers are becoming less and less expensive* (=they are continuing to become less expensive).

no less than used to emphasize that an amount is large: *No less than 70% of this forest has been destroyed.*

USAGE less, fewer

Use **less** before a noun that has no plural: *We've had less sunshine this year than last year.* Use **fewer** before a plural noun: *In those days there were fewer cars on the streets.*

less·en /'lesən/ *verb formal* to become smaller in amount, or to make something become smaller: *The pain had lessened slightly.* | *Exercise lessens the risk of heart disease.*

les·son /'lesən/ *noun*

1 a period of time in which someone is taught a subject or skill. You have or take lessons in something: *I've only had two driving lessons.*

2 an experience from which you can learn something useful, or the thing that you learn: *This experience taught me an important lesson: don't judge people too quickly.*

let /let/ *verb*, *past tense and past participle* let, letting

GRAMMAR
let someone/something do something
let someone/something in/out/through
let something to someone

1 to allow someone to do something, or to allow something to happen: *Will your parents let you go to America alone?* | *We wanted to go outside but our teacher wouldn't let us.* | *Don't let yourself be hurt by their attitude.* | *They've let the garden become very untidy.* ⇨ see usage note at ALLOW

2 to make it possible for someone or something to go in, out, or through somewhere, for example by opening

a door: *Open the door and let me in!* | *Don't forget to let the cat out of the house at night.* | *The crowds stood back to let the doctor through.*

3 if you let a room or house, you allow someone to use it and they pay you: *We went to France, and let our house to some students.*

PHRASES

let's, let's not *spoken* used to suggest doing something or not doing something: *"Let's go to the cinema tonight." "Oh, let's not."*

let someone know *informal* to tell someone something that they need or want to know: *Let me know if you need any help.* | *Will you let us know what time your plane's arriving?*

let someone/something go, let go to stop holding someone or something: *Let me go! You're hurting me!* | *Hold onto the rope and don't let go.* | *Jamie accidentally let go of the dog's lead.*

let me do something *spoken* used to offer to help someone: *Let me open that bottle for you.*

PHRASAL VERBS

let down
let someone down to not do what you promised you would do or what you were expected to do: *You can trust Jim – he'd never let you down.*

let in on
let someone in on something *spoken* to tell someone something that is a secret: *Shall we let Liz in on the plan?*

let off
let someone off to not punish someone when they have done something wrong: *"I'll let you off this time," the policeman said.*

let on
spoken if you do not let on that something is true, you do not tell anyone, because it is a secret: *He didn't let on that he'd met her before.*

let·down /'letdaʊn/ *noun informal* something that disappoints you: *The film was rather a letdown – I expected it to be more exciting.*

le·thal /'li:θəl/ *adjective* something that is lethal can kill you: *a lethal weapon*

L

let's /lets/ the short form of 'let us'

let·ter /'letə $ 'letɚ/ noun

1 a written message that you put in an envelope and send to someone: *I got a letter from my friend Anne yesterday.* | *I'll post the letter to him today.*
2 one of the signs that you use to write words: *the letter A*

let·ter·box /'letəbɒks $ 'letɚˌbɑks/ noun BrE, plural **letterboxes** 1 a hole in a door through which letters are put when they are delivered ⇨ *see picture on page 343* 2 a box in a post office or in the street, where you post letters; MAILBOX AmE

let·tuce /'letɪs/ noun a round green vegetable whose leaves you eat without cooking them: *lettuce and tomato salad* ⇨ *see picture on page 345*

lev·el¹ /'levəl/ noun

> **GRAMMAR**
> **the level of something**

1 the amount of something: *The noise level in the building has increased.* | *the high level of crime | students with the same level of ability*
2 the height of a liquid: *Changes in sea levels may result in flooding.*
3 a position in a system or structure that has different ranks or layers: *This decision can only be taken at a higher level.*

> **PHRASE**

at eye level, at ground level at the same height as your eyes or the ground: *All the controls are at eye level.*

level² adjective

> **GRAMMAR**
> **level with something**

1 flat, with no part higher than any other part: *Make sure that the ground is level before sowing the grass seed.*
2 at the same height or as far forward as something else: *The top of her head was level with his chin.* | *The two cars were almost level.*

level³ verb **levelled, levelling** BrE, **leveled, leveling** AmE 1 written if something such as a storm levels buildings, it destroys them completely: *The earth-*

quake has levelled this area of the city.
2 **level off, level out** to become steady after rising quickly: *House prices are beginning to level off.*

level cross·ing /ˌ.. '../ noun BrE a place where a road and a railway cross ⇨ *see picture on page 349*

level-head·ed /ˌ.. '../ adjective calm and sensible: *He's a firm and level-headed leader.*

le·ver /'liːvə $ 'levɚ/ noun 1 a bar that you use to lift a heavy object by putting one end under the object and pushing the other end of the bar down 2 a handle on a machine that you move to make the machine work

li·a·bil·i·ty /ˌlaɪəˈbɪləti/ noun [no plural] formal legal responsibility for something: *We accept no liability for cars that are left here overnight.*

li·a·ble /'laɪəbəl/ adjective be liable to do something to be likely to do something: *This film is liable to upset some viewers.*

li·ar /'laɪə $ 'laɪɚ/ noun someone who tells lies: *Are you calling me a liar?*

lib·e·ral /'lɪbərəl/ adjective someone who is liberal thinks that people should be allowed to do what they want ⇨ *same meaning* TOLERANT: *a liberal attitude towards drugs*

lib·e·rate /'lɪbəreɪt/ verb written to free someone from a situation or place that they cannot get out of: *US soldiers liberated the prisoners.*

lib·e·ra·tion /ˌlɪbəˈreɪʃən/ noun [no plural] when people are freed from a situation or place that they could not get out of: *the black liberation movement*

lib·er·ty /'lɪbəti $ 'lɪbɚti/ noun formal, plural **liberties** when you are free to live how you want without being told what to do: *This new law is a threat to our liberty.*

li·brar·i·an /laɪˈbreəriən $ laɪˈbreriən/ noun someone who works in a library

li·bra·ry /'laɪbrəri $ 'laɪˌbreri/ noun, plural **libraries** a room or building containing books that you can borrow, and other information on computers that you can use

li·cence BrE, **license** AmE /'laɪsəns/ noun an official document that gives you permission to do something: *Can I see your driving licence?*

L

license plate /'.. ,./ the American word for NUMBER PLATE

lick /lɪk/ *verb* to move your tongue across something: *The dog licked my face.*

lid /lɪd/ *noun* a cover for the top of a container: *Put the lid on the paint tin.*

lie¹ /laɪ/ *verb* **lay** /leɪ/ **lain** /leɪn/ **lying**

GRAMMAR
lie on something

1 also **lie down** if you are lying somewhere, your body is flat on a surface, for example the floor or a bed: *She was lying on the grass.* | *I feel a bit ill – I think I'll go and lie down.* | *I lay awake for ages.*

2 if something is lying somewhere, it is on something in a flat position: *She picked up the parcel lying on the table.*

PHRASES
lie ahead to be going to happen in the future: *Who knows what lies ahead?*

lie in wait *written* to remain hidden in order to attack someone: *The robbers had been lying in wait for him.*

PHRASAL VERBS
lie around also **lie about** *BrE*

1 **lie around, lie around something** if things are lying around, they have been left in the wrong place, in an untidy way: *He always left letters and papers lying around.* | *It's not sensible to have that amount of money lying around the house!*

2 **lie around, lie around something** to spend time sitting or lying in a relaxed way: *He just lies around doing nothing all day.*

lie behind
lie behind something to be the true reason for an action: *What lay behind Keith's criticism of Tony?* ⇨ see usage note at LAY¹

lie² *verb, present participle* **lying** to tell someone something that you know is not true: *He says he's rich but I think he's lying.* | *You lied to me!*

lie³ *noun* something that you say that you know is not true: *We found out that she'd been telling lies.*

lieu·ten·ant /lef'tenənt $ luː'tenənt/ *noun* an officer who has a middle rank in the army, navy, or AIR FORCE

life /laɪf/ *noun, plural* **lives** /laɪvz/

1 the period of time during which someone is alive: *I have lived in England all my life.* | *Do you want to spend the rest of your life being unhappy?* | *My father had a very hard life.*

2 the state of being alive: *They filmed the baby's first moments of life.* | *The animal showed no signs of life* (=it looked dead).

3 the activities of someone, especially someone who is in a particular place or situation: *Life in the city is very busy.* | *Are you enjoying married life?* | *He doesn't like questions about his private life.*

4 [no plural] living things such as people, animals, or plants: *Is there life on Mars?* | *the sea life of the Great Barrier Reef*

5 [no plural] activity or movement: *Young children are always so full of life.*

PHRASES
save someone's life to stop someone from being killed: *The fireman saved her life by carrying her from the burning building.*

be for life if something is for life, it continues until you are dead: *Marriage is supposed to be for life.*

way of life the typical or usual things that someone does: *They enjoy a simple way of life in the country.*

real life what really happens, rather than what happens in stories or in your imagination: *In real life there is not always a happy ending.*

life·boat /'laɪfbəʊt $ 'laɪfboʊt/ *noun* a boat that is used to save people who are in danger at sea: *They sent the lifeboat to search for the missing sailors.*

life guard /'. ./ *noun* someone whose job is to help swimmers who are in danger at the beach or at a swimming pool

life jack·et /'. ,../ *noun* a piece of clothing that you wear around your chest so that you float if you fall into water

life jacket

life·like /'laɪflaɪk/ *adjective* a picture or model that is lifelike looks very much like a real person or thing: *The statue is quite lifelike.*

life·long /ˈlaɪflɒŋ $ ˈlaɪflɔŋ/ adjective continuing all through your life: *She was my mother's lifelong friend.*

life-size /ˈ. ./ adjective a life-size picture or model is the same size as the real thing: *She painted a life-size picture of her dog.*

life·style /ˈlaɪfstaɪl/ noun the way that someone lives, including the things they do and the things they own: *They have a very exciting lifestyle.*

life·time /ˈlaɪftaɪm/ noun the period of time during which someone is alive: *There may not be a cure for cancer in my lifetime.*

lift¹ /lɪft/ verb

GRAMMAR
lift something/someone somewhere

1 also **lift up** to move something or someone to a higher position: *I can't lift this table on my own.* | *Paul lifted the lid from the box.* | *My father lifted me up on his shoulders.* ⇨ *see picture on page 340*

2 to end a rule or law that stops people from doing something: *We hope they will lift the ban and allow us to play in the competition.*

lift² noun 1 BrE a machine that takes you up and down in a building; ELEVATOR AmE: *I took the lift to the tenth floor.* 2 BrE a ride in a car; RIDE AmE: *I'll give you a lift to the station.*

light¹ /laɪt/ noun

1 [no plural] the brightness that comes from the sun or from a lamp, which allows you to see things: *There isn't much light in this room because the window is small.*

2 an electric lamp that gives light. You switch on or turn on a light to make it work, and you switch off or turn off a light to make it stop working: *Remember to turn the lights off before you go to bed.* | *the bright lights of Las Vegas*

3 lights a set of red, green, and yellow lights that tell drivers when to stop and when to go: *Turn right at the lights.*

PHRASES
see something in a new light, see something in a different light to have a different idea about some-

thing because of something that happens: *After talking to my mother, I saw things in a different light.*

shed light on something, throw light on something to explain something or make it easier to understand: *They got some new information that shed light on the accident.*

light² adjective

1 if it is light, it is daytime and there is enough light to see: *We need to finish the game while it is still light.*

2 a light colour is not very strong or not very dark: *a light grey shirt*

3 a light room is full of light from the sun: *The living room is very light because it has a large window.*

4 not heavy: *These small computers are light and easy to carry.* ⇨ *see picture at* HEAVY

5 not very thick or warm: *Just bring a light jacket.*

6 if traffic is light, there are not many cars and other vehicles on the road

7 gentle or without much force: *A light rain began to fall.* | *I gave him a light tap on the shoulder.*

light³ verb, past tense and past participle **lit** /lɪt/ or **lighted**

1 to start burning, or to make something start burning: *I can't get this wood to light.* | *He lit his pipe and began to smoke.*

2 also **light up** to make a place become light or bright: *Orange lights lit the stage.* | *A sudden flash of lightning lit up the whole sky.*

light bulb /ˈ. ./ noun a round glass and metal object that produces light from electricity: *Sue changed the light bulb* (=put in a new one).

light·er /ˈlaɪtə $ ˈlaɪtɚ/ noun a small object that produces a flame to light a cigarette

light·house /ˈlaɪthaʊs/ noun a tower with a bright light that warns ships of danger ⇨ *see picture on page 348*

lighthouse

lightning

light·ing /'laɪtɪŋ/ *noun* the lights in a place, or the way a place is lit: *Soft lighting creates a romantic mood.*

light·ly /'laɪtli/ *adverb* without using a lot of force: *I tapped him lightly on the shoulder.*

light·ning /'laɪtnɪŋ/ *noun* [no plural] a bright flash of electrical light in the sky during a storm: *There was thunder and lightning.* ⇨ *see picture at* LIGHTHOUSE

lik·a·ble /'laɪkəbəl/ *adjective* LIKEABLE

like¹ /laɪk/ *verb* **liked, liking, have liked**

> **GRAMMAR**
> **like doing something**
> **like to do something**
> **like something about someone/ something**

to think that someone or something is nice or good: *Katie **likes** John a lot.* | *I think you would really **like** this movie.* | *I really **like to** travel.* | *Katherine **likes** playing basketball* | *What **do** you **like** best **about** teaching?* | *I don't **like it when** Dave doesn't come home on time.*

> **USAGE**
> Do not say *I am liking* or *I am liking to do it.* Say *I like it* or *I like to do it.* Do not say *I like very much Anna.* Say *I like Anna very much.*

> **PHRASES**
> **I would like, I'd like...** *spoken* say this to tell someone politely what you want or what you want to do: *I'd like a glass of milk, please.* | *I'd **like to** talk to Jim first.* | *I **would** really **like to** get some sleep.* | *Mr. Robbins **would like** you **to** come to the meeting.*
>
> **would you like...?** *spoken* say this to ask someone politely if they want something: *Would you **like** a cup of tea?* | *Would Dana **like to** come with us?* | *What **would you like** for dinner?*

> **USAGE**
> When you are asking someone for something, do not say **I want** because it is not polite. Instead, say **I would like** or **May I have?/Could I have?** People often say **Can I have?** but many teachers think this is incorrect. When you are offering someone something, you can say **Do you want?** especially to your friends or your family, but it is more polite to say **Would you like?**

like² *preposition*

1 if one thing or person is like another, it is almost the same as the other person or thing: *I'd love to have a car **like** Diane's.* | *His new film is a lot **like** his last one.* | *It **tastes** a little **like** chicken.* | *Harry **looks like** his dad.* | *I **felt like** I was getting a cold.*

2 use **like** to give examples about something you are talking about: *Vegetables **like** broccoli and carrots are very good for you.* | *Games **like** chess take a long time to learn.* ⇨ *same meaning* SUCH AS

> **USAGE**
> Many teachers think that using **like** in this way is wrong. It is better to use **such as**: *Games **such as** chess take a long time to learn.*

3 what is someone/something like? say this to ask someone to describe a person, place, or thing: *They asked **what it was like** to work for an MP.* | ***What does** Robby **look like**? Is he tall?* | ***What was** the movie **like**?*

like³ *noun* someone's likes and dislikes the things someone likes and the things they do not like: *What are your girlfriend's likes and dislikes?*

like⁴ *spoken* **1** as if: *He talks like he's American.* **2** in the same way as: *Do it just like I said.*

like·a·ble also **likable** /'laɪkəbəl/ *adjective* likeable people are nice and easy to like: *Jo's a very likeable girl.*

like·li·hood /'laɪklihʊd/ *noun* [no plural] how likely something is to happen: *What's the likelihood of you passing your exams?*

like·ly /'laɪkli/ *adjective* **likelier, likeliest**

> **GRAMMAR**
> **likely to do something**
> **it is likely (that)**

1 if something is likely to happen, it will probably happen: *Rain is likely this afternoon.* | *Ruth **is** not **likely to** make many mistakes.* | *It's **likely that** he will have to miss Tuesday's game.*

2 if something is likely, it is probably true: *She thinks he has stolen her*

L

purse, but that's not very likely. | Is it
likely that *John is lying?*

like·ness /ˈlaɪknəs/ *noun* [no plural] if
there is a likeness between two people,
they look similar to each other: *The likeness between Sara and her mother is incredible.*

limb /lɪm/ *noun* an arm or leg: *Have you
ever broken a limb?*

lime /laɪm/ *noun* a bright green fruit with
a sour taste

lime·light /ˈlaɪmlaɪt/ *noun* be in the
limelight *informal* if you are in the limelight, you have the attention of a lot of
people: *Geri loves being in the limelight.*

lim·it¹ /ˈlɪmɪt/ *noun*

GRAMMAR
a limit on/to something
the greatest amount, number, or
speed that is allowed or possible: *Is
there a limit on the amount of
money you can borrow? | The speed
limit is 30 miles per hour on this
road.*

limit² *verb*

GRAMMAR
limit something to something
limit someone to something
be limited to something
1 to keep something at or below a particular amount or number: *Try to
limit the amount of salt you eat. | We
are limiting the working week to 35
hours.*
2 to allow someone to have or use
only a particular amount of something: *She has limited us to only
one piece of cake each. | Fans will
be limited to two tickets each.*
3 if something is limited to a place,
it only exists or happens there:
*Her injuries were limited to her
back.*

lim·i·ta·tions /ˌlɪməˈteɪʃəns/ *plural
noun* the limits of what someone or
something is able to do: *You have to
understand the limitations of the software.*

lim·it·ed /ˈlɪmətɪd/ *adjective* small in
amount or number: *There are only a
limited number of tickets.*

lim·ou·sine /ˈlɪməziːn/ *noun* a big expensive car in which someone is driven

somewhere: *He arrived at the party in a
black limousine.*

limp /lɪmp/ *verb* to walk with difficulty
because one leg is hurt: *He had hurt his
leg and was limping badly.*
– limp *noun*: *Sue walks with a limp.*

line¹ /laɪn/ *noun*
1 a long thin mark that someone has
drawn or painted on a surface: *Draw
a line under the title. | Someone had
put a line through (=crossed out) my
name. | Which runner crossed the
finishing line first?*
2 a number of people or things behind
or next to each other: *Ian went
straight to the front of the line. | A
line of cars were waiting to move.*
3 a long piece of rope, string, or wire
that is used for a particular purpose:
*Sally hung the wet clothes on the
line.*
4 the connection between two telephones: *Stay on the line while I try
and find Maxine. | I have been hold-
ing the line (=waiting to speak to
someone) for twenty minutes.*
5 a track for trains to travel along: *the
main line between London and Edinburgh*
6 a group of words in a poem, play, or
song: *Actors spend a long time
learning their lines.*

PHRASE
on line if you are on line, you have a
computer or you are using your
computer: *Soon the whole office will
be on line.*

line² *verb* 1 to cover the inside of
something with a material: *Line the
drawers with paper.* 2 if people or
things line something, they are in rows
along the edges: *Cheering children lined
the streets.* 3 line up if people line up,
they move to form a line: *The children
lined up at the door.*

lined /laɪnd/ *adjective* lined paper has straight lines printed on it

lin·en /'lɪnən/ *noun [no plural]* a high quality cloth like thick strong cotton: *a blue linen jacket*

lin·ger /'lɪŋɡə $ 'lɪŋɡɚ/ *verb* to stay somewhere for a long time: *The smell of cigarettes lingered in the room.*

lin·guis·tic /lɪŋ'ɡwɪstɪk/ *adjective* related to how well someone speaks or understands a language: *The children had different linguistic abilities.*

lin·ing /'laɪnɪŋ/ *noun* a piece of material that covers the inside of a piece of clothing: *The lining of her coat was torn.*

link¹ /lɪŋk/ *verb* **1** to join one place or thing to another: *The bridge links the two sides of the town.* **2** to decide that there is a connection between different situations, events, or people: *Scientists have linked cancer with smoking.*

link² *noun* **1** a relationship or connection between different situations, events, or people: *There is a link between crime and unemployment.* **2** one of the rings in a chain

li·on /'laɪən/ *noun* a large African and Asian wild cat: *The male lion has long thick hair around his neck.* ⇨ *see picture on page 339*

lip /lɪp/ *noun* one of the two edges of your mouth where the skin is redder or darker: *My lips are sore.* ⇨ *see picture at* HEAD¹

lip·stick /'lɪp,stɪk/ *noun* a coloured substance that some women wear on their lips: *She put on some red lipstick.* ⇨ *see picture at* MAKE-UP

liq·uid /'lɪkwɪd/ *noun* a substance such as water which flows and is not solid or a gas: *The nurse cleaned the wound with a clear liquid.*

liq·uor /'lɪkə $ 'lɪkɚ/ *noun AmE* a strong alcoholic drink such as WHISKY: *I could smell liquor on his breath.*

list¹ /lɪst/ *noun*

GRAMMAR
a list of things
a number of different things that you write one below the other: *I need a **list of** the people coming to the party.* | *What is the first item **on** your list?* | *Why don't you **make a shopping list**?*

list² *verb* to write a list: *List all the subjects you are studying.*

lis·ten ⇨ *see box on next page*

lis·ten·er /'lɪsənə $ 'lɪsənɚ/ *noun* someone who listens to something or someone: *Most of the radio station's listeners are young people.* | *Mary's a good listener.*

lit the past tense and past participle of LIGHT³

liter the American spelling of LITRE

lit·e·ral·ly /'lɪtərəli/ *adverb* **1** according to the basic or first meaning of a word: *'Television' literally means 'seeing at a distance'.* **2** used to emphasize that what you are saying is true even if it seems unlikely: *I was literally weak with hunger.*

lit·e·ra·ry /'lɪtərəri $ 'lɪtə,reri/ *adjective* related to literature: *She won a literary prize for her first book.*

lit·e·ra·ture /'lɪtərətʃə $ 'lɪtərətʃɚ/ *noun [no plural]* books, poems, and plays that are well written and considered to be good and important: *I'm interested in French literature.*

li·tre *BrE*, **liter** *AmE* /'liːtə $ 'litɚ/ *noun* a unit for measuring liquid: *a litre of water*

lit·ter¹ /'lɪtə $ 'lɪtɚ/ *noun [no plural]* waste paper, cans etc that people leave on the ground: *The streets were covered in litter.*

litter² *verb* if a lot of things litter a place, they are spread all over it in an untidy way: *The desk was littered with old letters.*

lit·tle¹ /'lɪtl/ *adjective*

1 small in size: *Look at that little baby.* | *a **tiny little** insect*
2 continuing for a short time: *There might be a little while before you can see the doctor.* | *We'll be back in a **little while** (=a short time).*
3 not very far: *Let's go for a little walk.*
4 not important: *We only had one little problem.*

little² less /les/ least /liːst/
formal not much: *Little has been done to improve the situation.* | *There's **very little** work to do.*

PHRASE
a little, a little bit **a)** a small amount of something: *Can I have a **little bit of** cheese?* | *"Would you*

➤ LISTEN or HEAR?

LISTEN you **listen** when you hear and pay attention to what someone says or to sounds or music

HEAR you **hear** a sound that has been made

*We were **listening** to the radio.*

*I **heard** the phone ringing.*

➤ LISTEN

listen

❶ to try to hear and understand sounds or what someone is saying
*I **was listening to** the news on the car radio. | What did you want to tell me? I'm **listening** now. | **Have** you **listened to** that tape Carl gave you yet? | People don't always **listen** carefully **to** children.*

> **GRAMMAR**
> **listen to someone/something**
>
> ✗ Don't say ➤ *listen music* or *listen him.*
> ✓ Say ➤ *listen to music, listen to him.*

❷ say this when you want someone to listen when you say something *spoken*
***Listen**, did you ever call Michelle back? | Okay, **listen**, Amanda, it's time to clean your room.*

PHRASAL VERBS

listen for someone, listen for something
to try to hear a particular sound: *He stopped by the door and **listened for** the sound of footsteps.*

L

▼ like some cake?" "Just *a **little**.*" b)
slightly: *My back still hurts a **little**.*

USAGE
Use **little** when you mean 'not much': *I've got very little money left.* Use **a little** when you mean 'a small amount': *I'm afraid I've spilt a little wine on the carpet.* **(A) little** is always used with nouns that have no plural. For plural nouns look at the note at **few**.

live¹ /lɪv/ *verb*

GRAMMAR
live in/at a place

1 if you live in a place, that place is your home: *Where do you live?* | *I **live at** 12 Queen Street.* | *She **lives in** London.*
2 to continue to be alive: *He doesn't seem to care if I live or die.* | *My grandfather lived until he was ninety.*
3 to have a particular kind of life: *Rock stars live exciting lives.*

PHRASAL VERBS
live on also **live off**
1 live on/off something if you live on or off a small amount of money, you only have that amount to buy all the things that you need: *How can I **live on** £10 a week?*
2 live on/off something to eat only a particular kind of food: *These animals **live on** leaves and fruit.* | *She **lives on** pizza.*
live together
if two people live together, they live in the same house and have a sexual relationship, but they are not married: *We **lived together** for two years before getting married.*
live with
1 live with someone to live in the same house as someone: *How long have you **lived with** your brother?*
2 live with someone to live in the same house as someone and have a sexual relationship with them, without being married: *He's my boyfriend, but I don't want to **live with** him yet.*

live² /laɪv/ *adjective*

1 live animals are alive: *I've never seen a live snake.*
2 if a television or radio programme is live, you see it or hear it at the same

▼ time as it happens: *Many things can go wrong in a live broadcast.*
3 live music is perfomed for people who are watching and listening in the same place: *You can see the band live tomorrow night.*

live·li·hood /ˈlaɪvlihʊd/ *noun* the job that you do to earn money in order to live: *Painting is my livelihood.*
live·ly /ˈlaɪvli/ *adjective* **livelier, liveliest** full of activity: *a group of lively six-year-olds* | *The town becomes livelier at night when people go out to clubs.*
liv·en /ˈlaɪvən/ *verb* **liven something up** to make something more interesting or exciting: *We need some music to liven the party up.*
liv·er /ˈlɪvə $ˈlɪvɚ/ *noun* **1** a large part inside your body that cleans your blood **2** [no plural] the liver of an animal that people eat as food: *lamb's liver*
lives the plural of LIFE
liv·id /ˈlɪvɪd/ *adjective* extremely angry: *My mother was livid when she saw the mess.*
liv·ing¹ /ˈlɪvɪŋ/ *adjective* **1** alive now: *Who is your favourite living author?*
2 living things things that are alive, such as animals and plants
living² *noun* the way that you earn money in order to live: *She earns a living by giving music lessons.*
living room /ˈ.. ˌ./ *noun* the main room in a house, where you relax by watching television, listening to music, reading etc: *Jay's in the living room watching TV.*
liz·ard /ˈlɪzəd $ˈlɪzɚd/ *noun* a type of REPTILE that has four short legs, a long tail, and skin like a snake

load¹ /ləʊd $loʊd/ *noun*

GRAMMAR
a load of something

an amount of something that a vehicle carries: *a train carrying a load of coal* | *A lorry has shed its load on the motorway* (=its load has fallen off).

PHRASES
a load of something *spoken* a lot of something: *We have a load of prizes to give away.*
loads (of something) *spoken* a lot of something: *His father earns loads of money.* | *There were loads of*
▼ people there.

L

load

a load of rubbish, a load of nonsense *spoken* used to say that something is completely wrong or very stupid: *Don't listen to what she says – it's a load of nonsense.*

load² *verb*

GRAMMAR
load something onto/into something

1 also **load up** to put a lot of things into a vehicle: *Will you help me load the car?* | *We loaded the wood onto the back of the truck.* | *The boxes are then loaded into vans.* | *It took us ages to load up the van.*
2 to put a PROGRAM into a computer: *You need to load the software onto your computer.*
3 to put a film into a camera: *I just need to load a new film and then I'll be ready to take the pictures.*
4 to put bullets into a gun

load·ed /'ləʊdɪd $ 'loʊdɪd/ *adjective*
1 a loaded weapon is one that contains bullets: *Is the gun loaded?* 2 if something is loaded with things, it has a lot of them on it or in it: *The shelves were loaded with books.*

loaf /ləʊf $ loʊf/ *noun, plural* loaves /ləʊvz $ loʊvz/ bread that has been baked in one large piece: *I bought a loaf of bread.*

loan¹ /ləʊn $ loʊn/ *noun*

an amount of money that you borrow. You take out a loan when you borrow the money and repay it, pay it back, or pay it off when you give the money back: *We took out a loan to buy our new car.* | *We're never going to be able to pay back this loan.*

PHRASE
be on loan if something is on loan, you have borrowed it from somewhere: *This book is on loan from the library.*

loan² *verb* to lend someone something, especially money: *I'll loan you the money.*

loathe /ləʊð $ loʊð/ *verb* to hate someone or something very much: *I loathe shopping.*

loaves the plural of LOAF

lob·by /'lɒbi $ 'lɑbi/ *noun, plural* lobbies a large area inside the entrance of a building: *I'll meet you in the theatre lobby.*

lo·cal¹ /'ləʊkəl $ 'loʊkəl/ *adjective*
1 a local place is one near to the place where you live: *You can now get these fruit in your local supermarket.* 2 a local person lives in the same town or area as you: *They think the murderer is a local man.*
– **locally** *adverb*: *People who live locally can also attend the college.*

local² *noun* someone who lives in a place: *It's a lovely village and the locals are very friendly.*

lo·cate /ləʊ'keɪt $ 'loʊkeɪt/ *verb formal*
1 to find the exact position of something: *We need to locate the gas pipe.*
2 be located to be in a particular place or position: *The engine is located in the front of the car.*

lo·ca·tion /ləʊ'keɪʃən $ loʊ'keɪʃən/ *noun formal* the place or position where someone or something is: *What is your exact location?*

lock¹ /lɒk $ lɑk/ *verb*

GRAMMAR
lock someone in somewhere
lock someone out of somewhere

1 to fasten something with a lock: *He closed the door and then locked it.* | *I accidentally locked myself in the bathroom* (=I locked the door and was unable to get out). | *She locked me out of the house* (=she locked the door so I could not get in).
2 if a part of a machine locks, it becomes fixed in one position and unable to move: *The brakes locked, causing him to crash.*

PHRASAL VERBS
lock up
1 lock up, lock something up to make a building safe by locking all the doors: *Don't forget to lock up before you go home.* | *They had locked the house up and gone away.*
2 lock someone up to put someone in prison: *They should lock him up for what he did.*

lock² *noun*

GRAMMAR
a lock of something

1 a metal part of a door that you use to

▼ keep the door closed. You usually open a lock with a key: *Was there a lock on the door?*

2 *formal* a small number of hairs that are growing together on your head: *She cut off a lock of her hair and gave it to Sam.*

lock·er /'lɒkə $ 'lɑkɚ/ *noun* a small cupboard where you leave books, clothes etc, for example at school: *I've left my pen in my locker.*

lodg·er /'lɒdʒə $ 'lɑdʒɚ/ *noun* BrE someone who lives in someone else's house and pays rent

loft /lɒft $ lɔft/ *noun* BrE a room or space under the roof of a house ⇨ *same meaning* ATTIC: *Our old photographs are in the loft.*

log¹ /lɒg $ lɔg/ *noun* a thick piece of wood that has been cut from a tree: *Put another log on the fire.*

log² *verb* **logged, logging 1** to make an official record of events or facts: *We log all our telephone calls.* **2 log off, log out** to stop using a computer: *I logged off half an hour ago.* **3 log on, log in** to start using a computer: *I logged on and read my emails.*

lo·gic /'lɒdʒɪk $ 'lɑdʒɪk/ *noun [no plural]* a sensible way of thinking: *There does not seem to be any logic in what they are planning to do.*

lo·gic·al /'lɒdʒɪkəl $ 'lɑdʒɪkəl/ *adjective* reasonable and sensible ⇨ *opposite* ILLOGICAL: *There's no logical reason for you to be jealous.*
–logically /-kli/ *adverb*: *Let's think about this logically.*

lo·go /'ləʊgəʊ $ 'loʊgoʊ/ *noun* a design that is the official sign of a company or organization and goes on their products, letters etc

lone·ly /'ləʊnli $ 'loʊnli/ *adjective* **lonelier, loneliest**
1 unhappy because you are alone: *I felt really lonely while my parents were away.* | *Don't you ever get lonely living by yourself?* ⇨ *see usage note at* ALONE
2 *written* a lonely place is somewhere that very few people visit: *They arranged to meet on a lonely road near the beach.*

lon·er /'ləʊnə $ 'loʊnɚ/ *noun* someone who likes being alone

long¹ /lɒŋ $ lɔŋ/ *adjective*
1 something that is long measures a large distance from one end to the other ⇨ *opposite* SHORT¹ (2): *She's tall and slim, with long legs.* | *a long piece of string* | *It's a long way from here to the beach.*
2 continuing for a great amount of time ⇨ *opposite* SHORT¹ (1): *The chemistry lesson seemed very long.* | *We had to wait quite a long time.*
3 used to talk about the length of something: *Our garden is about fifty metres long.* | *How long is the film?*

long² *adverb*
a great amount of time: *Have you lived here long?* | *They hadn't been married for long.* | *Where have you been? I've been waiting so long!* | *I'm going to the shops but I'll try not to be long.*

PHRASES
as long as used to say that one thing is possible or will happen if another thing happens too: *We're going to the beach tomorrow, as long as the weather's nice.*
no longer, not any longer used to say that something has stopped happening or cannot continue: *My brother no longer goes to the same school as me.* | *We can't wait any longer.*

long³ *verb formal* to want something very much: *I longed to go to America.*

long-dis·tance /ˌ. '../ *adjective* travelling or happening between places that are a long distance apart: *She made a long-distance phone call.*

long·ing /'lɒŋɪŋ $ 'lɔŋɪŋ/ *noun* written when you want something very much: *Her longing to see her mother increased.*
–longingly *adverb*: *She looked longingly at the ice-cream.*

long jump /'. ./ *noun* a sport in which you jump as far as possible: *She's quite good at the long jump.*

long·sight·ed /ˌlɒŋ'saɪtɪd $ ˌlɔŋ'saɪtɪd/ *adjective* BrE someone who is longsighted can only see things clearly when they are far away; FARSIGHTED AmE

long-stand·ing /ˌ. '../ *adjective* a long-standing problem or situation has existed for a long time: *The two companies have a long-standing business relationship.*

long-term /ˌ. './ *adjective* a long-term plan or situation is connected with a time that is a long time in the future: *We don't know about the long-term effects of using drugs.*

loo /luː/ *noun BrE informal* a toilet

look¹ ⇨ *see box on next page*

look² /lʊk/ *noun* **1** when you look at something: *Take a look at this photo.* | *What's in the box – can I have a look?* **2** when you search for something: *Will you have a look for my keys?* **3** an expression on your face which shows how you feel: *He gave her a surprised look.* **4** a particular fashion or type of appearance: *How do you like my new look?* **5 looks** how attractive someone is: *You shouldn't judge a person by their looks.* | *a young man with charm and good looks*

look·out /'lʊk-aʊt/ *noun* **be on the lookout for something** to pay attention to things around you because you hope to see or find something: *I'm always on the lookout for good, cheap clothes.*

loom /luːm/ *verb* **1** *written* to appear as a large unclear shape: *The church loomed ahead of us.* **2** if a difficult situation looms, it is likely to happen soon: *Exams are looming.*

loop¹ /luːp/ *noun* a shape like a circle in a piece of string, wire etc: *Make a loop with the wire.*

loop² *verb* to make a loop or to tie something with a loop: *He looped the rope over the cow's head.*

loop·hole /'luːphəʊl $ 'luphoʊl/ *noun* a small mistake in a law that makes it possible to legally avoid doing what the law says: *Because of a loophole in the law, he pays no tax.*

loose /luːs/ *adjective*

1 clothes that are loose are big and do not fit you tightly: *These jeans are a bit loose. Have you got a smaller size?* | *She was wearing trousers and a loose sweater.*
2 not firmly fixed in place: *There's a loose button on my jacket that needs sewing on.* | *Some of the screws had **come loose**.*
3 not fastened together or kept together in a container: *His desk was covered with loose pieces of paper.*

loos·en /'luːsən/ *verb* to make something less tight: *I loosened my belt.*

loot /luːt/ *verb* to steal things during a war or another time of violence: *They looted shops and burned cars.*

lop·sid·ed /ˌlɒp'saɪdɪd $ ˌlɑp'saɪdɪd/ *adjective* something that is lopsided has one side that is heavier or lower than the other

Lord /lɔːd $ lɔrd/ *noun* a title for God or Jesus Christ: *Praise the Lord.*

lord /lɔːd $ lɔrd/ *noun* a man who has a high social rank in Britain

lorry /'lɒri $ 'lɔri/ *noun BrE, plural* **lorries** a large heavy vehicle for carrying things; TRUCK *AmE: The lorry was carrying logs of wood.* ⇨ *see picture on page 349*

lose /luːz/ *verb, past tense and past participle* **lost** /lɒst $ lɔst/

GRAMMAR
lose to/against someone

1 if you lose something, you stop knowing where it is and cannot find it: *I was worried I might lose my camera if I took it on the trip.* | *I've lost my pen – have you seen it anywhere?*
2 if you lose something, you stop having it: *When the factory closed, five hundred people **lost** their **jobs**.* | *He **lost** a lot of **money** by making bad business decisions.*
3 to not win a game, competition, or fight ⇨ *opposite* WIN¹ (1): *The government **lost** the **election**.* | *We've only **lost** three **games** all season.* | *Manchester United **lost to** Leeds.*

PHRASES
lose weight *You **lose weight** (=become lighter) by eating less and exercising more.*
lose your temper. *Dad **lost** his **temper** (=became angry) and started to shout.*
lose interest *Kate's sixteen now and she's **lost interest in** horses (=is not interested in horses any more).*
lose touch with someone to not meet or talk to someone any more: *I **lost touch with** my old friends when I moved to a new school.*

los·er /'luːzə $ 'luzɚ/ *noun* **1** someone who loses a competition or game: *The loser has to buy everyone a drink.* **2** *informal* someone who is never successful in life, work, or relationships

L

➤ LOOK AT, SEE, or WATCH?

LOOK AT you **look at** a picture, photo, person, or thing because you want to: *He was **looking at** something on the ground.*

SEE you **see** something, a person, or event without planning to: *We **saw** some beautiful clothes.*

WATCH you **watch** TV, a film, a person, or an event for a period of time: *We spent the evening **watching** TV.*

➤ LOOK

❶ to turn your eyes towards something or someone in order to see them
*"You're late!" he said, **looking at** his watch.* | ***Look**, there's Mark and the kids.* | *Mrs. Mitchell stood **looking through** the window.* | *Zack **looked up** (=turned his head upwards) in surprise as she walked in.* | *Tina came into the restaurant and **looked around** (=turned her head and looked in all directions).*

> GRAMMAR
> look at something/someone
> look through/up/around etc

> ✗ Don't say ➤ *look something/someone*
> ✓ Say ➤ ***look at** something/someone*

❷ to use your eyes to find something
*Stella was here a few minutes ago – she was **looking for** Max.* | ***Look in** the red box – I think it's in there.* | *I spent a long time **looking**, but I couldn't find anything I really liked.*

> GRAMMAR
> look for something/
> someone
> look in something

look

❸ look happy, look nice, look tired, look dirty etc
to have a particular appearance: *"How does Jeannie **look**?" "She **looks** tired."* | *The rooms **looked** really dirty.* | *David **looks** a lot like his grandfather.* | *He **looks** like he's about fifty years old.* | *They **look** like bananas, but they're not.*

> ✗ Don't say ➤ *He is looking like his grandfather.*
> ✓ Say ➤ *He **looks** like his grandfather.*

PHRASAL VERBS

look after
to do things to make sure that someone or something is safe and well (⇨ *same meaning* TAKE CARE OF): *She **looks after** her sister's children during the week.* | *Their son is **looking after** the farm while they're away.*

look around
to look at different things in a place, in order to find out more about it: *We spent a few hours **looking around** the museum.* | *Kelly and Maria went* to the mall to **look around**.

look back (on)
to think about something that happened in the past: ***Looking back**, I think I made the wrong decision.* | *She **looks back on** her ten years of marriage with sadness.*

look up
to find information in a book, on a computer etc: *Frances **looked up** his telephone number in the phone book.* | *If you don't know the meaning of a word, **look it up** in a dictionary.*

L

loss /lɒs $lɔs/ *noun, plural* **losses**

GRAMMAR
the loss of something/someone

1 when you stop having something: *There have been many job losses in banking. | How will he cope with the loss of his sight?*
2 *[no plural]* the death of someone: *They couldn't bear to talk about the loss of their son.*
3 if a business makes a loss, it spends more money than it gets ⇨ *opposite* **PROFIT¹**: *The company made a loss of about $43,000 in 2001.*

lost¹ /lɒst $lɔst/ *adjective*

1 if you are lost, or get lost, you do not know where you are: *After walking for several hours, we realized that we were lost. | It was such a big building that I got lost in it!*
2 if something is lost, or gets lost, you cannot find it: *My suitcase got lost and I had no more money or clothes.*

PHRASE
Get lost! *spoken* used to rudely tell someone to go away

lost² the past tense and past participle of LOSE

lot /lɒt $lɑt/ *noun*

1 a lot also lots *informal* a) a large amount or number: *He had drunk a lot of wine. | Lots of my friends smoke. | I've learned a lot in the last few months.* b) very much: *He's a lot nicer than he used to be. | I like Kelly a lot.*
2 the lot *informal* the whole of an amount: *If I don't put these crisps away, I'll eat the lot!*

USAGE a lot, much, many

In negative sentences, you can use **much** or **many** instead of **a lot**. **Much** is used to talk about nouns that you cannot count: *There isn't much wine left.* **Many** is used to talk about nouns that you can count: *I didn't see many people there that I knew.* **A lot** can be used to talk about both: *I don't have a lot of money. | She doesn't have a lot of friends.*

lo·tion /ˈləʊʃən $ˈloʊʃən/ *noun* a liquid that you put on your skin in order to make it soft or to protect it: *a bottle of suntan lotion*

lot·te·ry /ˈlɒtəri $ˈlɑtəri/ *noun, plural*

lotteries a competition in which people choose a set of numbers and win money if they have chosen the winning numbers: *What would you do if you won the lottery?*

loud¹ /laʊd/ *adjective*

something that is loud makes a lot of noise ⇨ *opposite* QUIET¹ (1): *Turn that music down! It's too loud! | I could hear loud voices, arguing.*
 –**loudly** *adverb*: *"Stop!" she shouted loudly.*

loud² *adverb* 1 loudly: *Can you speak louder?* 2 **out loud** if you read or say something out loud, you say it so that people can hear you: *I asked her to read the poem out loud.*

loud·speak·er /ˌlaʊdˈspiːkə $ˈlaʊdˌspikɚ/ *noun* a piece of equipment that makes sound louder: *the loudspeakers of his stereo system*

lounge¹ /laʊndʒ/ *noun* 1 a room in a hotel or airport, where people can sit and relax: *He's in the TV lounge.* 2 *BrE* a LIVING ROOM

lounge² *verb* 1 to stand or sit somewhere in a relaxed way: *I was just lounging on the sofa.* 2 **lounge about, lounge around** *BrE* to be lazy and waste your time doing nothing: *Stop lounging around and do some work!*

lou·sy /ˈlaʊzi/ *adjective informal* **lousier, lousiest** very bad: *The food was lousy.*

lov·a·ble or **loveable** /ˈlʌvəbəl/ *adjective* a lovable person or animal is very nice and easy to love

love¹ /lʌv/ *verb*

GRAMMAR
love doing something
love to do something

1 to like someone and care about them a lot: *Anna says she loves Steve and wants to marry him. | I really love my mum and dad.*
2 to like something a lot: *I love that dress you're wearing!*
3 to enjoy doing something very much: *Adam loves playing computer games. | I'd love to go clubbing.*

love² *noun*

GRAMMAR
love for someone
a love of something

1 *[no plural]* a very strong feeling that you

have for someone you like and care about a lot: *Her **love for** her children was obvious.*

2 when you like or enjoy doing something very much: *Tom has a great **love of** travel.*

PHRASES

be in love, fall in love if you are in love with someone, you love them in a romantic way: *Everyone could see that she **was in love with** Nick.* | *Simon realized that he **was falling in love with** Maria* (=starting to love Maria).

make love to have sex with someone

love from, love you use this at the end of a letter to a friend or a member of your family: *I'll write again soon. **Love from** Mum.*

love·ly /ˈlʌvli/ *adjective* very nice, attractive, or pleasant: *She has a lovely face.* | *I've had a lovely day.*

lov·er /ˈlʌvə $ ˈlʌvɚ/ *noun* **1** someone who has a sexual relationship with another person: *She was killed by a jealous lover.* **2** someone who enjoys something very much: *Rick is a film lover.*

lov·ing /ˈlʌvɪŋ/ *adjective* behaving in a gentle kind way that shows you love someone: *His loving wife looked after him while he was ill.*
–**lovingly** *adverb*: *He looked lovingly into her face.*

low /ləʊ $ loʊ/ *adjective*

1 something that is low is not high, or not far above the ground: *The house was surrounded by a low wall.* | *There was a low branch that I could climb onto.*

2 below the usual level, amount, or standard ⇨ opposite HIGH[1] (4): *It was an unpleasant job and the pay was low.* | *My exam results were lower than usual.*

3 a low voice or sound is quiet or deep ⇨ opposite HIGH[1] (5): *They were in the kitchen, talking in low voices.*

low·er[1] /ˈləʊə $ ˈloʊɚ/ *adjective*

at the bottom of something ⇨ opposite UPPER: *The lower half of the building was made of stone.* | *She had pains in her lower back.*

lower[2] *verb* **1** to make an amount less: *I wish they'd lower the price.* **2** to move something down: *The men lowered the ship's lifeboats into the water.*

lower case /ˌ.. ˈ./ *noun [no plural]* letters written in their small form, for example a, b, c: *Her email address is written in lower case.*

loy·al /ˈlɔɪəl/ *adjective* always supporting someone or something ⇨ opposite DISLOYAL: *She's very loyal to her friends.*

loy·al·ty /ˈlɔɪəlti/ *noun [no plural]* when someone is loyal ⇨ opposite DISLOYALTY: *I expect loyalty from my family.*

Ltd the written abbreviation of LIMITED, used after the names of companies

luck /lʌk/ *noun [no plural]*

something good that happens by chance: *We won, but I think it was luck, not skill!* | *You **haven't had much luck** this year, have you?*

PHRASES

good luck, bad luck the good or bad things that happen to you by chance: *The whole family **has had a lot of bad luck** recently.*

with any luck, with a bit of luck *spoken* used to say that you think something good will probably happen: ***With any luck** we should be home before it gets dark.*

good luck, best of luck *spoken* used to say to someone that you hope they will be successful: ***Good luck with** your exams tomorrow.*

wish someone luck to tell someone that you hope they will be successful: *Sarah **wished** me **luck with** my exams.*

bad luck, hard luck *spoken* used to tell someone that you are sorry something bad has happened to them: *"I've got to stay late at school tonight." "Oh, **bad luck**!"*

luckily /ˈlʌkəli/ *adverb* used to say that you are glad that something happened or did not happen: *Luckily, it didn't rain all day.*

luck·y /ˈlʌki/ *adjective* luckier, luckiest

GRAMMAR
lucky to do something
lucky that

1 if you are lucky, something good happens to you by chance ⇨ opposite

UNLUCKY: *"I'm going to Florida this summer." "Oh, you are lucky!"* | *He's* **lucky to** *have such a good job.* | *I look at you and think I'm the luckiest man in the world.*
2 something that is lucky is good and happens for no particular reason ⇨ opposite UNLUCKY: *It was* very **lucky that** *you weren't hurt in the accident.*
3 if something is lucky, some people think it causes good luck ⇨ opposite UNLUCKY: *6 is my lucky number.*

lu·di·crous /'luːdəkrəs/ *adjective* stupid, wrong, and unreasonable: *That's a ludicrous idea.*

lug·gage /'lʌgɪdʒ/ *noun* [no plural] the bags that you carry when you are travelling: *You must not bring more than one item of luggage.*

> **USAGE**
> **Luggage** does not have a plural form. You can say **some luggage**, **any luggage**, or a **piece of luggage**: *Do you have any more luggage? She only took one small piece of luggage with her.*

luke·warm /ˌluːk'wɔːm $ ˌluk'wɔrm/ *adjective* slightly warm: *a cup of lukewarm tea*

lull /lʌl/ *noun* a short period when there is less activity or noise than usual: *There has been a slight lull in the fighting.*

lul·la·by /'lʌləbaɪ/ *noun, plural* **lullabies** a song that you sing to babies to make them sleep

lum·ber¹ /'lʌmbə $ 'lʌmbɚ/ *noun* AmE wood that is used for building or making things; TIMBER BrE

lum·ber² *verb informal* if you lumber someone with a job, you give it to them when they do not want it: *They lumbered me with the job of cleaning the floor.*

lu·mi·nous /'luː-mənəs/ *adjective* able to shine in the dark: *The clock has luminous hands.*

lump /lʌmp/ *noun*
1 a small piece of something solid: *I put two lumps of sugar in my tea.*
2 an unusual raised area on someone's

lump

body: *She discovered a lump in her neck.*

lump·y /'lʌmpi/ *adjective* **lumpier, lumpiest** something that is lumpy has lumps or raised areas: *I sat on the lumpy sofa.*

lu·nar /'luːnə $ 'lunɚ/ *adjective* formal related to the moon: *the lunar surface*

lu·na·tic /'luːnətɪk/ *noun* someone who behaves in a stupid or very strange way that can be dangerous: *He drives like a lunatic.*

lunch /lʌntʃ/ *noun, plural* **lunches** a meal that you eat in the middle of the day: *I'm having soup* **for lunch**. | *She bought me lunch.* | *We* **had** *a light* **lunch** *at the bar.*

lunch·time /'lʌntʃtaɪm/ *noun* the time in the middle of the day when people usually eat lunch: *I usually just have a sandwich at lunchtime.*

lung /lʌŋ/ *noun* your lungs are the two parts in your body that you use for breathing

lurch /lɜːtʃ $ lɚtʃ/ *verb* to move in an unsteady or uncontrolled way: *The car lurched forward.*

lure /luə $ lur/ *verb* to persuade someone to do something by making it seem attractive or exciting: *He lured her into his home by pretending to be an artist.*

lurk /lɜːk $ lɚk/ *verb written* to wait somewhere secretly, usually before doing something bad: *He lurked by the house, waiting to attack his enemy.*

lust /lʌst/ *noun* [no plural] a very strong sexual feeling towards someone

lux·u·ri·ous /lʌg'zjuəriəs $ lʌg'ʒuriəs/ *adjective* very comfortable, beautiful, and expensive: *He has a luxurious apartment in the south of France.*

lux·u·ry /'lʌkʃəri/ *noun, plural* **luxuries**
1 [no plural] great comfort and pleasure that you get from having beautiful or expensive things: *She married a rich man and lived in luxury.* **2** something that you do not really need but that you buy because you will enjoy it: *We don't have as much money now, so we can't afford as many luxuries.*

ly·ing /'laɪ-ɪŋ/ the present participle of LIE

lyr·ics /'lɪrɪks/ *plural noun* the words of a song: *I write the music and Max writes the lyrics.*

Mm

m the written abbreviation of METRE

MA or **M.A.** /ˌem ˈeɪ/ noun Master of Arts, a higher university degree: *She is studying for an MA in music.*

ma·chine /məˈʃiːn/ noun
a piece of equipment that uses electricity to do a job: *We've just bought a new washing machine.* | *I wanted to buy a cola from the drinks machine.* | *The goods are all packed by machine now.*

> **USAGE machine, tool, instrument, device**
> Machine, tool, instrument, and device are all words for something you use to do a particular job. A **machine** usually uses electricity, and you do not hold it in your hands: *factory machines*. A **tool** is something that you hold in your hands and use for making things from wood, metal etc, or for doing jobs in the house or garden: *basic tools such as a hammer and saw*. An **instrument** is something that you use for doing very careful or exact work, for example measuring things: *geometry instruments* | *Clocks are instruments for measuring time.* A **device** is a word for any object that does a particular job: *clever electronic devices*

machine gun /ˈ. ͵./ noun a gun that fires a lot of bullets very quickly: *We heard the sound of machine-gun fire.*

ma·chin·e·ry /məˈʃiːnəri/ noun [no plural] large machines: *The factory is full of engineering machinery.*

mach·o /ˈmætʃəʊ $ ˈmɑtʃoʊ/ adjective informal a man who is macho likes to show people that he is strong and brave: *You think you're so macho!*

mad /mæd/ adjective madder, maddest

> **GRAMMAR**
> **mad at/with someone**
> **mad to do something**

1 stupid or silly: *You'd be mad to give up a good job like that.* | *Paul's mad – he gets into trouble all the time.* | *That's a mad idea!* | *You must be mad if you think I'm going to do the work for you!*
2 mentally ill: *He's always talking to himself – I think he's a bit mad.*
3 informal angry: *My teacher will be mad at me if I don't do this work.* | *My dad's mad with me because I spent so much money.* ↪ see usage note at ANGRY

> **PHRASES**
> **go mad** BrE spoken to become very angry or excited: *Dad went mad when I got home so late.* | *At last the band walked on and the audience went mad.*
> **be mad about someone/something** BrE informal to like someone or something very much: *Jack's always been mad about football.*

mad·am /ˈmædəm/ noun used to show respect when talking or writing to a woman who you do not know: *Yes, madam – what would you like?* | *Dear Madam, I am writing to you about my son.*

mad·den·ing /ˈmædn-ɪŋ/ adjective extremely annoying: *It's maddening when you can't find a pen.*

made¹ /meɪd/ the past tense and past participle of MAKE

made² adjective **be made of, be made from** to be built from something: *The shelves are made of wood.*

mad·ly /ˈmædli/ adverb **1** in a wild excited way: *The dogs ran madly around him.* **2** madly in love very much in love: *I'm madly in love with Tim.*

mad·man /ˈmædmən/ noun, plural madmen /-mən/ a man who behaves in a very dangerous or stupid way: *He was driving like a madman.*

mad·ness /'mædnəs/ *noun* very stupid and dangerous behaviour: *It would be madness to try to cross the desert on your own.*

mag·a·zine /ˌmægə'ziːn $'mægəˌzin/ *noun* a large thin book with a paper cover, which is sold every week or every month: *I bought a magazine to read on the train.* ⇨ *see picture on page 342*

ma·gic /'mædʒɪk/ *noun* [no plural] a special power that makes strange or impossible things happen: *By magic, she turned the frog into a prince.* | *I can do magic tricks.*

ma·gic·al /'mædʒɪkəl/ *adjective* very enjoyable and exciting, in a strange or special way: *There's something magical about his music.*

ma·gi·cian /mə'dʒɪʃən/ *noun* someone who entertains people by doing magic tricks

ma·gis·trate /'mædʒəstreɪt/ *noun* someone who decides if people are guilty in a court of law that deals with less serious crimes

magnet

mag·net /'mægnət/ *noun* a piece of iron that makes other metal objects move towards it

mag·net·ic /mæg'netɪk/ *adjective* having the power of a magnet

mag·net·is·m /'mægnətɪzəm/ *noun* [no plural] the power that a magnet has to make metal things move towards it

mag·ni·fi·ca·tion /ˌmægnəfə'keɪʃən/ *noun* when something is MAGNIFIED

mag·nif·i·cent /mæg'nɪfəsənt/ *adjective* very impressive: *a magnificent palace* | *What a magnificent performance!*

magnify

mag·ni·fy /'mægnəfaɪ/ *verb* magnified, magnifies to make something look bigger by putting it under a piece of special glass: *Once the glass is fitted it will magnify any hairs that are on the skin.*

maid /meɪd/ *noun* a female servant

maid·en /'meɪdn/ *adjective* maiden flight, maiden voyage the first trip that a plane or ship makes

maiden name /'.. ˌ./ *noun* the family name that a woman has before she marries

mail¹ /meɪl/ *noun* [no plural]

1 the letters and packages that are delivered to your house or office; POST BrE: *Was there any mail for me this morning?*

2 the system of delivering letters and packages to people's houses and offices; POST BrE: *The invitation arrived by mail this morning.*

3 messages that you receive by E-MAIL: *I'm just logging on to read my mail.*

mail² *verb* to send a letter or package to someone; POST BrE: *Will you mail this letter for me?*

mail·box /'meɪlbɒks $'meɪlbɑks/ *noun, plural* mailboxes 1 a box where letters are put when they are delivered to your house or office 2 a FILE on a computer where you store E-MAIL messages

mail·man /'meɪlmæn/ the American word for POSTMAN

maim /meɪm/ *verb* to injure someone very badly: *The bomb killed and maimed many innocent people.*

main /meɪn/ *adjective* biggest or most important: *Maths is the main subject I am studying.* | *The main problem is lack of money.*

main·land /'meɪnlənd/ *noun* the mainland the main part of a country, not the islands near it: *People living on the islands come over to the mainland at least once a month to do shopping.*
– mainland *adjective*: *mainland China*

main·ly /'meɪnli/ *adverb* mostly: *The students are mainly from Europe.* | *Tomorrow will be mainly cloudy but dry.*

main road /ˌ. './ *noun* a large important road

main·tain /meɪn'teɪn/ verb

1 to continue to have or do something as much as you did in the past: *We managed to* **maintain contact with** *the astronauts all the time.* | *The college must maintain its very high standards.*

2 to keep a building, road, or machine in good condition: *The government is responsible for maintaining our roads.*

main·te·nance /'meɪntənəns/ noun [no plural] work that is done to keep something working properly: *Who will pay for all the computer maintenance?*

maize /meɪz/ noun [no plural] BrE a tall plant with yellow seeds that can be cooked and eaten; CORN AmE

maj·es·ty /'mædʒəsti/ noun **Your Majesty** a formal title that is used to talk to a king or queen

ma·jor¹ /'meɪdʒə $ 'meɪdʒɚ/ adjective

large and important; ⇨ opposite MINOR: *There has been a major earthquake in the south of the country.* | *This is one of our major problems.*

major² noun **1** an officer in the army **2** AmE the main subject that you study at college or university: *His major is science.*

major³ verb **major in something** AmE to study something as your main subject at college or university: *She majored in history.*

ma·jor·i·ty /mə'dʒɒrəti $ mə-'dʒɔrəti/ noun

GRAMMAR
the majority of people/things
a majority of people/things

most of the people or things in a group: *The majority of our students come from Europe and Asia.* | *A majority of countries still support the idea.*

make¹ ⇨ see box on next page

make² /meɪk/ noun a type of product made by a company: *"What make is your PC?" "It's a Dell."*

mak·er /'meɪkə $ 'meɪkɚ/ noun a person or company that makes something:

Honda is a Japanese car maker. | *a furniture maker*

make·shift /'meɪkʃɪft/ adjective made quickly from things that you have available: *They slept in a makeshift tent made from a sheet.*

make-up

mascara
eye-shadow
lipstick

make-up or **make·up** /'meɪkʌp/ noun [no plural] coloured creams and powders that a woman puts on her face to make herself look more attractive: *Do you ever wear make-up?*

ma·lar·i·a /mə'leəriə $ mə'leriə/ noun [no plural] a serious disease that is spread by MOSQUITOES

male¹ /meɪl/ adjective

1 someone who is male is a man or a boy: *There are still very few male nurses.* | *Young boys often feel happier with a male teacher.*

2 male animals belong to the sex which cannot have babies: *The male bird is bigger than the female.*

male² noun

a male person or animal: *Is your dog a male or a female?*

mal·ice /'mælɪs/ noun [no plural] a feeling of wanting to hurt someone: *Her eyes were full of malice.*

ma·li·cious /mə'lɪʃəs/ adjective intended to hurt or upset someone: *a malicious lie*

ma·lig·nant /mə'lɪgnənt/ adjective containing CANCER cells: *They are doing tests to see if the growth is malignant.*

➤ MAKE or DO?

MAKE you make something:
*I **made** a cake.*

DO you do an action or activity:
*I **did** my homework last night.*

➤ MAKE

1 to produce
*Do you want to **make** some cookies this afternoon? | The sofas **are made of** leather. | Sammy **made** me a cup of tea.*

GRAMMAR
be made of something
make someone something

2 make a mistake, make a decision, make a suggestion etc
*We lost because we **made** a lot of **mistakes**. | Ben and Joe were **making** too much **noise** and couldn't hear me. | Call this number to **make an appointment**.*

3 to cause
*The heat **made** her feel sleepy. | I'm sorry I **made** you cry. | The disease **makes** it **difficult** for him to walk.*

GRAMMAR
make someone do something
make something do something

make

4 to earn money
*She **makes** about £30,000 a year now. | The main goal of any business is to **make money**.*

5 Most common words used with **make**:

make a mistake	make a suggestion	make an effort
make a statement	make a difference	make progress
make a noise	make a note	make a choice
make an appointment	make a decision	make breakfast/lunch etc

PHRASES

make sure
to do something so that you are certain about something: *Make sure that you understand the test question before you begin answering it.*

make up your mind
to decide something after you have thought about it: *I **made up my mind** to go to the party after all.*

PHRASAL VERBS

make into
to change something so that it becomes something else: *They're **making** the book **into** a movie. | The corn is **made into** a type of bread.*

make up
To think of a story, explanation, excuse

etc that is not true: *I couldn't think of an answer, so I just **made** something **up**. | The children **made up** stories and drew pictures to go with them.*

M

mall /mɔːl/ *noun* a covered area that contains a lot of shops: *a huge shopping mall*

mam·mal /'mæməl/ *noun* a type of animal that gives birth to live babies rather than eggs. Humans and cows are examples of mammals

mam·moth /'mæməθ/ *adjective* very big: *We had the mammoth task of organising the concert.*

man¹ /mæn/ *noun, plural* **men** /men/

1 an adult male person: *Two men were standing at the door.* | *My father was a very attractive man.*

2 [*no plural*] all people, including men, women, and children: *This is one of the most deadly poisons known to man.*

man² *verb* **manned, manning** to be in charge of a machine or a place: *The spacecraft was manned by Russian astronauts.*

man·age /'mænɪdʒ/ *verb*

GRAMMAR
manage to do something

1 to succeed in doing something: *Nobody knows how the prisoners **managed to** escape.* | *I thought we would never get the door open, but in the end we managed.*

2 if you can manage, you can do a job or deal with a situation without help: *"Would you like some help?" "No, It's all right, I **can manage.**"*

3 to be in charge of a company or shop, and the people who work there: *His son now manages the restaurant.*

man·age·ment /'mænɪdʒmənt/ *noun* the job of organizing the work of a company or shop, and the people who work there: *He is responsible for the day-to-day management of the company.* | *The banks blamed the situation on bad management.*

man·ag·er /'mænɪdʒə $'mænɪdʒɚ/ *noun* someone who is in charge of an organization, sports team, shop etc: *The hotel manager asked if we were happy with the service.* | *a bank manager*

maneuver the American spelling of MANOEUVRE

mangled /'mæŋgəld/ *verb* if something

is mangled, it is badly damaged by something crushing or twisting it: *Rescuers managed to reach the mangled car and help the driver.*

man·go /'mæŋgəʊ $'mæŋgoʊ/ *noun, plural* **mangoes** a sweet tropical fruit with red or green skin and yellow flesh

man·han·dle /'mæn,hændl/ *verb* to move someone roughly: *He claimed the police manhandled him.*

ma·ni·ac /'meɪniæk/ *noun informal* someone who behaves in a stupid or dangerous way: *You drive like a maniac.*

man·i·cure /'mænɪkjʊə $'mænɪ,kjʊr/ *noun* a treatment for the hands and nails that includes cutting and painting the nails
—**manicure** *verb*: *She spends hours manicuring her nails.*

ma·nip·u·late /mə'nɪpjəleɪt/ *verb* to make someone do what you want by secretly tricking them: *He is willing to manipulate his friends if it will help his career.*

man·kind /,mæn'kaɪnd/ *noun* [*no plural*] all humans, considered as a group: *the history of mankind*

man-made /ˌ. './ *adjective* not made of natural materials: *All these clothes are made of man-made fibres.*

man·ner /'mænə $'mænɚ/ *noun*

1 your manner is the way in which you behave towards other people: *His manner was cold and unfriendly.*

2 the way in which something is done: *He reacted to the news **in a** very strange **manner.***

3 **manners** ways of behaving, eating, and speaking that people consider to be polite or not polite: *It's **bad manners** (=not polite) to speak with your mouth full.* | *Her children have very **good manners**.* | *It's important to teach children good **table manners** (=polite ways of behaving when eating).*

ma·noeu·vre *BrE*, **maneuver** *AmE* /mə'nuːvə $mə'nuːvɚ/ *verb* to move something skilfully into a different position: *I manoeuvred the car into a parking space.*
—**manoeuvre** *noun*: *She performed a difficult manoeuvre on her skis.*

man·sion /'mænʃən/ *noun* a very big house

M

mantelpiece

fireplace

man·tel·piece /'mæntlpiːs/ also **man·tel** /'mæntl/ *AmE, noun* the shelf above a fire in someone's house: *A clock was ticking on the mantelpiece.*

man·u·al¹ /'mænjuəl/ *adjective* done with your hands: *He has always worked on the farm, doing manual work.*
– **manually** *adverb*: *Adjust the controls manually.*

manual² *noun* a book that explains how to use a machine: *Consult your computer's user manual.*

man·u·fac·ture /ˌmænjə'fæktʃə $ ˌmænjə'fæktʃɚ/ *verb* to make large quantities of goods, using machines: *The factory manufactures plastic goods.*
– **manufacture** *noun* [no plural]: *the manufacture of textiles*

man·u·fac·tur·er /ˌmænjə'fæktʃərə $ ˌmænjə'fæktʃərɚ/ *noun* a company that makes large quantities of goods, using machines: *an aircraft manufacturer*

man·u·script /'mænjəskrɪpt/ *noun* a piece of writing that has been written, not printed: *a medieval manuscript*

many /'meni/

a large number of people or things. Use **many** about things that you can count, such as people, things, cars, books etc, especially in questions and negative sentences: *Were there **many** people left at Jill's party.* | *There aren't **many** tickets left.* | ***Many of** the houses were very old.* | *Some people came, but **not many**.* | *She has worked there **for many** years.* | *You can use this tool **in many ways**.* ⇨ compare MUCH

PHRASES
how many? use this to ask what number of people or things there are: *How many people are in your class?* | *How many eggs do you need?*
too many, so many use these when the number of something is larger than you want or need: *You've eaten **too many** sweets already.* | *We've had **so many** problems with the neighbours.*
as many use this to talk about a number of people or things, especially when you are comparing two numbers: *I don't have as **many** students in my class this year as I did last year.* | *Look at the picture, and find as **many** things beginning with the letter 'T' as you can.*

map /mæp/ *noun* a drawing of an area or country, showing rivers, roads, cities etc: *a map of the US*

mar·a·thon /'mærəθən $ 'mærəˌθɑn/ *noun* a race in which people run 26 miles 385 YARDS along roads: *He's going to run the New York marathon.*

mar·ble /'maːbəl $ 'marbəl/ *noun* **1** [no plural] a hard rock that can be polished and used to make floors, STATUES etc **2** a small coloured glass ball that children play with: *Who wants to play marbles?*

March /maːtʃ $ martʃ/ *written abbreviation* **Mar.** *noun* the third month of the year

march¹ /maːtʃ $ martʃ/ *verb*

GRAMMAR
march into/through etc a place

1 when soldiers march, they walk together with regular steps: *We watched the soldiers marching past.* | *The King's armies **marched into** the capital.* ⇨ see picture on page 340

2 to walk somewhere quickly, often because you are angry: *"I hate you," she shouted, and she **marched out of** the room.*

3 if people march, they walk together in a large group in order to protest about something: *The students **marched through** the city centre and called for the President to resign.*

march² *noun, plural* **marches 1** an event in which people walk together to protest about something: *We went on a march to protest about nuclear tests.* **2** when soldiers walk together with regular steps

mar·ga·rine /ˌmɑːdʒəˈriːn $ˈmɑrdʒə-rɪn/ *noun [no plural]* a food similar to butter, made from animal or vegetable fat

mar·gin /ˈmɑː- **margin** dʒɪn $ˈmɑrdʒɪn/ *noun* the empty space at the side of a printed page: *The teacher wrote 'Good' in the margin.*

mar·i·jua·na /ˌmær-əˈwɑːnə/ *noun [no plural]* an illegal drug that people smoke

ma·ri·na /məˈriːnə/ *noun* a small area of water near the sea where people keep boats

ma·rine /məˈriːn/ *adjective* related to the sea: *marine life*

mark¹ /mɑːk $mɑrk/ *verb*

1 when a teacher marks a student's work, he or she decides how good it is and gives it a number or letter showing this; GRADE *AmE*: *Haven't they finished marking the exam papers yet?*
2 to put a word or sign on something to give information: *The door was marked 'Private'.*
3 to show where something is: *A white post marked the turning in the road.*
4 to be a sign of an important event: *This fight marked the end of his boxing career. | There will be a festival to mark the anniversary of the writer's birth.*

mark² *noun*

1 a spot or cut on something, which spoils its appearance: *There were dirty marks all over the floor. | The wine glass had left a mark on the table.*
2 *BrE* a letter or number given by a teacher to show how good a student's work is; GRADE *AmE*: *If I get good marks in my exams, my dad will buy me a computer game. | She was the only student who got full marks in the test.*
3 a sign that is written or printed on something: *The customs official put*

a mark on the case to show it had been checked.
4 a mark of something a sign of something: *The crowd was silent for two minutes as a mark of respect.*

mar·ket¹ /ˈmɑːkɪt $ˈmɑrkɪt/ *noun*

1 an area where people bring food and other things to sell: *I usually buy fruit and vegetables at the market. | I bought some fish from the market. | Are you going to the market tomorrow?*
2 all the people who buy goods: *The market for mobile phones is increasing all the time. | Tobacco companies are looking for new markets.*

PHRASE

on the market available for people to buy: *There are hundreds of computer games on the market. | A new drink has just come onto the market. | They have decided to put their house on the market.*

market² *verb* to try to persuade people to buy something by advertising it: *IBM is marketing the new computer as a business tool.*

mar·ket·ing /ˈmɑːkɪtɪŋ $ˈmɑrkɪtɪŋ/ *noun [no plural]* the job of deciding how to advertise and sell a product: *Stella works in marketing.*

mark·ing /ˈmɑːkɪŋ $ˈmɑrkɪŋ/ *noun* **1** the work a teacher does when he or she reads a student's work and gives a mark: *I've got some marking to do tonight.* **2** **markings** coloured shapes or patterns on something: *The road markings aren't very clear. | The young birds have paler markings on their wings.*

mar·ma·lade /ˈmɑːməleɪd $ˈmɑr-mə,leɪd/ *noun [no plural]* a sweet food made from fruit and sugar, that you spread on bread

ma·roon /məˈruːn/ *noun, adjective* a dark red colour

mar·quee /mɑːˈkiː $mɑrˈki/ *noun BrE* a very big tent used for shows and parties: *We hired a marquee for the wedding.*

mar·riage /ˈmærɪdʒ/ *noun* **1** the relationship between a husband and wife: *We have a happy marriage.* **2** a wedding ceremony: *Your marriage should be a day you remember forever.*

M

mar·ried /'mærid/ adjective

GRAMMAR
married to someone

someone who is married has a husband or a wife: *She is **married to** a famous footballer.* | *a married couple*

mar·ry /'mæri/ verb married, marries

if a man and a woman marry, they become husband and wife: *I asked her to marry me.* | *John and I are **getting married** in May.* | *He is married, with three children.*

marsh /maːʃ $ marʃ/ noun, plural marshes an area of soft wet land

martial art /ˌmaːʃəl 'aːt $ ˌmarʃəl 'art/ noun a sport in which you fight using your hands and feet: *Kung Fu is a popular martial art.*

mar·vel /'maːvəl $ 'marvəl/ verb written marvelled, marvelling BrE, marveled, marveling AmE if you marvel at something, you find it very good and surprising: *I marvel at his ability to learn.*

mar·vel·lous BrE, **marvelous** AmE /'maːvələs $ 'marvələs/ adjective very good or enjoyable: *I thought it was a marvellous film.*

mas·ca·ra /mæ'skaːrə $ mæ'skærə/ noun [no plural] a dark substance that women use to colour their EYELASHES: *She was wearing mascara.* ⇨ see picture at MAKE-UP

mas·cot /'mæskət $ 'mæskat/ noun an animal or toy that a team has, which they think will bring them good luck

mas·cu·line /'mæskjələn/ adjective 1 like a man or typical of a man: *a deep masculine voice* 2 belonging to a group of nouns and adjectives in some languages that is different from the FEMININE and the NEUTER groups

mash /mæʃ/ verb to crush food until it is soft ⇨ see picture on page 344
– **mashed** adjective: *mashed potatoes*

mask /maːsk $ mæsk/ noun something you wear over your face to hide or protect it: *The thief wore a mask to hide his face.*

Mass /mæs/ noun the main religious ceremony in some Christian churches: *a Roman Catholic Mass*

mass¹ /mæs/ noun, plural masses

GRAMMAR
a mass of something

1 a large amount of something all in a group: *There was a mass of letters and reports on my desk.*

2 masses BrE informal a large number or amount of something: *There were masses of people there.* | *We've got masses of time.*

mass² adjective involving a large number of people: *The bomb caused mass panic.*

mas·sa·cre /'mæsəkə $ 'mæsəkər/ noun when a lot of people who cannot defend themselves are killed: *a massacre of innocent women and children*
– **massacre** verb: *The whole village was massacred.*

mas·sage /'mæsaːʒ $ mə'saʒ/ verb to press and rub someone's body to stop their muscles hurting or to help them relax: *He gently massaged my neck.*
– **massage** noun: *Will you give me a massage?*

mas·sive /'mæsɪv/ adjective very big: *Their house is massive.* | *a massive earthquake*

mast /maːst $ mæst/ noun a tall pole that supports the sails on a ship

mas·ter¹ /'maːstə $ 'mæstər/ verb to learn a skill or language very thoroughly so that you can use it well: *It takes years to master a game like chess.*

master² noun 1 a male school teacher 2 someone who is very good at doing something: *He is one of the best known masters of the sport.* 3 a document from which people can make copies

mas·ter·piece /'maːstəpiːs $ 'mæstərˌpis/ noun a work of art or piece of writing that is the best that someone has produced: *The 'Mona Lisa' is Leonardo's masterpiece.*

mat /mæt/ noun 1 a piece of thick material that covers part of a floor 2 a piece of material that you put under a plate or glass to protect a table

match¹ /mætʃ/ noun, plural matches

GRAMMAR
a match against/with someone

1 a small wooden stick that produces a flame when you rub it against

something. You light or strike a match: *He struck a match to find his way through the dark room.* | *a box of matches*

2 *BrE* a game between two people or teams: *John played his first football match on Saturday.* | *We need to win this match.* | *He lost the match against Sampras.* | *They've got a match with Peterborough United next week.*

match² *verb*

GRAMMAR
match something to/with something

1 if one thing matches another, the two things look attractive together because they are similar: *Her blue dress matched her eyes.* | *The patterns don't match.*

2 also **match up** to find something that is similar to another thing or belongs with another thing: *See if you can match the names to the voices you will hear.* | *Match up each sentence with the right picture.*

PHRASAL VERB
match up to
match up to something to be as good as something: *The experience of flying certainly matched up to his expectations.*

match·ing /ˈmætʃɪŋ/ *adjective* matching things have the same colour, style, or pattern and so look attractive together: *black shoes and a matching handbag*

mate¹ /meɪt/ *noun* **1** *BrE informal* a friend: *This is my mate Jim.* **2** the sexual PARTNER of an animal

mate² *verb* if animals mate, they have sex: *Birds mate in the spring.*

ma·te·ri·al /məˈtɪəriəl/ $məˈtɪriəl/ *noun*

1 cloth: *She sewed the pieces of material together.*

2 any solid substance: *Plastic is a very easy material to work with.* | *All our products are made from recycled materials.*

3 *[no plural]* information that you can use when you are writing about something: *I think I've got enough material for my essay now.*

4 **materials** the things you use in

order to do a job or an activity: *teaching materials*

ma·ter·ni·ty /məˈtɜːnəti $məˈtɜːnəti/ *adjective* used by or given to a woman who is going to have a baby or who has recently had a baby: *a maternity dress* | *She didn't get any maternity pay.*

math /mæθ/ the American word for MATHS

math·e·mat·i·cal /ˌmæθəˈmætɪkəl/ *adjective* related to mathematics

math·e·ma·ti·cian /ˌmæθəməˈtɪʃən/ *noun* someone who studies or teaches mathematics

math·e·mat·ics /ˌmæθəˈmætɪks/ *noun* *[no plural]* the study of numbers and shapes

maths /mæθs/ *BrE* mathematics

mat·ter¹ /ˈmætə $ˈmætər/ *noun*

1 a subject or situation: *Your education is an important matter.* | *We can discuss this matter at the next meeting.* | *I'm no good at dealing with financial matters.*

2 **matters** the situation you are talking about: *Matters became complicated when he fell in love with his brother's girlfriend.* | *That would only make matters worse.*

3 **the matter** *spoken* if something is the matter, something is making a person feel upset or worried: *You look upset. What's the matter?* | *Is there something the matter with Jane?*

4 **no matter how/where/what etc** *spoken* used to say that a situation remains the same whatever happens or whatever someone does: *No matter how hard he worked, he always failed his exams.*

5 **as a matter of fact** *spoken* used when you are telling someone something that is surprising: *"Will you be here in August?" "Well, as a matter of fact I'm thinking of spending the whole summer here."*

6 **be a matter of opinion** used to say that not everyone agrees that something is true: *"He's a great singer." "That's a matter of opinion."*

matter² *verb*

GRAMMAR
matter what/how etc
matter to someone

to be important: *"You've put the*

wrong date." "Does it matter?" | **It doesn't matter what** the score is – as long as you've done your best. | Nothing **matters to** her except music.

mat·tress /ˈmætrəs/ noun, plural **mattresses** the soft part of a bed, that you lie on

ma·ture /məˈtʃʊə $ məˈtʃʊr/ adjective **1** someone who is mature behaves sensibly and like an adult ⇨ opposite IMMATURE (1): She's very mature for her age. **2** fully grown or developed ⇨ opposite IMMATURE (2): mature trees –**mature** verb: It takes seven years for the wine to mature

mature stu·dent /ˌ.. ˈ../ noun BrE a student at college or university who starts studying after they are 21 years old

max·i·mum /ˈmæksəməm/ adjective

the maximum amount is the largest that is possible ⇨ opposite MINIMUM[1]: He scored the maximum number of points. | The train was travelling at its maximum speed. –**maximum** noun: Each group may have **a maximum of** eight members.

May /meɪ/ noun the fifth month of the year

may /meɪ/ modal verb, negative **may not**

1 likely to happen in the future: If I stand on this box, I **may** be able to reach the shelf. | Ring the door bell again – they **may** not have heard us the first time.

USAGE
May is not used in questions with this meaning.

2 giving someone permission to do something formal: You **may** leave at 5.00 pm. | Students **may** not (=are not allowed to) remove cassette tapes from the library.
3 asking very politely for something: **May** I see your passport, sir?
4 giving advice very politely: You **may** find it quicker to go by train.

may·be /ˈmeɪbi/ adverb
1 used when saying what might be true or what might happen: Maybe they haven't got your letter yet. | Maybe the switch is broken. | "Can we go to the beach tomorrow?" "Maybe (=we might go, or we might not)."
2 used when making a suggestion: Maybe we could meet up some time.

may·on·naise /ˌmeɪəˈneɪz $ ˈmeɪə-ˌneɪz/ noun [no plural] a thick white SAUCE that you put on cold food

mayor /meə $ ˈmeɪər/ noun someone who is the head of the local government in a town or city

maze /meɪz/ noun a set of small roads or passages where you have difficulty finding where to get out: I was lost in a maze of long dark corridors

me /mi; strong miː/ pronoun

the person who is speaking: Tom hit me! | You never listen to me. | Jill's taller than me. | Tell me what happened.

mead·ow /ˈmedəʊ $ ˈmedoʊ/ noun a field with wild grass and flowers

mea·gre BrE, **meager** AmE /ˈmiːgə $ ˈmiːgər/ adjective very small in amount: They paid him a meagre salary.

meal /miːl/ noun

a time when you eat food, or the food that you eat then: Would you like to come to our place on Sunday for a meal? | Let's **go out for a meal** tonight. | I went to get Grandpa while Mum finished preparing the meal. | What a delicious meal!

USAGE
The main meals we have are **breakfast** in the morning, **lunch** in the middle of the day, and **dinner** in the evening. Some people call this evening meal **supper** or, in Britain, **tea**.

mean[1] ⇨ see box on next page

mean[2] /miːn/ adjective

GRAMMAR
mean to someone

1 unkind: Why are you always so **mean to** him? | That was a very mean thing to do.
2 BrE not willing to spend money: He was so mean that he didn't buy his girlfriend a birthday present.

mean /miːn/ *verb* **meant** /ment/ **meant**

1 to have a meaning
to represent a particular idea or thing: *'Start' and 'begin' **mean** basically the same thing.* | *Oh, I thought you **meant** Tuesday the 14th, not the 21st.* | *What do you think the writer **means** when she says the house is sad?*

> ✗ **Don't say** ➤ *What is it meaning?*
> ✓ **Say** ➤ *What does it mean?*

2 to want and plan to do something
*Sorry, I didn't **mean** to scare you.* | *I've been **meaning** to go see Stephanie.*

mean

3 used to explain something
*He wants to be a doctor, which **means that** he'll have at least six years of training after university.* | *When I change schools, it will **mean** leaving the house 20 minutes earlier.*

> **GRAMMAR**
> mean (that)
> mean doing something

4 be meant to be something, be meant for something
to be for a particular purpose: *It **was meant to be** a joke, but no one laughed.* | *These books **are meant for** children who are learning to read.*

PHRASES

I mean *spoken*
a say this when you want to explain something: *I mean, can I get there in an hour or so?* | *The piano will be hard to move – I mean it's really heavy.* | *I like Tony a lot – I mean he's a really nice person.*
b say this when you want to correct what you have just said: *I think the papers are in the red folder ... I mean the yellow one.*

Do you mean...?, You mean...? *spoken*
say this when you want to check that you understand something: *"I'm looking for a tall guy, with red hair." "Oh, do you mean Dave?"* | *"I really miss this." "Walking in the woods, you mean?"*

What do you mean? *spoken*
say this when you want someone to explain what they have said: *"Sorry, you can't go in there." "What do you mean? Why not?"* | *What do you mean they won't accept my credit card? Why?*

M

mean·ing /ˈmiːnɪŋ/ *noun*
1 the idea or message that something gives you: *This word has several meanings.* | *I couldn't understand the meaning of his remark.*
2 [no plural] the purpose of something: *He had lost everything that gave meaning to his life.*

mean·ing·ful /ˈmiːnɪŋfəl/ *adjective* serious and important: *a meaningful discussion about religion*

mean·ing·less /ˈmiːnɪŋləs/ *adjective* without any purpose or meaning: *Most song lyrics are practically meaningless.*

means /miːnz/ *noun, plural* **means**

GRAMMAR
a means of something
a means of doing something
a way of doing something: *Email is becoming an important **means of** communication.* | *The police had **no means of** proving that Harris was guilty of the murder.*

PHRASES
by means of something using something: *Their movements were recorded **by means of** a video camera.*
by all means used to emphasize that you are willing for someone to do something: ***By all means** check the measurements for yourself.*

meant /ment/ the past tense and past participle of MEAN¹

mean·time /ˈmiːntaɪm/ *noun* **in the meantime** until something happens: *The film starts in 10 minutes. In the meantime, here's some music.*

mean·while /ˈmiːnwaɪl/ *adverb*
in the period while something is happening or before something happens: *William took the dog for a walk. Meanwhile Jack fed the rabbits.* | *Jill will be here soon. Meanwhile you can tell me about your holiday.*

mea·sles /ˈmiːzəlz/ *also* **the measles** *noun* [no plural] an illness which makes you feel very hot and gives you small red spots on your face and body: *Did you have measles as a child?*

mea·sure¹ /ˈmeʒə $ ˈmeʒɚ/ *verb*
1 to find out the size or amount of something, using a piece of equipment: *I **measured** the window **with** a ruler.* | *How can we measure the temperature of the water?*
2 *formal* to be a particular size or amount: *His feet measure over 45 cm in length.*

PHRASAL VERB
measure up
to be as good as you expected or wanted: *Did New York **measure up to** your idea of it?*

measure² *noun*

GRAMMAR
a measure to do something
an official action that someone takes to deal with a problem: *The government must **take measures to** reduce the number of young people who are homeless.*

mea·sure·ment /ˈmeʒəmənt $ ˈmeʒɚmənt/ *noun* the length, height etc of something: *What are the exact measurements of the room?*

meat /miːt/ *noun* [no plural] the flesh of animals and birds that you eat: *I don't eat very much meat.*

me·chan·ic /mɪˈkænɪk/ *noun* someone whose job is to repair vehicles and machinery

me·chan·i·cal /mɪˈkænɪkəl/ *adjective* related to machines, or using power from a machine: *His car developed mechanical problems.* | *a mechanical toy*

mech·a·nis·m /ˈmekənɪzəm/ *noun* the part of a machine that does a particular job: *The door has a special locking mechanism.*

med·al /ˈmedl/ *noun* a round flat piece of metal that is given to someone as a prize or reward: *He received a medal for bravery.*

med·al·list *BrE*, **medalist** *AmE* /ˈmedl-ɪst/ *noun* someone who has won a medal in a competition: *She's an Olympic medalist.*

med·dle /ˈmedl/ *verb* to try to change or influence a situation, even though you should not because it does not involve you: *Stop meddling in my affairs.*

M

me·di·a /'miːdiə/ *noun* **1** the media television, radio, and newspapers: *The crime was reported by the media.* **2** the plural of MEDIUM

mediaeval a British spelling of MEDIEVAL

med·i·cal¹ /'medɪkəl/ *adjective* related to medicine and treating diseases or injuries: *medical qualifications | She needs medical care.*
–**medically** /-kli/ *adverb*

medical² *noun* BrE an examination of your body by a doctor to find out whether you are healthy; PHYSICAL² AmE: *You must have a medical before you join the army.*

med·i·ca·tion /ˌmedə'keɪʃən/ *noun* formal medicine: *"Are you taking any medication at present?" asked the nurse.*

medi·cine /'medsən $ 'medəsən/ *noun* **1** a substance for treating an illness, especially one that you drink: *cough medicine | Keep medicines away from children.* **2** [no plural] the treatment and study of illnesses and injuries: *Sue wants to study medicine.*

med·i·e·val also **mediaeval** BrE /ˌmedi'iːvəl $ ˌmɪd'ivəl/ *adjective* related to the MIDDLE AGES, the period of European history from about 100 to 1500 AD: *a medieval castle*

me·di·o·cre /ˌmiːdi'əʊkə $ ˌmidi'oʊkɚ/ *adjective* formal not very good in quality: *Tim got mediocre grades in his exams.*

med·i·tate /'medəteɪt/ *verb* to stay silent and calm for a period of time as part of your religion or to help you relax: *Buddhist priests were meditating in the park.*

meditate

med·i·ta·tion /ˌmedə'teɪʃən/ *noun [no plural]* when you stay silent and calm for a period of time as part of your religion or to help you relax: *We spent 15 minutes in meditation.*

me·di·um¹ /'miːdiəm/ *adjective* something that is medium in size or amount is not very big and not very small, but in the middle: *He's of medium height, with brown eyes.*

medium² *noun, plural* **media** /-diə/ something that is used to communicate information or ideas: *Electronic media such as the Internet and the Web have changed the way we work.*

medium-sized also **medium-size** /ˌ... '.../ *adjective* not very small and not very large: *a medium-sized bed*

meet /miːt/ *verb, past tense and past participle* **met** /met/
1 to see and talk to someone for the first time: *They first met at university. | Have you ever met her husband? | Pleased to meet you* (=used to say hello to someone when you meet them). | *It was nice meeting you* (=used when you say goodbye to someone you have just met).
2 to come to the same place as someone else because you have arranged it: *We'll meet at eight o'clock outside the theatre. | Her mother came to the airport to meet her.*
3 to see someone by chance when you are out somewhere: *She was walking to the library when she met Vicky.*
4 formal if something meets someone's standards or needs, it is good enough: *All the rooms **meet the standard** required.*
5 written if two things meet, they join or touch: *the point where the two roads meet*

PHRASAL VERB
meet with formal
meet with someone to have a meeting with someone: *The tutor **met with** students to discuss the problem.*

meet·ing /'miːtɪŋ/ *noun* an organized event where people discuss something. You organize, arrange, or call a meeting. Then you have or hold it somewhere. You cancel a meeting if you decide not to have it: *Mr Thompson is **in a meeting**. | She **called a meeting** to discuss the future of the company. | We're **having a meeting** next week to discuss this problem.*

meg·a·byte /'megəbaɪt/ *written abbreviation* **MB** *noun* a unit for measuring computer information, equal to one million BYTES

M

mel·low /'meləʊ $ 'meloʊ/ adjective relaxed, gentle, and calm: *After my bath, I felt really mellow.* | *The club has a lovely mellow atmosphere.*

mel·o·dy /'melədi/ noun, plural melodies a tune: *She sang to a series of traditional melodies.*

mel·on /'melən/ noun a large round fruit with yellow, orange, or green skin and a lot of flat seeds ➪ see picture on page 345

melt

melt /melt/ verb to change from solid to liquid, or to make something do this by heating it: *The sun had melted the snow.* | *The candle started to melt.*

mem·ber /'membə $ 'membɚ/ noun someone who has joined a club, group, or organization: *We want our members to feel involved in our work.* | *a member of the college staff*

Member of Par·lia·ment /ˌ.. . '.../ abbreviation **MP** noun in the UK, someone who the people elect to speak and act for them in parliament

mem·ber·ship /'membəʃɪp $ 'membɚ-ˌʃɪp/ noun [no plural] **1** when you are a member of a group or organization: *He was criticized for his membership of the Communist Party.* | *How much is the membership fee?* **2** all the people who belong to a club or organization: *There has been a fall in membership* (=fewer members) *this year.*

me·men·to /mə'mentəʊ $ mə'mentoʊ/ noun, plural mementos or mementoes a small object that you keep to remind you of someone or something: *The photograph is a memento of my school days.*

mem·o /'meməʊ $ 'memoʊ/ noun, plural memos a short official note that you write to another person working in the same organization as you

mem·oirs /'memwɑːz $ 'memwɑrz/ plural noun a book that someone writes about their life and experiences: *The ex-Prime Minister has published his memoirs.*

mem·o·ra·ble /'memərəbəl/ adjective very good and likely to be remembered: *a memorable film*

me·mo·ri·al[1] /mə'mɔːriəl/ adjective

done to remind people of someone who has died: *We held a memorial ceremony for people who died in the war.*

memorial[2] noun a building or other structure that is built to remind people of someone who has died: *a war memorial*

mem·o·rize also **memorise** BrE /'meməraɪz/ verb to learn and remember words, music, or other information: *She memorised her speech.*

mem·o·ry /'meməri/ noun, plural memories

GRAMMAR
a memory of something

1 the ability to remember things: *She's got a good memory.*
2 something that you remember from the past: *She had very happy memories of her time at college.* | *She has no memory of the accident* (=she cannot remember it at all).
3 the part of a computer where information is stored: *How much memory does your computer have?*

PHRASES
from memory if you can do something from memory, you can do it without needing to read anything or look at anything: *She can play the whole piece of music from memory.*
in memory of someone if you do something in memory of someone who has died, you do it in order to remember them: *This statue was put up in memory of the soldiers who died.*

men the plural of MAN

men·ace /'menɪs/ noun something or someone that is dangerous: *Leaking gas ovens are a menace to old people.*

mend /mend/
verb
to repair something that is broken or damaged: *If they can't mend the TV, we'll have to get a new one.* | *We'll have to get the roof mended* (=ask someone to mend it).

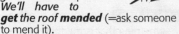
mend

men's room /'. ./ the American word for the GENTS

men·tal /'mentl/ *adjective* related to the mind, or happening in the mind: *mental health | I did a quick mental calculation.*
– **mentally** *adverb*: *a mentally ill patient*

men·tion /'menʃən/ *verb*

> **GRAMMAR**
> **mention (that)**
> **mention something to someone**
> **mention what/how/whether etc**

if you mention something, you say something about it, but you do not give a lot of information: *She **mentioned that** she'd just got back from the US. | I'll **mention** it **to** Rob. | Did Phil **mention whether** he'd come to the party? | He never mentioned his illness.*

> **PHRASE**

not to mention used when you are adding something better, bigger, or more surprising: *He stole my money, **not to mention** my girlfriend.*

men·u /'menjuː/ *noun* **1** a list of all the food that is available to eat in a restaurant: *Is steak on the menu tonight?* **2** a list of things that is shown on a computer screen: *Select 'Programs' from the menu.*

mer·cu·ry /'mɜːkjəri $ 'mɚkjəri/ *noun* [no plural] a silver-coloured liquid metal

mer·cy /'mɜːsi $ 'mɚsi/ *noun* [no plural] **1** kindness and willingness to forgive people: *The hostages pleaded for mercy.* **2 be at the mercy of someone/ something** to be unable to protect yourself from someone or something: *We were at the mercy of the killers.*

mere /mɪə $ mɪr/ *adjective* only or not more than; used to emphasize how small or unimportant something is: *We had a mere 10 minutes to do the test. | He won by a mere 3 points.*

mere·ly /'mɪəli $ 'mɪrli/ *adverb formal* only: *Smoking is not merely unpleasant, it's unhealthy.*

merge /mɜːdʒ $ mɚdʒ/ *verb* to join together to form one thing: *Havering College is merging with the University.*

mer·it /'merɪt/ *noun* a good quality or feature: *The long holidays are one of the biggest merits of the job. | Job applicants are chosen on merit.*

mer·maid /'mɜːmeɪd $ 'mɚmeɪd/ *noun* an imaginary creature with a woman's body and a fish's tail instead of legs

mer·ry /'meri/ *adjective* **Merry Christmas!** used to greet someone at CHRISTMAS

mesh /meʃ/ *noun* [no plural] material made of threads or wires that have been fastened together like a net: *The windows were protected by metal mesh.*

mess¹ /mes/ *noun*

1 [no plural] if a place is a mess, it is very untidy: *I'm afraid my room's a bit of a mess.*
2 a situation in which there are a lot of problems: *I've got to sort out this mess.*

> **PHRASES**

in a mess if a place is in a mess, it is very untidy: *The house was **in a** terrible **mess**.*
make a mess of something *spoken informal* to spoil something or do something badly: *I knew you'd **make a mess of** things!*

mess² *verb*

> **PHRASAL VERBS**

mess around also **mess about** *BrE informal*
1 mess around to do things that are silly or not useful: *We were just **messing around** on the computer. | Don't **mess around with** my books.*
2 mess someone around to treat someone badly, for example by not doing what you promised to do: *Sorry to **mess** you **around**, but could I come over tomorrow instead of tonight?*
mess up *informal*
mess something up to do something bad or make a mistake: *I **messed up** the exam.*

mes·sage /'mesɪdʒ/ *noun*

1 a piece of information that you send or give to another person: *I've got a message for you from Sammy. | I'm afraid Mr Jacobs isn't here at the moment. Would you like to **leave a message** for him? | I had 19 **email messages** this morning.*
2 the main idea in a film, speech, book etc that the writer is trying to make people understand: *The message is clear: don't drink and drive.*

M

mes·sen·ger /'mesəndʒə $'mesən-dʒɚ/ *noun* someone who takes messages to other people, especially as a job: *a motorbike messenger service*

mess·y /'mesi/ *adjective* **messier, messiest** dirty or untidy: *Your bedroom is very messy.*

met the past tense and past participle of MEET

met·al /'metl/ *noun* a substance such as iron, gold, or steel: *a metal gate*

me·te·or /'miːtiə $'miːtiɚ/ *noun* a small piece of rock or metal that is moving through space

me·te·o·rite /'miːtiərait/ *noun* a small meteor that has landed on the Earth's surface

me·ter /'miːtə $'miːtɚ/ *noun* **1** the American spelling of METRE **2** a machine that measures the amount of power such as gas or electricity you have used

meth·od /'meθəd/ *noun*

GRAMMAR
a method of doing something

a way of doing something: *What is the best method of teaching children to read?* | *There are many different methods of payment* (=ways of paying).

me·thod·i·cal /mə'θɒdɪkəl $mə'θɑd-ɪkəl/ *adjective* done carefully and in the right order, or doing things in this way: *a well-planned, methodical piece of writing* | *My father's very methodical when he's working.*

me·tre *BrE*, **meter** *AmE* /'miːtə $'miːtɚ/ written abbreviation **m** *noun* a unit for measuring length, equal to 100 CENTIMETRES

met·ric /'metrik/ *adjective* using the system of weighing and measuring that is based on the KILOGRAM and the METRE

mg the written abbreviation of MILLIGRAM

mice the plural of MOUSE (1)

mi·cro·chip /'maɪkrəʊˌtʃɪp $'maɪ-kroʊˌtʃɪp/ *noun* a small part of a computer or a machine, containing the electronic parts that control what the machine does

mi·cro·phone /'maɪkrəfəʊn $'maɪkrə-ˌfoʊn/ *noun* a piece of equipment that you use to record sounds or to make a sound louder

mi·cro·pro·ces·sor /'maɪkrəʊˌprəʊ-sesə $ˌmaɪkroʊ'prɑsesɚ/ *noun* the main MICROCHIP in a computer

mi·cro·scope /'maɪkrəskəʊp $'maɪ-krəˌskoʊp/ *noun* a scientific instrument that makes it possible to see very small things: *I examined the virus under a microscope.*

mi·cro·wave /'maɪkrəweɪv/ also **microwave ov·en** /ˌ... '../ *noun* a machine that cooks food very quickly, using electric waves instead of heat
– **microwave** *verb*: *It takes only 3 minutes to microwave a potato.*

mid /mɪd/ *adjective* in the middle of a time or place: *They went to Boston in mid June.* | *She was born in the mid-1980s.*

mid·air /ˌmɪd'eə $ˌmɪd'er/ *noun* **in midair** in the sky or in the air: *The ball seemed to stop in midair.*
– **midair** *adjective*: *The planes were involved in a mid-air collision.*

mid·day /ˌmɪd'deɪ $'mɪd-deɪ/ *noun* [no plural] 12 o'clock in the middle of the day ⇨ same meaning NOON

mid·dle¹ /'mɪdl/ *noun*

GRAMMAR
the middle of something

1 **the middle** the part of something that is in the centre, furthest from the edges: *He put the cake in the middle of the table.*
2 the part that is between the beginning and the end of a period of time: *We're going on holiday in the middle of June.* | *It was the middle of the night by the time we got home.*

PHRASES
in the middle between other people or things: *The three boys sat on the bench, with Sam in the middle.*
be in the middle of doing something to be busy doing something: *I can't talk now – I'm in the middle of doing my homework.*

middle² *adjective*

1 the middle one of a number of things is the one between the others: *The scissors are in the middle drawer.*
2 half of the way between the beginning and the end of an event or period of time: *The middle part of the film was a bit boring.*

M

middle-aged /ˌ.. './ adjective a middle-aged person is between about 40 and 60 years old

Middle Ag·es /ˌ.. '../ noun the Middle Ages the period in European history between about 1100 and 1400 AD

middle class /ˌ.. './ noun the middle class, the middle classes people such as teachers, doctors, and managers, who are neither very rich nor very poor – **middle-class** adjective: a middle-class family

Middle East /ˌ.. './ noun the Middle East the part of Asia that includes Iran and Egypt and the countries between them

middle name /'.. ˌ./ noun the name that comes between your first name and your SURNAME (=your family name)

middle school /'.. ˌ./ noun in Britain, a school for children between the ages of 9 and 13, and in the US for children between 11 and 14

mid·night /'mɪdnaɪt/ noun [no plural] 12 o'clock at night: We stayed up until midnight.

mid·way /ˌmɪd'weɪ/ adjective, adverb at the middle point between two places, or in the middle of a period of time: We scored at the midway stage of the game. | The Comoro islands lie midway between Madagascar and the coast of Tanzania.

mid·week /ˌmɪd'wiːk/ adjective, adverb in the middle of the week: I never go to parties midweek. | a midweek match

mid·wife /'mɪdwaɪf/ noun, plural midwives /-waɪvz/ a nurse who has been trained to help women when they are having a baby

might /maɪt/ modal verb, negative might not or mightn't /'maɪtnt/
1 likely to happen in the future a) if something **might** happen, it is possible that it will happen in the future: Be careful! You might hurt yourself! | I might not be back until much later. b) if something **might have** happened, it is possible that it did happen in the past: The thieves **might have** broken in through the window.
2 likely to be true: You **might be** right. | He **might not be** living here anymore.

3 giving advice carefully and politely: You **might try** ringing her at home. | You **might not need** a coat today.

might've /'maɪtəv/ the short form of 'might have': This might've been a bad idea.

mi·graine /'miːɡreɪn $ 'maɪɡreɪn/ noun a very bad HEADACHE

mi·grant /'maɪɡrənt/ noun a person, bird, or animal that regularly moves from one place to another – **migrant** adjective: The farm employs a large number of migrant workers.

mi·grate /maɪ'ɡreɪt $ 'maɪɡreɪt/ verb 1 if birds or animals migrate, they travel to a warmer part of the world in winter and return in the spring 2 to go to live in another place, usually to find work: Thousands of workers migrated west.

mi·gra·tion /maɪ'ɡreɪʃən/ noun when a large group of birds, animals, or people move from one place to another

mike /maɪk/ informal a MICROPHONE

mild /maɪld/ adjective 1 not too severe, strong, or serious: Dean had a mild case of the flu. | a mild punishment 2 not having a strong taste: The sauce is very mild. 3 mild weather is not too cold: It's very mild for January.

mile /maɪl/ noun a unit for measuring distance, equal to 1760 YARDS or 1609 METRES: Our school is about three miles away.

mile·age or **milage** /'maɪlɪdʒ/ noun [no plural] 1 the total number of miles a vehicle has travelled: The mileage is very low for the age of the vehicle. 2 the distance a car or other vehicle can travel using a particular amount of fuel: Diesel engines get better mileage but they are noisier.

mil·i·ta·ry¹ /'mɪlətəri $ 'mɪlə,teri/ adjective related to the army, navy etc: military vehicles | military conflicts

military² noun the military the army, navy etc: Jeff decided to join the military.

mi·li·tia /mə'lɪʃə/ noun an organized group of soldiers who are not members of an official army

milk¹ /mɪlk/ noun [no plural] a white liquid produced by female animals and humans to feed their babies: a glass of milk

milk² verb to take milk from a cow or goat

milk·man /'mɪlkmən/ *noun, plural* milkmen /-mən/ someone who delivers milk to people's houses

milk·shake /ˌmɪlk'ʃeɪk $ 'mɪlkʃeɪk/ *noun* a cold drink made from milk mixed with fruit or chocolate

mill /mɪl/ *noun* **1** a building containing a large machine for crushing grain **2** a factory that produces paper, steel, or cloth: *a paper mill*

mil·len·ni·um /mɪ'leniəm/ *noun, plural* millennia /-niə/ a period of 1000 years: *the start of a new millennium*

mil·li·gram /'mɪləgræm/ *written abbreviation* **mg** *noun* a unit for measuring weight, equal to 1/1000th of one GRAM

mil·li·li·tre *BrE*, **milliliter** *AmE* /'mɪləˌliːtə $ 'mɪləˌlitɚ/ *written abbreviation* **ml** *noun* a unit for measuring liquids, equal to 1/1000th of one LITRE

mil·li·me·tre *BrE*, **millimeter** *AmE* /'mɪləˌmiːtə $ 'mɪləˌmitɚ/ *written abbreviation* **mm** *noun* a unit for measuring length, equal to 1/1000th of one METRE

mil·lion /'mɪljən/ *noun* **1** 1,000,000: *$75 million | ten million people* **2** also **millions** *spoken informal* a very large number of people or things: *I have millions of things to do today.*

mil·lion·aire /ˌmɪljə'neə $ ˌmɪljə'ner/ *noun* someone who is very rich and has a million pounds or a million dollars

mime /maɪm/ *verb* to show something using movements, but no words: *Dana mimed pouring a glass of water.* – **mime** *noun*

mim·ic /'mɪmɪk/ *verb* mimicked, mimicking to copy someone's speech or actions: *Jodie mimicked the teacher's voice.*

mince /mɪns/ *noun* [no plural] *BrE* meat that has been cut into very small pieces; GROUND BEEF, HAMBURGER *AmE*

mind¹ /maɪnd/ *verb*

1 Do you mind...?, Would you mind...? *spoken* **a)** say this to politely ask if you can do something: *Do you mind if I call my mom? | I have to ask you a couple of questions – do you mind? | Would you mind if I borrowed your blue dress?* **b)** say this to politely ask if someone can do something for you: *Do you mind signing these forms? | Would you mind turning up the*

heat a little? | I hate to ask you to wait, but **would you mind**? I'm not ready.

2 never mind *spoken* say this to tell someone that something does not matter: *"Do you want the big box or the little one?" "Never mind, I'll get it myself." | "What did you say?" "Oh, never mind. It's not important." | Never mind, that mud will wash off.*

3 I wouldn't mind... *spoken* say this when you would like to do something: *I wouldn't mind another cup of coffee. Do you want one too? | It's supposed to be a good movie. I wouldn't mind seeing it.*

4 I don't mind *spoken* say this when you will be happy with whatever happens or with whatever someone decides: *"Do you want pasta or chicken tonight?" "I don't mind." | I just need a drink – I don't mind what it is. | You can put it in the box or over there, I don't mind which.*

5 mind your own business *spoken* say this when you are annoyed and want to tell someone not to ask questions. This is not a polite expression: *"Can't you keep that baby quiet?" "Why don't you mind your own business?" | "So, are you married?" "Mind your own business."*

6 mind something *BrE spoken* used to tell someone to be careful, so that they do not hit something or fall: *Mind your head – the ceiling is very low. | Mind the step! Everyone trips over it.*

mind² *noun*

the part of your brain that you use to think and imagine things: *New ideas were always coming into her mind. | He tried to push these worries out of his mind* (=he tried to think about them). | *I kept picturing what would happen in my mind.*

change your mind to change your opinion or decision about something: *I changed my mind about going to college.*

make up your mind to decide about something: *The desserts all looked so good I couldn't make up my mind which one to have. | He still has not made his mind up which club he will play for next season.*

have something in mind to be thinking about something and have a plan about it: *Most of the students did not have a particular career in mind.*

be on your mind if something is on your mind, you are thinking or worrying about it a lot: *You look worried. What's on your mind?*

have something on your mind to be thinking or worrying about something a lot: *I don't want to bother him. He has a lot on his mind right now.*

keep something in mind, bear something in mind if you tell someone to bear something in mind, you tell them to remember an important piece of information: *You must keep in mind that the weather changes quickly in the mountains. | Bear in mind that young children will not sit still during a long plane flight.*

come to mind, spring to mind if something comes to mind, you begin to think of it or remember it: *As I read, two questions kept coming to mind. | "Do you have any ideas?" "Nothing that springs to mind, I'm afraid."*

mine¹ /maɪn/ *pronoun*

a thing belonging to the person who is speaking: *Could I borrow your pen? I've lost mine. | Hey, that's mine! Give it back! | A friend of mine* (=one of my friends) *gave it to me.*

mine² *noun*

1 a place where people have dug deep holes in the ground in order to find coal, gold etc

2 a type of bomb that someone hides under the ground or in water, that

explodes when something touches it: *The ship hit a mine and sank. | Many children have been killed by land mines.*

mine³ *verb* to dig into the ground to find gold, coal etc: *People came to mine for gold.*

mine·field /'maɪnfiːld/ *noun* **1** an area of land or sea where bombs have been hidden **2** a situation in which there are many hidden difficulties and dangers: *The whole process is a legal minefield.*

min·er /'maɪnə $ 'maɪnɚ/ *noun* someone who works in a mine: *a coal miner*

min·e·ral /'mɪnərəl/ *noun* a natural substance such as iron or salt that is in the earth and some foods

mineral wa·ter /'... ,.../ *noun* water that comes from the ground naturally and that you can buy in bottles

min·gle /'mɪŋgəl/ *verb* if sounds or smells mingle, they mix together: *The smells of flowers and spices mingled in the hot air.*

min·ia·ture /'mɪnətʃə $ 'mɪniətʃɚ/ *adjective* much smaller than normal: *a miniature camera*

min·i·mal /'mɪnəməl/ *adjective* very small, and therefore not something you should worry about: *The accident caused only minimal damage to the car.* – **minimally** *adverb*

min·i·mize also **minimise** *BrE* /'mɪnəmaɪz/ *verb* to make something as small as possible: *We hope to minimize the effects of pollution.*

min·i·mum¹ /'mɪnəməm/ *adjective*

the minimum number or amount is the smallest that is possible ⇨ *opposite* MAXIMUM: *The government wants to increase the minimum wage for workers.*

minimum² *noun*

GRAMMAR
a/the minimum of something
the smallest amount that is possible: *Quickly, and with the minimum of noise, the police surrounded the house. | The airline tried to keep delays to a minimum.*

min·ing /'maɪnɪŋ/ *noun* [no plural] the job

or process of digging gold, coal etc out of the ground

min·is·ter /'mɪnəstə $ 'mɪnəstɚ/ *noun* **1** a religious leader in some Christian churches **2** a politician who is the head of a government department in some countries: *the Minister of Agriculture*

min·is·try /'mɪnəstri/ *noun* **1** plural **ministries** a government department in some countries: *the Ministry of Defence* **2** the ministry some parts of the Christian church, or the work done by those parts: *Sam planned to join the ministry.*

mi·nor /'maɪnə $ 'maɪnɚ/ *adjective*
not very important or serious ⇨ opposite MAJOR[1]: *You have made only a few **minor mistakes**. | The driver suffered **minor injuries** in the accident.*

mi·nor·i·ty /maɪ'nɒrəti $ mə'nɔrəti/ *noun*

GRAMMAR
a minority of something
be in a/the minority

1 a small part of a larger group of people or things: *Only **a minority of** students passed the exam. | The changes in the law were supported by only **a small minority**.*
2 *plural* **minorities** a group of people whose race or religion is different from the race or religion of most people in a country: ***Ethnic minorities** have many problems in this country.*

PHRASE
be in the minority, be in a minority: *Smokers **are in the minority** in our office* (=there are fewer people who do smoke cigarettes than people who do not).

mint /mɪnt/ *noun* **1** a type of sweet that tastes of PEPPERMINT **2** a place where the official coins of a country are made

mi·nus[1] /'maɪnəs/ *preposition* used in mathematics when you SUBTRACT one number from another: *12 minus 7 equals 5 (12 − 7 = 5)*

minus[2] *noun, plural* **minuses** also **minus sign** /'.. ,./ a sign (−) showing that a number is less than zero, or that

you must SUBTRACT one number from another

min·ute[1] /'mɪnɪt/ *noun*

1 a measure of time that is equal to 60 seconds. There are 60 minutes in an hour: *I waited 20 minutes for the bus. | Sharon was a few minutes late for the meeting. | Beckham scored in the 84th minute of the game. | It's a two-minute walk to the train station.*
2 **minutes** an official written record of the things that people say during a meeting

PHRASES
a minute a very short period of time: *Wait there **a minute**. | Leave me alone **for a minute**. | Mum will be back **in a minute**. | I'm going to the shop – **I won't be a minute** (=I won't be away for very long at all).*
any minute (now) very soon: *Hurry up – the play starts **any minute**. | Don't worry, the doctor will be here **any minute now**.*
this minute immediately: *Stop that **this minute** and come here! | You don't have to decide **this minute** – you can tell me tomorrow.*
the last minute the latest possible time: *I was planning to go to the party, but I changed my mind **at the last minute**. | Diane never leaves for work **until the last minute**.*

mi·nute[2] /maɪ'njuːt $ maɪ'nut/ *adjective* formal very small: *I made a few minute changes to my essay.*

mir·a·cle /'mɪrəkəl/ *noun* **1** something good that you did not expect to happen or did not think was possible: *It's a miracle she wasn't killed in the accident.* **2** an action or event that seems impossible and that people think has been done by God

mi·rac·u·lous /mɪ'rækjələs/ *adjective* very good and surprising
– miraculously *adverb*: *He has recovered miraculously from his illness.*

mir·ror /'mɪrə $ 'mɪrɚ/ *noun* an object made of special glass in which you can see yourself when you look in it: *Anna looked at her reflection in the mirror.* ⇨ *see picture at* CAR

mis·be·have /ˌmɪsbɪ'heɪv/ *verb* to behave badly: *Anyone who misbehaves will have to leave the room.*

mis·cel·la·ne·ous /ˌmɪsə'leɪnɪəs/ adjective formal of many different kinds: There were a few miscellaneous books on the shelf.

mis·chief /'mɪstʃɪf/ noun [no plural] formal bad behaviour, especially by children, that is annoying but causes no serious harm: The girls always caused a lot of mischief on the farm.

mis·chie·vous /'mɪstʃəvəs/ adjective formal a mischievous child behaves badly, but in a way that makes people laugh

mis·e·ra·ble /'mɪzərəbəl/ adjective 1 very unhappy: Paula looked miserable yesterday. 2 very bad: miserable weather

–**miserably** adverb: Our team played miserably.

mis·e·ry /'mɪzəri/ noun [no plural] when someone is very unhappy: Andy remembered the misery of his childhood.

mis·judge /ˌmɪs'dʒʌdʒ/ verb formal to make a wrong decision about what someone or something is like: We seriously misjudged the students' views.

mis·lead /mɪs'liːd/ verb, past tense and past participle **misled** /-'led/ to deliberately give someone incorrect information: They misled us about the quality of this car.

–**misleading** adjective: a misleading advertisement

misled the past tense and past participle of MISLEAD

mis·print /'mɪs-prɪnt/ noun a mistake in the way a word is spelled in a book, magazine etc

Miss /mɪs/ noun used in front of the name of a girl or unmarried woman when you are speaking or writing to her: Our teacher is Miss Rogers.

miss¹ /mɪs/ verb

GRAMMAR
miss doing something

1 to feel sad because someone that you like is not with you, or because you can no longer have something you enjoyed in the past: I really miss Mum and Dad now I'm at university. | Sue misses the long walks she used to go on. | Paul missed seeing Jenny after she left work.

2 to be too late for something: We missed the train, so we had to catch the next one. | If you don't hurry, we'll miss the start of the movie.

3 to not notice something: I think we must have missed the road for the airport.

4 to not hit or catch something: Dani missed a really easy goal. | The bullet missed and hit the wall.

5 to not be able to do something: Graham will miss the next match because he has hurt his leg.

PHRASAL VERBS
miss out

1 spoken to not have the chance to do something that you would enjoy: I saw other students going to parties and felt that I was **missing out**. | Don't **miss out** on the fun – join the sports club!

2 miss something out to forget to include a fact or detail: I **missed out** two questions on the test paper.

miss² noun

1 give something a miss BrE spoken to decide not to do something: I'm not feeling very well, so I think I'll **give** the party **a miss**.

2 when you do not hit or catch something: That was Southgate's second penalty miss this year. | The plane was involved in a **near miss** (= when one plane nearly hits another plane in the air).

mis·sile /'mɪsaɪl $ 'mɪsəl/ noun a weapon that can fly over long distances and that explodes when it hits the thing it is aiming at: The army has been firing missiles across the border.

missile

miss·ing /'mɪsɪŋ/ adjective 1 someone or something that is missing is not in the place where you expect it to be: The police keep records of missing children. | My keys have gone missing. 2 not included: Jane's name was missing from the list.

mis·sion /'mɪʃən/ noun an important job that someone has been sent to do: The men were on an important mission from their government. | The soldiers' mission was to destroy the bridge.

M

mis·sion·a·ry /'mɪʃənəri $ 'mɪʃə,neri/ noun, plural **missionaries** someone who goes to a foreign country in order to teach people about the Christian religion

mis·spell /,mɪs'spel/ verb **misspelled, misspelt** BrE /-'spelt/ to spell a word wrongly: *They misspelled my name on the list.*
– **misspelling** noun

misspelt a past tense and past participle of MISSPELL

mist /mɪst/ noun very small drops of rain in the air, that make it difficult for you to see very far ⇨ *see usage note at* FOG

mis·take¹ /mɪ'steɪk/ noun

GRAMMAR
be a mistake to do something

1 if you make a mistake, you do, say, or write something that is not correct: *You **made** two **mistakes** in the spelling test.* | *It **was a mistake** to invite Tom to the party because he always argues with the other guests.* | *This computer program **corrects** your **mistakes** automatically.*

2 **by mistake** if you do something by mistake, you do something wrong without meaning to: *I took another student's bag **by mistake**.*

mistake² **mistook** verb /-'stʊk/ **mistaken** /-'steɪkən/

GRAMMAR
mistake someone for someone
if you mistake one person for another, you think wrongly that one person is someone else: *She **mistook** the man **for** a policeman and asked him for help.*

mis·tak·en¹ /mɪ'steɪkən/ adjective formal someone who is mistaken is wrong about something: *No, I think you must be mistaken.*
– **mistakenly** adverb

mistaken² the past participle of MISTAKE²

Mis·ter /'mɪstə $ 'mɪstɚ/ MR.

mistook the past tense of MISTAKE

mis·trust¹ /mɪs'trʌst/ noun [no plural] the feeling that you cannot trust someone: *Susan has a mistrust of strangers.*

mistrust² verb to not trust someone: *Jenny mistrusts salesmen.*

mist·y /'mɪsti/ adjective **mistier, mistiest** covered by mist or having a lot of mist: *a cold, misty day*

mis·un·der·stand /,mɪsʌndə'stænd $,mɪsʌndɚ'stænd/ verb, past tense and past participle **misunderstood** /-'stʊd/ to not understand something correctly: *He must have misunderstood my instructions.*

mis·un·der·stand·ing /,mɪsʌndə-'stændɪŋ $,mɪsʌndɚ'stændɪŋ/ noun
1 when someone does not understand something correctly: *We need to be clear in order to avoid any misunderstanding.*
2 an argument that is not very serious: *It was just a small misunderstanding.*

mit·ten /'mɪtn/ noun a type of GLOVE that does not have separate parts for each finger

mix¹ /mɪks/ verb

GRAMMAR
mix something with something
mix something into something
mix things together

1 also **mix in** if you mix two different substances, you put them together so that they combine and become a single substance: ***Mix** two eggs in a bowl **with** some flour.* | *Sal **mixed in** (=added) some sugar to make the sauce taste better.* | ***Mix together** the powder **and** water.* ⇨ *see picture on page 344*

2 if two substances mix, they combine and become a single substance: *Oil and water will not mix.*

3 to put different activities, ideas, or styles together: *Jude likes to **mix** her studies **with** her interest in sport.*

4 if a DJ mixes two records, he or she plays one record after another with no stops between them, or plays them both at the same time

PHRASAL VERB
mix up
1 **mix someone/something up** to think wrongly that one person or thing is someone or something else: *I **mixed** Alan **up with** his brother, Pete.* | *I **got** the days **mixed up** and went on Tuesday instead of Thursday.*
2 **mix something up** if you mix things up, you put them in the wrong order: *I arranged these books, and now you've **mixed** them **up**!*

mix² noun, plural **mixes** 1 [no plural] all the different people or things that are in a place: *There was a good mix of people*

at the party. **2** a recording of a record that is different to the original, or when it has been mixed with another record **3** a powder that is added to liquid to make something: *Put the cake mix into a bowl and add water.*

mixed /mɪkst/ *adjective* **1** consisting of a lot of different types of things, people, ideas etc: *a package of mixed nuts* | *Kelly had mixed feelings about going to college.* **2** *BrE* for both males and females: *Simon goes to a mixed school.*

mixed up /ˌ. ˈ./ *adjective* confused: *Tony got mixed up and went to the wrong house.*

mix·er /'mɪksə $ 'mɪksɚ/ *noun* **1** a piece of kitchen equipment that you use for mixing food **2** a piece of electronic equipment that a DJ uses to mix different pieces of music together

mix·ing /'mɪksɪŋ/ *noun* when a DJ plays one record after another without any stops between them, or plays two records at the same time

mix·ture /'mɪkstʃə $ 'mɪkstʃɚ/ *noun*

> **GRAMMAR**
> **mixture of something**

1 a substance that is made of several different substances that are mixed together: *Stir the mixture with a spoon until it is smooth.* | *a bottle of cough mixture*
2 a mixture of things is several different ones that exist together: *Singapore has an exciting mixture of Chinese, Malay, and Indian cultures.* | *Noah felt a mixture of fear and disgust.*

mix-up /'. ./ *noun informal* a mistake or problem that happens when people get confused or do not understand each other: *There was a mix-up with our bags at the airport.*

ml the written abbreviation of MILLILITRE

mm the written abbreviation of MILLI-METRE

moan /məʊn $ moʊn/ *verb* **1** to make a long low sound, especially because a part of your body hurts **2** *BrE* to complain about something in an annoying way: *I wish she'd stop moaning.*
–**moan** *noun*

mob /mɒb $ mɑb/ *noun* a large noisy crowd of angry violent people: *a mob of demonstrators*

mo·bile /'məʊbaɪl $ 'moʊbəl/ *adjective* able to move quickly and easily: *A mobile health clinic travels to all the towns in the area.*

mobile phone /ˌ.. ˈ./ also **mobile** *BrE*, *noun* a telephone that you can carry with you and use anywhere; CELL PHONE *AmE*: *Call me on my mobile.* ⊃ see picture on page 342

mock¹ /mɒk $ mɑk/ *verb formal* to laugh at someone or say unkind things about them in order to make them seem stupid: *Farley's ideas were mocked by many scientists.*

mock² *adjective* a mock thing or feeling is not real, but is intended to look real: *They're mock fights and the actors never get hurt.* | *They expressed mock horror at Sara's costume.*

mo·dal verb /ˌməʊdl 'vɜːb $ ˌmoʊdl 'vɚb/ also **modal** *noun* in grammar, a verb such as 'can', 'might', or 'must' that you use to show ideas such as possibility, permission, or intention

models

mod·el¹ /'mɒdl $ 'mɑdl/ *noun*

> **GRAMMAR**
> **a model of something**

1 a small copy of a large object such as a car, plane, or building: *He had a model of the Eiffel Tower on his desk.* | *My brother made these aircraft models.*
2 someone whose job is to show people different clothes or HAIRSTYLES by wearing them and being photographed
3 someone who wears new clothes at special shows so that people will see them and want to buy the clothes
4 one type of car or machine that a company makes: *The Golf is the most popular model in the VW range.*

M

model² *adjective* **1** a model plane, train, car etc is a small copy of a real one **2** a model student, worker etc does everything perfectly: *Nita has been a model student.*

model³ *verb* **modelled, modelling** BrE, **modeled, modeling** AmE **1** to wear new clothes at special shows so people will see them and want to buy them: *Claudia was modeling a long blue dress.* **2** model something on something to make one thing similar to another thing: *Luis modeled the characters in his story on real people.*

mod·el·ling BrE, **modeling** AmE /'mɒdl-ɪŋ $ 'mɑdl-ɪŋ/ *noun* [no plural] the work of wearing new clothes to show them to people: *She moved from modelling into acting.*

mo·dem /'məʊdem $ 'moʊdəm/ *noun* a piece of electronic equipment used for sending information such as EMAILS from one computer to another

mod·e·rate /'mɒdərət $ 'mɑdərət/ *adjective* **1** neither very big nor very small, very fast nor very slow etc: *Cook the mixture over moderate heat.* **2** having political opinions or beliefs that are not extreme: *Moderate Republicans support his ideas.*

mod·e·ra·tion /ˌmɒdə'reɪʃən $ ˌmɑdə-'reɪʃən/ *noun* if you do something in moderation, you do not do it too much: *Eat fatty foods only in moderation.*

mod·ern /'mɒdn $ 'mɑdərn/ *adjective*
1 using new methods, new equipment, or new ideas: *modern farming methods | a modern hotel | an exhibition of modern art*
2 about recent or present times, rather than the past: *a degree in modern history | modern Britain*

mod·ern·ize also **modernise** BrE /'mɒdənaɪz $ 'mɑdərˌnaɪz/ *verb* to change something so that is uses new methods, new equipment, or new ideas: *The airline has modernized its airplanes. | The new president hopes to modernize society.*

mod·est /'mɒdɪst $ 'mɑdɪst/ *adjective* **1** not talking too proudly about your own skills or the things you have done: *We are taught to be modest and not to brag about things.* **2** formal not very big

in size, amount, value etc: *The economy is growing at a modest rate.* **3** shy and embarrassed about showing your body – **modestly** *adverb*

mod·es·ty /'mɒdəsti $ 'mɑdəsti/ *noun* [no plural] **1** not talking too proudly about your own skills or the things you have done **2** when someone is shy and embarrassed about showing their body

mod·i·fy /'mɒdəfaɪ $ 'mɑdəˌfaɪ/ *verb* **modified, modifies** **1** to make small changes to something: *You can modify the rules to play the game with younger children. | The computer wouldn't allow me to modify the file.* **2** in grammar, if one word modifies another, it gives more information about it

moist /mɔɪst/ *adjective* slightly wet, in a pleasant way: *Keep the soil around the plant moist. | a moist chocolate cake*

moist·en /'mɔɪsən/ *verb* to make something slightly wet: *Add milk to moisten the mixture.*

mois·ture /'mɔɪstʃə $ 'mɔɪstʃər/ *noun* [no plural] small amounts of water in the air, on a surface etc: *Moisture in the wood will make the paint come off.*

mois·tur·iz·er also **moisturiser** BrE /'mɔɪstʃəraɪz $ 'mɔɪstʃəˌraɪzər/ *noun* a cream you put on your skin to keep it soft and stop it being too dry

mo·lar /'məʊlə $ 'moʊlər/ *noun* one of the large teeth at the back of your mouth

mold the American spelling of MOULD

moldy the American spelling of MOULDY

mole /məʊl $ moʊl/ *noun* **1** a small dark brown mark on your skin **2** a small animal with black fur that cannot see well and lives under the ground

mol·e·cule /'mɒlɪkjuːl $ 'mɑləˌkjul/ *noun* the smallest amount of a substance that can exist: *a molecule of water*

mo·lest /mə'lest/ *verb* to sexually attack or harm someone, especially a woman or a child
– **molester** *noun*: *a child molester*

molt the American spelling of MOULT

mom /mɒm $ mɑm/ the American word for MUM

mo·ment /'məʊmənt $ 'moʊmənt/ *noun*
1 a very short time: *After a moment, Lou returned. | We waited for a few*

Y **moments** before going into the house.

2 a particular point in time: *At that moment, the teacher walked in.* | *Winning the school prize was an emotional moment for me.*

PHRASES

at the moment now: *At the moment, the hospital is caring for 17 patients.* | *What are you reading at the moment?*

in a moment very soon: *In a moment, I will explain how the machine works.*

moments later a short time later: *Moments later, we saw Sally getting on the bus.*

mo·men·tar·i·ly /'məʊməntərəli $,moʊmən'terəli/ *adverb written* for a very short time: *He paused momentarily, then began speaking again.*

mo·men·ta·ry /'məʊməntəri $ 'moʊmən,teri/ *adjective formal* continuing for a very short time: *The class was surprised into a momentary silence.*

mo·men·tous /məʊ'mentəs $ moʊ-'mentəs/ *adjective* a momentous event, decision etc is very important: *The birth of my first child was a momentous occasion.*

mo·men·tum /məʊ'mentəm $ moʊ-'mentəm/ *noun* [no plural] **1** the force that makes a moving object continue to move: *The ball lost momentum and stopped rolling.* **2** when something keeps increasing, developing, or becoming more successful: *We've won three games in a row now, so we need to keep up the momentum.*

mom·my /'mɒmi $ 'mami/ the American word for MUMMY

mon·arch /'mɒnək $ 'manək/ *noun* a king or queen

mon·ar·chy /'mɒnəki $ 'manəki/ *noun, plural* **monarchies 1** [no plural] a country that is ruled by a king or queen: *In spite of many changes, the UK remains a monarchy.* **2 the monarchy** the king or queen of a country and their family

mon·as·tery /'mɒnəstri $ 'manəs,teri/ *noun, plural* **monasteries** a building where MONKS live

Mon·day /'mʌndi/ *written abbreviation* **Mon** *noun* the day of the week between SUNDAY and TUESDAY

mon·ey /'mʌni/ *noun* [no plural]
the coins and paper notes that you use to buy things: *Billy spent lots of money in town today.* | *How much money did your Nintendo cost?* | *He wants to become a footballer and earn lots of money.* | *I'm going to save money* (=not spend money) *by going out less often.*

mon·i·tor¹ /'mɒnitə $ 'manətər/ *noun* a piece of computer equipment with a screen that shows information or pictures

monitor² *verb written* to watch or measure something carefully for a period of time to see how it changes: *The study monitored the health of 87,000 women for many years.*

monk /mʌŋk/ *noun* a man who is a member of a religious group that lives in a MONASTERY

mon·key /'mʌŋki/ *noun* an animal that lives in hot countries and uses its long tail, feet, and hands to climb trees

mo·nop·o·ly /mə'nɒpəli $ mə'napəli/ *noun, plural* **monopolies** a situation in which one person or organization controls all of a particular business or industry and there is no competition: *AT&T once had a monopoly on telephone services in the US.*

mo·not·o·nous /mə'nɒtənəs $ mə-'natn-əs/ *adjective* boring and not changing very often: *a low-paid, monotonous job*

mon·soon /,mɒn'suːn $,man'sun/ *noun* the time of year in southern Asia and India when it rains a lot

mon·ster /'mɒnstə $ 'manstər/ *noun* a large ugly frightening creature in stories

mon·strous /'mɒnstrəs $ 'manstrəs/ *adjective* very wrong, bad, or unfair: *a monstrous lie*

month /mʌnθ/ *noun*
one of the 12 periods of time that a year is divided into, for example February or December: *I'm visiting the States next month.* | *We stayed in Thailand for nearly two months.*

month·ly /'mʌnθli/ *adjective, adverb* happening or done every month: *a monthly magazine* | *The club meets monthly.*

M

mon·u·ment /ˈmɒnjəmənt $ ˈmɑːnjə-mənt/ *noun* a building or other structure that is built to remind people of an important event or famous person: *an ancient monument*

mood /muːd/ *noun*

your feelings and emotions at a particular time: *Dad's **in a bad mood*** (=cross and bad-tempered) *today. | Sam **seems in a very good mood**. | A good actor can always sense **the mood of** his audience. | Mina's sudden changes of mood annoyed Joe.*

PHRASES

be in the mood for doing something to feel that you want to do something: *I'm **in the mood for** dancing.*

be in no mood for doing something, be in no mood to do something to feel strongly that you do not want to do something: *Selena **was in no mood for** joking. | Taki **was in no mood to** listen to my advice.*

mood·y /ˈmuːdi/ *adjective* **moodier, moodiest** a moody person becomes angry or unhappy quickly and without any warning: *After his divorce, he became moody and began drinking too much.*

moon /muːn/ *noun*

the moon the large white object that you can see shining in the sky at night ⇨ see picture at CRATER

moon·light /ˈmuːnlaɪt/ *noun [no plural]* the light of the moon

moon·lit /ˈmuːn,lɪt/ *adjective* a moonlit place or night is made bright by the light of the moon

moor /mʊə $ mʊr/ *noun BrE* an area of high land covered with rough grass or low bushes

mop

mop¹ /mɒp $ mɑːp/ *noun* a stick with a soft end that you use for cleaning floors

mop² *verb* **mopped, mopping 1** to

clean a floor with a mop **2** **mop something up** to use a piece of soft material to clean liquid from a surface: *Sara used some paper towels to mop up the milk she spilled.*

mope /məʊp $ moʊp/ *also* **mope around** *verb* to feel unhappy and not try to become cheerful again

mo·ped /ˈməʊped $ ˈmoʊped/ *noun* a vehicle like a bicycle with a small engine

mor·al¹ /ˈmɒrəl $ ˈmɔːrəl/ *adjective*

moral behaviour is right and good ⇨ opposite IMMORAL: *We all have to live by certain **moral standards**. | We have **moral duty** to help these people.*
–**morally** *adverb: I think killing animals is **morally wrong**.*

moral² *noun* **1** morals standards of good behaviour, such as honesty and kindness: *Parents want to teach their children good morals.* **2** something you learn from the moral of a story is about how you should or should not behave: *The moral of the story is that you can't believe everything people tell.*

mo·rale /məˈrɑːl $ məˈræl/ *noun [no plural]* the confidence and hope that a person or group feels: *The team's morale is low after losing several games.*

mo·ral·i·ty /məˈræləti/ *noun [no plural]* ideas about what is right and wrong: *Some religious leaders questioned the morality of the war.*

more /mɔː $ mɔr/ *adverb, pronoun*

1 a larger amount or number: *You look much more attractive with long hair. | We ought to meet more often. | I think physics is **much more** interesting than history. | It's not fair – you've got more people in your team than we have! | You should spend more time checking your spelling. | We want **more of** our students to go to university. | **More than** 50 people died in the fire.*
2 an additional amount or number: *Can I have some more cake? | I have fifteen more cards to write.*

PHRASES

more and more: *As the storm got worse, he became **more and more** anxious* (=he continued to become more anxious).
more or less nearly, but not exactly:

M

▼ We've **more or less** finished now. |
That's **more or less** what she said.

USAGE
More is used to form the comparative of
adjectives with more than two syllables:
more attractive | more intelligent. **More** is
also the opposite of both **less** and **fewer**:
more wine | more people.

more·o·ver /mɔːrˈəʊvə $ mɔrˈoʊvɚ/
adverb *formal* used when you give more
information to support something that
you have just said: *I have always lived
here, and moreover, I do not plan to
move.*

morn·ing /ˈmɔːnɪŋ $ ˈmɔrnɪŋ/
noun
1 the time from when the sun rises to
the middle of the day: *I saw Steve
this morning. | I get up at 7.00 most
mornings. | I'll see you in the
morning. | Ruth and I are going into
town on Saturday morning.*
2 the part of the night from 12 at night
until the sun rises: *I heard a loud
bang at 2 o'clock in the morning.*

PHRASE
(Good) Morning *spoken* used when
you meet someone in the morning:
Good morning, Class 5.

mort·gage /ˈmɔːgɪdʒ $ ˈmɔrgɪdʒ/ *noun*
money you borrow from a bank in order
to buy a house

mor·ti·cian /mɔːˈtɪʃən $ mɔrˈtɪʃən/ an
American word for UNDERTAKER

mo·sa·ic /məʊˈzeɪ-ɪk $ moʊˈzeɪ-ɪk/
noun a design made from small pieces of
coloured stone and glass that is fixed to
a surface

Mos·lem /ˈmɒzləm $ ˈmɑzləm/ another
word for MUSLIM

mosque /mɒsk $ mɑsk/ *noun* a build-
ing where MUSLIMs go to pray

mos·qui·to /məˈskiːtəʊ $ məˈskitoʊ/
plural **mosquitoes** *noun* a small flying insect that bites and sucks blood

moss /mɒs $ mɔs/ *noun [no plural]* a small
flat green plant that looks like fur and
grows on trees and rocks

most /məʊst $ moʊst/ *adverb,
pronoun*
1 the largest amount: *This is the most
expensive perfume in the world. |
The most important thing is to stay
calm. | What scares me the most is*
▼

▼ the thought of being injured. | *Who's
got the most money? | The most I
ever scored was 100.*
2 nearly all: *I like most kinds of
food. | Most people have heard of
him. | Most of my friends live
nearby. | Gary did most of the hard
work.*

USAGE most, most of
For this meaning, use **most** immediately
before a noun: *Most new computers have
a DVD drive.* Use **most of** before 'the',
'this', 'my' etc + noun: *I got most of the
answers right. | He does most of his work
at home.*

PHRASES
at most, at the most: *This test won't
take long – half an hour at the most*
(=the largest amount of time it will take
is half an hour).
make the most of something to
use or enjoy something as much as
possible: *This good weather won't
last, so we'd better make the most
of it.*

most·ly /ˈməʊstli $ ˈmoʊstli/ *adverb* in
most cases or most of the time: *The
players were mostly men.*

mo·tel /məʊˈtel $ moʊˈtel/ *noun* a hotel
where people who are travelling by car
can stay

moth /mɒθ $ mɔθ/ *noun* an insect with
wings that flies around lights at night

moth·er /ˈmʌðə $ ˈmʌðɚ/ *noun*
your female parent: *My mother
taught me how to cook.*

moth·er·hood /ˈmʌðəhʊd $ ˈmʌðɚ-
hʊd/ *noun [no plural]* when someone is a
mother

mother-in-law /ˈ.. . ,./ *noun* the
mother of your husband or wife

mo·tion /ˈməʊʃən $ ˈmoʊʃən/
noun
when something moves: *He photographs animals while they are in
motion* (=moving). | *The slightest
motion could have sent him tum-
bling over the edge of the cliff.*

mo·tion·less /ˈməʊʃənləs $ ˈmoʊʃən-
ləs/ *adjective written* not moving at all:
Rick lay motionless on the ground.

mo·ti·vate /ˈməʊtəveɪt $ ˈmoʊtəˌveɪt/
verb to make someone want to do

something: *Teachers should motivate students to stay in school.*
– **motivated** *adjective*: *a group of highly motivated students*

mo·ti·va·tion /ˌməʊtə'veɪʃən $ˌmoʊ-tə'veɪʃən/ *noun* **1** *[no plural]* when you want to achieve something: *Pam has plenty of motivation, but she needs to improve her language skills.* **2** the reason why you want to do something: *The motivation for the change is money.*

mo·tive /'məʊtɪv $'moʊtɪv/ *noun formal* the reason why you do something: *I wonder what his motives really are?*

mo·tor[1] /'məʊtə $'moʊtə/ *noun* the part of a machine that uses electricity, petrol etc to make it move

motor[2] *adjective* **1** a motor vehicle uses an engine to make it move **2** related to cars: *the motor industry*

mo·tor·cy·cle /'məʊtəˌsaɪkəl $'moʊ-tə,saɪkəl/ also **mo·tor·bike** /'məʊtə-ˌbaɪk $'moʊtə,baɪk/ *BrE, noun* a vehicle with two wheels and an engine, that you sit on ⇨ *same meaning* BIKE ⇨ *see picture on page 349*

mo·tor·cy·clist /'məʊtəˌsaɪklɪst $'moʊtə,saɪklɪst/ *noun* someone who rides a motorcycle

mo·tor·ist /'məʊtərɪst $'moʊtərɪst/ *noun formal* someone who drives a car ⇨ *same meaning* DRIVER

mo·tor·way /'məʊtəweɪ/ *noun BrE* a wide road on which you can drive fast for long distances; FREEWAY *AmE*

mot·to /'mɒtəʊ $'mɑtoʊ/ *noun, plural* **mottoes** or **mottos** a short statement that says what the aims or principles of a person or organization are: *The Nike shoe advertising motto is "Just do it."*

mould[1] *BrE,* **mold** *AmE* /məʊld $moʊld/ *noun* **1** an unpleasant green or black substance that grows on old food or on wet things: *Mold was growing on the walls of the bathroom.* **2** a container with a special shape that you pour liquid into, so that when the liquid becomes solid it will have that shape: *a teddy bear mould for cakes*

mould[2] *BrE,* **mold** *AmE verb* to make a substance have a particular shape by pressing it or by putting it in a mould: *chocolate molded into heart shapes*

mould·y *BrE,* **moldy** *AmE* /'məʊldi $'moʊldi/ *adjective* covered with mould: *The bread was mouldy.*

moult *BrE,* **molt** *AmE* /məʊlt $moʊlt/ *verb* when an animal or bird moults, it loses hair or feathers so that new ones can grow

mound /maʊnd/ *noun* a large pile of something: *a mound of stones*

Mount /maʊnt/ *noun* used in the names of mountains: *Mount Everest*

mount /maʊnt/ *verb* **1** *written* to organize and begin an event: *The museum mounted a show of Egyptian art.* | *We want to mount a campaign against racism.* **2** also **mount up** *written* to gradually increase: *Concern for the girl's safety is mounting.* **3** to get on a horse or bicycle

moun·tain /'maʊntən/ *noun* a very high hill: *the Caucasus mountains in Russia* ⇨ *see picture on page 348*

moun·tain·eer /ˌmaʊntə'nɪə $ˌmaʊntə'nɪr/ *noun* someone who climbs mountains

moun·tain·eer·ing /ˌmaʊntə'nɪərɪŋ $ˌmaʊntə'nɪrɪŋ/ *noun [no plural]* the sport of climbing mountains

moun·tain·ous /'maʊntənəs/ *adjective* having a lot of mountains: *a mountainous region*

mourn /mɔːn $mɔrn/ *verb* to feel very sad because someone has died: *Friends and relatives mourned Anita's death.*

mourn·er /'mɔːnə $'mɔrnə/ *noun* someone who is at a FUNERAL

mourn·ing /'mɔːnɪŋ $'mɔrnɪŋ/ *noun [no plural]* when you feel very sad because someone has died: *In the Jewish religion, there are seven days of mourning after someone dies.*

mouse /maʊs/ *noun* **1** *plural* **mice** /maɪs/ a small animal with smooth fur, a long tail, and a pointed nose **2** *plural* **mouses** a small object connected to a computer, that you move with your hand and press to make the computer do things ⇨ *see picture on page 342*

mouse mat *BrE,* **mouse pad** *AmE* /'. ./ *noun* a small piece of material that you use with a computer MOUSE

mousse /muːs/ *noun* **1** a substance that you put in your hair to hold it in position **2** a cold sweet food made from cream, eggs, and fruit or chocolate

mous·tache *BrE,* **mustache** *AmE* /mə'stɑːʃ $'mʌstæʃ/ *noun* hair that a man grows on his upper lip ⇨ see picture on page 353

mouth /maʊθ/ noun, plural **mouths** /maʊðz/
the part of your face, including your lips, teeth, and tongue, that you use for speaking and eating ⇨ see picture at HEAD¹

mouth·ful /ˈmaʊθfʊl/ noun the amount of food or drink that you put into your mouth at one time: *Steve took another mouthful of fish.*

mouth·wash /ˈmaʊθwɒʃ $ ˈmaʊθwɑʃ/ noun, plural **mouthwashes** a liquid that you use to make your mouth clean and your breath smell fresh

move¹ /muːv/ verb

> **GRAMMAR**
> **move to/from a place**
> **move towards someone**

1 to go from one position or place to another: *Just then, the shape behind the curtain moved.* | *The dog **moved** slowly **towards** us.* | *Tony **was moving around** slowly.*
2 to take something and put it in a different place or position: *I can't move my arm – I think it's broken.*
3 to go to live in a different place: *Teenagers need to **move away from** home and be independent.* | *She **moved to** France in 2000.* | *When are you **moving house** (=going to live in a different house)?*

> **PHRASAL VERBS**
> **move in**
> to start living in a different house: *The day after we **moved in**, the roof started to leak.* | *I **moved in with** my cousin.*
> **move off**
> if a vehicle moves off, it starts its journey by going forward: *Our friends waved as the train started **moving off**.*
> **move out**
> to leave the house where you are living to go and live somewhere else: *Dad sold the house and we **moved out**.*

move² noun
something that you do in order to achieve something: *Accepting the job was **a good move**.*

move·ment /ˈmuːvmənt/ noun
when someone or something moves: *With an awkward movement, Nick turned his head.* | *We could hear movement in the room above us.*

mov·ie /ˈmuːvi/ **1 a** FILM¹ **2 the movies** the American word for the CINEMA

movie thea·ter /ˈ.. ˌ../ the American word for a CINEMA

mov·ing /ˈmuːvɪŋ/ adjective making you feel strong emotions, especially sadness or sympathy: *a moving story*

mow /məʊ $ moʊ/ verb, past participle **mown** /məʊn $ moʊn/ or **mowed** to cut grass with a machine: *Our son mows the lawn for us.*

MP /ˌem ˈpiː/ the abbreviation of MEMBER OF PARLIAMENT

mph the written abbreviation of 'miles per hour'; used to say how fast a vehicle goes: *The car was traveling at 85 mph when it crashed.*

Mr. /ˈmɪstə $ ˈmɪstɚ/ noun used in front of a man's family name when you are speaking or writing to him

Mrs. /ˈmɪsɪz/ noun used in front of a married woman's family name when you are speaking or writing to her

Ms. /mɪz/ noun used in front of a woman's family name when you are speaking or writing to her

MSc /ˌem es ˈsiː/ also **M.S.** /ˌem ˈes/ AmE noun the abbreviation of Master of Science; a higher university degree in science

Mt. the written abbreviation of MOUNT

much /mʌtʃ/
a large amount of something. Use **much** about things that you cannot count, such as work, time, food, information etc, or after a verb, especially in questions and negative sentences: *I don't have much time – can I call you back later?* | *Was there much traffic?* | *There wasn't much difference between the two pictures.* | *I didn't have **much of** a chance to talk to her.* | *Has Bobby grown much since you last saw him?* | *"Did you enjoy the film?" "Not much."* ⇨ compare MANY

In positive sentences, use **a lot of** rather than **much**: *There was a lot of traffic.* Do not say: *There was much traffic.*

PHRASES

how much? use this to ask about the amount or cost of something: *How much was your new stereo?* | *How much ice cream do you want?*

too much, so much use these when an amount of something is larger than you want or need: *He ate too much last night.* | *There was so much noise I couldn't hear her at all.*

too much, so much, very much use these to show how much someone does something or how much something happens: *Thank you very much!* | *He has grown so much this year.* | *I can't walk on it – it hurts too much.*

as much use this to talk about an amount of something, especially when you are comparing two amounts: *I don't like this book as much as his other novels.* | *Abby earns as much money as her husband.*

much better, much worse, much bigger etc use **much** when you are comparing things, to mean a lot: *I'm feeling much better today.* | *Kevin is much older than Debbie.* | *It is much warmer now.*

much too big, much too tired, much too old etc: *Sara was driving much too fast.* | *It was much too cold to stay outside.* | *The coat was much too small for him.*

much more expensive, much more important, much more easily etc: *He could see her much more clearly now.* | *Lamb is much more expensive than chicken.* | *The classwork is much more difficult now.*

muck¹ /mʌk/ *noun [no plural] informal* dirt or mud: *There's some muck on the carpet.*

muck² *verb* **muck about, muck around** *BrE spoken informal* to behave in a silly way and waste time: *Don't muck about while I'm working.*

mud /mʌd/ *noun [no plural]* wet earth: *Joe got mud on his shoes.*

mud·dle¹ /'mʌdl/ *noun* a situation in which things are badly organized or confusing: *My notes are in a bit of a muddle.*

muddle² *verb* **1** also **muddle up** to put things in the wrong order: *Someone's muddled up my socks.* **2 get someone/something muddled up** *informal* to wrongly think that one person or thing is someone or something else: *I always get their names muddled up.*

mud·dy /'mʌdi/ *adjective* **muddier, muddiest** covered with mud: *Take your muddy boots off!*

muf·fle /'mʌfəl/ *verb written* to make a sound less loud or less clear: *The falling snow muffled all sounds.*
–**muffled** *adjective*: *I heard muffled laughter behind the door.*

mug¹ /mʌg/ *noun* a large cup with straight sides: *a mug of coffee*

mug² *verb* **mugged, mugging** to attack someone in a public place and steal their money: *Anne was mugged last night.*
–**mugger** *noun*: *The mugger ran off when the police arrived.*

mug·gy /'mʌgi/ *adjective* **muggier, muggiest** muggy weather is unpleasantly wet and warm

Mu·ham·med /mu'hæməd/ also **Mo·ham·med** /məʊ'hæməd $moʊ'hæməd/ a PROPHET who taught the ideas that the Islamic religion is based on

mule /mjuːl/ *noun* an animal that has a DONKEY and a horse as parents

mull /mʌl/ *verb* **mull over** to think about something carefully: *He wanted to be left alone to mull things over.*

mul·ti·cul·tur·al /ˌmʌlti'kʌltʃərəl/ *adjective* involving people and ideas from many different countries: *America is a multicultural society.*

mul·ti·me·di·a /ˌmʌltɪ'miːdiə/ *adjective* multimedia computer products use sound, pictures, films, and writing: *multimedia software*

mul·ti·ple /'mʌltəpəl/ *adjective* involving many parts, people, events etc: *The driver died from multiple injuries.*

multiple choice /ˌ... './ *adjective* a multiple choice test or question shows several possible answers and you must choose the correct one

mul·ti·pli·ca·tion /ˌmʌltəplə'keɪʃən/ *noun [no plural]* a calculation in which you add a number to itself a particular number of times

mul·ti·ply /'mʌltəplaɪ/ *verb* **multiplied, multiplies 1** to do a calculation in which you add a number to itself a particular number of times: *6 multiplied by 2 equals 12* (=6 x 2 = 12). **2** to increase greatly in number: *The number of people with mobile phones has multiplied incredibly in the last year.*

mul·ti·ra·cial /ˌmʌltiˈreɪʃəl/ *adjective* involving people from many different races

mul·ti·tude /ˈmʌltətjuːd $ ˈmʌltəˌtud/ *noun written* a very large number of things or people: *She's kept busy by a multitude of projects.*

mum *BrE*, **mom** *AmE* /mʌm $ mɑːm/ *noun informal* a word for mother: *How old is your mom? | Mum, can you drive me to college?*

mum·ble /ˈmʌmbəl/ *verb* to speak in a quiet way that is difficult to understand: *He mumbled an excuse.*

mum·my *BrE*, **mommy** *AmE* /ˈmʌmi $ mɑːmi/ *noun* a word for mother, used by children: *Mummy, can I have some sweets?*

mumps /mʌmps/ also **the mumps** *noun [no plural]* an illness that makes your throat and neck hurt

munch /mʌntʃ/ *verb* to eat food that is hard and makes a noise as you eat it: *He was munching an apple.*

mu·ni·ci·pal /mjuːˈnɪsəpəl/ *adjective* related to the government of a city: *municipal elections*

mu·ral /ˈmjʊərəl $ ˈmjʊrəl/ *noun* a picture that is painted onto a wall

mur·der¹ /ˈmɜːdə $ ˈmɚdɚ/ *noun*

the crime of deliberately killing someone: *There were four murders here last year. | Her jealousy led her to commit murder.*

murder² *verb*

to kill someone deliberately: *I was frightened he might murder me. | She was murdered by terrorists.*

murk·y /ˈmɜːki $ ˈmɚki/ *adjective* **murkier, murkiest** dark and difficult to see through: *a murky river*

mur·mur¹ /ˈmɜːmə $ ˈmɚmɚ/ *noun written* a soft low continuous sound: *the murmur of distant traffic*

murmur² *verb* to speak in a quiet soft way: *Miguel murmured goodbye.*

mus·cle /ˈmʌsəl/ *noun*

your muscles are the pieces of flesh inside your body that you use to move your body: *Running gives you strong leg muscles.*

mus·cu·lar /ˈmʌskjələ $ ˈmʌskjələɚ/ *adjective* having a lot of big muscles: *muscular legs* ➪ *see picture on page 353*

mu·se·um /mjuːˈziːəm/ *noun* a building where people can go and see objects connected with art, history, science etc: *She is planning a class trip to the museum.*

mush·room /ˈmʌʃruːm/ *noun* a grey or white plant with a short stem and a round top. You can eat certain mushrooms: *pizza with pepperoni and mushrooms* ➪ *see picture on page 345*

mu·sic /ˈmjuːzɪk/ *noun [no plural]*

an attractive pattern of sounds that people make by singing or playing musical instruments: *Do you like this music? | They were **playing** very loud **music**. | Would you like to **listen** to some **music**? | a music teacher*

mu·sic·al¹ /ˈmjuːzɪkəl/ *adjective* related to music: *Do you play a musical instrument?*

musical² *noun* a play or film that uses songs to tell a story

mu·si·cian /mjuːˈzɪʃən/ *noun* someone who plays a musical instrument, especially as their job

Mus·lim /ˈmʊzləm/ also **Moslem** *noun* someone whose religion is ISLAM

must /məst; *strong* mʌst/ *modal verb, negative* **mustn't** or **must not**

1 necessary or important to happen: *You **must be** careful. | You **mustn't give up** now. | I **must leave** or I'll miss the bus. | Students **must pass** the exam to continue on the course.*

2 must not to say strongly that someone is not allowed to do something: *You **must not smoke** in the house. | This telephone **must not be used** by members of the public.*

3 very likely to be true **a)** use **must** to say that you are sure something is true: *Her eldest child **must be** about 12 now. | I suppose he **must know** what he's doing.* **b)** use **must have** to say that you are sure something happened in the past: *I **must have left** my essay at home. | Roy and Anna **must have** already **left**.*

▼4 giving advice strongly: *You **must try** this soup – it's delicious.*

mustache the American spelling of MOUSTACHE

mus·tard /'mʌstəd $ 'mʌstəd/ *noun* [no plural] a yellow or brown SAUCE with a strong taste that people eat with meat: *a hamburger with ketchup and mustard*

must·n't /'mʌsənt/ the short form of 'must not': *You mustn't be late for school.*

must've /'mʌstəv/ *spoken* the short form of 'must have': *She must've left already.*

mu·ti·lat·ed /'mjuːtəleɪtɪd/ *adjective* a mutilated body has been very badly damaged, for example by having pieces cut off

mut·ter /'mʌtə $ 'mʌtə/ *verb* to say something quietly in a way that is difficult to understand, especially when you are annoyed: *"Leave me alone," Jay muttered.*

mut·ton /'mʌtn/ *noun* the meat from an adult sheep

mu·tu·al /'mjuːtʃuəl/ *adjective* **1** used to say that people have the same feelings about each other: *a marriage based on mutual love and respect* **2** shared by two or more people: *We have a mutual friend.*

my /maɪ/
belonging to the person who is speaking: *My bedroom is quite large.* | *I'd better phone my mother.* | *My feet are cold.*

my·self /maɪ'self/ *pronoun*
1 used when the same person who is speaking does an action and receives an action: *I've cut myself!* | *I can look after myself.* | *I'm making myself a sandwich.*
2 used to emphasize the person
▼ speaking: *People tell me it's a lovely*

place, but I haven't been there myself.

PHRASE
3 by myself alone, or with no one helping: *I'm quite happy to be by myself.* | *I had to do all the packing by myself.*

mys·te·ri·ous /mɪ'stɪəriəs $ mɪ-'stɪriəs/ *adjective*
something that is mysterious seems strange and is difficult to understand or explain: *Police are puzzled by his mysterious disappearance.*
–mysteriously *adverb*: *She left as mysteriously as she had arrived.*

mys·te·ry /'mɪstəri/ *noun, plural* mysteries
something that seems very strange and is difficult to explain or understand: *The cause of her illness is a mystery.* | *The mystery was solved when we found the bike behind a tree.*

mys·tic·al /'mɪstɪkəl/ *adjective* something that is mystical is connected with religions or magical powers that people cannot understand: *Many saints had mystical experiences.*

mys·ti·fy /'mɪstəfaɪ/ *verb formal* **mystified, mystifies** if you are mystified by something, you do not understand it or you are confused by it: *His parents are mystified by his behaviour.*

myth /mɪθ/ *noun* **1** something that is not true, although many people believe it: *It's a myth that Elvis Presley is still alive.* **2** an old story about gods and people: *Greek myths about the creation of the world*

myth·i·cal /'mɪθɪkəl/ also **mytho·logical** /ˌmɪθə'lɒdʒɪkəl $ ˌmɪθə-'lɑdʒɪkəl/ *adjective* in imaginary stories: *mythical monsters and dragons*

myth·o·log·i·cal another word for MYTHICAL

M

Nn

N the written abbreviation of NORTH or NORTHERN

nag /næg/ *verb* **nagged, nagging** to keep asking someone to do something in an annoying way: *My friends have been nagging me to join their football team.*

nag·ging /'nægɪŋ/ *adjective* making you worry or feel pain all the time: *a nagging headache*

nail¹ /neɪl/ *noun* **1** a thin pointed piece of metal with a flat end that you hit with a hammer: *I hammered a nail into the wall.* **2** the thin hard parts that grow at the end of your fingers and toes: *She had long nails.*

nail² *verb* to fasten something to something else with a nail: *The windows were nailed shut.*

nail-bit·ing /'. ,../ *adjective* very exciting: *The race had a nail-biting finish.*

nail·brush /'neɪlbrʌʃ/ *noun, plural* **nailbrushes** a small brush for cleaning your nails

nail var·nish *BrE* also **nail pol·ish** /'. ,../ *noun* [no plural] paint for women's nails: *She wore pink nail varnish.*

na·ive /naɪ'iːv $ nɑ'iːv/ *adjective* if someone is naive, they believe that people are nicer and things are easier than they really are, because they have not had much experience of life: *I was young and naive then.*
– **naively** *adverb*: *Naively, I trusted him.*

na·ked /'neɪkɪd/ *adjective* not wearing any clothes ⇨ *same meaning* NUDE: *The baby was crawling around in the sand naked.*

name¹ /neɪm/ *noun*

what someone or something is called: *What's his brother's name?* | *Hello, my name's Clare.* | *I've forgot-*
ten **the name of** the school he goes to.

first name, Christian name: *Mrs Lee's **first name** is Sara.*
last name, family name the name that all the people in your family have ⇨ *same meaning* SURNAME: *Smith is a very common **last name** in England.*
a good name, a bad name the good or bad opinion that people have about a person, school, company etc: *This kind of behaviour gives the school **a bad name**.*

name² *verb*

1 to give someone or something a name: *They named their new baby Thomas.* | *She was **named** after her grandmother.* | *The college was **named for** Edward Kennedy.*
2 to say what the name of someone or something is: *Can you name three American presidents?*
3 *written* to officially choose someone for a job: *Miss Taylor **was named as** the new school principal.*

name·ly /'neɪmli/ *adverb written* used to add more information about the people or things that you have just mentioned: *He was arrested for possessing a weapon, namely a knife.*

name·sake /'neɪmseɪk/ *noun* your namesake is someone who has the same name as you: *Mr Yeats, like his famous namesake, is also a poet.*

nan·ny /'næni/ *noun, plural* **nannies** a

N

woman whose job is to take care of a family's children: *The young princes are looked after by a nanny.*

nap /næp/ *noun* a short sleep during the day: *I had a quick nap before work.*

nap·kin /'næpkɪn/ *noun* a square of cloth or paper that you use at meals to keep your clothes, hands, and mouth clean

nap·py /'næpi/ *noun* BrE, *plural* **nappies** a piece of cloth or paper that a baby wears on its bottom; DIAPER AmE: *Who's going to change the baby's nappy?*

nar·cot·ic /nɑː'kɒtɪk $ nɑr'kɑtɪk/ *noun* a drug that stops pain and makes people want to sleep: *Morphine is a powerful narcotic.*

nar·ra·tive /'nærətɪv/ *noun* the narrative of a film or book is its story: *The narrative is hard to follow.*

nar·ra·tor /nə'reɪtə $ 'næˌreɪtɚ/ *noun* someone who tells a story or explains what is happening in a book or a film: *At the start of the film you hear the voice of the narrator.*

nar·row¹ /'nærəʊ $ 'næroʊ/ *adjective*

something that is narrow measures a short distance from one side to the other: *the narrow streets of the old town*

PHRASE

a narrow escape when you just manage to avoid danger or trouble: *We had a narrow escape when a bus hit the car.*

narrow² *verb* **1** to become more narrow ⇨ *opposite* WIDEN: *The river narrows as we go under the bridge.* **2 narrow something down** to reduce the number of people or things that you can choose from: *I've narrowed down the choice of courses to just three.*

nar·row·ly /'nærəʊli $ 'næroʊli/ *adverb* only by a small amount: *They narrowly avoided being killed.*

narrow-mind·ed /ˌ.. '.. $ '.. ˌ../ *adjective* someone who is narrow-minded is not willing to accept ideas that are new and different from their own

na·sal /'neɪzəl/ *adjective* **1** a nasal sound or voice comes mostly through your nose: *She had a high nasal voice.* **2** for your nose: *a nasal spray*

nas·ty /'nɑːsti $ 'næsti/ *adjective* **nastier, nastiest** unpleasant or unkind: *The letter gave me a nasty shock.* | *Stop being so nasty to your sister.*

na·tion /'neɪʃən/ *noun* a country and its people: *America is the richest nation in the world.*

na·tion·al¹ /'næʃənəl/ *adjective*

related to all of a country, not just one part of it: *Drugs are a national problem.*

national² *noun* formal a British national, French national etc is a British person, French person etc: *Only Japanese nationals are employed by the firm.*

national an·them /ˌ... '../ *noun* a country's official song: *The crowd sang their national anthem before the match started.*

na·tion·al·is·m /'næʃənəlɪzəm/ *noun* [no plural] the feeling that you are proud of your own country and believe that it is better than other countries: *We are worried about the growth of nationalism.*

na·tion·al·ist /'næʃənəlɪst/ *noun* someone who is very proud of their country and believes that it is better than other countries

na·tion·al·i·ty /ˌnæʃə'næləti/ *noun*, *plural* **nationalities** your nationality is the country that you belong to: *We have students of many different nationalities.*

na·tion·al·ize also **nationalise** BrE /'næʃənəlaɪz/ *verb* if a government nationalizes an organization, it takes control of it: *Cardenos was the president who nationalized Mexico's oil industry in 1938.* ⇨ *opposite* PRIVATIZE

na·tion·al·ly /'næʃənəli/ *adverb* in all of a country: *a TV show that is broadcast nationally*

na·tion·wide /ˌneɪʃən'waɪd/ *adjective, adverb* happening in every part of a country: *There was a nationwide search for the missing girl.* | *adverts that appear nationwide*

na·tive¹ /'neɪtɪv/ *adjective* of the country where you were born: *Her native language is Spanish.*

native² *noun* someone who was born in a particular country: *a native of Brazil*

Native A·mer·i·can /ˌ.. '..../ *noun* a member of the group of people who were living in North America before the Europeans arrived

native speak·er /ˌ.. ˈ../ noun someone who learned to speak a language when they were a baby, as their first language: *Laurence is not a native speaker of English.*

nat·ter /ˈnætə $ ˈnætɚ/ verb BrE informal to talk a lot about unimportant things: *What are you two nattering about?*
− **natter** noun: *I stopped and had a natter with Jo.*

nat·u·ral /ˈnætʃərəl/ adjective
1 normal and usual: *Anger is a natural reaction when someone criticizes you.* | *It's only natural that you feel shy at first.* | *It's not natural for teenagers to agree with their parents.*
2 natural things are found in nature rather than being made by humans: *Water is a natural resource.* | *She doesn't wear make-up because she prefers to look natural.*

nat·u·ral·ist /ˈnætʃərəlɪst/ noun someone who studies plants and animals

nat·u·ral·ize also **naturalise** BrE /ˈnætʃərəlaɪz/ verb **be naturalized** to be given the official right to live in a country where you were not born
− **naturalized** adjective: *a naturalized Australian*

nat·u·ral·ly /ˈnætʃərəli/ adverb
1 used to say that something is what you would expect: *Naturally, we wanted to win.*
2 if something happens naturally, it happens on its own, without people doing anything to make it happen: *The tomatoes are left to dry naturally in the sun.* | *Is your hair naturally blonde?*

natural re·sourc·es /ˌ... .ˈ. $ ˌ... .ˈ./ plural noun the oil, coal, metals etc in a place that are available for the people who live there to use: *Japan has few natural resources of its own.*

na·ture /ˈneɪtʃə $ ˈneɪtʃɚ/ noun
1 [no plural] everything in the world that is not made or caused by humans, for example animals, plants, and the weather: *Storms remind us of the power of nature.* | *I love watching nature programmes on television.*
2 someone's character: *Terry has a kind nature.*

naugh·ty /ˈnɔːti $ ˈnɒti/ adjective naughtier, naughtiest a naughty child behaves badly: *Barney has been naughty today.*

nau·se·a /ˈnɔːziə/ noun [no plural] formal the feeling that you are going to be sick: *As I got off the bus, I had a terrible feeling of nausea.*

nau·se·a·ting /ˈnɔːzieɪtɪŋ/ adjective very unpleasant, and making you feel like you are going to be sick: *the nauseating smell of rotting flesh*

nau·ti·cal /ˈnɔːtɪkəl/ adjective related to ships and sailing: *England's nautical history*

na·val /ˈneɪvəl/ adjective related to a country's navy: *a naval battle*

na·vel /ˈneɪvəl/ noun the small hole in your stomach ⇨ same meaning BELLY BUTTON

nav·i·gate /ˈnævəgeɪt/ verb to decide which way a car or ship should go, using maps: *I'll drive and you can navigate.*
− **navigator** noun

nav·i·ga·tion /ˌnævəˈgeɪʃən/ noun [no plural] when you decide which direction your car or ship should go: *Navigation is difficult without a compass.*

na·vy /ˈneɪvi/ noun, plural **navies** the people and ships that a country has for fighting a war at sea: *At 18 he joined the navy.*

navy blue /ˌ.. ˈ./ also **navy** adjective very dark blue: *a navy blue car*
− **navy blue** noun [no plural]: *a woman dressed in navy blue*

NB or **N.B.** /ˌen ˈbiː/ used for telling someone to pay attention to something important you have written: *NB: unplug the machine before removing the cover.*

near¹ /nɪə $ nɪr/ adverb, preposition
a short distance away from something: *He lives near Bristol.* | *Don't stand too near the fire.* | *I watched as the car came nearer.*

USAGE near, close
Near and **close** are both used to describe short distances. But **close** is followed by **to**, and **near** is not: *We wanted a hotel close to the beach.* | *Is there a service station near here?*

N

near² *adjective*
a short distance away: *The nearest beach is only a mile away.*

PHRASE
in the **near** future *formal* soon: *The school hopes to offer more subjects in the near future.*

near·by /'nɪəbaɪ $ 'nɪrbaɪ/ *adjective, adverb* not far away: *Her cousins live in a nearby village.* | *My mother stood nearby.*

near·ly /'nɪəli $ 'nɪrli/ *adverb*
almost: *I could answer nearly all the questions.* | *I've nearly finished.* | *Dinner is nearly ready.* | *It's nearly time to go home.*

near·sight·ed /ˌnɪə'saɪtɪd $ 'nɪr-ˌsaɪtɪd/ *adjective* unable to see things clearly unless they are close to you; SHORTSIGHTED *BrE*

neat /niːt/ *adjective*
1 arranged in a tidy and careful way: *Ros has very neat handwriting.* | *His bedroom is always neat and tidy.*
2 *AmE spoken informal* very good: *The concert was really neat!*

neat·ly /'niːtli/ *adverb* in a tidy and careful way: *The clothes were neatly folded.*

ne·ces·sar·i·ly /'nesəsərəli $,nesə-'serəli/ *adverb* not necessarily used to say that something may not be true, or may not always happen: *Expensive restaurants do not necessarily have the best food.*

ne·ces·sa·ry /'nesəsəri $ 'nesə-ˌseri/ *adjective*

GRAMMAR
necessary to do something
necessary for someone to do something

if something is necessary, you need it: *"Do I need to bring some money with me?" "No, that won't be necessary."* | *Will it be necessary to bring spare clothes?* | *It is not necessary for you to spend the whole day there.* | *You can take the test again if necessary.* | *Her parents made all the necessary arrangements* (=did everything that needed to be done) *for the wedding.*

ne·ces·si·ty /nə'sesəti/ *noun* 1 *plural* necessities something that you need: *A car is a necessity for this job.* 2 *[no plural]* when you must do something: *They did it out of necessity* (=because they had to).

neck /nek/ *noun*
1 the part of your body that joins your head to your shoulders: *She wore a gold chain around her neck.* ➪ see pictures at BODY, HEAD¹
2 the part of a piece of clothing that goes around your neck
3 the narrow part near the top of a bottle

neck·lace /'nek-ləs/ *noun* a piece of jewellery that you wear around your neck: *a diamond necklace* ➪ see picture at JEWELLERY

neck·tie /'nektaɪ/ a formal American word for TIE²

need¹ /niːd/ *verb*

GRAMMAR
need to do something
needn't do something
something needs doing

1 if you need something, you must have it: *These plants need plenty of light and water.* | *I live in the city, so I don't really need a car.* | *How much money do you need?*
2 if you need to do something, it is necessary for you to do it: *I need to speak to Mike urgently.* | *Do you think he needs to see a doctor?* | *We don't need to get up early tomorrow.* | *You needn't worry* (=don't worry) – *everything will be fine.*
3 if something needs doing, you should do it because it is necessary: *Does this shirt need washing?* | *The house needs painting this year.*

need² *noun* 1 *[no plural]* something that is necessary: *There is an urgent need for more qualified nurses.* 2 needs your needs are the things that you need: *We try to meet the needs of all the children here.*

nee·dle /'niːdl/ *noun*
1 a small thin piece of steel that you use for sewing: *Have you got a needle and thread – I need to mend my trousers.*

2 a very thin metal tube that a doctor uses to put medicine into your body through your skin ➾ *see picture at* INJECTION
3 a thin pointed object that points to a number or sign on an instrument for measuring something: *a compass needle*

need·less/'niːdləs/ *adjective* **1** needless to say used when you are telling someone about something that they probably already know: *Needless to say, Jon loved his new bike.* **2** not necessary: *We must stop this needless suffering.*
–**needlessly** *adverb*: *Children are dying needlessly.*

need·n't /'niːdnt/ *spoken* the short form of 'do not need to': *You needn't call me back.*

need·y/'niːdi/ *adjective* needier, neediest having very little food or money: *a needy family*

neg·a·tive¹ /'negətɪv/ *adjective*

> **GRAMMAR**
> **negative about someone/something**

1 if something has a negative effect, it has a bad or harmful effect ➾ *opposite* POSITIVE (3): *Smoking has a very negative effect on health.*
2 considering only the bad things about a situation or person ➾ *opposite* POSITIVE (2): *My mother is always so negative about my friends.*
3 if you give a negative answer, you say no: *When people were asked if they liked the ad, the response was negative.*
4 a scientific or medical test that is negative shows that someone does not have a disease or chemical in their body ➾ *opposite* POSITIVE (4)
5 less than zero ➾ *opposite* POSITIVE (5): *Do you know how to multiply negative numbers?*

negative² *noun* the film from which a photograph is printed, which shows dark areas as light, and light areas as dark: *Do you have the negatives for these photos?*

ne·glect¹ /nɪ'glekt/ *verb* to fail to look after someone or something as well as you should: *You mustn't neglect your family.*
–**neglected** *adjective*: *a neglected house*

neglect² *noun* [no plural] when someone or something does not get enough care or attention: *children suffering from neglect*

neg·li·gence /'neglɪdʒəns/ *noun* [no plural] when someone does not do their job properly, causing a mistake or accident: *They have accused the doctor of negligence.*

neg·li·gent /'neglɪdʒənt/ *adjective* not doing your job properly, causing a mistake or accident: *Was the pilot negligent?*

neg·li·gi·ble /'neglɪdʒəbəl/ *adjective* very small and unimportant: *The damage was negligible.*

ne·go·ti·ate /nɪ'gəʊʃieɪt $nɪ'gəʊʃi-,eɪt/ *verb* to discuss something in order to reach an agreement: *He is in Japan negotiating an important business deal.*

ne·go·ti·a·tion /nɪ,gəʊʃi'eɪʃən $nɪ-,gəʊʃi'eɪʃən/ *noun* discussion between groups of people who are trying to reach an agreement: *After months of negotiation, the two sides agreed to a treaty.*

neigh /neɪ/ *verb* if a horse neighs, it makes a loud noise

neigh·bour *BrE*, **neighbor** *AmE* /'neɪbə $'neɪbɚ/ *noun* **1** someone who lives in a house very near you: *All our friends and neighbours are coming to the party.*
2 a person or country that is next to another one: *Write your name on the list and then pass it to your neighbor.* | *Poland's neighbours*

neigh·bour·hood *BrE*, **neighborhood** *AmE* /'neɪbəhʊd $'neɪbɚ,hʊd/ *noun* a small area of a town: *This is a poor neighbourhood.*

neigh·bour·ing *BrE*, **neighboring** *AmE* /'neɪbərɪŋ/ *adjective* near the place you are talking about: *people who live in London and neighbouring towns*

nei·ther¹ /'naɪðə $'niːðɚ/ *pronoun*
not one of two things or people: *Neither team played well* (=both teams played badly). | *Neither of us could drive.* | *I tried on two pairs of shoes, but neither fitted.*

> **USAGE neither, neither of**
> **Neither** is always used with a singular noun and verb: *Neither answer is right.* **Neither of** is used with a plural noun or pronoun, and the verb can be singular or plural: *Neither of us has/have ever been to America before.*

neither² *adverb*
used in negative statements, when adding something else: *"I'm not tired." "Neither am I* (=and I'm not tired)." | *I can't swim, and neither can my brother.*

neither³ neither... nor... used to emphasize that something is not true about two people or things: *Neither Sue nor Colin were clever.*

ne·on /'niːɒn $ 'niɑn/ *noun* [no plural] a gas that is used in tubes in electric lights and signs
– **neon** *adjective: flashing neon lights*

neph·ew /'nefjuː/ *noun* the son of your brother or sister

nerd /nɜːd $ nɚd/ *noun informal* a boring or unfashionable man

nerve /nɜːv $ nɚv/ *noun*
1 your nerves are the parts of your body that send information to your brain from different parts of your body. If your nerves are damaged, you cannot feel pain or move part of your body properly
2 **nerves** the feeling of being nervous: *Most people suffer from nerves before an exam.*

PHRASES
get on someone's nerves to annoy someone: *His singing is getting on my nerves.*
have the nerve to do something to be brave enough to do something dangerous or difficult
lose your nerve to no longer feel brave enough to do something dangerous or difficult: *She lost her nerve and decided not to jump.*

nerve-rack·ing also **nerve-wrack·ing** /'nɜːvˌrækɪŋ $ 'nɚvˌrækɪŋ/ *adjective* very worrying or frightening: *Appearing on TV was a nerve-racking experience.*

ner·vous /'nɜːvəs $ 'nɚvəs/ *adjective*
GRAMMAR
nervous about something
if you are nervous, you feel worried and frightened, and cannot relax: *Julie looked nervous before the test.* | *I get very nervous about*

speaking in public. | *His driving makes me nervous.*
– **nervously** *adverb: "Are you Tim Kelly?" she asked nervously.*

nervous break·down /ˌ.. '../ *noun* when someone becomes so worried and unhappy that they are unable to live a normal life for a while: *He had a nervous breakdown last year.*

nervous sys·tem /'.. ˌ../ *noun* the system of NERVES in your body: *The human nervous system is very complex.*

nest /nest/ *noun* a place made by a bird to lay its eggs in: *The young birds are still in their nest.*

nes·tle /'nesəl/ *verb* to be in a safe place among a group of hills, trees, buildings etc: *a cabin nestling among the pine trees*

Net /net/ *noun informal* **the Net** the INTERNET

nets

net¹ /net/ *noun* **1** a piece of material with large spaces between the threads, which you use in some sports: *The ball went into the back of the net.* | *a volleyball net* **2** a piece of material with spaces between the threads, which you use for catching fish **3** a type of light thin cloth: *The dancers' skirts were made of pink net.* **4** **the Net** the INTERNET: *He's been on the Net all afternoon.*

net² also **nett** *BrE* /net/ *adjective* a net amount of money is the amount that remains after you have paid taxes and other amounts have been taken away: *Our net profit for that year was £200,000.*

net·work /'netwɜːk $ 'netwɚk/ *noun* **1** a system of things that are connected with each other: *a network of computers* | *the railway network* **2** a group of companies that broadcast the same television or radio programmes

neu·rot·ic /njʊˈrɒtɪk $ nʊˈrɑtɪk/ *adjec-*

tive very worried or frightened about something in a way that does not seem normal: *My mother's neurotic about her health.*

neu·tral /'njuːtrəl $'nutrəl/ *adjective* someone who is neutral does not support any of the sides in a competition or war: *Switzerland was a neutral country during the war.*

nev·er /'nevə $'nevɚ/ *adverb*
not at any time: *I've never flown in a plane before.* | *He'll never be successful.* | *I never sign anything without reading it through first.*

nev·er·the·less /ˌnevəðə'les $ˌnevɚ-ðə'les/ *adverb* in spite of what has just been said: *He is unreliable, but I love him nevertheless.*

new /njuː $nu/ *adjective*

GRAMMAR
new to someone
1 something that is new has been made, built, or developed recently: *Have you heard the band's new album?* | *New technology is changing our lives.* | *He bought a brand new (=very new) motorbike.*
2 different or changed: *Her new boyfriend is a policeman.* | *Do you like their new apartment?*
3 not used or owned by anyone before: *Did you get a second-hand computer or a new one?*
4 if something is new to you, you did not know it before or have never used it before: *The Internet is completely new to me.*

new·born /'njuːbɔːn $'nubɔrn/ *adjective* a newborn baby has just been born: *newborn lambs*

new·com·er /'njuːkʌmə $'nuˌkʌmɚ/ *noun* someone who has recently arrived in a place: *We're newcomers to this town.*

new·ly /'njuːli $'nuli/ *adverb* very recently: *a newly married couple*

news /njuːz $nuz/ *noun* [no plural]

GRAMMAR
news about someone/something
news of something/someone
1 information about something that has happened recently: *I heard some interesting news about*

Charlie. | *The teacher gave the class a surprising piece of news.* | *I've got some good news for you – you've passed all your exams.* | *We were told the bad news that grandma had died.*
2 the news a regular television or radio programme that gives you reports of recent events: *I usually watch the news.* | *The President was interviewed on the news this morning.*

PHRASE
in the news if someone is in the news, they are mentioned in newspapers and on the television because they have done something important recently

USAGE
News is always followed by a singular verb: *The news was very exciting.* You can say some news, any news etc, or a piece of news: *Is there any interesting news in the paper?*

news·a·gent /'njuːzˌeɪdʒənt $'nuz-ˌeɪdʒənt/ *noun* BrE 1 newsagent's a shop that sells newspapers and magazines: *There's a newsagent's at the end of our street.* 2 someone who owns or works in a shop selling newspapers and magazines

news bul·le·tin /'. ˌ.../ *noun* a NEWSFLASH

news·cast·er /'njuːzˌkɑːstə $'nuz-ˌkæstɚ/ *noun* someone who reads the news on television or radio

news·flash /'njuːzflæʃ $'nuzflæʃ/ *noun, plural* newsflashes a special short news programme about something important that has just happened: *There was a newsflash about her death.*

news·let·ter /'njuːzˌletə $'nuzˌletɚ/ *noun* a sheet of printed news about an organization that is sent regularly to its members: *The school newsletter comes out each month.*

news·pa·per also **paper** /'njuːsˌpeɪpə $'nuzˌpeɪpɚ/ *noun* a set of folded sheets of paper containing news and advertisements: *I read about it in the newspaper.*

news·read·er /'njuːzˌriːdə $'nuz-ˌridɚ/ *noun* BrE someone who reads the news on television or radio; ANCHOR AmE

New Year /ˌ. './ *noun* the time when you

N

celebrate the beginning of the year: *Happy New Year!*

New Year's Day /ˌ. . '. / *noun* 1st January

New Year's Eve /ˌ. . '. / *noun* 31st December: *a New Year's Eve party*

next /nekst/ *adjective, adverb, pronoun*

1 after this thing or person: *What time is the next train to York? | I hope the next head teacher we have is less strict than this one! | What's next on the list? | The first house they looked at was too small, and the next was on a busy road. | I'll clean the bathroom next, after I've finished cleaning the kitchen. | He couldn't decide what to do next.*

2 nearest to the place or thing mentioned: *There's a pharmacy in the next village. | Turn left at the next traffic lights.*

PHRASES

next to someone/something very close to someone or something: *Come and sit next to me. | At the restaurant, they were given a table next to the window.*

next week, next Tuesday etc: *We're having a day in London next week* (=during the week after this one). | *We'll see you next Saturday.*

the next day the day after: *I didn't feel very well the next day.*

the week after next, the year after next etc during the week, year etc after the one that will come after this one: *I'm going to apply to college the year after next* (=in two years time).

next time on the next occasion that something happens: *Never mind, I'm sure you'll pass the test next time. | I'll ask him next time I see him.*

next door /ˌ. '. / *adverb, adjective* in the building that is next to another building: *We live next door to a police station. | my next-door neighbour*

next of kin /ˌ. . '. / *noun formal, plural* **next of kin** your closest relative who is still alive: *His next of kin was informed about the accident.*

nib·ble /'nɪbəl/ *verb* to take small bites from a piece of food: *Cindy was sitting at the table, nibbling a sandwich.*

nice /naɪs/ *adjective*

GRAMMAR
nice to do something
nice of someone
nice to someone

1 pleasant or enjoyable: *We had a really nice time at the party. | She's got a nice car. | You look nice in that hat. | It is nice to see old friends.*

2 friendly and kind: *He's a really nice man. | It was nice of you to help Ken with his homework. | Please be nice to your cousin.*

PHRASES

nice to meet you, nice meeting you *spoken* used when you meet someone for the first time

nice-look·ing /ˌ. '../ *adjective* attractive: *Your brother's really nice-looking.*

nice·ly /'naɪsli/ *adverb* in a pleasant or attractive way: *Ask me nicely! | a nicely decorated house*

nick¹ /nɪk/ *noun* a small cut on the surface of something: *a tiny nick on her hand*

nick² *verb* **1** to accidentally cut the surface of something: *I nicked my chin when I was shaving.* **2** *BrE spoken informal* to steal something: *Someone's nicked my purse!*

nick·el /'nɪkəl/ *noun* a coin used in the US and Canada worth 5 cents: *I put a nickel in the slot.*

nick·name /'nɪkneɪm/ *noun* a funny name your friends or family give you: *My nickname at school was 'Spike'.*
– **nickname** *verb*: *His teammates nicknamed him 'Ginger'.*

nic·o·tine /'nɪkətiːn/ *noun* [no plural] a substance contained in tobacco

niece /niːs/ *noun* the daughter of your brother or sister

nig·gle /'nɪgəl/ *verb* to annoy or worry you slightly: *This pain has been niggling me for days.*
– **niggle** *noun*: *I began to feel a niggle of doubt.*

night /naɪt/ *noun*

1 the time when it is dark, when people usually sleep: *It snowed in the night. | She doesn't like being alone in the house at night. | The party went on all night.*

2 the evening: *We went out for a meal last night. | Shall we go out tomor-*

row night? | *There's a good film on TV on **Friday night.***

PHRASES

a late night, an early night when you go to bed later or earlier than usual: *You shouldn't have so many **late nights** during the school week.*

a night out when you go out for the evening, to the cinema, for a meal etc: *You need **a night out.***

Good night spoken used to say good-bye to someone when it is late in the evening or when they are going to bed: *Good night. See you in the morning!*

USAGE

You can use different prepositions with night. We use **in the night** and **during the night** to talk about the night that has just passed: *I woke up twice **in the night**.* Use **at night** to talk about night time in general: *I hate driving **at night**.* Use **on** to talk about one particular night: *We're going to a club **on** Saturday **night**.*

night·club /'naɪtklʌb/ *noun* a place where people go late in the evening to drink and dance ⇨ *same meaning* CLUB[1]: *London has some great nightclubs.*

night·dress /'naɪtdres/ *noun, plural* **nightdresses** also **nightgown** /'naɪt-gaʊn/ a loose dress that a woman wears in bed

night·ie /'naɪti/ *noun informal* a NIGHT-DRESS

night·life /'naɪtlaɪf/ *noun [no plural]* all the entertainment that is available in the evening in a town: *The big attraction in Berlin is the nightlife.*

night·ly /'naɪtli/ *adjective, adverb* happening every night: *The bar is open nightly from 9.30.*

night·mare /'naɪtmeə $ 'naɪtmer/ *noun* a very frightening dream: *I had a nightmare about nuclear war.*

night school /'. ./ *noun [no plural]* classes that you go to in the evening: *I'm studying Spanish at night school.*

night·time /'naɪt-taɪm/ *noun [no plural]* the time during the night when it is dark ⇨ opposite DAYTIME: *It was night-time when we arrived.*

nil /nɪl/ *noun [no plural]* zero: *Brazil won the match two–nil (=2–0).*

nim·ble /'nɪmbəl/ *adjective* able to move quickly and easily: *She sewed with nimble fingers.*

–nimbly *adverb*: *She landed nimbly on her toes.*

nine /naɪn/ *number* 9

nine·teen /ˌnaɪn'tiːn/ *number* 19
–nineteenth *number*: *the nineteenth century*

nine-to-five /ˌ. . '. / *adverb* **work nine-to-five** to work every day from nine o'clock in the morning until five o'clock in the evening

nine·ty /'naɪnti/ *number, plural* **nineties** **1** 90 **2** **the nineties** the years between 1990 and 1999: *They met in the early nineties.* **3** **be in your nineties** to be aged between 90 and 99
–ninetieth *number*

ninth /naɪnθ/ *number* **1** 9th **2** one of the nine equal parts of something; 1/9

nip /nɪp/ *verb* **nipped, nipping** **1** if an animal or person nips you, they bite you, using the teeth at the front of their mouth: *The dog nipped her on the ankle.* **2** BrE informal to go somewhere for a short time: *I need to nip out to the shops.*

nip·ple /'nɪpəl/ *noun* **1** one of the two small dark circles on your chest. Babies suck milk through their mother's nipples ⇨ *see picture at* BODY **2** the American word for TEAT (2)

ni·tro·gen /'naɪtrədʒən/ *noun [no plural]* a gas that is the main part of the Earth's air

no[1] /nəʊ $ noʊ/ *adverb*

a word you say when you do not agree with something or do not think that something is true ⇨ opposite YES: *"Is that your bag?" "No."* | *"Do you need any help?" "No thanks."*

USAGE

You can use **no** when you want to agree with something negative that someone has just said: *"I don't like this type of music, do you?" "No, I don't."*

no[2]

not any: *I have no brothers or sisters.* | *There had been no rain for three months.*

no[3] *noun, plural* **noes** a negative answer or decision: *I need a yes or no before the end of the day.*

N

no. *plural* **nos.** the written abbreviation of 'number': *page nos. 12 to 16*

no·bil·i·ty /nəʊ'bɪləti $ noʊ'bɪləti/ *noun* **the nobility** the group of people with the highest social rank

no·ble /'nəʊbəl $ 'noʊbəl/ *adjective written* morally good or generous: *It was noble of you to share your prize.*
– **nobly** *adverb*: *"Keep the money," Jay said nobly.*

no·bo·dy /'nəʊbədi $ 'noʊ,bɑdi/ *pronoun* not anyone

nod

nod   shake

nod /nɒd $ nɑd/ *verb* **nodded, nodding**
1 to move your head up and down, to show that you understand something or agree with someone: *"Good," said Laura, nodding.* | *Ben nodded his head.*
2 **nod off** to begin to sleep: *I nodded off during the lecture.*

noise /nɔɪz/ *noun*
a loud or annoying sound: *The children were **making** too much **noise**.* | *I heard a strange noise.*

nois·y /'nɔɪzi/ *adjective* **noisier, noisiest**
1 noisy people are making a lot of noise: *You're being too noisy.*
2 a noisy place is full of noise: *a noisy city street*

nom·i·nate /'nɒmɪneɪt $ 'nɑmə,neɪt/ *verb* to officially suggest that someone should be given a job or prize: *The team nominated Harry as captain.*

nom·i·na·tion /,nɒmɪ'neɪʃən $,nɑmə-'neɪʃən/ *noun* when people officially suggest that someone should be given a job or prize: *the Oscar nominations*

non-al·co·hol·ic /,. ..'../ *adjective* a non-alcoholic drink has no alcohol in it

none /nʌn/ *pronoun*
not any: ***None of** the other children could speak Italian.* | ***None of** the information they gave us was correct.* |

By the time I phoned for tickets, there were none left.

none·the·less /,nʌnðə'les/ *adverb formal* in spite of what you have just said ⇨ *same meaning* NEVERTHELESS: *Martin was not well, but nonetheless he came to school.*

non·ex·ist·ent /,nɒnɪg'zɪstənt $,nɑn-ɪg'zɪstənt/ *adjective formal* not existing at all: *The boyfriend she talked about was nonexistent.*

non-fic·tion /,. '../ *noun* [no plural] books about real facts or events ⇨ *opposite* FICTION: *I read a lot of non-fiction.*

non·flam·ma·ble /,nɒn'flæməbəl $,nɑn'flæməbəl/ *adjective formal* something that is nonflammable is very difficult to burn ⇨ *opposite* INFLAMMABLE

no-non·sense /,. '../ *adjective* working in a practical way, making decisions quickly and not spending too much time discussing things: *a no-nonsense approach to teaching*

non·sense /'nɒnsəns $ 'nɑnsens/ *noun* [no plural]
1 things that someone says that are stupid and not true: *You're talking nonsense.*
2 speech or writing that you cannot understand because it has no meaning: *When she first heard English it sounded like nonsense.*

non·smok·ing /,nɒn'sməʊkɪŋ $,nɑn-'smoʊkɪŋ/ *adjective* a nonsmoking area is one where people are not allowed to smoke

non·stan·dard /,nɒn'stændəd $,nɑn-'stændəd/ *adjective* not the usual size or type: *Dialects are a form of non-standard English.*

non·start·er /,nɒn'stɑːtə $,nɑn-'stɑrtɚ/ *noun informal* an idea or plan that is very unlikely to succeed: *The whole idea sounds like a nonstarter.*

non·stop /,nɒn'stɒp $,nɑn'stɑp/ *adverb, adjective* without stopping: *Over dinner, we talked nonstop.* | *a nonstop flight to Bangkok*

noo·dles /'nuːdlz/ plural noun food made from flour, eggs, and water, cut into long thin pieces and cooked in boiling water: *chicken with noodles*

noon /nuːn/ noun [no plural] 12 o'clock in the middle of the day ⇨ same meaning MIDDAY: *Lunch will be served at noon.*

no one /'. ./ pronoun
not anyone ⇨ same meaning NOBODY: *The telephone rang but no one answered.*

noose /nuːs/ noun a circle at the end of a long piece of rope that can be pulled tight to catch animals or hang people

nor /nɔː $ nɔr/
1 used in negative statements, when adding something else: *"I don't want to go." "Nor do I* (=and I don't want to go)." | *I didn't tell Mum, and nor did John.*
2 saying that two things are not true written: *He was **neither** handsome **nor** ugly.* | *The government has **neither** confirmed **nor** denied the report.*

norm /nɔːm $ nɔrm/ noun **the norm** what is usual or normal: *Going to university is becoming the norm.*

nor·mal /'nɔːməl $ 'nɔrməl/ adjective

GRAMMAR
normal to do something
normal for someone to do something
something that is normal is how you would usually expect it to be: *It started out as a normal day.* | *She's just a normal 15-year-old girl.* | *The library will be open at the normal times next week.* | *It's quite **normal to** feel nervous before you go into hospital.* | *It is normal for women to work in this country.*

nor·mal·i·ty /nɔːˈmæləti $ nɔrˈmæləti/ noun [no plural] formal when things happen in the usual or normal way: *After the war, normality gradually returned.*

nor·mal·ly /'nɔːməli $ 'nɔrməli/ adverb usually: *I normally cycle to college.*

north /nɔːθ $ nɔrθ/ noun 1 [no plural] the direction towards the top of a map
2 **the north** the northern part of a country: *It will be windy in the north.*

–north adverb, adjective: *The army was marching north.* | *We climbed the north face of the mountain.*

north·bound /'nɔːθbaʊnd $ 'nɔrθbaʊnd/ adjective travelling towards the north: *I took the northbound train to Chicago.*

north·east /ˌnɔːθˈiːst $ ˌnɔrθˈist/ noun [no plural] the direction that is between north and east: *Towns in the northeast have been badly affected by the storms.*
–northeast adverb, adjective

north·er·ly /'nɔːðəli $ 'nɔrðɚli/ adjective towards the north: *The wind is blowing in a northerly direction.*

nor·thern /'nɔːðən $ 'nɔrðɚn/ adjective in or from the north: *northern California*

nor·thern·er /'nɔːðənə $ 'nɔrðɚnɚ/ noun someone who comes from the north of a country

North Pole /ˌ. './ noun the place on Earth that is farthest north

north·ward /'nɔːθwəd $ 'nɔrθwɚd/ also **northwards** /'nɔːθwədz $ 'nɔrθwɚdz/ adverb, adjective towards the north: *We headed northwards.*

north·west /ˌnɔːθˈwest $ ˌnɔrθˈwest/ noun [no plural] the direction that is between north and west
–northwest adverb, adjective

nose /nəʊz $ noʊz/ noun
the part of your face that you use for smelling things and for breathing: *She had a spot on her nose.* ⇨ see picture at HEAD[1]

nose·bleed /'nəʊzbliːd $ 'noʊzblid/ noun if you have a nosebleed, blood comes out of your nose

nose·dive /'nəʊzdaɪv $ 'noʊzdaɪv/ verb if an aircraft nosedives, it flies fast towards the ground with its front end pointing down, usually before crashing
–nosedive noun: *The plane did a sudden nosedive.*

nosey another spelling of NOSY

nos·tal·gia /nɒˈstældʒə $ nɑˈstældʒə/ noun [no plural] the slightly sad feeling you have when you think about nice things that happened in the past: *Dad feels nostalgia for his college days.*

nos·tril /'nɒstrəl $ 'nɑstrəl/ noun one of the two holes in your nose, which you breathe through ⇨ see picture at HEAD[1]

nos·y also **nosey** /'nəʊzi $ 'noʊzi/ adjective nosier, nosiest a nosy person is

N

always trying to find out about things that other people want to keep secret: *Don't be so nosy!*

not /nɒt $ nɑt/ *adverb*

used to give a negative meaning: *That would not be a good idea* (=that would be a bad idea). | *They had not been there before.* | *There were not many people there.* | *I read a lot because I want to, not because I have to.* | *"Have the others gone?" "I hope not."*

no·ta·ble /ˈnəʊtəbəl $ ˈnoʊtəbəl/ *adjective* important, interesting, or unusual: *This area is notable for its forests.*

no·ta·bly /ˈnəʊtəbli $ ˈnoʊtəbli/ *adverb* used when you are giving an especially important or interesting example: *She failed in several subjects, notably English.*

notch /nɒtʃ $ nɑtʃ/ *noun, plural* **notches** a cut in a surface that is in the shape of a V: *The arrow has a notch in the end for the bowstring.*

note¹ /nəʊt $ noʊt/ *noun*

1 a short letter: *Mum wrote a note to my teacher saying that I was sick.*
2 a musical sound, or the sign in written music that means this: *He played a few notes on the piano.*
3 BrE a piece of paper money; BILL AmE: *Milly paid with a five-pound note.*
4 **notes** information that you write down during a lesson or from a book so that you will remember it: *While the teacher talked, the students took notes.*

PHRASES

make a note of something to write something down so that you remember it: *She made a note of his birthday.*

take note (of something) to pay careful attention to something: *You should take note of what your grandmother says.*

note² *verb* **1** to notice or pay careful attention to something: *Please note that visiting time is 2 until 3.* **2** also **note down** to write something down so that you will remember it: *I noted down the time of the train.*

note·book /ˈnəʊtbʊk $ ˈnoʊtbʊk/ ▼

noun a small book in which you can write things that you need to remember

note·pa·per /ˈnəʊtˌpeɪpə $ ˈnoʊtˌpeɪpɚ/ *noun* [no plural] paper that you use for writing letters

noth·ing¹ /ˈnʌθɪŋ/ *pronoun*

1 not anything: *Nothing surprises me any more.* | *"What did Tessa say on the phone?" "Nothing important."* | *There's nothing we can do.*
2 no money: *We got into the concert for nothing!* | *She likes buying people presents but spends nothing on herself.*

PHRASES

for nothing without achieving or getting anything: *I did all that work for nothing!*

have nothing to do with someone/ something a) to not be connected with someone or something: *Their argument had nothing to do with work.* b) if something has nothing to do with someone, they do not have a right to know about it or get involved with it: *Go away – this has nothing to do with you.*

there's nothing to it *spoken* it's very easy: *I'll show you how to work the coffee machine – there's nothing to it really.*

nothing² *adverb* **be nothing like someone/something** *informal* to have no qualities that are similar to someone or something: *My brother is nothing like me.*

no·tice¹ /ˈnəʊtɪs $ ˈnoʊtɪs/ *verb* to see, feel, or hear someone or something: *I didn't notice you come in.*

notice² *noun*

a piece of writing that you put on a wall to give information to people: *They put up a notice saying 'No Smoking'.*

PHRASES

not take any notice, take no notice to not give any attention to someone or something because you do not think that they are important: *He shouted something at me, but I took no notice of him.*

a day's notice, a week's notice etc a warning about something that is going to happen, that you receive only a day, a week etc before it happens: *We only had **two days' notice** about the exam.*

at short notice if something happens at short notice, it happens without very much warning, so that you have only a short time to prepare for it: *I can't get time off work at such **short notice**.*

hand in your notice, give in your notice to tell your employer that you are leaving your job

no·tice·a·ble /'nəʊtɪsəbəl $ 'nəʊtɪsəbəl/ *adjective* easy to notice: *There's been a noticeable improvement in your work.*
–**noticeably** *adverb*: *He was noticeably thinner.*

no·tice·board /'nəʊtɪs,bɔːd $ 'nəʊtɪs,bɔrd/ *noun* BrE a board on a wall, where you can put information or pictures; BULLETIN BOARD AmE: *The exam results will be put up on the noticeboard.*

no·ti·fy /'nəʊtɪfaɪ $ 'nəʊtə,faɪ/ *verb* formal **notified, notifies** to tell someone something officially ⇨ *same meaning* INFORM: *She immediately notified the police.*

no·tion /'nəʊʃən $ 'nəʊʃən/ *noun* an idea or belief about something: *I had a notion that you were looking for a new job.*

no·to·ri·ous /nəʊˈtɔːriəs $ nəʊˈtɔriəs/ *adjective* famous for something bad: *This stretch of road is notorious for accidents.*
–**notoriously** *adverb*: *Phrasal verbs are notoriously difficult for students.*

nought /nɔːt/ *noun* BrE the number 0 ⇨ *same meaning* ZERO

noun /naʊn/ *noun* a word that is the name of a person, place, thing, or idea. *'Money' and 'table' are nouns*

nour·ish /'nʌrɪʃ $ 'nɜ·ɪʃ/ *verb* formal to give a person, animal, or plant the food etc they need in order to live and grow: *The cream contains vitamins A and E to nourish the skin.*
–**nourishing** *adjective*: *good nourishing food*

nov·el /'nɒvəl $ 'nɑvəl/ *noun* a book that tells a story: *He is writing a novel about a boy's life.*

nov·el·ist /'nɒvəlɪst $ 'nɑvəlɪst/ *noun* someone who writes novels: *the English novelist Charles Dickens*

nov·el·ty /'nɒvəlti $ 'nɑvəlti/ *noun*, *plural* **novelties** when something is new and unusual: *Using e-mail is no longer a novelty for me.*

No·vem·ber /nəʊˈvembə $ nəʊˈvembə·/ *written abbreviation* **Nov** *noun* the eleventh month of the year

nov·ice /'nɒvɪs $ 'nɑvɪs/ *noun* someone who has just begun learning how to do something: *I am a novice at chess.*

now¹ /naʊ/ *adverb*
1 at the present time: *They now live in Yorkshire. | He was ill, but he's better now. | I'll do it later – I'm busy **right now**. | Sam's late – I thought he'd be back **by now**. | If you wanted to get there by noon, you should have left **before now**.*
2 immediately: *We'd better go now, before the weather gets any worse.*
3 used when starting to talk to someone: *Now, be quiet everyone! | Now, what did you want to ask me?*

PHRASES
now and then, now and again spoken sometimes, not regularly: *I still see him **now and then**.*
from now on starting at this time and continuing: *From now on I'm going to work really hard!*

now² also **now that**
used when saying what will happen because something else has happened: *Now he's got a car, he'll be able to take us everywhere. | Now that you've seen the town, do you think you'll be happy there?*

now·a·days /'naʊədeɪz/ *adverb* informal used to talk about what happens now, compared to the past: *More people have cars nowadays.*

no·where /'nəʊweə $ 'nəʊwer/ *adverb*
not in any place: *He's got **nowhere to** sleep tonight. | There's **nowhere else to** put the computer, so it will have to go in my bedroom.*

PHRASES
get nowhere to have no success or make no progress: *I'm **getting nowhere** with this work – it's too difficult.*
nowhere near a) not at all: *She is **nowhere near** as tall as her sister.* b) not near at all: *You can't walk to the cinema – it's **nowhere near** your house.*

N

nu·cle·ar /'nju:kliə $'nukliɚ/ adjective
1 using the energy that is produced when an atom is split or joined to another atom: *nuclear power* | *nuclear weapons* **2** related to the NUCLEUS (=central part) of an atom: *nuclear physics*

nuclear re·ac·tor /ˌnju:kliə ri'æktə $ˌnukliɚ ri'ætɚ/ noun a large machine that produces energy by splitting or joining atoms

nu·cle·us /'nju:kliəs $'nukliəs/ noun, plural **nuclei** /-kliaɪ/ **1** the central part of an atom **2** the central part of a cell

nude /nju:d $nud/ adjective not wearing any clothes ⇨ same meaning NAKED: *a painting of a nude man*

nudge /nʌdʒ/ verb to push someone or something gently with your elbow: *Ken nudged me and said, "Look!"*
–**nudge** noun: *She gave me a nudge when it was my turn.*

nu·di·ty /'nju:dəti $'nudəti/ noun [no plural] when people are not wearing any clothes: *There's too much nudity on TV.*

nui·sance /'nju:səns $'nusəns/ noun something or someone that annoys you or causes problems: *What a nuisance! I forgot to buy milk.*

numb /nʌm/ adjective not able to feel anything: *It was so cold that my fingers went numb.*
–**numbness** noun [no plural]: *The disease causes numbness in the legs.*

num·ber¹ /'nʌmbə $'nʌmbɚ/
noun

GRAMMAR
a number of people/things
the number of people/things

1 a word or written sign that shows a quantity: *2, 4, 6 – what number comes next?* | *even number* (=2, 4, 6, 8 etc) | *odd number* (=1, 3, 5, 7 etc)
2 the set of numbers that you use to telephone someone: *She gave me her number and asked me to call her.*
3 an amount of something that you can count: *We don't know the exact number of people yet.* | *The number of girls at the school has increased.* | *A large number of people could not get tickets for the concert.* ⇨ see usage note at AMOUNT¹

number² verb to give a number to something that is part of a set or list: *I numbered all the photographs.*

number plate /'.. ˌ./ noun BrE the sign on the front and back of a vehicle that shows its official number; LICENSE PLATE AmE ⇨ see picture at CAR

nu·me·rous /'nju:mərəs $'numərəs/ adjective formal many: *He has visited Japan on numerous occasions.*

nun /nʌn/ noun a woman who lives as part of a group of religious women, away from other people

nurse¹ /nɜ:s $nɚs/ noun
someone whose job is to look after people who are ill or injured, usually in a hospital

nurse² verb to look after someone who is ill or injured: *His wife nursed him at home.*

nur·se·ry /'nɜ:səri $'nɚsəri/ noun, plural **nurseries 1** BrE a place where people look after young children during the day: *Does your son go to nursery?* **2** a place where plants and trees are grown and sold

nursery school /'... ˌ./ noun a school for children between three and five years old

nurs·ing /'nɜ:sɪŋ $'nɚsɪŋ/ noun [no plural] the job of looking after people who are ill, injured, or very old: *Nursing is a tough job.*

nut /nʌt/ noun **1** a large seed that you can eat, that usually grows in a hard brown shell: *a cashew nut* **2** a small piece of metal with a hole in the middle that is used with a BOLT for fastening things together

nu·tri·ent /'nju:triənt $'nutriənt/ noun formal a chemical that helps plants, animals, or people to live and grow: *Plants take nutrients from the soil.*

nu·tri·tious /nju:'trɪʃəs $nu'trɪʃəs/ adjective food that is nutritious contains a lot of things that your body needs to be healthy: *Bananas are very nutritious.* | *a nutritious diet*

nuts /nʌts/ adjective spoken informal crazy or very angry: *When I told her what happened, she went nuts.*

ny·lon /'naɪlɒn $'naɪlɑn/ noun [no plural] a strong material that is used for making clothes, rope etc: *nylon stockings* | *a carpet made of wool and nylon*

O o

oak /əʊk $ oʊk/ *noun* a type of large tree, or the wood that comes from it: *an oak table*

oar /ɔː $ ɔr/ *noun* a long pole that is wide at one end, that you use for moving a boat through water

o·a·sis /əʊˈeɪsɪs $ oʊˈeɪsɪs/ *noun, plural* **oases** /-siːz/ a place in a desert where there is water and plants

oath /əʊθ $ oʊθ/ *noun* an official promise: *He swore an oath to tell the truth in court.*

oats /əʊts $ oʊts/ *plural noun* a grain that is used in cooking: *Porridge is made with oats and milk.*

o·be·di·ence /əˈbiːdiəns/ *noun* [no plural] when someone does what a person or rule tells them to do: *Her father expects complete obedience.*

o·be·di·ent /əˈbiːdiənt/ *adjective* someone who is obedient does what a person or rule tells them to do ⇨ *opposite* DISOBEDIENT: *She expects children to be quiet and obedient.* | *a very obedient dog*
– **obediently** *adverb*: *"Yes, father," he said obediently.*

o·bese /əʊˈbiːs $ oʊˈbiːs/ *adjective formal* much too fat, in a way that is dangerous to your health: *The doctor told her she was obese and had to go on a diet.* ⇨ *see usage note at* FAT¹

o·bey /əʊˈbeɪ $ əˈbeɪ/ *verb* to do what a person or rule tells you to do ⇨ *opposite* DISOBEY: *Students must obey the school rules.*

ob·ject¹ /ˈɒbdʒɪkt $ ˈɑbdʒɪkt/ *noun*

> **GRAMMAR**
> **the object of something**

1 a thing that you can see and hold: *She had several strange-looking objects in her bag.*

2 the noun that says which person or thing is affected by a verb ⇨ *see also* DIRECT OBJECT, INDIRECT OBJECT: *In the sentence 'He kissed the girl', the object of the verb is 'the girl'.*

3 the thing that you are trying to do: *The object of the game is to throw the ball into the basket.*

ob·ject² /əbˈdʒekt/ *verb*

> **GRAMMAR**
> **object to something**

to say that you do not like something or do not want it to happen: *A lot of people objected to the ideas expressed in the book.* | *I said we should share the cost, and no one objected.*

ob·jec·tion /əbˈdʒekʃən/ *noun*

> **GRAMMAR**
> **an objection to something**

if you make an objection to something, you say that you do not like it or do not want it to happen: *Do you have any objection to smoking?* | *If the local people do not make an objection, we can start building the new houses.*

ob·jec·tive /əbˈdʒektɪv/ *noun* something that you are trying to achieve: *Our main objective is to raise money.*

ob·li·ga·tion /ˌɒbləˈɡeɪʃən $ ˌɑblə-ˈɡeɪʃən/ *noun formal* something that you must do because it is the law or it is your duty: *You have an obligation to inform the police of any accident on the road.*

ob·lig·a·to·ry /əˈblɪɡətəri $ əˈblɪɡə-tɔri/ *adjective formal* if something is obligatory, you must do it because of a law or rule: *Attending school is obligatory.*

o·blige /əˈblaɪdʒ/ *verb* **1** *formal* if you are obliged to do something, you must do it because it is the law or it is your

duty: *Doctors are obliged to offer the best possible treatment to their patients.*
2 to do something that someone has asked you to do: *We asked for her help, and she was happy to oblige.*

o·blit·er·ate /ə'blɪtəreɪt/ *verb formal* to destroy something completely: *The whole city was obliterated by bombing.*

o·bliv·i·ous /ə'blɪviəs/ *adjective formal* not noticing what is happening around you: *The children were fast asleep, oblivious to the noise.*

ob·long /'ɒblɒŋ $'ɑblɔŋ/ *noun* a shape with four corners that has two long sides and two shorter sides ➪ *same meaning* RECTANGLE
– **oblong** *adjective*: *an oblong table*

ob·nox·ious /əb'nɒkʃəs $əb'nɑkʃəs/ *adjective* extremely unpleasant or rude: *What an obnoxious man!*

o·boe /'əʊbəʊ $'oʊboʊ/ *noun* a long thin wooden musical instrument that you play by blowing and pressing holes with your fingers

ob·scene /əb'siːn/ *adjective* showing or talking about sex in an offensive and shocking way: *obscene photographs | obscene language*

ob·scure /əb'skjʊə $əb'skjʊr/ *adjective* not familiar or well known: *The play is full of obscure jokes.*

ob·ser·vant /əb'zɜːvənt $əb'zɚvənt/ *adjective* good at noticing things: *It was very observant of you to notice his shoes.*

ob·ser·va·tion /ˌɒbzə'veɪʃən $ˌɑbzɚ'veɪʃən/ *noun* **1** *[no plural]* when you watch someone or something carefully: *You can learn a lot about animals just by observation.* **2** *formal* a spoken or written remark: *She made some interesting observations in her article.*

ob·serve /əb'zɜːv $əb'zɚv/ *verb* **1** to watch someone or something carefully: *An inspector came to observe the lesson.* **2** to obey a law, agreement, or religious custom: *Both sides are observing the ceasefire.*

ob·sess /əb'ses/ *verb* if you are obsessed with something, you think about it too much, in a way that is not normal: *Julie is obsessed with losing weight.*

ob·ses·sion /əb'seʃən/ *noun* something that you think about too much, in a way that is not normal: *He has an obsession with money.*

ob·so·lete /'ɒbsəliːt $ˌɑbsə'lit/ *adjec-*

tive old, and no longer used: *Our computer system will soon be obsolete.*

ob·sta·cle /'ɒbstɪkəl $'ɑbstɪkəl/ *noun* **1** something that makes it difficult to do something: *Her parents are a major obstacle to her going to university.* **2** something that blocks a road or path: *The entrance was blocked by a chair and other obstacles.*

ob·sti·nate /'ɒbstənət $'ɑbstənət/ *adjective formal* refusing to change your opinions or behaviour ➪ *same meaning* STUBBORN: *Lucy can be very obstinate.*

ob·struct /əb'strʌkt/ *verb formal* to block a road or path: *A van was obstructing the entrance.*

obstruction

ob·struc·tion /əb'strʌkʃən/ *noun formal* something that blocks a road or path: *The accident caused an obstruction.*

ob·tain /əb'teɪn/ *verb formal*
to get something: *You can obtain more information by phoning our main office.*

ob·tain·a·ble /əb'teɪnəbəl/ *adjective formal* if something is obtainable, you can get it: *Fresh fish is easily obtainable.*

ob·vi·ous /'ɒbviəs $'ɑbviəs/ *adjective*

GRAMMAR
obvious to someone
obvious (that)
if something is obvious, you can see it or understand it easily: *It was **obvious to** me that Joe was unhappy. | There is an obvious reason why Sam wanted to leave. | **It is obvious that** you don't like each other.*
– **obviously** *adverb*: *He was obviously upset.*

oc·ca·sion /ə'keɪʒən/ *noun*
1 *formal* a time when something happens: *I have been there **on** many occasions.*

2 an important event or ceremony: *A 16th birthday is a special occasion.*

oc·ca·sion·al /əˈkeɪʒənəl/ adjective

happening sometimes but not very often: *We have occasional arguments.*
- **occasionally** adverb: *I still see my ex-boyfriend occasionally.*

oc·cu·pant /ˈɒkjəpənt $ˈɑkjəpənt/ noun formal someone who lives in or is using a building or room: *The occupants of the house were away.*

oc·cu·pa·tion /ˌɒkjəˈpeɪʃən $ˌɑkjə-ˈpeɪʃən/ noun formal a job or profession: *Please state your name and occupation.*
⇨ see usage note at JOB

oc·cu·pied /ˈɒkjəpaɪd $ˈɑkjəˌpaɪd/ adjective **1** if a room, bed, or seat is occupied, someone is using it: *All the seats in the row were occupied.* **2** busy doing or thinking about something: *The game kept us occupied all afternoon.*

oc·cu·py /ˈɒkjəpaɪ $ˈɑkjəˌpaɪ/ verb occupied, occupies **1** to be using a building or room: *Three companies now occupy this building.* **2** to go into a place and take control of it by force: *Enemy soldiers occupied the city.* **3** occupy yourself spoken to do things so that you do not become bored: *Can you occupy yourselves for half an hour?*

oc·cur /əˈkɜː $əˈkɝ/ verb formal occurred, occurring

to happen, without being planned: *When did the accident occur?*

PHRASAL VERB
occur to
occur to someone if an idea occurs to you, you think of it: *It didn't occur to me that she could be lying.*

oc·cur·rence /əˈkʌrəns $əˈkɝ·əns/ noun formal something that happens: *What could explain this unusual occurrence?*

o·cean /ˈəʊʃən $ˈoʊʃən/ noun
the ocean a sea: *the Pacific Ocean | Our house is right beside the ocean.*

o'clock /əˈklɒk $əˈklɑk/ adverb one o'clock, two o'clock etc used to say what time of day it is. You can only use

o'clock with full hours: *Dinner will be ready at 8 o'clock, but get here by 7.30.*

oc·ta·gon /ˈɒktəgən $ˈɑktəˌgɑn/ noun a flat shape with eight sides ⇨ see picture at SHAPE¹

Oc·to·ber /ɒkˈtəʊbə $ɑkˈtoʊbɚ/ written abbreviation **Oct** noun the tenth month of the year: *The arts festival will be in October.*

oc·to·pus /ˈɒktəpəs $ˈɑktəpəs/ noun, plural octopuses or octopi a sea creature with a soft body and eight long arms ⇨ see picture on page 339

odd /ɒd $ɑd/ adjective
strange or unusual: *Her behaviour seemed a bit odd. | It's odd that he still hasn't come home. | What an odd name!*

PHRASES
odd number an odd number is a number that you cannot divide exactly by two. For example, 1, 3, 5, and 7 are all odd numbers ⇨ opposite EVEN NUMBER
odd jobs small jobs that need to be done in the house and garden: *I earn a bit of money doing odd jobs for people.*

odd·ly /ˈɒdli $ˈɑdli/ adverb in a strange or unusual way: *He's been behaving very oddly recently.*

odds /ɒdz $ɑdz/ plural noun how likely it is that something will happen, often expressed using numbers: *The odds of winning the lottery are about 14 million to 1.*

odds and ends /ˌ. . ˈ./ plural noun informal small things that are not important or valuable: *She made a doll out of a few odds and ends.*

o·dour BrE, **odor** AmE /ˈəʊdə $ˈoʊdɚ/ noun formal a smell, especially an unpleasant one: *He noticed a strange odour in the room.*

of /əv; strong ɒv $ʌv/ preposition
1 belonging to someone: *A friend of my brother's offered to lend me his car. | We stayed in one of my aunt's houses.*
2 used when describing one part of something: *The door of the car was open. | I didn't notice the colour of her eyes. | This is a lovely part of the city.*
3 containing something: *There was a*

O

vase of flowers on the table. | a packet of sweets | a cup of coffee
4 showing an amount of something: I bought two kilos of apples.
5 what a picture shows: a photograph of my mother | a picture of the cathedral
6 showing how old someone is: an old man of seventy

PHRASE
it is nice of someone to do something, that is brave of someone etc used to say that someone's action is nice, brave etc: **It was nice of** her to phone. | **That was kind of** him.

off¹ /ɒf $ ɔːf/ adverb, preposition

1 showing that something is removed from a place: He brushed the crumbs off the table. | She took her coat off. | He knocked a glass off the table. ⇨ see picture on page 354
2 leaving a place: The boy rang the door bell and then ran off. | He got into his car and drove off.
3 when a machine or electrical equipment is not being used or not working: All the lights in the house were off. | **Switch** the television **off**.
4 not at school or at work: Robert's been off school for a week because he's ill. | I think Mr Turner is off today. | Can I have a day off?

PHRASE
off and on, on and off sometimes stopping and then starting again, in an irregular way: It had been raining **off and on** for a week.

off² adjective

1 food or drink that is off is not fresh any more: Don't use that milk – it's off.
2 an event that is off is not going to happen any more: The picnic's off because of the rain. | We had to **call** the game **off** because so many of our players were ill.

off-chance /'. ˌ./ noun **on the off-chance** informal because you hope that something will happen, although it is unlikely: I went to the library on the off-chance that I might see Harry.

of·fence BrE, **offense** AmE /ə'fens/ noun
formal a crime: Taking drugs is an

offence. | If he has **committed** an **offence**, we will arrest him.

PHRASE
take offence to feel upset or annoyed by something someone does or says to you: She **took offence** when I refused her invitation.

of·fend /ə'fend/ verb
to make someone feel upset or annoyed: I hope I haven't offended you. | His remarks offended many Scottish people.

of·fend·er /ə'fendə $ ə'fendər/ noun
formal someone who is guilty of a crime: a prison for young offenders

offense¹ the American spelling of OFFENCE

of·fense² /'ɒfens $ 'ɔːfens/ noun AmE
the players in a game such as American football who try to get points

of·fen·sive¹ /ə'fensɪv/ adjective
1 likely to make people feel upset or annoyed: She said some very offensive things. **2** formal used for attacking people: an offensive weapon

offensive² noun **1** an attack on a place by an army: a military offensive **2 go on the offensive** to attack or criticize people: We have to go on the offensive if we are going to win this election.

of·fer¹ /'ɒfə $ 'ɔːfər/ verb

GRAMMAR
offer someone something
offer something to someone
offer to do something

1 to ask someone if they would like something: He came over and offered me a drink. | She **offered** biscuits **to** the children.
2 to say that you will do something for someone if they want you to: Simon **offered to** take me to the station.
3 to say that you will give something to someone, if they want it: They've offered me a job! | I'll offer him £5000 for the car.

offer² noun

GRAMMAR
an offer of something
an offer to do something
when you say that you will do something for someone or give them

something if they want it: *Thanks for your kind* **offer** *of help.* | *I'm willing to* **make** *you* **an offer** *of $300.* | *I accepted his* **offer to** *clean the house for me.*

a good offer, a special offer a lower price than usual in the shops: *If you buy in January, there are usually some* **good offers.**

off·hand /ˌɒfˈhænd $ ˌɔːfˈhænd/ *adverb* if you do not know something offhand, you do not know it immediately, but need time to think or check it: *I don't know his address offhand.*

of·fice /ˈɒfɪs $ ˈɔːfɪs/ *noun*
a room or building with desks where people work: *The manager's office is on the second floor.* | *I'm afraid Mr Stokes isn't in his office at the moment.*

of·fi·cer /ˈɒfəsə $ ˈɔːfəsər/ *noun*
1 someone who has a position of authority in the army, navy etc: *an army officer* **2** a policeman or policewoman

of·fi·cial¹ /əˈfɪʃəl/ *adjective*
done or given by someone in authority: *The official report will be published next month.* | *The chairman has given his official support to the idea.*

official² *noun*
a person who has an important job in an organization or a government: *Senior government officials were waiting to greet the President.*

of·fi·cial·ly /əˈfɪʃəli/ *adverb* in an official or formal way: *We will announce the results officially next week.*

off·li·cence /ˈɒf ˌlaɪsəns/ *noun BrE* a shop that sells alcoholic drinks; LIQUOR STORE *AmE*

off·peak /ˌɒf ˈpiːk/ *adjective, adverb BrE* off-peak services are cheaper because they are used at less busy times: *an off-peak bus ticket for evenings and weekends* | *Save money by surfing the Net off-peak.*

off·side /ˌɒfˈsaɪd $ ˌɔːfˈsaɪd/ *adjective, adverb* in games such as football, a player who is offside is in a position that is not allowed by the rules when the ball is passed to them

of·ten /ˈɒfən $ ˈɔːfən/ *adverb*
many times: *I often go through the park on my way home from school.* | *I don't watch television very often.* | *Quite often there is no obvious cause of the pain.* | **How often** *do you wash your hair?*

Often usually comes before the main verb, and after words like 'is', 'have', 'don't' etc: *Dad often gets home late.* | *I don't often go to the cinema.* **Very often** is used at the end of a negative sentence: *He doesn't telephone very often.*

oh /əʊ $ oʊ/ *spoken* **1** used before replying: *"How was the film?" "Oh, it was OK."* **2** used to express strong emotions: *Oh, isn't she cute!*

oil¹ /ɔɪl/ *noun* [no plural]
1 a thick liquid used for making petrol, or for making machines work smoothly: *Kuwait is one of the countries that exports oil.* | *The engine needs some more oil.*
2 a liquid used for cooking, made from plants or animal fat: *Heat a little oil in a pan.*

oil² *verb* to put oil onto part of a machine: *He needs to oil the wheels of his bike.*

oil paint·ing /ˈ. ˌ../ *noun* a picture painted with paint that contains oil

oil rig /ˈ. ./ *noun* a large structure with equipment for getting oil out of the ground

oil slick /ˈ. ./ *noun* a layer of oil on the sea or a river which has come out of a ship carrying oil

oil well /ˈ. ./ *noun* a deep hole made to get oil out of the ground

oil·y /ˈɔɪli/ *adjective* **oilier, oiliest** covered with oil, or containing a lot of oil: *He wiped his oily hands on a rag.*

oint·ment /ˈɔɪntmənt/ *noun* a soft substance that you rub into your skin as a medical treatment

OK or **okay** /əʊˈkeɪ $ oʊˈkeɪ/ *adjective, adverb informal*
1 satisfactory or acceptable ⇨ same meaning ALL RIGHT (1): *Is it OK if I phone you tonight?* | *Does this dress look OK?*
2 safe and not ill, hurt, or upset

O

⇨ *same meaning* ALL RIGHT (2): *Are you feeling OK?*

3 used to say that you agree with something or are willing to do something ⇨ *same meaning* ALL RIGHT (3): *"Can you come round at about eight o'clock?" "Okay."*

old /əʊld $oʊld/ *adjective*

1 someone who is old has lived a long time: *an old woman* | *He was very old when he died.*

2 used when talking or asking about the age of a person or thing: *My sister's three years old.* | *How old are you?* | *Do you know how old the building is?*

3 not modern or new: *We lived in an old house in the country.* | *This is an old dress – I've had it for years.*

4 used when talking about something that you used to have but do not have any more: *I liked my old school better than this one.*

PHRASES

an old friend a friend that you have known for a long time: *Laura's an old friend of mine.*

older brother, older sister a brother or sister who is older than you

old age /ˌ. './ *noun* [no plural] the time in your life when you are old: *You should save some money for your old age.*

old-fash·ioned /ˌ. '../ *adjective* not modern or fashionable: *Her clothes are a bit old-fashioned.*

ol·ive /'ɒləv $'ɑlɪv/ *noun* a small bitter black or green fruit, often used for making oil

O·lym·pic /ə'lɪmpɪk/ *adjective* related to the Olympic Games: *She won two Olympic gold medals.*

Olympic Games /.ˌ.. './ also **Olympics** *plural noun* **the Olympic Games**, **the Olympics** an international sports event held every four years

ome·lette BrE, **omelet** AmE /'ɒmlət $'ɑmlət/ *noun* eggs mixed together and cooked in a pan, often with other foods added: *a cheese omelette*

om·i·nous /'ɒmənəs $'ɑmənəs/ *adjective* making you feel that something bad is going to happen: *There was an ominous knock at the door.*

—**ominously** *adverb*: *Everywhere was ominously quiet.*

o·mit /əʊ'mɪt $oʊ'mɪt/ *verb* formal **omitted, omitting** to not include something: *They had omitted his name from the list.*

om·ni·bus /'ɒmnɪbəs $'ɑmnɪbəs/ *noun* a book or television programme that consists of several previous books or programmes put together: *I missed an episode so I'll have to watch the omnibus.*

on¹ /ɒn $ɔn/ *preposition*

1 the surface where something is resting or where it is put: *Gloria was lying on the grass.* | *He put his mug of coffee down on the table.* | *There was a mirror on the wall.* | *Look at the picture on page 23.* ⇨ see picture on page 354

2 showing which part of your body is touching the ground: *She was lying on her back.* | *He was on his hands and knees, looking for the missing button.*

3 next to a road, river, or sea: *The hotel is on the main road to Oxford.* | *a small town on the River Thames*

4 showing the day or date when something happens: *I'll see you on Saturday.* | *I was born on 17th June 1986.* | *I called her on Tuesday afternoon.*

5 the subject of a book or talk etc: *She loves reading books on animals.* | *a talk on the history of the cinema*

6 travelling by bus, train, boat, or plane: *I've never been on a ship before.* | *A woman with two dogs got on the bus.*

7 using a machine or instrument: *I've added up the figures on my calculator.* | *Rosie was playing a tune on the piano.*

PHRASES

on television, on the radio being broadcast, by television or radio: *Did you see that film on television last night?*

on holiday, on vacation: *We went on holiday to Jamaica last year* (=Jamaica was the place we went to for a holiday last year).

on page 1, 2, 3 etc appearing on page one, two etc

have something on you informal to have something in your pocket or bag: *I have his address on me somewhere.*

on² *adverb, adjective*

1 if a machine or piece of equipment is on, it is working and someone is using it ⇨ *opposite* OFF: *The washing machine's still on.* | *Do you want the TV on?*

2 if a television programme or film is on, it is possible to watch it: *There's a good programme on tonight.* | *What's on at the cinema?*

3 an event that is on is going to happen ⇨ *opposite* OFF: *There's an outdoor concert on at the weekend.* | *Is the football match still on this Saturday?*

PHRASES

have something on, put something on to wear something: *She had on jeans and a T-shirt.* | *Put your coat on.*

from now on, from then on after this or that time: *From now on I'm going to be more careful.* | *From then on I never saw him again.*

once¹ /wʌns/ *adverb*

1 one time: *I've only been there once.* | *Press the switch once.* | *She goes out clubbing once a week* (=one night every week).

2 at a time in the past: *The house was once owned by a famous film star.* | *She must have been beautiful once.* | *He once gave a party for 2000 people.*

PHRASE

at once **a)** at the same time: *It will save time if we make several copies at once.* | *I can't understand you if you all talk at once!* **b)** immediately: *If he starts causing trouble, you must tell me at once.* | *I could see at once that something was wrong.*

once²

from the time when something happens: *Once someone lies to you, you can never trust them again.*

one /wʌn/ *number, pronoun*

1 the number 1: *I have one brother and two sisters.* | *Only one of them can be right.* | *One of the children was crying.*

2 used when talking about a thing that is the same as something you have

already mentioned: *Jim's got a puppy – can I have one too* (=can I have a puppy too)? | *My shoes are totally worn out – I'll have to get some new ones* (=some new shoes). | *All my presents were good, but I liked the one from my granddad best.* | *That one's too expensive.*

3 only: *This is my one chance to become famous!* | *That's the one thing I forgot.*

4 people in general *formal*: *One doesn't often* (=people don't often) *get the chance to talk to a President.*

PHRASES

one day, one afternoon etc at a time in the past or future: *One day last week the bus was 40 minutes late!* | *Why don't you come round one evening?*

one after the other, one after another if things happen one after the other, there is not much time between them: *He ate ten biscuits, one after the other.*

one another: *They try to help one another when they can* (=they each try to help the other person).

one or two *spoken* a few: *I've got one or two things to sort out.*

USAGE

One of is followed by a plural noun but a singular verb: *One of the computers isn't working.*

one-off /ˌ. ˈ./ *adjective* one-off things only happen once: *a one-off payment*

one-to-one /ˌ. . ˈ./ *adjective* a one-to-one talk or lesson involves only two people: *You will be given one-to-one training.*

one-way /ˌ. ˈ./ *adjective* **1** in a one-way street, cars can travel in only one direction **2** a one-way ticket is for travelling to a place, but not for coming back ⇨ *same meaning* SINGLE¹ (4)

on·ion /ˈʌnjən/ *noun* a round white vegetable that has a thin brown skin and a very strong smell ⇨ *see pictures on pages 344 and 345*

on·line or **on-line** /ˈɒnlaɪn $ ˈɔːnlaɪn/ *adjective, adverb* using a computer, especially one that is connected to the INTERNET: *an online information service* | *We do most of our work online.*

on·look·er /ˈɒnˌlʊkə $ ˈɔːnˌlʊkɚ/ *noun*

someone who watches something happening but is not involved in it: *A crowd of onlookers had gathered.*

on·ly¹ /'əʊnli $ 'oʊnli/ *adverb*

1 showing that an amount is very small: *William lived only half a mile away from the school.* | *She got married when she was only seventeen.*
2 showing that something is not important: *Don't get upset – it's only a game.*
3 not anyone or anything else: *Only Richard knew the answer.* | *She only likes cornflakes for breakfast.* | *There's only one thing we can do: say we're sorry.* | *You can only get there by car.*
4 showing that something happened a very short time ago: *He only bought that computer on Monday.* | *I saw her only last week.*

PHRASES
only just a) a very short time ago: *Martin's only just left.* **b)** used to show that you achieve something, but almost do not manage: *I could only just reach the top shelf.*
if only *spoken*: *If only I'd kept a copy of the letter* (=I wish I'd kept a copy, but I didn't).

only² *adjective*
one single person or thing: *You're the only person I can trust.* | *It was the only ticket they had left.* | *It was the only vegetarian meal on the menu.* | *His only problem is his lack of confidence.*

PHRASE
an only child someone who has no brothers or sisters

only³ *spoken* but; used especially to talk about a problem that makes it difficult for you to do something: *I want to go the party only I don't have anything to wear.*

on·to /'ɒntə $ 'ɒntə; *before vowels* 'ɒntʊ $ 'ɒntʊ; *strong* 'ɒntuː $ 'ɒntu/ *preposition*
showing the surface that something is put on goes on: *The car fell from the bridge onto the railway line.* | *He dropped two coins onto the table.*
⇨ *see picture on page 354*

on·wards /'ɒnwədz $ 'ɔnwɚdz/ also **onward** *adverb* forward in space or time: *The army marched onwards.* | *I'll be free from two o'clock onward.*

ooze /uːz/ *verb, present participle* **oozing** if a liquid oozes, it flows slowly: *Fat oozed out of the cooked chicken.*

o·pal /'əʊpəl $ 'oʊpəl/ *noun* a white stone used in jewellery

open¹ /'əʊpən $ 'oʊpən/ *adjective*
GRAMMAR
open to someone
open with someone
1 not closed: *The door was open, so I went in.* | *An open book lay on the desk.* | *Please could you* **leave** *the window* **open**? ⇨ opposite CLOSED ⇨ *see picture at* CLOSED
2 if a shop, restaurant etc is open, people can come into it and use it: *The Indian restaurant is only open in the evening.* | *Is the new swimming-pool open yet?* | *The library is not* **open to** *the public this week.*
3 an open person is honest and willing to talk about things: *Parents should try to be* **open with** *their children.*
4 if something is open to people, it is available for them to do: *A lot of interesting jobs are* **open to** *people with science qualifications.*

PHRASE
in the open air outside: *In summer, we often eat* **in the open air.**

open² *verb*
1 to move something so that it is open: *She opened her bag and took out some money.*
2 to become open: *At that moment the door opened.*
3 when a shop, bank etc opens, people can go in and use it: *Most shops open at 9.30 on Saturday.* | *The new hospital will open in September.*

PHRASES
open fire to start shooting at someone: *The soldiers were ordered to* **open fire.**
open an account, open a bank account if you open a bank account, you put money into the bank and start to use the bank's services

O

USAGE
Don't use **open** and **close** to talk about things that use electricity, or things that provide water or gas. Use **turn on** and **turn off** or **switch on** and **switch off** instead: *Shall I turn on the TV?* | *Can you turn off the taps?*

open³ noun **1** (out) in the open outside, not in a building: *We slept out in the open last night.* **2** be out in the open to be no longer a secret: *I want the truth to be out in the open.*

open-air /ˌ.. './ adjective outside, not in a building: *an open-air concert* | *an open-air swimming pool*

open day /'.. ˌ./ noun BrE a day when people can visit a school or company and see what is done there

o·pen·ing¹ /'əʊpənɪŋ $'oʊpənɪŋ/ noun **1** when the public can start using a new place: *He invited them to the opening of his new restaurant.* **2** the beginning of something: *The opening of the book is very exciting.* **3** a hole or space that something can go through: *The dog managed to get through an opening in the fence.*

opening² adjective happening first or coming at the beginning: *Dixon scored in the opening minutes of the game.*

o·pen·ly /'əʊpənli $'oʊpənli/ adverb without keeping anything secret: *She spoke openly about her feelings.*

o·pen·ness /'əʊpnən-nəs $'oʊpən-nəs/ noun [no plural] when someone does not keep things secret: *Should there be more openness in government?*

open plan /ˌ.. './ adjective an open plan building does not have walls dividing it into separate rooms: *an open-plan office*

op·e·ra /'ɒpərə $'ɑprə/ noun a play in which all the words are sung

op·e·rate /'ɒpəreɪt $'ɑpəˌreɪt/ verb

GRAMMAR
operate on someone

1 if you operate a machine or piece of equipment, you make it work: *How do you operate this machine?* | *My job was to operate the lighting for the concert.*
2 formal if a machine or piece of equipment operates, it works: *The computers weren't operating properly.*

3 if a doctor operates on someone, he or she cuts open their body to remove or repair a part that is damaged: *Doctors operated on him and removed one of his kidneys.*

op·e·ra·tion /ˌɒpə'reɪʃən $ˌɑpə-'reɪʃən/ noun

GRAMMAR
an operation on something

1 if someone has an operation, doctors cut open their body in order to remove or repair a part that is damaged: *Doug's got to have an operation on his back.*
2 an organized activity in which people work together in order to do something: *The police organized a big search operation.*

op·e·ra·tor /'ɒpəreɪtə $'ɑpəˌreɪtɚ/ noun **1** formal someone whose job is to use a machine or piece of equipment: *a computer operator* **2** someone whose job is to connect telephone calls

o·pin·ion /ə'pɪnjən/ noun

GRAMMAR
an opinion of someone
an opinion about someone/something

your opinion of someone or something is what you think about them: *What's your opinion of the new head teacher?* | *George has strong opinions about divorce.*

PHRASES
in my opinion used to tell someone what you think about something: *In my opinion, you should go to America if you have the chance.*
have a high opinion of something/someone to think that something or someone is very good: *I have a very high opinion of Sarah's work.*
have a low opinion of something/someone to think that something or someone is not very good: *He has a rather low opinion of Jenny.*

opinion poll /.'.. ˌ./ noun when a lot of people are asked what they think about something, done in order to find out how popular someone or something is: *The opinion polls show that the Labour party is the most popular in this area.*

op·po·nent /ə'pəʊnənt $ ə'poʊ-nənt/ *noun*
someone who is competing against you in a sport or competition: *Our opponents seemed to be much bigger and stronger than us.*

op·por·tun·ist /ˌɒpə'tjuːnɪst $ ˌɑpɚ-'tunɪst/ *noun* someone who uses every opportunity to get things they want, without caring whether their actions are right or wrong

op·por·tu·ni·ty /ˌɒpə'tjuːnəti $ ˌɑpɚ'tunəti/ *noun, plural* **opportunities**

> **GRAMMAR**
> **an/the opportunity to do something**
> if you have an opportunity to do something, you get a chance to do it: *I'd love to **have the opportunity to** study abroad. | A job in Paris? What a wonderful opportunity!*

> **PHRASE**
> **take the opportunity (to do something)** to do something when you get the chance to do it: *He was alone, so I **took the opportunity to** ask him some questions.*

op·pose /ə'pəʊz $ ə'poʊz/ *verb* to disagree with something and try to stop it happening: *Many local people oppose the plan.*

op·posed /ə'pəʊzd $ ə'poʊzd/ *adjective* if you are opposed to something, you believe that it is wrong and should not be allowed: *He is strongly opposed to animal testing.*

op·po·site¹ /'ɒpəzɪt $ 'ɑpəzɪt/ *adjective*
1 completely different: *They were travelling in opposite directions.*
2 furthest away: *On the opposite side of the road was the hospital. | Her desk was in the **opposite** corner of the room **from** Carol's.*

opposite² *preposition*
facing someone or something: *She sat next to her sister, opposite her parents. | The school is opposite the church.* → see picture on page 354

opposite³ *noun* something that is completely different from something else: *They think I hit Bill but the opposite is true – he hit me.*

op·po·si·tion /ˌɒpə'zɪʃən $ ˌɑpə'zɪʃən/ *noun* **1** [no plural] when people disagree strongly with something: *There was a lot of opposition to the plan.* **2 the opposition** the person or team that you are trying to defeat in a game or competition **3 the Opposition** *BrE* the second biggest political party in parliament, which is not in the government

op·press /ə'pres/ *verb* if a government oppresses people, it treats them in an unfair and cruel way: *We have been oppressed for too long.*
– **oppressor** *noun*

op·pres·sion /ə'preʃən/ *noun* [no plural] when a government treats people in an unfair and cruel way: *They suffered years of oppression.*

op·pres·sive /ə'presɪv/ *adjective* cruel and unfair: *an oppressive military government*

opt /ɒpt $ ɑpt/ *verb* **1** to choose something or choose to do something: *I opted for the cheaper car. | You can opt to do two extra subjects.* **2 opt out** to choose not to be involved in something: *Several students opted out of this class.*

optical il·lusion /ˌ... .'../ *noun* something that you think you are seeing, because your eyes are being tricked

op·ti·cian /ɒp'tɪʃən $ ɑp'tɪʃən/ *noun* *BrE* someone who tests people's eyes and sells GLASSES; OPTOMETRIST *AmE*

op·ti·mis·m /'ɒptəmɪzəm $ 'ɑptə-ˌmɪzəm/ *noun* [no plural] the belief that good things will happen → *opposite* PESSIMISM

op·ti·mist /'ɒptəmɪst $ 'ɑptəˌmɪst/ *noun* someone who believes that good things will happen → *opposite* PESSIMIST

op·ti·mis·tic /ˌɒptə'mɪstɪk $ ˌɑptə-'mɪstɪk/ *adjective* believing that good things will happen → *opposite* PESSIMISTIC: *She was optimistic about her chances of passing the exam.*

op·tion /'ɒpʃən $ 'ɑpʃən/ *noun* **1** something that you can choose to do: *We have three options.* **2 keep your options open, leave your options open** to not make a definite decision yet, so that you can still choose what to do: *I'm keeping my options open until I hear what Helen's decided to do.*

op·tion·al /'ɒpʃənəl $ 'ɑpʃənl/ *adjective* if something is optional, you can choose to do it but you do not have to: *All children have to study maths and English, but French is optional.*

op·tom·e·trist /ɒp'tɒmətrɪst $ ɑp-'tɑmətrɪst/ the American word for OPTICIAN

or /ə $ ɚ; *strong* ɔː $ ɔr/
1 used when you are showing a choice: *Do you like this one or the blue one best?* | *You can work on your own or in teams.* | *You must take French or German, or both.*
2 used in negative sentences, when you are adding something: *He hasn't invited Kevin or Mark.* | *She can't read or write.* | *I'm not angry or upset about it.*
3 used when giving a warning or threat: *Be careful, or you might get hurt.* | *Stop that or I'll tell Mom!*

PHRASE
two or three, thirty or forty etc used when giving a number that is not exact: *You made **two or three** spelling mistakes.* | *We're expecting **thirty or forty** people to come to the party.*

o·ral¹ /'ɔːrəl/ *adjective* an oral examination, report etc is spoken, not written: *an oral test*

oral² *noun* an examination in which questions and answers are spoken, not written

or·ange¹ /'ɒrɪndʒ $ 'ɔrɪndʒ/ *noun* **1** a round fruit that is a colour between red and yellow and has a thick skin: *a sweet, juicy orange* ⇨ *see picture on page 345* **2** a colour that is between red and yellow

orange² *adjective* something that is orange is the colour that is between red and yellow

or·bit¹ /'ɔːbɪt $ 'ɔrbɪt/ *noun* the circle that a PLANET or space vehicle moves in as it travels around another object in space: *the Earth's orbit of the sun*

orbit² *verb* to travel around an object in space: *The moon orbits the Earth.*

or·chard /'ɔːtʃəd $ 'ɔrtʃɚd/ *noun* an area of land where fruit trees grow

or·ches·tra /'ɔːkɪstrə $ 'ɔrkɪstrə/ *noun* a large group of people who play musical instruments together: *She plays violin in the school orchestra.*

or·deal /ɔː'diːl $ ɔr'dil/ *noun* a very difficult and unpleasant experience: *The journey took twelve hours – and it was a real ordeal.*

or·der¹ /'ɔːdə $ 'ɔrdɚ/ *noun*
1 the way in which you arrange things so that they follow each other in a particular way: *Please put the books back on the shelf **in the right order.*** | *The pieces of paper were all **in the wrong order.*** | *This list should be **in alphabetical order.***
2 something that a person in authority tells you to do: *The general **gave the order** to fire.* | *Soldiers must **obey orders** at all times.*
3 something that a customer has asked a company to make or send them: *The company has just **received an order** for another 300 chairs.*
4 the food and drink that you ask for in a restaurant: *A waitress came and **took our order** (=asked us what we would like to eat and drink).*

PHRASES
in order to do something so that you can do something: *I went to the shop **in order to** buy some stamps.*
be out of order if a machine is out of order, it is not working because something is wrong with it: *The telephone **is out of order** again.*

order² *verb*
GRAMMAR
order someone to do something
1 to ask for food or drink in a restaurant: *"Are you ready to order?" the waiter asked.* | *We ordered a bottle of red wine with our meal.*
2 to ask a company to send you something that you want to buy: *To order one of our computers, just telephone the number below.*
3 if someone orders you to do something, they say that you must do it: *The police officer **ordered** the man **to** stay where he was.*

or·der·ly /'ɔːdəli $ 'ɔrdɚli/ *adjective* arranged or organized in a neat way ⇨ *opposite* DISORDERLY: *Her wardrobe is very neat and orderly.*

or·di·na·ri·ly /'ɔːdənərəli $,ɔːrdn-
'erəli/ *adverb* *spoken* usually: *Ordinarily, I
don't like listening to classical music.*

or·di·na·ry /'ɔːdənəri $'ɔːrdn,eri/
adjective
normal or usual, and not different
from other people or things: *Nothing
much has happened – it's been a
very ordinary day.*

ore /ɔː $ɔːr/ *noun* rock or earth from
which you can get metal: *iron ore*

or·gan /'ɔːgən $'ɔːrgən/ *noun* **1** a
part inside your body that has a particular purpose, for example your heart: *the
stomach and other internal organs* **2** a
musical instrument like a piano that is
often played in churches: *Mr Reed will
play the organ.*

or·gan·ic /ɔː'gænɪk $ɔːr'gænɪk/ *adjec-
tive* organic vegetables and other foods
are grown using natural substances, not
chemicals: *organic carrots*
– **organically** *adverb*: *organically grown
fruit*

or·gan·i·sa·tion /,ɔːgənaɪ'zeɪʃən
$,ɔːrgənə'zeɪʃən/ a British spelling of
ORGANIZATION

organise a British spelling of ORGANIZE

or·gan·is·m /'ɔːgənɪzəm $'ɔːrgə-
,nɪzəm/ *noun formal* a living thing: *fish,
plants, and other living organisms*

or·gan·i·za·tion also **organ-
isation** *BrE* /,ɔːgənaɪ'zeɪʃən $,ɔːr-
gənə'zeɪʃən/ *noun*
1 a group of people, companies, or
countries that meet and work together in order to do something: *a
political organization* | *The United
Nations is an organization of many
countries.*
2 when you plan and arrange how
something happens: *Who was responsible for the organization of the
party?*

or·gan·ize also **organise** *BrE*
/'ɔːgənaɪz $'ɔːrgə,naɪz/ *verb*
to plan and arrange an event or activity: *The school has organized a trip
to the sea.*

or·gan·i·zed also **organised** *BrE*
/'ɔːgənaɪzd $'ɔːrgə,naɪzd/ *adjective*
1 well organized, badly organized

a) planned and arranged well or badly: *a
well-organized party, with plenty of food
and drink* **2** good at planning and
doing the things that you have to do:
*Lucy's very organized and always does
her homework on time.*

or·gan·i·zer also **organiser** *BrE*
/'ɔːgənaɪzə $'ɔːrgə,naɪzɚ/ *noun* some-
one who plans and arranges an event:
the organizers of the race

o·ri·en·tal or **Oriental** /,ɔːri'entl/
adjective connected with Asia, or coming
from Asia: *an oriental rug*

or·i·gin /'ɒrɪdʒɪn $'ɔːrədʒɪn/ *noun*
1 the beginning or cause of something:
the origin of Christianity **2** *formal* the
country or type of family that someone
comes from: *children of Asian origin*

o·rig·i·nal¹ /ə'rɪdʒɪnəl/ *adjective*
1 an original thing or idea is the one
that existed first, before any changes
were made: *The original price that
he wanted was far too high.* | *The
castle still had some of its original
doors.*
2 new, different, and interesting: *He's
a great teacher, full of original
ideas.* | *Her music is very original.*
3 an original painting or document is
the real one, not a copy of it: *an
original Van Gogh*

original² *noun* a painting or document
that is the real one, not a copy: *This
painting is an original.*

o·rig·i·nal·i·ty /ə,rɪdʒə'næləti/ *noun [no
plural]* when something is new, different,
and interesting: *His movies were famous
for their originality and style.*

o·rig·i·nal·ly /ə'rɪdʒɪnəli/ *adverb* in the
beginning: *My family are originally from
Ireland.*

o·rig·i·nate /ə'rɪdʒəneɪt/ *verb formal*
to start to exist in a particular place
or at a particular time: *This type of
music originated in the fifteenth
century.*

or·na·ment /'ɔːnəmənt $'ɔːrnəmənt/
noun an attractive object that you put on
a table, shelf etc in your house

or·phan /'ɔːfən $'ɔːrfən/ *noun* a child
whose parents are dead

or·phan·age /'ɔːfənɪdʒ $'ɔːrfənɪdʒ/
noun a home for children whose parents
are dead

or·tho·dox /'ɔːθədɒks $'ɔːrθədɑːks/ adjective orthodox ideas or methods are the ones that most people accept as right and normal: *Mr Bristow's teaching methods were not very orthodox.*

oth·er /'ʌðə $'ʌðər/ adjective, pronoun

1 different things or people: *I don't like any other kinds of music – only pop music. | She's not like other girls.*
2 **others** other people or things: *Some mistakes are easier to correct than others.*
3 additional things or people: *Are there any other questions?*
4 the rest of a group: *He's cleverer than the other kids in his class. | Why don't you go and play in the garden with the others?*
5 the second thing of a pair: *I've lost my other glove! | Her best friend lived on the other side of town. | He arrived with a bunch of flowers in one hand and a bottle of wine in the other.*

PHRASES

other than something except for something: *I've got a cold. Other than that, I'm fine.*

the other day, the other week etc informal recently: *I saw her the other day and she seemed OK.*

every other day, every other week etc every second day, week etc: *I wash my hair every other day.*

someone or other, something or other, somehow or other spoken informal used when you are not certain about something: *He wanted to ask me about something or other (=something, but I don't know what). | Somehow or other her parents found out what she'd done.*

USAGE
Don't use **other** after 'an'. Look at **another**.

oth·er·wise /'ʌðəwaɪz $'ʌðər-ˌwaɪz/ adverb

1 used when saying that something bad will happen if someone does not do what you have said they should do: *Hurry up! Otherwise we'll miss the bus.*
2 in all other ways: *The weather was bad but otherwise we enjoyed ourselves.*

ought /ɔːt/ modal verb, negative **ought not** or **oughtn't**

1 saying that something is a good thing to do **a)** if you **ought to do** something, it is the right thing to do: *You ought to work harder at school. | Something ought to be done about car pollution.* **b)** if something **ought to have** happened, it did not happen although it was the right thing to happen: *I ought to have bought a return ticket, not a single. | The authorities ought to have known that there was going to be an earthquake.*
2 expecting something to happen or be true **a)** use **ought to** to say that you expect something to happen: *When I press this button, the computer **ought to start**. | Rowena's party **ought to be good** tomorrow.* **b)** if something **ought to have** happened, you expect that it has happened already: *Class 2 **ought to have** finished their exam by now.*
3 making a suggestion or giving advice strongly: *You **ought to play** chess – you'd like it. | This is an opportunity you **oughtn't miss**.*

ounce /aʊns/ noun written abbreviation **oz** a measure of weight, equal to 28.35 grams or 1/16 of a pound

our /aʊə $aʊər/ determiner belonging to the person who is speaking and others: *Our house is not far from the river. | Our work is very important.*

ours /aʊəz $aʊərz/ pronoun a thing belonging to the person who is speaking and others: *His house is bigger than ours. | Their car is like ours.*

our·selves /aʊə'selvz $aʊər-'selvz/ pronoun

1 used when the same person who is speaking and others do an action and receive an action: *We have to protect ourselves.*
2 used to emphasize the person speaking and others: *We ourselves must find a solution.*

O

by ourselves with no one else there, or with no one helping: *We're spending Christmas by ourselves.*

out /aʊt/ *adverb, adjective*

1 leaving a room or place: *She turned and walked out.* | *George got out of the car.* | *Smoke was coming out of the chimney.* ⇨ *see picture on page 354*

2 removing something from a place or container: *She opened her suitcase and took out a pair of shoes.* | *He took all his books out of his bag.*

3 not in your home: *Mum and Dad are out, so we can turn the music up really loud.*

4 no longer burning or shining: *The fire was out.* | *Suddenly all the lights went out.*

PHRASE
be out of something to have none of something left: *We seem to be out of milk.*

out·break /'aʊtbreɪk/ *noun* when something bad suddenly starts: *We were living in Austria at the outbreak of the war.*

out·come /'aʊtkʌm/ *noun* the final result of an event or situation: *What was the outcome of the meeting?*

out·dat·ed /ˌaʊt'deɪtɪd/ *adjective* not modern or useful any more ⇨ *same meaning* OLD-FASHIONED: *outdated equipment.*

outdid the past tense of OUTDO

out·do /aʊt'duː/ *verb* **outdid** /-'dɪd/ **outdone** /-'dʌn/ to be better or more successful than someone else: *The two brothers were always trying to outdo each other.*

outdone the past participle of OUTDO

out·door /'aʊtdɔː $ 'aʊtdɔr/ *adjective* happening or used outside, not inside a building ⇨ *opposite* INDOOR: *outdoor sports*

out·doors /ˌaʊt'dɔːz $ ˌaʊt'dɔrz/ *adverb* outside, not inside a building ⇨ *opposite* INDOORS: *In the summer we often eat outdoors.*

out·er /'aʊtə $ 'aʊtər/ *adjective* on or near the outside of something, away from the middle ⇨ *opposite* INNER: *We live on the outer edge of the town.*

outer space /ˌ.. './ *noun* [no plural] the area outside the Earth's air, where the stars are

out·fit /'aʊtfɪt/ *noun* a set of clothes that you wear together: *I'll have to buy myself a new outfit for their wedding.*

out·go·ing /ˌaʊt'gəʊɪŋ $ 'aʊt,goʊɪŋ/ *adjective* someone who is outgoing enjoys meeting and talking to people: *a girl with a very outgoing personality*

outgrew the past tense of OUTGROW

out·grow /aʊt'grəʊ $ aʊt'groʊ/ *verb* **outgrew** /-'gruː/ **outgrown** /-'grəʊn $ -'groʊn/ if children outgrow their clothes, they grow too big for them: *John's outgrown all the trousers he wore last year.*

outgrown the past participle of OUTGROW

out·ing /'aʊtɪŋ/ *noun* a day trip to a place for you to enjoy yourself: *We're going on a school outing to the seaside.*

out·law /'aʊtlɔː/ *verb* to officially say that something is illegal: *The new law will outlaw abortion.*

out·line /'aʊtlaɪn/ *noun* a line around the edge of something that shows its shape: *In the distance I could just see the outline of a ship.*

out·live /aʊt'lɪv/ *verb* to live longer than someone: *Women usually outlive men.*

out·look /'aʊtlʊk/ *noun* your attitude to life and the world: *I think I have a positive outlook on life.*

out·num·ber /aʊt'nʌmbə $ aʊt'nʌmbər/ *verb* if the people or things in one group outnumber those in another group, there are more of them: *Girls greatly outnumber boys in our class.*

out of bounds /ˌ.. '. './ *adjective* if a place is out of bounds, people are not allowed to go there: *The pub is out of bounds to students.*

out-of-date /ˌ.. . './ *adjective* old-fashioned, and not useful or attractive any more: *I can't wear those shoes – they're completely out-of-date!*

out of work /ˌ.. . './ *adjective* someone who is out of work does not have a job ⇨ *same meaning* UNEMPLOYED: *Mark's been out of work since he lost his job last year.*

out·pa·tient /'aʊtˌpeɪʃənt/ *noun* someone who goes to a hospital for treatment and then goes home on the same day

out·put /'aʊtpʊt/ *noun* the amount of goods that a country, company etc produces: *Britain's industrial output fell by 2% in January,*

out·ra·geous /aʊt'reɪdʒəs/ *adjective* something that is outrageous makes you feel very angry or shocked: *His drunken behaviour was completely outrageous. | That's an outrageous price to pay.*

out·side¹ /aʊt'saɪd/ *preposition, adverb*
1 not in a building or room ⇨ *opposite* INSIDE¹, IN¹: *I'll wait for you outside the cinema. | It was a nice sunny day, so we had lunch outside. | I ran outside to see what was going on.* ⇨ *see picture on page 354*
2 not in a city or country: *My grandparents live just outside Oxford. | people from outside the United Kingdom*
3 not in a particular group or organization: *She didn't want to discuss the problem with anyone outside the family.*

out·side² *noun* **the outside** the part of something that surrounds the rest of it: *The outside of the box is covered with gold.*

out·side³ /'aʊtsaɪd/ *adjective* an outside wall, light etc is not inside a building

out·sid·er /aʊt'saɪdə/ *noun* someone who does not belong to a group, organization etc: *I felt like an ousider when I first started at the college.*

out·skirts /'aʊtskɜːts $ 'aʊtskɚts/ *plural noun* **the outskirts** the parts of a town that are furthest from the centre: *My parents have an apartment on the ouskirts of Paris.*

out·spo·ken /aʊt'spəʊkən $ aʊt'spoʊkən/ *adjective* an outspoken person says what they think even though it may shock or offend people: *She has been very outspoken in her opposition to the plan.*

out·stand·ing /aʊt'stændɪŋ/ *adjective* very good ⇨ *same meaning* EXCELLENT: *Eddie got outstanding results in his exams.*

out·stretched /ˌaʊt'stretʃt/ *adjective* written outstretched arms or hands are stretched towards someone: *She ran into her father's outstretched arms.*

out·ward /'aʊtwəd $ 'aʊtwɚd/ *adjective* an outward journey takes you away from the place where you live: *The outward flight took five hours.*

out·wards /'aʊtwədz $ 'aʊtwɚdz/ also **outward** *AmE, adverb* towards the outside of something or away from its centre ⇨ *opposite* INWARDS: *The town had grown and spread outwards since I left home.*

o·val /'əʊvəl $ 'oʊvəl/ *noun* a shape like an egg ⇨ *see picture at* SHAPE¹
– **oval** *adjective*: *She had a pretty oval face.*

o·va·ry /'əʊvəri $ 'oʊvəri/ *noun, plural* ovaries the part of a woman or a female animal that produces eggs

ov·en /'ʌvən/ *noun* a piece of cooking equipment with a door that you open when you want to cook food in it. An oven is a square shape like a large box and is part of a cooker: *Heat the oven to 200 degrees.*

o·ver¹ /'əʊvə $ 'oʊvɚ/ *preposition*
1 going from one side of something to the other: *He jumped over the fence. | the bridge over the river* ⇨ *see picture on page 354*
2 above something: *There was a large mirror over the fireplace.* ⇨ *see picture on page 354*
3 on the other side of a road: *There's a supermarket just over the road.*
4 when something covers an object or a person: *They put old sheets over the furniture | Spread the glue over the top of the box* (=so that it covers the top of the box).
5 more than: *There were over 5000 people at the concert. | This book is over two hundred years old.*
6 during a period of time: *I'll think about it over the weekend.*
7 showing what people are arguing about: *They were arguing over who should pay for the tickets.*

PHRASE
all over everywhere in a place: *The disease has now spread **all over** the world.*

over² *adverb*
more than the amount or age mentioned: *This film is for people aged 18 **and over** (=people aged 18 or more than 18).*

PHRASES
over here, over there used when pointing to a place: *"Where's*

Oliver?" "Over there." | Come over here!

over and over again very many times: *I've told you **over and over again** – I don't know where the money is.*

over³ adjective if something is over or all over, it is finished: *We were sad when the holiday was over.*

o·ver·all /,əυvər'ɔːl $,oυvə'ɔl/ adjective considering or including everything: *The overall price of the holiday is $700.*

o·ver·alls /'əυvərɔːlz $ 'oυvə,ɔlz/ plural noun **1** BrE a piece of clothing covering your legs and body that you wear over your usual clothes in order to keep them clean: *a clean pair of overalls* ⇨ see picture on page 352 **2** the American word for DUNGAREES

o·ver·board /'əυvə- overboard bɔːd $ 'oυvə- ,bɔrd/ adverb over the side of a boat or ship into the water: *The little boy had fallen overboard and nearly drowned.*

overcame the past tense of OVER-COME

o·ver·cast /,əυvə'kɑːst $ 'oυvə,kæst/ adjective if it is overcast, the sky is dark and cloudy: *an overcast November day*

o·ver·coat /'əυvəkəυt $ 'oυvə,koυt/ noun a long warm coat that you wear when it is cold

o·ver·come /,əυvə'kʌm $,oυvə'kʌm/ verb **overcame** /-'keɪm/ **overcome** to succeed in controlling a feeling or solving a problem: *Ally was struggling to overcome her disappointment.*

o·ver·crowd·ed /,əυvə'kraυdɪd $,oυvə'kraυdɪd/ adjective a place that is overcrowded has too many people in it: *Britain's overcrowded cities*

overdid the past tense of OVERDO

o·ver·do /,əυvə'duː $,oυvə'du/ verb **overdid** /-'dɪd/ **overdone** /-'dʌn/ to do or use too much of something: *It's good to take some exercise, but don't overdo it.*

overdone the past participle of OVERDO

o·ver·draft /'əυvədrɑːft $ 'oυvə- ,dræft/ noun an arrangement with your bank that allows you to spend more money than you have in your account: *The bank have agreed to give me a £1000 overdraft.*

o·ver·drawn /,əυvə'drɔːn $,oυvə- 'drɔn/ adjective if you are overdrawn, you have spent more money than you have in your bank account: *If I go overdrawn again, the bank will charge me twice.*

o·ver·due /,əυvə'djuː $,oυvə'du/ adjective late in arriving or being done: *I must finish this essay – it's already overdue.*

o·ver·es·ti·mate /,əυvər'estəmeɪt $,oυvə'estə,meɪt/ verb to think that something is bigger, longer etc than it really is: *I overestimated how long the journey would take.*

o·ver·flow /,əυvə- overflow 'fləυ $,oυvə'floυ/ verb if a liquid overflows, it goes over the edges of its container: *I forgot to turn the tap off and the water overflowed.*

overflow

o·ver·head¹ /,əυvə'hed $,oυvə'hed/ adverb, adjective high up in the air, above your head: *Several planes flew overhead.* | *overhead electricity wires*

overhead² AmE noun [no plural] **overheads** BrE plural noun the money that a business has to spend regularly on rent, electricity, SALARIES etc: *The company will have to reduce its overheads.*

o·ver·hear /,əυvə'hɪə $,oυvə'hɪr/ verb, past tense and past participle **overheard** /-'hɜːd $ 'hɜ·d/ to hear what someone is saying when they are talking to another person and do not know you are listening: *I overheard what you were saying on the phone.*

o·ver·lap /,əυvə'læp $,oυvə'læp/ verb **overlapped**, **overlapping** if two things overlap, part of one thing covers part of the other: *I want you to draw two circles that overlap each other at the edge.*

o·ver·load /,əυvə'ləυd $,oυvə'loυd/ verb to put too many people or things into a vehicle: *It's dangerous to overload your car.*

o·ver·look /,əυvə'lυk $,oυvə'lυk/

overtake

verb **1** if a building or room overlooks something, you can see that thing from the building or room: *Our hotel overlooked the sea.* **2** to not notice something or to not realize how important it is: *I overlooked the fact that prices have gone up since last year.*

o·ver·night /,əʊvə'naɪt $,ouvɚ'naɪt/ *adverb, adjective* **1** for or during the night: *Is it all right if I stay overnight at Tom's house?* **2** if something happens overnight, it happens very quickly: *He became a star overnight.* | *The play was an overnight success.*

o·ver·pop·u·lat·ed /,əʊvə'pɒpjəleɪtɪd $,ouvɚ'pɑpjə,leɪtɪd/ *adjective* a place that is overpopulated has too many people living in it

o·ver·pow·er·ing /,əʊvə'paʊərɪŋ $,ouvɚ'paʊərɪŋ/ *adjective formal* a feeling or smell that is overpowering is very strong: *Sam woke up with a feeling of overpowering excitement.*

o·ver·priced /,əʊvə'praɪst $,ouvɚ'praɪst/ *adjective* something that is overpriced is more expensive than it should be: *It's a nice restaurant, but it's a little overpriced.*

o·ver·rat·ed /,əʊvə'reɪtɪd $,ouvɚ'reɪtɪd/ *adjective* something that is overrated is not as good as some people think: *I think the band is overrated.*

o·ver·seas /,əʊvə'siːz $,ouvɚ'siːz/ *adverb, adjective formal* from or in a foreign country that is across the sea: *My father had to travel overseas several times each year.* | *overseas students*

o·ver·sight /'əʊvəsaɪt $ 'ouvɚ,saɪt/ *noun* a small mistake made because you did not notice something or forgot to do something

o·ver·sleep /,əʊvə'sliːp $,ouvɚ'slip/ *verb, past tense and past participle* **overslept** /-'slept/ to sleep for longer than you intended to, especially so that you are late for something: *Matt overslept this morning and missed the bus.*

overslept the past tense and past participle of OVERSLEEP

o·ver·take /,əʊvə'teɪk $,ouvɚ'teɪk/ *verb* **overtook** /-'tʊk/ **overtaken** /-'teɪkən/ to pass another vehicle or person because you are moving faster than them: *A police car overtook us.*

overtaken the past participle of OVERTAKE

overthrew the past tense of OVERTHROW

o·ver·throw /,əʊvə'θrəʊ $,ouvɚ'θroʊ/ *verb* **overthrew** /-'θruː/ **overthrown** /-'θrəʊn $ -'θroʊn/ to remove a leader or government from power, by using force: *The country's military leaders plan to overthrow the government.*

overthrown the past participle of OVERTHROW

o·ver·time /'əʊvətaɪm $ 'ouvɚ,taɪm/ *noun [no plural]* hours that you work in addition to your usual working hours: *How much do you get paid for overtime?*

o·ver·took the past tense of OVERTAKE

o·ver·turn /,əʊvə'tɜːn $,ouvɚ'tɚn/ *verb* if something overturns, it turns over completely or falls onto its side: *A truck carrying wood had overturned on the freeway.*

o·ver·weight /,əʊvə'weɪt $,ouvɚ'weɪt/ *adjective* a person who is overweight is too fat and heavy: *an overweight businessman* ⇨ *see picture on page 353* ⇨ *see usage note at* FAT¹

o·ver·whelm /,əʊvə'welm $,ouvɚ'welm/ *verb* if a feeling overwhelms you, you feel it very strongly

o·ver·whelm·ing /,əʊvə'welmɪŋ $,ouvɚ'welmɪŋ/ *adjective* **1** if a feeling is overwhelming, you feel it very strongly: *He felt an overwhelming desire to leave.* **2** big in number or amount: *An overwhelming majority voted against the government.*

o·ver·worked /,əʊvə'wɜːkt $,ouvɚ'wɚkt/ *adjective* someone who is overworked works too much

owe /əʊ $ oʊ/ *verb*

GRAMMAR
owe someone something
owe something to someone

1 if you owe money to someone, you need to give it back to them because you borrowed it from them: *I owe James £5.* | *They owe money to the bank.*

2 if you owe someone something, you feel that you should give it to them or do it for them: *I owe you an apology.*

3 if you owe your success to someone or something, you were successful because of someone or something: *I owe my success to my parents.*

owing to /'... / preposition *formal* because of: *He could not play in the match, owing to an injury.*

owl /aʊl/ *noun* a bird that hunts at night and has large eyes and a loud call

own¹ /əʊn $oʊn/ *adjective, pronoun*

belonging to a particular person: *He has his own way of doing things.* | *She borrowed a friend's car because her own was being repaired.* | *I'm going to start looking for a place of my own.*

PHRASE

on your own without anyone with you or helping you: *She was quite* happy living **on** her **own.** | *Do you think you'll be able to carry it* **on** *your* **own?**

own² *verb* **1** if you own something, it belongs to you: *He was the only person I knew who owned a van.* **2 own up** to admit that you did something wrong: *She didn't want to own up to her mistake.*

own·er /'əʊnə $'oʊnɚ/ *noun* someone who owns something: *Who is the owner of this car?*

ox·y·gen /'ɒksɪdʒən $'ɑksɪdʒən/ *noun* [no plural] a gas in the air that all living things need

oy·ster /'ɔɪstə $'ɔɪstɚ/ *noun* a small sea animal that has a shell and makes a jewel called a PEARL

oz the written abbreviation of OUNCE or ounces

o·zone lay·er /'əʊzəʊn ˌleɪə $'oʊzoʊn ˌleɪɚ/ *noun* [no plural] a layer of gases around the Earth that stops harmful heat from the sun reaching the Earth

Pp

p /piː/ BrE the abbreviation of PENNY or PENCE

PA /ˌpiː 'eɪ/ noun BrE PERSONAL ASSISTANT; someone in an office who writes letters, answers the telephone, and arranges meetings for an important person

pace¹ /peɪs/ noun **1** [no plural] how quickly you do something, or how quickly something happens: *They walked along at a fairly slow pace.* **2 keep pace with something/someone** to move or change as fast as something or someone: *He walked so quickly that she found it difficult to keep pace with him.*

pace² verb written to walk around a lot when you are waiting or when you are worried about something: *She paced up and down the corridor, waiting for news.*

pac·i·fi·er /ˈpæsəfaɪə $ ˈpæsəˌfaɪɚ/ the American word for DUMMY

pac·i·fist /ˈpæsəfɪst/ noun someone who believes that all wars are wrong

pack¹ /pæk/ verb **1** also **pack up** to put things into bags or boxes so that you can take them somewhere: *Did you remember to pack your swimming costume?* | *She went upstairs to pack.* | *He helped Kelly pack up all her books.* **2 pack up** informal **a)** BrE if a machine packs up, it stops working **b)** to finish doing something: *We packed up and went home.*

pack² noun **1 a pack of things** a number of things that are kept together in a container: *a pack of envelopes | an information pack* **2** a group of animals that hunt together: *a pack of dogs* **3** a set of playing cards; DECK AmE

pack·age¹ /ˈpækɪdʒ/ noun **1** something that has been put in a box or wrapped in paper and sent somewhere by post ⇨ same meaning PARCEL **2** AmE the box or bag that food is put in so that it can be sold: *a package of butter*

package² verb to put something in a box or bag so that it can be sold: *They packaged the biscuits in cardboard boxes.*

pack·ag·ing /ˈpækɪdʒɪŋ/ noun [no plural] the bag or box that a product is in when you buy it

packed /pækt/ also **packed out** /ˌ ˈ ./ adjective informal full of people: *The hall was absolutely packed.*

pack·et /ˈpækɪt/ noun a bag or box of things that you can buy: *a packet of crisps* ⇨ see picture at CONTAINER

pack·ing /ˈpækɪŋ/ noun [no plural] when you put things into bags or boxes so that you can take them somewhere: *I'll help you do the packing.*

pad /pæd/ noun **1** a book of sheets of paper, that you use for writing or drawing: *She wrote something down on her pad.* **2** a thick piece of material that you use to protect something: *The boy on the skateboard was wearing elbow pads.*

pad·ded /ˈpædɪd/ adjective something that is padded has soft material inside it, to make it thicker and bigger or more comfortable: *a padded chair*

pad·dle¹ /ˈpædl/ noun a short pole with a flat end, that you use for moving a small boat along

paddle² verb **1** to move a small boat through water, using a paddle **2** BrE to walk around in water that is not very deep

pad·lock¹ /ˈpædlɒk $ ˈpædlɑːk/ noun a strong lock that you put on a bicycle or a door

padlock² verb to fasten something, using a padlock: *I padlocked my bike to the fence.*

padlock

page /peɪdʒ/ *noun* a sheet of paper in a book, newspaper etc: *I tore a page out of my notebook.* | *What's on the next page?*

pag·er /'peɪdʒə $ 'peɪdʒɚ/ *noun* a small machine you carry with you that makes a noise when it receives a message, for example when someone telephones you

paid the past tense and past participle of PAY[1]

P

pain

pain /peɪn/ *noun*

GRAMMAR
a pain in something
the pain of something

1 the unpleasant feeling you have when part of your body hurts: *She had a pain in her chest.* | *Do you feel any pain?* | *He was in terrible pain.*

2 a feeling of sadness: *the pain of seeing someone you love die*

PHRASE

be a pain, be a pain in the neck *spoken informal* to be very annoying: *It's a pain having to look after my little brother.* | *My boss is a right pain in the neck.*

pain·ful /'peɪnfəl/ *adjective* **1** something that is painful causes you physical pain: *Her sore throat was very painful.* | *a painful injury* **2** something that is painful makes you feel very unhappy: *Breaking up with her boyfriend had been a painful experience.*

pain·kill·er /'peɪnˌkɪlə $ 'peɪnˌkɪlɚ/ *noun* a drug that makes you feel less pain

pain·less /'peɪnləs/ *adjective* not making you feel any pain: *Having my tooth pulled out was quite painless.*

pains·tak·ing /'peɪnzˌteɪkɪŋ/ *adjective* done very carefully: *the painstaking work of the research team*

paint[1] /peɪnt/ *noun* [no plural] a coloured liquid that you use to cover surfaces or make pictures: *Be careful – the paint on the door is still wet.*

paint[2] *verb* **1** to put paint on a surface: *They painted the walls green.* **2** to make a picture of someone or something using paint: *She was painting a picture of some flowers.*

paint·brush /'peɪntbrʌʃ/ *noun, plural* **paintbrushes** a brush that you use to paint pictures or to paint walls ⇨ see picture at BRUSH[1]

paint·er /'peɪntə $ 'peɪntɚ/ *noun* **1** someone who paints pictures: *My favourite painter is Monet.* **2** someone whose job is painting houses

paint·ing /'peɪntɪŋ/ *noun* a painted picture: *a painting of a horse*

pair /peə $ per/ *noun*

GRAMMAR
a pair of things

1 something that is made of two similar parts that are joined together: *a pair of trousers* | *a sharp pair of scissors*

2 two similar things that you use together: *a pair of socks*

3 two people who do something together: *We all had to work in pairs.*

pajamas the American spelling of PYJAMAS

pal /pæl/ *noun informal* a friend

pal·ace /'pælɪs/ *noun* a very large house where a king or queen lives: *Buckingham Palace*

pale /peɪl/ *adjective* **1** light in colour: *a pale blue shirt* **2** someone who is pale has skin that looks white, for example because they are ill or frightened: *You look pale – are you alright?*

palm /pɑːm/ *noun* the surface of the inside of your hand: *The palms of her hands were sweaty.*

palm tree /'. ./ *noun* a tall tree that grows in hot dry places

pal·try /'pɔːltri/ *adjective* a paltry amount is too small: *We work long hours for paltry pay.*

pam·per /'pæmpə $ 'pæmpɚ/ *verb* to treat someone too kindly, by giving them everything they want: *Some people pamper their children too much.*

pam·phlet /'pæmflɪt/ *noun* a thin book

that contains information about something

pan /pæn/ *noun* **1** a round metal container with a long handle that you cook things in: *There was a pan of soup on the cooker.* **2** *AmE* a metal container for baking things: *a pie pan*

pan·cake /'pænkeɪk/ *noun* a thin round food that you make by mixing flour, milk, and eggs and cooking the mixture in a pan

pan·da /'pændə/ *noun* a large black and white bear that lives in China

pan·de·mo·ni·um /ˌpændə'məʊniəm $ ˌpændə'məʊniəm/ *noun [no plural] formal* when there is a lot of noise and excitement

pan·der /'pændə $ 'pændɚ/ *verb* to give someone what they want, even though you know it is not good for them: *You shouldn't pander to the children when they ask you for sweets.*

pane /peɪn/ *noun* a piece of glass in a window or door

pan·el /'pænl/ *noun* **1** a group of people who are chosen to discuss something: *A panel of teachers will choose the best story.* **2 instrument panel, control panel** the part inside a plane, boat etc where the controls are fixed

pang /pæŋ/ *noun* a sudden strong feeling of pain, sadness, or hunger: *I had a pang of guilt about leaving Sally alone.*

pan·ic¹ /'pænɪk/ *noun [no plural]* a sudden very strong feeling of fear or worry: *The bomb warning caused panic.* | *In a panic, he searched all his pockets for the keys.*

panic² *verb* **panicked, panicking** to feel so frightened or worried that you cannot think clearly: *When I saw him lying on the ground, I just panicked.*

pant /pænt/ *verb* to breathe quickly because you have been running

pan·ties /'pæntiz/ *plural noun* underwear for women that covers the area between the waist and the top of the legs; KNICKERS *BrE*

pan·to·mime /'pæntəmaɪm/ *noun* a funny play for children that is performed at Christmas in Britain

pants /pænts/ *plural noun* **1** *BrE* a piece of underwear that covers the area between your waist and your legs; UNDERPANTS *AmE* **2** the American word

for TROUSERS: *I need to buy a new pair of pants.*

pan·ty·hose /'pæntihəʊz $ 'pæntiˌhoʊz/ the American word for TIGHTS

pa·per /'peɪpə $ 'peɪpɚ/ *noun*

1 *[no plural]* a thin material that you use for writing on or for wrapping things in: *She wrote the address on a **piece of paper**.* | *a paper bag*

2 a newspaper: *The story was in all the papers.*

3 **papers** documents: *He was sorting through the papers on his desk.*

4 a piece of writing or a talk about a particular subject: *She is **giving** a **paper on** the Spanish civil war.*

5 an examination: *He found the maths paper very hard.*

pa·per·back /'peɪpəbæk $ 'peɪpɚˌbæk/ *noun* a book with a soft paper cover

paper clip /'.. ˌ./ *noun* a small piece of curved wire that you use for holding pieces of paper together

pa·per·work /'peɪpəwɜːk $ 'peɪpɚˌwɚk/ *noun [no plural]* work such as writing letters or reports: *I have to do a lot of paperwork in my job.*

par /pɑː $ pɑr/ *noun* **be on a par with something** to be of the same standard as something: *This qualification is on a par with a degree.*

par·a·chute¹ /'pærəʃuːt/ *noun* a large piece of cloth that people use when they jump out of a plane, to make them fall through the air slowly and come to the ground safely

parachute

parachute² *verb* to jump from a plane, using a parachute

pa·rade¹ /pə'reɪd/ *noun* an event in which people walk through the streets and play music to celebrate something

parade² *verb* to walk through the streets in a large group in order to celebrate something: *The children paraded through the town.*

par·a·dise /'pærədaɪs/ *noun* a perfect place where some people think good people go after they die

par·a·dox /'pærədɒks $'pærə,dɑks/ *noun, plural* **paradoxes** something that seems strange because it contains two very different ideas: *It is a paradox that when you do more exercise, you feel less tired.*

par·af·fin /'pærəfɪn/ *noun BrE* a kind of oil that you use for heating and in lamps; KEROSENE *AmE*

par·a·graph /'pærəɡrɑːf $'pærə,ɡræf/ *noun* one part of a long piece of writing containing one or more sentences. A paragraph starts on a new line

par·al·lel /'pærəlel/ *adjective* lines that are parallel go in the same direction and are the same distance apart all the way along: *The two streets are parallel to each other.*

par·a·lysed *BrE*, **paralyzed** *AmE* /'pærəlaɪzd/ *adjective* if you are paralysed, you cannot move part of your body, for example because you have injured it

pa·ral·y·sis /pə'ræləsɪs/ *noun [no plural]* when you cannot move part of your body, for example because you have injured it

par·a·med·ic /,pærə'medɪk/ *noun* someone who is not a doctor or nurse but is trained to help people who are ill or injured until they get to hospital

par·a·mil·i·ta·ry /,pærə'mɪlətəri $,pærə'mɪlə,teri/ *adjective* a paramilitary organization is organized like an army, but is not part of a country's official army: *a paramilitary terrorist group*

par·a·mount /'pærəmaʊnt/ *adjective formal* more important than anything else: *The safety of the children is paramount.*

par·a·noi·a /,pærə'nɔɪə/ *noun [no plural]* when you wrongly think that everyone is against you or wants to hurt you

par·a·phrase /'pærəfreɪz/ *verb* to write or say in different words what someone else has written or said: *We had to paraphrase what the teacher said.*

par·a·site /'pærəsaɪt/ *noun* a plant or animal that lives on another plant or animal and gets food from it

par·a·troop·er /'pærə,truːpə $'pærə,truːpɚ/ *noun* a soldier who is trained to jump out of planes, using a PARACHUTE

par·cel /'pɑːsəl $'pɑrsəl/ *noun* something that has been wrapped in paper so that it can be sent somewhere ➔ *same meaning* PACKAGE[1]

par·don[1] /'pɑːdn $'pɑrdn/ *verb* to officially decide not to punish someone for a crime
— **pardon** *noun*

pardon[2] *also* **pardon me** /,.. '. / *spoken* **1** used to ask someone to repeat something because you have not heard them properly **2** another way of saying "Excuse me."

par·ent /'peərənt $'perənt/ *noun* your parents are your father and mother: *I didn't want to disappoint my parents.*

pa·ren·the·ses /pə'renθəsiːz/ *plural noun* the small curved lines (), that you sometimes use in writing: *Put the dates in parentheses.*

par·ent·hood /'peərənthʊd $'perənt,hʊd/ *noun [no plural]* when you are a parent: *They were really enjoying parenthood.*

par·ish /'pærɪʃ/ *noun* an area that has its own church

park[1] /pɑːk $pɑrk/ *noun* an area with grass and trees, where people can walk, play games etc

park[2] *verb* to leave your car somewhere: *We parked behind the school.*

park·ing /'pɑːkɪŋ $'pɑrkɪŋ/ *noun [no plural]* when you park your car: *Parking is not allowed in front of the gates.*

parking lot /'.. ,./ the American word for a CAR PARK

parking me·ter /'.. ,../ *noun* a machine that you put money into when you park your car

parking tick·et /'.. ,../ *noun* a piece of paper that is put on your car to tell you that you must pay an amount of money because you have parked your car in an illegal place

par·lia·ment /'pɑːləmənt $'pɑrləmənt/ *noun* a group of people who make or change a country's laws. A parliament is chosen by all the people in a country who are able to vote: *Laws are made by parliament.*

par·lia·men·ta·ry /,pɑːlə'mentəri $,pɑrlə'mentri/ *adjective* related to parliament: *a parliamentary committee*

par·o·dy[1] /'pærədi/ *noun, plural* **parodies** a piece of writing or a film that copies someone else's style in a funny way: *The song is a parody of '70s music.*

parody² verb parodied, parodies to copy someone's style or behaviour in a funny way: *He can parody Gary's voice very well.*

par·rot /'pærət/ noun a brightly coloured bird that you can teach to speak

pars·ley /'pɑːsli $'pɑrsli/ noun [no plural] a plant with small curled leaves that you eat

pars·nip /'pɑːsnɪp $'pɑrsnɪp/ noun a white or yellow vegetable that is the root of a plant

part¹ /pɑːt $pɑrt/ noun

GRAMMAR
(a) part of something
someone's part in something

1 one piece or amount of something: *Part of the roof was missing.* | *The best part of the job is meeting lots of different people.* | *in the early part of the nineteenth century*

2 if an actor plays a part in a play or film, they pretend to be a particular person in it: *I've always wanted to play the part of Juliet.*

3 your part in an action or event is what you do in it: *She was given a medal for her part in the rescue.*

PHRASES

take part to be involved in an event or activity: *Hundreds of children took part in the festival.*

play a part in something to be one of several things that makes something happen: *The death of his wife played a part in his decision to leave London.*

on someone's part, on the part of someone formal by someone: *Organizing the concert will mean a lot of work on my part.*

part² verb

GRAMMAR
be parted from someone

to be separated from someone or something that you love: *She didn't want to be parted from her family.*

PHRASAL VERB

part with

part with something to give away or sell something that you like very much: *He refused to part with his collection of old records.*

part³ adverb if something is part one thing and part another thing, it is partly the first thing and partly the second: *The creature was part horse and part cow.*

par·tial /'pɑːʃəl $'pɑrʃəl/ adjective not complete: *She suffers from partial blindness.*

par·tial·ly /'pɑːʃəli $'pɑrʃəli/ adverb partly, but not completely: *The window was partially covered by a curtain.*

par·tic·i·pant /pɑː'tɪsəpənt $pɑr-'tɪsəpənt/ noun formal someone who is involved in an activity with other people: *Mark was a willing participant in the study.*

par·tic·i·pate /pɑː'tɪsəpeɪt $pɑr'tɪsə-ˌpeɪt/ verb formal to do an activity with other people: *The whole class participated in the play.*

par·tic·i·pa·tion /pɑːˌtɪsə'peɪʃən $pɑrˌtɪsə'peɪʃən/ noun [no plural] formal when you do an activity with other people: *We want to encourage more participation by women in sport.*

par·ti·ci·ple /'pɑːtəsɪpəl $'pɑrtə-ˌsɪpəl/ noun the form of a verb that is used to form some verb tenses

par·ti·cle /'pɑːtɪkəl $'pɑrtɪkəl/ noun a very small piece of something: *particles of dust*

par·tic·u·lar¹ /pə'tɪkjələ $pə'tɪk-jələ/ adjective **1** used to talk about one thing and not any other: *If a particular food makes you ill, avoid it.* **2** special: *You need to pay particular attention to your spelling.*

particular² noun in particular especially: *I like all subjects, but maths in particular.*

par·tic·u·lar·ly /pə'tɪkjələli $pə-'tɪkjələli/ adverb especially: *Crime is increasing, particularly in the cities.* | *We are particularly concerned about the effect on the young children.*

PHRASE

not particularly spoken not very much: *"Are you hungry?" "Not particularly."*

part·ing /'pɑːtɪŋ $'pɑrtɪŋ/ BrE, **part** AmE, noun the line on your head that you make when you separate your hair with a comb: *She has a centre parting.*

par·ti·tion /pɑː'tɪʃən $pɑr'tɪʃən/ noun a thin wall that separates one part of a room from another: *There's a partition between the two offices.*

the mixture in hot water. Pasta is usually eaten with a SAUCE ⇨ *see picture on page 344*

paste¹ /peɪst/ *noun* thick glue: *wallpaper paste*

paste² *verb* to stick one thing to another using paste: *Cut the pictures out and paste them on the chart.*

pas·tel /'pæstl $ pæ'stel/ *adjective* a pastel colour is pale and light, not dark or bright: *a pastel blue dress*

pas·time /'pɑːstaɪm $ 'pæstaɪm/ *noun* something that you enjoy doing when you are not working: *The game of chess became her favourite pastime.*

past par·ti·ci·ple /ˌ. '..../ *noun* a form of a verb that you use in PERFECT tenses or as an adjective. You usually form it by adding '-ed' to a REGULAR verb

past per·fect /ˌ. '../ *noun* the past perfect the tense of a verb that shows that an action was completed before another event or time in the past. In the sentence 'I had finished my breakfast before Rick phoned', 'had finished' is in the past perfect

pas·try /'peɪstri/ *noun* **1** [no plural] a mixture of flour, fat, and water that you fill with other food and bake **2** plural **pastries** a small sweet cake

pas·ture /'pɑːstʃə $ 'pæstʃɚ/ *noun* land that is covered with grass which cows and sheep can eat

pat /pæt/ *verb* **patted, patting** to touch someone or something lightly with your hand flat in a friendly way: *Don't pat your dogs while they're eating.* –**pat** *noun*: *She gave me a pat on the shoulder.*

patch /pætʃ/ *noun, plural* **patches** **1** a small area of something that looks different from the rest: *a wet patch on the carpet* **2** a piece of material that you use for covering a hole in your clothes: *a pair of jeans with a patch on one knee*

patch·work /'pætʃwɜːk $ 'pætʃwɚk/ *noun* [no plural] when you sew many different coloured pieces of cloth together to make a larger piece of cloth: *a patchwork quilt*

pa·tent·ly /'peɪtntli $ 'pætntli/ *adverb* patently obvious, patently false etc completely obvious, false etc, in a way that anyone can notice: *That's patently untrue!*

pa·ter·ni·ty /pə'tɜːnəti $ pə'tɚnəti/ *noun* [no plural] formal being a father

path /pɑːθ $ pæθ/ *noun, plural* **paths** /pɑːðz, pɑːθs $ pæðz, pæθs/ a track for people to walk along: *A narrow path led down to the stream.* ⇨ *see picture on page 348*

pa·thet·ic /pə'θetɪk/ *adjective* very bad, useless, or weak: *Stop crying – you're being pathetic!* | *That's a pathetic excuse.* –**pathetically** /-kli/ *adverb*

pa·tience /'peɪʃəns/ *noun* [no plural] the ability to stay calm and not get angry when you have to wait for a long time or when someone is behaving badly: *You have to have a lot of patience to be a teacher.* | *I **don't have the patience** to look after young children.*

PHRASE

lose your patience, run out of patience to no longer be patient: *People have been queuing up for hours and are beginning to **lose their patience.** | I'm **running out of patience** with you, Lance.*

pa·tient¹ /'peɪʃənt/ *noun* someone who is getting medical treatment

patient² *adjective* able to stay calm and not get angry when you have to wait for a long time or when someone is behaving badly ⇨ *opposite* IMPATIENT: *My father is a kind and patient man.* | *Please be patient. Mr Smith will be here soon.* –**patiently** *adverb*: *David waited patiently in the corridor.*

pat·i·o /'pætiəʊ $ 'pæti,oʊ/ *noun* an area of a garden next to a house, that has a surface of flat stones ⇨ *see picture on page 343*

pat·ri·ot /'pætriət $ 'peɪtriət/ *noun* someone who is very proud of their country

pat·ri·ot·ic /ˌpætri'ɒtɪk $ ˌpeɪtri'ɑtɪk/ *adjective* very proud of your country: *I'm not very patriotic.*

pat·ri·o·tis·m /'pætriətɪzəm $ 'peɪtriə,tɪzəm/ *noun* [no plural] when someone is very proud of their country

pa·trol¹ /pə'trəʊl $ pə'troʊl/ noun
1 when police or soldiers go regularly around a place in order to protect it: *There were two policemen on patrol in the High Street.* **2** a group of police officers or soldiers who go regularly around an area to protect it: *the California Highway Patrol*

patrol² verb **patrolled, patrolling** BrE, **patroled, patroling** AmE if police or soldiers patrol a place, they go regularly around it in order to protect it: *Soldiers patrol the prison camp every hour.*

pa·trol·man /pə'trəʊlmən $ pə'troʊl-mən/ noun AmE, plural **patrolmen** /-mən/ a police officer who goes regularly around an area in order to protect it

pat·ron·ize also **patronise** BrE /'pætrənaɪz $ 'peɪtrə,naɪz/ verb to speak to someone in a way that shows you think they are less important or intelligent than you

pat·ro·niz·ing also **patronising** BrE /'pætrənaɪzɪŋ $ 'peɪtrə,naɪzɪŋ/ adjective talking to someone in a way that shows you think they are less important or intelligent than you: *I thought his remarks were very patronizing to women.*

pat·ter /'pætə $ 'pætɚ/ verb written to make a light knocking noise: *A child's feet pattered along the hallway.*
–patter noun [no plural]: *the patter of rain on the windows*

pat·tern /'pætn $ 'pætɚn/ noun
GRAMMAR
a pattern of things
1 a design made from shapes or lines that are arranged in a regular way: *The wallpaper has a very modern pattern.* | *a flag with a pattern of stars and stripes*
2 the regular way in which something happens: *Is there any pattern to his bad behaviour?* | *We are studying people's sleeping patterns.*

pat·terned /'pætnd $ 'pætɚnd/ adjective decorated with a pattern: *a patterned skirt*

pause¹ /pɔːz/ verb
GRAMMAR
pause to do something
written to stop doing something for a short time before you start again: *He paused a moment and then added*

"I meant what I said yesterday." | *Sue paused to check her watch.*

pause² noun
GRAMMAR
a pause in something
a short time when you stop doing something: *There was a pause in the conversation, and then it continued again.*

pave /peɪv/ verb to cover a path or road with a surface of flat stones

pave·ment /'peɪvmənt/ noun **1** BrE the path you walk on at the side of a road; SIDEWALK AmE ⇨ see picture on page 343 **2** [no plural] AmE the hard surface of a road

paving stone /'.. ,./ noun a flat piece of stone that you use to make a surface for walking on

paw /pɔː/ noun an animal's foot: *The cat licked its paws.*

pawn /pɔːn/ noun a weak person who is controlled by other people

pay¹ /peɪ/ verb, past tense and past participle **paid** /peɪd/
GRAMMAR
pay for something
pay something for something
pay someone for something
pay someone something
pay someone to do something
pay for doing something
1 to give someone money for something that you are buying from them: *You pay over there.* | *Have you paid for that CD?* | *I paid ten pounds for this book.* | *You haven't paid me for your ticket yet.*
2 to give someone money that you owe them: *I don't have enough money to pay the rent.*
3 to give someone money for doing work for you: *They don't pay me enough in this job.* | *When do you get paid?* | *I will pay you to take my old car away.* | *Waiters aren't very well paid.* | *a highly paid businessman*
4 if you pay for something bad you have done, someone punishes you for it: *You're going to pay for ruining our concert!*

PHRASES
pay attention to listen or watch

pay

pay

carefully: *You must pay more attention in class.*

pay someone a visit, pay a visit to someone to visit a person or place: *Why don't you pay me a visit while you're in Chicago.*

pay someone a compliment to tell someone that you think they are nice, attractive, or intelligent

PHRASAL VERB

pay someone/something back to give someone the money that you borrowed from them: *Can I borrow $10? I'll pay you back tomorrow. | When will you pay back that money you borrowed?*

pay² *noun [no plural]*
money that you get for working ⇨ *same meaning* SALARY: *They are always asking for more pay. | I asked for a pay rise.*

USAGE pay, income, salary, wage
Pay, income, salary, and wage are all words for money that you earn. **Pay** is a general word for money that you get for working: *It's an interesting job and the pay's good.* **Income** is all the money that you get from working and in other ways too: *I increased my income by renting the house to students.* A **salary** is the money a professional person or office worker earns every month or year: *He has a salary of £50,000 a year.* **Wages** are the money that someone who works with their hands earns every hour or week: *The factory workers worked long hours for very low wages.*

pay·a·ble /'peɪəbəl/ *adjective formal*
1 an amount of money that is payable must be paid: *A deposit of £50 is payable when you order the goods.*
2 make a cheque payable to someone to write someone's name on a cheque etc to show that the money must be paid to them: *Please make the cheque payable to Millennium Editions Ltd.*

pay·day /'peɪdeɪ/ *noun [no plural]* the day on which you receive your wages

pay·ment /'peɪmənt/ *noun*
an amount of money that you pay to someone, especially one of several amounts: *You can make payments by cash or credit card. | Your first payment will be £50.*

pay phone /'. ./ *noun* a public telephone that you pay to use

pay·roll /'peɪrəʊl $ 'peɪroʊl/ *noun* **the payroll** a list of the people who work in an organization: *They have over 500 staff on the payroll.*

PC¹ /ˌpiː'siː/ *noun* a computer that you can use in your home

PC² POLITICALLY CORRECT

PE /ˌpiː 'iː/ *noun [no plural]* physical education; sports and exercises that you do as a school subject

pea /piː/ *noun* peas are small round green vegetables ⇨ *see picture on page 345*

peace /piːs/ *noun [no plural]*
1 when there is no war: *When will there be peace in Northern Ireland? | Both sides are at the peace talks.*
2 when everything is very calm and quiet: *I'm going out to get some peace. | If you want peace and quiet, go to your room.*

PHRASES
leave someone in peace to not interrupt someone, and allow them to rest or do something quietly: *Leave your mother in peace – she's tired.*

peace of mind the feeling you have when you are not worried: *Insurance gives you peace of mind when you are on holiday.*

peace·ful /'piːsfəl/ *adjective*
1 calm and quiet: *I just want a peaceful weekend with my family.*
2 not violent: *This is a peaceful protest.*
–peacefully *adverb*: *The children were all sleeping peacefully.*

peace·keep·ing /'piːsˌkiːpɪŋ/ *adjective* **peacekeeping forces, peacekeeping operations etc** soldiers or military activities that are in a place where there is a war, to try to stop the fighting

peace·time /'piːstaɪm/ *noun [no plural]* when a country is not fighting a war

peach /piːtʃ/ *noun, plural* **peaches** a round fruit with soft yellow and red skin and a large seed inside ⇨ *see picture on page 345*

pea·cock /'piːkɒk $ 'piːkɑk/ *noun* a

large male bird with long blue and green tail feathers that it can spread out

peak¹ /piːk/ *noun* **1** the peak of something is the time when it is biggest or most successful: *She is now at the peak of her career.* **2** the pointed top of a mountain

peak² *adjective* peak times are when the largest number of people are travelling somewhere, using something etc: *July and August are the peak holiday periods.*

peak³ *verb written* if something peaks, it reaches its highest or most successful level: *Blondie's singing career peaked in the 1980s.*

pea·nut /ˈpiːnʌt/ *noun* **1** a small nut with a soft light brown shell **2** peanuts *informal* a very small amount of money: *$2 an hour is peanuts!*

peanut but·ter /ˌ.. ˈ.. $ˈ.. ˌ../ *noun* [no plural] a soft food made from crushed peanuts that you spread on bread

pear /peə $per/ *noun* a sweet juicy yellow or green fruit that is round at the bottom and becomes thinner at the top ⇨ *see picture on page 345*

pearl /pɜːl $pɜrl/ *noun* a valuable small white round object that is used in jewellery: *pearl earrings*

pear-shaped /ˈ. ./ *adjective* go pear-shaped *BrE informal* if something you try to do goes pear-shaped, it fails because things do not happen in the way you planned: *Our trip to the beach went pear-shaped when the car broke down.*

peas·ant /ˈpezənt/ *noun* someone who lives in the country and works on the land, used especially about people in a poor country or people who lived a long time ago

peb·ble /ˈpebəl/ *noun* a small smooth stone ⇨ *see picture on page 348*

peck¹ /pek/ *verb* if a bird pecks something, it hits or bites it with its beak: *A bird was pecking at some breadcrumbs.*

peck

peck² *noun* a peck on the cheek a quick light kiss on someone's cheek

pe·cu·li·ar /pɪˈkjuːliə $pɪˈkjuljɚ/ *adjective* strange and surprising: *The car was making a peculiar noise.*

– peculiarly *adverb*: *She's been behaving peculiarly for weeks.*

pe·cu·li·ar·i·ty /pɪˌkjuːliˈærəti/ *noun formal, plural* **peculiarities** an unusual habit that only one person has: *One of her peculiarities is sleeping on the floor.*

ped·al¹ /ˈpedl/ *noun* **1** the part of a bicycle that you push with your foot in order to make it move forward: *I'll have to lower the seat so my feet can reach the pedals.* **2** the part of a car or machine that you press with your foot to control its movements: *the brake pedal*

pedal² *verb* **pedalled, pedalling** *BrE,* **pedaled, pedaling** *AmE* to ride a bicycle by pushing the pedals with your feet: *Pedal harder!*

ped·dle /ˈpedl/ *verb* to sell something, especially something illegal: *He was found guilty of peddling drugs.*

ped·es·tal /ˈpedəstəl/ *noun* a base for something such as a STATUE

pe·des·tri·an /pəˈdestriən/ *noun* someone who is walking in the streets, rather than driving a car or riding a bicycle: *He almost knocked down a pedestrian.*

pedestrian cross·ing /ˌ.... ˈ../ *noun BrE* a place where people who are walking can safely cross a road; CROSSWALK *AmE*

ped·i·gree /ˈpedəgriː/ *noun* an animal's pedigree is its parents and its family

– pedigree *adjective*: *pedigree puppies* (=puppies whose parents are dogs of the same special breed)

pee /piː/ *verb informal* to URINATE

– pee *noun*

peek /piːk/ *verb* to look at something quickly and secretly: *Don't peek – I want this to be a surprise.*

– peek *noun informal*: *I took a peek at my present when he wasn't looking.*

peel¹ /piːl/ *verb* **1** to remove the skin of a fruit or vegetable: *Will you peel the potatoes, please?* ⇨ *see picture on page 344* **2** peel something off to remove something that is stuck to a surface: *Peel the label off carefully.*

peel² *noun* the skin of a fruit or vegetable that you remove before eating it: *orange peel*

peep¹ /piːp/ *verb* to look at something quickly and secretly: *I peeped through the keyhole to see what was happening.*

peep² *noun* **1** a quick or secret look at something: *She took a peep at the answers in the back of the book.* **2** not hear a peep out of someone if you do not hear a peep out of someone, they do not make any noise: *I didn't hear a peep out of the kids all afternoon*

peer /pɪə $ pɪr/ *verb* to look at something very carefully and for a long time, especially because you cannot see it well: *Someone was peering at us through the window.*

peers /pɪəz $ pɪrz/ *plural noun* also **peer group** /'. ./ **1** your peers or your peer group are the people who are the same age as you or who have the same type of job or social position: *Teenagers prefer to spend their time with their peers.* **2** peer (group) pressure the feeling that you should do the same things as other people who are the same age as you: *There is a lot of peer group pressure to wear fashionable clothes.*

peeved /piːvd/ *adjective informal* slightly annoyed: *He'll be peeved if you don't call around and see him.*

pegs

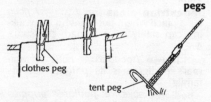

clothes peg

tent peg

peg¹ /peg/ *noun* **1** a piece of wood or metal on a wall that you hang coats on **2** also **clothes peg** *BrE* a small object that you use for fastening wet clothes to a line where they can dry; CLOTHES PIN *AmE*

peg² *verb* **pegged, pegging** to fasten something with pegs: *Peg the clothes on the washing line.*

pe·li·can cross·ing /ˌpelɪkən 'krɒsɪŋ $ ˌpelɪkən 'krɔsɪŋ/ *noun BrE* a place on the road where you can push a button that makes TRAFFIC LIGHTS turn red, so you can cross the road safely ⇨ *see picture on page 343*

pel·let /'pelɪt/ *noun* a small hard ball made from something such as paper or metal: *a gun that fires plastic pellets*

pelt¹ /pelt/ *verb informal* if someone pelts you with things, they attack you by throwing a lot of things at you: *They pelted us with snowballs.*

pelt² *noun* at full pelt *informal* running as fast as you can: *She came running down the road at full pelt.*

pen /pen/ *noun*
a thing you use for writing and drawing in ink: *I need a pen and some paper.*

pe·nal·ize also **penalise** *BrE* /'piːnl-aɪz/ *verb* to punish a player or sports team by giving an advantage to the other team: *The referee penalized our team for wasting time.*

pen·al·ty /'penlti/ *noun, plural* **penalties** **1** a punishment for not obeying a law or rule: *There will be a penalty of £50 for anyone who does not pay their bill.* **2** in SOCCER, an occasion when a player from one team can place the ball directly in front of the other team's GOAL and kick the ball towards the goal. A penalty is taken when the other team has broken the rules

pence /pens/ *abbreviation* **p** *BrE* the plural of PENNY: *Can I borrow 10 pence for the phone?*

pen·cil /'pensəl/ *noun*
a wooden stick with a black or coloured substance inside which you use for writing and drawing: *Can I borrow your pencil? | Sally sharpened her pencil. | First, he drew the picture in pencil* (=using a pencil). ⇨ *see picture at* BLUNT

pen·dant /'pendənt/ *noun* a jewel or small decoration that hangs from a chain around your neck

pen·du·lum /'pen-djələm $ 'pen-dʒələm/ *noun* a long object with a weight at the bottom that moves from side to side inside a large clock

pendulum

pen·e·trate /'penətreɪt/ *verb* to enter something or pass through it: *bullets that can penetrate metal*

pen·e·trat·ing /'penətreɪtɪŋ/ *adjective* a penetrating look, a penetrating stare a look that makes you feel uncomfortable because the other person seems to know what you are thinking

pen friend /'. ./ *BrE noun* a PEN PAL

pen·guin /'peŋgwɪn/ noun a large black and white bird that lives in ANTARCTICA. Penguins cannot fly and use their wings for swimming ⇨ see picture on page 339

pen·i·cil·lin /ˌpenə'sɪlən/ noun [no plural] a medicine that destroys BACTERIA that are in your body and making you ill

pe·nin·su·la /pə'nɪnsjələ $ pə'nɪnsələ/ noun a long thin piece of land that is almost completely surrounded by water but is joined to a larger area of land

pe·nis /'piːnɪs/ noun the male sex organ

pen·i·ten·tia·ry /ˌpenə'tenʃəri/ noun, plural penitentiaries a prison in the US: He was sent to the state penitentiary.

pen·knife /'pen-naɪf/ noun, plural pen-knives /-naɪvz/ a small knife with a blade that you can fold into its handle

pen name /'. ./ noun a name used by a writer instead of their real name

pen·ni·less /'penɪləs/ adjective informal someone who is penniless has no money: I'll be penniless if I keep giving you money.

pen·ny /'peni/ noun, plural pennies or pence abbreviation p 1 a coin worth 1/100 of a pound: I found a penny on the floor. 2 a CENT

pen pal /'. ./ noun someone living in another country who you write friendly letters to, but who you have never met

pen·sion /'penʃən/ noun money that a company or the government pays regularly to someone after they have stopped working because they are old or ill

pen·sion·er /'penʃənə $ 'penʃənɚ/ noun BrE someone who is receiving a pension because they are old and have stopped working

pen·sive /'pensɪv/ adjective formal thinking about something a lot and seeming slightly worried or sad: He sat by the river, looking pensive.

pen·ta·gon /'pentəgən $ 'pentə,gɑn/ noun a flat shape with five straight sides and five angles

peo·ple /'piːpəl/ plural noun men, women, or children. 'People' is the plural of 'person': There are too many people in this room. | I don't like people who smoke.

pep·per /'pepə $ 'pepɚ/ noun 1 [no plural] a hot-tasting powder made from the seeds of a plant: The soup needs a little more salt and pepper 2 a red, yellow, or green vegetable with a sweet or hot taste: chili peppers ⇨ see picture on page 345

per /pɜː $ pɚ/ preposition for each: There will be one book per child. | He charges £20 per lesson.

per·ceive /pə'siːv $ pɚ'siv/ verb formal 1 to understand or think about something in a particular way: They perceive us as being troublemakers. 2 to notice something that is not easy to notice: It is difficult to perceive the difference between the two sounds.

per·cent also **per cent** BrE /pə'sent $ pɚ'sent/ adjective, adverb, noun 5 percent, 10 percent etc used after a number to show how many in every hundred. 'Percent' is often written as %: Thirty percent of people think that taxes should be reduced. | Sales are up 30 percent. | He needs 70% of the vote to win.

per·cen·tage /pə'sentɪdʒ $ pɚ'sentɪdʒ/ noun an amount that is part of a larger amount: A high percentage of teenagers (=a large number of teenagers) play computer games.

per·cep·tion /pə'sepʃən $ pɚ'sepʃən/ noun formal your opinion of what something is like: You have a strange perception of marriage.

per·cep·tive /pə'septɪv $ pɚ'septɪv/ adjective good at noticing and understanding things: She is very perceptive for a young girl.

perch¹ /pɜːtʃ $ pɚtʃ/ noun a branch or stick where a bird sits

perch² verb written to be on the top or edge of something, or to put something there: The hotel was perched high on a cliff. | She perched herself on the stool.

per·cus·sion /pə'kʌʃən $ pɚ'kʌʃən/ noun [no plural] drums and other musical instruments that you hit

per·fect¹ /'pɜːfɪkt $ 'pɚfɪkt/ adjective

GRAMMAR
perfect for something

1 something that is perfect is so good that it could not be any better: She speaks perfect English. | The car is in perfect condition.

perfect

2 exactly right for a particular purpose: *The conditions were **perfect** for sailing.*

the perfect tenses the perfect tenses in English are the PRESENT PERFECT, the PAST PERFECT, and the FUTURE PERFECT

per·fect² /pə'fekt $pɚ'fekt/ *verb* to make something perfect: *I'm always trying to perfect my skills.*

per·fect³ /'pɜːfɪkt $'pɚfɪkt/ *noun* the PRESENT PERFECT, the PAST PERFECT, or the FUTURE PERFECT. In the sentence 'Joe has stolen money', 'has stolen' is in the present perfect.

per·fec·tion /pə'fekʃən $pɚ'fekʃən/ *noun* [no plural] when something is so good that it cannot be any better: *She tries to achieve perfection in her work.*

per·fec·tion·ist /pə'fekʃənəst $pɚ'fekʃənɪst/ *noun* someone who likes to do things so well that they cannot be any better: *Jo is a perfectionist and her work is always beautifully presented.*

per·fect·ly /'pɜːfɪktli $'pɚfɪktli/ *adverb* **1** in a perfect way: *She speaks English perfectly.* **2** used to emphasize what you are saying, especially when you are annoyed: *You know perfectly well what I'm talking about!*

per·fo·rat·ed /'pɜːfəreɪtɪd $'pɚfəˌreɪtɪd/ *adjective* perforated paper has a line of small holes in it so that you can tear part of it off easily

per·form /pə'fɔːm $pɚ'fɔrm/ *verb*
1 to entertain people, for example by being in a play, singing, or dancing: *Many students performed in the school play.* | *I have never performed in public before.*
2 *formal* to do a job or a piece of work: *Surgeons have never performed this operation before.* | *a computer that can perform complicated tasks*
3 if something or someone performs well, they work well. If they perform badly, they work badly: *In tests, the computer **performed** very **well**.* | *She began to **perform badly** at school.*

per·form·ance /pə'fɔːməns $pɚ'fɔrməns/ *noun*

GRAMMAR
a performance of something
1 an event when one person or a group entertains people, for example by acting or singing: *We watched a **performance** of Hamlet.* | *Robbie Williams **gave** a brilliant **performance** at the concert.*
2 how successful someone has been or how well a person or machine does a job: *The company's performance has been very good this year.* | *I'm quite pleased with the car's performance.*

per·form·er /pə'fɔːmə $pɚ'fɔrmɚ/ *noun* someone such as an actor or musician who does things to entertain people: *a circus performer*

per·fume /'pɜːfjuːm $'pɚfjum/ *noun* a liquid with a strong pleasant smell that you put on your skin: *She never wears perfume.*

per·haps /pə'hæps $pɚ'hæps/ *adverb*
1 used when saying what might be true or what might happen: *Perhaps you'll win next time.* | *I can't find Jessica. Perhaps she's upstairs.*
2 used when making a suggestion: *Perhaps we could go to a club.*

per·il /'perəl/ *noun formal* great danger: *Our soldiers are in great peril.*

per·il·ous /'perələs/ *adjective written* very dangerous: *a perilous journey*

pe·ri·od /'pɪəriəd $'pɪriəd/ *noun*
1 an amount of time: *Do not sit at a computer for long periods.* | *She has been at the school for only a short **period of time**.*
2 one of the parts of a school day in which you have a particular class: *We have history last period on Friday.*
3 the American word for a FULL STOP
4 a woman's period is the flow of blood from her body every month

pe·ri·od·ic /ˌpɪəri'ɒdɪk $ˌpɪri'ɑdɪk/ also **pe·ri·od·ic·al** /ˌpɪəri'ɒdɪkəl $ˌpɪri'ɑdɪkəl/ *adjective* regular but not very frequent: *one of her periodic visits to the dentist*

–periodically /-kli/ *adverb*: *The river floods the valley periodically.*

pe·riph·e·ral /pə'rɪfərəl/ *adjective* a peripheral idea or activity is less important than the main one

per·ju·ry /'pɜːdʒəri $ 'pɚdʒəri/ *noun* [no plural] the crime of telling a lie in a law court: *He was found guilty of perjury.*

perk /pɜːk $ pɚk/ *noun* something such as a car or free meals that you get from your work in addition to your pay: *Free travel is one of the perks of the job.*

perm

straight hair

permed hair

perm /pɜːm $ pɚm/ *verb* to put special chemicals on straight hair so that it will have curls: *Debbie's had her hair permed.* ⇨ see picture on page 353
–perm *noun*: *I've decided to have a perm.*

per·ma·nent /'pɜːmənənt $ 'pɚmə-nənt/ *adjective* something that is permanent continues for a long time or for all time ⇨ *opposite* TEMPORARY: *His injury left a permanent scar.* | *Will the job be permanent?*

per·ma·nent·ly /'pɜːmənəntli $ 'pɚ-mənəntli/ *adverb* for all time ⇨ *opposite* TEMPORARILY: *Why don't you come and live with us permanently?*

per·mis·sion /pə'mɪʃən $ pɚ'mɪ-ʃən/ *noun* [no plural]

> **GRAMMAR**
> **permission to do something**
>
> if you have permission to do something, someone allows you to do it: *Do you **have permission to** park your car here?* | *Who **gave** you **permission to** work in this room?* | *Do not use the telephone before **asking** the owner's **permission**.*

per·mit¹ /pə'mɪt $ pɚ'mɪt/ *verb formal* **pemitted, permitting** to allow something to happen: *Smoking is not permitted inside the hospital.* | *The visa permits you to stay for three weeks.* ⇨ see usage note at ALLOW

per·mit² /'pɜːmɪt $ 'pɚmɪt/ *noun* an official document that allows you to do something: *You can't park here without a permit.* | *Do you have a work permit?*

per·pe·trate /'pɜːpətreɪt $ 'pɚpə-ˌtreɪt/ *verb formal* to do something that is wrong: *people who perpetrate crimes*

per·plexed /pə'plekst $ pɚ'plekst/ *adjective formal* very confused: *He looked totally perplexed.*

per·se·cute /'pɜːsɪkjuːt $ 'pɚsɪˌkjut/ *verb* to treat someone cruelly and unfairly: *These people are persecuted because of their beliefs.*

per·se·ver·ance /ˌpɜːsə'vɪərəns $ ˌpɚ-sə'vɪrəns/ *noun* [no plural] when you keep trying to do something difficult because you want to succeed: *She succeeded through hard work and perseverance.*

per·se·vere /ˌpɜːsə'vɪə $ ˌpɚsə'vɪr/ *verb* to keep trying to do something difficult because you want to succeed: *My father wants me to persevere with my studies.*

per·sist /pə'sɪst $ pɚ'sɪst/ *verb formal* to continue to do something or to happen: *Why do you persist in disobeying me?* | *If the rain persists, we'll cancel the game.*

per·sis·tent /pə'sɪstənt $ pɚ'sɪstənt/ *adjective* **1** continuing for a long time: *There have been persistent rumours that he is leaving.* **2** a persistent person keeps trying to do something even when it is annoying for other people: *He's called me four times today – he's very persistent.*

per·son /'pɜːsən $ 'pɚsən/ *noun*, plural **people** /'piːpəl/
a man, woman, or child: *Diana is a very kind person.* | *How many people live in England?*

> **PHRASE**
> **in person** if you do something in person, you go there yourself and do it: *I wanted to come and thank you **in person**.*

per·son·al /'pɜːsənəl $ 'pɚsənəl/ *adjective*
1 your personal things are things that belong to you and no one else: *The students have lockers to keep their **personal belongings** in.* | *Each child has their own personal bank account.*

P

2 your personal experiences or views are your own and are not heard or copied from someone else: *Is this story based on personal experience? | My personal opinion is that it is a bad idea.*
3 involving your health, relationships, or feelings: *The doctor will ask you a lot of personal questions. | Does he have any personal problems?*
4 involving rude criticism: *They kept making personal remarks about my age.*

personal com·pu·ter /ˌ... .ˈ../ a PC

per·son·al·i·ty /ˌpɜːsəˈnæləti $ˌpɚsə-ˈnæləti/ *noun*, *plural* **personalities**
1 the type of person someone is, and the way they behave towards other people: *He's not good-looking but he has a great personality.* **2** a famous person, especially in sport or television: *a TV personality*

per·son·a·lized also **personalised** BrE /ˈpɜːsənəlaɪzd $ˈpɚsənəˌlaɪzd/ *adjective* personalized objects have the name or INITIALS of the owner on them: *a car with personalized number plates*

per·son·al·ly /ˈpɜːsənəli $ˈpɚsənəli/ *adverb* **1** *spoken* used to emphasize that you are only giving your own opinion: *Personally, I don't like war movies.* **2** if you know someone personally, you have met them: *I know who she is, but I don't know her personally* **3** if you do something personally, you do it yourself instead of letting someone else do it: *The teacher thanked us personally.*

personal or·ga·niz·er /ˌ... ˈ.../ personal organizer
noun a small book or a very small computer for recording addresses, times of meetings etc

personal pro·noun /ˌ... ˈ../ *noun* in grammar, a PRONOUN, such as 'I', 'you', and 'they'

personal ster·e·o /ˌ... ˈ.../ *noun* a small machine that plays CASSETTES or CDS. You carry it with you and listen through EARPHONES (=thin wire with a special piece that you put in each ear) ⇨ *see picture on page 342*

per·son·nel /ˌpɜːsəˈnel $ˌpɚsəˈnel/ *plural noun* the people who work in an organization: *military personnel*

per·spec·tive /pəˈspektɪv $pɚˈspektɪv/ *noun* a way of thinking about something: *Foreign travel gives you a whole new perspective on life.*

per·spi·ra·tion /ˌpɜːspəˈreɪʃən $ˌpɚspəˈreɪʃən/ *noun* [no plural] *formal* liquid that comes from your skin when you are very hot ⇨ *same meaning* SWEAT[2]

per·suade /pəˈsweɪd $pɚˈsweɪd/ *verb*

> **GRAMMAR**
> **persuade someone to do something**
> **persuade someone that**

1 to make someone do something by explaining to them why it is a good idea: *I managed to persuade Tom to come to the party.*
2 to make someone believe something: *Can you persuade Sue that this is a good idea?*

per·sua·sion /pəˈsweɪʒən $pɚˈsweɪʒən/ *noun* [no plural] when you persuade someone to do something: *With a little persuasion, I'm sure she'll agree.*

per·sua·sive /pəˈsweɪsɪv $pɚˈsweɪsɪv/ *adjective* good at persuading people to do things: *Salesmen can be very persuasive.*

per·vert /ˈpɜːvɜːt $ˈpɚvɚt/ *noun* someone whose sexual behaviour is unnatural and unacceptable

pes·si·mis·m /ˈpesəmɪzəm/ *noun* [no plural] the belief that bad things will happen ⇨ *opposite* OPTIMISM

pes·si·mist /ˈpesəmɪst/ *noun* someone who always expects that bad things will happen ⇨ *opposite* OPTIMIST: *Don't be such a pessimist – you're sure to pass your exam.*

pes·si·mis·tic /ˌpesəˈmɪstɪk/ *adjective* someone who is pessimistic always expects that bad things will happen ⇨ *opposite* OPTIMISTIC: *I am pessimistic about my chances of winning.*

pest /pest/ *noun* **1** a small animal or insect that destroys crops **2** *informal* an annoying person: *Stop being a pest.*

pes·ter /ˈpestə $ˈpestɚ/ *verb* if you pester someone, you ask them for something so often that they get annoyed: *I'm busy – stop pestering me.*

pes·ti·cide /'pestəsaɪd/ *noun* a chemical substance that you put on plants to kill insects that cause damage to the plants

pet /pet/ *noun* an animal that you keep at home: *Do you have any pets?*

pet·al /'petl/ *noun* one of the coloured parts of a flower: *rose petals*

pet·er /'piːtə $ 'pitɚ/ **peter out** *verb* if something peters out, it gradually becomes smaller or less and finally disappears: *After a few days our food supplies petered out.*

pe·ti·tion /pə'tɪʃən/ *noun* a piece of paper that a lot of people sign, which asks someone in authority to do something: *Will you sign a petition to save the library from closing?*

pet·ri·fied /'petrəfaɪd/ *adjective* very frightened: *I'm petrified of spiders.*

pet·rol /'petrəl/ *noun* [no plural] *BrE* a liquid that you put in a car or other vehicle to make the engine work; GAS *AmE*: *I had to stop to fill the car up with petrol.*

pe·tro·le·um /pə'trəʊliəm $ pə'trouliəm/ *noun* [no plural] oil from under the ground that is used to make petrol and other chemical substances

petrol sta·tion /'.. ,../ *noun BrE* a place where you can buy petrol to put in your car; GAS STATION *AmE*

pet·ti·coat /'petikəʊt $ 'peti,kout/ *noun* a piece of clothing like a thin dress or skirt that a woman wears under a dress or skirt

pet·ty /'peti/ *adjective* **1** petty things are not important: *a petty argument* **2** if someone is petty, they care too much about small unimportant things: *She can be very petty about money.*

pew /pjuː/ *noun* a long wooden seat in a church

pha·raoh /'feərəʊ $ 'ferou/ *noun* a ruler of ancient Egypt

phar·ma·cist /'fɑːməsɪst $ 'fɑrmə-sɪst/ *noun* someone whose job is to prepare drugs and medicines ⇨ *same meaning* CHEMIST *BrE*

phar·ma·cy /'fɑːməsi $ 'fɑrməsi/ *noun* **1** *plural* **pharmacies** a store where you can buy medicine ⇨ *same meaning* CHEMIST *BrE*, DRUGSTORE *AmE* **2** the study of drugs and medicines

phase[1] /feɪz/ *noun* one part of a process: *Phase 1 of the project will start next week.*

phase[2] *verb* **1** **phase something in** to gradually start using something or doing something: *The government is phasing in new smoking laws.* **2** **phase something out** to gradually stop using something or doing something: *The old car design will be phased out over the next few years.*

PhD or **Ph.D.** /,piː eɪtʃ 'diː/ *noun* Doctor of Philosophy; the highest university degree

phe·nom·e·nal /fɪ'nɒmənəl $ fɪ'nɑm-ənl/ *adjective* very unusual and impressive: *This was a phenomenal success for our team.*
– **phenomenally** *adverb*: *a phenominally successful film*

phe·nom·e·non /fɪ'nɒmənən $ fɪ'nɑm-ənən/ *noun, plural* **phenomena** /-nə/ something that happens or exists, especially something unusual: *Earthquakes and hurricanes are natural phenomena.*

phi·los·o·pher /fɪ'lɒsəfə $ fɪ'lɑsəfɚ/ *noun* someone who studies philosophy: *ancient Greek philosophers*

phil·o·soph·i·cal /,fɪlə'sɒfɪkəl $,fɪlə-'sɑfɪkəl/ *adjective* related to philosophy

phi·los·o·phy /fɪ'lɒsəfi $ fɪ'lɑsəfi/ *noun* [no plural] the study of ideas about life and how people should live: *Eastern philosophy*

pho·bi·a /'fəʊbiə $ 'foubiə/ *noun* a strong fear of something: *She had a phobia of spiders.*

phone[1] /fəʊn $ foun/ *noun* a telephone: *A woman **answered the phone**. | I wish someone would **pick up** (=answer) the phone. | I wrote down her **phone number**. | You can contact me **by phone** or email.*

PHRASES
be on the phone to be talking to someone, using a telephone: *Could you be a little quieter – I'm **on the phone**.*
put the phone down on someone *BrE* to end a telephone conversation immediately because you are angry with the person you are talking to: *When I mentioned the money she **put the phone down on** me.*

phone² also **phone up** verb

to speak to someone, using a telephone ⇨ *same meaning* TELEPHONE²: *Steve phoned me seven times last week.* | *You can* **phone up** *and book tickets.*

> **USAGE phone, ring, call, telephone**
> **Phone**, **ring**, **call**, and **telephone** all mean 'to use the telephone to speak to someone'. **Phone** and **ring** are the most usual words in British English, and **call** is the most usual word in American English. **Telephone** is only used in fairly formal situations.

phone booth also **phone box** BrE /'. ../ noun a small covered area containing a public telephone ⇨ *see picture on page 343*

phone-in /'. ../ noun a radio or television programme in which people telephone the presenter to give their opinions or ask questions: *Call our phone-in now and give us your views.*

pho·ney BrE, **phony** AmE /'fəʊni $ 'foʊni/ adjective informal false and not real ⇨ *same meaning* FAKE²: *a phoney American accent*

pho·to /'fəʊtəʊ $ 'foʊtoʊ/ noun informal, plural **photos** a PHOTOGRAPH: *I took some photos of the wedding.*

pho·to·cop·i·er /'fəʊtəʊ͵kɒpiə $ 'foʊtə͵kɑpiə/ noun a machine that makes copies of documents; COPIER AmE

pho·to·cop·y¹ /'fəʊtəʊ͵kɒpi $ 'foʊtə͵kɑpi/ noun, plural **photocopies** a copy of a document that you make using a photocopier: *Send a photocopy of your certificate to the college.*

photocopy² verb photocopied, photocopies to make a copy of a document using a photocopier: *Could you photocopy this article, please?*

pho·to·graph¹ /'fəʊtəɡrɑːf $ 'foʊtə͵ɡræf/ also **photo** informal noun a picture that you make using a camera: *I took a photograph of the beach.*

photograph² verb to make a picture of someone or something using a camera: *Jill hates being photographed.*
– **photographer** noun: *a fashion photographer*

pho·to·graph·ic /͵fəʊtəˈɡræfɪk $ ͵foʊtəˈɡræfɪk/ adjective connected with photographs and photography: *expensive photographic equipment*

pho·tog·ra·phy /fəˈtɒɡrəfi $ fəˈtɑɡrəfi/ noun [no plural] taking photographs: *He developed an interest in photography.*

phras·al verb /͵.. ˈ./ noun a verb that is used with an adverb or preposition, which has a different meaning from the verb used alone. 'Set off' and 'put up with' are examples of phrasal verbs

phrase /freɪz/ noun a group of words without a main verb: *He always starts the class with the phrase "Good morning!"*

phys·i·cal¹ /'fɪzɪkəl/ adjective

1 related to someone's body, not their mind: *Do you do much physical exercise?* | *Their child has a physical disability.*
2 physical things are objects that you can touch and see: *We need some physical evidence to prove our case.*
– **physically** adverb: *He was physically attractive.*

physical² the American word for MEDICAL²

phys·ics /'fɪzɪks/ noun [no plural] the study of things that happen naturally in the world, such as heat, light, and movement

physiotherapist

phys·i·o·ther·a·pist /͵fɪziəʊˈθerəpɪst $ ͵fɪzioʊˈθerəpɪst/ noun someone whose job is doing physiotherapy

phys·i·o·ther·a·py /͵fɪziəʊˈθerəpi $ ͵fɪzioʊˈθerəpi/ noun [no plural] medical treatment, especially exercises, for people who cannot move a part of their body

phy·sique /fəˈziːk/ noun the shape and size of your body: *a tall man with a powerful physique* (=a strong body with big muscles)

pi·a·nist /'piːənɪst $ piˈænɪst/ noun someone who plays the piano

pi·an·o /pɪ'ænəʊ $ pɪ'ænoʊ/ *noun* a large musical instrument that you play by pressing small black and white bars

piano

pick¹ /pɪk/ *verb*

1 to choose some thing or someone: *Pick which jumper you want to wear.* | *I picked Sara to be my partner.*
2 to take a flower or fruit from a plant: *Let's go to the farm and pick strawberries.*
3 to pull small pieces from something: *He was picking food from his teeth.*

PHRASE

pick a fight, pick an argument to behave in an unpleasant way towards someone so that they will fight you or argue with you: *It is always the older children who pick fights.*

PHRASAL VERBS

pick on
pick on someone to keep criticizing or upsetting someone unfairly: *Why do you always pick on me?*

pick up
1 **pick something/someone up** to lift something or someone: *I picked up a stick that was lying on the path.* | *You are too heavy for me to pick you up.* ⇨ see picture on page 340
2 **pick someone/something up** to collect someone or something: *Could you pick up my clothes from the cleaner's.* | *Can you pick me up from school today?*
3 **pick something up** *informal* to learn something by watching or listening to other people: *She picked up a bit of German from her Swiss cousins.*
4 **pick someone up** *informal* to talk to someone and try to start a sexual relationship with them

pick² *noun* something that you choose: *What would you like to drink? Take your pick.*

pick·axe *BrE*, **pickax** *AmE* /'pɪk-æks/ *noun* a large metal tool with a long handle, used to break up hard ground

pick·et /'pɪkɪt/ also**picket line** /'.. ../ *noun* a group of people who stand in front of a factory or other building to protest about something or to stop people from going in during a STRIKE: *They've been on the picket line for two months.*
– **picket** *verb*: *About 200 people picketed outside the courthouse.*

pick·le /'pɪkəl/ *noun* 1 *BrE* a cold SAUCE made with vegetables that have been preserved in VINEGAR or salt 2 *AmE* a CUCUMBER preserved in VINEGAR and salt or sugar: *Could I have pickles on my hamburger?*

pick·pock·et /'pɪk-ˌpɒkɪt $ 'pɪkˌpɑ-kɪt/ *noun* someone who steals from people's pockets in public places

pickpocket

pick·y /'pɪki/ *adjective informal* **pickier, pickiest** a picky person only likes a few things and is difficult to please ⇨ *same meaning* FUSSY: *Jeremy's a very picky eater.*

pic·nic /'pɪknɪk/ *noun* a meal that you eat outside, away from home: *Let's have a picnic on the beach.*

pic·ture¹ /'pɪktʃə $ 'pɪktʃɚ/ *noun*

GRAMMAR
a picture of something/someone

1 a painting, drawing, or photograph: *That's a nice picture of Oscar.* | *I drew a picture of a vase of flowers.* ⇨ see picture on page 342
2 **the pictures** *BrE* the cinema: *Do you want to go to the pictures on Saturday?*

PHRASE
take a picture of someone/something, take someone's picture to take a photograph of someone or something: *Will you take a picture of us?*

pic·ture² *verb written* 1 to imagine something: *I pictured myself swimming in the warm ocean.* 2 to show someone or something in a photograph in a newspaper: *Mr. Parker, pictured above, plays the part of a doctor in the play.*

pic·tur·esque /ˌpɪktʃəˈresk/ *adjective* a picturesque place is very attractive: *the picturesque villages of southern Spain*

pie /paɪ/ *noun* a food made with fruit, meat, or vegetables baked inside PASTRY: *apple pie*

piece /piːs/ *noun*

> **GRAMMAR**
> **a piece of something**

1 a part of something that has been separated or broken off from the rest of it: *a **piece of** cheese | I need a new **piece of** paper. | The broken glass lay **in pieces** on the floor. | It had been smashed **to pieces**.*

2 a piece of music, poetry etc is a song, poem etc that someone has written or produced: *What is your favourite **piece of music**? | Choose your three best pieces of work.*

3 a piece of furniture, clothing, equipment etc is an object of that kind: *The table in the dining room is my favourite **piece of furniture**.*

> **PHRASES**

a piece of advice, a piece of evidence etc some advice, evidence etc: *The most important piece of advice of all is to trust your own instincts.*

a piece of land a small area of land: *We want to buy a piece of land and build a house.*

pier /pɪə $ pɪr/ *noun* a structure that is built out into the sea so that people can walk along it ⇨ *see picture on page 348*

pierce /pɪəs $ pɪrs/ *verb* to make a hole in something, using a sharp object: *The blade of the knife pierced his arm. | pierced ears*

pierc·ing /ˈpɪəsɪŋ $ ˈpɪrsɪŋ/ *adjective* a piercing sound is high, loud, and unpleasant: *a piercing scream*

pig /pɪg/ *noun* a farm animal with short legs, a fat usually pink body, and a curled tail

pi·geon /ˈpɪdʒən/ *noun* a grey bird that is common in cities

pig·head·ed /ˌpɪgˈhedɪd/ *adjective informal* a pigheaded person refuses to change their opinion about something, even when they are wrong: *I've never met a woman so obstinate and pigheaded.*

pig·let /ˈpɪglət/ *noun* a young pig

pig·sty /ˈpɪgstaɪ/ also **pig·pen** /ˈpɪgpen/ *AmE, noun* a place where pigs are kept

pig·tail /ˈpɪgteɪl/ *noun* hair that has been twisted together and tied ⇨ *same meaning* BRAID: *a fat child with hair in pigtails*

pile¹ /paɪl/ *noun*

> **GRAMMAR**
> **a pile of something**

a lot of similar things put one on top of the other: *There was **a huge pile of** dirty washing. | Put those books **in a pile** on my desk.*

pile² *verb* to put things together in a pile, or to be in a pile: *Clothes were piled up on Lilly's bed. | My plate was piled with food.*

pile-up /ˈ. ./ *noun informal* a road accident involving several vehicles: *a 16-car pile-up*

pil·grim /ˈpɪlgrəm/ *noun* someone who travels to a holy place for religious reasons

pil·grim·age /ˈpɪlgrəmɪdʒ/ *noun* a trip to a holy place for religious reasons

pill /pɪl/ *noun* 1 a small solid piece of medicine that you swallow ⇨ *same meaning* TABLET 2 **the Pill** a pill that women can take to stop them becoming PREGNANT

pil·lar /ˈpɪlə $ ˈpɪlər/ *noun* a tall solid piece of stone, wood, or metal used to support part of a building

pil·low /ˈpɪləʊ $ ˈpɪloʊ/ *noun* the soft object you put under your head when you sleep

pi·lot /ˈpaɪlət/ *noun* someone who flies a plane

pillar

pin¹ /pɪn/ noun

a short thin piece of metal with a sharp point, used especially for holding pieces of cloth together

pin² verb pinned, pinning **1** to fasten something or join things together with a pin: *Karen pinned a flower to her hat.* **2** to press someone against something, stopping them from moving: *He grabbed me and pinned my arms behind my back.*

pinch¹ /pɪntʃ/ verb

1 to press a part of someone's skin tightly between your finger and thumb: *I pinched his arm.* ⇨ *see picture on page 341*
2 BrE informal to steal something that is not valuable: *Who's pinched my pencil?*

pinch² noun **1** an act of pressing someone's flesh between your finger and thumb **2** a very small amount: *Add a pinch of salt to the sauce.* ⇨ *see picture on page 344* **3** **at a pinch** BrE, **in a pinch** AmE, spoken informal only with difficulty or only if it really necessary: *At a pinch, I could fit six people in the car.*

pine¹ /paɪn/ noun a tall tree with very thin leaves, or the wood from this tree: *a pine table*

pine² also **pine away** verb to become ill because you are sad or lonely: *I found myself pining for home.*

pine·ap·ple /'paɪnæpəl/ noun a large tropical fruit with pointed leaves and sweet yellow flesh ⇨ *see picture on page 345*

pink /pɪŋk/ adjective, noun pale red

pins and nee·dles /ˌ. '.. / plural noun the sharp slightly uncomfortable pain you get in your arms or legs after you have been sitting in an awkward position: *I woke up with pins and needles in my foot.*

pint /paɪnt/ noun a unit for measuring liquid, equal to 0.473 litres in the US or 0.568 litres in Britain

pin·up /'pɪnʌp/ noun a large picture of someone famous or attractive that is put up on a wall

pi·o·neer /ˌpaɪə'nɪə $ ˌpaɪə'nɪr/ noun one of the first people to do something that other people then develop: *the pioneers of interactive video*

– **pioneer** verb: *the company that pioneered genetic fingerprinting*

pi·ous /'paɪəs/ adjective a pious person has strong religious beliefs: *He grew up to be a quiet, pious man.*

pip /pɪp/ noun BrE a small seed of a fruit such as an apple or orange

pipe¹ /paɪp/ noun

1 a tube that liquid or gas flows through: *There is something blocking the water pipe.*
2 an object shaped like a tube with a round container on the end which is used for smoking tobacco: *My father smokes a pipe.*

pipe² verb to send a liquid or gas through a pipe to another place: *Our water is piped from the Colorado River.*

pipe·line /'paɪp-laɪn/ noun **1** pipes used for carrying a liquid or gas over long distances **2** **be in the pipeline** informal if something is in the pipeline, it will happen soon: *The band's third album is in the pipeline.*

pi·ping /'paɪpɪŋ/ adjective **piping hot** very hot: *piping hot soup*

pi·rate¹ /'paɪərət $ 'paɪrət/ noun **1** someone who illegally copies a VIDEO, book, computer game etc and sells it: *video pirates* **2** someone who attacks other boats and steals things from them

pirate² verb to illegally copy a video, book, computer game etc in order to sell it

pis·tol /'pɪstl/ noun a small gun

pit /pɪt/ noun **1** a coal mine **2** a deep hole in the ground **3** **be the pits** spoken informal to be very bad: *Isn't work the pits?* **4** AmE the large hard seed in some fruits: *a cherry pit*

pitch¹ /pɪtʃ/ verb **1** to throw the ball to the BATTER in a game of BASEBALL: *Who's pitching in tonight's game?* **2** to present something so that it is suitable for a particular group of people: *Compaq are pitching their new PC at the teenage market.*

pitch² noun, plural pitches **1** BrE an area of ground used for playing a sport: *a football pitch* **2** the pitch of a sound is how high or low it is: *Jean's voice rose to a higher pitch.* **3** a throw of the ball in a game of BASEBALL

pitch black also **pitch dark** /ˌ. '. /

pitcher

adjective completely black or dark: *It's pitch dark outside.*

pitch·er /'pɪtʃə $ 'pɪtʃɚ/ *noun* **1** a container used for pouring liquids: *a pitcher of beer* **2** the BASEBALL player who throws the ball to the BATTER

pit·i·ful /'pɪtɪfəl/ *adjective* making you feel very sorry for someone: *the pitiful sight of homeless children*

pit·y¹ /'pɪti/ *noun*

GRAMMAR
pity for someone
sadness that you feel for someone who is suffering or sad: *I felt a lot of* **pity for** *the dead man's family.*

PHRASES
it's a pity (that), that's a pity used when you are disappointed about a situation and wish it was different: *It's a pity that we don't live nearer to each other.* | *"I'll have to miss your party." "That's a pity."*
out of pity *spoken* if you do something out of pity, you do it because you feel sorry for someone: *I don't want you to stay with me* **out of pity**.
take pity on someone, have pity on someone to try to help someone who is suffering or in trouble because you feel sorry for them: *James* **had pity on** *the beggar and gave him $10.*

pity² *verb* **pitied, pities** to feel sympathy for someone who is suffering or in a bad situation: *These poor children should be pitied.*

piv·ot /'pɪvət/ *noun* a central point that something balances or turns on

pix·el /'pɪksəl/ *noun* the smallest unit of an image on a computer screen

pix·ie /'pɪksi/ *noun* a small imaginary person who has magic powers

piz·za /'piːtsə/ *noun* a thin flat round bread, baked with cheese, meat, vegetables etc on top

plac·ard /'plækɑːd $ 'plækɚd/ *noun* a large sign that is carried by a person: *Protestors were carrying placards.*

place¹ ⇨ see box on next page

place² /pleɪs/ *verb* to put something carefully somewhere ⇨ *same meaning* PUT: *Kevin placed his books on the shelf.*

plac·id /'plæsɪd/ *adjective* calm and peaceful: *He is a very placid baby.* | *the placid waters of the lake*

– **placidly** *adverb*: *She smiled placidly.*

pla·gia·ris·m /'pleɪdʒərɪzəm/ *noun* when someone uses another person's words or ideas in their writing and pretends that they are their own: *Ms. Burns suspected Carol of plagiarism.*

plague /pleɪg/ *noun* a disease that spreads quickly, killing a lot of people

plaice /pleɪs/ *noun* a flat sea fish that people eat

plaid /plæd/ the American word for TARTAN

plain¹ /pleɪn/ *adjective*

1 all one colour, with no pattern or design: *Do you have any plain white envelopes?*
2 without a lot of decoration; simple: *Mark likes good plain cooking.* | *Their house is neat and plain.*
3 easy to see or understand ⇨ *same meaning* CLEAR¹ (1): *The facts were plain.* | *She* **made** *her feelings* **plain** (=she told everyone how she felt).
4 a plain woman is not very attractive

plain² *noun* a large area of flat land: *the plains of North America.*

plain·ly /'pleɪnli/ *adverb* **1** easily seen or recognized: *He's plainly unhappy.* **2** simply or without decoration: *a plainly dressed young girl*

plait /plæt/ *verb* BrE to twist three long pieces of hair, rope etc together to make one long piece; BRAID AmE: *I combed and plaited my hair.*
– **plait** *noun*

plan¹ /plæn/ *noun*

GRAMMAR
a plan to do something
a plan for something
an idea or arrangement for doing something in the future: *Their* **plan** *is* **to** *travel around Europe by train.* | *Do you* **have** *any* **plans for** *your future?*

PHRASE
make plans to arrange to do something: *I can't come on Saturday night – I've already made plans.*

plan² *verb* **planned, planning**

GRAMMAR
plan what/who/when etc
plan to do something
plan on doing something
1 to think about something you want

P

1 **area, building, town, shop, restaurant etc**
*I like this **place** a lot – they have really good food. | There's a **place** in town where they sell bikes. | We go back to the same **place** for a holiday every year. | Everyone had to find a **place** to sleep on the floor. | It's a great **place for** the kids to play.*

> **GRAMMAR**
> place to do something
> place for something

5 **team, course, university** *BrE*
if you have a place on a team or course, you are able to be a part of that team or course: *She got a **place on** the swimming team. | He has applied for a **place at** the university. | There are no **places** left at the school.*

place

2 **where something is or where you put it**
*Keep your passport in a safe **place**. | Is this a good **place** to put the TV? | Please sign the form in these two **places**.*

3 **where you are sitting or standing**
*When I got back, someone had taken my **place**. | Save me a **place** next to you, okay? | Please stay in your **places** while I call your names.*

4 **where someone lives** *informal*
*I'm going over to Bill's **place** later. | You've got a nice **place** here.*

PHRASES

take place
to happen, especially after being planned to happen: *The wedding **took place** outside, in the gardens of the hotel. | A lot of changes had **taken place** since I had last visited Paris.*

in the first place *spoken*
say this when talking about what was done or should have been done at the beginning of a situation: *If you'd done it right **in the first place**, we wouldn't have to do it again.*

first place, second place etc
the person who finishes a race, competition etc in first place is the winner; the person who finishes in second place finishes next etc: *Daniel Wallace won **third place**. | Last year, the team finished **in second place**.*

all over the place *informal*
if things or people are all over the place, there are a lot of them in many different parts of an area: *There were cans and bottles **all over the place**.*

take someone's place, take something's place
to do something instead of someone or something else: *When George left, Lucy **took** his **place** as team captain.*

to do, and how you will do it: *Kathy is already planning her wedding.* | *Have you **planned what** you're going to do at the weekend?* | *I've **planned where** we will go to eat.*

2 to intend to do something: *She **plans to** get a part-time job.* | *Julia **plans on** being a lawyer.* | *I didn't **plan on** telling you that.*

plane /pleɪn/ *noun* a vehicle that flies ⇨ *same meaning* AEROPLANE *BrE*, AIRPLANE *AmE*

plan·et /'plænət/ *noun* **1** a large round object in space that moves around a star: *Mercury is the smallest planet in our solar system.* **2** the planet the world: *the environmental future of the planet*

plank /plæŋk/ *noun* a long flat piece of wood

plant¹ /plɑːnt $ plænt/ *noun*

1 a living thing that has leaves and roots and is usually smaller than a tree: *She likes to have lots of plants in the house.*
2 a factory and all its equipment: *a nuclear plant*

plant² *verb* **1** to put plants or seeds in the ground to grow: *We planted an apple tree in the yard.* **2** to hide something, especially a bomb, somewhere: *Terrorists planted a bomb in the city centre.*

plan·ta·tion /plæn'teɪʃən/ *noun* a large farm, especially in a hot country, where a single crop is grown: *a tobacco plantation*

plas·ter¹ /'plɑːstə $ 'plæstɚ/ *noun*
1 [no plural] a smooth substance used for covering walls and ceilings **2** *BrE* a piece of sticky material used to cover small wounds; BAND-AID *AmE* **3** be in plaster *BrE* if someone's leg, arm etc is in plaster, it is covered with a hard white substance to protect a broken bone: *Greg returned from his skiing holiday with his leg in plaster.*

plas·ter² *verb informal* to spread or stick something all over a surface: *Her bedroom was plastered with posters.*

plaster cast /ˌ.. './ *noun* a hard cover made from a special type of plaster, used to protect a broken bone

plas·tic¹ /'plæstɪk/ *noun* a light material made from chemicals, which is used for making many different objects: *garden furniture made of plastic*

plastic² *adjective* made of plastic: *a plastic cup*

plastic sur·ge·ry /ˌ.. '.../ *noun* [no plural] medical operations to improve the way someone looks: *She needed plastic surgery after she was badly burnt in a fire.*

plate /pleɪt/ *noun*

GRAMMAR
a plate of something

1 a flat dish that you use for eating or serving food
2 also **plateful** the amount of food that a plate will hold: *Lunch was a plate of sandwiches.*

plat·form /'plætfɔːm $ 'plætfɔrm/ *noun*

1 the part of a station where you get on and off trains: *The train for Brighton leaves from Platform 4.* | *I was standing on platform eleven at London's Liverpool Street station.* ⇨ *see picture on page 349*
2 a raised structure for people to stand or work on: *The teacher stood on a platform at the front of the classroom.*

plat·i·num /'plætənəm/ *noun* [no plural] an expensive white metal, used for making jewellery

pla·ton·ic /plə'tɒnɪk $ plə'tɑnɪk/ *adjective* if you have a platonic relationship with someone, it is friendly but not sexual: *Their friendship was purely platonic.*

plau·si·ble /'plɔːzəbəl/ *adjective* likely to be true ⇨ *opposite* IMPLAUSIBLE: *That's not a plausible excuse for being late.*

play¹ /pleɪ/ *verb*

GRAMMAR
play (against) something/some-one
play with something/someone
play for something/someone

1 to take part in a sport or game: *Do you know how to play tennis?* | *The boys were playing computer games.* | *England **played against** France in the final.* | *The USA will* *play Norway.* | *He* **plays for** *the Chicago Bulls* (=he is on their team).

2 if you play a musical instrument, you use it to produce music: *I'm learning to play the piano.* | *He played me a tune on his guitar.*

USAGE
Always use 'the' after the verb **play** and before the names of musical instruments: *Anna plays the piano, and Sam plays the trumpet.* Never use 'the' after the verb **play** and before the name of a particular sport: *In the winter I play football, and in the summer I play tennis.*

3 if children play, they have fun doing things with toys or with their friends: *Henry loves* **playing with** *his toy cars.* | *When you've finished your lunch, you can go and play.*

4 if you play a record, radio etc, or it plays, it produces music or sounds: *The DJ played some great records.* | *My favourite song was playing on the radio.*

5 to take part in a film, programme, or play as one of the characters in it: *Brad Pitt played the hero in the film.*

PHRASES
play a part, play a role if something plays a part or role in something, it is one of several causes that makes it happen: *Alcohol* **played a part in** *the accident.*

play a trick, play a joke to do something to surprise or trick someone: *They* **played** *a stupid* **trick on** *me.*

PHRASAL VERBS
play around
1 to do silly things when you should be serious: *Stop* **playing around** *there at the back!*
2 play around with something to try different ways of doing something: *You can* **play around with** *the picture on the computer screen.*

play at
play at something   a) to not do something seriously or properly: *They're just* **playing at** *running a business.*   **b)** *BrE* to pretend to be something as part of a game: *The kids are* **playing at** *soldiers.*

play back
play something back to play a TAPE or VIDEO so that you can hear or see something again: *When they played*

back *the goal again, you could see it was offside.*

play down
play something down to try to make something seem less important than it really is: *He tried to* **play down** *the fact that there had been a fight.*

play up *BrE informal*
if children play up, they behave badly; ACT UP *AmE*

play² *noun*

1 a story that is written to be performed by actors: *'Hamlet' is a play by Shakespeare.* | *My class at school is going to* **put on a play** (=perform a play).
2 the activity of doing things you enjoy for fun, especially when you are a child: *We all need time for work and play.*

play·er /'pleɪə $ 'pleɪər/ *noun*   **1** someone who plays a game or sport: *one of the top tennis players*   **2** someone who plays a musical instrument: *a horn player*

play·ful /'pleɪfəl/ *adjective* very active and happy: *a playful little kitten*

play·ground /'pleɪɡraʊnd/ *noun* an outdoor area connected to a school where children play

play·group /'pleɪɡruːp/ *noun BrE* a place where children can go to play and learn in the years before they go to school

play·ing field /'.. ,./ *noun* an area used for playing sports

play·time /'pleɪtaɪm/ *noun* the time when children at school can play

play·wright /'pleɪraɪt/ *noun* someone who writes plays

plea /pliː/ *noun*   **1** an urgent request for something: *Neighbours ignored her desperate pleas for help.*   **2** *formal* in a law court, the answer someone gives when they are asked whether they are guilty or not guilty of a crime: *a plea of not guilty*

plead /pliːd/ *verb, past tense and past participle* **pleaded** or **pled** /pled/   **1** to ask for something in a very strong way, with a lot of emotion ⇨ *same meaning* BEG (1): *Sarah pleaded with him to stay.*
2 *formal* to say officially in a law court whether or not you are guilty of a crime: *"How do you plead?" "Not guilty."*

pleas·ant /'plezənt/ adjective
1 enjoyable or nice ⇨ opposite UN-PLEASANT: *The village is a pleasant place to live.* | *The weather in June is very pleasant.*
2 polite and friendly ⇨ opposite UN-PLEASANT: *Our boss is always very pleasant to us.*
– **pleasantly** adverb: *I was pleasantly surprised to see Max.*

please¹ /pliːz/
used when you are politely asking for something: *Please don't be late.* | *Can I have a drink of water, please?*

PHRASE
yes, please spoken used to politely say that you want something that someone offers you: *"Another cookie?" "Yes, please!"*

please² verb
to make someone feel happy or satisfied: *She tries hard to please her parents.*

PHRASE
whatever you please, as you please, as she pleases etc used to say that someone can do anything they want: *When you've finished your work, you can do whatever you please.* | *Women should be able to dress as they please.*

pleased /pliːzd/ adjective

GRAMMAR
pleased with someone/something
pleased to do something
pleased (that)
happy or satisfied: *Mom was pleased with me for cleaning my room.* | *I'm really pleased with my new haircut.* | *I'm so pleased to hear that you're coming.* | *Are you pleased that Joe got the job?*

PHRASE
(I'm) pleased to meet you spoken something that you say to be polite when you meet someone for the first time ⇨ see usage note at GLAD

plea·sur·a·ble /'pleʒərəbəl/ adjective formal enjoyable: *Preparing a meal should be a pleasurable experience.*

plea·sure /'pleʒə $'pleʒɚ/ noun
[no plural]
a feeling of happiness, satisfaction, or enjoyment that something gives you: *Seeing her grandchildren gives her a lot of pleasure.* | *He draws and paints for pleasure.*

PHRASE
it's a pleasure, it's my pleasure spoken used to reply politely to someone who has thanked you: *"Thanks for your help." "It's a pleasure."*

pleat /pliːt/ noun a narrow flat fold in a piece of clothing
pleat·ed /'pliːtɪd/ adjective a pleated skirt, dress etc has lots of pleats
pled a past tense and past participle of PLEAD
pledge /pledʒ/ verb formal to make a formal promise to do something: *The mayor is pledging to reduce crime.* | *Different nations pledged $1 billion to help the eathquake victims.*
plen·ti·ful /'plentɪfəl/ adjective if something is plentiful, there is a large amount of it: *plentiful supplies of fresh water*
– **plentifully** adverb: *The bar was plentifully stocked with wine.*

plen·ty¹ /'plenti/ noun [no plural]
quite a lot or more than enough: *We've got plenty of time left.* | *She has plenty of confidence.* | *You'll have plenty to talk about.* | *They've got plenty more work to keep them busy.*

plenty² adverb
plenty more spoken informal a lot more, so that there is enough or more than enough: *There's plenty more pizza if anyone's still hungry.*

pli·ers /'plaɪəz $'plaɪɚz/ plural noun a tool for cutting wire or pulling nails out of wood: *a pair of pliers*
plight /plaɪt/ noun when someone is in a difficult or dangerous situation: *the plight of homeless young people*
plod /plɒd $plɑd/ verb plodded, plodding to move or do something slowly, because you are tired or bored: *Neil plodded through the snow.*
plot¹ /plɒt $plɑt/ noun 1 a secret

plan to do something bad: *a plot to kill the king* **2** the main events in a book, film, or play: *The plot is difficult to follow.*

plot² *verb* **plotted, plotting** to plan secretly to do something bad: *The three men had plotted to rob a bank.*

plough¹ *BrE,* **plow** *AmE* /plaʊ/ *noun* a large machine that is used on farms to turn over the soil before crops are planted

plough² *BrE,* **plow** *AmE, verb* **1** to turn over the soil with a plough so that seeds can be planted: *They ploughed the field near the river this morning.* **2** to hit something with a lot of force: *The plane ploughed into electricity lines.* **3 plough on** to continue doing something, even though it is difficult: *We were tired but ploughed on anyway.*

ploy /plɔɪ/ *noun* a dishonest but clever way of getting what you want: *He's not really ill – it's just a ploy to avoid going to school.*

pluck /plʌk/ *verb* **1** *written* to pull something quickly to remove it from its place: *She plucked a rose from her garden.* **2 pluck up the courage** to decide to do something difficult or unpleasant, which you were not brave enough to do before: *I finally plucked up the courage to audition for the play.*

plugs

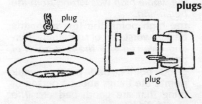

plug

plug

plug¹ /plʌg/ *noun* **1** the thing that you use to connect a piece of electrical equipment to the electricity supply **2** a round flat piece of rubber used for blocking the hole in a bath or SINK

plug² *verb* **plugged, plugging 1** also **plug up** to fill or block a hole: *I managed to plug most of the leaks round the bath.* **2 plug something in, plug something into something** to connect a piece of equipment to the electricity supply, or to another piece of equipment ⇨ *opposite* UNPLUG: *Plug the modem into the back of the PC.*

plug·hole /'plʌghəʊl $'plʌghoʊl/ *noun BrE* a hole in a bath or SINK, where the water can flow out; DRAIN *AmE*

plum /plʌm/ *noun* a soft round fruit, which is purple, red, or yellow, and has a large seed in the middle ⇨ *see picture on page 345*

plumb·er /'plʌmə $'plʌmɚ/ *noun* someone whose job is to repair water pipes, toilets etc

plumb·ing /'plʌmɪŋ/ *noun [no plural]* the system of water pipes in a building

plume /pluːm/ *noun* **1** a small cloud of smoke or dust that is moving upwards: *a plume of smoke* **2** a large feather: *ostrich plumes*

plump /plʌmp/ *adjective* slightly fat: *Dora's not fat – she's just a little plump.* ⇨ *see usage note at* FAT¹

plun·der /'plʌndə $'plʌndɚ/ *verb written* to steal or take large amounts of money or things from somewhere: *Foreign armies plundered and burned the city.*

plunge¹ /plʌndʒ/ *verb* to fall or move quickly down with a lot of force, especially into water: *The workman plunged 200 feet from the bridge.*

plunge² *noun* when something suddenly becomes much lower in value: *a plunge in the price of shares in some companies*

plu·per·fect /pluː'pɜːfɪkt $,pluː'pɚfɪkt/ *noun* **the pluperfect** the PAST PERFECT

plu·ral /'plʊərəl $'plʊrəl/ *noun* the form of a word that shows you are talking about more than one person, thing, etc, which is usually formed by adding 's'. For example, 'dogs' is the plural of 'dog', and 'children' is the plural of 'child'

plus¹ /plʌs/ *preposition* used when one number or amount is added to another. In calculations, plus is written as +: *Three plus six equals nine. (3 + 6 = 9)*

plus² *adjective* **1** more than a particular number or amount: *Donna makes £30,000 a year plus.* **2 plus or minus** used to say how much an amount can vary: *The margin of error is plus or minus 5%.*

plus³ *noun* something that is an advantage, or a quality that you think is good: *Politeness is always a plus when you first meet someone.*

plu·to·ni·um /pluː'təʊniəm $pluː'toʊniəm/ *noun [no plural]* a metal used for producing NUCLEAR power

P

ply·wood /ˈplaɪwʊd/ *noun* [no plural] a board made from several layers of thin wood

pm or **p.m.** /ˌpiː ˈem/ **2 pm, 11 pm** etc 2 or 11 o'clock in the afternoon or evening, not in the morning: *We should get back by 8:30 pm.*

pneu·mo·ni·a /njuːˈməʊniə $ nʊ-ˈməʊnjə/ *noun* [no plural] a serious lung disease

pock·et¹ /ˈpɒkɪt $ ˈpɑkɪt/ *noun*
part of a piece of clothing that is like a small flat bag, for keeping small things in: *He took some money out of the pocket of his jeans.* | *I put my hands in my coat pockets.*

pocket² also **pocket-sized** /ˈ.. ˌ./ *adjective* small enough to fit into a pocket: *a pocket knife*

pocket mon·ey /ˈ.. ˌ./ *noun* BrE money given to children by their parents to spend on things such as sweets; ALLOWANCE AmE

pod /pɒd $ pɑd/ *noun* the long thin object containing seeds that grows on some plants: *a pea pod*

po·di·um /ˈpəʊdiəm $ ˈpoʊdiəm/ *noun* a small raised area on which a performer or speaker stands: *The orchestra's conductor stepped up to the podium.*

po·em /ˈpəʊəm $ ˈpoʊəm/ *noun* a piece of writing in which the words are chosen for their sound or beauty, and arranged in short lines: *a poem by John Keats*

po·et /ˈpəʊɪt $ ˈpoʊɪt/ *noun* someone who writes poems

po·et·ic /pəʊˈetɪk $ poʊˈetɪk/ *adjective* related to or typical of poetry: *poetic language*

po·et·ry /ˈpəʊətri $ ˈpoʊətri/ *noun* [no plural] poems in general: *Emily Dickinson's poetry*

poi·gnant /ˈpɔɪnjənt/ *adjective* formal making you have strong feelings of sadness: *a poignant farewell*

point¹ /pɔɪnt/ *noun*
1 a fact or idea that someone talks or writes about: *What were the main points in the article?* | *That's a very good point.*
2 **the point** what is really important in a situation: *The point is, we can't go because we weren't invited.* | *I don't want to marry him – that's the point.*
3 a time in a process or series of events when something happens: *At that point, I decided to leave.* | *Things have reached the point where they won't even talk to each other.*
4 an exact position or place: *You can cross the river easily at this point.*
5 the purpose or reason for doing something: *The point of going to college is to learn.*
6 the sharp end of something: *The point of a needle*
7 a unit used for showing the SCORE in a game or competition: *You get one point for each correct answer.*
8 *spoken* the sign (.) used for separating a whole number from the DECIMALS that follow it: *He weighs 65 point 5 (=65.5)* kilos.

PHRASES

there's no point, what's the point used to say that an action will not succeed or will not achieve anything useful: *There's no point asking him – he doesn't know.* | *What's the point in talking to you when you don't listen?*

miss the point to not understand what is really important in a situation: *You're missing the point – the whole plan was wrong from the beginning.*

the high point, the low point the best or worst part of something: *Getting divorced was the low point of my life.*

good points, bad points, weak points etc things about a person or thing that are good, bad etc: *The movie did have some good points.*

boiling point, freezing point the temperature at which something boils or freezes: *The water has reached boiling point.*

make a point (about something) to show that your idea or opinion is right: *I was exaggerating to make a point.*

make a point of doing something to do something deliberately or carefully: *She made a point of telling everyone that I had failed my driving test.*

to the point mentioning only the most important thing, and not anything else: *His speech was short and to the point.*

point² *verb*

→ see picture on page 341

GRAMMAR
point to/at/towards something
point something at/towards someone/something

1 to move your finger in the direction of something in order to show it to someone: *He **pointed to** a blonde girl and said, "That's my girlfriend."* | *Everyone **pointed at** the car and laughed.* | *The teacher **pointed** her pen **at** me and said, "Stand up."*

2 to be facing a particular direction, or to move something so that it faces a particular direction: *He saw a sign **pointing towards** the motorway.*

PHRASAL VERB

point out
1 point something out to tell someone about a mistake that they had not noticed or a fact they had not thought about: *She **pointed out** that I had made a mistake.*
2 point something/someone out to point at a person or thing so that people will know who they are or where they are: *Geoff **pointed out** his sister on the dance floor.*

point-blank /ˌ. './ *adverb* **1** if you say something point-blank, you do it directly without trying to explain your reasons: *I asked him point-blank where he'd been.* **2** a gun fired point-blank is fired very close to the person or thing it is aimed at
– point-blank *adjective*: *Ken was shot at point-blank range.*

point-ed /'pɔɪntɪd/ *adjective* having a point at the end: *a dog with pointed ears*

point-er /'pɔɪntə $ 'pɔɪntɚ/ *noun* a helpful piece of advice ⇨ *same meaning* TIP¹ (2): *Sharon may be able to give you some pointers about public speaking.*

point-less /'pɔɪntləs/ *adjective* without any sense or purpose: *pointless violence on TV*

point of view /ˌ. . './ *noun* your personal opinion about something: *We share the same point of view on music.* | *The story is told from a 14-year-old's point of view.*

poised /pɔɪzd/ *adjective* ready to move or do something: *The army was poised to attack.*

poi·son¹ /'pɔɪzən/ *noun*
a substance that can kill or harm you if you eat it, drink it etc: *The plant's leaves contain a poison.* | *rat poison* (=a substance used to kill rats)

poison² *verb* **1** to kill or harm someone by giving them poison: *His friend tried to poison him.* **2** to damage or harm water, land, air etc by adding dangerous chemicals to it: *Toxic waste has poisoned many rivers in the area.*

poi·son·ing /'pɔɪzənɪŋ/ *noun* when someone swallows, touches, or breathes a substance that contains poison and it makes them ill: *lead poisoning*

poi·son·ous /'pɔɪzənəs/ *adjective* containing poison: *poisonous chemicals*

poke /pəʊk $ poʊk/ *verb* **1** to press something quickly, using your finger or a pointed object: *He poked at his food with a knife.* ⇨ *see picture on page 341* **2** to appear, or make something appear, through an opening: *Her toe poked through a hole in her sock.* | *David poked his head around the door.*
– poke *noun*: *He gave me a poke in the shoulder.*

pok·er /'pəʊkə $ 'poʊkɚ/ *noun* **1** [no plural] a card game that people usually play for money **2** a metal stick that you use for moving wood in a fire

pok·y or **pokey** /'pəʊki $ 'poʊki/ *adjective informal* too small: *a poky apartment*

po·lar /'pəʊlə $ 'poʊlɚ/ *adjective* related to the North or South Pole: *the polar ice caps*

polar bear /ˌ.. '. $ '.. ˌ./ *noun* a large white bear that lives near the North Pole
⇨ *see picture on page 339*

pole /pəʊl $ poʊl/ *noun* **1** a long piece of wood or metal: *tent poles* | *a fishing pole* **2** **North Pole, South Pole** the most northern and southern point on Earth

pole vault /'. ./ *noun* [no plural] a sport in which you jump over a high bar using a special long pole

po·lice¹ /pə'liːs/ *noun*
the police the official organization whose job is to catch criminals and make sure that people obey the law: *Have the police caught the person who stole your car?* | *a police car*

police² *verb* if the police or the army police an area or an event, they make sure that people obey the law: *A United Nations' force is policing the area.*

police force /.'. ,./ *noun* the official police organization in a country or area: *The city is proud of its police force.*

po·lice·man /pə'liːsmən/ *noun, plural* **policemen** /-mən/ a man who is a member of the police

police of·fi·cer /.'. ,.../ *noun* a member of the police

police sta·tion /.'. ,../ *noun* the building used by police who work in an area

po·lice·wom·an /pə'liːs,wʊmən/ *noun, plural* **policewomen** /-,wɪmɪn/ a woman who is a member of the police

po·li·o /'pəʊliəʊ $ 'poʊli,oʊ/ *noun [no plural]* a serious disease that makes you unable to move your muscles

pol·ish¹ /'pɒlɪʃ $ 'pɑlɪʃ/ *noun* a liquid, cream etc used for polishing things: *shoe polish*

polish² *verb* **1** to make something clean and shiny by rubbing polish into it with a cloth or brush: *Dad polished his shoes.* **2** **polish something off** *informal* to quickly eat or finish all of something: *Jim polished off the rest of the cake.*

po·lite /pə'laɪt/ *adjective*
someone who is polite speaks or behaves in a way that is not rude and shows respect for other people: *Kevin is a very polite young man.* | *It is polite to stand up so that older people can sit down.*
— **politely** *adverb*: *"Excuse me," she said politely.*

po·lit·i·cal /pə'lɪtɪkəl/ *adjective*
1 related to politics and the government: *The US has two main political parties.* **2** interested in or involved in politics: *I'm not a political person.*
— **politically** /-kli/ *adverb*

political a·sy·lum /.,... .'../ *noun [no plural]* the right to stay in another country because your political activities make it dangerous for you to live in your own country

politically cor·rect /.,.... .'../ also **PC** *adjective* speaking in a way that shows you are being careful not to offend people who belong to a particular group

pol·i·ti·cian /,pɒlə'tɪʃən $,pɑlə'tɪʃən/ *noun* someone who works in politics, especially a member of a parliament (=the group of people elected to make a country's laws etc): *I don't trust politicians.*

pol·i·tics /'pɒlətɪks $ 'pɑlətɪks/ *noun [no plural]*
ideas and activities that are concerned with government and power in a country or area: *Are you interested in politics?* | *She wanted a career in politics.*

poll /pəʊl $ poʊl/ also **opinion poll** *noun* when a lot of people are asked a question in order to find out what they think about it: *Recent polls show that the mayor is still popular.*

pol·len /'pɒlən $ 'pɑlən/ *noun [no plural]* a powder produced by flowers, which is carried by the wind or insects to make other flowers produce seeds

pol·li·nate /'pɒləneɪt $ 'pɑlə,neɪt/ *verb* to make a flower or plant produce seeds by giving it pollen

polling day /'.. ,./ *noun* the day when people vote in an election

pol·lute /pə'luːt/ *verb* to make the air, water, or land dirty or dangerous: *The oil has polluted many beaches.*

pol·lut·ed /pə'luːtɪd/ *adjective* polluted air, water, or land is dirty and dangerous because harmful chemicals are in it: *polluted rivers*

pollution

noise pollution

air pollution

water pollution

pol·lu·tion /pə'luːʃən/ noun [no plural]
harmful chemicals and waste, and the damage they cause to the environment: *Plants and fish are dying because of pollution.* | *Air pollution is worst in big cities.*

polo neck /'pəʊləʊ ˌnek $ 'poʊloʊ ˌnek/ noun BrE a SWEATER with a high band at the top that covers most of your neck; TURTLENECK AmE

pol·y·sty·rene /ˌpɒlɪ'staɪriːn $ ˌpɑli-'staɪrin/ noun [no plural] a very light plastic material, used especially to make containers

pom·pous /'pɒmpəs $ 'pɑmpəs/ adjective someone who is pompous behaves or speaks in a formal way so that people think they are more important than they really are: *a pompous professor*
– **pompously** adverb

pond /pɒnd $ pɑnd/ noun a small area of water that someone has made in a field or garden

pon·der /'pɒndə $ 'pɑndər/ verb formal to think carefully and seriously about something: *He pondered the problem for a long time.*

po·ny /'pəʊni $ 'poʊni/ noun, plural ponies a small horse

po·ny·tail /'pəʊniteɪl $ 'poʊniˌteɪl/ noun long hair tied at the back of your head so that it hangs down: *Kim's hair was pulled back in a ponytail.* ⇨ see picture on page 353

poo·dle /'puːdl/ noun a type of dog with thick curly hair

pool¹ /puːl/ noun

> **GRAMMAR**
> **a pool of something**
> 1 a place that has been made for people to swim in: *They have a pool in their back garden.*
> 2 a pool of water, blood etc is a small area of it somewhere: *There was a pool of oil under the motorbike.*
> 3 [no plural] a game in which you use a long stick to hit numbered balls into holes at the edge of a table. You play or shoot pool.

pool² verb if people pool their money, knowledge etc, they put it all together in order to share it: *We pooled our money and got a pizza.*

poor /pʊə $ pʊr/ adjective
1 someone who is poor has very little money and does not own many things ⇨ opposite RICH (1): *My family was very poor.* | *I came from a poor background* (=from a family that has very little money or an area with a lot of poor people).
2 something that is poor is not as good as it should be: *His schoolwork has been poor recently.*
3 spoken used to show that you feel sorry for someone: *Poor Ted had no idea what was happening.*

poor·ly¹ /'pʊəli $ 'pʊrli/ adverb badly: *a poorly paid job*

poorly² adjective BrE informal ill: *Are you feeling poorly?*

pop¹ /pɒp $ pɑp/ verb popped, popping
1 to make a sound like a small explosion: *The balloon popped.* 2 **pop out, pop up** to suddenly appear from somewhere: *I saw Sergio's head pop out of the water.* 3 spoken to go somewhere for a short time: *I'm just popping out to my friend's house.*

pop² noun 1 [no plural] modern music that is popular with young people: *a pop singer* 2 a sound like a small explosion: *The cork came out of the bottle with a loud pop.* ⇨ see picture on page 350 3 [no plural] a sweet FIZZY drink such as LEMONADE

pop·corn /'pɒpkɔːn $ 'pɑpkɔrn/ noun [no plural] corn that is heated until it swells and bursts open and then is eaten

Pope /pəʊp $ poʊp/ noun **the Pope** the leader of the Roman Catholic Church

pop·py /'pɒpi $ 'pɑpi/ noun, plural poppies a bright red flower with small black seeds

pop·u·lar /'pɒpjələ $ 'pɑpjələr/ adjective

> **GRAMMAR**
> **popular with someone**
> liked by a lot of people ⇨ opposite UNPOPULAR: *He's one of the most popular boys in the school.* | *The cafe is popular with young people.*

pop·u·lar·i·ty /ˌpɒpjə'lærəti $ ˌpɑpjə'lærəti/ noun [no plural] when a lot of people like someone or something: *Skiing has increased in popularity.*

pop·u·lar·ly /'pɒpjələli $ 'pɑpjələrli/

adverb **popularly believed, popularly known as etc** believed to be the case or called a particular name by many people: *Crime in this part of town is much more common than is popularly believed.*

pop·u·lat·ed /'pɒpjəleɪtɪd $ 'pɑpjə-ˌleɪtɪd/ *adjective* used to describe the type of people or the number of people that live in an area: *England is a densely populated country.*

pop·u·la·tion /ˌpɒpjə'leɪʃən $ ˌpɑpjə-'leɪʃən/ *noun* the number of people who live in a country or area: *What's the population of Tokyo?*

porce·lain /'pɔːslən $ 'pɔrsəlɪn/ *noun* [no plural] a hard shiny white material that is used to make plates, cups etc: *a porcelain vase*

porch /pɔːtʃ $ pɔrtʃ/ *noun* an entrance to a building, that has a roof and walls

por·cu·pine /'pɔːkjəpaɪn $ 'pɔrkjə-ˌpaɪn/ *noun* an animal with long needles on its back and sides

pore¹ /pɔː $ pɔr/ *noun* one of the small holes in your skin that SWEAT can pass through

pore² *verb* **pore over** to read or look at something very carefully for a long time: *He spent hours poring over the photographs.*

pork /pɔːk $ pɔrk/ *noun* [no plural] meat from a pig: *roast pork*

po·rous /'pɔːrəs/ *adjective* with small holes that allow liquid, air etc to pass through slowly: *It's best to keep your plants in pots made of porous material, such as clay.*

port /pɔːt $ pɔrt/ *noun*

an area or town where ships arrive and leave from: *Liverpool is a large port.*

por·ta·ble /'pɔːtəbəl $ 'pɔrtəbəl/ *adjective* portable televisions etc are small and easy to carry: *a portable stereo*

por·ter /'pɔːtə $ 'pɔrtɚ/ *noun* someone whose job is to carry bags at an airport, station, or hotel

port·hole /'pɔːthəʊl $ 'pɔrthoʊl/ *noun* a small round window in the side of a ship

por·tion /'pɔːʃən $ 'pɔrʃən/ *noun* an amount of food for one person: *Two portions of fries, please.*

por·trait /'pɔːtrɪt $ 'pɔrtrɪt/ *noun* a painting, drawing, or photograph of a person: *a portrait of the Queen*

por·tray /pɔː'treɪ $ pɔr'treɪ/ *verb* written to describe or show something or someone in a story, film etc: *The film portrayed him as evil.*

pose /pəʊz $ poʊz/ *verb* **1 pose a problem, pose a danger etc** to cause a problem or danger: *The chemicals pose a risk to people.* **2** to sit or stand in a particular position in order to be photographed or painted: *In the photograph, a woman poses with her sleeping child.*

posh /pɒʃ $ pɑʃ/ *adjective* informal **1** expensive and used by rich people: *a posh hotel* **2** typical of people from a high social class: *a posh voice*

po·si·tion /pə'zɪʃən/ *noun*

1 a good or bad situation that someone is in: *She is **in a strong position**.* | *It's your fault that we are **in this position**.*
2 the way someone stands or sits: *Her back hurt because she was sitting in an uncomfortable position.*
3 the place that someone or something is in relation to other things: *If you get sore eyes, try changing the position of your computer.*
4 the official opinion or attitude of a person or group about a subject: *What is the school's **position on** students wearing make-up?*

PHRASES

be in a position to do something to be able to do something: *We **are** not **in a position to** give you financial help.*
be in position if something or someone is in position, they are in the place where they should be: *Troops **were in position** on the border.*

pos·i·tive /'pɒzətɪv $ 'pɑzətɪv/ *adjective*

GRAMMAR
positive (that)

1 very sure that something is true: *I'm **positive that** this is the right way home.* | *"Are you sure you saw Tim and Suzy together?" "Yes, positive."*
2 considering the good qualities of a situation or person and expecting

success ⇨ *opposite* NEGATIVE¹ (2): *It's important to have a positive attitude towards your work.* | *His reaction to our suggestion was very positive.*

3 having a good or useful effect, especially on someone's character ⇨ *opposite* NEGATIVE¹ (1): *Living abroad has been a positive experience for Jim.*

4 a scientific or medical test that is positive shows signs that something is present or has happened ⇨ *opposite* NEGATIVE¹ (4): *She had a pregnancy test and the result was positive.*

5 greater than zero ⇨ *opposite* NEGA-TIVE¹ (5)

pos·i·tive·ly /ˈpɒzətɪvli $ ˈpɑːzətɪvli/ *adverb spoken* used to emphasize what you are saying: *This is positively the worst party I've ever been to.*

pos·sess /pəˈzes/ *verb formal* to own or have something: *We lost everything we possessed in the fire.*

pos·ses·sion /pəˈzeʃən/ *noun* something that belongs to you: *Don't bring any valuable possessions with you on holiday.* | *His car is his favourite possession.*

pos·ses·sive¹ /pəˈzesɪv/ *adjective*
1 not wanting to share someone's love or attention with other people: *He is very possessive about his wife.* 2 not wanting to share the things you own with other people

possessive² *noun* a word such as 'my', 'mine', 'your', or 'their', used to show who something belongs to

pos·si·bil·i·ty /ˌpɒsəˈbɪləti $ ˌpɑːsəˈbɪləti/ *noun, plural* **possibilities**

GRAMMAR
a possibility (that)
a possibility of something

1 something that may happen: *There's a possibility that we might go to America in the summer.* | *Do you think there's any possibility of another world war?*

2 something that may be true: *I think there's a possibility that George is lying to you.*

3 one of the things that you might try or choose to do: *I'm not sure what I want to study, but medicine is one possibility.*

pos·si·ble /ˈpɒsəbəl $ ˈpɑːsəbəl/ *adjective*

GRAMMAR
possible to do something
possible (that)

1 if something is possible, people can do it ⇨ *opposite* IMPOSSIBLE: *Is it possible to get a train to Bristol from here?*

2 something that is possible may happen ⇨ *opposite* IMPOSSIBLE: *It's possible that Rod will be at the party too.*

3 something that is possible may be true ⇨ *opposite* IMPOSSIBLE: *So you think Fiona is in London? Well, it's certainly possible.*

PHRASES
if possible: *If possible* (=if you can), *could you phone me later today?*
as quickly as possible, as soon as possible etc: *You should see a doctor as soon as possible* (=as soon as you can).

pos·si·bly /ˈpɒsəbli $ ˈpɑːsəbli/ *adverb*
perhaps: *"Are you going to the beach tomorrow?" "Possibly. It depends on the weather."*

PHRASES
can't possibly do something: *I can't possibly get there* (=used to emphasize that you can't get there) *before six o'clock.*
as quickly as you possibly can, as much as you possibly can etc: *I ran as fast as I possibly could* (=used to emphasize that you ran as fast as you could).

post¹ /pəʊst $ poʊst/ *noun*
1 [no plural] *BrE* letters or packages that are delivered to your house, office etc; MAIL *AmE*: *What time does the post come?* | *There's no post for you today.*

2 [no plural] *BrE* the system of sending and delivering letters, packages etc; MAIL *AmE*: *A big parcel arrived by post.* | *I'll put these photographs in the post.*

3 a wooden or metal pole that sticks

up out of the ground: *Wooden posts supported the roof.*
4 formal a job: *Simon's applied for a teaching post.*

post² verb

GRAMMAR
post something to someone
post someone something
BrE to send a letter or package to someone; MAIL AmE: *Don't forget to **post** that letter **to** Mum. | I've posted Sally a birthday card.*

post·age /'pəʊstɪdʒ $ 'poʊstɪdʒ/ noun [no plural] the money you pay to send a letter or package by post

post·al /'pəʊstl $ 'poʊstl/ adjective related to sending letters or packages by post: *postal charges*

post·box /'pəʊstbɒks $ 'poʊstbɑks/ noun BrE, plural **postboxes** a box in a public place where you put letters that you want to send; MAILBOX AmE

post·card /'pəʊstkɑːd $ 'poʊstkɑrd/ noun a card with a picture on the front that you send without an envelope: *Mary sent us a postcard from Spain.*

post·code /'pəʊstkəʊd $ 'poʊstkoʊd/ noun BrE a group of letters and numbers that you put at the end of someone's address; ZIP CODE AmE

post·er /'pəʊstə $ 'poʊstɚ/ noun a large notice or picture used to advertise something or as a decoration ⇨ see picture on page 342

pos·ter·i·ty /pɒ'sterəti $ pɑ'sterəti/ noun [no plural] formal the people who will live after you are dead: *I photographed the scene for posterity.*

post·grad·u·ate /ˌpəʊst'grædjuət $ ˌpoʊst'grædʒuət/ noun BrE someone who is studying at a university who has already done a DEGREE; GRADUATE STUDENT AmE

post·man /'pəʊstmən $ 'poʊstmən/ noun BrE, plural **postmen** /-mən/ someone whose job is to collect and deliver letters; MAILMAN AmE

post·mark /'pəʊstmɑːk $ 'poʊstmɑrk/ noun a mark on an envelope that shows the place and time it was sent

post·mor·tem /ˌpəʊst'mɔːtəm $ ˌpoʊst'mɔrtəm/ noun an official medical examination of a dead body to discover why the person died

post of·fice /'. ˌ../ noun a place where you can buy stamps and send letters and packages

post·pone /pəʊs'pəʊn $ poʊs'poʊn/ verb to change an event to a later time or date: *The concert was postponed because of rain.*

pos·ture /'pɒstʃə $ 'pɑstʃɚ/ noun the way that you sit or stand: *Good posture is important if you want to avoid backache.*

pot /pɒt $ pɑt/ noun
a round container, especially one for storing food or growing plants: *a pot of jam | a plant pot*

PHRASE
a pot of tea, a pot of coffee a container with hot tea or coffee in it: *I sat down and ordered **a pot of tea.***

po·ta·to /pə'teɪtəʊ $ pə'teɪtoʊ/ noun, plural **potatoes** a round vegetable with a pale brown or yellow skin that grows under the ground ⇨ see pictures on pages 344 and 345

potato chip /.'.. ˌ./ the American word for CRISP²

po·tent /'pəʊtnt $ 'poʊtnt/ adjective formal strong or powerful: *This homemade wine is very potent. | Advertising has a potent influence on what we buy.*

po·ten·tial¹ /pə'tenʃəl/ adjective possible but not yet achieved: *We believe that Rob is a potential tennis champion.*
–**potentially** adverb: *a potentially dangerous situation*

potential² noun [no plural] **1** when someone or something has natural qualities which could make them very successful in the future: *She has great potential as a dancer.* **2** the possibility that something will develop or happen in a particular way: *There is always a potential for trouble at football games.*

pot·ter /'pɒtə $ 'pɑtɚ/ also **potter around/about** verb BrE to spend time doing unimportant but pleasant things: *I like just pottering around at home.*

pot·ter·y /'pɒtəri $ 'pɑtəri/ noun [no plural] pots, dishes etc made out of baked earth

pot·ty /'pɒti $ 'pɑti/ noun informal, plural **potties** a plastic pot that a very young child uses as a toilet

pouch /paʊtʃ/ noun, plural **pouches** **1** a small bag **2** a pocket of skin that animals such as KANGAROOS carry their babies in

poul·try /'pəʊltri $ 'poʊltri/ *noun* [no plural] birds such as chickens and ducks that are kept on farms, or their meat

pounce /paʊns/ *verb* to suddenly jump towards a person or animal in order to catch them: *The cat pounced on a mouse.*

pound¹ /paʊnd/ *noun* **1** *written abbreviation* **lb**; a unit for measuring weight, equal to 16 OUNCES or 453.6 grams: *a pound of apples* **2** *written sign* £; the standard unit of money in Britain and some other countries: *The ticket cost me ten pounds.*

pound² *verb* **1** to hit something hard many times, making a lot of noise: *The police were pounding on the door.* **2** if your heart pounds, it beats very quickly: *My heart was pounding as I walked towards her.*

pour /pɔː $ pɔr/ *verb*

> **GRAMMAR**
> **pour something into/onto/over something**
> **pour someone something**
> **pour from/out of something**

1 to make a liquid flow out of a container, often into another container: *Jane poured some more coffee into our mugs.* | *Simon poured drinks for everyone.* | *Shall I pour you a glass of wine?* ⇨ *see picture on page 344*
2 if liquid pours somewhere, it flows very quickly: *Blood was pouring from a cut on his head.* | *Water was pouring out of the tank.*

> **PHRASE**
> it's pouring, it's pouring with rain
> BrE it's raining a lot: *It's pouring with rain outside!*

pov·er·ty /'pɒvəti $ 'pɑvərti/ *noun* [no plural] when people do not have enough money: *Millions of people are living in poverty.*

POW /ˌpiː əʊ 'dʌbəljuː $ ˌpi oʊ 'dʌbəljuː/ the abbreviation of PRISONER OF WAR

pow·der /'paʊdə $ 'paʊdər/ *noun* a dry substance in the form of very small grains: *washing powder*

pow·er¹ /'paʊə $ 'paʊər/ *noun*

1 [no plural] someone who has power is important and is able to control

people and events: *All his life he'd wanted power and money.* | *a position of power* | *Parliament has the power to make new laws.*
2 [no plural] energy that is used to make a machine work, or to give light, heat etc: *We use solar power* (=energy from the sun) *to heat the house.*

> **PHRASE**
> be in power : *Which political party is in power* (=has political control) *in the US?*

power² *verb* to supply power to a machine: *The camera is powered by a small battery.*

pow·er·ful /'paʊəfəl $ 'paʊərfəl/ *adjective*
1 a powerful person is important and has a lot of control and influence over people or situations: *The king was the most powerful person in the country.*
2 something that is powerful is very strong or has a strong effect: *a powerful engine* | *It's a very powerful poem.*

pow·er·less /'paʊələs $ 'paʊərləs/ *adjective* unable to stop or control something: *I was powerless to stop the car as it rolled down the hill.*

power sta·tion /'.. ˌ../ also **power plant** /'.. ˌ./ *AmE, noun* a building where electricity is made

pp the written abbreviation of 'pages': *Read pp 20–35.*

PR /ˌpiː 'ɑː $ ˌpi 'ɑr/ PUBLIC RELATIONS

prac·ti·cal¹ /'præktɪkəl/ *adjective*
1 work that is practical involves doing things rather than thinking or talking about them: *Science involves a lot of practical work in the laboratory.* | *practical skills such as carpentry*
2 sensible and likely to be effective ⇨ *opposite* IMPRACTICAL: *Don't ask Peter to help – he's not very practical!* | *We need a practical solution.*
3 useful and suitable for a particular purpose ⇨ *opposite* IMPRACTICAL: *You'll need plenty of clothes that are practical for cold wet weather.*

practical² *noun* BrE a lesson or test where you do or make something, rather than reading, writing, or answering questions: *a physics practical*

practical joke /ˌ... ˈ./ *noun* a trick to surprise someone and make other people laugh at them

prac·ti·cally /ˈpræktɪkli/ *adverb* **1** *spoken* almost: *These shoes are practically new.* **2** in a sensible way: *You need to think about this more practically.*

prac·tice /ˈpræktɪs/ *noun*

[no plural] when you do something regularly in order to improve your skill at it: *We go to football practice every week.* | *Learning a musical instrument takes a lot of practice.*

PHRASE

be out of practice to have not done something for a long time, so that you cannot do it well or easily now: *I'm not sure that I can run ten kilometres now – I'm very out of practice.*

prac·tise *BrE*, **practice** *AmE* /ˈpræktɪs/ *verb*

GRAMMAR
practise doing something
practise for something

to do something in order to improve your skill at it: *I have to practice playing the trumpet every day.* | *The students are busy practising for the Christmas play.*

prac·tis·ing *BrE*, **practicing** *AmE* /ˈpræktəsɪŋ/ *adjective* practising Catholic, practising Jew etc someone who obeys the rules of a particular religion

prai·rie /ˈpreəri $ ˈpreri/ *noun* a large area of flat land in North America that is covered in grass

praise¹ /preɪz/ *verb*

GRAMMAR
praise someone for something
praise someone for doing something

to say that someone has done something well, or that something is good: *General Simms praised the men for their bravery.* | *Mrs Watts praised all the children for working so hard.*

praise² *noun* [no plural] things you say to

praise someone or something: *Her novel has won the praise of critics.*

pram /præm/ *noun* *BrE* a thing that a small baby lies in, with wheels so you can push it around; BABY CARRIAGE *AmE*

prawn /prɔːn/ *noun* a small pink sea animal that you can eat

pray /preɪ/ *verb* **1** to ask or thank God for something: *Let us pray for peace.* **2** to hope for something very strongly: *We're praying for good weather for the wedding.*

pray·er /preə $ prer/ *noun* words that you say to God: *We used to say our prayers every night.*

preach /priːtʃ/ *verb* to give a religious speech, usually in a church: *He preached about love.*
–**preacher** *noun*: *The preacher spoke out against war.*

pre·cau·tion /prɪˈkɔːʃən/ *noun* something that you do to prevent something bad or dangerous from happening: *I took the precaution of locking the door before I left.*

pre·cede /prɪˈsiːd/ *verb* *formal* to happen or exist before something else: *Mr Clark preceded Miss Lee as head teacher.*
–**preceding** *adjective* *formal*: *Her new album had been number one the preceding week.*

pre·ce·dence /ˈpresədəns/ *noun* take precedence over *formal* to be more important than something else: *For me, education takes precedence over everything else.*

pre·ce·dent /ˈpresədənt/ *noun* *formal* an action or decision that is an example of something, and which can be used to say that similar actions or decisions that happen later are correct: *The trial set a precedent for civil rights legislation.*

pre·cinct /ˈpriːsɪŋkt/ *noun* **1** shopping precinct, pedestrian precinct *BrE* an area with shops in a town where cars are not allowed **2** *AmE* a part of a city that has its own police force, local government etc: *the 12th precinct*

pre·cious /ˈpreʃəs/ *adjective* extremely valuable: *Gold and silver are precious metals.* | *Your time is precious.*

pre·ci·pice /ˈpresəpɪs/ *noun* a very steep side of a mountain or cliff

pre·cise /prɪˈsaɪs/ *adjective*

exact and correct: *He gave us precise details of how to get there.* | *I* think it was nine or ten o'clock – I'm sorry I can't be more precise.

pre·cise·ly /prɪ'saɪsli/ adverb exactly: *That's precisely what I mean.* | *The judge came into the courtroom at precisely 8:55 am.*

pre·ci·sion /prɪ'sɪʒən/ noun [no plural] when something is measured or described very exactly: *This watch keeps time with incredible precision.*

pre·con·ceived /ˌpriːkən'siːvd/ adjective if you have preconceived ideas about something, you have decided what you think about it before you know what it is really like: *He has a lot of preconceived opinions about girls.*

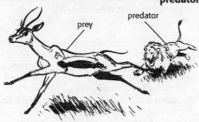

predator

prey

pred·a·tor /'predətə $'predətɚ/ noun an animal that kills and eats other animals

pre·de·ces·sor /'priːdəsesə $'predə-ˌsesɚ/ noun your predecessor is the person who had your job before you: *My predecessor worked here for ten years.*

pre·dic·a·ment /prɪ'dɪkəmənt/ noun if you are in a predicament, you are in a difficult situation and you do not know what to do

pre·dict /prɪ'dɪkt/ verb to say that something will happen: *His teachers predicted that he would get high grades.*

pre·dict·a·ble /prɪ'dɪktəbəl/ adjective behaving or happening in the way that you expect, and not at all interesting: *The ending of the film was so predictable.*
– **predictably** adverb: *Predictably, a crowd gathered to watch the fire.*

pre·dic·tion /prɪ'dɪkʃən/ noun when you say what you think will happen in the future: *Here are our predictions for next year's fashions.*

pre·dom·i·nant·ly /prɪ'dɒmənəntli $prɪ'dɑmənəntli/ adverb formal mostly or mainly: *The students here are predominantly boys.*

pref·ace /'prefəs/ noun an introduction at the beginning of a book

pre·fect /'priːfekt/ noun BrE an older student who has special powers and duties in a school

pre·fer /prɪ'fɜː $prɪ'fɚ/ verb preferred, preferring

> **GRAMMAR**
> prefer someone/something to someone/something
> prefer doing something
> prefer to do something

to like someone or something more than someone or something else: *I **prefer** football **to** cricket.* | *Do you prefer travelling by train or car?* | *I'd **prefer to** stay at home today.*

pref·e·ra·ble /'prefərəbəl/ adjective better or more suitable: *Even a short walk is preferable to no exercise.*

pref·e·ra·bly /'prefərəbli/ adverb used to say what would be the best or most suitable: *The form needs to be signed by an adult, preferably your teacher.*

pref·e·rence /'prefərəns/ noun formal when someone likes one thing more than other things: *There are several movies we could see tonight – do you have a preference?*

pre·fix /'priːfɪks/ noun, plural prefixes a group of letters added to the beginning of a word to make a new word

preg·nan·cy /'pregnənsi/ noun, plural pregnancies when someone is pregnant: *The study shows that most teenage pregnancies are accidents.*

preg·nant /'pregnənt/ adjective if a woman or female animal is pregnant, she has a baby growing in her body: *She got pregnant soon after they were married.*

pre·his·tor·ic /ˌpriːhɪ'stɒrɪk $ˌpriː-hɪ'stɔrɪk/ adjective related to the time a long way in the past before anything was written down: *prehistoric cave drawings*

prej·u·dice /'predʒədɪs/ noun an unfair opinion about someone that is not based on facts or reason: *There's still a lot of prejudice against disabled people.*

prej·u·diced /'predʒədɪst/ adjective

P

having an unfair attitude towards someone or something, so that you dislike them without any good reason: *She is prejudiced against me just because I am young.*

pre·lim·i·na·ry /prɪˈlɪmənəri $ prɪˈlɪməˌneri/ *adjective* formal happening or done at the beginning of a process, usually to prepare for what will come later: *During preliminary discussions, the teacher encouraged students to talk about their ideas.*

pre·ma·ture /ˈpremətʃə $ ˌpriːməˈtʃʊr/ *adjective* happening too early: *Smoking causes premature death.*
–**prematurely** *adverb*: *The baby was born prematurely.*

pre·med·i·tat·ed /priːˈmedəteɪtɪd/ *adjective* a premeditated crime has been planned before it happens

prem·i·er /ˈpremiə $ prɪˈmɪr/ *noun* written the leader of a government

prem·i·ere /ˈpremieə $ prɪˈmɪr/ *noun* the first public performance of a film or play: *All the stars were at the premiere.*

prem·is·es /ˈpreməsɪz/ *plural noun* the buildings and land that a shop or company uses: *No children are allowed on the premises.*

pre·mo·ni·tion /ˌpreməˈnɪʃən/ *noun* a feeling that something bad is going to happen: *I had a premonition that the plane was going to crash.*

pre·oc·cu·pied /priːˈɒkjəpaɪd $ priːˈɑkjəˌpaɪd/ *adjective* thinking or worrying about something a lot, so that you do not pay attention to other things: *I was so preoccupied with my work that I didn't hear him.*

prep·a·ra·tion /ˌprepəˈreɪʃən/ *noun*

GRAMMAR
preparation of something
preparation for something

1 [no plural] getting something ready, or getting yourself ready for something: *He sometimes spends hours on the* **preparation of** *one meal.* | *You need to do plenty of* **preparation for** *your exams.*
2 **preparations** the things that you do in order to get ready for something: *Our* **preparations for** *the party took several days.* | *We are* **making preparations for** *the King's visit.*

pre·pare /prɪˈpeə $ prɪˈper/ *verb*

GRAMMAR
prepare for something
prepare to do something
prepare someone for something
prepare something for someone/ something

1 to make yourself ready for something: *I went home early to* **prepare for** *my holiday.* | *Craig stood up and* **prepared to** *go.*
2 to make something ready, so that it can be used: *At the moment we're busy* **preparing** *some new courses* **for** *our students.* | *It took us several hours to* **prepare** *the room* **for** *the party.*
3 to make another person ready for something: *As a teacher it's your job to* **prepare** *the children* **for** *their exams.*

pre·pared /prɪˈpeəd $ prɪˈperd/ *adjective* 1 ready to deal with a situation: *I wasn't prepared for his questions.* 2 **be prepared to do sth** to be willing to do something: *She is not prepared to discuss her personal life.*

prep·o·si·tion /ˌprepəˈzɪʃən/ *noun* a word such as 'at' or 'into' that is used before a noun to show the place or position of something, or to talk about time

pre·pos·ter·ous /prɪˈpɒstərəs $ prɪˈpɑstərəs/ *adjective* formal completely unreasonable or silly: *What a preposterous idea!*

prep school /ˈprep skuːl/ *noun* 1 a private school in Britain for children aged between 8 and 13 2 a private school in the US that prepares students for college

pre·school /ˈpriːskuːl/ *noun* a school for children aged between two and five

pre·school /ˌ. ˈ./ *adjective* related to children who are not old enough to go to school: *a group for pre-school children*

pre·scribe /prɪˈskraɪb/ *verb* to say what medicine or treatment someone should have: *The doctor prescribed an antibiotic.*

pre·scrip·tion /prɪˈskrɪpʃən/ *noun* a piece of paper on which a doctor writes what medicine someone should have

pres·ence /ˈprezəns/ *noun* [no plural] 1 when someone or something is in a particular place at a particular time: *His presence in the classroom upset the* students. **2 presence of mind** the ability to deal with a dangerous or difficult situation quickly and calmly: *She had the presence of mind to jump out of the way.*

pres·ent¹ /'prezənt/ adjective

present events or situations exist now, rather than in the past or the future: *Prices have increased a lot during the present year.* | *Our present situation is very difficult.*

PHRASES

be present (at something) to be in a particular place, or at a particular event: *Only half the class was present at the talk.*

the present tense the form of a verb which shows what is happening now

pre·sent² /prɪ'zent/ verb

GRAMMAR
present someone with something
present something to someone

1 to give something to someone at a formal ceremony: *The children presented their teacher with some flowers.* | *When he retired, Professor Fletcher was presented with a gold watch.* | *She presented the trophy to the winning team.*

2 if something presents a problem, a new opportunity etc, it causes or provides it: *If it rains, it will present a serious problem.*

3 to introduce a radio or television programme: *David Attenborough presented a new wildlife programme.*

pres·ent³ /'prezənt/ noun

GRAMMAR
a present for someone

something that you give to someone ⇨ same meaning GIFT (1): *I went into town to buy a present for my dad.* | *They gave me a lovely present for my birthday.* | *a Christmas present*

PHRASES

the present the time that we live in now: *The present is more important than the past.*

at present: *Debbie's working in London, at present* (=at this time).

pre·sen·ta·tion /ˌprezən'teɪʃən $ˌprizən'teɪʃən/ noun **1** an event at

which someone explains an idea to a group of people: *I gave a presentation to the class about my history project.* **2** when someone is given a prize or present at a formal ceremony: *the presentation of the medal* **3** [no plural] the way something looks because of how it has been arranged: *Your essay contains some good ideas, but the presentation is poor.*

pre·sent·er /prɪ'zentə $prɪ'zentɚ/ noun someone who introduces a television or radio programme

pres·ent·ly /'prezəntli/ adverb formal **1** now: *They are presently on holiday.* **2** after a short time: *Presently, he became aware he was being watched.*

present par·ti·ci·ple /ˌ.. '..../ noun the form of a verb that ends in '-ing'

present per·fect /ˌ.. '../ noun the present perfect is the verb tense that you use to talk about a time up to and including the present, which is formed with 'have' and the PAST PARTICIPLE, as in 'he has gone'

pre·ser·va·tive /prɪ'zɜːvətɪv $prɪ'zɜːvətɪv/ noun a chemical that is added to food to keep it in good condition

pre·serve /prɪ'zɜːv $prɪ'zɜːv/ verb to keep something safe or in good condition: *It is important to preserve your culture.* | *The group is working to preserve rain forests.*

pres·i·den·cy /'prezədənsi/ noun, plural **presidencies** the job or time of being president: *towards the end of his presidency*

pres·i·dent /'prezədənt/ noun **1** the leader of a country that does not have a king or queen: *President Kennedy* | *the President of France* **2** someone who is in charge of an organization: *the president of the chess club*

pres·i·den·tial /ˌprezə'denʃəl/ adjective related to the president of a country: *the presidential election*

press¹ /pres/ verb

GRAMMAR
press something into/against something

1 if you press a button, SWITCH etc, you push it in order to make something work: *You press this button to turn the TV on.*

2 to push something firmly: *She*

pressed the money **into** his hand. | Kate **pressed** her shoulder **against** the door and it opened.

press² noun

the press newspapers and magazines: The accident was reported **in the local press.** | **The press** has a lot of influence over what people think.

press con·fer·ence /'. ,.../ noun a meeting at which someone answers questions asked by people who work for newspapers, radio, and television: The police dealing with the murder held a press conference today.

press re·lease /'. .,./ noun an official statement giving information to newspapers, radio, and television

press-up /'. ./ noun BrE an exercise in which you lie facing the ground and push your body up using your arms ⇨ same meaning PUSH-UP: He does 20 press-ups every day before breakfast.

pres·sure¹ /'preʃə $ 'preʃɚ/ noun

GRAMMAR
pressure on someone
pressure from someone
pressure for something
pressure to do something
the pressure(s) of something

1 [no plural] when other people try to make someone do something: There's a lot of **pressure on** her to get married now. | His family **put pressure on** him **to** go to university. | I get a lot of **pressure from** my family **to** do well in exams. | There's **pressure for** a change in the law.

2 when something makes you feel anxious or unhappy, for example because you have too much to do: John eventually became ill because of **the pressure of** his work.

3 [no plural] the force that one thing causes when it presses on another thing: **The pressure of** his hand on her shoulder was annoying her.

PHRASES
be under pressure to be in a difficult situation: A lot of small businesses **are under pressure** at the moment.
be under pressure to do something to feel that you must try hard

to do something, because of the situation you are in: The minister **is under pressure to** resign. | I felt **under pressure to** earn more and more money.

pressure² verb AmE to make someone do something: Carrie's friends pressured her into going to the dance.

pressure group /'.. ,./ noun a group of people who try to make the government, a company etc do a particular thing: an environmental pressure group

pres·sur·ize also **pressurise** BrE /'preʃəraɪz/ verb to try to make someone do something by threatening them, arguing with them etc: Her parents tried to pressurize her into going to college.

pres·tige /pre'stiːʒ/ noun [no plural] when you are respected and admired because of what you have achieved

pres·ti·gious /pre'stɪdʒəs $ pre'stiːdʒəs/ adjective a prestigious job, school etc makes you respected and admired

pre·su·ma·bly /prɪ'zjuːməbli $ prɪ'zuːməbli/ adverb used when you think that something is probably true: The burglars presumably knew he was out.

pre·sume /prɪ'zjuːm $ prɪ'zuːm/ verb to think that something is probably true: I presume we'll be finished by two o'clock.

pre·tence BrE, **pretense** AmE /prɪ'tens $ 'pritens/ noun when you pretend that something is true: He seemed confident, but I knew it was just a pretence.

pre·tend /prɪ'tend/ verb

GRAMMAR
pretend to do something
pretend (that)

to behave in a particular way in order to make people believe something is true, although it is not: Helen **pretended to** be ill so that she could stay at home. | The kids lay on the floor **pretending that** they were dead.

pre·ten·tious /prɪ'tenʃəs/ adjective trying to seem more important or clever than you really are

pre·text /'priːtekst/ noun a false reason that you give for doing something: He stayed at home on the pretext of having some homework to do.

pret·ty¹ /'prɪti/ adverb

spoken fairly or quite: *Their house is pretty big.* | *It was a pretty quick journey, really.*

pretty² adjective **prettier, prettiest**

pleasant and attractive to look at: *Alison was sixteen, and very pretty.* | *a pretty garden*

USAGE pretty, beautiful, good-looking, handsome
When you are describing people, use **pretty** or **beautiful** about girls and women. Use **good-looking** or **handsome** about boys and men.

pre·vent /prɪ'vent/ verb

GRAMMAR
prevent someone from doing something
to stop something from happening, or to stop someone from doing something: *There was nothing we could do to prevent the war.* | *She tried to prevent me from leaving.*

pre·ven·ta·tive /prɪ'ventətɪv/ PREVENTIVE

pre·ven·tion /prɪ'venʃən/ noun [no plural] when something is prevented: *the prevention of tooth decay*

pre·ven·tive /prɪ'ventɪv/ also **preventative** adjective intended to prevent something bad from happening: *preventive medicine* (=medicine that prevents people from becoming ill)

pre·view /'pri:vju:/ noun **1** an occasion when you see a film or show before the rest of the public **2** an advertisement for a film or television programme, which consists of short parts from it

pre·vi·ous /'pri:viəs/ adjective

a previous time or event happened in the past: *We've already discussed that idea at a previous meeting.* | *Last year we went to Spain on holiday. The previous year, we went to Majorca.*

pre·vi·ous·ly /'pri:viəsli/ adverb before a particular time in the past: *The car had previously belonged to his dad.*

prey /preɪ/ noun [no plural] an animal that is hunted and eaten by another animal: *The cat pounced on its prey.* ⇨ see picture at PREDATOR

price /praɪs/ noun

GRAMMAR
the price of something
the amount of money that you must pay in order to buy something: *The price of petrol has increased a lot.* | *It's a lovely shop but their prices are quite high.* | *You can get meals there at quite low prices.* | *Everything in the shop is being sold at half price.*

PHRASE
at any price even if there are a lot of problems or difficulties: *I was determined to get into the team at any price.*

price·less /'praɪsləs/ adjective worth a very large amount of money: *a priceless diamond necklace*

pric·ey /'praɪsi/ adjective informal expensive

prick /prɪk/ verb to make a small hole in the surface of something

prick·ly /'prɪkli/ adjective covered with sharp points: *a prickly cactus*

pride¹ /praɪd/ noun [no plural]

GRAMMAR
pride in someone/something
the feeling you have when you are pleased and proud that you have achieved something or own something: *His pride in his son was obvious to everyone.* | *Jason showed us his new sports car with great pride.*

PHRASE
take pride in something to get pleasure from doing something well: *Richard took pride in his tennis, and practised every day.*

pride² verb **pride yourself on something** to be very proud of something: *Allen prides himself on being the fastest swimmer on the team.*

priest /pri:st/ noun someone who performs religious duties and ceremonies, especially in the Christian church

pri·ma·ri·ly /'praɪmərəli $ praɪ'merəli/ adverb mainly: *The club is used primarily by teenagers.*

pri·ma·ry /'praɪməri $ 'praɪ,meri/ adjective first or most important: *The police's primary goal is to prevent crime.*

P

P

primary school /'... ,./ noun a school for children between the ages of 5 and 11; ELEMENTARY SCHOOL AmE

prime[1] /praɪm/ adjective **1** main or most important: *Vincent is the prime suspect in the murder case.* **2** of the very best quality or kind: *The office is in a prime location on the river.*

prime[2] noun **be in your prime, be in the prime of life** to be at the time in your life when you are strongest and most active

prime min·is·ter /,. '.../ noun the leader of the government in some countries with a PARLIAMENT

prim·i·tive /'prɪmətɪv/ adjective **1** primitive people have a simple way of life, without modern machines **2** very simple or old-fashioned, and therefore not very good: *The washing facilities were a bit primitive.*

prince /prɪns/ noun the son of a king or queen, or one of their male relations: *Prince Charles*

prin·cess /,prɪn'ses $ 'prɪnsɪs/ noun, plural princesses the daughter of a king or queen, one of their female relations, or the wife of a prince: *Princess Margaret*

prin·ci·pal[1] /'prɪnsəpəl/ adjective most important: *Coffee is Brazil's principal export.*

principal[2] noun the person in charge of a school or college

prin·ci·pally /'prɪnsəpli/ adverb mainly: *The money will be spent principally on new books for the school.*

prin·ci·ple /'prɪnsəpəl/ noun

an idea that you believe is right, and that you use to guide the way you behave: *The old lady had very strong principles.*

PHRASES

be against someone's principles: *Any cruelty to animals is against our principles* (=we believe it is wrong).

on principle: *I don't work on Sundays, on principle* (=because I believe it is wrong).

print[1] /prɪnt/ verb

1 to produce words or pictures on paper, using a machine: *They had to print more copies of the book.*
2 to write words without joining the letters: *Print your name at the top of your entry form.*

▼ PHRASAL VERB

print off also **print out**
print something off/out to print information from a computer onto paper: *She printed off the list of names.*

print[2] noun **1** [no plural] writing that has been printed in books, newspapers etc: *We bought grandma a book in large print.* **2** a picture or photograph that has been printed: *She has a Renoir print on her wall.* **3** **be in print, be out of print** if a book is in print, it is available to buy; if a book is out of print, it is not available to buy **4** a mark made on a surface when you press something onto it: *The dog left paw prints in the sand.*

print·er /'prɪntə $ 'prɪntɚ/ noun **1** a machine that prints a document from a computer onto paper ⇨ see picture on page 342 **2** someone who works for a company that prints books, newspapers etc

print·out /'prɪnt,aʊt/ noun paper with information from a computer printed on it

pri·or /'praɪə $ 'praɪɚ/ adjective formal **1 prior to** before: *Prior to this, we had never had any trouble.* **2** existing or happening before something else: *The bomb exploded without any prior warning.*

pri·or·i·ty /praɪ'ɒrəti $ praɪ'ɔːrəti/ noun, plural priorities
the thing that you think is most important and should be dealt with first: *The government's priority is education.*

PHRASES

take priority, have priority to be treated as more important than other people or things: *His family took priority over everything else.*

give priority to someone/something to treat one person or thing as more important than others: *Hospitals must give priority to people who are seriously ill.*

prise /praɪz/ verb BrE to force something open or away from something else; PRY AmE: *I tried to prise open the door.*

pris·on /'prɪzən/ noun a building where criminals are kept: *He's been in prison for two years.*

pris·on·er /ˈprɪzənə $ˈprɪzənɚ/ *noun*
1 someone who is in prison **2** someone who is kept somewhere by someone: *The rebels have released their prisoners.* | *Her father was taken prisoner in the war.*

priv·a·cy /ˈprɪvəsi $ˈpraɪvəsi/ *noun [no plural]* when other people cannot see or hear you, or know what you are doing: *You must respect your father's privacy.*

pri·vate¹ /ˈpraɪvət/ *adjective*
1 owned by one person or group and not available for others to use ➪ *opposite* PUBLIC¹ (1): *This is private land.*
2 not owned or paid for by the government: *a private school* | *a private hospital*
3 if something is private, you do not want other people to know about it: *I can't tell you – that information is private.*
4 a private place is one where you can be alone ➪ *opposite* PUBLIC¹ (4): *Can we talk about this somewhere more private?*

private² *noun* **1** in private without other people listening or watching: *Kevin waited after class, so he could speak to the teacher in private.* **2** a soldier who has the lowest rank in the army

pri·vat·ize *also* **privatise** *BrE* /ˈpraɪvətaɪz/ *verb* if a government privatizes an organization which it owns, it sells it ➪ *opposite* NATIONALIZE: *The railways have been privatized.*

priv·i·lege /ˈprɪvəlɪdʒ/ *noun* a special advantage or right that only a small number of people are given: *The older students were given special privileges.*

prize /praɪz/ *noun*
something that is given to someone who is successful in a competition, race etc: *She **won first prize** in a poetry competition.*

prob·a·bil·i·ty /ˌprɒbəˈbɪləti $ˌprɑbəˈbɪləti/ *noun [no plural]* how likely it is that something will happen: *What's the probability of the disease coming back?*

prob·a·ble /ˈprɒbəbəl $ˈprɑbəbəl/ *adjective* very likely to happen, exist, or be true: *A gas leak was the probable cause of the explosion.*

prob·a·bly /ˈprɒbəbli $ˈprɑbəbli/ *adverb*
used when saying what is likely to be true or what is likely to happen: *They've probably got lost.* | *I haven't been working very hard, so I'll probably fail all my exams.*

pro·ba·tion /prəˈbeɪʃən $proʊˈbeɪʃən/ *noun [no plural]* a system of keeping an official check on criminals, instead of keeping them in prison: *He has to go to the police station every week while he's on probation.*

probe /prəʊb $proʊb/ *verb written* to ask a lot of questions in order to find out information: *I don't want people probing into my private life!*
– probing *adjective*: *My boss always asks the most probing questions.*

prob·lem /ˈprɒbləm $ˈprɑbləm/ *noun*

> **GRAMMAR**
> **a problem with something**

something bad or difficult that you have to deal with: *She's **had** a lot of personal **problems** recently.* | *I've been **having problems with** my car.* | *the **problem of** how to deal with crime* | *There's **a problem with** the computer* | *We must try to **solve** this **problem**.* | *This is a very **serious problem**.*

pro·ce·dure /prəˈsiːdʒə $prəˈsiːdʒɚ/ *noun* the correct or normal way of doing something: *What's the procedure for getting a driver's licence?*

pro·ceed /prəˈsiːd/ *verb formal* to continue: *The police have decided not to proceed with the case.*

pro·ceed·ings /prəˈsiːdɪŋz/ *plural noun formal* a series of events: *She sat down and took no further part in the proceedings.*

pro·ceeds /ˈprəʊsiːdz $ˈproʊsiːdz/ *plural noun* the money that you get from selling something or holding an event: *They sold their car and spent the proceeds on a boat.*

pro·cess¹ /ˈprəʊses $ˈprɑses/ *noun, plural* **processes**
something that happens over a period of time: *Learning a new language is a long process.*

P

be in the process of doing something to have started doing something and not finished doing it: *I'm in the process of choosing which universities to apply to.*

process² *verb* 1 to deal with information by putting it through a system or computer: *Your application hasn't been processed yet.* 2 to add chemicals to food before it is used or sold: *The meat is processed in huge factories.*

pro·ces·sion /prə'seʃən/ *noun* a line of people or vehicles moving slowly along as part of a ceremony

pro·claim /prə'kleɪm $ proʊ'kleɪm/ *verb formal* to formally tell people something: *The country proclaimed its independence in 1956.*

prod /prɒd $ prɑd/ *verb* **prodded, prodding** to push someone or something with your finger or a long object: *She prodded the girl next to her and asked what was going on.*
– **prod** *noun*: *He gave the meat a prod.*

prod·i·gy /'prɒdɪdʒi $ 'prɑdədʒi/ *noun, plural* **prodigies** a young person who is unusually good at doing something

pro·duce¹ /prə'djuːs $ prə'dus/ *verb*
1 to grow or make something: *The tree produces red berries in the autumn.* | *The company produced 30,000 cars last year.*
2 to make something happen: *Which method will produce the results we want?*
3 to bring something out so that someone can see it: *He put his hand in his pocket and produced his ticket.*
4 to be in charge of the making of a film, show, or record: *The film was produced by Nick Staines.*

prod·uce² /'prɒdjuːs $ 'prɑdus/ *noun* [no plural] food that is grown on a farm and sold

pro·duc·er /prə'djuːsə $ prə'dusər/ *noun* someone who is in charge of making a film, record etc: *a film producer*

prod·uct /'prɒdʌkt $ 'prɑdʌkt/ *noun* something that is made and sold by a company: *The company produces a range of household products.*

pro·duc·tion /prə'dʌkʃən/ *noun* [no plural] the process of making or growing things, or the amount that you make or grow: *How can we increase our production?*

pro·duc·tive /prə'dʌktɪv/ *adjective* producing a lot or producing a good result: *That was a very productive meeting.*

pro·duc·tiv·i·ty /ˌprɒdʌk'tɪvəti $ ˌproʊdʌk'tɪvəti/ *noun* [no plural] the speed at which goods are produced and the amount that is produced: *Productivity at the factory has increased by 5% over the last year.*

Prof. the written abbreviation of PROFESSOR

pro·fes·sion /prə'feʃən/ *noun* a job for which you need special education and training, such as being a doctor or a teacher: *the legal profession* ⇨ see usage note at JOB

pro·fes·sion·al¹ /prə'feʃənəl/ *adjective*
1 a professional football player, artist etc does a sport or activity as their job: *a professional photographer*
2 made or done well: *The magazine produced by the students looked very professional.*

professional² *noun* someone who earns money by doing a sport that other people do for enjoyment ⇨ *opposite* AMATEUR

pro·fes·sor /prə'fesə $ prə'fesər/ *noun*
1 *BrE* a teacher with the highest job in a university department: *Professor Sinclair*
2 *AmE* a teacher at a university or college who has a PHD

pro·fi·cien·cy /prə'fɪʃənsi/ *noun* [no plural] *formal* the ability to do something well: *her proficiency in French*

pro·file /'prəʊfaɪl $ 'proʊfaɪl/ *noun* a side view of someone's head: *I could see the profile of her face.*

prof·it¹ /'prɒfɪt $ 'prɑfɪt/ *noun* if you make a profit when you sell something, you get more money for it than you spent on it ⇨ *opposite* LOSS (3): *The company made a good profit this year.*

profit² *verb formal* to get money or something useful from a situation: *Some groups profited from the war.*

prof·it·a·ble /ˈprɒfɪtəbəl $ ˈprɑːfɪt-əbəl/ *adjective* producing a profit: *a profitable business*

pro·found /prəˈfaʊnd/ *adjective* a profound shock, effect etc is a very great one: *a profound disappointment*

pro·gram¹ /ˈprəʊɡræm $ ˈproʊɡræm/ *noun* **1** the American spelling of PROGRAMME **2** a set of instructions given to a computer or other machine: *a computer program*

> **USAGE program, programme**
> When we are talking about computers, the British and the American spelling is **program**. For every other meaning, the British spelling is **programme** and the American spelling is **program**.

program² *verb* **programmed, programming** the American spelling of PROGRAMME

pro·gramme¹ *BrE*, **program** *AmE* /ˈprəʊɡræm $ ˈproʊɡræm/ *noun*

> **GRAMMAR**
> **a programme about/on something**

1 a show on television or radio: *Did you see that TV programme about earthquakes? | Do you want to watch this programme?*
2 a set of planned actions or activities: *a four-year research programme*
3 a small book that you get at a concert or play which gives information about it

programme² *BrE*, **program** *AmE*, *verb* to set controls so that a machine will work a particular way: *Have you programmed the video to record the football match tonight?*

pro·gram·mer /ˈprəʊɡræmə $ ˈproʊ-ˌɡræmɚ/ *noun* someone whose job is to write sets of instructions for computers: *a computer programmer*

pro·gress¹ /ˈprəʊɡres $ ˈprɑːɡrəs/ *noun* [no plural] if you make progress, you get better or get closer to achieving something: *Parents want to be told about their child's progress at school. | The patient is making good progress after the operation.*

pro·gress² /prəˈɡres/ *verb* **1** to develop and become better or more complete: *The students' drawing skills have progressed quickly.* **2** to continue or move forward: *As Sarah's career progressed, she earned more money.*

pro·gres·sive¹ /prəˈɡresɪv/ *adjective* a progressive change is gradual and continuous

progressive² *noun* the progressive a verb form that consists of 'be' and the PRESENT PARTICIPLE, as in 'She was reading'

pro·hib·it /prəˈhɪbət $ proʊˈhɪbɪt/ *verb formal* if people in authority prohibit something, they do not allow it: *Skateboarding is prohibited in the town centre.*

proj·ect /ˈprɒdʒekt $ ˈprɑːdʒekt/ *noun*
1 a piece of planned work that is done over a period of time: *This is part of a project to make this area of the city more attractive.*
2 a piece of school work in which students have to collect information about a subject: *Cindy's in the library working on her history project. | We're doing a project on global warming.*

pro·jec·tor /prəˈdʒektə $ prəˈdʒektɚ/ *noun* a piece of equipment for showing film or pictures on a screen

pro·lif·ic /prəˈlɪfɪk/ *adjective* producing a lot of things: *a prolific writer*

pro·long /prəˈlɒŋ $ prəˈlɔːŋ/ *verb* to make something continue for longer: *Heart transplants have prolonged many people's lives.*

pro·longed /prəˈlɒŋd $ prəˈlɔːŋd/ *adjective* continuing for a long time: *a prolonged period of silence*

prom·i·nent /ˈprɒmənənt $ ˈprɑːm-ənənt/ *adjective* well known or important: *a prominent supporter of animal rights*

prom·ise¹ /ˈprɒmɪs $ ˈprɑːmɪs/ *verb*

> **GRAMMAR**
> **promise to do something**
> **promise (that)**
> **promise someone (that)**
> **promise someone something**

to say that you will definitely do or give something: *She promised to* write to me. | I **promise that** I'll be there. | He **promised** me **that** he wouldn't be late. | His parents had promised him a camera for his birthday.

promise² noun

GRAMMAR
the promise of something
a promise to do something
if you make a promise, you say that you will definitely do or give something: He came to England last year with **the promise of** a good job. | I reminded my aunt of her **promise to** take us to the zoo. | He **made** all sorts of **promises** before he left. | I knew she would **keep her promise** (=do what she said she would do). | He said he would wait for me, but he **broke his promise** (=did not do what he said he would do).

prom·is·ing /'prɒmɪsɪŋ $'prɑmɪsɪŋ/ adjective likely to be successful in the future: a very promising student

pro·mote /prə'məʊt $prə'moʊt/ verb **1** to give someone who works for you a higher job: He is hoping to be promoted to manager soon. **2** to try to make something happen or help something be successful: a campaign promoting the use of cycle helmets | She's been on lots of talk shows, promoting her latest film.

pro·mo·tion /prə'məʊʃən $prə'moʊ-ʃən/ noun **1** when you are given a higher job: She felt she deserved promotion. **2** an advertisement or special attempt to sell something: a big promotion campaign on national television

prompt¹ /prɒmpt $prɑmpt/ verb to make someone decide to do something, especially something they were already thinking about doing: John's leaving prompted me to look for a new job.

prompt² adjective **1** done quickly or immediately: I expect a prompt reply to my letter. **2** arriving at the right time: The meeting starts at 11, so please be prompt.
– **promptly** adverb

prone /prəʊn $proʊn/ adjective likely to do something bad, or likely to suffer from something: He was prone to

jealousy. | Young drivers are more accident-prone than older ones.

pro·noun /'prəʊnaʊn $'proʊnaʊn/ noun a word such as 'he' or 'themselves' that is used instead of using a noun

pro·nounce /prə'naʊns/ verb

1 to say a word using particular sounds: He always pronounces my name wrong.
2 formal to state something officially: The doctor pronounced him dead at 11 p.m.

pro·nun·ci·a·tion /prə,nʌnsi'eɪ-ʃən/ noun

the way in which you say a word: Is that the correct pronunciation?

proof /pruːf/ noun

GRAMMAR
proof of something
proof that
something that proves something is true: She needed **proof of** her theory. | This letter is **proof that** Higson knew about the robbery.

prop¹ /prɒp $prɑp/ verb **propped, propping** **1** to lean or rest something on something: He propped his feet on the table. **2** **prop something up** to support something so that it does not fall or hang down: We propped the fence up with some old bits of wood.

prop² noun an object that is used in a play or film

prop·a·gan·da /,prɒpə'gændə $,prɑpə-'gændə/ noun [no plural] false information that a political organization gives to the public to influence them: This is just government propaganda.

pro·pel·ler /prə-'pelə $prə'pelɚ/ noun the part of a boat or aircraft that spins round and makes it move along

propeller

prop·er /'prɒpə $'prɑpɚ/ adjective

1 correct for a particular situation: Have you filled in the proper form?
2 BrE real, with every necessary feature: I wanted a proper job where I got paid. | I always try to eat a proper meal in the evenings.

prop·er·ly /'prɒpəli $ 'prɑpɚli/ adverb
in a correct or satisfactory way: *The computer printer isn't working properly.*

proper noun /ˌ.. './ *noun* a noun such as 'Mike' or 'Paris' that is the name of a person, place, or thing and is spelled with a capital letter

prop·er·ty /'prɒpəti $ 'prɑpɚti/ *noun formal* **1** [no plural] something that you own: *Make sure you take all your property with you when you leave the train.* **2** *plural* **properties** a building: *We have quite a lot of properties for sale.* | *Is this a good time to buy property?* **3** *plural* **properties** a natural quality that a substance has: *What are the properties of mercury?*

proph·e·cy /'prɒfəsi $ 'prɑfəsi/ *noun, plural* **prophecies** a statement in which you say what you believe will happen in the future

proph·et /'prɒfɪt $ 'prɑfɪt/ *noun* someone who people believe God has chosen to be a religious leader or teacher

pro·por·tion /prə'pɔːʃən $ prə'pɔr-ʃən/ *noun* **1** part of an amount or group: *A large proportion of the students go on to college after leaving school.* **2** the relationship between two amounts: *What is the proportion of girls to boys in the class?* **3** **proportions** the size of something: *a problem of huge proportions*

pro·pos·al /prə'pəʊzəl $ prə'poʊzəl/ *noun* **1** a suggested plan: *I have a proposal to make.* **2** when you ask someone to marry you

pro·pose /prə'pəʊz $ prə'poʊz/ *verb* **1** to officially suggest a plan: *The President proposed a 5% cut in income tax.* | *I propose we discuss this at a later meeting.* **2** to ask someone to marry you: *Tom proposed to me last night.* **3** *formal* to intend to do something: *Where do you propose to put the television?*

prop·o·si·tion /ˌprɒpə'zɪʃən $ ˌprɑpə-'zɪʃən/ *noun* **1** an offer or suggestion, especially in business or politics: *They came to me with a business proposition.* **2** *AmE* a suggestion for a new law that people in a state vote on

pros /prəʊz $ proʊz/ *plural noun* **the pros and cons** the good and bad points of something: *I spent some time considering the pros and cons, but eventually decided to accept the job.*

prose /prəʊz $ proʊz/ *noun* [no plural] ordinary written language, not poetry: *a great prose writer*

pros·e·cute /'prɒsəkjuːt $ 'prɑsə-ˌkjut/ *verb* to say officially that you think someone is guilty of a crime and must be judged by a court of law: *The police decided to prosecute him for dangerous driving.*

pros·e·cu·tion /ˌprɒsə'kjuːʃən $ ˌprɑsə'kjuʃən/ *noun* **the prosecution** the lawyers who are trying to prove that someone is guilty of a crime in a court of law: *The prosecution have a good case.* ⇨ opposite DEFENCE (3)

pros·pect /'prɒspekt $ 'prɑspekt/ *noun* the chance that something will happen soon: *Laura was dreading the prospect of Christmas without her family.*

pro·spec·tive /prə'spektɪv/ *adjective formal* likely to do or be something in the future: *Find out as much as you can about your prospective employer before the interview.*

pro·spec·tus /prə'spektəs/ *noun, plural* **prospectuses** a small book in which a university, school, or company gives information about itself

pro·sper·i·ty /prɒ'sperəti $ prɑ'sper-əti/ *noun* [no plural] when people have a lot of money: *years of prosperity*

pros·per·ous /'prɒspərəs $ 'prɑs-pərəs/ *adjective* rich and successful: *a prosperous businessman*

pros·ti·tute /'prɒstətjuːt $ 'prɑstə-ˌtut/ *noun* someone who earns money by having sex with people

pros·ti·tu·tion /ˌprɒstə'tjuːʃən $ ˌprɑs-tə'tuʃən/ *noun* [no plural] when someone earns money by having sex with people

pro·tect /prə'tekt/ *verb*

GRAMMAR
protect someone/something from someone/something
protect someone/something against something
to prevent someone or something from being harmed or damaged:

*The police should **protect** people from dangerous men like him. | Wear a hat to **protect** yourself against the sun.*

pro·tec·tion /prə'tekʃən/ noun
[no plural]

> **GRAMMAR**
> **protection from/against something**

if something gives protection, it prevents someone or something from being harmed or damaged: *The trees **gave** them some **protection** against the rain.*

pro·tec·tive /prə'tektɪv/ adjective
1 intended to protect someone or something from damage: *The players wear protective helmets.* **2** wanting to protect someone from harm: *She was very protective towards her children.*

pro·tein /'prəʊtiːn $'proʊtin/ noun a substance in food such as meat and eggs, which helps your body to grow and be healthy

pro·test¹ /'prəʊtest $'proʊtest/ noun

> **GRAMMAR**
> **a protest against something**

an action by which a group of people show publicly that they think something is wrong: *He took part in a **protest against** the government's treatment of refugees. | She resigned **in protest at** his behaviour* (=because she thought his behaviour was wrong).

pro·test² /prə'test/ verb

> **GRAMMAR**
> **protest against/about something**

if people protest against something, they show publicly that they think it is wrong. In American English, you say that people protest something: *Thousands of people gathered to **protest against** the new law. | The students were protesting the war.*

Prot·es·tant /'prɒtəstənt $'prɑt-əstənt/ noun a Christian who is not a Roman Catholic
–**Protestant** adjective: *a Protestant church*

pro·test·er /prə'testə $'proʊtestər/

noun one of a group of people who are showing publicly that they think something is wrong or unfair: *a demonstration by anti-war protesters*

pro·trac·tor /prə'træktə $proʊ'træktər/ noun a flat object shaped like a half circle, used for measuring and drawing angles

proud /praʊd/ adjective

> **GRAMMAR**
> **proud of something/someone**
> **proud to do something**
> **proud that**

if you feel proud, you feel pleased because you think that something you have achieved or are connected with is very good: *He is **proud of** his son's achievement. | A success like this makes you **proud to** be British. | She was **proud that** her work was chosen for the exhibition.*

> **PHRASE**
> **be too proud to do something** to not do something because you feel that it would make you look foolish: *She **was too proud to** ask her family for money.*

prove /pruːv/ verb proved, proved or proven /'pruːvən/

> **GRAMMAR**
> **prove (that)**
> **prove to be something**

1 to show that something is definitely true: *You can't **prove that** I took the money. | The scientists are trying to prove the theory by doing an experiment.* **2** if something proves useful, difficult etc, it is found to be useful, difficult etc: *Getting a job proved difficult. | This information **proved to be** extremely useful.*

> **PHRASE**
> **prove someone right, prove someone wrong** to show that what someone said was true or not true: *I said he would be successful, and I **was proved right.***

prov·en a past participle of PROVE

prov·erb /'prɒvɜːb $'prɑvərb/ noun an old, well-known sentence that tells you something about life, such as 'Many hands make light work.'

pro·vide /prə'vaɪd/ verb

GRAMMAR
provide someone with something
provide something for someone
to give someone something they need: *This book will provide all the information you need.* | *I can provide you with a place to stay.* | *We provide financial help for students.*

pro·vid·ed /prə'vaɪdɪd/ also **pro·vid·ing** /prə'vaɪdɪŋ/ used to say that something will only happen if another thing happens: *You'll get good marks, provided you do the work.*

prov·ince /'prɒvɪns $ 'prɑvɪns/ noun one of the large areas into which some countries are divided: *the Canadian province of Ontario*

pro·vi·sion /prə'vɪʒən/ noun **1** when people provide something: *the provision of health care* **2** provisions supplies of food: *After a week they were running short of provisions.*

pro·vi·sion·al /prə'vɪʒənəl/ adjective likely to be changed: *A provisional date for the meeting had been agreed.*

prov·o·ca·tion /ˌprɒvə'keɪʃən $ ˌprɑvə-'keɪʃən/ noun an action that is likely to make someone attack you: *He attacked me totally without provocation.*

pro·voke /prə'vəʊk $ prə'voʊk/ verb **1** to deliberately make someone attack you: *Ignore him – he's just trying to provoke you.* **2** to cause a feeling: *Her comments provoked a lot of anger.*

prowl /praʊl/ verb to move around an area quietly: *A cat prowled the streets.*

pru·dent /'pruːdənt/ adjective sensible and careful

prune /pruːn/ verb to cut some of the branches of a tree or bush

pry /praɪ/ verb pried, pries **1** to try to find out about someone's private life, when the person does not want you to: *I don't mean to pry, but are you still seeing Tom?* **2** to force something open or away from something else ⇨ *same meaning* PRISE: *He pried off the lid.*

PS /ˌpiː 'es/ used at the end of a letter when you want to add something after you have signed your name: *PS Don't forget Jane's birthday.*

pseu·do·nym /'sjuːdənɪm $ 'sudn,ɪm/ noun a false name used by a writer: *She wrote under a pseudonym.*

psy·chi·at·ric /ˌsaɪki'ætrɪk/ adjective related to mental illness: *a psychiatric hospital*

psy·chi·a·trist /saɪ'kaɪətrɪst/ noun a doctor for people who have a mental illness: *She needs to see a psychiatrist.*

psy·chi·a·try /saɪ'kaɪətri/ noun [no plural] the treatment of mental illness

psy·chic /'saɪkɪk/ adjective related to strange events or things such as GHOSTS that cannot be explained by science: *a fortune-teller who claimed to have psychic powers*

psy·cho·log·i·cal /ˌsaɪkə'lɒdʒɪkəl $ ˌsaɪkə'lɑdʒɪkəl/ adjective related to people's minds: *Many soldiers suffer from psychological problems.*
–**psychologically** /-kli/ adverb: *The crash affected her psychologically.*

psy·chol·o·gist /saɪ'kɒlədʒɪst $ saɪ-'kɑlədʒɪst/ noun someone who studies the way people's minds work

psy·chol·o·gy /saɪ'kɒlədʒi $ saɪ'kɑl-ədʒi/ noun [no plural] the study of the mind

psy·cho·path /'saɪkəpæθ/ noun someone who is very violent because of mental illness

pub /pʌb/ noun a place where you can buy and drink alcohol: *I'll meet you at the pub for a drink.*

pu·ber·ty /'pjuːbəti $ 'pjubɚti/ noun [no plural] the time when your body changes from a child's to an adult's: *Has she reached puberty yet?*

pub·lic¹ /'pʌblɪk/ adjective

1 available for anyone to use or take part in ⇨ *opposite* PRIVATE¹ (1): *public transport* | *a public meeting*
2 related to the government and the services that it provides for people: *The government wants to reduce public spending.*
3 related to all the people in a country: *Car theft is a matter of great public concern.*
4 done in a place where anyone can see or hear you ⇨ *opposite* PRIVATE¹ (4): *a series of public arguments*
–**publicly** adverb: *He had to apologise publicly.*

PHRASES
become public if a piece of information becomes public, it becomes

P

known to everyone: *News of their wedding soon became public.*
make something public to give people information: *We don't want this information to be made public.*

public² *noun*

the public *also* the general public all the people in a country: *The public have a right to know what the government is doing.*

PHRASE

in public in a place where anyone can see or hear you: *It was the first time she had sung in public.*

pub·li·ca·tion /ˌpʌbləˈkeɪʃən/ *noun*
1 [no plural] when a book becomes available to the public: *The date of publication is May 1st.* 2 *formal* a book or magazine: *scientific publications*
public hol·i·day /ˌ.. ˈ.../ the American word for BANK HOLIDAY
pub·lic·i·ty /pʌˈblɪsəti/ *noun* [no plural] attention from newspapers and television: *Murder trials always get a lot of publicity.*
pub·li·cize *also* **publicise** *BrE* /ˈpʌbləsaɪz/ *verb* to tell people about an event or a new film, book etc, especially in the newspapers and on television: *She appeared on TV to publicize her new film.*
public re·la·tions /ˌ.. .ˈ../ *also* **PR** *noun* [no plural] the work of keeping a good relationship between a company and its customers and with the public: *Giving money to local schools is good for the company's public relations.*
public school /ˌ.. ˈ./ *noun* 1 *BrE* a school that parents pay to send their children to 2 *AmE* a free school that is paid for by the government
pub·lish /ˈpʌblɪʃ/ *verb* to print a book or information and make it available for people to read: *a company that publishes children's books*
pub·lish·er /ˈpʌblɪʃə $ ˈpʌblɪʃɚ/ *noun* a company that produces books: *a publisher of scientific journals*
pub·lish·ing /ˈpʌblɪʃɪŋ/ *noun* [no plural] the business of producing books: *a career in publishing*
pud·ding /ˈpʊdɪŋ/ *noun* a sweet food that you eat as the last part of a meal: *Christmas pudding*

pud·dle /ˈpʌdl/ **puddle**
noun a small pool of rain
puff¹ /pʌf/ *verb*
1 to breathe quickly and with difficulty: *Max was puffing after running for the bus.*
2 to breathe smoke from a cigarette or pipe: *an old man puffing on his pipe*
puff² *noun* a small amount of air, smoke, or wind: *Puffs of smoke came from the chimney.*

pull¹ /pʊl/ *verb*
to move something towards you: *She pulled the chair forward.* | *He pulled a small table towards him.* | *He pulled the door closed behind him.* | *Pull harder!* ⇨ see picture on page 340

PHRASES
pull a gun, pull a knife to take out a gun or knife and threaten someone with it: *He suddenly pulled a gun on me.*
pull a face to make your face have a funny or ugly expression
pull your weight to do your share of the work: *The others said he wasn't pulling his weight.*
pull someone's leg to tell someone something that is not true, as a joke: *He must have been pulling your leg!*

PHRASAL VERBS
pull down
pull something down to destroy a building that is no longer needed: *The old factory was pulled down in 1995.*
pull in
to drive to the side of the road and stop: *I pulled in just past the school.*
pull out
1 to not take part in something that you have agreed to do: *He pulled out of the competition because he was ill.*
2 if a car pulls out, it moves towards the middle of the road: *A van pulled out in front of me.*
pull over
to drive to the side of the road and

stop: *I saw Jenny on the pavement, so I **pulled over**.*

pull through *informal*
to stay alive after a serious injury or illness: *The doctors thought he might not **pull through**.*

pull up
if a car pulls up, it stops: *A taxi **pulled up** outside the house.*

pull² *noun* when you pull something towards you: *He gave the rope a good pull, but it wouldn't move.*

pul·ley /'pʊli/ *noun* a piece of equipment for lifting things, that has a wheel and a rope

pull·o·ver /'pʊl,əʊvə $ 'pʊl,oʊvɚ/ *noun* a SWEATER

pulp /pʌlp/ *noun [no plural]* a soft substance, especially one made by crushing something: *Mash the potatoes to a pulp.*

pul·pit /'pʊlpɪt/ *noun* a high place where a priest stands to speak to people in a church

pulse /pʌls/ *noun* the regular beat made by your heart when it is moving blood around your body: *A nurse took my pulse.*

pump¹ /pʌmp/ *noun* **1** a machine that forces liquid or gas into or out of something: *a fuel pump* **2** a type of plain light shoe for women

pump² *verb*

GRAMMAR
pump something into/out of something
to make liquid or gas flow somewhere using a machine: *They **pumped** the water **out of** the boat.*

PHRASAL VERB
pump up
pump something up to fill a tyre, ball etc with air: *I **pumped up** some balloons for the party.*

pump·kin /'pʌmpkɪn/ *noun* a large round orange vegetable ⇨ *see picture on page 345*

pun /pʌn/ *noun* a joke that is based on two words that sound the same but have different meanings

punch¹ /pʌntʃ/ *verb* to hit something hard with your closed hand: *I'll punch you on the nose!* ⇨ *see picture on page 341*

punch² *noun* **1** *plural* **punches** when someone hits something with their closed hand: *a punch in the stomach* **2** *[no plural]* a drink that contains fruit juice, water, and often alcohol: *a glass of fruit punch*

punch·line /'pʌntʃlaɪn/ *noun* the last few words of a joke or story, that make it funny or clever: *I've forgotten the punchline.*

punc·tu·al /'pʌntʃuəl/ *adjective* arriving at exactly the right time: *She's usually so punctual.*
–**punctually** *adverb*: *We expect you to arrive puntually for school.*

punc·tu·a·tion /,pʌntʃu'eɪʃən/ *noun [no plural]* the use of COMMAS (,), FULL STOPS (.) etc in a piece of writing: *You must use the correct punctuation.*

punc·ture¹ /'pʌntʃə $ 'pʌntʃɚ/ *noun* a small hole made by a sharp point: *The glass made a puncture in my tyre.*

puncture² *verb* to make a small hole in something: *A piece of broken bone had punctured his lung.*

pun·ish /'pʌnɪʃ/ *verb*

GRAMMAR
punish someone for (doing) something
to do something unpleasant to someone because they have done something wrong or illegal: *His dad **punished** him **for** lying by not letting him go out for two weeks.* | *He must **be punished for** this terrible crime.* | *The people who did this will be **severely punished**.*

pun·ish·ment /'pʌnɪʃmənt/ *noun* an action taken to punish someone: *He was made to clear up rubbish as a punishment.*

punk /pʌŋk/ *noun [no plural]* a type of loud violent music popular in the late 1970s and early 1980s

pu·ny /'pjuːni/ *adjective* **punier, puniest** small, thin, and weak: *a puny little kid*

pu·pil /'pjuːpəl/ *noun* a child in a school: *There are 30 pupils in my class.*

pup·pet /'pʌpɪt/ *noun* a MODEL of a person or animal that you can move by pulling wires, or by putting your hand inside it

pup·py /ˈpʌpi/ *noun, plural* **puppies** a young dog

pur·chase[1] /ˈpɜːtʃəs $ ˈpɜtʃəs/ *verb formal* to buy something: *I'd like to purchase a bus ticket please.*

purchase[2] *noun formal* **1** when you buy something: *the purchase of new computers* **2** something you have bought: *This car is my most expensive purchase.*

pure /pjʊə $ pjʊr/ *adjective*

1 not mixed with anything else: *This shirt is made of pure silk.*

2 pure water or air does not contain anything harmful: *The air is very pure in the mountains.*

PHRASE

pure chance, pure luck if something happens by pure chance, it happens completely by chance: *We found the right place by **pure luck**.*

pu·ree /ˈpjʊəreɪ $ pjʊˈreɪ/ *noun* a soft food, made by boiling or crushing: *tomato puree*

pur·ple /ˈpɜːpəl $ ˈpɜpəl/ *adjective, noun* a colour made by mixing red with blue: *They were both dressed in purple.* | *purple flowers*

pur·pose /ˈpɜːpəs $ ˈpɜpəs/ *noun*

GRAMMAR

the purpose of something

1 the thing that you want to achieve when you do or use something: *My purpose today is to explain how the Internet works.* | *What is **the purpose of** this meeting?* | *We are keen to expand the business, and have already started investing money **for this purpose**.* | *Exercises from this book can be used **for** teaching **purposes**.*

2 on purpose if you do something bad on purpose, you intend to do it and do not do it by accident: *Geoff went the wrong way **on purpose**.*

purr /pɜː $ pɜ/ *verb* if a cat purrs, it makes a low soft sound
– **purr** *noun*

purse /pɜːs $ pɜs/ *noun* **1** *BrE* a small container that women use to carry money: *I had very little money in my purse.* **2** the American word for HAND-BAG

pur·sue /pəˈsjuː $ pɜˈsu/ *verb formal* to chase someone: *A police car pursued them for 5 miles.*

pur·suit /pəˈsjuːt $ pɜˈsut/ *noun* **1** *[no plural]* when you chase someone: *The pursuit lasted 20 minutes.* **2** pursuits things that you spend time doing: *outdoor pursuits such as climbing and sailing*

push[1] /pʊʃ/ *verb*

GRAMMAR

push something along/over/open etc

push past someone

1 to press something using your hands, often to make it move away from you: *He **pushed** the wheelchair **along**.* | *He **pushed** her **into** the car.* | *Joey **pushed** me **over** in the playground.* | *Push this button to turn the computer on.* | *Gary **pushed** the door **open**.* ⇨ see pictures on pages 340 and 341

2 to move forward by pushing people away from you: *Rod **pushed past** Sal very rudely.* | *Joe **pushed his way** to the front of the queue.*

3 push someone into doing something to make someone do something that they do not really want to do: *Phil **was pushed into** joining the Marines by his dad.*

push[2] *noun, plural* **pushes** **1** when you push someone or something: *Give the gate a push.* **2** when people try very hard to achieve something: *a push to get more money for schools*

push·chair /ˈpʊʃ-tʃeə $ ˈpʊʃˌtʃer/ *noun BrE* a chair on wheels that is used for pushing a child somewhere; STROLLER *AmE*

push-up

push-up /ˈ. ./ *noun* an exercise in which you lie on the floor and push yourself up with your arms ⇨ same meaning PRESS-UP

push·y /'pʊʃi/ *adjective* pushier, pushiest determined to get what you want, in a way that seems rude: *a pushy salesman*

put /pʊt/ *verb* put, putting, have put

GRAMMAR
put something in/on/into etc
to move something to a place and leave it there: *Where did I put my keys?* | *Harry put the pen in his pocket.* | *I thought I put my purse on the table, but it's not there now.* | *Did you put the cat outside?*

PHRASAL VERBS
put away
put something away to put something in the place where you usually keep it: *The kids never put anything away!* | *Mom is upstairs, putting away the clothes.*
put back
put something back to put something back in the place where it was before: *Sandy always forgets to put the milk back in the refrigerator.*
put down
put something down to put something you are holding onto a table or the floor: *Just put it down on the floor over there.* | *Brianna put down her glass* ⇨ see picture on page 340
put off
put something off to not do something at the time when you should do it, and instead decide to do it later: *I had to put off the meeting until next week.*
put on
put something on to put clothes on your body: *Put your coat on – it's cold outside!* | *Let me put on my glasses – I can't read this.* ⇨ opposite TAKE OFF

put together
put something together to make something by joining all the different parts together: *You can buy really nice furniture there, but you have to put it together yourself.*
put up
1 put something up to put something on a wall or in a high position: *The teachers had put the children's paintings up on the walls.*
2 put up with to accept an annoying situation or someone's annoying behaviour, without trying to stop it or change it: *I don't get paid enough to put up with customers being rude to me.* | *How do you put up with all this noise?*

puz·zle¹ /'pʌzəl/ *noun* 1 a game or toy that is difficult to do: *a crossword puzzle* | *a jigsaw puzzle*
2 something that is difficult to understand: *Why the plane crashed is a complete puzzle.*

puzzle² *verb* if something puzzles you, it makes you feel confused: *It puzzles me why you don't like him.*

puz·zled /'pʌzəld/ *adjective* confused: *You look puzzled.*

puz·zling /'pʌzlɪŋ/ *adjective* difficult to understand: *I find his reaction puzzling.*

py·ja·mas *BrE*, **pajamas** *AmE* /pə'dʒɑː-məz/ *plural noun* light trousers and a shirt that you wear in bed: *a pair of pyjamas*

pyr·a·mid /'pɪrəmɪd/ *noun* a solid shape which is square at the base and pointed at the top: *a paperweight in the shape of a pyramid*

py·thon /'paɪθən $ 'paɪθɑːn/ *noun* a large snake that kills the animals it eats by crushing them

P

Qq

quack /kwæk/ *verb* if a duck quacks, it makes a loud noise from its throat
– **quack** *noun*

quad·ru·ple /'kwɒdrupəl $ kwɑ'dru-pəl/ *verb* to increase by four times: *Sales of digital televisions have quadrupled.*

quaint /kweɪnt/ *adjective* attractive in an old-fashioned way: *a quaint little village*

quake /kweɪk/ *informal* an EARTHQUAKE

qual·i·fi·ca·tion /ˌkwɒləfə'keɪʃən $ ˌkwɑləfə'keɪʃən/ *noun* an official examination that you have passed, which shows what level of education you have reached or what training you have had: *What qualifications do you have? | You need to get a qualification in nursing.*

qual·i·fied /'kwɒləfaɪd $ 'kwɑlə‚faɪd/ *adjective* someone who is qualified has passed an official examination that shows they are trained to do a particular job: *a qualified football trainer | Are you qualified to be a life guard?*

qual·i·fi·er /'kwɒləfaɪə $ 'kwɑlə‚faɪɚ/ *noun* **1** a game that you have to win to take part in a sports competition: *a world-cup qualifier* **2** a person or team who achieves the standard that is needed to enter a sports competition: *Johnson was the fastest qualifier.*

qual·i·fy /'kwɒləfaɪ $ 'kwɑlə‚faɪ/ *verb* **qualified, qualifies** **1** to pass an official examination that shows you are trained to do a particular job: *It takes a long time to qualify as a doctor.* **2** to be successful at one stage of a sports competition so that you can continue to the next stage: *She's hoping to qualify for the Olympic Games.*

quality /'kwɒləti $ 'kwɑləti/ *noun, plural* **qualities**

> **GRAMMAR**
> **the quality of something**
> **1** *[no plural]* how good something is: *The*

quality of *the food in that restaurant is very high* (=very good). *| a **good quality** hi-fi system | Some of the work was **of** very **poor quality**. | **top quality** (=highest quality) products*
2 a good thing such as honesty that someone has as part of their character: *What qualities do you look for in a student?*

quan·ti·fi·er /'kwɒntəfaɪə $ 'kwɑntə-‚faɪɚ/ *noun* a word or phrase such as 'much', 'few', or 'a lot of', which is used with a noun to show an amount

quantity /'kwɒntəti $ 'kwɑn-təti/ *noun, plural* **quantities**

> **GRAMMAR**
> **a quantity of something**
> an amount of something that you can measure or count: *We brought a **large quantity of** food with us. | a **small quantity of** butter. | The police discovered huge **quantities of** drugs hidden in the old building.*

quar·an·tine /'kwɒrəntiːn $ 'kwɔrən-‚tin/ *noun [no plural]* when someone with a disease must stay apart from other people so that other people do not get the disease too: *The hospital kept her in quarantine for a week.*

quar·rel[1] /'kwɒrəl $ 'kwɔrəl/ *noun* an angry argument: *I've had a quarrel with my father.*

quar·rel[2] *verb* **quarrelled, quarrelling** *BrE,* **quarreled, quarreling** *AmE* to have an angry argument: *I'm always quarrelling with my sister.*

quar·ry /'kwɒri $ 'kwɔri/ *noun, plural* **quarries** a place where sand or stone is dug out of the ground ➪ *see picture on page 348*

quart /kwɔːt $ kwɔrt/ *written abbreviation* **qt** *noun* a unit for measuring liquid, the same as 2 PINTS

quar·ter /ˈkwɔːtə $ˈkwɔrtɚ/ noun

GRAMMAR
a quarter of something

1 one of four equal parts that you can divide something into: *She cut the cake into quarters.*

2 25 per cent: *About **a quarter of** the students here are Chinese.* | *Over **three-quarters of** the forest (=75 per cent) was destroyed in the fire.*

3 a coin in the US and Canada worth 25 cents: *Can you lend me a quarter?*

4 AmE one of the four periods of time into which the school year is divided

PHRASES
a quarter of an hour fifteen minutes: *We waited **a quarter of an hour** for the bus.*

quarter to two, quarter to three etc BrE, **quarter of two, quarter of three** etc AmE: *We leave school at **quarter to four** (=at fifteen minutes before four o'clock).*

quarter past two, quarter past three etc BrE, **quarter after two, quarter after three** etc AmE: *It's **quarter after eight** (=it's fifteen minutes after eight o'clock).*

quar·ter·back /ˈkwɔːtəbæk $ˈkwɔrtɚ‚bæk/ noun the most important player in American football, who throws the ball

quar·ter·fi·nal /ˌkwɔːtəˈfaɪnl $ˌkwɔrtɚˈfaɪnl/ noun one of the last four games at the end of a sports competition. The winners play in the two SEMIFINALS

quar·ter·ly /ˈkwɔːtəli $ˈkwɔrtɚli/ adjective, adverb produced or happening four times a year: *a quarterly magazine* | *We pay our electricity bill quarterly.*

quartz /kwɔːts $kwɔrts/ noun [no plural] a type of hard rock used for making electronic clocks

quash /kwɒʃ $kwɑʃ/ verb formal **1** to officially say that a decision is not legal or correct any more: *The Court of Appeal quashed his conviction for murder.* **2** to use force to stop fighting or protests: *Troops were sent in to quash the rebellion.*

quay /kiː/ noun a place beside the sea or a big river for loading and unloading boats

quea·sy /ˈkwiːzi/ adjective **queasier, queasiest** if you feel queasy, you feel as if you are going to be sick: *The awful smell was making me feel queasy.*

queen /kwiːn/ noun **1** the female ruler of a country, or the wife of a king: *Queen Victoria* **2** a playing card with a picture of a queen on it: *the queen of hearts*

queer /kwɪə $kwɪr/ adjective **1** strange and not normal: *His behaviour seemed a bit queer.* **2** informal an offensive word meaning HOMOSEXUAL

quench /kwentʃ/ verb **quench your thirst** to drink something so that you no longer feel thirsty: *I had a drink of water to quench my thirst.*

que·ry¹ /ˈkwɪəri $ˈkwɪri/ noun, plural **queries** a question asking for more information: *Does anyone have any queries?*

query² verb formal **queried, queries** to check that something is correct by asking questions about it: *My mother queried the bill.*

quest /kwest/ noun formal a long and difficult search: *the quest for life on Mars*

ques·tion¹ /ˈkwestʃən/ noun

GRAMMAR
a question about something

1 something that you say or write when you are asking about something: *Does anyone want to **ask** any **questions** before we begin?* | *The police **asked** him a lot of **questions about** the car.* | *The teacher could not **answer** my **question**.*

2 a part of a test that asks you to give information: *I didn't understand some of the questions in the exam.* | *We had to **do** 30 **questions** in an hour.*

PHRASES
be out of the question: *Dad says that having the party here **is out of the question** (=is definitely not allowed).*

good question! spoken used to say in an amusing way that you do not know the answer to a question: *"How many paintings did Picasso actually do?" "**Good question!** I have no idea!"*

question² *verb*

GRAMMAR
question someone about something
to ask someone a lot of questions about something: *The police questioned him about the robbery.*

ques·tion·a·ble /ˈkwestʃənəbəl/ *adjective* something that is questionable does not seem to be completely true, correct, or honest: *It's questionable whether she's telling the truth.*

question mark /ˈ.. ,./ *noun* the sign (?), that you write at the end of a question

ques·tion·naire /ˌkwestʃəˈneə $ ˌkwestʃəˈner/ *noun* a set of written questions that you answer in order to give information about something: *Could you fill in this questionnaire?*

queue¹ /kjuː/ *noun* BrE a line of people or vehicles that are waiting for something; LINE AmE: *I joined the back of the queue. | There's a long queue at the bank.*

queue² also **queue up** *verb* BrE to wait in a line of people; LINE UP AmE: *How long have you been queueing for tickets?*

quib·ble /ˈkwɪbəl/ *verb* to argue about something that is not very important: *Let's not quibble about 10p.*

quick /kwɪk/ *adjective*

GRAMMAR
quick to do something
1 something that is quick does not take very much time to do: *Can I make a quick telephone call? | Do you know the quickest way to the station? | We need a quick decision on this.*
2 someone who is quick moves or does something fast: *The dog chased me, but I was too quick. | Children are very **quick to** learn.*

quick·ly /ˈkwɪkli/ *adverb*

1 if you move quickly, you move fast: *Rick ran quickly to the car.*
2 if you do something quickly, you do it in a short amount of time: *We must leave quickly or we'll miss the coach.*

quick·sand /ˈkwɪksænd/ *noun* [no plural] wet sand that is dangerous to walk on because you sink into it

quid /kwɪd/ *noun* BrE informal, plural **quid** a pound in British money: *Will you lend me a quid?*

qui·et¹ /ˈkwaɪət/ *adjective*

1 something that is quiet does not make a lot of noise ⇨ opposite LOUD¹: *She spoke in a quiet voice. | The music became quieter.*
2 someone who is quiet does not talk very much: *Emily was a quiet, shy girl. | "Be quiet!" (=stop talking) said the teacher.*
3 if a place is quiet, there is not very much noise there and not many things happen there: *They live in a quiet little village. | a quiet country road | It was very quiet in town today.*

PHRASE
keep something quiet, keep quiet about something to not talk about something because you do not want other people to know about it: *I've found a job, but I want to **keep it quiet** for now. | It's typical of Roy to **keep quiet about** winning.*

quiet² *noun* [no plural] when there is not very much noise and not many things are happening: *We sat outside, enjoying the quiet of the night.*

qui·et·en /ˈkwaɪətn/ BrE, **quiet** AmE also **quieten down** BrE, **quiet down** AmE, *verb* to become quiet after making a lot of noise: *After a while the children quietened down.*

qui·et·ly /ˈkwaɪətli/ *adverb* without making much noise: *She quietly turned the key. | "I'm sorry," he said quietly.*

quilt /kwɪlt/ *noun* a bed cover filled with soft warm material

quirk·y /ˈkwɜːki $ ˈkwɚki/ *adjective* **quirkier, quirkiest** slightly strange: *a quirky sense of humour*

quit /kwɪt/ *verb* informal, past tense and past participle **quit, quitting** 1 to leave a place or job permanently: *Dad was furious when he found out I'd quit college.* 2 to close a computer PROGRAM: *If the* program won't run, try quitting and restarting. **3** to stop doing something: *My doctor told me I have to quit smoking.*

quite /kwaɪt/ *adverb*

1 fairly large: *It can be quite cold at night.* | *I was quite surprised when Sandy turned up.* | *We had to wait for quite a long time.* | *I quite liked the book.* | *I've saved up quite a lot of money already.*
2 completely: *I'm afraid that's quite impossible.* | *The special effects in the film were quite amazing!*

PHRASE

not quite almost, but not completely or not exactly: *I **haven't quite** finished.* | *I'm **not quite** sure where the sports centre is.* | *I **don't quite** understand.*

quiv·er /'kwɪvə $ 'kwɪvɚ/ *verb* to shake slightly, especially because you are angry, upset, or nervous: *His voice was quivering with rage.*

quiz /kwɪz/ *noun, plural* **quizzes** a competition in which you have to answer questions: *Ten teams entered the quiz.*

quo·ta /'kwəʊtə $ 'kwoʊtə/ *noun* an amount of something that someone is allowed to have: *The city has already had its quota of financial help from the government.*

quo·ta·tion /kwəʊ'teɪʃən $ kwoʊ'teɪʃən/ *noun* 1 words that come from a book, poem etc: *a quotation from one of Shakespeare's plays* 2 a statement showing how much money it will cost to do something: *This is the cheapest quotation.*

quotation mark /.'.. ,./ *noun* a sign ("," or ',') that you write before and after someone's speech

quote¹ /kwəʊt $ kwoʊt/ *verb* 1 to say some of the words that are written in a book, poem etc, or that someone else has said: *He's always quoting from the Bible.* 2 to tell a customer the price you will charge them for something: *They quoted us £20 for delivering the bed.*

quote² a QUOTATION

Q

Rr

rab·bi /ˈræbaɪ/ *noun* a Jewish religious leader

rab·bit /ˈræbɪt/ *noun* a small animal with long ears and soft fur that lives in holes in the ground

rab·ble /ˈræbəl/ *noun* [no plural] a noisy crowd of people who are behaving badly: *Get this rabble to be quiet.*

ra·bies /ˈreɪbiːz/ *noun* [no plural] a disease that kills animals and people that are bitten by an infected animal

race¹ /reɪs/ *noun*

race

1 a competition in which people try to run or drive faster than each other: *Very few of the British athletes **won** their **races**. | She came second in her race.*
2 one of the main groups that people can be divided into because they look similar and have the same colour skin: *We employ people of every race and religion.*

race² *verb* 1 to run or drive somewhere very quickly: *I raced to catch up with them. | A fire engine raced past.*
2 to compete in a race: *She will be racing against athletes from all over the world.*

race·course /ˈreɪs-kɔːs $ ˈreɪs-kɔrs/ *noun* a place where horses compete in races

race·horse /ˈreɪshɔːs $ ˈreɪshɔrs/ *noun* a horse that competes in races

race·track /ˈreɪs-træk/ *noun* a track (=special area or surface) where runners, cars, or horses race

ra·cial /ˈreɪʃəl/ *adjective* relating to the colour of someone's skin and the race that they belong to: *people from different racial groups | The company was accused of racial discrimination* (=treating people unfairly because of their skin colour etc).
–**racially** *adverb*: *a racially motivated attack*

rac·ing /ˈreɪsɪŋ/ *noun* [no plural] a sport in which horses or cars race: *horse racing*

ra·cis·m /ˈreɪsɪzəm/ *noun* [no plural] unfair treatment of someone because of their skin colour or the race that they belong to: *We will not tolerate racism in this school.*

rac·ist /ˈrɪsɪst/ *noun* someone who treats people unfairly because of their skin colour or the race that they belong to: *I'm not a racist.*
–**racist** *adjective*: *Some of the other children were unkind and made racist remarks.*

racks

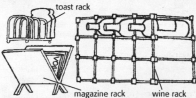

toast rack

magazine rack   wine rack

rack /ræk/ *noun* a shelf or frame for holding things: *a luggage rack | a wine rack*

rack·et /ˈrækɪt/ *noun* 1 also **racquet** the thing you use for hitting the ball in games such as tennis: *a tennis racket* 2 *informal* a lot of loud noise: *Who's making that racket?*

ra·dar /'reɪdɑː $'reɪdɑr/ noun a piece of equipment that finds the position of things such as planes and ships by sending out radio signals

ra·di·ant /'reɪdiənt/ adjective happy and beautiful: *Sarah, you look radiant.*

ra·di·ate /'reɪdieɪt/ verb **1** to show a feeling very strongly in your appearance or behaviour: *She radiated confidence.* **2** to send out light or heat: *A huge fire radiated warmth around the room.*

ra·di·a·tion /ˌreɪdi'eɪʃən/ noun [no plural] very powerful dangerous energy that some substances send out: *The process produces high levels of radiation.*

ra·di·a·tor /'reɪdieɪtə $'reɪdiˌeɪtɚ/ noun **1** a piece of equipment that heats a room: *Hang your shirt on the radiator to dry.* **2** a piece of equipment that stops a vehicle's engine from getting too hot

rad·i·cal¹ /'rædɪkəl/ adjective a change that is radical is big and very noticeable: *They are planning radical changes in education.* | *Don't do anything too radical with my hair.*
 – **radically** /-kli/ adverb: *It's not radically different.*

radical² noun someone who wants to change a political system completely

ra·di·o¹ /'reɪdiəʊ $'reɪdiˌoʊ/ noun
1 a piece of electronic equipment that you use to listen to programmes that are broadcast: *Al* **switched the radio on** *to hear his favourite music programme.* | *I've just bought myself a new radio.*
2 if something is broadcast on radio, it is done so that people can listen to it using radios: *Bob Geldof was interviewed* **on Irish radio.** | *What sort of music do you listen to* **on the radio?**

radio² verb to send a message to someone using a radio: *The ship's captain radioed for help.*

ra·di·o·ac·tive /ˌreɪdiəʊ'æktɪv $ˌreɪdioʊ'æktɪv/ adjective something that is radioactive contains or sends out RADIATION: *Plutonium is highly radioactive.* | *radioactive nuclear waste*

ra·di·o·ac·tiv·i·ty /ˌreɪdiəʊæk'tɪvəti $ˌreɪdiʊæk'tɪvəti/ noun [no plural] when a substance produces or sends out RADIATION

ra·di·o·ther·a·py /ˌreɪdiəʊ'θerəpi $ˌreɪdioʊ'θerəpi/ noun [no plural] the treatment of illnesses such as CANCER, using RADIATION: *She may have to have radiotherapy.*

ra·di·us /'reɪdiəs/ noun, plural **radii** /-diaɪ/ **1** the distance from the centre of a circle to the edge **2** within a two mile radius, within a ten mile radius etc within a particular distance from a place in any direction: *Police searched houses within a two-mile radius of the crime.*

raf·fle /'ræfəl/ noun a competition in which people buy tickets with numbers on them and win a prize if one of their numbers is chosen: *Would you like to buy some raffle tickets?*

raft /rɑːft $ræft/ noun a flat structure that floats on water, made from long pieces of wood tied together

rag /ræg/ noun a piece of old cloth: *Clean the lamp with a rag.*

rage¹ /reɪdʒ/ noun extreme anger: *She went wild with rage.*

rage² verb if fighting, a storm etc rages, it continues with a lot of force or violence: *The war raged for five years.*

rag·ged /'rægɪd/ adjective clothes that are ragged are old and torn: *an old pair of ragged jeans.*

raid /reɪd/ noun **1** a sudden military attack on a place: *Several buildings were destroyed in the air raid.* **2** a sudden visit by police who are looking for something: *Police found a large number of stolen guns during a raid on the house.* **3** a crime in which thieves enter a bank, shop etc and steal something: *a daring bank raid*
 – **raid** verb: *Thieves broke in and raided the post office.*

rail /reɪl/ noun **1** a metal bar that prevents you from moving forward or falling: *We stood at the rails and waved as the ship began to move.* **2** a metal bar that you hang things on: *a towel rail* **3 the rails** the two long metal tracks that trains move along **4 by rail** by train: *It would be quicker to go by rail.*

rail·ings /'reɪlɪŋz/ plural noun a fence that is made of metal bars: *The gates were shut, so we climbed over the railings.*

rail·way /'reɪlweɪ/ BrE, **rail·road** /'reɪlrəʊd $'reɪlroʊd/ AmE, noun a track for trains to travel along

R

rain¹ /reɪn/ *noun* [no plural]

water that falls in small drops from the sky: *If the **rain stops**, we'll go out.* | *The **rain** continued to **fall** overnight.* | *There was **heavy rain** (=a lot of rain) last night.*

rain² *verb*

when it rains, small drops of water fall from the sky: *If it's **raining**, we'll have to do something indoors.* | *Take an umbrella in case **it rains**.* | *It started to **rain** just as we were leaving.*

rain·bow /'reɪnbəʊ $ 'reɪnboʊ/ *noun* a curve of different colours in the sky that you see when there is sun and rain at the same time

rain·coat /'reɪnkəʊt $ 'reɪnkoʊt/ *noun* a coat that you wear to protect you from the rain

rain·drop /'reɪndrɒp $ 'reɪndrɑp/ *noun* a single drop of rain

rain·fall /'reɪnfɔːl/ *noun* the total amount of rain that falls on an area in a period of time: *Sri Lanka has an annual rainfall of 200–510 cm.*

rain for·est /'. ,../ *noun* a tropical forest with tall trees that are very close together: *the Amazon rainforests*

rain·y /'reɪni/ *adjective* rainier, rainiest a rainy day, afternoon etc is a day when it rains a lot

raise¹ /reɪz/ *verb*

GRAMMAR
raise something for someone/ something

1 to move something so that it is higher: *She raised her head to look at him.* | *The batter raised his bat, ready to hit the ball.*

2 to increase the amount or level of something: *The company has raised its prices.* | *This drug will raise your temperature.*

3 if you raise money, you collect money from other people so that you can help people who are hungry, ill, poor etc: *The class **raised** $500 dollars **for** cancer patients.* | *We are **raising funds** (=money) **for** children in Africa.*

PHRASES
raise your voice to speak more loudly than usual, often because you are annoyed with someone: *The teacher had to raise her voice to make the children listen.*

raise a question to mention something to someone because you want them to think about it: *When I **raised the question of** getting a new car, Rick got quite angry.*

raise the standard of something, **raise standards** to improve the quality or standard of something: *The government wants to **raise the standard of** animal care in zoos.*

raise fears, **raise hopes**: *The bomb has **raised fears** (=made people feel afraid) of more terrorist attacks.* | *I didn't want to **raise** their **hopes** (=make them feel hopeful).* ➪ see usage note at RISE¹

raise² the American word for RISE²

rai·sin /'reɪzən/ *noun* a small dried fruit that is often used in cakes

rake¹ /reɪk/ *noun* a garden tool that you use for gathering dead leaves together or making the earth level

rake² *verb* **1** to pull a rake over the ground in order to gather dead leaves together or make the earth level: *Rake the soil thoroughly before planting the seeds.* **2** be raking it in *informal spoken* to be earning a lot of money: *Hank's really raking it in with his new job!*

rally¹ /'ræli/ *noun*, plural rallies **1** a very large public meeting that shows support for a political idea: *30,000 workers attended a rally in the capital, Buenos Aires.* **2** a race for cars or MOTORCYCLES

rally² *verb* rallied, rallies **1** to come together to support someone or something: *In the end, everyone rallied to the President's support.* **2** rally around also rally round *BrE* to support someone when they are in a difficult situation: *My family always rallied round each other in a crisis.*

RAM /ræm/ *noun* [no plural] the part of a computer that keeps information for a short time so that you can use it immediately

ram¹ /ræm/ *verb* rammed, ramming also **ram into** to crash into something: *The driver lost control and rammed into the back of my car.*

ram² *noun* a male sheep

ramble[1] /ˈræmbəl/ also **ramble on**
verb to talk in a boring or confused way:
*The teacher was rambling on at the
front of the class.*

ramble[2] noun a long walk

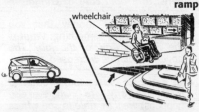

ramp

wheelchair

ramp /ræmp/ noun **1** a slope that is
put somewhere so that you can get from
one level to another: *They walked up the
ramp and onto the ship.* **2** the American word for SLIPROAD .

ram·page /ræmˈpeɪdʒ/ verb if people
rampage, they behave in a noisy and violent way: *Football fans rampaged
through the town.*
– **rampage** /ˈræmpeɪdʒ/ noun: *drunken
tourists on the rampage*

ram·pant /ˈræmpənt/ adjective something bad that is rampant is increasing
quickly and is difficult to control: *The
disease is rampant throughout the
population.* | *rampant inflation*

ram·shack·le /ˈræmʃækəl/ adjective a
ramshackle building is in bad condition
and looks as if it might fall down: *a ramshackle old shed*

ran the past tense of RUN

ranch /rɑːntʃ $ræntʃ/ noun, plural
ranches a big farm in the US where
cows, horses, or sheep are kept

ran·cid /ˈrænsɪd/ adjective food that is
rancid smells or tastes unpleasant because it is no longer fresh: *the smell of
rancid butter*

ran·dom /ˈrændəm/ adjective at random if you choose something or someone at random, you choose them in no
particular order: *Ten people were
chosen at random from the audience.*

rang the past tense of RING[2]

range[1] /reɪndʒ/ noun

1 a number of different things that all
belong to the same general type of
thing: *Mitsubishi has brought out
a new range of small cars.* | *Our*

survey of students collected *a wide
range of* views. | *The shop sells
videos, and there's a huge range to
choose from.*
2 the amounts or numbers between
two limits: *The water temperature
should be in the range of 76 to 89
degrees.* | *The school has children in
the 5 to 11 age range.*

range[2] verb range from something to
something to be between two limits:
*The children ranged in age from 5 to
14.* | *Prices range from about £100 to
£500.*

rang·er /ˈreɪndʒə $ˈreɪndʒər/ noun
someone whose job is to look after a
large area of public land: *She works as a
park ranger at Yellowstone National
Park.*

rank[1] /ræŋk/ noun
1 the position that someone has in the
army, the police etc, that shows how
important they are: *He held the
rank of colonel in the British army.*
2 the ranks the ordinary soldiers in an
army: *Morale in the ranks was low
after the defeat.*
3 a line of people or things: *a taxi
rank* | *Ranks of newspaper reporters
lined the streets.*

rank[2] verb to have a particular position in
a list that shows how good someone or
something is: *The team ranks third in
the nation.*

ran·sack /ˈrænsæk/ verb to damage a
place and make it very untidy, often because you are looking for something:
*The thieves ransacked the house and
stole jewellery worth £2000.*

ran·som /ˈrænsəm/ noun the money
that criminals ask you to pay before they
will free a prisoner: *The kidnappers demanded a ransom of £175,000 for the
child.*

rant /rænt/ also **rant on** verb to talk for
a long time in an angry way: *My father
was ranting on about me coming home
too late.*

rap[1] /ræp/ noun **1** a quick light knock
on a door or window **2** a type of popular music in which the words are spoken
not sung

R

rap² *verb* **rapped, rapping** **1** to hit something quickly and lightly: *A policeman came and rapped on my car window.* **2** to speak the words of a song very quickly in the type of popular music called rap

rape¹ /reɪp/ *verb* to force someone to have sex when they do not want to

rape² *noun* the crime of raping someone

rap·id /ˈræpɪd/ *adjective* very quick: *I did some rapid calculations in my head.* —**rapidly** *adverb*: *He walked rapidly away.*

rap·ids /ˈræpɪdz/ *plural noun* a part of a river where the water is moving very fast over rocks

rap·ist /ˈreɪpɪst/ *noun* someone who forces someone else to have sex with them when they do not want to

rare /reə $rer/ *adjective*
if something is rare, it does not often happen or there are not many things of that type: *Mary was born with a rare heart disease.* | *He was excited to see such a rare bird.*

rare·ly /ˈreəli $ˈrerli/ *adverb*
not very often: *I rarely see my parents now.*

rar·ing /ˈreərɪŋ $ˈrerɪŋ/ *adjective* **be raring to go** *informal* to be eager to start doing something: *Come on! We're all raring to go!*

ras·cal /ˈrɑːskəl $ˈræskəl/ *noun* a child who behaves slightly badly, but not in a very serious way

rash¹ /ræʃ/ *adjective* done too quickly, without enough thought: *Giving up my job was a rash decision.*

rash² *noun, plural* **rashes** a lot of small red spots on someone's skin that is often a sign of illness: *Tom had a temperature, and a rash all over his chest.*

rasp·ber·ry /ˈrɑːzbəri $ˈræzˌberi/ *noun, plural* **raspberries** a small soft sweet red fruit that grows on bushes ⇨ *see picture on page 345*

rat /ræt/ *noun* an animal like a large mouse with a long tail

rate¹ /reɪt/ *noun*

GRAMMAR
the rate of something
1 the number of times that something happens over a period of time: *The*

exam has a very **high** failure **rate** (=a lot of people fail it). | *The crime* **rate rose** (=increased) *by 3% last year.* **2** the speed at which something happens: *the rapid* **rate of** *change in technology* **3** the amount of money that you earn or pay for something: *What is the* **rate of pay** *for the job?* | *The government has increased the tax rate.* **4** **at any rate** *spoken*: *Tom brought a torch, so* **at any rate** (=whatever else happens) *we'll be able to see where we are.*

rate² *verb* to say how good or bad you think someone or something is: *Each video game is rated on a scale of 1 to 4, with four being best.*

ra·ther /ˈrɑːðə $ˈræðɚ/ *adverb*
1 a fairly large amount *BrE*: *I think you're being rather unfair.* | *It's rather cloudy – do you think it's going to rain?* | *That's rather an odd thing to do.* **2** **or rather** used to give different information to what you have just said: *She's at university, or rather she was until last week.* | *You should not boil the leaves, rather you should steam them.*

PHRASES
rather than something/someone not something or someone else: *The pupils wear their ordinary clothes* **rather than** *a school uniform.* | *We could walk to the station* **rather than** *waiting for a taxi.*
would rather if you would rather do something, you would prefer to do it: *I'd rather be outside on a lovely sunny day like this.* | *He said he* **would rather** *not talk about his problems.*

rat·ing /ˈreɪtɪŋ/ *noun* a measurement of how good or popular something or someone is: *The hotel had a five-star rating, and was very expensive.*

ra·ti·o /ˈreɪʃiəʊ $ˈreɪʃiˌoʊ/ *noun* the difference in size between two numbers or amounts that you are comparing: *In our school, the ratio of boys to girls is about 2:1.*

ra·tion¹ /'ræʃən/ *noun* the amount of food, petrol etc that you are allowed to have when there is not very much available: *During the war the weekly meat ration was very small.*

ration² *verb* to limit the amount of something that people are allowed to have because there is not very much available: *On the ship, water had to be strictly rationed.*

ra·tion·al /'ræʃənəl/ *adjective* **1** rational decisions are based on real facts or knowledge, not on your feelings: *Don't just do the same as everyone else – make a rational decision of your own.* **2** someone who is rational is able to think clearly about things: *Lucy was upset, and was not being very rational.*

rat race /'. ./ *noun* **the rat race** *informal* the way people live when they are always competing against each other in order to be richer or more successful: *I was tired of the rat race – so I gave up my job and went to live in the country.*

rat·tle¹ /'rætl/ *verb* if something rattles, or if it is rattled, it shakes and makes a noise: *The earthquake only lasted a few seconds, but it rattled all the doors and windows.*

rattle² *noun* **1** a baby's toy that makes a noise when you shake it **2** the noise something makes when it rattles: *the rattle of cups and plates* ⇨ *see picture on page 350*

rattle·snake /'rætlsneɪk/ *noun* a poisonous American snake that makes a noise with its tail

rav·age /'rævɪdʒ/ *verb* to destroy or badly damage a town or an area: *The enemy soldiers attacked, ravaging villages and towns.*

rave¹ /reɪv/ *noun* a large party where young people dance to electronic music

rave² also **rave on** *verb spoken* **1** to talk in an excited way about something because you think it is very good: *Sam's always raving about this music, but I don't like it much.* **2** to talk for a long time in an angry way: *Mum raved on at me about the state of my bedroom.*

rave³ *adjective* **rave reviews** if a new film, book, or play gets rave reviews, people praise it a lot in newspapers, on the television etc

rav·e·nous /'rævənəs/ *adjective* extremely hungry

ra·vine /rə'viːn/ *noun* a deep narrow valley with steep sides ⇨ *see picture on page 348*

rav·ing /'reɪvɪŋ/ *adjective informal* crazy: *He was acting like a raving lunatic.*

raw /rɔː/ *adjective*

1 raw food has not been cooked: *a salad of raw vegetables* | *You can cook apples, or eat them raw.*

2 raw materials or substances are still in their natural state and have not been changed or used for making anything yet: *France imports raw materials such as coal and steel.* | *raw cotton*

ray /reɪ/ *noun* a narrow line of light from the sun: *A ray of light shone through the window and onto my bed.*

razors

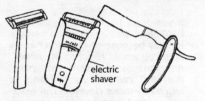

electric shaver

ra·zor /'reɪzə $ 'reɪzər/ *noun* a sharp tool that you use for removing hair from your face or body

Rd. *noun* the written abbreviation of 'road', used in addresses: *406, Cranberry Rd.*

reach¹ /riːtʃ/

verb

reach

GRAMMAR
reach for something

1 to arrive at a place: *We reached the village just after lunchtime.* | *Your email took three hours to reach me.*

2 to move your hand in order to touch something or pick it up: *The man reached for his gun.* | *She had to reach up to close the window.* | *Ann reached out her hand and caught the ball.*

3 if you can reach something, you are able to touch it or pick it up by stretching towards it: *Can you reach that book on the top shelf?*

R

4 to get to a particular level or standard: *We reached the quarter-final of the competition.* | *The number of deaths from the disease has reached 700.*
5 to speak to someone, especially by telephone: *You can reach me on my mobile.*

reach² *noun* **1 out of reach, out of someone's reach** too far away for someone to pick up or touch by stretching out their hand: *Keep the medicine out of children's reach.* **2 within reach, within someone's reach** near enough for someone to pick up or touch when they stretch out their hand: *The key was just within my reach.*

re·act /ri'ækt/ *verb*

GRAMMAR
react to something
react by doing something

if you react to something that has happened, you behave in a particular way because of it: *I didn't know how you would react to my news.* | *After the new rules were announced, the staff reacted by refusing to teach any more classes.* | *The workers reacted angrily when smoking was banned in the factory.*

PHRASAL VERB
react against something/someone

to show that you do not accept something that someone is telling you to do by deliberately doing the opposite: *My parents were very strict, and I reacted against them.*

re·ac·tion /ri'ækʃən/ *noun*

GRAMMAR
a reaction to something
the reaction of someone

1 what you do, feel, or say because of something that happens, something you see etc: *What was her reaction when you told her the school was going to close?* | *I was very surprised by John's reaction to the news.* | *What was the reaction of the audience when she came onto the stage?*
2 reactions your ability to move quickly when something happens suddenly: *This computer game tests your reactions.*

read /riːd/ *verb, past tense and past participle* **read** /red/

GRAMMAR
read about something
read (something) to someone
read someone something

1 to look at something that is written down and understand what it means: *Dad sat in his chair, reading the paper.* | *My little brother is learning to read.* | *I like reading about space travel.*
2 to say words that are written down in a book, newspaper etc so that other people can hear: *Fathers now have more time to read to their kids.* | *Mum, will you read me a story?*

PHRASAL VERBS
read out
read something out to say the words that are written in a message, list etc so that other people can hear them: *I will now read out the names of the winners.*
read through also **read over**
read something through, read something over to read something carefully from the beginning to the end, especially in order to check it: *Would you mind reading through my essay?* | *I read over my notes the night before the exam.*
read up on
read up on something to read a lot about something so that you can learn about it: *Catherine read up on the company before her job interview.*

read·a·ble /'riːdəbəl/ *adjective* interesting and enjoyable to read: *His second book is more readable than the first.*
read·er /'riːdə $ 'ridɚ/ *noun* someone who reads books, magazines etc: *These books are aimed at adult readers*
read·er·ship /'riːdəʃɪp $ 'ridɚˌʃɪp/ *noun* the number or type of people who read a newspaper, magazine etc: *The newspaper has a readership of 460,000.*
read·i·ly /'redəli/ *adverb* quickly and easily: *Jack readily agreed.*
read·i·ness /'redinəs/ *noun* [no plural] willingness to do something: *Small children have a natural readiness to learn.*

read·ing /ˈriːdɪŋ/ noun [no plural] when you read books, magazines etc: *Do you enjoy reading?*

read·y /ˈredi/ adjective

> **GRAMMAR**
> **ready to do something**
> **ready for something**

1 if you are ready, you have done everything that you need to do in order to prepare for something: *Are you **ready to** go yet? | I need to go home and **get ready for** the party.*
2 something that is ready is prepared and available for someone to use, eat, have etc: *Your dinner will be ready soon. | When will my shoes be **ready for** collection? | The fire was **ready to** light.*
3 if you are ready for something, you are old enough or sensible enough to do it: *I don't think I'm **ready for** a full-time job yet. | He doesn't **feel ready to** get married.*

ready-made /ˌ.. ˈ./ adjective ready-made meals, clothes etc have been prepared or made before you buy them and are ready for you to use: *ready-made pasta dishes*

real /rɪəl/ adjective

1 something that is real is not imagined, because it actually exists or is true: *The story is based on real events. | None of the characters in this film are real. | Is Joe Brown his real name?*
2 not false or artificial: *The necklace was made of real gold.*
3 used to emphasize what you are saying: *At this price, the tickets are a real bargain.*

real es·tate /ˈ. .ˌ./ noun [no plural] property such as houses or land

real estate a·gent /ˈ. ...ˌ../ the American word for ESTATE AGENT

rea·lis·tic /rɪəˈlɪstɪk/ adjective someone who is realistic accepts the facts about a situation and realizes what is possible and what is not possible: *Be realistic! We can't possibly afford to buy that car!*

re·al·i·ty /riˈæləti/ noun [no plural] the way life really is, not the way you would like it to be: *School starts tomorrow – it's back to reality again!*

re·a·li·za·tion also **realisation** BrE /ˌrɪəlaɪˈzeɪʃən $ ˌrɪələˈzeɪʃən/ noun [no plural] when you realize something that you did not know before: *The realization that Dan had lied to me was a terrible shock.*

rea·lize also **realise** BrE /ˈrɪəlaɪz/ verb

> **GRAMMAR**
> **realize (that)**
> **realize how/what/who etc**

to notice or understand something that you did not notice or understand before: *I suddenly realized it was getting late. | The school acted quickly once it **realized that** the problem was serious. | Nobody **realized how** unhappy she was. | I finally **realized what** I had done.*

real·ly /ˈrɪəli/ adverb

1 very or very much: *She's been really ill. | I really enjoyed our holiday there.*
2 if something really happens or is really true, it does happen or is true and is not imagined: *You're not really sleeping – you're just pretending. | Are you really going to America for your holidays?*
3 **Really?** spoken used when you are surprised about what someone has said: *"Sandra's having a party on Friday night." "Really?"*

re·ap·pear /ˌriːəˈpɪə $ ˌriːəˈpɪr/ verb to appear again: *At that moment the door opened and Anna reappeared.*

rear¹ /rɪə $ rɪr/ noun **the rear** the back part of a vehicle, building etc: *I went round to the rear of the house but there was no one there.*
– **rear** adjective: *the car's rear window*

rear² verb to look after a person or animal until they grow up

re·ar·range /ˌriːəˈreɪndʒ/ verb **1** to change the position or order of things: *We could rearrange these chairs to make a little more space.* **2** to change the time of a meeting or event: *The match has been rearranged for April 28th.*

rear·ward /ˈrɪəwəd $ ˈrɪrwəd/ adverb AmE towards the back of something: *I'd prefer a seat facing rearward on the train.*

rea·son¹ /'riːzən/ noun

> **GRAMMAR**
> **the reason for something**
> **the reason (that)**
> **the/any reason why**
> **a reason to do something**

1 why someone does something, or why something happens: *One reason the team played so badly was that Malcolm was injured.* | *What was the reason for the delay?* | *Did he give you any reason why he called?*
2 a fact that makes it sensible or fair for you to do something or think something: *I had no reason to think he was lying.* | *You have every reason to feel angry.*

reason² verb **1** to decide that something is true by thinking carefully about the facts: *I reasoned that I had at least half an hour before the others got back.* **2** reason with someone to talk to someone in order to persuade them to be more sensible: *I've tried reasoning with him, but he won't listen.*

rea·son·a·ble /'riːzənəbəl/ adjective
1 a reasonable amount or number is not too much or too big: *The hotel has good food, and the prices are reasonable.*
2 fair and sensible: *It seems like a reasonable idea to me.*

rea·son·a·bly /'riːzənəbli/ adverb
1 fairly: *I felt reasonably sure that I knew the way.* **2** in a way that is fair or acceptable: *a reasonably priced hotel*

rea·son·ing /'riːzənɪŋ/ noun [no plural] the reasons that make you decide or think something: *What was the reasoning behind the decision?*

re·as·sure /ˌriːə'ʃʊə $ ˌriːə'ʃʊr/ verb to make someone feel less worried: *"It'll be all right," Tim said, reassuring her.*
–**reassuring** adjective: *New students should make a reassuring phone call home.*

re·bel¹ /'rebəl/ noun someone who fights against the government or opposes a person in authority: *There has been further fighting between the army and the rebels in the south.*

re·bel² /rɪ'bel/ verb rebelled, rebelling to fight against the government or oppose a person in authority: *Jim hated school and rebelled against his teachers.*

re·bel·lion /rɪ'beljən/ noun fighting against the government or opposing a person in authority: *There was widespread rebellion and eventually civil war.*

re·bel·lious /rɪ'beljəs/ adjective deliberately disobeying someone in authority: *At fifteen, Karl began to get very rebellious.*

re·build /ˌriː'bɪld/ verb, past tense and past participle rebuilt /-'bɪlt/ to build something again, after it has been damaged or destroyed: *The cathedral had to be rebuilt after the war.*

rebuilt the past tense and past participle of REBUILD

re·buke /rɪ'bjuːk/ verb formal to tell someone that something they have done is wrong: *My mother rebuked me for being unkind.*

re·call /rɪ'kɔːl/ verb to remember something: *I'm afraid I don't recall his name.*

re·cap /'riːkæp/ noun when you repeat the main points of something you have already said: *It's time for a quick recap of tonight's main news.*

re·cede /rɪ'siːd/ verb if something you can hear or see recedes, it gets further away from you: *The sound of his footsteps receded down the stairs.* ⇨ see picture on page 353

re·ceipt /rɪ'siːt/ noun a piece of paper which shows how much you have paid for something: *I paid the bill and the waiter brought me a receipt.*

re·ceive /rɪ'siːv/ verb

> **GRAMMAR**
> **receive something from someone**

to get something that is given or sent to you: *You should receive the package by Saturday.* | *I received a letter from my aunt.*

re·ceiv·er /rɪ'siːvə $ rɪ'siːvɚ/ noun the part of a telephone that you hold to your ear

re·cent /'riːsənt/ adjective
something recent happened or was done only a short time ago: *This is John Irving's most recent book.*

re·cent·ly /'riːsəntli/ adverb
not very long ago: *I saw James quite recently.* | *Have you talked to Anna recently?* | *James recently changed schools.*

re·cep·tion /rɪ'sepʃən/ noun 1 [no plural] a desk in the entrance of a hotel or other organization where you go when you first arrive: *Please sign your name at reception when you arrive.* 2 a big formal party to celebrate a wedding or welcome an important visitor

re·cep·tion·ist /rɪ'sepʃənɪst/ noun someone who works at a desk near the entrance of a hotel or other organization, and helps people when they arrive

re·cep·tive /rɪ'septɪv/ adjective willing to listen to new ideas or opinions: *The other members of staff were quite receptive to my ideas.*

re·cess /rɪ'ses $ 'riːses/ noun, plural recesses 1 a period of time when a parliament is not working: *The bill will not be passed before Congress begins its autumn recess.* 2 [no plural] AmE a short period of time between classes at school

re·ces·sion /rɪ'seʃən/ noun a time when businesses and trade are not successful: *During the recession there were more than three million people unemployed.*

re·charge /ˌriː'tʃɑːdʒ $ ˌriː'tʃɑrdʒ/ verb to put more electricity into a BATTERY (=an object that provides the electrical power for a toy, machine, car etc): *I need to recharge the car's battery.*

re·charge·a·ble /ˌriː'tʃɑːdʒəbəl $ ˌriː'tʃɑrdʒəbəl/ adjective able to be recharged: *rechargeable batteries*

re·ci·pe /'resəpi/ noun a list of the things you need in order to cook something, and instructions how to cook it: *a recipe for strawberry ice-cream*

re·cip·ro·cal /rɪ'sɪprəkəl/ adjective a reciprocal arrangement or relationship involves two people, groups, or countries who each do something for the other: *It's a reciprocal arrangement – our students visit their school, and their students visit ours.*

re·cite /rɪ'saɪt/ verb to repeat the words of something you have learned, such as a poem, in front of an audience: *Susan recited the whole poem without a single mistake.*

reck·less /'rekləs/ adjective doing something in a dangerous way, without thinking about the risks: *Hazlett was fined £80 for reckless driving.*

reck·on /'rekən/ verb 1 informal to think or guess something: *I reckon you have a very good chance of winning.* 2 reckon something up to add together an amount or cost: *Pat sat down and reckoned up the cost of everything in her mind.*

re·claim /rɪ'kleɪm/ verb formal to ask for something that is yours to be given back to you: *If you pay now, you can reclaim the money later.*

re·cline /rɪ'klaɪn/ verb formal to lie or sit back in a relaxed way: *Alice was reclining on the sofa, reading a magazine.*

re·clin·ing /rɪ'klaɪnɪŋ/ adjective a reclining chair has a back that you can move, so that it slopes backwards

rec·og·ni·tion /ˌrekəg'nɪʃən/ noun [no plural] 1 when a lot of people admire or respect someone or something: *These examinations have worldwide recognition.* 2 being recognized by people: *It's impossible for someone like Madonna to avoid recognition.*

rec·og·nize also **recognise** BrE /'rekəgnaɪz/ verb

GRAMMAR
recognize that

1 to know someone or something because you have seen them before and remember them: *I recognized quite a few people in the crowd.* | *I hadn't seen her for years – I hardly recognized her.*
2 formal to accept that something is true: *The school has recognized the need for improvement.* | *I recognize that this will be difficult.*

re·coil /rɪ'kɔɪl/ verb to move back suddenly, away from something that is unpleasant or that you are afraid of: *Lisa recoiled from the spider, and screamed.*

rec·ol·lect /ˌrekə'lekt/ verb formal to remember something: *I don't recollect the name of the hotel.*

rec·ol·lec·tion /ˌrekə'lekʃən/ noun formal when you are able to remember something, or something that you remember: *I woke up in the morning with no recollection of where I was.* | *We listened to his recollections of life during the war.*

R

rec·om·mend /ˌrekəˈmend/ *verb*

GRAMMAR
recommend something to someone
recommend (that)

1 to tell someone that something is good or enjoyable: *I've recommended the book to all my friends.*
2 to tell someone that they should do something: *Doctors recommend that people eat more fresh fruit and vegetables.*

rec·om·men·da·tion /ˌrekəmenˈdeɪʃən/ *noun formal* a suggestion of what someone should do: *The report made several recommendations on how schools can imporve their teaching.*

rec·on·cile /ˈrekənsaɪl/ *verb formal* be reconciled to become friendly with someone again after you have had a serious argument: *They were finally reconciled with each other, after two years of not speaking.*

re·con·sid·er /ˌriːkənˈsɪdə $ˌriːkənˈsɪdɚ/ *verb formal* to think about something again so that you can decide whether you should change your opinion: *Do you think you might reconsider your decision in the future?*

re·con·struct /ˌriːkənˈstrʌkt/ *verb formal* to build something again after it has been destroyed ⇨ same meaning RE-BUILD: *There are plans to reconstruct the old bridge.*

rec·ord¹ /ˈrekɔːd $ˈrekɚd/ *noun*

GRAMMAR
a record of something
the record for something

1 information that you write down and keep so that you can look at it later: *Keep a record of all the money you spend. | The police keep records of all crimes, even minor ones.*
2 the best that anyone has ever achieved, especially in a sport: *She holds the current world record for downhill skiing. | Powell broke the record in the long jump* (=he got a better result than the last world record).
3 a round flat black piece of plastic that music is stored on: *He's got a wonderful collection of old Beatles records.*

PHRASE
on record information that is on record has been written down and kept: *This winter was the warmest on record* (=the warmest since temperatures have been written down).

re·cord² /rɪˈkɔːd $rɪˈkɔrd/ *verb*

1 to put films, events, or music on TAPE so that you can watch them or listen to them again: *We've recorded the match on video.*
2 to write down information and keep it so that you can look at it later: *We have been recording information about the weather for over a hundred years now.*

re·cord·er /rɪˈkɔːdə $rɪˈkɔrdɚ/ *noun* a simple musical instrument, which you play by blowing into it and covering the holes with your fingers

re·cord·ing /rɪˈkɔːdɪŋ $rɪˈkɔrdɪŋ/ *noun* a piece of music, film etc that has been recorded: *an early recording of the Beatles*

record play·er /ˈ.. ˌ../ *noun* a piece of equipment that you use for playing and listening to records

re·count /rɪˈkaʊnt/ *verb formal* to describe an event or to tell a story: *Jeremy was in the kitchen, recounting the events of the day.*

re·cov·er /rɪˈkʌvə $rɪˈkʌvɚ/ *verb*

GRAMMAR
recover from something

1 to become healthy again after you have been ill or hurt: *Gordon is recovering from a knee injury.*
2 to become strong again: *It will be years before the country recovers from the war.*

re·cov·er·y /rɪˈkʌvəri/ *noun* [no plural]

1 when someone becomes healthy again after being ill or hurt: *She will make a full recovery after the operation.*
2 when something becomes strong again after it has been weak: *Creating more jobs should help the country's economic recovery.*

re·cre·ate /ˌriːkriˈeɪt/ *verb* to make something like it was in the past, or like something in another place: *The zoo aims to recreate the animals' natural habitats as closely as possible.*

rec·re·a·tion /ˌrekri'eɪʃən/ *noun formal* the things you do for pleasure when you are not working: *The town has excellent facilities for recreation and leisure.*

recruit¹ /rɪ'kruːt/ *verb* to find new people to work in a company or join an organization: *Many companies are keen to recruit young people during their last year at university.*

recruit² *noun* someone who has recently joined an organization, especially the army: *New recruits are sent on a training course.*

rec·tan·gle /'rektæŋgəl/ *noun* a shape with four straight sides, with two longer sides and two shorter sides ⇨ see picture at SHAPE¹

rec·tan·gu·lar /rek'tæŋgjələ $rek-'tæŋgjələr/ *adjective* shaped like a rectangle: *a rectangular room*

rec·ti·fy /'rektəfaɪ/ *verb formal*, **rectified**, **rectifies** to change something that is wrong and make it right: *We need to rectify all the problems with the system.*

re·cu·pe·rate /rɪ'kjuːpəreɪt/ *verb formal* to spend time resting after an illness or injury until you feel better again ⇨ *same meaning* RECOVER (1): *Atherton spent the summer recuperating after a back operation.*

re·cur /rɪ'kɜː $rɪ'kɜr/ *verb formal* **recurred**, **recurring** to happen again: *The doctor told me to come back if the problem recurred.*

re·cy·cle /ˌriː'saɪkəl/ *verb* if people recycle things that have been used, they use them again, after putting them through a special process: *Things like used bottles, paper and cans are collected for recycling.*

red¹ /red/ *adjective* **redder**, **reddest** **1** something that is red is the colour of blood: *a red car* **2** red hair is an orange-brown colour ⇨ see picture on page 353

red² *noun* the colour of blood: *The painting has many different shades of red in it.*

red-hand·ed /ˌ. '../ *adjective* **catch someone red-handed** *informal* to catch someone at the moment when they are doing something wrong: *The police caught the burglars red-handed, climbing in the window.*

red·head /'redhed/ *noun* someone who has red hair, especially a woman

red-hot /ˌ. '../ *adjective* something that is red-hot has become so hot that it is red in colour: *red-hot coals*

redid the past tense of REDO

re·do /riː'duː/ *verb* **redid** /-'dɪd/ **redone** /-'dʌn/ to do something again: *I've just cleaned this room, and I don't want to have to redo it.*

redone the past participle of REDO

red tape /ˌ. './ *noun* [no plural] official rules that seem unnecessary and prevent people from doing things quickly and easily: *There's so much red tape – it took me ages to get my visa.*

re·duce /rɪ'djuːs $rɪ'dus/ *verb*

> **GRAMMAR**
> **reduce something from something to something**
> to make the amount or size of something less than it was before: *We had to reduce the price of our house in order to sell it.* | *The number of employees has been **reduced from** 30 **to** only 22.*

re·duc·tion /rɪ'dʌkʃən/ *noun*

> **GRAMMAR**
> **a reduction in something**
> when the amount or size of something becomes less than it was before: *There's been **a reduction in** the number of deaths from car accidents.*

re·dun·dant /rɪ'dʌndənt/ *adjective* **make someone redundant** *BrE* to stop employing someone because there is not enough work for them any more: *Part of the factory was closed, and one hundred workers were made redundant.*

reed /riːd/ *noun* a plant like tall grass that grows in or near water

reef /riːf/ *noun* a long line of rocks or CORAL (=a hard substance formed from dead sea animals): *a coral reef*

reek /riːk/ *verb* to smell strongly of something unpleasant: *He came in reeking of cigarettes and beer.*

reel¹ /riːl/ *noun* a round object that you wind something long onto, for example thread or camera film: *a cotton reel*

reel² *verb* **1** to walk in an unsteady way: *The man was reeling a little, as if he was drunk.* **2** **reel something off** to say a list of things quickly and easily, using your memory: *Sally reeled off the names of everyone who she had invited to the party.*

refer /rɪ'fɜː $ rɪ'fɚ/ *verb* **referred, referring**

PHRASAL VERB
refer to
refer to someone/something to talk about a person or thing without giving very many details: *Moran referred to her parents several times. | I talked to him all evening, but he never referred to his fight with Henry.*

ref·e·ree /ˌrefə'riː/ *noun* someone who makes people obey the rules when they are playing a game such as football: *Just at that moment the referee blew his whistle.*
–**referee** *verb*: *He refereed last year's World Cup final.*

ref·er·ence /'refərəns/ *noun* **1** when you mention another person or thing: *There was no reference to his family in his letter.* **2 for reference** so that you can find information when you need it: *You should keep all your old letters, for reference.* **3** a letter that says whether someone is suitable for a new job, course etc: *Your employer will normally give you a reference.*

reference book /'... ./ *noun* a book that you use for finding information, for example a dictionary

ref·e·ren·dum /ˌrefə'rendəm/ *noun* an occasion when the people of a country vote on one particular political subject, not on who will govern the country: *The government has promised that there will be a referendum to decide whether Britain should remain in the EU.*

re·fill /ˌriː'fɪl/ *verb* to fill something again: *Waitresses kept coming round refilling our glasses.*

re·fine /rɪ'faɪn/ *verb* to make a natural substance pure by using a special process: *methods of refining oil*

re·fined /rɪ'faɪnd/ *adjective* **1** made pure by using a special process: *refined sugar* **2** *old-fashioned* polite and educated: *a very refined young lady*

re·fin·e·ry /rɪ'faɪnəri/ *noun, plural* **refineries** a factory where something such as oil, sugar, or metal is made pure by using a special process: *an oil refinery*

re·flect /rɪ'flekt/ *verb* **1 be reflected in something** if something is reflected in a mirror or in water, you can see an image of it in the mirror or the water: *The mountains around us were reflected in the lake.* **2** if a surface reflects heat, light, or sound, heat, light, or sound is sent back from it, instead of passing through it: *Dark glasses reflect the light and make driving safer.* **3 reflect on** *formal* to think carefully about something: *I went home and reflected on what Sally had just told me.*

re·flec·tion /rɪ'flekʃən/ *noun* **1** the picture that you see when you look in water or a mirror: *She stared at her own reflection in the mirror.* **2** careful and serious thinking: *After days of reflection, she decided to leave.*

reflection

re·flec·tive /rɪ'flektɪv/ *adjective* a reflective object is made of material that reflects light, so that it looks very bright when light shines on it: *If you're cycling at night you should wear a reflective belt.*

re·flex /'riːfleks/ *noun, plural* **reflexes** a quick physical reaction that your body makes without you thinking about it: *Goalkeepers need to have good reflexes.*

re·flex·ive /rɪ'fleksɪv/ *adjective* a reflexive verb or PRONOUN shows that an action affects the person or thing that does the action. In the sentence 'I enjoyed myself', 'myself' is a reflexive pronoun

re·form¹ /rɪ'fɔːm $ rɪ'fɔrm/ *verb formal* to change a system or an organization in order to make it better: *We need to reform some parts of our education system.*

reform² *noun formal* a change that is made to a system or organization in order to make it better: *government reforms*

re·frain /rɪ'freɪn/ *verb formal* to stop yourself from doing something: *She politely refrained from saying what she really thought.*

re·fresh /rɪ'freʃ/ *verb* to make someone feel less tired or hot: *We went to refresh ourselves in the swimming-pool.*

re·fresh·ing /rɪˈfreʃɪŋ/ adjective
1 making you feel less tired or less hot: a long cool refreshing drink **2** interesting and different in a pleasant way: It was refreshing to be working on something completely new.

re·fresh·ments /rɪˈfreʃmənts/ plural noun food and drinks that are provided at a cinema, theatre, or public event: Refreshments are available in the coffee shop downstairs.

re·fri·ge·rate /rɪˈfrɪdʒəreɪt/ verb to put food or drinks in a refrigerator in order to keep them cold

re·fri·ge·ra·tor /rɪˈfrɪdʒəreɪtə $rɪ-ˈfrɪdʒəˌreɪtɚ/ also **fridge** /frɪdʒ/ noun a metal kitchen cupboard that is kept cold by electricity, and that you put food in to keep it cool

ref·uge /ˈrefjuːdʒ/ noun a safe place that people can go to, for example to escape from violence: The old hospital became a refuge for homeless people.

ref·u·gee /ˌrefjʊˈdʒiː/ noun someone who has had to leave their country to escape from danger or war. The refugees fled across the border.

re·fund /ˈriːfʌnd/ noun money that is given back to you in a shop, restaurant etc, for example because you are not satisfied with what you bought: The shop assistant gave me a refund.
−**refund** /rɪˈfʌnd/ verb: Your money will be refunded if you are not entirely satisfied.

re·fur·bish /ˌriːˈfɜːbɪʃ $rɪˈfɚbɪʃ/ verb formal to improve a building by decorating it and buying new equipment for it: The old cinema has been completely refurbished.

re·fus·al /rɪˈfjuːzəl/ noun when someone refuses to do or accept something: I was disappointed by her refusal to come.

re·fuse¹ /rɪˈfjuːz/ verb

1 to say firmly that you will not do something: I asked Steve to help me, but he refused. | Carl absolutely **refuses to** eat vegetables.
2 to say that you will not allow someone to do something: The chairman refused him permission to speak. | He tried to get into the club, but the owner refused him entry.

ref·use² /ˈrefjuːs/ noun [no plural] formal waste material such as old food or paper ⇨ same meaning RUBBISH

re·gain /rɪˈgeɪn/ verb formal to get something back after you have lost it: It took me a few minutes to regain my self-control.

re·gal /ˈriːgəl/ adjective suitable for a king or queen: He looked at her with a very regal expression.

regard¹ /rɪˈgɑːd $rɪˈgɑrd/ noun

1 [no plural] formal if you have regard for other people, you respect them and care about how they feel: He always does exactly what he wants, with **no regard for** anyone else.
2 **regards** a word used in polite greetings

PHRASE
with regard to formal used to say what subject you are talking about: With regard to the cost − it will be a little more expensive than we first thought.

regard² verb formal **1** regard someone/something as something to think about someone or something in a particular way: I've always regarded science as a fascinating subject. **2** formal to look at someone or something, especially in a particular way: "What do you think?" she asked, regarding me carefully.

re·gard·ing /rɪˈgɑːdɪŋ $rɪˈgɑrdɪŋ/ preposition formal about a particular subject: I went to see my boss regarding a pay rise.

reg·gae /ˈregeɪ/ noun [no plural] a type of music from Jamaica with a strong regular beat

re·gime /reɪˈʒiːm/ noun a system or way of doing something: my new exercise regime

re·gi·ment /ˈredʒəmənt/ noun a group of soldiers in an army

re·gi·men·ted /ˈredʒəmentɪd/ adjective strictly controlled: Her lessons are always highly regimented.

re·gion /ˈriːdʒən/ noun

a fairly large area within a country: We don't get very much snow in this region.

re·gion·al /ˈriːdʒənəl/ adjective

related to a particular region: the regional government

re·gis·ter¹ /'redʒəstə $ 'redʒəstɚ/
noun an official list: *Our classroom register contains the names of all the students.*

register² verb **1** to put a name on an official list: *I need to register with a doctor.* **2** if an instrument registers an amount, it shows it: *The thermometer registered 84°F.*

re·gis·tra·tion /,redʒə'streɪʃən/ noun [no plural] when names are put on an official list

registration num·ber /..'.. ,../ noun BrE the numbers and letters on a car's NUMBER PLATE; LICENSE NUMBER AmE

re·gret¹ /rɪ'gret/ verb regretted, regretting

GRAMMAR
regret doing something
regret that
if you regret something, you feel sorry that you did it and wish you had not done it: *I really regret leaving school so young.* | *I now regret that I didn't travel more when I was younger.*

regret² noun sadness that you feel when you wish you had not done something: *I don't have any regrets about the choices I've made in life.*

re·gret·ta·ble /rɪ'gretəbəl/ adjective a regrettable thing is something you wish had never happened: *This was a regrettable mistake.*

reg·u·lar¹ /'regjələ $ 'regjələr/ adjective
1 happening often, every day, every week etc: *We have regular weekly meetings.* | *She still has to go for regular check-ups to the hospital.* | *Regular exercise is good for you.* | *We check all the babies at regular intervals.*
2 something that is regular happens with the same amount of time between each event: *The patient's breathing was slow and regular.*
3 doing something or going somewhere often: *She's a regular customer at the coffee shop* (=she uses the coffee shop often).
4 normal, usual, or ordinary: *It looks like a regular phone, but you can get e-mail on it.*
5 a regular verb or noun changes its

forms in the same way as most verbs or nouns. The verb 'walk' is regular, but 'be' is not

regular² noun informal someone who goes to the same shop, restaurant etc very often

reg·u·lar·ly /'regjələli $ 'regjələrli/ adverb
often, for example every day, every week, every month etc: *The Glasers regularly travel all over the world.* | *Water the plant regularly.*

reg·u·late /'regjəleɪt/ verb **1** to control an activity or process with rules: *The Bank of England regulates the printing of banknotes.* **2** to keep something at a particular speed, temperature etc: *Special equipment regulates the swimming pool's temperature.*

reg·u·la·tion /,regjə'leɪʃən/ noun an official rule: *There are too many rules and regulations.* | *safety regulations*

re·ha·bil·i·ta·tion /,riːhəbɪlə'teɪʃən/ noun [no plural] treatment to help someone stop taking drugs or drinking alcohol

re·hears·al /rɪ'hɜːsəl $ rɪ'hɚsəl/ noun a practise for a performance: *Please don't be late for the rehearsal.*

re·hearse /rɪ'hɜːs $ rɪ'hɚs/ verb to practise a song, play etc for a performance: *We need to rehearse a couple of songs.*

reign /reɪn/ noun a period of time during which a king or queen rules a country: *the reign of Queen Victoria*
–**reign** verb: *King Henry VIII reigned from 1491 to 1547.*

re·in·car·na·tion /,riːɪnkɑː'neɪʃən $,riːɪnkɑr'neɪʃən/ noun [no plural] the belief that people are born again in another body after they have died

re·in·force /,riːɪn'fɔːs $,riːɪn'fɔrs/ verb to make something stronger: *They used concrete to reinforce the walls.* | *reinforced glass*

re·in·force·ments /,riːɪn'fɔːsmənts $,riːɪn'fɔrsmənts/ plural noun more soldiers or police that go to help other soldiers or police: *It's time to send in reinforcements.*

reins /reɪnz/ plural noun long narrow bands of leather that you use to control a horse

re·in·state /ˌriːɪnˈsteɪt/ *verb* to give a job back to someone: *They lost their jobs but the company later reinstated them.*

re·it·e·rate /riːˈɪtəreɪt/ *verb* formal to say something again: *Let me reiterate that smoking is not allowed anywhere on the school premises.*

re·ject /rɪˈdʒekt/ *verb*
to say that you will not accept something or someone: *The committee rejected the plan.* | *She applied to the college, but they rejected her.*

re·jec·tion /rɪˈdʒekʃən/ *noun* 1 when someone refuses to accept something: *He felt disappointed by the publisher's rejection of his first novel.* 2 [no plural] when someone stops giving you love or attention: *I can't take any more rejection.*

re·joice /rɪˈdʒɔɪs/ *verb* to be very happy because something good has happened

re·lapse /rɪˈlæps $ ˈriːlæps/ *noun* when someone becomes ill again after they were getting better: *Unfortunately, he had a relapse and had to return to the hospital.*

re·late /rɪˈleɪt/ *verb* 1 if you relate one thing to another, you show that they are similar or connected in some way: *Police have tried to relate this murder to others in the area.* 2 formal to tell a story or talk about something that happened: *She couldn't wait to relate the day's events to her friends.* 3 relate to something to be about something or connected with it: *I collect anything that relates to baseball.*

re·lat·ed /rɪˈleɪtɪd/ *adjective*
GRAMMAR
related to something/someone
1 if two things are related, there is a connection between them: *Norwegian and Danish are closely related languages.* | *Today's traffic problems are related to the heavy rain we had last night.*
2 if two people are related, they are members of the same family: *Are you related to Jean Benson?* | *We look alike, but we're not related.*

re·la·tion /rɪˈleɪʃən/ *noun*
GRAMMAR
a relation between things
1 a connection between events or facts: *Is there a relation between drinking coffee and health problems?*
2 a member of your family: *She is staying with some relations in Canada.*
3 relations the way in which two countries or groups behave towards each other, for example whether they are friendly or not: *Relations between the two countries have got better recently.*

PHRASE
in relation to something used when comparing two things: *The picture shows the size of the gray whale in relation to humans.*

re·la·tion·ship /rɪˈleɪʃənʃɪp/ *noun*
GRAMMAR
a relationship with someone/something
a relationship between people/things
1 the way in which two people or groups feel and behave towards each other, for example whether they like each other or not: *Her relationship with her father has always been difficult.* | *I had a very good relationship with my mother.* | *The relationship between the two countries is friendly.*
2 the way in which two things are connected: *The relationship between health and exercise is clear.*

rel·a·tive¹ /ˈrelətɪv/ *noun*
a member of your family: *We'll be visiting relatives at Christmas.*

relative² *adjective* true to some degree, especially when compared with other things: *The park is somewhere the children can play in relative safety.*

relative clause /ˌ... ˈ./ *noun* a part of a sentence that has a verb in it and is joined to the rest of the sentence by a relative pronoun such as 'which'

rel·a·tive·ly /ˈrelətɪvli/ *adverb* fairly: *Our house is relatively small.*

relative pro·noun /ˌ... ˈ../ *noun* a PRONOUN such as 'who', 'which', or 'that', which connects a relative clause to the rest of the sentence

R

re·lax /rɪˈlæks/ verb
to feel more calm and less worried, by resting or doing something you enjoy: *I decided just to stay home and relax.* | *A hot bath should help to relax you after a day's work.*

re·lax·a·tion /ˌriːlækˈseɪʃən/ noun [no plural] when you relax: *It's a great place to go for relaxation.*

re·laxed /rɪˈlækst/ adjective calm and not worried about anything: *She looked happy and relaxed on her wedding day.*

re·lax·ing /rɪˈlæksɪŋ/ adjective something that is relaxing makes you feel calm and comfortable: *a relaxing bath* | *relaxing music*

re·lay /ˈriːleɪ/ also **relay race** /ˈ.. ˌ./ noun a race in which each member of a team runs or swims part of the distance: *the 100 metre relay*

re·lease¹ /rɪˈliːs/   release
verb
GRAMMAR
release someone from something

1 to allow someone to be free again after keeping them as a prisoner: *When will he be released from prison?*
2 to stop holding something: *He grabbed her arm and refused to release it.*
3 to make a film or music available for people to buy or see: *Disney released a new Fantasia film in 2000.*
4 to give information to people after keeping it secret: *The names of the victims were not released.*

release² noun **1** when someone is allowed to be free and no longer a prisoner: *They have demanded the release of political prisoners.* **2** a new film or music that is available for people to see or buy: *a review of the new film releases*

rel·e·gate /ˈreləɡeɪt/ verb if a sports team is relegated, it has to play in a lower group of teams because it has finished in the bottom place of the higher group

re·lent /rɪˈlent/ verb formal to let someone do something that you would not let them do before: *His parents relented, and allowed his friends to stay.*

re·lent·less /rɪˈlentləs/ adjective never stopping: *I'm fed up with your relentless complaining.*

rel·e·vance /ˈreləvəns/ noun [no plural] how relevant something is: *That is of no relevance to what we're talking about.*

rel·e·vant /ˈreləvənt/ adjective directly related to the subject or problem that you are discussing → opposite IRRELEVANT: *Is that information really relevant?*

re·li·a·ble /rɪˈlaɪəbəl/ adjective
if someone or something is reliable, you can trust them to do what you want them to do → opposite UNRELIABLE: *Rick is a good, reliable worker.* | *We need a computer system that is reliable and fast.*

re·li·ance /rɪˈlaɪəns/ noun [no plural] when you depend on something: *our reliance on the car*

re·li·ant /rɪˈlaɪənt/ adjective formal if you are reliant on someone or something, you depend on them: *I'm still reliant on my family for money.*

rel·ic /ˈrelɪk/ noun something from the past that still exists

re·lief /rɪˈliːf/ noun [no plural]
the feeling you have when you are no longer worried that something bad might happen: *It **was a great relief** when Ben finally called to tell me where he was.* | *This news will **come as a great relief to** his family.* | *I **breathed a sigh of relief** (=felt great relief) when I saw the little boat enter the harbour.*

re·lieve /rɪˈliːv/ verb to make something bad seem better: *drugs for relieving pain* | *We sang songs to relieve the boredom.*

re·lieved /rɪˈliːvd/ adjective happy because something bad did not happen: *We were all relieved when she returned home safely.*

re·li·gion /rɪˈlɪdʒən/ noun a system of beliefs in God: *the Islamic religion*

re·li·gious /rɪˈlɪdʒəs/ adjective **1** related to religion: *a religious ceremony* **2** believing strongly in your religion: *a very religious man*

re·li·gious·ly /rɪˈlɪdʒəsli/ adverb if you do something religiously, you always do it: *I clean my teeth religiously every night.*

rel·ish /'relɪʃ/ verb if you relish the thought that something is going to happen, you want it to happen and are happy that it is going to happen: *I don't relish the thought of another argument.*

re·live /ˌriː'lɪv/ verb to remember something so well that it seems to happen again: *I relived that first kiss over and over in my mind.*

re·lo·cate /ˌriːləʊ'keɪt $riː'loʊˌkeɪt/ verb formal to move to a new place: *The company is relocating to London.*

re·luc·tant /rɪ'lʌktənt/ adjective if you are reluctant to do something, you do not want to do it: *I'm reluctant to tell my parents about this.*

re·ly /rɪ'laɪ/ verb relied, relies

PHRASAL VERB
rely on
1 rely on someone/something if you rely on someone or something, you need them and always use them: *She relies on relatives to drive her to the store.* | *He relies on his parents for money.* | *We rely very heavily on our car.*
2 can rely on someone/something if you can rely on someone or something, you know they will do what you want or expect them to do: *You can rely on Toby to do the work well.*

re·main /rɪ'meɪn/ verb formal

GRAMMAR
remain in/at a place
1 to stay in the same place, or position: *Harris remained in jail for ten years.* | *I decided to remain at home.* | *Please remain seated* (=stay sitting down).
2 to continue to do something: *Children can't remain quiet* (=continue to be quiet) *for long.* | *He remained in power for over forty years.*

re·main·der /rɪ'meɪndə $rɪ'meɪndər/ noun the part of something that is left after everything else has gone: *Most of us took the train and the remainder went by bus.*

re·main·ing /rɪ'meɪnɪŋ/ adjective left when others have gone or the rest has been used: *The remaining two children went to live with their grandparents.*

re·mains /rɪ'meɪnz/ plural noun the

parts of something that are left after the rest has disappeared: *the remains of an ancient theatre*

re·mand /rɪ'mɑːnd $rɪ'mænd/ verb BrE **be remanded in custody** to be kept in prison until your TRIAL

re·mark¹ /rɪ'mɑːk $rɪ'mɑrk/ noun
GRAMMAR
a remark about someone/something
something that you say: *Several of the men made rude remarks about the way she was dressed.*

remark² verb **1** to say something ⇨ same meaning COMMENT²: *My sister remarked that she thought Celia looked unhappy.* **2 remark on/upon** to say something about a thing that you have noticed: *Several people remarked on the horrible smell.*

re·mark·a·ble /rɪ'mɑːkəbəl $rɪ'mɑrkəbəl/ adjective very unusual and good: *That's a remarkable achievement.*

re·mark·a·bly /rɪ'mɑːkəbli $rɪ'mɑrkəbli/ adverb extremely: *You boys look remarkably similar.*

re·mar·ry /ˌriː'mæri/ verb remarried, remarries to marry again: *He said he would never remarry after his wife died.*

rem·e·dy¹ /'remədi/ noun, plural remedies something that makes an illness or bad situation go away: *an effective remedy for headaches* | *What is the remedy for rising crime?*

remedy² verb remedied, remedies to make a bad situation get better: *Engineers are trying to remedy the problem now.*

re·mem·ber /rɪ'membə $rɪ'membər/ verb
GRAMMAR
remember doing something
remember to do something
remember that
1 if you remember something, it comes back into your mind: *I couldn't remember her name.* | *I don't remember seeing John at the party.* | *Do you remember going to the fair with her when we were little?* | *I suddenly remembered that I had promised to meet my mother for lunch.*
2 if you remember to do something,

you do not forget to do it: **Remember to** buy Anne a card when you go to town.

re·mind /rɪ'maɪnd/ verb **1** to make someone remember something that they must do: Remind me to take the cake out of the oven. **2 remind someone of someone** if someone reminds you of another person, they make you think of that person because they are similar to them: You remind me of my sister.

re·mind·er /rɪ'maɪndə $ rɪ'maɪndə/ noun something that makes you remember something

rem·i·nisce /ˌremə'nɪs/ verb to talk about pleasant events in your past: They sat reminiscing about the old days.

rem·i·nis·cent /ˌremə'nɪsənt/ adjective formal making you think of something similar: The garden was reminiscent of a jungle.

rem·nant /'remnənt/ noun a small part of something that remains after the rest is gone

re·morse /rɪ'mɔːs $ rɪ'mɔrs/ noun [no plural] formal a feeling that you are sorry for something bad that you have done: He showed no remorse for his crime.

re·mote /rɪ'məʊt $ rɪ'moʊt/ adjective **1** far away: a remote farm **2** very small: There's a remote possibility that we'll finish early.
—**remotely** adverb: I'm not remotely interested in computer games.

remote con·trol /ˌ. .'./ noun a piece of equipment that you use for controlling a television, VIDEO etc

re·mov·al /rɪ'muːvəl/ noun [no plural] formal when you take something away: A lot of people protested about the removal of so many trees.

re·move /rɪ'muːv/ verb formal

GRAMMAR
remove something/someone from somewhere

1 to take something away from a place: Please do not **remove** these books **from** the library.
2 to take off a piece of clothing: He removed his hat and sat down.

re·name /riː'neɪm/ verb to give something a new name: The new owners renamed the company.

ren·dez·vous /'rɒndɪvuː $ 'rɑndeɪˌvu/ noun, plural **rendezvous** an arrangement to meet someone: He had arranged a secret rendezvous with his girlfriend.

re·new /rɪ'njuː $ rɪ'nu/ verb **1** to arrange for an official document or agreement to continue: I need to renew my passport. **2** to begin to do something again: We will renew our search in the morning.

re·nounce /rɪ'naʊns/ verb to say publicly that you no longer support or want something: Why will you not renounce violence?

ren·o·vate /'renəveɪt/ verb to repair a building so that it looks new

re·nowned /rɪ'naʊnd/ adjective formal famous for something: The restaurant is renowned for its excellent food.

rent¹ /rent/ verb

GRAMMAR
rent something to someone
rent something from someone

1 to pay money to live in a place or to use something such as a car: We **rent** the flat **from** my uncle. | We rented bicycles and rode along the beach.
2 also **rent out** if you rent something that you own, you allow someone else to use it, and they pay you money: Some people don't like to **rent** rooms to students. | They **rent** the house **out to** tourists in the summer.

rent² noun money that you pay to use a house, car etc that belongs to someone else: I pay the rent at the beginning of the month.

rent·al /'rentl/ noun an arrangement to use something that belongs to someone else in return for money: a car rental agreement | Bike rental is £8.00.

re·or·gan·ize also **reorganise** BrE /riː'ɔːgənaɪz $ ri'ɔrgəˌnaɪz/ verb to organize something in a new and better way: I think I'll reorganize my bedroom.

rep /rep/ noun informal someone who sells products for a company: a sales rep

re·pair¹ /rɪ'peə $ rɪ'per/ verb
to fix something that is damaged or not working properly: How much will it cost to repair the video? | We need

▼ to **get** the car **repaired** (=arrange for someone to fix it).

repair² noun something that you do to fix something that is damaged or not working properly: *He's just doing a few repairs on my car.* | *The school buildings are badly in need of repair.*

re·pay /rɪ'peɪ/ verb, past tense and past participle **repaid** /-'peɪd/ **1** to give money back to someone after you have borrowed it from them: *You can repay the loan over 2 years.* **2** to reward someone for helping you: *How can I ever repay you?*

re·pay·ment /rɪ'peɪmənt/ noun an amount of money that you pay to someone who you have borrowed money from: *Your first repayment is due next week.*

re·peal /rɪ'piːl/ verb to officially end a law

re·peat¹ /rɪ'piːt/ verb

1 to say or do something again: *Could you repeat what you just said?* | *If the operation is not successful the first time, we may have to repeat it.*
2 if a television or radio programme is repeated, it is broadcast again: *The programme will be repeated on Saturday afternoon.*

repeat² noun **1** a situation or event that has happened before: *We don't want a repeat of the fires that destroyed so many houses.* **2** a television or radio programme that is broadcast again

re·peat·ed /rɪ'piːtɪd/ adjective done several times: *Despite repeated efforts, they failed to save the child.*
– **repeatedly** adverb: *I've told you about this repeatedly.*

re·pel /rɪ'pel/ verb repelled, repelling to force someone or something away: *sprays that repel insects*

re·pel·lent¹ /rɪ'pelənt/ noun a substance that keeps insects away: *mosquito repellent*

re·pent /rɪ'pent/ verb formal to be sorry for something bad that you have done: *If you repent, you will be forgiven.*

re·per·cus·sions /ˌriːpə'kʌʃnz $ ˌrɪpɚ'kʌʃənz/ plural noun bad things that happen as a result of something that you do: *Children are afraid of repurcussions if they report bullies.*

rep·e·ti·tion /ˌrepə'tɪʃən/ noun when something happens again or is done again many times: *Avoid repetition by using different words.*

re·pet·i·tive /rɪ'petətɪv/ adjective something that is repetitive is boring because the same thing is repeated many times: *Typing is a very repetitive job.*

re·phrase /ˌriː'freɪz/ verb to say or write something using different words: *Can you rephrase the question?*

re·place /rɪ'pleɪs/ verb formal

GRAMMAR
replace someone/something with someone/something
to get a new person or thing to use instead of the one you use now: *When the TV broke, we didn't replace it.* | *He left in June, and they still haven't replaced him with anyone* (=employed someone else to do his job).

re·place·ment /rɪ'pleɪsmənt/ noun a new person or thing that you can use instead of the one you used before: *This battery is dead – I need to get a replacement.*

re·play /'riːpleɪ/ noun **1** a piece of action in a sports game on television that is shown again immediately after it happens: *The replay clearly shows that it was a foul.* **2** BrE a sports game that is played again because there was not a winner in the first game

rep·li·ca /'replɪkə/ noun an exact copy of something

re·ply¹ /rɪ'plaɪ/ verb replied, replies

GRAMMAR
reply to something/someone
reply that
to answer: *"Yes, that's true," she replied.* | *He didn't reply to my question.* | *I asked George whether he enjoyed the film, and he replied that he found it disappointing.*

reply² noun, plural replies

GRAMMAR
a reply to something
something that you say or write as an answer: *I am still waiting for a reply to my letter.* | *I asked Helen if she was all right, but she made no*

R

▼ *reply* (=did not answer). | *Jeff said very little **in reply to** my questions.*

re·port¹ /rɪˈpɔːt $rɪˈpɔrt/ *noun*

GRAMMAR
a report on something
a report of something

something that gives facts about a situation or event: *Each child wrote a **report on** their visit to the museum. | a weather report | There have been **reports of** more fighting on the streets of the capital.*

report² *verb*

GRAMMAR
report that
report on something
report something/someone to someone

1 to tell people about something that has happened: *The pilot **reported that** he had trouble with one engine. | I've been asked to **report on** how the meeting goes.*
2 to tell someone that a crime or accident has happened: *Have you **reported** the burglary **to** the police?*
3 to give someone's name to a person in authority because they have done something wrong: *One of the older children saw Jake smoking and **reported** him **to** the headteacher.*

report card /ˈ. ˌ./ *noun AmE* a written statement showing how well a student has worked

reported speech /.ˌ.. ˈ./ *noun [no plural]* the style of writing that is used for telling people what someone says, without repeating the actual words

re·port·er /rɪˈpɔːtə $rɪˈpɔrtɚ/ *noun* someone who writes news stories: *a newspaper reporter*

rep·re·sent /ˌreprɪˈzent/ *verb*
1 if someone represents you, they officially speak for you or do a job for you because you cannot do it yourself: *You will need a good lawyer to represent you in court. | Tina Collins will represent the students in the meetings with parents and teachers.*
2 to show or mean something: *This line on the graph represents temperature.*

rep·re·sen·ta·tive¹ /ˌreprɪˈzentətɪv/ *noun* someone who people have chosen to do things for them: *Jean Mason will be the student representative on the committee.*

representative² *adjective* typical of a group of people or things: *Sally isn't representative of teenagers as a whole.*

re·press /rɪˈpres/ *verb* 1 to stop yourself from saying something or showing your feelings: *It's not good to repress your feelings.* 2 to control people by force: *a brutal leader who repressed his people*

re·pres·sive /rɪˈpresɪv/ *adjective* cruel and very strict: *a repressive government*

re·prieve /rɪˈpriːv/ *noun* when something bad that was going to happen does not happen: *I got a last minute reprieve.*

rep·ri·mand /ˈreprəmɑːnd $ˈreprəˌmænd/ *verb formal* to tell someone officially that they have done something wrong: *His manager reprimanded him for being late.*
– **reprimand** *noun*

re·pri·sal /rɪˈpraɪzəl/ *noun* something that is done to punish an enemy: *He's afraid to help the police for fear of reprisals against his family.*

re·proach /rɪˈprəʊtʃ $rɪˈproʊtʃ/ *verb formal* to blame or criticize someone for something: *I don't reproach you for wanting to leave.*

re·pro·duce /ˌriːprəˈdjuːs $ˌriprəˈdus/ *verb* to produce young animals, people, or plants

re·pro·duc·tion /ˌriːprəˈdʌkʃən/ *noun* 1 *[no plural]* when animals or humans produce young 2 a copy of something such as a work of art

rep·tile /ˈreptaɪl/ *noun* an animal such as a snake or LIZARD

re·pub·lic /rɪˈpʌblɪk/ *noun* a country that elects its government and does not have a king or queen

re·pub·li·can /rɪˈpʌblɪkən/ *noun* someone who believes in having a republic

re·pul·sive /rɪˈpʌlsɪv/ *adjective* extremely unpleasant: *What a repulsive smell!*

rep·u·ta·ble /ˈrepjətəbəl/ *adjective* respected for being honest and doing good work: *a reputable builder*

rep·u·ta·tion /ˌrepjəˈteɪʃən/ *noun* the opinion that people have of someone or something: *This school has a very good reputation.*

re·quest[1] /rɪ'kwest/ noun when someone asks for something: *Can I make a request?* | *Send us your requests for your favourite songs.*

request[2] verb formal to ask for something: *They requested some drinks.* | *We request that you do not smoke.* ⇨ see usage note at ASK

re·quire /rɪ'kwaɪə $ rɪ'kwaɪər/ verb **1** to need something: *Pets require a lot of care.* **2** formal to officially say that someone must do something: *The law requires all drivers to wear seatbelts.*

re·quire·ment /rɪ'kwaɪəmənt $ rɪ'kwaɪərmənt/ noun formal something that you need: *Do you have any special dietary requirements?*

re·run /'riːrʌn/ noun a television programme that is shown again; REPEAT BrE: *endless reruns of old comedy programmes*

resat the past tense and past participle of RESIT

res·cue[1] /'res kjuː/ verb

GRAMMAR
rescue someone from something

to save someone when they are in danger: *Roberts **rescued** a two-year-old girl **from** the burning car.*

rescue

rescue[2] noun when someone is saved from danger: *The storm made the rescue difficult.*

re·search[1] /rɪ'sɜːtʃ $ 'riːsɜːrtʃ/ noun [no plural] detailed study of a subject in order to find out new information: *research into the causes of cancer* | *She's doing research on tropical diseases.*

USAGE
Research does not have a plural form: *I need to do some research before writing the paper.* | *Research shows that reading to children improves their development.*

research[2] verb to study a subject in detail so you can discover new facts about it: *He spent several days researching the company.*
– **researcher** noun

re·sem·blance /rɪ'zembləns/ noun when two people or things look similar to each other: *We're brothers – can you see the resemblance?*

re·sem·ble /rɪ'zembəl/ verb to look similar to someone or something: *You don't resemble your father at all.*

re·sent /rɪ'zent/ verb to feel angry and upset about something that someone has done to you: *I always resented my mother for leaving us.*

re·sent·ful /rɪ'zentfəl/ adjective angry and upset about something that someone has done: *I'm very resentful about losing my job.*

re·sent·ment /rɪ'zentmənt/ noun [no plural] a feeling of anger about something that someone has done to you

res·er·va·tion /ˌrezə'veɪʃən $ ˌrezər'veɪʃən/ noun **1** an arrangement to have a seat on a plane, a table in a restaurant etc ready for you: *I'd like to make a reservation for dinner tonight.* **2** a feeling of doubt about something: *I still have reservations about leaving home.*

re·serve[1] /rɪ'zɜːv $ rɪ'zɜːrv/ verb

GRAMMAR
reserve something for something/someone

1 to arrange that a seat on a plane, a table in a restaurant etc will be available for you to use: *Tom reserved a table at the hotel restaurant.* | *It's best to reserve your seat in advance.* **2** to keep something for a particular purpose: *This parking area has been **reserved for** buses.*

reserve[2] noun a supply of something that is kept to be used when it is needed: *The country has huge reserves of grain.*

re·served /rɪ'zɜːvd $ rɪ'zɜːrvd/ adjective unwilling to show or talk about your thoughts and feelings

res·er·voir /'rezəvwɑː $ 'rezər,vwɑːr/ noun an artificial lake used for storing water

res·i·dence /'rezədəns/ noun formal **1** a house where someone lives: *the Prime Minister's official residence* **2** [no plural] when someone lives in a particular place: *They have applied to take up residence* (=start living) *in the US.*

res·i·dent /'rezədənt/ noun someone who lives in a particular place: *a park for local residents*

res·i·den·tial /ˌrezə'denʃəl/ adjective

R

consisting of houses, not offices or factories: *a residential area of the city*

res·i·due /'rezədju: $'rezə,du/ *noun* a substance that remains after something else has disappeared

re·sign /rɪ'zaɪn/ *verb* **1** to officially say that you are going to leave your job: *I've decided to resign from the bank.* **2** if you resign yourself to something, you accept it because you cannot change it: *He's resigned himself to a few more years studying.*

res·ig·na·tion /,rezɪg'neɪʃən/ *noun* when someone officially says they are going to leave their job: *Her resignation was a big surprise.*

re·sil·i·ent /rɪ'zɪliənt/ *adjective* strong enough to be able to deal with problems

re·sist /rɪ'zɪst/ *verb* **1** to refuse to accept something and try to prevent it: *He resists any kind of change.* **2** to stop yourself doing something you would like to do but should not: *I managed to resist looking in the bag.*

re·sist·ance /rɪ'zɪstəns/ *noun* [no plural] when someone refuses to accept something and tries to prevent it: *There is strong resistance to the scheme.*

re·sis·tant /rɪ'zɪstənt/ *adjective* **1** not harmed or damaged by something: *Some diseases are resistant to antibiotics.* **2** unwilling to accept new ideas or changes: *Old people can be very resistant to change.*

re·sit /,ri:'sɪt/ *verb BrE, past tense and past participle* **resat** /-'sæt/ **resitting** to take a test or examination again
− **resit** /'ri:sɪt/ *noun*: *He failed some of his exams, so he's doing resits.*

res·o·lu·tion /,rezə'lu:ʃən/ *noun* **1** an official decision, especially after a vote: *The United Nations passed a resolution calling for an end to the fighting.* **2** a promise that you make to yourself to do something: *I made a New Year resolution to stop smoking.*

re·solve /rɪ'zɒlv $rɪ'zɑlv/ *verb* **1** to deal with a problem or end a disagreement: *Everyone wants to resolve this as soon as possible.* **2** *formal* to make a definite decision to do something: *He resolved to work harder.*

resolve *noun* [no plural] *formal* strong determination to do something: *I admire your resolve.*

re·sort /rɪ'zɔːt $rɪ'zɔrt/ *noun* **1** a place where a lot of people go for a holiday: *a popular tourist resort* **2** as a last resort if everything else fails: *I could borrow the money, but only as a last resort.*

resort *verb* **resort to something** to do something that you do not want to do, in order to achieve something: *In the end he resorted to borrowing money from his parents.* | *We will not resort to violence.*

re·sound·ing /rɪ'zaʊndɪŋ/ *adjective* **1** used for emphasizing that something is very successful: *a resounding victory* **2** very loud: *a resounding crash*

re·source /rɪ'zɔːs $'rizɔrs/ *noun* something that is available for people to use: *The library is a useful resource.* | *the country's natural resources* (=oil, coal, gold etc)

re·source·ful /rɪ'zɔːsfəl $rɪ'sɔrsfəl/ *adjective* good at finding ways to deal with problems

respect¹ /rɪ'spekt/ *noun* [no plural]

GRAMMAR
respect for someone/something
1 if you have respect for someone, you admire them and have a very good opinion of them: *He was a very good teacher – I **had** great **respect for** him.* | *I've got **a lot of respect for** Henry.*
2 a polite way of behaving towards other people: *We expect everyone at this school to treat each other **with respect**.* | *You must learn to **show respect for** other people* (=treat them in a polite way).
3 if you have respect for something, you believe that it is important: *Many people **have** no **respect for** religion any more.*

respect² *verb*

GRAMMAR
respect someone for (doing) something
1 to admire someone and have a good opinion of them: *Everyone loved and respected Mother Teresa.* | *I **respected** him **for** saying exactly what he thought.*
2 if you respect other people's feelings or ideas, you show that you understand and care about them: *I respect how you feel, but I don't think you really need to worry.*

3 if you respect a law or rule, you obey it

re·spec·ta·ble /rɪˈspektəbəl/ adjective
1 someone who is respectable is good and honest: *a respectable businessman*
2 neatly dressed and not dirty or untidy: *Do I look respectable?*

re·spect·ful /rɪˈspektfəl/ adjective showing respect for someone or something

re·spec·tive /rɪˈspektɪv/ adjective used to talk about each different person or thing in order: *I invited three friends and their respective boyfriends.*
—**respectively** adverb: *For English and French I got 58% and 59% respectively.*

re·spi·ra·to·ry /rɪˈspɪrətəri $ ˈresprə-ˌtɔri/ adjective formal related to breathing: *Smoking causes respiratory illnesses.*

res·pite /ˈrespaɪt $ ˈrespɪt/ noun [no plural] formal when something unpleasant stops happening for a short time: *There was no respite from the rain.*

re·spond /rɪˈspɒnd $ rɪˈspand/ verb formal **1** to answer: *How did she respond to your questions?* **2** to do something because of something that has happened: *The police responded to the violence by using water canons.*

re·sponse /rɪˈspɒns $ rɪˈspans/ noun formal a reply or reaction to something: *Every time I asked her a question I got no response.* | *I am writing in response to your advertisement.*

re·spon·si·bil·i·ty /rɪˌspɒnsəˈbɪl-əti $ rɪˌspansəˈbɪləti/ noun, plural **responsibilities**

GRAMMAR
responsibility to do something
responsibility for (doing) something

1 if something is your responsibility, it is your job to do it: *In the holidays it is Jim's responsibility to feed all the animals.* | *The manager explained what my responsibilities were.* | *The treasurer has responsibility for the club's budget.*
2 accept responsibility, take responsibility if you accept responsibility for something bad that has happened, you admit that you did it or caused it: *The hospital has accepted responsibility for the mistake.*

re·spon·si·ble /rɪˈspɒnsəbəl $ rɪ-ˈspansəbəl/ adjective

GRAMMAR
responsible for (doing) something

1 if you are responsible for something, it is your job to do it: *Mrs Hendrick is responsible for all the cooking.* | *I am responsible for putting the books away at the end of the lesson.*
2 a young person who is responsible always behaves in a sensible way: *You can trust Mary – she's very responsible.*
3 if you are responsible for something bad that has happened, you did it or caused it: *The boy said that he was not responsible for the attack on the girl.*

re·spon·si·bly /rɪˈspɒnsəbli $ rɪˈspan-səbli/ adverb in a sensible way: *I don't trust them to behave responsibly.*

re·spon·sive /rɪˈspɒnsɪv $ rɪˈspansɪv/ adjective paying attention to what people need, and doing something to help them: *The government needs to be responsive to people's needs.*

rest¹ /rest/ noun

GRAMMAR
the rest of something

1 the part of something that still remains: *I'll keep the rest of the cake until tomorrow.* | *What shall we do for the rest of the day?*
2 the other people or things: *Some people were in the house and the rest were in the garden.*

PHRASES
have a rest, need a rest, get some rest to have some time when you are quiet and can relax or sleep: *I went upstairs to have a rest before dinner.*

rest² verb

GRAMMAR
rest something on something

1 to spend some time being quiet and relaxing or sleeping: *Tessa lay down on the sofa to rest.* | *We spent the afternoon resting.*
2 to put something in a position where it is supported by something else: *Kyle was drinking a beer and resting his feet on the table.* | *She rested her bicycle against the wall.*

R

res·tau·rant /'restərɒnt $ 'res,trɑnt/
noun a place where you can buy and eat
a meal: *They had dinner in a Chinese
restaurant.*

rest·ful /'restfəl/ adjective peaceful and
quiet

rest·less /'restləs/ adjective unable to
relax and keep still: *The children were
getting restless.*

re·store /rɪ'stɔː $ rɪ'stɔr/ verb 1 to
repair something so that it looks new
2 to get back something that had disappeared: *How can we restore his confidence?*

re·strain /rɪ'streɪn/ verb to stop someone from doing something, usually by
holding them: *I put my hand on Jim's
arm to restrain him*

re·straint /rɪ'streɪnt/ noun 1 [no plural]
when you act calmly even though a situation is very difficult: *The police showed
great restraint.* 2 something that limits
what you can do: *The government has
introduced new restraints on free
speech.*

re·strict /rɪ'strɪkt/ verb to limit something: *laws that restrict people's freedom*

re·strict·ed /rɪ'strɪktɪd/ adjective
limited to a small group of people or
things: *Cancer is not restricted to old
people.*

re·stric·tion /rɪ'strɪkʃən/ noun a rule
that limits what you are allowed to do:
*There are a lot of travel restrictions on
people in some countries.*

rest·room /'restruːm/ noun AmE a room
containing a toilet, in a public place such
as a restaurant

re·sult¹ /rɪ'zʌlt/ noun

GRAMMAR
a result of something

1 something that happens because of
something else: *The whole situation
was **the result of** (=was caused by) a
silly mistake.* | *Bill died **as a result of**
(=because of) the accident.*
2 the number of points or votes that
each person or team has at the end
of a game or competition: ***The result
of** the match was 3–0.* | *I wonder
what **the result of** the election will
be.*
3 the information you get from studying something carefully or doing a
scientific test: *You will get **the result***

of your blood test next week. | *I de-
cided to show **the results of** my
survey by drawing a graph.*
4 a number or letter that shows how
well you have done in an exam;
SCORE AmE: *Dave got excellent results
in his exams this year.*

result² verb 1 **result in** something to
make something happen: *The extremely
cold weather resulted in the deaths of
three people.* 2 **result from** something to happen because of something:
*Her illness resulted from smoking and
drinking too much.*

re·sume /rɪ'zjuːm $ rɪ'zum/ verb formal
to start again: *Normal service will re-
sume soon.*

rés·u·mé /'rezjʊmeɪ $,rezʊ'meɪ/ the
American word for CV

re·sus·ci·tate /rɪ'sʌsəteɪt/ verb to
make someone start breathing again:
*Doctors tried to resuscitate her but it was
too late.*

re·tail /'riːteɪl/ noun [no plural] the activity
of selling things to people in shops: *Re-
tail sales are rising steadily.*

re·tail·er /'riːteɪlə $ 'ri,teɪlɚ/ noun a
person or company that sells things to
people in shops

re·tain /rɪ'teɪn/ verb formal to keep
something: *The village has retained its
old charm.*

re·tal·i·ate /rɪ'tælieɪt/ verb to do
something unpleasant to someone because they have done something unpleasant to you: *Don't retaliate if he hits
you.*

re·tal·i·a·tion /rɪ,tæli'eɪʃən/ noun [no
plural] when someone retaliates

ret·i·cent /'retəsənt/ adjective formal not
wanting to say what you know or think
about something

re·tire /rɪ'taɪə $ rɪ'taɪɚ/ verb to stop
working at the end of your working life:
I'm going to retire when I'm 60.

re·tire·ment /rɪ'taɪəmənt $ rɪ'taɪɚ-
mənt/ noun when you stop working at
the end of your working life: *It's important to save money for your retirement.*

re·tir·ing /rɪ'taɪərɪŋ/ adjective someone
who is retiring is shy and nervous with
other people: *a shy retiring type of man*

re·treat /rɪ'triːt/ verb 1 to move
away from someone or something that

R

is unpleasant or frightening: *The shouting made her retreat into the house.* **2** if an army retreats, it moves back to avoid fighting
–**retreat** *noun*: *the army's retreat from Kosovo*

ret·ri·bu·tion /ˌretrəˈbjuːʃən/ *noun* [no plural] *formal* when someone is hurt or punished for doing something: *They would not give evidence against the men for fear of retribution.*

re·trieve /rɪˈtriːv/ *verb* to get something and bring it back from the place where you left it: *I retrieved my bags from the car.*

ret·ro·spect /ˈretrəspekt/ *noun* in retrospect used when you are thinking about something that happened in the past, and you know more about it now than you knew then: *In retrospect, I shouldn't have sold my computer.*

re·turn¹ /rɪˈtɜːn $ rɪˈtɚn/ *verb*

GRAMMAR
return to something
return from somewhere
return something to someone

1 to come back or go back to a place: *At eleven o'clock I was still waiting for Simone to return.* | *Years later I* **returned to** *the house I used to live in.* | *He's been much happier since* **returning from** *the States.* | *He* **returned home** *just after midnight.*
2 to give or send something back to someone: *I decided to* **return** *the jeans* **to** *the shop where I had bought them.* | *The letter was returned to me without being opened.*
3 if something returns, it starts to happen again: *By the evening my headache had returned.*
4 if you return to something, you start to do it again: *The doctor said I was well enough to* **return to** *work.* | *Ten years later I decided to* **return to** *teaching.*

PHRASES
return to normal: *It was a long time before the situation at work* **returned to normal** (=became normal again).
return someone's call to telephone someone after they have tried to telephone you: *Lyn's not here at the moment. Shall I ask her to* **return your call**?

return² *noun* **1** [no plural] when someone comes back or goes back to a place: *After three years abroad he was looking forward to his return to England.* **2** in return if you do something in return for what someone has done for you, you do it because they did that thing for you: *She offered to help, but wouldn't take anything in return.* **3** *BrE* a return ticket is a ticket for a journey to a place and back again

re·u·nion /riːˈjuːnjən/ *noun* a meeting of people who have not met for a long time: *a college reunion*

re·u·nite /ˌriːjuːˈnaɪt/ *verb* to bring people together again: *He was at last reunited with his family.*

rev /rev/ *verb* revved, revving also **rev up** to make an engine work faster: *Rev the engine by pressing on the accelerator.*

re·veal /rɪˈviːl/ *verb* **1** to tell people information that was secret: *He finally revealed the name of his partner.* **2** to show something that you could not see before: *The door opened to reveal a large hall.*

re·veal·ing /rɪˈviːlɪŋ/ *adjective* **1** showing someone's true character or feelings: *a revealing interview* **2** revealing clothes show parts of your body that are usually kept covered: *a revealing blouse*

rev·el /ˈrevəl/ *verb* revelled, revelling *BrE*, reveled, reveling *AmE* **revel in something** to enjoy something very much

rev·e·la·tion /ˌrevəˈleɪʃən/ *noun* a fact that people did not know before: *newspaper revelations about her private life*

re·venge /rɪˈvendʒ/ *noun* [no plural] when you hurt or punish someone because they have done something bad to you: *She was determined to get her revenge.*

rev·e·nue /ˈrevənjuː $ ˈrevəˌnuː/ *noun* [no plural] money that a company or organization earns: *Most of the theatre's revenue comes from ticket sales.*

re·verse¹ /rɪˈvɜːs $ rɪˈvɜrs/ *verb* **1** to drive a car backwards: *I'll reverse the car into the garage.* **2** to make something the opposite of what it was: *We will never reverse our decision.* **3** reverse the charges *BrE* to make the person you are telephoning pay for the call; CALL COLLECT *AmE*

reverse² *noun* [no plural] **1** if a car is in

R

reverse, it is ready to drive backwards: *Put the car in reverse.* **2** the opposite: *In fact, the reverse is true.*

reverse³ *adjective* in the opposite way to usual: *I will read the winners' names in reverse order.*

re·vers·i·ble /rɪ'vɜːsəbəl $ rɪ'vɚsəbəl/ *adjective* **1** something that is reversible can be changed ⇨ *opposite* IRREVERSIBLE: *Any bad effects from the treatment are easily reversible.* **2** a reversible piece of clothing can be worn with the inside part on the outside

re·vert /rɪ'vɜːt $ rɪ'vɚt/ *verb* to go back to what something was before: *Leningrad reverted to the name of St Petersburg.*

re·view¹ /rɪ'vjuː/ *noun* **1** when someone thinks about something again and decides how to change it: *We are having a review of all our safety procedures.* **2** a report about a new book, film, or television show: *The latest Star Wars film got very good reviews.*

review² *verb* **1** to think about something again and decide how to change it: *The school is reviewing its policy on homework.* **2** to write a report about a new book, film, or television show: *He reviews films for a Sunday newspaper.* **3** the American word for REVISE²

re·vise /rɪ'vaɪz/ *verb* **1** to change something to make it better: *We need to revise our plans.* **2** *BrE* to prepare for a test by learning work again; REVIEW *AmE*: *I need to revise for my maths test.*

re·vi·sion /rɪ'vɪʒən/ *noun [no plural] BrE* when you learn work again before a test: *Have you done enough revision?*

re·vi·val /rɪ'vaɪvəl/ *noun* when something becomes popular or successful again: *the revival of seventies music*

re·vive /rɪ'vaɪv/ *verb* **1** to make something popular or strong again: *Attempts to revive the economy have failed.* **2** to make someone conscious again: *The doctors could not revive him.*

re·volt¹ /rɪ'vəʊlt $ rɪ'voʊlt/ *verb* to refuse to obey a government and use violence in order to try to change it: *The people revolted against the government.*

revolt² *noun* when people refuse to obey a government and use violence against it: *a peasants' revolt*

re·volt·ing /rɪ'vəʊltɪŋ $ rɪ'voʊltɪŋ/

adjective very unpleasant: *The revolting smell of dead fish.*

rev·o·lu·tion /ˌrevə'luːʃən/ *noun* **1** when the people of a country change the political system completely, using force: *the French Revolution* **2** a complete change in the way people do something: *a revolution in scientific thinking*

rev·o·lu·tion·a·ry¹ /ˌrevə'luːʃənəri $ ˌrevə'luːʃə,neri/ *adjective* completely new and different: *a revolutionary new product*

revolutionary² *noun, plural* **revolutionaries** someone who is involved in a political revolution

rev·o·lu·tion·ize *also* **revolutionise** *BrE* /ˌrevə'luːʃənaɪz/ *verb* to completely change the way people do something: *E-mail has revolutionized the way we work.*

re·volve /rɪ'vɒlv $ rɪ'vɑlv/ *verb* **1** *formal* to move around in a circle: *The wheel revolved slowly.* **2 revolve around something** to have something as the most important part: *Our lives revolve around the school.*

re·volv·er /rɪ'vɒlvə $ rɪ'vɑlvɚ/ *noun* a type of small gun

re·ward¹ /rɪ'wɔːd $ rɪ'wɔrd/ *noun* something, especially money, that is given to someone to thank them for doing something: *She offered a reward to anyone who could find her cat.*

reward² *verb* if you are rewarded for what you have done, something good happens to you or is given to you: *He was rewarded for all his hard work.*

re·ward·ing /rɪ'wɔːdɪŋ $ rɪ'wɔrdɪŋ/ *adjective* a job that is rewarding makes you feel happy and satisfied: *Teaching can be rewarding work.*

re·wind /riː'waɪnd/ *verb, past tense and past participle* **rewound** /-'waʊnd/ to make a TAPE go back towards the beginning

re·wound the past tense and past participle of REWIND

re·write /ˌriː'raɪt/ *verb* **rewrote** /-'rəʊt $ 'roʊt/ **rewritten** /-'rɪtn/ to write something again in a different way: *They rewrote the ending of the film.*

rewritten the past participle of REWRITE

rewrote the past tense of REWRITE

rhe·tor·i·cal ques·tion /rɪ,tɒrɪkəl 'kwestʃən $ rɪ,tɔrɪkəl 'kwestʃən/ *noun*

R

a question that you ask in order to make a statement, without expecting an answer

rheu·ma·tis·m /'ruːmətɪzəm/ *noun [no plural]* a disease that makes your muscles and joints painful and difficult to move

rhi·no·ce·ros /raɪ'nɒsərəs $raɪ'nɑːsərəs / also **rhi·no** /'raɪnəʊ $'raɪnoʊ/ *noun* a large heavy animal with a horn on its nose ⇨ see picture on page 339

rhyme¹ /raɪm/ *verb* if two words or phrases rhyme, they end with the same sound: *'Car' rhymes with 'far'.*

rhyme² *noun* **1** a short poem or song that uses words that rhyme **2** when someone uses words that rhyme: *a letter all in rhyme*

rhyth·m /'rɪðəm/ *noun* a regular repeated pattern of sounds: *the rhythm of the music*

rib /rɪb/ *noun* one of the curved bones in your chest

rib·bon /'rɪbən/ *noun* a narrow piece of coloured cloth that you use to make your clothes or hair look attractive: *She wore ribbons in her hair.*

rice /raɪs/ *noun [no plural]* food that consists of small white or brown grains that are cooked in water: *We had chicken with boiled rice.*

rich /rɪtʃ/ *adjective*

1 someone who is rich has a lot of money or owns a lot of things: *He became rich and powerful. | She's one of the richest people in the world.*

2 rich food has a lot of fat or sugar in it, so you cannot eat very much of it: *The food was delicious, but very rich. | a rich sauce*

3 a rich smell, taste, or colour is strong and pleasant: *I love the rich colours in that painting. | the rich smell of fresh coffee*

PHRASE
rich in something containing a lot of something good: *It's a beautiful country, **rich in** natural resources.*

rick·et·y /'rɪkəti/ *adjective informal* in bad condition and likely to break: *a rickety old chair*

ric·o·chet /'rɪkəʃeɪ/ *verb* if a bullet or stone ricochets off a surface, it hits the surface and moves away from it in a different direction

rid /rɪd/ *adjective*

1 get rid of something **a)** to throw away or sell something because you do not want it any more: *I'm going to **get rid of** this car and buy a new one.* **b)** to make something that you do not want go away: *We couldn't **get rid of** the smell in the house.*

2 get rid of someone to make someone leave a place or job: *Most people were glad to **get rid of** the old president. | Andy stayed for hours – we couldn't **get rid of** him!*

rid·dle /'rɪdl/ *noun* **1** an event that people cannot understand or explain: *The riddle of Len's death was never solved.* **2** a joke or question that you must guess the answer to

rid·dled /'rɪdld/ *adjective* riddled with something containing a lot of something bad: *His essay was riddled with mistakes.*

ride¹ /raɪd/ *verb* **rode** /rəʊd $roʊd/ **ridden** /'rɪdn/ **riding**

1 to move along on a horse or bicycle: *I learnt to ride a horse when I was five. | Can you ride a bicycle? | Paul jumped on his bike and **rode off**. | We decided to **ride through** the woods.*

2 *AmE* to travel in a bus, car etc: *This was the first time she had ridden in a train.*

ride² *noun* **1** a trip in a car or train, or on a bicycle or horse: *I went for a ride on my bike. | Dad took us for a ride in his new car.* **2** a large moving machine that people go on for fun: *children's fairground rides*

rid·er /'raɪdə $'raɪdər/ *noun* someone who rides a horse, bicycle, or MOTORCYCLE

ridge /rɪdʒ/ *noun* a long narrow area of high land along the top of a mountain: *We could see climbers on the ridge.*

rid·i·cule /'rɪdəkjuːl/ *verb formal* to laugh and say unkind things about someone or something: *They ridiculed his appearance.*
–**ridicule** *noun [no plural] formal*: *My idea was greeted with ridicule.*

ri·dic·u·lous /rɪ'dɪkjələs/ *adjective* very silly: *That's a ridiculous idea!*

ri·dic·u·lous·ly /rɪ'dɪkjələsli/ *adverb*

R

too much, in a way that seems silly: *Their clothes are ridiculously expensive.*

rid·ing /ˈraɪdɪŋ/ *noun* [no plural] the sport of riding horses

rife /raɪf/ *adjective* if something bad is rife, it is very common: *Burglary is rife in large cities.*

ri·fle /ˈraɪfəl/ *noun* a long gun that you hold against your shoulder to shoot

rift /rɪft/ *noun* a serious disagreement between people: *The argument created a rift between them.*

rig[1] /rɪg/ *verb* **rigged, rigging** to make an election or competition have the result that you want, by doing something dishonest: *They claim the election was rigged.*

rig[2] *noun* a large structure that is used for getting oil or gas from under the bottom of the sea

right[1] /raɪt/ *adjective*

> **GRAMMAR**
> **right about something**
> **right to do something**
> **right for something/someone**

1 correct ⇨ opposite WRONG[1] (1): *In the test, all my answers were right.* | *Are you sure this is the right way?* | *You were right about the weather – it's raining now.*

2 the right side is the side nearest your right hand, which is the hand most people write with ⇨ opposite LEFT[1]: *Dan's broken his right leg.*

3 fair or morally good ⇨ opposite WRONG[1] (2): *I think it's right that you should pay for your own ticket.* | *It's never right to steal.*

4 suitable ⇨ opposite WRONG[1] (3): *Make sure you wear something that's right for the occasion.*

> **PHRASE**
> **that's right** *spoken* something you say when someone is correct about something: *"You live in London, don't you?" "Yes, that's right."*

right[2] *adverb*

1 exactly in a place or at a time: *A child was standing right in the middle of the road.* | *They arrived right at the end of the show.*

2 *spoken* used when you want to make someone listen or get ready to do something: *Right, everyone! It's time to go!*

3 correctly ⇨ opposite WRONG[1] (1): *Have I done this question right?*

> **PHRASES**
> **turn right, look right etc** to turn, look etc towards your right side ⇨ opposite LEFT[2]: *Turn right by the traffic lights.*
> **right now, right away** *spoken* immediately: *I'll go and talk to him right now.*

right[3] *noun*

> **GRAMMAR**
> **the right to do something**
> **the right to something**

1 something that you are allowed to do by law: *In Britain everyone has the right to vote when they are eighteen.* | *All children have the right to free education.* | *Of course men and women should have equal rights* (=the same rights).

2 behaviour that is good and fair: *It's important to teach children the difference between right and wrong.*

> **PHRASES**
> **on the right, to the right** on or near your right side: *Walk straight on and you'll see a post-office on the right.*
> **the Right** political groups that believe that the government should not own any business or try to control business by making too many rules

right an·gle /ˈ. ˌ./ *noun* an angle of 90°, like the angles at the corners of a square

right-angled /ˈ. ˌ./ *adjective* a right-angled TRIANGLE has two sides that join each other at 90°

right·ful /ˈraɪtfəl/ *adjective* formal according to what is legally and morally right: *He is the rightful owner of the house.*
−**rightfully** *adverb*: *The money should rightfully be hers.*

right-hand /ˈ. ./ *adjective* on or near your right side: *Their house is on the right-hand side of the road.*

right-hand·ed /ˌ. ˈ../ *adjective* someone who is right-handed uses their right hand rather than their left hand to do most things

right·ly /ˈraɪtli/ *adverb* correctly or for a good reason: *Her father quite rightly said that she was too young to drive.*

right of way /ˌ. . ' ./ noun [no plural] the right to drive into or across a road before other vehicles

right-wing /ˌ. ' ./ adjective someone with right-wing views does not like changes in society, and supports CAPITAL-ISM rather than SOCIALISM

ri·gid /'rɪdʒɪd/ adjective 1 rules or ideas that are rigid are strict and difficult to change: *a society with rigid traditions* 2 something that is rigid is stiff and does not move or bend easily: *His body was rigid with fear.*

rig·or·ous /'rɪgərəs/ adjective done in a careful and thorough way: *Some people are demanding a more rigorous driving test.*
—**rigorously** adverb: *The new rules will be rigorously enforced.*

rile /raɪl/ verb informal to make someone angry: *Don't let him rile you.*

rim /rɪm/ noun the outside edge of something round, such as a glass or a wheel

rind /raɪnd/ noun the thick skin on the outside of some foods or fruits: *lemon rind*

ring¹ /rɪŋ/ noun

1 a round piece of silver, gold etc that you wear on your finger: *a gold wedding ring* ⇨ see picture at JEWELLERY
2 a circle: *The kids sat in a ring in the middle of the room.* | *There was a ring of policemen around the building.*

PHRASES

give someone a ring BrE informal to telephone someone: *I'll give you a ring at the weekend.*

a ring at the door the sound that a door bell makes: *At that moment there was a ring at the door.*

ring² verb **rang** /ræŋ/ **rung** /rʌŋ/

1 if a bell or telephone rings, it makes a sound: *I could hear the church bells ringing.* | *We were just going out when the telephone rang.* ⇨ see picture on page 350
2 if you ring a bell, you press it so that it makes a sound: *The postman rang the front door bell.*
3 BrE also **ring up** to telephone someone: *Jim rang me up and asked me to go to a party.* ⇨ see usage note at PHONE²

PHRASAL VERB
ring back
ring someone back BrE to telephone someone later; CALL BACK AmE: *Mr Todd's busy at the moment. Can he ring you back?*

ring·lead·er /'rɪŋˌliːdə $ 'rɪŋˌlidɚ/ noun someone who leads a group that is doing something wrong: *He is the ringleader of the gang.*

rink /rɪŋk/ noun an area where you can ICE SKATE

rinse /rɪns/ verb to wash something in clean water in order to remove soap or dirt from it: *Rinse the shampoo out of your hair.*
—**rinse** noun: *He gave the glass a quick rinse.*

ri·ot¹ /'raɪət/ noun when a crowd of people behaves very violently in a public place: *The demonstration became a riot.*

riot² verb if a crowd of people riot, they behave violently in a public place: *People rioted against the new law.*
—**rioting** noun [no plural]: *There was rioting in the streets of the city.*

ri·ot·ous /'raɪətəs/ adjective noisy and excited: *riotous New Year's celebrations*

rip¹ /rɪp/ verb **ripped, ripping** 1 to tear something, or become torn: *He ripped the letter open.* | *My sleeve ripped.* 2 **rip something up** to tear something into a lot of pieces: *I ripped up all his love letters.* 3 **rip someone off** informal to charge someone too much money for something: *The taxi driver really ripped me off.*

rip² noun a hole in a piece of clothing or material where it has torn: *There's a rip in your skirt.*

ripe /raɪp/ adjective fruit that is ripe is ready to pick and eat: *a ripe red apple* | *Those bananas aren't ripe yet.*

rip·en /'raɪpən/ verb formal to become ripe: *As the tomatoes ripen, they change from green to red.*

rip·off /'rɪpɒf $ 'rɪpɔf/ noun in-formal something that is much too expensive: *Some designer clothes are a ripoff.*

rip·ple¹ /'rɪpəl/ verb when water ripples, it moves in small waves: *The pond rippled in the breeze.*

ripple

ripple² *noun* a small wave: *I watched the ripples on the lake.*

rise¹ /raɪz/ *verb* **rose** /rəʊz $ roʊz/ **risen** /'rɪzən/

> **GRAMMAR**
> **rise by something**
> **rise from something, rise to something**

1 if an amount rises, it increases ⇨ *opposite* FALL¹ (2): *The amount of crime in our cities is rising all the time.* | *The cost has risen from £100 to £200.* | *Unemployment has now risen to 2 million.* | *House prices have risen by 10% this year.*
2 also **rise up** *formal* to move upwards: *Suddenly the bird rose up in the sky and disappeared.*
3 to stand up: *We all rose when the president entered.* | *Mr Millet rose from his chair and walked across the room.*
4 when the sun or moon rises, it appears in the sky ⇨ *opposite* SET¹ (4): *We got up early to watch the sun rising.*

> **USAGE rise, raise**
> **Rise** is not followed by an object: *The balloon rose high in the air.* **Raise** is always followed by an object: *Please raise your hand if you know the answer.*

rise² *noun* **1** an increase ⇨ *opposite* FALL² (2): *There has been a rise in food costs.* | *We haven't had a pay rise this year.* **2** when someone or something becomes more successful or more powerful ⇨ *opposite* FALL² (3): *Hitler's rise to power*

ris·en the past participle of RISE¹

risk¹ /rɪsk/ *noun*

> **GRAMMAR**
> **a/the risk of something**
> **a/the risk of doing something**
> **a/the risk (that)**
> **a risk to something**

1 a possibility that something bad may happen: *Most sports involve the risk of injury.* | *There is always a risk of dying during an operation.* | *Is there a risk that I will become ill too?*
2 something that may be dangerous: *Smoking cigarettes is a risk to your health.*

> **PHRASES**
> take a risk to do something even though you know it is dangerous or

you may not succeed: *It's best not to take risks with your money.*
at risk (from something) likely to suffer because of something: *Children are most at risk from pollution.* | *Hundreds of jobs are at risk if we lose the contract.*

risk² *verb*

> **GRAMMAR**
> **risk doing something**

1 to do something which may be dangerous or may cause something bad to happen: *He didn't want to risk travelling in such bad weather.*
2 if you risk your life, money etc, you do something which may make you lose it: *Thousands of men and women risked their lives in the war.*

risk·y /'rɪski/ *adjective* **riskier, riskiest** dangerous: *Travelling alone can be risky.*

rit·u·al¹ /'rɪtʃuəl/ *noun* a ceremony or set of actions that is always done in the same way: *The priest began the ritual of lighting the candles.*

ritual² *adjective* ritual actions are done as part of a ritual: *a ritual sacrifice*

ri·val¹ /'raɪvəl/ *noun* a person or group that you compete with: *The two sisters have always been rivals.*
− **rival** *adjective*: *rival gangs*

rival² *verb* **rivalled, rivalling** *BrE*, **rivaled, rivaling** *AmE* if one thing rivals another, it is as good as the other thing: *The city's nightlife rivals London's.*

ri·val·ry /'raɪvəlri/ *noun, plural* **rivalries** when people or groups try to show that they are better than each other: *There's a lot of rivalry between our schools.*

riv·er /'rɪvə $ 'rɪvɚ/ *noun* a long area or water that flows into a sea: *the River Ganges* ⇨ *see picture on page 348*

riv·et /'rɪvɪt/ *verb* be riveted if you are riveted by something, you cannot stop looking at it or listening to it because it is very interesting: *We sat riveted to the TV news.*
− **riveting** *adjective*: *a riveting story*

roach /rəʊtʃ $ roʊtʃ/ *AmE* a COCKROACH

road /rəʊd $ roʊd/ *noun*

> **GRAMMAR**
> **the road to somewhere**

a hard surface that cars and other vehicles travel on: *Is this the road to Stratford?* | *You're too young to cycle on the road.* | *A police car was com-*

R

▼ ing **along the road.** | We live just **down the road.** | I live at 73, Middle Road. ⇨ see picture on page 343

PHRASES

by road in a car, bus etc: If we go **by road** it will take at least seven or eight hours.

cross the road to walk across a road in order to get to the other side: Look left and right before you **cross the road.**

USAGE

A **road** in a town, city etc with buildings at the side is often called a **street.** Don't use **street** for roads outside towns. A very wide road for driving fast over long distances is called a **motorway** in British English. It is called a **highway** or a **freeway** in American English.

road·block /ˈrəʊdblɒk $ ˈroʊdblɑk/ noun a place where the police or army have blocked the road: Police have set up roadblocks to stop the terrorists escaping.

road rage /ˈ. ./ noun [no plural] when drivers become angry and start shouting at or attacking other drivers

road·side /ˈrəʊdsaɪd $ ˈroʊdsaɪd/ noun [no plural] the land at the edge of a road: We stopped at the roadside to eat our picnic.

road·works /ˈrəʊdwɜːks $ ˈroʊdwɜːks/ noun work that is being done to repair a road

roam /rəʊm $ roʊm/ verb to walk around all over a place: Gangs of thieves roam the city.

roar /rɔː $ rɔr/ verb to make a very loud deep noise: We heard a lion roar.
– **roar** noun: a roar of laughter

roar·ing /ˈrɔːrɪŋ/ adjective **roaring fire** a fire that burns with a lot of flames and heat

roast¹ /rəʊst $ roʊst/ verb to cook food such as meat or vegetables in an OVEN: Shall I roast or boil the potatoes?
– **roast** noun: We always have a roast on Sunday.

roast² adjective roast meat or vegetables have been cooked in an OVEN: roast beef

rob /rɒb $ rɑb/ **robbed, robbing** verb

GRAMMAR

rob someone of something

▼ to steal money or other things from a

▼ bank, shop, or person: They decided to rob a bank. | Two men broke into the house, and **robbed** the old lady **of** all her jewellery.

USAGE rob, steal

Use **rob** to talk about the person or place that money or other things are taken from: They tried to rob a bank. | Help! I've been robbed! Use **steal** to talk about the things that are taken: The men stole £2000.

rob·ber /ˈrɒbə $ ˈrɑbɚ/ noun someone who steals money or other things from a bank, shop etc: a gang of armed robbers

rob·ber·y /ˈrɒbəri $ ˈrɑbəri/ noun, plural robberies the crime of stealing money or other things from a bank, shop etc: Barker spent two years in jail for robbery.

robe /rəʊb $ roʊb/ noun **1** a long loose piece of clothing that people wear especially for formal ceremonies: a judge's robe **2** the American word for DRESSING GOWN

rob·in /ˈrɒbɪn $ ˈrɑbɪn/ noun a small brown bird with a red chest

ro·bot /ˈrəʊbɒt $ ˈroʊbɑt/ noun a machine that can move and do jobs like a person: Most of the work in the factory is now done by robots.

ro·bust /rəˈbʌst $ roʊˈbʌst/ adjective strong and not likely to become ill or be damaged: She is 75, but still robust.

rock¹ /rɒk $ rɑk/ noun **1** [no plural] the hard substance in the Earth's surface that cliffs and mountains are made of: They had to drill through solid rock. **2** a large piece of stone: We sat on a large rock. ⇨ see picture on page 348 **3** [no plural] a type of popular modern music with a strong loud beat: Their music is a mixture of rock and disco.

PHRASE

be on the rocks informal if someone's marriage is on the rocks, it is likely to fail

rock² verb if something rocks, or if you rock it, it moves gently from side to side: The boat rocked slowly. | I rocked the baby to sleep.

rock and roll /ˌ. . ˈ./ ROCK 'N' ROLL

rock bot·tom /ˌ. ˈ../ noun **hit rock bottom, reach rock bottom** informal to become as bad as it is possible to be: His musical career has now hit rock bottom.

R

R

rock-bottom *adjective* *informal* rock-bottom prices are as low as they can be: *The houses are being sold for rock-bottom prices.*

rock·et[1] /'rɒkɪt $'rɑkɪt/ *noun* **1** a long thin vehicle that carries people or scientific equipment into space **2** a long thin weapon that carries a bomb and is fired from a plane, ship etc **3** a FIREWORK that goes high into the air and explodes

rocket[2] *verb* *informal* to increase very quickly: *Sales of CDs have rocketed.*

rock·ing chair /'.. ,./ *noun* a chair with curved pieces of wood on the bottom that allow it to move backwards and forwards when you sit on it

rock 'n' roll /,rɒk ən 'rəʊl $,rɑk ən 'roʊl/ *noun* [no plural] a type of music with a strong loud beat for dancing

rock·y /'rɒki $'rɑki/ *adjective* **rockier**, **rockiest** covered with rocks or made of rock: *a rocky coastline*

rod /rɒd $rɑd/ *noun* a long thin pole or stick: *a fishing rod*

rode the past tense of RIDE[1]

ro·dent /'rəʊdənt $'roʊdnt/ *noun* *formal* an animal such as a rat or a mouse that has long sharp front teeth

rogue /rəʊg $roʊg/ *noun* a man or boy who is not honest or who behaves badly

role /rəʊl $roʊl/ *noun* **1** the jobs that someone has to do: *The mother of the family has an important role. | What is the role of the sales manager?* **2** a character in a play or film: *Rob played the role of the king.*

role mod·el /'. ,../ *noun* someone you admire and try to copy: *A father should be a good role model for his sons.*

roll[1] /rəʊl $roʊl/ *verb*

> **GRAMMAR**
> **roll down/across/over etc something**
> **1** to move somewhere smoothly, by turning over many times like a ball: *The coin fell out of my hands and rolled across the floor.*
> **2** if a vehicle rolls, it moves on its own, with no one driving it: *The car was starting to roll down the hill.*
> **3** also **roll over** to turn your body over when you are lying down: *Dan rolled over onto his back and fell asleep.*

▼ PHRASAL VERBS

roll in
informal if people or things roll in, large amounts of them arrive: *Letters soon rolled in complaining about the show.*

roll out
roll something out to make something flat after it has been in the shape of a ball or a tube: *I rolled out my sleeping bag on the floor.*

roll up
1 *informal* to arrive late: *We'd arranged to meet at eight, but he didn't roll up till nine o'clock!*
2 **roll something up** to bend something so that it is in the shape of a ball or a tube: *He stood up and rolled up his newspaper.*

roll[2] *noun* **1** a piece of paper, plastic etc that has been curled into the shape of a tube: *I only had one roll of film left.* **2** a small round LOAF of bread for one person

roll call /'. ./ *noun* when someone reads out all the names on a list to check who is there: *We must take a roll call to make sure everyone is here.*

rollerblade

roller skate   Rollerblade

Rol·ler·blade /'rəʊləbleɪd $'roʊlɚ-,bleɪd/ *noun* *trademark* a boot with a single row of wheels fixed under it that you wear for SKATING

rol·ler·blad·ing /'rəʊləˌbleɪdɪŋ $'roʊlɚˌbleɪdɪŋ/ *noun* [no plural] SKATING when you are wearing rollerblades: *We went rollerblading in the park.*

roller coast·er /'.. ,../ *noun* a small railway which carries people up and down a steep track very fast for fun

roller skate /'.. ,./ *noun* a boot with four wheels fixed under it that you wear for SKATING ⇨ *see picture at* ROLLERBLADE

roller skat·ing /'.. ,../ *noun* [no plural]

SKATING when you are wearing roller skates

roll·ing /'rəʊlɪŋ $'roʊlɪŋ/ *adjective* be rolling in it*informal* to be very rich

Ro·man[1] /'rəʊmən $'roʊmən/ *adjective* related to ancient Rome: *the Roman Empire*

Roman[2] *noun* the Romans were the people of ancient Rome

ro·mance /rəʊ'mæns $'roʊmæns/ *noun* **1** an exciting relationship between two people who love each other: *I don't think their relationship will last – it was just a summer romance.* **2** a story or film about two people who love each other

ro·man·tic /rəʊ'mæntɪk $roʊ'mæn-tɪk/ *adjective* connected with love and with treating the person you love in a special way: *I wish my boyfriend was more romantic.* | *a romantic novel*

roof /ruːf $rʊf/ *noun*

> **GRAMMAR**
> **the roof of something**
> the part of a building or vehicle that covers the top of it: *The roof of the church had been damaged in a storm.* ➪ see picture on page 343

> **PHRASES**
> **the roof of your mouth** the top part of the inside of your mouth: *The soup was hot and burnt the roof of my mouth.*
> **hit the roof** *BrE informal* to become very angry: *Dad hit the roof when he found out what I'd done.*

roof·top /'ruːftɒp $'rʊftɑp/ *noun* the top surface of a roof

room[1] /ruːm/ *noun*

> **GRAMMAR**
> **room for something**
> **1** a part of a building that has its own walls, floor, and ceiling: *This is the room I work in.* | *My brother was sleeping in the next room.* | *the living room*
> **2** [no plural] space for something or someone: *Is there room for my camera in your bag?*

> **PHRASES**
> **make room for someone/something** to move so that there is enough space for someone or some-

thing: *Please move along and make room for Jerry.*

leg room, head room etc the amount of space in front of you, or above you in a vehicle: *There's never much leg room in aeroplanes.*

room[2] *verb* **room with someone** *AmE* to live in the same room, apartment, or house as someone

room·mate /'ruːmˌmeɪt/ *noun* someone you share a room, apartment, or house with: *We were roommates at college.*

room·y /'ruːmi/ *adjective* **roomier, roomiest** a roomy building has plenty of space inside: *a nice roomy apartment*

roost·er /'ruːstə $'rʊstɚ/ *noun* a male chicken

root[1] /ruːt/ *noun* **1** the part of a plant that grows under the ground and takes water from the soil **2** the basic cause of a problem: *Family problems are at the root of his behaviour.* **3** the part of a tooth or hair that is under the skin **4 roots** where something first started or where someone was born: *She has never forgotten her roots in Ireland.*

root[2] *verb* **1** also **root around** to search for something by moving things around: *I rooted around in my bag for my key.* **2 root something out** to find out if a problem exists and get rid of it: *We will root out drugs from our school.*

rope[1] /rəʊp $roʊp/ *noun* **1** very strong thick string: *They tied up the boat with rope.* **2 know the ropes** *informal* to know how something works or how to do a job

rope[2] *verb* **1** to tie things or people together, using rope: *The climbers roped themselves together.* **2 rope someone in** *informal* to persuade someone to help you: *I was roped in to help organize the party.*

rose[1] /rəʊz $roʊz/ *noun* a garden flower that smells sweet and has sharp parts called THORNS

rose[2] the past tense of RISE[1]

ro·sé /'rəʊzeɪ $roʊ'zeɪ/ *noun* [no plural] pink wine

ros·ter /'rɒstə $'rɑstɚ/ *noun* a list showing the jobs people must do and when they must do them

ros·trum /'rɒstrəm $'rɑstrəm/ *noun* a

R

small raised area that someone stands on, for example to make a speech

ros·y /'rəʊzi $ 'roʊzi/ *adjective* **rosier, rosiest** pink: *a baby with rosy cheeks*

rot /rɒt $ rɑt/ **rotted, rotting** *verb* if something rots, it goes bad and soft because it is old or wet: *The apple had started to rot.*

ro·ta /'rəʊtə $ 'roʊtə/ a British word for ROSTER

ro·tate /rəʊ'teɪt $ 'roʊteɪt/ *verb formal* if something rotates, or if you rotate it, it turns round: *Try to rotate the joint to loosen it.*

rote /rəʊt $ roʊt/ *noun* **learn something by rote** to learn something by repeating it many times until you remember it

rot·ten /'rɒtn $ 'rɑtn/ *adjective* **1** rotten food or wood has gone bad and soft: *rotten apples* **2** *informal* very bad, unpleasant, or unfair: *What a rotten thing to do!*

rough /rʌf/ *adjective*
1 not smooth or even: *The road up the mountain was steep and rough.* | *an old man with rough skin*
2 using too much force, and not gentle or careful enough: *Don't be so rough! Someone will get hurt.* | *Rugby can be a rough game.*
3 if the sea is rough, there are large waves because there are strong winds: *The little boat was tossed about on the rough seas.*
4 a rough description or idea is not exact and does not have very many details: *Can you give me a rough idea of where the station is?*
5 if your life is rough, it is unpleasant or difficult: *She's had a bit of a rough time recently.*
6 a rough place has a lot of violence and crime in it

rough·ly /'rʌfli/ *adverb* **1** not exactly ⇨ *same meaning* ABOUT² (1): *Roughly 100 people came.* **2** not gently or carefully: *He pulled me along roughly.*

round¹ /raʊnd/ *adjective*
something that is round is the same shape as a circle or ball: *The baby has big round eyes.*

round² *noun* **1** a set of events that are connected: *the latest round of peace talks* **2** one of the parts of a sports competition that you have to finish before you go to the next part: *Dallas will play Atlanta in the first round of the competition.* **3** a round of applause when people hit their hands together to show that they enjoyed a performance: *Let's give tonight's performers a big round of applause.* **4** alcoholic drinks that one person buys for all the people in a group: *Joe bought us a round of drinks.*

round³ *adverb, preposition* BrE
1 surrounding something: *There's a path round the lake.* | *He had a woollen scarf round his neck.*
2 in many parts of a place: *Come on – I'll show you round the office* (=I'll take you to every part of the office).
3 to someone's home: *We're going round to Bill's.*
4 somewhere in a place *spoken*: *Do you live round here?*
5 moving in a circle: *The cars raced round the track.* | *The dancers spun round and round.* ⇨ see picture on page 354

PHRASE
round about *spoken* used when giving an amount or time that is nearly right, but not exact: *The school was built round about 1930.*

round⁴ *verb* **round people up** to find and bring together a group of people: *Will someone go and round up all the children?*

round·a·bout /'raʊndəbaʊt/ *noun* BrE a circle where several roads meet, which you have to drive around until you reach the road you want to go on; TRAFFIC CIRCLE AmE ⇨ see picture on page 349

round·ed /'raʊndɪd/ *adjective* curved, not pointed or sharp: *We recommend rounded scissors for small children.*

round trip /ˌ. './ *noun* a journey to a place and back again

round·up /'. ./ *noun* **1** when a lot of people or animals are brought together, often by force: *a roundup of criminals by the FBI* **2** a short description of the most important pieces of news: *Here's a roundup of today's news.*

rous·ing /'raʊzɪŋ/ adjective making people feel excited and eager to do something: *The song has a rousing chorus.*

route /ruːt $ rut, raʊt/ noun **1** the way from one place to another: *This is the shortest route to school.* **2** the way in which someone's life changes and develops over time: *She does not know which route her career will take.*

rou·tine¹ /ruː'tiːn/ noun **1** the usual way in which you do things: *My daily routine starts with breakfast at 7.* **2** a set of actions, songs, or jokes that someone performs to entertain people: *They're learning a new dance routine.*

routine² adjective ordinary and usual: *The interview began with a few routine questions.*

row¹ /rəʊ $ roʊ/ noun

GRAMMAR
a row of people/things

1 a line of people or things: *There were **rows of** videos to choose from.* | *The children were all **standing in a row**, waiting for their parents.*

2 a line of seats in a cinema or theatre: *I always prefer to sit in **the back row**.*

PHRASE
three times in a row, four days in a row etc three times, one after the other or four days, one after the other etc: *The bus was late four days **in a row**.*

row² /rəʊ $ roʊ/ verb to make a boat move through water using OARS: *We rowed over to the island.*

row³ /raʊ/ noun BrE an angry argument: *The neighbours were having a row.*

row·dy /'raʊdi/ adjective **rowdier, rowdiest** behaving in a noisy and uncontrolled way: *a rowdy class*

roy·al /'rɔɪəl/ adjective connected with or belonging to a king or queen: *the royal family*

roy·al·ty /'rɔɪəlti/ noun [no plural] members of a royal family: *These seats are reserved for royalty.*

RSVP /ˌɑːr es viː' piː/ an abbreviation that is written on invitations to ask someone to reply

rub /rʌb/ verb **rubbed, rubbing**

GRAMMAR
rub something into/onto/over something
rub against something

1 to move your hand or a cloth backwards and forwards on a surface: *You'll have to rub a bit harder if you want to get those shoes clean.* | *Andy got out his sunscreen and **rubbed** it **into** his skin.*

2 also **rub against** if something rubs against your skin, it presses and moves against it in a way that is uncomfortable: *It was hot and my shirt collar was **rubbing against** my neck.*

PHRASE
rub it in informal to make someone remember something embarrassing or stupid that they have done: *I made a mistake, but you don't need to keep **rubbing it in**!*

PHRASAL VERBS
rub out
rub something out to remove something that you have written or drawn with a pencil: *I quickly **rubbed out** what I had written.*

rub·ber /'rʌbə $ 'rʌbɚ/ noun **1** [no plural] a substance that is used for making tyres, boots etc: *a toy made of rubber* | *rubber gloves* **2** a British word for ERASER

rubber band /ˌ.. '../ noun a thin circular piece of rubber used for holding things together

rub·bish /'rʌbɪʃ/ noun [no plural] BrE

1 things such as old food, empty bottles etc that you do not need any more and that you throw away; GARBAGE AmE: *Could you put this rubbish outside in the bin?* | *a pile of rubbish*

2 informal something that you think is silly or wrong: *I don't agree with that – it's rubbish!*

rub·ble /'rʌbəl/ noun [no plural] broken stones or bricks from a building that has been destroyed: *After the explosion, the house was just a pile of rubble.*

ru·by /'ruːbi/ noun, plural **rubies** a valuable dark red jewel

ruck·sack /'rʌksæk/ a British word for BACKPACK ⇨ see picture at BAG

R

rud·der /ˈrʌdə $ˈrʌdɚ/ *noun* a part at the back of a boat or plane that helps it change direction

rude /ruːd/ *adjective* **1** not polite: *She was rude to the teacher.* **2** talking about things to do with sex, in a way that may offend people: *The boys were telling rude jokes.*
–rudely *adverb*: *"Go away," she said rudely.*
–rudeness *noun* [no plural]: *I've had enough of your rudeness!*

ru·di·men·ta·ry /ˌruːdəˈmentəri/ *adjective formal* very simple and basic: *I have only a rudimentary knowledge of grammar.*

ruf·fle /ˈrʌfəl/ *verb* to make something that was smooth uneven or untidy: *He gently ruffled my hair.*

rug /rʌg/ *noun* a piece of thick material that you put on the floor: *a beautiful Turkish rug*

rug·by /ˈrʌgbi/ *noun* [no plural] a game played by two teams who carry and kick a ball that is the shape of a large egg ➪ *see picture on page 351*

rug·ged /ˈrʌgɪd/ *adjective* **1** rugged land is rough and uneven, with large rocks: *a rugged coastline* **2** if a man has a rugged appearance, he is attractive and looks strong and quite rough

ru·in¹ /ˈruːɪn/ *verb* to spoil or destroy something completely: *Her behaviour ruined the party.*

ruin² *noun* **1** also **ruins** part of a building that is left after the rest of it has been destroyed: *the ruins of an old abbey* **2** be in ruins to be completely spoiled or destroyed: *Their relationship was in ruins.* **3** [no plural] a situation in which someone loses all their money and possessions: *He faced ruin when his business failed.*

rule¹ /ruːl/ *noun*

something that tells you what you are allowed to do or what you cannot do, for example at school or in a game: *Jamie explained the rules of the game to us.* | *We were given a long list of school rules.*

PHRASES
against the rules not allowed by the rules: *Smoking at school is against the rules.*
break a rule, break the rules to do

something that is not allowed by the rules: *You're breaking the rules if you touch the ball with your hands.*
as a rule *formal* usually: *As a rule, I go to the gym three times a week.*

rule² *verb* **1** the people who rule a country control the country: *An Islamic government has ruled Iran since 1979.* **2** to make an official decision about a legal problem: *A judge ruled that Thompson had been fired from his job illegally.* **3** rule something out to decide that something is not possible: *Doctors have ruled out an operation at this time.*

ruled /ruːld/ *adjective* ruled paper has lines printed across it for writing on

rul·er /ˈruːlə $ˈruːlɚ/ *noun* **1** someone such as a king who has the official power to control a country **2** a flat narrow piece of plastic, wood, or metal that you use for measuring and drawing straight lines

rul·ing¹ /ˈruːlɪŋ/ *noun* an official decision that is made by a law court: *The company is refusing to accept the court's ruling.*

ruling² *adjective* having the most power in a country or organization: *The ruling class still get the best education.*

rum /rʌm/ *noun* a strong alcoholic drink made from sugar

rum·ble /ˈrʌmbəl/ *verb* to make a continuous low sound: *Traffic rumbled in the distance.*
–rumble *noun* [no plural]: *a rumble of thunder*

rum·mage /ˈrʌmɪdʒ/ *verb informal* to search for something by moving things around in an untidy way: *I rummaged through my bag for a pen.*

rummage sale /ˈ.. ˌ./ *noun AmE* an event at which old clothes, toys etc are sold; JUMBLE SALE *BrE*

ru·mour *BrE*, **rumor** *AmE* /ˈruːmə $ˈruːmɚ/ *noun* information that one person tells another which may not be true: *I heard a rumour that Joe and Liz were getting married.*

ru·moured *BrE*, **rumored** *AmE* /ˈruːməd $ˈruːmɚd/ *adjective* if something is rumoured to be true, people are saying that it may be true but no one is sure: *The band is rumoured to be splitting up.*

rump /rʌmp/ noun formal the part of an animal at the top of its back legs

run¹ ⇨ see box on next page

run² /rʌn/ noun

1 **go for a run, do a run** to run for pleasure or for exercise: *I try to go for a run at least twice a week.* | *We had to do a three-kilometre run at school.*

2 **in the long run** not immediately, but after some time: *If you buy good quality clothes it's cheaper in the long run.*

3 a point in the games of CRICKET and BASEBALL: *New Zealand won by 81 runs.*

run·a·way¹ /'rʌnəweɪ/ adjective **1** a runaway vehicle is moving fast and is out of control: *a runaway train* **2** happening quickly and in a way that is difficult to control: *Their first record was a runaway success.*

runaway² noun a young person or child who has left home without telling anyone

run·down /'rʌndaʊn/ noun [no plural] a quick description or explanation: *I gave him a rundown on what had happened.*

run-down /ˌ. './ adjective **1** in very bad condition: *run-down school buildings* **2** if you are run-down, you feel tired and ill

rung¹ the past participle of RING²

rung² noun **1** one of the steps of a LADDER **2** informal a level in an organization: *She started on the bottom rung in the company.*

run·ner /'rʌnə $ 'rʌnər/ noun someone who runs as a sport: *He's a brilliant long-distance runner.*

runner-up /ˌ.. './ noun, plural **runners-up** the person or team that finishes second in a competition: *The judge chose one winner and two runners-up.*

run·ning¹ /'rʌnɪŋ/ noun [no plural] **1** when you run for pleasure or as a sport: *Would you like to go running?* **2** **be in the running** to have a chance of winning: *We were never really in the running for the finals.*

running² adjective **1** **running water** water that flows from a TAP: *Some people had no running water or electricity.* **2** **a running total** a total that increases gradually as new amounts

are added to it: *Keep a running total of the amount you have spent.*

running³ adverb **three years running, five times running etc** for three years, five times etc without changing: *I was late for the third day running.*

run·ny /'rʌni/ adjective **runnier, runniest** a runny nose or runny eyes have liquid coming out of them: *a sore throat and a runny nose*

run·way /'rʌnweɪ/ noun a long wide road that planes use when they are landing or taking off ⇨ see picture on page 349

ru·ral /'rʊərəl $ 'rʊrəl/ adjective related to the country rather than the city: *Do you think you will enjoy rural life?*

rush¹ /rʌʃ/ verb

GRAMMAR
rush to/from somewhere
rush to do something

1 to go somewhere or do something quickly: *Maria rushed out of the room, crying.* | *The telephone rang, and we all rushed to answer it.*

2 to do something too quickly, without taking enough care: *Don't rush your homework.* | *If you rush your dinner, you'll get a stomachache.*

3 if you rush someone, you try to make them hurry: *I'm sorry to rush you, but we're going to miss the bus.*

PHRASE
rush someone to hospital to take someone to hospital very quickly: *An ambulance arrived and rushed her to hospital.*

PHRASAL VERBS
rush around
to be very busy going to different places or doing a lot of things: *Sally rushed around, making sure everyone had plenty to eat.*
rush into
rush into something if you rush into something, you do it without thinking about it carefully enough: *I don't think you should rush into buying a house.*

rush² noun [no plural]

GRAMMAR
a rush to do something
a rush for something

1 a situation in which you need to

R

1 to move quickly, going faster than when you walk

I can **run** faster than Tom. | A small boy grabbed my bag and **ran** out of the shop. | My dog loves to **run** after cats. | The girls came **running** towards me.

2 run a business, run an organization etc

to manage or control a business, organization, or country: The same family has been **running** the company for years. | They **run** a small restaurant in the centre of town.

5 run software, run a program etc

to make a computer PROGRAM work: If I **run** that software on my computer, it crashes.

run

3 road, river, wall etc

if a road, river, wall etc runs somewhere, it goes or passes there: Which river **runs** through Paris? | A high wall **ran** along the back of the house.

4 bus, train etc

if buses or trains run at particular times, they travel at those times: How often do trains **run** from Oxford to Birmingham?

PHRASES

run into problems, run into trouble
to start to have problems or trouble: The business **ran into trouble**, and eventually had to close.

run late, run on time
to happen or arrive late or at the right time: Are the trains **running on time**? | I'm afraid we're **running** a bit **late**.

run on coal, run on electricity etc
if a machine runs on coal, electricity etc, it uses coal etc to make it work: Most modern cars **run on lead-free petrol**.

run for office, run for President AmE
to try to get elected or become President: Al Gore and George W. Bush **ran for President** in 2000.

PHRASAL VERBS

run away
to leave a place without telling anyone because you are unhappy there: Danny had **run away from** home several times.

run into
1 run into someone informal to meet someone by chance: I **ran into** Miguel in town yesterday.

2 run into something if a vehicle runs into something, it hits it: Our car

went off the road and **ran into** a tree.

run out
to have no more of something left because you have used it all: Oh no! I've **run out of** coffee! | Hurry up! We're **running out of** time!

run over
if a vehicle runs over someone or something, it hits them and drives over them: A lorry had **run over** the dog and killed it.

hurry: *Can I phone you later? I'm in a rush to catch the bus.* | *Enjoy your meal. There's no rush.*

2 a situation in which a lot of people are trying to do something or get something: *There's always a rush for the bathroom in the morning.*

rushed /rʌʃt/ *adjective* **1** a piece of work that is rushed has been done too quickly and carelessly: *His lecture notes were rushed and almost unreadable.* **2 be rushed off your feet** *informal* to be very busy: *Mum's always rushed off her feet these days.*

rush hour /'. ./ *noun* the time of day when there is a lot of traffic because people are going to and from work: *If you leave by 7, you should miss the rush hour.*

rust[1] /rʌst/ *noun* [no plural] a brown substance that forms on metal when it gets wet: *Check your car each month for signs of rust.*

rust[2] *verb* if metal rusts, a brown substance forms on it: *The hinges on the box had rusted.*

rus·tle /'rʌsəl/ *verb* to make a soft light sound like the sound of paper moving: *leaves rustling in the wind*

rust·y /'rʌsti/ *adjective* **rustier, rustiest** **1** covered with rust: *a heap of rusty metal* **2** if someone's skill or knowledge is rusty, it is not as good it used to be because they have not used it for a long time: *My French is a bit rusty.*

rut /rʌt/ *noun* **1 be in a rut** *informal* to be living or working in a boring situation that you cannot easily change: *Many office workers feel they are in a rut after a few years.* **2** a deep narrow track made by a wheel

ruth·less /'ruːθləs/ *adjective* cruel and not caring about other people: *The judge described Marshall as a ruthless killer.*

–ruthlessly *adverb*: *The soldiers ruthlessly destroyed anything in their way.*

rye /raɪ/ *noun* [no plural] a type of grain, used for making bread and WHISKY

R

Ss

S the written abbreviation of SOUTH or SOUTHERN

's /z, s/ **1** is: *What's the time?* **2** has: *She's got a cold.* **3** used to show who owns something

sab·o·tage /'sæbətɑːʒ/ *verb* to secretly damage or destroy something: *He tried to sabotage her plans.*
–**sabotage** *noun*: *The bridge was destroyed in a deliberate act of sabotage.*

sach·et /'sæʃeɪ $ sæˈʃeɪ/ *noun* a small packet containing a liquid or powder: *a sachet of salt*

sack¹ /sæk/ *noun* **1** a large bag made of strong material: *We store the potatoes in sacks.* | *a sack of flour* **2 get the sack** *BrE informal* to be told that you must leave your job: *I worked for a while in a shop, but I got the sack.* **3 give someone the sack** *BrE informal* to tell someone that they must leave their job

sack² *verb BrE informal* if your employer sacks you, they tell you that you cannot work for them any longer ⇨ *same meaning* FIRE² (2): *If you continue to be late, the company will sack you.*

sa·cred /'seɪkrɪd/ *adjective* important and special according to a religion: *To Hindus, the River Ganges is sacred.*

sac·ri·fice¹ /'sækrəfaɪs/ *noun* **1** something important that you give up in order to help someone or get something that is more important: *Her parents made many sacrifices so that they could pay for their daughter's education.* **2** an animal or person that is killed in order to please a god

sacrifice² *verb* **1** to give up something important in order to help someone or get something that is more important: *I sacrificed my family for my career.* **2** to kill an animal or person in order to please a god

sad /sæd/ *adjective* **sadder, saddest**

1 unhappy ⇨ *opposite* HAPPY: *The movie had a very sad ending.* | *Why are you so sad?* | *I liked him and I was sad to say goodbye.* | *Of course the team felt sad that they had lost the match.*
2 *informal* boring and not fashionable: *He wears really sad clothes.*

sad·den /'sædn/ *verb formal* if something saddens you, it makes you feel sad: *We are all very saddened by her death.*

saddles

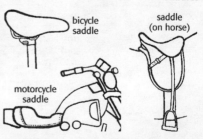

bicycle saddle

saddle (on horse)

motorcycle saddle

sad·dle¹ /'sædl/ *noun* a leather seat on a horse or bicycle

saddle² *verb* **saddle someone with something** *informal* to give someone a difficult or boring job: *I've been saddled with organising the party.*

sad·ly /'sædli/ *adverb* **1** in a sad way: *She smiled sadly.* **2** used when you are saying something that you wish were not true: *Sadly, the museum will have to close next year.*

sa·fa·ri /sə'fɑːri/ *noun* a trip through wild areas of Africa to hunt or watch wild animals: *We spent three weeks on safari in Kenya.*

safe¹ /seɪf/ *adjective*

> **GRAMMAR**
> **safe to do something**
> **safe for someone**
> **safe from something/someone**

1 something that is safe will not hurt people: *You can walk on the bridge – it's perfectly safe.* | *Walking is the safest form of travel.* | *Is the water here* **safe to** *drink?* | *We need more play areas that are* **safe for** *young children.*
2 if you are safe, you are not likely to be hurt: *I knew that when we got across the river we would be safe.* | *I didn't* **feel safe** *in the house on my own.* | *Stay indoors, where you will be* **safe from** *the fighting.*

> **PHRASES**
> **a safe place** a place where something is not likely to be stolen or lost: *You'd better put that money* **in a safe place.**
> **safe and sound, safe and well** not harmed or damaged in any way: *The horse was returned to its owner,* **safe and sound.**
> **to be on the safe side,** just to be safe in order to be very careful and avoid any problems: *We got to the airport very early,* **just to be on the safe side.**
> **in safe hands** if something is in safe hands, it is with a person who will look after it carefully: *Don't worry – the kids* **are in safe hands.**
> **–safely** *adverb*: *Drive safely.* | *Make sure that medicines are safely locked away.*

safe² *noun* a strong metal box with a lock on it, where you keep money and valuable things

safe·ty /'seɪfti/ *noun* [no plural]

when people are safe and not likely to be hurt: *Thousands of people left their homes and tried to escape to safety.* | *We were very concerned for* **the safety of** *the children.* | *There*

are new laws to **improve safety** on aircraft.

safety belt /'.. ,./ a SEAT BELT

safety pin /'.. ,./ *noun* a metal pin with a cover, used for fastening clothes together

safety pin

sag /sæg/ *verb* **sagged, sagging** to hang down loosely: *The bed sags in the middle.*

sa·ga /'sɑːgə/ *noun* a long complicated story

sage /seɪdʒ/ *noun* [no plural] a plant with grey-green leaves that you use in cooking

said the past tense and past participle of SAY

sail¹ /seɪl/ *verb*

> **GRAMMAR**
> **sail to/for/from somewhere**

1 to travel across water in a ship or boat: *The next day we* **sailed from** *Malta* **to** *Cairo.* | *We* **sail for** *America next week.*
2 to make a boat with sails move across water, especially as a sport: *I spent the summer learning to sail.* | *Do you want to have a go at sailing the boat?*

sail² *noun* **1** a large piece of strong cloth used to catch the wind and make a boat move **2 set sail** to begin a trip on a boat: *They set sail for America.*

sail·ing /'seɪlɪŋ/ *noun* [no plural] when people sail boats as a sport: *The sailing season starts in February.*

sail·or /'seɪlə $ 'seɪlɚ/ *noun* someone who works on a ship or sails a ship

saint /seɪnt/ *written abbreviation* **St** *noun* someone who is remembered because their life was very good and holy: *March 1 is Saint David's Day.*

sake /seɪk/ *noun* **1 for someone's sake** in order to help or please someone: *I did it for your sake, because I love you.* **2 for heaven's sake** *spoken* used when you are very annoyed about something: *For heaven's sake, switch that music off!*

sal·ad /'sæləd/ *noun* a mixture of vegetables, eaten cold: *a tomato salad* | *Meals are served with chips and salad.*

S

sa·la·mi /sə'lɑːmi/ *noun* a type of SAUS-AGE that is eaten cold

sal·a·ry /'sæləri/ *noun, plural* **salaries** the pay you receive from the organization you work for: *She gets a salary of at least £60,000 a year.* ⇨ *see usage note at* PAY²

sale /seɪl/ *noun*

> **GRAMMAR**
> **the sale of something**
> 1 when you sell something to someone: *He made a lot of money from* **the sale of** *his house.*
> 2 an event when a shop sells things for lower prices than usual: *The summer sales start next week.* | *I bought this shirt for £15* **in the sale***.*

> **PHRASES**
> **for sale** if something is for sale, someone is trying to sell it: *The house next door is* **for sale***.*
> **on sale** if something is on sale, you can buy it: *Tickets for the concert will be* **on sale** *next week.*

sales·man /'seɪlzmən/ *noun, plural* **salesmen** /-mən/ a man whose job is to sell things for a company

sales·per·son /'seɪlzpɜːsən $ 'seɪlz-ˌpɜ·sən/ *noun, plural* **salespeople** /-ˌpiːpl/ someone whose job is to sell things for a company

sales·wom·an /'seɪlzˌwʊmən/ *noun, plural* **saleswomen** /-ˌwɪmɪn/ a woman whose job is to sell things for a company

sa·li·va /sə'laɪvə/ *noun* [no plural] the liquid that you produce naturally in your mouth

salm·on /'sæmən/ *noun, plural* **salmon** a large silver fish with pink flesh that you can eat

sal·on /'sælɒn $ sə'lɑn/ *noun* a place where you can get your hair cut, have your nails cut etc: *a beauty salon*

sa·loon /sə'luːn/ *noun* 1 a place where alcoholic drinks were served in the US in the past 2 *BrE* a car with a separate space at the back for bags, cases etc; SEDAN *AmE*: *a five-seater family saloon*

salt /sɔːlt/ [no plural] *noun* 1 a white substance that is found naturally in sea water and that is used in cooking to make food taste better: *This sauce* needs more salt. 2 **take something with a pinch of salt** *informal* to not completely believe what someone tells you: *You have to take some of Jill's stories with a pinch of salt.*

salt·y /'sɔːlti/ *adjective* **saltier, saltiest** containing salt or tasting of salt: *The meat is too salty.*

sa·lute /sə'luːt/ *verb* to hold your right hand to your head to show respect for someone: *The soldiers saluted General Fox as he approached.* – **salute** *noun*: *His arm was raised in a salute.*

salute

sal·vage /'sælvɪdʒ/ *verb* to save something from a situation in which other things have been damaged or lost: *They managed to salvage a few of their things from the fire.*

same /seɪm/ *adjective, pronoun*

1 similar: *Your shoes are* **the same as** *mine!* | *All their songs sound the same.* | *The two girls have the same posters on their bedroom walls.* | *Yes, I had the same problem with my computer.*
2 the exact one, not a different one: *They go to the same school.* | *He lives in* **the same** *street* **as** *me.* | *Her new car is* **the same** *colour* **as** *her old one.*

> **USAGE**
> Do not say 'a same'. Say **the same sort of**: *I'd like* **the same sort of** *car as that.*

sam·ple¹ /'sɑːmpəl $ 'sæmpəl/ *noun* a small amount of something that shows what the rest of it is like: *Take samples of your work to the interview.* | *A small sample of blood is tested for the virus.*

sample² *verb* to try something to see what it is like: *Would you like to sample the wine?*

sanc·tion /'sæŋkʃən/ *verb formal* to officially allow something to happen: *The college has sanctioned the use of calculators in examinations.*

sanc·tions /'sæŋkʃənz/ *plural noun* laws that stop trade with another country, as a punishment when the country has behaved badly: *They agreed to end the sanctions against China.*

sanc·tu·a·ry /'sæŋktʃuəri $'sæŋktʃu-ˌeri/ *noun, plural* **sanctuaries** a place where people or animals are protected from danger: *The refugees sought sanctuary in a nearby church.* | *a bird sanctuary*

sand¹ /sænd/ *noun [no plural]* the mixture of very small grains of rock that you find in deserts and on beaches: *The children played on the sand.* ⇨ *see picture on page 348*

sand² *verb* to make a wooden surface smooth by rubbing it with SANDPAPER

san·dal /'sændl/ *noun* a light open shoe that you wear in warm weather: *a pair of leather sandals* ⇨ *see picture on page 352*

sand·cas·tle /'sænd,kɑːsəl $'sænd-ˌkæsəl/ *noun* a pile of sand in the shape of a castle, that children make on the beach

sand·pa·per /'sændpeɪpə $'sænd-ˌpeɪpə/ *noun [no plural]* strong rough paper that you rub on a wooden surface in order to make it smooth

sand·trap /'sændtræp/ *noun* the American word for BUNKER

sand·wich¹ /'sænwɪdʒ/ *noun, plural* **sandwiches** two pieces of bread with cheese, meat, egg etc between them: *We had chicken sandwiches for lunch.*

sandwich² *verb* **be sandwiched between** to be in a very small space between two things: *I was sandwiched between two fat ladies.*

sand·y /'sændi/ *adjective* **sandier, sandiest** covered with sand: *a sandy beach*

sane /seɪn/ *adjective* **1** able to think in a normal reasonable way ⇨ *opposite* INSANE: *They have to decide whether the murderer was sane when he committed his crimes.* **2** sensible and reasonable ⇨ *opposite* INSANE: *Leaving home seemed the only sane thing to do.*

sang the past tense of SING

san·i·ty /'sænəti/ *noun [no plural]* the ability to think normally and reasonably: *Kate was having doubts about her own sanity.*

sank the past tense of SINK¹

San·ta Claus /'sæntə ˌklɔːz/ also

Santa *noun* an old man with red clothes and white hair. Children believe that Santa Claus brings presents at Christmas; FATHER CHRISTMAS *BrE*

sar·cas·m /'sɑːkæzəm $'sɑrˌkæzəm/ *noun [no plural]* when you say something that seems to be kind and friendly but really means the opposite and is used to hurt or offend someone

sar·cas·tic /sɑː'kæstɪk $sɑr'kæstɪk/ *adjective* using sarcasm: *I was really upset by his sarcastic comments.*
– **sarcastically** /-kli/ *adverb*: *"Nice dress," he said sarcastically.*

sar·dine /sɑː'diːn $sɑr'din/ *noun* a small silver fish that you can eat

sa·ri /'sɑːri/ *noun* a type of loose dress worn by Asian women ⇨ *see picture on page 352*

sash /sæʃ/ *noun, plural* **sashes** a long piece of cloth that you wear around your waist or across one shoulder: *a red satin sash*

sas·sy /'sæsi/ *adjective informal* **sassier, sassiest** the American word for CHEEKY

sat the past tense and past participle of SIT

Sa·tan /'seɪtn/ *noun* the DEVIL

sat·el·lite /'sætəlaɪt/ *noun* a machine that has been sent into space to receive and send radio or television signals

satellite dish /'... ˌ./ *noun, plural* **satellite dishes** a large circular piece of metal on a building, that receives television or radio signals from a satellite ⇨ *see picture on page 343*

sat·in /'sætɪn $'sætn/ *noun [no plural]* a type of smooth shiny cloth: *a red satin dress*

sat·ire /'sætaɪə $'sætaɪə/ *noun* amusing speech or writing that shows how silly or wrong something is: *The play is a satire on modern American life.*

sat·ir·i·cal /sə'tɪrɪkəl/ *adjective* using satire: *a satirical TV show*

sat·is·fac·tion /ˌsætɪs'fækʃən/ *noun* the happiness you feel when you succeed or get what you want: *I get a lot of satisfaction from my job.*

sat·is·fac·to·ry /ˌsætɪs'fæktəri/ *adjective*
quite good, or good enough: *Liam's work has been satisfactory this term.* | *The arrangement was not really very satisfactory.*

sat·is·fied /'sætɪsfaɪd/ *adjective*

GRAMMAR
satisfied with something
pleased with something that you have done or got: *I didn't feel satisfied with my exam results. | We try to keep our customers satisfied.*

sat·is·fy /'sætɪsfaɪ/ *verb* **satisfied, satisfies** to make someone happy by giving them what they want: *We always try to satisfy our guests. | I offered him £50, but that didn't satisfy him.*

sat·is·fy·ing /'sætɪsfaɪ-ɪŋ/ *adjective* something that is satisfying makes you feel pleased because you have achieved something or got what you want: *Photography is a satisfying hobby.*

sat·u·rate /'sætʃəreɪt/ *verb* formal to make something completely wet: *The back of his shirt was saturated with sweat.*

Sat·ur·day /'sætədi $ 'sætərdi/ *written abbreviation* **Sat** *noun* the day of the week between Friday and Sunday: *What are you doing on Saturday?*

sauce /sɔːs/ *noun* a thick liquid that you eat with food: *cheese sauce*

sauce·pan /'sɔːspæn/ *noun* a metal pot with a handle that you use for cooking

sau·cer /'sɔːsə $ 'sɔːsər/ *noun* a small round plate that you put a cup on

sau·na /'sɔːnə/ *noun* if you have a sauna, you sit in a hot room that is filled with steam

saun·ter /'sɔːntə $ 'sɔːntər/ *verb* to walk slowly and confidently: *The door opened and Guy sauntered in.*

saus·age /'sɒsɪdʒ $ 'sɔːsɪdʒ/ *noun* a small tube of skin filled with a mixture of meat and SPICES that you can eat hot or cold

sav·age /'sævɪdʒ/ *adjective* very cruel and violent: *a savage war*
–**savagely** *adverb*: *The woman was savagely beaten.*

save¹ /seɪv/ *verb*

GRAMMAR
save someone/something from something
save for something
save something for someone
save someone something
save someone from doing something

1 to prevent someone from being hurt or killed: *Mark ran into the burning building to save the child. | She saved me from drowning.*
2 to prevent something from being damaged or destroyed: *Many people are fighting to save the rainforests from destruction.*
3 also **save up** to keep money instead of spending it, so that you can use it later: *You should try and save some money each month. | I'm saving up for a new computer game. | My brother's saving his money to buy a car.*
4 to keep something instead of using it or throwing it away: *We'd better save some of the cake for Dad. | Can you save me some food for later?*
5 if you save someone from doing something, you do it for them so that they do not have to do it: *If you could meet Tom from school, it would save me a journey.*
6 to press a special button that makes a computer store information that you want to keep: *Don't forget to save your work before you log off.*
7 to stop the ball from going into the GOAL in a game such as football or HOCKEY: *It was a great shot, but Jack saved it.*

PHRASE
save time, save energy etc to use less time, energy etc: *It'll save time if we both do some of the work. | In a small house, you need to find ways of saving space.*

save² *noun* when a GOALKEEPER in football, HOCKEY etc stops the ball from going into their GOAL

sav·ings /'seɪvɪŋz/ *plural noun* all the money that you have saved: *My aunt withdrew all her savings from the bank.*

sa·vour·y *BrE*, **savory** *AmE* /'seɪvəri/ *adjective* savoury food has a pleasantly sharp taste: *savoury snacks such as crisps*

saw¹ the past tense of SEE

saw² /sɔː/ *noun* a flat metal blade with a series of sharp points on it, that you use for cutting wood ⇨ *see picture at* TOOL

saw³ *verb, past tense* **sawed**, *past participle* **sawed** or **sawn** /sɔːn/ to cut something, using a saw: *Cyril sawed some logs for the fire.*

sax·o·phone /'sæksəfəun $'sæksə-ˌfoʊn/ *noun* a large metal musical instrument that you play by blowing into it and pressing buttons

say¹ ⇨ *see box on next page*

say² /seɪ/ *noun* [no plural] if you have a say in something, you can give your opinion about it and help decide it: *The kids have a say in which jobs they do to help at home.*

say·ing /'seɪ-ɪŋ/ *noun* a well-known statement that gives good advice about something ⇨ *same meaning* PROVERB

scab /skæb/ *noun* a layer of dried blood that forms over a wound

scaf·fold·ing /'skæfəldɪŋ/ *noun* [no plural] a structure made from poles and boards that workers can stand on when they are working on the outside walls of a building

scald /skɔːld/ *verb* to burn someone with hot liquid: *The water was so hot that it scalded his hand.*

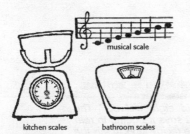

musical scale

kitchen scales   bathroom scales

scales

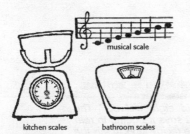

scale¹ /skeɪl/ *noun*

GRAMMAR
the scale of something

1 the scale of something is how big, serious, or important it is: *We don't yet know **the scale of** her injuries. | This is a **large-scale** project.*

2 a set of numbers that you use to measure how big something is: *The earthquake measured 3.5 on the Richter scale.*

3 the scale of a map, drawing, or MODEL is the relationship between its size and the actual size of the thing that it shows: *a map with a scale of 1 centimetre to 1 kilometre*

4 scales a piece of equipment that you use to weigh people or objects:

a set of kitchen scales | The doctor asked me to stand on the scales.

5 a series of musical notes that you play or sing in a fixed order, getting higher or lower

scale² *verb* formal if you scale a mountain, you climb to the top of it

scalp /skælp/ *noun* the skin on the top of your head, where your hair grows

scal·y /'skeɪli/ *adjective* an animal that is scaly is covered with small flat pieces of hard dry skin: *Birds have tough, scaly skin on their legs.*

scam·per /'skæmpə $'skæmpɚ/ *verb* to run somewhere with short quick steps: *The children scampered back to bed.*

scan /skæn/ *verb* scanned, scanning
1 to read something very quickly: *She scanned the lists, looking for her name.*
2 if you scan a picture into a computer, you use a machine called a scanner to copy it into the computer: *Once the image has been scanned, you can make it bigger or smaller.*
–**scan** *noun*: *The scan produces a picture of the baby in its mother's womb.*

scan·dal /'skændl/ *noun* something that shocks people because it is very bad or wrong: *His behaviour caused a political scandal.*

scan·ner /'skænə $'skænɚ/ *noun* a piece of equipment that copies a picture into a computer ⇨ *see picture on page 342*

scar¹ /skɑː $skɑr/ *noun* a permanent mark on someone's skin, caused by a cut or burn

scar

scar² *verb* scarred, scarring if something such as a knife or fire scars you, it makes a permanent mark on your skin: *The fire scarred her quite badly.*

scarce /skeəs $skers/ *adjective* if something is scarce, there is not enough of it: *Fresh water and food were scarce.*

scarce·ly /'skeəsli $'skersli/ *adverb* hardly at all: *I scarcely go out these days.*

scare¹ /skeə $sker/ *verb* informal
to frighten someone: *The movie really scared the children. | Your dad*

S

➤ SAY, TELL, or TALK?

SAY you **say** words to someone:
*She **said that** she was going home.*

TELL you **tell** someone facts or information:
*She **told** me **that** she was going home.*

TALK you **talk** about a particular subject:
*Each student had to **talk about** their family.*

➤ SAY

say

1 **to speak words in order to give information or show your thoughts, feelings etc**
*What did you **say**? I couldn't hear you. | Sandra **said that** Stuart wasn't feeling well. | "Just a minute," **said** Francesca. | Mrs. Robbins came over and **said** something **to** her daughter. | Did she **say what** they were going to do?*

> **GRAMMAR**
> **say (that)**
> **say something to someone**
> **say what/where/how etc**

2 **to give information in writing, pictures, or numbers**
*My watch **said** eight o'clock. | The weather report **says** it's going to rain tomorrow. | The recipe **says** to mix the sugar and eggs.*

✗ Don't say ➤ *say someone that.*
✓ Say ➤ **say that** or **tell someone that**: *Barbara **said that** she was tired. | Barbara **told** me **that** she was tired.*

✗ Don't say ➤ *say someone to do something.*
✓ Say ➤ **tell someone to do something**: *My mother **told** me **to** clean my room.*

✗ Don't say ➤ *say about something.*
✓ Say ➤ **tell someone about something** or **talk about something**: *He **told** me **about** his family or He **talked about** his family.*

✗ Don't say ➤ *say someone no, say someone hello etc.*
✓ Say ➤ **say hello, say no** etc.

▼ *scares me to death* (=makes me feel very frightened).

PHRASAL VERB
scare off
scare away
scare someone off
scare someone away to frighten someone so that they go away: *A barking dog scared the attackers away.*

scare² *noun* **1** a sudden feeling of fear: *You gave me a terrible scare!* **2** a situation in which many people become frightened because it is possible that something bad might happen: *There was a bomb scare at the airport.*

scared /skeəd $ skerd/ *adjective*

GRAMMAR
scared of something
scared to do something
scared (that)
frightened: *My brother is scared of dogs.* | *Hazel was scared to tell Mum what had happened.* | *I'm scared that the car might break down.* | *I was scared stiff* (=very scared) *that someone would find us.*

scarf /skɑːf $ skɑrf/ *noun, plural* **scarves** /skɑːvz $ skɑrvz/ or **scarfs** a piece of material that you wear around your neck to keep you warm ⇨ *see picture on page 352*

scar·let /'skɑːlət $ 'skɑrlət/ *adjective, noun* bright red

scar·y /'skeəri $ 'skeri/ *adjective informal* **scarier, scariest** frightening: *It's a really scary movie.*

scat·ter /'skætə $ 'skætɚ/ *verb* **1** to throw or drop things all over an area: *The children had scattered mud everywhere!* | *Scatter the seeds evenly over the ground.* **2** if people scatter, they go quickly in different directions: *The crowd scattered in terror.*

scene /siːn/ *noun*
1 one part of a play or film: *I loved the scene where the children arrived home.* | *The battle scenes were very exciting.*
2 a picture: *a Christmas card with a winter scene on the front*
3 when something violent or exciting happens and people react to this:
▼

▼ *There were scenes of confusion and panic at the airport after the bomb exploded.*
4 the scene of an accident or crime is the place where it happens: *Several people were at the scene of the crash.*

sce·ne·ry /'siːnəri/ *noun* [no plural] the natural things such as woods and rivers that you see around you in the country-side: *the spectacular scenery of the Alps*

sce·nic /'siːnɪk/ *adjective* a scenic place has very beautiful scenery

scent /sent/ *noun* **1** a pleasant smell: *the scent of fresh flowers* **2** a liquid with a pleasant smell that you put on your skin ⇨ *same meaning* PERFUME

scent·ed /'sentɪd/ *adjective* something that is scented has a pleasant smell: *scented soap*

scep·ti·cal *BrE,* **skeptical** *AmE* /'skeptɪkəl/ *adjective* if you are sceptical about something, you have doubts about whether it is true or right: *Many doctors are sceptical about this new treatment.*

sched·ule¹ /'ʃedjuːl $ 'skedʒəl/ *noun*
1 a list of things that people will do and when they will do them: *Draw up* (=write) *a schedule of all the things you need to do.*
2 the American word for TIMETABLE

PHRASES
have a busy schedule to have a lot of things to do: *Jacqui has a very busy schedule today.*
on schedule if something is on schedule, everything is happening at the right time: *The train is on schedule.*
behind schedule if something is behind schedule, things are happen-ing later than you had planned: *The building work is already eight months behind schedule.*

schedule² *verb* to plan when something will happen: *We have scheduled the competition for March 8.*

scheme¹ /skiːm/ *noun*
BrE a plan that you use to try to achieve something: *This new gov-ernment scheme will help young people to find jobs.* | *Have you heard*
▼

S

scheme 546

S

about Michael's latest money-making scheme?

scheme² *verb formal* to secretly make plans to do something bad or illegal ⇨ *same meaning* PLOT²: *He schemed to kill his wife for the insurance money.*

schol·ar /'skɒlə $'skɑlɚ/ *noun* someone who has studied a subject and knows a lot about it: *Most scholars agree that the bird came from North America.*

schol·ar·ship /'skɒləʃɪp $'skɑlɚˌʃɪp/ *noun* money that is given to a student so that they can go to college: *Pat was awarded a Fulbright scholarship to study in the US.*

school /skuːl/ *noun*
1 a place where children are taught: *Mr Mamood is a teacher at my school.* | *Are the children at school today?* | *Dad drives us to school in the morning.* | *I was late for school this morning.* | *When do the school holidays start?* | *I'll meet you after school.*
2 a place where one particular subject or skill is taught: *I'm going to a language school this summer.* | *He's at drama school.*
3 *AmE* a university

USAGE

Don't use **the** before **school** if you are thinking about it as a place where someone studies or teaches: *What time do you leave for school in the morning?* Use **the** before **school** if you go there for some other reason, not to study or teach: *We all went to see the play at the school.* You must also use **the** if you describe exactly which school you are talking about: *the local school*

school·boy /'skuːlbɔɪ/ *noun* a boy who goes to school

school·child /'skuːltʃaɪld/ *noun, plural* **schoolchildren** /-ˌtʃɪldrən/ a child who goes to school

school·days /'skuːldeɪz/ *plural noun* the time during your life when you go to school

school·girl /'skuːlɡɜːl $'skuːlɡɚl/ *noun* a girl who goes to school

school·teach·er /'skuːlˌtiːtʃə $'skuːlˌtiːtʃɚ/ *noun* a teacher in a school

sci·ence /'saɪəns/ *noun [no plural]* the study of nature and the way that natural things happen and the knowledge we get by testing and proving facts: *We've been learning about electricity in our science lessons.* | *Science made great progress in the 17th century.*

science fic·tion /ˌ.. '../ *noun [no plural]* books and films about imaginary things that happen in the future or in other parts of the universe

sci·en·tif·ic /ˌsaɪən'tɪfɪk/ *adjective* related to science or using the methods of science: *a scientific experiment*

sci·en·tist /'saɪəntɪst/ *noun* someone who studies science

sci-fi /ˌsaɪ 'faɪ/ *informal* SCIENCE FICTION

scis·sors /'sɪzəz $'sɪzɚz/ *plural noun* a small tool with two blades that you use for cutting paper, hair, or material: *a pair of sharp scissors*

scissors

scoff /skɒf $skɔf/ *verb* to speak to someone in a way that shows that you do not respect them or you think they are stupid: *Andy's friends scoffed at his plans to become famous.*

scold /skəʊld $skoʊld/ *verb* to tell someone angrily that they have done something wrong: *Her father scolded her for staying out late.*

scoop¹ /skuːp/ *noun* 1 a deep spoon for picking up or serving food such as ICE CREAM 2 an important news story that appears in only one newspaper: *This story was a real scoop for the Sunday Times.*

scoop² *verb* to lift something up using a spoon or your hands: *She scooped the baby up and put him on the chair.*

scoot·er /'skuːtə $'skuːtɚ/ *noun* a vehicle like a small MOTORCYCLE with a low seat

scope /skəʊp $skoʊp/ *noun* the scope of a piece of work is the range of subjects it deals with or discusses: *Looking at the airline's safety records will be within the scope of this inquiry.*

scorch /skɔːtʃ $skɔrtʃ/ *verb* to burn the surface of something, leaving a brown mark: *The ceiling and the walls were badly scorched by fire.*

scorch·ing /'skɔːtʃɪŋ $'skɔrtʃɪŋ/ *adjective informal* if the weather is scorching, it is very hot: *It's been a scorching summer.*

score¹ /skɔː $skɔr/ *verb*

to win points in a game or competition: *Jim scored 2 goals in the game last night.* | *Who scored the most points?*

score² *noun*

GRAMMAR
scores of people/things

1 the number of points that a team or player gets in a game or competition: *The final score was 3–1.* | *I got a score of 700.*

2 the printed copy of a piece of music

3 scores a very large number of people or things: *Scores of people were injured in the crash.*

score·board /'skɔːbɔːd $'skɔrbɔrd/ *noun* a large sign showing the score of a game

scor·er /'skɔːrə $'skɔrəʳ/ *noun* someone who scores a point in a game or competition: *the club's top goal scorer*

scorn /skɔːn $skɔrn/ *noun* [no plural] *formal* if you treat something with scorn, you show that you think it is very stupid: *My ideas were treated with scorn.*
– **scornful** *adjective*: *He made some very scornful remarks about my work.*

scor·pi·on /'skɔːpiən $'skɔrpiən/ *noun* a small brown creature that uses its tail to sting

Scotch /skɒtʃ $skɑtʃ/ *noun* [no plural] a strong alcoholic drink made in Scotland ⇨ *same meaning* WHISKY: *a bottle of Scotch*

Scotch tape /ˌ. './ *trademark* the American word for SELLOTAPE

scour /skaʊə $skaʊəʳ/ *verb* if you scour a place, you search everywhere in it very carefully and thoroughly: *I scoured the library for more information.*

scout /skaʊt/ *noun* **1** a soldier who is sent to search an area of land in front of an army to find out information about an enemy **2** someone whose job is to find good sports players, musicians etc in order to employ them: *a football scout* **3** also **boy scout, girl scout** a member of an organization called the Scouts that teaches young people practical skills

scowl /skaʊl/ *verb* to look at someone in a way that shows you are angry: *She scowled and turned away.*
– **scowl** *noun*: *That girl has a permanent scowl on her face.*

scram·ble¹ /'skræmbəl/ *verb* **1** to climb up or over something quickly, using your hands: *I scrambled up onto the roof of the house.* **2** to compete with other people in order to try to get or do something: *Fans scrambled to buy tickets for the concert.*

scramble² *noun informal* when people compete against each other to get something: *There was a scramble for the best seats.*

scrambled eggs /ˌ. './ *plural noun* eggs mixed together and cooked in butter

scrap¹ /skræp/ *noun*

GRAMMAR
a scrap of something

1 a small piece of something: *I wrote her phone number on a scrap of paper.*

2 materials that are no longer suitable for the purpose they were made but can be used another way: *scrap metal*

scrap² *verb informal* **scrapped, scrapping** to decide not to use or do something: *We have now scrapped this idea.*

scrap·book /'skræpbʊk/ *noun* a book with empty pages for sticking pictures in

scrape¹ /skreɪp/ *verb*

GRAMMAR
scrape something off/away/ from something

1 to remove something from a surface: *Scrape the skin off the potatoes.* | *She bent down and scraped away the soil.* | *Bill was scraping the mud from his boots.*

2 to damage something by rubbing against it: *The tree branches scraped her cheek.* | *You've scraped the floor with your shoe.*

scrape² *noun* **1** a small injury that you get when you rub a part of your body against a rough surface: *She had a few scrapes on her knees.* **2** *informal* a difficult or dangerous situation: *I knew that I was now in a bit of a scrape.*

scratch

scratch¹ /skrætʃ/ *verb*   **1** to rub your skin with your nails: *He scratched his head in surprise.*   **2** to make a long thin cut or mark on something with a sharp object: *Bill's dad was furious when he scratched the car door.*

scratch² *noun, plural* **scratches**   **1** a long thin cut on something: *Nicole had several scratches on her face.*   **2 from scratch** if you do something from scratch, you do it without using anything that was done or made before: *My computer crashed, and I had to start my essay again from scratch.*

scrawl /skrɔːl/ *verb informal* to write something in a careless or untidy way: *She scrawled her phone number on the back of an envelope.*
— **scrawl** *noun informal*: *I can't read your scrawl.*

scream¹ /skriːm/ *verb*

> **GRAMMAR**
> **scream at someone**
> **scream for something/someone**
> to shout very loudly because you feel frightened, angry, or very excited: *Sally screamed when she saw the rat.* | *The children were screaming with excitement.* | *"Don't touch me!" she screamed.* | *Sometimes I* **scream at** *the kids.* | *I tried to* **scream for** *help.* | *I screamed out her name.*

scream² *noun*
a loud shout that you give when you are frightened, angry, or very excited: *We heard screams outside.*

screech /skriːtʃ/ *verb* to make a high loud unpleasant sound: *Our tyres screeched as we turned the corner.*
— **screech** *noun*: *Jodie let out an ear-splitting screech.*

screen¹ /skriːn/ *noun*   **1** the glass part of a television or computer that you look at: *a television with a 26" screen*   **2 on screen** if you work on screen, you do written work using a computer rather than writing on paper

screen² *verb*   **1** to do medical tests on people to find out whether any of them have an illness: *People who are at risk for the disease should be screened.*   **2** to show a film or programme at the cinema or on television: *Many new films will be screened at the festival.*

screw¹ /skruː/ *noun* a pointed piece of metal like a nail that you use to fix things together. You fix it into something by pushing it and turning it round and round

screw² *verb*   **1** to fix something somewhere, using screws: *I screwed the mirror to the wall.*   **2 screw up** *informal* to spoil a plan or arrangement: *The car broke down, so that screwed up our holiday.*

screw·driv·er /ˈskruːˌdraɪvə $ ˈskruːˌdraɪvər/ *noun* a tool that you use for turning screws ⇨ see *picture at* TOOL

scrib·ble /ˈskrɪbəl/ *verb* to write something in a quick and untidy way: *I scribbled down the number of the license plate.*

script /skrɪpt/ *noun*   **1** the words of a speech, play, film etc that have been written down: *He began his career writing scripts for daytime TV shows.*   **2** *formal* the letters used to write a language: *Arabic script*

scrip·ture /ˈskrɪptʃə $ ˈskrɪptʃər/ *noun* [no plural] the holy books of a religion, for example the Bible

scroll /skrəʊl $ skroʊl/ *verb* **scrolled, scrolling** to move information up or down a computer SCREEN: *Scroll down until you reach the end of the file.*

scrounge /skraʊndʒ/ *verb informal* to get something you want by asking someone to give it to you, instead of buying it yourself: *I scrounged a cigarette off the girl sitting next to me.*

scrub¹ /skrʌb/ *verb* to rub something hard in order to clean it: *We scrubbed and polished the floors until they shone.*

scrub² *noun* [no plural] plants that grow in a dry place: *We walked through the scrub and long grass.*

scruf·fy /ˈskrʌfi/ *adjective* **scruffier, scruffiest** dirty and untidy: *a scruffy old man*

scrub

scru·pu·lous /'skru:pjələs/ adjective formal if you do something in a scrupulous way, you do it in a very careful or exact way
–**scrupulously** adverb: We try to be scrupulously fair.

scru·ti·nize also **scrutinise** BrE /'skru:tənaɪz/ verb formal to examine something very carefully and thoroughly: The customs official scrutinized his passport.

scru·ti·ny /'skru:təni/ noun [no plural] formal when something is very carefully watched or examined: The police are keeping the men under close scrutiny.

scu·ba div·ing /'sku:bə ˌdaɪvɪŋ/ noun [no plural] the sport of swimming under water using a container of air to help you breathe

sculp·tor /'skʌlptə $ 'skʌlptɚ/ noun someone who makes sculptures

sculp·ture /'skʌlptʃə $ 'skʌlptʃɚ/ noun a work of art made from stone, wood, or metal, or the art of making these: a bronze sculpture | She studied sculpture at art college.

scum /skʌm/ noun [no plural] 1 an unpleasant dirty layer on the surface of a liquid: The pond was covered with scum. 2 informal people you have a very low opinion of

scur·ry /'skʌri $ 'skɚi/ verb scurried, scurries to move very quickly with small steps: A couple of chipmunks scurried about, collecting seeds.

sea /si:/ noun
the sea the salt water that covers large parts of the Earth: We swam in the sea. | The ship was lost at sea. | The Red Sea lies between Arabia and North Africa. ⇨ see picture on page 348

sea·bed or **sea bed** /'si:bed/ noun the land at the bottom of the sea

sea·food /'si:fu:d/ noun [no plural] fish and other creatures from the sea that you can eat

sea·front /'si:frʌnt/ noun [no plural] a part of a town that is next to the sea: I went into a shop on the seafront.

sea·gull /'si:gʌl/ also **gull** noun a common grey and white bird that lives near the sea

seal¹ /si:l/ noun a large animal that lives in the sea in cold areas

seal² verb 1 to close something very tightly or firmly: He addressed the envelope and sealed it. 2 seal something off to stop people entering an area or building, especially because it is dangerous: The police have sealed off the area.

sea li·on /'. ˌ../ noun a large type of SEAL

seam /si:m/ noun the line where two pieces of cloth have been sewn together

search¹ /sɜːtʃ $ sɚtʃ/ noun

GRAMMAR
a search for something/someone
an attempt to find someone or something: The police led the **search for** the missing boy.

PHRASE
go in search of something to try to find something: I went **in search of** a present for grandma.

search² verb

GRAMMAR
search for something
search something for something
search through something
to try to find someone or something: We **searched for** you everywhere! | The police searched his car and found the gun. | We **searched** the room **for** money. | He was **searching through** the drawers. | **Search around** and see if you can find an envelope.

sea·shore /'si:ʃɔː $ 'si:ʃɔr/ noun the seashore the land next to the sea

sea·sick /'si:ˌsɪk/ adjective if you feel seasick, you feel ill because of the movement of a boat

sea·side /'si:saɪd/ noun the seaside a place or area next to the sea, especially

S

where people go on holiday: *I love being at the seaside.* | *a seaside holiday*

sea·son¹ /'siːzən/ *noun*

1 the seasons are the periods of time into which a year is divided, based on changes in the weather. In Britain, the seasons are spring, summer, autumn, and winter: *Spring is my favorite season.*

2 a period of time in a year when something usually happens: *The football season starts in September.*

PHRASES

the holiday season, the high season etc the time of year when most people take their holiday: *Prices range from £30 a night in the **low season*** (=the time when fewer people than normal go on holiday) *to £45 per night in the **high season**.*

in season vegetables and fruit that are in season are ready to pick and eat

season² *verb* to add salt, pepper etc to food to make it taste better: *She seasoned the chicken with a few herbs and spices.*

sea·son·ing /'siːzənɪŋ/ *noun* salt, pepper etc that you add to food to make it taste better

season tick·et /'.. ,.. $,.. '../ *noun* a ticket that you can use for a lot of journeys or events during a fixed period of time

seat¹ /siːt/ *noun*

a chair or something else that you can sit on: *I couldn't **get a seat** on the bus this morning.* | *I rang the theatre and booked two seats for tonight's show.* | *This isn't a very comfortable seat.*

PHRASE

take a seat to sit down: *Please **take a seat** and the doctor will see you soon.*

seat² *verb* **1 be seated** **a)** to be sitting down: *A nurse was seated behind the desk.* **b)** *spoken formal* used to ask someone politely to sit down: *Please be seated, Ms. Williams.* **2** to have enough seats for a particular number of people: *The hall seats 500 people.*

seat belt /'. ./ *noun* a strong belt that

holds you in your seat in a car or plane
⇨ *same meaning* SAFETY BELT

seat·ing /'siːtɪŋ/ *noun [no plural]* the seats in a public place

sea·weed /'siːwiːd/ *noun [no plural]* a plant that grows in the sea

se·clud·ed /sɪ'kluːdɪd/ *adjective* a secluded place is very quiet and private: *a secluded beach*

sec·ond¹ /'sekənd/ *number, adverb, adjective*

1 someone or something that is after the first one: *There are two keys – the first is for the main door and the second is for the office.* | *We only saw **the second half** of the match.* | *John came **second** in the race.*

2 **have second thoughts** to have doubts about whether you are making the right decision: *Mary was going to study physics, but now she's **having second thoughts**.*

second² *noun*

1 one of the sixty parts that a minute is divided into: *He ran the race in 2 minutes 35 seconds.* | *This computer can move data at 800 Mb **per second*** (=in each second).

2 *informal* a very short period of time: *Wait **a few seconds** for the computer to start.* | *For a second I thought I'd broken my leg.* | *I'll be back **in a second**.*

second³ *verb* to say that you agree with a suggestion made by another person at a meeting: *Parker seconded the idea.*

sec·ond·a·ry /'sekəndəri $ 'sekən‑,deri/ *adjective* secondary education is the education of children between the ages of 11 and 18: *a secondary school*

secondary school /'.... ,../ *noun* a school for children between the ages of 11 and 18

second best /,.. './ *adjective* not as good as the best thing: *He got the second best exam results in the school.*

second class /,.. './ *adverb* if someone travels or sends something second-class, they do it using a service that is cheaper and less expensive than FIRST CLASS: *I sent the letter second class.*

second-class /,.. './ *adjective* **1** cheaper than FIRST-CLASS and with service that is not quite as good: *I only*

S

put a second-class stamp on the letter.
2 less important than other people or things: *Old people should not be treated as second-class citizens.*

sec·ond·hand /ˌsekənd'hænd/ *adjective, adverb* previously owned by someone else: *a cheap secondhand computer* | *I bought the car secondhand.*

second lan·guage /ˌ.. '../ *noun* a language that you speak in addition to the language that you learned to speak as a child

sec·ond·ly /'sekəndli/ *adverb* used to introduce a second fact, reason etc: *And secondly, we must consider the cost.*

second na·ture /ˌ.. '../ *noun* [no plural] something you have done so often that you do it almost without thinking: *Lying had become second nature to him.*

second per·son /ˌ.. '../ *noun* the second person the form of a verb that you use with 'you'

se·cre·cy /'si:krəsi/ *noun* [no plural] when you keep something secret

secret¹ /'si:krət/ *adjective*

if something is secret, only a few people know about it and they deliberately do not tell anyone else: *We held a secret meeting after school.* | *Keep your computer password secret* (=don't tell it to anyone).
– **secretly** *adverb*: *The rebels were secretly planning to take control.*

secret² *noun*

1 something that you do not tell other people about: *Don't tell anyone our secret.* | *Can you **keep a secret**?* | *The peace talks were held **in secret*** (=without other people knowing).
2 the secret of something *Informal* the way to achieve something: *What's the secret of a happy marriage?*

secret a·gent /ˌ.. '../ *noun* a SPY

sec·re·ta·ry /'sekrətəri $ 'sekrə,teri/ *noun, plural* **secretaries 1** someone whose job is to write letters, arrange meetings, answer telephone calls etc in an office **2 Secretary** someone who is in charge of a large government department: *the Defence Secretary*

se·cre·tive /'si:krətɪv/ *adjective* unwilling to tell people about something: *John was very secretive about his new girlfriend.*

sect /sekt/ *noun* a group of people with its own religious beliefs, that has separated from a larger religious group

sec·tion /'sekʃən/ *noun*

one of the parts that something is divided into: *Does the library have a children's section?* | *Some **sections** of this road are very busy.*

sec·tor /'sektə $ 'sektər/ *noun* part of an economic system, such as business, industry, or trade: *the nation's manufacturing sector* (=all the companies that make goods)

se·cure¹ /sɪ'kjʊə $ sɪ'kjʊr/ *adjective* **1** fixed and not likely to change: *The company now has a secure future.* **2** a secure place is one which people cannot get into or out of if you do not want them to: *Make sure the building is secure before you leave.*
– **securely** *adverb*: *She kept the room securely locked.*

secure² *verb formal* **1** to get something important, especially after a lot of effort: *He managed to secure a job in a university.* **2** to fasten or tie something firmly: *They secured the bookcase to the wall.*

se·cu·ri·ty /sɪ'kjʊərəti $ sɪ'kjʊrəti/ *noun* [no plural] **1** the things that you do to protect a place: *He is in charge of security at the airport.* **2** if you have security, you are not likely to suffer or lose something: *The new contract will give you more security in your job.* **3** the feeling that you are safe and cannot be hurt: *Children need security.*

se·date /sɪ'deɪt/ *verb* to give someone a drug to make them feel sleepy and calm

sed·a·tive /'sedətɪv/ *noun* a drug that makes someone sleepy or calm

se·duc·tive /sɪ'dʌktɪv/ *adjective* attractive, especially in a sexual way: *her soft, seductive voice*

see ⇨ *see box on next page*

seed /si:d/ *noun* a small hard thing produced by a plant, from which a new plant will grow

seed·y /'si:di/ *adjective informal* **seedier, seediest** a seedy person or place looks dirty and poor: *a seedy nightclub*

seeing eye dog /ˌ.. '. ˌ./ the American word for GUIDE DOG

seek /si:k/ *verb formal, past tense and past*

S

S

➤ SEE, LOOK AT, or WATCH?

SEE you **see** something, a person, or event without planning to

Have you seen my bag anywhere?

LOOK AT you **look at** a picture, photo, person, or thing because you want to

Here, look at this painting!

WATCH you **watch** TV, a film, a person, or an event for a period of time

We spent the evening watching TV

➤ SEE

① to use your eyes
It was too dark to see anything. | *Did you see what Patrick did?* | *I couldn't see who was at the door.* | *Did you see Jean leave?* | *I saw Steven playing basketball at the school.*

> **GRAMMAR**
> **see someone doing something**
> **see someone do something**
> **see who/what/where etc**

② to know or understand
Do you see how it works? | *He's really difficult to talk to, if you see what I mean.* | "*Then you just add these two numbers together.*" "*Oh, I see.*"

> **GRAMMAR**
> **see how/why/what etc**

③ to meet or visit
I see Pam every Saturday. | *Ken hasn't seen his daughters for a month.* | *You should see a doctor.*

⑤ to see a film, concert, television programme
He's seen 'Star Wars' six times. | *Let's go to see a movie.*

see

④ to find out information or facts
Alison, can you see who is at the door? | *Let's see how much it costs.* | *Plug in the TV and see if it's working.*

> **GRAMMAR**
> **see how/who/why etc | see if/whether**

PHRASES

see you, see you later *spoken*
say this to friends when saying goodbye: "*Bye, Ben.*" "*See you.*" | *I'll see you later.* | *See you tomorrow, Cathy.*

participle **sought** /sɔːt/ **1** to try to find or get something: *She sought the help of several organizations.* **2** to try to do something: *We are always seeking to improve our results.*

seem /siːm/ *verb*

> **GRAMMAR**
> **seem to be something**
> **seem to someone**
> **seem that**
> **seem as if**
> **seem like**

how something seems is how it appears to you: *The house seemed very quiet after everyone had left.* | *She seemed to be upset.* | *It seems to me that we're lost.* | *It seemed strange that she wasn't at home.* | *It seemed as if everything was going wrong.* | *Toronto seems like such a nice place to live.*

seem·ing·ly /'siːmɪŋli/ *adverb* used to say how something seems: *a seemingly endless list of jobs*

seen the past participle of SEE

seep /siːp/ *verb* if a liquid seeps somewhere, it flows there slowly through small holes: *Water was seeping into the boat.*

see·saw /'siːsɔː/ *noun* a long board on which children play outdoors, that is balanced in the middle so that when one end goes up the other end goes down

seethe /siːð/ *verb* to be very angry, but not show it: *By this time I was quietly seething.*

seg·ment /'segmənt/ *noun* one of the parts that something is divided into: *a segment of orange*

seg·re·gate /'segrɪgeɪt/ *verb* to separate one group of people from others: *They were segregated from the rest of the prisoners.*

seize /siːz/ *verb* **1** to take something in your hand quickly and roughly: *Frannie suddenly seized the gun from me.* **2** if someone seizes power or control, they take it using force: *He seized power in 1995.*

sel·dom /'seldəm/ *adverb formal* not very often: *He seldom goes out.*

se·lect¹ /sɪ'lekt/ *verb* to choose something or someone: *It wasn't easy to select a winner.*

select² *adjective formal* a select group is a small group of special people: *a select group of students*

se·lec·tion /sɪ'lekʃən/ *noun* **1** [no plural] when something or someone is chosen: *Selection of the jury for the trial will begin tomorrow.* **2** a group of things that someone has chosen: *He read a selection of his favourite poems.* **3** a group of things that you can choose from: *The shop has a wide selection of books for all ages.*

se·lec·tive /sɪ'lektɪv/ *adjective* careful about the things that you choose: *If you don't have much money, you have to be selective when you are shopping.*

self /self/ *noun, plural* **selves** /selvz/ your nature and character: *You'll soon be back to your old self.*

self-cen·tred *BrE*, **self-centered** *AmE* /ˌ. '../ *adjective* only interested in yourself ⇨ *same meaning* SELFISH

self-con·fi·dence /ˌ. '.../ *noun* [no plural] the belief that you can do things successfully

self-con·fi·dent /ˌ. '.../ *adjective* feeling sure that you are able to do things successfully

self-con·scious /ˌ. '../ *adjective* uncomfortable and worried about how you seem to other people: *He felt self-conscious in his new suit.*

self-de·fence *BrE*, **self-defense** *AmE* /ˌ. .'./ *noun* [no plural] the use of force to protect yourself when you are attacked: *He said he killed the man in self-defence.*

self-em·ployed /ˌ. .'./ *adjective* someone who is self-employed has their own business rather than being employed by a company

self-es·teem /ˌ. .'./ *noun* [no plural] how you feel about yourself and whether, for example, you feel that you are a nice or successful person: *Many of our patients suffer from low self-esteem* (=feel that they are not nice or successful people).

self-in·dul·gent /ˌ. .'../ *adjective* allowing yourself to have or do something that you do not need but which you enjoy having or doing

self·ish /'selfɪʃ/ *adjective* caring only about yourself and not about other people ⇨ *opposite* UNSELFISH: *That was a very selfish thing to do.*

S

self-made /ˌ. './ *adjective* a self-made person has become rich and successful by working hard: *He was proud of being a self-made man.*

self-pit·y /ˌ. '../ *noun* [no plural] when you feel sorry for yourself and there is not a good reason

self-portrait

self-por·trait /ˌ. '../ *noun* a picture of yourself, painted by you

self-re·spect /ˌ. '../ *noun* [no plural] a feeling of respect that you have for yourself

self-serv·ice /ˌ. '../ *adjective* a self-service restaurant is one where you get the food for yourself before paying for it

sell /sel/ *verb, past tense and past participle* **sold** /səʊld $ soʊld/

> **GRAMMAR**
> **sell someone something**
> **sell something to someone**
> **sell something for something**

1 to give something to someone and accept money from them in return: *I sold Joe my computer.* | *She sold her bike for £50.* | *I sold two tickets to Mary.*
2 to offer something for people to buy: *The shop sells computer games.*

> **PHRASAL VERBS**
> **sell off**
> **sell something off** to sell goods quickly and cheaply: *The library is selling off some of its old books.*
> **sell out**
> if a shop sells out of something, or if something sells out, the shop sells all of it and there is none left: *I'm sorry – we've sold out of bread.* | *All the tickets for the evening performance have sold out.*

sell-by date /'. . ˌ./ *noun* BrE the date printed on a food product after which a shop should not sell it; EXPIRATION DATE AmE: *This yoghurt's past its sell-by date.*

Sel·lo·tape /'seləteɪp/ *noun* [no plural] BrE trademark TAPE that you use for sticking ▼

pieces of paper or card together; SCOTCH TAPE AmE

selves the plural of SELF

se·mes·ter /səˈmestə $ səˈmestər/ *noun* AmE one of two periods into which the school or college year is divided: *I'm taking three classes this semester.*

sem·i·cir·cle /'semiˌsɜːkəl $ 'semiˌsɚkəl/ *noun* half a circle ⇨ *see picture at* SHAPE¹

sem·i·co·lon /ˌsemiˈkəʊlən $ 'semiˌkoʊlən/ *noun* the mark (;) that you use in writing to separate different parts of a sentence or list

semi-de·tached /ˌ.. .'./ *adjective* BrE a semi-detached house is joined on one side to another house ⇨ *see picture on page 343*

sem·i·fi·nal /ˌsemiˈfaɪnl/ *noun* one of the two games that are played in a competiton before the last game. The winners of the two semi-finals play each other in the last game to find the winner

sem·i·nar /'semənɑː $ 'seməˌnɑr/ *noun* a meeting in which a group of people discuss a subject

sen·ate /'senɪt/ *noun* the smaller of the two parts of government in countries such as the US and Australia

sen·a·tor /'senətə $ 'senətər/ *noun* a member of a senate: *Senator Dole*

send /send/ *verb, past tense and past participle* **sent** /sent/

> **GRAMMAR**
> **send someone something**
> **send something to someone**
> **send someone to a place**

1 to arrange for something to go to a place or a person: *I sent some money to my sister.* | *When did you send the parcel?* | *I sent you an e-mail yesterday.*
2 to make someone go somewhere: *I sent Jo to buy some food.* | *Al was sent to prison for stealing.*

> **PHRASAL VERBS**
> **send for**
> **send for someone/something** to ask someone to come to you: *We must send for an ambulance.*
> **send off**
> 1 **send something off** to send something somewhere by mail: *I sent off a job application.*
> 2 **send someone off** BrE to order a sports player to leave a game be-

cause they have behaved badly: *Vincent **was sent off** for fighting.*

send out

1 send something out to send things to several people so that they receive one each: *I **sent out** all the party invitations.* | *The school is **sending** a letter **out** to all the parents.*

2 if a machine sends out light, sound etc, it produces it: *The ship's radio **sends out** a powerful signal.*

send-off /'. ./ *noun informal* when a group of people say goodbye to someone who is leaving: *They gave her a good send-off when she retired.*

se·nile /'si:naɪl/ *adjective* mentally confused because of old age

se·ni·or[1] /'si:niə $ 'sinjɚ/ *adjective* a senior person has an important position or rank ⇨ *opposite* JUNIOR[1]: *senior members of staff*

senior[2] *noun AmE* a student in the last year of HIGH SCHOOL or college

senior cit·i·zen /,... '.../ *noun* a person who is over the age of 65

senior high school /,... '. ./ HIGH SCHOOL

sen·sa·tion /sen'seɪʃən/ *noun* **1** a feeling or experience: *It was an odd sensation, like going down in an elevator.* | *She had a tingling sensation in her hands.* **2** *informal* extreme excitement or interest, or something that causes this: *The film was a sensation.*

sen·sa·tion·al /sen'seɪʃənəl/ *adjective* very interesting, exciting, or good: *Her performance in that film was sensational.*

sense[1] /sens/ *noun*

1 one of the five physical abilities of sight, hearing, touch, taste, and smell: *Dogs have a good **sense of smell**.*

2 the meaning of a word, phrase, sentence etc: *The word 'bank' has two main senses.*

PHRASES

make sense if something makes sense, it has a clear meaning that you can understand: *This essay does not **make sense**.*

make sense of something if you can make sense of something, you can understand it: *Can you **make sense of** the instructions?*

it makes sense to do something if it makes sense to do something, it is a reasonable and sensible thing to do: *It would **make sense to** leave early, so that we miss the traffic.*

have some sense, have good sense to be able to make good decisions: *Come on – **have some sense**. We can't possibly have a picnic in this rain!*

not have any sense to be unable to make good decisions

have the sense to do something to do the thing that is most sensible: *She **had the sense to** call the police.*

sense of humour someone who has a sense of humour enjoys things that are funny: *I want to meet a boy with a **good sense of humour**.*

sense[2] *verb* to feel or know something without being told: *Rebecca sensed that something was wrong.*

sense·less /'sensləs/ *adjective* **1** a senseless action is bad and will not achieve anything: *senseless violence* | *The destruction of the rainforest is senseless.* **2** if someone is beaten senseless, they are hit until they are not conscious

sen·si·ble /'sensəbəl/ *adjective*

GRAMMAR
sensible to do something

1 someone who is sensible is able to make good decisions: *You can trust Julia – she's a very sensible girl.*

2 something that is sensible is a good idea: *My friend gave me some sensible advice.* | *It seemed sensible to move to London.*

–**sensibly** *adverb*: *If you won't behave sensibly, you must leave.*

USAGE
You use **sensible** to describe people who are able to make good decisions or behave properly: *The sensible thing is to live in that part of town.* You use **sensitive** about people's feelings, or their ability to consider other people's feelings: *A teacher has to be sensitive to all the students in their class.*

sen·si·tive /'sensətɪv/ *adjective*

GRAMMAR
sensitive about something
sensitive to someone/something

S

S

1 thinking of how other people will feel about something: *He was very* **sensitive to** *other people's needs.*
⇨ opposite INSENSITIVE

2 easily offended or upset: *Billy is such a sensitive child.* | *She's* **sensitive about** *her big nose.*

3 if you have sensitive skin, it is easily affected by something such as water, wind, soap etc: *The skin around my eyes is very sensitive.* ⇨ *see usage note at* SENSIBLE

sen·su·al /'senʃuəl/ *adjective* related to physical pleasure: *sensual pleasures such as sunbathing*

sen·su·ous /'senʃuəs/ *adjective* making you feel physical pleasure: *the sensuous feel of silk*

sent the past tense and past participle of SEND

sen·tence¹ /'sentəns/ *noun*

1 a group of words that are written with a capital letter at the beginning and a FULL STOP at the end

2 a punishment that a judge gives to someone who is guilty of a crime: *The judge gave him a six-month* **prison sentence** (=the judge sent him to prison for six months).

sentence² *verb* when a judge sentences someone, he or she gives them a punishment for a crime: *The judge sentenced Larsen to six years in prison.*

sen·ti·ment·al /ˌsentə'mentl/ *adjective* showing emotions such as love, pity, and sadness too strongly or in a silly way: *an old-fashioned, sentimental movie*

sen·try /'sentri/ *noun, plural* **sentries** a soldier who stands outside a building, guarding it

sep·a·rate¹ /'sepərət/ *adjective*

GRAMMAR
separate from something

1 separate things are different ones, not the same one: *Two drivers were injured in the race, in two separate accidents.*

2 if two things are separate, they are not touching or connected to each other: *Keep the wires separate.* | *The science building was* **separate from** *the main school building.*
–**separately** *adverb*: *He spoke to each child separately.*

sep·a·rate² /'sepəreɪt/ *verb*

GRAMMAR
separate something into something
separate something from something

1 to divide something into different parts or groups: *The teacher* **separated** *the children* **into** *three groups.* | *Separate the male rabbits* **from** *the female ones.*

2 if something separates one thing from another, it is between the two things so they do not touch or are not connected: *A high fence separated the two gardens.*

3 if people who are married separate, they start living apart: *My parents separated when I was 10 years old.*

sep·a·rat·ed /'sepəreɪtɪd/ *adjective* not living with your husband, wife, or partner any more: *My husband and I are separated.*

sep·a·ra·tion /ˌsepə'reɪʃən/ *noun* when two people stop being together: *She found the separation from her boyfriend hard to bear.*

Sep·tem·ber /sep'tembə $ sep-'tembɚ/ *written abbreviation* **Sept** *noun* the ninth month of the year: *Lisa's birthday is September 21st.*

sep·tic /'septɪk/ *adjective* BrE if a cut or wound is septic, it is infected by disease

se·quel /'siːkwəl/ *noun* a film, book etc that continues the story of an earlier one

se·quence /'siːkwəns/ *noun* a series of events that are connected to each other: *A long sequence of events has led up to this crisis.*

ser·geant /'sɑːdʒənt $ 'sɑrdʒənt/ *noun* an officer in the army or police

se·ri·al¹ /'sɪəriəl $ 'sɪriəl/ *noun* a story that is shown on television, broadcast on radio, or printed in a magazine in several separate parts

serial² *adjective* a serial killer, RAPIST etc has attacked several people over a period of time

se·ries /'sɪəriːz $ 'sɪriz/ *noun, plural* **series** **1** several events of the same kind that happen one after the other: *The police are investigating a series of robberies.* **2** a set of television or radio programmes with the same characters or about the same subject

se·ri·ous /'sɪəriəs $'sɪriəs/ *adjective*

GRAMMAR
serious about something

1 a serious problem or situation is very bad: *There's been a serious road accident.*

2 if you are serious about something, you are sincere about what you are saying: **Are** *you **serious about** wanting to come with me?* | *I didn't know if it was a serious offer.*

3 a serious person thinks carefully about things and does not laugh very often: *Philip was a very serious child.*

se·ri·ous·ly /'sɪəriəsli $'sɪriəsli/ *adverb*

1 very: *My mother is seriously ill.*

2 if you say or think about something seriously, you do it in a sincere way: *I am seriously thinking of leaving school.*

PHRASE
take something seriously to believe that something is important: *You're not **taking** our friendship **seriously**!*

ser·mon /'sɜːmən $'sɚmən/ *noun* a religious talk that someone gives at a church

ser·pent /'sɜːpənt $'sɚpənt/ *noun written* a snake

ser·vant /'sɜːvənt $'sɚvənt/ *noun* someone who works for someone in a large house, doing jobs such as cleaning and cooking

serve¹ /sɜːv $sɚv/ *verb*

1 if you serve food or drink, you give it to people: *Could you serve the vegetables?* | *This pie can be served hot or cold.*

2 if you serve people in a shop, you give them the things they want to buy and take the money they pay: *I couldn't find anyone to serve me.*

3 to work in the army or another public organization: *He served in the army for three years.*

4 if you serve in a game such as tennis, you start the game by throwing the ball in the air and hitting it to the other person

PHRASE
it serves someone right *spoken* used

to say that someone deserves something unpleasant that happens to them: *"Sarah won't speak to me." "It serves you right for telling lies about her!"*

serve² *noun* when you serve in a game such as tennis: *That was a brilliant serve!*

serv·er /'sɜːvə $'sɚvɚ/ *noun* the main computer in a NETWORK

ser·vice¹ /'sɜːvɪs $'sɚvɪs/ *noun*

1 an organization that provides help for people or does a job for people: *The new government has promised to improve local services in all areas.* | *the **health service** (=the government department that organizes hospitals, doctors etc for people)*

2 *[no plural]* the help that people who work in a restaurant, hotel, shop etc give you: *It was a lovely meal, and the service was excellent.* | *The bill includes a 12% charge for service.*

3 a formal religious ceremony in a church: *Everyone stood around chatting after the service.* | *a funeral service (=a ceremony for someone who has died)*

4 a regular examination of a machine or vehicle to make sure it works correctly: *You should take your car for a service every six months.*

5 bus service, train service a bus or train that regularly travels to a particular place: *There's a very good train service between London and Peterborough.*

service² *verb* to examine a machine or vehicle and fix it if necessary: *Bill offered to service my car for me.*

service sta·tion /'.. ,../ *noun* a place beside a road that sells petrol, food etc

ser·vi·ette /,sɜːvi'et $,sɚvi'et/ *noun BrE* a NAPKIN

serv·ing /'sɜːvɪŋ $'sɚvɪŋ/ *noun* an amount of food that is enough for one person

ses·sion /'seʃən/ *noun* a period of time when people work or do an activity: *a football training session*

set¹ /set/ *verb, past tense and past participle* set, setting

GRAMMAR
set something to do something

S

▼ **set something for/at something**
set something to do something
set something (down) some-
where
set someone something

1 if you set a date, price, or amount, you decide what it will be: *Shall we* **set a date** *for the next meeting?* | *We've set a limit of £15,000 on the building costs.*

2 if you set a machine, you put the control on it in a particular position so that the machine will do something you want it to do: *I've* **set** *my alarm clock* **for** *six o'clock.* | *The heating* **is set at** *18 degrees.* | *The oven* **was set to** *come on at four o'clock.*

3 if a story or film is set in a particular time or place, the events in it happen in that time or place: *The film is set in the future – about 2080 AD.*

4 when the sun sets, it moves lower in the sky until you cannot see it any more* ⇨ *opposite* RISE¹ (4): *The sun doesn't set until nine o'clock in the summer.*

PHRASES

set a record to do something better or faster than anyone has ever done it before: *He has* **set a** *new* **record for** *the high jump.*

set an example to behave in a good way that shows other people how they should behave: *You should always* **set an example** *by being polite.*

set fire to something, set light to something to make something start burning: *Someone had dropped a cigarette, which* **set fire to** *a piece of paper.*

set someone free to allow someone to leave a place after they have been a prisoner: *All the prisoners have now been* **set free**.

set a trap to make a clever plan to catch someone: *The police* **set a** **trap** *for the thieves.*

PHRASAL VERBS

set about
set about doing something to start doing something that will take a long time: *Tim* **set about** *raising money for his trip to Africa.*

set aside
▼ **set something aside** if you set

aside money or time, you keep it so that it is available for a particular purpose: *You should* **set aside** *an hour each evening for homework.*

set back
set something/someone back if something sets back a piece of work, it delays it: *This problem could* **set** *the project* **back** *by several months.* | *The bad weather* **set** *us* **back** *a bit.*

set off
to start a journey somewhere: *If we* **set off** *early, we should get there by five o'clock.*

set out
1 **set out** to start a journey: *In the autumn the two men* **set out for** *Egypt again.*

2 **set out to do something** to start trying to achieve something: *He* **set out to** *write a best-selling novel.*

3 **set something out** to say or write something in a clear and organized way: *The rules of the competition* **are set out** *below.*

set up
set something up to start a company or organization: *The government wants to encourage people to* **set up** *new businesses.*

set² noun

GRAMMAR
a set of things

a group of things that belong together: *She packed a spare* **set of** *clothes.* | *a* **chess set**

set³ adjective 1 a set time, price, amount etc is fixed and does not change: *You can have a full meal for a set price of £10.* 2 informal if you are set to do something, you are ready to do it: *Are you all set to go?*

set·back /'setbæk/ noun a bad event that stops you from being successful for a while: *Losing the headteacher was a big setback for the school.*

set·tee /se'tiː/ noun BrE a SOFA

set·ting /'setɪŋ/ noun 1 the place where something happens: *It was the perfect setting for a romantic meal.* 2 one of the positions that the controls on a machine can be turned to: *Use your hairdryer on its lowest setting.*

set·tle /'setl/ verb

GRAMMAR
settle in
settle on

1 to make a decision that ends an argument or disagreement: *How can we settle this argument?* | *That's settled then – we're going to France for our holiday.*
2 to start living in a place where you intend to live for a long time: *His parents came to America from Ireland and settled in Boston.*
3 if dust or snow settles on something, it falls onto it and stays there: *The snow had settled on the ground.*

PHRASE
settle a bill, settle a debt to pay money that you owe: *They settled the bill and left the restaurant.*

PHRASAL VERBS
settle down
1 to stop travelling around and start living in one place: *Isn't it time you got married and settled down?*
2 to sit down quietly: *They settled down to watch the match on TV.*
settle for
settle for something to accept something that is less than what you wanted: *I'd like to win, but I'll settle for second place.*
settle in
to start to feel happy after moving to a new house, job, or school: *It's difficult starting a new school, but you'll soon settle in.*

set·tled /'setld/ adjective 1 happy in your new house, job, or school: *I'm beginning to feel a bit more settled.* 2 if the weather is settled, it is dry and warm and not likely to change ⇨ opposite meaning UNSETTLED: *The weather should stay settled for the next few days.*

set·tle·ment /'setlmənt/ noun 1 an official agreement that ends fighting: *The two sides have agreed on a settlement.* 2 a place where a group of people live: *a small settlement high up in the mountains*

set-up /'. ./ noun informal 1 the way that something is organized: *I didn't understand the set-up at the college.* 2 a trick or trap: *I should have realized it was a set-up.*

sev·en /'sevən/ number 7

sev·en·teen /ˌsevən'tiːn/ number 17
– **seventeenth** number

sev·enth /'sevənθ/ number 1 7th
2 one of the seven equal parts of something; 1/7

sev·en·ty /'sevənti/ number, plural **seventies** 1 70 2 the seventies the years between 1970 and 1979 3 be in your seventies to be aged between 70 and 79
– **seventieth** number

sev·er /'sevə $'sevɚ/ verb formal to cut through something completely: *His hand was completely severed in the accident.*

sev·er·al /'sevərəl/ quantifier
a few: *The journey took several days.* | *She applied to several different universities.* | *Several of the apples were rotten.*

se·vere /sə'vɪə $sə'vɪr/ adjective a severe thing is very bad: *They suffered severe hardship.* | *a severe earthquake*

se·vere·ly /sə'vɪəli $sə'vɪrli/ adverb very badly: *Her mother was severely injured in the crash.*

se·ver·i·ty /sə'verəti/ noun [no plural] formal how bad something is: *We didn't understand the severity of the problem.*

sew /səʊ $soʊ/ verb **sewed, sewn** /səʊn $soʊn/ or **sewed** to use a needle and thread to join pieces of cloth together: *Next she sewed on the sleeves of the dress.* | *I need to sew a button on my shirt.*

sew

sew·age /'sjuːɪdʒ $'suːɪdʒ/ noun [no plural] dirty water that is carried away from buildings through pipes

sew·er /'sjuːə $'suːɚ/ noun a pipe under the ground that carries away sewage

sew·ing /'səʊɪŋ $'soʊɪŋ/ noun [no plural] making or mending clothes, using a needle and thread: *Are you any good at sewing?*

sewn a past participle of SEW

sex /seks/ noun 1 [no plural] the activity that a male and female do together to produce children or that two people do together for pleasure 2 [no plural] the sex of a person or animal is whether they are male or female: *What sex is your cat?* | *Write down your name, sex, age, and occupation on the form.* | *He is shy with the opposite sex* (=women).

sex·is·m /'seksɪzəm/ *noun* [no plural] when people, especially women, are treated unfairly because of their sex

sex·ist /'seksɪst/ *adjective* treating people unfairly because of what sex they are: *Her boss has a very sexist attitude.*
– **sexist** *noun*

sex·u·al /'sekʃuəl/ *adjective* **1** related to sex: *I'm not ready for a sexual relationship.* **2** related to whether someone is male or female: *Sexual discrimination at work is illegal.*
– **sexually** *adverb*: *I don't find him sexually attractive.*

sexual har·ass·ment /ˌ... '.../ *noun* [no plural] when someone you work with speaks to you or touches you in a sexual way when you do not want them to

sex·u·al·i·ty /ˌsekʃu'æləti/ *noun* [no plural] someone's sexual feelings

sex·y /'seksi/ *adjective* **sexier, sexiest** sexually attractive: *He had sexy brown eyes.*

sh or **shh** /ʃ/ used to tell someone to be quiet

shab·by /'ʃæbi/ *adjective* **shabbier, shabbiest** old and in bad condition: *shabby clothes*
– **shabbily** *adverb*: *a shabbily dressed man*

shack /ʃæk/ *noun* a small building that has not been built very well

shade¹ /ʃeɪd/ *noun*
1 [no plural] a pleasant area that is away from the heat and light of the sun: *I'd rather sit in the shade.* ⇨ *see picture at* SHADOW
2 one particular type of a colour: *They painted the ceiling a darker shade of blue.*

shade² *verb* to cover something so that the light from the sun cannot reach it: *The tables were shaded from the sun by a tree.*

shades /ʃeɪdz/ *informal* SUNGLASSES

shad·ow /'ʃædəʊ $ 'ʃædoʊ/ *noun*
1 a dark shape that appears on a surface when the light cannot shine

on it because something is in the way: *The leaves made shadows on the wall.*
2 [no plural] if something is in shadow, it is dark because light cannot reach it: *His face was in shadow.*

shadow

in the shade

shadow

shad·y /'ʃeɪdi/ *adjective* **shadier, shadiest** a shady place is outside, but away from the direct heat and light of the sun: *a shady corner of the garden*

shaft /ʃɑːft $ ʃæft/ *noun* a deep straight hole: *an elevator shaft*

shake¹ /ʃeɪk/ *verb* **shook** /ʃʊk/ **shaken** /'ʃeɪkən/
1 if something shakes, it moves quickly up and down or from side to side: *His hands were shaking.* ⇨ *see picture at* NOD
2 to move something about quickly and roughly: *She shook the bottle of medicine.*
3 also **shake up** if you are shaken by something, it makes you feel shocked and upset: *She was shaken by her parents' divorce.*

PHRASES

shake your head to move your head from side to side as a way of saying no: *When I asked her if she was all right, she just shook her head.*

shake hands if you shake hands with someone, you hold their hand and move it up and down, as a greeting or when you have made an agreement: *The two men shook hands.* | *He refused to shake hands with me.* ⇨ *see picture on page 341*

shake² *noun* when someone shakes something: *He held my hand and gave it a friendly shake.*

shaken the past participle of SHAKE¹

shake-up /'. ./ *noun* when big changes are made to the way that something is organized: *There's going to be a big shake-up in the company where she works.*

shak·y /'ʃeɪki/ *adjective* **shakier, shaki-est** upset and weak because something has shocked or hurt you: *I was still feeling a bit shaky after the accident.*

shall /ʃəl; *strong* ʃæl/ *modal verb*, *negative* **shan't** or **shall not**
1 offering to do something politely: *Shall I give you a lift home? | Shall we fetch the bags from the car while you make a drink?*
2 suggesting something: *What time **shall we start**? | **Shall we** stop for a beer? | Come on – let's get on with it, **shall we**?*

shal·low /'ʃæləʊ $ 'ʃæloʊ/ *adjective* not deep: *They paddled in the shallow water. | a shallow stream*

sham·bles /'ʃæmbəlz/ *noun* **be a shambles** *informal* to be very untidy or badly organized: *The place was a shambles.*

shame /ʃeɪm/ *noun* [no plural] the feeling that you have when you know that you have done something bad or embarrassing: *He felt **a great sense of shame** about leaving her.*

PHRASE
it's a shame, what a shame *spoken* used to say that something is disappointing: *It's a shame you can't come with us. | "He was too ill to play." "Oh, what a shame!"*

shame·ful /'ʃeɪmfəl/ *adjective* if something you do is shameful, you should be ashamed of it: *It's shameful the way he treats his wife!*

shame·less /'ʃeɪmləs/ *adjective* behaving badly and not caring that other people do not approve: *This was a shameless attempt to cheat.*

sham·poo /ʃæm'puː/ *noun* a liquid that you use for washing your hair: *I like that lemon shampoo.*

shan't /ʃɑːnt $ ʃænt/ *BrE* the short form of 'shall not': *I shan't be long.*

shape¹ /ʃeɪp/ *noun* the shape of something is whether it is a circle, square etc: *What shape is the box? | a card **in the shape of** a heart*

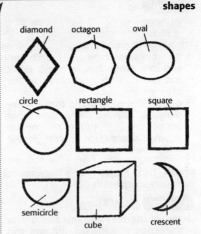

shapes

diamond　octagon　oval
circle　rectangle　square
semicircle　cube　crescent

PHRASES
be in good shape, be in bad shape to be in good condition or in bad condition: *The boxer was obviously **in bad shape**.*
get in shape, keep in shape to become fit or stay fit by doing exercise: *What do you do to **keep in shape**?*
take shape if an idea takes shape, it develops and becomes clear and definite: *The plans for the show **are taking shape**.*

shape² *verb* if something is shaped like a particular thing, it has the same shape as that thing: *cookies shaped like snowmen*

share¹ /ʃeə $ ʃer/ *verb*

GRAMMAR
share something with someone
share something between/among people

1 if two people share something, they both have it or use it: *The two secretaries share an office. | He **shares** a room **with** his brother.*
2 also **share out** to give part of something to each person in a group: *We **shared** the work **between** us. | The children **shared out** the sweets. | The money will be **shared out among** all the members of the family.*
3 if you share something with someone, you tell them about it: *Would you like to **share** your thoughts **with** us?*

S

share² noun

GRAMMAR
a share of something
shares in something

1 a part of something which each person in a group has received: *What will you do with your* **share of** *the money?*
2 one of the equal parts that a company is divided into and that people can buy: *A lot of people are* **buying shares in** *mobile phone companies.*

shark /ʃɑːk $ʃɑrk/ noun a large sea fish with very sharp teeth

sharp¹ /ʃɑːp $ʃɑrp/ adjective

1 something that is sharp has a very thin edge or narrow point and can cut things easily ⇨ opposite BLUNT (1) ⇨ see picture at BLUNT: *Cut off the leaves with a sharp knife.* | *The dog's teeth were sharp.*
2 a sharp increase is large and sudden: *There has been a sharp increase in the number of accidents.*
3 a sharp pain is bad and sudden: *He felt a sharp pain in his stomach.*
4 good at noticing things or thinking quickly: *Her* **sharp eyes** *missed nothing.*
5 a sharp line or shape is very clear: *the sharp outline of the mountain*
6 a sharp taste is strong and slightly sour
7 A sharp, B sharp etc the musical note that is slightly higher than A, B etc ⇨ opposite FLAT¹ (5): *He played F sharp instead of F.*

sharp² adverb at 8 o'clock sharp, at two-thirty sharp etc at exactly 8:00, 2:30 etc: *Class starts at 9 a.m. sharp.*

sharp·en /ˈʃɑːpən $ˈʃɑrpən/ verb to make something sharp: *I sharpened my pencil.*

shat·ter /ˈʃætə $ˈʃætɚ/ verb 1 to break into very small pieces: *The glass hit the floor and shattered.* 2 to break something into very small pieces: *The explosion shattered the window.*

shat·tered /ˈʃætəd $ˈʃætɚd/ adjective
1 very shocked and upset: *They were shattered when they heard the news.*
2 BrE informal very tired

shave¹ /ʃeɪv/ verb to cut off the hair on your face, legs etc: *He washed and shaved.*

shave² noun 1 [no plural] an act of shaving: *He needs a shave.* 2 a close shave informal a situation in which you only just avoid something bad: *Nobody was injured, but it was a close shave.*

shav·er /ˈʃeɪvə $ˈʃeɪvɚ/ noun an electric tool that a man uses for shaving ⇨ see picture at RAZOR

shawl /ʃɔːl/ noun a large piece of cloth that a woman wears around her shoulders or head: *She wore a red shawl.*

she /ʃiː/ pronoun

a woman or girl: *Fiona knew she would pass the exam.* | *Has she got any sisters?* | *She's nice, isn't she?*

shear /ʃɪə $ʃɪr/ verb, past tense **sheared**, past participle **sheared** or **shorn** /ʃɔːn $ʃɔrn/ to cut the wool off a sheep: *We watched him shearing sheep.*

shears /ʃɪəz $ʃɪrz/ plural noun large scissors for cutting plants or grass: *a pair of garden shears*

she'd /ʃiːd/ the short form of 'she had' or 'she would': *She'd already left.* | *I knew she'd like it.*

shed¹ /ʃed/ noun a small building that you use for storing things: *a tool shed* ⇨ see picture on page 343

shed² verb, past tense and past participle **shed**, **shedding** 1 when a tree sheds its leaves, the leaves drop off 2 shed light on something to explain something: *Can you shed any light on what he was doing there?* 3 shed tears to cry: *Nobody shed any tears when she left.*

sheep /ʃiːp/ noun, plural **sheep** a farm animal that is kept for its wool and meat: *There was a flock of sheep in the field.*

sheep·ish /ˈʃiːpɪʃ/ adjective informal embarrassed because you have done something silly or wrong: *She came back looking sheepish.*

sheer /ʃɪə $ʃɪr/ adjective 1 sheer luck, sheer chance etc complete luck etc: *I only heard about it by sheer chance.* 2 a sheer slope goes straight up or down: *the sheer cliffs*

sheet /ʃiːt/ noun 1 a large piece of thin cloth that you put on a bed: *I prefer* *cotton sheets.* **2** a flat piece of paper, metal, glass etc: *a sheet of paper*

shelf /ʃelf/ *noun, plural* **shelves** /ʃelvz/ a board to put things on, fixed to a wall or in a cupboard: *He put the jar back on the shelf.* ⇨ see picture on page 342

she'll /ʃiːl/ the short form of 'she will': *She'll go crazy when she finds out!*

shell¹ /ʃel/ *noun* **1** the hard outside part of a nut or egg **2** the hard part that covers some animals, for example SNAILS and CRABS: *We took the shells off the shrimps.* **3** a bomb which is fired from a large gun: *Shells fell on the city all night.*

shell² *verb* **1** to fire bombs at something from a large gun: *The town was shelled during the war.* **2 shell out** *informal* to pay a lot of money for something: *I had to shell out fifty pounds to have my bike mended.*

shell·fish /ˈʃelˌfɪʃ/ *noun, plural* **shellfish** a small creature that lives in water and has a shell

shel·ter¹ /ˈʃeltə $ ˈʃeltɚ/ *noun*

GRAMMAR
shelter from something

1 a small building in which you are safe from bad weather or from attack: *They built themselves a shelter out of branches.*
2 *[no plural]* protection from bad weather or from danger: *These people need food and shelter.* | *The line of trees provides **shelter from** the wind.*

PHRASE
take shelter to go into or under something so that you are safe from bad weather or from danger: *The rain forced them to **take shelter** under a tree.*

shelter² *verb* **1** to give someone a safe place to stay: *Relatives offered to shelter the family until it was safe for them to go home.* **2** to go into or under a place so that you are safe from bad weather or danger: *We sheltered from the sun under a tree.*

shelve /ʃelv/ *verb* if you shelve a plan, you decide not to continue with it immediately, although you might continue with it later: *They have shelved plans to expand the college.*

shelves the plural of SHELF

shep·herd /ˈʃepəd $ ˈʃepɚd/ *noun* someone whose job is to take care of sheep

sher·iff /ˈʃerɪf/ *noun* an elected chief police officer in the US

sher·ry /ˈʃeri/ *noun* *[no plural]* a strong Spanish wine: *a glass of sherry*

she's /ʃiːz/ the short form of 'she is' or 'she has': *She's very upset.* | *She's never been abroad.*

shh /ʃ/ SH

shield¹ /ʃiːld/ *noun* a large flat object which a soldier or police officer holds in front of their body to protect themselves

shield² *verb* to protect someone from something unpleasant: *I just wanted to shield her from the truth.*

shift¹ /ʃɪft/ *noun* **1** a change in what people think or do: *There has been a shift in attitudes towards women at work.* **2** one of the periods of work in a factory, hospital etc: *She's on the night shift this week.*

shift² *verb* *informal* **1** to move something from one place to another: *I asked him to shift his car.* **2** to move slightly: *Could you shift up a bit, please?*

shim·mer /ˈʃɪmə $ ˈʃɪmɚ/ *verb* to shine with a soft unsteady light: *The moonlight shimmered on the water.*

shin /ʃɪn/ *noun* the front part of your leg between your knee and your foot: *He got kicked on the shin.*

shine /ʃaɪn/ *verb, past tense and past participle* **shone** /ʃɒn $ ʃoʊn/
1 to produce light or look bright: *The sun was shining.* | *The cat's eyes shone in the car's headlights.*
2 to point a light in a particular direction: *Can you shine your torch over here?*

shin·y /ˈʃaɪni/ *adjective* **shinier, shiniest** something that is shiny has a very bright surface: *a shiny new coin*

ship¹ /ʃɪp/ *noun* a large boat: *I was terrified that the ship might sink.* ⇨ see picture on page 349

ship² *verb* **shipped, shipping** to send goods a long distance, especially in a ship: *The animals were shipped over from France.*

S

ship·ping /'ʃɪpɪŋ/ *noun [no plural]* ships in general, or when things are moved by ships: *The bad weather has caused delays to shipping.*

ship·wreck¹ /'ʃɪp-rek/ *noun* an accident in which a ship is destroyed at sea: *Many sailors lost their lives in the shipwreck.*

shipwreck² *verb* be shipwrecked if people are shipwrecked, the ship they are travelling on is destroyed in an accident at sea, but they manage to reach land

shirk /ʃɜːk $ ʃɚk/ *verb* to avoid doing something you should do: *George worked hard and never shirked his responsibilities.*

shirt /ʃɜːt $ ʃɚt/ *noun* a piece of clothing that covers the top part of your body, and has buttons down the front: *He wore a shirt and tie.* ⇨ *see picture on page 352*

shiv·er /'ʃɪvə $ 'ʃɪvɚ/ *verb* if you shiver, your body shakes a little because you are cold or frightened: *I was cold and wet and I couldn't stop shivering.*
shiver *noun*: *"I'm scared," she said with a shiver.*

shoal /ʃəʊl $ ʃoʊl/ *noun* a large group of fish that swim together

shock¹ /ʃɒk $ ʃɑk/ *noun [no plural]*
1 if you get a shock, something bad happens which you did not expect, and you feel very surprised and upset: *I got a terrible shock when I saw how ill Simon looked.* | *I'm still in a state of shock.*
2 if someone is suffering from shock after an accident, their body is very weak because they have been frightened and upset: *The driver was taken to hospital and treated for shock.*

PHRASE
be a shock, come as a shock if something bad that happens is a shock or comes as a shock, it is very unexpected and upsets you a lot: *The news that she had cancer came as a terrible shock.*

shock² *verb*
to make someone feel very surprised and upset: *The terrible crime shocked even the police.* | *The children's attitude really shocked me.*
shocked *adjective*: *She was shocked to find out that her husband had been in prison.*

shock·ing /'ʃɒkɪŋ $ 'ʃɑkɪŋ/ *adjective* something that is shocking is so bad that it makes you feel very upset or angry: *It's shocking that so many young people are homeless in this country.*

shod·dy /'ʃɒdi $ 'ʃɑdi/ *adjective* **shoddier, shoddiest** shoddy work is badly done, and shoddy goods are badly made: *markets selling cheap shoddy goods*

shoe /ʃuː/ *noun* 1 a piece of clothing that you wear on your feet, which is made of leather or some other strong material: *a pair of running shoes* ⇨ *see picture on page 352* 2 be in someone's shoes to be in the situation that someone else is in: *I wouldn't want to be in her shoes.*

shoe·lace /'ʃuːleɪs/ *noun* a thin piece of string or leather that you use to tie your shoes: *Your shoelace is undone.*

shone the past tense and past participle of SHINE

shook the past tense of SHAKE

shoot¹ /ʃuːt/ *verb, past tense and past participle* **shot** /ʃɒt $ ʃɑt/
1 to kill or injure someone with a gun: *He shot the man in the back.* | *Fifteen people were shot dead.*
2 to fire a gun: *Don't shoot!*
3 to make a film or take photographs: *It takes several weeks to shoot a pop video.*

PHRASAL VERBS
shoot down
shoot something down to destroy an enemy plane while it is flying: *Three planes were shot down.*
shoot up
to increase very quickly: *The number of car thefts has shot up.*

shoot² *noun* 1 a new part of a plant that is starting to grow: *A few green shoots appeared in the ground.* 2 a time when someone makes a film or takes photographs: *The film shoot lasted three months.*

shoot·ing /'ʃuːtɪŋ/ noun **1** a situation in which someone is killed or injured by a gun: *Two men have died after a shooting at a pub in Liverpool.* **2** [no plural] the sport of killing animals and birds with guns

shop¹ /ʃɒp $ ʃɑp/ noun

a building where you can buy things: *The town has some good clothes shops.* | *I got these shoes **in a shop** near the town centre.*

shop² verb **shopped, shopping**

GRAMMAR
shop for something

to go to a shop or several shops to buy things: *We shop once a week.* | *I'm **going shopping** this afternoon.* | *Where do you **shop for** food?*

PHRASE
shop around to compare the price and quality of things in different shops before you decide which to buy: ***Shop around** to find the best computer you can afford.*

shop as·sis·tant /'. .,../ noun BrE someone who works in a shop selling things and helping customers; SALES CLERK, SALES ASSISTANT AmE

shop·keep·er /'ʃɒp,kiːpə $ 'ʃɑp,kipɚ/ noun someone who owns or manages a small shop; STOREKEEPER AmE

shop·lift /'ʃɒplɪft $ 'ʃɑp,lɪft/ verb to steal things from shops: *All his friends used to shoplift.*
– **shoplifter** noun: *More and more shoplifters are now being caught by the police.*

shop·lift·ing /'ʃɒp,lɪftɪŋ $ 'ʃɑp,lɪftɪŋ/ noun [no plural] the crime of stealing things from shops: *She was arrested for shoplifting.*

shop·ping /'ʃɒpɪŋ $ 'ʃɑpɪŋ/ noun [no plural]
1 when you go to shops to buy things: *I'll **do the shopping** this week.*
2 things that you have just bought: *Maggie was carrying bags of shopping.*

shopping cen·tre BrE, **shopping cen·ter** AmE /'.. ,../ noun a group of shops that are built together in one area, often inside one large building

shore /ʃɔː $ ʃɔr/ noun the land along the edge of the sea or a large lake: *the southern shore of Lake Geneva.*

shorn the past participle of SHEAR

short¹ /ʃɔːt $ ʃɔrt/ adjective
1 happening for only a little time: *It's quite a short film.* | *We made a short visit to his parents.*
2 a short distance or length is not long: *It's only a short walk to my school.* | *His hair is short and black.*
3 a short person is not tall: *Her father was a short fat man.* | *Louise is shorter than me.* ⇨ see picture on page 353

PHRASES
be short of something to not have enough of something that you need: *Ken **is** always **short of** money.*
be short for something to be a shorter way of saying a name: *Liz **is short for** Elizabeth.*

short² noun **in short** used to say something in only a few words: *In short, we're lost.*

short·age /'ʃɔːtɪdʒ $ 'ʃɔrtɪdʒ/ noun when there is not enough of something that people need: *There is now a serious shortage of hospital beds.*

short cut /,. './ noun a quicker more direct way of going somewhere or doing something: *We took a short cut over the fields to the station.*

short·hand /'ʃɔːthænd $ 'ʃɔrthænd/ noun [no plural] a fast method of writing down what people say, using signs instead of words: *Candidates for the job must know shorthand.*

short·list¹ /'ʃɔːtlɪst $ 'ʃɔrtlɪst/ noun BrE a list of the most suitable people for a job or prize, chosen from a larger group: *Her first novel was on the shortlist for an important literary prize.*

short·list² /'. ./ verb **be short-listed** BrE to be chosen for a shortlist: *No women were short-listed for the job.*

short·ly /'ʃɔːtli $ 'ʃɔrtli/ adverb soon: *Liz left home shortly after 8 a.m.*

shorts /ʃɔːts $ ʃɔrts/ plural noun
1 short trousers that only reach to your knees: *Jack was wearing a pair of shorts and a T-shirt.* ⇨ see picture on page 352
2 the American word for UNDERPANTS

short·sight·ed /,ʃɔːt'saɪtɪd $,ʃɔrt'saɪtɪd/ adjective **1** if you are shortsighted, you cannot see things very

S

clearly if they are a long way away from you **2** thinking only about the effect that something will have immediately, rather than thinking about the effect it will have over a longer period of time: *The government's policy on the environment is short-sighted.*

short-term /ˌ. './ *adjective* continuing for only a short time: *We have had some short-term financial problems.*

shot¹ /ʃɒt $ʃɑt/ *noun* **1** when someone fires a gun, or the sound that this makes: *I heard a shot and the animal fell to the ground.* **2** when someone hits the ball in a game such as BASEBALL, or kicks the ball towards the GOAL in a game of football: *Renaldo's shot hit the goalpost and went in.* **3** a photograph or piece of film: *The film opens with a shot of Central Park.*

shot² the past tense and participle of SHOOT

shot·gun /'ʃɒtgʌn $'ʃɑtgʌn/ *noun* a long gun that shoots small metal balls, and is used especially for shooting animals and birds

should /ʃəd; *strong* ʃʊd/ *modal verb*, *negative* **shouldn't** or **should not**
1 saying that something is a good thing to do **a)** if something **should** happen, it is a good thing to happen: *People shouldn't use their cars so often.* | *Alan really should do something about his weight.* | *Disabled people should have the same rights as everyone else.* **b)** if something **should have** happened it did not happen: *Some scenes in the film should have been shorter.* | *I shouldn't have lost my temper with Tim.*
2 expecting something to happen or be true: *You should be able to find vegetarian meals in most restaurants.* | *Tickets should be on sale next week.*
3 making a suggestion or giving advice strongly: *We should call an ambulance.* | *You shouldn't worry about your exams.*
4 asking for advice: *What should we do?* | *Do you think I should change my shoes?*

shoul·der /'ʃəʊldə $'ʃoʊldɚ/ *noun*
your shoulders are the two parts of your body at the side of your neck where your arms join your body: *Sam patted me **on the shoulder**.* | *She carried her bag **over her shoulder**.* ➪ see picture at BODY

PHRASE
shrug your shoulders to raise your shoulders to show that you do not know something or do not care about it: *I asked what happened and he just **shrugged his shoulders**.*

shoulder bag /'.. ˌ./ *noun* a bag that you carry over your shoulder

shoulder blade /'.. ˌ./ *noun* one of the two flat bones below your shoulders on your back

should·n't /'ʃʊdnt/ *verb* the short form of 'should not': *You shouldn't leave your desk in such a mess.*

should've /'ʃʊdəv/ *verb* the short form of 'should have': *I should've worn a coat.*

shout¹ /ʃaʊt/ *verb*

GRAMMAR
shout at someone
to say something very loudly, usually in an angry way: *"Stop!" he shouted.* | *Mrs Keane is always **shouting at** us.*

shout² *noun*
something that someone says very loudly: *I heard a shout outside my window.* | *There was a shout of "Hooray!"*

shove /ʃʌv/ *verb informal* to push someone or something in a rough or careless way: *People were shoving each other, trying to get on the bus.* | *He shoved the clothes into his bag.*
– **shove** *noun*

shovel¹ /'ʃʌvəl/ *noun* a tool made of a wide piece of metal on a long handle, that you use for moving earth and stones

shovel² *verb* **shovelled, shovelling** *BrE*, **shoveled, shoveling** *AmE* to move earth, stones etc with a shovel

show¹ /ʃəʊ $ ʃoʊ/ verb showed, shown /ʃəʊn $ ʃoʊn/

GRAMMAR
show something to someone
show someone something
show that
show how/what/whether etc
show someone what/how/where etc
show someone to a place

1 to let someone see something: *You have to show your ticket at the door.* | *I **showed** the teacher's note to my mother.* | *Will you show me the photos?*
2 to provide facts or information that tells you that something is true: *The report showed an increase in sales of CDs.* | *His letter **showed that** he was still in love with her.* | *The statistics will **show whether** the advertising campaign is working.*
3 to tell someone how to do something: *Joan **showed** me **how** to use the computer.*
4 to take someone to a place: *Will you **show** the new students **to** their classroom?*
5 if you show a feeling or it shows, people can see it when they look at you: *He couldn't help showing his embarrassment.* | *Her tiredness showed on her face.*
6 if a film or picture shows something, you can see it on the film or picture: *The photo showed surfers on a beach.*
7 if a film or programme is showing at a cinema or on television, people are able to see it: *They are showing "Star Wars" on TV on Saturday.*

PHRASAL VERBS
show around
show someone around to go with someone around a place and show them the important or interesting parts: *I offered to **show** the new boy **around** the school.*
show off
1 to do things to try to make people think you are clever, attractive, funny etc: *The boys all started **showing off** because Kate was there.*
2 show something off to show something to people because you are very proud of it: *I want to go out tonight and **show off** my new dress.*

show² noun
1 a programme on television or radio: *What's your favourite show on TV?* | *He has his own **radio show**.*
2 a performance involving singing, dancing etc in a theatre: *She is **in a show** on Broadway.*

PHRASE
be on show to be available for the public to look at: *His paintings **are on show** at the Museum of Modern Art.*

show busi·ness /'. ,.../ also **show biz** /'ʃəʊ bɪz $ 'ʃoʊ bɪz/ noun [no plural] informal the industry that deals with providing entertainment for people: *a career in show business*

show·er¹ /'ʃaʊə $ 'ʃaʊɚ/ noun 1 a flow of water that you stand under to wash your whole body: *a bedroom with a private shower* 2 when you wash your body in a shower: *I'm going to have a quick shower before dinner.* 3 a short period of rain: *It will be mainly sunny with a few showers.* 4 AmE a party at which people give presents to a woman who is going to get married or have a baby

shower² verb to wash your body by having a shower: *He showered and dressed quickly.*

show·er·y /'ʃaʊəri/ adjective showery weather has a lot of short periods of rain: *Tomorrow will be brighter but showery.*

shown the past participle of SHOW¹

show-off /'. ./ noun someone who tries to show how clever, funny etc they are in order to make other people admire them

show·room /'ʃəʊruːm $ 'ʃoʊrum/ noun a large room where you can look at large goods such as cars or electrical goods that are for sale: *Everything in the car showroom was too expensive for us.*

shrank the past tense of SHRINK

shred¹ /ʃred/ noun a small thin piece that has been torn from something: *She picked up his letter and tore it to shreds.*

shred² verb shredded, shredding to cut or tear something into small pieces: *The burger comes with shredded lettuce.*

shrewd /ʃruːd/ adjective good at understanding people or situations and knowing how to get what you want from them: *a shrewd politician*

S

shriek /ʃriːk/ *verb written* to make a sudden high cry, especially because you are afraid or amused: *"Go away!" she shrieked.*
– **shriek** *noun*: *We heard shrieks of laughter.*

shrill /ʃrɪl/ *adjective* a shrill sound is very high and unpleasant: *She was a small thin woman with a shrill voice.*

shrimp /ʃrɪmp/ *noun* a small pink sea animal that you can eat, with ten legs and a shell

shrine /ʃraɪn/ *noun* a holy place that people visit: *This temple is a shrine for Sikhs.*

shrink

shrink /ʃrɪŋk/ *verb* **shrank** /ʃræŋk/ **shrunk** /ʃrʌŋk/
to become smaller: *My dress shrank when I washed it.*

shriv·el /ˈʃrɪvəl/ *verb* **shrivelled, shrivelling** *BrE*, **shriveled, shriveling** *AmE* also **shrivel up** if something shrivels, it gets smaller and its surface becomes covered with lines because it is dry or old: *A lot of the plants had shrivelled up in the heat.*

shroud¹ /ʃraʊd/ *noun* a cloth that is wrapped around a dead person's body before it is buried

shroud² *verb* **be shrouded in** *written* if something is shrouded in mist or smoke, it is covered and hidden by the mist or smoke: *It was early morning and the hills were shrouded in mist.*

shrub /ʃrʌb/ *noun* a plant that is smaller than a tree and has a lot of branches coming up from the ground

shrug /ʃrʌɡ/ *verb* **shrugged, shrugging** to raise your shoulders to show that you do not know some thing or do not care about it: *"Sorry, I've no idea," she said, shrugging.*

shrug

– **shrug** *noun*: *Luke gave a casual shrug.*

shrunk the past participle of SHRINK

shud·der /ˈʃʌdə $ ˈʃʌdɚ/ *verb* to shake because you dislike something very much or are afraid of it: *The memory of that day makes me shudder.*

shuf·fle /ˈʃʌfəl/ *verb* **1** to walk in a slow or lazy way without lifting your feet off the ground: *Grandad got up and shuffled across the room.* **2** to mix playing cards into a different order before playing a game: *Shall I shuffle?*

shut¹ /ʃʌt/ *verb, past tense and past participle* **shut, shutting**
1 to close something ⇨ opposite OPEN² (1): *Will you shut the door please? | I shut my eyes and went to sleep.*
2 to become closed ⇨ opposite OPEN² (2): *She let the gate shut behind her.*
3 if a shop, bank, or other public place shuts, it is not available for people to use ⇨ opposite OPEN² (3) ⇨ same meaning CLOSE¹ (2): *What time do the shops shut? | The banks here shut for two hours at lunchtime.*

PHRASE
shut your mouth, shut your face! *spoken* used to tell someone rudely and angrily to stop talking

PHRASAL VERBS
shut down
if a company or factory shuts down, it stops doing any work: *The company shuts down for a week at Christmas.*
shut up *informal*
1 to stop talking: *Will you please shut up and listen!*
2 **shut someone up** to make someone stop talking: *We gave Joey some sweets to shut him up.*

shut² *adjective*
closed ⇨ opposite OPEN¹ (1): *The gate was shut but not locked.*

shut·ter /ˈʃʌtə $ ˈʃʌtɚ/ *noun* shutters are wooden or metal covers that you can close in front of a window

shut·tle /ˈʃʌtl/ *noun* **1** a plane, bus, or train that makes regular short trips between two places: *I arrived at Heathrow and caught the shuttle to Gatwick.* **2** a vehicle that can travel into space and return to Earth more than once: *They have*

had to delay the launch of the space
shuttle.

shy /ʃaɪ/ adjective someone who is shy is
nervous and finds it difficult to talk to
other people: a shy child | Come on,
don't be shy.
 —**shyly** adverb: Shyly she told me her
name.
 —**shyness** noun [no plural]: He suffers from
terrible shyness.

sib·ling /ˈsɪblɪŋ/ noun formal your
brother or sister

sick /sɪk/ adjective

1 someone who is sick is ill or has a
disease: I couldn't go to school be-
cause I was sick. | He looks after his
sick mother.
2 interested in things that are strange,
cruel, and unpleasant: Whoever
made that movie must be sick. |
Everyone was telling sick jokes
about the murder.

PHRASES
be sick BrE if you are sick, food
comes up from your stomach
through your mouth ⇨ same meaning THROW UP, VOMIT: The baby has
been sick on me.
feel sick to feel as if you are going to
be sick: She ate so much pizza she
felt sick.
be sick of something to be annoyed about a situation that has
happened too often or for too long: I
am absolutely sick of you being
late every day.
make someone sick if something
makes you sick, it makes you very
angry: It makes me sick to hear him
lying like that.

sick·ly /ˈsɪkli/ adjective **sicklier, sickli-
est** someone who is sickly is weak and
often ill: She was a pale sickly woman.

sick·ness /ˈsɪknəs/ noun [no plural] when
people are ill: He misses a lot of school
because of sickness.

side¹ /saɪd/ noun

GRAMMAR
the side of something

1 one half of something: She has a
scar on the left side of her face. | I
realized I was driving on the wrong
side of the road. | He grew up on the
city's west side.
2 one surface of something: Write on

both sides of the paper. | A voice
came from the other side of the
fence. | A cube has six sides.
3 a surface of something that is not
the front, back, top, or bottom: The
company name is painted on the
side of the truck. | I keep a glass of
water by the side of my bed.
4 the side of the road is the part at the
edge, furthest from the middle: She
stopped her car at the side of the
road.
5 one part of a situation or argument,
which may be different to other
parts: I need to hear her side of the
story. | I saw a different side to his
character that day.
6 one person, group, or team in a fight
or sports game: They were on the
winning side in the war. | England
were the first side to score a goal.
7 one side of your family is the grandparents and other people that are related to either your mother or your
father: I am half Irish on my
mother's side.

PHRASES
**at someone's side, by someone's
side** with someone, especially when
they need you to help them: My boyfriend was by my side the whole
time I was sick.
side by side next to each other: We
sat side by side.
from side to side from left to right
and right to left many times: The bird
kept moving its head from side to
side.
be on someone's side to support
someone in an argument, fight, or
war: Mom is always on my side.
take sides to say that you support
one person or group in an argument:
A teacher cannot take sides in a
fight between students.

side² adjective

1 on the side of something: Students
come into school by the side entrance.
2 side street, side road a small street
or road that is near a main street:
The restaurant is on a little side
road.

side³ verb **side with someone** to support one person or group of people in an

argument or fight: *Dad always sides with Mum when we argue.*

side·board /'saɪdbɔːd $ 'saɪdbɔrd/ *noun* **1** a long low piece of furniture in which you keep plates and glasses **2 sideboards** *BrE* sideburns

side·burns /'saɪdbɜːnz $ 'saɪdbɜ·nz/ also **sideboards** *BrE*, *noun* hair that grows down the sides of a man's face ⇨ *see picture on page 353*

side-effect /'. .,./ *noun* a bad effect that a drug has on your body, while you are using it to cure an illness: *Antibiotics can have serious side-effects.*

side·track /'saɪdtræk/ *verb* if you are sidetracked, you become interested in something that is not important and stop doing or thinking about something that is important: *I was determined to get an answer and I refused to be sidetracked.*

side·walk /'saɪdwɔːk/ the American word for PAVEMENT

side·ways /'saɪdweɪz/ *adjective* towards one side: *I stepped sideways to let the bicycle pass.*

siege /siːdʒ/ *noun* when an army surrounds a place and stops any food, weapons etc from getting into it: *The city was under siege for six months.* | *the siege of Sarajevo*

sieve /sɪv/ *noun* a piece of kitchen equipment that looks like a net, and that you use for separating solid food from liquid or small pieces of food from larger pieces: *I put the soup through a sieve.*

sift /sɪft/ *verb* to put flour, sugar etc through a sieve in order to remove any large pieces

sigh /saɪ/ *verb* to breathe out loudly because you are tired, annoyed or bored: *"I'll never finish this essay," she sighed.* –**sigh** *noun*: *He sat down with a sigh of relief.*

sight /saɪt/ *noun*

GRAMMAR
the sight of something/someone
1 [no plural] when you see something: *I hate **the sight of** blood.* | *She turned pale **at the sight of** (=when she saw) Harry.*
2 [no plural] the ability to see: *He is 85 and losing his sight.*
3 **sights** places that are interesting to see, and which many people visit:

*Will you have time to **see the sights** while you are in London?*

PHRASES
catch sight of someone/something to suddenly see someone or something: *I **caught sight of** Chris getting on a bus.*
in sight a) if something is in sight, you can see it: *I looked for Terry, but he was nowhere **in sight**.* **b)** going to happen soon: *The end of the exams is **in sight**.*
out of sight if something is out of sight, you cannot see it: *We parked the car behind the house, **out of sight**.*

sight·ing /'saɪtɪŋ/ *noun* when someone sees something unusual or completely new: *This was the first sighting of this bird in Britain.*

sight·see·ing /'saɪt,siːɪŋ/ *noun* [no plural] visiting famous or interesting places, especially as a tourist: *In the afternoon we all went sightseeing round the town.*

sign¹ /saɪn/ *noun*

GRAMMAR
a sign of something
a sign that
1 something with words or pictures on it that gives you information or tells you which way to go: *There was a 'No Entry' sign on the door.* | *We followed the signs for Birmingham.*
2 a fact that shows that something is true or is starting to happen: *Headaches can be **a sign of** stress.* | *She came out smiling, which was **a good sign**.*
3 a picture or shape that has a particular meaning: *a plus sign* | *dollar signs*

sign² *verb*
1 to write your name on a letter or document: *She signed the letter 'Dr Kay Hill'.* | *I showed them the contract and they all signed.*
2 to agree to give someone a job in a sports team or musical group: *Liverpool have signed a new player.*

PHRASAL VERB
sign up
1 sign someone up to agree to give someone a job in a sports team or musical group: *He **was signed up***

by the Bulls as soon as he finished college.
2 sign up to put your name on a list because you want to do something: *You should **sign up for** a computer course.*

sig·nal[1] /'sɪgnəl/ *noun* **1** a movement or sound which gives information or tells someone to do something: *Don't move until you hear the signal.* **2** a light that tells a train driver whether to go or stop: *The train stopped at a signal.*

signal[2] *verb* **signalled, signalling** *BrE*, **signaled, signaling** *AmE* **1** to move your hand or head as a way of telling someone something: *I put up my hand to signal that I knew the answer.* | *I looked at Dad, but he signalled to me to be quiet.* **2** the American word for IN-DICATE (3)

sig·na·ture /'sɪgnətʃə $ 'sɪgnətʃɚ/ *noun* your usual way of writing your name, for example on a cheque: *His signature was on the letter.*

sig·nif·i·cance /sɪg'nɪfɪkəns/ *noun [no plural]* the importance or meaning of something: *Could you explain the significance of this ceremony?*

sig·nif·i·cant /sɪg'nɪfɪkənt/ *adjective* **1** important ⇨ *opposite* INSIGNIFICANT: *This is a very significant change.* **2** a significant amount is a large amount: *She received a significant pay increase.*
–**significantly** *adverb*: *Exam results were significantly better this year.*

sig·ni·fy /'sɪgnəfaɪ/ *verb formal* **signified, signifies** to be a sign of something: *Losing weight can signify a variety of health problems.*

sign lan·guage /'. ,../ *noun* a language for people who cannot hear, where you move your hands instead of using words

sign·post[1] /'saɪnpəʊst $ 'saɪnpoʊst/ *noun* a sign at the side of the road that shows people which way to go and how far it is to a place

signpost[2] *verb BrE* **be signposted** if a place is signposted, there are signs that show you how to get there: *The castle is signposted off the main road.*

Sikh /siːk/ *noun* someone who belongs to an Indian religious group
–**Sikh** *adjective*: *a Sikh temple*

si·lence /'saɪləns/ *noun* **1** when there is no sound: *There was complete silence*

in the house. **2 in silence** without talking or making a noise: *The class sat in silence.*

si·lent /'saɪlənt/ *adjective* if a person is silent, they do not say anything or make any sound. If a place is silent, there is no sound there: *I asked her what happened but she was silent.* | *I came home to a silent, empty house.* | *The crowd **fell silent** (=became silent) as he began to speak.*
–**silently** *adverb*: *He walked silently across the grass.*

sil·hou·ette /ˌsɪlu'et/ *noun* a dark shape or shadow on a light background: *The silhouette of a man appeared on the wall.*

sil·i·con /'sɪlɪkən/ *noun [no plural]* a chemical substance that is used for making glass, bricks, and computer parts: *All computers have silicon chips.*

silk /sɪlk/ *noun [no plural]* very soft material that is made from the threads produced by an insect and used for making clothes: *a silk dress*

silk·y /'sɪlki/ *adjective* **silkier, silkiest** soft and smooth: *silky hair*

sil·ly /'sɪli/ *adjective* **sillier, silliest** stupid and not sensible: *That was a silly thing to do!*

sil·ver[1] /'sɪlvə $ 'sɪlvɚ/ *noun [no plural]* a valuable shiny white metal that is used for making jewellery, coins etc

silver[2] *adjective* made of silver or the colour of silver: *a silver ring*

sim·i·lar /'sɪmələ $ 'sɪmələr/ *adjective*

> **GRAMMAR**
> **similar to something/someone**
> things that are similar are almost the same: *Martine and her sister **look** very **similar**.* | *Your taste in music is **similar to** mine.*

sim·i·lar·i·ty /ˌsɪmə'lærəti/ *noun, plural* **similarities** if there is a similarity between two things, they are the same in some way: *There are some similarities between the two towns.*

sim·mer /'sɪmə $ 'sɪmɚ/ *verb* if food that you are cooking simmers, it boils very gently: *Let the sauce simmer for about ten minutes.*

S

sim·ple /'sɪmpəl/ *adjective*
1 not difficult or complicated: *She explained her work in simple language.* | *Using the software is very simple.*
2 plain and ordinary, without a lot of special things: *I made a simple tomato soup.*
3 **simple past, simple present, simple future** a tense of a verb in English that is formed without using a PARTICIPLE that ends in '-ing': *'Went' is the **simple past** of 'go'.*

sim·pli·fy /'sɪmpləfaɪ/ *verb* **simplified, simplifies** to make something easier to do or understand: *The college hopes to simplify its procedure for admissions.*

sim·ply /'sɪmpli/ *adverb* **1** used to emphasize what you are saying: *We simply can't afford a holiday this year.* | *It was simply wonderful!* **2** in a way that is easy to understand: *I'll try to explain it more simply.* **3** in a plain way, without any decoration: *She was dressed simply, in a white blouse and black skirt.*

sim·u·late /'sɪmjəleɪt/ *verb* to do something that seems real, but is not: *The machine simulates conditions in space.*

sim·u·la·tion /ˌsɪmjə'leɪʃən/ *noun* an activity that is not real, but looks or feels like it is: *The computer simulation game lets you drive 100 miles per hour.*

sim·ul·ta·ne·ous /ˌsɪməl'teɪniəs $ ˌsaɪməl'teɪniəs/ *adjective* happening at exactly the same time as something else: *Two simultaneous explosions rocked the city centre.*
−**simultaneously** *adverb*: *They both spoke simultaneously.*

sin /sɪn/ *noun* something that breaks a religious law: *They believe that jealousy is a sin.*

since /sɪns/ *preposition, adverb*
use **since** with a past date, time, or event to say how long something has been happening: *We've lived in London since 1992* (=we began living in London in 1992, and we still live there now).| *I haven't eaten anything since yesterday* (=yesterday is the last time I ate). | *Since he arrived in England, Philippe has been staying with friends.* | *Since leaving*

college, *Rodrigo has worked in a burger bar.* | *"How long is it since you visited Spain?" "It's nearly 10 years since I was here."* ⇨ see usage note at AGO

sin·cere /sɪn'sɪə $ sɪn'sɪr/ *adjective* someone who is sincere is honest and means what they say ⇨ *opposite* INSINCERE: *He said he loved the painting, but he didn't seem sincere.* | *Please accept my sincere apologies.*

sin·cere·ly /sɪn'sɪəli $ sɪn'sɪrli/ *adverb*
1 used to emphasize that you really mean what you are saying: *I do sincerely hope that things improve for Sammy.*
2 **Yours sincerely** *BrE* something you write at the end of a formal letter before you sign your name; **Sincerely (yours)** *AmE*

sing /sɪŋ/ *verb* **sang** /sæŋ/ **sung** /sʌŋ/
to produce musical sounds with your voice: *a mother singing to her baby* | *Kerry sings in a band.* | *Will you sing that song again?*
−**singing** *noun* [no plural]: *I heard beautiful singing.*

sing·er /'sɪŋə $ 'sɪŋɚ/ *noun* someone who sings, especially as a job: *a pop singer*

sin·gle¹ /'sɪŋgəl/ *adjective*
1 only one: *Ten thousand people visited the exhibition in a single day.* | *Not one single person* (=no one at all) *offered to help me.*
2 not married or in a serious relationship: *Brad's gorgeous – is he single?*
3 intended to be used by only one person: *a single bed*
4 *BrE* a single ticket is for a trip to a place but not back again ⇨ *same meaning* ONE-WAY (2)

PHRASE
every single used to emphasize that you are talking about every person or thing: *She phones him **every single day**.* | *I kept **every single** letter she sent me.*

single² *noun* **1** a musical record, CD etc with only one or two songs on it: *Have you heard the new Madonna single?* **2** *BrE* a ticket to travel to a place but not back again: *a single to London*

single³ verb single someone/something out to choose one person or thing from a group because they are different to the others: *Our college was singled out for praise in a report.*

single file /ˌ.. ˈ./ noun [no plural] in a line with one person behind the other: *Please walk in single file.*

single-hand·ed·ly /ˌ.. ˈ.../ also **single-hand·ed** /ˌ.. ˈ../ adverb if you do something difficult single-handedly, you do it alone, without any help: *I single-handedly moved all the furniture out of the room.*

single-mind·ed /ˌ.. ˈ../ adjective very determined to achieve one particular thing: *Clare has always been very single-minded about her career.*

single par·ent /ˌ.. ˈ../ noun a mother or father who looks after their children alone, without the other parent

sin·gly /ˈsɪŋgli/ adverb separately or one at a time: *You can buy stamps singly or in books of ten.*

sin·gu·lar¹ /ˈsɪŋgjələ $ˈsɪŋgjəlɚ/ adjective the singular form of a word is the form you use when you are talking or writing about one person or thing

singular² noun the singular the form of a word that you use when you are talking or writing about one person or thing

sin·is·ter /ˈsɪnɪstə $ˈsɪnɪstɚ/ adjective unpleasant or frightening in a way that seems bad or evil: *She moved toward me with a sinister laugh.*

sink¹ /sɪŋk/ verb, past tense **sank** /sæŋk/ or **sunk** /sʌŋk/ past participle **sunk**

1 to go down below the surface of water: *His bike fell in the river and sank.* | *The boat sank to the bottom of the sea.* ⇨ see picture at FLOAT¹

2 to make something go down below the surface of water: *They sank fifteen enemy ships.*

PHRASE

your heart sinks *My heart sank* (=I felt suddenly sad, worried, or annoyed) *when I saw that Mum was waiting for me.*

PHRASAL VERB

sink in

informal if information sinks in, you finally understand it and realize the effect it will have: *The news of my* ▼ *father's death was finally beginning to sink in.*

sink² noun

the thing in a kitchen or bathroom that you fill with water to wash dishes or wash your hands: *He put the dirty dishes in the sink.*

sink·ing /ˈsɪŋkɪŋ/ adjective **a sinking feeling** a feeling you have when you realize that something bad is going to happen: *I opened the letter with a sinking feeling.*

sip /sɪp/ verb **sipped**, **sipping** to drink something slowly, taking only small amounts into your mouth: *Maria sat at the table, sipping her coffee.*

– **sip** noun: *Can I have a sip of your wine?*

si·phon¹ or **syphon** /ˈsaɪfən/ noun a tube that you use to take liquid out of a container

siphon² or **syphon** verb to remove liquid from a container using a siphon: *She caught him siphoning petrol out of her car.*

sir /sə; strong sɜː $sɚ/ noun **1** spoken a polite way of speaking to a man, for example a customer in a shop: *Can I help you, sir?* **2 Dear Sir** used at the beginning of a formal letter to a man when you do not know his name

si·ren /ˈsaɪərən $ˈsaɪrən/ noun a machine in police cars, fire engines etc which makes a very loud noise to warn people that they are coming: *We heard an ambulance siren.*

siren

sis·ter /ˈsɪstə $ˈsɪstɚ/ noun

1 a girl or woman who has the same parents as you: *I share a bedroom with my sister.* | *Do you get on well with your big sister* (=older sister)? | *He's always fighting with his little sister* (=younger sister).

2 BrE a nurse who is in charge of a group of patients in a hospital: *The sister told me to lie down.*

sister-in-law /ˈ... ˌ../ noun **1** the sister of your husband or wife **2** the wife of your brother

sit /sɪt/ verb, past tense and past participle **sat** /sæt/ **sitting**

> **GRAMMAR**
> **sit on something**
> **sit down**

1 if you are sitting somewhere, you are resting there with your weight on your bottom: *The children were all **sitting on** the floor.* | *Who is that **sitting next to** Mary?* | *He can't **sit still** (=sit and not move) for a minute.*
2 also **sit down** to lower yourself down so that you are sitting: *She walked over and sat on my desk.* | *Come in Mr Fox and **sit down**.*
3 if something is sitting somewhere, it is in that place: *The letters were still **sitting on** the table.*
4 BrE to do an examination: *You will be ready to **sit the exam** in June.*

> **PHRASAL VERBS**

sit around also **sit about** BrE to sit and not do very much: *I spent the whole day **sitting around** reading magazines.*

sit in on
sit in on something to watch a meeting or activity but not get involved in it: *Sometimes the school principal **sits in on** lessons.*

sit through
sit through something to stay until the end of something that is long or boring: *I can't **sit through** that awful film again.*

sit up
to move to a sitting position after you have been lying down: *He **sat up** and got out of bed.*

sit·com /'sɪtkɒm $ 'sɪtkɑm/ noun a funny television programme that is shown regularly and has the same characters but a different story each time

site /saɪt/ noun 1 a piece of land where buildings are being built: *Children must stay off the building site.* 2 a place where something important happened in the past: *the site of the battle*

sitting room /'.. ˌ./ a British word for LIVING ROOM

sit·u·at·ed /'sɪtʃueɪtɪd/ adjective be situated formal to be in a particular place: *The house is situated on a cliff overlooking the sea.*

sit·u·a·tion /ˌsɪtʃu'eɪʃən/ noun
the things that are happening at a particular time and place: *We are **in** a very difficult **situation**.* | *I think the situation is improving.*

sit-ups /'. ./ plural noun an exercise in which you lie down and then lift the top part of your body towards your feet while keeping your legs flat on the floor: *He does sit-ups every morning.*

six /sɪks/ number 6

six·teen /ˌsɪk'stiːn/ number 16
– sixteenth number

sixth¹ /sɪksθ/ number 1 6th 2 one of the six equal parts of something; 1/6

sixth form /'. ./ noun the classes for young people at school in Britain between the ages of 16 and 18: *You don't have to wear school uniform when you are in the sixth form.*

six·ty /'sɪksti/ number, plural **sixties** 1 the number 60 2 the sixties the years from 1960 to 1969 3 be in your sixties to be aged between 60 and 69
– sixtieth number

size /saɪz/ noun

> **GRAMMAR**
> **the size of something**

1 how big or small something is: *Nigel and I are about **the same size**.* | *The animal was **the size of** a large cat.* | *People's bodies vary **in size** and shape.*
2 a number, letter etc that shows how big clothes and shoes are: *What **size** shoes do you **take**?* | *These shoes are size 6.* | *Do you have this shirt in a bigger size?*

siz·zle /'sɪzəl/ verb to make the sound of food cooking in oil: *The sausages were sizzling in the pan.* ⇨ see picture on page 350

skate¹ /skeɪt/ noun 1 an ICE SKATE 2 a ROLLER SKATE

skate² verb to move around on skates: *Can you skate?* | *She skated over to him.*

skate·board /'skeɪtbɔːd $ 'skeɪtbɔrd/ noun a board on wheels, that you stand on and ride for fun or sport: *All the kids come here with their skateboards.*

skate·board·ing /'skeɪtˌbɔːdɪŋ 'skeɪtˌbɔrdɪŋ/ noun [no plural] riding on a skateboard: *Skateboarding is very popular at my school.*

skat·ing /'skeɪtɪŋ/ noun [no plural] moving around on skates: *We all love skating.*

skel·e·ton /ˈskelətən/ *noun* the bones of a whole dead person or animal: *the skeleton of a sheep*

skep·ti·cal /ˈskeptɪkəl/ the American spelling of SCEPTICAL

sketch¹ /sketʃ/ *noun, plural* **sketches** a drawing of something that is done quickly and without very many details: *He made a sketch of the building.*

sketch² *verb* to make a drawing of something quickly: *He sketched my face.*

sketch·y /ˈsketʃi/ *adjective* **sketchier, sketchiest** sketchy information does not include a lot of details: *The police could only give us some very sketchy information.*

ski¹ /skiː/ *noun* skis are long narrow pieces of wood or plastic that you fasten to boots so you can move easily on snow: *He put on his skis.*

ski² *verb, past tense and past participle* **skied, skiing** to move over snow on skis: *I've never learnt to ski.*

skid /skɪd/ *verb* **skidded, skidding** if a vehicle skids, it suddenly slides sideways and you cannot control it: *The truck skidded on the ice and crashed.*
– **skid** *noun*: *He fell off his bike after a skid.*

ski·ing /ˈskiː-ɪŋ/ *noun* [no plural] the sport of moving over snow on skis: *We went skiing in Switzerland.* ⇨ *see picture on page 351*

skil·ful *BrE*, **skillful** *AmE* /ˈskɪlfəl/ *adjective* **1** someone who is skilful is able to do something very well: *There are some very skilful players in our team.* **2** very good and clever: *It was a skilful speech.*
– **skilfully** *adverb*

skill /skɪl/ *noun*

> **GRAMMAR**
> **skill in doing something**
> **skill at something**
> **skill as something**
> an ability to do something well, especially because you have practised it: *His **skill in** dealing with people makes him a good manager.* | *It takes great **skill** to score goals like that.* | *I was impressed by her **skill at** tennis.* | *his **skill as** a sailor* | *This is an opportunity for you to **learn** new skills.* | *You need to **improve** your typing **skills**.*

skilled /skɪld/ *adjective* **1** a skilled person has the training and experience that is necessary to do a particular job: *a highly skilled cameraman* **2** skilled work needs special training to do it

skill·ful /ˈskɪlfəl/ the American spelling of SKILFUL

skim /skɪm/ *verb* **skimmed, skimming** to read something very quickly and not very carefully: *I only had time to skim through the newspaper.*

skimmed milk *BrE*, **skim milk** *AmE* /ˌ. ˈ./ *noun* [no plural] milk with most of the fat removed from it

skin¹ /skɪn/ *noun*

1 the outside part of your body: *That jumper makes my skin itch.* | *Babies have such lovely soft skin.* | *He's got skin cancer.*
2 the outside part of a fruit, that you take off before you eat it: *a banana skin*

skin² *verb* **skinned, skinning** to remove the skin from an animal

skin·ny /ˈskɪni/ *adjective* **skinnier, skinniest** a skinny person is too thin ⇨ *see usage note at* THIN

skip¹ /skɪp/ *verb* **skipped, skipping**
1 to jump up and down over a rope that you keep turning over your head and under your feet **2** to run with a little jump on each step: *The children skipped along the path.* ⇨ *see picture on page 340*

skip

skip² *noun* *BrE* a large open metal container in which you can put large heavy things that you do not want any more

skirt /skɜːt $skɚt/ *noun*
a piece of clothing for girls and women that fits around the waist and hangs down like a dress: *She wore a white blouse and a blue skirt.* ⇨ *see picture on page 352*

skive /skaɪv/ also **skive off** *BrE, verb informal* to not go to school or work when you should: *The boys skived off school and went down to the shops.*

skull

skull /skʌl/ *noun* the bones which form a person's or animal's head

sky /skaɪ/ *noun* [no plural]
the space above the earth where the sun and clouds are: *The sky is blue and the sun is shining.* | *There wasn't a cloud in the sky.*

sky·scrap·er /'skaɪˌskreɪpə $ 'skaɪˌskreɪpɚ/ *noun* a very tall building in a city ➪ *see picture on page 343*

slab /slæb/ *noun* a thick flat piece of something: *a big slab of chocolate*

slack /slæk/ *adjective* not pulled or fastened tightly: *These trousers are a bit slack at the waist.* ➪ *see picture at* TAUT

slam /slæm/ *verb* **slammed, slamming** to shut a door or gate quickly and loudly, usually because you are angry: *Milly ran up to her bedroom and slammed the door behind her.*
–slam *noun*: *She shut the door with a slam.*

slang /slæŋ/ *noun* [no plural] very informal words and expressions that are not considered to be part of the ordinary language

slant /slɑːnt $ slænt/ *verb* to slope in a particular direction: *His handwriting slants backwards.*

slap /slæp/ *verb* **slapped, slapping** to hit someone with the flat part of your hand: *She was so angry that she slapped his face.* ➪ *see picture on page 341*
–slap *noun*: *She gave the child a slap on the leg.*

slap-up /'. ./ *adjective* **slap-up meal, slap-up dinner** *BrE informal* a big and good meal

slash /slæʃ/ *verb* to cut something in a violent way, making a long deep cut: *A gang of boys slashed our tyres.*

slate /sleɪt/ *noun* [no plural] a type of dark grey rock, or a thin piece of this rock that is used for covering roofs

slaugh·ter /'slɔːtə $ 'slɔːtɚ/ *verb* **1** to kill an animal for its meat **2** to kill a lot of people in a violent way: *Enemy soldiers slaughtered thousands of men, women and children.*
–slaughter *noun* [no plural]: *the slaughter of innocent women and children*

slaugh·ter·house /'slɔːtəhaʊs $ 'slɔːtɚˌhaʊs/ *noun* a building where animals are killed for their meat

slave¹ /sleɪv/ *noun* someone who is owned by another person and must work for them without any pay: *Slaves were used to build the pyramids.*

slave² *verb informal* to work very hard: *I've been slaving away at this essay all morning.*

sla·ve·ry /'sleɪvəri/ *noun* [no plural] using people as slaves: *The United States ended slavery after the Civil War.*

sledge /sledʒ/ also **sled** /sled/ *noun* a vehicle for travelling on snow, or sliding down snow for fun

sledge ham·mer /'. ˌ../ *noun* a large heavy hammer

sleek /sliːk/ *adjective* sleek hair or fur is smooth and shiny

sleep¹ /sliːp/ *verb*, *past tense and past participle* **slept** /slept/
if you are sleeping, you are resting with your eyes closed and your mind and body are not active: *Tom is sleeping – don't wake him.* | *Did you sleep well last night?* | *I sometimes sleep on the floor.*

PHRASE

not sleep a wink *informal* to be unable to sleep at all: *I didn't sleep a wink last night with that party going on next door.*

sleep rough *BrE* to sleep outdoors because you have no home: *Many young people sleep rough in London.*

PHRASAL VERBS

sleep in
to sleep until later than your usual time in the morning: *I slept in and was late for school.*

sleep through
sleep through something to continue to sleep while things are happening around you: *How did you sleep through all that noise?*

sleep together
if two people are sleeping together, they are having a sexual relationship with each other but are not married

sleep with
sleep with someone to have sex with someone

USAGE
Do not use the verb **sleep** to talk about starting to sleep. Use **go to sleep** or **fall**

asleep: *What time do you usually go to sleep?* | *I fell asleep while I was watching television.*

sleep² *noun* [no plural]

when you are sleeping: *Are you getting plenty of sleep?* | *I'm going to have a little sleep.* | *I closed my eyes and fell into a deep sleep.*

PHRASES

go to sleep to start sleeping: *I went to sleep in the chair.*

in your sleep if you do something in your sleep, you do it when you are sleeping: *Sometimes he talks in his sleep.*

sleeping bag /'.. ,./ *noun* a large warm bag that you sleep in when you are camping

sleep·less /'sli:pləs/ *adjective* **a sleepless night** a night when you cannot sleep, for example because you are worried

sleep·y /'sli:pi/ *adjective* **sleepier, sleepiest** tired and ready to sleep: *I felt so sleepy that I went straight to bed.*

sleet /sli:t/ *noun* [no plural] a mixture of rain and snow

sleeve /sli:v/ *noun* the part of a piece of clothing that covers your arm ⇨ see picture on page 352

sleeve·less /'sli:vləs/ *adjective* without sleeves: *a sleeveless shirt*

slen·der /'slendə $ 'slendɚ/ *adjective* thin in an attractive way: *a tall slender girl* ⇨ see usage note at THIN

slept the past tense and past participle of SLEEP¹

slice¹ /slaɪs/ *noun*

GRAMMAR
a slice of something
a thin piece of bread, meat etc that you cut from a larger piece: *Would you like a slice of pizza?* | *Cut the bread in thin slices.*

slice² *verb*

GRAMMAR
slice something off
slice through something
1 also **slice up** to cut meat, bread etc into thin pieces: *David sliced the turkey.* | *Did you slice up all the ham?* ⇨ see picture on page 344

2 to cut through something quickly and easily: *They sliced off his head with a sword.* | *a knife that slices through metal*

slid the past tense and past participle of SLIDE¹

slide¹ /slaɪd/ *verb, past tense and past participle* **slid** /slɪd/
1 to move smoothly: *Ducks were sliding about on the frozen pond.*
2 to move something smoothly: *She slid my drink along the bar.* | *I slid the letter into my bag.*

slide² *noun* 1 a photograph in a frame. You shine light through it to show the photograph on a screen: *Mr Hall showed us some slides of his trip.* 2 a long metal slope with steps at one end, that children can climb up and slide down

slight /slaɪt/ *adjective*

small and not very important: *There's a slight problem.* | *He had only slight wounds.*

slight·ly /'slaɪtli/ *adverb*

a little, but not very much: *I am slightly annoyed about this.* | *"Does it hurt?" "Slightly."*

slim¹ /slɪm/ *adjective* **slimmer, slimmest** thin in an attractive way: *a slim pretty girl* ⇨ see picture on page 353 ⇨ see usage note at THIN

slim² *verb* **slimmed, slimming** if you are slimming, you are trying to become thinner by eating less: *I'd better not have an ice-cream – I'm slimming.*

slime /slaɪm/ *noun* [no plural] any thick sticky liquid that looks or smells unpleasant: *The sink was covered in slime.*

slim·y /'slaɪmi/ *adjective* **slimier, slimiest** covered with slime: *a slimy dead fish*

sling¹ /slɪŋ/ *verb informal, past tense and past participle* **slung** /slʌŋ/ to throw or put something somewhere carelessly: *Don't just sling your jacket on the sofa – hang it up!*

sling² *noun* a piece of cloth that you put under your arm and then tie around your neck in order to support your arm or hand when it is injured

S

slip¹ /slɪp/ *verb* **slipped, slipping**

GRAMMAR
slip through/on etc something
slip something into/through etc
something

1 if you slip, your feet move accidentally and you fall: *Be careful not to slip – the floor is wet.* ⇨ see picture on page 340
2 to go somewhere quickly and quietly: *She must have **slipped out through** the back door.*
3 to put something somewhere quietly or secretly: *He **slipped** a sleeping pill **into** her drink.*
4 if something slips, it drops out of your hand or it moves accidentally: *My cup slipped and dropped on the floor.*

PHRASES
slip your mind *spoken* if something slips your mind, you forget about it: *She asked me to phone you, but it **slipped** my **mind**.*
let something slip *informal* to say something that is supposed to be a secret without intending to: *Mary **let it slip** about John's surprise party.*

PHRASAL VERB
slip into
slip into something *informal* to put on a piece of clothing quickly and easily: *She **slipped into** her pyjamas.*
slip off
slip something off *informal* to take off a piece of clothing quickly and easily: *Just **slip off** your jacket.*
slip on
slip something on *informal* to put on a piece of clothing, quickly and easily: *Jean got out of bed and **slipped on** her dressing gown.*
slip out
informal if something slips out, you say it without intending to: *Before she could stop herself, the words had **slipped out**.*

slip² *noun* **1** a small piece of paper: *She wrote the number on a slip of paper.* **2** a small mistake: *You made a few slips in your last piece of work.*

slip·per /ˈslɪpə $ˈslɪpɚ/ *noun* a soft shoe that you wear indoors

slip·per·y /ˈslɪpəri/ *adjective* something that is slippery is difficult to walk on or hold because it is wet, oily, or covered in ice: *It had snowed in the night and the roads were very slippery.*

slit¹ /slɪt/ *noun* a long narrow cut or opening: *a long dress with a slit up one side*

slit² *verb, past tense and past participle* **slit, slitting** to make a long narrow cut in something: *I slit open the envelope with a knife.*

slob /slɒb $slɑb/ *noun informal* someone who is lazy, dirty, or untidy

slo·gan /ˈsləʊgən $ˈsloʊgən/ *noun* a short clever phrase that is used in advertising and politics

slope¹ /sləʊp $sloʊp/ *noun* a piece of ground that gradually gets higher or lower: *Go up the slope till you get to the top of the hill.*

slope² *verb* if a road or path slopes down or up, it gradually gets lower or higher: *a garden that slopes down to the river*

slop·py /ˈslɒpi $ˈslɑpi/ *adjective informal* **sloppier, sloppiest** not tidy or careful: *a sloppy piece of work*

slot /slɒt $slɑt/ *noun* a long narrow hole in something, especially one for putting coins in: *Lift the telephone's receiver and put your money in the slot.*

slot ma·chine /ˈ. .ˌ./ *noun* a machine that you put coins into to play a game and try to win money

slouch /slaʊtʃ/ *verb* to stand, sit, or walk in a lazy way, with your shoulders bent forward: *My mother's always telling me not to slouch.*

slow¹ /sləʊ $sloʊ/ *adjective*

1 not moving or happening quickly ⇨ *opposite* FAST¹ (1): *This computer's very slow! | It was quite a slow journey because the roads were very busy. | Jamie's a very slow worker.*
2 a clock that is slow shows a time earlier than the true time ⇨ *opposite* FAST¹ (2): *My watch is two minutes slow.*
3 someone who is slow does not understand things very quickly or easily: *Some of the children in her class are a bit slow.*

slow² also **slow down** *verb* to become slower or make something slower: *The car slowed down and stopped. | It* started to rain, which slowed down the rescue.

slow·ly /'sləuli $'slouli/ adverb
at a slow speed: *I drove slowly into the drive.* | *Can you speak more slowly?*

slow mo·tion /ˌ. '../ noun [no plural] if part of a film or television programme is shown in slow motion, it is shown at a slower speed than the real speed: *Let's look at the end of the race again in slow motion.*

slug /slʌg/ noun a small creature with a soft body that moves very slowly along the ground

slum /slʌm/ noun a house that is in very bad condition, where poor people live

slump /slʌmp/ verb if a price or value slumps, it suddenly becomes less: *House prices slumped last year.*
– **slump** noun: *Many people are now expecting a slump in the economy.*

slung the past tense and past participle of SLING¹

slurp /slɜːp $sləˈp/ verb informal to drink in a noisy way

slush /slʌʃ/ noun [no plural] snow that has partly melted and looks wet and dirty

sly /slaɪ/ adjective someone who is sly tries to get what they want by lying to people or not being completely honest: *He's sly and greedy.*

smack¹ /smæk/ verb to hit someone with the inside part of your hand as a punishment: *I don't agree with smacking children.*
– **smack** noun: *When I was young, teachers were allowed to give you a smack.*

smack² adverb informal exactly in a place: *She was standing smack in the middle of the road.*

small /smɔːl/ adjective
1 not big: *There's a small hole in the roof.* | *A small number of students behaved badly.* | *My mom is smaller than me.* ⇨ *see picture on page 353*
2 not important ⇨ opposite BIG (2): *It's only a small problem.*

small·pox /'smɔːlpɒks $'smɔlpaks/ noun [no plural] a serious disease that killed a lot of people in the past

smart /smɑːt $smɑrt/ adjective
1 intelligent: *John's much smarter*

than his brother. | *Lucy is a smart kid.*
2 if you look smart, you are dressed in a neat and attractive way: *She looked very smart in her new uniform.* | *Alan was dressed in a smart suit.*
– **smartly** adverb: *It's important to dress smartly for interviews.*

smash¹ /smæʃ/ verb to break into a lot of small pieces, or to make something break in this way: *When I dropped the cup it smashed.* | *A stone smashed the car windscreen.*

smash² also **smash hit** /ˌ. './ noun a very successful new song, film, or play: *The film is expected to be a smash hit at the box office.*

smear¹ /smɪə $smɪr/ verb 1 to spread a soft substance on a surface: *Someone had smeared mud on the walls.* 2 be smeared with something to be partly covered with a soft substance, especially in a way that looks unpleasant: *His hands were smeared with blood.*

smear² noun a dirty mark: *There were smears of paint on his face.*

smell¹ /smel/ verb, past tense and past participle **smelled** or **smelt** /smelt/

GRAMMAR
smell like something
smell of something

1 how something smells is what you notice about it, using your nose: *That soup smells delicious!* | *a perfume that **smells like** fresh flowers* | *The room **smelled of** cigarette smoke.*
2 if something smells, it has an unpleasant smell ⇨ same meaning STINK: *Your feet smell!*
3 if you can smell something, you can notice or recognize it with your nose: *I'm sure I **can smell** gas.*
4 if you smell something, you put your nose close to it to discover what kind of smell it has: *Smell this sauce – it's delicious.*

USAGE
Do not use **smell** in the continuous tense. For example, you cannot say: *I am smelling something burning.* Use **can smell** instead: *I can smell something burning.*

smell² noun

GRAMMAR
the smell of something

1 the smell of something is what you notice about it, using your nose: *Some of the flowers have quite a* **strong smell**. | *I love* **the smell of** *clean sheets.*

2 an unpleasant smell: *There's a* **terrible smell** *in the kitchen.* | *What's that* **awful smell**?

3 sense of smell your sense of smell is your ability to notice and recognize smells: *I've got a cold, so my* **sense of smell** *isn't very good.*

smell·y /'smeli/ adjective **smellier**, **smelliest** something that is smelly has a strong unpleasant smell: *This fish is a bit smelly.* | *smelly socks*

smelt a past tense and past participle of SMELL¹

smile¹ /smaɪl/ verb

GRAMMAR
smile at someone

if you smile, the sides of your mouth curve upwards because you are happy: *Come on – smile for the camera!* | *Sue* **smiled at** *the children in a friendly way.* | *"It's lovely to see you again," she smiled.*

smile² noun

when the sides of your mouth curve upwards because you are happy: *"Hello," she said, with a smile.* | *Dan had a big* **smile on his face**.

smirk /smɜːk $ smɚk/ verb to smile in an unpleasant way, as though you are laughing at someone: *The other girls pointed at her and smirked.*

smog /smɒg $ smɑg/ noun [no plural] unhealthy air in cities that is a mixture of smoke, gases, chemicals etc

smoke¹ /sməʊk $ smoʊk/ noun [no plural]

the white or grey gas that comes from something that is burning: *Clouds of smoke* came from the chimney. | *I could smell* **cigarette smoke** *on his clothes.*

smoke² verb to breathe in smoke from a cigarette or pipe: *Are you allowed to smoke at work?* | *a man who smokes 30 cigarettes a day*
–**smoker** noun

smok·ing /'sməʊkɪŋ $ 'smoʊkɪŋ/ noun [no plural] the habit of smoking cigarettes or a pipe: *Smoking is very bad for you.*

smok·y /'sməʊki $ 'smoʊki/ adjective **smokier**, **smokiest** full of smoke: *The room was crowded and smoky.*

smol·der /'sməʊldə $ 'smoʊldɚ/ the American spelling of SMOULDER

smooth¹ /smuːð/ adjective

1 something that is smooth has an even surface: *Your skin* **feels** *so* **smooth**. | *It's a beautiful cat – its fur is so lovely and smooth.* | *Make sure the walls are smooth before you paint them.*

2 a smooth substance has no big pieces in it: *Stir the mixture into a smooth paste.*

3 a smooth movement is graceful and has no sudden changes: *With a smooth turn, he caught the ball.*

smooth² verb to make something flat by moving your hands over it: *He carefully smoothed his hair.*

smooth·ly /'smuːðli/ adverb if something happens smoothly, it happens without any problems: *I hope everything goes smoothly when you move house.*

smoth·er /'smʌðə $ 'smʌðɚ/ verb to kill someone by putting something over their face so that they cannot breathe

smoul·der BrE, **smolder** AmE /'sməʊldə $ 'smoʊldɚ/ verb if a fire is smouldering, it is burning slowly, with smoke but without flames: *The fire was still smouldering when I went to bed.*

smudge¹ /smʌdʒ/ noun a dirty mark made by a pencil mark or ink: *The teacher complained that there were smudges all over my homework.*

smudge

smudge² verb if you smudge ink or paint, it makes a dirty mark

smug /smʌg/ adjective very pleased with yourself, in a way that is annoying to other people: *"I told you that would happen," she said trying not to sound too smug.*

smug·gle /'smʌgəl/ verb to secretly bring something or someone into a country, when it is illegal to do this: *She was accused of smuggling drugs.* | *Some friends smuggled him into the country.*
–**smuggler** noun: *a drug smuggler*

snack /snæk/ noun a small quick meal

snack bar /'. ./ noun a place where you can buy quick meals and drinks

snag /snæg/ noun informal a small difficulty or problem

snail /sneɪl/ noun a small garden creature that has a round shell on its back and moves very slowly

snake /sneɪk/ noun a long thin animal that slides across the ground and sometimes bites people ➪ see picture on page 339

snap¹ /snæp/ verb snapped, snapping
1 if something snaps, it breaks suddenly with a short loud noise: *Just at that moment the branch snapped.* **2** to speak suddenly in an angry way: *"I don't agree at all," she snapped.*

snap² noun **1** a sudden loud noise of something breaking: *The branch broke with a snap.* ➪ see picture on page 350 **2** also **snapshot** informal a photograph: *holiday snapshots*

snap³ adjective **snap decision, snap judgement** a decision or judgement that is made quickly and not very carefully

snarl /snɑːl $ snɑrl/ verb **1** to say something in an angry way: *"Go away!" he snarled.* **2** if an animal snarls, it makes a low angry sound and shows its teeth: *The dog started snarling at me.*
–**snarl** noun

snatch¹ /snætʃ/ verb to take something from someone with a quick sudden movement: *I snatched the letter from him.*

snatch² noun, plural **snatches** a **snatch of conversation** a short part of a conversation that you hear: *I could only hear snatches of their conversation.*

sneak /sniːk/ verb **1** to go somewhere quietly and secretly: *I managed to sneak into her bedroom.* **2** **sneak up on** to move close to someone without them noticing you: *Stop sneaking up on me like that!*

sneak·er /'sniːkə $ 'sniːkɚ/ noun AmE a sports shoe

sneak·ing /'sniːkɪŋ/ adjective **have a sneaking suspicion, have a sneaking feeling** to think that something is true but not feel sure: *I have a sneaking suspicion that she's lying.*

sneak·y /'sniːki/ adjective **sneakier, sneakiest** doing things in a secret and clever but unfair way

sneer /snɪə $ snɪr/ verb to look at someone or speak to them in a way that show you have no respect for them: *She sneers at people who are poor.*

sneeze /sniːz/ 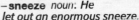 verb when you sneeze, air suddenly comes out of your nose and mouth in a noisy way: *Cats make me sneeze.*
–**sneeze** noun: *He let out an enormous sneeze.*

sniff /snɪf/ verb **1** to breathe in quickly through your nose: *She couldn't stop sniffing and coughing.* **2** to smell something: *I sniffed the milk to see if it was sour.*
–**sniff** noun: *Take a sniff at these socks.*

snig·ger /'snɪgə $ 'snɪgɚ/ BrE
snick·er /'snɪkə $ 'snɪkɚ/ AmE, verb to laugh quietly in an unpleasant way: *What are you sniggering at?*

snip /snɪp/ verb snipped, snipping to cut something with quick small cuts, using scissors: *Snip the corner off the packet.*

snip·pet /'snɪpɪt/ noun informal a small piece of information or news: *I heard snippets of the story from my sister.*

snob /snɒb $ snɑb/ noun someone who thinks they are better than other people

snoo·ker /'snuːkə $ 'snʊkɚ/ noun [no plural] a game in which you hit coloured balls into holes around the edge of a green table, using a long stick called a CUE

snoop /snuːp/ verb to go into someone's room and look at their private things: *I caught Jo snooping around my room.*

snooze /snuːz/ verb informal to sleep for a short time: *Jack was snoozing by the fire.*
– **snooze** noun: *I think I'll have a snooze.*

snore /snɔː $ snɔr/ verb to make a loud noise as you sleep: *Stop snoring!*
– **snore** noun: *Loud snores were coming from the bedroom.*

snort /snɔːt $ snɔrt/ verb to make a loud noise by forcing air out through your nose because you think something is unpleasant or funny: *He read the letter and snorted in disgust.*

snot /snɒt $ snɑt/ noun [no plural] informal an impolite word for the thick liquid in your nose

snout /snaʊt/ noun an animal's long nose: *a pig's snout*

snow¹ /snəʊ $ snoʊ/ noun [no plural]

soft white pieces of frozen water that fall like rain when the weather is very cold: *The fields were **covered with snow**. | Several roads were blocked by **deep snow**.*

snow² verb

when it snows, snow falls from the sky: *Children love it when **it snows**. | Mum, look – **it's snowing**!*

PHRASE

be snowed in, get snowed in to be unable to leave a place because so much snow has fallen: *Maybe we'll **get snowed in** and not be able to go to school.*

snow·ball /'snəʊbɔːl $ 'snoʊbɔl/ noun a small ball made out of snow: *Who threw that snowball?*

snow·board·ing /'snəʊˌbɔːdɪŋ $ 'snoʊˌbɔrdɪŋ/ noun [no plural] a sport in which you move over the snow on a long wide board

snow·flake /'snəʊfleɪk $ 'snoʊfleɪk/ noun one small piece of snow that falls from the sky

snow·man /'snəʊmæn $ 'snoʊmæn/ noun, plural snowmen /-men/ the shape of a person, made out of snow

snow·plough BrE, **snowplow** AmE /'snəʊplaʊ $ 'snoʊplaʊ/ noun a vehicle for removing snow from roads

snow·y /'snəʊi $ 'snoʊi/ adjective snowier, snowiest if it is snowy, there is a lot of snow: *a snowy day*

snub /snʌb/ verb snubbed, snubbing to

deliberately not talk to someone or not be friendly towards them: *She always snubs me when she sees me.*

snug /snʌg/ adjective warm and comfortable: *a snug little bed*

snug·gle /'snʌgəl/ verb to get into a warm comfortable position: *Ed and Sara snuggled up on the sofa.*

so¹ /səʊ $ soʊ/

1 because of something: *I had a headache, so I couldn't go to the party. | It was a lovely day, so we went to the beach.*

2 also **so that** in order to make something possible: *Can you draw a map so that I can find your house? | Mum gave me some money so I could buy Dad a present.*

3 spoken use **so** to start a conversation or start talking about something different: *So, what did you do on your birthday? | So, after arguing for half an hour, we all agreed to go to Gino's Pizza.*

so² adverb

1 use **so** in place of what someone has just asked you, to avoid repeating it: *"Has Jo got a dog?" "I think so."* (=I think Jo has got a dog) *| Are you interested in films? If so* (=if you are interested in films)*, join our Film club. | "Will you be going on holiday this year?" "Yes, I expect so."*

2 too; as well. In negative sentences with this meaning, use neither: *"I'm studying German." "So am I."* (=I'm studying German too) *| "I like heavy metal music." "So do I."* (=I like heavy metal music too) *| "I've spent too much money today." "So have I." | She's fair-haired, and so is her father.*

USAGE

For negative sentences, look at **neither**.

3 use **so** with an adjective or an adverb to make it stronger or to explain why something happened: *The bag was so heavy the handle broke. | He was driving so fast I thought we'd crash. | The English are so polite! | You've been so kind to us during our stay. | The tutor talked so quickly I couldn't understand her.*

PHRASES

and so on used at the end of a list to show that you could add more things of the same type: *Bring a towel, sun-glasses, suntan oil and so on.*

so many, so much used to emphasize the amount, number, or extent of things: *She had so many things to do, she didn't know where to start.* | *You shouldn't drink so much.* | *I didn't realise so many people would turn up.* | *Carrie has changed so much since she went to college.*

or so used with an amount to show that it could be slightly bigger or slightly smaller: *There were 20 or so people in the room.* | *Geoff is staying with us for a week or so.*

so much for something *informal spoken* used to say that something was not as good or successful as you had hoped: *So much for your map-reading – we're lost!*

so ... that used with an adjective or adverb to give a reason or result: *I was so tired that I went straight to bed.* | *We played so badly that we lost 10–nil.*

So what?, So? *informal spoken* used to show that you do not care about what someone has just said: *"You're drunk again." "So what?"* | *"Hurry, we'll be late for college." "So? It's boring there anyway."*

USAGE

In more formal English, use **do so** in place of a statement: *Copying essays from the Internet is not allowed. Any student doing so (=copying essays from the Internet) will be punished.* | *We were asked to leave, and we did so (=we left).*

---

soak /səʊk $ soʊk/ *verb*

GRAMMAR
soak into something
soak through something

1 if you soak something, or let it soak, you cover it with water and leave it for a period of time: *It's best to soak clothes before you wash them.* | *Leave those dishes to soak.*

2 if a liquid soaks something, it makes it completely wet: *The rain has soaked her clothes.* | *The water had soaked through my shoes.* | *The oil slowly soaks into the wood.*

PHRASAL VERB
soak up
soak something up if something

soaks up a liquid, it takes the liquid into itself: *He used some newspaper to soak up the spilt drinks.*

soaked /səʊkt $ soʊkt/ *adjective* very wet: *I'm completely soaked.*

soak·ing /'səʊkɪŋ $ 'soʊkɪŋ/ also **soaking wet** /ˌ.. './ *adjective* completely wet: *The washing's still soaking wet.*

soap /səʊp $ soʊp/ *noun* 1 [no plural] a substance that you use to wash yourself: *a bar of soap* 2 *informal* a soap opera

soap op·e·ra /'. ˌ.../ *noun* a television story about the ordinary lives of a group of people

soap·y /'səʊpi $ 'soʊpi/ *adjective* soapy water has soap in it

soar /sɔː $ sɔr/ *verb* to increase quickly: *The price of houses has soared in recent months.*

sob /sɒb $ sɑb/ *verb* **sobbed, sobbing** to cry with quick noisy breaths: *She just wouldn't stop sobbing.* | *"I want him back," she sobbed.*
– **sob** *noun*: *Melanie couldn't hide her sobs.*

so·ber¹ /'səʊbə $ 'soʊbɚ/ *adjective* not drunk: *I can't tell if he's drunk or sober.*

sober² *verb* **sober up** to stop being drunk: *You need to sober up before you go home.*

so-called /'. ./ *adjective* used when you think that a person or thing is not what people say they are: *That so-called expert has completely ruined my hair.*

soc·cer /'sɒkə $ 'sɑkɚ/ *noun* [no plural] a game in which two teams try to kick a ball into a net at each end of a field;
⇨ *same meaning* FOOTBALL *BrE*

so·cia·ble /'səʊʃəbəl $ 'soʊʃəbəl/ *adjective* someone who is sociable is friendly and enjoys being with people: *a very sociable child*

so·cial /'səʊʃəl $ 'soʊʃəl/ *adjective* 1 related to the way people live in society: *people from different social backgrounds* 2 social activities are the things that you do with other people for enjoyment: *When's the next social event?*
– **socially** *adverb*: *We never go out socially.*

so·cial·is·m /'səʊʃəlɪzəm $ 'soʊʃə-ˌlɪzəm/ *noun* [no plural] a political system that tries to give equal opportunities to

S

all people, and in which many industries are owned by the state

so·cial·ist /'səʊʃəlɪst $'soʊʃəlɪst/ *noun* someone who believes in socialism – **socialist** *adjective*: *a society built on socialist ideas*

so·cial·ize also **socialise** BrE /'səʊ-ʃəlaɪz $'soʊʃəlaɪz/ *verb* to go out with people for enjoyment: *I never socialize with people from work.*

social work /'.. ,./ *noun* [no plural] the job of helping people who are poor or have problems with their families

social work·er /'.. ,../ *noun* someone whose job is doing social work

so·ci·e·ty /sə'saɪəti/ *noun, plural* **soci·eties** all the people who live in the same country and share the same way of life: *We live in a multi-racial society.*

so·ci·ol·o·gy /ˌsəʊsi'ɒlədʒi $ˌsoʊsi-'aládʒi/ *noun* [no plural] the study of the relationships between different groups of people in society

sock /sɒk $sak/ *noun* a piece of clothing that you wear on your foot: *a pair of woollen socks* ⇨ see picture on page 352

sock·et /'sɒkɪt $'sakɪt/ *noun* **1** the place in a wall where you can connect electrical equipment to the supply of electricity **2** the place where one thing fits into another: *You nearly pulled my arm out of its socket!*

so·da /'səʊdə $'soʊdə/ also **soda wa·ter** /'.. ,../ *noun* water that contains BUBBLES, that you mix with other drinks

so·fa /'səʊfə $'soʊfə/ *noun* a comfortable seat that is wide enough for two or three people ⇨ see picture on page 342

soft /sɒft $sɔft/ *adjective*

1 if something is soft, you can press it easily because it is not hard or firm ⇨ opposite HARD[1] (1): *a soft chair | The ground was quite soft. | The biscuits have gone soft.*

2 something that feels soft feels smooth and pleasant when you touch it: *the cat's soft fur | Your skin is lovely and soft. | The wool felt soft against my skin.*

3 soft sounds are quiet: *She spoke in a lovely soft voice.*

soft drink /'. ./ *noun* a cold drink that does not contain alcohol

soft·en /'sɒfən $'sɔfən/ *verb* to become softer: *Your shoes will soften as you wear them.*

soft·ware /'sɒftweə $'sɔft-wer/ *noun* [no plural]
the PROGRAMS (=sets of instructions) that a computer uses to do different jobs: *First you need to load the software onto your computer. | It will take a while for you to get used to the new software.*

sog·gy /'sɒgi $'sagi/ *adjective* wet and soft in an unpleasant way: *My sandwiches are all soggy.*

soil /sɔɪl/ *noun*
the earth in which plants grow: *Water the soil well when you plant out the young lettuces.*

so·lar /'səʊlə $'soʊlɚ/ *adjective* related to or using the sun: *solar power*

solar sys·tem /'.. ,../ *noun* the sun and all the PLANETs that move around it: *the biggest planet in our solar system*

sold the past tense and past participle of SELL

sol·dier /'səʊldʒə $'soʊldʒɚ/ *noun* someone who is in the army

sold-out /ˌ. './ *adjective* if a concert or other event is sold out, all the tickets have been sold

sole[1] /səʊl $soʊl/ *adjective* only: *He was the sole survivor of the accident.*

sole[2] *noun* the bottom surface of your foot or shoe: *I had a huge blister on the sole of my foot.*

sole·ly /'səʊl-li $'soʊli/ *adverb* formal only: *This club is solely for students.*

sol·emn /'sɒləm $'saləm/ *adjective* serious and slightly sad: *I knew from the solemn expression on his face that something was wrong.*

sol·i·ta·ry /'sɒlətəri $'salə,teri/ *adjective* a solitary person or thing is the only one: *a solitary cottage on the side of the hill*

so·lo[1] /'səʊləʊ $'soʊloʊ/ *adjective, adverb* a solo activity is one that you do alone: *a solo parachute jump*

solo[2] *noun* a piece of music for one performer

so·lo·ist /'səʊləʊɪst $'soʊloʊɪst/ *noun* a musician who performs a solo

so·lu·tion /sə'luːʃən/ *noun* **1** the answer to a difficult question or problem: *Have you found the solution to that maths problem? | The only solution was* to share the money. **2** a liquid mixed with a solid or a gas: *a solution of salt and water*

solve /sɒlv $salv/ *verb*

1 to find a successful way to deal with a problem: *Students and teachers need to **solve** this **problem** by working together.*
2 to find the answer to something: *The police have been unable to **solve** the **murder**.*

som·bre *BrE*, **somber** *AmE* /'sɒmbə $'sɑmbɚ/ *adjective* sad and serious: *He was in a sombre mood.*

some¹ /səm; *strong* sʌm/

1 an amount or number of something, but not a large amount or number. Use this when you are not saying exactly what the number or amount is: *"Would you like some cake?" "Yes, I'd love some."* | *There were some children playing in the street.* | *He brought some pictures of his holiday to show us.*

USAGE some or any?
Use **some** in questions when you think the answer will be 'yes': *Would you like **some** coffee?* Use **any** when you do not know what the answer will be: *Were there **any** letters for me?*

2 a few people or things from a group, or part of an amount, but not all: *I've met **some of** Jack's friends.* | *Some babies start walking before they are a year old.* | *Anne has spent **some of** the money she got for her birthday.*

USAGE
Do not say *We're going to London for some days*. Say *We're going to London for a few days*.

3 *spoken* use this to talk about a person or thing when you do not know their name or details about them, or when it is not important to say the name or details: *Some guy asked me for the time.* | *I read about it in some magazine.* ⇨ compare ANY

some² *adverb* **1** some more an additional amount of something: *Would you like some more tea?* **2** a little more or less than a particular number: *Some 30 students have already completed the course.*

some·bod·y /'sʌmbɒdi, $'sʌmbadi/ SOMEONE

some·day /'sʌmdeɪ/ *adverb* at an unknown time in the future: *Maybe someday I'll get married!*

some·how /'sʌmhaʊ/ *adverb* *informal*
in some way, although you do not know how: *You need to make the speech funnier somehow.*

some·one /'sʌmwʌn/ *also* **somebody** *pronoun*
used to mention a person without saying who the person is: *Someone phoned you this morning.* | *She always tries to blame **someone else** (=a different person) when something goes wrong.*

USAGE
In questions and negative sentences we usually use **anyone** and not **someone**.

some·place /'sʌmpleɪs/ *AmE* SOMEWHERE

somersault

som·er·sault /'sʌməsɔːlt $'sʌmɚ-ˌsɔlt/ *noun* a movement in which you roll forwards until your feet go over your head and touch the ground again: *She did a somersault in the air.*

some·thing /'sʌmθɪŋ/ *pronoun*
a thing: *I'm just going out to get something to eat.* | *There's something sticky on the bottom of my shoe.* | *Steven told me something very interesting.* | *Don't just stand there – do something!* | *Can't you use **something else** (=some other thing) instead?*

PHRASE
something like used when giving a number or amount that is not exact: *The journey will take **something like** four hours.*

S

sometime

USAGE

In questions and negative sentences we usually use **anything** and not **something**. But if you are offering someone some food, a drink etc, it sounds more polite to use **something**: *Would you like something to eat?*

some·time /'sʌmtaɪm/ *adverb* spoken at an unknown time in the past or future: *I'll call you sometime tomorrow.*

some·times /'sʌmtaɪmz/ *adverb*
on some occasions, but not always: *I go there for lunch sometimes.*

some·what /'sʌmwɒt $ 'sʌmwʌt/ *adverb* formal a little, but not very much: *The weather improved somewhat in the second week.*

some·where /'sʌmweə $ 'sʌmwer/ also **someplace** AmE, *adverb*
in a place, although you do not know exactly where: *I put my keys down somewhere and now I can't find them.* | *Diane lives somewhere in London.* | *Let's sit somewhere else* (=somewhere different) – *it's too noisy here.*

PHRASE
somewhere around, somewhere between a little more or a little less than a particular number: *There will be somewhere between forty and fifty people there.* | *It'll cost somewhere around £200.*

USAGE
In questions and negative sentences we usually use **anywhere** and not **somewhere**.

son /sʌn/ *noun* your male child: *I have two sons and a daughter.*

song /sɒŋ $ sɔŋ/ *noun*
a short piece of music with words that you can sing: *The kids were singing songs.*

son-in-law /'. . ,./ *noun* the husband of your daughter

soon /suːn/ *adverb*
after a short time: *We'll have to leave soon if we want to catch the bus.* | *We'll see you again soon!* | *I want the information as soon as*

possible. | *He soon realized that he was in the wrong job.*

PHRASES
as soon as immediately after something has happened: *I'll call you as soon as I get any news from the hospital.* | *As soon as I saw him, I recognized his face.*
sooner or later spoken if something will happen sooner or later, it will definitely happen but you are not sure when: *Sooner or later he's going to find out the truth.*

soot /sʊt/ *noun* [no plural] black powder that is produced when something burns

soothe /suːð/ *verb* to make someone feel better: *Music will often soothe a crying baby.*

so·phis·ti·cat·ed /sə'fɪstəkeɪtɪd/ *adjective* **1** someone who is sophisticated has a modern fashionable life: *a sophisticated city girl* **2** a sophisticated machine is designed in a very clever way and is more modern than similar machines: *a sophisticated computer*

sop·py /'sɒpi $ 'sɑpi/ *adjective* BrE informal **soppier, soppiest** expressing sadness or love in a silly way; SAPPY AmE: *a soppy film*

so·pra·no /sə'prɑːnəʊ $ sə'prænoʊ/ *noun* a female singer with a high voice

sor·did /'sɔːdɪd $ 'sɔrdɪd/ *adjective* unpleasant and dishonest: *He told me all the sordid details of his love affair.*

sore¹ /sɔː $ sɔr/ *adjective*
painful: *My legs are sore from running so far.* | *Sophie was tired, and her arm still felt sore.* | *I woke up with a sore throat.*

sore² *noun* a painful infected wound on your body: *His body was covered with sores.*

sor·row /'sɒrəʊ $ 'sɑroʊ/ *noun* formal a feeling of great sadness

sor·ry /'sɒri $ 'sɑri/ *adjective*
GRAMMAR
sorry about something
sorry for doing something
sorry (that)
sorry to do something
1 if you are sorry, you feel bad about something that you have done and

wish you had not done it: *I'm sorry, I didn't mean to scare you.* | *I'm* **sorry** **about** *the food being late.* | **Sorry**, *did I hurt you?* | **I'm sorry for** *calling you so late.* | *Bill, I'm* **sorry to** *wake you, but Jennifer's on the phone.* | *Sarah said she* **was sorry that** *she lost her temper.* | *I think you need to* **say you're sorry** (=apologize).

2 disappointed or sad about something: *I'm sorry now that I stopped taking piano lessons.* | *I* **am sorry to** *hear that your mother is ill.*

PHRASES

be sorry for someone, feel sorry for someone to feel sadness and sympathy for someone who has problems: *I* **feel** *really* **sorry** **for** *Chloe, but she won't let me help her.*

Sorry? used to ask someone to repeat something because you have not heard them properly ⇨ *same meaning* PARDON?: *Sorry? What did you say?*

sort¹ /sɔːt $ sɔrt/ *noun*

GRAMMAR
a sort of thing
a type of thing: *What* **sort of** *car are you going to buy?* | *It's not the* **sort of** *thing you want to talk to your parents about.* | *There are* **all sorts of** (=many different types of) *reasons for not taking drugs.*

PHRASE
sort of *spoken informal* used when what you say is partly true but not exactly true: *It tasted really good –* **sort of** *sweet, but also spicy.* | *She's not really sick, just* **sort of** *tired.*

sort² *verb*

GRAMMAR
sort something into something
to put things in the right order or group: *She* **sorted** *the books* **into** *three piles.* | *The glass is sorted by color for recycling.*

PHRASAL VERBS
sort out
sort something out *informal* if you sort something out, you deal with it or organize it: *We need to* **sort things out** *before the new term starts.* | *Have you* **got** *the food* **sorted out** *yet?*

sort through
sort through something to look at a lot of things in order to organize them: *Stella* **sorted through** *all the old letters.*

SOS /ˌes əʊ 'es $ ˌes oʊ 'es/ *noun* a message saying that someone is in danger: *The ship sent out an SOS.*

so-so /'. ./ *adjective, adverb* spoken informal not very good: *"How was the film?" "So-so."*

sought the past tense and past participle of SEEK

soul /səʊl $ soʊl/ *noun* your thoughts and feelings rather than your body, which some people believe continue to exist after your body dies

sound¹ /saʊnd/ *noun*

GRAMMAR
the sound of something
something that you hear: *We could hear* **the sound of** *traffic outside.* | *The picture on the TV was okay, but there was no sound.*

sound² *verb*
the way something sounds is how it seems to you when you listen to it or hear about it: *The class sounded really interesting.* | *He sounds really depressed.* | *The band sounded really good tonight.*

sound³ *adjective* **1** sound advice is sensible and likely to produce good results: *The guide gives sound advice to young travellers.* **2** strong and in good condition: *The doors are old, but sound.* | *The doctors say my heart is basically sound.*

sound ef·fects /'. .ˌ./ *plural noun* the sounds that someone makes for a film or radio show

sound·ly /'saʊndli/ *adverb* **1** if you sleep soundly, you sleep well and peacefully **2** something that is soundly made is strong and unlikely to break: *The house is very soundly built.*

sound·proof /'saʊndpruːf/ *adjective* a soundproof wall does not allow sound to get through it

sound·track /'saʊndtræk/ *noun* the recorded music from a film

soup /suːp/ *noun* a hot liquid food: *chicken soup*

sour /saʊə $ saʊɚ/ adjective **1** food that is sour is not sweet but has an unpleasant acid taste: *I don't like this apple – it's too sour.* **2** milk that is sour is not fresh and has an unpleasant taste

source /sɔːs $ sɔrs/ noun the place that something comes from: *An encyclopedia is a good source of information.*

south /saʊθ/ noun **1** [no plural] the direction towards the bottom of a map **2** the south the southern part of a country: *It's warmer in the south* – **south** adverb, adjective: *The garden faces south.* | *the south coast of England*

south·bound /'saʊθbaʊnd/ adjective going towards the south: *Southbound traffic is busy in summer.*

south·east /ˌsaʊθ'iːst/ noun [no plural] the direction that is between south and east: *a town to the southeast of Oxford* – **southeast** adverb, adjective: *We drove east and then headed southeast.*

south·er·ly /'sʌðəli $ 'sʌðɚli/ adjective towards the south: *We drove in a southerly direction.*

south·ern /'sʌðən $ 'sʌðɚn/ adjective in the south of a place: *southern Texas*

south·ern·er /'sʌðənə $ 'sʌðɚnɚ/ noun someone who comes from the south of a country

South Pole /ˌ. './ noun the place on Earth that is farthest south

south·ward /'saʊθwəd $ 'saʊθwɚd/ also **south·wards** /'saʊθwədz $ saʊθwɚdz/ adverb, adjective towards the south: *We travelled southwards for three days.*

south·west /ˌsaʊθ'west/ noun [no plural] the direction between south and west: *the southwest of China* – **southwest** adverb, adjective

sou·ve·nir /ˌsuːvə'nɪə $ ˌsuvə'nɪr/ noun something you keep to help you remember a place

sove·reign /'sɒvrən $ 'sɑvrɪn/ adjective a sovereign country is independent and rules itself

sow /səʊ $ soʊ/ verb, past tense **sowed** past participle **sown** /səʊn $ soʊn/ or **sowed** to plant seeds in the ground: *Sow tomatoes in February or March.*

sowed the past tense and a past participle of SOW

sown a past participle of SOW

soy·a bean /'sɔɪə biːn/ also **soy·bean** /'sɔɪbiːn/ noun a bean that you can cook and eat or use to make other foods

space¹ /speɪs/ noun

GRAMMAR
space in something
space for something

1 an area that is empty: *There isn't* **enough space in** *the suitcase.* | *Can you* **leave space for** *my clothes too?* | *I moved the furniture around, trying to* **make space for** *the extra chairs.* | *I couldn't find a* **parking space.**
2 [no plural] the area around the Earth where the stars and PLANETS are: *I love the idea of travelling* **through space.** | *The astronauts will spend two weeks* **in space.** | *a creature from* **outer space** (=far away in space)

space² also **space out** verb to arrange things so that they have an equal amount of space between them: *Space the fence posts 3 feet apart.*

space·ship /'speɪsʃɪp/ also **space-craft** /'speɪskrɑːft $ 'speɪsˌkræft/ noun a vehicle that can travel into space

space shut·tle /'. ,../ noun a vehicle that can travel into space and return to Earth more than once

spa·cious /'speɪʃəs/ adjective a place that is spacious is large and has a lot of space: *a spacious apartment*

spade /speɪd/ noun **1** a tool that you use for digging earth **2** spades a group of playing cards with black shapes like pointed leaves on them: *the queen of spades*

spa·ghet·ti /spə'geti/ noun [no plural] long thin pieces of PASTA that look like pieces of string

span¹ /spæn/ noun **1** attention span, concentration span the amount of time for which someone can CONCENTRATE on something: *Children have a short attention span.* **2** wing span the distance from one side of a plane's or bird's wing to the other: *The plane has a wing span of forty feet.*

span² verb spanned, spanning to include all of a period of time: *His career spanned 40 years.*

spank /spæŋk/ verb to hit a child on the bottom as a punishment

span·ner /'spænə $ 'spænɚ/ noun BrE a tool that you use for making NUTS tighter; WRENCH AmE ➪ see picture at TOOL

spare¹ /speə $sper/ adjective
a spare object is one that you do not usually use, but that you keep for when you might need it: *Have you got a spare key?* | *Della can sleep in the spare room.* | *The spare tyre is in the boot of the car.*

PHRASE
spare time time when you are not working: *I have so much homework that I don't have much spare time.*

spare² verb to be able to give someone something because you do not need it: *Can you spare a cigarette?*

spark¹ /spɑːk $spark/ noun a very small piece of brightly burning material from a fire: *Even a small spark from a fire can be very dangerous.*

spark² verb **spark something off** to make something start happening: *The speech sparked off a political crisis.*

spar·kle /'spɑːkəl $'sparkəl/ verb to shine with small bright flashes: *Her eyes sparkled with delight.*

spar·row /'spærəʊ $'spæroʊ/ noun a small brown or grey bird

sparse /spɑːs $spars/ adjective existing only in small amounts: *a rocky area with sparse vegetation*
– **sparsely** adverb: *a sparsely populated area*

spas·m /'spæzəm/ noun when a muscle in your body becomes suddenly tight in a way you cannot control

spat the past tense and past participle of SPIT

spate /speɪt/ noun [no plural] a number of similar events that happen in a short time: *There has been a spate of burglaries in the town recently.*

speak ⇨ see box on next page

speak·er /'spiːkə $'spikɚ/ noun **1** someone who speaks: *He asked the speaker's name.* **2** the part of a radio, computer etc where sound comes out ⇨ see picture on page 342

spear¹ /spɪə $spɪr/ noun a long thin weapon with a blade at one end, which you throw or push at someone

spear² verb to push a pointed object into something: *I speared the steak with my fork.*

spear·head /'spɪəhed $'spɪrhed/ verb to lead an attack or an organized action: *British soliders spearheaded the attack.*

spe·cial¹ /'speʃəl/ adjective
1 something that is special is slightly different to other things and better or more important: *We have a very special guest with us this evening.* | *I want to do something special for your birthday.*
2 a special thing is used by one particular person: *Winnie has her own special plate.*

special² noun **1** a television programme that is made for a particular purpose: *a two-hour rock music special* **2** a meal in a restaurant that has been made for that day only: *Today's special is roast lamb.*

special ef·fects /ˌ.. .'./ plural noun pictures and sounds that make the action in a film seem real: *a movie with brilliant special effects*

spe·cial·ist /'speʃəlɪst/ noun someone who knows a lot about a subject: *a heart specialist*

spe·ci·al·i·ty /ˌspeʃi'æləti/ noun BrE, plural **specialities 1** a subject that you know a lot about; SPECIALTY AmE: *My speciality is European history.* **2** the speciality of a restaurant is the food that is cooked there in a special way and is always good; SPECIALTY AmE: *Fish is the speciality of the restaurant.*

spe·cial·ize also **specialise** BrE /'speʃəlaɪz/ verb to study only one subject or do only one activity: *a lawyer who specializes in divorce*

spe·cial·ly /'speʃəli/ adverb for one particular purpose or person: *The dance costumes are specially made for the dancers.*

spe·cial·ty /'speʃəlti/ noun AmE, plural **specialties** SPECIALITY

spe·cies /'spiːʃiːz/ noun, plural **species** a type of animal or plant: *a rare species of bird*

spe·cif·ic /spə'sɪfɪk/ adjective **1** a specific thing is one particular thing: *The books are designed for this specific age group.* **2** detailed and exact: *Please be more specific.*

spe·cif·ic·ally /spə'sɪfɪkli/ adverb **1** for a particular type of person or thing: *a book specifically for teenagers* **2** if you specifically say something, you say it clearly because it is important: *I specifically told you to be here by ten o'clock!*

S

speak /spiːk/ verb spoke /spəʊk $ spoʊk/ spoken /ˈspəʊkən $ ˈspoʊkən/

➤ SPEAK or TALK?

- If just one person is talking, use either **speak** or **talk**: *He **spoke about** his friends in India.* | *He **talked about** his friends in India.*
- When two or more people are having a conversation, use **talk**: *We **talked** for hours after the film.* | *The two men were **talking about** their families.*

➤ SPEAK

❶ to talk to someone or to a group about something
*Each leader **spoke** for about fifteen minutes.* | *Hello, can I **speak to** Mrs. Allyson, please?* | *She had never **spoken of** her brother's death.* | *Moore **spoke about** his books on the radio.* | *Leland **spoke with** his friend Tony before the game.*

GRAMMAR
speak to someone
speak to someone about something
speak of something
speak with someone *AmE*

speak

❸ to use your voice to say words
*No one **spoke** for about five minutes, then everyone started talking at once.* | *It was difficult for him to **speak** while he was ill.* | *She **spoke** in a quiet, tired voice.*

❷ to be able to say and understand words in a particular language
*My grandfather **spoke** four languages.* | *Susanna Kim **speaks** perfect English.* | *Do you **speak** Russian?* | *I **speak** a little Italian.*

- When you mean that someone is able to speak a language, use **speak**: *I speak a little Spanish.*
- When you mean that someone is speaking a language at a particular time, use **speak in**: *I won't understand him if he speaks in Japanese.*
- Don't confuse *She is speaking English* (=she is speaking it now) and *She speaks English* (=she is able to speak English).

PHRASES

speak up
1 *spoken* say this to tell someone to speak more loudly: *Could you **speak up**? I can't hear you very well.*
2 to say publicly what you think about something: *When I was young, I was afraid to **speak up** in class.*

spe·ci·fy /'spesəfaɪ/ verb specified, specifies to give exact details about something: Did he specify which route he would take?

spe·ci·men /'spesəmən/ noun something from your body that is tested or examined: a blood specimen

speck /spek/ noun a very small piece of something: a speck of dust

spec·ta·cle /'spektəkəl/ noun an unusual or strange thing to see: the bizarre spectacle of Tom dressed as a woman

spec·ta·cles /'spektəkəlz/ noun formal GLASSES: an expensive pair of spectacles

spec·tac·u·lar /spek'tækjələ $ spek-'tækjələ/ adjective very impressive or exciting: We got a spectacular view of Niagra Falls.

spec·ta·tor /spek'teɪtə $ 'spekteɪtə/ noun someone who watches an event

spec·u·late /'spekjəleɪt/ verb formal to guess the reason for something: Everyone speculated about why he left.

sped the past tense and past participle of SPEED

speech /spiːtʃ/ noun, plural speeches

> **GRAMMAR**
> a speech on something
> a speech to someone

1 a talk about a subject that you give to a group of people: He **gave a speech to** the conference. | Gore **made a speech on** the environment.
2 when someone speaks: Only humans are capable of speech. | He was drunk, and his speech was unclear.

> **PHRASE**
> freedom of speech, free speech the right to say or print whatever you want: The protestors are demanding the right to **freedom of speech**.

speech·less /'spiːtʃləs/ adjective formal unable to speak because you are too shocked: She was speechless when I told her the news.

speech marks /'. ./ plural noun the marks (",") or (',') that you write to show when someone starts and stops speaking

speed¹ /spiːd/ noun

1 how fast something moves: What speed were you travelling at? | Try to **keep** your **speed down** (=not go too fast) on small roads.
2 [no plural] how quickly something happens: The speed of the changes has surprised many people.

> **PHRASES**
> speed limit a limit on how fast you are allowed to drive: The **speed limit** is 30 miles an hour.
> top speed the top speed of a vehicle is its fastest possible speed: This car has a **top speed** of 80 miles an hour.
> at high speed very fast: The police car drove away **at high speed**.

speed² verb, past tense and past participle sped /sped/ or speeded 1 to move very quickly: We sped up the stairs. | The van sped along the motorway. 2 speed by if time speeds by, it seems to pass very quickly: The weeks sped by. 3 speed up to move more quickly: Come on – speed up or we'll be late! 4 speed something up to make something happen more quickly

speed·boat /'spiːdbəʊt $ 'spidbout/ noun a small fast boat with a powerful engine ⇨ see picture on page 349

speed·ing /'spiːdɪŋ/ noun [no plural] the crime of driving too fast: The police stopped me for speeding.

spell¹ /spel/ verb, past tense and past participle spelled or spelt /spelt/ BrE to form a word by writing or saying the letters in the correct order: Can you spell your name for me?

spell² noun 1 a piece of magic: They say that a witch cast a spell on her. 2 a short period of time: She had a short spell in hospital.

spell·ing /'spelɪŋ/ noun 1 [no plural] the ability to spell words correctly: My spelling is terrible. 2 the way that you spell a word: There are two different spellings for this word.

spelt a past tense and past participle of SPELL¹

spend /spend/ verb, past tense and past participle spent /spent/

> **GRAMMAR**
> spend something on something

1 to use your money to pay for

S

something: *I spent all my money.* | *Brendan* **spent** *over £600* **on** *his new mountain bike.*

2 to use time doing something: *Joe spends hours on the phone with her.* | *I spent the afternoon doing my homework.*

spent the past tense and past participle of SPEND

sperm /spɜːm $ spɝːm/ *noun* a cell produced inside a man that joins with an egg and produces new life

sphere /sfɪə $ sfɪr/ *noun* the shape of a ball

spher·i·cal /ˈsferɪkəl/ *adjective* formal round in shape like a ball

spice¹ /spaɪs/ *noun* a substance that you add to food to give it a special strong taste

spice² *verb* **spice something up** to make something more interesting or exciting: *I need a few jokes to spice up my speech.*

spic·y /ˈspaɪsi/ *adjective* **spicier, spiciest** spicy food has a strong taste because it contains a lot of spices

spi·der /ˈspaɪdə $ ˈspaɪdɚ/ *noun* a small creature with eight legs

spike¹ /spaɪk/ *noun* a long thin object with a sharp point: *a fence with spikes along the top*

spike² *verb* to add alcohol or a drug to someone's drink without telling them: *She thinks that someone must have spiked her drink.*

spik·y /ˈspaɪki/ *adjective* **spikier, spikiest** something that is spiky has a lot of sharp points: *She had short spiky hair.* ⇨ *see picture on page 353*

spill¹ /spɪl/
verb, past tense and past participle **spilled** or **spilt** /spɪlt/ *BrE*

GRAMMAR
spill something over/on something
spill over/on something

1 if you spill a liquid, you let it fall out of a container by accident: *I spilled paint all over the floor.* | *Mind you don't spill coffee on your shirt.*

spill

2 if a liquid spills, it pours out of a container by accident: *My wine spilled all over the carpet.*

spill² *noun* an amount of liquid that pours out of a container by accident: *An oil spill would kill all the fish in the area.*

spilt a past tense and past participle of SPILL¹

spin¹ /spɪn/ *verb, past tense and past participle* **spun** /spʌn/, **spinning**

1 if something spins, or if you spin it, it turns around and around very quickly: *The dancers spun round and round on the ice.* | *He spun the rope around above his head.*

2 if an insect spins a WEB or a COCOON, it produces the thread to make it: *a spider spinning a web*

spin² *noun* when something turns around and around very quickly: *The plane went into a spin.*

spin·ach /ˈspɪnɪdʒ $ ˈspɪnɪtʃ/ *noun* [no plural] a vegetable with large dark green leaves

spin·al /ˈspaɪnl/ *adjective* related to your SPINE: *a spinal injury*

spin doc·tor /ˈ. ˌ./ *noun* someone who gives advice to politicians and members of large organizations about what things they should say to make the public like and respect them

spine /spaɪn/ *noun* the row of bones down the centre of your back: *She fell and injured her spine.*

spine·less /ˈspaɪnləs/ *adjective* not brave: *He's too spineless to speak for himself.*

spin-off /ˈ. ./ *noun* a product that a person or company develops from something else: *The film's spin-offs include toys, clothes and a magazine.*

spin·ster /ˈspɪnstə $ ˈspɪnstɚ/ *noun* old-fashioned a woman who has never married

spi·ral /ˈspaɪərəl $ ˈspaɪrəl/ *noun* a shape that goes round and round as it goes up: *a spiral staircase*

spire /spaɪə $ spaɪɚ/ *noun* a tower on a church that rises steeply to a point ⇨ *see picture on page 343*

spir·it /ˈspɪrɪt/ *noun* 1 the part of you that many people think continues to live after you die: *He said he could talk to the* spirit of his dead mother. **2** a strong alcoholic drink: *I never drink spirits.* **3 high spirits** if someone is in high spirits, they are happy and excited: *Why are the children in such high spirits?*

spir·i·tu·al /ˈspɪrətʃuəl/ *adjective* **1** related to your thoughts and feelings, rather than to your body and the things you own **2** related to religion: *spiritual songs*

spit¹ /spɪt/ *verb, past tense* **spat** /spæt/ or **spit** *AmE, past participle* **spat, spitting** **1** to push liquid or food out of your mouth: *He tasted the meat then spat it out.* | *One of the boys spat at me as I walked past.* **2** *BrE* if it is spitting, it is raining very lightly: *It's only spitting – you don't need an umbrella.*

spit² *noun* **1** SALIVA **2** a long thin stick for cooking meat over a fire

spite /spaɪt/ *noun*

[no plural] the feeling of wanting to hurt or upset someone: *She only told Jim what had happened **out of spite**.*

PHRASE

in spite of something although something else is also true; ⇨ *same meaning* DESPITE: *We enjoyed the trip **in spite of** the bad weather.*

spite·ful /ˈspaɪtfəl/ *adjective* unkind or cruel to someone: *That was a spiteful thing to do.*
–spitefully *adverb*: *"You can't come," Jane said spitefully.*

splash¹ /splæʃ/ *verb*

1 if a liquid splashes, it moves through the air and falls on something: *Rain splashed into the pond.* | *Some wine had splashed onto his shirt.* **2** if you splash a liquid, you hit it or throw it so that it moves through the air and falls on something: *He splashed some cold water onto his face.*

splash² *noun, plural* **splashes** **1** the sound that something makes when it hits water: *The stone fell in the water with a loud splash.* ⇨ *see picture on page 350* **2** a small amount of a liquid that falls onto a surface: *splashes of paint*

splat·ter /ˈsplætə $ ˈsplætər/ *verb* if a ▼

liquid splatters, it hits loudly against a surface: *Rain splattered against the window.*

splen·did /ˈsplendɪd/ *adjective* old-fashioned very good: *What a splendid idea!*

splint /splɪnt/ *noun* a flat piece of wood or plastic that stops a broken bone from moving: *I have to wear a splint until my leg gets better.*

splin·ter¹ /ˈsplɪntə $ ˈsplɪntər/ *noun* a small sharp piece of wood, glass, or metal

splinter² *verb* to break into thin sharp pieces: *The window frames had begun to splinter.*

split¹ /splɪt/ *verb, past tense and past participle* **split, splitting**

GRAMMAR
split something between people/ things
split something into something
split something open

1 to break something into two or more parts: *Meg dropped the pumpkin, which **split open** on the floor.* | *The wire had **split in half.*** **2** to divide something into different groups or parts: *Nathan and I **split** the £25 **between** us.* | ***Split** the class **into** four groups.*

PHRASAL VERB
split up
if two people split up, their marriage or relationship ends: *Eve's parents **split up** when she was three.*

split² *noun* **1** a long thin cut or hole in something: *He had a painful split on his lip.* **2** a serious disagreement that divides an organization or group of people: *Ministers are denying that there is any split in the party.*

split sec·ond /ˌ. ˈ../ *noun* a very short period of time: *For a split second, I thought I'd won.*

spoil /spɔɪl/ *verb, past tense and past participle* **spoiled** or **spoilt** /spɔɪlt/ *BrE*

1 to make something less good or less enjoyable: *I didn't want to spoil the surprise.* | *Being ill spoiled the trip for me.* **2** to let a child have or do whatever they want, with the result that they behave badly: *Grandparents*

S

sometimes spoil their grandchildren.
3 if food spoils, it becomes bad and you cannot eat it

spoiled /spɔɪld/ also **spoilt** /spɔɪlt/ BrE, *adjective* a spoiled child behaves badly because they always get what they want

spoil·sport /'spɔɪlspɔːt $'spɔɪlspɔrt/ *noun informal* someone who spoils other people's fun: *Don't be a spoilsport – please let us go swimming.*

spoilt a past tense and past participle of SPOIL

spoke the past tense of SPEAK

spoken[1] the past participle of SPEAK

spok·en[2] /'spəʊkən $'spoʊkən/ *adjective* spoken English/Spanish etc the form of language that you speak rather than write

spokes·man /'spəʊksmən $'spoʊksmən/ *noun, plural* **spokesmen** /-mən/ someone who speaks for a group, especially a man

spokes·per·son /'spəʊks,pɜːsən $'spoʊks,pɜsən/ *noun, plural* **spokespeople** /-,piːpəl/ someone who speaks for a group

spokes·wo·man /'spəʊks,wʊmən $'spoʊks,wʊmən/ *noun, plural* **spokeswomen** /-,wɪmɪn/ a woman who speaks for a group

sponge /spʌndʒ/ *noun* a soft object full of small holes that takes in and holds water and is used to wash things ⇨ see picture at ABSORB

spong·y /'spʌndʒi/ *adjective* **spongier, spongiest** soft and full of air or liquid, like a sponge: *spongy wet earth*

spon·sor[1] /'spɒnsə $'spɑnsɚ/ *verb* **1** to provide the money to pay for an event: *Coca-Cola have offered to sponsor the tournament.* **2** to give someone money for a CHARITY if they manage to do something difficult: *I'm doing a walk for charity – will you sponsor me?*

sponsor[2] *noun* a company that provides the money to pay for an event

spon·sor·ship /'spɒnsəʃɪp $'spɑnsɚ,ʃɪp/ *noun* [no plural] when someone sponsors an event or person: *We are still trying to get sponsorship for the competition.*

spon·tan·e·i·ty /,spɒntə'neɪɪti $,spɑntə'neɪɪti/ *noun* [no plural] when you decide to do things very quickly,

without thinking about them or planning them: *He brings enthusiasm and spontaneity to our work.*

spon·ta·ne·ous /spɒn'teɪniəs $spɑn'teɪniəs/ *adjective* if something is spontaneous, you do it without thinking about it or planning it: *The audience gave a spontaneous cheer.*
– **spontaneously** *adverb*: *The crowd spontaneously started clapping.*

spook·y /'spuːki/ *adjective informal* **spookier, spookiest** strange and frightening: *a spooky old house*

spool /spuːl/ *noun* a small object that you wind something around: *a spool of thread*

spoon[1] /spuːn/ *noun* something that you use for eating food, shaped like a small bowl with a long handle

spoon[2] *verb* to lift food with a spoon: *Spoon the sauce over the meat.*

spoon·ful /'spuːnfʊl/ *noun* the amount that a spoon can hold: *a spoonful of medicine*

sport /spɔːt $spɔrt/ *noun*
a game or competition such as football or tennis, in which you use your body to play: *I like to **play** most **sports**, but basketball is my favorite.* | *I think children should **do** more **sport** at school.*

sport·ing /'spɔːtɪŋ $'spɔrtɪŋ/ *adjective* relating to sports: *sporting activities*

sports car /'. ./ *noun* a fast car with only two seats

sports cen·tre /'. ,. ./ *noun* BrE a place where you can do sports

sports·man /'spɔːtsmən $'spɔrtsmən/ *plural* **sportsmen** /-mən/ *noun* a man who plays sports

sports·wom·an /'spɔːts,wʊmən $'spɔrts,wʊmən/ *noun, plural* **sportswomen** /-,wɪmɪn/ a woman who plays sports

sport·y /'spɔːti $'spɔrti/ *adjective* BrE good at sport: *I'm not very sporty.*

spot[1] /spɒt $spɑt/ *noun*
1 a place: *This is a great spot for a holiday.*
2 a small round mark on a surface: *There were some **spots of** blood on the carpet.*
3 BrE a small red mark on someone's

skin: *If you eat too much chocolate you'll get spots.*

PHRASE

on the spot **a)** at the place where something is happening: *One victim was taken to hospital; the other was treated on the spot.* **b)** immediately: *She gave him some money on the spot.*

spot² *verb* **spotted, spotting** to notice or see something: *I spotted my friend Anna in the audience.*

spot check /ˌ. ˈ. $ˈ. ./ *noun* a check that is done without warning: *Paul will be making spot checks on your work.*

spot·less /ˈspɒtləs $ˈspɑːtləs/ *adjective* completely clean: *a spotless kitchen*
– **spotlessly** *adverb*: *Her house is always spotlessly clean.*

spot·light /ˈspɒtlaɪt $ˈspɑːtlaɪt/ *noun* **1** a very powerful light that you can point at different things **2 in the spotlight** receiving a lot of attention from newspapers or television

spot·ty /ˈspɒti $ˈspɑːti/ *adjective* BrE **spottier, spottiest** someone who is spotty has a lot of spots on their face: *a fat, spotty young boy*

spouse /spaʊs/ *noun* formal, plural **spouses** someone's husband or wife

spout¹ /spaʊt/ *noun* a part on the side of a container that you use for pouring out liquid: *a teapot with a broken spout*

spout² *verb* if a liquid spouts, it comes out of something with a lot of force: *Water spouted from the burst pipe.*

sprain /spreɪn/ *verb* to injure your wrist, knee etc by suddenly twisting it: *I think I've sprained my ankle.*
– **sprain** *noun*: *Your wrist isn't broken – it's just a bad sprain.*

sprang the past tense of SPRING¹

sprawl /sprɔːl/ *verb* to lie or sit with your arms and legs stretched out: *Jo lay sprawled on the sofa.*

spray

aerosol

spray¹ /spreɪ/ *verb*

GRAMMAR
spray something on/onto something
spray something with something

to force a lot of very small drops of liquid out of a container onto something: *Someone had sprayed paint on the walls.* | *She sprayed the children with cold water.*

spray² *noun* liquid in a special container that is forced out in very small drops: *a can of hair spray*

spread¹ /spred/ *verb*, past tense and past participle **spread**

GRAMMAR
spread something on/over/across something
spread something with something
spread over/through something

1 to put a layer of something over a surface so that the surface is covered: *Spread the icing on the top of the cake.* | *He spread the bread with the soft cheese.* ⇨ see picture on page 344

2 if things are spread over an area, they are all over that area: *Dirty clothes were spread all across the floor.*

3 if something spreads, it affects a larger area or more people: *The fire spread quickly through the house.* | *Colds are spread when people cough or sneeze.*

4 if information spreads, a lot of people learn about it: *The rumours spread quickly.* | *You shouldn't spread gossip.*

PHRASAL VERBS
spread out
1 to open something so that it is flat: *Sally spread out the beach towels on the sand.*
2 if a group of people spread out, they move apart from each other: *The children spread out across the playground.*

spread² *noun* when something affects a larger area or more people: *We must do more to stop the spread of this virus.*

spread·sheet /ˈspredʃiːt/ *noun* a computer PROGRAM that you use for showing and calculating lists of numbers

S

spree /spriː/ noun when you spend a short time doing a lot of something you enjoy: *I went on a spending spree.*

spring¹ /sprɪŋ/ verb **sprang** /spræŋ/ **sprung** /sprʌŋ/

GRAMMAR
spring into/out of/back etc
to jump suddenly and quickly: *Tim's cat sprang into my lap.* | *She sprang back in surprise.* | *Josie sprang out of bed.* | *He sprang to his feet* (=stood up quickly).

PHRASAL VERB
spring up
to suddenly appear: *New companies have sprung up to start businesses on the Internet.*

spring² noun
the season between winter and summer: *I planted an apple tree this spring.* | *We're hoping to move house in the spring.* | *I first met Simon in the spring of 1998.*

spring-clean /ˌ. ˈ./ verb to clean a place thoroughly: *I'm going to spring-clean the bedrooms today.*
– **spring-cleaning** noun [no plural]: *Do you need help with the spring-cleaning?*

spring·on·ion /ˌ. ˈ../ noun BrE a small white onion with a long green stem; GREEN ONION AmE

spring·time /ˈsprɪŋtaɪm/ noun [no plural] the time of year when it is spring

sprin·kle /ˈsprɪŋkəl/ verb to scatter small drops of liquid or small pieces of something onto something else: *Finally, sprinkle grated chocolate on top of the cake.* ⇨ see picture on page 344

sprint /sprɪnt/ verb to run very fast for a short distance: *She sprinted past the other runners.*
– **sprint** noun: *Her jogging turned into a sprint.*

sprout¹ /spraʊt/ verb if a plant sprouts, it starts to grow new leaves

sprout² also **brus·sels sprout** /ˌbrʌsəlz ˈspraʊt/ noun a round green vegetable like a very small CABBAGE

sprung the past participle of SPRING¹

spun the past tense and past participle of SPIN¹

spur¹ /spɜː $ spɚ/ noun **on the spur of the moment** if you do something on the spur of the moment, you suddenly decide to do it: *On the spur of the moment, she decided to take a holiday.*

spur² verb **spurred, spurring; spur someone on** to encourage someone to try harder: *The fear of failure spurred him on.*

spurt¹ /spɜːt $ spɚt/ verb to flow out suddenly with a lot of force: *Juice spurted out over her fingers.*

spurt² noun a sudden short increase in effort, speed etc: *With one final spurt, she reached the top of the hill.*

spy¹ /spaɪ/ verb **spied, spies** 1 to secretly get information for a government: *He was found guilty of spying for the Americans.* 2 **spy on** to secretly watch someone: *Have you been spying on me?*

spy² noun, plural **spies** someone whose job is to find out secret information for a government

squab·ble /ˈskwɒbəl $ ˈskwɑbəl/ verb to argue about something unimportant
– **squabble** noun: *She's having another squabble with her sister.*

squad /skwɒd $ skwɑd/ noun 1 a group of soldiers or police officers who work together: *the anti-terrorist squad* 2 BrE the group of players that a sports team is chosen from

squad·ron /ˈskwɒdrən $ ˈskwɑdrən/ noun a group of military planes or vehicles

squal·or /ˈskwɒlə $ ˈskwɑlɚ/ noun [no plural] formal extremely dirty conditions: *They lived in squalor.*

squan·der /ˈskwɒndə $ ˈskwɑndɚ/ verb formal to waste time or money in a stupid way: *He had squandered all his money on clothes.*

square¹ /skweə $ skwer/ adjective
1 something that is square has four straight sides of equal length and four angles of 90 degrees: *a square table* ⇨ see picture at SHAPE¹
2 a square INCH, square metre etc is a measurement of an area which is a square with sides an inch long, a metre long etc: *The park covers two square miles of the city.*

square² noun
1 a shape with four straight sides of equal length and four angles of 90 degrees: *The cloth has a pattern of squares.*

2 an open area with buildings around it in the middle of a town: *The Police Station is in the main square.*

squash¹ /skwɒʃ $ skwɑʃ/ *verb*

> **GRAMMAR**
> **squash something into something**

1 to damage something by pressing on it so that it becomes flat: *He sat on the bananas and squashed them.*
2 to push someone or something into a space that is too small: *Move – you're squashing me!* | *I squashed a towel into my bag.*

squash² *noun* [no plural] a game that is played indoors by two people who hit a small rubber ball against the walls of a small room

squat¹ /skwɒt $ skwɑt/ *noun* BrE a building people live in without permission and without paying rent

squat² *verb* **squatted, squatting** to live in a building without permission and without paying rent: *There are many people squatting in London because houses are so expensive.*

squeak /skwiːk/ *verb* to make a very high sound: *As he crept up the stairs, a floorboard squeaked.* ⇨ see picture on page 350
– **squeak** *noun: the squeak of a mouse*

squeak·y /ˈskwiːki/ *adjective* **squeakier, squeakiest** making a very high sound: *a squeaky voice*

squeal /skwiːl/ *verb* to make a long loud high sound: *The children squealed and giggled.*
– **squeal** *noun: squeals of laughter*

squeam·ish /ˈskwiːmɪʃ/ *adjective* easily upset by seeing unpleasant things

squeeze

squeeze /skwiːz/ *verb*

> **GRAMMAR**
> **squeeze into/through something**
> **squeeze something into/through something**
> **squeeze something out of something**

1 to press something firmly with your hand: *Mike squeezed my hand and said, "Don't worry."* ⇨ see picture on page 344
2 to remove something from a container by pressing it firmly: *She squeezed some glue out onto the paper.*
3 to push yourself into or through a small space: *Tom squeezed through a gap in the hedge.* | *There's a seat free next to me, if you can squeeze in.*
4 to press or push something into a small space: *We managed to squeeze the desk into my small office.*

squid /skwɪd/ *noun, plural* **squid** a sea creature with a long soft body and ten soft arms

squint¹ /skwɪnt/ *verb* to look at something with your eyes partly closed so that you can see it better: *She squinted at the name on the envelope.*

squint² *noun* [no plural] a condition in which each eye looks in a different direction

squirm /skwɜːm $ skwɚm/ *verb* to twist your body from side to side: *Gary squirmed, trying to get free.*

squir·rel /ˈskwɪrəl $ ˈskwɚəl/ *noun* a small animal with a long furry tail that lives in trees and eats nuts

squirt /skwɜːt $ skwɚt/ *verb* if you squirt liquid, or if it squirts out, it is forced out of a narrow hole: *He squirted mustard on his burger.*

St. **1** the written abbreviation of STREET: *Oxford St.* **2** the written abbreviation of SAINT: *St. Peter*

stab¹ /stæb/ *verb* **stabbed, stabbing** to push a knife into someone: *The boy stabbed him in the leg.*

stab² *noun* [no plural] *informal* an attempt to do something: *I wouldn't mind having another stab at playing the guitar.*

S

stab·bing /ˈstæbɪŋ/ *adjective* a stabbing pain is very sudden and strong

sta·bil·i·ty /stəˈbɪləti/ *noun* [no plural] when a situation does not change for a long time

sta·bil·ize also **stabilise** *BrE* /ˈsteɪbəlaɪz/ *verb* if something stabilizes, it stops changing: *The patient's condition has stabilized.*

sta·ble¹ /ˈsteɪbəl/ *adjective* not likely to move or change ⇨ *opposite* UNSTABLE: *Make sure the ladder is stable before you go up it.*

stable² *noun* a building where horses are kept

stack¹ /stæk/ *noun* a pile of things one on top of the other: *a stack of dirty plates*

stack² also **stack up** *verb* to make a pile of things one on top of the other: *She stacked the old magazines on the floor.*

sta·di·um /ˈsteɪdiəm/ *noun* a large area for playing sports, surrounded by rows of seats: *a football stadium*

staff¹ /stɑːf $ stæf/ *noun* [no plural] the people who work for an organization: *If you need help, ask a member of our staff.*

staff² *verb* if a place is staffed by people, they work there: *The shop is staffed by volunteers.*

stag /stæg/ *noun* an adult male DEER

stage¹ /steɪdʒ/ *noun*

1 one part of a long process: *Different books are suitable for different* **stages of** *your education.* | *At this* **stage** *in my life, I am not interested in a serious relationship.*
2 the raised part in a theatre where people perform: *I stood* **on the stage** *and sang.* | *The star of the show came* **on stage.**

stage² *verb* to organize an event or performance: *We were planning to stage an end-of-term show.*

stag·ger /ˈstægə $ ˈstægɚ/ *verb* to walk in a very unsteady way: *He staggered to the phone.*

stag·gered /ˈstægəd $ ˈstægɚd/ *adjective* extremely surprised: *I was staggered to hear you're leaving.*

stag·ger·ing /ˈstægərɪŋ/ *adjective* extremely surprising: *a staggering amount of money*

stag night /ˈ. ./ *noun* an evening when a man goes out with his male friends just before his wedding

stain¹ /steɪn/ *verb* to make a mark on something that is difficult to remove: *The coffee had stained her skirt badly.*

stain

stain² *noun* a mark that is difficult to remove: *The carpet was covered in wine stains.*

stair /steə $ ster/ *noun* 1 stairs a set of steps that you use to go from one level of a building to another: *I ran up the stairs to get my jacket.* | *The office is at the top of the stairs.* 2 one of the steps in a set of stairs: *Mia was sitting on the top stair.*

stair·case /ˈsteəkeɪs $ ˈsterkeɪs/ *noun* a set of stairs inside a building

stair·way /ˈsteəweɪ $ ˈsterweɪ/ *noun* a wide set of stairs

stake /steɪk/ *noun* 1 be at stake if something is at stake, you will lose it if an action is not successful: *There's a lot at stake in this game.* 2 stakes money that you risk losing as the result of a game, race etc: *Gamblers in Las Vegas often play for high stakes.*

stale /steɪl/ *adjective* no longer fresh: *stale bread*

stalk¹ /stɔːk/ *noun* the main stem of a plant

stalk² *verb* to follow a person or animal in order to watch or attack them

stalk·er /ˈstɔːkə $ ˈstɔːkɚ/ *noun* a person who keeps following someone in a way that upsets them or frightens them

stall¹ /stɔːl/ *noun* the main stem of a large table on which you put things you want to sell: *the fruit and vegetable stall in the market* 2 *AmE* a small enclosed area for washing or using the toilet 3 the stalls the seats on the lowest level in a theatre;

stall² *verb* 1 if an engine stalls, it suddenly stops 2 *informal* to prevent something from happening or prevent someone from doing something until a later time: *I kept stalling.* | *"He wants to know now." "Stall him."*

stal·lion /'stæljən/ *noun* an adult male horse

stam·i·na /'stæmənə/ *noun* [no plural] the physical or mental strength to continue doing something for a long time

stam·mer /'stæmə $ 'stæmɚ/ *verb* to repeat the first sound of a word when you speak: *"N-no," he stammered.*
–**stammer** *noun*: *She's got quite a stammer.*

stamp¹ /stæmp/ *noun*

1 a small piece of paper that you stick on a letter before you post it to show that you have paid to send it
2 an official mark that is printed on a document using a small block covered with ink: *They put a stamp in his passport.*

stamp² *verb*

GRAMMAR
stamp into/out of etc a place
stamp something on something
stamp something with something

1 to put your feet down very hard on the ground when you walk: *Andy stamped out of the room.*
2 to print an official mark on a document by pressing a small block covered with ink onto it: *They stamped the date on my passport.* | *The letter was stamped with the word 'Urgent'.*

PHRASE
stamp your foot to put your foot down very hard on the ground: *Tess stamped her foot and shouted "No!"*

PHRASAL VERB
stamp out
stamp something out to stop something bad from continuing: *We will stamp out racism in this school.*

stam·pede /stæm'piːd/ *noun* when a large number of animals or people suddenly run somewhere: *There was a stampede for the door.*

stance /staːns $ stæns/ *noun formal* someone's public attitude to something: *The Church will not change its stance on divorce.*

stand¹ /stænd/ *verb, past tense and past participle* **stood** /stʊd/

1 if you are standing, you are on your feet in an upright position: *Miss Fell was standing in front of the class.* | *I stood and watched him play.* | **Stand still** while I do your hair.
2 also **stand up** to get up so that you are standing after you have been sitting or lying down: *He stood up when I came into the room.*
3 if something stands somewhere, it is there: *This is where the castle once stood.*

PHRASES
can't stand *spoken* to hate something or someone: *I can't stand that man!* | *She can't stand loud music.*
stand a chance to be likely to succeed: *I don't stand a chance of getting that job.*

PHRASAL VERBS
stand back
to move back so that you are standing a little further away: *Everyone stood back while Dad lit the fireworks.*
stand by
stand by someone to support someone when they are in trouble: *She stood by him when he went to jail.*
stand for
stand for something to be a short form of a word or phrase: *PTO stands for 'please turn over'.*
stand in
to do someone else's job for them while they are away: *He is standing in for Mrs Lewis while she has her baby.*
stand out
to be very easy to see or notice: *Wear something bright so that you stand out.*
stand up
stand up to get up so that you are standing after you have been sitting or lying down: *Louise stood up and left the room.*
stand up for someone/something
to defend someone or something when people criticize them: *Pete always stands up for his younger brother.*

S

stand² *noun*   **1** a piece of equipment that holds or supports something: *a music stand*   **2** a small structure that you put things on to sell them or show them to people   **3** a building at a sports ground where people sit or stand to watch a game

stan·dard¹ /'stændəd $'stæn-dərd/ *noun*
a level that measures how good something is or how well someone does something: *The work was done to a very **high standard**. | We must do more to **raise** academic **standards** in the college. | He believes that **standards** in schools are **falling**. | Candidates must **reach** this **standard** in order to pass the exam.*

PHRASE
by someone's standards compared to what a person normally does or achieves: *I stayed up until 11.00, which is late by my standards.*

standard² *adjective* normal or usual: *The doors are all a standard size.*

stan·dard·ize also **standardise** *BrE* /'stændədaız $'stændər,daız/ *verb* to make things all the same as each other

stand·by /'stændbaı/ *noun* **on standby** ready to do something if needed: *There are medical staff on standby at the stadium.*

stand·ing /'stændıŋ/ *noun* [no plural] people's opinion of someone: *The President's standing has never been higher.*

stand·point /'stændpɔınt/ *noun* a particular way of thinking about something ⇨ *same meaning* POINT OF VIEW: *Obviously, from my standpoint it's a brilliant idea.*

stand·still /'stænd,stıl/ *noun* [no plural] a situation in which things are not moving, or no one is doing anything: *All the traffic came to a standstill. | Work on the new bridge is at a standstill.*

stank the past tense of STINK

sta·ple¹ /'steıpəl/ *noun* a small U-shaped piece of metal wire that you push through pieces of paper to fasten them together

staple² *verb* to fasten pieces of paper

together with staples: *She stapled the pages together.*

sta·pler /'steıplə $'steıplər/ *noun* a machine for putting staples through paper

star¹ /stɑː $stɑr/ *noun*
1 a point of light that you see in the sky at night: *Stars were shining above us.*
2 a shape with a lot of points sticking out of it: *The American flag has stars and stripes on it.*
3 a famous actor, singer, sports player etc: *She has posters of **pop stars** on her wall. | a **movie star***

star² *verb* **starred, starring** if a film or play stars someone, or if someone stars in it, they are the main character in it: *The film stars Hugh Grant. | She has starred in more than twenty movies.*

star³ *adjective* a star pupil, player etc is the best in a group: *Liz is one of our star pupils.*

starch /stɑːtʃ $stɑrtʃ/ *noun* [no plural] a substance in foods such as bread, rice, and potatoes

star·dom /'stɑːdəm $'stɑrdəm/ *noun* [no plural] when someone is very famous as an actor, singer, sports player etc

stare /steə $ster/ *verb*
GRAMMAR
stare at someone/something
to look at someone or something for a long time without moving your eyes: *The boy just stood there staring at me!*
−**stare** *noun*: *She gave me a cold stare.*

stark¹ /stɑːk $stɑrk/ *adjective*   **1** a stark place is very plain and not attractive: *The building was stark and unwelcoming.*   **2** very clear and unpleasant: *The government faces a stark choice.*

stark² *adverb* **stark naked** not wearing any clothes

star sign /'. ./ *noun* one of the twelve signs that show the part of the year when you were born, which some people believe influence your character: *"What star sign are you?" "Libra."*

start¹ /stɑːt $ stɑrt/ verb

GRAMMAR
start doing something
start to do something

1 to begin doing something: *Suddenly Sue started to cry.* | *I started writing my essay this morning.* | *My brother is starting school in September.*
2 to begin happening: *What time does the party start?*
3 to make something begin: *It was Kevin who started the argument.*
4 if a car or an engine starts, it begins to work: *Dad's car wouldn't start this morning.*
5 also **start up** to make a new company or organization: *My friends and I decided to start a band.*

PHRASE
to start with *spoken* **a)** used before you mention the first thing in a list: *To start with, you need a map.* **b)** happening for a while at the beginning, and then stopping: *I didn't understand him to start with.*

PHRASAL VERBS
start off
1 **start off** to begin doing something: *Let's start off by introducing ourselves.*
2 **start something off** to make something start happening: *Linda read her report to start off the discussion.*
start on
start on something to begin doing something: *Have you started on your homework yet?*
start over *AmE*
to start doing something again from the beginning: *It's no good – you'll have to start over.*

start² noun

GRAMMAR
the start of something
the beginning of something: *He appears at the start of the movie.* | *I knew from the start that she was lying.*

PHRASES
get off to a good start, get off to a bad start to start with something good or something bad happening: *The party got off to a bad start when someone broke a chair.*
for a start *spoken* used when you mention the first in a list of things: *You're not going out – you've got too much homework for a start.*

start·er /ˈstɑːtə $ ˈstɑrtɚ/ noun BrE the first part of a meal

start·le /ˈstɑːtl $ ˈstɑrtl/ verb to surprise someone by suddenly appearing in an unexpected way: *Oh – you startled me!*
– **startled** adjective: *She looked up with a startled expression on her face.*

starv·a·tion /stɑːˈveɪʃən $ stɑrˈveɪʃən/ noun [no plural] when someone has little or no food to eat: *People there are dying of starvation.*

starve /stɑːv $ stɑrv/ verb 1 to become ill or die because you do not have enough to eat: *He got lost in the desert and starved to death.* 2 to not give a person or animal enough food: *They starved her and let her die.*

starv·ing /ˈstɑːvɪŋ $ ˈstɑrvɪŋ/ adjective 1 someone who is starving is ill or dying because they have not had enough food for a long time 2 informal also **starved** AmE very hungry

stash /stæʃ/ verb informal to keep something in a secret place: *He stashed the money under his pillow.*

state¹ /steɪt/ noun

1 the condition that something is in: *Your bedroom is in a terrible state.* | *Look at the state of your clothes! They're filthy!*
2 one of the parts that the US and some other countries are divided into: *the state of Texas*
3 formal a country that has its own government: *the former state of Yugoslavia*

PHRASE
be in a state to be very upset or nervous: *She was in a real state about her missing cat.* | *I always get into a state before an exam.*

state² verb formal to say something publicly or officially: *The President stated that he would introduce new laws to protect children.*

state·ment /ˈsteɪtmənt/ noun

GRAMMAR
a statement about/on something
something that a person says or writes publicly and officially: *The*

S

band *made a statement* to the press *about* their reasons for cancelling the concert. | *The Prime Minister will* **issue a statement on** *the economy this afternoon.*

state-of-the-art /ˌ . . . ˈ ./ *adjective* something that is state-of-the-art is very good because it is made in the most modern way

States /steɪts/ *noun* the States *spoken* the United States

state school /ˈ. ˌ./ *noun BrE* a school which provides free education and is paid for by the government

states·man /ˈsteɪtsmən/ *noun, plural* statesmen /-mən/ an experienced and respected politician

stat·ic /ˈstætɪk/ also **static e·lec·tri·ci·ty** /ˌ . . . .ˈ .ˈ . ./ *noun* [no plural] electricity produced when two surfaces rub together

sta·tion /ˈsteɪʃən/ *noun* **1** a place where trains or buses stop so that people can get on and off: *I'm getting off at the next station.* | *the railway station* ⇨ see picture on page 349 **2** a company that broadcasts on radio or television: *your local radio station* **3** a building where the police or people who stop fires are based: *a police station* | *a fire station*

sta·tion·a·ry /ˈsteɪʃənəri $ ˈsteɪʃəˌneri/ *adjective formal* not moving: *The traffic was almost stationary.*

sta·tion·e·ry /ˈsteɪʃənəri $ ˈsteɪʃəˌneri/ *noun* [no plural] things such as paper and envelopes that you use for writing

station wag·on /ˈ.. ˌ../ *noun AmE* a large car with space at the back for carrying things; ESTATE CAR *BrE*

sta·tis·tics /stəˈtɪstɪks/ *plural noun* a set of numbers that give information about something: *These statistics show that the population is still increasing.*

stat·ue /ˈstætʃuː/ *noun* a stone or metal model of a person or animal: *a statue of King Charles on a horse*

stat·ure /ˈstætʃə $ ˈstætʃɚ/ *noun* [no plural] *formal* the importance that someone has because of their work or achievements

sta·tus /ˈsteɪtəs $ ˈsteɪtəs/ *noun* [no plural] **1** the position that someone has in a country or organization: *She fought to improve the status of women in*

society. **2** special importance that someone has because of their job, achievements, or social position: *He wanted a job with status.*

staunch /stɔːntʃ/ *adjective* very loyal: *All you need is one staunch friend.*

stave /steɪv/ *verb* **stave off something** to prevent something bad from happening: *The team did their best to stave off defeat.*

stay¹ /steɪ/ *verb*

GRAMMAR
stay in/at a place
stay with someone

1 to continue to be in the same place and not leave: *I'll* **stay in** *the car and wait for you.* | *Do you want to go over to Kathy's or* **stay here***? | I've decided to* **stay at** *this school. | Do you think he will* **stay with** *his wife?*
2 if something stays the way it is, it continues to be the same and does not change: *The door won't* **stay open***. | I* **stayed awake** *all night.*
3 to spend a short period of time in a place: *We are* **staying in** *London for a few days. | He* **stayed at** *the Ritz hotel. | They went to* **stay with** *Ed's parents.*

PHRASE
stay put *spoken* to remain in the same place and not move: *Stay put and I'll get someone who can help you.*

PHRASAL VERBS
stay away
to not go near someone or get involved with something: *You should* **stay away from** *drugs.*
stay behind
to stay in a place after other people have left: *Bob* **stayed behind** *after the party and helped me clear up.*
stay in
to stay in your home and not go out: *I hate* **staying in** *on Saturday night.*
stay on
to continue to study: *Are you* **staying on** *at school next year?*
stay out of
to not become involved in something: *I try to* **stay out of** *their arguments.*
stay up
to not go to bed: *I* **stayed up** *late trying to finish my homework.*

S

stay² *noun* a period of time that you spend somewhere: *an overnight stay in New York*

stead·fast /ˈstedfɑːst $ ˈstedfæst/ *adjective written* refusing to change your beliefs: *his steadfast loyalty to his country*

stead·y¹ /ˈstedi/ *adjective* **steadier, steadiest**
1 something that is steady does not move or shake: *His hand was very steady as he signed his name.* | *It's important to hold the camera steady.*
2 something that is steady continues at the same speed or level: *We drove along at a steady 50 miles per hour.*
–**steadily** *adverb*: *His work has improved steadily.*

PHRASES
a steady job a job that pays you regular money and is likely to continue for a long time: *My parents want me to find a steady job.*
a steady girlfriend, a steady boyfriend someone that you have a relationship with for a long time: *Rob was her first steady boyfriend.*

steady² *verb* **steadied, steadies** to stop something from moving: *He steadied the ladder against the wall.*

steak /steɪk/ *noun* a thick flat piece of meat or fish

steal /stiːl/ *verb* **stole** /stəʊl $ stoʊl/ **stolen** /ˈstəʊlən $ ˈstoʊlən/

GRAMMAR
steal something from someone/somewhere
to take something that belongs to someone else: *Someone stole $5 from her pocket.* | *She stole money from her parents.* | *My bike was stolen.* ⇨ *see usage note at* ROB

stealth·y /ˈstelθi/ *adjective* **stealthier, stealthiest** a stealthy action is quiet and secret
–**stealthily** *adverb*: *Andy crept stealthily up to the window.*

steam¹ /stiːm/ *noun*
the gas that hot water produces: *The bathroom was full of steam.*

steam² *verb* to use steam to cook food:

It's healthier to steam vegetables rather than boil them.

steamed up /ˌ. ˈ./ *adjective* covered with very small drops of water: *My glasses were all steamed up.*

steel /stiːl/ *noun* [no plural] a strong metal that is used for making knives, cars etc

steep /stiːp/ *adjective*
a steep road or hill goes down or up very quickly: *I can't ride my bike here – it's too steep.* | *The garden is on quite a steep slope.* | *We had to climb up a steep hill.*

steer /stɪə $ stɪr/ *verb*

GRAMMAR
steer something into/out of etc a place
to control which way a vehicle goes: *He steered the car into the car park.* | *I steered my bike out of her way.*

PHRASE
steer clear of someone/something to avoid someone or something: *I'm going to steer clear of Henry until he's in a better mood.*

steering wheel /ˈ.. ˌ./ *noun* the wheel that you turn to make a vehicle go right or left

stem¹ /stem/ *noun* the long thin part of a plant, from which leaves or flowers grow

stem² *verb* **stemmed, stemming; stem from** to happen as a result of something: *All their problems stemmed from their lack of money.*

stench /stentʃ/ *noun* [no plural] a very strong unpleasant smell

sten·cil /ˈstensəl/ *noun* a piece of card or plastic with shapes cut out of it, which you can use to paint a design on something

step¹ /step/ *noun*
1 a movement in which you put one foot down in front of or behind the other: *She took a step backwards from the edge of the water.*
2 one of a series of things that you do in order to achieve something: *The next step is to attach the wheels.*
3 a surface that you step onto so that you can go up or down to another level: *There were three steps leading up to the door.* | *She ran down the flight of steps.*

S

one step ahead to have done something or thought of something before someone else: *We've got to stay one step ahead of the competition.*

step by step steadily, in stages: *Step by step, you will become more confident in using the language.*

take steps to do something in order to deal with a problem: *We must take steps to prevent any more accidents.*

step² *verb* **stepped, stepping** **1** to put one foot down in front of or behind the other: *He stepped forward to collect his prize.* | *She stepped carefully over the dog.* **2 step down** to leave an important job **3 step out of line** to break the rules **4 step something up** to increase something: *Security at the hospital is being stepped up.*

step·broth·er /'step,brʌðə $ 'step-,brʌðɚ/ *noun* someone who is not your brother but is the son of someone who is married to one of your parents

step·child /'steptʃaɪld/ *noun, plural* **stepchildren** /-,tʃɪldrən/ a child that your husband or wife has from a previous relationship

step·daugh·ter /'step,dɔːtə $ 'step-,dɔtɚ/ *noun* a daughter that your husband or wife has from a previous relationship

step·fa·ther /'step,fɑːðə $ 'step-,fɑðɚ/ *noun* a man who is married to your mother but is not your father

step·lad·der /'step,lædə $ 'step-,lædɚ/ *noun* a LADDER with two sloping parts joined at the top

step·moth·er /'step,mʌðə $ 'step-,mʌðɚ/ *noun* a woman who is married to your father but is not your mother

step·sis·ter /'step,sɪstə $ 'step,sɪstɚ/ *noun* someone who is not your sister but is the daughter of someone who is married to one of your parents

step·son /'stepsʌn/ *noun* a son that your husband or wife has from a previous relationship

ster·e·o /'steriəʊ $ 'steri,oʊ/ *noun* a machine for playing music TAPES, CDs etc that produces sound from two SPEAKERS ⇨ *see picture on page 342*

ster·e·o·type¹ /'steriətaɪp,taɪp/ *noun* the usual and well-known idea of what a type of person is like, which is probably not correct

stereotype² *verb* to think that someone is a particular type of person, especially when this is not correct: *Blonde women are stereotyped as stupid.*

ster·ile /'steraɪl $ 'sterəl/ *adjective* **1** completely clean and not containing any BACTERIA **2** unable to have children

ster·il·ize also **sterilise** *BrE* /'sterəlaɪz/ *verb* **1** to make something completely clean and contain no BACTERIA: *a sterilized needle* **2** to perform a medical operation on someone so that they cannot have any children

ster·ling /'stɜːlɪŋ $ 'stɚlɪŋ/ *noun* [no plural] the standard unit of money in the UK; the pound

stern¹ /stɜːn $ stɚn/ *adjective* very serious or strict: *The teacher gave me a stern look.*

stern² *noun* the back part of a ship

stew¹ /stjuː $ stu/ *noun* pieces of meat and vegetables that are cooked slowly in liquid

stew² *verb* to cook something slowly in liquid

stew·ard /'stjuːəd $ 'stuɚd/ *noun* a man who serves food and drinks to people on a ship or plane

stew·ard·ess /'stjuːədes $ 'stuɚdɪs/ *noun, plural* **stewardesses** a woman who serves food and drinks to people on a ship or plane

stick¹ /stɪk/ *verb, past tense and past participle* **stuck** /stʌk/

stick something on/to/into etc something
stick on/to something

1 to join two things together using glue: *I stuck a label on the bottle.* | *Stick the ticket to the car windscreen.*
2 if something sticks to a surface, it stays on it, for example because it has glue on it: *These stamps won't stick on the envelope.* | *The leaves were sticking to my shoes.*
3 to push a pointed object into something: *She accidentally stuck the sewing needle into her finger.*
4 if something sticks, it becomes difficult to move: *The window sometimes sticks.*

PHRASAL VERBS

stick out

1 stick out if something sticks out, it comes out from a surface: *Michael's ears **stick out**.*

2 stick something out to deliberately make a part of your body come forward: *He **stuck** his leg **out** and I fell over it.* | *The boy **stuck** his tongue **out** at me.*

stick to

stick to something to continue doing something in the way you planned to do it: *I think we should **stick to** what we decided.*

stick together

if people stick together, they stay together and help each other: *The two sisters have always **stuck together**.*

stick up

if something sticks up, it is not flat but comes up above a surface: *Your hair is **sticking up**.*

stick² *noun* a long thin piece of wood: *a bundle of sticks*

stick·er /'stɪkə $'stɪkɚ/ *noun* a small piece of paper or plastic with a picture or writing on it, which you can stick to something

stick·y /'stɪki/ *adjective* **stickier, stickiest**
covered with a substance like glue that sticks to surfaces: *Your hands are all sticky.*

sties the plural of STY

stiff /stɪf/ *adjective*

1 something that is stiff is hard and difficult to bend: *a sheet of stiff paper*

2 if a part of your body is stiff, it is difficult to move because your muscles hurt: *I've got a stiff neck.*

3 **stiff competition** people or teams that are difficult to defeat: *The team will face **stiff competition** this season.*

4 a stiff sentence, a stiff punishment a severe punishment: *The judge gave him a **stiff sentence**.*

sti·fle /'staɪfəl/ *verb* to stop something from happening or developing: *Living with my parents is stifling my social life.*

stif·ling /'staɪflɪŋ/ *adjective* if it is stifling in a place, it is very hot, so that you feel uncomfortable: *It's stifling in here – can I open a window?*

sti·let·to /stɪ'letəʊ $stɪ'letoʊ/ *noun* a woman's shoe with a high thin heel

still¹ /stɪl/ *adverb*

1 use still to say that a situation has not changed: *Are there any sandwiches left? I'm still hungry.* | *Is Dad still asleep?* | *It's still raining.* | *I think you should go back to college.* | *You still haven't given me the money you owe me.*

2 use still to say that something continues to be possible: *We've still got time to catch that film, if we hurry.* | *You could still change your mind.* | *Can you still walk?*

3 use still to say that there is a particular amount of something left: *It's still a week before we get paid.* | *I've still got some cigarettes from last night.* | *There are still three days to go before the final.*

4 use still with 'but' or 'although' to say that something did happen, even though something else might have stopped it: *Although Shelley hates cleaning, she still came and helped us.* | *Cliff had a bad cold, but he still performed.*

still² *adjective*
not moving: ***Keep still** while I comb your hair.* | *He was **standing** perfectly **still**.* | *I wish those children would **sit still**.*

still·born /'stɪlbɔːn $,stɪl'bɔrn/ *adjective* a stillborn baby is born dead

stim·u·late /'stɪmjəleɪt/ *verb* **1** to make something grow, develop, or happen: *The light stimulates the plants to grow.* **2** to make someone interested and excited: *toys that stimulate children*

stim·u·lat·ing /'stɪmjəleɪtɪŋ/ *adjective* interesting and giving you new ideas: *a stimulating conversation*

stim·u·lus /'stɪmjələs/ *noun* formal, plural **stimuli** /-laɪ/ **1** [no plural] something that makes a thing develop or happen **2** something that makes you feel interested or excited: *Children need the visual stimulus of pictures in a book.*

sting

sting¹ /stɪŋ/ verb, past tense and past participle **stung** /stʌŋ/
1 if an insect or plant stings you, it hurts you by putting poison into your skin: *A wasp stung me on the leg.*
2 if something stings, it gives you a sharp pain on your skin: *It stung when they cleaned the wound.* | *The salt from the sea made my eyes sting.*

sting² noun a wound on your skin where an insect or plant has stung you: *a wasp sting*

stin·gy /'stɪndʒi/ adjective informal **stingier, stingiest** not generous with your money

stink /stɪŋk/ verb informal **stank** /stæŋk/ **stunk** /stʌŋk/ to have a very strong and unpleasant smell: *Ugh – you stink of smoke!* | *These socks stink!*
–**stink** noun: *the stink of dead fish*

stir¹ /stɜː $ stɚ/ verb **stirred, stirring**

GRAMMAR
stir something with something
stir something in
stir something into something
to mix something by moving a spoon around in it: *Kate stirred her tea with a spoon.* | *Next, stir in the milk.* | *Stir the grated cheese into the sauce.* ⇨ *see picture on page 344*

stir² noun **1 create a stir, cause a stir** to make people very excited, angry, or surprised: *Her first speech really caused a stir.* **2 give something a stir** to stir liquid or food: *Give the paint a good stir before using it.*

stir-fry /'. ./ verb **stir-fried, stir-fries** to cook vegetables or meat quickly in a little hot oil

–**stir-fry** noun: *Shall we have a stir-fry tonight?*

stir·ring /'stɜːrɪŋ/ adjective making people feel very excited, proud, or eager to do something: *a stirring speech*

stir·rup /'stɪrəp $ 'stɚəp/ noun one of the two metal things that you put your feet in when you are riding a horse

stitch¹ /stɪtʃ/ noun, plural **stitches**
1 a single line of thread that has been sewn on material: *a black dress with white stitches around the collar* **2** one of the small circles of wool you make when you KNIT **3 in stitches** informal laughing a lot: *We were all in stitches!*

stitch² verb to sew something: *Can you stitch this button on?*

stock¹ /stɒk $ stɑk/ noun **1** a supply of things that a shop has available to sell or that someone has ready to use: *The store now has a large stock of computer games.* **2 in stock** if a shop has something in stock, it has it available for people to buy there: *I'm afraid we haven't got that video in stock at the moment.* **3 stocks (and shares)** if you buy stocks in a company, you buy and own a small part of it, so that when the company's profits increase you make more money too: *A lot of people invest in stocks and shares.*

stock² verb **1** to have something available for people to buy: *We don't stock that brand of cereal any more.* **2 stock up** to buy a supply of things in order to have them ready to use later: *I need to stock up on tea and coffee.*

stock·brok·er /'stɒk,brəʊkə $ 'stɑk-brəʊkɚ/ noun someone whose job is to buy and sell company SHARES for other people

stock ex·change /'. .,./ also **stock mar·ket** /'. .,./ noun **1** a place where people buy and sell the SHARES of many different companies **2 the stock exchange, the stock market** the buying and selling of SHARES: *He made a lot of money on the stock exchange.*

stock·ing /'stɒkɪŋ $ 'stɑkɪŋ/ noun a very thin piece of clothing that fits closely over a woman's foot and leg: *a pair of stockings*

stock mar·ket /'. .,./ a STOCK EXCHANGE

stock·pile /'stɒkpaɪl $'stɑkpaɪl/ verb to collect a large supply of something because you think that it may not be available later: *People have been stockpiling food in case there is a bad winter.*

stock·y /'stɒki $'stɑki/ adjective **stockier, stockiest** someone who is stocky is short and has a heavy strong body

stole the past tense of STEAL

stolen the past participle of STEAL

stom·ach¹ /'stʌmək/ noun **1** the part inside your body where food is DIGESTED **2** the front part of your body, below your chest: *These exercises should help to keep your stomach flat.*

stomach² verb **can't stomach something** to be unable to watch or listen to something because it is so unpleasant or upsetting

stone /stəʊn $stoʊn/ noun
1 a small piece of rock: *There's a stone in my shoe.* | *We were told off for throwing stones.*
2 [no plural] rock: *The fireplace is made of stone.* | *a stone wall*
3 plural **stone** a measurement of weight that is used in Britain and is equal to 14 pounds or 6.35 KILOGRAMS: *Sue weighs eight stone.*
4 BrE a large hard seed in the centre of a fruit; PIT AmE

stoned /stəʊnd $stoʊnd/ adjective informal someone who is stoned is behaving in a strange way because they have used illegal drugs

ston·y /'stəʊni $'stoʊni/ adjective **stonier, stoniest** covered with stones or containing a lot of stones: *the stony ground*

stood the past tense and past participle of STAND¹

stool /stuːl/ noun a chair with no back ⇨ see picture at CHAIR¹

stoop /stuːp/ verb to bend your head and shoulders down: *Try not to stoop when you walk.*

stop¹ /stɒp $stɑp/ verb **stopped, stopping**

GRAMMAR
stop doing something
stop for something

stop to do something
stop someone from doing something
1 if you stop doing something, you do not continue to do it: *Suddenly she stopped laughing and looked serious.* | *Stop making so much noise!* | *I stopped smoking several years ago.*
2 if something stops, it ends: *Suddenly the laughter stopped.* | *We all want the fighting to stop.* | *It's stopped raining* (=it is not raining any more).
3 if you stop something, you make it end: *The referee stopped the game.*
4 if a vehicle or machine stops, it does not continue to move or work: *The train stopped at the station.* | *Stop the car – I need to get out.* | *Has this clock stopped?*
5 to pause for a short time: *Shall we **stop for** a break? | Let's **stop to** get something to eat.*
6 to prevent someone from doing something: *I'm going out and you can't stop me! | I tried to **stop** her **from** leaving.*
7 if you stop someone, you ask them to stand still and talk to you: *A woman stopped me and asked me the way to the bank.*

PHRASE
stop it, stop that spoken used to tell someone not to do something: *I told him to **stop it** but he kept on hitting me.* | *Ian, **stop that** immediately!*

stop² noun
1 a place where a bus or train regularly stops for its passengers: *She got off the bus at the first stop.* | *This is my stop – goodbye!* ⇨ see picture on page 349
2 a place that you visit during a trip: *Our first stop will be the Eiffel Tower.*

PHRASES
come to a stop to stop moving: *The plane finally **came to a stop** at the end of the runway.*
put a stop to something to prevent something from continuing to happen: *I'm going to **put a stop to** all this nonsense.*

stop·light /'stɒplaɪt $'stɑplaɪt/ the American word for a TRAFFIC LIGHT

S

stop·watch /'stɒpwɒtʃ $ 'stɑpwɑtʃ/ noun, plural **stopwatches** a watch for measuring the exact time it takes to do something

stor·age /'stɔːrɪdʒ/ noun [no plural] when you keep things somewhere until you need them: *All our furniture is in storage.*

store¹ /stɔː $ stɔr/ noun

GRAMMAR
a store of something

1 a building where you can buy things; shop *BrE*: *There's a big furniture store near here.* | *a new clothes store*
2 a supply of things that you can use later: *She has **a secret store of** sweets.*

store² verb

GRAMMAR
store something in/at a place

1 also **store away** to put things somewhere and keep them there until you need them: *I **store** all my old books **in** this room.* | *My summer clothes are all **stored away**.*
2 to keep information in a computer: *The hard disk stores a large amount of information.*

store·keep·er /'stɔːˌkiːpə $ 'stɔrˌkipɚ/ the American word for a SHOP-KEEPER

store·room /'stɔːruːm/ noun a room where you store things: *We use this bedroom as a storeroom.*

sto·rey *BrE*, **story** *AmE* /'stɔːri/ noun one level of a tall building: *a building with 32 stories*

storm¹ /stɔːm $ stɔrm/ noun

if there is a storm, there is a lot of wind and rain, and sometimes snow: *It looks like there's going to be a storm.* | *She got lost in a **snowstorm** (=a storm with a lot of snow).* | *We had a huge **thunderstorm** (=a storm with* THUNDER *and* LIGHTNING*) last night.*

storm² verb 1 if people storm a place, they attack it: *The army stormed the city last night.* 2 to walk somewhere in a way that shows you are very angry: *The tutor stormed in and asked why we weren't getting on with our work.*

storm·y /'stɔːmi $ 'stɔrmi/ adjective **stormier, stormiest** if the weather is stormy, there is a lot of wind and rain or snow: *stormy weather* | *a stormy day*

sto·ry /'stɔːri/ noun, plural **stories**

GRAMMAR
the story of something
a story about something

1 a description of a set of events that can be real or imaginary: *Do you know **the story of** Peter Pan?* | *I'm going to **tell** you **a story about** two cats.* | *Will you **read** me **a story**?*
2 a report of a real event in a newspaper or news programme: *There's an interesting story on the front page of the newspaper.*
3 an explanation about something that happened, which may be untrue: *The police didn't believe his story.*

stout /staʊt/ adjective rather fat: *a stout 40-year-old man*

stove /stəʊv $ stoʊv/ noun a piece of kitchen equipment that you cook on; COOKER *BrE*: *She heated a pan of milk on the stove.*

strad·dle /'strædl/ verb to sit or stand with your legs on either side of something: *He sat straddling the gate.*

strag·gly /'strægli/ adjective **stragglier, straggliest** growing or spreading out in an untidy way: *straggly hair*

straight¹ /streɪt/ adjective

1 not bent or curved: *Draw a straight line across the page.*
2 level or upright, and not leaning: *That picture isn't straight.* | *Try and keep your writing straight.*
3 straight hair does not have curls in it: *She had long straight hair.*
4 honest and direct: *I just want a **straight answer**.* | *Do you think he's being straight with us?*

PHRASES
get straight A's to get the highest possible mark in all your school subjects: *Elizabeth always **got straight A's** at school.*

get something straight *spoken* to make sure that people completely understand the true facts about a situation: *We need to **get this***

▼ *straight. Do you want to live here or not?*

keep a straight face to not laugh or smile even though something is funny: *I managed to keep a straight face even when he fell over.*

straight² *adverb*

1 in a straight line: *Jon was sitting straight in front of me.* | *Keep looking straight ahead.* | *Go straight on* (=continue in the same direction), *and turn left at the church.*

2 immediately: *When I got home, I went straight to my room.* | *I've got French straight after lunch.*

PHRASES

straight away immediately: *I knew straight away that I had made a mistake.*

sit up straight, stand up straight to sit or stand with your body in an upright position: *It's good for your back to stand up straight.*

cannot think straight, could not think straight if you cannot think straight, you cannot think clearly because you are excited or upset

straight·en /'streɪtn/ *verb* to make something straight: *Let me straighten your tie.*

straight·for·ward /ˌstreɪt'fɔːwəd $ ˌstreɪt'fɔrwəd/ *adjective* easy to do or understand: *It's a straightforward question.*

straightjacket another spelling of STRAITJACKET

strain¹ /streɪn/ *noun* **1** worry and pressure caused by a difficult situation: *She found it hard to cope with the strain of being a teacher.* | *His work put a strain on our marriage.* **2** [no plural] when something is pulled too tightly or has to hold a lot of weight: *The cable broke under the strain* (=because of the strain). **3** an injury to part of your body, caused by using it too much: *Many nurses suffer from back strain.*

strain² *verb* **1** to use a lot of effort to do something: *I had to strain to hear the music.* **2** to separate solid things from a liquid by pouring the mixture through a strainer: *Will you strain the vegetables?* ⇨ *see picture on page 344* **3** to injure part of your body by using it too much: *I've strained my neck.* **4** to make a

relationship more difficult: *His job is straining our relationship.*

strain·er /'streɪnə $ 'streɪnɚ/ *noun* a kitchen tool used for separating solid food from a liquid

strait·jack·et also **straightjacket** /'streɪtˌdʒækɪt/ *noun* a very tight piece of clothing that is sometimes put on a violent or mentally ill person to stop them from moving their arms

strand /strænd/ *noun* a single thin piece of hair, wire, or thread

strand·ed /'strændɪd/ *adjective* unable to get away from a place, for example because of bad weather: *I was stranded at the airport.*

strange /streɪndʒ/ *adjective*

1 unusual or surprising: *I could hear strange noises.* | *Kevin has some strange ideas.* | *It's strange that Sarah hasn't called.*

2 a strange place is a place where you have never been before: *She was all alone in a strange city.*

strang·er /'streɪndʒə $ 'streɪndʒɚ/ *noun* someone who you do not know: *A stranger approached him and asked for a cigarette.*

stran·gle /'stræŋgəl/ *verb* to kill someone by tightly pressing their throat: *Her attacker had strangled her with a rope.*

strap¹ /stræp/ *noun* a band of cloth or leather for carrying or fastening something: *a bag with a leather strap* | *a watch strap*

strap² *verb* **strapped, strapping** to fasten something or someone, using straps: *They strapped the bags onto their bikes.* | *His two-year-old son was strapped in the back seat of the car.*

stra·te·gic /strə'tiːdʒɪk/ *adjective* done as part of a military, business, or political plan: *The President made an important strategic decision.*

strat·e·gy /'strætədʒi/ *noun, plural* **strategies** a set of plans to achieve something: *What's your strategy going to be for winning the election?*

straw /strɔː/ *noun* **1** [no plural] dried stems of wheat: *We put down clean straw for the animals to sleep on.* **2** a thin tube of plastic used for drinking

S

through **3 the last straw, the final straw** the last problem in a series of problems that finally makes you become angry or stop trying to do something: *It was the last straw when my car broke down.*

straw·ber·ry /'strɔːbəri $'strɔ,beri/ *noun, plural* **strawberries** a small red juicy fruit that grows on plants near the ground ⇨ *see picture on page 345*

stray¹ /streɪ/ *verb* to move away from a safe or familiar area: *The kitten had strayed from its mother.*

stray² *noun* an animal that is lost or has no home
– **stray** *adjective*: *a stray dog*

streak /striːk/ *noun* a thin line of colour that is different to the colour around it: *He had streaks of grey in his hair.*

stream¹ /striːm/ *noun* **1** a small river ⇨ *see picture on page 348* **2** a moving line of things: *There was a steady stream of traffic through the town centre.*

stream² *verb* to move somewhere quickly and continuously, in large amounts: *Tears were streaming down his face.* | *People streamed into the building.*

stream·line /'striːmlaɪn/ *verb* **1** to make something work in a simpler and more effective way: *We are streamlining our business.* **2** if you streamline a vehicle, you improve its shape so that it moves more easily through air or water
– **streamlined** *adjective*: *the streamlined shape of modern planes*

street /striːt/ *noun*

a road in a town or city with houses or shops on it: *Go to the end of the street and turn left.* | *The two boys live* **in** *the same* **street.** | *I live at 75 Queen Street.* ⇨ *see usage note at* ROAD

street·car /'striːtkɑː $'striːtkɑr/ the American word for a TRAM

street·light or **street light** /'striːtlaɪt/ *noun* a light on a long pole in a street ⇨ *see picture on page 343*

strength /streŋθ/ *noun*

GRAMMAR
strength to do something
1 *[no plural]* someone's strength is their ability to lift or carry heavy objects: *You need a lot of* **strength to** *be a*

▼ weightlifter. | *She didn't* **have the strength to** *lift the fridge on her own.*

2 your strengths are the things that you are good at: *Make a list of your strengths and weaknesses.*

3 *[no plural]* being brave and determined in difficult situations: *She has shown a lot of strength in dealing with her son's illness.* | *He didn't* **have the strength to** *carry on living.*

---

strength·en /'streŋθən/ *verb* to make something stronger: *an exercise to strengthen your legs*

stren·u·ous /'strenjuəs/ *adjective* a strenuous activity needs a lot of effort or strength: *a strenuous exercise routine*

stress¹ /stres/ *noun, plural* **stresses** **1** continuous feelings of worry that prevent you from relaxing: *I don't cope well with stress.* | *She's under a lot of stress at work.* **2** the force or loudness with which you say a part of a word: *The stress is on the first syllable.*

stress² *verb* **1** to say how important something is: *She stressed the importance of homework.* **2** to say a word or part of a word more loudly or with more force than other words: *He stressed the word 'everyone'.*

stressed /strest/ also **stressed out** /ˌ. './ *adjective informal* worried and unable to relax: *Don't get stressed about exams.*

stress·ful /'stresfəl/ *adjective* making you worried and unable to relax: *Pilots have a stressful job.*

stretch

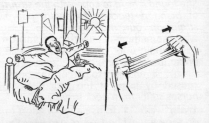

stretch¹ /stretʃ/ *verb*

GRAMMAR
stretch (something) somewhere
1 to make something bigger by pulling it: *Don't pull my sweater – you'll stretch it.*

2 if something stretches, it becomes bigger when you pull it: *Tights stretch when you put them on.*

3 to push your arms or legs out as far as they can go: *He yawned and stretched.* | **Stretch** *your arms* **above** *your head.* ⇨ see picture on page 340

4 to spread over a large area: *The beach* **stretched down to** *the sea.* | *The traffic jam stretched for over two miles.*

5 to pull something so that is straight and tight: *They* **stretched** *the net* **between** *the two posts.*

> **PHRASAL VERB**
> **stretch out**
> **1** stretch out, stretch yourself out to lie down: *He* **stretched out** *on the bed and went to sleep.*
> **2** stretch your hand out, stretch your arm out to move your hand or arm forwards so that you can reach something: *She* **stretched out** *her hand towards the sugar pot.*

stretch² *noun, plural* **stretches** an area of land or water: *a dangerous stretch of water*

stretch·er /'stretʃə $'stretʃɚ/ *noun* a covered frame that you use for carrying an injured person: *He was carried off the pitch on a stretcher.*

strewn /struːn/ *adjective* if objects are strewn somewhere, they have been thrown or dropped there in an untidy way: *Toys were strewn all over the floor.*

strict /strɪkt/ *adjective*

> **GRAMMAR**
> **strict about something**
> **strict with someone**

1 a strict person has a lot of rules and makes people obey them: *Most of the teachers here are quite strict.* | *The bosses are very* **strict about** *people arriving on time.* | *Some parents are very* **strict with** *their children.*

2 a strict rule or instruction must be obeyed: *There are strict rules about who is allowed in the country.* | *I have strict orders not to let you leave.*

3 always following your beliefs or religion very carefully: *Margaret is a strict Catholic who goes to mass every day.* | *a strict vegetarian*

strict·ly /'strɪktli/ *adverb* **1** if something is not strictly true, it is not exactly true **2** in a strict way: *My father raised us very strictly.*

stridden the past participle of STRIDE¹

stride¹ /straɪd/ *verb* **strode** /strəʊd $strəʊd/ **stridden** /'strɪdn/ to walk with quick long steps: *He strode down the hall.*

stride² *noun* **1** a long step: *He walks with great big strides.* **2** take something in your stride to deal with a problem easily and calmly: *Kids seem to take everything in their stride.*

strike¹ /straɪk/ *verb, past tense and past participle* **struck** /strʌk/

> **GRAMMAR**
> **strike someone as something**

1 to hit something or someone: *His spade struck a stone.* | *The church tower was struck by lightning.*

2 if an idea strikes you, you suddenly think of it: *It suddenly struck me that Peter was keeping very quiet.*

3 how something strikes you is how it seems to you: *Her attitude* **struck** *me* **as** *odd.*

4 if a clock strikes, its bell makes a number of sounds to show the time: *The clock struck four.*

strike² *noun*

when a group of workers stop working because they want better pay or working conditions: *Railway workers are planning a one-day strike next week.*

> **PHRASE**
> **be on strike, go on strike** if a group of workers are on strike, they have stopped working because they want better pay or working conditions: *The workers at the factory* **went on strike.** | *They've* **been on strike** *for three weeks now.*

strik·er /'straɪkə $'straɪkɚ/ *noun* **1** someone who has stopped working in order to get better pay or working conditions: *Strikers stopped cars entering the factory.* **2** a football player whose main job is to try to get GOALS: *Shearer is the team's best striker.*

S

strik·ing /'straɪkɪŋ/ *adjective* **1** unusual and noticeable: *There's a striking similarity between them.* **2** very attractive, often in an unusual way: *She's a very striking woman.*

string /strɪŋ/ *noun*

GRAMMAR
a string of things

1 a thin rope that you use for tying things: *He tied some string round the package.*
2 the strings on a GUITAR or other musical instrument are the long thin pieces of wire that are stretched across it
3 a number of similar things that happen one after the other: *There's been a string of complaints about you.*

strip¹ /strɪp/ *verb* **stripped, stripping** also **strip off** **1** to take off your clothes: *He stripped and got into the shower.* **2** to remove something that is covering a surface: *We stripped the paint off the walls.*

strip² *noun* a long narrow piece of something: *a strip of paper*

stripe /straɪp/ *noun* a long narrow area of colour: *a shirt with red stripes*

striped /straɪpt/ also **strip·y** /'straɪpi/ *adjective* something that is striped has a pattern of stripes on it: *a striped dress*

strive /straɪv/ *verb formal* **strove** /strəʊv $ stroʊv/ **striven** /'strɪvən/ to try very hard to do something: *He always strives to do his best.*

striven the past participle of STRIVE

strode the past tense of STRIDE¹

stroke¹ /strəʊk $ stroʊk/ *noun* **1** an illness in which a part of your brain becomes damaged, often with the result that you become unable to move a part of your body: *My grandad's had a stroke.* **2** a way of swimming: *back stroke*

stroke² *verb* to move your hand gently over something: *The cat likes it when you stroke her.* ⇨ see picture on page 341

stroll /strəʊl $ stroʊl/ *verb* to walk in a slow relaxed way: *We strolled along the beach.*
— **stroll** *noun*: *Are you coming for a stroll?*

stroll·er /'strəʊlə $ 'stroʊlɚ/ the American word for a PUSHCHAIR

strong /strɒŋ $ strɔŋ/ *adjective*

1 someone who is strong has strength and energy ⇨ *opposite* WEAK (1): *He was not strong enough to lift the rock up.* | *a big man with strong arms*
2 something that is strong cannot be broken or damaged easily: *She carried the bottles in a strong plastic bag.*
3 a strong wind is blowing with a lot of force: *a strong wind*
4 a strong feeling or belief is one that you feel or believe a lot: *I had a strong desire to hit him.* | *There is strong evidence that smoking makes you ill.*
5 a strong drink contains a lot of a substance ⇨ *opposite* WEAK (4): *a cup of strong coffee*
6 if someone is strong, they are not made too upset by problems and are not easily persuaded by other people ⇨ *opposite* WEAK (2): *You have to be strong to cope with the death of a child.*

PHRASE
a strong chance, a strong possibility if there is a strong chance or possibility of something happening, it is very likely: *There's a strong possibility that he will be chosen for the school team.*

strong·ly /'strɒŋli $ 'strɔŋli/ *adverb* **1** if you believe in something strongly, you think it is important or care a lot about it: *I believe strongly in the importance of education.* **2** tasting or smelling a lot of something: *The house smelled strongly of gas.*

strove the past tense of STRIVE

struck the past tense of STRIKE¹

struc·tur·al /'strʌktʃərəl/ *adjective* related to the structure of a building, bridge etc: *The storm caused structural damage.*

struc·ture¹ /'strʌktʃə $ 'strʌktʃɚ/ *noun* **1** the way in which the parts of something are put together or organized: *the structure of society* **2** something that has been built, especially a building: *a huge wooden structure*

structure² *verb* to arrange something in a clear way: *The teacher taught us how to structure a piece of writing.*

strug·gle /'strʌgəl/ *verb* **1** to try very hard to achieve something difficult: *Susie's really struggled to pass these exams.* **2** to fight someone who is attacking or holding you: *She struggled but could not get away from him.*
– **struggle** *noun: He broke his glasses in the struggle.*

strut /strʌt/ *verb* **strutted, strutting** to walk in a very proud and annoying way: *He struts around the school as if he owns it.*

stub /stʌb/ *noun* the part of a cigarette that is left after the rest has been used

stub·ble /'stʌbəl/ *noun [no plural]* the very short hairs on a man's face when he has not SHAVEd for a few days ⇨ *see picture on page 353*

stub·born /'stʌbən $ 'stʌbə·n/ *adjective* someone who is stubborn refuses to change their opinions or beliefs in a way that seems unreasonable: *Stop being so stubborn.*

stuck¹ the past tense and past participle of STICK¹

stuck² /stʌk/ *adjective* spoken **1** not able to move: *John's stuck up the tree! | The door's stuck!* **2** if you are stuck, you cannot continue with your work because it is too difficult: *Jane helps me when I get stuck with my homework.*

stud /stʌd/ *noun* a small round piece of metal that is stuck into the surface of something: *You need football shoes with studs in this wet weather.* ⇨ *see picture at JEWELLERY*

stu·dent /'stjuːdənt $ 'studnt/ *noun* someone who studies at a school or university

stu·di·o /'stjuːdiəʊ $ 'studi,oʊ/ *noun* **1** a room where a painter or photographer works **2** a place where films, records, or television or radio programmes are made

stu·di·ous /'stjuːdiəs $ 'studiəs/ *adjective* someone who is studious spends a lot of time studying: *a studious young boy*

stud·y¹ /'stʌdi/ *noun, plural* **studies**

GRAMMAR
a/the study of something

1 a piece of work in which someone collects facts and information so that they can find out more about something: *They carried out a study of the types of food that children eat.* **2** *[no plural]* when you learn about a subject: *Biology is the study of living things.* **3** a room in your house where you write or study **4** your studies, his studies etc the work someone does at school or college: *You've got to continue with your studies.*

study² *verb* **studied, studies**
1 to learn about a subject: *She wants to study law at university.* **2** to look at something carefully: *He studied the map.*

stuff¹ /stʌf/ *noun [no plural]* informal **1** any substance or material: *What's that green stuff on the wall?* **2** things in general: *Do you need all this stuff on holiday? | It's the same old stuff on TV every night.*

stuff² *verb* to push something into a place quickly and carelessly: *I quickly stuffed some clothes into a bag. | He stuffed the letter into his pocket.*

stuff·ing /'stʌfɪŋ/ *noun [no plural]* material that is used to fill something: *All the stuffing's come out of the mattress.*

stuff·y /'stʌfi/ *adjective* **stuffier, stuffiest** places that are stuffy do not have enough fresh air: *It's very stuffy in here.*

stum·ble /'stʌmbəl/ *verb* to almost fall: *She stumbled over the rocks.*

stump /stʌmp/ *noun* the part of something that is left when the rest has been cut off: *a tree stump*

stun /stʌn/ *verb* **stunned, stunning** to surprise or shock someone very much: *Everyone was stunned by the news.*

stung the past tense and past participle of STING

stunk the past participle of STINK

stun·ning /'stʌnɪŋ/ *adjective* **1** very beautiful: *You look absolutely stunning.* **2** very surprising: *stunning news*

stunt¹ /stʌnt/ *noun* **1** a dangerous thing that someone does to entertain people, especially in a film: *There's a great stunt in which his car has to jump across a 15 metre gap.* **2** something

S

that people do to get attention: *The photograph was just a publicity stunt.*

stunt² *verb* to stop something from growing or developing properly: *a disease that stunts your growth*

stu·pid /'stju:pɪd $'stupɪd/ *adjective*

1 not intelligent or sensible: *You're so stupid – you haven't switched the machine on! | I made a stupid mistake.*

2 *spoken* used to talk about something that annoys you: *The stupid machine's broken!*

stu·por /'stju:pə $'stupɚ/ *noun* a state in which you are almost unconscious: *He was lying on the bed in a drunken stupor.*

stur·dy /'stɜ:di $'stɚdi/ *adjective* **sturdier, sturdiest** thick and strong: *sturdy shoes*

stut·ter /'stʌtə $'stʌtɚ/ *verb* to have difficulty speaking so that you repeat the first sound of a word: *"I w-w-want to g-g-go too," he stuttered.*
– **stutter** *noun*: *I didn't always speak with a stutter.*

sty /staɪ/ *noun, plural* **sties** *noun* a PIGSTY

style /staɪl/ *noun*

GRAMMAR
a style of something

1 a way of doing something: *He developed his own **style** of painting. | The two poems are written **in** different **styles**.*

2 the shape or design of a piece of clothing: *Does this **style of** jacket suit me?*

3 the shape in which your hair is cut: *I think a shorter style would suit you.*

styl·ish /'staɪlɪʃ/ *adjective* attractive and fashionable: *Joe always wears very stylish clothes.*
– **stylishly** *adverb*: *She always dresses stylishly.*

sub /sʌb/ *informal* **1** a SUBMARINE **2** a SUBSTITUTE¹

sub·con·scious¹ /sʌb'kɒnʃəs $sʌb-'kɑnʃəs/ *adjective* subconscious feelings affect your behaviour although you do not realize that they exist
– **subconsciously** *adverb*: *Maybe subconsciously you feel trapped.*

subconscious² *noun* [no plural] your subconscious is the part of you that has thoughts and feelings that you do not know about, but which influence your behaviour

sub·due /səb'dju: $səb'du/ *verb* to stop someone from behaving violently: *Police were sent in to subdue the crowd.*

sub·dued /səb'dju:d $səb'dud/ *adjective* **1** quiet, especially because you are worried: *You seem a bit subdued.*
2 not as bright or loud as usual: *subdued lighting*

sub·ject /'sʌbdʒɪkt/ *noun*

GRAMMAR
the subject of something

1 one of the things such as literature or science that you study at school or university: *My favourite subject is English.*

2 the thing that you are talking or writing about: *I don't think we should talk about this subject in front of the children. | They discussed **the subject of** money. | I tried to **change the subject** (=start talking about something else).*

3 the word that usually comes before the verb in a sentence and shows who is doing the action. In the sentence 'Jean loves cats', 'Jean' is the subject

sub·jec·tive /səb'dʒektɪv/ *adjective* influenced by your own opinions and feelings rather than by facts: *Beauty is a very subjective thing.*

sub·junc·tive /səb'dʒʌŋktɪv/ *noun* a verb form that you use to express a doubt, wish, or possibility. In the sentence 'He suggested we leave early', 'leave' is in the subjunctive

sub·ma·rine /'sʌbməri:n/ *noun* a ship that can travel under water ⇨ *see picture on page 349*

sub·merge /səb'mɜːdʒ $səb'mɚdʒ/ *verb* to put something below the surface of water: *The town was completely submerged by the floods.*

sub·mis·sion /səb'mɪʃən/ *noun* [no plural] when you are forced to agree to do what someone tells you to: *The soldiers beat them into submission.*

sub·mit /səb'mɪt/ *verb* formal **submitted, submitting** **1** to write something formal and give it to someone to look at or consider: *I've been asked to submit a report to the committee.* | *Have you submitted your job application yet?* **2** to agree to do something because someone is forcing you to do it

sub·or·di·nate /sə'bɔːdənət $ sə'bɔrdənət/ *noun formal* someone who has a less important job than another person in an organization: *It's important to get on well with both your colleagues and subordinates.*

sub·scribe /səb'skraɪb/ *verb* to pay money so that you receive a newspaper or magazine regularly: *I've always subscribed to the National Geographic magazine.*

sub·scrip·tion /səb'skrɪpʃən/ *noun* an amount of money that you pay to regularly get a newspaper or magazine

sub·se·quent /'sʌbsəkwənt/ *adjective formal* coming after something else: *His illness and subsequent death were a terrible shock to us all.*

– **subsequently** *adverb*: *We met on holiday and subsequently became good friends.*

sub·side /səb'saɪd/ *verb formal* if a feeling or noise subsides, it becomes less strong or loud: *Her grief eventually subsided.*

sub·sid·i·a·ry[1] /səb'sɪdiəri $ səb'sɪdiˌeri/ *noun, plural* **subsidiaries** a company that another company owns or controls: *Ford has subsidiaries all over the world.*

subsidiary[2] *adjective formal* less important than something else: *We have to study two subsidiary subjects as well as our main subject.*

sub·si·dize also **subsidise** *BrE* /'sʌbsədaɪz/ *verb* to pay part of the cost of something: *The government subsidizes school meals.*

sub·si·dy /'sʌbsədi/ *noun, plural* **subsidies** *noun* money a government pays to help with the cost of something: *government subsidies to farmers*

sub·stance /'sʌbstəns/ *noun*

> any type of solid or liquid: *Honey is a sweet substance made by bees.* | *There might be poisonous substances in the water.*

sub·stan·tial /səb'stænʃəl/ *adjective* large in amount or size: *A substantial amount of money is missing.* | *We ate a substantial breakfast before setting off.* ▼

sub·stan·tial·ly /səb'stænʃəli/ *adverb* by a large amount: *Costs have risen substantially.*

sub·sti·tute[1] /'sʌbstətjuːt $ 'sʌbstəˌtut/ *noun* someone who takes the place of someone else: *a substitute goalkeeper*

substitute[2] *verb* to use something new or different instead of something else: *You can substitue olive oil for butter.*

sub·ti·tles /'sʌbˌtaɪtlz/ *plural noun* words on a film or television SCREEN that translate what the actors are saying: *a French film with English subtitles*

sub·tle /'sʌtl/ *adjective* not very noticeable, strong, or bright: *a subtle change* | *a subtle smell of roses*

sub·tract /səb'trækt/ *verb* to take one number away from another number: *If you subtract 10 from 45 you get 35.*

sub·trac·tion /səb'trækʃən/ *noun* when you take one number away from another: *Subtraction is more difficult than addition.*

sub·urb /'sʌbɜːb $ 'sʌbɜrb/ *noun* an area on the edge of a big city where people live: *a suburb of New York*

sub·ur·ban /sə'bɜːbən $ sə'bɜrbən/ *adjective* a suburban area is outside the main part a big city: *suburban districts of London*

sub·way /'sʌbweɪ/ *noun* **1** *BrE* a path that goes under a road or railway; UNDERPASS *AmE*: *If you need to cross the road, use the subway.* **2** *AmE* a railway that runs under the ground; UNDERGROUND *BrE*: *I took the subway up to Ninth Avenue.*

suc·ceed /sək'siːd/ *verb*

GRAMMAR
succeed in doing something
to achieve what you have been trying to do ➪ *opposite* FAIL: *By pushing hard, he **succeeded in** opening the window.* | *I tried to light a fire, but didn't succeed.*

suc·cess /sək'ses/ *noun, plural* **successes**
1 when you achieve what you have been trying to do ➪ *opposite* FAILURE: *They were pleased with their success at the tournament.* | *I tried to persuade Josh to come with us, but I didn't **have** much success.*

S

2 if a film, event, product etc is a success, many people like it ⇨ opposite FAILURE: *The film was a great success.*

suc·cess·ful /sək'sesfəl/ *adjective*

GRAMMAR
successful in doing something
1 if you are successful in doing something, you achieve what you have been trying to do ⇨ opposite UNSUCCESSFUL: *They were successful in persuading him to join their team.*
2 something that is successful achieves what you want it to achieve: *The treatment was successful, and she is able to walk again now.*
3 something that is successful is liked by many people and makes a lot of money: *He has written two successful books.*
—successfully *adverb*: *She successfully applied for a place at university.*

suc·ces·sion /sək'seʃən/ *noun* [no plural] a number of things that happen one after the other: *They finally managed to win a game after a succession of failures.*

suc·ces·sive /sək'sesɪv/ *adjective* happening one after the other: *I had to go to London on three successive days.*

suc·ces·sor /sək'sesə $sək'sesɚ/ *noun* the person who has someone's job after they leave: *Who will be his successor?*

suc·cinct /sək'sɪŋkt/ *adjective* clear and not containing many words: *a succinct answer to the question*

suc·cu·lent /'sʌkjələnt/ *adjective* succulent food has a lot of juice and tastes very good: *a succulent steak*

suc·cumb /sə'kʌm/ *verb formal* to be unable to stop yourself from doing something: *She finally succumbed and had a chocolate biscuit.*

such /sʌtʃ/ *adverb*
1 use **such** with an adjective and noun to make the adjective stronger, or to give a reason for something: *Sophia Loren is such a beautiful woman.* | *I didn't realise you worked in such a big building.* | *That was such a good film I'd like to see it again.* | *There was such a lot of noise outside I couldn't hear.*
2 *formal* also **such ... as** use **such** in place of something that has just been mentioned or seen: *There are more violent shows on TV each year, and such shows are damaging our children.* | *Such behaviour as we saw this morning must never be repeated.*

PHRASES
such as used to give an example of the type of thing you mean: *I enjoy sports, such as swimming, football and golf.* | *Illegal drugs such as cocaine cause many deaths each year.*
such ... that used with a noun that describes something to give a reason or result: *Gran has such bad hearing that she has the TV on full volume.* | *I made such a delicious meal that my guests ate all of it.*
no such thing used to say that something doesn't exist: *I don't believe in aliens – there's no such thing.* | *I tried ringing her, but the operator said there was no such number.*

suck /sʌk/ *verb* **1** to hold something in your mouth and pull on it with your tongue and lips: *children sucking their thumbs* **2** if water or air sucks someone or something in a particular direction, the force of it pulls them there: *She tried to swim, but the water sucked her down.*

sud·den /'sʌdn/ *adjective*
something that is sudden happens quickly, when you are not expecting it: *A sudden change in your life can cause stress.* | *His death was very sudden.*

sud·den·ly /'sʌdnli/ *adverb*
if something happens suddenly, it happens quickly, when you are not expecting it: *Jim suddenly stopped the car.* | *I suddenly remembered that I had to phone Jane.*

suds /sʌdz/ *plural noun* the BUBBLES you get when you mix soap and water: *soap suds*

sue /sjuː $su/ *verb* to start a legal process to get money from someone who has harmed you: *They're suing us for $10,000.*

S

suede /sweɪd/ noun [no plural] soft leather with a slightly rough surface: a suede jacket

suf·fer /'sʌfə $'sʌfɚ/ verb

1 to experience pain: It was a quick death – he didn't suffer much.

2 to feel very upset: Children often suffer a lot when their parents get divorced.

3 formal to be harmed or made weaker by something: A lot of small businesses suffered badly during the economic recession.

4 to become worse because of something: His school work is suffering because he goes out every evening.

PHRASAL VERB

suffer from

suffer from something to have an illness or health problem: Do you **suffer from** headaches?

suf·fi·cient /sə'fɪʃənt/ adjective as much as you need: The police do not have sufficient evidence.

suf·fix /'sʌfɪks/ noun, plural **suffixes** letters that you add to the end of a word to make a new word, for example 'ness' at the end of 'kindness'

suf·fo·cate /'sʌfəkeɪt/ verb to kill someone by not allowing them to breathe air: He suffocated her with a pillow.

sug·ar /'ʃʊgə $'ʃʊgɚ/ noun [no plural] a sweet substance that you add to food: Do you take sugar in your tea?

sug·gest /sə'dʒest $səg'dʒest/ verb

GRAMMAR
suggest doing something
suggest (that)

1 to say what you think someone should do: I **suggest that** you make a list of things that you will need on your trip. | Paul suggested looking for the information on the Internet.

2 to mention someone or something that would be suitable for a particular purpose: They were looking for a new goalkeeper, so I suggested Callum.

3 to say or show that something might be true: Are you **suggesting that**

she cheated in the test? | The evidence **suggests that** red wine may be good for your health.

sug·ges·tion /sə'dʒestʃən $səg-'dʒestʃən/ noun

GRAMMAR
a suggestion about something
a suggestion for something
a suggestion that
a suggestion of something

1 an idea that someone suggests: The teacher **made** some helpful **suggestions about** where to find the information. | I **have a suggestion**. Why don't we share the cost between us? | Luke's **suggestion for** a present was a CD. | There was a **suggestion that** we needed a new team captain.

2 a sign or posssibility that something might be true: When was the first **suggestion of** a link between smoking and cancer? | **One suggestion is that** dinosaurs died out because of a change in the Earth's climate.

su·i·cid·al /ˌsuːə'saɪdl/ adjective people who are suicidal feel so unhappy that they want to kill themselves: I felt almost suicidal when my mother died.

su·i·cide /'suːəsaɪd/ noun when someone deliberately kills himself or herself: More and more young men are committing suicide.

suit¹ /suːt/ noun

1 a JACKET and trousers or skirt that are made of the same material: a businessman in a dark blue suit ➪ see picture on page 352

2 a set of clothes that you wear for a particular activity: a ski suit

3 one of the four types of playing card. The four suits are called CLUBS, DIA-MONDS, HEARTS, and SPADES

suit² verb

1 if something suits you, it makes you look attractive: That blue dress suits you.

2 if something suits you, it is acceptable for you and does not cause any problems for you: "I'd like to make an appointment." "Would Monday morning suit you?"

S

suit·a·ble /'su:təbəl/ adjective right for a particular purpose or situation: This movie's not suitable for children.

suit·case /'su:tkeɪs/ noun a case for carrying clothes and other things when you travel

suite /swi:t/ noun 1 a set of expensive rooms in a hotel: the honeymoon suite 2 a set of furniture: a dining room suite

sulfur the American spelling of SULPHUR

sulk /sʌlk/ verb to show that you are annoyed by being silent and looking unhappy: She'll sulk if you don't let her go to the party.
– sulk noun [no plural]: He's in a sulk again.

sulk·y /'sʌlki/ adjective sulkier, sulkiest often sulking: a sulky child

sul·len /'sʌlən/ adjective quiet and looking angry: Simon sat in the corner, looking sullen.

sul·phur BrE, **sulfur** AmE /'sʌlfə $ 'sʌlfɚ/ noun [no plural] a yellow chemical powder that smells unpleasant

sul·tan /'sʌltən/ noun a ruler in some Muslim countries

sul·ta·na /sʌl'tɑ:nə $ sʌl'tænə/ noun BrE a dried white GRAPE

sum /sʌm/ noun 1 an amount of money: They've spent huge sums of money on that house. 2 BrE if you do a sum, you add, divide, multiply etc numbers: I'm terrible at doing sums 3 the total you get when you add two or more numbers together: The sum of 3 and 7 is 10.

sum·mar·ize also **summarise** BrE /'sʌməraɪz/ verb to give only the main information about something without all the details: I'll summarize the main points of his speech.

sum·ma·ry /'sʌməri/ noun, plural summaries a short statement that gives the main information about something without all the details: Write a summary of the article.

sum·mer /'sʌmə $ 'sʌmɚ/ noun
the season between spring and autumn, when the weather is hottest: Last summer we went on vacation to Florida. | We often eat outside in summer. | We'll come and visit you in the summer.

sum·mer·time /'sʌmətaɪm $ 'sʌmɚ-,taɪm/ noun [no plural] the time of year when it is summer: It gets very hot in summertime.

sum·mit /'sʌmɪt/ noun 1 a meeting between the leaders of several governments: an economic summit 2 the top of a mountain: It took them 3 weeks to reach the summit.

sum·mon /'sʌmən/ verb formal to officially order someone to come to a place: The head teacher summoned me to his office.

sun /sʌn/ noun the thing in the sky that gives us light and heat: The sun's gone behind a cloud. | She lay in the sun reading.

sun·bathe /'sʌnbeɪð/ verb to sit or lie outside in the sun so that your skin will become brown: This is a good place to sunbathe.

sun·burn /'sʌnbɜ:n $ 'sʌnbɚn/ noun [no plural] when your skin has become red and painful because you have stayed too long in the sun

sun·burnt /'sʌnbɜ:nt $ 'sʌnbɚnt/ also **sun·burned** /'sʌnbɜ:nd $ 'sʌnbɚnd/ adjective if you are sunburnt, your skin is red and painful because you have stayed too long in the sun: Be careful not to get sunburnt.

sun cream /'. ./ SUNSCREEN

Sun·day /'sʌndi/ written abbreviation **Sun** noun the day of the week between Saturday and Monday: I'll see you on Sunday. | Last Sunday it snowed.

sun·flow·er /'sʌnflaʊə $ 'sʌn,flaʊɚ/ noun a tall plant with a large yellow flower

sung the past participle of SING

sun·glass·es /'sʌn,glɑ:sɪz $ 'sʌn,glæsɪz/ plural noun dark glasses that protect your eyes from the sun: She was wearing sunglasses. ⇨ see picture at GLASSES

sunk the past participle of SINK[1]

sun·light /'sʌnlaɪt/ noun [no plural] light from the sun: The room was full of sunlight.

sun·ny /'sʌni/ adjective sunnier, sunniest a sunny day or place has a lot of sunlight

sun·rise /'sʌnraɪz/ noun [no plural] the time when the sun appears in the morning

sunrise

sunrise   sunset

sun·screen /'sʌnskriːn/ also **sun cream** BrE, noun a cream that you put on your skin to stop the sun from damaging your skin

sun·set /'sʌnset/ noun [no plural] the time when the sun disappears at night ⇨ see picture at SUNRISE

sun·shine /'sʌnʃaɪn/ noun [no plural] light and heat from the sun: We spent the afternoon sitting in the sunshine.

sun·tan /'sʌntæn/ also **tan** noun if you have a suntan, your skin is brown because you have been in the sun: She came back from Barbados with a wonderful suntan.

su·per /'suːpə $ 'suːpɚ/ adverb spoken extremely: He's super fit.

su·perb /sjuː'pɜːb $ sʊ'pɚb/ adjective very good: a superb four-course meal

su·per·fi·cial /ˌsuːpə'fɪʃəl $ ˌsuːpɚ'fɪʃəl/ adjective 1 done quickly, and not in a thorough or careful way: The police carried out only a superficial examination of the body. 2 a superficial wound or superficial damage is not very deep or serious: Our car escaped with only superficial damage. 3 someone who is superficial does not think about serious or important things

su·per·in·tend·ent /ˌsuːpərɪn'tendənt $ ˌsuːpɚɪn'tendənt/ noun 1 someone who is officially responsible for looking after a building 2 a British police officer

su·pe·ri·or¹ /suː'pɪəriə $ sə'pɪriɚ/ adjective better than something or someone else ⇨ opposite INFERIOR: He seems to think that he's superior to the rest of us.

superior² noun someone who has a higher position than you at work: You should never be rude to your superiors.

su·per·la·tive /suː'pɜːlətɪv $ sʊ'pɚlətɪv/ noun the superlative the form of an adjective or adverb that you use

when saying that something is the biggest, best, most expensive etc

su·per·mar·ket /'suːpəˌmɑːkɪt $ 'suːpɚˌmɑrkɪt/ noun a large shop that sells food, drink, cleaning products etc

su·per·mod·el /'suːpəˌmɒdl $ 'suːpɚˌmɑdl/ noun a very famous fashion model

su·per·nat·u·ral /ˌsuːpə'nætʃərəl $ ˌsuːpɚ'nætʃərəl/ noun the supernatural strange events that cannot be explained by science: Do you believe in the supernatural?
– **supernatural** adjective: They believed that cats had supernatural powers.

su·per·son·ic /ˌsuːpə'sɒnɪk $ ˌsuːpɚ'sɑnɪk/ adjective supersonic aircraft travel faster than the speed of sound

su·per·star /'suːpəstɑː $ 'suːpɚˌstɑr/ noun someone who is extremely famous and popular: a footballing superstar

su·per·sti·tion /ˌsuːpə'stɪʃən $ ˌsuːpɚ'stɪʃən/ noun a belief that some things are lucky or unlucky

su·per·sti·tious /ˌsuːpə'stɪʃəs $ ˌsuːpɚ'stɪʃəs/ adjective believing that some things are lucky or unlucky: She's so superstitious she stays home every Friday 13th.

super·store /'suːpəstɔː $ 'suːpɚˌstɔr/ noun BrE a very large shop: a computer superstore

su·per·vise /'suːpəvaɪz $ 'suːpɚˌvaɪz/ verb to make sure someone is doing their work or behaving correctly: There is always someone there to supervise the children in the pool.

su·per·vi·sion /ˌsuːpə'vɪʒən $ ˌsuːpɚ'vɪʒən/ noun [no plural] when you supervise people

su·per·vis·or /'suːpəvaɪzə $ 'suːpɚˌvaɪzɚ/ noun someone whose job is to supervise people who are doing a job

sup·per /'sʌpə $ 'sʌpɚ/ noun a meal that you eat in the evening

sup·ple /'sʌpəl/ adjective able to bend or move your body easily: You have to be quite supple in order to do these exercises.

sup·ple·ment /'sʌpləmənt/ noun 1 an additional part of a newspaper or magazine: This week's magazine contains a free fashion supplement. 2 a special food or drink that contains substances that are good for your body: *He takes vitamin supplements every morning.*

sup·pli·er /sə'plaɪə $sə'plaɪɚ/ *noun* a company that provides goods for shops and businesses: *an office equipment supplier*

sup·ply¹ /sə'plaɪ/ *noun, plural* supplies

GRAMMAR
a supply of something
1 an amount of something that you have available to use: *While he was ill in bed, we made sure he had a supply of magazines and videos.*
2 supplies food, clothes, and other things that people need: *Emergency food supplies were flown out to the area.*

PHRASE
be in short supply if people or things are in short supply, there are not many of them available: *Good maths teachers are in short supply.*

supply² *verb formal* supplied, supplies to provide people with something that they need: *We were supplied with paper and pens for the test.*

sup·port¹ /sə'pɔːt $sə'pɔrt/ *verb*
1 to like a particular team or person and want them to win in a game, election etc: *Which football team do you support?* | *65% of voters still support the president.*
2 to help and encourage someone: *Whatever you decide to do, I will support you.*
3 to be under something, holding it up: *the pieces of wood that support the roof*
4 to provide someone with money for food, clothes, and other things they need: *You will have to support yourself one day.*

support² *noun* [no plural] help and encouragement: *I want to thank my teachers for all the support they gave me.* | *Poor families receive financial support from the government.*

sup·port·er /sə'pɔːtə $sə'pɔrtɚ/ *noun* someone who supports a particular person, team, or plan: *loyal supporters of the president* | *a crowd of football supporters*

sup·por·tive /sə'pɔːtɪv $sə'pɔrtɪv/ *adjective* giving help and encouragement: *My parents are usually very supportive.*

sup·pose /sə'pəʊz $sə'poʊz/ *verb* to think that something is probably true: *I suppose he's still in London.*

PHRASES
I suppose so, I suppose not *spoken* used to agree with someone in an uncertain or unwilling way: *"Can I come too?" "I suppose so."* | *"It's not a bad film, is it?" "I suppose not."*
be supposed to do something a) if something is supposed to happen, people expect it or have planned it, although it may not actually happen: *The fence is supposed to keep animals out.* | *He was supposed to meet me at the station, but he didn't arrive.* b) if you are supposed to do something, a rule or instruction says you should do it: *You're supposed to turn the computer off when you've finished.* c) if something is supposed to be true, many people say it is true: *This is supposed to be his best book.*

sup·pos·ed·ly /sə'pəʊzɪdli $sə'poʊzɪdli/ *adverb* if something is supposedly true, people say it is true but it may not be true: *These chemicals are supposedly harmless.*

sup·press /sə'pres/ *verb* 1 to stop people from opposing the government, especially by using force: *The police suppressed the riots.* 2 to not show a feeling

su·preme /suː'priːm $sə'prim/ *adjective formal* the most important: *the Supreme Court*

sure¹ /ʃɔː $ʃʊr/ *adjective*
GRAMMAR
sure (that)
sure about/of something
sure to do something
not sure what/where/why etc
1 certain about something: *I'm sure that everything will be all right.* | *Are you sure about that?* | *Monica will be late – I'm sure of it.* | *She's not sure where she put her keys.*

2 if something is sure to happen, it is certain to happen: *She's **sure to** find out.*

PHRASES

make sure a) to check that something has been done: *I'll just **make sure** the TV's switched off.* **b)** to be careful to do something: ***Make sure** you read the exam questions carefully.*

be sure to do something *spoken*: ***Be sure to** lock the door* (=remember to lock the door)*!*

sure² *adverb spoken*

used to say yes or to agree with someone: *"Is it OK if I sit here?" "Sure."*

PHRASE

for sure *informal* if you know something for sure, you are certain about it: *Now I **know for sure** who stole my wallet.*

sure·ly /'ʃɔːli $ 'ʃʊrli/ *adverb* used to show that you are very surprised about something: *Surely you're not going to invite Harry? | Surely you remember?*

surf¹ /sɜːf $ sɚf/   **surf**
verb **1** to balance on ocean waves as they move towards the shore, standing on a SURFBOARD **2** surf the net to look for information on the INTERNET
–**surfing** *noun [no plural]*: *We went surfing every day when we were in Australia.*

surfboard

surf² *noun* the white water that forms when waves get near to the shore

sur·face¹ /'sɜːfɪs $ 'sɚfɪs/ *noun*

GRAMMAR
the surface of something

1 the top part of an area of land or water: *There were dead fish floating **on the surface of** the river. | I could see some tiny fish just **beneath the surface of** the water. | Two-thirds of the Earth's surface is covered by water.*

2 a flat area: *You need a nice smooth surface for skating.*

surface² *verb* to appear from under water after being hidden: *A shark surfaced from beneath the water.*

surf·board /'sɜːfbɔːd $ 'sɚfbɔrd/ *noun* a long board that you stand on to SURF ⇨ *see picture at* SURF¹

surge¹ /sɜːdʒ $ sɚdʒ/ *verb* if people surge forward, they suddenly move forward

surge² *noun* a sudden large increase in something: *He felt a sudden surge of anger.*

sur·geon /'sɜːdʒən $ 'sɚdʒən/ *noun* a doctor who cuts open people's bodies in order to repair or remove something inside

sur·ge·ry /'sɜːdʒəri $ 'sɚdʒəri/ *noun*
1 [no plural] medical treatment in which a doctor cuts open your body to repair or remove something inside: *She had surgery to remove a lump from her neck.*
2 plural **surgeries** *BrE* a place where you go to see a doctor or DENTIST

sur·gi·cal /'sɜːdʒɪkəl $ 'sɚdʒɪkəl/ *adjective* related to or used for medical operations: *surgical instruments*

sur·name /'sɜːneɪm $ 'sɚneɪm/ *noun* the name you share with other people in your family ⇨ *same meaning* LAST NAME

sur·plus /'sɜːpləs $ 'sɚpləs/ *plural* **surpluses** *noun* more of something than you need: *We've got a surplus of milk.*
–**surplus** *adjective*: *They sold their surplus books.*

sur·prise¹ /sə'praɪz $ sɚ'praɪz/ *noun*
1 something that you did not expect: *This is a surprise! I thought you weren't coming till tomorrow! | a surprise visit | I've **got a surprise for** you – I'm getting married!*
2 [no plural] the feeling you have when something you did not expect happens: *She expressed surprise when I told her my plans. | **To my surprise**, Dad wasn't angry.*

PHRASES

take someone by surprise, catch someone by surprise if something takes or catches you by surprise, you did not expect it: *His suggestion **took** us all **by surprise**.*

S

come as a surprise if something comes as a surprise, you did not expect it: *The news came as a complete surprise to me.*

surprise² *verb* if something surprises you, you did not expect it: *The result of the election surprised me.*

sur·prised /sə'praɪzd $ sə-'praɪzd/ *adjective*

GRAMMAR
surprised (that)
surprised at/by something

if you are surprised by something, you did not expect it and it seems strange: *I'm surprised you haven't been there before. | Bill was surprised that we were leaving so early. | He seemed surprised at my question. | She was surprised to find Sally waiting for her.*

sur·pris·ing /sə'praɪzɪŋ $ sə-'praɪzɪŋ/ *adjective*

GRAMMAR
it is surprising that
it is surprising how/what

1 something that is surprising seems strange and makes you feel surprised: *This is a very surprising result. | A surprising number of adults cannot read. | It's surprising that so many people offered to help. | It's surprising how little a computer costs now.*
2 not surprising, hardly surprising if something is not surprising, it seems very normal and you expect it: *It's not surprising she was annoyed.*
–surprisingly *adverb*: *The food was surprisingly good.*

sur·ren·der /sə'rendə $ sə'rendə/ *verb* to stop fighting and put yourself under the control of your enemies: *The hijackers surrendered to the government forces.*
–surrender *noun [no plural]*

sur·round /sə'raʊnd/ *verb* 1 if people surround someone or something, they go all around them: *Soldiers surrounded the building. | He was surrounded by his fans.* 2 be surrounded by something to have something all around: *The house was surrounded by a tall fence.*

sur·round·ings /sə'raʊndɪŋz/ *plural noun formal* the place where you are and the things around you: *He will be more relaxed at home in familiar surroundings.*

sur·veil·lance /sə'veɪləns $ sə'veɪləns/ *noun [no plural]* when the police or the army carefully watch a person or place: *The police kept the group under surveillance.*

sur·vey /'sɜːveɪ $ 'sə-veɪ/ *noun* a set of questions that you ask a lot of people in order to find out about their opinions: *The company carried out a survey of people's attitudes to housework.*

sur·vey·or /sə'veɪə $ sə-'veɪə/ *noun* someone whose job is to examine land or buildings

sur·viv·al /sə'vaɪvəl $ sə-'vaɪvəl/ *noun [no plural]* when someone or something continues to live or exist after being in a dangerous situation: *Because of the cold, our chances of survival were low.*

sur·vive /sə'vaɪv $ sə-'vaɪv/ *verb*
1 to continue to live after an accident or illness: *The driver survived the accident. | Only one of the children survived.*
2 to continue to exist: *Only a small number of the town's old buildings survive.*

sur·vi·vor /sə'vaɪvə $ sə-'vaɪvə/ *noun* someone who continues to live after an accident or illness: *The survivors of the crash are in hospital.*

sus·cep·ti·ble /sə'septəbəl/ *adjective formal* likely to be affected by an illness or problem: *Young children are susceptible to colds.*

sus·pect¹ /'sʌspekt/ *noun* someone that the police think may be guilty of a crime

sus·pect² /sə'spekt/ *verb* to think that someone may have done something bad: *I suspect that one of the boys took the money. | He is suspected of murder.*

sus·pend /sə'spend/ *verb formal* 1 to officially stop or delay something for a short time: *They had to suspend the rescue operation because of bad weather.* 2 to officially stop someone from working or going to school for a fixed time, because they have broken the rules

sus·pen·ders /sə'spendəz $ sə-'spendə-z/ *plural noun* 1 BrE STRAPS that hold up a woman's STOCKINGS 2 the American word for BRACES

sus·pense /sə'spens/ *noun* [no plural] the feeling you have when you are waiting for something exciting to happen: *They all wanted to know if I'd passed the exam, but I kept them in suspense.*

sus·pen·sion /sə'spenʃən/ *noun* **1** when someone is not allowed to work or go to school for a fixed time because they have broken the rules: *The players received a three-match suspension for fighting.* **2** [no plural] the part of a vehicle that makes it move up and down more gently when the surface of the road is uneven, so that it is more comfortable to ride in

sus·pi·cion /sə'spɪʃən/ *noun* **1** the belief that someone may have done something wrong: *Until someone admits stealing the money, everyone is under suspicion.* **2** a feeling that something may be true: *I've a suspicion she already knows about our relationship.*

sus·pi·cious /sə'spɪʃəs/ *adjective* **1** something that is suspicious appears to involve a crime: *She died in suspicious circumstances.* **2** if you are suspicious of someone, you do not trust them: *I'm suspicious of anyone who comes to the house selling things.*
–**suspiciously** *adverb*: *"Who are you?" the old woman asked suspiciously.*

sus·tain /sə'steɪn/ *verb formal* **1** to make something continue to exist: *Can the team sustain their lead in the competition?* **2** **sustain an injury, sustain damage** to be injured or damaged: *Mr Turner sustained serious head injuries in the attack.*

swag·ger /'swægə $'swægɚ/ *verb* to walk in a way that seems too proud and confident

swal·low /'swɒləʊ $'swɑloʊ/ *verb*
to make food or drink go down your throat and into your stomach: *Don't chew the pills, just swallow them.* | *My throat is sore and it's hard to swallow.*
–**swallow** *noun*: *She took a swallow of tea.*

swam the past tense of SWIM

swamp /swɒmp $swɑmp/ *noun* an area of land that is always very wet

swan /swɒn $swɑn/ *noun* a large white bird with a long neck that lives on lakes and rivers

swap or **swop** /swɒp $swɑp/ *verb* **swapped, swapping** to exchange something you have for something that someone else has: *He swapped his torch for a CD.* | *We swapped places so that I could look out of the window.*
–**swap** *noun*: *Let's do a swap.*

swarm¹ /swɔːm $swɔrm/ *verb* **swarm with** to be full of a lot of people moving about: *The place was swarming with tourists.*

swarm² *noun* a large group of insects moving together: *a swarm of bees*

swat /swɒt $swɑt/ *verb* **swatted, swatting** to hit a flying insect with your hand or a flat object

sway /sweɪ/ *verb* to move slowly from one side to another: *The wooden bridge swayed as they walked across it.*

swear /sweə $swer/ *verb* **swore** /swɔː $swɔr/ **sworn** /swɔːn $swɔrn/ **1** to use very rude words: *He was sent home for swearing at the teacher.* **2** to make a promise or statement very seriously: *I swear I didn't do it!*

swear word /'. ./ *noun* a very rude word

sweat¹ /swet/ *verb* when you sweat, liquid comes out through your skin because you are hot or nervous: *I always sweat a lot when I exercise.*

sweat² *noun* [no plural] liquid that comes out through your skin when you are hot or nervous: *He wiped the sweat from his forehead.*

sweat·er /'swetə $'swetɚ/ *noun* a piece of warm woollen clothing that you wear on the top half of your body ➪ see picture on page 352

sweat·shirt /'swet-ʃɜːt $'swet-ʃɚt/ *noun* a thick soft cotton shirt without buttons: *He was dressed casually, in a sweatshirt and jeans.*

sweat·y /'sweti/ *adjective* **sweatier, sweatiest** covered with sweat

sweep¹
/swiːp/ *verb past tense and past participle* **swept** /swept/

GRAMMAR
sweep something up
sweep something into/from etc a place

1 to clean the dirt

sweep

broom

from a floor using a brush: *I swept the kitchen floor.* | *Could you* **sweep** *the leaves* **up** *please?* | *I swept the broken glass* **into** *the corner of the room.*

2 to push something off a surface so that it falls to the ground: *She* **swept** *the glasses angrily* **from** *the table.*

3 **sweep over/across/through** if a fire, wind, or storm sweeps over an area, it moves or spreads over it quickly: *The fire* **swept over** *the dry hills.*

PHRASAL VERB

sweep away
sweep something away to destroy or remove something by force: *The floods have* **swept away** *80 homes.*

sweep² *noun* a smooth swinging movement: *He knocked the glasses from the table with a sweep of his hand.*

sweet¹ /swiːt/ *adjective*

1 sweet food or drink contains sugar or tastes like sugar: *This chocolate sauce is very sweet.*

2 kind and friendly: *Jeff's a sweet boy.*

3 small and attractive: *Her baby is so sweet!* | *What a* **sweet little** *house!*

sweet² *noun BrE* 1 a small sweet thing that you eat; CANDY *AmE: Don't let the kids eat too many sweets.* 2 something sweet that you eat at the end of a meal; DESSERT *AmE: What are you having as a sweet?*

sweet·en /'swiːtn/ *verb* to make a food or drink taste sweeter

sweet·ener /'swiːtnə $ 'switnɚ/ *noun* a substance used instead of sugar to make food and drink taste sweeter

swell /swel/ *verb* **swelled, swollen** /'swəʊlən $ 'swoʊlən/ also **swell up** if a part of your body swells, it becomes bigger: *His ankle swelled to twice its normal size.*

swell·ing /'swelɪŋ/ *noun* an area on your body that has become bigger because of injury or illness

swept the past tense and past participle of SWEEP¹

swerve /swɜːv $ swɝv/ *verb* if a car swerves, it suddenly goes to the left or right in a way that is not controlled: *The car in front suddenly swerved across the road.*

swift /swɪft/ *adjective* happening or moving very quickly: *We had to make a swift decision.*

swim¹ *verb* /swɪm/ **swam** /swæm/ **swum** /swʌm/
to move through water using your arms and legs: *We swam in the lake.* | *George is just learning to swim.* | *Can you swim yet?*
–**swimmer** *noun: I'm not a very good swimmer.*

swim² *noun* a time when you swim: *We're going for a swim after school.*

swim·ming /'swɪmɪŋ/ *noun* [no plural]
when you swim: *Do you want to* **go** *swimming?* | *We* **took** *the children swimming.* ⇨ see picture on page 351

swimming cos·tume /'.. ,../ *noun BrE* a piece of clothing that girls and women wear for swimming

swimming pool /'.. ./ also **pool** *noun* a large hole full of water that is built for swimming in

swimming trunks /'.. ./ also **trunks** *plural noun* a piece of clothing that boys and men wear for swimming: *He was wearing a pair of bright blue swimming trunks.*

swim·suit /'swɪmsuːt/ *noun* a piece of clothing that girls and women wear for swimming

swin·dle /'swɪndl/ *verb* to get money from someone by tricking them: *Sherman had swindled the woman out of thousands of dollars.*
–**swindle** *noun: a tax swindle*
–**swindler** *noun*

swing¹ /swɪŋ/ *verb, past tense and past participle* **swung** /swʌŋ/

1 to move something backwards and forwards or round and round: *Children sat on the bench, swinging their legs.*

2 to move smoothly and easily: *The door swung shut behind him.*

PHRASAL VERB

swing at
swing at someone to try to hit someone: *Dean swung at me and missed.*

swing² *noun* a seat that hangs from ropes or chains, for children to play on

swipe /swaɪp/ verb informal to steal something: Who's swiped my pencil?

swirl /swɜːl $ swɝl/ verb to turn around and around: Leaves swirled to the ground.

switch¹ /swɪtʃ/ verb

> **GRAMMAR**
> switch to something
> switch from something to something
> switch something with someone

to change from one thing to a different one: Davis switched the day of the meeting – it's on Monday now. | **Switch to** sugar-free drinks if you want to lose weight. | We've **switched from** using the old system **to** a newer one. | Would you mind **switching** places **with** me?

> **PHRASAL VERBS**
> **switch off**
> switch something off to make a machine or light stop working by moving a button ⇨ same meaning TURN OFF: Did you **switch off** the light in the kitchen?
> **switch on**
> switch something on to make a machine or light start working by moving a button ⇨ same meaning TURN ON: Jen **switched on** the radio.
> **switch over**
> to change from one television station to another: Do you mind if I **switch over**?

switch² noun, plural **switches**

a button that you move to make a machine or light start or stop working: Where's the light switch?

switch·board /'swɪtʃbɔːd $ 'swɪtʃbɔrd/ noun the place in a large organization where telephone calls are answered and connected to the people who work there: Hello, you're through to the switchboard.

swiv·el /'swɪvəl/ verb swivelled, swivelling BrE, swiveled, swiveling AmE to turn around while staying in the same place: You can swivel the computer screen to the right position.

swollen¹ the past participle of SWELL

swol·len² /'swəʊlən $ 'swoʊlən/ adjective a part of your body that is swollen is bigger than usual because of illness or injury: Her lips are so swollen she can't eat.

swoop /swuːp/ verb to move down through the air suddenly: The bird swooped on the rabbit.

swop /swɒp $ swɑːp/ another spelling of SWAP

sword /sɔːd $ sɔrd/ noun a weapon with a long sharp blade and a short handle

swore /swɔː $ swɔːr/ the past tense of SWEAR

sworn /swɔːn $ swɔːrn/ the past participle of SWEAR

swot¹ /swɒt $ swɑːt/ noun BrE informal someone who studies too hard

swot² verb BrE informal, **swotted, swotting** also **swot up** to study hard: I need to swot up on my maths before the exam.

swum the past participle of SWIM¹

swung the past tense and past participle of SWING¹

syl·la·ble /'sɪləbəl/ noun a part of a word that contains a single vowel sound. 'Dad' has one syllable and 'butter' has two syllables

syl·la·bus /'sɪləbəs/ noun, plural **syllabuses** a list of all the things that students will study on a course

sym·bol /'sɪmbəl/ noun **1** a simple shape or picture that has a meaning: That symbol means the truck is carrying a dangerous chemical. **2** something that shows or represents something else: A big car is a symbol of how much money you have.

sym·bol·ic /sɪm'bɒlɪk $ sɪm'bɑːlɪk/ adjective formal if something is symbolic, it means more than its simple appearance because it shows or represents something else: The new bridge is symbolic of the link between the two countries.

sym·bol·ize also **symbolise** BrE /'sɪmbəlaɪz/ verb formal to be a symbol that shows or represents something

sym·met·ri·cal /sɪ'metrɪkəl/ also **sym·met·ric** /sɪ'metrɪk/ adjective if something is symmetrical, its two halves or sides are the same size and shape. ⇨ see picture on page 626

sym·me·try /'sɪmətri/ noun [no plural] when both halves or sides of something are the same size and shape

sym·pa·thet·ic /ˌsɪmpə'θetɪk/ adjective kind and understanding to someone

S

symmetrical

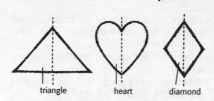

triangle   heart   diamond

who is sad ⇨ *opposite* UNSYMPATHETIC: *My parents weren't very sympathetic when I told them I had no money left.*

sym·pa·thize also **sympathise** BrE /'sɪmpəθaɪz/ *verb* **1** to be kind to someone who is sad by showing that you understand their problems **2** to support someone's ideas or actions: *On the whole, I sympathize with their aims.*

sym·pa·thy /'sɪmpəθi/ *noun* [no plural] **1** the feeling you have when you understand why someone is sad and want to help them feel better: *I have no sympathy for you – you knew what you were doing.* **2** support for someone's ideas or actions: *I have a lot of sympathy for the workers who are on strike.*

sym·pho·ny /'sɪmfəni/ *noun, plural* **symphonies** a long piece of music that is written for an ORCHESTRA

symp·tom /'sɪmptəm/ *noun* a sign of a disease: *Sneezing is often the first symptom of a cold.*

syn·a·gogue /'sɪnəgɒg $ 'sɪnə,gɑg/ *noun* a building where Jewish people meet for religious services

sync /sɪŋk/ *noun* **be out of sync, be in sync** *informal* if two things are out of sync, they are not working together correctly as they should. If they are in sync, they are: *The sound was out of sync with the pictures.*

syn·di·cate /'sɪndəkət/ *noun* a group of people or companies that have joined together for business reasons

syn·drome /'sɪndrəʊm $'sɪndroʊm/ *noun formal* a medical condition that produces a particular set of problems

syn·o·nym /'sɪnənɪm/ *noun* a word with the same meaning as another word in the same language: *'Enormous' is a synonym of 'huge'.*

syn·the·siz·er also **synthesiser** BrE /'sɪnθəsaɪzə $'sɪnθə,saɪzɚ/ *noun* an electronic musical instrument that can produce many kinds of sound

syn·thet·ic /sɪn'θetɪk/ *adjective* a synthetic material or substance is not natural but has been made in a factory

sy·ringe /sə'rɪndʒ/ *noun* a hollow tube and needle that a doctor uses for taking blood from people or for giving people medicine through their skin

syr·up /'sɪrəp $'sɚəp/ *noun* [no plural] a thick sticky liquid made from sugar

sys·tem /'sɪstəm/ *noun*

> **GRAMMAR**
> **a system for something**
> **a system of something**

1 a way of organizing something that is carefully planned according to a fixed set of rules: *We need a better* **system for** *dealing with complaints.* | *We have a very good education system in this country.* | *We now have a new filing system.* | *The present* **system of** *funding is not really ideal.*
2 several pieces of equipment that are connected to each other and work together: *We're having a new computer system installed at college.* | *a central heating system* | *an expensive stereo system*

sys·te·mat·ic /,sɪstə'mætɪk/ *adjective formal* using a planned and organized method: *a systematic search of the building*
 – systematically /-kli/ *adverb*

S

Tt

tab /tæb/ *noun* **1 pick up the tab** *informal* to pay for something, especially a meal in a restaurant **2 keep tabs on someone** *informal* if you keep tabs on someone, you make sure you always know where they are and what they are doing

ta·ble /'teɪbəl/ *noun*
1 a piece of furniture which has a flat top resting on legs: *We eat breakfast at the kitchen table.* | *A book lay open on the table.*
2 a table in a restaurant that you arrange to use at a particular time: *I'd like to book a table for two at 8.00 pm, please.*
3 a set of numbers or facts that are arranged in rows: *This table shows the city's monthly rainfall.*

PHRASES
set the table also **lay the table** *BrE* to put knives, forks, dishes etc on a table, ready for a meal: *John, will you set the table, please?*
the table of contents a list of the parts of a book and what page they are on: *The table of contents is on page iii.*

ta·ble·cloth /'teɪbəlklɒθ $'teɪbəl-ˌklɔːθ/ *noun* a cloth for covering a table

ta·ble·spoon /'teɪbəlspuːn/ *noun* a large spoon, or the amount it holds: *Add a tablespoon of flour.*

tab·let /'tæblət/ *noun* a small hard piece of medicine that you swallow ⇨ *same meaning* PILL: *She took two sleeping tablets.*

table ten·nis /'.. ,../ *noun* [no plural] a game in which people hit a ball to each other over a net that is stretched across a table

tab·loid /'tæblɔɪd/ *noun* a newspaper with small pages, short reports, and not very much serious news

ta·boo /tə'buː/ *noun* something that you must not do or talk about because it offends or embarrasses people

tack /tæk/ *noun* a small nail with a sharp point and a flat top

tack·le¹ /'tækəl/ *verb* **1** to deal with a difficult problem: *How should the police tackle the problem of crime by young people?* **2** to try to take the ball away from another player in a game such as football

tackle² *noun* an attempt to take the ball away from another player in a game such as football

tact /tækt/ *noun* [no plural] the quality that you show when you are careful not to say or do things that will upset people

tact·ful /'tæktfəl/ *adjective* careful not to say or do anything that will upset someone ⇨ *opposite* TACTLESS

tac·tic /'tæktɪk/ *noun* an action that you plan carefully in order to achieve what you want: *The team have prepared their tactics for the game.*

tact·less /'tæktləs/ *adjective* carelessly saying or doing something that upsets someone ⇨ *opposite* TACTFUL: *That was a rather tactless remark.*

tad·pole /'tædpəʊl $'tædpoʊl/ *noun* a small creature that will become a FROG

tag¹ /tæg/ *noun* a small piece of paper, plastic etc that is fastened to something and gives information about it: *All the staff wore name tags.*

tag² *verb* **tagged, tagging; tag along** *informal* to go somewhere with someone, although they have not asked you to: *The others were going to the cinema, so I decided to tag along.*

tail /teɪl/ *noun* **1** the long thin part on the back end of an animal's body: *The*

TAKE or BRING?

TAKE use **take** when you have something with you when you go to a place: *Are you taking your camera to Ben's party?* | *I took some cakes to class on my birthday.*

BRING use **bring** when someone has something with them when they come to the place where you are: *Elena brought some photographs to show us.* | *Will everyone please bring a packed lunch on Thursday.*

TAKE

1 move something or someone
*I always **take** too many clothes when I go on holiday.* | *Don't forget to **take** you bag!* | *Jim **took** some Playstation games **to** John's party.* | *I have to **take** my sister **to** the dentist.* | *She's always **taking** work home **with** her.*

> **GRAMMAR**
> take something to somewhere
> take something with you

2 go with someone
*I **took** Susan to the station.* | *Why don't you **take** Sarah with you **to** the store?* | *Dad **took** me **with** him **to** the football game.*

> **GRAMMAR**
> take someone to somewhere
> take someone with you

8 use a car, bus etc
*Do you mind if we **take** your car? Mine's not working.* | *I'll **take** the bus home.*

3 take a look, take a picture, take a holiday etc
*We've **taken** a lot of **pictures** of the baby (=photographed the baby).* | *I **took** my driving **test** last October.* | *Sandra **took** a **look** at the menu (=she read it).* | *Leo and his wife are hoping to **take** a **holiday** in Spain this summer.*

7 eat or drink medicine, drugs
***Take** an aspirin if you've got a headache.* | *It is easier for small children to **take** liquid medicine*

take

6 steal
*The burglars **took** £500 that she had hidden in her bedroom.* | *I left my bag on the chair, and someone **took** it.*

4 hold something
*I **took** Nick's pen and wrote down my phone number.* | ***Take** my hand to cross the street.* | *Jeff **took** Diana's bags **from** her and carried them to the car.*

> **GRAMMAR**
> take something from someone

5 time
if something takes a particular amount of time, you need that amount of time to do it: *This chicken recipe only **takes** twenty minutes to make.* | *It **takes** about 10 hours on the plane to get from London to Los Angeles.* | *It **takes** me ten minutes to get to school.*

Most common words used with **take**:			
take a bath	take risks	take a rest	take a bite
take an exam	take effect	take a breath	take a walk
take a break	take notes	take action	take a step

PHRASES

take place
to happen, especially after being planned to happen: *The wedding took place outside, in the gardens of the hotel.*

take part
to be involved in something such as an activity or event with other people: *Teachers and students from six schools will take part in the competition.*

take care of someone
to watch and help someone, and make sure they stay safe and well: *Melanie has no idea what it's like to take care of a baby all day long.*

take care of something
to do things to keep something in good condition: *My brother usually takes care of the house when my parents are away.*

take a message
to write down information that someone gives you on the telephone, so that you can give the information to someone else: *Mrs Pattie isn't here – may I take a message?*

take milk, take sugar etc
to use milk, sugar etc in your coffee or tea: *Do you take cream in your coffee?*

PHRASAL VERBS

take away
to move something from a place: *The waitress took the plates away.* | *The police took away the knife for examination.*

take back
to move something back to the place or person it came from: *Shelley took the dress back to the store because it didn't fit.* | *We have to take back the library books today*

take off
1 to move clothes off your body: ⋄ *opposite* PUT ON: *Jane took off her coat and hung it up.* | *I bent down and took my shoes off.*

2 if a plane takes off, it leaves the ground and goes into the air: ⋄ *opposite* LAND: *The plane took off at 8:45.*

3 to not go to work for a period of time: *Emma took three days off school last week when she was ill.*

*The plane **took off** at 8:45.*

take out
1 to move something so that it is outside of the place where it was: *Lucy took out her books and started doing her homework?* | *Take the butter out of the refrigerator.* | *"Can you take the cake out of the oven for me?"*

*"Can you **take** the cake **out of** the oven for me?"*

2 to go with someone to a restaurant, film etc and pay for them: *He took Sabina out for dinner.*

take over
to do something that someone else did before: *Machines have taken over much of the work people used to do in factories.* | *Mrs Hudson took over as head teacher last term.*

T

horse *was brown with a black tail.*
2 the back part of a plane   **3 tails** the side of a coin that does not have a picture of someone's head on it ⇨ *opposite* HEADS

tail-light or **tail light** /ˈ. ./ *noun* one of the two red lights at the back of a car or plane

tai·lor /ˈteɪlə $ˈteɪlɚ/ *noun* someone whose job is to make men's clothes. Tailors usually measure their customers so that the clothes fit exactly

tailor-made /ˌ.. ˈ./ *adjective* very suitable for someone or something: *The job seems tailor-made for him.*

tail·pipe /ˈteɪlpaɪp/ the American word for EXHAUST PIPE

take ⇨ *see box on pages 628 and 629*

take·a·way /ˈteɪkəweɪ/ *noun BrE* a meal that you buy from a restaurant to eat at home, or a restaurant that sells these meals; TAKEOUT *AmE*: *a Chinese takeaway*

take-off or **takeoff** /ˈteɪkɒf $ˈteɪkɔːf/ *noun* when a plane moves off the ground and into the air

take·out /ˈteɪkaʊt/ the American word for TAKEAWAY

tale /teɪl/ *noun* a story about things that happened long ago, or things that did not really happen: *We used to listen to his tales of life in the army.*

tal·ent /ˈtælənt/ *noun* a natural ability to do something well: *That boy has a lot of talent.*

tal·ent·ed /ˈtæləntɪd/ *adjective* having a natural ability to do something well: *a talented musician*

talk¹ ⇨ *see box on next page*

talk² /tɔːk/ *noun*

GRAMMAR
a talk with someone
a talk about something
a talk on something

1 when people talk to each other about a subject: *I had a long talk with Kelly today. | We've had a talk about the problem.*
2 a speech on a particular subject: *Davies gave a talk on his work at the university.*
3 talks formal discussions between different countries, organizations, leaders etc: *The peace talks are making good progress.*

talk·a·tive /ˈtɔːkətɪv/ *adjective* a talkative person talks a lot

tall /tɔːl/ *adjective*

1 a tall person, building, tree etc has great height: *a tall, beautiful woman | It is one of the tallest trees in the world.* ⇨ *see picture on page 353*
2 used to talk about the height of someone or something: *My mother's only 5 feet tall. | How tall is Ricky?*

tal·on /ˈtælən/ *noun* one of the sharp curved nails of a bird that hunts other animals

tame¹ /teɪm/ *adjective* a tame animal is not afraid of people and does not attack people ⇨ *opposite* WILD¹ (1)

tame² *verb* to train a wild animal to obey people and not be afraid of them

tam·per /ˈtæmpə $ˈtæmpɚ/ *verb* **tamper with** to change something without permission, especially in order to damage it: *Someone had tampered with the car's brakes.*

tan¹ /tæn/ *noun* brown skin that someone gets by spending time in the sun ⇨ *same meaning* SUNTAN: *She's come back from Spain with a great tan.*

tan² *adjective* pale yellow-brown in colour: *a tan bag*

tan³ *verb* **tanned, tanning** to get brown skin by spending time in the sun: *I'm trying to tan my legs.*
–tanned *adjective*: *He looked tanned and healthy.*

tan·ge·rine /ˌtændʒəˈriːn/ *noun* a small sweet orange

tan·gle¹ /ˈtæŋɡəl/ *noun* a lot of hair, string, wires etc that are twisted together in an untidy way

tangle

tangle² *verb* to become twisted together in an untidy way: *My hair's all tangled!*

tank /tæŋk/ *noun* **1** a large container for holding liquid or gas: *The tank's nearly empty – we'd better stop at the next petrol station.* **2** a heavy military vehicle with a large gun and a belt around the wheels on each side

➤ TALK, SPEAK, or TELL?

- If just one person is talking, use either **speak** or **talk**: *He **spoke** about his friends in India.* | *He **talked about** his friends in India.*
- When two or more people are having a conversation, use **talk**: *We **talked** for hours after the film.*

*I **talked to** Ruth on the phone yesterday.* | *They **were talking** about a television programme*

- When you want someone to know something, you **tell** them **about** it: *I **told** Jenny **about** a television programme I saw.*

➤ TALK

to speak, or to have a conversation

*Sorry, I can't **talk** now – I have to go to a meeting.* | *Mr Samuels **talked to** the police for an hour.* | *Each student stood in front of the class and **talked about** a book they had read.* | *Lucy sat on the sofa, **talking with** Camille.*

> **GRAMMAR**
> **talk about something**
> **talk to someone**
> **talk with someone** AmE

| ✗ | Don't say ➤ *I want to talk you about my homework.* |
| ✓ | Say ➤ *I want to **talk to** you about my homework.* |

| ✗ | Don't say ➤ *I talked him about my holiday.* |
| ✓ | Say ➤ *I **told** him **about** my holiday.* |

*Each student **talked about** a book they had read.*

| ✗ | Don't say ➤ *I talk French/ English/Japanese.* |
| ✓ | Say ➤ *I **speak** French/ English/Japanese.* |

PHRASAL VERBS

talk back
if a child talks back to an adult, they answer the adult rudely: *He's been **talking back to** his teachers and getting into trouble.*

talk into
to make someone agree to do something that they do not really want to do: *I **talked** my mother **into**

buying me the shoes.* | *Diane didn't really want to go, but Bill **talked** her **into** it.*

talk out of
to make someone agree not to do something that they wanted to do: *I wanted to buy a car, but my dad **talked** me **out of** it.* | *His friends **talked** him **out of** trying drugs.*

tank

tanker

tank·er /'tæŋkə $'tæŋkɚ/ *noun* a ship or vehicle that carries liquid or gas: *an oil tanker* ⇨ *see picture at* TANK

tan·noy /'tænɔɪ/ *noun BrE trademark* a system of LOUDSPEAKERS that people use to announce things in public places: *I heard my name called over the tannoy.*

tan·trum /'tæntrəm/ *noun* when a young child suddenly becomes very angry: *She had a tantrum when I refused to buy her any sweets.*

tap¹ /tæp/ **tapped, tapping** *verb*

GRAMMAR
tap on something

1 to gently hit something with your hand or an object: *Paul tapped her on the shoulder.* | *Someone tapped on the window.*
2 if you tap your feet, you move them gently up and down in time to music

tap² *noun*

GRAMMAR
a tap on something

1 *BrE* something that you turn to make water come out of a pipe. You turn a tap on to make the water come out and turn it off to make the water stop coming out; FAUCET *AmE: Water was dripping from the kitchen tap.* | *I turned the tap on.* | *Could you turn off the taps in the bathroom for me?*
2 the sound that someone makes by hitting something gently with their hand or an object: *I heard a tap on the window.*

tape¹ /teɪp/ *noun*

1 a thin band of plastic inside a box that you use to record sounds, music, or television pictures: *Keith has hundreds of tapes and CDs.*
2 [no plural] a band of sticky material that you use to stick paper together: *You*

don't need to use that much tape to wrap up presents!

tape² *verb* **1** to record sounds or pictures on a tape: *You must not tape the concert without permission.* | *Can you tape the football for me, please?* **2** to fasten something to a surface using tape: *He taped the poster above his desk.*

tape deck /'. ./ *noun* the part of a STEREO which you use to play and record music on tapes

tape mea·sure /'. ‚../ *noun* a very long piece of cloth or metal with INCHes or CENTIMETRES marked on it, which you use for measuring things

tape re·cord·er /'. .‚../ *noun* a piece of equipment that you use for recording and playing sounds on TAPES

tap·es·try /'tæpəstri/ *noun, plural* **tapestries** a piece of heavy cloth that is covered with a picture made of coloured threads

tar /tɑː $tɑr/ *noun* a black sticky substance that is used to cover roads, roofs etc

tar·get¹ /'tɑːgɪt $'tɑrgɪt/ *noun*

GRAMMAR
a target for something/someone
a/the target of something

1 a person or place that people attack or criticize: *Military buildings are an obvious target for terrorists.* | *Smith has been the target of a lot of criticism recently.*
2 a particular person or group of people that you are trying to affect or influence: *Young people are the target of these advertisements.*
3 an amount or level that you are trying to achieve: *The company has reached its sales targets.*
4 a board with circles on it that you try to hit when you are shooting: *The arrow hit the middle of the target.*

target² *verb* **1** to aim a weapon at a place: *They targeted their missiles on American cities.* **2** to choose a particular place to attack: *The bombers targeted popular tourist areas.* **3** to try to sell a product or give information about something to a particular group of people: *The company targets its clothing at teenagers.*

tar·mac /'tɑːmæk $'tɑrmæk/ *noun*
1 Tarmac *[no plural] trademark* a material made of tar and small stones that is used to cover the surface of a road; BLACKTOP *AmE*   **2** the tarmac the part of an airport where the planes stand: *There were two planes on the tarmac.*

tart /tɑːt $tɑrt/ *noun* a small PIE without a top, usually containing fruit

tar·tan /'tɑːtn $'tɑrtn/ *noun* a traditional Scottish pattern with coloured lines and squares

task /tɑːsk $tæsk/ *noun*

a piece of work that someone has to do: *Machines **do** most of the simple **tasks** in the factory. | The teacher **set** us some really difficult **tasks**.*

taste¹ /teɪst/ *noun*

1 your sense of taste is your ability to know what sort of food or drink you have in your mouth, and whether it is sweet, sour, bitter etc
2 the taste of a food or drink is the quality that you notice when you put it in your mouth: *I don't like **the taste of** fish. | The coffee had **a strong**, bitter **taste**.*
3 a taste a small amount of a food or drink that you have in order to find out what it is like: *Do you want **a taste of** my curry?*
4 your taste in something is what kind of that thing you like: *What are your **tastes in** music?*

PHRASES
have taste, have good taste to be good at knowing what things are attractive or of good quality: *Kaufman **has good taste in** clothes.*
be in bad taste to be likely to upset people: *That joke **was in** very **bad taste**.*

taste² *verb*

GRAMMAR
taste of something
taste like something

1 to have a particular taste: *This coffee tastes great! | The sauce **tasted of** cheese. | Chillies **taste like** peppers, but they're much hotter.*
2 to eat or drink a small amount of

something in order to find out what it is like: *Gabby tasted the soup and added a little salt.*

USAGE
Do not use **taste** in the continuous tense. For example, you cannot say: *I am tasting onion in this sauce.* Use **can taste** instead: *I **can taste** onion in this sauce.*

taste·ful /'teɪstfəl/ *adjective* attractive and of good quality: *a tasteful birthday card*

taste·less /'teɪstləs/ *adjective*   **1** not attractive and not of good quality: *Some of her clothes are really tasteless!*   **2** likely to offend people: *tasteless jokes*   **3** tasteless food is not nice because it does not have a very strong taste

tast·y /'teɪsti/ *adjective* tastier, tastiest tasty food has a good strong taste: *This pizza is really tasty.*

tat·tered /'tætəd $'tætərd/ *adjective* old and torn: *a tattered flag*

tat·too /tə'tuː/ *noun* a picture that is put onto someone's skin using a needle and ink
–tattoo *verb*: *He had a lion tattooed on his chest.*

tattoo

taught the past tense and past participle of TEACH

taunt /tɔːnt/ *verb* to say unkind things to someone in order to upset them ⇨ *same meaning* TEASE: *The other kids taunted her about her clothes.*
–taunt *noun*: *The taunts about his father upset him.*

taut /tɔːt/ *adjective* stretched tight: *They pulled the rope until it was taut.*

taut

taut

slack

tax¹ /tæks/ *noun, plural* **taxes**

> **GRAMMAR**
> **a tax on something**

money that you have to pay to the government: *There is no **tax on** food.* | *You have to **pay tax on** everything you earn.* | *Most people would like to see **lower taxes**.* | *People are protesting about the **high taxes**.*

tax² *verb* to make someone pay a particular amount of money to the government

tax-free /ˌ. ˈ./ *adjective* if something is tax-free, you do not have to pay tax on it: *a tax-free savings account*

tax·i /ˈtæksi/ also **tax·i·cab** /ˈtæksiˌkæb/ *noun* a car with a driver that you pay to drive you somewhere: *We took a taxi to the station.* ⇨ *see picture on page 349*

tea /tiː/ *noun* **1** a drink that you make by pouring hot water onto dried leaves, or the leaves that you use to make this drink: *I'm going to make a cup of tea.* **2** *BrE* a meal that you eat in the afternoon or early evening

tea·bag /ˈtiːbæg/ *noun* a small paper bag containing dried leaves which you pour hot water on to make tea

teach /tiːtʃ/ *verb, past tense and past participle* **taught** /tɔːt/

> **GRAMMAR**
> **teach something to someone**
> **teach someone something**
> **teach someone how to do something**
> **teach someone to do something**
> **teach someone what to do**

1 to give lessons in a subject: *She teaches history.* | *He teaches at a secondary school.* | *She **teaches** French **to** primary school children.* | *Mr Howard teaches me maths.* **2** to show someone how to do something: *My grandmother **taught** me **how to** bake cakes.* | *It's important to **teach** children to swim.* | *Will you **teach** me **what to** do?* ⇨ *see usage note at* LEARN

teach·er /ˈtiːtʃə $ ˈtiːtʃɚ/ *noun* someone whose job is to teach: *Miss Lind is my English teacher.*

teach·ing /ˈtiːtʃɪŋ/ *noun* [no plural] the work of being a teacher: *Teaching is not easy.*

team¹ /tiːm/ *noun*

> **GRAMMAR**
> **a team of people**

1 a group of people who play a game together against another group: *a football team* **2** a group of people who work together: *a **team of** doctors*

team² *verb* **team up** to join another person or group in order to do something together: *Why don't we team up with class 5 for the school trip?*

team·mate /ˈtiːm-meɪt/ *noun* someone who is in the same team as you: *His teammates cheered as he scored.*

team·ster /ˈtiːmstə $ ˈtiːmstɚ/ the American word for TRUCK DRIVER

tea·pot /ˈtiːpɒt $ ˈtiːpɑt/ *noun* a container that you use for making and pouring tea

tear¹ /teə $ ter/ *verb* **tore** /tɔː $ tɔr/ **torn** /tɔːn $ tɔrn/

> **GRAMMAR**
> **tear something down/off etc**

1 if you tear cloth or paper, or if it tears, you make a hole in it or pull it into pieces ⇨ *same meaning* RIP¹ (1): *I fell down and tore my trousers.* | *The bag tore on the way home.* | *The kids **tore open** their Christmas presents.* **2** to remove something quickly by pulling it violently: *She **tore** the pictures **down**.* | *Strong winds **tore** the roofs **off** several houses.* | *He **tore off** his shirt.*

> **PHRASAL VERBS**
> **tear down**

tear something down *informal* to deliberately destroy a building: *The old houses will **be torn down**.*

tear up

tear something up to pull paper into lots of pieces: *I **tore up** Neil's letter.*

tear² /tɪə $ tɪr/ *noun* **1** one of the drops of water that come from your eyes when you cry: *She had tears in her eyes by the end of the movie.* **2** **be in tears** to be crying: *Sally was in tears when she heard the news.*

tear³ /teə $ ter/ *noun* a hole in paper or cloth where it has been torn ⇨ *same meaning* RIP²: *There's a tear in your jacket.*

T

tear·ful /'tɪəfəl $ 'tɪrfəl/ *adjective* crying or almost crying: *She looked very tearful.*

tease /tiːz/ *verb* to say amusing but unkind things about someone in order to embarrass or annoy them: *The other girls tease me because I haven't got a boyfriend.*

tea·spoon /'tiːspuːn/ *noun* a small spoon, or the amount it holds: *Add a teaspoon of salt.*

teat /tiːt/ *noun* **1** the part of a female animal that baby animals suck to get milk **2** *BrE* the soft rubber part of a baby's bottle that a baby sucks; NIPPLE *AmE*

tea tow·el /'. ,../ *noun BrE* a piece of cloth that you use for drying cups, plates etc after washing them; DISH TOWEL *AmE*

tech·ni·cal /'teknɪkəl/ *adjective* related to the knowledge and skills of people who know about science or know how to make something: *We had to learn all the technical words used in computing.*

tech·ni·cian /tek'nɪʃən/ *noun* someone whose job is to do practical work connected with science or technology: *a laboratory technician*

tech·nique /tek'niːk/ *noun* a special skill or way of doing something: *He showed us different guitar-playing techniques.*

tech·no·log·i·cal /ˌteknə'lɒdʒɪkəl $ ˌteknə'lɑdʒɪkəl/ *adjective* related to technology: *the latest technological developments*

tech·nol·o·gy /tek'nɒlədʒi $ tek-'nɑlədʒi/ *noun, plural* **technologies** the knowledge, equipment, and methods that are used in scientific or industrial work: *the development of modern computer technology | new technologies, such as the Internet and mobile phones*

ted·dy bear /'tedi beə $ 'tedi ˌber/ also **teddy** *BrE noun, plural* **teddies** a soft toy that looks like a bear

te·di·ous /'tiːdiəs/ *adjective* boring, and seeming to continue for a long time: *a tedious lesson*

teem /tiːm/ *verb* **teem with** to be full of people or animals that are moving around: *The ground was teeming with ants.*

teen·age /'tiːneɪdʒ/ *adjective* aged between 13 and 19, or suitable for people of this age: *She teaches teenage girls. | a teenage magazine*

teen·ag·er /'tiːneɪdʒə $ 'tiːnˌeɪdʒɚ/ *noun* someone who is aged between 13 and 19 ⇨ *see usage note at* CHILD

teens /tiːnz/ *plural noun* the time in your life when you are aged between 13 and 19: *The club is for people in their teens. | She was in her late teens* (=17, 18, or 19).

tee shirt /'. ,./ a T-SHIRT

teeth the plural of TOOTH

tee·to·tal /tiː'təʊtl $ tiː'toʊtl/ *adjective* someone who is teetotal never drinks alcohol

tel·e·com·mu·ni·ca·tions /ˌtelikə-mjuːnə'keɪʃənz/ *noun* the process of sending and receiving messages by telephone, radio, SATELLITE etc

tel·e·gram /'teləgræm/ *noun* a message sent by telegraph

tel·e·graph /'teləgrɑːf $ 'teləˌgræf/ *noun* an old-fashioned way of sending messages along electrical wires

tel·e·phone¹ /'teləfəʊn $ 'teləˌfoʊn/ *noun*
a piece of electrical equipment that you use to speak to someone who is in another place and has a similar piece of equipment ⇨ *same meaning* PHONE¹: *Can I use your telephone? | What's your telephone number? | I've got to make a quick telephone call. | The telephone rang and Vicky answered it.*

PHRASE

be on the telephone a) to be talking using the telephone: *I was on the telephone for 20 minutes.* **b)** to have a telephone at your house or office: *Are you on the telephone?*

telephone² *verb formal* to use a telephone to speak to someone: *I telephoned the shop several times.* ⇨ *see usage note at* PHONE²

tel·e·scope /'teləskəʊp $ 'teləˌskoʊp/ *noun* a piece of equipment like a long tube that you use to look at things that are far away

telescope

tel·e·vise /'teləvaɪz/ *verb* to broadcast something on television: *The concert will be televised.*

tel·e·vi·sion /'telə,vɪʒən/ *noun*
an object with a SCREEN which shows moving pictures and produces sounds. You turn on or switch on a television to watch it, and turn it off or switch it off when you have finished watching it: *Many children **watch** too much **television.** | Is there anything good **on television** tonight? | It's time to **turn off the television.*** ⇨ see picture on page 342

tell ⇨ see box on next page

tel·ly /'teli/ *noun BrE informal*, *plural* **tellies** a television: *What's on telly tonight?*

temp /temp/ *noun* a secretary who works for different companies for short periods of time: *We will need a temp while the secretary is away.*

tem·per /'tempə $'tempɚ/ *noun*
a sudden angry state, or a tendency to become angry suddenly: *Lucy **gets in a temper** if she can't have what she wants. | Julie's certainly **got a temper.***

PHRASES
in a good temper, in a bad temper: *David is **in a** very **good temper** today* (=he is feeling happy). *| Why are you **in such a bad temper*** (=feeling so unhappy and angry)?
lose your temper to suddenly become very angry: *I **lose my temper** very quickly when I'm tired.*

tem·pe·ra·ment /'tempərəmənt/ *noun* your basic character, which controls whether you are usually happy, sad, friendly etc: *a baby with a sweet temperament*

tem·pe·ra·men·tal /,tempərə'mentl/ *adjective* someone who is temperamental changes suddenly from being happy to being angry, sad etc: *She is so temperamental, I never know how she's going to act.*

tem·pe·rate /'tempərət/ *adjective formal* a temperate country has weather that is never very hot or very cold

tem·pe·ra·ture /'tempərətʃə $'temprətʃɚ/ *noun*

GRAMMAR
the temperature of something
how hot or cold something is: *The*

temperature drops at night to 2°C. | Check **the temperature of** the water before you get into the bath.

PHRASES
take someone's temperature to measure the temperature of someone's body, to find out whether they are ill: *The nurse **took** her **temperature** with a thermometer.*
have a temperature to be hot because you are ill: *Danny **had a temperature of** 39°C.*

tem·plate /'templeɪt/ *noun* **1** a piece of paper, plastic etc in a particular shape that you use to help you cut other things in the same shape **2** a computer FILE that you use as a model for producing many similar documents: *a template for writing business letters*

tem·ple /'tempəl/ *noun* **1** a building where people in some religions go to pray: *a Hindu temple* **2** the area on the side of your head, between your eye and your ear

tem·po·ra·ri·ly /'tempərərəli $,tempə'rerəli/ *adverb* for a short limited period of time ⇨ opposite PERMANENTLY: *The school has been closed temporarily.*

tem·po·ra·ry /'tempərəri $'tempə,reri/ *adjective* existing or happening for a short limited period of time ⇨ opposite PERMANENT: *She got a temporary job. | This is only a temporary arrangement.*

tempt /tempt/ *verb* to make someone want something that they should not have: *She tried to tempt me to have a cigarette.*

temp·ta·tion /temp'teɪʃən/ *noun* a strong feeling of wanting something that you should not have: *I resisted the temptation to have another cookie.*

tempt·ing /'temptɪŋ/ *adjective* something that is tempting seems attractive because you would like to have it: *a tempting job offer*

ten /ten/ *noun* 10

ten·ant /'tenənt/ *noun* someone who pays rent to live in a room or house

tend /tend/ *verb*

GRAMMAR
tend to do something
to be likely to do a particular thing, or to often do it: *Older students **tend***

➤ SAY, TALK, or TELL?

SAY you **say** words to someone: *She **said that** she was going home.*

TALK you **talk to** someone or **talk about** something when you are having a conversation: *We **talked about** our families.*

TELL you **tell** someone facts or information about something: *She **told** me **that** she was going home.*

Tell can have two objects: *Uncle Ben **told** <u>the children</u> <u>a story</u>.*

➤ TELL

1 to give someone facts or information by speaking to them
*I **can't tell** you – it's a secret.* | *She wrote to **tell** us **that** she was getting married.* | *Jim will **tell** you everything you need to know.* | ***Tell** me **about** your trip to New York.* | *Can you **tell** me **what** is going on?*

GRAMMAR
tell someone something
tell someone about something
tell someone (that)
tell someone what/where/when etc

✗ Don't say ➤ He told that he was going.
✓ Say ➤ He **told me that** he was going or He **said that** he was going.

✗ Don't say ➤ She told about it.
✓ Say ➤ She **told me about** it or She **talked about** it.

tell

2 to say that someone must do something
*She's going to **tell** Jim not to call her anymore.* | *His doctor **told** him **that** he needs to take more exercise.* | *Josh **told** me **what** to get Chris for her birthday.*

GRAMMAR
tell someone to do something
tell someone what to do
tell someone (that)

✗ Don't say ➤ He told to me to stop.
✓ Say ➤ He **told me to** stop.

3 can tell, could tell
to know that something is true, because you can see something that shows you it is true: *You **can tell that** they're sisters – they look so much alike.* | *I **could tell** you didn't like him.*

T

PHRASES

tell the truth
to say what really happened: *I wasn't sure if Bobby was **telling the truth**.* | *I know Catherine **told** me the **truth** about what happened.*

tell a story, tell a joke etc
to write or speak a story, joke etc: *Grandpa used to **tell** us **stories** about when he was little.*

tell the difference
to be able to know that two things are different: *It's easy to **tell the difference between** real coffee and instant coffee.*

ˇ *to ask more questions in class.* | *I*
tend to *wake up early.*

ten·den·cy /'tendənsi/ *noun, plural*
tendencies if you have a tendency to do
something, you often do it: *He has a
tendency to shout.*

ten·der /'tendə $ 'tendər/ *adjective*
1 gentle and loving: *a tender kiss*
2 soft and easy to cut and eat ⇨ *opposite* TOUGH (3): *a lovely tender piece of
meat*

ten·ner /'tenə $ 'tenər/ *noun* BrE *spoken
informal* £10 or a ten pound note

ten·nis /'tenɪs/ *noun [no plural]* a game in
which two or four people use RACKETs *to
hit a ball to each other over a net* ⇨ *see
picture on page 351*

ten·or /'tenə $ 'tenər/ *noun* a male
singer with a fairly high voice

tense¹ /tens/ *adjective*

1 nervous and anxious: *John* **looked**
really **tense.** | *I don't know why I* **feel**
so **tense.**
2 a tense situation makes people feel
anxious: *It was a tense game.*

tense² *noun* in grammar, one of the
forms of a verb that shows whether you
are talking about the past, the present,
or the future. For example, 'he studied' is
in the past tense and 'he studies' is in the
present tense

ten·sion /'tenʃən/ *noun* a nervous
feeling that you have when you do not
know what is going to happen: *You
could feel the tension in the room as
the teacher slowly read out the exam
results.*

tent /tent/ *noun* a thing that you sleep
in when you are camping, which is
made of cloth and held up by poles and
ropes: *We had to put up our tent in the
dark.*

ten·ta·cle /'tentəkəl/ *noun* one of the
long soft arms of a sea creature such as
an OCTOPUS

ten·ta·tive /'tentətɪv/ *adjective* not definite or certain: *We had tentative plans to
meet for lunch.*

tenth /tenθ/ *number* **1** 10th **2** one
of the ten equal parts of something; 1/
10

tep·id /'tepɪd/ *adjective* tepid liquid is
slightly warm

term /tɜːm $ tɜrm/ *noun*

1 BrE one of the parts of a school year:
*We'll be learning about maps this
term.* | *The exams are at the end of
the summer term.*
2 terms the things that you accept or
agree to do as part of a legal agreement: *Both sides have accepted* **the
terms of** *the peace agreement.*
3 a scientific or technical word: *Doctors should explain difficult medical
terms.*
4 a period of time during which
someone does a job: *The President
is hoping to win a second* **term of
office** (=a second period of time as
president).

in the long term, in the short term
during a long or short period from
now: *We're not sure what effect the
changes will have* **in the long
term.** | **In the short term** *I can bor-
row money from my parents, but* **in
the longer term** *I'll have to get a
job.*
in terms of something used to
show what part of something you
are talking about: **In terms of**
*musical quality, his last album was
better.*
be on good terms to have a good,
friendly relationship with someone:
Joe and Jim **are on good terms** *now
that they sit together in class.* | *I'm
afraid my uncle* **is not on** *very* **good
terms with** *the rest of the family.*
come to terms with something to
fully understand and accept a difficult situation: *He couldn't* **come to
terms with** *losing his job.*

ter·mi·nal¹ /'tɜːmənəl $ 'tɜrmənəl/
noun **1** a building where people get
onto planes, buses, or ships: *Our plane
leaves from terminal 4.* ⇨ *see picture
on page 349* **2** a SCREEN and KEYBOARD
that are connected to a computer

terminal² *adjective* a terminal illness
cannot be cured, and causes death
– **terminally** *adverb: Her mother is terminally ill.*

ter·mi·nol·o·gy /,tɜːmə'nɒlədʒi $,tɜr-
mə'nɑlədʒi/ *noun formal, plural* **termin-
ologies** the technical words that are

used in a subject: *a dictionary of medical terminology*

ter·mi·nus /'tɜːmənəs $'tɜ˞mənəs/ *noun, plural* **terminuses** the place at the end of a railway line or bus service where the trains and buses end their journeys

ter·race /'terɪs/ *noun* a flat area next to a building or on a roof, where you can sit: *We sat and had drinks on the terrace.* ⇨ *see picture on page 343*

terraced house also **terrace house** /ˌ.. './ *BrE noun* a house that is one of a long row of houses that are joined together; ROW HOUSE *AmE* ⇨ *see picture on page 343*

ter·ri·ble /'terəbəl/ *adjective* very bad: *I have a terrible headache.* | *a terrible accident*

ter·ri·bly /'terəbli/ *adverb* **1** very badly: *She sang terribly.* **2** *BrE* very: *I'm terribly late.*

ter·ri·er /'teriə $'teriə˞/ *noun* a type of small dog

ter·rif·ic /tə'rɪfɪk/ *adjective informal* very good: *I love your new hairstyle – it's terrific!*

ter·ri·fied /'terəfaɪd/ *adjective* very frightened: *I'm terrified of flying.*

ter·ri·fy /'terəfaɪ/ *verb* **terrified, terrifies** to make someone very frightened: *That dog terrifies me.*
– **terrifying** *adjective*: *a terrifying film*

ter·ri·to·ry /'terətəri $'terəˌtɔri/ *noun, plural* **territories** land that a country, person, or animal controls: *We knew that we were now in enemy territory.*

ter·ror /'terə $'terə˞/ *noun* a feeling of great fear: *He screamed in terror.*

ter·ror·is·m /'terərɪzəm/ *noun [no plural]* the use of violent actions, usually against ordinary people, to try to force a government to do something: *The government said the bombing was an evil act of terrorism.*

ter·ror·ist /'terərɪst/ *noun* someone who uses violent actions, usually against ordinary people, to try to force a government to do something

test¹ /test/ *noun*
1 a set of questions or activities that you do to show how much you know or how well you can do something. You take a test ⇨ *same meaning* EXAM: *I passed my history test.* | *Michelle had to take her driving test three times before she passed.* | *I'm afraid I might fail my maths test.*
2 a short medical check on part of your body: *The children will be given eye tests.* | *a blood test*

test² *verb*

GRAMMAR
test someone on something
test someone for something

1 to ask someone questions or make them do things to show how much they know or how well they can do something: *The teacher tested us on chapters 7 to 11.*
2 to use something to find out whether it works: *The school is testing some new educational software.*
3 to do a medical check on part of someone's body: *They tested him for malaria and other illnesses.*

tes·ti·fy /'testəfaɪ/ *verb* **testified, testifies** to formally say in a law court what you know about something: *She testified that she had seen the man leaving the bank.*

tes·ti·mo·ny /'testəməni $'testəˌmoʊni/ *noun, plural* **testimonies** a formal statement that someone makes in a law court

test tube /'. ./ *noun* a small narrow glass container that is used in scientific tests

tet·a·nus /'tetənəs/ *noun [no plural]* a serious disease that you can get when you are cut, which makes you unable to move the muscles in your body

text /tekst/ *noun* the writing in a book, magazine etc, rather than the pictures

text·book /'tekstbʊk/ *noun* a book about a subject which students use: *a history textbook*

tex·tile /'tekstaɪl/ *noun formal* any material that you make by crossing threads over and under each other

tex·ture /'tekstʃə $'tekstʃə˞/ *noun* the way that something feels when you touch it: *a material with a rough texture*

than /ðən; strong ðæn/ *preposition* used when comparing people or things: *These shoes are cheaper than the other ones.* | *My brother's older than me.* | *She's thinner than* she used to be (=she used to be fatter).

thank /θæŋk/ verb

GRAMMAR
thank someone for something
thank someone for doing something
to tell someone that you are grateful to them for something: *Have you written to **thank** Grandma **for** your present yet?* | *She **thanked** the boy **for** helping her.*

PHRASE
thank God, thank goodness spoken
used to say that you are very glad about something: ***Thank God I** didn't send the letter before noticing the mistake!*

thank·ful /'θæŋkfəl/ adjective glad about something: *We're thankful nobody was hurt in the accident.*
–**thankfully** adverb: *Thankfully, nobody lost their job* (=I'm glad nobody lost their job).

thanks¹ /θæŋks/ informal

GRAMMAR
thanks for something
thanks for doing something
thank you: *"Lunch is ready." "Thanks, Mom."* | ***Thanks for** the ride home.* | *Bye, **thanks for** coming.* | *"Do you want any help, Bob?" "No, thanks."*

PHRASE
thanks to something because of something: *Dealing with information is much easier now, **thanks to** modern computers.*

thanks² plural noun something that you say to thank someone: *I helped him a lot, but did I get any thanks? No.*

Thanks·giv·ing /ˌθæŋksˈɡɪvɪŋ/ noun a holiday in the US and Canada in autumn, when families have a large meal together

thank you /'. ./

GRAMMAR
thank you for something
thank you for doing something
1 used when someone does or says something kind to you: *"What a beautiful dress!" "Thank you."* | *Oh, this is just what I wanted. **Thank you**

very much.* | ***Thank you for** dinner – it was really good.* | ***Thank you for** sending me those books.*
2 used to say yes or no to something that someone is offering you: *"Do you want a drink?" "No, thank you."*

thank-you /'. ./ noun something that you say or do to thank someone: *They gave her some flowers as a thank-you.*

that¹ pronoun
1 /ðæt/ plural **those** /ðəʊz $ ðoʊz/ a thing or person which is farther away from you, often in a place you point at: *He lives in that house on the corner.* | *"Which piece would you like?" "I'd like that one, please."* | *Look at those cute little rabbits.* | *Can you park in that space over there, please, sir.*
2 /ðæt/ plural **those** /ðəʊz $ ðoʊz/ used to say something about the thing you are already talking about: *That was the hardest exam so far.* | *Have you got those old photographs of Dad?* | *"Are they related?" "Yes, that is his sister."* | *We drove to Brighton, and later that day we went for a walk along the beach.*
3 /ðət/ 'who' or 'which': *He's the boy that hit me.* | *There are lots of things that I need to do before I leave.*
4 /ðət/ used to join two parts of a sentence together: *I hope that you get better soon.* | *He's the most handsome guy that I've ever seen.* | *I need to be sure that you're not lying.*

that² /ðæt/ adverb spoken
that long, that much, that big etc as long, much, big etc as you show, using your hands: *The car missed us by about that much.*

thatched /θætʃt/ adjective a thatched roof on a house is made of dried plant stems

thaw /θɔː/ also **thaw out** verb if something frozen thaws, it becomes warmer until all the ice is gone: *The freezer broke and all the food thawed out.* | *In spring, the river thaws and sometimes floods the valleys.*

the /ðə; before vowels, and strong ðiː/
1 before a noun to show that you talking about a particular person or

▼ thing: *The boy was riding the blue bicycle.* | *That's the dress I want to buy.* | *He went to the shop to buy some milk.* | *The movie wasn't very good.*

USAGE
Don't use **the** when you are talking about something in general: *I like ice cream.* | *Cats often hunt at night.* Use **the** when you are talking about a particular thing: *I like the ice cream I bought.* | *The cats on our street make a lot of noise.* Don't use **the** before street names or before the names of airports or railway stations: *We arrived at Gatwick Airport.* | *The train leaves from Euston Station.* | *She lives in Spencer Way.* Use **the** when you are talking about airports or stations in general: *We arrived at the airport. The train leaves from the new station.* | *She lives in the same street as me.*

2 before the names of rivers, oceans, and seas and before the names of groups of mountains: *the Ganges* | *the Atlantic Ocean* | *the Mediterranean Sea*
3 before the names of countries if they are plural or have the word 'state', 'union', 'republic', or 'kingdom' in them: *the Philippines* | *the United States* | *The People's Republic of China*
4 to talk about all the people in a country: *The British like fish and chips.* | *The Japanese have a good school system.*
5 to talk about all people who are blind, deaf, disabled etc: *parking spaces for the disabled* | *a school for the deaf*
6 use **the** about a particular period of time: *The sixties* (=1960s) *were a time of great change.* | *In the 1800s, millions of people came to America.*
➪ compare A, AN

thea·tre *BrE*, **theater** *AmE* /ˈθɪətə $ ˈθiːətər/ *noun* 1 a building with a stage where plays are performed: *Would you like to go to the theater?* | *the Royal Gala Theatre* 2 also **movie theater** the American word for a CINEMA 3 the room in a hospital where doctors do operations

the·at·ri·cal /θiˈætrɪkəl/ *adjective* related to the theatre: *She makes theatrical costumes* (=clothes for actors to wear).

theft /θeft/ *noun formal* the crime of steal-ing something: *There is a lot of car theft around here.*

their /ðə $ ðər; strong ðeə $ ðer/ *adjective*
1 belonging to a group of two or more people: *Someone stole their car.* | *Their plan was not successful.*
2 his or her: *Someone's left their coat behind.*

theirs /ðeəz $ ðerz/ *pronoun*
a thing belonging to a group of two or more people: *Our house is bigger than theirs.*

them /ðəm; strong ðem/ *pronoun*
1 a group of people or things: *Some boys were talking, so the teacher told them to be quiet.* | *The magazines were old, so I threw them away.*
2 him or her: *If anyone calls, tell them I'll be back at 4 o'clock.*

theme /θiːm/ *noun* 1 the main subject or idea in a book, film etc: *The theme of the novel is the effect that war has on people.* 2 **theme music, theme song** music that is always played with a particular television or radio programme

theme park /ˈ. ./ *noun* a place where people pay to ride on machines that is based on one particular thing, such as space travel or animals

them·selves /ðəmˈselvz/ *pronoun*
1 used when the same group does an action and receives an action: *The children might hurt themselves if they play on the rocks.* | *My parents are old and no longer able to look after themselves.*
2 used to emphasize that you are talking about a particular group: *The students themselves said that the exam was too easy.* | *The products themselves are good, but they are too expensive.*
3 himself or herself: *The person who wrote this obviously has a high opinion of themselves.*

PHRASE
by themselves with no one else there, or with no one helping: *They spent the day by themselves.* | *They did all the work by themselves.*

then /ðen/ adverb

1 at a time in the past or future: *It happened in 1972, and things were different then.* | *"I'll come round at about 8." "OK, I'll see you then."*

2 after something else: *I'll get changed and then we can go out.* | *Fry the onions. Then add the mushrooms.*

3 used when saying something because of what has been said before *spoken*: *"There are no seats here." "Then we'll have to go somewhere else." | "It's nearly ten." "Come on, then. We'd better go."*

the·ol·o·gy /θi'ɒlədʒi $θi'ɑlədʒi/ noun [no plural] the study of religion

theo·ry /'θɪəri $'θiəri/ noun, plural **theories** an idea that explains why something happens: *But can you prove your theory?* | *My theory is that he's behaving like this because his parents are always arguing.*

ther·a·py /'θerəpi/ noun, plural **therapies** the treatment of mental or physical illness without using drugs or operations: *She's having therapy to help with her fear of birds.*

there¹ /ðeə $ðer/ pronoun

1 there is, there are used to say that something exists or happens: *There are some great photographs in the book.* | *At the beginning of the film, there's a robbery.* | *There has been a lot of rain recently.*

2 is there?, are there? used to ask whether something exists: *Is there a telephone in your office?* | *Are there any girls in the team?*

there² adverb

1 in another place, not the place where you are: *You can sit over there.* | *I wish I had been there – it sounds so exciting!* | *If we leave home in the morning, we should get there by lunch time.*

2 available or ready to help: *The offer's there if you want it.* | *We'll always be there for you when you need us.*

PHRASE
there's, there it is, there he is etc something you say when you are pointing at something or someone: *Look – there's our hotel!* | *We're still waiting for Jack – look, there he is.*

there·a·bouts /ˌðeərə'baʊts $ˌðerə'baʊts/ adverb near the number, amount, time etc that you have just mentioned: *We should arrive at 9 o'clock or thereabouts.*

there·fore /'ðeəfɔː $'ðerfɔr/ adverb *formal* for the reason that you have just mentioned: *These shoes are made of the best materials and are therefore very expensive.*

ther·mal /'θɜːməl $'θɚməl/ adjective *formal* related to or caused by heat: *thermal energy*

ther·mom·e·ter /θə'mɒmətə $θɚ'mɑmətɚ/ noun a piece of equipment that measures the temperature of the air, your body etc

ther·mo·stat /'θɜːməstæt $'θɚmə-ˌstæt/ noun a piece of equipment that controls the temperature of a house

the·sau·rus /θɪ'sɔːrəs/ noun, plural **thesauruses** a book containing lists of words that have similar meanings

these the plural form of THIS¹

they /ðeɪ/ pronoun

1 a group of people or things: *Her parents said they would be out that evening.* | *He had some paints but they were the wrong colour.*

2 he or she: *Anyone can learn to play the piano if they want to.*

they'd /ðeɪd/ **1** the short form of 'they had': *They'd seen him earlier.* **2** the short form of 'they would': *They said they'd love to come.*

they'll /ðeɪl/ the short form of 'they will': *They'll be late – they always are.*

they're /ðə $ðɚ strong ðeə $ðer/ the short form of 'they are': *They're lovely earrings.*

they've /ðeɪv/ the short form of 'they have': *They've gone out.*

thick /θɪk/ adjective

1 something that is thick has a wide distance between its two opposite sides ⇨ opposite THIN (2): *a thick heavy book* | *I drew a thick line around the edge of the page.* | *a thick warm coat*

2 used to talk about the distance between the two opposite sides of something: *The castle walls are about one metre thick* (=the walls are one metre from front to back).

3 thick smoke or cloud is difficult to see through: *The ship could not sail because of thick fog.*

4 a thick liquid does not have much water in it: *Heat the mixture until it is quite thick.*

5 if you have thick hair, it grows closely together on your head

6 *BrE informal* stupid: *He's really thick!*

thick·ness /'θɪknəs/ *noun* how thick something is: *Cut the bread the same thickness as your finger.*

thief /θiːf/ *noun, plural* **thieves** /θiːvz/ someone who steals things: *a car thief*

thigh /θaɪ/ *noun* the top part of your leg above your knee: *She smiled and patted his thigh.*

thin /θɪn/ *adjective* **thinner**, **thinnest**

1 someone who is thin has very little fat on their body ⇨ *opposite* FAT¹ (1): *a tall thin man* | *Her face was thin and pale.* ⇨ *see picture on page 353*

2 something that is thin has very little distance between its opposite sides ⇨ *opposite* THICK (1): *thin slices of ham* | *a thin layer of dust*

3 if someone's hair is thin, it does not grow closely together: *John looks older, and his hair is getting a bit thin.*

USAGE thin, slim, slender, skinny
Thin, slim, slender, and skinny all have a similar meaning. **Thin** is a general word for describing people who have very little fat on their bodies. **Slim** or **slender** are used to describe people who are thin in an attractive way: *She's tall and slim with blonde hair.* | *a slender waist.* **Skinny** is an informal word and describes someone who is very thin, often in a way that is not attractive: *You need to eat more – you're too skinny.*

thing ⇨ *see box on next page*

think ⇨ *see box on page 645*

think·ing /'θɪŋkɪŋ/ *noun [no plural]* someone's opinions and ideas about something: *What is your latest thinking on the future of the college?*

thin·ly /'θɪnli/ *adverb* **1** thinly sliced cut into thin pieces **2** thinly popu-

lated with few people in a large area: *a thinly populated mountain area*

third /θɜːd $ θɝd/ *number* **1** 3rd: *Josh came third in the race.* **2** one of three equal parts of something; 1/3: *One third of the students are girls.*

third per·son /ˌ. '../ *noun* the third person a form of a verb that you use with 'he', 'she', 'it', or 'they'

thirst /θɜːst $ θɝst/ *noun [no plural]* when you need a drink very much: *People are dying of thirst.*

thirst·y /'θɜːsti $ 'θɝsti/ *adjective* **thirstier, thirstiest**
if you are thirsty, you want or need to drink something: *I'm really thirsty – let's get a drink.*

thir·teen /ˌθɜːˈtiːn $ ˌθɝˈtin/ *number* 13 – **thirteenth** *number*

thir·ty /'θɜːti $ 'θɝti/ *number, plural* **thirties 1** 30 **2** the thirties the years from 1930 to 1939 **3** be in your thirties to be aged between 30 and 39 – **thirtieth** *number*

this¹ /ðɪs/ *pronoun, plural* **these** /ðiːz/

1 a thing or person that is near you: *This coffee's cold.* | *These trousers are a bit tight.* | *I've lived in this town all my life.* | *"What's this?" "A present."* | *This is Janet* (=used to introduce someone).

2 used to mention a period of time that is happening now or will happen very soon: *I've been pretty busy this week.* | *This year has been a difficult one.* | *Shall we go to the cinema this weekend* (=during the weekend that will come next)?

3 used to say something about the thing you are already talking about: *Barry was late. This didn't surprise her because he was often late.* | *This is very bad news.*

this² *adverb*
this late, this cold, this difficult etc as late, cold, difficult etc as something is at the present time: *It's never been this cold in October before.*

this·tle /'θɪsəl/ *noun* a wild plant with sharp points on its leaves

thorn /θɔːn $ θɔrn/ *noun* a sharp pointed part on a plant such as a rose

thing /θɪŋ/ *noun*

❶ object

use **thing** when you are talking about something without saying its name or when you do not know what it is called: *What's this little round **thing** for?* | *Just put all those **things** in a pile on the table.* | *Turn that **thing** off! You've watched enough TV today.*

❷ event, idea, statement, action

use **thing** when you are talking about something without saying its name or without giving any details: *It was a stupid **thing** to do.* | *My brother says some really funny **things** sometimes.* | *I've heard some good **things** about that film.* | *This is the hardest **thing** I've ever done.*

> ✗ **Don't say** ➤ *I know many things* or *He has learned many things.*
> ✓ **Say** ➤ *I know **a lot*** or *He has learned **a great deal.***

> ✗ **Don't say** ➤ *I have a thing to ask you.* | *Do you have a thing to do?*
> ✓ **Say** ➤ *I have **something** to ask you.* | *Do you have **anything** to do?*

thing

❹ my/your/their etc things
spoken

the 'things' that you own or are carrying with you, such as books, clothes etc: *Just put **your things** over there for now.* | *Have you brought **your** swimming **things**?*

❸ events in someone's life

use **things** to talk about the events that are happening in someone's life, without naming any of the events: *"Hi, Jason, how are **things** with you?" "Fine, thanks."* | *Dad's finally found another job, so **things** are getting better.* | *We've been in business for fifteen years, and **things** have really changed since we started.*

PHRASES

all sorts of things, all kinds of things
a lot of different types of things: *We talked about **all kinds of things.*** | *They sell **all sorts of things** – everything from sweets to videos.*

for one thing
use this to give a reason why you think something is true or will happen: *She's not a great basketball player. **For one thing**, she can't jump.* | ***For one thing**,* smoking makes your breath smell horrible.

the last thing somebody wants, the last thing somebody needs, the last thing on your mind etc
use this to say that someone does not want or need something at all, that you are not thinking about something at all etc: ***The last thing I wanted*** was to miss the class. | *Marriage was **the last thing on her mind.***

T

❶ to use your mind

*I need some time to **think**. | Alison **thought about** what he had said. | George is **thinking about** changing jobs. | **Think carefully** before you make any decisions.*

GRAMMAR
think about something | think about doing something

think

❸ to believe

*I **think** Sarah is in the garden (=I believe she is in the garden, but I am not completely sure). | Jim **thinks that** something might be wrong with the car. | I **thought** you liked carrots (=I believed you liked carrots, but now I know that you do not). | She's sixteen? I **thought** she was a lot older.*

GRAMMAR
think (that)

❷ to have an opinion

*I **thought** it was one of the best books I'd ever read. | Everyone **thought that** the new teacher was really nice. | **What did you think** of Joe? Did you like him?*

GRAMMAR
think (that)

PHRASES

I think so *spoken*
say this to answer yes to a question, when you are almost sure about the answer: *"Is there any cake left?" "I think so."*

I don't think so *spoken*
say this to answer no to a question, when you are almost sure about the answer: *"Will Ben be coming to the party?" "I don't think so."*

PHRASAL VERBS

think of
1 to use your mind in order to produce an idea, plan suggestion etc: *I couldn't **think of** anything I could do to help.*
2 to remember something or someone: *The flowers made Peter **think of** his mother's garden.*

think over
to think about something very carefully

before you decide what to do: *I needed some time to **think** things **over**. | Take a few days to **think over** any job offers.*

think through
to think very carefully about all the things that might happen if you do something: *Students need to **think through** their job and college decisions. | Make sure you **think** it **through** before you do it.*

thor·ough /ˈθʌrə $ ˈθɝ·ou/ *adjective*

if someone is thorough, they do things very carefully: *She's always very thorough in her work.* | *The doctor gave me a thorough examination.*

thor·ough·ly /ˈθʌrəli $ ˈθɝ·ouli/ *adverb*
1 very much: *He thoroughly enjoyed the meal.* 2 carefully and completely: *Check your work thoroughly.*

those the plural of THAT[1]

though /ðəu $ ðou/ *adverb*
1 in spite of something: *Though I was tired, I still decided to go out and meet the others.* | *I seem to be gaining weight even though I'm exercising regularly.*
2 but: *He's a nice dog, though he doesn't always obey me.* | *I don't know if I'll be able to fix it – I'll try though* (=but I'll try).

thought[1] the past tense and past participle of THINK

thought[2] /θɔːt/ *noun*

GRAMMAR
a/the thought that
a/the thought of someone/something
thoughts on something

something that you think, for example an idea or opinion: *I've just had a thought – why don't we ask Steve to help?* | *I was upset by the thought that Mary might have been lying to me.* | *The thought of Simon made me want to scream.* | *Rachel, what are your thoughts on this?*

PHRASE
give something some thought, give some thought to something to think about something: *That's a good idea. I'll give it some thought.*

thought·ful /ˈθɔːtfəl/ *adjective*
1 serious and quiet because you are thinking: *She looked thoughtful.*
2 thinking of and doing kind things to make people happy: *It was thoughtful of you to remember my birthday.*
–**thoughtfully** *adverb*: *He thoughtfully gave me his chair.*

thought·less /ˈθɔːtləs/ *adjective* not thinking about how other people will

feel about something: *How can you be so thoughtless?*
–**thoughtlessly** *adverb*: *She thoughtlessly told everyone my secret.*

thou·sand /ˈθauzənd/ *noun* 1000

thrash /θræʃ/ *verb* 1 *informal* to easily win a game against someone: *We thrashed them 10–0.* 2 to hit someone violently, usually as a punishment

thread[1] /θred/ *noun* a long thin string of cotton, silk etc that you use to sew cloth: *a needle and thread*

thread[2] *verb* to put thread, string etc through a small hole: *He threaded the wire carefully through the holes.*

threat /θret/ *noun* 1 when you tell someone that you will hurt them if they do not do what you want: *He had made threats against his teachers.* 2 someone or something that may cause harm or damage: *This method of farming is a threat to birds and animals.*

threat·en /ˈθretn/ *verb*

GRAMMAR
threaten to do something
be threatened with something

1 to tell someone that you will do something unpleasant to them if they do not do what you want: *The boys threatened him until he gave them all his money.* | *He had threatened to kill her if she didn't keep quiet.*
2 to be likely to harm or destroy something: *This new law threatens the rights of all of us.* | *Many of the animals in the area are threatened with extinction* (=are likely to stop existing).

three /θriː/ *number* 3

three·di·men·sion·al /ˌ..ˈ...ˌ/ *adjective* a three-dimensional object has length, width, and height: *The computer game makes you feel you are in a three-dimensional space.*

threw the past tense of THROW[1]

thrill /θril/ *noun* a strong feeling of excitement and pleasure: *I get such a thrill from driving fast.*

thrilled /θrild/ *adjective* very excited, pleased, or happy: *I was thrilled when he told me he liked me.*

thrill·er /ˈθrilə $ ˈθrilɝ/ *noun* an exciting film or book about murder or crime

thud

thril·ling /'θrɪlɪŋ/ adjective very exciting: *a thrilling game*

throat /θrəʊt $ θroʊt/ noun the back part of your mouth and the inside of your neck: *I have a sore throat.*

throb /θrɒb $ θrɑːb/ verb throbbed, throbbing to hurt with a strong regular pain: *My finger was throbbing.*

throne /θrəʊn $ θroʊn/ noun **1** the large chair that a king or queen sits on **2** on the throne: *This happened when Queen Victoria was on the throne* (=when she was queen).

throt·tle¹ /'θrɒtl $ 'θrɑːtl/ verb to hold someone's throat tightly, stopping them from breathing ➪ same meaning STRANGLE: *He tried to throttle me.*

throttle² noun a part of a vehicle that controls the speed of the engine by controlling the amount of FUEL going into it

through¹ /θruː/ preposition, adverb
1 going from one side of a thing or place to the other: *They drove through the tunnel under the mountain. | We went through Belgium on our way to Germany. | This knife can cut through metal. | If we don't mend that hole in the roof, the rain will come through.* ➪ see picture on page 354
2 looking from one side of something to the other: *A man was looking at them through the window.*
3 from the beginning to the end: *She slept through the night without waking up. | The people in front of us talked all the way through the film.*
4 until the end of a particular day or month AmE: *I'm busy from Monday through Thursday.*

through² adjective
be through with something informal to have finished using something or doing something: *Are you through with my lecture notes yet?*

through·out /θruːˈaʊt/ preposition, adverb
1 in every part of a place: *It's a large company, with offices throughout the world.*
2 during all of a period of time: *The school runs language courses throughout the year.*

throw¹ /θrəʊ $ θroʊ/ verb threw /θruː/ thrown /θrəʊn $ θroʊn/

GRAMMAR
throw something to someone
throw something into/at etc something
throw someone something
throw something at someone/something

1 if you throw something you are holding, you make it go through the air: *He **threw** the empty bottle **into** the bin. | Dad **threw** the ball **to** Alex* (=threw it so that Alex could catch it). | *Could you **throw** me my sweater? | One of the boys **threw** a stone **at** the dog* (=threw it to try to hit the dog). ➪ see pictures at CATCH¹ and on page 340
2 to suddenly move yourself or part of your body somewhere: *She **threw** herself **onto** the bed. | "Don't go," he said, **throwing** his arms **around** her.*

PHRASAL VERBS
throw away
throw something away if you throw away something that you do not want, you put it in a container where it will be removed: *This bread looks rather old – shall I **throw** it **away**?*
throw out
throw something out if you throw out something that you do not want, you get rid of it: *Are you **throwing out** those old clothes?*
throw up
informal if you throw up, the food you have eaten comes back out of your mouth: *I'll **throw up** if I eat any more pizza!*

throw² noun when you throw something or how you throw it: *That was a good throw!*

thrown the past participle of THROW

thru /θruː/ another spelling of THROUGH that is sometimes used in notes, written signs etc

thrust /θrʌst/ verb, past tense and past participle **thrust** to push something somewhere with quite a lot of force: *She thrust a letter into my hand.*

thud /θʌd/ noun the low sound of something heavy hitting something else: *He fell out of bed with a thud.*

thug /θʌg/ *noun* a rough violent person: *A gang of thugs attacked him.*

thumb¹ /θʌm/ *noun*

the short thick finger at the side of your hand: *He broke his thumb playing rugby.*

thumb² *verb* **thumb through** to quickly look at the pages in a book, magazine etc: *I thumbed through the guidebook, looking for a map.*

thumb·tack /ˈθʌmtæk/ the American word for a DRAWING PIN

thump /θʌmp/ *verb* **1** to hit someone or something hard with your hand closed: *I'll thump you if you say that again!* **2** if your heart is thumping, it is beating strongly and quickly because you are afraid or excited
– **thump** *noun*: *Paul gave him a thump in the stomach.*

thun·der /ˈθʌndə $ ˈθʌndɚ/ *noun* [no plural] the loud noise that you hear during a storm: *Thunder roared and lightning flashed.*

thun·der·ous /ˈθʌndərəs/ *adjective* extremely loud: *thunderous applause*

Thurs·day /ˈθɜːzdi $ ˈθɚzdi/ *written abbreviation* **Thurs** *noun* the day of the week between Wednesday and Friday: *Claire goes to hospital on Thursday.*

tick¹ /tɪk/ *noun* **1** the sound that a clock makes every second: *The only sound was the tick of a clock.* ⇨ *see picture on page 350* **2** *BrE* a mark that you write to show that something is correct; CHECK *AmE*: *She put a tick next to Louise's name.*

tick² *verb* **1** if a clock ticks, it makes a short sound every second: *His watch ticked loudly.* **2** *BrE* to mark something with a tick to show that it is correct: *Tick the box if you want to receive our magazine.*

tick·et /ˈtɪkɪt/ *noun*

GRAMMAR
a ticket for something

a piece of paper that you buy in order to travel somewhere or go to an event: *How much is a **bus ticket** to London?* | ***Tickets for** the concert are £15.*

tick·le /ˈtɪkəl/ *verb* **1** to move your fingers over part of someone's body in order to make them laugh: *I tickled the baby's chin.* ⇨ *see picture on page 341* **2** if something tickles, it touches your body lightly in an uncomfortable way: *This sweater really tickles.*

tide¹ /taɪd/ *noun* **1** the regular movement of the sea as it comes up to cover the land and goes down away from the land: *The tide is coming in* (=towards the land). **2** **high tide, low tide** when the level of the sea is high or low: *You can walk to the island at low tide.*

tide² *verb* **tide someone over** to give someone money to help them while they are waiting to get money from somewhere else: *Mum lent me £20 to tide me over until I got paid.*

ti·dy¹ /ˈtaɪdi/ *adjective* **tidier, tidiest**

1 neat ⇨ *opposite* UNTIDY: *Your grandmother's coming, so make sure your room is tidy!* | *Please leave the house tidy when you go.*
2 *BrE* someone who is tidy likes to keep things neat and in the right place; NEAT *AmE*: *Sarah is very tidy.*
– **tidily** *adverb*

tidy² *verb BrE* **tidied, tidies**

also **tidy up** to make a place look tidy by picking things up and putting them in their correct place: *It took us two hours to **tidy up** after the party.* | *Don't forget to tidy your room.*

PHRASAL VERB
tidy away *BrE*

tidy something away to put something back in its correct place or into a container: *Can you **tidy away** your papers please?*

tie¹ /taɪ/ *verb, present participle* **tying**

GRAMMAR
tie something/someone to something
tie things together
tie something around something
tie with someone
tie for something

1 to fasten things together using rope, string etc: *George got out of the boat and **tied** it **to** a tree.* | *The soldier took some rope and **tied** Ken's hands **together**.*

2 to fasten something in a particular position by making a knot in it: *Jack tied his sweater around his waist and went out.* | *He had forgotten to tie his shoelaces.*
3 if two people or teams tie with each other, they have the same number of points at the end of a competition: *Tom tied for first place with Craig.*

PHRASAL VERB

tie up
1 tie someone up to tie someone's arms and legs with rope so that they cannot move: *They tied us up and left us in a dark room.*
2 tie something up to fasten something with rope, string etc: *a box of chocolates tied up with pink ribbon*

---

tie² *noun* **1** a long narrow piece of cloth that you wear around your neck with a shirt: *He has to wear a shirt and tie for work.* ⇨ *see picture on page 352* **2** when a competition ends with two people or teams getting the same number of points: *The match ended in a tie.*

tier /tɪə $ tɪr/ *noun* a row of seats that has other rows above or below it: *We were in the first tier of seats.*

ti·ger /ˈtaɪgə $ ˈtaɪgɚ/ *noun* a large wild cat with yellow and black lines on its fur ⇨ *see picture on page 339*

tight¹ /taɪt/ *adjective*
1 clothes are tight fit your body very closely ⇨ *opposite* LOOSE (1): *She was wearing a tight white T-shirt.* | *This skirt's a bit too tight.*
2 firmly fixed and difficult to move ⇨ *opposite* LOOSE (2): *The lid's too tight – I can't get it off.* | *I fastened my hair up in a tight knot.*
3 tight laws or rules are very strict: *We need tighter controls on the burning of coal, gas and oil.*

tight² *adverb* if you hold something tight, you hold it with a lot of force: *I held on tight as the bus started to move.*

tight·en /ˈtaɪtn/ *verb* **1** to become tighter, or to make something tighter: *How do I tighten my seat belt?* **2** also **tighten something up** to make a rule or law stricter: *They are tightening up the rules on smoking at school.*

tight·rope /ˈtaɪt-rəʊp $ ˈtaɪt-roʊp/ *noun* a wire high above the ground that a performer walks along in a CIRCUS

tights /taɪts/ *plural noun* a thin piece of clothing that fits around a woman's feet and legs, and up to her waist: *a pair of black tights*

tile /taɪl/ *noun* a thin square piece of a hard material that is used for covering roofs, walls, or floors: *Dad is fixing some new tiles in the bathroom.*

till¹ /tɪl/ *preposition* until: *Let's wait till later.*

till² *noun* a machine that is used in a shop to keep money in and show how much customers have to pay: *There was over a thousand pounds in the till.*

tilt /tɪlt/ *verb* if something tilts, or if you tilt it, it moves so that one side or edge is higher: *Jackie tilted the mirror slightly so that she could see herself better.*

tim·ber /ˈtɪmbə $ ˈtɪmbɚ/ *noun* [no plural] *BrE* wood that you use to build or make things; LUMBER *AmE*

time¹ ⇨ *see box on next page*

time² /taɪm/ *verb* **1** to arrange for something to happen at a particular time: *The bomb was timed to explode at 6.00 pm.* **2** to measure how long it takes to do something: *The coach timed us as we ran around the track.*

time·less /ˈtaɪmləs/ *adjective* not affected by changes over time: *the timeless beauty of the sea*

time off /ˌ. ˈ./ *noun* [no plural] time when you do not have to be at work or school: *I'd like some time off this week.*

time out /ˌ. ˈ./ *noun* a short break during a sports game to let the players rest or plan how they will play the rest of the game

tim·er /ˈtaɪmə $ ˈtaɪmɚ/ *noun* a part of a machine or system that you use to make it stop or start at a particular time: *You can set the timer to switch the cooker off.*

time·ta·ble /ˈtaɪmˌteɪbəl/ *noun* a list of times or dates, showing when things will happen: *the train timetable*

tim·id /ˈtɪmɪd/ *adjective* shy and nervous: *a timid girl who never spoke*

tin /tɪn/ *noun* **1** a metal container in which you can store food: *a biscuit tin* **2** *BrE* a small metal container in which food is sold; CAN *AmE*: *a tin of baked beans* ⇨ *see picture at* CONTAINER

time

1 **'time' is what we measure in minutes, hours, years etc**

*A machine that can travel through **time** is impossible.* | *As you get older, **time** seems to **go by** more quickly.* | *A lot of **time** has **passed**, and not much has been done.*

> ✗ Don't say ➤ *Times passed quickly.*
>
> ✓ Say ➤ ***Time** passed quickly.*

2 **'the time' is the particular minute or hour of the day**

*The **time** is ten to five.* | *"**What time is it?**" asked Meg, sleepily.* | *"Excuse me, **have you got the time?**" "Yes, it's ten past four."* | ***What time** do you want to start?*

"What **time** is it please?"

3 **an amount of time**

*The building had been empty **for a long time**.* | *Most of the homework can be finished **in a short time**.* | *She left **a short time** ago.* | *After a **period of time**, the children were asked to do the task again.* | *Harrison had been ill **for some time** (=for a long time).*

4 **an occasion when you do something or when something happens**

*Your mother called you five **times** today.* | *I'll tell you about it the next **time** that I see you.* | *Do you remember the **time** when Dad lost his car keys?* | *Every **time** I see her, her hair is a different color.* | *Okay, play the song louder this **time**.* | *This is the first **time** the kids have seen snow.*

T

PHRASES

spend time
to use time to do something: *He wants to spend more time with his kids.* | *Jackie spent a lot of time on this report for school.*

waste time, a waste of time
if you waste time, or if something is a waste of time, you do not do anything in the time you have, or you do something that is not successful or useful: *Studying Latin seems like a waste of time.* | *Why are you wasting your time just watching TV?*

take time
if something takes time, you need a long time to do it: *Learning a language well takes time.*

have (the) time
to have enough time to do something: *You don't have time to change your clothes now!* | *I don't have enough time to do all the things I need to do.*

at the time, at that time
if something happened at the time or at that time, it happened during a particular time in the past: *At that time, Paul was only five years old.* | *I was living in Detroit at the time.*

it's time
use this to say that something should happen now: *It's time for dinner.* | *I'll come get you when it's time to go.*

by the time
(=when) use this to show that one thing happened later than another thing: *By the time I got home, everyone else had finished dinner.*

By the time I got here, everyone else had finished dinner.

on time
if something happens on time, it happens at the correct time: *Most of the students finished their homework on time.* | *Is the train on time?*

Is the train on time?

in time
if something happens in time, it happens early or at the right time: *Make sure you get back in time for dinner.* | *Jon wants to get home in time to watch the football.*

all the time
always or very often: *I used to play tennis all the time.* | *He just wears his glasses for reading – he doesn't have to wear them all the time.*

most of the time, some of the time
usually or sometimes: *Ken gets home by six o'clock most of the time.* | *Katie feeds the cats some of the time, and I do it other times.*

have a good time, have a great time
to enjoy yourself: *We had a really good time on our holiday.*

take your time
to do something carefully, without hurrying: *Take your time during the exam, and check your answers.*

T

tin·gle /'tɪŋgəl/ verb if a part of your body tingles, the skin feels slightly uncomfortable: *Her lips tingled from the cold air.*

tin·ker /'tɪŋkə $ 'tɪŋkɚ/ verb informal if you tinker with a machine, you make small changes to it: *He spends Sundays tinkering with his bike.*

tin·kle /'tɪŋkəl/ verb to make a sound like small bells: *A piano tinkled in the distance.*

tinned /tɪnd/ adjective BrE tinned food is sold in tins; CANNED AmE: *tinned tomatoes*

tin o·pen·er /'. ,.../ noun BrE a tool that you use for opening tins of food; CAN OPENER AmE

tin·sel /'tɪnsəl/ noun [no plural] Christmas decorations made of thin pieces of silver paper: *They hung tinsel on the Christmas tree.*

tint /tɪnt/ noun a small amount of a colour: *His eyes had a yellow tint.*

tint·ed /'tɪntɪd/ adjective tinted glass is slightly coloured

ti·ny /'taɪni/ adjective tinier, tiniest very small: *They live in a tiny house.*

tip¹ /tɪp/ noun

GRAMMAR
the tip of something
a tip on something

1 the end of something long, narrow, and pointed: *He touched the flower with **the tip of** his finger.* | *the southern **tip of** the island*
2 a useful piece of advice: *Can you **give** me any **tips on how to** lose weight?* | *fashion tips*
3 an additional amount of money that you give to someone who has done a job for you as a way of thanking them: *Do you usually **leave a tip** in a restaurant?*
4 BrE informal a very dirty or untidy place; DUMP AmE: *His flat is a complete tip!*

tip² verb tipped, tipping

GRAMMAR
tip something up/back

1 to move, or to move something, so that one side, end etc is higher: *The boat kept **tipping** to one side.* | *"Could you just **tip** your head **back**?" the dentist said.* | *Tip the bottle **up** slightly.*
2 to make something flow or fall out of a container, by moving the con-

tainer: *I **tipped** all the shopping **onto** the table.*
3 to give an additional amount of money to someone who has done a job for you as a way of thanking them

PHRASAL VERBS
tip over
tip over, tip something over if something tips over, or if you tip it over, it falls over: *I **tipped** the paint pot **over** by accident.*

tip·toe /'tɪptəʊ $ 'tɪptoʊ/ noun on tiptoe if you stand or walk on tiptoe, you stand or walk just on your toes: *We couldn't see the stage, even when we stood on tiptoe.* ➔ see picture on page 340

tire¹ the American spelling of TYRE

tire² /taɪə $ taɪɚ/ also **tire out** verb if something tires you, it makes you feel very tired: *All that dancing has tired me out.*
– **tiring** adjective: *Teaching is a very tiring job.*

tired /taɪəd $ taɪɚd/ adjective

GRAMMAR
tired of something/someone
tired of doing something

1 someone who is tired feels that they want to sleep or rest: *By the end of the day, I **felt** so **tired** that I had to lie down.* | *Young children **get tired** very quickly.*
2 if you are tired of something, you have become bored with it, and you do not want to do or have that thing any more: *He says he's **tired of** school and wants to get a job!* | *I'm **tired of** football now.* | *They soon **got tired of** watching television.*

PHRASE
tired out very tired: *I can't dance any more – I'm tired out.*

tire·some /'taɪəsəm $ 'taɪɚsəm/ adjective formal annoying or boring: *I'm sick of hearing your tiresome excuses.*

tis·sue /'tɪʃuː/ noun a piece of soft thin paper that you use to blow your nose: *a box of tissues*

ti·tle /'taɪtl/ noun 1 the name of a book, painting, play etc: *The title of his last book was 'Easy Computing'.* 2 a word such as Mr, Mrs, or Sir, that you use before someone's name

title-hold·er /'.. ,../ noun someone who has won an important sports competition that happens each year

T-junc·tion /'ti: ,dʒʌŋkʃən/ noun BrE a place where two roads meet and form the shape of the letter T

to¹ /tə; before vowels, and strong tu:/
used with verbs: He decided to stay at home. | She asked the teacher to help her. | Sarah seems to be very happy. | I phoned her to say sorry.

to² preposition
1 where someone or something goes: He ran to the door. | We're going on holiday to Iceland. | I went to a party last night.
2 who receives or is given something: I gave my old jacket to my sister. | He sent presents to the children.
3 the person you are telling something: Mark is talking to Steve. | She whispered something to the girl beside her.
4 when something ends: The museum is open from 10.30 to 5 (=it opens at 10.30 and closes at 5).
5 used when telling the time: It's ten to five (=it's ten minutes before five). | We left at a quarter to twelve.
6 showing who has an idea or opinion: It looks OK to me (=I think it's OK). | The idea seemed ridiculous to Stan.

PHRASES
be nice to someone, be cruel to someone etc: She's always **been nice to** me (=she's always treated me nicely).
have something/someone to yourself to be alone in a place or with someone, and not sharing that place or person: At last she **had** the house **to** herself.

toad /təʊd $ toʊd/ noun a brown animal like a large FROG

to and fro /,tu: ənd 'frəʊ $,tu: ənd 'froʊ/ adverb if someone or something moves to and fro, they move in one direction and then another

toast /təʊst $ toʊst/ noun [no plural] bread that has been heated until it is brown

toast·er /'təʊstə $ 'toʊstɚ/ noun a machine that you use to make toast: I put some bread in the toaster.

to·bac·co /tə'bækəʊ $ tə'bækoʊ/ noun [no plural] dried brown leaves that people smoke in cigarettes and pipes

to·bog·gan /tə'bɒgən $ tə'bɑgən/ noun a curved wooden board, used for going down hills that are covered in snow

to·bog·gan·ing /tə'bɒgənɪŋ $ tə'bɑgənɪŋ/ noun [no plural] the activity or sport of going down hills that are covered in snow while on a toboggan: We went tobogganing in the park.

to·day /tə'deɪ/ adverb, noun [no plural]
1 this day: It's Linda's birthday today. | What's today's date?
2 the present period of time: Today's teenagers have a lot more freedom than teenagers in the past. | A lot of the crime that happens today is in poor areas of the city.

tod·dler /'tɒdlə $ 'tɑdlɚ/ noun a young child who has just learned to walk ⇨ see usage note at CHILD

toe /təʊ $ toʊ/ noun one of the five parts at the end of your foot: These shoes hurt my toes. ⇨ see picture at BODY

toe·nail /'təʊneɪl $ 'toʊneɪl/ noun the hard flat part at the end of your toe

tof·fee /'tɒfi $ 'tɔfi/ noun a sticky brown sweet: Would you like a piece of toffee?

to·geth·er /tə'geðə $ tə'geðɚ/ adverb
1 when people do something with each other: They wrote all the songs together. | We must all work together to solve this problem.
2 when you join or mix things: I stuck the pieces of wood together with glue. | Mix the eggs and the cream together.
3 when people or things are next to each other: The girls were all standing together in a group. | I put all the books together at one end of the table.

toi·let /'tɔɪlɪt/ noun 1 a large bowl that you sit on when you get rid of waste substances from your body 2 BrE a small room with a toilet: The toilet is upstairs, on the right. 3 go to the toilet

BrE to use the toilet: *Mum, I want to go to the toilet!*

toilet pa·per /'.. ,../ *noun [no plural]* soft thin paper that you use to clean yourself after you have used the toilet

toi·let·ries /'tɔɪlətriz/ *plural noun* things such as soap that you use when you wash yourself

toilet roll /'.. ,./ *noun* toilet paper that is wound around a small tube: *We need some more toilet rolls.*

to·ken /'təʊkən $ 'toʊkən/ *noun* a special piece of paper that you can use to buy certain things, instead of using money: *I gave her a record token for her birthday.*

told the past tense and past participle of TELL

tol·e·rant /'tɒlərənt $ 'tɑlərənt/ *adjective* letting other people do or say what they want, even if you do not approve of it ➔ *opposite* INTOLERANT: *We should be tolerant of other people's beliefs.*

tol·e·rate /'tɒləreɪt $ 'tɑlə,reɪt/ *verb* to accept behaviour or a situation that you do not like, and not do anything about it: *I will not tolerate this sort of behaviour.*

toll /təʊl $ toʊl/ *noun* 1 the number of people that have been killed by something: *The death toll from the crash has risen to twenty.* 2 money that you pay so that you can use a road, bridge etc

to·ma·to /tə'mɑːtəʊ $ tə'meɪtoʊ/ *noun, plural* tomatoes a soft round red vegetable: *tomato salad* ➔ *see picture on page 345*

tomb /tuːm/ *noun* a large grave: *the tomb of an Egyptian king*

tom·boy /'tɒmbɔɪ $ 'tɑmbɔɪ/ *noun* a young girl who likes to play or dress like a boy

tomb·stone /'tuːmstəʊn $ 'tumstoʊn/ *noun* a stone on a grave, showing the name of the dead person

to·mor·row /tə'mɒrəʊ $ tə-'mɑroʊ/ *adverb, noun [no plural]* the day after this day: *Shall we go shopping tomorrow?* | *Do you have any plans for tomorrow?*

ton /tʌn/ *noun* a unit for measuring weight, equal to 2240 pounds or 1016 kilos in Britain, and 2000 pounds in the US

tone /təʊn $ toʊn/ *noun*

GRAMMAR
the tone of something
1 the way that something sounds, especially a person's voice: *"Hi, Jane," Rod called out in a friendly tone.* | *Her **tone of voice** was definitely a bit angry.*
2 *[no plural]* the general feeling or quality that something has: *It's important to keep **the tone of** the meeting relaxed.*
3 one of the sounds that you hear on the telephone: *Please leave your name and number after the long tone.* | *Can you hear a **dialling tone*** (=the sound you hear when you pick a phone up and it is ready to use)?

tongs /tɒŋz $ tɑŋz/ *plural noun* a tool for picking things up, which has two thin pieces of metal joined together at the top: *She picked up the coal with a pair of tongs.*

tongue /tʌŋ/ *noun*
the soft part inside your mouth that moves when you eat and speak

PHRASES
stick your tongue out at someone to point your tongue at someone in order to be rude
mother tongue, native tongue the language that you learn as a baby: *Many Canadians have French as their **mother tongue**.*

tongue-tied /'. ./ *adjective* unable to speak because you are nervous: *I always feel tongue-tied when I have to answer in class.*

to·night /tə'naɪt/ *adverb, noun [no plural]*
this evening or night: *What are you doing tonight?* | *Tonight's weather will be clear and cold.*

tonne /tʌn/ *noun* a unit for measuring weight, equal to 1000 kilograms

too /tuː/ *adverb*
1 use **too** when you want to add a new fact or to show that something is true about two people or things: *Jan plays the guitar, and she plays the piano **too**.* | *I would like some water **too**.* | *The sports centre has a large swimming pool, and it has a*

small pool for children, **too.** | "I'm really hungry." "Me **too.**"

2 use **too** to show that something is more than you need or more than you want: It's **too** hot in here. | I'm **too** tired to go out tonight. | He was driving **much too** fast. | This house is **too** small for six people. ⇨ compare ALSO

PHRASES

too much use this before things you cannot count, such as amounts or costs: I drank **too much** coffee. | I put **too much** salt in the soup. | He spent **too much** on that car.

too many use this before things that you can count, such as numbers of people or things: I drank **too many** cups of coffee. | There were **too many** people in the room. | Don't eat **too many** biscuits – it's nearly dinnertime.

took the past tense of TAKE

tools

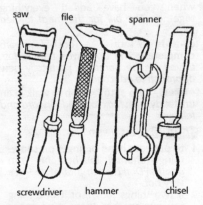

saw　file　spanner

screwdriver　hammer　chisel

tool /tuːl/ noun
any object that you hold in your hand and use for doing a particular job: I didn't have the right tools to fix the car. | gardening tools ⇨ see usage note at MACHINE

tooth /tuːθ/ noun, plural **teeth** /tiːθ/
one of the hard white things in your

mouth that you use for biting food: Don't forget to **brush your teeth**.

tooth·ache /'tuːθ-eɪk/ noun a pain in a tooth: I've got terrible toothache.

tooth·brush /'tuːθbrʌʃ/ noun, plural toothbrushes a small brush for cleaning your teeth ⇨ see picture at BRUSH¹

tooth·paste /'tuːθpeɪst/ noun [no plural] a substance that you use for cleaning your teeth: Use a small amount of toothpaste.

top¹ /tɒp $ tɑp/ noun

GRAMMAR
the top of something

1 the highest part of something ⇨ opposite BOTTOM¹ (1): I'm going to try and climb to **the top of** that tree! | My name was at **the top of** the list.

2 the lid or cover for a container, pen etc: Can you get the top off this jar?

3 **the top** the best or most important position in a company etc: He worked hard and got to **the top of** his profession.

4 a piece of clothing that you wear on the top part of your body: I've bought a blue top to wear with this skirt.

PHRASES

on top on something, or on the highest part of something: ice cream with chocolate sauce **on top** | They built the castle **on top of** a hill.

on top of something as well as something else: **On top of** all our other problems, my mother has been very ill.

from top to bottom including every part of a place: The police came in and searched the house **from top to bottom.**

over the top informal too extreme: I thought George's reaction was a bit **over the top.**

get on top of someone informal if something gets on top of you, it makes you feel unhappy because it is too difficult for you to deal with: My work's **been getting on top of** me recently.

top² adjective

1 best or most successful: Rick won the top prize of £500. | top tennis players like Tim Henman and Greg Rusedski

2 highest ⇨ *opposite* BOTTOM²: *My family lived on the top floor of the building.*

top³ *verb* topped, topping **1** to be more than a particular amount: *Audience figures topped 14 million last year.* **2** to be the best in a list of similar things: *The Spice Girls have topped the charts again* (=their record is the most popular). **3** if food is topped with something, it has that thing on top: *pizza topped with cheese*

top·ic /'tɒpɪk $ 'tɑpɪk/ *noun* a subject that people talk or write about: *The main topic of conversation was the party.*

top·ic·al /'tɒpɪkəl $ 'tɑpɪkəl/ *adjective* related to events that are happening now: *Racism is a very topical issue.*

top·less /'tɒpləs $ 'tɑpləs/ *adjective* a woman who is topless is not wearing any clothes on the top part of her body

top·ping /'tɒpɪŋ $ 'tɑpɪŋ/ *noun* food that you put on top of other food: *cake with a chocolate topping*

top·ple /'tɒpəl $ 'tɑpəl/ *verb* to fall over: *The lamp toppled over and broke.*

top-se·cret /ˌ. '../ *adjective* top-secret documents or information must be kept completely secret

torch /tɔːtʃ $ tɔrtʃ/ *noun, plural* torches *BrE* a small electric lamp that you carry in your hand; FLASHLIGHT *AmE*

tore the past tense of TEAR

tor·ment /tɔː'ment $ tɔr'ment/ *verb* to deliberately hurt, upset, or annoy someone: *Stop tormenting your sister!*

torn the past participle of TEAR

tor·na·do /tɔː'neɪdəʊ $ tɔr'neɪdoʊ/ *noun, plural* tornadoes a violent storm with strong winds that go round and round: *A tornado destroyed the building.*

tor·pe·do /tɔː'piːdəʊ $ tɔr'pidoʊ/ *noun, plural* torpedoes a weapon that is fired from a ship or SUBMARINE and travels under the sea: *The ship was sunk by a torpedo.*

tor·rent /'tɒrənt $ 'tɔrənt/ *noun* a large amount of water moving very fast: *a torrent of cold water*

tor·so /'tɔːsəʊ $ 'tɔrsoʊ/ *noun formal* the main part of your body, not including your arms, legs, or head: *He had injuries to his head and torso.*

tor·ture /'tɔːtʃə $ 'tɔrtʃɚ/ *verb* to deliberately hurt someone a lot for a long time, especially in order make them tell

you something: *They tortured many of their prisoners.*
– **torture** *noun* [no plural]: *victims of torture*

toss /tɒs $ tɔs/ *verb* to throw something somewhere in a careless way: *He tossed the keys to me.*

to·tal¹ /'təʊtl $ 'toʊtl/ *adjective*

1 *spoken* used to describe something as complete, in a strong way: *My date with John was a total disaster.* | *I have total confidence in the teachers.*

2 including everything: *What was the total cost of the holiday?*

total² *noun*

GRAMMAR
a total of something
the number that you get when you have added everything together: *Our teacher gave us ten numbers and told us to find the total.* | *The team played a total of 36 matches.*

PHRASE
in total including everything: *In total, I spent at least £100.*

total³ *verb* totalled, totalling *BrE*, totaled, totaling *AmE* to be a particular amount, when you have added everything together: *The bill for the meal totaled $45.*

tot·al·ly /'təʊtl-i $ 'toʊtl-i/ *adverb* completely: *The town was totally destroyed by the bombing.* | *a totally new approach to education*

tot·ter /'tɒtə $ 'tɑtɚ/ *verb* to walk in an unsteady way: *Max tottered forward and fell over.*

touch¹ /tʌtʃ/ *verb*

1 to put your hand or finger on something: *Chantal touched his arm gently.* | *Don't touch that plate – it's very hot.*

2 if two things touch, or if one thing touches another, there is no space between the things: *Their lips touched.* | *Lie on your back with your arms touching the floor.*

PHRASAL VERB
touch down
when a plane touches down, it lands safely on the ground: *The plane **touched down** in Dubai to take on more fuel.*

touch² *noun, plural* **touches**
1 your ability to know what something is like when you feel it with your fingers: *The children were learning about the senses of taste and touch.*
2 when something or someone touches you: *At the touch of her hand he turned round.*

PHRASES

get in touch, be in touch to write to someone or telephone them: *George decided to get in touch with an old friend of his.*

keep in touch, stay in touch to continue to speak or write to someone who does not live near you: *Jane and I have kept in touch since we left school.*

lose touch to stop speaking or writing to someone who does not live near you: *Sally moved to South Africa and I lost touch with her.*

out of touch if you are out of touch with something, it has changed and you no longer know about it or understand it: *I was out of touch with British pop music after living abroad for so long.*

touch·down /'tʌtʃdaʊn/ *noun*
1 when a plane lands safely on the ground 2 when a team playing RUGBY or American football gets points by taking the ball over the other team's line

touch·ing /'tʌtʃɪŋ/ *adjective* making you feel sad or sorry for someone: *The movie has some touching moments.*

touch·y /'tʌtʃi/ *adjective* **touchier, touchiest** easily annoyed or upset: *Are you always touchy about your work?*

tough /tʌf/ *adjective*
1 difficult and causing you a lot of problems: *Leaving home was a tough decision. | The match will be tough, but I'm sure we can win. | Life can be very tough sometimes.*
2 someone who is tough is strong, brave, or determined: *In business you have to be tough. | Hollywood's tough guys, like Arnold Schwarzenegger*
3 hard, and not easy to cut or bite ⇨ *opposite* TENDER (2): *This meat is tough.*

4 tough laws or rules are very strict: *We need tough new laws in order to fight crime.*

tough·en /'tʌfən/ also **toughen up** *verb* to make someone or something stronger: *The government wants to toughen up the law on drugs.*

tour¹ /tʊə $ tʊr/ *noun*

GRAMMAR
a tour of something
1 a journey to several different places in a country, area etc: *In the summer we went on a tour of North America.*
2 a trip around the different parts of a building, city etc: *Would you like a guided tour of the castle? | Steve took us on a tour of the university.*

PHRASE
be on tour to be travelling to different places in order to give concerts, perform plays etc: *The band is on tour in Europe at the moment.*

tour² *verb* to travel around an area, visiting different places: *The band will tour the States next year.*

tour·is·m /'tʊərɪzəm $ 'tʊrɪzəm/ *noun* [no plural] the business of providing tourists with places to stay and things to do: *The island's main industry is tourism.*

tour·ist /'tʊərəst $ 'tʊrɪst/ *noun* someone who visits a place for pleasure: *a group of Japanese tourists*

tour·na·ment /'tʊənəmənt $ 'tʊrnəmənt/ *noun* a competition in which many players compete against each other until there is one winner: *a tennis tournament*

tow

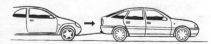

tow /təʊ $ toʊ/ *verb* if one vehicle tows another one, it pulls the other vehicle along behind it

to·wards /tə'wɔːdz $ tɔrdz/ also
toward /tə'wɔːd $ tɔrd/ *preposition*
1 going in the direction of someone or

▼ something: *Helen came running towards them.* | *Plants grow towards the light.* ⇨ *see picture on page 354*

2 at a particular time, that is getting close: *The weather should get better towards the end of the week.*

3 showing how you behave to someone: *He's always been quite friendly towards me.*

tow·el /'taʊəl/ *noun* a large piece of thick soft cloth that you use to dry your body: *I went swimming and forgot my towel.*

tow·er /'taʊə $ 'taʊɚ/ *noun* a tall narrow building or part of a building: *the bells at the top of the church tower*

town /taʊn/ *noun*

a place with many buildings and streets, where people live and work: *We lived in a small town on the south coast.* | *I think I'll go into town* (=the main part of the town where the shops are) *this afternoon.*

tox·ic /'tɒksɪk $ 'tɑksɪk/ *adjective* poisonous: *toxic chemicals*

toy /tɔɪ/ *noun* a thing for children to play with: *Polly was playing with her toys upstairs.*

trace¹ /treɪs/ *verb* **1** to find someone or something that is lost and may be far away: *Police are trying to trace her family.* **2** to copy a picture by drawing on a thin piece of paper that you put over it

trace² *noun* a sign that someone or something has been in a place: *There was no trace of the missing child.*

track¹ /træk/ *noun*

1 a small path or road, without a smooth surface: *The farm was at the end of a rough track.* ⇨ *see picture on page 348*

2 one of the songs or pieces of music on a CD etc: *This is my favourite track.*

3 the two metal lines that a train travels on: *The sign said 'Keep away from the track.'*

4 tracks marks on the ground that were made by an animal, person, or vehicle going over that ground: *It was easy to follow the lion's tracks.*

▼

PHRASES

keep track of something to have all the most recent information about something: *I try to keep track of the situation by reading the newspapers.*

lose track of something to not have all the most recent information about something any more: *I've lost track of how many children he has.*

track² *verb* track someone down to find someone after searching for them in different places: *The police are determined to track down the robbers.*

track·suit /'træksuːt/ *noun* BrE loose trousers and a loose top, which you wear for sport ⇨ *see picture on page 352*

trac·tor /'træktə $ 'træktɚ/ *noun* a strong vehicle with large wheels that is used on farms

trade¹ /treɪd/ *noun*

GRAMMAR
trade with someone
trade between people

1 [no plural] the business of buying and selling things, especially between countries: *Last year we increased our trade with Saudi Arabia.* | *There has been an increase in trade between the two countries.*

2 the car trade, the tourist trade etc is the business of producing and selling a particular type of thing, or providing particular services: *It's been a very bad year for the book trade.*

trade² *verb*

GRAMMAR
trade with someone
trade in something

when people, companies, or countries trade, they do business by buying and selling things: *Britain continued to trade with Cuba.* | *The company trades in high quality children's clothing.*

PHRASAL VERB
trade in

trade something in to give something that you own as part of the payment when you buy something similar: *You can trade your old computer games in for new ones.*

trade·mark /'treɪdmɑːk $'treɪdmɑrk/ noun a special word or picture on a product that shows it is made by a particular company: *'Coca-Cola' is a trademark.*

tra·di·tion /trə'dɪʃən/ noun

> **GRAMMAR**
> **a tradition to do something**
> **a/the tradition of doing something**

something that people have done for a long time, and continue to do ⇨ *same meaning* CUSTOM: *It's a tradition to celebrate the new year.* | *She wanted her daughter to carry on the family tradition of studying at Oxford.*

tra·di·tion·al /trə'dɪʃənəl/ adjective traditional beliefs or activities are shared by a group of people and have existed for a long time: *traditional folk music* | *It's traditional for the bride's father to pay for her wedding.*

traf·fic /'træfɪk/ noun [no plural] cars etc that are moving on the road: *There isn't as much traffic on the roads on Sunday.* | *The traffic's really bad* (=busy and slow) *in the morning.* | *I got to work late because of the heavy traffic* (=the large number of cars etc on the roads).

traffic cir·cle /'.. ,../ the American word for ROUNDABOUT

traffic jam /'.. ,../ noun a long line of cars etc on the road. moving very slowly: *We got stuck in a traffic jam.*

traffic light /'.. ,../ also **traffic sig·nal** /'.. ,../ noun a set of coloured lights at the side of the road, which show when cars etc are allowed to move: *Turn left at the traffic lights.*

traffic war·den /'.. ,../ noun BrE someone whose job is to check that cars are parked only where parking is allowed

tra·ge·dy /'trædʒədi/ noun, plural tragedies
1 a very sad event: *The fishing trip ended in tragedy when one of the men drowned.* | *This is a terrible tragedy.*
2 a play or book that ends very sadly: *We are studying Shakespeare's tragedies*

tra·gic /'trædʒɪk/ adjective very sad: *a tragic accident*
–**tragically** /-kli/ adverb: *Tragically, she died young.*

trail[1] /treɪl/ noun 1 something that shows the direction in which someone or something is moving: *a trail of muddy footprints* 2 a rough path: *a woodland trail*

trail[2] verb 1 to follow someone: *The three men trailed the old woman back to her house.* 2 if a player or team in a competition is trailing, they are losing: *By half-time, Germany was trailing by three goals.*

trail·er /'treɪlə $'treɪlɚ/ noun 1 a vehicle without an engine that can be pulled behind another vehicle 2 a short part of a film or television programme, which is shown to advertise it: *We saw a trailer for the new James Bond film.*

train[1] /treɪn/ noun a line of vehicles that are connected together, which travels along a railway and carries people or things. You take, catch, or get a train when you want to travel in it: *I caught the nine o'clock train to Boston.* | *He was late and nearly missed his train.* | *Shall we drive or go by train?* | *You have to change trains* (=get on a different train) *at Cambridge.* ⇨ *see picture on page 349*

train[2] verb

> **GRAMMAR**
> **train (someone) to do something**
> **train (someone) as something**
> **train (someone) for something**

1 to teach someone the skills that they need to do something difficult: *We could train nurses to do these tests on patients.*
2 to learn how to do something that needs a particular skill: *Jeff trained as a pilot when he left school.* | *I'd like to train to become a teacher.*
3 to prepare for a sports competition by exercising and practising, or to help someone to prepare: *Vicky's been training for the race for the past nine months.*

train·ee /ˌtreɪ'niː/ noun someone who is being trained for a job: *a trainee nurse*

train·er /'treɪnə $ 'treɪnɚ/ noun
1 someone whose job is to train people to do a job: *a teacher trainer* **2** BrE a kind of shoe that you wear for sports such as running; SNEAKER AmE: *a pair of new trainers*

train·ing /'treɪnɪŋ/ noun [no plural] activities that help you learn how to do a job or play a sport: *a training programme for new employees | She was injured while in training for the Olympics.*

trait /treɪ $ treɪt/ noun a way of behaving or thinking that is typical of someone: *Honesty is one of his best traits.*

trai·tor /'treɪtə $ 'treɪtɚ/ noun someone who helps the enemies of their country or of a group that they belong to

tram /træm/ noun an electric vehicle which moves along the street on metal tracks; STREETCAR AmE

tramp /træmp/ noun someone poor who has no home or job and moves from place to place

tram·ple /'træmpəl/ verb to step heavily on something, damaging it: *Don't trample on the flowers!*

tram·po·line /'træmpəli:n $ ˌtræmpə'li:n/ noun a flat piece of material that is fastened in a metal frame with springs, which you jump up and down on as exercise or as a sport

trance /trɑːns $ træns/ noun if you are in a trance, you seem to be asleep, but you are still able to hear and understand things: *The children watched TV as if they were in a trance.*

tran·quil /'træŋkwəl/ adjective calm and peaceful: *the tranquil waters of the lake*

tran·quil·liz·er also **tranquilliser** BrE, **tranquilizer** AmE /'træŋkwəlaɪzə $ 'træŋkwəˌlaɪzɚ/ noun a medicine that makes someone calm or sleepy: *Since his mother's death, he has been taking tranquillizers.*

trans·at·lan·tic /ˌtrænzət'læntɪk/ adjective on a transatlantic journey, you cross the Atlantic Ocean: *a transatlantic flight from London to New York*

trans·fer /træns'fɜː $ 'trænsfɚ/ verb formal **transferred, transferring** to move someone or something from one place to another: *They are transferring him to another hospital.*
–**transfer** /'trænsfɜː $ 'trænsfɚ/ noun: *the transfer of money between bank accounts*

trans·form /træns'fɔːm $ træns'fɔrm/ verb to change something completely: *The new owners have transformed the building into a smart hotel.*

trans·fu·sion /træns'fjuːʒən/ noun formal if you are given a transfusion, doctors put blood into your body: *She needed to have a blood transfusion.*

tran·sis·tor /træn'zɪstə $ træn'zɪstɚ/ noun a small piece of electronic equipment that is used in radios, televisions etc

tran·si·tive /'trænsətɪv/ noun a transitive verb can have a noun or a pronoun after it. In the sentence 'She makes her own clothes', 'makes' is a transitive verb

trans·late /træns'leɪt/ verb

> **GRAMMAR**
> **translate something from something**
> **translate something into something**
> if you translate something that someone has said or written, you change it from the language they used into another language: *It's easy to **translate** things **from** Spanish **into** English. | His books **have been translated into** ten different languages.*

trans·la·tion /træns'leɪʃən/ noun the process of translating something into a different language, or something that has been translated: *The poem was a translation of a poem in Latin.*

trans·la·tor /træns'leɪtə $ 'trænsˌleɪtɚ/ noun someone whose job is to translate things from one language into another: *She works as a translator at the UN.*

trans·mis·sion /trænz'mɪʃən $ træns'mɪʃən/ noun [no plural] formal the sending out of radio or television signals: *The announcer apologised for the break in transmission.*

trans·mit /trænz'mɪt $ træns'mɪt/ verb formal **transmitted, transmitting** to send out radio or television signals: *We will be transmitting live from the cricket ground.*

trans·mit·ter /trænz'mɪtə $ træns'mɪtɚ/ noun equipment that sends out radio or television signals: *a radio transmitter*

trans·par·ent /træn'spærənt/ *adjective*

if something is transparent, you can see through it: *The paper was so thin that it was transparent.* | *transparent plastic*

trans·plant /'trænsplɑːnt $ 'trænsplænt/ *noun* a medical operation in which doctors remove a part of someone's body and replace it with a part from another person's body: *a heart and lung transplant*

trans·port¹ /'trænspɔːt $ 'trænspɔrt/ *noun* [no plural] *BrE*

1 vehicles that people use to travel from one place to another: *Bicycles are the best form of transport in the city centre.* | *It's a poor country, with very little **public transport** (=buses, trains etc that everyone can use).*

2 moving things or people from one place to another in a vehicle: *the transport of grain by ship*

trans·port² /træn'spɔːt $ træns'pɔrt/ *verb formal* to move things or people from one place to another in a vehicle: *The coal is transported by train to all parts of the country.*

trans·por·ta·tion /ˌtrænspɔː'teɪʃən $ ˌtrænspɚ'teɪʃən/ the American word for TRANSPORT¹

trap¹ /træp/ *noun*

1 a piece of equipment that you use for catching animals or birds: *Farmers used to put down traps for rabbits.* | *a mouse trap*

2 something that you do in order to catch or trick someone: *She asked him to meet her, but it was a trap.*

trap² *verb* trapped, trapping

GRAMMAR
trap someone in/at a place

1 to make it impossible for someone to escape from a place: *Water came up as far as the door, trapping us.* | *The boys **were trapped in** the bedroom by fire.*

2 to catch an animal or a person using a trap: *They trapped rabbits for food.* | *Police managed to trap the criminals.*

trash /træʃ/ an American word for RUBBISH

trash·can /'træʃkæn/ *noun AmE* a container for putting waste material in

trau·ma /'trɔːmə/ *noun* a very upsetting experience which has a strong effect on someone: *the trauma of seeing his dog run over by a car*

trau·mat·ic /trɔː'mætɪk/ *adjective* very shocking and upsetting: *A death in the family is a traumatic event.*

trav·el¹ /'trævəl/ *verb* travelled, travelling *BrE*, traveled, traveling *AmE*

GRAMMAR
travel from/to somewhere

if you travel, you go from one place to another, usually in a vehicle: *It's quicker if you **travel by** train.* | *My ambition is to **travel round the world.** | I've been traveling all day and I'm exhausted! | We **travelled from** Birmingham **to** London in two hours.*

travel² *noun* [no plural] when you travel: *Air travel is safe and cheap.*

USAGE travel, journey, trip, voyage
Travel, journey, trip, and voyage all have a similar meaning. Travel is a general word for going from one place to another, especially outside your own country: *During that time, the government introduced limits on foreign travel.* Use journey to talk about going from one particular place to another: *How long does your journey to school take? | It's a 12-hour journey from here to Tokyo.* Use trip to talk about a journey somewhere, as well as the time you spend in that place: *Did you enjoy your trip to Scotland? | a business trip.* A voyage is a long journey in a ship.

travel a·gen·cy /'.. ˌ.../ *noun* a business that arranges holidays for people

travel a·gent /'.. ˌ../ *noun* 1 also **travel agent's** a travel agency: *We went to a travel agent's on the High Street.* 2 someone who works in a travel agency

trav·el·ler *BrE*, **traveler** *AmE* /'trævələ $ 'trævələ/ *noun* someone who is on a journey or who travels a lot: *She is an experienced traveller.*

traveller's cheque *BrE*, **traveler's check** *AmE* /'... ˌ./ *noun* a special cheque that can be exchanged in a foreign country for the money of that country: *Do you cash traveller's cheques?*

trawl·er /'trɔːlə $'trɔlɚ/ noun a large boat that is used for fishing in the sea

tray /treɪ/ noun a flat piece of plastic, wood, or metal with raised edges, which you use to carry plates, food etc: *He brought in a tray of cakes.*

trea·cle /'triːkəl/ noun [no plural] BrE a dark sweet sticky liquid that is made from sugar plants; MOLASSES AmE

tread¹ /tred/ verb **trod** /trɒd/ $trɑd/ **trodden** /'trɒdn/ $'trɑdn/

GRAMMAR
tread on/in something
to put your foot on or in something: *I trod on the cat's tail by mistake.* | *Don't tread in that mud!*

tread² noun the pattern of deep lines on the surface of a tyre: *This tyre has lost its tread.*

trea·son /'triːzən/ noun [no plural] the crime of helping your country's enemies and putting your country in danger: *He had committed treason.*

trea·sure¹ /'treʒə $'treʒɚ/ noun a collection of valuable things such as gold or jewellery that has been hidden: *They searched the beach for buried treasure.*

treasure² verb if you treasure something, you think it is very special or important: *I will always treasure the time we spent together.*

treat¹ /triːt/ verb

GRAMMAR
treat someone like/as something
treat something as something
treat someone for something
treat someone to something
treat yourself

1 to behave towards a person or animal in a particular way: *He treated his wife and children really badly.* | *These animals need to be treated with care.* | *I wish you'd treat me like an adult* (=treat me as though I was an adult). | *The teachers here treat us as equals.*
2 to deal with something in a way that shows what you think about it: *Police are treating the death as an accident.*
3 if a doctor treats someone, he or she gives them medical care or medicine in order to make them well again: *Mr Griffith is being treated for shock in hospital.* | *There are several drugs available for treating this condition.*
4 to buy something special for someone: *Come on! I'll treat you to burgers and chips.* | *You need to treat yourself occasionally.*

treat² noun

GRAMMAR
a treat for someone
something special that you buy or do in order to give someone pleasure: *We're taking all the kids to see a film as a treat.* | *I bought some sweets as a treat for the children.*

treat·ment /'triːtmənt/ noun

GRAMMAR
treatment for something
treatment of someone/something
1 the medical care that you receive from doctors, nurses etc, or the medicine that they give you: *I was sent to hospital for immediate treatment.* | *There is no treatment for this type of snake bite.*
2 a way of behaving towards a person or animal: *We were shocked by his cruel treatment of the dog.*

treat·y /'triːti/ noun, plural **treaties** a formal written agreement between two or more countries: *a peace treaty*

treb·le /'trebəl/ verb another word for TRIPLE²

tree /triː/ noun a large plant with branches, leaves, and a TRUNK (=thick strong stem): *a cherry tree*

trek /trek/ verb **trekked, trekking** to walk a very long way, especially across rough ground: *We trekked across the mountains.*
– trek noun: *They went on a 22-day trek.*

trem·ble /'trembəl/ verb to shake because you are afraid or excited: *The child trembled with fear.*

tre·men·dous /trɪ'mendəs/ adjective **1** very great or very large: *There was a tremendous crash.* **2** very good: *You've done a tremendous job.*

trench /trentʃ/ noun, plural **trenches** a long narrow hole that is dug along the ground, usually to put pipes or wires in

trend /trend/ noun the way that a situation is changing or developing: *the latest fashion trends*

trend·y /'trendi/ *adjective informal* **trendier, trendiest** modern and fashionable: *trendy shoes*

tres·pass /'trespəs $ 'trespæs/ *verb* to go onto someone's land without permission: *Two men were arrested for trespassing on the railway line.*
— **trespasser** *noun*

tri·al /'traɪəl/ *noun*
when people in a court of law listen to information about a crime and then decide whether someone is guilty: *The trial ended, and he was sent to prison.* | *She was on trial for murdering a child* (=a court of law was trying to decide whether she murdered a child).

tri·an·gle /'traɪæŋgəl/ *noun* a shape with three straight sides and three angles ⇨ *see picture at* SYMMETRICAL

tri·an·gu·lar /traɪ'æŋgjələ $ traɪ'æŋgjələr/ *adjective* shaped like a triangle

trib·al /'traɪbəl/ *adjective* connected with a tribe: *tribal dances*

tribe /traɪb/ *noun* a group of people with the same language and customs who live together in the same area, for example in the forests of South America or Africa: *The Masai are one of the largest tribes in Kenya.*

tri·bu·nal /traɪ'bjuːnl/ *noun* a special court of law whose purpose is to deal with a particular problem: *an employment tribunal*

trib·u·ta·ry /'trɪbjətəri $ 'trɪbjə,teri/ *noun, plural* **tributaries** a river that flows into a larger river

trib·ute /'trɪbjuːt/ *noun* something that people do to show how much they admire and respect someone: *The concert was arranged as a tribute to the queen on her birthday.*

trick¹ /trɪk/ *noun*
1 something that you do in order to deceive someone and get what you want: *It was a trick. He never intended to give me the money.* | *Let's play a trick on the girls* (=deceive them as a joke).
2 a clever action that entertains people because they cannot see how you do it: *a magic trick* | *card tricks*

trick² *verb*

to make someone do something by deceiving them: *He **tricked** her **into** signing the letter.* | *They **tricked** the old lady **out of** all her money* (=they made her give them all her money).

trick·le /'trɪkəl/ *verb* if liquid trickles somewhere, a small amount of it flows there slowly: *Water was trickling down the walls.*
— **trickle** *noun*: *A trickle of sweat ran down his back.*

trickle

trick·y /'trɪki/ *adjective informal* **trickier, trickiest** difficult: *That's a very tricky question.*

tried the past tense and past participle of TRY¹

trig·ger¹ /'trɪgə $ 'trɪgər/ *noun* the part of a gun that you pull with your finger to fire it: *She raised the gun and pulled the trigger.*

trigger² *also* **trigger off** *verb* to make something start to happen: *His speech has triggered protests from some students.*

tril·o·gy /'trɪlədʒi/ *noun, plural* **trilogies** a set of three books, plays, films etc, which all have the same subject or characters

trim¹ /trɪm/ *verb* **trimmed, trimming** to cut a small amount off something to make it look neater: *Dad was outside, trimming the lawn.*
— **trim** *noun*: *I'm going to the barber's for a trim* (=a haircut).

trim² *adjective* **trimmer, trimmest** thin and healthy looking: *You need exercise to keep trim.*

tri·mes·ter /trɪ'mestə $ 'traɪmestər/ *noun AmE* one of the three periods in a year at school or college: *I'm taking history this trimester.*

trin·ket /'trɪŋkɪt/ *noun* a cheap pretty object or piece of jewellery

tri·o /'tri:əʊ $'trioʊ/ noun a group of three people, especially musicians

trip¹ /trɪp/ noun

GRAMMAR
a trip to a place

a journey to a place and back again, especially when you only stay in the place for a short time: *Dad's promised us a **trip to** Disneyland.* | *The school **went on** a **day trip to** France* (=they went to France and back in the same day). ⇨ *see usage note at* TRAVEL²

trip² verb tripped, tripping also **trip up**

GRAMMAR
trip over/on something

1 to hit your foot against something while you are walking so that you fall or almost fall: *He **tripped up** and broke his ankle.* | *I **tripped over** the telephone wire and hit my head.* | *Be careful not to **trip on** that step.* ⇨ *see picture on page 340*
2 to make someone fall by putting your foot in front of them as they are walking: *Mum! Jake **tripped** me up!*

trip·le¹ /'trɪpəl/ adjective consisting of three parts: *The prison has a triple barrier around it.*

triple² verb if something triples, it becomes three times as big as it was before: *The number of students getting the highest grade has tripled.*

trip·let /'trɪplət/ noun one of three children who are born at the same time and have the same mother: *Di gave birth to triplets last year.*

tri·pod /'traɪpɒd $'traɪpɑd/ noun a piece of equipment with three legs that you use to support something such as a camera

tri·umph /'traɪəmf/ noun an important success or win: *Brazil celebrated their World Cup triumph last night.*
–**triumph** verb: *England triumphed yet again.*

tri·um·phant /traɪˈʌmfənt/ adjective very pleased because you have succeeded or won: *the triumphant team*

triv·i·al /'trɪviəl/ adjective not important or serious: *a trivial mistake*

trod the past tense of TREAD¹

trodden the past participle of TREAD¹

trol·ley /'trɒli $'trɑli/ noun 1 BrE a large metal container on wheels that you use for carrying things, for example in a SUPERMARKET; CART AmE 2 the American word for TRAM

trom·bone /trɒmˈbəʊn $trɑmˈboʊn/ noun a metal musical instrument that you play by blowing into it and moving a long tube backwards and forwards

troop /tru:p/ verb if people troop somewhere, they walk in an organized group: *A group of tourists trooped out of the hotel.*

troops /tru:ps/ plural noun soldiers: *There were 12,000 American troops in Panama.*

tro·phy /'trəʊfi $'troʊfi/ noun, plural trophies an object such as a silver cup that you get as a prize when you win a race or competition: *Stella won the Rosebowl Trophy for best young female singer.*

trop·i·cal /'trɒpɪkəl $'trɑpɪkəl/ adjective in or from the hottest and wettest parts of the world: *tropical rainforests*

trop·ics /'trɒpɪks $'trɑpɪks/ noun the tropics the hottest and wettest parts of the world

trot /trɒt $trɑt/ verb trotted, trotting if a horse trots, it runs with quick short steps

troub·le¹ /'trʌbəl/ noun

GRAMMAR
trouble with something

1 problems or difficulties: *We **had** a lot of **trouble** parking the car.* | *There's often **trouble with** the computers at work.* | *financial troubles*
2 a situation in which people fight or argue: *The police are ready to deal with any trouble at the football match.* | *If I complain, it will only **cause trouble**.*
3 [no plural] illness or pain in part of your body: *Mum's been **having** some **trouble with** her back.*

PHRASES
be in trouble, get into trouble if you are in trouble, you have done something wrong, so that someone in authority is likely to punish you: *I'll **be in trouble** at school if I'm late again.* | *As a teenager, Joey often **got into trouble with** the police.*

be in trouble to be in a difficult situation: *You should always try and help someone who is in trouble.*

trouble² *verb* to make you feel worried or upset: *We talked over some of the things that were troubling her.*

troub·led /ˈtrʌbəld/ *adjective* having a lot of problems or difficulties: *one of the most troubled areas of the world*

troub·le·mak·er /ˈtrʌbəlˌmeɪkə $ˈtrʌbəlˌmeɪkɚ/ *noun* someone who deliberately causes trouble

troub·le·some /ˈtrʌbəlsəm/ *adjective* causing a lot of trouble: *a troublesome back injury*

trough /trɒf $trɔf/ *noun* a long container for animals to drink or eat from

trou·sers /ˈtraʊzəz $ˈtraʊzɚz/ *plural noun*
a piece of clothing that you wear on the lower part of your body, with a separate part for each leg; PANTS *AmE*: *These trousers are too big.* | *I bought a new pair of trousers in the sale.*
⇨ see picture on page 352

trout /traʊt/ *noun, plural* trout a brown or silvery fish that lives in rivers

trowel /ˈtraʊəl/ *noun* a small garden tool that you use for digging

tru·ant /ˈtruːənt/ *noun* 1 a student who stays away from school without permission 2 **play truant** to stay away from school without permission: *Nearly every child plays truant at some time in their life.*

truce /truːs/ *noun* an agreement between two enemies to stop fighting or arguing for a short time: *The two countries have called a truce.*

truck /trʌk/ *noun* a large road vehicle that is used for carrying things

trudge /trʌdʒ/ *verb* to walk with slow heavy steps because you are tired: *An old man was trudging up the hill.*

true /truː/ *adjective*

GRAMMAR
true that
1 correct and based on facts or things that really happened ⇨ opposite FALSE: *Is it true that she's only 30 years old?* | *"There will be less traffic*

if we leave early." "That's true." | *The film was based on a true story.*
2 real: *true love* | *a true friend*

PHRASE
come true if your dream or wish comes true, what you hope for actually happens: *She had hoped for a place at college, and now her dream had come true.*

tru·ly /ˈtruːli/ *adverb* formal used to emphasize that what you are saying is really true: *He was a truly great man.*

trum·pet /ˈtrʌmpɪt/ *noun* a metal musical instrument that you play by blowing into it, and that plays quite high notes

trun·cheon /ˈtrʌnʃən/ *noun* BrE a stick that police officers carry as a weapon

trunks

trunk /trʌŋk/ *noun* 1 the main part of a tree, which the branches grow from 2 the American word for the BOOT of a car 3 the very long nose of an ELEPHANT

trunks /trʌŋks/ *plural noun* a piece of clothing that boys and men wear when they go swimming: *a pair of swimming trunks*

trust¹ /trʌst/ *verb*

GRAMMAR
trust someone to do something
trust someone with something
to believe that someone is good and will do what they say, or what is right: *Trust me. I'll look after you.* | *I'm afraid I don't trust politicians.* | *Can I trust you to lock the door when you go out?* | *Do you think I can trust David with my new car* (=believe that he will be careful with it)?

trust² *noun* [no plural]
when you believe that someone is good and will do what they say, or what is right: *Trust is very important in a marriage.*

trust·wor·thy /'trʌst,wɜːði $'trʌst-,wɚði/ *adjective* a trustworthy person can be trusted: *Don't tell Clare; she isn't very trustworthy.*

truth /truːθ/ *noun*

1 **the truth** the real facts about something: *Will we ever find out the truth? | I don't believe he's telling us the truth.*

2 *[no plural]* the quality of being correct and true: *There's no truth in what he said.*

truth·ful /'truːθfəl/ *adjective* honest: *a truthful answer | He hasn't been very truthful about his past.*
– **truthfully** *adverb*

try /traɪ/ *verb* **tried, tries**

GRAMMAR
try to do something
try doing something
be tried for something

1 if you try to do something, you make an effort to do it: *I've been trying to remember where I left my jacket. | Try not to worry. | The teacher told me that I had to try harder* (=make more effort) *in class.*

2 to do, use, or taste something in order to find out whether it is successful or good: *I'd tried eating less but I was still fat. | I tried turning the computer off and on again, but it still wouldn't work. | Would you like to try some of this soup?*

3 if someone is tried for a crime, people in a court of law listen to information about the crime and then decide whether the person is guilty: *The three men will be tried for robbery.*

PHRASAL VERB
try on
try something on to put on a piece of clothing in order to find out whether you like it, especially before buying it: *I tried on three dresses but none of them fitted me.*

try² *noun, plural* **tries** 1 an attempt to do something: *I passed my driving test on my first try.* 2 when a team gets points in RUGBY by placing the ball behind the other team's GOAL line

tsar also **tzar** or **czar** /zɑː $zɑr/ *noun* a ruler of Russia before 1917

T-shirt or **tee-shirt** /'tiː ʃɜːt $'tiː ʃɚt/ *noun* an informal shirt with short SLEEVES, and no buttons or collar ⇨ *see picture on page 352*

tub /tʌb/ *noun* 1 a deep round container: *The yard was full of tubs of brightly coloured flowers.* 2 a small plastic container for food: *a one-litre tub of ice-cream*

tu·ba /'tjuːbə $'tubə/ *noun* a large metal musical instrument that you play by blowing into it, and that has a wide opening that points upwards

tube /tjuːb $tub/ *noun* 1 a long thin pipe made of plastic, glass, or metal that liquids or gases go through: *He was very ill, and had to be fed through a tube.* 2 a small narrow container that you press in order to make the substance inside come out of the end: *a tube of toothpaste* ⇨ *see picture at* CONTAINER 3 **the Tube** *BrE informal* another word for UNDERGROUND²

tuck /tʌk/ *verb* **tuck something in** to push the bottom of your shirt inside your trousers or the end of a sheet under a bed, so that it looks neat: *Keep still while I tuck your shirt in.*

Tues·day /'tjuːzdi $'tuzdi/ *written abbreviation* **Tues** *noun* the day of the week between MONDAY and WEDNESDAY: *Our next meeting is on Tuesday the 10th of March.*

tuft /tʌft/ *noun* a group of hairs, pieces of grass etc growing closely together

tug /tʌg/ *verb* **tugged, tugging** to pull something suddenly and hard: *I tugged at the door but it wouldn't open.*
– **tug** *noun: John gave the rope a tug.*

tu·i·tion /tjuː'ɪʃən $tu'ɪʃən/ *noun [no plural]* teaching, especially of small groups or only one person: *The school offers excellent tuition in most sports.*

tum·ble /'tʌmbəl/ *verb* to suddenly fall: *He slipped and tumbled down the stairs.*
– **tumble** *noun: She took a tumble on the ice.*

tum·bler /'tʌmblə $'tʌmblɚ/ *noun* a drinking glass with straight sides and no handle

tum·my /'tʌmi/ *noun informal, plural* **tummies** a word for stomach, used especially by children

tu·mour *BrE,* **tumor** *AmE* /'tjuːmə $'tumɚ/ *noun formal* a group of cells in the body that grow more quickly than normal and that can cause serious illness or death: *a brain tumour*

tu·na /'tjuːnə $'tunə/ *noun* a large fish that lives in the sea, or the meat from this fish: *tuna sandwiches*

tune¹ /tjuːn $tun/ *noun*

the series of musical notes in a song or piece of music: *He was whistling a cheerful tune.*

tune² *verb* **1** also **tune up** to make small changes to a musical instrument or a car engine so that it works better: *I need to tune my guitar before I start playing.* | *How much will it cost to tune up my car?* **2 tune to something** to change the controls of your radio so that you are listening to a particular radio STATION: *I tuned to the BBC for the news.* **3 tune in** to watch or listen to a particular television or radio programme: *14 million viewers tuned in for the big match.*

tun·nel /'tʌnl/ *noun* a long passage through a hill, under the ground, or under the sea for cars or trains to go through: *Trains go through the Channel Tunnel between Britain and France.*

tur·ban /'tɜːbən $'tɚbən/ *noun* a type of head covering that is made from a long piece of cloth, which Sikh men and some Hindu and Muslim men wear ⇨ *see picture on page 352*

turf /tɜːf $tɚf/ *noun* [no plural] short grass and the earth under it

tur·key /'tɜːki $'tɚki/ *noun* **1** a bird that is like a chicken, but larger **2** [no plural] the meat from this bird. Many people eat warm turkey at Christmas in Britain and the US

turn¹ ⇨ *see box on next page*

turn² /tɜːn $tɚn/ *noun*

GRAMMAR
someone's turn to do something
1 if it is your turn to do something, it is the time when you can or should do it, not anyone else: *It's your turn to wash the dishes.* | *Whose turn is it to do the shopping?* | *Sam, you have to wait your turn* (=wait until it is your turn).
2 a change in the direction you are moving in: *Go up to Lindley Avenue and make a right turn.*

3 a road that joins the road you are on: *Take the next turn on the right.*

PHRASES
take turns also **take it in turns** BrE if a group of people take turns doing something, first one person does it, then another: *We took turns riding the skateboard.* | *Jill and Sandy will take it in turns to drive.*
the turn of the century formal the beginning of a century: *This house was built at the turn of the century.*

turn·ing /'tɜːnɪŋ $'tɚnɪŋ/ *noun* BrE a road that joins the road you are on; TURN: *Go past the church and it's the next turning on your left.*

turning point /'.. ./ *noun* a time when an important change starts to happen: *Meeting Rick was a turning point in my life.*

tur·nip /'tɜːnɪp $'tɚnɪp/ *noun* a round white vegetable that grows under the ground

turn·out /'tɜːnaʊt $'tɚnaʊt/ *noun* [no plural] the number of people who go to an event such as a party, meeting, or election: *There was an excellent turnout at the meeting* (=a lot of people came).

tur·quoise /'tɜːkwɔɪz $'tɚkwɔɪz/ *adjective, noun* a bright blue-green colour

tur·tle /'tɜːtl $'tɚtl/ *noun* an animal with a hard shell that lives in the sea but lays its eggs on land ⇨ *see picture on page 339*

tur·tle·neck /'tɜːtlnek $'tɚtl,nek/ the American word for POLO NECK

tusk /tʌsk/ *noun* one of the two long pointed teeth that grow outside the mouth of some animals: *an elephant's tusks*

tu·tor /'tjuːtə $'tutɚ/ *noun* **1** someone who teaches one person or a small group of people: *a private tutor* **2** a teacher at a British university
– **tutor** *verb*

tu·to·ri·al /tjuː'tɔːriəl $tu'tɔriəl/ *noun* a class in which a small group of students discuss a subject with their tutor: *Most of the teaching is done in small tutorials.*

tux·e·do /tʌk'siːdəʊ $tʌk'sidoʊ/ the American word for DINNER JACKET

TV /,tiː 'viː/ *noun* informal TELEVISION ⇨ *see picture on page 342*

1 to move your body so that you are looking in a different direction

Pat **turned** and looked at me. | Joyce **turned around** and walked out of the room. | Joe **turned towards** us and started to walk back. | I **turned to** Steve and whispered, "Let's go – now!"

GRAMMAR
turn (something)
around/towards/to etc

2 to move something so that it is facing in a new direction
He **turned** his head **away** from me. | Turn your chair **towards** me.

7 to become different
The traffic lights **turned** red as we approached them. | In autumn, the weather **turns** colder. | He might **turn** violent.

3 to start going in a new direction
The car **turned** a corner. | **Turn right** on Baldwin Street, and then **turn left** onto Grissom Avenue.

turn

4 to move around in a circle
The wheels began to **turn** slowly. | Dee **turned** the key in the lock.

6 to reach and pass a particular age or time
Leanne **turned** 18 on Thursday (=it was her 18th birthday on Thursday). | "What time is it?" "It's just **turned** 2 o'clock."

5 also **turn over**
to move a page of a book or magazine so that you can see the next one: He sat in the waiting room, **turning over the pages** of a magazine. | **Turn to** page 31 in your books.

PHRASAL VERBS

turn away
to not allow someone to enter a place: *The soldiers at the border **turned away** some of the refugees.*

turn back
to go in the opposite direction to the one you were going in before: *He stopped and **turned back** toward the desk.*

turn down
1 turn something down to make a machine produce less sound, heat etc, using its controls ◊ *opposite* TURN UP: *Could you **turn** the TV **down** a bit?*

2 turn someone/something down to say no when someone offers you something: *She was offered the job, but she **turned** it **down**.*

turn in
the American phrase for HAND IN

turn into
1 turn into something to become something different: *The party **turned into** a complete disaster. | The rain **turned into** snow later that day (=it stopped raining and started snowing).*

2 turn someone/something into something to change someone or something so that they become something different: *We **turned** this bedroom **into** an office. | His experiences in the war **turned** him **into** a violent man.*

turn off
1 turn off to leave the road you are on and to start going along a different road: *We need to **turn off** at the next road on the left.*

2 turn something off to make a machine, light etc stop working, using its controls ◊ *opposite* TURN ON: *Sal **turned off** the tap when the bucket was full.*

*Sal **turned off** the tap when the bucket was full.*

turn on
to make a machine, light etc start working, using its controls ◊ *opposite* TURN OFF: *Paul **turned on** the TV to watch his favourite programme. | Can you **turn** the light **on**, please?*

*Paul **turned on** the TV to watch his favourite programme.*

turn out
1 turn out to happen in a particular way, so that there is a particular result: *You can make plans, but things don't always **turn out** the way you want. | The cake didn't **turn out** very well.*

2 turn something out to make a light stop working by pressing a button ◊ *opposite* TURN ON: ***Turn out** the lights before you go to bed.*

turn over
1 if something turns over, or if you turn it over, it moves so that the top part faces down: *The car hit the bridge, **turned over** and burst into flames. | When the toast is cooked on one side, **turn** it **over**.*

2 turn over to press a button to change the television programme on your television: *Quick, **turn over**! The film's starting! | Shall I **turn over** to the news?*

turn up
1 turn something up to make a machine produce more sound, heat etc, using its controls: ◊ *opposite* TURN DOWN: ***Turn up** the heat – I'm freezing.*

2 turn up *informal* to arrive: *Her mother **turned up** about ten minutes later. | Did Joe **turn up for** classes today?*

3 turn up *informal* if something turns up after you have been looking for it, you suddenly find it: *I'd been looking for work for months when this job **turned up**.*

T

tweed /twiːd/ *noun* [no plural] a thick wool cloth that is used especially for making clothes such as coats and suits

twee·zers /'twiː-zəz $ 'twizɚz/ *plural noun* a small tool consisting of two thin pieces of metal joined at one end. You use tweezers for pulling out hairs or picking up small things: *a pair of tweezers*

tweezers

twelfth /twelfθ/ *number* **1** 12th **2** one of the twelve equal parts of something; 1/12

twelve /twelv/ *number* 12

twen·ti·eth /'twentiəθ/ *number* 20th

twen·ty /'twenti/ *number, plural* **twenties** **1** 20 **2 the twenties** the years from 1920 to 1929 **3 be in your twenties** to be aged between 20 and 29 **—twentieth** *number*: *the twentieth of June*

twice /twaɪs/ *adverb* two times: *I've been to America twice this year.*

twig /twɪg/ *noun* a very thin branch that grows on a larger branch of a tree

twin /twɪn/ *noun* one of two children who are born at the same time and have the same mother: *Denny and Daniel are identical twins* (=twins that look exactly the same as each other). | *my twin brother*

twinge /twɪndʒ/ *noun* a sudden slight pain

twin·kle /'twɪŋkəl/ *verb* to shine very brightly but not continuously: *stars twinkling in the night sky*

twist¹ /twɪst/ *verb*

1 to turn something around quickly when holding it with your hand: *I twisted the lid off the jar.*
2 to bend something around several times and change its shape: *He twisted the wire around the fence post.* | *Sharon twisted her hair into a rope and pinned it up.*
3 to hurt a part of your body by suddenly turning it: *He twisted his ankle playing football.*

twist² *noun* **1** a shape that you make by twisting or bending something: *Decorate the cake with twists of lemon peel.* **2** a sudden change in a story or situation that you did not expect: *There's an unusual twist at the end of the film.*

twitch /twɪtʃ/ *verb* if a part of your body twitches, it suddenly moves slightly and you cannot control it: *The muscles in his legs began to twitch.*

two /tuː/ *number* **1** 2 **2 in two, into two** if you break or cut something in two, it becomes two pieces instead of one: *June broke her cookie in two and gave the dog half.*

two-way /ˌ. ˈ./ *adjective* moving in two opposite directions: *two-way traffic*

ty·coon /taɪˈkuːn/ *noun* someone who is very successful in business and has a lot of money

tying the present participle of TIE¹

type¹ /taɪp/ *noun*

a group of people or things that are similar to each other in some way ⇨ *same meaning* KIND¹, SORT¹: *I think you should try a **different type of** exercise.* | ***What type of** job are you looking for?* | *We grow **various types of** grass.*

type² *verb* **1** to write something using a computer or a TYPEWRITER: *Jill can type really fast.* **2 type into, type in** if you type information into a computer, or if you type it in, you press the keys so that the computer records the information: *Type in your name and password to log on.*

type·writ·er /'taɪpˌraɪtə $ 'taɪpˌraɪtɚ/ *noun* a machine that prints letters, numbers etc on paper when you press keys

ty·phoon /ˌtaɪˈfuːn/ *noun* a tropical storm with very strong winds

typ·i·cal /'tɪpɪkəl/ *adjective*

something that is typical has the usual features or qualities of that type of thing: *a typical British school* | *On a typical day, I watch television for about three hours.* | *Spaghetti **is typical of** Italian cooking.*

typ·i·cally /'tɪpɪkli/ *adverb* used to say that something is typical: *The atmosphere was happy and bright – typically Irish.*

typ·ing /'taɪpɪŋ/ *noun [no plural]* writing that you do using a TYPEWRITER: *Are you good at typing?*

typ·ist /'taɪpɪst/ *noun* someone whose job is to type letters and other documents in an office

ty·rant /'taɪrənt $ 'taɪrənt/ *noun* someone who uses their power in a cruel and unfair way: *My boss is a real tyrant!* | *The country was ruled by tyrants for many years.*

tyre *BrE*, **tire** *AmE* /taɪə $ taɪɚ/ *noun* the round piece of rubber that fits around a wheel of a car, bicycle etc and is filled with air: *My bicycle needs new tyres.* | *The car had a flat tyre* (=the air had gone out of one tyre). ⇨ *see picture at* CAR

Uu

UFO /ˈjuːfəʊ $ ˌju ef ˈoʊ/ *noun* an abbreviation for Unidentified Flying Object; a moving object in the sky that some people believe could be carrying creatures from another world

ug·ly /ˈʌgli/ *adjective* **uglier, ugliest** very unattractive or unpleasant to look at: *an ugly animal with a fat body and short legs*

ul·cer /ˈʌlsə $ ˈʌlsɚ/ *noun* a painful area on your skin or inside your body: *a mouth ulcer*

ul·ti·mate /ˈʌltəmət/ *adjective* formal
1 used to say that something is the most important final result in a series of things: *Our ultimate aim is to be the best women's football team in the country.*
2 used to say that something is the best, greatest, or worst of its kind: *It has been described as the ultimate pop video.*

ul·ti·mate·ly /ˈʌltəmətli/ *adverb* finally: *Ultimately, after a long trial, he was sent to prison for life.*

ul·tra·vi·o·let /ˌʌltrəˈvaɪələt/ *abbreviation* **UV** *adjective* ultraviolet light makes your skin darker: *the risks of exposure to ultraviolet light*

um·brel·la /ʌm-ˈbrelə/ *noun* a thing that you hold over your head to protect yourself from the rain

umbrella

um·pire /ˈʌmpaɪə $ ˈʌmpaɪɚ/ *noun* the person in a game such as tennis who makes sure that the players obey the rules

un·a·ble /ʌnˈeɪbəl/ *adjective* formal

GRAMMAR
unable to do something
if you are unable to do something, you are not able to do it: *Some of the* children were **unable to** read. | *I'm sorry, I'm **unable to** help you.*

un·ac·cept·a·ble /ˌʌnəkˈseptəbəl/ *adjective* formal something that is unacceptable is bad or wrong and people should not do it or allow it: *The amount of traffic on these roads is completely unacceptable.* | *The standard of your work is unacceptable.*

u·nan·i·mous /juːˈnænəməs/ *adjective* a unanimous decision or vote is one in which everyone agrees: *The vote was unanimous and Mr Edwards was re-elected.*

un·armed /ˌʌnˈɑːmd $ ˌʌnˈɑrmd/ *adjective* someone who is unarmed is not carrying any weapons: *The soldiers attacked unarmed civilians.*

un·at·tend·ed /ˌʌnəˈtendɪd/ *adjective* something that is unattended is not being watched, and so may be stolen, lost etc: *Please do not leave your suitcases unattended.* | *Unattended baggage will be removed.*

un·a·vail·a·ble /ˌʌnəˈveɪləbəl/ *adjective* **1** someone who is unavailable is not able to meet or speak to you because they are doing something else: *I'm afraid Mrs Brewer is unavailable this morning; she's in a meeting.* **2** if something is unavailable, you cannot buy it or get it: *The new Sega computer game will be unavailable until Christmas.*

un·a·ware /ˌʌnəˈweə $ ˌʌnəˈwer/ *adjective* formal someone who is unaware of something does not know about it or does not see it: *Lucy seemed to be unaware of the dangers that we faced.* | *I was unaware that I was being watched.*

un·bear·a·ble /ʌnˈbeərəbəl $ ʌn-ˈberəbəl/ *adjective* very unpleasant, painful etc: *In summer, the heat was unbearable.*

un·beat·a·ble /ʌnˈbiːtəbəl/ adjective much better than other things: *Their prices are unbeatable!*

un·be·liev·a·ble /ˌʌnbəˈliːvəbəl/ adjective extreme or surprising, and therefore difficult to believe: *Jack's had some unbelievable bad luck in the last few years.*

un·cer·tain /ʌnˈsɜːtn $ ʌn-ˈsɜːtn/ adjective formal

> **GRAMMAR**
> **uncertain about/of something**
> **uncertain what/where/how etc**

if you are uncertain, you are not sure about something ⇨ opposite CERTAIN: *Sylvia was **uncertain about** how much money the trip would cost.* | *I'm **uncertain of** the date of the next meeting.* | *We were **uncertain what** to do next.*

un·cer·tain·ly /ʌnˈsɜːtnti $ ʌnˈsɜːtnti/ noun formal, plural **uncertainties** when something is not known or not definite: *There is uncertainty over the future of the project.*

un·cle /ˈʌŋkəl/ noun the brother of your mother or father, or the husband of your AUNT: *Uncle Mike always visits us at Christmas.*

un·clear /ˌʌnˈklɪə $ ʌnˈklɪr/ adjective formal difficult to understand or know: *It was unclear exactly what he meant.*

un·com·fort·a·ble /ʌnˈkʌmft-əbəl/ adjective
1 if you are uncomfortable, you do not feel physically relaxed ⇨ opposite COMFORTABLE (1): *I'm always so uncomfortable on long plane journeys.*
2 something that is uncomfortable makes you unable to feel physically relaxed ⇨ opposite COMFORTABLE (2): *an uncomfortable chair* | *These shoes are terribly uncomfortable to wear.*
3 if you feel uncomfortable, you feel embarrassed or worried ⇨ opposite COMFORTABLE (3): *She felt really **uncomfortable** because the man was standing so close to her.* | *Alice is uncomfortable about being photographed.*

un·con·scious /ʌnˈkɒnʃəs $ ʌn-ˈkɑnʃəs/ adjective someone who is unconscious is not awake and cannot hear, feel, or see ⇨ opposite CONSCIOUS (1): *The doctor said that she was still unconscious after the operation.*
– **unconsciousness** noun [no plural]

un·con·trol·la·ble /ˌʌnkənˈtrəʊləbəl $ ˌʌnkənˈtroʊləbəl/ adjective impossible to control or stop: *Everyone ran for the exits in uncontrollable panic.*

un·count·a·ble /ʌnˈkaʊntəbəl/ adjective in grammar, an uncountable noun has no plural. 'Water', 'gold', and 'furniture' are examples of uncountable nouns ⇨ opposite COUNTABLE

un·cov·er /ʌnˈkʌvə $ ʌnˈkʌvɚ/ verb to discover something secret or illegal: *The police uncovered evidence that the killer was living in Spain.*

un·de·cid·ed /ˌʌndɪˈsaɪdɪd/ adjective formal if you are undecided about something, you have not made a decision about it yet: *I'm still undecided which subjects I want to study.*

un·der¹ /ˈʌndə $ ˈʌndɚ/ preposition, adverb
1 directly below something: *Clare found the letter under a pile of papers.* | *She keeps her shoes under her bed.* | *He was sitting under a tree* (=below its branches). ⇨ see picture on page 354
2 below the surface of water: *She dived under the water.*
3 less than an amount: *Can you get a good computer for under £1000?* | *children under five* (=children less than five years old) *travel free.*

under² adverb
1 below the surface of something: *He dived into the water and stayed under for over a minute.*
2 less than the age, number, or amount that is mentioned: *These presents cost £10 and under.*

under-age /ˌ.. ˈ./ adjective too young to legally buy alcohol, drive a car etc: *under-age smokers*

un·der·go /ˌʌndəˈɡəʊ $ ˌʌndɚˈɡoʊ/ verb formal **underwent** /-ˈwent/ **undergone** /-ˈɡɒn $ -ˈɡɔn/ if you undergo something such as medical treatment, it is done to you or it happens to you: *Mr Buckley underwent a five-hour emergency operation.*

undergone the past participle of UNDERGO

un·der·grad·u·ate /ˌʌndəˈgrædʒuət $ˌʌndəˈgrædʒuət/ *noun* a student who is at university, studying for his or her first degree

un·der·ground¹ /ˌʌndəˈgraʊnd $ˌʌndəˈgraʊnd/ *adjective, adverb* under the surface of the ground: *an underground tunnel* | *animals that stay underground during the day*

un·der·ground² /ˈʌndəgraʊnd $ˈʌndəˌgraʊnd/ *noun* BrE **the Underground** the railway system that runs under the city of London. Similar systems in American cities are called the SUBWAY ⇨ *same meaning* TUBE (3) *informal*: *Shall we go by bus or use the Underground?*

un·der·growth /ˈʌndəgrəʊθ $ˈʌndəˌgroʊθ/ *noun* [no plural] low bushes and plants that grow around trees

un·der·line /ˌʌndəˈlaɪn $ˈʌndəˌlaɪn/ *verb* to draw a line under a word or sentence: *Underline the name of the book.*

un·der·neath¹ /ˌʌndəˈniːθ $ˌʌndəˈniθ/ *preposition, adverb*
1 directly below something: *She kept her diary in a box underneath her bed.* | *If we don't cut the trees back, the grass underneath will die.*
2 covered by something: *What's underneath that sheet?* | *They found their skis under a layer of snow.*

underneath² *noun*
GRAMMAR
the underneath of something
the bottom part of something: *the underneath of the car*

un·der·pants /ˈʌndəpænts $ˈʌndəˌpænts/ *plural noun* 1 BrE a short piece of clothing that men or boys wear under their other clothes on the lower part of their body ⇨ *same meaning* PANTS: *a pair of underpants* 2 AmE a short piece of clothing that both men and women wear under their clothes on the lower part of their body

un·der·pass /ˈʌndəpɑːs $ˈʌndəˌpæs/ *noun, plural* **underpasses** a road or path that goes under another road or a railway

un·der·stand /ˌʌndəˈstænd $ˌʌndəˈstænd/ *verb, past tense and past participle* **understood** /-ˈstʊd/
GRAMMAR
understand what/how/why etc
1 if you understand something that is spoken or written, you know what it means: *Does Jim understand Spanish?* | *I couldn't understand what the men were saying.* | *Do you understand this computer manual?*
2 to know how something works or why something happens: *Do you understand how this machine works?* | *Judy is too young to understand why her mom isn't here.*
3 to know what someone's feelings are and why they behave in a particular way: *Suddenly, I understood how Angela felt.* | *I don't understand my children anymore.*

un·der·stand·a·ble /ˌʌndəˈstændəbəl $ˌʌndəˈstændəbəl/ *adjective* understandable behaviour or feelings are normal and what you expect: *It is understandable that you are nervous before such an important examination.*

un·der·stand·ing¹ /ˌʌndəˈstændɪŋ $ˌʌndəˈstændɪŋ/ *noun* [no plural] 1 your understanding of something is how well you understand it: *My understanding of computers is very limited.* 2 sympathy and kindness that you show towards someone with problems or worries: *Teenagers need plenty of understanding and support.*

understanding² *adjective* an understanding person is kind and shows sympathy towards someone with problems or worries: *I'll talk to Alex – he's always very understanding.*

understood the past tense and past participle of UNDERSTAND

un·der·take /ˌʌndəˈteɪk $ˌʌndəˈteɪk/ *verb* *formal* **undertook** /-ˈtʊk/ **undertaken** /-ˈteɪkən/ to start to do something that is difficult or will take a long time: *The university is undertaking a 10-year research programme.*

undertaken the past participle of UNDERTAKE

un·der·tak·er /ˈʌndəteɪkə $ˈʌndəˌteɪkə/ *noun* BrE someone whose job is to arrange funerals; MORTICIAN AmE

undertook the past tense of UNDERTAKE

un·der·wa·ter /ˌʌndəˈwɔːtə $ ˌʌndə-ˈwɔtəʳ/ adverb, adjective below the surface of the water: *How long can you stay underwater?* | *the underwater explorer Jacques Cousteau*

un·der·wear /ˈʌndəweə $ ˈʌndəʳˌweəʳ/ noun [no plural] clothes that you wear next to your body, under your other clothes

underwent the past tense of UNDERGO

un·de·vel·oped /ˌʌndɪˈveləpt/ adjective undeveloped land has not been built on or used for anything: *undeveloped areas of the city*

undid the past tense of UNDO

un·do /ʌnˈduː/ verb **undid** /-ˈdɪd/ **undone** /-ˈdʌn/
to make something looser, so that it is no longer tied or fastened: *I couldn't undo the knot.* | *Mel slowly undid the buttons on his shirt.*
– **undone** adjective: *Your shoelaces are undone.*

undone the past participle of UNDO

un·dress /ʌnˈdres/ verb to remove your clothes
– **undressed** adjective: *I got undressed and had a quick shower.*

un·eas·y /ʌnˈiːzi/ adjective **uneasier, uneasiest** worried or afraid about something: *I began to feel uneasy when he still wasn't home by ten.*

un·em·ployed /ˌʌnɪmˈplɔɪd/ adjective someone who is unemployed does not have a job ⇨ same meaning OUT OF WORK: *I'm unemployed at the moment, but I'm looking for work*

un·em·ploy·ment /ˌʌnɪmˈplɔɪmənt/ noun [no plural] when people do not have jobs, or the number of people who do not have jobs: *the problems of unemployment* | *the latest unemployment figures*

un·e·ven /ʌnˈiːvən/ adjective not flat, smooth, or level: *The surface of the road was very uneven.*

un·ex·pect·ed /ˌʌnɪkˈspektɪd/ adjective formal something that is unexpected is surprising because you did not expect it: *We had an unexpected visit from my parents.*
– **unexpectedly** adverb

un·fair /ˌʌnˈfeə $ ˌʌnˈfeʳ/ adjective

1 something that is unfair is not right or acceptable because it does not treat people in a fair and equal way: *It's unfair to give sweets to her and not to me.* | *Black people still sometimes get unfair treatment.* | *I think it's unfair that she got the job instead of me.*
2 someone who is unfair does not treat all people in a fair and equal way: *"Our tutor is useless at teaching." "Oh come on – you're being a bit unfair aren't you?"*
– **unfairly** adverb: *I felt the teacher had punished me unfairly.*

un·faith·ful /ʌnˈfeɪθfəl/ adjective someone who is unfaithful has sex with someone who is not their wife, husband etc

un·fa·mil·i·ar /ˌʌnfəˈmɪliə $ ˌʌnfəˈmɪl-jəʳ/ adjective formal if someone or something is unfamiliar, you do not recognize them: *The handwriting on the envelope was unfamiliar.* | *He felt like a stranger, lost in a crowd of unfamiliar faces.*

un·fash·ion·a·ble /ʌnˈfæʃənəbəl/ adjective not popular or fashionable: *an unfashionable part of New York*

un·fas·ten /ʌnˈfɑːsən $ ʌnˈfæsən/ verb to undo a piece of clothing, rope etc so that it is not tied or fastened: *Can you unfasten my dress?*

un·fit /ʌnˈfɪt/ adjective **1** not healthy because you have not had enough exercise ⇨ opposite FIT² (2): *I'm so unfit – I could only run half the race!* **2** not good enough or suitable for something: *The water here is unfit to drink.*

un·fold /ʌnˈfəʊld $ ʌnˈfoʊld/ verb if you unfold something, or if it unfolds, it opens out and becomes bigger and flatter: *Jim carefully unfolded the piece of paper.* | *The buds of the flower had started to unfold.*

un·for·tu·nate /ʌnˈfɔːtʃənət $ ʌnˈfɔrtʃənət/ adjective formal

unlucky ⇨ opposite FORTUNATE: *It's unfortunate that she was hurt.* | *a very unfortunate accident*

un·for·tu·nate·ly /ʌnˈfɔːtʃənətli
$ ʌnˈfɔrtʃənətli/ *adverb* used to say that
you feel sad or disappointed about
something: *Unfortunately, we had to go
home early.*

un·friend·ly /ʌnˈfrendli/ *adjective* not
friendly and often unkind: *Some of the
kids in my class are really unfriendly towards me.*

un·grate·ful /ʌnˈɡreɪtfəl/ *adjective*
someone who is ungrateful does not
thank someone who has been kind or
helpful to them ⇨ *opposite* GRATEFUL: *You
must write and thank her, or she'll think
you're ungrateful.*

un·hap·py /ʌnˈhæpi/ *adjective*
unhappier, unhappiest

GRAMMAR
unhappy about something
unhappy with something

1 not happy: *Barbara had a very un-
happy childhood.* | *The kids were
really unhappy about moving away
from their friends.* | *Sam, you seem
terribly unhappy – is something
wrong?* | *It was the unhappiest year
of my life.*
2 if you are unhappy with something,
you do not think it is good enough:
*We were unhappy with the rooms
in the hotel, which were small and
dirty.*
–unhappiness *noun [no plural]*: *her
unhappiness at school*
–unhappily *adverb*: *His first marriage ended unhappily.*

un·health·y /ʌnˈhelθi/ *adjective* un-
healthier, unhealthiest **1** not healthy:
Louise always looks so unhealthy.
2 things that are unhealthy are likely to
make you ill or less healthy: *unhealthy
food such as burgers and chips* ⇨ *see
picture at* HEALTHY

un·help·ful /ʌnˈhelpfəl/ *adjective* not
willing to help someone, in a way that
seems rude and unfriendly: *The
shop assistants were completely un-
helpful.*

u·ni·form /ˈjuːnəfɔːm $ ˈjuːnə-
ˌfɔrm/ *noun*
a set of clothes that people wear so
that they all look the same: *the
school uniform* | *The soliders were in
uniform* (=wearing their uniforms).

un·im·por·tant /ˌʌnɪmˈpɔːtənt
$ ˌʌnɪmˈpɔrtnt/ *adjective* not important

un·in·hab·it·ed /ˌʌnɪnˈhæbɪtɪd/ *adjective formal* an uninhabited place is one
where no one lives: *We think the island
is probably uninhabited.*

un·in·terest·ed /ʌnˈɪntrəstɪd/ *adjective* not interested: *The whole class
seemed completely uninterested in the
lesson.*

union /ˈjuːnjən/ *noun*
1 an organization that a group of
workers form in order to protect
their rights at work: *the National
Union of Teachers* | *Employees have
the right to join a union.*
2 a country or state that is made up of
two or more countries that have
joined together: *the Soviet Union*

u·nique /juːˈniːk/ *adjective* something
that is unique is very special because
there are no others like it: *Everyone's
personality is totally unique.*

u·ni·sex /ˈjuːnɪseks/ *adjective* for both
men and women: *a unisex hairdresser's*

u·nit /ˈjuːnɪt/ *noun*

GRAMMAR
a unit of something

1 something that is one whole part of
a larger thing: *The coursebook is div-
ided into 6 units.* | *the police de-
partment's crime prevention unit*
2 an amount of something that is used
as a way of measuring how much
there is: *A 'bit' is the smallest unit of
information in a computer.*

u·nite /juːˈnaɪt/ *verb formal*

GRAMMAR
unite with someone/something

1 if people unite, they join together as
a group: *The workers united to de-
mand better pay.* | *East Germany
united with West Germany in 1990.*
2 if something unites people, it makes
them join together or work together
as a group: *The war united everyone
in the country.*

u·nit·ed /juːˈnaɪtɪd/ *adjective* **1** if a
group of people or countries is united,
they all agree with each other about
something: *The people in the town were
united in their opposition to the plans.*
2 a united country is one that consists of

two or more countries or states that have joined together: *hopes for a united Ireland*

u·ni·ver·sal /ˌjuːnəˈvɜːsəl $ ˌjunə-ˈvɝsəl/ *adjective* for or related to everyone: *the need for universal health care and education*

u·ni·verse /ˈjuːnəvɜːs $ ˈjunəˌvɝs/ *noun* the universe the whole of space and all the stars and PLANETS

university /ˌjuːnəˈvɜːsəti $ ˌjunə-ˈvɝsəti/ *noun, plural* universities
a place where students study for a degree in a subject at a high level: *"Did you go to university?" "Yes, I went to Oxford."*

un·just /ˌʌnˈdʒʌst/ *adjective* not fair or reasonable: *an unjust ruler | unjust laws*

un·kind /ˌʌnˈkaɪnd/ *adjective*
GRAMMAR
unkind to someone/something
if someone is unkind, they say or do things that are not pleasant or friendly: *She said some very unkind things. | Don't be so unkind! | Children are sometimes very **unkind to** each other.*

un·known /ˌʌnˈnəʊn $ ˌʌnˈnoʊn/ *adjective* not known or not famous: *The number of people who died in the earthquake is still unknown. | an unknown singer*

un·lead·ed /ˌʌnˈledɪd/ *adjective* unleaded petrol does not contain any LEAD (=a harmful substance)

un·less /ʌnˈles, ən-/
showing that one thing must happen so that another thing can happen: *You aren't allowed to drive a car unless you have a licence* (=you are only allowed to drive a car if you have a licence). *| I won't tell you unless you promise to keep it a secret. | I'll meet you at 8 unless you phone me to say you can't go out* (=if you phone me. I won't meet you).

un·like /ˌʌnˈlaɪk/ *preposition* completely different from someone or something else: *Unlike beef, chicken has very little fat. | Our new house was quite unlike the old cottage.*

un·like·ly /ʌnˈlaɪkli/ *adjective*
GRAMMAR
unlikely that
unlikely to do something
something that is unlikely will probably not happen: *It is **unlikely that** you will get your money back. | Holt is **unlikely to** play in Saturday's game.*

un·lim·it·ed /ʌnˈlɪmətɪd/ *adjective* as much as you want: *The rail ticket allows students to have unlimited travel for a month.*

un·lit /ˌʌnˈlɪt/ *adjective* dark because there are no lights on: *a small, unlit road*

un·load /ˌʌnˈləʊd $ ʌnˈloʊd/ *verb* to take things out of a car, off a ship etc, after bringing them from somewhere: *We arrived home late, and unloaded the car the next morning.*

un·lock /ʌnˈlɒk $ ʌnˈluːk/ *verb* to open the lock on a door, car etc, using a key

un·luck·y /ʌnˈlʌki/ *adjective*
unluckier, unluckiest
GRAMMAR
unlucky to do something
unlucky that
1 if you are unlucky, bad things happen to you for no particular reason ⇨ opposite LUCKY: *We played pretty well but lost – I guess we were just unlucky. | Michael Owen was **unlucky** not to score a goal.*
2 something that is unlucky is unpleasant and happens for no particular reason ⇨ opposite LUCKY: *It isn't your fault – it was just **unlucky that** we missed the plane.*
3 if something is unlucky, some people think it causes bad luck ⇨ opposite LUCKY: *It's **unlucky to** walk under a ladder. | 13 is an unlucky number.*

un·mar·ried /ˌʌnˈmærid/ *adjective* not married ⇨ same meaning SINGLE[1] (2)

un·ne·ces·sa·ry /ʌnˈnesəsəri $ ʌnˈnesəˌseri/ *adjective* if something is unnecessary, you do not need to have it or do it: *Having two cars is an unnecessary luxury. | Testing cosmetics on animals is unnecessary.*

un·oc·cu·pied /ʌnˈɒkjəpaɪd $ ʌnˈɑːkjəˌpaɪd/ *adjective* formal an unoccupied seat, house, room etc does not have anyone in it or using it: *The top floor of the house was completely unoccupied.*

un·of·fi·cial /ˌʌnəˈfɪʃəl/ *adjective* not accepted or approved by anyone in authority: *There were unofficial reports that the President was seriously ill.*
– **unofficially** *adverb*

un·pack /ʌnˈpæk/ *verb* to take everything out of your cases, bags etc after travelling: *We arrived at the hotel, unpacked and had dinner.*

un·paid /ˌʌnˈpeɪd/ *adjective* **1** someone who is unpaid works without receiving any money: *We have several unpaid helpers at the school.* **2** an unpaid bill or debt has not been paid

un·pleas·ant /ʌnˈplezənt/ *adjective*

GRAMMAR
unpleasant to someone

1 not pleasant or enjoyable: *an unpleasant smell* | *The weather was really unpleasant.*
2 someone who is unpleasant behaves in an unkind or rude way: *What an unpleasant man!* | *She was extremely unpleasant to me.*

un·plug /ʌnˈplʌg/ *verb* unplugged, unplugging to take the PLUG on a piece of electrical equipment out of the SOCKET (=the place in a wall where you can connect electrical equipment to an electricity supply)

un·pop·u·lar /ʌnˈpɒpjələ $ʌnˈpɑpjələ/ *adjective* not liked by many people ⇨ opposite POPULAR: *Billy was unpopular at school and very unhappy.* | *She was the most unpopular politician in England.*

un·rea·lis·tic /ˌʌnrɪəˈlɪstɪk/ *adjective* formal if you are unrealistic, you expect things to be better than they really are: *Teachers sometimes have unrealistic expectations of their students.*

un·rea·son·a·ble /ʌnˈriːzənəbəl/ *adjective* unreasonable behaviour, ideas, prices etc are not fair, sensible, or acceptable: *I thought that what he said was very unreasonable.*

un·re·li·a·ble /ˌʌnrɪˈlaɪəbəl/ *adjective* unreliable people or things cannot be trusted to do what they should do ⇨ opposite RELIABLE: *These builders are very unreliable; they never arrive on time.* | *an unreliable bus service*

un·ru·ly /ʌnˈruːli/ *adjective* unruly people are difficult to control: *an unruly crowd*

un·safe /ˌʌnˈseɪf/ *adjective* formal dangerous and likely to harm people: *That car is unsafe to drive.*

un·sat·is·fac·to·ry /ˌʌnsætɪsˈfæktəri/ *adjective* not good enough and not acceptable: *an unsatisfactory explanation*

un·screw /ʌnˈskruː/ *verb* to open or undo something by twisting it: *I unscrewed the top of the jar.*

unscrew

un·self·ish /ʌnˈselfɪʃ/ *adjective* unselfish person is kind and cares more about other people than they do about themselves: *a mother's unselfish devotion to her children*

un·set·tle /ʌnˈsetld/ *verb* if something unsettles you, it makes you feel nervous or worried: *All the changes at work unsettled her.*
– **unsettling** *adjective*: *an unsettling experience*

un·set·tled /ʌnˈsetld/ *adjective* **1** unsettled weather is wet and changes often ⇨ opposite meaning SETTLED: *The forecast is for more unsettled weather.* **2** feeling worried or unsure: *Children often feel unsettled by divorce.*

un·so·phis·ti·cat·ed /ˌʌnsəˈfɪstɪkeɪtɪd/ *adjective* simple and not modern: *Farmers were still using unsophisticated methods.*

un·sta·ble /ʌnˈsteɪbəl/ *adjective* likely to change suddenly and cause problems ⇨ opposite STABLE: *The country is unstable and tourists have been warned not to go there.*

un·suc·cess·ful /ˌʌnsəkˈsesfəl/ *adjective* not achieving what you wanted to achieve: *an unsuccessful attempt to break the world record*
– **unsuccessfully** *adverb*: *She tried unsuccessfully to open the door.*

un·suit·a·ble /ʌnˈsuːtəbəl/ *adjective* formal not acceptable or right for a particular purpose: *Her shoes were unsuitable for a long walk.*

un·sure /ˌʌnˈʃʊə $ˌʌnˈʃʊr/ *adjective* not certain or confident about some-

U

thing: *Rob was unsure about passing the exam.*

un·sym·pa·thet·ic /ˌʌnsɪmpəˈθetɪk/ *adjective* not kind or helpful towards people who have problems ⇨ *opposite* SYMPATHETIC: *a stern, unsympathetic policeman*

un·ti·dy /ʌnˈtaɪdi/ *adjective* **untidier, untidiest 1** not neat: *Why is your bedroom always so untidy?* | *Jim always left his clothes in an untidy heap on the floor.* **2** an untidy person does not care whether things are neat or arranged correctly: *You really are the untidiest person I have ever met!*

un·tie /ʌnˈtaɪ/ *verb, present participle* **untying** to undo something so that it is not tied or fastened: *I untied the knot and opened the parcel.*

un·til /ʌnˈtɪl/ *also* **till** *preposition*

showing when something stops: *The football practice session will start at 4 o'clock and go on until 6.* | *We lived in Oxford until I was ten.* | *I'm allowed to stay out until 12 o'clock.*

PHRASE

not until a) only when something has been done: *You can't go out until you've done you're homework* (=you can only go out when you've done your homework). **b)** at a particular time, after a long delay: *The next train is **not until** 4 o'clock.*

USAGE until, till, as far as, up to
Use **till/until** to talk about the time when something stops: *They stayed till/until after midnight.* Use **as far as** to talk about the place where something stops: *Does the bus go as far as the station?* Use **up to** to talk about the final number in a series of numbers: *The children had to count up to fifty.*

un·true /ʌnˈtruː/ *adjective* not true

un·used /ˌʌnˈjuːzd/ *adjective* not being used, or never used: *an unused £20 note*

un·u·su·al /ʌnˈjuːʒʊəl/ *adjective*

GRAMMAR
unusual for someone to do something
something that is unusual does not happen often or is different from what you would normally expect: *He*

has an unusual name.* | *It's* very **unusual for** *Mandy* **to** *be ill.*
–**unusually** *adverb*: *The train was unusually late this morning.*

un·veil /ʌnˈveɪl/ *verb* formal to officially let people know about something that was a secret: *BMW will unveil their latest car at the Motor Show.*

un·well /ʌnˈwel/ *adjective* formal ill: *Judy left, saying she felt unwell.*

un·will·ing /ʌnˈwɪlɪŋ/ *adjective* if you are unwilling to do something, you do not want to do it: *Customers are unwilling to pay for poor service.*

un·wind /ʌnˈwaɪnd/ *verb, past tense and past participle* **unwound** /-ˈwaʊnd/ to relax and stop feeling worried: *Watching TV helps me unwind.*

unwound the past tense and past participle of UNWIND

un·wrap /ʌnˈræp/ *verb* **unwrapped, unwrapping** to remove the paper that is covering something: *The children unwrapped their presents excitedly.*

unwrap

up /ʌp/ *adverb, preposition*

1 towards a higher place: *He climbed up the ladder to the tree house.* | *I always put medicines up on a high shelf where children can't reach them.* ⇨ *see picture on page 354*

2 not in bed: *Is Martin up yet, or is he still in bed?* | *We stayed up to watch the late film.*

3 increasing in amount: *Prices are going up quickly.* | *His temperature's up* (=it's higher than normal).

4 further along a road: *I was going up Vine Street when I met Luke.* | *The school's just up the road.*

5 towards the north: *She's going up to Scotland tomorrow.*

PHRASES
up to something a) used to mention the largest number or size that is possible: *The car can carry **up to** six people.* | *These fish can grow **up to** seven feet long.* **b)** if you go up to a person or place, you go towards them and stop when you are next to

them: *This man came **up to** me in the street and asked where the police station was.* | *I walked **up to** the front door and rang the bell.*

be up to something *informal* if someone is up to something, they are secretly doing something bad: *I know he's **up to** something, and I'm going to find out what it is.*

be up to doing something *informal* to be strong enough and healthy enough to do something: *I'm not **up to** seeing anyone right now.*

be up to someone if something is up to you, you can choose what to do or have: *It's **up to** him whether he takes the exam or not.*

up·bring·ing /ˈʌpˌbrɪŋɪŋ/ *noun* the way your parents treated you when you were a child, and the things they taught you: *I had a strict religious upbringing.*

up·date[1] /ʌpˈdeɪt/ *verb* to add new parts or the most recent information to something so that it stays modern: *We need to update our computers every 12 months.*

up·date[2] /ˈʌpdeɪt/ *noun formal* the most recent news about something: *a news update from the BBC*

up·front /ʌpˈfrʌnt/ *adjective informal* speaking honestly and openly: *He's very ambitious, but at least he's upfront about it.*

up·grade /ʌpˈgreɪd/ *verb* to change something so that it is better or more modern: *We need to upgrade our computer system.*

– **upgrade** /ˈʌpgreɪd/ *noun*: *a software upgrade*

up·heav·al /ʌpˈhiːvəl/ *noun formal* a very big change that causes problems: *the upheaval of moving house*

upheld the past tense and past participle of UPHOLD

up·hill /ˌʌpˈhɪl/ *adverb, adjective* towards the top of a hill ⇨ *opposite* DOWN-HILL: *We pulled the sled uphill.* | *an uphill slope*

up·hold /ˌʌpˈhəʊld $ ʌpˈhoʊld/ *verb formal, past tense and past participle* **up·held** /-ˈheld/ to support a law or decision and make sure it continues to exist: *We must uphold the rights of all people.*

up·lift·ing /ʌpˈlɪftɪŋ/ *adjective formal* making you feel happy: *an uplifting piece of music*

up·on /əˈpɒn $ əˈpɑn/ *preposition formal* on: *She laid a cloth upon the table.*

up·per /ˈʌpə $ ˈʌpɚ/ *adjective* in a higher position ⇨ *opposite* LOWER[1]: *the upper parts of the body* | *a room on the upper floor*

up·per·case /ˌʌpəˈkeɪs $ ˌʌpɚˈkeɪs/ *adjective* uppercase letters are written in CAPITAL LETTERS, for example A, B, C etc

upper class /ˌ.. ˈ./ *noun* the upper class, the upper classes the people in society who belong to the highest social class

– **upper-class** *adjective*: *She spoke with an upper-class accent.*

up·right /ˈʌp-raɪt/ *adjective, adverb* pointing straight up: *It's rude to place your chopsticks upright in the bowl.*

up·ris·ing /ˈʌpˌraɪzɪŋ/ *noun* when a large group of people fight against the people who are in power in their country: *the Polish uprising of 1830*

up·roar /ˈʌp-rɔː $ ˈʌp-rɔr/ *noun [no plural] formal* a lot of shouting and noise: *The school was in uproar.*

up·root /ʌpˈruːt/ *verb* to make someone leave their home: *The war has uprooted whole families.*

up·set[1] /ʌpˈset/ *adjective*

GRAMMAR
upset about something

unhappy because something unpleasant has happened: *She's a bit upset because her cat has died.* | *John **feels upset** because he wasn't invited to the party.* | *My mother **got really upset** when I didn't get home on time.* | *Joe **was** very **upset about** losing his wallet.*

up·set[2] *verb, past tense and past participle* **upset, upsetting** to make someone feel unhappy or worried: *Her remarks about my hair really upset me.* | *The pressure of exams is upsetting some students.*

– **upsetting** *adjective*: *a very upsetting film*

up·side·down also **upside-down** /ˌʌpsaɪd ˈdaʊn/ *adverb, adjective* if something is upside down, the part that should be at the top is at the bottom: *He turned the bag upside down and everything fell out.* | *The pattern is upside-down.*

up·stairs /ˌʌp'steəz $ ˌʌp'sterz/ adverb, adjective

on or going towards a higher floor of a building ⇨ opposite DOWNSTAIRS: *Julie is upstairs in her room.* | *Go upstairs and fetch my glasses.* | *We live in the upstairs flat.*

up·state /'ʌpsteɪt/ adjective, adverb AmE in or towards the northern part of a state: *upstate New York*

up-to-date /ˌ. . './ adjective recent, modern, or fashionable: *Websites hold all the up-to-date information.*

up·town /ˌʌp'taʊn/ adjective, adverb AmE in or towards the northern part of a city and where rich people usually live

up·wards /'ʌpwədz $ 'ʌpwɚdz/ also **up·ward** /'ʌpwəd $ 'ʌpwɚd/ adverb

towards a higher position or level ⇨ opposite DOWNWARDS: *I pulled the rope upwards.*

u·ra·ni·um /jʊ'reɪniəm/ noun [no plural] a RADIOACTIVE metal used to produce NUCLEAR energy

ur·ban /'ɜːbən $ 'ɚbən/ adjective related to a town or city: *urban development*

urge¹ /ɜːdʒ $ ɚdʒ/ verb formal to advise someone very strongly to do something: *We urged her to accept the job.*

urge² noun formal a strong desire: *He had a very strong urge to laugh.*

ur·gen·cy /'ɜːdʒənsi $ 'ɚdʒənsi/ noun [no plural] when something is urgent: *The minister stressed the urgency of the situation.*

ur·gent /'ɜːdʒənt $ 'ɚdʒənt/ adjective

if something is urgent, it is important and someone must deal with it immediately: *I must speak to Mr Hill – it's urgent.* | *John had to leave on urgent business.* | *"Can't this typing wait?" "No, it's urgent."*
–**urgently** adverb: *Food and medicine are urgently needed.*

us /əs; strong ʌs/ pronoun
the person who is speaking and others: *Can you help us?*

us·a·ble /'juːsəbəl/ adjective available or in a good enough condition for you to use: *The PC comes with 128Mb of usable memory.*

us·age /'juːsɪdʒ/ noun [no plural] formal 1 the way that words are used in a language: *modern English usage* 2 the amount of something that is used, or the way it is used: *Drug usage is increasing.*

use¹ /juːz/ verb

GRAMMAR
use something to do something
use something for something
use something as something

1 if you use something, you do something with it: *Can I use your phone?* | *Have you been using my makeup again?* | *Neil **used** his cigarette lighter **to** start the fire.* | *What do you want to **use** the computer **for**?* | *Don't **use** your illness **as** an excuse for being lazy.*
2 also **use up** to finish all of something so that there is nothing left: *Sorry, I've **used up** all of the milk.*
3 if someone uses illegal drugs, they take them regularly
4 you can say that someone uses the toilet or bathroom as a polite way of saying that they go to the toilet: *Could I use the bathroom please?*

use² /juːs/ noun

GRAMMAR
use of something

1 [no plural] when people use something: *The use of sunscreens can help prevent skin cancer.* | *Our use of paper is increasing every year.*
2 the purpose that you use something for: *The new drug **has** many uses.*
3 [no plural] formal if you have the use of something, you are allowed to use it: *Students **have** the use of school computers at evenings and weekends.*

PHRASES
make use of something to use something that is available: *These recipes **make use of** leftover turkey.*
▼ **be in use** if something is in use,

U

someone is using it: *I'm sorry, this room is in use.* | *These methods of making wine have been in use for hundreds of years.*

be of no use to someone if something is of no use to you, you do not need it: *You can have this old washing machine – it's of no use to me now.*

it's no use, what's the use *spoken* used to say that doing something will not have any effect, so you should not do it: *It's no use. The door won't open.* | *What's the use of arguing? It won't solve our problems.*

used¹ /juːst/ *adjective*

1 be used to (doing) something if you are used to something, it is not unusual or surprising for you, because you have done it or experienced it so often: *Sam is used to living in a city.*

2 get used to (doing) something if you get used to something, you do it or experience it several times so that it no longer seems unusual or surprising to you: *We soon got used to living in London.*

used² /juːzd/ *adjective* used cars or clothes are not new because someone else owned them before ⇨ *same meaning* SECONDHAND: *We decided to save money by buying a used car.*

use·ful /'juːsfəl/ *adjective* helping you do or get what you want: *a useful map of the town centre*

use·less /'juːsləs/ *adjective* not useful at all: *This knife is useless for cutting meat.*

us·er /'juːzə $ 'juːzɚ/ *noun* someone who uses something such as a product or service: *PC users*

user-friend·ly /ˌ.. '../ *adjective* something that is user-friendly is designed to be easy for people to use: *Manufacturers should make their equipment more user-friendly.*

u·su·al /'juːʒuəl/ *adjective*

the same as happens most of the time: *I couldn't park my car in the usual place* (=the place where I park it most often). | *I'll see you at the usual time* (=the time that I most often see you). | *I ate more than usual* (=more than I would normally eat). | *Henry was late, as usual* (=Henry is often late).

u·su·al·ly /'juːʒuəli/ *adverb*

if something usually happens, it almost always happens: *I usually get up at about 8.* | *Saturday is usually our busiest day.*

u·ten·sil /juːˈtensəl/ *noun formal* a tool that you use for cooking: *kitchen utensils*

ut·most /'ʌtməʊst $ 'ʌtmoʊst/ *adjective formal* the most that is possible: *You must take the utmost care.*

ut·ter¹ /'ʌtə $ 'ʌtɚ/ *adjective formal* complete or total: *a sense of utter helplessness*

–utterly *adverb*: *That exam was utterly impossible.*

utter² *verb* to say something: *He looked at me without uttering a word.*

U-turn /'juː tɜːn $ 'juː tɚn/ *noun* if the driver of a car does a U-turn, they turn the car round and go back in the direction they came from

Vv

v a written abbreviation of VERSUS

va·can·cy /'veɪkənsi/ *noun, plural* **vacancies** **1** a room that is available in a hotel: *I'm sorry, we have no vacancies tonight.* **2** a job that is available for someone to do: *The company has a vacancy for a driver.*

va·cant /'veɪkənt/ *adjective* not being used: *We tried to find some vacant seats.*

va·ca·tion /və'keɪʃən $veɪ'keɪʃən/ the American word for HOLIDAY

vac·cin·ate /'væksəneɪt/ *verb* if you are vaccinated, a doctor gives you a vaccine to stop you getting a disease: *Have you been vaccinated against TB?*

vac·cine /'væksiːn $væk'sin/ *noun* a substance given to people to stop them getting a disease, which contains a very small amount of the GERM that causes the disease: *the measles vaccine*

vac·u·um¹ /'vækjuəm/ *noun* **1** a vacuum cleaner **2** a space that has no air in it

vacuum² *verb* to clean a place using a vacuum cleaner: *I need to vacuum the carpet.*

vacuum clean·er /'... .../ *noun* a machine that cleans floors by sucking up dirt

vague /veɪg/ *adjective* not clear or definite: *His plans are rather vague at the moment.*
– **vaguely** *adverb*: *I know vaguely where he lives.*

vain /veɪn/ *adjective* too proud of your appearance: *a vain, arrogant young man*

val·id /'vælɪd/ *adjective* **1** a valid ticket or document can be used and is officially correct: *a valid passport* **2** if something someone says is valid, it is reasonable and likely to be right: *I can think of many valid reasons not to talk to her again.*

val·ley /'væli/ *noun* a low area of land between two hills or mountains ⇨ see picture on page 348

val·ua·ble /'væljəbəl/ *adjective*
1 worth a lot of money: *a very valuable painting*
2 very useful: *She gave me some very valuable advice.*

val·ua·bles /'væljəbəlz/ *plural noun* small things that you own that are worth a lot of money

val·ue¹ /'væljuː/ *noun*

> **GRAMMAR**
> **the value of something**

1 how much money something is worth: *What is **the** total **value of** the paintings in the collection?* | *Do you have anything **of value** (=worth a lot of money) in your bag?*
2 how important something is: *John puts a **high value on** honesty (=he thinks honesty is very important).*

value² *verb* to think that something is important: *I really value the time I spend with my friends.*

valve /vælv/ *noun* something that controls the flow of liquid or air passing through a tube: *There's a leak in the radiator valve in my bedroom.*

vam·pire /'væmpaɪə $'væmpaɪɚ/ *noun* a person in stories who bites people's necks and sucks their blood

van /væn/ *noun* a large vehicle that is used for carrying goods ⇨ see picture on page 349

van·dal /'vændl/ *noun* someone who deliberately damages public property

van·dal·is·m /'vændəlɪzəm/ *noun* [no plural] the crime of deliberately damaging public property

van·dal·ize also **vandalise** *BrE* /'vændəlaɪz/ *verb* to deliberately damage public property: *The phone box has been vandalized.*

va·nil·la /vəˈnɪlə/ *noun* [no plural] a substance with a slightly sweet taste, that you use to add taste to food: *vanilla ice cream*

van·ish /ˈvænɪʃ/ *verb*

GRAMMAR
vanish from somewhere
to disappear suddenly and in a way that people cannot explain: *My bike vanished from the shed overnight. | When I came outside again, the girl had vanished.*

van·i·ty /ˈvænəti/ *noun* [no plural] when someone is too proud of their appearance, their abilities etc: *Melony's friends respect her talent but dislike her vanity.*

va·pour BrE, **vapor** AmE /ˈveɪpə $ ˈveɪpər/ *noun* many small drops of liquid that float in the air: *a cloud of water vapour*

var·i·a·ble /ˈveəriəbəl $ ˈveriəbəl/ *adjective* likely to change often: *The weather is quite variable at this time of year.*

var·i·ant /ˈveəriənt $ ˈveriənt/ *noun* formal something that is slightly different from the usual form: *This tree is a variant of the English oak.*
−**variant** *adjective: 'Color' is a variant spelling of 'colour'.*

var·i·a·tion /ˌveəriˈeɪʃən $ ˌveriˈeɪʃən/ *noun* a change or difference: *We noticed huge price variations between different shops. | The variation in results might be due to a fault in the experiment.*

var·ied /ˈveərid $ ˈverid/ *adjective* consisting of many different types: *Try to eat a varied diet.*

va·ri·e·ty /vəˈraɪəti/ *noun, plural* varieties

GRAMMAR
a variety of things
1 a type of something: *We tried three different varieties of cheese. | a new variety of apple*
2 [no plural] a lot of different kinds of things: *We sell a wide variety of books.*
3 [no plural] when things are different from each other and not all the same: *A good cinema should offer plenty of variety.*

var·i·ous /ˈveəriəs $ ˈveriəs/ *adjective*
several different kinds: *There are various ways of sending money abroad. | I left my job for various reasons.*

var·nish /ˈvɑːnɪʃ $ ˈvɑrnɪʃ/ *noun* a clear liquid that you paint onto wood to protect it and make it shine
−**varnish** *verb: He varnished the front door.*

var·y /ˈveəri $ ˈveri/ *verb* varied, varies
if things vary, they are all different from each other: *The rules vary from state to state.*

vase /vɑːz $ veɪs/ *noun* a container for flowers ⇨ see picture at VIBRATE

vast /vɑːst $ væst/ *adjective* very large: *a vast area of desert*

vat /væt/ *noun* a very large container for holding liquids: *a vat of wine*

vault¹ /vɔːlt/ *noun* a room in a bank with strong walls and doors, in which money, jewels etc can be kept safe

vault² *verb* to jump over something in one movement: *The thieves vaulted the wall and escaped.*

VCR /ˌviː siː ˈɑː $ ˌvi si ˈɑr/ a VIDEO CASSETTE RECORDER

VDU /ˌviː diː ˈjuː/ *noun* visual display unit; a machine with a SCREEN that shows the information from a computer

veal /viːl/ *noun* [no plural] meat from a young cow

veer /vɪə $ vɪr/ *verb* to change direction suddenly: *The car veered off the road and crashed.*

ve·gan /ˈviːgən/ *noun* someone who does not eat anything that is produced from animals

vege·ta·ble /ˈvedʒtəbəl/ *noun* a plant such as a potato or onion which is grown as food

veg·e·tar·i·an /ˌvedʒəˈteəriən $ ˌvedʒəˈteriən/ *noun* someone who does not eat meat or fish

veg·e·ta·tion /ˌvedʒəˈteɪʃən/ *noun* [no plural] the plants, flowers, and trees that grow in a particular area

ve·hi·cle /ˈviːɪkəl/ *noun* a thing such as a car or bus that is used for carrying people or things

veil /veɪl/ *noun* a piece of thin material that a woman wears to cover her face

V

vein /veɪn/ noun one of the tubes that carries blood around your body

Vel·cro /'velkrəʊ $'velkroʊ/ noun [no plural] trademark a material you use for fastening things, made from two pieces of cloth that stick together

vel·vet /'velvɪt/ noun [no plural] a type of material that is very thick and soft: red velvet curtains

ven·det·ta /ven'detə/ noun [no plural] a serious argument between people which continues a long time and often involves them trying to harm each other: They were involved in a spiteful vendetta against their neighbours.

ven·i·son /'venəzən/ noun [no plural] the meat of a DEER

ven·om /'venəm/ noun [no plural] poison produced by snakes, insects etc

ven·o·mous /'venəməs/ adjective a venomous snake or insect is poisonous: a venomous spider

vent /vent/ noun a hole in something that lets air in or lets smoke out

ven·ti·late /'ventəleɪt $'ventl̩ˌeɪt/ verb formal to allow air to come into and go out of place
– **ventilated** adjective: a well-ventilated room

ven·ture[1] /'ventʃə $'ventʃɚ/ noun a new business activity that might earn money but involves taking risks: an exciting new business venture

venture[2] verb to go somewhere or do something that may involve risks because you are not sure what will happen: Many old people are afraid to venture out alone.

ven·ue /'venjuː/ noun a place where a public event takes place: a popular concert venue

ve·ran·da also **verandah** /və'rændə/ noun a structure with a floor and a roof that is built outside a house's front or back door; PORCH AmE

verb /vɜːb $vɝb/ noun a word that describes an action, for example 'go', 'eat', or 'finish'

verb·al /'vɜːbəl $'vɝbəl/ adjective spoken rather than written: He received a verbal warning.

ver·dict /'vɜːdɪkt $'vɝdɪkt/ noun an official decision in a court of law about whether someone is guilty

verge /vɜːdʒ $vɝdʒ/ noun **be on the verge of something, be on the verge of doing something** to be about to do something: Anita was on the verge of tears.

ver·sa·tile /'vɜːsətaɪl $'vɝsətl̩/ adjective having many different skills or uses: a versatile tool

verse /vɜːs $vɝs/ noun a set of lines that form one part of a poem or song: We will sing the first and third verses.

ver·sion /'vɜːʃən $'vɝʒən/ noun a form of something that is slightly different from others of the same type: I prefer the original version of that song.

ver·sus /'vɜːsəs $'vɝsəs/ written abbreviation **vs** or **v** preposition used to say that two teams or players are competing against each another: Romania versus Hungary | England v Brazil

ver·ti·cal /'vɜːtɪkəl $'vɝtɪkəl/ adjective pointing straight upwards ⇨ opposite HORIZONTAL: a vertical line ⇨ see picture at LINE[1]

ver·ti·go /'vɜːtɪgəʊ $'vɝtɪˌgoʊ/ noun [no plural] when you feel ill because you are looking down from a very high place: Do you suffer from vertigo?

ve·ry /'veri/ adverb

used to emphasize an adjective or adverb: We finished the job very quickly. | Joe looks very happy. | That test was very difficult. | I'm **not very good at maths** (=not good at maths at all). | We all felt very hungry.

USAGE

Do not use **very** with adjectives and adverbs that already have a strong meaning, for example **huge** or **terrible**: It was a terrible war (NOT 'very terrible'). Use **really** instead: a really awful film. Do not use **very** with the comparative form of adjectives. Use **much** instead: This school's much better (NOT 'very better').

ves·sel /'vesəl/ noun formal **1** a ship or large boat **2** a container for keeping liquids in

vest /vest/ noun **1** BrE a piece of underwear that you wear to keep the top part of your body warm **2** the American word for WAISTCOAT

vet /vet/ noun someone who is trained to give medical treatment to sick animals

vet·e·ran /'vetərən/ noun someone who fought in a war: a Vietnam veteran

vet·e·ri·na·ri·an /ˌvetərəˈneəriən $ ˌvetərəˈneriən/ *noun* a vet

ve·to /ˈviːtəʊ $ ˈvitoʊ/ *verb* **vetoed, ve-toes** if someone in authority vetoes something, they refuse to allow it to happen: *The government has vetoed the proposals.*
– **veto** *noun*: *France has threatened to use its veto to stop these reforms.*

vi·a /ˈvaɪə, ˈviːə/ *preposition* through a place: *The train goes via Washington.* | *Groups can now release their albums via the Internet.*

vi·a·duct /ˈvaɪədʌkt/ *noun* a long high bridge across a valley

vi·brant /ˈvaɪbrənt/ *adjective* full of excitement and energy: *New York is a very vibrant city.*

vi·brate /vaɪˈbreɪt $ ˈvaɪbreɪt/ *verb* to shake with small fast movements: *The windows vibrated in the wind.*

vibrate
vase

vi·bra·tion /vaɪˈbreɪʃən/ *noun* a continuous shaking movement

vic·ar /ˈvɪkə $ ˈvɪkɚ/ *noun* a priest in the Church of England

vice /vaɪs/ *noun* a bad habit or a bad part of someone's character: *Greed is not one of my vices.*

vice ver·sa /ˌvaɪs ˈvɜːsə $ ˌvaɪs ˈvɝːsə/ *adverb* used to talk about the opposite of a situation you have just described: *Films that the boys like don't appeal to the girls, and vice versa.*

vi·cious /ˈvɪʃəs/ *adjective* violent and dangerous: *a vicious dog*

vic·tim /ˈvɪktɪm/ *noun* someone who has been hurt or killed: *the victims of the bomb attack*

vic·to·ri·ous /vɪkˈtɔːriəs/ *adjective* successful in a battle or competition: *The victorious team were celebrating a great win.*

vic·to·ry /ˈvɪktəri/ *noun, plural* **victories** when someone wins a game or competition ⇨ *opposite* DEFEAT[2]: *Jenson Button is aiming for victory in this year's British Grand Prix.*

vid·e·o[1] /ˈvɪdiəʊ $ ˈvɪdioʊ/ *noun* **1** a TAPE on which a film or television pro-

gramme has been recorded: *Have you got a video of 'Robocop 3'?* **2** *BrE* a video cassette recorder

video[2] *verb* to record something, using a video cassette recorder or a camera: *My father videoed the game so we could watch it later.*

video cas·sette re·cord·er /ˌ... .ˈ. ˌ.../ *also* **video re·cord·er** /ˈ... ˌ.../ *abbreviation* **VCR** *noun* a machine used for recording television programmes or playing videotapes ⇨ *see picture on page 342*

video game /ˈ... ˌ./ *noun* a computer game you play by pressing buttons to move pictures on a SCREEN ⇨ *see picture on page 342*

vid·e·o·tape /ˈvɪdiəʊˌteɪp $ ˈvɪdioʊˌteɪp/ *noun* a long narrow band of material in a plastic container, on which you can record films, television programmes etc

view /vjuː/ *noun*

1 an opinion or belief about something: *What are your views on animal rights?* | *John has very strong views about education.* | *In my view, the government is right.* | *Teachers should listen to the views of their students.* | *Helen's view is that stealing is always wrong.*
2 the things that you can see from a place, especially when this is very beautiful or interesting: *We bought a house with a view of the beach.* | *There are great views from the mountain.*

view·er /ˈvjuːə $ ˈvjuɚ/ *noun* someone who watches television: *The programme attracted over 2 million viewers.*

vig·il /ˈvɪdʒəl/ *noun* when people stand or sit quietly somewhere as a way of showing their feelings of sadness: *Her family kept a vigil by her hospital bed.*

vig·i·lant /ˈvɪdʒələnt/ *adjective formal* watching what happens carefully, so that you notice anything dangerous or illegal: *Policemen in Northern Ireland have to be especially vigilant.*

vig·o·rous /'vɪgərəs/ adjective using a lot of effort and energy: a vigorous walk in the mountains

vile /vaɪl/ adjective very unpleasant: That's a vile colour!

vil·la /'vɪlə/ noun a large house in the countryside or near the sea, used especially for holidays

vil·lage /'vɪlɪdʒ/ noun a place in the countryside where people live, that is smaller than a town

vil·lain /'vɪlən/ noun a bad person in a book or film: Dennis Hopper plays the villain in 'Speed'.

vin·dic·tive /vɪn'dɪktɪv/ adjective deliberately cruel and unfair: Sometimes, she can be very vindictive.

vine /vaɪn/ noun a climbing plant, especially one that produces GRAPES

vin·e·gar /'vɪnɪgə $'vɪnɪgɚ/ noun [no plural] a very sour liquid that you use to add FLAVOUR to food: oil and vinegar salad dressing

vine·yard /'vɪnjəd $'vɪnjɚd/ noun an area of land where people grow GRAPES to make wine

vin·tage /'vɪntɪdʒ/ adjective 1 vintage wine is good quality wine: a 1941 vintage wine 2 a vintage car is one that was made a long time ago but is still in good condition and is still used today

vi·nyl /'vaɪnl/ noun [no plural] a type of strong plastic

vi·o·la /vi'əʊlə $vi'oʊlə/ noun a wooden musical instrument, similar to a VIOLIN, but bigger

vi·o·lence /'vaɪələns/ noun [no plural]
when people attack, hurt, or kill other people: There is too much violence shown on television. | We always said that we would never **resort to violence** (=use violence). | The police deal with many cases of **domestic violence** (=when one member of a family deliberately hurts another) each week.

vi·o·lent /'vaɪələnt/ adjective
1 a violent person attacks, hurts, or kills other people: The man was **becoming violent**, so I called the police. | a **violent attack** on an old woman

2 a violent film or television programme shows people trying to hurt or kill each other: The film contains some very violent scenes.

vi·o·lin /ˌvaɪə'lɪn/ noun a wooden musical instrument that you hold under your chin and play by pulling a special stick across four strings

violin

VIP /ˌviː aɪ 'piː/ noun a very important person; someone who receives special treatment because they are famous or powerful

vi·per /'vaɪpə $'vaɪpɚ/ noun a small poisonous snake

vir·gin[1] /'vɜːdʒɪn $'vɚdʒɪn/ noun someone who has never had sex

virgin[2] adjective virgin land has never been used or spoiled by people: 300 acres of virgin forest

vir·ile /'vɪraɪl $'vɪrəl/ adjective a virile man has a strong sexually attractive body

vir·tu·al /'vɜːtʃuəl $'vɚtʃuəl/ adjective
1 very close to being something: Even a virtual beginner can use this computer.
2 using virtual reality: a virtual library

vir·tu·al·ly /'vɜːtʃuəli $'vɚtʃuəli/ adverb almost completely: The town was virtually empty.

virtual re·al·i·ty /ˌ... .'.../ noun [no plural] when a computer makes you feel as though you are in a real situation or place by showing pictures and sounds

vir·tue /'vɜːtʃuː $'vɚtʃu/ noun a good quality in someone's character: Honesty is a virtue I really admire.

vir·tu·o·so /ˌvɜːtʃu'əʊsəʊ $ˌvɚtʃu'oʊsoʊ/ noun formal someone who has great skill in music: Nigel Kennedy, the violin virtuoso

vir·tu·ous /'vɜːtʃuəs $'vɚtʃuəs/ adjective behaving in a way that is morally good or kind: a decent, virtuous man

vi·rus /'vaɪərəs $'vaɪrəs/ noun, plural viruses 1 a very small living thing that causes diseases: the flu virus 2 a computer PROGRAM that can destroy or damage information stored in the computer: Many viruses are spread by software downloaded from the Internet.

V

vi·sa /'viːzə/ noun an official document that allows you to enter or leave a country: *You need a visa to visit the U.S. | Have you got your entry visa yet?*

vis·i·bil·i·ty /ˌvɪzə'bɪləti/ noun [no plural] the distance you are able to see ahead of you: *The pilot reported poor visibility before the crash.*

vis·i·ble /'vɪzəbəl/ adjective if something is visible, you can see it: *The house was only just visible behind the trees.*
– **visibly** adverb: *She was visibly upset.*

vi·sion /'vɪʒən/ noun
1 your ideas or hopes about what the world could be like in the future: *Gandhi had a vision of a better, more peaceful society.*
2 [no plural] your ability to see: *An airline pilot needs to have good vision.*

vis·it¹ /'vɪzɪt/ verb
1 to go and spend time with someone: *Granny is visiting us next weekend. | I went to visit Simon in hospital. | You must come and visit me some time.*
2 to go and spend a short time in a place: *We're hoping to visit Rome while we're in Italy.*

visit² noun

GRAMMAR
a visit to somewhere/someone
a visit from someone
when someone visits a place or a person: *The President made a speech during his visit to China. | I've just had a visit from Mr Heaney* (=Mr Heaney has just visited me).

vis·it·or /'vɪzətə $ 'vɪzətɚ/ noun someone who visits a place or person: *I came to Tokyo as a visitor in 1979. | Visitors to the building must wear a name tag.*

vi·sor /'vaɪzə $ 'vaɪzɚ/ noun the front part of a HELMET (=hard hat) that comes down in front of your eyes to protect them ⇨ see picture at GLASSES

vi·su·al /'vɪʒuəl/ adjective related to your ability to see and things that you see: *an exhibition of visual arts*

visual aid /ˌ... './ noun something that people can see, such as a picture or film, that is used to help them learn something

vi·su·al·ize also **visualise** BrE /'vɪʒuəlaɪz/ verb formal to imagine something:

I tried to visualize myself winning the race.

vi·tal /'vaɪtl/ adjective very important: *It's vital to concentrate when you are driving.*

vit·a·min /'vɪtəmən $ 'vaɪtəmɪn/ noun a natural chemical in food that keeps you healthy: *Oranges contain a lot of Vitamin C.*

vi·va·cious /vɪ'veɪʃəs/ adjective a vivacious person has a lot of energy and enjoys life

viv·id /'vɪvɪd/ adjective vivid descriptions or memories are very clear: *a vivid description of the accident*
– **vividly** adverb: *I can remember my childhood vividly.*

vo·cab·u·la·ry /və'kæbjələri $ vou'kæbjə,leri/ noun, plural **vocabularies**
1 your vocabulary is all the words you know: *Our teacher wants us to improve our vocabulary.* 2 all the words in a language: *English has a very large vocabulary.*

vo·cal /'vəukəl $ 'voukəl/ adjective related to the human voice

vo·cal·ist /'vəukəlɪst $ 'voukəlɪst/ noun someone who sings with a group playing popular music: *She was a vocalist in a successful band.*

vo·cals /'vəukəlz $ 'voukəlz/ plural noun the part of a popular song that someone sings, rather than the part played by instruments: *The vocals were recorded separately.*

vo·ca·tion /vəu'keɪʃən $ vou'keɪʃən/ noun if you have a vocation, you have a strong feeling that you should do a particular job, especially a job that involves helping people: *He discovered his vocation as a nurse in a large hospital.*

vo·ca·tion·al /vəu'keɪʃənəl $ vou'keɪʃənəl/ adjective concerned with teaching or learning the skills you need to do a job: *vocational education and training*

vod·ka /'vɒdkə $ 'vɑdkə/ noun [no plural] a strong alcoholic drink from Russia that has no colour and looks like water

vogue /vəug $ voug/ noun **be in vogue** to be fashionable and popular: *Fur coats are in vogue this year.*

voice /vɔɪs/ noun
your voice is the sound you make when you speak or sing: *I could hear*

▼ *voices outside.* | *Lynda has a beautiful voice when she sings.*

keep your voice down informal to speak quietly: *Keep your voice down, can't you? She'll hear us!*

lose your voice to not be able to speak, for example because of an illness: *The concert was cancelled when the lead singer **lost** his voice.*

voice·mail /'vɔɪsˌmeɪl/ *noun* [no plural] a system that records telephone calls so that you can listen to them later: *I left a message on your voicemail.*

void /vɔɪd/ *adjective* formal not legally or officially acceptable: *The result of the race was declared void.*

vol·a·tile /'vɒlətaɪl $ 'vɑlətl/ *adjective* **1** someone who is volatile often changes suddenly from being happy to being angry or upset **2** a volatile situation is one that is likely to change suddenly and become worse

vol·ca·no /vɒl-'keɪnəʊ $ vɑl'keɪnoʊ/ *noun, plural* **volcanoes** or **volcanos** a mountain that sometimes explodes, sending out fire and hot rocks

volcano

vol·ley /'vɒli $ 'vɑli/ *noun* a volley of bullets or stones is a large number of them moving through the air at the same time

vol·ley·ball /'vɒlibɔːl $ 'vɑliˌbɔl/ *noun* [no plural] a game in which two teams hit a ball to each other across a high net with their hands and try to keep the ball off the ground

volt /vəʊlt $ voʊlt/ *abbreviation* **v** *noun* a unit for measuring the force of an electric current: *a 12-volt battery*

vol·ume /'vɒljuːm $ 'vɑljəm/ *noun* [no plural] the amount of sound a television, radio etc produces: *Turn up the volume – I really like this song.*

vol·un·ta·ri·ly /'vɒləntərəli $ ˌvɑlən-'terəli/ *adverb* if you do something voluntarily, you do it because you want to, not because you have to: *She left the country voluntarily.*

vol·un·ta·ry /'vɒləntəri $ 'vɑlənˌteri/ *adjective* voluntary activities are ones that you do because you want to, not because you are being paid or forced to: *Have you thought of doing some voluntary work at the hospital?*

vol·un·teer¹ /ˌvɒlən'tɪə $ ˌvɑlən'tɪr/ *verb* to offer to do something without being told to: *I volunteered to clean the house.*

volunteer² *noun* someone who offers to do a job without being paid or forced to do it: *The shop is run by volunteers.*

vom·it /'vɒmɪt $ 'vɑmɪt/ *verb* formal if you vomit, food comes up from your stomach and out of your mouth –**vomit** *noun* [no plural]: *The car seats were covered in vomit.*

vote¹ /vəʊt $ voʊt/ *noun*

a vote on something
a vote for someone/something
a vote against someone/something

1 a choice that you make to support a particular person or group of people by making a mark on a piece of paper or raising your hand in the air: *There were 603 **votes for** Mr Jameson, and only 16 **against**.* | *We spent three hours counting the votes.* | *The Communists won 22% of **the vote*** (=won 22% of the votes).
2 when people decide something by voting: *We **held a vote** to decide who would lead the team.* | *Since we can't agree, let's **take a vote** on it.*
3 **have the vote, get the vote** people who have the vote are allowed to vote: *It was years before women **got the vote**.*

vote² *verb* to choose which person you want to elect or which plan you support by making a mark on a piece of paper or raising your hand: *Who are you going to vote for in the student elections?* | *The government has voted to increase taxes.*

vot·er /'vəʊtə $ 'voʊtɚ/ *noun* someone who votes or has the right to vote

vot·ing /'vəʊtɪŋ $ 'voʊtɪŋ/ *noun* [no plural] when people vote in an election or in a meeting: *Voting ends at 10.00 pm tonight.*

vouch /vaʊtʃ/ *verb* **vouch for** a) if you vouch for something, you say that you know it is correct or true **b)** if you vouch for someone, you say that you know they are a good and honest person and people can trust them

vouch·er /'vautʃə $'vautʃɚ/ noun a ticket that you can use instead of money: *free cinema vouchers*

vow /vaʊ/ verb formal to promise something: *After he lost, Agassi vowed he would return for next year's championship.*
−**vow** noun: *She made a vow to give up drinking.*

vow·el /'vauəl/ noun one of the sounds shown by the letters a, e, i, o, or u

voy·age /'vɔɪ-ɪdʒ/ noun a long trip in a ship or space vehicle: *a round-the-world voyage | the long voyage from Ireland to America* ⇨ see usage note at TRAVEL²

vs a written abbreviation of VERSUS

vul·gar /'vʌlgə $'vʌlgɚ/ adjective rude and likely to offend people: *Judy has a very vulgar sense of humour.*

vul·ne·ra·ble /'vʌlnərəbəl/ adjective not protected and therefore likely to be hurt or damaged: *Elderly people living alone are very vulnerable. | The town is very vulnerable to attack.*

vul·ture /'vʌltʃə $'vʌltʃɚ/ noun a large wild bird that eats dead animals

W w

W the written abbreviation of WEST or WESTERN

wade /weɪd/ verb to walk through deep water: *We waded across the river.*

waft /wɑːft/ verb to move gently through the air: *Smoke wafted in through the open window.*

wag /wæg/ verb **wagged, wagging** if a dog wags its tail, it moves it from side to side

wage /weɪdʒ/ noun also **wages** the money that a worker gets for doing their job: *They promised us a wage increase. | The wages are low, but I love the job.* ⇨ see usage note at PAY²

wag·on /'wægən/ noun a strong vehicle with four wheels that is pulled by a horse

wail /weɪl/ verb to cry loudly: *The children started to wail with hunger.*
−**wail** noun: *the wails of the baby*

waist /weɪst/ noun the narrow part around the middle of your body: *Carole has a slim waist.*

waist·coat /'weɪskəʊt $'weskət/ noun BrE a piece of clothing with buttons down the front and no arms, which you usually wear over a shirt; VEST AmE ⇨ see picture on page 352

wait¹ /weɪt/ verb

GRAMMAR
wait for someone/something
wait to do something
to stay in one place because you are

expecting a particular thing to come or happen: *Three people were **waiting for** the bus. | **Wait for** me! | I read a magazine while I was waiting. | We had to **wait until** the police arrived. | Ella **waited** a few minutes **to** see what would happen.*

PHRASES
can't wait spoken: *I **can't wait to** get back home* (=I want to get home very much).

wait tables AmE to serve food in a restaurant to people who are sitting at the tables: *He got an evening job **waiting tables**.*

PHRASAL VERBS
wait around
to do nothing because you are waiting for a particular thing to happen: *We spent the afternoon **waiting around** at the airport.*

wait on
wait on someone to serve food to someone at the table where they are sitting: *Life must be great if you've got servants to **wait on** you.*

wait up
to not go to bed because you are waiting for someone to come home: *I'll be late, so don't **wait up**. | When I got back at midnight, my dad was **waiting up for** me.*

wait² noun [no plural] a period of time when you wait for something to happen:

You'll have a long wait for the next bus.

wait·er /'weɪtə $ 'weɪtɚ/ *noun* a man who serves food in a restaurant

wait·ing list /'.. ./ *noun* a list of people who are waiting to have something that is not available for them now: *There's a long waiting list for eye operations. | We've been on the waiting list for a new flat for six months.*

waiting room /'. . ./ *noun* a room where people wait to see someone or do something: *the doctor's waiting room*

wait·ress /'weɪtrəs/ *noun*, *plural* waitresses a woman who serves food in a restaurant

wake¹ /weɪk/ *verb* woke /wəʊk $ woʊk/ **woken** /'wəʊkən $ woʊkən/ also **wake up** if you wake, or if something wakes you, you stop sleeping: *Wake up, Sam, your breakfast is ready. | Guy was woken by a loud noise. | Can you wake me up at 7.00 tomorrow?*

wake² *noun* the waves that a ship leaves behind as it moves along

walk¹ /wɔːk/ *verb*

GRAMMAR
walk to/across/from etc a place
to move forwards by putting one foot in front of the other: *I usually walk to college. | She walked across the room towards him. | I walked up the steps to the front door.*

PHRASAL VERBS
walk away
to leave a difficult situation or problem and not try to deal with it: *Henry's marriage was not happy, but he couldn't just walk away and leave his children. | You can't deal with your problems by walking away from them.*

walk off with *informal*
walk off with something to steal something: *Someone has walked off with my camera.*

walk out on
walk out on someone to leave your family suddenly and go to live somewhere else: *Dad walked out on us when I was five.*

walk² *noun*
1 a journey that you make by walking: *We always go for a walk on Sundays. | The students went on a long walk. | The hotel is a 10-minute walk away* (=it takes 10 minutes to walk there). *| It's only a short walk to the station from here.*
2 a path that people can walk along for pleasure: *There are some lovely walks in the area.*

walk·ing stick /'.. ,./ *noun* a long stick that people who are old or ill use to help them walk

Walk·man /'wɔːkmən/ *noun* trademark a small machine that plays CASSETTES. You carry it with you and listen through EAR-PHONES (=thin wire with a special piece that you put in each ear) ⇨ *same meaning* PERSONAL STEREO ⇨ *see picture on page 342*

wall /wɔːl/ *noun*
1 one of the sides of a room or building: *We stuck pictures on the classroom walls. | The room had blue walls and a white ceiling.*
2 a narrow brick or stone structure that is built around an area of land or between two areas: *He crashed his car into a brick wall.*

wal·let /'wɒlɪt $ 'wɑlɪt/ *noun* a small flat case that you use for carrying paper money

wall·pa·per /'wɔːlˌpeɪpə $ 'wɔlˌpeɪpɚ/ *noun* [no plural] paper that you stick on the walls of a room to decorate it –**wallpaper** *verb*: *Dad's wallpapering my bedroom this weekend.*

wal·nut /'wɔːlnʌt/ *noun* a type of tree that produces nuts, which are called walnuts

waltz /wɔːls $ wɒlts/ *noun*, *plural* waltzes a dance with sets of three steps, or a piece of music for this dance: *the last waltz of the evening* –**waltz** *verb*: *They waltzed around the room.*

wan /wɒn $ wɑn/ *adjective* written looking pale, weak, or tired

wand /wɒnd $ wɑnd/ *noun* a long thin stick that you hold in your hand when you are doing magic tricks: *He waved his wand, and a rabbit appeared.*

wan·der /ˈwɒndə $ ˈwɑːndɚ/ verb

GRAMMAR
wander around/to etc a place
wander to something

1 to walk somewhere quite slowly and with no particular purpose: *A group of tourists* **wandered around** *the museum.* | *Derek stood up and* **wandered over to** *the window.*

2 if your mind or your thoughts wander, you stop paying attention to something and think about other things instead: *His* **thoughts wandered to** *his wife and children.* | *The students'* **attention** *was beginning to* **wander.**

wane /weɪn/ verb if someone's power, support, or interest wanes, it becomes less: *The students' interest was starting to wane.*
–wane noun [no plural]: *His popularity is on the wane* (=becoming less).

wan·na·be /ˈwɒnəbi $ ˈwɑːnəbi/ noun informal someone who tries to be like a famous person, although this is not sensible: *a Madonna wannabe*

want /wɒnt $ wʌnt/ verb

GRAMMAR
want to do something
want someone to do something

to wish or need to have or do something: *Do you want something to eat, Nancy?* | *The kids want a computer for Christmas.* | *Paul* **wanted to** *move to a bigger house.* | *I* **want you to** *clean up your rooms for dinner.* | *Does Mike* **want** *me* **to** *call him?*

USAGE want, wish, or **desire?**
Use **want** to talk about things you would like to do or have: *I want a drink of water.* | *Libby wants to go to France.* | *Carol really wants to win this match.* Use **wish** when you want something to happen, but it is very unlikely or is impossible: *I wish I had more time to do this.* | *I wish William were here too.* Use **desire** to mean 'want' only in formal writing: *She has everything she desires.* When you are asking someone for something, don't say **I want**, because it is not polite. Instead say, **I would like** or **May I have?/Could I have?** People often say **Can I have?**, but many teachers think this is incorrect. When you are offering someone something, you can say **Do you want?** especially to your friends or

your family, but it is more polite to say **Would you like?**
Do not say *I want visit England.* Say **I want to** *visit England.* Do not say *I want that you do it.* Say **I want you to** *do it.* Do not say *I'm wanting a new bicycle.* Say **I want** *a new bicycle.*

want·ed /ˈwɒntɪd $ ˈwʌntɪd/ adjective if someone is wanted, the police are looking for them because they may have done something illegal: *He is wanted for murder.*

war /wɔː $ wɔːr/ noun

GRAMMAR
war with someone
war between people
a war against something

1 a period of fighting between two or more countries or states: *He was a prisoner during the Vietnam War.* | *The two countries* **have been at war** (=have been fighting) *for three years.* | *France* **went to war with** *England.* | *the* **war between** *Greece and Troy* | *The* **war broke out** (=started) *on August 4th.*

2 when people try to stop something bad from happening: *The police are losing the* **war against** *crime.*

ward¹ /wɔːd $ wɔːrd/ noun a room in a hospital with beds in it, where sick people stay

ward² verb **ward something off** to stop something bad from affecting you: *Keep warm in winter to ward off colds.*

war·den /ˈwɔːdn $ ˈwɔːrdn/ noun someone whose job is to look after an area or the people who live in a large building: *He is warden of a block of flats for old people.*

ward·er /ˈwɔːdə $ ˈwɔːrdɚ/ noun BrE someone whose job is to guard people in prison

ward·robe /ˈwɔːdrəʊb $ ˈwɔːrdroʊb/ noun BrE a large cupboard where you keep your clothes; CLOSET AmE ⇨ see picture on page 342

ware·house /ˈweəhaʊs $ ˈwerhaʊs/ noun a large building for storing materials or things that will be sold

war·fare /ˈwɔːfeə $ ˈwɔːrfer/ noun [no plural] formal the fighting in a war: *We are all aware of the dangers of nuclear warfare.*

war·like /ˈwɔːlaɪk $ ˈwɔːrlaɪk/ adjective

warlike countries or people who like fighting wars

warm¹ /wɔːm $ wɔrm/ adjective
1 quite hot: *It's lovely and warm in this room.* | *Cover the bowl to keep the soup warm.* | *It was a warm day, so we sat outside.*
2 warm clothes stop you from feeling cold: *I must buy a warm coat to wear this winter.*
3 friendly: *We gave the visiting students **a warm welcome.***

warm² verb 1 also **warm up** to make something warm, or to become warmer: *I can warm some soup if you're hungry.* | *The weather is expected to warm up this weekend.* 2 warm up to do gentle exercises to prepare your body before doing a sport or exercising: *It's important to warm up before you start running.*

warm-heart·ed /ˌ. '../ adjective kind

warmth /wɔːmθ $ wɔrmθ/ noun [no plural] the heat that something produces: *the warmth of the sun*

warm-up /'. ./ noun a set of gentle exercises that you do to prepare for a sport: *We always do a ten-minute warm-up before the game.*

warn /wɔːn $ wɔrn/ verb

> **GRAMMAR**
> warn someone (that)
> warn that
> warn someone about/of something
> warn someone (not) to do something

1 to tell someone about a danger, so that they can be careful or can prepare for it: *The police **have warned** drivers **that** the roads are dangerous.* | *Scientists **have warned that** there will be more storms in future.* | *It is important that we **warn** young people **about** the dangers of drugs.* | *No one **warned** me **of** the risks of this treatment.*
2 to tell someone to do something or not to do something, because there is danger: *They **warned** us **not to** go out at night.* | *I **warned** you **to** be careful!*

warn·ing /'wɔːnɪŋ $ 'wɔrnɪŋ/ noun
something that tells you that some-

thing bad or dangerous is likely to happen: *The police **received a warning** just before the bomb exploded.* | *The wall collapsed **without warning**.*

warp /wɔːp $ wɔrp/ verb if wood or metal warps, it becomes bent or twisted

war·rant /'wɒrənt $ 'wɔrənt/ noun an official document that allows the police to search someone's house or take someone to a police station: *The police have a warrant for his arrest.*

war·ren /'wɒrən $ 'wɔrən/ noun a group of holes underground where wild rabbits live

war·ri·or /'wɒriə $ 'wɔriɚ/ noun a very brave person who fought in battles in the past

war·ship /'wɔːˌʃɪp $ 'wɔrˌʃɪp/ noun a ship with guns that is used in wars

wart /wɔːt $ wɔrt/ noun a small hard raised spot that grows on your skin

war·y /'weəri $ 'weri/ adjective warier, wariest careful because you think that someone or something may harm you: *Children should be wary of strangers.*

was /wəz; strong wɒz $ wʌz/ the past tense of BE which you use after 'I', 'he', 'she', and 'it'

wash¹ /wɒʃ $ wɑʃ/ verb

> **GRAMMAR**
> wash something with/in something

1 to clean something using soap and water: *Have you washed my shirt?* | ***Wash** your hands **with** soap after touching raw meat.* | *I had to **wash** my hair **in** cold water.* | *It's your turn to **wash the dishes** (=wash the plates etc after a meal).*
2 if you wash or get washed, you clean your body with soap and water: *My brother **got washed** quickly and left for work.*

> **PHRASAL VERBS**
> **wash away**
> wash something away if water washes something away, it removes it: *The heavy rains **washed away** the river bank.*
> **wash down**
> wash something down if you wash down food, you drink something

while you eat to help you swallow it: *Ari took a big bite of his sandwich, and **washed** it **down** with a mouthful of tea.*

wash up
1 wash up, wash something up *BrE* to wash the plates, dishes etc after a meal: *It's your turn to **wash up**. | Carrie was **washing** the cups **up**.*
2 wash up *AmE* to wash your hands

wash² *noun*

1 **have a wash** to wash your body with soap and water: *Isn't it time you had a wash?*
2 **give something a wash** to clean something with soap and water: *I'll **give** the car a **wash** later.*
3 **be in the wash** if your clothes are in the wash, they are being washed: *I can't wear my best shirt because it **is in the wash**.*

wash·ba·sin /'wɒʃˌbeɪsən $'wɑʃ-ˌbeɪsən/ *noun* a SINK that you use for washing your hands and face

washing

washing   washing-up

wash·ing /'wɒʃɪŋ $'wɑʃɪŋ/ *noun*
1 *[no plural]* clothes, sheets etc that you need to wash or have just washed: *There were piles of dirty washing all over the flat.* 2 **do the washing** to wash dirty clothes, sheets etc

washing ma·chine /'.. .ˌ./ *noun* a machine that washes clothes

washing-up /ˌ.. './ *noun BrE* **do the washing-up** to wash the plates, dishes etc after a meal: *It's your turn to do the washing-up.* ⇨ *see picture at* WASHING

was·n't /'wɒzənt $'wʌzənt/ the short form of 'was not': *He wasn't happy.*

wasp /wɒsp $wɑsp/ *noun* a flying insect with a black and yellow body, which can sting

waste¹ /weɪst/ *verb*

GRAMMAR
waste something on something
waste something doing something

if you waste something, you use more than you need to, or you do not use it in a sensible way: *I **wasted** £500 **on** that piano! | I don't want to **waste money** buying books I won't read. | Let's not **waste** any more **time** arguing. | Don't **waste** your **energy** worrying about things you can't change.*

PHRASAL VERB
waste away
to slowly become thinner and weaker because of an illness: *Her muscles became weaker and gradually **wasted away**.*

waste² *noun*

GRAMMAR
a waste of something

1 *[no plural]* when you use more of something than you need to, or you do not use it in a sensible way: *My parents think CDs are **a waste of money**. | It's **a waste of time** asking Roger for help. | Are you throwing that food away? What a waste!*
2 the parts of something that you have not used and do not need: *You can feed chickens on kitchen waste.*

waste·bas·ket /'weɪstˌbɑːskɪt $'weɪstˌbæskɪt/ a WASTEPAPER BASKET

waste·ful /'weɪstfəl/ *adjective* using much more of something than you should: *a wasteful use of water*

waste·land /'weɪstlænd/ *noun* an area of unattractive land that is not being used for anything

waste·pa·per bas·ket /ˌweɪst'peɪpə ˌbɑːskɪt $'weɪstˌpeɪpɚ ˌbæskɪt/ *noun* a container, especially one in a CLASSROOM or office, where you put paper and other small things that you no longer want

watch¹ ⇨ *see box on next page*

watch² /wɒtʃ $wɑtʃ/ *noun, plural* watches

1 a small clock that you wear on your wrist: *I checked the time on my watch. | What time is it? I think my **watch has stopped** (=is not working at the moment).*

➤ WATCH, LOOK AT, or SEE?

WATCH you **watch** something that is happening or moving for a period of time

LOOK AT you **look at** a picture, photo, person, or thing because you want to

SEE you **see** something, a person, or event without planning to

They **watched** the football game from the sidelines.

He **was looking at** something on the ground.

We **saw** some beautiful clothes.

➤ WATCH

① **to look for some time at something that is happening or moving**

We **watched** a movie on TV. | A lot of kids **watch** too much television. | Do you want to play too, or just sit and **watch**? | I went to **watch** Jason play volleyball. | **Watch**, Dad, I can do a handstand!

> **GRAMMAR**
> watch someone do something
> watch someone doing something

② **to take care of someone or something for a short time**

Carrie is going to **watch** the kids for me this afternoon. | Would you mind **watching** my bag for me? I'll be right back.

watch

③ **to be careful and pay attention to what you are doing**

Watch your head – the ceiling's low. | "Hey, **watch it!**" the truck driver yelled.

PHRASES

watch out
use this when someone should pay attention to what they are doing and be careful: Charlie, **watch out!** The oven's hot. | **Watch out for** kids playing in the street.

watch your weight
to be careful about what you eat, so that you do not become fat: "Would

you like some cake?" "No, thanks, I'm **watching my weight.**"

watch your language
if you watch your language, you do not swear, especially because you do not want to offend the people you are with: Mark! **Watch your language** in front of Becky!

2 when you carefully watch a place or pay close attention to a situation: *Rosie stayed **on watch** while her friends slept.* | *The President **is keeping a close watch on** the progress of the war.*

wa·ter¹ /'wɔːtə $'wɔtɚ/ *noun*

1 [no plural] the clear liquid that falls from the sky as rain, and is in rivers and the sea: *a glass of water* | *I boiled some water to make tea.* | *The boat sank slowly under the water.*
2 waters the sea, especially when it is close to a particular country: *The ship was not allowed to pass through French waters.*

water² *verb* **1** to pour water on a plant to help it grow: *George waters his roses every day.* **2** if your eyes water, they fill with tears because they are hurting: *The smoke made my eyes water.* **3** if food makes your mouth water, you want to eat it because it looks and smells good: *The smell of sausages made his mouth water.*

wa·ter·fall /'wɔːtəfɔːl $'wɔtɚ͵fɔl/ *noun* water that is flowing over the edge of high rocks into a river or the sea ⇨ *see picture on page 348*

wa·ter·ing can /'... ͵./ *noun* a container that you use for pouring water on plants

wa·ter·logged /'wɔːtəlɒgd $'wɔtɚ͵lɔgd/ *adjective* waterlogged land is very wet: *After the rain, the football pitch was waterlogged.*

wa·ter·mel·on /'wɔːtə͵melən $'wɔtɚ͵melən/ *noun* a large round green fruit which is red inside with black seeds ⇨ *see picture on page 345*

wa·ter·proof /'wɔːtəpruːf $'wɔtɚ͵pruf/ *adjective* waterproof clothing or material does not let water in

water-ski·ing /'.. ͵../ *noun* [no plural] a sport in which someone wearing SKIS on their feet is pulled behind a boat over water

wa·ter·tight /'wɔːtətaɪt $'wɔtɚ͵taɪt/ *adjective* a container that is watertight does not allow any water to get in or out

watt /wɒt $wɑt/ *noun* a unit for measuring electrical power: *a 60 watt light bulb*

wave¹ /weɪv/ *verb*

GRAMMAR
wave to/at someone

1 to move your hand from side to side

in the air so that someone will see you: *We **waved goodbye to** Dad.* | *The children **waved at** the Queen as her car passed.* | *The crowd waved and cheered when the singer appeared on stage.* | *His girlfriend came to **wave** him **off** (=wave to him as he was leaving a place).* ⇨ *see picture on page 341*
2 if you wave something, or it waves, it moves from side to side: *"Stop!" shouted Neil, waving his arms.* | *trees waving in the wind*

wave² *noun*

GRAMMAR
a wave of things

1 a raised line of water that moves across the surface of a large area of water: *Big waves crashed against the side of the boat.* ⇨ *see picture on page 348*
2 the movement that you make with your hand when you wave to someone: *Dave **gave** us **a wave** as he passed.*
3 a sudden increase in a particular activity, especially one that is bad: *a crime wave* | *Who is responsible for the recent **wave of** bombings?*
4 the way that energy such as light and sound moves: *sound waves* | *radio waves*

wave·length /'weɪvleŋθ/ *noun* **1** the size of radio wave that a radio company uses to broadcast its programmes: *What wavelength is Radio 1 on?* **2** be on the same wavelength *informal* if two people are on the same wavelength, they think about things in the same way: *We've never been on the same wavelength about music.*

wa·ver /'weɪvə $'weɪvɚ/ *verb* to be uncertain about a decision for a short time: *Paul wavered for a few moments before accepting the offer.*

wav·y /'weɪvi/ *adjective* wavier, waviest **1** wavy hair has gentle curves and is not straight or curly: *wavy grey hair* ⇨ *see picture on page 353* **2** a wavy line has a series of curves in it

wax /wæks/ *noun* [no plural] a solid substance made of fats and oils which becomes soft when it is warm: *Wax polish protects your car against the weather.*

way ⇨ *see box on page 698*

way of life /ˌ. . './ *noun, plural* **ways of life** the typical or usual things that someone does: *The way of life in the countryside is quite different from the way that city people live.*

way out /ˌ. './ *noun* **the way out** a door through which you can leave a place ⇨ *same meaning* EXIT¹

WC /ˌdʌbəljuː 'siː/ *noun BrE* a word for a toilet, which is used on signs

we /wiː/ *pronoun*

the person who is speaking and others: *We had a great time on holiday.* | *We had a maths test at school today.* | *We must protect the environment.*

weak /wiːk/ *adjective*

1 someone who is weak does not have much strength or energy ⇨ *opposite* STRONG (1): *At the end of the race he felt weak.*
2 if someone is weak, it is easy for other people to persuade them to do things ⇨ *opposite* STRONG (6): *He was too weak to say no.*
3 a weak student is not good at a subject: *The teacher gave special help to the weaker students.* | *Maths is my weakest subject* (=the one I am worst at).
4 a weak drink contains a lot of water and does not have a strong taste ⇨ *opposite* STRONG (5): *Do you like your coffee strong or weak?*

weak·en /'wiːkən/ *verb* to become less strong, or to make someone or something less strong: *Her long illness had weakened her.*

weak·ness /'wiːknəs/ *noun* 1 [no plural] when someone is not physically strong: *Weakness is one sign of the illness.* 2 when someone is not determined enough: *Children think behaviour like that is a sign of weakness.* 3 if you have a weakness for something, you like it very much even though it may not be good for you: *I have a weakness for chocolate.*

wealth /welθ/ *noun* [no plural]

the large amount of money and things that a rich person has: *She wanted to share her wealth with her friends.*

wealth·y /'welθi/ *adjective* **wealthier, wealthiest** very rich: *a wealthy businessman*

weap·on /'wepən/ *noun* something that you use to fight with: *The weapon that he used was a knife.*

wear¹ /weə $wer/ *verb* **wore** /wɔː $wɔr/ **worn** /wɔːn $wɔrn/

if you wear clothes, shoes, glasses etc, you have them on your body: *I decided to wear my blue dress.* | *Do you ever wear lipstick?*

PHRASAL VERBS
wear away
wear away, wear something away if something wears away, it slowly becomes thinner and disappears because something has rubbed it a lot: *The design on the necklace has worn away.* | *Their feet wore the steps away.*
wear off
if a feeling or effect wears off, it slowly stops: *The drug takes a few hours to wear off.*
wear out
1 **wear out, wear something out** if something wears out, or if you wear it out, it becomes damaged and useless because you have used it a lot: *One of the parts of the washing machine had worn out.* | *How do you manage to wear out your shoes so quickly?*
2 **wear someone out** *informal* to make someone very tired: *All these parties are wearing me out!*

wear² *noun* 1 **children's wear, women's wear** etc clothes for children, women etc: *The shop now has a very good women's wear department.* 2 [no plural] the damage that you cause to something when you use it a lot: *These old blankets are showing signs of wear.*

wear·y /'wɪəri $'wɪri/ *adjective* very tired

wea·sel /'wiːzəl/ *noun* a small wild animal that looks like a long rat

weath·er /'weðə $'weðər/ *noun* [no plural]

the weather in a place is the temperature and other conditions such as sun, rain, or wind: *Did you have good weather on your trip?* | *The*

W

1 how you do or make something

*I'm not sure I'm doing this the **right way**. | The Internet is a **great way** to get information quickly. | Can you think of a **good way of** raising money for the school? | This chapter explains the **way that** the computer program works.*

GRAMMAR
way to do something
way of doing something
the way (that) someone/
something does something

2 how someone behaves, talks, feels etc

*Losing a job affects people in different **ways**. | Marge was looking at him **in a** strange **way**. | It was his **way of** saying he was sorry. | That's an awful **way** to treat his own daughter. | The **way that** he walks is just like the way his father walks.*

GRAMMAR
the way (that) somebody
does something
someone's way of doing
something
way to do something

5 the distance between two places

*Becky ran **all the way** home. | People don't always realize that San Francisco is a **long way** from Los Angeles. | The park is just a **little way** up the road.*

way

3 the road, path etc that you must follow in order to get to a place

*Are you sure that this is the **way**? | Excuse me, is this the **way to** the station? | We must have gone **the wrong way** – we should have taken St. John's Road. | Why don't you drive, since you **know the way**. | John went into a shop to **ask the way**.*

4 the direction that someone or something is moving or pointing towards

*"Which **way** should we turn when we get to Redmond Road?" "Turn left" | Come on, the shops are **this way**. | If you go **that way**, the hospital will be on the left side of the street. | I was facing **the wrong way**, so I didn't see her.*

*I was facing **the wrong way**, so I didn't see her.*

*John went into a shop to **ask the way**.*

PHRASES

by the way *spoken*
say this when you want to tell someone about something you have just remembered: *By the way, have you heard from Tanya since she left? | Oh, Michael, by the way, Jim called about an hour ago.*

no way! *spoken*
say this when you will not do or allow something: *You're not staying overnight at Ben's house. No way!*

in a way, in some ways
say this when you want to say something is true about a part of an event, a part of your feelings etc: *The holiday was great, but in a way I'll be glad to go back to work. | In some ways, we're a lot alike.*

on the way, on someone's way
if you do something on the way or on your way to somewhere, you stop somewhere and do it when you are going to another place: *He stopped for a cup of coffee on the way to work. | I can pick Kerry up – her house is on my way.*

on your way, on her way, on their way etc
if someone is on their way somewhere, they are travelling to somewhere: *Jack's on his way; he called to say he'd be here by ten.*

Jack's on his way; he called to say he'd be here by ten.

get your (own) way
to be able to do what you want, even when other people want to do something different: *If Hannah doesn't get her own way, she cries.*

get in the way
if something gets in the way, it stops you doing what you want to do: *Hunger and tiredness can get in the way of learning anything at school.*

out of the way
if something or someone is out of the way, it is not stopping you from going somewhere or seeing something: *She shouted, "Get out of the way!" | Here, let me move this bag out of the way.*

Here, let me move this bag out of the way.

in the way, in someone's way
if something is in the way or in your way, it is in front of you and stops you from going somewhere or seeing something: *A lot of people were standing in the way.*

A lot of people were standing in the way.

W

*weather was great! | You should drive more slowly in **wet weather**. | We had a week of lovely **hot weather**.*

weather-beat·en /'.. ˌ../ *adjective* made rough by the wind and the sun: *a weather-beaten face*

weather fore·cast /'.. ˌ../ *noun* a report that says what the weather is expected to be like: *The weather forecast for tomorrow isn't very good.*

weather fore·cast·er /'.. ˌ../ also **weath·er·man** /'weðəmæn $ 'weðə-mæn/, **weath·er·girl** /'weðəgɜːl $ 'weðəgəl/ *noun* someone whose job is to read the weather forecast on the television or radio

weave /wiːv/ *verb, past tense* **wove** /wəʊv $ woʊv/ or **weaved** *past participle* **woven** /'wəʊvən $ 'woʊvən/ or **weaved**   **1** to make material by crossing threads under and over each other: *The women sit together and weave rugs.* **2** to reach a place by moving around and between things: *Phil weaved through the crowd.*

web /web/ *noun*   **1** a net of thin threads that a SPIDER makes   **2** **the Web** the WORLD WIDE WEB; a system that connects computers around the world so that people can use the INTERNET

webbed /webd/ *adjective* webbed feet have skin between the toes: *Ducks have webbed feet.*

web·site /'websaɪt/ *noun* a place on the INTERNET where you can find out information about something: *Visit our website at www.awl-elt.com/dictionaries.*

we'd /wiːd/ the short form of 'we had' or 'we would': *We'd met her brother before. | We'd like to see a film tonight.*

wed·ding /'wedɪŋ/ *noun* a marriage ceremony: *I've been invited to Janet and Peter's wedding.*

wedding ring /'.. ˌ./ *noun* a ring that you wear to show that you are married

wedge¹ /wedʒ/ *noun* a piece of something that is thick at one end and pointed at the other end: *a wedge of chocolate cake*

wedge² *verb* to force something into a small space: *I wedged the book in at the end of the shelf.*

Wednes·day /'wenzdi/ *written abbrevi-* ation **Wed** *noun* the day of the week between Tuesday and Thursday: *Sorry, I can't go – I'm busy on Wednesday evening.*

weed¹ /wiːd/ *noun* a wild plant that grows in gardens, where it is not wanted

weed² *verb* to remove weeds from a place: *Mum was outside, weeding the flower bed.*

week /wiːk/ *noun*

1 a period of seven days. A week is usually considered to start on Monday in Britain, and on Sunday in the US: *I won't have time to finish it **this week**. | The exams start **next week**. | She's been seeing her new boyfriend for three weeks. | I'll talk to you **later in the week** (=in a few days).*

2 the days from Monday to Friday, when people work or study: *My parents don't let me go out **during the week**. | I don't have much free time **in the week**.*

USAGE

In British English, another word for **two weeks** is a **fortnight**.

week·day /'wiːkdeɪ/ *noun* any day of the week except Saturday and Sunday: *I work on weekdays.*

week·end /ˌwiːk'end $ 'wikend/ *noun*

Saturday and Sunday. In British English you do things at the weekend, and in American English you do things on the weekend: *Did you have a good weekend? | We always go to a club **at the weekend**. | They play tennis **on the weekend**.*

week·ly /'wiːkli/ *adjective, adverb* happening or done every week: *You will be paid weekly. | a weekly newspaper*

weep /wiːp/ *verb, past tense and past participle* **wept** /wept/ to cry: *Relatives were weeping outside the church.*

weigh /weɪ/ *verb*

1 if something weighs a particular amount, it is that weight: *How much does she weigh? | My suitcase weighed 20 kilos.*

2 to use a machine to find out how much something or someone weighs: *They weigh all the parcels*

before loading them into vans. | He weighs himself every morning.

PHRASAL VERB
weigh down
weigh someone down if something heavy weighs you down, it stops you from moving easily: *I moved slowly along the street with my bags weighing me down.*

weight /weɪt/ noun

GRAMMAR
the weight of something
1 how heavy someone or something is: *She worries about her weight. | What's the average weight of the parcels?*
2 weights heavy pieces of metal that people lift to make their muscles stronger

PHRASES
lose weight if you lose weight, you become lighter: *You need to lose some weight.*
put on weight if you put on weight, you become heavier: *John's put on a lot of weight since I last saw him.*

weight·lift·ing /'weɪt,lɪftɪŋ/ noun [no plural] the sport of lifting heavy weights

weir /wɪə $ wɪr/ noun a wall that is built across a river to control the flow of water

weird /wɪəd $ wɪrd/ adjective informal unusual and strange: *It was quite a weird experience.*

wel·come¹ /'welkəm/ adjective

GRAMMAR
welcome to do something
1 if you are welcome in a place, other people want you to be there and are friendly to you: *Strangers do not feel welcome in this town. | Everyone was kind and made me welcome* (=made me feel welcome).
2 if someone tells you that you are welcome to do something, they are telling you politely that you can do it: *You are all welcome to stay the night.*

PHRASES
welcome! spoken a friendly thing that you say to someone who has just arrived in a new place: *Welcome to London!*
you're welcome spoken used to reply

politely to someone who has just thanked you: *"Thanks for the meal." "You're welcome."*

welcome² verb
1 to say hello in a friendly way to someone who has just arrived: *Josh welcomed us with a big smile.*
2 if you welcome something, you are happy if it happens because you think it is good: *The school always welcomes suggestions from parents.*

welcome³ noun the way that you behave towards someone when they arrive: *The Queen received a warm welcome from the people of Japan.*

weld /weld/ verb to join metal objects together by heating them and pressing them together

wel·fare /'welfeə $ 'welfer/ noun [no plural] 1 formal your welfare is your health, comfort, and happiness: *The teachers were concerned about the child's welfare.* 2 AmE money that the government gives to people who cannot work

we'll /wiːl/ the short form of 'we will': *We'll be late.*

well¹ /wel/ adverb **better** /'betə $ 'betɚ/ **best** /best/
1 in a good or successful way ⇨ opposite BADLY: *I thought the whole team played well. | She did very well in her exams. | Did the meeting go well?* ⇨ see usage note at GOOD¹
2 a lot or completely: *Do you know him well? | I like my steak well cooked.*

PHRASES
as well also: *I bought a coat, and some shoes as well.*
as well as something in addition to something else: *He has been to Malaysia as well as Thailand.*
well done! used to tell someone that you are pleased with what they have done: *That was a great goal, Tim. Well done!*
may as well, might as well spoken used to say that you think you should do something because there is nothing else you can do: *We may as well go to the cinema.*
well after, well before spoken a long time after or before: *She didn't come home until well after eleven.*

W

well² *adjective* better, best

healthy and not ill: *I don't feel very well.* | *Is he well enough to go to school?*

PHRASES

very well thank you, very well thanks *spoken* used to reply when someone asks how you are: *"Hello Clare, how are you?" "Very well thanks, how are you?"*

it's just as well *spoken* used to say that something that happens is lucky or good, after or before saying why: *It's just as well you're not hungry, because we haven't got much to eat.*

well³

used when you want to pause before saying something, for example because you are not sure what to say: *"Who should I ask to the disco?" "Well, how about Carla?"*

PHRASE

oh well used to show that you accept a situation, even though it is not a good one: *Oh well, I can take the exam again next year.*

well⁴ *noun* a deep hole in the ground from which water or oil is taken

well-bal·anced /ˌ. '../ *adjective* someone who is well-balanced is sensible and not easily upset: *a happy, well-balanced child*

well-be·haved /ˌ. .'./ *adjective* a well-behaved child is polite and behaves well

well-be·ing /ˌ. '../ *noun* a feeling of being healthy and happy

well-built /ˌ. './ *adjective* someone who is well-built is big and strong ⇨ see picture on page 353

well-dressed /ˌ. './ *adjective* wearing good clothes: *a well-dressed TV presenter*

well-fed /ˌ. './ *adjective* getting plenty of good food: *The local cats look well-fed and healthy.*

wel·ling·tons /ˈwelɪŋtənz/ also **wellington boots** /ˈ... ˌ./ or **wellies** /ˈweliz/ *informal, plural noun* BrE long rubber boots that you wear to keep your feet dry; rubber boots AmE

well-kept /ˌ. './ *adjective* a well-kept place is neat and tidy: *a well-kept garden*

well-known /ˌ. './ *adjective* if someone or something is well-known, a lot of people know about them: *a well-known singer*

well-off /ˌ. './ *adjective* someone who is well-off has quite a lot of money: *She comes from quite a well-off family.*

well-paid /ˌ. './ *adjective* providing or getting a lot of money for a job: *Work in advertising is very well paid indeed.* | *a well-paid lawyer*

well-read /ˌwel 'red/ *adjective* someone who is well-read has read a lot and knows about many subjects

well-timed /ˌ. './ *adjective* done at the best moment: *Aldridge scored a well-timed goal – just before the final whistle.*

well-wish·er /ˈ. ˌ../ *noun* someone who shows that they want you to succeed or be happy and healthy: *Hundreds of well-wishers have left flowers at the hospital.*

went the past tense of GO

wept the past tense and past participle of WEEP

we're /wɪə $ wɪr/ the short form of 'we are': *We're late.*

were /wə; *strong* wɜː $ wɚ/ the past tense of BE which you use after 'you', 'we', and 'they'

weren't /wɜːnt $ wɚrnt/ the short form of 'were not': *We weren't very impressed by the concert.*

west /west/ *noun* 1 [no plural] the direction that you look in to see the sun go down 2 **the west** the western part of a country or area: *Rain is expected in the west.*
– **west** *adverb, adjective*: *The house faces west.* | *Los Angeles is on the west coast.*

west·bound /ˈwestbaʊnd/ *adjective* travelling towards the west: *westbound trains*

west·er·ly /ˈwestəli $ ˈwestɚli/ *adjective* 1 towards the west: *They travelled in a westerly direction.* 2 **westerly wind** a westerly wind blows from the west

west·ern¹ /ˈwestən $ ˈwestɚn/ *adjective* 1 in or from the west part of a country or area: *western Canada* 2 also **Western** in or from Europe or the United States: *the Western way of life*

western² noun a film about life in the 19th century in the western part of the US

west·ward /'westwəd $'westwəd/ also **west·wards** /'westwədz $'westwərdz/ adjective, adverb towards the west: *We travelled westwards for three days. | Go in a westward direction for three miles.*

wet¹ /wet/ adjective **wetter, wettest**
1 covered in water or another liquid: *Her hair was wet. | We got wet in the rain. | Try not to get your shoes wet.*
2 a wet day is a day when it is raining: *It was a horrible wet day.*
3 not yet dry: *My nail varnish is still wet.*

PHRASE
wet through, soaking wet very wet: *All my clothes were soaking wet.*

wet² verb, past tense and past participle **wet** or **wetted, wetting** to make something wet: *Paul wetted his lips and blew the trumpet as hard as he could.*

we've /wi:v/ the short form of 'we have': *We've been playing basketball.*

whale /weɪl/ noun a very large animal that lives in the sea

whale

wharf /wɔ:f $wɔrf/ noun, plural **wharves** /wɔ:vz $wɔrvz/ a structure that is built at the edge of a sea or river so that ships can stop next to it

what /wɒt $wʌt/ pronoun
1 asking about something: *What did you tell him? | What's that noise? | What colour is your new car? | What time is it?* ⇨ see usage note at WHICH
2 knowing or telling something: *I know what the answer is. | He told me what to do.*
3 the thing that: *I didn't like what he said. | What matters is that you tried.*
4 used to say very strongly what you think spoken: *What a great idea! | What a shame you were ill.*
5 used to show you did not hear what someone said, not very politely spoken: *"The game starts at 3."*

"What?" "I said the game starts at 3."
6 used when you are surprised or angry spoken: *"The key isn't in the door." "What? It must be!"*

PHRASES
what for? spoken why: *"Take your shoes off." "What for?" | What did you tell her for?*
what if spoken used to talk about something that might happen: *What if someone finds out about the money?*

what·ev·er¹ /wɒt'evə $wʌt'evər/ pronoun
anything, or any kind of thing: *We could do whatever we liked. | Give him whatever he wants. | Whatever problems you have (=it doesn't matter what they are), we are here to help.*

whatever² BrE, **what·so·ev·er** AmE /,wɒtsəʊ'evə $,wʌtsoʊ'evər/ adverb formal used to say strongly that there is none of something: *There is no evidence whatsoever of drug-taking at the college.*

wheat /wi:t/ noun [no plural] a plant that is used to produce grain for making flour

wheel¹ /wi:l/ noun
one of the round things under a car, bicycle etc that turn when it moves along: *A tricycle has three wheels.* ⇨ see picture at CAR

wheel² verb to push something that has wheels so that it moves along: *I had to wheel my bicycle home.*

wheel·bar·row /'wi:l,bærəʊ $'wil,bæroʊ/ noun a container with one wheel at the front that you use outdoors for carrying heavy things

wheel·chair /'wi:ltʃeə $'wil-tʃer/ noun a chair with wheels that is used by someone who cannot walk ⇨ see picture at RAMP

wheeze /wi:z/ verb to breathe with difficulty, making a whistling sound: *The old man coughed and wheezed.*

when /wen/ adverb
1 asking or saying what time something happens: *When did you get back? | When's the next train? | She didn't tell us when she would be leaving.*

W

2 at the time that something happens: *I was very tired when I got home.* | *Call me when the programme starts.* | *When I was younger I hated football.*

when·ev·er /wen'evə $ wen-'evɚ/ *adverb*
1 every time: *This picture will remind me of you whenever I look at it.*
2 at any time: *The students can use the music rooms whenever they like.* | *We can go whenever you're ready.*

where /weə $ wer/ *adverb*
1 asking or saying which place: *"Where's Rosa?" "Upstairs, I think."* | *Where are you going for your holiday?* | *I don't know where to put everything.* | *This is where we hold our meetings.* | *I showed the police the place where the accident happened.*
2 used when talking about one part of a story: *I liked the bit where they were sleeping in the tent and it fell down.*

where·a·bouts¹ /ˌweərə'bauts $ 'werə,bauts/ *adverb spoken* used to ask about a place: *Whereabouts are you going in Spain?*
whereabouts² /'weərəbauts $ 'wer↓əbauts/ *plural noun spoken* the place where someone is: *His exact whereabouts are unknown.*

wher·ev·er /weər'evə $ wer-'evɚ/ *adverb*
1 in every place: *They followed us wherever we went.* | *These plants grow wherever the ground is wet.*
2 in any place: *You can sit wherever you like.*

whet /wet/ *verb* **whetted, whetting; whet someone's appetite** to make someone want more of something by letting them try it or see what it is like: *This book has really whetted my appetite for science fiction.*

wheth·er /'weðə $ 'weðɚ/
asking if something is true or happens, or saying that something is true or happens: *I asked Harriet whether she was coming to the*

party **or not.** | *I'm not sure whether that would be a good idea.* | *I can't decide **whether to** go **or not.***

which /wɪtʃ/
1 asking or explaining about the particular thing you are talking about: *Which book did you like best?* | *Which is your car?* | *I'm not sure which class she's in.*
2 used when giving more information about something: *This is a new car which uses electricity, not petrol.* | *This is the book which I was talking about.* | *Sheila was looking for her keys, which she had put down somewhere.* | *He'll be able to stay for two whole weeks, which will be nice.*

USAGE which, what
Which and **what** are both used when you are trying to choose or decide something. Use **which** when you are choosing from a limited number of possibilities: *Which house does Tom live in?* | ***Which of** these dresses do you like best?* Use **what** when you are choosing from an unlimited number of possibilities: *What name have they given the baby?* | *What is the answer to question 12?* **Which** can be followed by 'of' but **what** cannot.

which·ev·er /wɪtʃ'evə $ wɪtʃ-'evɚ/ *pronoun*
any of the things or people in a group: *Use whichever shampoo suits you best.* | *I'll be happy whichever team wins* (=it does not matter which team wins).

whiff /wɪf/ *noun* a slight smell: *a whiff of cigarette smoke*

while¹ /waɪl/
1 during the time that something is happening: *He started a business while he was still at school.* | *You must have phoned while I was asleep.* | *She listens to music while she works.*
2 *formal* although: *While it is possible to make a lot of money from writing, it's not easy.*

while² *noun* **a while** a short period of time: *We waited a while, but Anna didn't arrive.*

whilst /waɪlst/ WHILE

whim /wɪm/ *noun* a sudden feeling that you want to do something, without any particular reason: *I went to see the film on a whim.*

whim·per /'wɪmpə $ 'wɪmpɚ/ *verb* to make gentle crying sounds: *The dog whimpered and looked at his master.*

whine /waɪn/ *verb* **1** to complain about something in an annoying voice: *Stop whining and get on with your work!* **2** to make a long, high, unhappy sound – **whine** *noun*: *The dog gave a small whine.*

whinge /wɪndʒ/ *verb* BrE to complain in an annoying way about something unimportant: *She's been whinging to the tutor about the amount of homework we get.*

whip¹ /wɪp/ *noun* a long thin piece of leather with a handle that is used for hitting people or animals

whip² *verb* **whipped, whipping** **1** to hit a person or animal with a whip **2** AmE informal to defeat someone easily: *The Dallas Cowboys whipped the Redskins last week.*

whir the American spelling of WHIRR

whirl /wɜːl $ wɝːl/ *verb* to turn around quickly, or to make something turn around quickly: *Snowflakes were whirling down from the sky.*

whirl·pool /'wɜːlpuːl $ 'wɝːlpul/ *noun* water that turns around and around very quickly, pulling things towards it and then down into it

whirl·wind¹ /'wɜːl,wɪnd $ 'wɝːl,wɪnd/ *noun* a strong wind that turns around and around very quickly and causes a lot of damage

whirlwind² *adjective* whirlwind events are exciting because they happen very quickly: *After a whirlwind romance, they got married.*

whirr BrE, **whir** AmE /wɜː $ wɝː/ *verb* if a machine whirrs, it makes a continuous low sound: *A helicopter whirred overhead.*

whisk¹ /wɪsk/ *verb* **1** to mix eggs or cream in a bowl very quickly so that air is mixed in: *Whisk the cream until it is thick.* ⇨ *see picture on page 344* **2** to take someone somewhere very quickly: *They whisked her to hospital.*

whisk² *noun* a small kitchen tool that you use to whisk eggs or cream ⇨ *see picture on page 344*

whis·ker /'wɪskə $ 'wɪskɚ/ *noun* **1** an animal's whiskers are the long stiff hairs that grow near its mouth **2 whiskers** the hair that grows on a man's face

whis·ky /'wɪski/ *noun* a strong alcoholic drink

whis·per¹ /'wɪspə $ 'wɪspɚ/ *verb*

> **GRAMMAR**
> **whisper something to someone**

to say something very quietly to someone, so that other people cannot hear: *The girls were whispering at the back of the class.* | *James whispered something **to** Susie and she laughed.* | *He **whispered** something **in** my ear.*

whisper² *noun* a very quiet voice: *I can hear whispers at the back of the room.*

whis·tle¹ /'wɪsəl/ *verb*

1 to make a high sound or tune by blowing air out through your lips: *Terry **whistled a tune** as he worked.* **2** if something whistles, it makes a high sound because it is moving very fast: *The wind whistled in the trees.*

whistle² *noun*

a small object that makes a high sound when you blow into it: *The teacher **blew** her **whistle** for the game to start.*

white¹ /waɪt/ *adjective* **1** something that is white is the colour of milk, snow, or salt **2** someone who is white has naturally pale skin: *white and black children playing together* **3** BrE white coffee has milk or cream in it

white² *noun* a white colour: *She was dressed completely in white.*

white-col·lar /ˌ. '../ *adjective* white-collar workers do jobs in offices, banks etc

whit·tle /'wɪtl/ *verb* **whittle something down** to gradually reduce a number or an amount: *I've whittled the list down to just four people now.*

whizz¹ BrE, **whiz** AmE, /wɪz/ *verb* informal to move very quickly: *A bullet whizzed past his ear.*

whizz² BrE, **whiz** AmE *noun* informal **be a whizz at something** to be very good at something: *Peter is a whiz at math.*

who /huː/ pronoun

1 asking or saying which person: *Who's your favourite singer?* | *Who told you that?* | *I know who the card is from.*

2 used when giving more information about someone: *That's the girl who was nasty to me.* | *She's visiting her friend Deborah, who lives in London.*

who'd /huːd/ the short form of 'who had' or 'who would': *Nobody knew who'd done it.*

who·ev·er /huːˈevə $ huˈevɚ/ pronoun

1 the person who: *Whoever did this must be crazy.* | *There will be a reward for whoever finds the missing money.*

2 any person: *My parents said I could invite whoever I liked to the party.*

whole¹ /həʊl $ hoʊl/ adjective

all of something ⇨ *same meaning* ENTIRE: *I ate a whole loaf of bread.* | *We spent the whole day on the beach.* | *The whole class was shouting.*

whole² noun

1 the whole of something all of something: *The whole of my body ached.*

2 on the whole generally or usually: *On the whole, girls grow up faster than boys.*

whole·heart·ed /ˌ. ˈ../ adjective formal wholehearted support or agreement is total

−wholeheartedly adverb: *I agree wholeheartedly with your mother.*

whole·meal /ˈhəʊlmiːl $ ˈhoʊlmiːl/ adjective *BrE* wholemeal flour, bread etc is made using all the parts of the grains of wheat ⇨ *same meaning* WHOLEWHEAT

whole·sale /ˈhəʊlseɪl $ ˈhoʊlseɪl/ adjective affecting a lot of things or people, often in a bad way: *the wholesale destruction that occurred during the war*

whole·sal·er /ˈhəʊlˌseɪlə $ ˈhoʊlˌseɪlɚ/ noun a person or company that buys things in large quantities and sells them to shops

whole·some /ˈhəʊlsəm $ ˈhoʊlsəm/ adjective good for your health: *We eat only wholesome, natural foods.*

whole·wheat /ˈhəʊlwiːt $ ˈhoʊlwit/ adjective the American word for WHOLEMEAL

who'll /huːl/ the short form of 'who will': *Who'll be next?*

whol·ly /ˈhəʊl-li $ ˈhoʊli/ adverb formal completely: *The mistake was wholly my fault.*

whom /huːm/ pronoun formal

used as the object of a verb or PREPOSITION to mean 'who': *To whom was the letter addressed?*

USAGE
It is very formal to use **whom**.

who're /ˈhuːə $ ˈhuːɚ/ the short form of 'who are': *Who're you going to vote for?*

who's /huːz/ the short form of 'who is' or 'who has': *Who's your favourite film star?* | *Who's taken my pen?*

who've /huːv/ the short form of 'who have': *people who've got problems*

why /waɪ/ adverb

asking or giving the reason for something: *Why are you so late?* | *"I can't come to lessons tomorrow." "Why not?"* | *He didn't know why they hated him.* | *I told her why I wanted to speak to her.*

PHRASES

why not, why don't you? informal used to make a suggestion: *Why not try giving up coffee?* | *Why don't you check the figures again − you might have made a mistake.*

why not spoken informal used to accept an invitation or suggestion: *"Coming to the park with us?" "Yes, why not."*

wick·ed /ˈwɪkɪd/ adjective **1** very bad or evil: *Who would do such a wicked thing?* **2** informal very good: *We had a wicked time!*

wick·et /ˈwɪkɪt/ noun one of the sets of sticks that the BOWLER tries to hit with the ball in a game of CRICKET

wide¹ /waɪd/ adjective

1 measuring a large distance from one side to the other ⇨ *opposite*

NARROW¹: *a wide bed* | *a shirt with wide sleeves* | *The street is not wide enough to park in.*

2 used to talk about the distance from one side of something to the other: *The river is over a mile wide here.* | **How wide** *is the path?*

3 including a lot of different people or things: *You can study a **wide range** of subjects.*

wide² *adverb*

1 **wide open, wide apart** open as far as possible, or as far as possible apart: *The window was **wide open**.* | *She held her arms **wide apart**.*

2 **wide awake** completely awake: *Suddenly I was **wide awake**.*

wide-eyed /ˌ. ˈ./ *adjective, adverb* with your eyes wide open because you are very surprised or interested: *The children stared wide-eyed at the magician.*

wide·ly /ˈwaɪdli/ *adverb* in a lot of different places or by a lot of people: *Johnson was widely expected to be made team captain.*

wid·en /ˈwaɪdn/ *verb* to become wider, or to make something wider ⇨ *opposite* NARROW²: *The river begins to widen here.* | *They had to widen the entrance.*

wide·spread /ˈwaɪdspred/ *adjective* happening in many places: *The use of computers in classrooms is becoming more widespread.*

wid·ow /ˈwɪdəʊ $ ˈwɪdoʊ/ *noun* a woman whose husband is dead

wid·owed /ˈwɪdəʊd $ ˈwɪdoʊd/ *adjective* if someone is widowed, their husband or wife is dead

wid·ow·er /ˈwɪdəʊə $ ˈwɪdoʊɚ/ *noun* a man whose wife is dead

width /wɪdθ/ *noun* the distance from one side of something to the other: *He measured the length and width of the desk.*

wield /wiːld/ *verb* **1** to have and use power and influence: *The United States wields enormous political influence.* **2** to hold or use a weapon: *a gang of young men wielding knives*

wife /waɪf/ *noun, plural* **wives** /waɪvz/ the woman that a man is married to: *My brother and his wife came to visit us last week.*

wig /wɪg/ *noun* something that is made to look like hair, which someone wears on their head

wig

wig·gle /ˈwɪgəl/ *verb informal* to move part of your body from side to side or up and down: *She wiggled her bottom as she danced.*

wild¹ /waɪld/ *adjective*

1 a wild animal or plant is living or growing in natural conditions, rather than being looked after by people: *A dingo is a kind of wild dog.* | *wild strawberries*

2 very excited, angry, or happy, so that you cannot control your behaviour: *The children are a bit wild today.* | *When she saw them together she went wild* (=behaved in a very angry way).

PHRASES

a wild guess a guess that you make without knowing any facts, so that it may be completely wrong: *He asked me how old I thought he was and I made a **wild guess**.*

be wild about something/someone *spoken* to like something or someone very much: *I'm not **wild about** rock music.*

wild² *noun* **1** **in the wild** in natural conditions, not looked after by people: *In the wild, lions hunt in groups.* **2** **the wilds** areas that are very far from towns and cities and where very few people live: *in the wilds of northern China*

wil·der·ness /ˈwɪldənəs $ ˈwɪldɚnəs/ *noun* [no plural] a large natural area of land with no buildings: *Fifty years ago, this area was just a wilderness.*

wild·life /ˈwaɪldlaɪf/ *noun* [no plural] animals that live in natural conditions

wild·ly /ˈwaɪldli/ *adverb* in a way that is careless and not controlled: *He drives rather wildly.*

wil·ful *BrE*, **willful** *AmE* /ˈwɪlfəl/ *adjective* **1** doing what you want even though people tell you not to: *His daughter became a wilful teenager.*

2 *formal* done deliberately and without caring about the possible harmful results: *This act of wilful damage could have caused an accident.*

will¹ /wɪl/ *modal verb,* shortened form **'ll** *negative* **will not** or **won't**

1 likely to happen in the future: *Russ will be back next Tuesday.* | *I think I'll go to Spain again next year.* | *The film will be showing at a cinema near you next week.* | *Greg won't manage to finish his course.*

2 planning to do something in the future: *"Someone's at the door." "I'll get it."* | *Sean won't play with the other boys.* | *I will explain how to perform the experiment next week.*

3 being able to do something: *The new plane will carry 550 passengers.* | *My car won't start.* | *I don't know if I'll be able to come to your party.*

4 telling someone to do something: *Will you be quiet please, class.* | *Will you take me back to the hotel?*

will² *noun*

a legal document in which you say who you want to have your money and property after you die: *Her grandfather left her some money **in** his **will**.*

PHRASES

against your will: *Nobody can make her get married **against** her **will*** (=if she does not want to get married).

of your own free will: *I came here **of** my **own** free **will*** (=because I wanted to, not because I was forced).

the/your will to do something if you have the will to do something, especially something difficult, you strongly want to do it: *She is very ill, but has not lost her **will to** live.*

will³ *verb* if you will something to happen, you try to make it happen by thinking about it very hard: *We were all willing England to win.*

willful the American spelling of WILFUL

will·ing /'wɪlɪŋ/ *adjective*

GRAMMAR
willing to do something

if you are willing to do something,

you will do it if someone wants you to do it: *I **am willing to** help in any way that I can.*
–**willingly** *adverb*: *I will willingly lend you the money for the car.*
–**willingness** *noun* [no plural]: *He wanted to show his willingness to change.*

wil·low /'wɪləʊ $ 'wɪloʊ/ *noun* a tree with very long thin branches that hang down

will·pow·er /'wɪl.paʊə $ 'wɪl.paʊɚ/ *noun* [no plural] the ability to make yourself do something even if it is difficult or unpleasant: *Losing weight takes a lot of willpower.*

wilt /wɪlt/ *verb* if a plant wilts, it becomes soft and bends because it needs water

wilt

wil·y /'waɪli/ *adjective* **wilier, wiliest** clever at getting what you want

wimp /wɪmp/ *noun informal* someone who is afraid to do things: *Oh, come on. Don't be such a wimp!*

win¹ /wɪn/ *verb, past tense and past participle* **won** /wʌn/ **winning**

GRAMMAR
win at something
win (something) by something

1 to be the best or first in a game, competition, or fight ⇨ *opposite* LOSE (3): *Mark's team won the basketball tournament.* | *Laurie always **wins at** cards.* | *We **won** the quiz **by** 12 points.* | *We always knew we would win the war.*

2 to get a prize in a game or competition: *I won a free trip to New York!* ⇨ *see usage note at* GAIN¹

PHRASAL VERB
win over
win someone over to persuade someone to like you or support you: *It took me quite a while to **win** the children **over**.*

win² *noun* when a team or player wins something: *We've only had two wins this year.*

wince /wɪns/ *verb* to suddenly change the expression on your face when you see or remember something painful or embarrassing: *He winced as he remembered his embarrassing mistake.*

wind¹ /wɪnd/ *noun*

1 air that you can feel moving around you: *It was hard to hear him because of the wind.* | *A cold wind was blowing.* | *The strong winds have caused quite a lot of damage.*
2 [no plural] air or gas in your stomach that feels uncomfortable

wind² /waɪnd/ *verb, past tense and past participle* **wound** /waʊnd/

> **GRAMMAR**
> **wind something round/around something**
> **wind up/down/along etc a place**

1 to wrap something long and thin around another thing many times: *I wound some sticky tape around the handle.*
2 also **wind up** to make a machine or clock work by turning a small handle around several times: *You wind the toy using this key.* | *We had to wind the clock up once a week.*
3 if a road or river winds somewhere, it goes in that direction and has many bends: *The path winds up the mountain.*

> **PHRASAL VERBS**
> **wind down**
> 1 to gradually end: *After he left, the party started to wind down.*
> 2 to relax: *Exercise can help you wind down after work.*
> **wind up**
> 1 wind something up to end something such as a meeting: *I think it's time to wind up the meeting.*
> 2 wind someone up *BrE informal* to make someone annoyed or angry: *He deliberately does that to wind me up!*

wind·fall /'wɪndfɔːl/ *noun* an amount of money that you get when you do not expect it

wind·mill /'wɪnd,mɪl/ *noun* a tall structure with parts that are turned by the wind, which is used to crush grain or make electricity

win·dow /'wɪndəʊ $ 'wɪndoʊ/ *noun*

1 a space in the side of a building or car with glass across it, where light can come in: *I looked out of the window.* | *You could see them through the window.* | *She was standing at the kitchen window.* ⇨ see pictures on pages 342 and 343
2 one of the areas on a computer SCREEN where you can do different types of work

window shop·ping /'.. ,../ *noun* [no plural] when you look at things in shops, without intending to buy them

win·dow·sill /'wɪndəʊ,sɪl $ 'wɪndoʊ-,sɪl/ *noun* a shelf at the bottom of a window

wind·screen /'wɪndskriːn/ *BrE*, **windshield** /'wɪndʃiːld/ *AmE, noun* the large window at the front of a vehicle ⇨ see picture at CAR

windscreen wip·er *BrE*, **windshield wiper** *AmE* /'.. ,../ *noun* a long object that moves across a windscreen to remove rain ⇨ see picture at CAR

wind·surf·er /'wɪnd,sɜːfə $ 'wɪnd-,sɜːfɚ/ *noun* someone who goes windsurfing

wind·surf·ing /'wɪnd,sɜːfɪŋ $ 'wɪnd-,sɜːfɪŋ/ *noun* [no plural] the sport of sailing across water by standing on a board and holding onto a sail: *I go windsurfing most weekends.*

wind·swept /'wɪndswept/ *adjective* a windswept place is very windy

wind·y /'wɪndi/ *adjective* **windier, windiest** if the weather is windy, there is a lot of wind: *It was too windy to go for a walk.*

wine /waɪn/ *noun* an alcoholic drink that is made from GRAPES: *a glass of red wine*

wing /wɪŋ/ *noun*

1 one of the two parts of a bird's or insect's body that it uses for flying: *The eagle spread its wings and flew away.*
2 one of the two flat parts that stick out of the sides of a plane: *I had a seat next to the wing.* ⇨ see picture on page 349

wing·span /'wɪŋspæn/ *noun* the distance from the end of one wing to the end of the other

wink /wɪŋk/ *verb*
to close and open
one eye quickly,
especially to show
that you are joking
or being friendly:
*He winked at
Eddie.*
– **wink** *noun*: *"You
might see Julie there," said Jon, with a
wink.*

win·ner /'wɪnə $'wɪnɚ/ *noun* the
person who wins a race, game, or
competition: *The winner of each race
will get a prize.*

win·nings /'wɪnɪŋz/ *plural noun* money
that you win in a game or competition:
She went to collect her winnings.

win·ter /'wɪntə $'wɪntɚ/ *noun*
the season between autumn and
spring, when the weather is coldest:
*It gets very cold here **in winter**. | This
has been the coldest winter since
1947. | We don't travel very much **in
the winter**.*

win·try /'wɪntri/ *adjective* wintry weather is cold or snowy weather

wipe /waɪp/ *verb*

GRAMMAR
**wipe something from/off some-
thing**

1 to move a cloth or your hand over
something, in order to clean it: *Sue
wiped the table. | He **wiped** the dirt
from his face with his hand. | **Wipe**
those crumbs **off** the table.*
2 to remove all the sound, film, or information from a TAPE or computer
DISK: *Make sure you don't wipe that
video.*

PHRASE
wipe your feet to clean the bottom
of your shoes by standing on something and rubbing your feet on it:
***Wipe** your **feet** before you come in
the house.*

PHRASAL VERBS
wipe out
wipe something out *informal* to destroy something completely: *The
floods **wiped out** whole areas.*
wipe up
wipe something up to remove
liquid from a surface using a cloth:
*I **wiped up** the water I had spilt.*

wip·er /'waɪpə $'waɪpɚ/ a WINDSCREEN
WIPER

wire¹ /waɪə $waɪɚ/ *noun*
1 metal that is long and thin like string
or thread: *We tied the posts together
with wire.*
2 a long thin piece of metal that is
used to carry electricity: *One of the
wires was not connected correctly.*

wire² also **wire up** *verb* to connect
electrical wires so that a piece of equipment will work: *Dad wired up the lights
in my flat for me.*

wir·y /'waɪəri/ *adjective* wirier, wiriest
1 someone who is wiry is thin but strong
2 wiry hair is stiff and curly

wis·dom /'wɪzdəm/ *noun* [no plural]
1 the ability to understand things and
make good decisions because you have
a lot of experience: *a man of great
wisdom* 2 whether an action is sensible: *I was not sure about the wisdom of
this plan.*

wise¹ /waɪz/ *adjective*

GRAMMAR
it is wise to do something

1 a wise decision or action is a sensible one: *Do you think that was a
wise decision? | I think **it would be
wise to** ask your parents for permission first.*
2 a wise person makes good decisions
and gives good advice because they
have a lot of experience: *Your grandfather is a very wise man.*
– **wisely** *adverb*: *She wisely chose to
ignore his advice.*

wise² *verb* wise up *informal* to realize
what is really true or what a situation is
really like: *If you think college life is all
drinking and partying, you'd better wise
up.*

wise·crack /'waɪzkræk/ *noun* informal
something funny that someone says,
especially when they should be more
serious

wish¹ /wɪʃ/ *verb*

GRAMMAR
wish (that)
to want something to happen even
though it is unlikely: *I wish we lived
in London. | Sally **wished that** she
had a sister like Kate.*

PHRASES

wish someone luck to tell someone that you hope they will have good luck and be successful: *I've got exams tomorrow – wish me luck!*

could wish for, couldn't wish for used to say strongly that something is as good as it could possibly be: *It was the best birthday that anyone could wish for.* | *I couldn't wish for a better friend.*

wish² *noun, plural* wishes

1 **make a wish** to secretly say to yourself that you hope that something happens: *I made a wish as I blew out the candles on my birthday cake.*

2 **against someone's wishes** if you do something against someone's wishes, you do it even though they do not want you to: *You took the car against my wishes.*

3 **have no wish to do something** to definitely not want to do something: *I have no wish to spend the summer holidays at home.*

4 **best wishes** a friendly phrase that you write before your name in cards and letters

wish·ful think·ing /ˌwɪʃfəl ˈθɪŋkɪŋ/ *noun [no plural]* when someone hopes that something good might happen, even though it is impossible

wisp /wɪsp/ *noun* 1 a small thin piece of hair 2 a small thin line of smoke or cloud: *They could see a wisp of smoke in the distance.*

wist·ful /ˈwɪstfəl/ *adjective written* a little sad because you know you cannot have something you want
–**wistfully** *adverb*: *She looked wistfully back at the dress in the shop window.*

wit /wɪt/ *noun* 1 *[no plural]* the ability to say things that are clever and funny 2 **wits** someone's ability to make good decisions quickly when they have to: *You have to use your wits in this job.* 3 **scare someone out of their wits** to frighten someone very much

witch /wɪtʃ/ *noun, plural* witches a woman who has magic powers

witch·craft /ˈwɪtʃkrɑːft $ ˈwɪtʃkræft/ *noun [no plural]* the use of magic, usually to do bad things

with /wɪð $ wɪθ/ *preposition*

1 when people are together: *Can I come with you?* | *Go and play with your sister.* | *I'm going to the cinema with Jack.*

2 when things are mixed together: *Mix the paint with a little water.* | *We had chicken with rice.*

3 arguing or fighting against someone: *He disagreed with me.* | *We used to fight with each other a lot.*

4 using something: *Cut round the shapes with scissors.* | *He pushed the door open with his foot.*

5 having something: *a girl with long blonde hair* | *a house with a garden* | *people with problems*

6 because of a feeling: *She was shaking with fear* (=she was shaking because she was so afraid).

with·draw /wɪðˈdrɔː $ wɪθˈdrɔ/ *verb formal* **withdrew** /-ˈdruː/ **withdrawn** /-ˈdrɔːn/ 1 to take something out or away: *He withdrew £100 from the bank.* 2 if soldiers withdraw from an area, they leave it 3 to not take part in something that you intended to take part in: *He withdrew from the race because of a back injury.*

with·draw·al /wɪðˈdrɔːəl $ wɪθˈdrɔːəl/ *noun* 1 when you take some of your money out of a bank: *You have made three withdrawals this month.* 2 when soldiers leave an area 3 *[no plural]* when someone who has been taking a drug regularly stops taking it and feels ill

with·drawn¹ /wɪðˈdrɔːn $ wɪθˈdrɔn/ *adjective* quiet and not wanting to talk to people: *He became very withdrawn after his father died.*

withdrawn² the past participle of WITHDRAW

withdrew the past tense of WITHDRAW

with·er /ˈwɪðə $ ˈwɪðɚ/ *verb* if a plant withers, its leaves become dry and it starts to die

withheld the past tense and past participle of WITHHOLD

with·hold /wɪðˈhəʊld $ wɪθˈhoʊld/ *verb formal, past tense and past participle* **withheld** /-ˈheld/ to not give something to someone: *The doctors decided to withhold treatment.*

W

with·in /wɪð'ɪn/ preposition

1 before the end of a period of time: *Your goods will be delivered within 28 days.*

2 inside a particular distance and not beyond it: *I stood within two feet of him!*

3 formal inside: *Only a few people within the company knew about the plans.*

with·out /wɪð'aʊt/ adverb, preposition

1 not having something: *I left home in the morning without my bag.* | *You can't travel on this train without a ticket* (=you must have a ticket to travel on this train). | *people without jobs*

2 not having someone with you: *Sammy was late, so we left without him.*

3 showing what someone does not do: *He left without saying goodbye.* | *Suddenly, without warning* (=not telling other people), *the soldiers started shooting.*

with·stand /wɪð'stænd $wɪθ'stænd/ verb formal, past tense and past participle **withstood** /-'stʊd/ to not be harmed or affected by something: *These dishes can withstand high temperatures.*

withstood the past tense and past participle of WITHSTAND

wit·ness¹ /'wɪtnəs/ noun, plural **witnesses 1** formal someone who saw an accident or a crime: *There were no witnesses to the murder.* **2** someone who gives information in a court of law

witness² verb formal to see something happen, especially an accident or a crime: *Did anyone witness the attack?*

witness box BrE, **witness stand** AmE /'.. ./ noun the place where someone stands to give information in a court of law

wit·ty /'wɪti/ adjective **wittier, wittiest** clever and funny: *He tried to think of a witty remark to make.*

wives the plural of WIFE

wiz·ard /'wɪzəd $'wɪzɚd/ noun **1** a man who has magic powers **2** informal someone who is very good at doing something: *a chess wizard*

wob·ble /'wɒbəl $'wɑbəl/ verb to move from side to side in an unsteady way: *She wobbled along the lane on her bicycle.*

wob·bly /'wɒbli $'wɑbli/ adjective **wobblier, wobbliest** moving from side to side in an unsteady way: *a wobbly chair*

wok /wɒk $wɑk/ noun a large round pan used in Chinese cooking

woke the past tense of WAKE

woken the past participle of WAKE

wolf /wʊlf/ noun, plural **wolves** /wʊlvz/ a wild animal that is like a large dog ⇨ see picture on page 339

wolves the plural of WOLF

wom·an /'wʊmən/ plural **women** /'wɪmɪn/ noun
an adult female person: *Diana was a very beautiful woman.*

wom·an·iz·er also **womaniser** BrE /'wʊmənaɪzə $'wʊmə,naɪzɚ/ noun a man who has sexual relationships with a lot of women

womb /wuːm/ noun the part of a woman's body where a baby grows before it is born

women the plural of WOMAN

won the past tense and past participle of WIN

won·der¹ /'wʌndə $'wʌndɚ/ verb

GRAMMAR
wonder why/where/what etc
to think about something you do not know, and want to know it: *We were wondering where you were.* | *I wonder what this switch does?*

wonder² noun **1** [no plural] a feeling of surprise or admiration: *I watched the performance with wonder.* **2** no wonder spoken used to say that something does not surprise you: *No wonder you're cold – you've got no shoes on!* **3** something that is very impressive: *the wonders of modern science*

won·der·ful /'wʌndəfəl $'wʌndɚfəl/ adjective extremely good: *It was wonderful to see him again.*

won't /wəʊnt $woʊnt/ the short form of 'will not': *This won't take long.*

wood /wʊd/ noun **1** the material that trees are made of, which is used to make

things: *All the furniture is made of wood.*
2 also **woods** a small forest: *We got lost in the woods.* ⇨ *see picture on page 348*

wood·ed /'wʊdɪd/ *adjective* covered with trees: *They walked through a wooded valley.*

wood·en /'wʊdn/ *adjective* made from wood: *a wooden door*

wood·land /'wʊdlənd/ *noun* an area of trees

wood·peck·er /'wʊd,pekə $ 'wʊd-,pekə/ *noun* a bird that uses its long beak to make holes in trees

wood·wind /'wʊd,wɪnd/ *noun* woodwind instruments are musical instruments shaped like straight tubes which you blow into

wood·work /'wʊdwɜːk $ 'wʊdwɚk/ *noun [no plural]* the parts of a building that are made of wood: *A lot of the woodwork was rotten and had to be replaced.*

wood·worm /'wʊdwɜːm $ 'wʊdwɚm/ *noun* an insect that makes holes in wood

wool /wʊl/ *noun [no plural]* the soft thick hair of a sheep, which is made into thread: *She bought five balls of red wool.*

wool·len *BrE*, **woolen** *AmE* /'wʊlən/ *adjective* made of wool: *woollen socks*

wool·ly *BrE*, **wooly** *AmE* /'wʊli/ *adjective informal* made of wool: *a woolly hat*

word /wɜːd $ wɚd/ *noun*
a group of sounds or letters that have a particular meaning: *The only word she said was "yes".* | *I don't understand all these long words.*

PHRASES
not say a word, **not understand a word** to say nothing at all or understand nothing at all: *She hasn't said a word all morning.*

a word of advice, **a word of warning** something that you say to advise or warn someone: *Here's a word of advice – never trust a salesman.*

have a word with someone *spoken* to talk to someone, usually about something that needs doing: *I'll have a word with my father, and ask if he can help you.*

in other words used when you are explaining what something means in a different way: *The car would cost £7000 – in other words half her salary.*

word for word if you repeat something word for word, you say it using exactly the same words: *I want you to tell me what she said word for word.*

word pro·cess·or /'. ˌ.../ *noun* a small computer that you use for writing

wore the past tense of WEAR

work[1] ⇨ *see box on next page*

work[2] /wɜːk $ wɚk/ *noun*
1 *[no plural]* activity that involves effort: *Thank you for all your hard work.* | *Come on – we've still got a lot of work to do.*
2 *[no plural]* something that you do in order to earn money: *What kind of work would you like to do when you leave school?* ⇨ *see usage note at JOB*
3 *[no plural]* the place where you do your job: *Paul isn't here – he's at work.* | *I go to work at eight o'clock.*
4 *[no plural]* the time when you are doing your job: *I'll meet you after work.*
5 *[no plural]* the things that you write or produce: *Your work is improving.*

PHRASES
work of art something such as a painting or SCULPTURE: *He has a collection of works of art.*
a piece of work something that you have written or produced: *This essay is an excellent piece of work.*
be in work to have a job: *Are you in work at the moment?*
be out of work, **be looking for work** to not have a job: *Bill has been out of work for six months.*

work·a·ble /'wɜːkəbəl $ 'wɚkəbəl/ *adjective* a workable plan or system will work effectively and be successful

work·a·hol·ic /ˌwɜːkə'hɒlɪk $ ˌwɚkə-'hɒlɪk/ *noun informal* someone who spends all their time working

worked up /ˌ. '. / *adjective informal* very upset or angry: *I don't see why you're getting so worked up about it.*

work·er /'wɜːkə $ 'wɚkə/ *noun* someone who works for a company or organization, but is not a manager: *The workers at the factory are asking for more money.*

work·force /'wɜːkfɔːs $ 'wɚkfɔrs/

W

①to do a job in order to earn money

I **work in** a bank. | Where do you **work**? | Do you like **working for** your father? | Steve gave up farming and now **works as** an engineer. | My father **worked at** the same place all his life.

GRAMMAR
work in/at a place
work for someone
work as something

②if a machine works, it is not broken

Does that old radio still **work**? | My computer isn't **working** – can you check what's wrong with it?

work

③if an idea or plan works, it gives you the results that you want

She went on a diet to lose weight, but it didn't **work**. | We have to think of another solution. This isn't **working**.

④to do something that needs effort in order to achieve a result

You have to **work** hard to pass your exams. | Tom was busy **working** in the garden.

W

PHRASAL VERBS

work on
to try to produce or repair something: The band are **working on** some new songs. | Can I watch you **work on** your car?

work out
1 to calculate an amount: I will **work out** how much money each person owes. | Give me the calculator and I'll **work** it **out** for you.

2 to find a solution to a problem or make a decision after thinking carefully: We need to **work out** where we're going to live.

3 if something works out, it gradually stops being a problem: Everything **worked out** fine in the end.

4 to do a series of physical exercises in order to keep your body strong and healthy: I **work out** three times a week.

work up to
to gradually do more of something so that finally you are doing a lot of it: I'm **working up to** exercising four days a week.

noun all the people who work somewhere: *A quarter of the workforce will lose their jobs.*

work·ing /'wɜːkɪŋ $ 'wɚkɪŋ/ *adjective* **1** working people have jobs: *Working mothers should get more support from their employers.* **2** related to work: *What are your working conditions like?*

working class /ˌ.. './ *noun* the working class, the working classes the people in society who do physical work or jobs for which they get low pay –working-class *adjective*: *He came from a working-class background.*

work·ings /'wɜːkɪŋz $ 'wɚkɪŋz/ *plural noun* the way in which something works: *They didn't understand the workings of the heating system.*

work·load /'wɜːkləʊd $ 'wɚkloʊd/ *noun* the amount of work that a person has to do: *My workload keeps increasing.*

work·man /'wɜːkmən $ 'wɚkmən/ *noun, plural* **workmen** /-mən/ someone who does physical work such as building

work·man·ship /'wɜːkmənʃɪp $ 'wɚkmənʃɪp/ *noun [no plural]* the skill with which something has been made: *a high standard of workmanship*

workmen the plural of WORKMAN

work·out /'wɜːkaʊt $ 'wɚkaʊt/ *noun* a series of physical exercises that you do to keep your body strong and healthy

work·sheet /'wɜːkʃiːt $ 'wɚkʃit/ *noun* a piece of paper with questions which helps students practise what they have learned

work·shop /'wɜːkʃɒp $ 'wɚkʃɑp/ *noun* **1** a room or building where people make or repair things **2** a meeting at which people try to improve their skills by working together

work·sta·tion /'wɜːkˌsteɪʃən $ 'wɚkˌsteɪʃən/ *noun* a desk and computer in an office

work·top /'wɜːktɒp $ 'wɚktɑp/ also **work-sur·face** /'. ˌ../ *noun* a flat surface in a kitchen on which you can prepare food

world¹ /wɜːld $ wɚld/ *noun*
1 the world the Earth and all the people and countries on it: *This is the best city in the world.* | *People all over the world are dying from cancer.*
2 things that are connected with a particular type of business or activity: *the world of professional football* | *people from the fashion world*

PHRASES
the whole world everyone: *The whole world is trying to get tickets for this concert.*
the outside world the people and places outside the area where you live: *She wouldn't leave her house – she was afraid of the outside world.*

world² *adjective* related to the whole world: *the world heavyweight boxing champion*

world-class /ˌ. './ *adjective* one of the best in the world: *He has the ability to become a world-class footballer.*

world-fa·mous /ˌ. '../ *adjective* famous all over the world: *a world-famous writer*

world·wide /ˌwɜːld'waɪd $ ˌwɚld-'waɪd/ *adjective, adverb* in every part of the world: *Pollution is a worldwide problem.*

World Wide Web /ˌ. . './ *written abbreviation* **WWW** *noun* the World Wide Web a system that makes people able to see information and pictures on computers in many parts of the world

worm¹ /wɜːm $ wɚm/ *noun* a small creature with a long soft body and no legs, which lives in the ground

worm² *verb* worm your way to move with difficulty through a narrow place: *Ron wormed his way into the tunnel.*

worn /wɔːn $ wɔːrn/ the past participle of WEAR

worn out also **worn-out** /ˌ. './ *adjective*
1 very tired, especially because you have been working hard: *I'm worn out – I need a holiday.* **2** too old or damaged to use any more: *We spent two weeks in a worn-out tent in the rain.*

wor·ried /'wʌrid $ 'wɚid/ *adjective*

GRAMMAR
worried (that)
worried about something/someone

if you are worried, you keep thinking about something bad that might happen and so do not feel happy or relaxed: *Her mother is worried that she might not get better.* | *I'm very worried about my exams.* | *I'm getting a bit worried about Jamie – he doesn't seem very happy.*

wor·ry¹ /ˈwʌri $ ˈwɚi/ *verb*
worried, worries

GRAMMAR
worry about something
worry (that)

1 to keep thinking about something bad that might happen so that you do not feel happy or relaxed: *Parents always worry about their children.* | *I worry that I won't have enough money for the things I need.*
2 if something worries you, it makes you feel worried: *It worries me that my father lives alone now.*

worry² *noun, plural* **worries** something that makes you feel worried, or the feeling of being worried: *It's a big worry when your children first leave home.* | *He couldn't sleep for worry.*

wor·ry·ing /ˈwʌri-ɪŋ $ ˈwɚi-ɪŋ/ *adjective* making you feel worried: *a worrying piece of news*

worse /wɜːs $ wɚs/ *adjective*
more bad or more unpleasant: *Your singing is even worse than mine!* | *The problem is getting worse.* | *If you feel worse* (=feel more ill) *tomorrow, go to the doctor.*

wors·en /ˈwɜːsən $ ˈwɚsən/ *verb* to become worse: *The hospital says his condition is worsening.*

worse off /ˌ. ˈ./ *adjective* poorer, or in a worse situation: *Cheer up, we could be worse off.*

wor·ship /ˈwɜːʃɪp $ ˈwɚʃɪp/ *verb* worshipped, worshipping *BrE* to express respect and love for God: *In my religion, we worship many gods.*
– **worship** *noun [no plural]*: *an occasion for worship and prayer*

worst¹ /wɜːst $ wɚst/ *adjective*
worse than any other person or thing: *Who is the worst player in the team?*

worst² *noun* **1** the worst someone or something that is worse than every other

person or thing: *Of all the exams, this one will be the worst.* **2 fear the worst** to be afraid that the worst possible thing has happened or will happen: *When Bob didn't come home, I began to fear the worst.*

worth¹ /wɜːθ $ wɚθ/ *preposition*
showing the value of something: *That old watch must be worth at least £100.*

PHRASES
be worth doing if something is worth doing, it would be useful or enjoyable: *This film is definitely worth seeing.* | *It's worth making sure you understand the question before answering it.*
be worth it, be worth your while if something is worth it, it is important enough or good enough to spend time and effort on: *I started running to catch the bus but then decided it wasn't worth it.* | *I think it would be worth your while to apply for the job.*

worth² *noun*
$10 worth, £500 worth etc an amount of something that has a value of $10, £500 etc: *I need £2 worth of stamps.*

worth·less /ˈwɜːθləs $ ˈwɚθləs/ *adjective* having no value: *It's just a worthless piece of rubbish.*

worth·while /ˌwɜːθˈwaɪl $ ˌwɚθˈwaɪl/ *adjective* if something is worthwhile, it is useful or enjoyable: *It's worthwhile checking the price of a camera in several shops.*

wor·thy /ˈwɜːði $ ˈwɚði/ *adjective* worthier, worthiest good enough to have your respect or attention: *He has made a worthy effort to improve his spelling.*

would /wʊd/ *modal verb, short form* **'d** *negative* **would not** or **wouldn't**

1 describing what someone said or thought in the past: *Joe said he would think again about leaving the company.* | *I never thought she'd marry him.* | *She wouldn't listen to my advice.*
2 saying what you hope or imagine will happen **a)** if you say that something **would** happen, you hope

that it will happen: *If I won the national lottery, I'd spend the money on a huge house.* | *It would be cheaper to go by bus.* | *I wouldn't ever want to leave London.* **b)** if something **would have** happened, it might have happened, but it did not happen: *Dad would have loved this if he'd still been alive.* | *I would have fetched you from the station, but you didn't ring me.*
3 asking for something politely: *Would you open the door please?*
4 offering someone something politely: *Would you like a beer?*
5 making a suggestion or giving advice politely: *I wouldn't worry too much about the test – it's easy.* | *I'd ask your teacher for help, if I were you.*

would·n't /'wʊdnt/ the short form of 'would not': *He wouldn't do a thing like that!*

would've /'wʊdəv/ the short form of 'would have': *You would've enjoyed the film.*

wound¹ /wuːnd/ *noun* a deep cut made in your skin by a knife or bullet: *He had a deep wound in his side.*

wound² *verb* to injure someone with a knife or gun ⇨ *see usage note at* HURT¹ **–wounded** *adjective*: *Is he badly wounded?*

wound³ /waʊnd/ the past tense and past participle of WIND²

wound up /ˌwaʊnd 'ʌp/ *adjective* very angry, nervous, or excited: *He gets really wound up when the other children tease him.*

wove the past tense of WEAVE

woven the past participle of WEAVE

wow /waʊ/ *spoken* used when you think something is impressive or surprising: *Wow, what a beautiful house!*

wran·gle /'ræŋgəl/ *verb* to argue with someone angrily for a long time

wrap /ræp/ *verb* wrapped, wrapping

1 to cover a present with attractive paper: *I haven't wrapped the Christmas presents yet.*

2 to put a piece of cloth or paper around something: *She wrapped the baby in a blanket.* | *She wrapped her scarf around her neck.*

PHRASAL VERBS
wrap up
1 wrap something up to completely cover something by putting paper or cloth around it: *They wrapped all the cups up in newspaper.*
2 wrap up to put on warm clothes: *Make sure you wrap up well if you're going out in the snow.*

wrap·per /'ræpə $ 'ræpɚ/ *noun* the paper or plastic that covers something you buy: *The ground was covered in sweet wrappers.*

wrap·ping /'ræpɪŋ/ *noun* paper or cloth that is put around something: *She took the present and tore off the wrapping.*

wrapping pa·per /'.. ,../ *noun* coloured paper that you use to wrap presents

wreath /riːθ/ *noun* a circle of flowers and leaves that is used as a decoration or to show respect for someone who has died

wreath

wreck¹ /rek/ *verb informal* to destroy something completely: *My drinking problem wrecked my marriage.*

wreck² *noun* **1** a car, plane, or ship that is very badly damaged **2** be a **wreck** *informal* to be very tired, unhealthy, or worried **3** *AmE* a bad car accident or plane accident; CRASH *BrE*

wreck·age /'rekɪdʒ/ *noun* [no plural] the broken parts of a vehicle or building that has been destroyed: *She managed to pull the driver from the wreckage.*

wrench¹ /rentʃ/ *verb* to twist and pull something from somewhere, using force: *Tom wrenched the nail out of the wall.*

wrench² *noun, plural* **wrenches** the American word for SPANNER

wres·tle /'resəl/ *verb* **1** to fight by holding someone and trying to push them to the ground **2** wrestle with

W

something to try to deal with something difficult: *I've been wrestling with this problem for days.*

wres·tler /'reslə $ 'reslə/ *noun* someone who wrestles as a sport

wres·tling /'reslɪŋ/ *noun* [no plural] a sport in which two people fight and try to push each other to the ground

wretch·ed /'retʃɪd/ *adjective* 1 very unhappy or unlucky: *He led a wretched life with his first wife.* 2 *informal* used when you feel angry with someone or something: *The wretched thing's broken again!*

wrig·gle /'rɪgəl/ *verb* to twist quickly from side to side: *She wriggled into the tight dress.*

wring /rɪŋ/ *verb, past tense and past participle* wrung /rʌŋ/ 1 also **wring out** to twist wet clothes etc to remove water from them 2 **wring something's neck** to kill an animal by twisting its neck

wrin·kle /'rɪŋkəl/ *noun* a small line on your face that you get when you are old

wrin·kled /'rɪŋkəld/ *adjective* if someone's skin is wrinkled, it has a lot of lines on it because they are old

wrist /rɪst/ *noun* the joint between your hand and your arm ⇨ *see picture at* BODY

wrist·watch /'rɪstwɒtʃ $ 'rɪst-wɑtʃ/ *noun, plural* wristwatches a watch that you wear on your wrist

write /raɪt/ *verb* wrote /rəʊt $ roʊt/ written /'rɪtn/

GRAMMAR
write something on/in something
write to someone
write something to someone
write someone something

1 to make letters or words on paper, using a pen or pencil: *We teach children how to **read and write**.* | *Write your name **on** this piece of paper.*
2 to produce a letter to send to someone: *Will you **write to** me when you've gone?* | *I'm **writing** a letter to my mother.* | *David **wrote** me a **letter** every week.*
3 to produce a book, song etc: *He wrote several books and many poems.* | *The article was very **well written**.*

PHRASE
write a cheque, write out a cheque to write information on a cheque as

a way of paying money: *I **wrote a cheque for** £30 to pay for the meal.*

PHRASAL VERBS
write back
to answer someone's letter by sending them a letter: *Do you think Sarah will **write back**?*
write down
write something down to write something on a piece of paper: *Can you **write** your phone number **down** for me?*
write off
to send a letter to an organization, especially to ask them to send you something: *I've **written off for** an application form.*

write-off /'. ./ *noun BrE* if a vehicle is a write-off, it is so badly damaged in an accident that it is not worth repairing

writ·er /'raɪtə $ 'raɪtər/ *noun* someone who writes books

writhe /raɪð/ *verb written* to twist your body, especially because you are in a lot of pain: *He lay on the ground, writhing in agony.*

writ·ing /'raɪtɪŋ/ *noun* [no plural] 1 words that are written by hand or printed: *I couldn't read the writing on the envelope.* | *I informed them in writing that I was going to leave.* 2 the activity of writing: *I'm hoping to do a course in creative writing.*

written the past participle of WRITE

wrong¹ /rɒŋ $ rɔŋ/ *adjective, adverb*

GRAMMAR
it is wrong to do something

1 not correct ⇨ *opposite* RIGHT¹ (1): *You're wrong – I don't live on London Road.* | *That is the **wrong answer**.* | *You've added the numbers up wrong.*
2 not morally right ⇨ *opposite* RIGHT¹ (3): *Killing is wrong.* | *Some people think **it's wrong to** kill animals for food.*
3 not suitable ⇨ *opposite* RIGHT¹ (4): *You're wearing the wrong shoes for an exercise class.*

PHRASES
go wrong if something goes wrong, it starts to have problems or it is unsuccessful: *My washing machine **has gone wrong**.* | *His plan **went wrong**.*

W

something is wrong with something. **Something's wrong with** my computer (=my computer is not working correctly). | **There's something wrong with** his heart. | **What's wrong with** you today (=why are you not all right)?

get something wrong to make a mistake and say something that is not correct: *Did you **get** all the answers **wrong**?*

wrong² noun **1** [no plural] behaviour that is not morally right: *Children need to learn the difference between right and wrong.* **2** a situation in which someone is treated badly or unfairly: *the wrongs that were done to these people during the war*

wrong·do·ing /ˈrɒŋ,duːɪŋ $,rɔŋˈduːɪŋ/ noun formal when someone does something illegal or wrong

wrote the past tense of WRITE

wrung the past tense and past participle of WRING

wry /raɪ/ adjective showing that you think that something is both funny and sad: *She made a wry comment about the state of his room.*

WWW the written abbreviation of WORLD WIDE WEB

Xe·rox¹ /ˈzɪərɒks $ˈzɪrɑks/ AmE trademark **1** also **Xerox machine** /ˈ.. .,./ a PHOTOCOPIER **2** a PHOTOCOPY¹

Xerox² AmE trademark to make a copy of a document using a PHOTOCOPIER; PHOTOCOPY²

X·mas /ˈkrɪsməs/ noun an informal way of writing 'Christmas'

X-ray /ˈeks reɪ/ noun a photograph of the inside of someone's body, that you make using a special kind of light
–X-ray verb: *The doctor X-rayed her broken leg.*

xy·lo·phone /ˈzaɪləfəun $ˈzaɪlə,foun/ noun a musical instrument with flat wooden bars that you hit with a stick

yacht /jɒt $jɑt/ noun a boat with sails that people use for races or sailing for pleasure ⇨ *see picture on page 349*

yachts·man /ˈjɒtsmən $ˈjɑtsmən/ noun, plural yachtsmen /-mən/ a man who sails a yacht

yachts·wom·an /ˈjɒtswumən $ˈjɑts-,wumən/ noun, plural yachtswomen /-,wɪmɪn/ a woman who sails a yacht

Yank /jæŋk/ noun informal someone from the US

yank /jæŋk/ verb informal to suddenly pull something hard: *The boy yanked at his mother's sleeve.*

yap /jæp/ verb yapped, yapping if a small dog yaps, it BARKS a lot

yard /jɑːd $jɑrd/ noun **1** written abbreviation **yd** a length equal to 3 feet or 0.9144 metres: *The room was four yards wide.* **2** the American word for GARDEN: *Joey's out in the yard.* **3** an area of land with a wall around it, next to a building

yarn /jɑːn $jɑrn/ noun [no plural] thick thread that you use for KNITTING

yawn /jɔːn/ verb
to open your mouth wide and breathe deeply because you are tired or bored

yawn

–**yawn** noun: "I'm going to bed," he said with a yawn.

yd the written abbreviation of YARD

yeah /jeə/ spoken informal yes

year /jɪə $ jɪr/ noun
a period of 12 months: I have lived here **for** two **years**. | We last saw Harry three **years ago**. | Insurance costs $100 per year. | She died **last year**. | **Next year** I will be sixteen.

PHRASES
for years informal for a long time: I haven't seen Ray **for years**.
ten years old, twelve years old etc used for saying how old someone is: My sister is only **two years old**
year four, year six etc BrE used for saying what class someone is in in a school or college: Ciara is in **year seven**.

year·book /'jɪəbʊk $ 'jɪrbʊk/ noun a book that an organization or school produces every year, giving information about its activities

year·ly /'jɪəli $ 'jɪrli/ adjective, adverb happening every year: her yearly visit to her aunt | You can pay weekly, monthly, or yearly.

yeast /jiːst/ noun [no plural] a substance that you use when you are making bread to make the bread rise

yell /jel/ also **yell out** verb to shout something very loudly: "Come back!" he yelled.
–**yell** noun: With a yell, she landed at the bottom of the stairs.

yel·low[1] /'jeləʊ $ 'jeloʊ/ adjective something that is yellow is the colour of a LEMON or BANANA

yellow[2] noun the colour of a LEMON: Yellow is my favourite colour.

yelp /jelp/ verb if a dog yelps, it makes a short high sound because it is in pain or excited

yes /jes/ adverb
a word you say when you agree with something or think that something is true ⇨ opposite NO[1]: "Are you Ann?" "Yes I am." | "This is great isn't it?" "Yes, it is." | If I ask her to marry me do you think that she will **say yes**?

yes·ter·day /'jestədi $ 'jestɚdi/ adverb
the day before today: I went swimming yesterday. | Yesterday, the weather was fine.

yet /jet/ adverb

GRAMMAR
have done something yet
be something yet
do something yet

1 also **as yet** formal use **yet** in questions and negative sentences to say that something has not happened up to the present time: Have you seen 'The Phantom Menace' yet? | Is Sharon back yet? | I haven't finished my essay yet. | The government has not as yet decided how to deal with the problem. | The train goes in two hours, so we haven't got leave yet. | Have you washed the car yet? | I can't ask Mum yet – she's busy.

2 use **yet** to say that something could still happen: There's time yet to catch the train. | I've got plenty of work to do yet, so I won't be home till late.

PHRASES
biggest yet, best yet, most important yet etc used to say that something is the biggest, best, most important etc that has existed up to the present time: Kevin Costner's best film yet. | This is the most exciting game the Red Sox have played yet. | the most difficult exam yet
yet another, yet more, yet again used to say that you are surprised that there is more of something or that something has happened again: You were late yet again this morning – that's the fourth time this week. | The first train broke down, and then yet another train was delayed. | I watched as Bob took yet another slice of chocolate cake.

yield¹ /jiːld/ *verb formal* to do what someone wants, although you do not want to: *The head teacher finally yielded to pressure and allowed students to wear casual clothes.*

yield² *noun* the amount that something produces: *Scientists are trying to find out how to produce higher yields from crops.*

yo·ga /'jəʊgə $ 'joʊgə/ *noun* [no plural] a system of exercises which relax you and make your muscles stronger

yog·hurt also **yogurt** /'jɒgət $ 'joʊgət/ *noun* a thick white food that is made from milk

yolk /jəʊk $ joʊk/ *noun* the yellow part of an egg

you /jə; *strong* juː/ *pronoun*
1 the person or people being spoken to: *Would you like some coffee?* | *I hate you!* | *What are you two doing?*
2 anyone: *Smoking is bad for you.* | *You can earn quite a lot of money being a salesman.*

you'd /jəd; *strong* juːd/ the short form of 'you would' or 'you had': *I know you'd like a drink.* | *I didn't think you'd finished.*

you'll /jəl; *strong* juːl/ the short form of 'you will': *You'll have to leave.*

young¹ /jʌŋ/ *adjective*
1 someone who is young has only lived for a short time: *You are too young to smoke.* | *When my father was young he was very handsome.* | *Do you enjoy working with young children?*
2 younger brother, younger sister a brother or sister who is younger than you

young² *plural noun* 1 the young young people: *The BBC is planning more programmes for the young.* 2 young animals: *The mouse is capable of producing 150 young a year.*

young·ster /'jʌŋstə $ 'jʌŋstɚ/ *noun* a young person

your /jə $ jɚ; *strong* jɔː $ jɔr/
1 belonging to the person or people being spoken to: *You can hang your coat up here.* | *Are your hands clean?* | *Have you all got your passports?*
2 belonging to anyone: *I believe you have to learn from your mistakes.*

you're /jə $ jɚ; *strong* jɔː $ jɔr/ the short form of 'you are': *You're silly.*

yours /jɔːz $ jɔrz/ *pronoun*
a thing belonging to the person or people being spoken to: *I wish I lived in a nice house like yours.*

your·self /jə'self $ jɚ'self/ *pronoun, plural* **yourselves** /jə'selvz $ jɚ'selvz/
1 used when the same person that you are speaking to does an action and receives the action: *Be careful you don't hurt yourself.* | *What do you see when you look at yourself in the mirror?* | *You should all feel ashamed of yourselves.*
2 emphasizing that you are talking about the person or people you are speaking to: *If you don't have a computer yourself, ask a friend if you can use theirs.* | *You have probably noticed this yourselves.*
3 used when talking about people in general, and they do an action and receive the action: *You can hurt yourself quite badly if you don't use the correct safety equipment.*

PHRASE
by yourself, by yourselves with no one else there, or no one else helping: *You'll have to wait there by yourself until the others get back.* | *See if you can manage to do it by yourselves.*

youth /juːθ/ *noun* 1 [no plural] your youth is the time when you are young: *I lived in London in my youth.* 2 a young man: *There were three youths waiting outside.* 3 [no plural] young people in general: *We must do more for the youth of this country.*

youth club /'. ./ *noun* a place where young people can meet, dance etc

youth·ful /'juːθfəl/ *adjective* seeming younger than you really are: *He has kept his youthful good looks.*

youth hos·tel /'. ,../ *noun* a place where people who are travelling can stay cheaply

you've /jəv; *strong* juːv/ the short form of 'you have': *You've eaten it all!*

yo-yo /'jəʊ jəʊ $ 'joʊjoʊ/ *noun* a toy made of a round piece of plastic or wood that moves up and down a string

Y

Zz

za·ny /ˈzeɪni/ *adjective* **zanier, zaniest** strange but amusing: *a zany comedian*

zeal /ziːl/ *noun* [no plural] *formal* great desire to do something: *He set off for Africa, full of religious zeal.*

ze·bra /ˈzebrə $ ˈzibrə/ *noun* a black and white African animal, similar to a horse ⇨ *see picture on page 339*

zebra cros·sing /ˌ.. ˈ../ *noun BrE* a set of black and white lines painted on the road where vehicles are supposed to stop so people can cross safely; CROSSWALK *AmE* ⇨ *see pictures on pages 343 and 349*

ze·ro /ˈzɪərəʊ $ ˈzɪroʊ/ *number*, plural **zeros** or **zeroes** the number 0

zig·zag¹ /ˈzɪgzæg/ *noun* a line that goes first in one direction and then in the other, and continues in this way: *a zigzag of lightning*

zigzag² *verb* **zigzagged, zigzagging** to move forward, going in straight lines first to one side, and then to the other: *The car zigzagged across the road.*

zip¹ /zɪp/ *verb* **zipped, zipping** also **zip up** to close or fasten something using a zip: *She zipped the bag shut.*

zip² *noun BrE* a type of fastener made of two lines of small metal teeth and a sliding piece that joins them together; ZIPPER *AmE*: *The zip on my pencil case has broken.* ⇨ *see picture on page 352*

zip code /ˈ. ./ the American word for POST CODE

zip·per /ˈzɪpə $ ˈzɪpɚ/ the American word for a ZIP

zone /zəʊn $ zoʊn/ *noun* an area where a particular thing happens or where there are particular rules: *People are advised not to live in earthquake zones.* | *You're in a no-parking zone.*

zoo /zuː/ *noun* a place where different types of wild animal are kept so that people can see or study them

zo·ol·o·gy /zuːˈɒlədʒi $ zoʊˈɑlədʒi/ *noun* [no plural] the scientific study of animals

zoom /zuːm/ *verb* *informal* to travel somewhere very quickly: *Cars zoomed past us on the freeway.*

zuc·chi·ni /zʊˈkiːni/ the American word for COURGETTE

zigzag

Z